Lecture Notes in Computer Science 523

Edited by G. Goos and J. Hartmanis

J. Hughes (Ed.)

Functional Programming Languages and Computer Architecture

5th ACM Conference
Cambridge, MA, USA, August 26-30, 1991
Proceedings

Springer-Verlag
Berlin Heidelberg New York
London Paris Tokyo
Hong Kong Barcelona
Budapest

Series Editors

Gerhard Goos
GMD Forschungsstelle
Universität Karlsruhe
Vincenz-Priessnitz-Straße 1
W-7500 Karlsruhe, FRG

Juris Hartmanis
Department of Computer Science
Cornell University
Upson Hall
Ithaca, NY 14853, USA

Volume Editor

John Hughes
Computing Science Department, University of Glasgow
Glasgow G12 8QQ, UK

CR Subject Classification (1991): C.1.2-3, D.1.1, D.3.1-4, F.3.2

ISBN 3-540-54396-1 Springer-Verlag Berlin Heidelberg New York
ISBN 0-387-54396-1 Springer-Verlag New York Berlin Heidelberg

Typesetting: Camera ready by auhtor
Printing and binding: Druckhaus Beltz, Hemsbach/Bergstr.
2145/3140-543210 - Printed on acid-free paper

Foreword

This book is the proceedings of the fifth conference on Functional Programming Languages and Computer Architecture, held at Harvard University, Cambridge, MA, August 26-30, 1991. Thirty papers were selected for presentation from a total of 126 submissions. The book offers a comprehensive view of the best and the latest work in functional programming.

A number of themes emerge from the papers. One is a growing interest in *types*. Some papers describe powerful type systems or type checkers supporting overloading, coercion, dynamic types, and incremental inference; others exploit linear types to optimise storage, and polymorphic types to optimise semantic analysis.

The hot topic of *partial evaluation* is well represented. Authors address techniques for higher-order binding-time analysis, assuring termination of partial evaluation, and improving the residual programs a partial evaluator generates. There are also accounts of a novel "online" partial evaluator, and the first self-applicable one for a strongly typed language.

The thorny problem of manipulating *state* in functional languages is addressed by several papers. One even argues that parallel programs with side-effects can be "more declarative" than purely functional ones!

Theoretical work covers a new model of types based on projections, parametricity, a connection between strictness analysis and logic, and a discussion of what it means for an implementation of the λ-calculus to be efficient. Surprisingly, none of the well known implementation techniques meets the natural criterion posed!

The connection with computer architecture is represented by work on high-performance implementations, both sequential and parallel, and techniques for multi-threaded code generation, unboxing, and cache-level garbage collection.

A variety of other topics are also addressed.

The conference was sponsored by ACM SIGPLAN and SIGARCH, IFIP WG2.8, and Harvard University. Their support is gratefully acknowledged.

June 1991 John Hughes

Programme Committee

Arvind (MIT, USA)
Lennart Augustsson (Chalmers University, Sweden)
Geoffrey Burn (Imperial College London, GB)
Warren Burton (Simon Fraser University, Canada)
Luca Cardelli (DEC SRC, USA)
Paul Hudak (Yale University, USA)
John Hughes (Glasgow University, GB)
Neil Jones (Copenhagen University, Denmark)
Michel Mauny (INRIA, France)
Lambert Meertens (CWI & Utrecht University, The Netherlands)
Robin Milner (Edinburgh University, GB)
Mike Reeve (ECRC, Germany)
Colin Runciman (York University, GB)
Mitch Wand (Northeastern University, USA)

Conference Chair

John Williams (IBM ARC, USA)

Local Arrangements Chair

Robert Muller (Harvard University, USA)

Contents

Type Classes and Overloading Resolution via Order-Sorted Unification

Tobias Nipkow*
University of Cambridge

Gregor Snelting†
Technische Hochschule Darmstadt

Abstract

We present a type inference algorithm for a Haskell-like language based on order-sorted unification. The language features polymorphism, overloading, type classes and multiple inheritance. Class and instance declarations give rise to an order-sorted algebra of types. Type inference essentially reduces to the Hindley/Milner algorithm where unification takes place in this order-sorted algebra of types. The theory of order-sorted unification provides simple sufficient conditions which ensure the existence of principal types. The semantics of the language is given by a translation into ordinary λ-calculus. We prove the correctness of our type inference algorithm with respect to this semantics.

1 Introduction

In a recent paper on order-sorted unification, Meseguer et al. [8] state

> An application of order-sorted unification that seems to have escaped prior notice is to polymorphism for typed functional languages, in the case where there are subtypes as well as polymorphic type constructors.

In the spirit of this remark we show that for languages like Haskell [6] which feature polymorphism, type classes and overloading, order-sorted unification can indeed be the basis of a type inference system which is much simpler than those which have been proposed previously.

The key idea of this paper is to introduce a three-level system of values, types and partially ordered *sorts* that classify types. This is in contrast to many type systems used in the area of term-rewriting, e.g. OBJ [4], where types[1] are partially ordered. Although we assume that the quotation above was meant to apply to these two-level systems, Haskell's combination of polymorphism and type classes cries out for a three-level treatment with ordered sorts. Sorts are useful even for Standard ML [9] where we find a distinction between general types and equality types. This can be described by a signature with only two sorts, Eq and Ω, where $Eq < \Omega$.

Figure 1 defines the abstract syntax of our language *Mini-Haskell* which is the focus of our investigations. Although it is not mandatory that the reader is familiar with either the Haskell Report [6] or the paper by Wadler and Blott [14], that is where he should turn for motivating examples. In addition to the well-known constructs of functional languages, Mini-Haskell offers *class* and *instance* declarations. A class declaration is a named collection of

*Author's address: University of Cambridge, Computer Laboratory, Pembroke Street, Cambridge CB2 3QG, England. E-mail: `Tobias.Nipkow@cl.cam.ac.uk`. Research supported by ESPRIT BRA 3245, *Logical Frameworks*.

†Author's address: Technische Hochschule Darmstadt, Praktische Informatik, Magdalenenstr. 11c, D-61 Darmstadt, Fed. Rep. of Germany. E-mail: `snelting@pi.informatik.th-darmstadt.de`.

[1] which are usually called *sorts* in that context, making the terminology somewhat confusing.

Type classes	γ
Type variables	α_γ
Type constructors	χ
Types	$\tau = \alpha_\gamma \mid \chi(\tau_1, \ldots, \tau_n)$
Type schemes	$\sigma = \tau \mid \forall\alpha_\gamma.\sigma$
Identifiers	x
Expressions	$e \;=\; x$
	$\mid\; (e_0\; e_1)$
	$\mid\; \lambda x.e$
	$\mid\;$ **let** $x = e_0$ **in** e_1
Declarations	$d \;=\;$ **class** $\gamma \le \gamma_1, \ldots, \gamma_m$ **where** $x_1 : \forall\alpha_\gamma.\tau_1, \ldots, x_k : \forall\alpha_\gamma.\tau_k$
	$\mid\;$ **inst** $\chi : (\gamma_1, \ldots, \gamma_n)\gamma$ **where** $x_1 = e_1, \ldots, x_k = e_k$
Programs	$p \;=\; d_1; \ldots d_n; e$

Ω is the universal type class

α means α_Ω

int, *float*, *char*, *list*(α), *pair*(α, β), $\alpha \rightarrow \beta$ are type constructors[2]

Figure 1: Syntax of Mini-Haskell types and expressions

function declarations. The types of these functions depend on a parameter, the instance type. Informally, a type belongs to some class γ if it provides the functions x_i associated with γ. This relationship is expressed formally in an instance declaration: it asserts that some type constructor χ returns a type of class γ if the arguments to χ are of class $\gamma_1, \ldots, \gamma_n$, and it defines the functions x_i introduced in the class declaration for γ. As there can be multiple instances of a class, there can be multiple definitions of the x_i. This provides for a kind of overloading where the type of each x_i is an instance of the generic type as defined in the class declaration. In addition, Mini-Haskell features multiple inheritance: a class γ may depend on superclasses $\gamma_1, \ldots, \gamma_n$, meaning that γ inherits all functions of the γ_i. In accordance with the Haskell report we require that all class and instance declarations must be top level; this avoids some subtle problems with nested classes.

Mini-Haskell enforces a restriction also present in the Haskell Report: classes express properties of individual types, not relationships between types. The latter, more general interpretation was introduced in [14], but we allow only type classes with one type parameter. Hence the type variable a in the Haskell notation[3] $(\gamma_1\ \mathtt{a}, \ldots, \gamma_m\ \mathtt{a})$ `=>` $\gamma\ \mathtt{a}$ and $(\gamma_1\ \mathtt{a}_1, \ldots, \gamma_n\ \mathtt{a}_n)$ `=>` $\gamma(\chi\ \mathtt{a}_1 \ldots \mathtt{a}_n)$, where χ is an n-ary type constructor, can be dropped. Instead we write $\gamma \le \gamma_1, \ldots, \gamma_n$ and $\chi : (\gamma_1, \ldots, \gamma_n)\gamma$.

For reasons of presentation, we have restricted the types of the functions x_i to be of the form $\forall\alpha_\gamma.\tau_i$, rather than $\forall\alpha_\gamma.\sigma_i$, where σ_i could again be quantified. This eliminates a certain amount of notational overhead, without being unreasonable: all of the examples in the Haskell Report fit the simpler scheme. In addition, several other context conditions must be satisfied, e.g. "No type constructor can be declared as an instance of a particular class more than once in the same scope"; these conditions are discussed later.

Wadler and Blott [14] present a type inference system for what appears to be a superset of Mini-Haskell. The main difference is that in their syntax, class definitions are no longer present.

[2] Except for $\alpha \rightarrow \beta$, the collection is arbitrary. Type constructors have global scope and are predefined.

[3] Note that each argument of χ is determined by a single class γ_i, rather than some finite list of classes as in Haskell. This is nonessential (see Section 5). We also assume that all $\mathtt{a}_i$ are distinct. We believe that this was the intention of the Haskell definers. It is not clear whether our ideas work without this linearity assumption.

Instead, they introduce so-called predicated types, as well as inference rules for the introduction and elimination of such types. The resulting inference system is rather complicated, and it is not clear whether it leads to a terminating algorithm.

Upon analysis of their article, we detected that a much simpler inference system for Mini-Haskell can be constructed, provided we replace ordinary unification in the Hindley-Milner system with order-sorted unification. Therefore, we first recall basic facts about order-sorted unification. We then present our type inference system, and provide some illuminating examples. In addition, we discuss conditions which ensure the existence of principal types. Finally, we define a translation from Mini-Haskell to Mini-ML [1] and show that the inferred types and the semantics given by the translation fit together.

2 Order-sorted terms and order-sorted unification

An *order-sorted signature* is a triple $(S, \leq, \Sigma)$, where S is a set of sorts, $\leq$ a partial order on S, and Σ a family $\{\Sigma_{w,s} \mid w \in S^*, s \in S\}$ of not necessarily disjoint sets of operator symbols. We assume that S and Σ are finite. For notational convenience, we often write $f : (w)s$ instead of $f \in \Sigma_{w,s}$; $(w)s$ is called an *arity*[4] and $f : (w)s$ a *declaration*. The signature $(S, \leq, \Sigma)$ is often identified with Σ. An S-sorted variable set is a family $V = \{V_s \mid s \in S\}$ of disjoint, nonempty sets. For $x \in V_s$ we also write $x : s$ or x_s.

The set of *order-sorted terms* of sort s freely generated by V, $T_\Sigma(V)_s$, is the least set satisfying

- if $x \in V_{s'}$ and $s' \leq s$, then $x \in T_\Sigma(V)_s$
- if $f \in \Sigma_{w,s'}$, $w = s_1..s_n$, $s' \leq s$, and $t_i \in T_\Sigma(V)_{s_i}$ for all $i = 1..n$, then $f(t_1, \ldots, t_n) \in T_\Sigma(V)_s$.

In contrast to sort-free terms and variables, order-sorted variables and terms always have a sort. Terms must be sort-correct, that is, subterms of a compound term must be of an appropriate sort as required by the arities of the term's operator symbol. Note that an operator symbol may have not just one arity (as in classical homogeneous or heterogeneous term algebras), but may have *several* arities. As a consequence, each term may have several sorts. $T_\Sigma(V) := \bigcup_{s \in S} T_\Sigma(V)_s$ denotes the set of all order-sorted terms over Σ freely generated by V. The set of all ground terms over Σ is $T_\Sigma := T_\Sigma(\{\})$.

A signature is called *regular*, if each term $t \in T_\Sigma(V)$ has a least sort. It is decidable if a signature is regular:

Theorem 2.1 (Smolka et al. [12, 15]) *A signature $(S, \leq, \Sigma)$ is regular iff for every $f \in \Sigma$ and $w \in S^*$ the set $\{s \mid \exists w' \geq w.\ f : (w')s\}$ either is empty or contains a least element.*

As an example of a simple non-regular signature, consider $(\{s_0, s_1, s_2\}, \{s_1 \leq s_0, s_2 \leq s_0\}, \Sigma_{\epsilon,s_1} = \{a\}, \Sigma_{\epsilon,s_2} = \{a\})$: the constant a has two sorts which are incomparable, hence it does not have a minimal sort.

A *substitution* θ from a variable set Y into the term algebra $T_\Sigma(V)$ is a mapping from Y to $T_\Sigma(V)$, which additionally satisfies $\theta(x) \in T_\Sigma(V)_s$ if $x \in V_s$ (that is, substitutions must be sort-correct). As usual, substitutions are extended canonically to $T_\Sigma(V)$. We write $\theta = \{x_1 \mapsto t_1, \ldots, x_n \mapsto t_n\}$. If, for $t, t' \in T_\Sigma(V)$, there is a substitution θ such that $t' = \theta(t)$, t' is called an *instance* of t. Similarly, a substitution θ' is called an instance of a substitution θ w.r.t. a set of variables W, written $\theta \succeq \theta'$ $[W]$, if there is a substitution γ such that $\theta'(x) = \gamma(\theta(x))$ for all $x \in W$.

[4] The term *type* and the notation $w \rightarrow s$ are reserved for the types in Mini-Haskell.

A *unifier* of a set of equations Γ is a substitution θ such that $\theta(s) = \theta(t)$ for all equations $s =^? t$ in Γ. A set of unifiers U of Γ is called *complete* (and denoted by CSU), if for every unifier θ' of Γ there exists $\theta \in U$ such that θ' is an instance of θ w.r.t. the variables in Γ. As usual, a signature is called *unitary (unifying)* if for all equation sets Γ there is a complete set of unifiers containing at most one element; it is called *finitary*, if there is always a finite and complete set of unifiers. For non-regular signatures, unification can be infinitary even if the signature is finite [11]. But we have the following

Theorem 2.2 (Schmidt-Schauß [11]) *In finite and regular signatures, finite sets of equations have finite, complete, and effectively computable sets of unifiers.*

Waldmann [15, Thm 9.5] provides a succinct characterization of unitary signatures. For our purposes the following sufficient conditions are more interesting. Call a signature *downward complete* if any two sorts have either no lower bound or an infimum, and *coregular* if for every f and s the set

$$D(f,s) = \{w \mid \exists s'.\ f:(w)s' \wedge s' \le s\}$$

either is empty or has a greatest element. Smolka et al. [12] show

Theorem 2.3 *Every finite, regular, coregular, and downward complete signature is unitary.*

From this theorem it is easy to derive the following specialization:

Corollary 2.4 *Every finite, regular, and downward complete signature is unitary if it is*

- injective*: $f:(w)s$ and $f(w')s$ imply $w = w'$, and*
- subsort reflecting*: $f:(w')s'$ and $s' \le s$ imply $f:(w)s$ for some $w \ge w'$.*

Injectivity and subsort reflection imply coregularity, but not the other way around. Nevertheless one can show that the two criteria are essentially equivalent [10].

For unitary signatures, order-sorted unification can be implemented in quasi-linear time [8]. For finitary signatures, order-sorted unification in general is NP-complete [11], but in most cases can be implemented efficiently. We do not intend to present algorithms for order-sorted unification; this has been done elsewhere [15, 8, 10]. We merely provide some examples which will be used later. Consider the sort hierarchy[5]

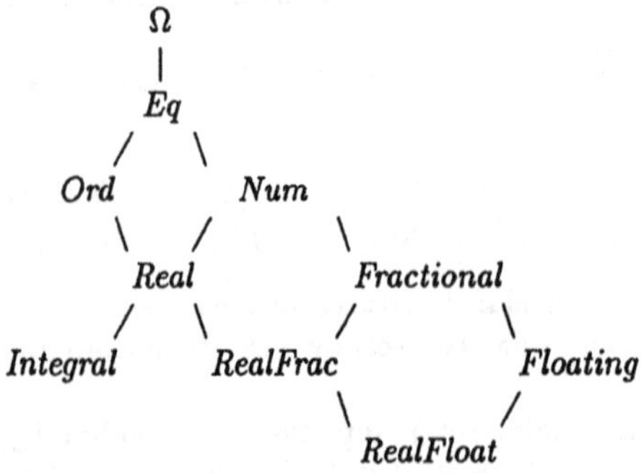

and the operator *list* with multiple declarations

$$\begin{array}{ll} list: & (\Omega)\Omega \\ list: & (Eq)Eq \\ list: & (Ord)Ord \\ list: & (Num)Num \end{array}$$

[5]It is not an accident that this sort hierarchy coincides with the Haskell numeric class hierarchy [6, p. 50].

Now we want to unify $x_{Eq} =^?_\Sigma list(y_\Omega)$. Since $list(y_\Omega)$ has sort Ω, we need a substitution θ such that $list(\theta(y))$ has a sort $\leq Eq$, by choosing a suitable arity for *list*. This process is known as *weakening*[6]. Choose $\theta = \{y \mapsto z_{Eq}, x_{Eq} \mapsto list(z_{Eq})\}$, which is sort-correct (because $list : (Eq)Eq$), and constitutes a complete (singleton) set of unifiers. But note what happens if the declaration $list : (Eq)Eq$ is removed from the signature: the above substitution is no longer sort-correct, since $list(z_{Eq})$ has only sort Ω. Instead, the weakening process must go even further down in the sort hierarchy, and we obtain the complete 2-element set of unifiers $\{\{y \mapsto z_{Ord}, x \mapsto list(z_{Ord})\}, \{y \mapsto z_{Num}, x \mapsto list(z_{Num})\}\}$. Now let us unify $x_{Ord} =^?_\Sigma y_{Num}$. We obtain the singleton CSU $\theta = \{x_{Ord} \mapsto z_{Real}, y_{Num} \mapsto z_{Real}\}$. If Ord and Num had no lower bound, these terms would not unify, unless we added a new constant a of sort both Ord and Num: the reader should convince herself that in this case the set $\{\{x \mapsto list^n(a), y \mapsto list^n(a)\} \mid n \in \mathbb{N}_0\}$ is a complete and minimal, yet infinite set of unifiers! This strange behaviour is due to the fact that the signature is not regular: $list(a)$ does not have a minimal sort.

3 The type inference system

Our type inference system for Mini-Haskell replaces ordinary unification in the Hindley-Milner system with order-sorted unification, where the signature of the order-sorted algebra of types is constructed from the class and instance declarations. The inference system described below is a simple extension of the system DM' due to Clément et al. [1], which in turn is a variant of the classical Damas-Milner system [3]. In fact, if we remove class and instance declarations from our syntax, our system reduces to DM': the order-sorted algebra of types is the trivial one with only one sort Ω, order-sorted unification reduces to classical Robinson unification, and the inference rules simplify to the original DM' rules. Overloading resolution is performed by order-sorted unification alone. Since we have already seen that order-sorted signatures allow multiple operator arities, and that the unification algorithm will select the right one(s) which must be used in order to unify two terms, the reader might already get an idea of what we are aiming for.

As usual, inferences in our system depend on type assumptions. A type assumption is a finite mapping from variables to types, just as in the ordinary Damas-Milner algorithm. The only difference is that in our system every type variable has a sort; in case there are no class declarations, all type variables have sort Ω. In addition, our inferences depend on the signature of an order-sorted algebra which can be seen as a compact representation of the class and instance declarations found so far. If there are no class definitions, this signature contains only declarations of the from $\chi : (\Omega^n)\Omega$ for all n-ary type constructors χ. A class declaration will add a new sort and subsort relations to the signature, an instance declaration will add a new arity for the type constructor involved.

The following convention is used: $\overline{\alpha_{\gamma_k}}$ denotes the list $\alpha_{\gamma_1}, \ldots, \alpha_{\gamma_k}$, with the understanding that the α_{γ_i} are distinct type variables.

The first four rules in the type inference system in Figure 2 are of the form $(A, \Sigma) \vdash e : \sigma$ and are almost identical to the DM' rules. There are two differences: all inferences depend on the signature Σ of the type algebra as well as the set of type assumptions A. Furthermore, generic instantiation in rule TAUT must respect Σ. This is written $\sigma \succeq_\Sigma \tau$, meaning that σ has the form $\forall \overline{\alpha_{\gamma_n}}.\tau_0$, there are τ_i of sort γ_i, and $\tau = \tau_0[\tau_1/\alpha_{\gamma_1}, \ldots, \tau_n/\alpha_{\gamma_n}]$. In the rule LET we use the notation $FV(\tau)$, which denotes the set of free type variables in τ; $FV(\tau, A)$ denotes $FV(\tau) - FV(A)$.

[6] In our setting, *strengthening* would be more appropriate: the lower we are in the sort hierarchy, the more we know.

TAUT	$\dfrac{A(x) \succeq_\Sigma \tau}{(A,\Sigma) \vdash x : \tau}$
APP	$\dfrac{(A,\Sigma) \vdash e_0 : \tau \to \tau' \qquad (A,\Sigma) \vdash e_1 : \tau}{(A,\Sigma) \vdash (e_0\ e_1) : \tau'}$
ABS	$\dfrac{(A + [x \mapsto \tau], \Sigma) \vdash e : \tau'}{(A,\Sigma) \vdash \lambda x.e : \tau \to \tau'}$
LET	$\dfrac{(A,\Sigma) \vdash e_0 : \tau \qquad FV(\tau, A) = \{\alpha_{\gamma_1}, \ldots, \alpha_{\gamma_k}\} \qquad (A + [x \mapsto \forall \overline{\alpha_{\gamma_k}}.\tau], \Sigma) \vdash e_1 : \tau'}{(A,\Sigma) \vdash \mathbf{let}\ x = e_0\ \mathbf{in}\ e_1 : \tau'}$
CLASS	$(A,\Sigma) \vdash \mathbf{class}\ \gamma \leq \gamma_1, \ldots, \gamma_n\ \mathbf{where}\ x_1 : \forall \alpha_\gamma.\tau_1, \ldots, x_k : \forall \alpha_\gamma.\tau_k :$ $(A + [x_i \mapsto \forall \alpha_\gamma.\tau_i \mid i = 1..k], \Sigma + \{\gamma \leq \gamma_j \mid j = 1..n\})$
INST	$\dfrac{A(x_i) = \forall \alpha_\gamma.\tau_i \qquad (A,\Sigma) \vdash e_i : \tau_i[\chi(\overline{\alpha_{\gamma_n}})/\alpha_\gamma] \qquad i = 1..k}{(A,\Sigma) \vdash \mathbf{inst}\ \chi : (\overline{\gamma_n})\gamma\ \mathbf{where}\ x_1 = e_1, \ldots, x_k = e_k : (A, \Sigma + \chi : (\overline{\gamma_n})\gamma)}$
PROG	$\dfrac{(A_{i-1}, \Sigma_{i-1}) \vdash d_i : (A_i, \Sigma_i) \qquad i = 1..n \qquad (A_n, \Sigma_n) \vdash e : \tau}{(A_0, \Sigma_0) \vdash d_1; \ldots; d_n; e : \tau}$

Figure 2: Type inference rules

If no class and instance declarations are present,

$$\Sigma_0 = (\{\Omega\}, \{\Omega \leq \Omega\}, \{int : \Omega, float : \Omega, char : \Omega, list : (\Omega)\Omega, pair : (\Omega^2)\Omega, \_ \to \_ : (\Omega^2)\Omega\})$$

is the trivial order-sorted signature, and from the facts mentioned above it is clear that we have

Lemma 3.1 *For a Mini-Haskell expression e without class and instance declarations, our system and Damas-Milner compute the same type:*

$$A_0 \vdash_{DM'} e : \tau \;\Leftrightarrow\; (A_0, \Sigma_0) \vdash_{NS} e : \tau$$

where A_0 is any initial set of type assumptions.

The rules CLASS and INST are of course at the heart of our inference system, although they are remarkably simple. Both rules are of the form $(A, \Sigma) \vdash d : (A', \Sigma')$, thus declarations do not have a type, but extend a given set of type assumptions and a given signature.

The declaration **class** $\gamma \leq \gamma_1, \ldots, \gamma_n$ **where** $x_1 : \forall \alpha_\gamma.\tau_1, \ldots, x_k : \forall \alpha_\gamma.\tau_k$ introduces a new class γ, which should not have been declared before. This class is added to Σ by extending the ordering with $\gamma \leq \gamma_i$ for all super-classes γ_i of γ. For all overloaded identifiers x_i introduced in the construct, their generic type scheme $\forall \alpha_\gamma.\tau_i$, where τ_i should be well-formed w.r.t. Σ, is added to the set of type assumptions A. As a consequence, the x_i may be used, for example, in subsequent let-definitions. But note that they cannot be applied to real data, unless an instance of γ is declared: by the definition of generic instantiation, the instance of α must by a type of sort γ. Without instance declarations for γ, the only types of this sort are type variables! It should be pointed out that because the context A associates at most one type with any identifier, different declarations of the same identifier overwrite each other. In particular it means that if there are two classes which share some of their method names x_i, only those of the latter class are visible — there is a limit to the amount of overloading that can be expressed.

```
class Eq a where (==) ::  a -> a -> bool
class Eq a => Num a where ...
instance Eq char where (==) = eqChar
instance Eq a => Eq [a] where
   [] == []        =  true
   [] == x:xs      =  false
   x:xs == []      =  false
   x:xs == y:ys    =  (x==y) & (xs == ys)
['a','b','c'] == ['d','e','f']
```

Figure 3: An example program

This is in contrast to some object-oriented languages, but agrees with the Haskell definition and in a canonical way resolves naming problems caused by multiple inheritance.

Typing **inst** $\chi : (\overline{\gamma_n})\gamma$ **where** $x_1 = e_1, \ldots, x_k = e_k$ requires that the x_i have some generic type $A(x_i) = \forall\alpha_\gamma.\tau_i$. Thus, no instance declaration is allowed without a corresponding class declaration. In Section 6 a stronger context condition is imposed: the x_i defined in an instance must be exactly those declared in the enclosing class declaration for γ. The type constructor χ is declared to be in class γ, provided its arguments are in classes $\gamma_1, \ldots, \gamma_n$. Hence the instance declaration extends Σ with the declaration $\chi : (\overline{\gamma_n})\gamma$. Note that w.r.t. the extended Σ there are now type terms of sort γ which are not type variables, hence the x_i can now be applied to values of type χ. The e_i need to have the type obtained by replacing the α_γ in their generic type $\forall\alpha_\gamma.\tau_i$ by $\chi(\overline{\alpha_{\gamma_n}})$. Note that our language does not have explicit recursion. If it did, the e_i could be referring to the very instances of the x_i they define. In that case each e_i would need to be typed in the extended signature as well:

$$(A, \Sigma + \chi : (\overline{\gamma_n})\gamma) \vdash e_i : \tau_i[\chi(\overline{\alpha_{\gamma_n}})/\alpha_\gamma] \tag{1}$$

Finally, the rule PROG simply states that the type of a program is the same as the type of its constituting expression, provided this expression is typed in the extended signature and type assumptions which have been produced by the declarations. Note that according to this rule a function definition in an instance declaration cannot refer to functions from subsequent classes. This is however allowed in Haskell and would require that all e_i in all instance declarations are typed in the final signature Σ_n; for the sake of readability, we stick to the simpler system.

4 Some examples

Figure 3 shows a small Haskell program (adapted from [14]) in concrete syntax. The translation into Mini-Haskell is straightforward.

The type constants $int : \Omega$ and $char : \Omega$ are assumed to be predefined, as well as *eqInt* and *eqChar*, which have type $int \to int \to bool$ resp. $char \to char \to bool$[7]. Upon analysis of the second instance declaration, the signature contains the sorts Ω, Eq and Num, where $Num < Eq < \Omega$, and *char* has the additional sort Eq. The type assumptions are just $[(==) \mapsto \forall\alpha_{Eq}.\alpha_{Eq} \to \alpha_{Eq} \to bool]$. The second instance declaration causes a new arity of the type constructor *list* to be added to the signature, namely $list : (Eq)Eq$.

[7] The standard Haskell prelude defines *char* to be an instance of *Enum* and *int* to be an instance of *Num*, but for reasons of presentation we assume that all type constructors have default sort Ω. Of course, our system can handle the real situation as well.

Before we look at the type inference for the second instance declaration in detail, we trace the simpler problem `['a','b','c'] == ['d','e','f']`. Since character literals have type *char* in Haskell, both lists have type *list*(*char*). The order-sorted nature of the problem becomes important only with the application of "==". According to TAUT, the type of "==" must be an instance of $\alpha_{Eq} \rightarrow \alpha_{Eq} \rightarrow bool$. According to APP, α_{Eq} must be unified with *list*(*char*). Since the current signature contains the declarations *char* : *Eq* and *list* : (*Eq*)*Eq*, *list*(*char*) is of sort *Eq* and the resulting CSU is the substitution $\{\alpha_{Eq} \mapsto list(char)\}$. A similar unification is needed for the second argument of "==", and we can infer that this particular use of "==" has type $list(char) \rightarrow list(char) \rightarrow bool$. Note that the actual overloading resolution is performed by the unification algorithm: the arities of type constructors used during unifications determine the instance to be used. In our example the second instance of "==" is identified, since the inferred instance of "=="'s generic type uses the arity of list which was introduced through the second instance declaration. If the second instance declaration were missing, *list*(*char*) could not have sort *Eq*, thus the above unification would fail and the last line would not be typable.

The body of the second instance declaration translates into something like the following Mini-Haskell definition:

```
(==) = fix(λeql.λx.λy.
            if(null x, null y, if(null y, false,
                                  hd x == hd y & eql (tl x) (tl y))))
```

The lack of pattern matching and recursion forces us to use the fixpoint combinator `fix`. This simplifies the typing problem, since there is no recursive use of "==". To make this example more interesting, we ignore the translation and type check the original code using the modified INST rule shown in (1). We must infer that the definition of "==" has type $list(\alpha_{Eq}) \rightarrow list(\alpha_{Eq}) \rightarrow bool$, which is the specific instance of the generic type of "==" required here. For the first three clauses this is immediate. Now consider the last one. From the use of ":" we can infer that *xs* and *ys* have type $list(\alpha_\Omega)$. A similar computation as above will then determine that in the second recursive call "==" has type $list(\alpha_{Eq}) \rightarrow list(\alpha_{Eq}) \rightarrow bool$. For the first recursive call, the situation is more tricky. Since we do not know anything about the types of x and y, their initial type is α_Ω. Unification with the argument type of the generic type of "==" will weaken this to α_{Eq}. Hence this use of "==" has type $\alpha_{Eq} \rightarrow \alpha_{Eq} \rightarrow bool$. As this type contains free type variables not of sort Ω, we cannot resolve overloading and do not know which instance of "==" to use for the comparison of list elements; this decision must be postponed until runtime. But we can at least successfully type the definition, because we now know that the arguments are lists with elements of sort *Eq*, and the result type is *bool*.

If we want to type `[1,2,3]==[4,5,6]`, we have a different situation. In Haskell, integer literals have any numeric type, and type inference will thus infer the type $list(\alpha_{Num})$ for both lists. Since *Num* is a subsort of *Eq*, the unification of α_{Eq} with $list(\alpha_{Num})$ is possible, and the expression can be typed. This mirrors the fact that a subclass inherits all functions of its superclasses (thus "==" is automatically defined for integer literals). In the absence of the second class declaration, there is no sort-correct unifier, and the expression is not typable.

Now consider the (illegal!) program

```
class γ1 ...
class γ2 ...
class δ1 a where f ::  a -> bool
class δ1 a => δ2 a where ...
instance γ1 a => δ1 [a] where f = ...
instance γ2 a => δ2 [a] where ...
λx.f [x]
```

Suppose *int* is a member of γ_2. Hence $list(int)$ is a member of δ_2 and hence of δ_1. According to the type system, f is defined on objects of type $list(int)$. But the program does not define its value, since the only f that is defined requires its argument to be of type $list(\alpha_{\gamma_1})$! This incoherence is reflected in our system as follows. The expression $\lambda x.f[x]$ has to be typed in the regular signature with sort ordering $\gamma_1 \leq \Omega$, $\gamma_2 \leq \Omega$, $\delta_2 \leq \delta_1$ and declarations $list : (\gamma_1)\delta_1$ and $list : (\gamma_2)\delta_2$, and under type assumption $[f \mapsto \forall\alpha_{\delta_1}.\alpha_{\delta_1} \rightarrow bool]$. This leads to the unification problem $list(\alpha_\Omega) =^? \beta_{\delta_1}$ which has the two solutions $\{\alpha_\Omega \mapsto \alpha_{\gamma_1}, \beta_{\delta_1} \mapsto list(\alpha_{\gamma_1})\}$ and $\{\alpha_\Omega \mapsto \alpha_{\gamma_2}, \beta_{\delta_1} \mapsto list(\alpha_{\gamma_2})\}$. These two solutions are incomparable (because γ_1 and γ_2 are), and there is no solution subsuming both of them. Hence $\lambda x.f[x]$ has the two types $\alpha_{\gamma_1} \rightarrow bool$ and $\alpha_{\gamma_2} \rightarrow bool$. This ambiguity is caused by the second instance declaration which also violates a Haskell context condition [6, p. 27]. Thus the above incoherence reveals itself by the absence of a principal type. The next section introduces restrictions similar to those in Haskell which ensure the existence of principal types. As Section 6 shows, principal types help to ensure semantic well-definedness.

5 Computing principal types

The type inference system gives rise to an algorithm, just by reading the rules backwards. In fact, we have implemented our overloading resolution in Prolog. If an expression has several incomparable types, our Prolog program will compute them one by one upon backtracking. The termination of this algorithm is obvious (provided unifications are finitary), since every rule decomposes an abstract syntax tree into its components. Instead of guessing the required instantiation in TAUT, it is inferred by order-sorted unification. This raises certain computability questions.

Theorem 2.2 states that regularity implies finiteness and decidability of order-sorted unification. Unfortunately, we have no guarantee that the signature built up during type inference is regular. In fact, in many cases it will not be. However, by going to the powerset of sorts, regularity can be achieved. Furthermore, we show that two semantically motivated context conditions lead to unitary signatures, i.e. principal types exist.

The main idea for regularity is quite trivial: two classes γ_1 and γ_2 can always be combined to form a subclass $\gamma = \gamma_1 \wedge \gamma_2$ of both of them which provides the union of the operations available in each of them. In fact, this can already be done inside the language by writing

$$\textbf{class}\ \gamma \leq \gamma_1, \gamma_2\ \textbf{where}\ ;$$

The idea of conjunctive sorts[8] can be integrated into the framework by defining a new set of sorts $\hat{S}$, the set of all non-empty sets of incomparable class names, and imposing the following ordering on them:

$$S_1 \preceq S_2 \Leftrightarrow \forall s_2 \in S_2\ \exists s_1 \in S_1.\ s_1 \leq s_2$$

This gives rise to a lower semi-lattice $(\hat{S}, \preceq)$, the free lower semi-lattice on the poset $(S, \leq)$, where $S_1 \wedge S_2 = S_1 \cup S_2$ if S_1 and S_2 are incomparable. In Haskell this extension is expressed by multiple class assertions for type variables.

Conjunctive sorts alone do not guarantee regularity. It is also necessary to realize that the behaviour of type constructors on $\gamma_1 \wedge \gamma_2$ is determined by their behaviour on γ_1 and γ_2. More precisely, we can add a closure condition to signatures:

$$\frac{\chi : (\overline{\gamma_n})\gamma \quad \chi : (\overline{\delta_n})\delta}{\chi : (\overline{\gamma_n \wedge \delta_n})\gamma \wedge \delta} \tag{2}$$

[8] By analogy with conjunctive *types*, first explored by Coppo et al. [2].

which tells us that type constructors are homomorphisms w.r.t. conjunction. Again, there is a corresponding construction inside the language. Given

$$\textbf{inst}\ \chi : (\gamma_1)\gamma\ \textbf{where}\ x = e;$$
$$\textbf{inst}\ \chi : (\delta_1)\delta\ \textbf{where}\ x' = e';$$

we can add **inst** $\chi : (\gamma_1 \wedge \delta_1)\gamma \wedge \delta$ **where** ;.

Conjunctive sorts together with the homomorphism condition (2) guarantee regularity: either the set defined in Theorem 2.1 is empty, or its least element is the conjunction of all its elements.

For reasons of space we do not present the type inference rules in terms of conjunctive sorts. Instead we assume that the user or the system provide the required additional class and instance declarations shown above.

Regularity alone does not ensure the existence of principal types, as we have seen in the last example of the previous section. According to Theorem 2.2, it at least guarantees finite complete sets of types, a familiar picture for languages with classes and inheritance [16]. The ambiguity in that example is ruled out by subsort reflection as defined in Section 2. It follows from Corollary 2.4 that the extended system with conjunctive sorts has principal types if injectivity and subsort reflection are enforced. In Haskell this is indeed the case. Section 4.3.2 of the Haskell Report states that "A type may not be declared as an instance of a particular class more than once in the same scope", which is equivalent to injectivity. The same section, at the bottom of page 27, introduces a context condition which amounts to the following: if $\gamma_1, \ldots, \gamma_m$ are the immediate super-classes of δ, a declaration **inst** $\chi : (\overline{\delta_n})\delta$ must be preceded by declarations **inst** $\chi : (\overline{\gamma_n^i})\gamma_i$ such that δ_j is a subclass of γ_j^i for all $i = 1 \ldots m$ and $j = 1 \ldots n$. Any signature built up from such a sequence of declarations is easily seen to be subsort reflecting. It follows that imposing these two conditions on Mini-Haskell guarantees the existence of principal types. However, we will see in Section 6 that principal types do not preclude semantic ambiguity.

6 Translation

So far nothing has been said about the semantics of our language. This will be given by a translation into a well-understood sub-language consisting just of identifiers, abstraction, application and **let** — essentially Mini-ML [1]. Type classes and instances are eliminated in favour of so called *(method) dictionaries* which contain all the functions associated with a class. The scheme presented below generalizes ideas from [14], and the reader should consult this article for intuition and examples.

The formal definition of the translation in terms of inference rules is given in Figure 4. For an expression e, the judgement $(A, \Sigma) \vdash e : \tau \leadsto e'$ should be pronounced "in the context (A, Σ) e has type τ and translates to e'". Declarations produce a **let**-expression without body, which introduces dictionaries and access functions. Thus, in the notation $(A, \Sigma) \vdash d : (A', \Sigma') \leadsto d'$, d' is of the form **let** $x_1 = e_1, ..., x_j = e_j$.

The effect of the translation can best be explained in terms of types. In the following we use the phrase "ML-type" to distinguish the translated types from the original ones which may contain sorted type variables. Below we show how the declaration of a class γ gives rise to an ML-type $\gamma(\alpha)$ of γ-dictionaries, where α is the instance type. Assuming $\gamma(\alpha)$ we define

$$ML(\forall \overline{\alpha_{\gamma_k}}.\tau) \;=\; \forall \overline{\alpha_k}.\gamma_1(\alpha_1) \to \cdots \to \gamma_k(\alpha_k) \to \tau[\alpha_1/\alpha_{\gamma_1}, \ldots, \alpha_k/\alpha_{\gamma_k}]$$

which translates order-sorted types to ML-types: type restrictions are turned into additional dictionary arguments. This means that the translation of a function definition has to provide abstractions for these new arguments and the application has to provide corresponding dictionary arguments.

TAUT $$\frac{A(x) = \forall\overline{\alpha_{\gamma_k}}.\tau}{(A,\Sigma) \vdash x : \tau[\tau_1/\alpha_{\gamma_1},\ldots,\tau_k/\alpha_{\gamma_k}] \leadsto (x\ \mathsf{dict}_\Sigma(\tau_1,\gamma_1)\ \ldots\ \mathsf{dict}_\Sigma(\tau_k,\gamma_k))}$$

APP $$\frac{(A,\Sigma)\vdash e_0 : \tau \to \tau' \leadsto e_0' \qquad (A,\Sigma)\vdash e_1 : \tau \leadsto e_1'}{(A,\Sigma)\vdash (e_0\ e_1) : \tau' \leadsto (e_0'\ e_1')}$$

ABS $$\frac{(A + [x \mapsto \tau],\Sigma)\vdash e : \tau' \leadsto e'}{(A,\Sigma)\vdash \lambda x.e : \tau \to \tau' \leadsto \lambda x.e'}$$

LET $$\frac{(A,\Sigma)\vdash e_0 : \tau \leadsto e_0' \quad FV(\tau,A) = \{\overline{\alpha_{\gamma_k}}\} \quad (A + [x \mapsto \forall\overline{\alpha_{\gamma_k}}.\tau],\Sigma)\vdash e_1 : \tau' \leadsto e_1'}{(A,\Sigma)\vdash \mathbf{let}\ x = e_0\ \mathbf{in}\ e_1 : \tau' \leadsto \mathbf{let}\ x = \lambda\overline{\alpha_{\gamma_k}}.e_0'\ \mathbf{in}\ e_1'}$$

CLASS
$$\begin{array}{l}(A,\Sigma)\vdash \mathbf{class}\ \gamma \le \gamma_1,\ldots,\gamma_n\ \mathbf{where}\ x_1 : \forall\alpha_\gamma.\tau_1,\ldots,x_k : \forall\alpha_\gamma.\tau_k : \\ \qquad (A + [x_i \mapsto \forall\alpha_\gamma.\tau_i \mid i = 1..k], \Sigma + \{\gamma \le \gamma_j \mid j = 1..n\}) \\ \qquad \leadsto \mathbf{let} x_1 = \pi_1^{k+n},\ldots,x_k = \pi_k^{k+n},\ \gamma_{1_\gamma} = \pi_{k+1}^{k+n},\ldots,\gamma_{n_\gamma} = \pi_{k+n}^{k+n}\end{array}$$

INST
$$\frac{\begin{array}{c}\mathsf{super}_\Sigma(\gamma) = \{\gamma^1,\ldots,\gamma^s\} \\ A(x_i) = \forall\alpha_\gamma.\tau_i \qquad (A,\Sigma)\vdash e_i : \tau_i[\chi(\overline{\alpha_{\gamma_n}})/\alpha_\gamma] \leadsto e_i' \qquad i = 1..k\end{array}}{\begin{array}{l}(A,\Sigma)\vdash \mathbf{inst}\ \chi : (\overline{\gamma_n})\gamma\ \mathbf{where}\ x_1 = e_1,\ldots,x_k = e_k : (A, \Sigma + \chi : (\overline{\gamma_n})\gamma) \\ \quad \leadsto \mathbf{let}\ \gamma_\chi = \lambda\overline{\alpha_{\gamma_n}}.\,(e_1',\ldots,e_k', \\ \qquad\qquad (\gamma_\chi^1\ \mathsf{cast}_\Sigma(\alpha_{\gamma_1},\gamma_1^1)\ \ldots\ \mathsf{cast}_\Sigma(\alpha_{\gamma_n},\gamma_n^1)), \\ \qquad\qquad \vdots \\ \qquad\qquad (\gamma_\chi^s\ \mathsf{cast}_\Sigma(\alpha_{\gamma_1},\gamma_1^s)\ \ldots\ \mathsf{cast}_\Sigma(\alpha_{\gamma_n},\gamma_n^s)))\end{array}}$$

PROG $$\frac{(A_{i-1},\Sigma_{i-1})\vdash d_i : (A_i,\Sigma_i) \leadsto d_i' \quad i = 1..n \qquad (A_n,\Sigma_n)\vdash e : \tau \leadsto e'}{(A_0,\Sigma_0)\vdash d_1;\ldots;d_n;e : \tau \leadsto d_1'\ \mathbf{in} \ldots \mathbf{in}\ d_n'\ \mathbf{in}\ e'}$$

Figure 4: Translation of expressions

The target language has the following special features: it contains all n-ary product types $\alpha_1 * \cdots * \alpha_n$, with values $(a_1,\ldots,a_n)$ and projection functions $\pi_i^n : \alpha_1 * \cdots * \alpha_n \to \alpha_i$. In addition to ordinary identifiers (x) the translation introduces α_γ (parameter representing γ-dictionaries), γ_χ (γ-dictionary for type χ), and γ_δ (function extracting the γ-dictionary from a δ-dictionary).

We go through the rules one by one.

Conceptually, a class declaration **class** $\gamma \le \gamma_1,\ldots,\gamma_n$ **where** $x_1 : \forall\alpha_\gamma.\tau_1,\ldots,x_k : \forall\alpha_\gamma.\tau_k$ introduces a new dictionary of ML-type

$$\gamma(\alpha) = \tau_1[\alpha/\alpha_\gamma] * \cdots * \tau_k[\alpha/\alpha_\gamma] * \gamma_1(\alpha) * \cdots * \gamma_n(\alpha) \tag{3}$$

The type parameter α stands for the type of the instance. The first k components of $\gamma(\alpha)$ are the functions added in the declaration of class γ. The next n components are the dictionaries for all immediate super-classes of γ. Note that $\Omega(\alpha)$ is the empty product type.

Instead of defining this ML-type explicitly, the translation just defines the relevant access functions: x_i accesses the i-th component and hence the instance of function x_i; γ_{j_γ} accesses the super-dictionary corresponding to the super-class γ_j, i.e. γ_{j_γ} takes a γ dictionary and returns a γ_j dictionary.

An instance declaration **inst** $\chi : (\overline{\gamma_n})\gamma$ **where** $x_1 = e_1,\ldots,x_k = e_k$ introduces γ_χ of ML-type

$$\forall\overline{\alpha_n}.\gamma_1(\alpha_1) \to \cdots \to \gamma_n(\alpha_n) \to \gamma(\chi(\overline{\alpha_n})).$$

Given the required dictionaries for the arguments $\overline{\alpha_n}$ of χ, γ_χ produces a dictionary of ML-type $\gamma(\chi(\overline{\alpha_n}))$. The λ-bound variables $\overline{\alpha_{\gamma_n}}$ represent the argument dictionaries. In case χ is a constant like *int* or *char*, γ_χ is a dictionary of ML-type $\gamma(\chi)$.

The first k components of the result type $\gamma(\chi(\overline{\alpha_n}))$ are the translated expressions defining the methods x_1 to x_k. Since e_i has type $\tau_i[\chi(\overline{\alpha_{\gamma_n}})/\alpha_\gamma]$, the expression e_i' depends on n dictionaries of ML-type $\gamma_j(\alpha_j)$, $j = 1..n$. By some mechanism that is explained in connection with the translation of identifiers, this implies that e_i' contains free variables $\overline{\alpha_{\gamma_n}}$ waiting to be instantiated with dictionaries.

The last s components are the dictionaries of the immediate super-classes of γ:

$$\mathsf{super}_\Sigma(\gamma) \;=\; \{\gamma' \mid \gamma < \gamma' \wedge \nexists \delta.\ \gamma < \delta < \gamma'\}$$

At this point we assume that the current expression is in the scope of χ instance declarations for all γ^1 to γ^s (context condition 3 below). Hence the dictionary generators γ^j_χ have been defined. However, they may not expect dictionaries for the classes $\overline{\gamma_n}$, but for some super-classes thereof. Therefore the relevant super-dictionaries need to be extracted from the $\overline{\alpha_{\gamma_n}}$: if $\gamma \leq_\Sigma \gamma'$, $\mathsf{cast}_\Sigma(\alpha_\gamma, \gamma')$ expands into an expression which does just that by inserting the appropriate sequence of coercers which have been defined by the translation of the class declarations for all the classes between γ and γ'.

$$\mathsf{cast}_\Sigma(\alpha_\gamma, \gamma') \;=\; \begin{cases} \alpha_\gamma & \text{if } \gamma = \gamma' \\ (\gamma'_\delta\ \mathsf{cast}_\Sigma(\alpha_\gamma, \delta)) & \text{if } \gamma \leq \delta \wedge \gamma' \in \mathsf{super}_\Sigma(\delta) \end{cases}$$

If there is more than one path from γ to γ' w.r.t. $\leq_\Sigma$, cast_Σ chooses an arbitrary fixed one.

Notice that the positional scheme used for arranging the methods and the super-dictionaries in a dictionary requires some fixed ordering on both the x_i and the γ_j, e.g. lexicographic. Otherwise it is not clear in which order the x_i and γ_j appear: the signature Σ does not record this information.

The translation of an identifier in rule TAUT is determined by its use. If x has type $\forall\overline{\alpha_{\gamma_k}}.\tau$, its definition has translated into an function of ML-type $ML(\forall\overline{\alpha_{\gamma_k}}.\tau)$ which requires k dictionaries. Exactly which dictionaries are passed with this call to x is determined by the τ_i. Expanding $dict_\Sigma(\tau, \gamma)$ produces the code representing the dictionary of ML-type $\gamma(\tau)$ as defined in (3).

$$\begin{aligned} \mathsf{dict}_\Sigma(\alpha_{\gamma'}, \gamma) &= \mathsf{cast}_\Sigma(\alpha_{\gamma'}, \gamma) \\ \mathsf{dict}_\Sigma(\chi(\tau_1, \ldots, \tau_n), \gamma) &= \gamma_\chi\ (\mathsf{dict}_\Sigma(\tau_1, \gamma_1))\ \ldots\ (\mathsf{dict}_\Sigma(\tau_n, \gamma_n)) \quad \text{where } \chi \in \Sigma_{\tau_1 \ldots \tau_n, \tau} \end{aligned}$$

It is a homomorphism which maps type constructors to their corresponding dictionary generators declared in the translation of the respective instance declarations. Type variables map to dictionary variables (with suitable coercers inserted by cast). In case x is a subexpression of e_0 in LET or of some e_i in INST, these type variables are λ-abstracted later on. Otherwise the represent a semantic ambiguity as in Example 6.1 below.

The rules APP and ABS do not need any explanation. Note that λ-bound identifiers cannot be polymorphic. Thus for such identifiers $k = 0$ in TAUT, and the identifier translates into itself.

The correctness of our translation depends on a number of context conditions:

1. No type constructor can be declared as an instance of a particular class more than once in the same scope. This is ruled out in Haskell as well [6, p. 29].
2. Each instance declaration lists exactly those x_i that the corresponding class declaration listed (and in the same order, which is simply a technical device). This means that operations of super-classes cannot be redefined in subclasses. A more sophisticated translation scheme can easily avoid this restriction.

3. Every instance declaration **inst** $\chi : (\overline{\gamma_n})\gamma$, where $\mathsf{super}_\Sigma(\gamma) = \{\gamma^1, \ldots, \gamma^s\}$ at that point, has to be nested inside instance declarations **inst** $\chi : (\overline{\gamma_n^i})\gamma^i$ for all $i = 1..s$. In particular $\overline{\gamma_n} \leq_\Sigma \overline{\gamma_n^i}$ must hold. It can be shown that this is equivalent to the context condition in Section 4.3.2 of the Haskell Report and implies subsort reflection and hence the existence of principal types.

If these conditions are violated, the translated expression may not be well-formed. Hence the original expression has no semantic meaning. But even if an expression conforms to the context conditions, can be typed and translated, it may still be regarded as ambiguous:

Example 6.1 Let $\Sigma = (\{\Omega, Eq\}, \{Eq < \Omega\}, \{list : (\Omega)\Omega, list : (Eq)Eq\})$ and $A = \{[] \mapsto \forall\alpha.list(\alpha), (==) \mapsto \forall\alpha_{Eq}.\alpha_{Eq} \to \alpha_{Eq} \to bool\}$, and $e =$ `[] == []`. Because the element type of `[]` is undetermined, it is not clear which Eq-dictionary should be passed to `==`, and hence e is ambiguous. Nevertheless, we have $(A, \Sigma) \vdash e : bool \leadsto$ `(==)` α_{Eq} `[] []` where the free variable α_{Eq} signifies an undetermined dictionary.

Haskell deals with this problem by inferring the type `Eq a => bool` for e, concluding that e is ambiguous because the class assumption `Eq a` contains a type variable `a` not present in the type `bool` [6, p. 30].

In our approach the ambiguity reveals itself by looking at the translation which contains the free variable α_{Eq} not present in *bool*.

The final theorem shows that the inferred types and the semantics given by the translation fit together. Let $ML(A) = \{x \mapsto ML(\sigma) \mid A(x) = \sigma\}$

Theorem 6.2 *Let all types in the range of A be closed. If* $(A, \Sigma) \vdash_{NS} e : \tau \leadsto e'$ *and* $FV(\tau) = FV(e') - FV(e) = \{\alpha_{\gamma_1}, \ldots, \alpha_{\gamma_n}\}$, *then* $ML(A) \vdash_{DM} \lambda\overline{\alpha_{\gamma_n}}.e' : ML(\forall\overline{\alpha_{\gamma_n}}.\tau)$.

Roughly speaking, this says that the if e has type τ, the translation e' of e has the translated type $ML(\tau)$. The implication is trivial if $FV(\tau) \neq FV(e') - FV(e)$. This is precisely the case if e' contains a free dictionary variable α_γ not free in τ, which in turn corresponds exactly to the Haskell ambiguity definition quoted in Example 6.1 above. Hence we know that the type of unambiguous expressions matches their semantics.

7 Conclusion

We have presented a type inference system and algorithm for a Haskell-like language, which is based on order-sorted unification. In contrast to the type system of Wadler and Blott [14] and a similar system by Kaes [7][9], our system is the first one to utilize full order-sorted unification. It grew out of efforts to integrate polymorphism into a generic theorem prover [10] which required more control over the instantiation of type variables than is available in ML. A weaker form of order-sorted unification is also used in the concept of context relations [13] which is a generic and incremental type inference mechanism and can be used for the resolution of user-defined overloading as for example in ADA [5]. But context relations do not allow user-defined classes: the signature must be fixed at language definition time.

Acknowledgements The first author would like to thank Uwe Waldmann for e-mail consultations and Eugenio Moggi and Larry Paulson for detailed comments. The second author would like to thank Stefan Kaes for stimulating discussions. We are grateful to Mark Lillibridge and Stephen Blott who pointed out some subtle errors in a previous version of this paper.

[9] Kaes' language does not have explicit type classes; such classes arise only implicitly.

References

[1] D. Clément, J. Despeyroux, T. Despeyroux, and G. Kahn. A simple applicative language: Mini-ML. In *Proc. ACM Conf. Lisp and Functional Programming*, pages 13–27, 1986.

[2] M. Coppo, M. Dezani-Ciancaglini, and B. Venneri. Principal type schemes and λ-calculus semantics. In R. Hindley and J. Seldin, editors, *To H.B. Curry: Essays on Combinatory Logic, Lambda Calculus and Formalisms.* Academic Press, 1980.

[3] L. Damas and R. Milner. Principal type schemes for functional programs. In *Proc. 9th ACM Symp. Principles of Programming Languages*, pages 207–212, 1982.

[4] K. Futatsugi, J. Goguen, J.-P. Jouannaud, and J. Meseguer. Principles of OBJ2. In *Proc. 12th ACM Symp. Principles of Programming Languages*, pages 52–66, 1985.

[5] F. Grosch and G. Snelting. Inference-based overloading resolution for ADA. In *Proc. 2nd Conf. Programming Language Implementation and Logic Programming*, pages 30–44. LNCS 456, 1990.

[6] P. Hudak and P. Wadler. Report on the programming language Haskell. Version 1.0, April 1990.

[7] S. Kaes. Parametric overloading in polymorphic programming languages. In *Proc. 2nd European Symposium on Programming*, pages 131–144. LNCS 300, 1988.

[8] J. Meseguer, J. Goguen, and G. Smolka. Order-sorted unification. *J. Symbolic Computation*, 8:383–413, 1989.

[9] R. Milner, M. Tofte, and R. Harper. *The Definition of Standard ML.* MIT Press, 1990.

[10] T. Nipkow. Higher-order unification, polymorphism, and subsorts. In *Proc. 2nd Int. Workshop Conditional and Typed Rewriting Systems.* LNCS ???, 1990.

[11] M. Schmidt-Schauß. A many-sorted calculus with polymorphic functions based on resolution and paramodulation. In *Proc. 9th Int. Joint Conf. Artificial Intelligence*, pages 1162–1168, 1985.

[12] G. Smolka, W. Nutt, J. Goguen, and J. Meseguer. Order-sorted equational computation. In H. Aït-Kaci and M. Nivat, editors, *Resolution of Equations in Algebraic Structures, Volume 2*, pages 297–367. Academic Press, 1989.

[13] G. Snelting. The calculus of context relations. *Acta Informatica*, 1991. To appear.

[14] P. Wadler and S. Blott. How to make *ad-hoc* polymorphism less *ad hoc*. In *Proc. 16th ACM Symp. Principles of Programming Languages*, pages 60–76, 1989.

[15] U. Waldmann. Unification in order-sorted signatures. Technical Report 298, Fachbereich Informatik, Universität Dortmund, 1989.

[16] M. Wand. Type inference for record concatenation and multiple inheritance. In *Proc. 4th IEEE Symp. Logic in Computer Science*, pages 92–97, 1989.

On the Complexity of ML Typability with Overloading

Dennis M. Volpano and Geoffrey S. Smith[1]

Department of Computer Science
Cornell University
Ithaca, New York 14853 USA

ABSTRACT

We examine the complexity of type checking in an ML-style type system that permits functions to be overloaded with different types. In particular, we consider the extension of the ML type system proposed by Wadler and Blott in the appendix of [WB89], with global overloading only, that is, where the only overloading is that which exists in an initial type assumption set; no local overloading via **over** and **inst** expressions is allowed. It is shown that under a correct notion of well-typed terms, the problem of determining whether a term is well typed with respect to an assumption set in this system is undecidable. We then investigate limiting recursion in assumption sets, the source of the undecidability. Barring mutual recursion is considered, but this proves too weak, for the problem remains undecidable. Then we consider a limited form of recursion called *parametric recursion*. We show that although the problem becomes decidable under parametric recursion, it appears harder than conventional ML typability, which is complete for DEXPTIME [Mai90].

1. Introduction

A rather obvious limitation of the Hindley-Milner type system [Hin69, Mil78, DM82] is that it does not allow an identifier to be *overloaded*, that is, to possess more than one assumption in a type assumption set. For example, we may want equality to possess precisely types $Int \rightarrow Int \rightarrow Bool$ and $Char \rightarrow Char \rightarrow Bool$, but in the Hindley-Milner type discipline, there is no type assumption set from which we can deduce all and only these types for equality. For this reason, languages whose type systems are based on the Hindley-Milner system are forced to avoid overloading altogether, as in Miranda

[1] The authors acknowledge joint support from the NSF and DARPA under grant ASC-88-00465.

[Tur86], or allow it but fix the set of overloaded operators, as in Standard ML [HMT88].

Wadler and Blott, in the appendix of [WB89], present an extension of the Hindley-Milner type system that incorporates overloading. The system is the basis for the type system of Haskell, a functional programming language aimed at providing a more standardized notation for the functional programming language community [HW90]. But unlike an earlier extension proposed by Kaes [Kae88], their type system has a new form of type, called a *predicated type*, and allows more expressive type assumption sets. The computational consequences of this increased expressiveness are explored in this paper.

The language considered by Wadler and Blott in the design of their type system is core ML [MH88] with two new kinds of expressions, **over** and **inst**, for overloading identifiers locally. The language we consider is just core ML, so all overloading has global scope, and is introduced through an initial type assumption set only. We call Wadler and Blott's type system without the inference rules for **over** and **inst** system WB.

2. System WB

Given a set of type variables $\{\alpha, \beta, \gamma, \ldots\}$ and type constructors $\{\chi$, *Int*, *Char*, *Set*, *List*, *Pair* ,... $\}$, the types of system WB are defined by

Types	$\tau \ ::= \alpha \mid \tau \to \tau' \mid \chi\,(\tau_1, \ldots, \tau_n)$
Predicated types	$\rho \ ::= (x :: \tau).\, \rho \mid \tau$
Type schemes	$\sigma \ ::= \forall\alpha.\, \sigma \mid \rho$

The parentheses of χ are omitted if it has no arguments. The term $(x :: \tau)$ is called a *predicate* and is viewed as a restriction stating that x has type τ . The τ-describable part of a type scheme is referred to as its type part, or body.

2.1. Type assumption sets

Type checking is done in the context of a set of assumptions which bind type information to the free identifiers in an expression. Wadler and Blott also require type assumptions to specify translations of overloaded identifiers, but we omit them here for they are not relevant to our discussion. An assumption set may contain multiple assumptions per identifier, called *instance assumptions*, each of which is designated $::_i$. All types appearing in the instance assumptions for an identifier are specializations of a single type given in an *overload assumption*, designated $::_o$, for the identifier. All assumption sets in WB must be *valid*, a property whose definition depends on a notion of overlapping type schemes.

Definition. (overlap). Two type schemes σ and σ' overlap if there exists a type τ and a valid set of assumptions A such that $\sigma \geq_A \tau$ and $\sigma' \geq_A \tau$. We write $\sigma \# \sigma'$ if σ and σ' do not overlap.

The definition of overlap is given in terms of the instance relation $\geq_A$, but it need not be, for it is equivalent, under a renaming of bound variables, to merely a test for whether the type parts of two schemes are unifiable.

Theorem 2.1. *Two type schemes, each with bound variables not occurring free or bound in the other, overlap if and only if their type parts are unifiable.*

Proof. Let $\sigma = \forall\alpha_1 \cdots \forall\alpha_m . \rho . \tau$ and $\sigma' = \forall\beta_1 \cdots \forall\beta_n . \rho' . \tau'$ such that α_i is not in σ' and β_i is not in σ.

(only if). Suppose σ and σ' overlap. Then there is a valid assumption set A and type γ such that $\sigma \geq_A \gamma$ and $\sigma' \geq_A \gamma$. By the definition of $\geq_A$, then, there are substitutions $S = [\alpha_1 := \tau_1, \ldots, \alpha_m := \tau_m]$ and $S' = [\beta_1 := \tau_1', \ldots, \beta_n := \tau_n']$ such that $\tau S = \gamma$ and $\tau' S' = \gamma$ (we write the application of a substitution to a term in postfix notation). Thus, $\tau S S' = \tau' S S'$, or τ and τ' are unifiable.

(if). Suppose there is a substitution S such that $\tau S = \tau' S = \gamma$. Let A be an assumption set formed by adding to it $x ::_o \forall\alpha.\alpha$ and $x ::_i \Pi$ for each $x :: \Pi$ in $(\rho \cup \rho')S$. $\Pi_i \# \Pi_j$, whenever $\Pi_i \neq \Pi_j$, so A is valid. Since $\tau S = \gamma$ and $A \vdash \rho S$, $\sigma \geq_A \gamma$. Likewise, $\tau' S = \gamma$ and $A \vdash \rho' S$, so $\sigma' \geq_A \gamma$. Thus, σ and σ' overlap.

Therefore we adopt a much simpler test for whether two type schemes overlap, one that only requires renaming their bound variables so that no bound variable of one occurs in the other and then checking to see if their type parts are unifiable.

Definition. (valid assumption set). The empty set is valid. Let A be a valid assumption set, x an identifier that does not appear in A, and σ a type scheme. Then $A, x :: \sigma$ is valid. If $\tau_1 ,\ldots, \tau_m$ are types and $\sigma_1 , \ldots , \sigma_n$ are type schemes such that

$$\sigma \geq_A \sigma_i \text{, for } 1 \leq i \leq n \text{, and}$$
$$\sigma \geq_A \tau_i \text{, for } 1 \leq i \leq m \text{, and}$$
$$\sigma_i \# \sigma_j \text{ for } i \neq j \text{ and } 1 \leq i, j \leq n$$

then

$$A,\ x ::_o \sigma\ ,$$
$$x ::_i \sigma_1 , \ldots , x ::_i \sigma_n\ ,$$
$$x :: \tau_1 , \ldots , x :: \tau_m$$

is a valid assumption set.

The types given to each overloaded identifier in a valid assumption set are pairwise nonoverlapping. This restriction guarantees that any type for an overloaded identifier has at most one derivation in WB, thus ensuring that each resolved occurrence of the identifier in an expression has a unique translation.

A predicated type enables one to assert, via an instance assumption, that an identifier has a certain type provided that the identifier itself has some other type. We characterize those assumption sets in which this capability is exploited as *recursive*.

Definition. (recursive assumption set). Let R be a binary relation on the identifiers of an assumption set A such that $g\ R\ h$ if and only if there is an instance assumption about g in A with a predicate involving h (g and h may be the same identifier). Then A is recursive if and only if R^+ is not irreflexive.

For example, the assumptions in Figure 1 form a valid, recursive assumption set. Under the assumptions in this set, it would be type correct to apply predicate eq to values of types such as $List(List(Int))$, $List(Pair(Int, Char))$ and so on.

2.2. Inference rules

The inference rules that we regard as part of system WB, for the purpose of this paper, are all but the rules for **over** and **inst** given in the appendix of [WB89]. These include basically the inference rules of Damas and Milner [DM82], and two new rules **PRED** and **REL**, which are given below without translation information.

$$\frac{A, (x :: \tau) \vdash e :: \rho}{A \vdash e :: (x :: \tau) . \rho} \qquad x ::_o \sigma \in A \qquad \textbf{(PRED)}$$

$$\frac{A \vdash e :: (x :: \tau) . \rho, \quad A \vdash x :: \tau}{A \vdash e : \rho} \qquad x ::_o \sigma \in A \qquad \textbf{(REL)}$$

$$\begin{aligned}
&eq ::_o \forall\alpha.\, \alpha \to \alpha \to Bool \\
&eq ::_i Int \to Int \to Bool \\
&eq ::_i Char \to Char \to Bool \\
&eq ::_i \forall\alpha.\, (eq :: \alpha \to \alpha \to Bool).\, List(\alpha) \to List(\alpha) \to Bool \\
&eq ::_i \forall\alpha.\, \forall\beta.\, (eq :: \alpha \to \alpha \to Bool).\, (eq :: \beta \to \beta \to Bool). \\
&\qquad\qquad Pair(\alpha, \beta) \to Pair(\alpha, \beta) \to Bool
\end{aligned}$$

Figure 1. A recursive assumption set.

The **PRED** rule allows an assumption about an identifier used to deduce a type for an expression to be shifted from the assumption set into the type of the expression. Eliminating, or releasing, a predicate $(x :: \tau)$ from a type relative to an assumption set A using rule **REL** requires showing $A \vdash x :: \tau$, that is, that the predicate can be *satisfied* with respect to A.

2.3. Well-typed expressions

The ability to move assumptions about overloaded identifiers from an assumption set into the type of an expression via **PRED** calls into question the notion of typability in WB. That is, when is an expression e well typed with respect to a valid assumption set A? The obvious condition is that e is well typed with respect to A if and only if

$$A \vdash e : \sigma, \quad \text{for some type scheme } \sigma. \tag{1}$$

However, this appears incorrect based on the objectives of system WB. In particular, the condition is too weak to force certain terms to be the source of type errors.

For example, let A be a valid, initial assumption set defined by

$$A = \left\{ \begin{array}{l} mult ::_o \forall\alpha.\, \alpha \to \alpha \to \alpha\,, \\ mult ::_i Int \to Int \to Int\,, \\ mult ::_i Float \to Float \to Float\,, \\ c :: Char \end{array} \right\}$$

In this set, *mult* (multiplication) is defined for, or has instances at, types *Int* and *Float* only. Suppose *square* is a function defined as $\lambda x.\, mult\ x\ x$. Wadler and Blott suggest that *square* applied to c should cause a type error under A since *mult* has no instance at type *Char* in A (see pg. 64 of [WB89]). Yet in their type system, according to condition (1), the application is well typed under A because a type scheme can be derived for it from A as follows.

by rules **TAUT** and **COMB**

$$A,\ mult :: Char \to Char \to Char,\ \ x :: Char \vdash (mult\ x\ x) :: Char$$

by rule **ABS**

$$A,\ mult :: Char \to Char \to Char \vdash (\lambda x.\, mult\ x\ x) :: Char \to Char$$

by rule **TAUT**

$$A,\ mult :: Char \to Char \to Char \vdash c :: Char$$

by rule **COMB**

$$A,\ mult :: Char \rightarrow Char \rightarrow Char \vdash ((\lambda x.\ mult\ x\ x)\ \ c) :: Char$$

by rule **PRED**

$$A \vdash ((\lambda x.\ mult\ x\ x)\ \ c) :: (mult :: Char \rightarrow Char \rightarrow Char) . Char$$

So under condition (1), the application is well typed with respect to A, for we are able to give it a type scheme. That is, it does not cause a type error. In order for it to be the source of a type error, a stronger condition is needed to judge whether terms are well typed. A suitable condition is that e is well typed if and only if it can be given a τ type.

Definition. (well-typed expression). An expression e is well typed with respect to A if and only if $A \vdash e : \tau$, for some τ.[2]

Under this condition, the preceding derivation is not enough to show that function *square* applied to c is well typed. The condition forces us to try to eliminate predicate $(mult :: Char \rightarrow Char \rightarrow Char)$ relative to A, which is impossible since *mult* does not have an instance at type *Char* in A. So the application is regarded as untypable in the context A, giving us the desired type error.

3. WB typability is undecidable

The power of recursion in assumption sets renders the typability problem in WB (determining whether a term is well typed under a given valid assumption set) undecidable.

Theorem 3.1. *Given a valid assumption set A and an expression e, it is undecidable whether e is well typed under A.*

Proof. We reduce PCP (Post's Correspondence Problem [HU79]) to WB typability. The reduction is presented through an example. Recall that an instance of PCP consists of two lists $x_1, \ldots, x_k$ and $y_1, \ldots, y_k$ of strings over some alphabet and has a solution if there is a sequence of integers $i_1, i_2, \ldots, i_m$, for $m \geq 1$, such that $x_{i_1} x_{i_2} \cdots x_{i_m} = y_{i_1} y_{i_2} \cdots y_{i_m}$. Suppose that the PCP instance we are given is

$$\begin{array}{ll} x_1 = 10 & y_1 = 101 \\ x_2 = 011 & y_2 = 11 \\ x_3 = 101 & y_3 = 011 \end{array}$$

Assume that there are type constants 0, 1, ε, and t_i, for $1 \leq i \leq 3$, and that $\rightarrow$ is

---

[2] Though the definition is adequate for the purpose of this paper, it is unsatisfactory for typing let [Smi89]. Actually rule **PRED** should be reformulated, allowing the introduction of only those predicates that are satisfiable.

right associative. Let A be an assumption set containing all and only the assumptions

$$pcp ::_o \forall\alpha.\alpha$$
$$pcp ::_i (1 \rightarrow 0 \rightarrow \varepsilon) \rightarrow (1 \rightarrow 0 \rightarrow 1 \rightarrow \varepsilon) \rightarrow t_1$$
$$pcp ::_i (0 \rightarrow 1 \rightarrow 1 \rightarrow \varepsilon) \rightarrow (1 \rightarrow 1 \rightarrow \varepsilon) \rightarrow t_2$$
$$pcp ::_i (1 \rightarrow 0 \rightarrow 1 \rightarrow \varepsilon) \rightarrow (0 \rightarrow 1 \rightarrow 1 \rightarrow \varepsilon) \rightarrow t_3$$
$$pcp ::_i \forall\alpha.\forall\beta.\forall\gamma.(pcp :: \alpha \rightarrow \beta \rightarrow \gamma).\ (1 \rightarrow 0 \rightarrow \alpha) \rightarrow (1 \rightarrow 0 \rightarrow 1 \rightarrow \beta) \rightarrow (t_1 \rightarrow \gamma)$$
$$pcp ::_i \forall\alpha.\forall\beta.\forall\gamma.(pcp :: \alpha \rightarrow \beta \rightarrow \gamma).\ (0 \rightarrow 1 \rightarrow 1 \rightarrow \alpha) \rightarrow (1 \rightarrow 1 \rightarrow \beta) \rightarrow (t_2 \rightarrow \gamma)$$
$$pcp ::_i \forall\alpha.\forall\beta.\forall\gamma.(pcp :: \alpha \rightarrow \beta \rightarrow \gamma).\ (1 \rightarrow 0 \rightarrow 1 \rightarrow \alpha) \rightarrow (0 \rightarrow 1 \rightarrow 1 \rightarrow \beta) \rightarrow (t_3 \rightarrow \gamma)$$

By the t_i components of the types of *pcp*, the assumptions do not overlap. Therefore, A is valid. Then the function $\lambda x.\, pcp\ x\ x$ is well typed with respect to A if and only if $A \vdash pcp :: \tau \rightarrow \tau \rightarrow \gamma$ for some τ and γ. But the assumptions for *pcp* allow it to have only types of the form $\tau \rightarrow \tau' \rightarrow \gamma$, where τ is obtained by concatenating various x_i's and τ' by concatenating the corresponding y_i's (recall that $\rightarrow$ is right associative). Hence $\lambda x.\, pcp\ x\ x$ is well typed with respect to A if and only if the PCP instance has a solution. **Q.E.D.**

We can also show that the instance relation of system WB is undecidable.

Theorem 3.2. *Given a valid assumption set A and two types* σ *and* σ', *it is undecidable whether* $\sigma \geq_A \sigma'$.

Proof. Let A be a valid assumption set encoding a PCP instance as in Theorem 3.1. Then

$$\forall\alpha.\forall\gamma.(pcp :: \alpha \rightarrow \alpha \rightarrow \gamma).\, int \geq_A int$$

if and only if the PCP instance has a solution. **Q.E.D.**

By Theorem 2.1, the instance relation is no longer needed to determine overlap, but the validity condition still depends on it. All types appearing in the instance assumptions for an identifier must be instances of the type given in the overload assumption. Thus we have the following immediate corollary.

Corollary. *It is undecidable whether an assumption set is valid.*

Proof. Given a valid assumption set A and two types σ and σ', let x be an identifier that does not appear in A. Then

$$A,\ x ::_o \sigma,\ \ x ::_i \sigma'$$

is valid if and only if $\sigma \geq_A \sigma'$. Q.E.D.

4. Limiting recursion

In light of Theorem 3.1, we wish to identify a restriction on type assumption sets with which WB typability becomes decidable. WB typability is decidable for nonrecursive assumption sets, but banning recursion altogether seems unacceptable since recursive assumption sets, like the set in Figure 1, arise naturally in practice. So we prefer to restrict it instead. First we consider a restriction that prohibits *mutual recursion.*

Definition. (mutually-recursive assumption set). An assumption set is mutually recursive if and only if it contains a sequence of distinct instance assumptions of the form

$$\begin{aligned} &h_0 ::_i \forall\alpha_1 \cdots \forall\alpha_{m_0} . (h_1 :: \tau_0) . \rho_0 \\ &h_1 ::_i \forall\alpha_1 \cdots \forall\alpha_{m_1} . (h_2 :: \tau_1) . \rho_1 \\ &\quad\vdots \\ &h_{n-1} ::_i \forall\alpha_1 \cdots \forall\alpha_{m_{n-1}} . (h_0 :: \tau_{n-1}) . \rho_{n-1} \end{aligned}$$

for $n > 1$ (the h_i's need not be distinct identifiers).

At first glance, it appears that limiting assumption sets to sets that are not mutually recursive is overly restrictive. The assumptions in Figure 1, for example, would be illegal. But, surprisingly, enough expressive power has been retained to permit an alternative formulation of them without mutual recursion. In fact, so much has been retained that assumption sets are still too expressive.

Theorem 4.1. *Given a valid assumption set A that is not mutually recursive and an expression e, it is undecidable whether e is well typed under A.*

Proof. Again we reduce PCP to WB typability. As in the proof of Theorem 3.1, the reduction is presented through an example. Suppose that the PCP instance we are given is the same one given in the proof of Theorem 3.1. Assume that there are type constants 0, 1, ε, and t_i, for $1 \leq i \leq 3$, and that $\rightarrow$ is right associative. Initially, let A be an assumption set containing only the assumptions $xy_j ::_o \forall\alpha . \alpha$, for $1 \leq j \leq 3$. Then add to A the assumptions

$$xy_1 ::_i (1 \to 0 \to \varepsilon) \to (1 \to 0 \to 1 \to \varepsilon) \to t_1$$
$$xy_2 ::_i (0 \to 1 \to 1 \to \varepsilon) \to (1 \to 1 \to \varepsilon) \to t_2$$
$$xy_3 ::_i (1 \to 0 \to 1 \to \varepsilon) \to (0 \to 1 \to 1 \to \varepsilon) \to t_3$$

For each j, $1 \le j \le 3$, add to A,

$$xy_j ::_i \forall\alpha.\ \forall\beta.\ \alpha \to \beta \to t_k$$

for all k such that $1 \le k \le 3$ and $j \ne k$. Next, add to A the assumptions

$$\begin{aligned}
&append ::_o \forall\alpha.\ \alpha \\
&append ::_i \forall\alpha.\ \varepsilon \to \alpha \to \alpha \\
&append ::_i \forall\alpha.\ \forall\beta.\ \forall\gamma.\ \forall\delta.\ (append :: \alpha \to \beta \to \gamma). \\
&\qquad (\delta \to \alpha) \to \beta \to (\delta \to \gamma)
\end{aligned}$$

The effect of $append : \alpha \to \gamma \to \pi$ is to bind to π, γ appended to the right of α.

The idea is to construct an assumption which effectively selects one of the x_i's and corresponding y_i's for concatenation. To this end, add to A,

$$\begin{aligned}
&pcp ::_o \forall\alpha.\ \alpha \\
&pcp ::_i \forall\gamma.\ \forall\rho.\ \forall\tau. \\
&\qquad\qquad (xy_1 :: \gamma \to \rho \to \tau). \\
&\qquad\qquad (xy_2 :: \gamma \to \rho \to \tau). \\
&\qquad\qquad (xy_3 :: \gamma \to \rho \to \tau). \\
&\qquad \gamma \to \rho \to t_1 \\
&pcp ::_i \forall\alpha.\ \forall\beta.\ \forall\gamma.\ \forall\rho.\ \forall\pi_1.\ \forall\pi_2.\ \forall\tau.\ \forall\sigma. \\
&\qquad\qquad (pcp :: \alpha \to \beta \to \sigma). \\
&\qquad\qquad (append :: \alpha \to \gamma \to \pi_1). \\
&\qquad\qquad (append :: \beta \to \rho \to \pi_2). \\
&\qquad\qquad (xy_1 :: \gamma \to \rho \to \tau). \\
&\qquad\qquad (xy_2 :: \gamma \to \rho \to \tau). \\
&\qquad\qquad (xy_3 :: \gamma \to \rho \to \tau). \\
&\qquad \pi_1 \to \pi_2 \to t_2
\end{aligned}$$

A is valid, but not mutually recursive, and $\lambda x.\ pcp\ x\ x$ is well typed with respect to A if and only if the PCP instance has a solution. **Q.E.D.**

4.1. Parametric recursion

Fortunately, there is a form of recursion under which WB typability is decidable and that allows the kind of mutual recursion exhibited in Figure 1. We call it *parametric recursion.* Before defining it, we need the definition of *parametric overloading.*

Definition. (parametric overloading). An identifier h is parametrically overloaded in an assumption set A if and only if it has an overload assumption in A of the form $h ::_o \forall\alpha . \tau$, for some τ, and for every instance assumption $h ::_i \forall\beta_1 \cdots \forall\beta_n . \rho . \tau'$ in A, where $n \geq 0$,

(a) $\rho = (h :: \tau[\alpha := \beta_1]), \ldots, (h :: \tau[\alpha := \beta_n])$, and

(b) $\tau' = \tau[\alpha := \chi(\beta_1, \ldots, \beta_n)]$, for some type constructor χ.

A desirable property of parametric overloading is its type-constructor property. For each identifier h overloaded this way in an assumption set A with $h ::_o \forall\alpha . \tau$ as its overload assumption, there is a finite set of type constructors that describes precisely the types τ' for which $A \vdash h :: \tau[\alpha := \tau']$. For example, *eq* of Figure 1 is parametrically overloaded as is *mult* in assumption set A defined in Section 2.3.

Definition. (parametric recursion). An assumption set is parametrically recursive if and only if its only source of recursion is that which comes from overloading identifiers parametrically.

The assumptions in Figure 1, for example, form a parametrically-recursive assumption set. Further, note that any nonrecursive assumption set is trivially parametrically recursive, for the definition merely states that if there is recursion then it must be the kind that comes from overloading identifiers parametrically.

WB typability is also decidable under a more flexible form of parametric overloading where equality in (a) is replaced by containment:

(a) $(h :: \tau[\alpha := \beta_1]), \ldots, (h :: \tau[\alpha := \beta_n]) \subseteq \rho$.

This form corresponds more closely to the parametric overloading notion of Kaes [Kae88]. It is needed to express certain assumptions, however it does not preserve the type-constructor property. An assumption for matrix multiplication, for example, has predicates involving the product and sum of matrix elements where the elements themselves may be matrices:

$$mult ::_i \forall\alpha . (add :: \alpha \to \alpha \to \alpha) . (mult :: \alpha \to \alpha \to \alpha) .$$
$$Matrix(\alpha) \to Matrix(\alpha) \to Matrix(\alpha)$$

The type-constructor set property can be exploited so that if every identifier with an overload assumption is parametrically overloaded, then WB typability is, from a complexity standpoint, as hard as but no harder than conventional ML typability, which is complete for DEXPTIME [Mai90]. However, for parametrically-recursive assumption sets, where some identifiers may not be parametrically overloaded, the problem appears harder than conventional ML typability. Though decidable, it is NEXPTIME hard with respect to polynomial-time reduction which implies that it requires exponential time, nondeterministically.

Theorem 4.2 . *Given a valid, parametrically-recursive assumption set A and an expression e, deciding whether e is well typed with respect to A is NEXPTIME hard.*

Proof. To show that every problem in NEXPTIME is reducible to WB typability, for each nondeterministic Turing machine (NTM) M that is time bounded by $2^{p(n)}$, for some polynomial p of the input length n, we give a polynomial-time algorithm that takes as input a string x and produces a set of type assumptions A_x and an expression e such that e is well typed under A_x if and only if M accepts x.

Let M be a $2^{p(n)}$ time-bounded, one-tape NTM. For each input $x = a_1 a_2 \cdots a_n$, the set A_x is constructed as follows.

Based on an encoding of instantaneous descriptions (ID's), assumptions are generated for an identifier, *move*, that describe M's next-move function δ. Suppose the states of M $(q_0, q_1, \ldots)$, its tape symbols $(X_1, X_2, \ldots)$, and the special symbol ε are type constants. Then an ID $X_1 X_2 \cdots X_{i-1} q X_i \cdots X_n$ is encoded as

$$(X_{i-1} \to \cdots \to X_2 \to X_1 \to \varepsilon) \to q \to (X_i \to \cdots \to X_n \to \varepsilon) .$$

Initially, let A_x contain only $move ::_o \forall\alpha . \alpha$. There are two possibilities, left (L) and right (R), for the direction of the tape head in a single move. If $\delta(q, X)$ contains (q', Y, L), for some states q and q' and tape symbols X and Y, then generate

$$move ::_i \forall\alpha . \forall\beta . \forall\gamma . ((\gamma \to \alpha) \to q \to (X \to \beta)) \to (\alpha \to q' \to (\gamma \to Y \to \beta)) .$$

In addition, if X is B, the blank symbol, then include

$$move ::_i \forall\alpha . \forall\beta . \forall\gamma . ((\gamma \to \alpha) \to q \to \varepsilon) \to (\alpha \to q' \to (\gamma \to Y \to \varepsilon)) .$$

Similarly, if $\delta(q, X)$ contains (q', Y, R), then generate

$$move ::_i \forall\alpha.\forall\beta.(\alpha \to q \to (X \to \beta)) \to ((Y \to \alpha) \to q' \to \beta)$$

and if $X = B$, also include

$$move ::_i \forall\alpha.\forall\beta.(\alpha \to q \to \varepsilon) \to ((Y \to \alpha) \to q' \to \varepsilon).$$

Next, assumptions are produced that together describe valid computations of M. For each j such that $1 \le j \le p(n)$, generate $c_j ::_o \forall\alpha.\alpha$. Then generate $p(n)+1$ assumptions, one for each of the identifers $c_1, c_2, \ldots, c_{p(n)+1}$:

$$c_1 ::_i \forall\alpha.\forall\beta.\forall\gamma.(move :: \alpha \to \beta).(move :: \beta \to \gamma).\alpha \to \gamma$$
$$c_k ::_i \forall\alpha.\forall\beta.\forall\gamma.(c_{k-1} :: \alpha \to \beta).(c_{k-1} :: \beta \to \gamma).\alpha \to \gamma \quad \forall k.1 < k \le p(n)$$
$$c_{p(n)+1} :: \forall\alpha.\forall\beta.(c_{p(n)} :: \alpha \to \beta).(final :: \beta).\alpha$$

For $1 \le k \le p(n)$, if τ and τ' encode ID's then c_k has type $\tau \to \tau'$ if and only if there is some sequence of exactly 2^k moves of M from τ to τ'. Since M may accept before making $2^{p(n)}$ moves, it is also necessary to generate

$$move ::_i \forall\alpha.\forall\beta.(\alpha \to q_f \to \beta) \to (\alpha \to q_f \to \beta)$$

for each final state q_f of M. The effect is to allow all accepting ID's to repeat so that every valid computation of M can be regarded as consisting of exactly $2^{p(n)}$ moves. So we see that if $c_{p(n)+1}$ has type τ, and τ encodes an ID, then there is an accepting ID that is reachable from τ in exactly $2^{p(n)}$ moves. That the ID is accepting is ensured by the predicate involving *final* and its assumptions, which include the overload assumption $final ::_o \forall\alpha.\alpha$, and an instance assumption of the form

$$final ::_i \forall\alpha.\forall\beta.\alpha \to q_f \to \beta$$

for each final state q_f of M.

Finally, with q_0 as M's start state, add to A_x the assumptions

$$ID_0 :: \varepsilon \to q_0 \to a_1 \to a_2 \to \cdots a_n \to \varepsilon$$
$$eq :: \forall\alpha.\alpha \to \alpha \to Bool$$

where ID_0 corresponds to the initial ID of M on input x. Then $eq(c_{p(n)+1}, ID_0)$ is well typed under A_x if and only if M accepts x. Moreover, A_x is valid, nonrecursive, and can be generated in time proportional to $p(n)$. **Q.E.D.**

Notice that the proof of Theorem 4.2 makes no use of recursion, so this complexity result applies to WB typability under valid, nonrecursive assumption sets as well.

5. Conclusion

Programs that use overloaded identifiers may apply to many types of inputs for they inherit the multiple types of these identifiers, a kind of polymorphism we call bounded polymorphism. Predicated types are useful for expressing the principal types of such programs. However when coupled with overloading in assumption sets they lead to a very powerful form of expression that must be limited if typability is to be decidable (we have been tempted to create a small library of useful functions encoded as type assumptions in system WB such as *append* in the proof of Theorem 4.1). One approach is to limit recursion in assumption sets to parametric recursion.

We have independently developed our own extension of the Hindley-Milner system that incorporates overloading. The extension preserves two important properties of the original system, namely decidable typability and principal types. It has a new type called a *constrained type* which corresponds to a predicated type in system WB but the inference rules for introducing and eliminating them are different as is the instance relation on types. The only restriction on assumption sets in our system is that they be parametrically recursive. This restriction appears reasonable and unobtrusive in practice based on our experience with an implementation of a type inference algorithm for the system. Other restrictions are considered in [Smi89].

References

[DM82] Damas, L. and Milner, R., Principal type-schemes for functional programs. *Proc. 9th Annual ACM Symp. on Principles of Prog. Lang.*, pp. 207-212, January 1982.

[HMT88] Harper, R., Milner, R. and Tofte, M., The definition of Standard ML. Version 2, ECS-LFCS-88-62, University of Edinburgh, August 1988.

[Hin69] Hindley, R., The principal type scheme of an object in combinatory logic. *Trans. Amer. Math. Soc.*, 146, pp. 29-60, December 1969.

[HU79] Hopcroft, J. and Ullman, J., Introduction to Automata Theory, Languages, and Computation. Addison-Wesley, 1979.

[HW90] Hudak, P. and Wadler, P., Report on the Programming Language Haskell. Version 1.0, Yale University, April 1990.

[Kae88] Kaes, S., Parametric overloading in polymorphic programming languages. In Lecture Notes in Comp. Sci., *Proc. of the 2nd European Symp. on Programming*, 300, pp. 131-144, 1988.

[Mai90] Mairson, H., Deciding ML typability is complete for deterministic exponential time. *Proc. 17th Annual ACM Symp. on Principles of Prog. Lang.*, pp. 382-401, January 1990.

[Mil78] Milner, R., A theory of type polymorphism in programming. *J. Comp. System Sci.*, 17, pp. 348-375, 1978.

[MH88] Mitchell, J. and Harper, R., The essence of ML. *Proc. 15th Annual ACM Symp. on Principles of Prog. Lang.*, pp. 28-46, January 1988.

[Smi89] Smith, G.S., Overloading and bounded polymorphism. TR 89-1054, Department of Computer Science, Cornell University, November 1989.

[Tur86] Turner, D.A., An overview of Miranda. *SIGPLAN Notices*, December 1986.

[WB89] Wadler, P. and Blott, S., How to make ad-hoc polymorphism less ad-hoc. *Proc. 16th Annual ACM Symp. on Principles of Prog. Lang.*, pp. 60-76, January 1989.

Coercive Type Isomorphism

Satish R. Thatte
Department of Mathematics and Computer Science
Clarkson University, Potsdam, NY 13699.
satish@sun.mcs.clarkson.edu

Abstract

There is a variety of situations in programming in which it is useful to think of two distinct types as representations of the same abstract structure. However, language features which allow such relations to be effectively expressed at an abstract level are lacking. We propose a generalization of ML-style type inference to deal effectively with this problem. Under the generalization, the (normally free) algebra of type expressions is subjected to an equational theory generated by a finite set of *user-specified* equations that express interconvertibility relations between objects of "equivalent" types. Each type equation is accompanied by a pair of conversion functions that are (at least partial) inverses. We show that so long as the equational theory satisfies a reasonably permissive syntactic constraint, the resulting type system admits a complete type inference algorithm that produces unique principal types. The main innovation required in type inference is the replacement of ordinary free unification by unification in the user-specified equational theory. The syntactic constraint ensures that the latter is *unitary*, *i.e.*, yields *unique* most general unifiers. The proposed constraint is of independent interest as the first known syntactic characterization for a class of unitary theories. Some of the applications of the system are similar to those of Wadler's *views* [Wad87]. However, our system is considerably more general, and more orthogonal to the underlying language.

1 Introduction

Promoting software reusability is one of the most important goals in the design of high level programming languages. Incidental differences in representation decisions are a mundane but rather potent barrier to such reusability in practice. Consider the problem of merging two programs that manipulate complex numbers and finite maps. It is quite possible that one program uses the polar representation for complex numbers and lists of pairs (assoc-lists) for finite maps while the other uses cartesian complex numbers and a pair of (domain and range) lists for finite maps. Short of rewriting one program to confirm to the representation choices of the other, and thereby abandoning reuse, the only way to overcome this conflict is to convert the representations in either direction as needed. This is not hard in principle since the representations are nearly isomorphic in an obvious way. However, the actual process of modifying the two programs where they interact is likely to be tedious and error-prone. The merger would be much simpler if one could simply add declarations to the effect that these representations are mutually convertible, and let the compiler insert conversions where needed[1]. Another application of implicit isomorphism concerns pattern-matching for abstract types. For instance, one may want to define functions on integers—a primitive, and therefore abstract, type—using patterns based on **zero** and **succ** as constructors. This relies on the isomorphism between non-negative integers and the algebraic type of Peano numerals. This paper describes an extension of the Hindley-Milner type reconstruction system used in languages like Standard ML to allow such *isomorphism* declarations. It turns out that the new notion of *type isomorphism* needed for such applications is viable in practice for a rather large and interesting class of isomorphisms, although an important theoretical issue related to the extension is still open.

The purpose of implicit isomorphism is to introduce coercions *implicitly* in order to unify conflicting representations. Any system of coercions always creates concern about loss of programmer control over both the meaning and the performance of a program. There is no doubt that any sufficiently powerful coercion system (such as the one in this paper) can be used in ways that lead to undesirable consequences. For instance, it would be foolish to define complex addition only for the cartesian form and multiplication only for the polar form and rely on implicit conversions to make both operations available for both forms if the program spends a large proportion of its time performing complex arithmetic. Also, implicit conversions will allow some applications to be well-typed that ought to lead to type errors. We believe that a combination of intelligent use (such as avoiding the complex arithmetic pitfall mentioned above) and the use of scoping and abstraction will largely eliminate such undesirable effects. For instance, an isomorphism between two finite-map abstractions is much less likely to lead to unwarranted coercions than a direct isomorphism between lists-of-pairs and pairs-of-lists.

The Hindley-Milner system uses Robinson's first-order unification as its main computation engine. The underlying assumption is that type expressions are *free*—distinct ground types are incompatible. This assumption is violated (for instance) when types satisfy inclusion relationships [Mit84, FM88, Tha88]. Free unification must then be replaced by algorithms for resolving subsumption constraints. When the inclusions are symmetric, as in the case of some systems of type reconstruction for labeled records [Wan87, Rém90], types are in effect subject to an equational theory, and free unification can be replaced by *equational* unification in the theory concerned. This also applies to symmetric coercions, as in the present case. Our reconstruction algorithm is therefore based on equational unification. The major new dimension is that the equational theory involved is user-specified instead of being predetermined, since the system would not be very useful unless users were allowed to decide which concrete types are to be used as representations of abstract structures. Thus, instead of a *specific* equational unification algorithm as in [Wan87, Rém90], we need a *universal* algorithm for the class of theories we choose to permit. An additional difficulty is the coercive nature of our (symmetric) subtype structures. Combining coercive subtyping with polymorphic type reconstruction in a satisfactory way is still an open problem—systems combining

[1]These remarks apply even if the representations involved have been encapsulated into abstract types.

coercions with parametric polymorphism either use *explicit* typing [BCGS89] or are seriously incomplete [Fuh89]. Fortunately, it turns out that our special case of symmetric subtyping with "sufficiently polymorphic" coercions avoids most of the difficulties of the general case including the need for run-time inference of coercions.

When considering type reconstruction using equational unification, the first concern usually is that this will lead to a combinatorial explosion in the number of most general unifiers and therefore in the number of principal types (*cf.*. [Wan89]). It turns out that, in our case, unique principal types (modulo isomorphism) are needed for ***semantic integrity*** and therefore the Hindley-Milner-like economy in typing comes "for free". The constraint arises because the semantics of an expression depends on the type assigned to it since the use of isomorphism relationships in typing involves the insertion of coercions. The need for unique principal types implies that unification in every permitted theory must be ***unitary***, *i.e.*, there must be a single most general unifier for every unifiable pair of terms (as in free unification). As an example of the contrary situation, consider the following isomorphism

$$\alpha \times (\beta \times \delta) \;\simeq\; (\alpha \times \beta) \times \delta$$

which makes the product constructor associative. The corresponding conversions are obvious. Now the fact that associative unification is not unitary—in fact it is infinitary [Sie89]: unification of a pair of terms may yield an infinite number of ***independent*** unifiers—leads to semantic ambiguity in expressions like *let* $f(x,y) \;=\; x$ *in* $f(1,(2,3))$ since there are *two* ways to unify the argument part $\alpha \times \beta$ of the (functional) type of f with the actual argument type int×(int×int) which is "equivalent" to (int×int)×int. Thus the expression could evaluate to either 1 or (1,2). Moreover, as [BCGS89] points out, the semantics of an expression subject to a coercive typing system is in general dependent not only on the typing judgement but also on the specific proof of that judgement. To avoid ambiguity, the typing system must be *coherent*, *i.e.*, the meaning associated with a specific judgement must be independent of its proof. In our case, this requires conversions between isomorphic types to be true inverses. This is natural in genuine cases of multiple representations but in cases of imperfect isomorphism of data structures, such as that between pairs of lists and lists of pairs, the zipping/unzipping conversions are only partial inverses since zipping is impossible for two lists of unequal length. Such cases require pragmatic annotations and other restrictions to ensure unambiguity (see Section 7).

The practical use of type isomorphism as a language feature depends on the existence of a decidable class of unitary equational theories subject to a universal unification algorithm. No sufficient syntactic conditions for unitary theories are known in the literature on equational unification (see [Sie89] for a recent survey). We have recently shown that the class of *finite acyclic* theories contains only unitary theories (finite acyclic theories and the unification procedure for them are described in Section 5). The decidability of the universal unification problem for the class is still open. Given that the decidability of unification in some of the simplest finite acyclic theories (the theories of one-sided distributivity) turned out to be quite difficult to establish [TA87], the general problem is unlikely to have a straightforward solution. In particular, the termination technique of [TA87] does not appear to generalize in a natural way for this purpose. However, it has been shown that the efficient *free* unification algorithm of [MM82] can be generalized to obtain a universal procedure for decomposable theories [Kir84] (a class that includes finite acyclic theories), and therefore, an efficient determinate unification procedure that succeeds whenever possible exists for finite acyclic theories.

Although interesting theoretically, an efficient semi-decision procedure is not usable in a practical type reconstruction system. On the other hand, even if the universal unification problem for finite acyclic theories turns out to be decidable, testing for termination is likely to be too expensive for use in type reconstruction. For practical purposes one must therefore find a heuristic that will allow the use of the simple and efficient semi-decision procedure. There is a simple heuristic based on limiting the number of coercions required for unification. We believe that a sufficiently large limit of this kind is unlikely to have any practical consequences since natural programs which use huge numbers of coercions in single function applications are extremely rare and would be impossible to understand in any case. This is the basis for the claim above that an extension of the Hindley-Milner system for a large class of isomorphism theories is workable in practice.

In the rest of the paper, we begin with a brief discussion of related work in Section 2 followed by a few examples in Section 3 to illustrate our approach. A formal description of the type system is given in Section 4. Section 5 describes the relevant results on equational unification. Sections 6 and 7 contain brief discussions of the implications of the system for type reconstruction and semantics. We conclude with a comparison with Wadler's system of *views* in Section 8.

2 Related Work

The work that comes closest in spirit to ours is Wadler's work on *views* [Wad87]. Wadler addresses the narrower problem of pattern matching for arbitrary types, for which he proposes a kind of asymmetric isomorphism in which an algebraic type with ephemeral constructors (a so-called *view*) is declared equivalent to an ordinary type (abstract or otherwise). Although there does not seem to be any compelling conceptual reason to treat view-constructors as being ephemeral, the implementation relies on treating them as such. The type system is not altered significantly by the addition of views, but the run-time behavior is made more complex. The generality of *views* is limited by lack of symmetry and transitivity, and also by the restriction that a view must be algebraic. A more detailed comparison between Wadler's proposal and ours is given in Section 8.

An interesting related application motivated by software reuse is the use of type isomorphism relationships in *library search* [RT89, Rit91, Rit90]. This usually uses equational *matching* rather than unification, and since the types involved are to be matched rather than discovered, it is possible to use a much broader class of isomorphisms (Rittri [Rit91] uses the canonical isomorphism for functions in cartesian-closed categories, which is algebraically identical with the theory of natural numbers with 1, multiplication and exponentiation). Nielson and Nielson [NN90] use a notion of isomorphism very similar to ours as a heuristic in program transformation, and (extensions of) the work presented here may be useful in such applications.

Notions of type equivalence have been considered in other contexts, for instance in Wand's work on type reconstruction for record types [Wan87], in Cardelli's discussion of structural subtyping [Car88] and in Reynolds' use of conjunctive types [Rey88]. In all these cases, the equational theories involved are predetermined. Our system is the first to consider *user-specified* theories. Moreover, in most previous cases, syntactic equivalence implies semantic equality—no conversions are involved when substituting equals for equals in typing. Thus, for instance, the lack of unique principal types is not a semantic problem in Wand's work, in contrast to our situation.

3 Examples

The purpose of this section is to use a few suggestive examples to illustrate the use of type isomorphism. Instead of designing special concrete syntax, we use the traditional double-arrow notation for isomorphism declarations. All the examples use *finite acyclic* theories (see Section 5) and all of them and in fact all their combinations admit unitary unification. The examples are necessarily rather simple. It should be clear that the same techniques can be used in more complex cases.

To introduce the feature, consider the equivalence between (nonnegative) integers and Peano numerals. The prerequisites for its declaration are a new algebraic type peano along with two conversion functions p_to_i and i_to_p that are partial inverses:

```
peano ::= Zero | Succ int

p_to_i Zero = 0
p_to_i (Succ x) = x+1

i_to_p 0 = Zero
i_to_p n = Succ (n−1), if n>0
```

Now the equivalence between peano and int could be declared by:

$$\textit{isomorphic}\ \ \mathsf{peano}\ \underset{\mathsf{i\_to\_p}}{\overset{\mathsf{p\_to\_i}}{\rightleftarrows}}\ \mathsf{int}$$

Note that although, for efficiency, peano is not quite the type of Peano numerals, the conversion i_to_p has been deliberately constrained to prevent the conversion of negative integers to peano since the pattern-matching style is most often used for well-founded recursive definitions. An attempt to apply i_to_p to a negative number will generate a run-time error.

When type isomorphism is used to model multiple representations, all representations are treated symmetrically. There is no need to choose one of the forms as primary, as in the case of Wadler's *views*. This is illustrated by the treatment of complex numbers in polar and cartesian form:

```
p_complex ::= Pole real real
c_complex ::= Cart real real

c_p (Cart x y) = Pole (sqrt(x↑2+y↑2)) (atan y x)
```

$$\mathsf{p\_c\ (Pole\ m\ a) = Cart\ (m * cos\ a)\ (m * sin\ a)}$$

$$\textit{isomorphic}\ \mathsf{p\_complex} \underset{\mathsf{c\_p}}{\overset{\mathsf{p\_c}}{\rightleftarrows}} \mathsf{c\_complex}$$

If complex addition is now defined using the cartesian form and complex multiplication using the polar form, both operations are immediately available for both forms. Note that polar complex numbers are not a free data type since all such numbers with zero length are identical. To make the isomorphism perfect, this needs to be enforced by algebraic "laws" [Tho86].

As another example of incidental differences causing problems for reusability, consider the case of some Standard ML implementations where a nonstandard representation of integers is used[2]. If such an implementation provides a foreign function facility which permits ML functions to call, say, C functions, the two different integer types ml_int and c_int would need to be converted in both directions. Given appropriate conversions ml_to_c and c_to_ml, we can declare:

$$\textit{isomorphic}\ \mathsf{ml\_int} \underset{\mathsf{c\_to\_ml}}{\overset{\mathsf{ml\_to\_c}}{\rightleftarrows}} \mathsf{c\_int}$$

making the distinction transparent to all programs.

The natural isomorphism between lists of pairs and pairs of lists is an example of near-isomorphic data structures that may be used in representing finite maps:

$$\textit{isomorphic}\ (\mathsf{list}\ \alpha)\times(\mathsf{list}\ \beta) \underset{\mathsf{unzip}}{\overset{\mathsf{zip}}{\rightleftarrows}} \mathsf{list}\ (\alpha \times \beta)$$

where the conversions zip and unzip have the obvious definitions. Note that *isomorphic* declarations may involve type variables, such as α and β in this case. Finiteness of a theory implies that the same variables must occur on both sides in each equation.

To illustrate the use of transitivity, Suppose we use $[x_1, \ldots, x_n]$ to denote a vector with elements $x_1, \ldots, x_n$, and we have the declaration

$$\textit{isomorphic}\ \mathsf{list}\ \alpha \underset{\mathsf{listify}}{\overset{\mathsf{vectorize}}{\rightleftarrows}} \mathsf{vector}\ \alpha$$

in addition to the isomorphism between lists-of-pairs and pairs-of-lists declared above. By the transitivity of isomorphism, we can now treat $[(1,2),(3,4),(5,6)]$ as if it were the pair $([1,3,5],[2,4,6])$ based on the implicit conversion of the vector-of-pairs to a list-of-pairs, the list-of-pairs to a pair-of-lists, and finally the pair-of-lists to a pair-of-vectors.

---

[2] In Standard ML of New Jersey the last bit is used to differentiate between pointers and non-pointers (so called *boxed* and *non-boxed* values).

4 Typing Judgements

The formal part of the paper uses a very austere language, which is assumed to be augmented with the usual primitive constants. Letting the metavariable e range over expressions in the language and x over identifiers, we have:

$$\begin{array}{rll} e ::= & x & \textit{variables} \\ & \mid \lambda x.\, e_{body} & \textit{abstractions} \\ & \mid e_{fun}\ e_{arg} & \textit{applications} \end{array}$$

For brevity, we assume that the environment contains primitives for the introduction and elimination of tupling and other data structures such as lists. We do not consider let-bound identifiers since they do not introduce anything new in this context. Given unique principal types for expressions, quantification and generic instantiation proceed exactly as in the standard case [DM82]. Our type language here will therefore contain only monomorphic types.

The type language contains type variables and function types. Letting the metavariable τ range over type expressions, and α over type variables:

$$\begin{array}{rll} \tau ::= & \mid \alpha & \textit{type variables} \\ & \mid \tau_1 \rightarrow \tau_2 & \textit{function types} \end{array}$$

Moreover, types may also contain base types such as int and bool, and type constructors such as product ($\times$) and list, introduced by constants in the environment.

The major new element in the typing rules is that types will now be subject to the equations introduced by *isomorphic* declarations. Moreover, whenever these equations are used during typing, the corresponding coercions must be inserted at the appropriate point in the original expression. We shall need two kinds of judgements: typing judgements and isomorphism judgements. Reasoning about the semantic role of typing judgements is easier if the insertion of coercions is made explicit. Typing/coercion judgements will therefore be sequents of the form:

$$TE,\, E \vdash e \Rightarrow e_{new} : \tau$$

which may be read as: "given the set TE of typing assumptions for free variables, and a set E of *isomorphic* declarations, the expression e can be coerced to an expression e_{new} with type τ". An isomorphism judgement will be a sequent of the form:

$$E \vdash \tau \underset{g}{\overset{f}{\rightleftarrows}} \sigma$$

which is read as: "One may infer from the set E of *isomorphic* declarations that the type expressions τ and σ are mutually convertible using the coercions $f : \tau \rightarrow \sigma$ and $g : \sigma \rightarrow \tau$".

There is one complication in the use of *isomorphic* declarations that we wish to avoid in the formalism: their scope. Of course, in reality one *isomorphic* declaration may be made in the scope of others, and the type reconstruction for its conversion functions may need to use isomorphism judgements, but it should be clear that if the system guarantees unique principal types and a proper semantics in its simplified form, then the extensions required for real languages will not pose new technical problems. We therefore assume that all *isomorphic* declarations occur in the global environment, and hence a fixed set E of *isomorphic* declarations is used as an environment in both typing and isomorphism judgements.

Isomorphism judgements will be derived from *isomorphic* declarations using the following *instantiation* rule

$$\frac{}{E \cup \{\textit{isomorphic}\ \tau \underset{g}{\overset{f}{\rightleftarrows}} \sigma\} \vdash \zeta\tau \underset{g}{\overset{f}{\rightleftarrows}} \zeta\sigma}$$

where ζ is an arbitrary substitution. This rule relies on the fact that the variables in an *isomorphic* declaration are implicitly universally quantified, and the conversion functions are required to be correspondingly polymorphic. Thus, if E contains the declaration

$$\textit{isomorphic}\ \mathsf{list}\ \alpha \underset{\mathsf{listify}}{\overset{\mathsf{vectorize}}{\rightleftarrows}} \mathsf{vector}\ \alpha$$

we can derive both

$$E \vdash \mathsf{list\ int} \underset{\mathsf{listify}}{\overset{\mathsf{vectorize}}{\rightleftarrows}} \mathsf{vector\ int}$$

and

$$E \vdash \mathsf{list}\ \alpha \times \beta \underset{\mathsf{listify}}{\overset{\mathsf{vectorize}}{\rightleftarrows}} \mathsf{vector}\ \alpha \times \beta$$

Since the declaration above requires vectorize and listify to possess the types $\forall\beta.\,\mathsf{list}\ \beta \rightarrow \mathsf{vector}\ \beta$ and $\forall\beta.\,\mathsf{vector}\ \beta \rightarrow \mathsf{list}\ \beta$ respectively, their use in all instantiations is appropriate. This implies that translations are substitution invariant. If we can prove $TE, E \vdash e \Rightarrow e' : \tau$ then we can also prove $TE, E \vdash e \Rightarrow e' : \zeta\tau$ for any substitution ζ. This property has two important consequences:

- A combination of principal type and coherence properties is sufficient for unambiguous semantics.
- All coercions can be determined at compile-time. The target language for the translation does not need to include type abstractions and applications for run-time computation of coercions.

The instantiation rule is supplemented with a set of rules for equivalence (we use *Id* to denote the identity function and the infix operator "$\bullet$" for function composition):

$$\frac{}{E \vdash \tau \underset{Id}{\overset{Id}{\rightleftarrows}} \tau} \qquad \frac{E \vdash \tau \underset{g}{\overset{f}{\rightleftarrows}} \sigma \qquad E \vdash \sigma \underset{k}{\overset{h}{\rightleftarrows}} \nu}{E \vdash \tau \underset{g \bullet k}{\overset{h \bullet f}{\rightleftarrows}} \nu} \qquad \frac{E \vdash \tau \underset{g}{\overset{f}{\rightleftarrows}} \sigma}{E \vdash \sigma \underset{f}{\overset{g}{\rightleftarrows}} \tau}$$

The rule for function types below illustrates the congruence laws for type constructors, which involve the application of isomorphism to *parts* of a type expression:

$$\frac{E \vdash \tau \underset{g}{\overset{f}{\rightleftarrows}} \sigma \qquad E \vdash \mu \underset{k}{\overset{j}{\rightleftarrows}} \nu}{E \vdash \tau \rightarrow \mu \underset{\lambda h.\, j \bullet h \bullet f}{\overset{\lambda h.\, j \bullet h \bullet g}{\rightleftarrows}} \sigma \rightarrow \nu}$$

Similar laws are needed for every type constructor in the system. For instance,

$$\frac{E \vdash \tau \underset{g}{\overset{f}{\rightleftarrows}} \sigma \qquad E \vdash \mu \underset{k}{\overset{j}{\rightleftarrows}} \nu}{E \vdash \tau \times \mu \underset{g \times k}{\overset{f \times j}{\rightleftarrows}} \sigma \times \nu} \qquad \frac{E \vdash \tau \underset{g}{\overset{f}{\rightleftarrows}} \sigma}{E \vdash \mathsf{list}\ \tau \underset{\mathsf{list}\ g}{\overset{\mathsf{list}\ f}{\rightleftarrows}} \mathsf{list}\ \sigma}$$

where $f \times g$ is the function that applies f and g to the left and right components of a pair, and $\mathsf{list}\ f$ is the function which applies f to every component of a list—*i.e.*, it is $\mathsf{map}\ f$. We shall similarly use the notation $\mathsf{con}(f_1, \ldots, f_k)$ to denote the function which applies the function f_i to the components of type τ_i in an object of type $\mathsf{con}(\tau_1, \ldots, \tau_k)$. This is, roughly speaking, the function to which $f_1 \times \cdots \times f_k$ is taken by the initial functor in the category of functors which take each k-ary product type $(\tau_1 \times \cdots \times \tau_k)$ to $\mathsf{con}(\tau_1, \ldots, \tau_k)$[3].

Of the typing rules, most are straightforward adaptations of the standard rules:

$$\frac{x \in Dom(TE)}{TE,\, E \vdash x \Rightarrow x : TE(x)}$$

$$\frac{TE[x \leftarrow \tau],\, E \vdash e_{body} \Rightarrow e_{newbody} : \sigma}{TE,\, E \vdash \lambda x.\ e_{body} \Rightarrow \lambda x.\ e_{newbody} : \tau \rightarrow \sigma}$$

[3]Assuming that con is covariant in all its arguments. Actual algebraic type constructors may even have arguments that are used in both covariant and contravariant ways in their definitions. In such cases the corresponding coercions need to be constructed with a complicated algorithm.

$$\frac{\begin{array}{c} TE, E \vdash e_{fun} \Rightarrow e_{newfun} : \sigma \rightarrow \nu \\ TE, E \vdash e_{arg} \Rightarrow e_{newarg} : \sigma \end{array}}{TE, E \vdash e_{fun}\ e_{arg} \Rightarrow e_{newfun}\ e_{newarg} : \nu}$$

The only *new* typing rule will be:

$$\frac{\begin{array}{c} TE, E \vdash e \Rightarrow e_{new} : \tau \\ E \vdash \tau \underset{g}{\overset{f}{\rightleftarrows}} \sigma \end{array}}{TE, E \vdash e \Rightarrow f(e_{new}) : \sigma}$$

Intuitively, this rule is similar to the familiar subsumption rule in subtype systems in which subsumption requires explicit coercion. The implications of this rule for semantics are discussed in Section 7. It is obvious that the implication for type reconstruction is that isomorphism judgements may be used in the process of resolving the equational constraints on types generated by applications. In other words, the *only* new factor in reconstruction is that unification must be performed within the equational theory presented by *isomorphic* declarations. We now turn to a discussion of this new problem.

5 Equational Unification

It seems useful to briefly review the standard concepts of equational unification, since this theory has not been widely used in typing in the past. For brevity and clarity, the notation and definitions omit some minor but essential details. The reader is referred to [BHSS90, JK91, Sie89] for more careful treatments.

We are interested in equational theories that are presented by finite sets of axioms. For instance, the standard theory of free monoids is presented by

$$\begin{aligned} f(x, f(y, z)) &= f(f(x, y), z) \\ f(x, 1) = f(1, x) &= x \end{aligned}$$

where f is the binary operator and 1 is the identity. A theory E of this kind defines a *least* congruence $=_E$ on terms that includes all instances of the axioms. The unification problem in E can then be defined as follows: given two terms s and t, an E-unifier for them is a substitution ξ such that $\xi s =_E \xi t$. Given two E-unifiers ξ and ξ' (with identical domains), ξ is more general than ξ' modulo E (written $\xi \leq_E \xi'$) iff there is a substitution ζ such that

$$\forall x. \xi' x =_E \zeta \xi x$$

The relation $\leq_E$ is a preorder. If $U_E(s,t)$ denotes the set of *all* E-unifiers of s and t, then $\mu U_E(s,t)$ is a *minimal complete* set of E-unifiers iff

1. $\mu U_E(s,t) \subseteq U_E(s,t)$
2. $\xi \in U_E(s,t) \Rightarrow \exists \xi' \in \mu U_E(s,t). \xi' \leq_E \xi$

3. $\forall \xi, \xi' \in \mu U_E(s,t). \xi \leq_E \xi' \Rightarrow \xi = \xi'$.

The three conditions can be thought of as *correctness, completeness* and *minimality* conditions respectively. Equational theories are classified as being *unitary, finitary, infinitary* or *nullary* depending on whether the corresponding minimal complete set of unifiers for a pair of unifiable terms is in general a *singleton, finite set, infinite set* or may not exist. Thus, unification in the *empty* theory (Robinson's free unification) is unitary, in commutative semigroups it is finitary, in free semigroups it is infinitary, and in idempotent semigroups it is nullary [Sie89]. Standard algebraic structures yield few theories with unitary unification problems. The simple theories of left and right distributivity and the theory of boolean rings, are some known examples. However, as the examples in Section 3 illustrate, there are many natural instances of type isomorphism in programming that can be expressed with unitary theories.

For the present, we will concentrate on the equational theory presented by the type equations in isomorphism declarations and ignore the corresponding coercions. Our main concern is to guarantee that theories presented by arbitrary collections of such declarations will be *unitary.* We therefore need an easily checked syntactic sufficient condition to detect unitary theories. The main new idea in this section is the definition of such a condition and the description of the corresponding unification procedure. As far as we are aware, this is the first such sufficient condition to be discovered. Interestingly, two of the known unitary theories (those of left and right distributivity) belong to the class defined below.

Briefly put, our basic result is that *all finite acyclic* theories are unitary. A theory E is *finite* if the congruence class (relative to $=_E$) for each term is finite. The following two conditions on E are *sufficient* to ensure finiteness and are liberal enough for most applications of type isomorphism:

1. E must be *regular, i.e.*, each equation in E must have the same variables on both sides.

2. The two sides of each equation in E must have the same *depth* (of nesting of function symbols).

One of the pleasant properties of these conditions is that they are invariant under combination (of theories) and therefore permit incremental verification of finiteness, unlike the acyclicity condition defined below. If E is presented by the set of equations:

$$f_1(t_{11}, \ldots, t_{1m_1}) = g_1(u_{11}, \ldots, u_{1n_1})$$

$$\vdots$$

$$f_k(t_{k1}, \ldots, t_{km_k}) = g_k(u_{k1}, \ldots, u_{kn_k})$$

then E is said to be *acyclic* if the *undirected* graph $\mathcal{G}_E = (\mathcal{V}_E, \mathcal{E}_E)$ with

- $\mathcal{V}_E = \{f_i, g_i : 1 \leq i \leq k\}$
- $\mathcal{E}_E = \{\{f_i, g_i\} : 1 \leq i \leq k\}$

is acyclic. Acyclicity of $\mathcal{G}_E$ implies (besides the usual meaning):

- $(f, f) \notin \mathcal{E}_E$ (No loops).
- $i \neq j \Rightarrow \{f_i, g_i\} \neq \{f_j, g_j\}$ (No double edges).

Thus, the following equation which promises "currying for free" is not acyclic since it creates a loop on the "$\rightarrow$" symbol:

$$(\alpha \times \beta) \rightarrow \gamma = \alpha \rightarrow (\beta \rightarrow \gamma)$$

This is fortunate since the equation implies associativity of $\times$ in certain contexts and thus yields an infinitary theory.

Theorem 1 *Every finite acyclic theory is unitary.*

The proof of this theorem is too complicated to give here. It will appear in a separate paper [Tha91]. The main insight is that acyclicity allows deterministic narrowing when the top symbols in the terms to be unified are different. This is not enough for unitariness since two additional properties—decomposability and strictness—must be ensured. Decomposability means that the usual decomposition of a unification problem

$$f(t_1, \ldots, t_k) \stackrel{?}{=}_E f(u_1, \ldots, u_k)$$

into k subproblems

$$t_i \stackrel{?}{=}_E u_i, \ 1 \leq i \leq k$$

preserves the space of solutions (E-unifiers). Regularity (the constraint that each equation must have the same variables on both sides) together with acyclicity is enough for decomposability. Strictness means that the occurs-check can be applied when binding a variable. Otherwise, simple regular acyclic systems such as

$$f(x) = g(f(x)) \qquad h(x) = g(h(x))$$

yield two independent solutions ($x \mapsto f(y)$ and $x \mapsto h(y)$) for $x \stackrel{?}{=}_E g(x)$. When regularity is strengthened to finiteness, both properties are obtained.

6 Unification and Type reconstruction

It is henceforth assumed that all theories under consideration are finite and acyclic. We now describe the unification procedure informally. The main difference between free unification and equational unification is that when there is a clash of outermost symbols in the terms to be unified, free unification fails but equational unification may succeed using *paramodulation* (also called *narrowing*) to bridge the gap. Equational unification has sometimes been called "semantic" unification for this reason, when the equational theory expresses semantic equivalence. For type reconstruction, we need a procedure *Unify* which, given types τ and ν and a set E of isomorphism declarations, will return a substitution ξ and coercions f and g such that

$$E \vdash \xi\tau \underset{g}{\overset{f}{\rightleftarrows}} \xi\nu$$

is the "most general" judgement that can be derived. As an example, suppose E contains the declarations

$$\textit{isomorphic}\ [\alpha \times \beta] \underset{\mathsf{unzip}}{\overset{\mathsf{zip}}{\rightleftarrows}} [\alpha]\times[\beta] \qquad\qquad \textit{isomorphic}\ [\alpha] \underset{\mathsf{unlink}}{\overset{\mathsf{link}}{\rightleftarrows}} \{\alpha\}$$

where "[ ]" and "{ }" are two outfix type constructors. Consider the execution of *Unify*$(\{\mathsf{int}\}\times\{\mathsf{bool}\}, \{\mathsf{int}\times\mathsf{bool}\}, E)$. Note first that there is a "path" in $\mathcal{G}_E$ between the clashing outermost constructors "$\times$" and "{ }". Moreover, given that $\mathcal{G}_E$ is acyclic, this path is ***unique***. Thus, the original problem reduces to the three new problems *Unify*$(\{\mathsf{int}\}\times\{\mathsf{bool}\}, [\gamma]\times[\epsilon], E)$, *Unify*$([\gamma\times\epsilon], [\delta], E)$, and *Unify*$(\{\delta\}, \{\mathsf{int}\times\mathsf{bool}\}, E)$, where the equations

$$[\gamma]\times[\epsilon] \;=\; [\gamma\times\epsilon] \quad \textit{and} \quad [\delta] \;=\; \{\delta\}$$

which link the subproblems together are instances of the two declarations in E which form the path between "$\times$" and "{ }" in $\mathcal{G}_E$. Of the new unification problems, the first one requires two further uses of the first isomorphism in E. *Unify*$(\{\mathsf{int}\}\times\{\mathsf{bool}\}, \{\mathsf{int}\times\mathsf{bool}\}, E)$ therefore succeeds and returns the judgement

$$E \vdash \{\mathsf{int}\}\times\{\mathsf{bool}\} \underset{(\mathsf{link}\times\mathsf{link})\,\bullet\,\mathsf{unzip}\,\bullet\,\mathsf{unlink}}{\overset{\mathsf{link}\,\bullet\,\mathsf{zip}\,\bullet\,(\mathsf{unlink}\times\ \mathsf{unlink})}{\rightleftarrows}} \{\mathsf{int}\times\mathsf{bool}\}$$

We give a technically precise but naive universal unification procedure along these lines (including the inference of coercions) in Figure 1 in the Appendix. A more sophisticated and efficient procedure can be derived from that of [Kir84] by incorporating the inference of coercions into the *paramodulation* phase. If E (minus coercions) is a finite acyclic theory, then the following theorem states one of the properties of the *Unify* procedure in Figure 1.

Theorem 2 *There is a procedure Unify such that, given a finite acyclic collection E of isomorphic declarations, and a pair of E-unifiable types τ and ν, Unify(τ, ν, E) succeeds and returns ζ, $f \leftrightarrow g$ such that*

1. $E \vdash \zeta\tau \underset{g}{\overset{f}{\rightleftarrows}} \zeta\nu.$

2. *if* $E \vdash \xi\tau \underset{k}{\overset{h}{\rightleftarrows}} \xi\nu$ *then* $\zeta \leq_E \xi$.

Unfortunately, *Unify*(τ, σ, E) is not guaranteed to terminate when τ and σ are *not* E-unifiable. For instance, if E consists of the declaration:

$$\textit{isomorphic}\ \{[\beta]\} \underset{\mathsf{flop}}{\overset{\mathsf{flip}}{\rightleftarrows}} [\{\beta\}]$$

then *Unify*$([\alpha], \{\alpha\}, E)$ will loop forever. It is easy to devise a termination criterion for this particular theory based on the technique of [TA87], but no *general* termination criterion for finite acyclic theories is known. However, it turns out that in all cases of nontermination isomorphism relationships are used infinitely often. This implies that the procedure *Coerce* of Figure 1 is called infinitely often and the number of coercions needed to accomplish the (impossible) unification grows without bound. The main use of unification is in reconciling the actual and expected argument types in an application. Intuitively, it seems highly unlikely that programmers will want to use huge numbers of coercions in single applications. Even if such programs could be written, they would be almost impossible to understand[4]. This suggests that imposing a (sufficiently high) fixed limit on the number of calls to *Coerce* during a single unification is unlikely to cause any practical reduction in expressive power. A realistic type reconstruction algorithm must be based on such a *coercion-limited* version of the unification procedure of Figure 1.

Given unitary unification, the type reconstruction algorithm of [DM82] can be used virtually unchanged. The only new factor is that unification is *coercive*. The modification for coercions is straightforward: the basic case where an equality constraint on types is resolved with unification is application where a coercion is applied to the argument part if required. When *isomorphic* declarations are allowed to use *partial* inverses as coercions, additional annotations described in Section 7 need to be taken into account. *We refer to the plain and coercion-limited versions of the reconstruction algorithm as* **Type** *and* **BoundedType** *respectively.*

7 Semantics

As in all coercive systems, the semantics is inseparable from typing. Given a typing judgement $TE, E \vdash e \Rightarrow e_1 : \tau$, the *standard* meaning of e_1 is one of the *coercive* meanings of e in the given environments. Clearly, since we expect a *unique* meaning for each expression subject to coercive typing, there must be a canonical typing judgement which characterizes it. Given that E is finite and acyclic, each expression e does possess a principal type τ in the usual sense (modulo type isomorphism), but there may be many distinct coerced versions e_i of e, corresponding to distinct judgements $TE, E \vdash e \Rightarrow e_i : \tau$. We need to be able to assert that all such e_i are semantically equivalent. This is the *coherence* property proposed by [BCGS89]. *Assuming* that the two-way conversions in each *isomorphic* declaration are true inverses, the typing system is indeed coherent:

[4]The point here is similar to the reason why the theoretically high complexity of ML typability [KM89] rarely occurs in practice.

Theorem 3 *If* $TE, E \vdash e \Rightarrow e_1 : \tau$ *then* **Type**(TE, E, e) *succeeds and returns* (χ, τ', e_2) *and there is a substitution* ζ *such that* $E \vdash \tau \underset{g}{\overset{f}{\rightleftarrows}} \zeta\tau'$ *and* $\forall \rho \in [\![\chi TE]\!].\ [\![e_1]\!]\rho = [\![g\ e_2]\!]\rho$.

where $[\![\chi TE]\!]$ denotes the domain of environments which satisfy the typing assumptions resulting from applying the substitution χ to TE, and $[\![e]\!]\rho$ denotes the (standard) semantics of e in environment ρ. The proof of the theorem rests on a *coherence of isomorphism* result that is proved using rewriting techniques along the same lines as the *coherence of subsumption* result in [Tha90b][5]. Note that **Type** does not necessarily terminate if the given expression is not typable. The only limitation of **BoundedType** in the context of Theorem 3 is that it will sometimes fail when it shouldn't. However, as we argued in Section 6, such situations are unlikely to arise in practice.

In many useful cases of type isomorphism, the assumption that the two-way conversions are true inverses fails—in other words, the types involved are nearly, but not quite isomorphic. For instance, the zipping/unzipping conversions between pairs of lists and lists of pairs and the conversions between c_int and ml_int are only partial inverses. An attempt to zip two lists of unequal length leads to a run-time error, and therefore unzip (zip ([1,2], [2,3,4])) does not return the original pair of lists.

For the pure language used in the formal parts of this paper, we could use the notion of *safe translations* to replace coherence by a weaker but practically sufficient *convergence* property [Tha90a] to ensure unambiguity. If *wrong* represents the semantic value of conversion errors, we can construct a natural partial order on semantic values induced by the base relation *wrong* $\sqsubseteq x$ for all x in the same way that the relation $\perp \sqsubseteq x$ is used in traditional denotational domains. Since every proof of a typing judgement corresponds uniquely to a translation of the original expression, this induces a "safety" order on proofs based on the semantics of the translation. The safest (least error-prone) proofs are the maximal proofs in this order and convergence states that coherence holds if proofs are constrained to be maximal. See [Tha90a] for more precise and detailed definition of convergence.

Convergence by itself turns out to be inadequate in practice since the addition of essential constants such as a conditional operator causes anomalies. For instance, an expression such as

if 2=2 *then* ([1,2,3], [4,5]) *else* [(1,2), (3,4)]

may or may not lead to run-time error depending on the type—pair-of-lists or list-of-pairs—we choose to assign to it. Thus, it is not always enough to say that we have a principal type modulo isomorphism. The choice of a specific type in the equivalence class may have semantic consequences if conversions between equivalent types are not true inverses. A good pragmatic solution to this problem is possible based on the following restrictions:

---

[5] The phrase *coherence of subsumption* is used in [CG90] in a related but distinct sense.

1. Whenever mutual conversions in an *isomorphic* declaration are not true inverses, one of the two isomorphic types must be declared as the *preferred* form. This induces a *preorder* on each isomorphism class of types (since the ordering between truly isomorphic types is symmetric).
2. The partial order in each isomorphism class (derived by identifying truly isomorphic types) must be join-complete (every pair of distinct types must have a join).

The system must rely on programmers to correctly identify situations of imperfect isomorphism. Given acyclicity, the second requirement is easy to check (in time proportional to $|\mathcal{V}_E|^3$) with a minor modification of the standard transitive closure algorithm.

With these restrictions, the convergence property mentioned above can be applied to realistic languages. In most cases of partial inverses, the "isomorphism" is in fact a monomorphism (instead of the conversions being a bijections, they are a projection pair) and the larger type (*e.g.*, pair-of-lists) is the natural preferred form.

8 Comparison with *Views*

This section assumes familiarity with Wadler's paper [Wad87]. The examples used are from that paper, and Section 3 of this paper, unless otherwise mentioned.

Wadler's *views* were originally motivated by the idea of using pattern matching for instances of abstract data types, and the details of their design were very closely tied to this application although it soon became apparent that many other applications required a similar construct, and several of the interesting examples in [Wad87] itself do not fit the original mold. All of Wadler's examples can be rendered naturally within our framework since a view can always be declared as a new algebraic type which can then be declared equivalent to the base type. In cases where the mutual conversions are not true inverses, the view is the less-preferred form in the isomorphism (see Section 7). Since views are never shared, acyclicity of the resulting theory is assured and both the requirements of Section 7 are satisfied. Although Wadler does not explicitly impose the finiteness condition, the need for the conversions to be at least partial inverses implies regularity (the same variables on both sides of each type equation) implicitly. Finiteness then follows from the fact that views are not shared.

On the other hand, all examples of type isomorphism cannot be rendered as views since (among other things) a view must be algebraic, while primitive types such as c_int and ml_int can be declared isomorphic. The ephemeral nature of view-constructors causes additional problems. Consider the isomorphism between lists and vectors. If lists are considered a view of vectors, list objects cannot exist independently. Vectors cannot be considered a view at all since they are not algebraic. The only way to work around this is to use a declaration such as

view list α ::= Links (vector α)

creating an artificial constructor Links. Similarly, the interconvertibility between lists of pairs and pairs of lists is expressed in [Wad87] by *view* list $\alpha \times \beta$ ::= Zip (list $\alpha \times$ list β)

using the artificial constructor Zip. The natural convertibility between vectors of pairs and pairs of vectors in our version of the example in Secion 3 (implied intuitively by transitivity) is not freely available through these relationships. In Wadler's system, the expression Links $[(1,2),(3,4),(5,6)]$ can be coerced to Zip (Links $[1,3,5]$, Links $[2,4,6]$), given suitable "coaxing" through applications of pattern-matching. There is no way to simply treat $[(1,2),(3,4),(5,6)]$ as if it were the pair $([1,3,5],[2,4,6])$.

Views are of course effective in their original application of treating abstract types as if they were algebraic types. Under certain conditions, views may enhance efficiency by eliminating view-constructors rapidly or even preventing their creation by optimization (see [Wad87] for a discussion of such optimizations). It may be possible to mimick this in the context of isomorphism by adapting the notion of preferred form introduced in Section 7. On the other hand, there are situations where persistence of view-constructors may be more efficient. Note that such persistence is difficult to achieve efficiently in Wadler's scheme, because the need for conversion to the "standard" form for the type must then be determined at *run-time* since the conversion does not amount to a *coercion* from one type to another. As an example, suppose we have the declaration

view int ::= Zero | Succ int

If we wanted to allow the Peano-like forms to persist, then the code for an expression such as "$x + 5$" where x is known to be of type int cannot simply consist of an integer addition, since it is possible that x is in Peano form (which is *not* a different type) and needs to be converted to binary form before addition can be performed. In the context of type isomorphism, this determination is made, and a coercion inserted, at compile-time since the two types are recognized to be distinct.

In summary, it is clear that the type isomorphism scheme of this paper is more general in expressive power than *views*. The practical tradeoffs (especially in efficiency of implementation) in using one or the other in a real language must be judged by experience with actual implementations.

9 Conclusions

We have described an orthogonal extension of the Hindley-Milner type reconstruction system with a new notion of type isomorphism, and illustrated its utility in solving a variety of problems, including automatic conversions between multiple representations of abstract values and isomorphic data structures, and pattern matching for arbitrary datatypes. The main technical innovation is a novel application of equational unification. A naive implementation of the feature is straightforward. A more sophisticated implementation would be expected to optimize multiple coercions by eliminating intermediate representations.

One issue not addressed directly in the paper is the compatibility of type isomorphism with constructs for hiding *multiple* representations, which might be useful in program merging. It is easy to show that an abstract type based on a collection of representations can be translated as a new pseudorepresentation, being in fact a variant type consisting of the actual representations. All the necessary conversions for the pseudorepresentation can be inferred automatically. The main price for using an abstract type rather than directly using the representations is the run-time overhead of attaching and checking variant tags. This seems unavoidable when multiple representations are hidden.

10 Acknowledgments

I am indebted to Prateek Mishra, Didier Rémy and especially to Benjamin Pierce and Philip Wadler for detailed comments on a previous version of the paper. Claude Kirchner provided valuable explanations and references to relevant work in equational unification.

References

[BCGS89] V. Breazu-Tannen, T. Coquand, C. Gunter, and A. Scedrov. Inheritance and explicit coercion. In *Proceedings of Fourth LICS Symposium*. IEEE Computer Society Press, June 1989.

[BHSS90] H.-J. Bürkert, A. Herold, and M. Schmidt-Schauß. On equational theories, unification and (un)decidability. In C. Kirchner, editor, *Unification*, pages 69–116. Academic Press, 1990.

[Car88] Luca Cardelli. Structural subtyping and the notion of power type. In *Proceedings of Fifteenth POPL Symposium*. ACM Press, January 1988.

[CG90] P-L. Curien and G. Ghelli. Coherence of subsumption. In A. Arnold, editor, *Proceedings of Fifteenth Colloquium on Trees in Algebra and Programming (CAAP'90)*. Springer-Verlag, 1990. LNCS 431.

[DM82] L. Damas and R. Milner. Principle type-schemes for functional programs. In *Proceedings of Ninth POPL Symposium*. ACM Press, 1982.

[FM88] Y-C. Fuh and P. Mishra. Type inference with subtypes. In *Proceedings of Second European Symposium on Programming*. Springer-Verlag, 1988. LNCS 300.

[Fuh89] You-Chin Fuh. *Design and Implementation of a functional language with subtypes.* PhD thesis, SUNY at Stony Brook, 1989.

[JK91] Jean-Pierre Jouannaud and Claude Kirchner. Solving equations in abstract algebras: A rule-based survey of unification. In J.-L. Lassez and G. Plotkin, editors, *Computational Logic: Essays in Honor of Alan Robinson*. MIT Press, Cambridge, MA, 1991. To appear.

[Kir84] Claude Kirchner. A new equational unification method: A generalization of Martelli-Montanari's algorithm. In *Proceedings of 7th Conference on Automated Deduction*, pages 224–247. Springer-Verlag, 1984. LNCS 170.

[KM89] Paris Kanellakis and John C. Mitchell. Polymorphic unification and ML typing. In *Proceedings of Sixteenth POPL Symposium*. ACM Press, January 1989.

[Mit84] John C. Mitchell. Coercion and type inference (summary). In *Proceedings of Eleventh POPL Symposium*, pages 175–185. ACM Press, 1984.

[MM82] A. Martelli and U. Montanari. An efficient unification algorithm. *ACM Transactions on Programming Languages and Systems*, 4(2):258–282, 1982.

[NN90] H. Riis Nielson and F. Nielson. Eureka definitions for free! In Neil Jones, editor, *Proceedings of Fourth European Symposium on Programming*. Springer-Verlag, 1990. LNCS 432.

[Rém90] Didier Rémy. *Algebres touffues. Application au typage polymorphe de objets enregistrements dans les langages fonctionnels.* PhD thesis, Université de Paris 7, 1990.

[Rey88] John C. Reynolds. Preliminary design of the programming language Forsythe. Technical Report CMU-CS-88-159, Carnegie-Mellon University, Computer Science Department, June 1988.

[Rit90] M. Rittri. Retrieving library identifiers via equational matching of types. In M. E. Stickel, editor, *10th Int. Conf. on Automated Deduction (CADE-10), Kaiserslautern, Germany*, pages 603–617. Springer-Verlag, July 1990. Lecture Notes in Artificial Intelligence, vol. 449.

[Rit91] M. Rittri. Using types as search keys in function libraries. *Journal of Functional Programming*, 1(1):71–89, 1991. (Earlier version in Func. Prog. Lang. and Comp. Arch. 1989, ACM Press.).

[RT89] C. Runciman and I. Toyn. Retrieving reusable software components by polymorphic type. In *Proceedings of Fourth International Conference on Functional Programming Languages and Computer Architecture (FPCA'89), London, U.K.* ACM Press, Addison-Wesley, 1989.

[Sie89] J.H. Siekmann. Unification theory. *Journal of Symbolic Computation*, 7:207–274, 1989.

[TA87] E. Tiden and S. Arnborg. Unification problems with one-sided distributivity. *Journal of Symbolic Computation*, 3:183–202, 1987.

[Tha88] Satish R. Thatte. Type inference with partial types. In Timo Lepistö and Arto Salomaa, editors, *Automata, languages and programming : 15th International Colloquium (ICALP'88)*, pages 615–629. Springer-Verlag, July 1988. LNCS 317.

[Tha90a] Satish R. Thatte. Quasi-static typing. In *Proceedings of Seventeenth POPL Symposium*, pages 367–381. ACM Press, 1990.

[Tha90b] Satish R. Thatte. Type inference and implicit scaling. In Neil Jones, editor, *Proceedings of Fourth European Symposium on Programming*, pages 406–420. Springer-Verlag, 1990. LNCS 432 (The full version will appear in a special issue of the journal Science of Computer Programming.).

[Tha91] Satish R. Thatte. Unification in finite acyclic theories is unitary. in preparation, 1991.

[Tho86] Simon Thompson. Laws in miranda. In *Proceedings of 1986 ACM Conference on LISP and Functional Programming*, pages 1–12. ACM Press, 1986.

[Wad87] Philip Wadler. Views: A way for pattern-matching to cohabit with data abstraction. In *Proceedings of Fourteenth POPL Symposium*, pages 307–313. ACM Press, 1987.

[Wan87] Mitchell Wand. Complete type inference for simple objects. In *Proceedings of Second LICS Symposium*, pages 37–44. IEEE Computer Society Press, 1987.

[Wan89] Mitchell Wand. Type inference for record concatenation and multiple inheritance. In *Proceedings of Fourth LICS Symposium*, pages 92–97. IEEE Computer Society Press, 1989.

Appendix: A Naive Unification Algorithm

Unify $(\tau, \nu, E) =$

Case 1: either τ or ν is a variable; let τ be the variable wlog

return $[\tau \mapsto \nu]\ Id \leftrightarrow Id$ if τ does not occur in ν and fail otherwise

Case 2: $\tau = C(\tau_1, \ldots, \tau_k),\ \nu = C(\nu_1, \ldots, \nu_k)$

let $S_0 = Id,\ S_i,\ c_i \leftrightarrow d_i = \mathit{Unify}(S_{i-1} \cdot\cdot S_0 \tau_i,\ S_{i-1} \cdot\cdot S_0 \nu_i,\ E),\ 1 \leq i < k$

return $S_k S_{k-1} \cdots S_1,\ C(c_1, \ldots, c_k) \leftrightarrow C(d_1, \ldots, d_k)$

Case 3: $\tau = C(\tau_1, \ldots, \tau_k),\ \nu = D(\nu_1, \ldots, \nu_m),\ C \neq D$

return $\mathit{Coerce}(\tau, \nu, E)$

Coerce $(\tau, \nu, E) =$

let $\tau = C(\tau_1, \ldots, \tau_k),\ \nu = D(\nu_1, \ldots, \nu_m)$

in if there is no path in $\mathcal{G}_E$ from C to D then return with failure

else let the unique path be C—B_1—$\cdots$—B_{n-1}—D and instantiate the corresponding n isomorphisms with new variables, yielding

$E \vdash \sigma_1 \underset{d_1}{\overset{c_1}{\rightleftarrows}} \nu_1, \ldots, E \vdash \sigma_n \underset{d_n}{\overset{c_n}{\rightleftarrows}} \nu_n$ where the equations are assumed to be oriented according to the orientation of the edges with C outermost in σ_1, D in ν_n and B_1 in ν_1 and σ_2, etc.

let $\nu_0 = \tau,\ \sigma_{n+1} = \nu,\ S_{-1} = Id$

and $S_i,\ a_i \leftrightarrow b_i = \mathit{Unify}(S_{i-1} \cdot\cdot S_{-1} \nu_i, S_{i-1} \cdot\cdot S_{-1} \sigma_{i+1}, E),\ 0 \leq i \leq n$ in

return $S_n S_{n-1} \cdot\cdot S_0,\ (a_n \bullet c_n \bullet \cdots \bullet a_1 \bullet c_1 \bullet a_0) \leftrightarrow (b_0 \bullet d_1 \bullet b_1 \bullet \cdots \bullet d_n \bullet b_n)$

Figure 1: *Procedures Unify and Coerce*

Compiler-Controlled Multithreading for Lenient Parallel Languages

Klaus Erik Schauser (schauser@cs.Berkeley.EDU)
David E. Culler (culler@cs.Berkeley.EDU)
Thorsten von Eicken (tve@cs.Berkeley.EDU)
Computer Science Division
University of California, Berkeley

Abstract: Tolerance to communication latency and inexpensive synchronization are critical for general-purpose computing on large multiprocessors. Fast dynamic scheduling is required for powerful non-strict parallel languages. However, machines that support rapid switching between multiple execution threads remain a design challenge. This paper explores how multithreaded execution can be addressed as a compilation problem, to achieve switching rates approaching what hardware mechanisms might provide.

Compiler-controlled multithreading is examined through compilation of a lenient parallel language, Id90, for a threaded abstract machine, TAM. A key feature of TAM is that synchronization is explicit and occurs only at the start of a thread, so that a simple cost model can be applied. A scheduling hierarchy allows the compiler to schedule logically related threads closely together in time and to use registers across threads. Remote communication is via message sends and split-phase memory accesses. Messages and memory replies are received by compiler-generated message handlers which rapidly integrate these events with thread scheduling.

To compile Id90 for TAM, we employ a new parallel intermediate form, dual-graphs, with distinct control and data arcs. This provides a clean framework for partitioning the program into threads, scheduling threads, and managing registers under asynchronous execution. The compilation process is described and preliminary measurements of its effectiveness are discussed. Dynamic execution measurements are obtained via a second compilation step, which translates TAM into native code for existing machines with instrumentation incorporated. These measurements show that the cost of compiler-controlled multithreading is within a small factor of the cost of control flow in sequential languages.

1 Introduction

Multithreaded execution appears to be a key ingredient in general purpose parallel computing systems. Many researchers suggest that processors should support multiple instruction streams and switch very rapidly between them in response to remote memory reference latencies or synchronization[AI87, Smi90, HF88, ALKK90, ACC$^+$90]. However, the proposed architectural solutions make thread scheduling invisible to the compiler, preventing it from applying optimizations that might reduce the cost of thread switching or improve scheduling based on analysis of the program. Inherently parallel languages, such as Id[Nik90] and Multilisp[Hal85], require that small execution threads be scheduled dynamically, even if executed on a uniprocessor[Tra88]. Traub's theoretical work demonstrates how to minimize thread switching for these languages on sequential machines. However, in compiling this class of languages for parallel machines, the goal is not simply to minimize the number of thread switches, but to minimize the total cost of synchronization while tolerating latency on remote references and making effective use of critical processor resources, such as registers and cache bandwidth. In this paper, we address this three-fold goal in compiling Id90 for execution on a threaded abstract machine, TAM, that exposes these costs to the compiler through explicit scheduling and storage hierarchies.

The lenient parallel language Id90 is taken as a starting point for the study, using the MIT compiler to produce dataflow program graphs[Tra86]. A new intermediate form, dual graphs, is introduced to provide a vehicle for integrated treatment of partitioning, thread scheduling and register usage. In dual graphs control and data dependences are separate, but stand on an equal footing. We show how dual graphs are produced for the basic constructs of the language and how partitioning and thread generation are performed. Finally, code quality is evaluated on several benchmarks.

2 Language Issues

Several studies have demonstrated that by exposing parallelism at all levels ample parallelism is available on a broad class of programs[ACM88, Cul90, AE88, AHN88]. Exposing parallelism at all levels requires that functions or arbitrary expressions be able to execute and possibly return results before all operands are computed. Data structures must be able to be accessed or passed around while components are still being computed. In language terms, this means functions, expressions, and data structures are non-strict, but not lazy. Traub has termed this class of languages *lenient*.

We begin with a several examples in Id90 to indicate the subtlety of compiling such a language and the need for multithreading. These are not intended to be indicative of important applications, but serve to demonstrate the compilation issues. The function `lookup_array`, as shown below, takes an array `A` of values and an ordered table `T` and returns an array of the table indexes corresponding to the values in `A` computed by `lookup`. Although there is little parallelism in the `lookup` function, all the lookups can be performed in parallel. Each access to `T[m]` in the lookup may require a remote access or may even suspend, if the table `T` is still being produced. Thus, we want to execute several lookups on each processor and be able to switch among them cheaply upon remote or deferred access. (The `lookup` function is used throughout the paper to illustrate the compilation process.) The function `flat` produces a list of the leaves of a binary tree using accumulation lists. If `cons` and `flat` are strict, this exhibits no parallelism. Under lenient execution, the list is constructed in parallel[Nik91]. The contrived function `two_things` returns a pair containing the square of its first argument and the product of its two arguments. It can compute and return `x*x` before `y` is available, which enhances parallelism. In fact, it must be able to do so, since the first result can be used as the second argument, as in the unusual function `cube`. The final example, due to Traub[Tra88], has three mutually recursive bindings, where the cyclic dependence through the conditional must be resolved dynamically.

```
def lookup_array A T = {(al,ah) = bounds A;  (tl,th) = bounds T
                        in {array (al,ah) of
                                 [i] = (lookup A[i] T tl th) || i <- al to ah}};
def lookup v T l h = {while l < h do
                        m = div (l + h) 2;
                        next l, next h = if (v <= T[m]) then (l,m) else (m+1,h)
                       finally l};
def flat tree acc = if (leaf tree) then (cons tree acc)
                        else flat (left tree) (flat (right tree) acc);
def two_things x y = (x*x, x*y);
def cube x = {a,b = two_things (x,a) in b};
def strange x p = {a,b,c = if p then (bb,x,aa) else (x,aa,bb);
                   aa = 3*a;
                   bb = 4*b
                  in c};
```

None of these examples present problems for a machine with dynamic instruction scheduling such as Monsoon[PC90]. At the same time, none require dynamic scheduling throughout. Thus, it makes sense to investigate hybrid execution models[Ian88, NA89], where statically ordered *threads* are scheduled dynamically. Our TAM model takes this idea one step further by exposing the scheduling of threads to the compiler as well, so that dynamic scheduling is done without hardware support. This means that register management can be closely tied to thread scheduling in order to minimize the overhead where dynamic scheduling is required.

3 TAM

To investigate compiler-controlled multithreading, a simple threaded abstract machine (TAM) has been developed. Synchronization, thread scheduling and storage management are explicit in the machine language and exposed to the compiler. TAM is presented elsewhere[CSS+91, vESC91]; in this section we describe the salient features of TAM as a compilation target. A primary design goal in TAM is to provide a means of exploiting locality, even under asynchronous execution, to minimize the overhead of multithreading.

A TAM program is a collection of *code-blocks*, typically representing functions in the program text. Each code-block comprises several *threads* and *inlets*. Invoking a code-block involves allocating an *activation frame* to hold its local variables, depositing argument values into the (possibly remote) frame and enabling threads within the code-block for execution in the context of the frame. Since an activation does not suspend when it invokes a subordinate, the dynamic call structure is represented by a tree of activation frames, rather than a stack. Instructions in a thread may refer to slots in the current frame and to processor registers. A frame is said to be *resident* when a processor is executing threads relative to the frame. A resident frame continues executing as long as it has enabled threads. A *quantum* is the set of threads executed during a single residency.

A thread is simply a sequence of instructions; it contains no jumps or suspension points; synchronization occurs only at the top of a thread. TAM control primitives initiate or terminate threads. *Fork* attempts to enable a thread in the current activation. *Stop* terminates its thread and causes some other enabled thread to begin execution. A synchronizing thread has associated with it a frame slot containing its *entry count*. The entry count is explicitly set prior to any fork of the thread. Each time the thread is forked, its entry count is decremented; the thread is enabled when the entry count reaches zero. Conditional execution is supported by a *cfork* operation, which forks one of two threads, based on a boolean operand. Merging of conditionally executed threads is implicit, since the arms of a conditional can both contain a fork to a common thread. Fork essentially puts a thread into a work pool that is serviced continuously, while multiple long latency requests and synchronization events are outstanding.

TAM assumes that an activation executes on a single processor; work is distributed over processors at the activation level. Thus, passing arguments and results between frames may involve interprocessor communication. The *Send* operation delivers a sequence of data values to an *inlet* relative to the target frame. An inlet is a restricted thread that extracts data from a message, deposits it into specific slots in the designated frame, and forks threads for the corresponding activation. Inlets are compiler generated message handlers that quickly integrate message data into the computation. An inlet may interrupt a thread, but does not disturb the current quantum; threads enabled by the inlet will run when their frame becomes resident.

TAM provides a specialized form of send to support split-phase access to data structures. The heap is assumed to be distributed over processors, so access to a data element may require interprocessor communication. In addition, accesses may be synchronizing, as with I-structures[ANP87] where a read of an empty element is deferred until the corresponding write takes place. I-structure operations generate a request for a particular heap location and the response is received by an inlet. Meanwhile, the processor continues with other enabled threads.

Scheduling in TAM is under compiler control and tied closely to the storage hierarchy. The first level of scheduling is static — grouping and ordering instructions into threads. Values defined and used within a thread can be retained in processor registers. The next level of scheduling is dynamic — a quantum. Threads enabled by fork or cfork operations execute within the same quantum as the fork. Values can be transmitted in registers between threads that the compiler can prove will execute in the same quantum. When no enabled threads remain, another activation with enabled threads must be made resident. This also is under compiler control. The scheduling queue is contained within the frames, and the last thread executed in a quantum, called the *leave thread*, includes code to locate the next activation and fork to a designated *enter thread* within that activation. Empirically, quanta often cross many points of possible suspension[CSS+91]. Thus, it is advantageous to keep values in registers between threads that the compiler cannot prove will execute in a single quantum. The compiler can construct leave and enter threads that save and restore specific registers if the guess proves incorrect.

The task of compiling for TAM has two aspects. First, a program must be partitioned into valid threads. This aspect is constrained partly by the language and partly by the execution model. The language dictates which portions of the program can be scheduled statically and which require dynamic synchronization. An elegant theoretical framework for addressing the language requirements is provided by Traub's work[Tra88]. The execution model places further constraints on partitioning, since synchronization only occurs at the entry to a thread and conditional execution occurs only between threads. These constraints simplify treatment of the language requirements. The second aspect is management of processor and storage resources in the context of dynamic scheduling to gain maximum performance. This involves analysis of expected quantum boundaries, frame and register assignment under asynchronous thread scheduling, and generation of inlets.

4 Dual Graphs

Compilation of Id90 to TAM begins after generation of dataflow program graphs[Tra86]. Program graphs are a hierarchical graphical intermediate form that facilitates powerful high level optimizations. The meaning of program graphs is given in terms of a dataflow firing rule, so control flow is implicitly prescribed by the dynamic propagation of values. In TAM, control is explicit and the flow of data is implicit in the use of registers and frame slots. In order to bridge this gap, we introduce a new graphical intermediate form, *dual graphs*, in which control and data flow are both explicit. Dual graphs are similar in form to data structures used in most optimizing compilers, but the key differences are that they describe parallel control flow and are in static single assignment form[CFR+89]. Compilation to TAM involves a series of transformations on the dual graph, described below.

A **dual graph** is a directed graph with three types of arcs: data, control and dependence.

- **Data arcs:** A data arc $(u, o) - -(v, i)$ specifies that the value produced by output o of node u is used as operand i by node v. A node may have several data output ports; each port represents a name (*i.e.*, a memory location) to which a value can be bound (one producer) and accessed (multiple consumers).
- **Control arcs:** A control arc $u \rightarrow v$ specifies that instruction u executes before instruction v and has direct responsibility for scheduling v. A node may have one or more control output ports, each with a bundle of control arcs.
- **Dependence arcs (split-phase long-latency arcs):** A dependence arc, $u \rightsquigarrow v$ specifies that inlet instruction v will be scheduled as an indirect consequence of executing outlet instruction u.

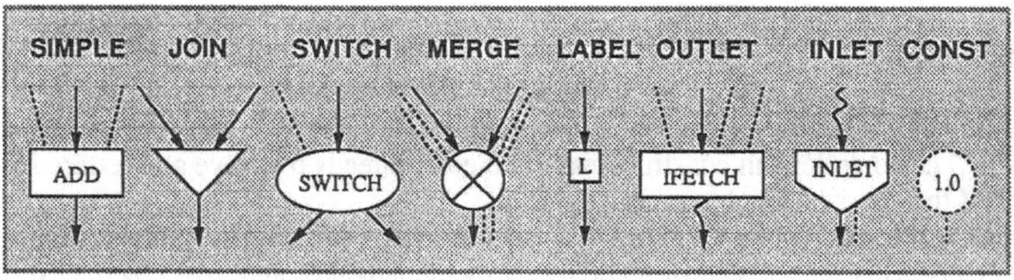

Figure 1: Dual Graph Nodes

Dual-graphs have well-defined operational semantics and can be executed directly. Control can be represented by tokens traveling along the control arcs. A node fires when control tokens are present on all its control inputs (merge nodes are the only exception to this rule). Upon firing, a node computes a result based on data values bound to its data inputs, binds the result to its data outputs, and propagates control tokens to its control outputs. In correct dual graphs, control will appear on control inputs only if corresponding data inputs have been produced. To ensure this, is the task of the compiler. As shown in Figure 1, there are eight types of nodes.

- A **simple node** describes an arithmetic or logic operation. It has a single control input, a data input for each operand, a single control output port (the successors), and typically a single data output port (the result). When control passes to a simple node, it reads the value bound to its data inputs, performs its operation, binds the result to the data outputs and produces a new token on the output control arcs.

- A **join** synchronizes control paths. It has multiple control inputs and a single control output port. Control passes to its control output once a token arrives on every control input.

- A **switch** conditionally steers control. It has a control input and a boolean data input; control passes on to one of its control outputs depending on the value of the data input.

- A **merge** complements the switch by steering control from one of many control inputs to a single control output. (It is the only node that is not strict in its control inputs.) It also unifies the data inputs associated with the active control input to the data outputs, *i.e.*, the input data is bound to the output name. A merge has multiple matching input sets, each with a control input and zero or more data inputs. The output ports have the same topology. In the final code generation for TAM, merge may expand into collections of data moves.

- A **label** indicates a separation constraint; the adjacent nodes must be in distinct threads. It has one control input port and one control output port. (In generating dual graphs, a label is placed on each output of a switch, reflecting the fork-based control primitives in TAM.)

- An **outlet** sends a message or initiates a request. These have an effect external to their code-block. An outlet has a single control input, a data input for each operand, and a dependence output connecting it to inlet nodes that receive responses.

- An **inlet** receives a message or split-phase response. It may have a dependence input and has one control output and zero or more data outputs. It will receive values corresponding to its data outputs and pass control to the operations connected to its control output. Usually its dependence input will be connected to the dependence output of a node that sends a split-phase request indicating that it will handle the response. Inlets that receive arguments are identified by convention.

- A **constant** node represents a manifest constant. It has a data output, but neither a control input nor a control output, since the value is known at compile time.

Dual graphs are generated by expanding dataflow program graph instructions. This is a local transformation described by expansion rules for individual program graph nodes. A program graph arc expands into a data arc and a control arc in the dual graph. In many cases, one or the other will prove unnecessary and be eliminated.

The program graph for the `lookup` example includes a function DEF node, enclosing a LOOP node, enclosing a IF node, as shown in Figure 2. The figure shows the corresponding dual graph representation, using a 1-bounded loop[Cul90]. The four arguments enter at the inlet nodes at the top of the graph. Since the function is strict in all its arguments, their control outputs are joined before the merge. The data arcs (shown dashed) for `l` and `h` connect to the merge nodes at the top of the loop. The other inlets are connected directly to

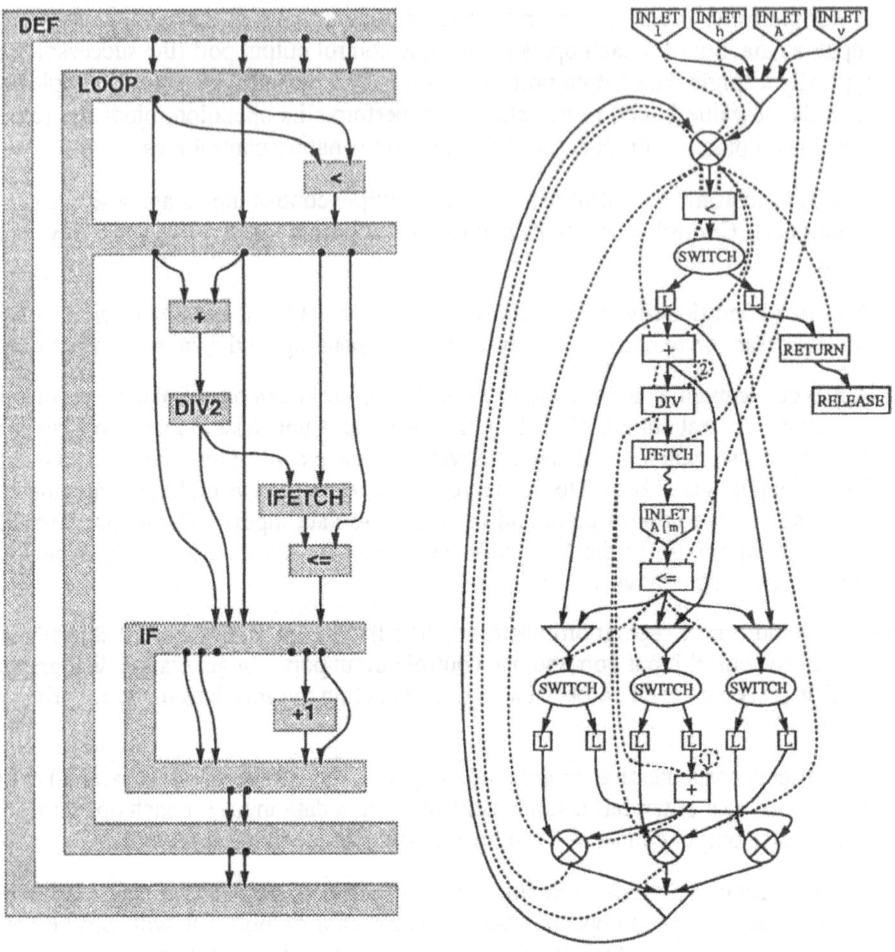

Figure 2: Program graph and dual graph for `lookup` example

their uses within the loop and the enclosed conditional, as do the data outputs of the loop merge. By separating the control and data arcs, the flow of information is not obscured by control constructs. In each iteration, control is directed to the loop body or exit based on the loop predicate. Within the body of the loop, the value of `m` is calculated and used in an I-fetch operation. The result of the I-fetch will eventually arrive at the inlet indicated by the dependence arc. This inlet feeds the conditional predicate, which controls three separate switches, one for each data value used in the conditional. The three switches cause the correct values to be routed to the merges, producing the next iteration values of `l` and `h`. The third merge has only control inputs and serves to indicate that all the switches have executed. Control is joined at the bottom of the loop and directed to the loop merge.

The dual-graph for an Id program could be executed directly, but the number of dynamic synchronizations per useful operation would be high. The compilation goal is to minimize this cost by employing the cheapest form of synchronization available in the synchronization hierarchy provided by TAM — the sequencing of instructions in a thread. Identifying portions of the dual graph that can be executed as a thread is called partitioning.

5 Partitioning

The key step in compiling a lenient language for a machine that executes instruction sequences is partitioning the program into statically schedulable entities[Tra88]. Fundamental limits on partitioning are imposed by dependence cycles that can only be resolved dynamically. In ID these arise due to conditionals, function calls, and access to I-structures. Partitioning for TAM involves identifying portions of the dual graph that can be executed as a TAM thread, *i.e.*, a partition must be linearizable with synchronization and control entry occurring only at the top. The number of entries to a thread must be statically determined. Partitioning uses only the control and dependence arcs of the dual graph. Assignment of storage to output ports is deferred until after partitioning; the critical information is retained in the data arcs.

Definition 1 A *TAM partition* is a subset of dual graph nodes and their incident control and dependence edges. In a valid partitioning, partitions are node-disjoint and cover the graph. A partition consists of an *input region* containing only inlet, merge, and label nodes and a *body* containing simple nodes, outlets, switches and joins. The *outputs* of a partition are its outlet nodes and all leaving control arcs. Control edges that connect two partitions belong to both partitions.

Definition 2 (Safe Partition) We call a TAM partition *safe* if (i) no output of the partition needs be produced before all inputs to the body are available, (ii) when the inputs to the body are available, all nodes in the body are executed, and (iii) no arc connects a body node to an input node of the same partition.

The first property says that the body of the partition can be treated as strict. The second says that there is no conditional execution within a partition; conditional execution occurs only between partitions. The third implies that a partition is acyclic, since all cycles include a switch and a merge, and can be linearized by a topological sort on control arcs. Also, all dependence arcs must cross partitions. Finally, the entry count for any valid execution of the partition is constant. These properties imply the following lemma. (We will omit proofs throughout this paper. The interested reader is referred to [Sch91].)

Lemma 1 *A safe partition can be mapped into a TAM thread.*

Our partitioning algorithm first identifies small safe partitions. Then, these *basic partitions* are iteratively *merged* into larger safe partitions by applying simple merge rules, eliminating redundant control arcs, and combining switches and merges until the process converges. Below, we describe creation of basic partitions and discuss the merge and elimination rules.

5.1 Basic Partitioning

A simple method basic partitioning observes that unary operations never need dynamic synchronization; thus, joins, inlets, merges and labels each start a new partition. Simple, switch and outlet nodes are placed into the partition of their control predecessor. We call this **dataflow partitioning** because each partition is like a dataflow actor, enabled by a binary match or arrival of a message. Note, that this form of partitioning puts fan-out trees into a partition.

Dependence sets partitioning is far more powerful. It finds safe partitions by grouping together nodes which depend on the same set of input nodes (inlets, merges and labels). This guarantees that there are no cyclic dependences within a partition. This is a variant of Iannucci's method of dependence sets [Ian88]. It groups overlapping fan-out trees into a partition. Dependence sets is powerful and practical to implement.

Definition 3 (Dependence Set) The *dependence set* for a dual graph node u is the set of input nodes i such that there exists a control path of length zero or more from i to u that does not go through any other input node.

To compute the dependence sets, assign each input node the dependence set containing only itself and for all other nodes assign the union of the dependence sets of the control predecessors. Our definition will not allow dependence to cross switches because every control output of a switch will be connected to a label.

One can propose many other partitioning schemes. For example, **dominance sets partitioning** finds safe partitions by grouping together nodes which dominate the same set of output nodes (outlet nodes and nodes that directly feed a control input of an merge or label).

Lemma 2 (Basic Partitioning) *Dataflow partitioning, dependence sets partitioning and dominance sets partitioning create only safe partitions.*

5.2 Merging partitions

After basic partitioning, partitions will be merged into larger safe partitions by iteratively applying two merge rules.

Merge up rule: Two partitions α and β can be merged into a larger partition if (i) all input arcs to β come from α, (ii) β contains no inlet nodes, and (iii) all output arcs from the body of α connect to body nodes of β.

Figure 3 shows this case graphically. The arcs connecting *alpha* to *beta* indicate that it is necessary for *alpha* to execute before *beta*. The first two points of the merge up rule imply that this is also sufficient. The last point ensures that no separation constraint is violated. The

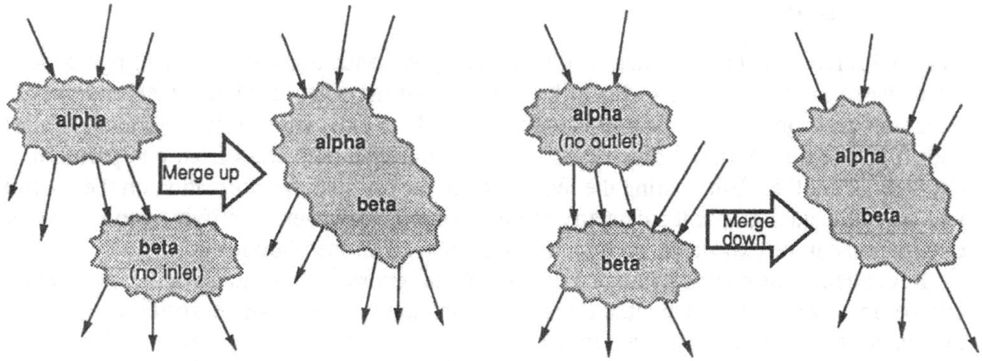

Figure 3: Merge rules: A partition with a single control predecessor can be *merged up* if no "separation constraints" are violated. A partition can be *merged down* into a successor, if the results of the partition feed strictly into the successor.

astute reader will notice that this rule cannot be applied after basic partitioning. Opportunities for this rule arise as a result of "merging down".

Merge down rule: Two partitions α and β can be merged into a larger partition if (i) all output arcs from α go to β, (ii) α contains no outlet nodes, and (iii) no output arc from the body of α goes to an input node of β.

The first two points ensure that *alpha* has no side-effect on an input of *beta*. The last point guarantees that no separation constraint is violated.

Lemma 3 (Merge) *If α and β are safe partitions meeting the conditions of the "merge up" rule, then the merged partition is safe, and similarly for the "merge down" rule.*

The synchronization cost for a partition is proportional to the number of control arcs that enter the body from other partitions plus the number of nodes in the input region that have control arcs going to the body. For a merged partition, this number can never be greater than the sum of the synchronization costs of the two unmerged partitions. Thus we have the following.

Lemma 4 *Applying the partitioning merge rules will never increase the synchronization cost.*

The quality of partitioning after merging depends strongly on basic partitioning. Dependence sets partitioning always produces better partitions than dataflow partitioning. The power of dependence sets and dominance sets partitioning lies in the fact that they can work across different fan-out or fan-in trees. It is possible to find examples where dependence sets partitioning is superior to dominance sets partitioning, and vice versa[Sch91]. A better choice may be to combine the two forms of basic partitioning.

5.3 Redundant Arc Elimination

The goal of redundant arc elimination is to reduce synchronization cost. Eliminating a control arc between two partitions avoids a fork and decreases the entry count of the target partition. A control arc from partition u to v is redundant if there exist another unconditional control path from u to v. A trivial case of this is where multiple arcs cross from one partition to the body of another. Eliminating the redundant arc is a simple transformation on the control portion of the dual graph; the data arcs are unchanged. However, identifying candidates for elimination can be expensive, so limitations are placed on the search.

Redundant control arcs within a partition can be ignored, since the partition will eventually be linearized into a sequential thread. Elimination of arcs between partitions improves the quality of partitioning, since it may enable additional merges. Thus, after each partition merge the incident arcs to the new partition should be checked for redundancy.

5.4 Switch and merge combining

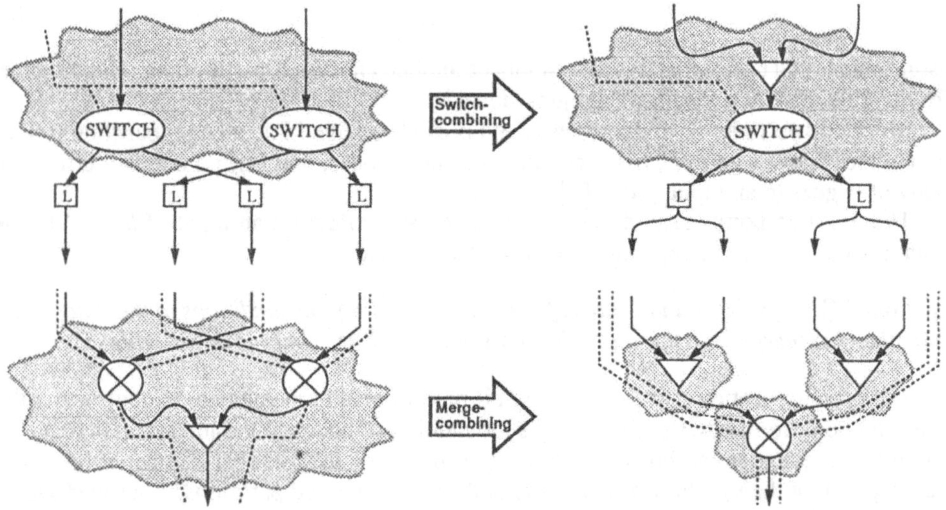

Figure 4: Switch and Merge Combining

Two switches that are in the same partition and are steered by the same predicate can be merged into a single switch. This optimization attempts to reduce the control transfer overhead where the full power of lenient conditionals is not required. Switch combining is a simple transformation on the control graph, as shown in the top part of Figure 4.

Merges that are in the same partition and are determined by the same predicate can be combined into a single merge that steers the union of the data arcs, as shown in the bottom part of Figure 4. This optimization serves primarily to reduce synchronization costs by enabling further merging of partitions within the arms of the conditional.

5.5 Partitioning algorithm

We can now summarize our partitioning algorithm for TAM:

Algorithm 1 (Dependence sets partitioning with merging)

- *Compute the dependence sets for all nodes,*
- *Put all nodes with the same dependence set into the same basic partition,*
- *iteratively apply the merge rules (and optionally redundant arc elimination, switch combining, and merge combining) until no rule applies.*

The previous lemmas imply the following correctness theorem.

Theorem 1 (Partitioning Algorithm) *The partitioning algorithm produces only safe partitions.*

Traub showed that optimal partitioning is NP-complete. Our algorithm is a heuristic, since starting with basic partitions, it will iteratively merge partitions as long as a merge rule can be applied. If mutually exclusive merge rules are applicable at some point, one is picked arbitrarily. Partitioning decisions imply trade-offs between parallelism, synchronization cost, and sequential efficiency. However, given the limits on thread size imposed by the language model, the use of split-phase accesses, and the control paradigm, we simply attempt to make partitions as large as possible and minimize the synchronization cost. In Section 7 we compare partitioning according to the algorithm above against dependence sets basic partitioning without merging and simple dataflow partitioning.

5.6 Partitioning the lookup example

To illustrate the partitioning process, we consider the `lookup` example from Figure 2. Grouping nodes with the same dependence set, we get 20 basic partitions. Iteratively merging partitions using the two merge rules, yields twelve partitions as shown in the left part of Figure 5. The example contains three redundant arcs connecting to the `joins` above the three `switches`. One comes from the control output of the `div`, the other two from the loop body `label`. These are redundant since the dependence arc between the `ifetch` and the corresponding `inlet` guarantees that the partition with the `ifetch` will always be executed before the partition with the three switches. The three switches can be combined into a single switch, replacing the three labels on each side with a new label. Similarly, the three merges can be combined, yielding the final partitioned dual graph shown in the right part of Figure 5.

6 Thread Generation

To produce TAM code, the dual graph partitions must be ordered, each must be linearized to form a thread, and data outputs must be replaced by specific registers and frame slots, so that subsequent operations can use them. This is done by the following steps: (1) lifetime and quantum analysis, (2) instruction scheduling, (3) frame slot and register assignment, (4)

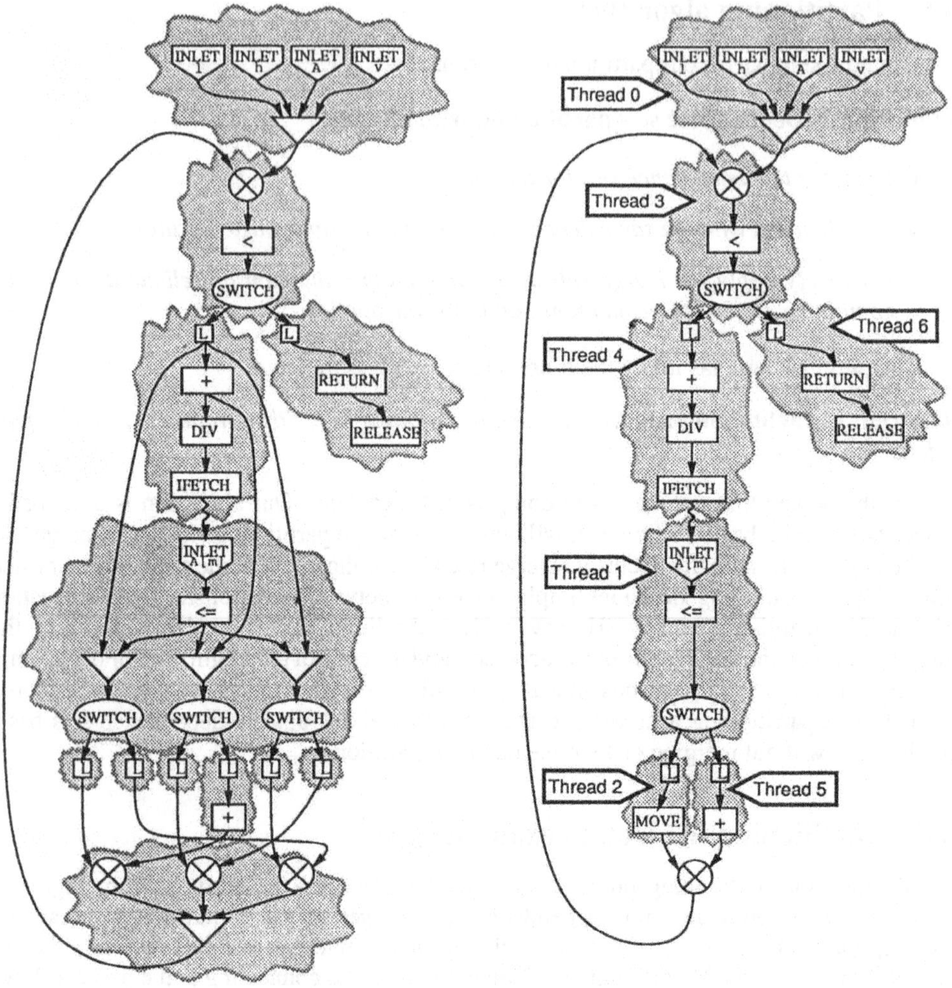

Figure 5: Dual Graph for `lookup` after dependence sets partitioning and merging. Right side shows graph after redundant arc elimination, switch and merge combining, move-insertion and thread ordering

move insertion, (5) entry count determination, (6) fork insertion, (7) thread ordering, and, finally, assembly.

Lifetime analysis: Determining whether a value can be stored in a register or needs to be placed in a frame slot involves a simple lifetime analysis using the data arcs of the dual graph. If all targets of a data output are in the same partition as the source node, the lifetime of the value is limited to a single thread. It can safely be placed in a register. More generally, values can be carried in registers across threads, as long as the threads are guaranteed to execute in the same quantum.

Instruction Scheduling: The dual graph partitions are a partial order and must be linearized. Linearization influences the lifetime of values and thus has an effect on the register and frame slot usage. Furthermore, optimal instruction scheduling depends on pipeline structure and register availability. Although dual graphs are well suited for this kind of optimization, our current heuristic merely attempts to minimize the overlap of the lifetimes of values.

Frame slot and register assignment: In order to reduce frame size and the number of registers required, storage is reused for distinct data outputs that have disjoint lifetimes. An appropriate interference graph is constructed for each storage class using the data arcs in the linearized dual graph. It contains a node for each value and an edge between two nodes if their lifetimes overlap. Coloring this graph so that all vertices connected by an edge have different colors gives a valid register and frame slot assignment. Whereas in sequential languages the uncertainty in interference arises because of multiple assignments under unpredictable control paths, in compiling ID to TAM the uncertainty arises because of dynamic scheduling.

Move insertion: A merge node has a single control output port and various control input ports, each with some number of data ports. The compiler must insure that for each control input, data port i will be assigned the same frame slot or register as the data port i for the control output. Basically, this constrains register coloring to use the same color for each of the data ports. Whenever this cannot be achieved a MOVE instruction is inserted in the partition providing input to the merge. If this predecessor is in the same partition as the merge, *e.g.*, if the merge is directly fed by a label or merge, a new partition must be created. Currently, we try to minimize the number of move insertions by unifying names at merges before coloring for register and frame slots.

Entry counts: Synchronizing threads in TAM have an associated frame slot where the entry counter is maintained. For each partition, the entry count of the corresponding thread is equal to the number of control arcs that enter the body from other partitions plus the number of nodes from the input region that have control arcs going to the body.

Fork insertion: A partitioned dual graph contains switches where conditional forks are required, but does not contain forks. These are only determined after partitioning is complete. Where a control arc crosses from one partition to another, other than from a switch, a *fork* to the target partition is inserted.

Thread ordering: The TAM control transfer primitives fork threads for later execution. This could be exploited to fetch the next thread while completing the current one. Even so, by placing threads contiguously, a fork and a stop can often be replaced by a simple fall-through. Since current processors cannot exploit fork-based control, the translator from TAM to target machine code moves the last fork or switch in a thread to the very bottom and replaces it by a branch. If the target is the next thread, this becomes a fall-through. Our current thread ordering scheme tries to maximize the number of fall-throughs.

Figure 5 shows how thread numbers are assigned for the lookup example. Note that thread 1 to 4 are placed contiguously. At machine code level the switch from thread 1 to threads 2 and 5, as well as the switch from thread 3 to 4 and 6 will be replaced by a single conditional branch, while the fork from thread 2 to 3 will turn into a fall-through.

7 Results

This section presents preliminary data on the quality of TAM code produced under our compilation paradigm. Previous to this work, execution of Id programs was limited to specialized architectures or dataflow graph interpreters. By compiling via TAM, we have achieved more than two orders of magnitude performance improvement over graph interpreters on conventional machines, making this Id implementation competitive with machines supporting dynamic instruction scheduling in hardware[PC90, SYH+89, GH90, Ian88]. By constraining how dual-graphs are partitioned, we can generate TAM code that closely models these other target architectures. It can be seen that the TAM partitioning described in this paper reduces the control overhead substantially and that more aggressive partitioning would yield modest additional benefit. There is, however, considerable room for improvement in scheduling and register management.

7.1 Benchmarks

Ten benchmark programs ranging from 50 to 1,100 lines are used. *Lookup* is the small example program discussed above. The input is an array and a table of 10,000 elements. *AS* is an array selection sort, where the key is a function passed to the sort routine. The input is an array of 500 numbers. *QS* is a simple quick-sort using accumulation lists. The input is a list of 1,000 random numbers. *MMT* is a simple matrix operation test; two double precision identity matrices are created, multiplied, and subtracted from a third. The matrix size is 100×100. *Wavefront* computes a sequence of matrices, using a variant of successive over-relaxation. Each element of the new matrix is computed by combining the three new values to the north and west with value of corresponding element of the old matrix. Thirty iterations are run on matrices of size 100×100. *DTW* implements a dynamic time warp algorithm used in discrete word speech recognition[Sah91]. The size of the test template and number of cepstral coefficients is 100. *Speech* is used to determine cepstral coefficients for speech processing. We take 10240 speech samples and compute 30 cepstral coefficients. *Paraffins*[AHN88] enumerates the distinct isomers of paraffins of size up to 14. *Gamteb* is a Monte Carlo neutron transport code[BCS+89]. It is highly recursive with many conditionals. *Simple* is a hydrodynamics and heat conduction code widely used as an application benchmark, rewritten in Id[CHR78, AE88]. One iteration is run on 50×50 matrices.

Our current compiler performs only a limited form of redundant arc elimination and does no switch or merge combining. Registers are used only for thread local values. TAM code can be expanded to run on MIPS, nCUBE, or (via C) several other platforms. The expansion can insert code to gather TAM-level statistics at run time. In this section we present only dynamic statistics, which were collected on one node of a multiprocessor nCUBE/2.

7.2 TAM vs Dataflow

To better understand the quality of TAM partitioning, we may constrain the compiler to produce code in the spirit of recent dataflow or hybrid architectures. These machines all provide a notion of execution thread and a specific synchronization mechanism. An instruction on these machines maps into multiple TAM instructions, providing a consistent cost metric for control, scheduling and message passing.

- Threads produced by dataflow partitioning without merging reflects the limited thread capability of most dataflow machines. Hardware provides two-way synchronization as token matching on binary operations; unary operations do not require matching, so they can be scheduled into the pipeline following the instruction on which they depend.
- Threads produced using dependence sets partitioning without merging correspond closely to Scheduling Quanta in Iannucci's hybrid architecture[Ian88]. Iannucci integrates thread generation and register assignment to a limited extent; registers are assumed to vanish at every possible suspension point or control transfer. This style of register usage is incorporated in recent dataflow machines, including Monsoon[PT91], Epsilon[GH90] and EM-4[SYH^+89], allowing partitioning similar to the hybrid model.
- For TAM we use our best partitioning: dependence sets partitioning with merging.

The distribution of instructions for the the ten benchmark programs is shown in Figure 6.a. For each program three columns are shown: dependence sets partitioning with merging (DE_ME), dependence sets partitioning without merging (DE), and dataflow partitioning without merging (DF). The final three columns give the arithmetic mean over all programs. The bar graphs show the distribution of instructions into classes: ALU, data moves, split-phase operations, instructions in inlets, control overhead, and moves needed to initialize or reset entry counts. For each program, the distributions are normalized with respect to DE_ME to better illustrate the relative costs. (Where possible numbers indicate size of containing box).

The number of ALU, data move, split-phase, and inlet instructions is independent of the type of partitioning. Under DE_ME, we have on average 20% ALU, 6% data moves, 10% split-phase, and 24% inlet instructions. An inlet will usually execute three instructions: one that receives the corresponding data value and stores it into the appropriate frame, a FORK which puts the corresponding thread into the remote continuation vector and enables the frame, and finally a STOP. The fraction of time spent in inlets may differ from instruction frequency, depending on how quickly the implementation can start the message handler, receive the message, and enable the corresponding thread.

The number of control instructions and entry count moves varies substantially under the different partitioning schemes. On average, 31% of the instructions are used for control under DE_ME, less than twice the fraction of control operations in sequential languages. Without merging nearly twice as many control instructions are needed, and three times as many with only dataflow partitioning. Entry count moves follow the same trend.

Without merging 1.33 times as many instructions are executed as with DE_ME. Dataflow partitioning yields about 1.85 times as many instructions executed. Comparing these partitioning styles highlights the effects of improved compilation. It is not meant to be a performance comparison between the three classes of machines, as merging could be employed to improve code quality for hybrid or dataflow machines to some extent, and actual

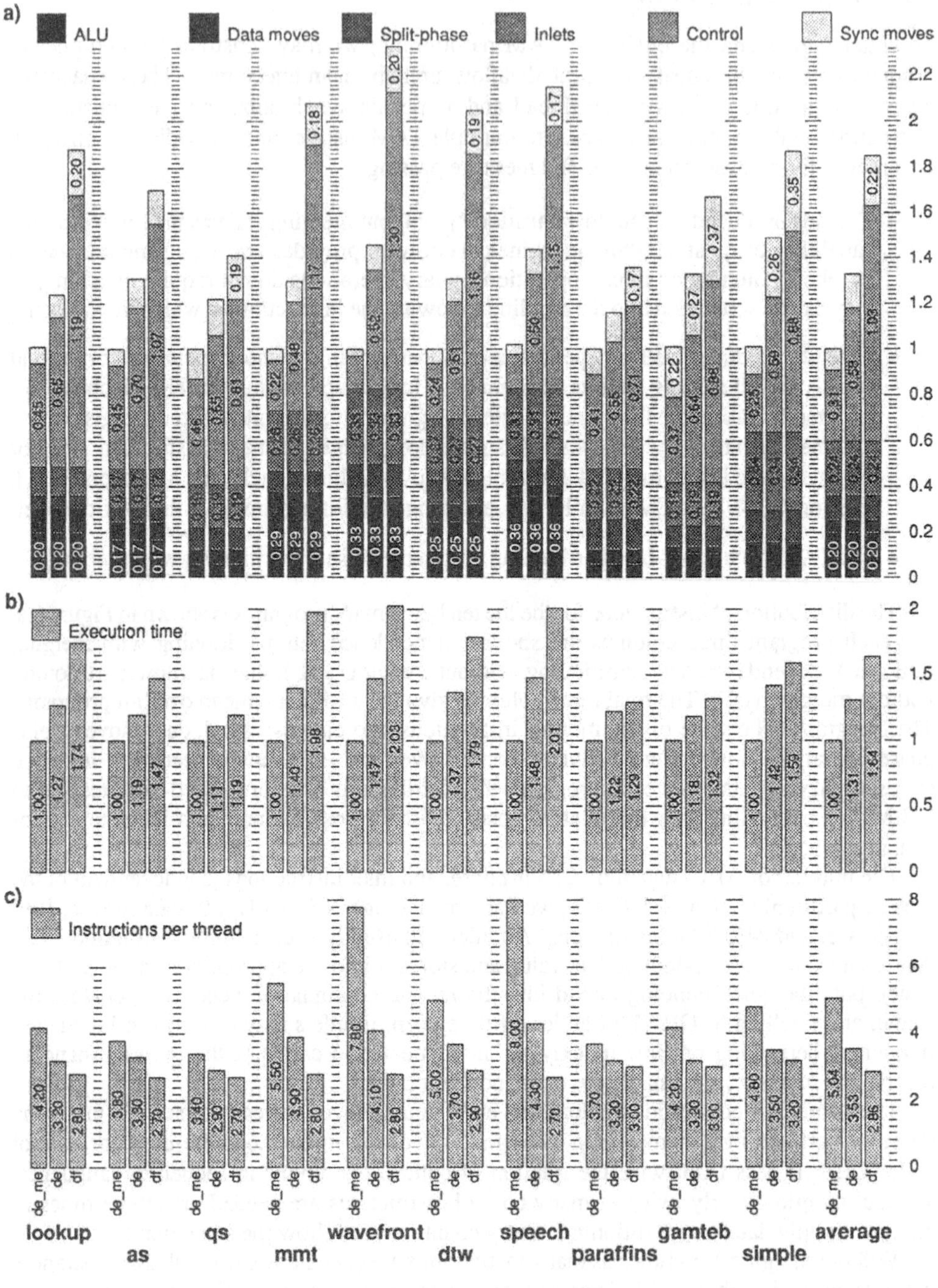

Figure 6: (a) Instruction distributions, (b) Relative execution times, (c) Thread sizes.

performance depends on cycle time, specifics of operand fetch, instruction issue, etc. The qualitative difference is that the control portion is reduced with better partitioning. This gain derives from two sources. By increasing the thread size, a greater fraction of explicit control and synchronization operations are made implicit through instruction ordering. Secondly, separating control and data flow allows redundant synchronization between partitions to be identified and eliminated.

The strong relationship between Figures 6.a and 6.b confirms that the reduction in control overhead translates into execution efficiency and that the TAM instruction as a cost unit is reasonable. For *AS*, *QS* and *MMT* running the same programs written in C is between 2 and 3 times as fast. *Simple* on the recent dataflow machine Monsoon is twice as fast as executing the TAM program on standard RISC, a MIPS R3000.

7.3 Thread Characteristics

Average thread lengths are shown in Figure 6.c. Using DE_ME the average thread length is slightly over 5 instructions. While this is not large, it should be noted that control primitives in TAM fork threads, so thread length is expected to be close to typical branch distances. Also, global accesses are split-phase, so they initiate threads. Finally, instruction count would increase if arithmetic instruction could only access registers. The larger thread sizes in wavefront and speech arise because many requests are issued in one thread and all the responses are received by another. Smaller threads result from conditionals, since no combining is performed.

Improved partitioning not only changes the size of threads, it changes their structure. The stacked bars in Figure 7.b show the breakdown of threads into synchronizing and non-synchronizing (*i.e.*, entry count is one) relative to DE_ME. Without merging, roughly twice as many threads are executed and four times using only dataflow partitioning. The number of threads executed does not grow inversely to thread size, since the overall instruction count is reduced by better partitioning. With the exception of *Gamteb*, two-thirds of the threads are non-synchronizing, regardless of partitioning. Better partitioning reduces the number of both kinds of threads, although the average entry count for synchronizing threads increases. For DE_ME the average entry count varies between 3 and 8. Forks from a thread to a non-synchronizing thread are essentially jumps, however, non-synchronizing threads can also be forked by inlets in handling an incoming message or response.

The effects of more sophisticated partitioning are more apparent in examining the fork operations. Figure 7.b shows the number of forks to synchronizing and non-synchronizing threads occurring in threads and inlets. The number of forks occurring in inlets is independent of partitioning, whereas the number of forks occurring in threads is reduced. However, as partitions are merged, inlet forks shift dramatically from non-synchronizing to synchronizing. Synchronizing messages in inlets means that frames are not activated until several operands have accumulated.

The data presented above was obtained without switch and merge combining. Implementing these will reduce the control portion further under TAM. Combining inlets, *i.e.*, sending multiple arguments as a single larger message, can be applied when the arguments feed the same partition; this will reduce the number of inlets instructions. Global strictness analysis could be applied to attempt to reduce these two components further, but the lower bound on control is the branch frequency and on inlets is the frequency of split-phase operations. Keeping in mind that the target is parallel execution, not complete sequentialization, it appears that DE_ME partitioning is approaching the "knee of the curve."

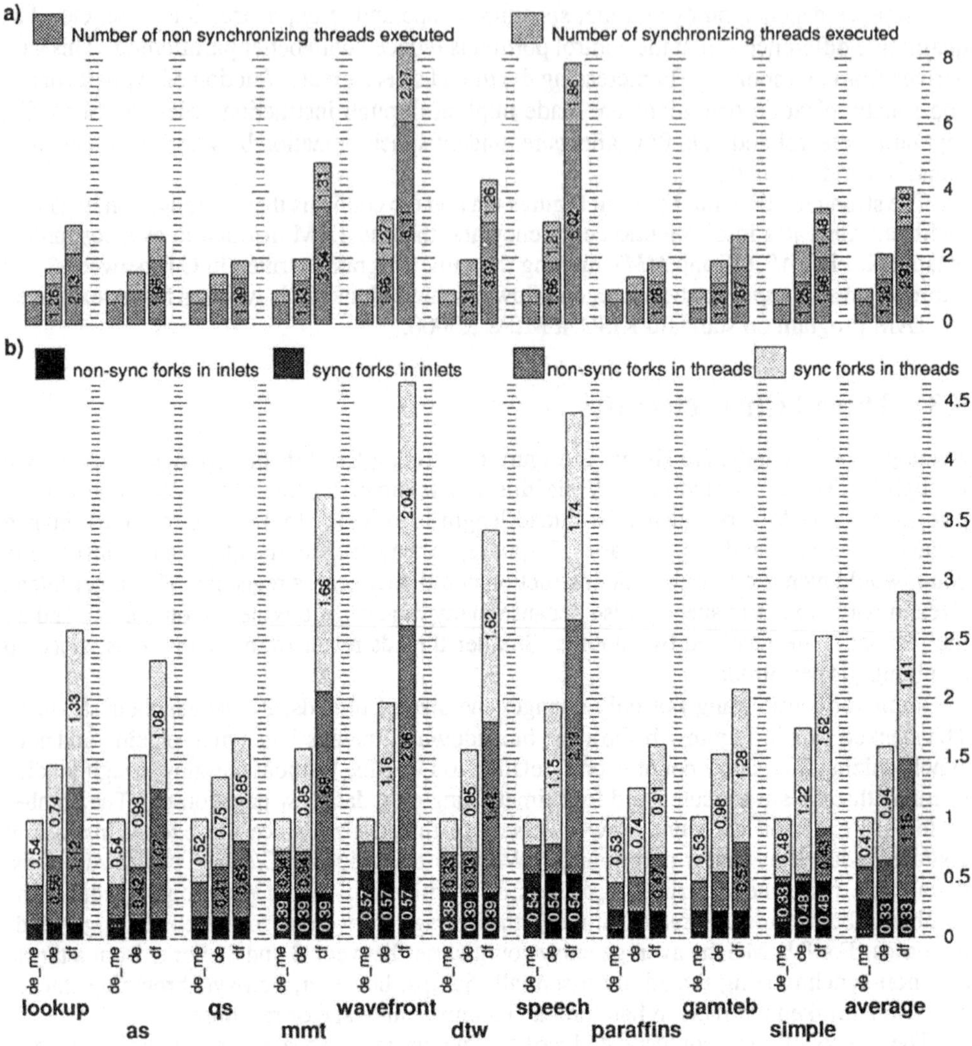

Figure 7: (a) Relative thread counts, (b) Control instruction distributions

7.4 Dynamic Scheduling

The second aspect of TAM compilation is management of processor and storage resources in the context of dynamic scheduling. Dual graphs were developed specifically to attack this problem, although our current compiler uses only registers in threads. Table 1 shows the dynamic scheduling behavior of programs under TAM using DE_ME. We assume zero latency, so I-Fetches return immediately, unless deferred. The table shows the number of code-block activations, quanta, threads and instructions executed. Also shown are ratios of these. The number of quanta per activation (QPA) is small, usually between 2 and 3. Thus, the cost of swapping to another code-block activation (roughly 10 instructions) is paid infrequently. Although thread sizes (IPT) are small, quanta generally contain many threads (TPQ), so quantum based register allocation stands to make much better use of registers. Where the compiler fails to discover that two computations can be put into the same thread, often the two computations will occur in the same quantum. The cost of synchronizing them is not large — it requires that the entry count be decremented and tested. This dynamic scheduling behavior — although collected on a sequential machine — indicates the value of TAM's scheduling hierarchy.

Program	Activations	Quanta	Threads	Instructions	QPA	TPQ	IPQ	IPT
lookup	10002	20003	1105342	4683207	2.0	55.3	234.1	4.2
as	503	1005	2386788	9046137	2.0	2374.9	9001.1	3.8
qs	6004	14007	408945	1393260	2.3	29.2	99.5	3.4
mmt	10506	21013	3285714	18161654	2.0	156.4	864.3	5.5
wavefront	3196	6485	966555	7512370	2.0	149.0	1158.4	7.8
dtw	30402	61400	3593989	18131827	2.0	58.5	295.3	5.0
speech	4362	11156	1342402	10802677	2.6	120.3	968.3	8.0
paraffins	2841	5750	203068	758808	2.0	35.3	132.0	3.7
gamteb	13081	34837	661931	2792257	2.7	19.0	80.2	4.2
simple	58674	182097	1560974	7529351	3.1	8.6	41.3	4.8

Table 1: Dynamic Scheduling Behaviour

In practice the full power of non-strict languages which requires dynamic scheduling of small threads is seldom used. The compiler has to be conservative, but TAM scheduling paradigm exploits the typical case by executing as many threads as possible for a frame in a single quantum. If a code-block is called in a strict manner and all the arguments arrive close together in time, all of the threads for the activation may execute within a single quantum. Only if it runs out of useful work after making split-phase requests or calls to other code-blocks, will it require execute in multiple quanta.

8 Conclusions

In this paper we demonstrate how a lenient parallel language, Id90, can be compiled for conventional processors using compiler-controlled multithreading. Our approach involves several large translation steps: Id90 to dataflow program graphs, program graphs to dual graphs, dual graphs to TAM threads, TAM to native machine code. Each of these intermediate forms plays a crucial role. Dataflow program graphs facilitate powerful, high-level transformations. They are compact and easy to manipulate, because they are hierarchical, employ a single kind of dependence arc, and assume scheduling is accomplished "as needed." Dual graphs facilitate the synthesis of control operations and management of storage. They make control and data flow explicit and, by retaining both in graphical form, allow transformations to be applied to one without prematurely constraining the other. In particular, unnecessary data movement and redundant control can be eliminated independently. TAM provides a means of describing a mixture of static and dynamic scheduling, makes scheduling costs apparent, exposes message handling, and emphasizes locality amongst dynamically scheduled entities. This approach has produced the first efficient implementation of Id90 on conventional machines.

We have shown that it is practical to implement lenient languages without fast dynamic scheduling in hardware. Reasonably sophisticated partitioning is required; we describe a partitioning algorithm that is practical to employ on real programs and results in control overhead within a small factor of the cost of control flow in sequential languages. Measurements under several partitioning strategies show that arithmetic, data movement, heap access, and message handling costs are invariant with respect to the partitioning strategy. However, partitioning has substantial impact on control overhead. Our implementation on conventional state-of-the-art processors provides a baseline against which novel multithreaded machines can be judged. Surprisingly, the compilation techniques developed for conventional machines can improve the performance of these novel architectures as well[PT91].

While these results are encouraging, there is considerable room for improvement. Partitioning of conditionals will improve significantly when switch and merge combining are implemented. Redundant arc elimination is currently quite primitive. On a larger scale, more extensive analysis, such as strictness analysis and propagation of dependence through conditionals and function calls, can be used in partitioning. Furthermore, much of the power of TAM has not yet been exercised, including the management of processor registers across threads.

TAM has been implemented on uniprocessors and shared memory multiprocessors. We are currently implementing TAM on a 1,024 node nCUBE/2 using very fine grain message passing. The results presented in this paper, combined with these TAM implementations, suggest that latency tolerance and cheap synchronization can be achieved with sophisticated compilation in lieu of extensive hardware support.

Acknowledgements

We would like to thank the contributors to TAM at UC Berkeley, including John Wawrzynek, Anurag Sah, Seth Goldstein, Mike Flaster, Meltin Bell, and Bertrand Irissou. We are grateful also to the Computation Structures Group led by Arvind at MIT for providing Id90, the compiler front-end, and many fruitful interactions. TAM builds upon Greg Papadopoulos' Monsoon and Nikhil's PRISC. Ken Traub's dissertation inspired much of the work presented here, "to understand it we had to build it", and we have benefited from his insights.

This work was supported by National Science Foundation PYI Award (CCR-9058342) with matching funds from Motorola Inc. and the TRW Foundation. Thorsten von Eicken is supported by J. Wawrzynek's PYI Award (MIP-8958568) and the Semiconductor Research Corporation. Computational resources were provided, in part, under NSF Infrastructure Grant CDA-8722788.

References

[ACC+90] R. Alverson, D. Callahan, D. Cummings, B. Koblenz, A. Porterfield, and B. Smith. The Tera Computer System. In *Proc. of the 1990 Int. Conf. on Supercomputing*, pages 1–6, Amsterdam, 1990.

[ACM88] Arvind, D. E. Culler, and G. K. Maa. Assessing the Benefits of Fine-Grain Parallelism in Dataflow Programs. *The Int. Journal of Supercomputer Applications*, 2(3), November 1988.

[AE88] Arvind and K. Ekanadham. Future Scientific Programming on Parallel Machines. *Journal of Parallel and Distributed Computing*, 5(5):460–493, October 1988.

[AHN88] Arvind, S. K. Heller, and R. S. Nikhil. Programming Generality and Parallel Computers. In *Proc. of the Fourth Int. Symp. on Biological and Artificial Intelligence Systems*, pages 255–286. ESCOM (Leider), Trento, Italy, September 1988.

[AI87] Arvind and R. A. Iannucci. Two Fundamental Issues in Multiprocessing. In *Proc. of DFVLR - Conf. 1987 on Par. Proc. in Science and Eng.*, Bonn-Bad Godesberg, W. Germany, June 1987.

[ALKK90] A. Agarwal, B. Lim, D. Kranz, and J. Kubiatowicz. APRIL: A Processor Architecture for Multiprocessing. In *Proc. of the 17th Ann. Int. Symp. on Comp. Arch.*, pages 104–114, Seattle, Washington, May 1990.

[ANP87] Arvind, R. S. Nikhil, and K. K. Pingali. I-Structures: Data Structures for Parallel Computing. Technical Report CSG Memo 269, MIT Lab for Comp. Sci., 545 Tech. Square, Cambridge, MA, February 1987. (Also in *Proc. of the Graph Reduction Workshop*, Santa Fe, NM. October 1986.).

[BCS+89] P. J. Burns, M. Christon, R. Schweitzer, O. M. Lubeck, H. J. Wasserman, M. L. Simmons, and D. V. Pryor. Vectorization of Monte-Carlo Particle Transport: An Architectural Study using the LANL Benchmark "Gamteb". In *Proc. Supercomputing '89*. IEEE Computer Society and ACM SIGARCH, New York, NY, November 1989.

[CFR+89] R. Cytron, J. Ferrante, B. K. Rosen, M. N. Wegman, and F. K. Zadeck. An Efficient Method of Computing Static Single Assignment Form. In *Proc. of the 16th Annual ACM Symp. on Principles of Progr. Lang.*, pages 25–35, Los Angeles, January 1989.

[CHR78] W. P. Crowley, C. P. Hendrickson, and T. E. Rudy. The SIMPLE code. Technical Report UCID 17715, Lawrence Livermore Laboratory, February 1978.

[CSS+91] D. Culler, A. Sah, K. Schauser, T. von Eicken, and J. Wawrzynek. Fine-grain Parallelism with Minimal Hardware Support: A Compiler-Controlled Threaded Abstract Machine. In *Proc. of 4th Int. Conf. on Architectural Support for Programming Languages and Operating Systems*, Santa-Clara, CA, April 1991. (Also available as Technical Report UCB/CSD 91/591, CS Div., University of California at Berkeley).

[Cul90] D. E. Culler. Managing Parallelism and Resources in Scientific Dataflow Programs. Technical Report 446, MIT Lab for Comp. Sci., March 1990. (PhD Thesis, Dept. of EECS, MIT).

[GH90] V. G. Grafe and J. E. Hoch. The Epsilon-2 Hybrid Dataflow Architecture. In *Proc. of Compcon90*, pages 88–93, San Francisco, CA, March 1990.

[Hal85] R. H. Halstead, Jr. Multilisp: A Language for Concurrent Symbolic Computation. *ACM Transactions on Programming Languages and Systems*, 7(4):501–538, October 1985.

[HF88] R. H. Halstead, Jr. and T. Fujita. MASA: a Multithreaded Processor Architecture for Parallel Symbolic Computing. In *Proc. of the 15th Int. Symp. on Comp. Arch.*, pages 443–451, Hawaii, May 1988.

[Ian88] R. A. Iannucci. Toward a Dataflow/von Neumann Hybrid Architecture. In *Proc. 15th Int. Symp. on Comp. Arch.*, pages 131–140, Hawaii, May 1988.

[NA89] R. S. Nikhil and Arvind. Can Dataflow Subsume von Neumann Computing? In *Proc. of the 16th Annual Int. Symp. on Comp. Arch.*, Jerusalem, Israel, May 1989.

[Nik90] R. S. Nikhil. Id (Version 90.0) Reference Manual. Technical Report CSG Memo, to appear, MIT Lab for Comp. Sci., 545 Tech. Square, Cambridge, MA, 1990.

[Nik91] R. S. Nikhil. The Parallel Programming Language Id and its Compilation for Parallel Machines. In *Proc. Workshop on Massive Parallelism, Amalfi, Italy, October 1989*. Academic Press, 1991. Also: CSG Memo 313, MIT Laboratory for Computer Science, 545 Technology Square, Cambridge, MA 02139, USA.

[PC90] G. M. Papadopoulos and D. E. Culler. Monsoon: an Explicit Token-Store Architecture. In *Proc. of the 17th Annual Int. Symp. on Comp. Arch.*, Seattle, Washington, May 1990.

[PT91] G. M. Papadopoulos and K. R. Traub. Multithreading: A Revisionist View of Dataflow Architectures. In *Proc. of the 18th Int. Symp. on Comp. Arch.*, pages 342–351, Toronto, Canada, May 1991.

[Sah91] A. Sah. Parallel Language Support for Shared memory multiprocessors. Master's thesis, Computer Science Div., University of California at Berkeley, May 1991.

[Sch91] K. E. Schauser. Compiling Dataflow into Threads. Technical report, Computer Science Div., University of California, Berkeley CA 94720, 1991. (MS Thesis, Dept. of EECS, UCB).

[Smi90] B. Smith. Keynote Address. Proc. of the 17th Annual Int. Symp. on Comp. Arch., May 1990.

[SYH+89] S. Sakai, Y. Yamaguchi, K. Hiraki, Y. Kodama, and T. Yuba. An Architecture of a Dataflow Single Chip Processor. In *Proc. of the 16th Annual Int. Symp. on Comp. Arch.*, pages 46–53, Jerusalem, Israel, June 1989.

[Tra86] K. R. Traub. A Compiler for the MIT Tagged-Token Dataflow Architecture. Technical Report TR-370, MIT Lab for Comp. Sci., 545 Tech. Square, Cambridge, MA, August 1986. (MS Thesis, Dept. of EECS, MIT).

[Tra88] K. R. Traub. Sequential Implementation of Lenient Programming Languages. Technical Report TR-417, MIT Lab for Comp. Sci., 545 Tech. Square, Cambridge, MA, September 1988. (PhD Thesis, Dept. of EECS, MIT).

[vESC91] T. von Eicken, K. E. Schauser, and D. E. Culler. TL0: An Implementation of the TAM Threaded Abstract Machine, Version 2.1. Technical Report, Computer Science Div., University of California at Berkeley, 1991.

Multi-thread Code Generation for Dataflow Architectures from Non-Strict Programs

Kenneth R. Traub
Motorola Cambridge Research Center
One Kendall Square, Bldg. 200
Cambridge MA 02139
kt@mcrc.mot.com

Abstract

This paper presents a new style of code generation for dataflow architectures, based on a view of such architectures as general multi-threaded von Neumann machines. Whereas the traditional picture of dataflow object code consists of tokens flowing along the arcs of a dataflow graph, the multi-threaded style treats a linear sequence of dataflow instructions as a sequential thread. Within a thread, data is passed by imperatively reading and writing an activation frame associated with a procedure invocation, just as in conventional architectures. Also, advanced dataflow architectures like Monsoon provide specific support for sequential threads, in the form of general registers for operand storage within a thread. Between threads, values are also communicated via the activation frame. The generation and synchronization of tokens, which in traditional dataflow is the primary means of communicating data, is relegated here to a purely control flow role, spawning new threads and gating their initiation, but themselves carrying no data.

Our results show that in many cases, the multi-thread style of code generation results in fewer total machine cycles to execute a given program as compared to the traditional dataflow style. Surprisingly, this remains true even if the general registers are not employed. The reason the multi-thread style is so successful is that by separating data flow from control flow, redundant control flow can be eliminated. In other words, fewer forking (token creation) and joining (token matching) operations are required. Central to eliminating redundant control flow is the compiler's ability to discover sequential threads that may be scheduled at compile time. While this is inherently difficult when starting from a non-strict language such as Id, even small threads have a beneficial effect. The most dramatic performance improvement comes about in compiling Id loops, where the language semantics specifies a greater degree of strictness, resulting in larger threads.

We demonstrate the comparative performance between the multi-thread and traditional dataflow styles of code generation through empirical observations on the Monsoon hardware, and also through a detailed analytic examination of the code generated under each paradigm.

1 Introduction

This paper brings together two recent advances in implicitly parallel implementations of functional programming languages. The first is the development of techniques for the efficient compilation of non-strict functional programs as a collection of sequential threads [CSS+91, Tra89]. These techniques were first developed to improve the performance of such languages on stock von Neumann hardware, or on von Neumann multiprocessors. The second advance is the development of explicit token store (ETS) dynamic dataflow architectures [PC90], and in particular a shift in the way such dataflow architectures are understood. Whereas dataflow machines were formerly understood to be specialized evaluators of dataflow graphs, it is now recognized that their machine language may be viewed as a collection of sequential threads [PT91]. Traditional dataflow object code is essentially composed of threads containing exactly one instruction each. But with suitable control over the order in which tokens are scheduled, a chain of dataflow instructions behaves like a von Neumann instruction stream. In particular, the compiler can use the sequential order to implicitly synchronize producers and consumers of data, and the hardware can provide a set of registers for temporary operand storage within a thread.

A compiler from the non-strict programming language Id [Nik90] for the Monsoon dataflow architecture [PC90] is presented here, which produces its object code not as a dataflow graph but as a collection of sequential threads. Within a thread, execution resembles conventional von Neumann code: each instruction proceeds to the next higher instruction memory address, and operands may be passed through registers, or through (imperative) reads and writes to the activation frame (stack frame) when the supply of registers is insufficient. Between threads, all values are passed in the activation frame, with tokens serving only to initiate and synchronize threads. In other words, control flow is *separated* from data flow. By taking a multi-threaded view of Monsoon, the compiler is able to exploit the hardware features provided for the efficient execution of sequential threads, including the aforementioned register set. What is surprising is that in many cases, the multi-thread style of code generation can result in more efficient code than traditional dataflow code, even when the registers are not used. For example, empirical observations of a matrix multiplication program reveal an approximately 15–20% improvement at all levels of loop nesting, without the use of registers.

The key to the performance improvement is the elimination of redundant control flow. In traditional dataflow code, an intermediate value that is to be used several times must be copied onto as many tokens, which must later be synchronized with other tokens via the token-matching hardware of the dataflow processor. While token matching is inexpensive, it is not free: each binary operation occupies two pipeline cycles, one for each token participating in the match. Neither is copying free: to produce n copies of a token a tree of $n-1$ *fanout* operators is needed. Token copying (forking) and matching (joining) are control flow operations, but in a style where all data is passed on tokens, these control flow operations inevitably accompany all data flow. In the multi-thread style, however, control flow operations need only be inserted when actual run-time scheduling decisions need be

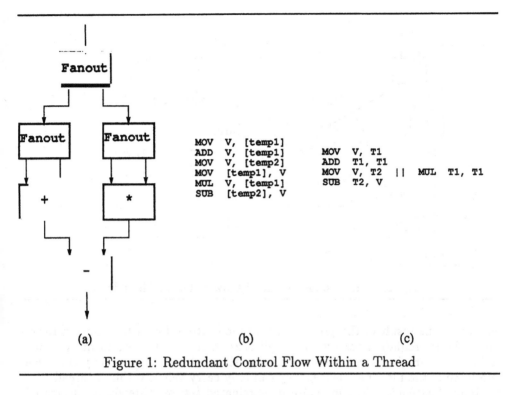

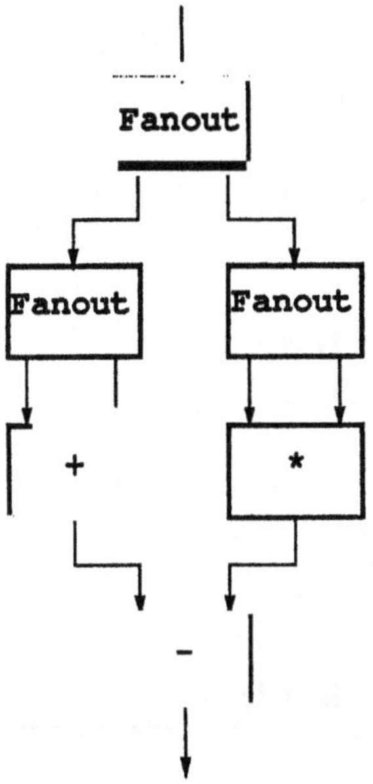


```
MOV  V, [temp1]
ADD  V, [temp1]
MOV  V, [temp2]
MOV  [temp1], V
MUL  V, [temp1]
SUB  [temp2], V
```

```
MOV  V, T1
ADD  T1, T1
MOV  V, T2   ||  MUL  T1, T1
SUB  T2, V
```

(a) (b) (c)

Figure 1: Redundant Control Flow Within a Thread

made, and a single control flow operation can implicitly carry several data items. The resulting reduction in forking and joining can be directly measured in the number of cycles to execute a piece of source code.

Figure 1 illustrates how redundant control flow may be eliminated. Figure 1a shows dataflow code for an expression where a single value is used several times. In Figure 1b, the same expression has been rendered in a multi-thread style, where the shared value has been moved into frame location `temp1` and fetched repeatedly as an operand. The lack of any matching operations in this sequence reduces the cycle count by a third compared to the dataflow code. Figure 1c shows the same code, using the temporary registers ("T-registers"). The more powerful register addressing modes result reduces the cycle count by another third (relative to the dataflow code). Both examples exploit the implicit sequential control flow to enforce the data dependence between the producer of `temp1` and the consumers later in the thread.

(In the machine, code sequences like this are executed by recirculating a token directly from the bottom of the pipeline to the top. The result of the previous instruction is carried on this token, but the compiler simply views this as a special register called `V`, as suggested by the assembly language. The result of any operation other than `MOV` is always written into `V`, with the other operand locations remaining unchanged. The T-registers are simply a small set of additional values recirculated in parallel with this token; an instruction may take one or both operands from T-registers rather than `V` or a frame location, and simultaneously

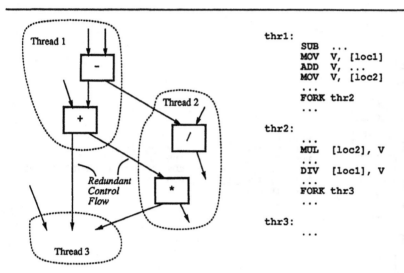

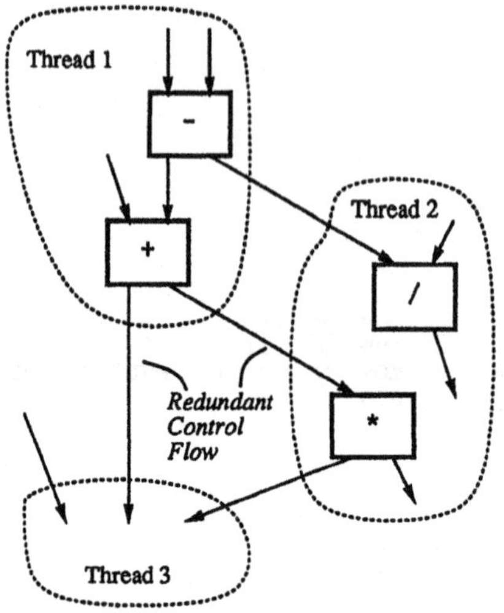


```
thr1:
        SUB  ...
        MOV  V, [loc1]
        ADD  V, ...
        MOV  V, [loc2]
        ...
        FORK thr2
        ...
thr2:
        ...
        MUL  [loc2], V
        ...
        DIV  [loc1], V
        ...
        FORK thr3
        ...
thr3:
        ...
```

Figure 2: Redundant Control Flow Between Threads

may move the result of the previous instruction into a T-register. Once a token leaves the recirculation path via an explicit `fork` or a split-phase memory transaction, the T-registers will be destroyed by the next thread to occupy the same interleave of the pipeline. Hence, they can only carry values within a thread.)

Redundant control flow may also be eliminated *between* threads, as illustrated in Figure 2. In the dataflow graph thread 1 must produce three tokens for threads 2 and 3, each carrying a distinct value. In the multi-thread version a single token serves to synchronize threads 1 and 2, and thread 3 need not explicitly synchronize on the completion of thread 1, as synchronizing on thread 2 is sufficient.

Central to the elimination of redundant control flow is the formation of *threads* which may be scheduled sequentially at compile time. Non-strictness in the source language makes this difficult [Tra89], as some scheduling decisions must inevitably be taken at run-time. In particular, it is often impossible to determine that a heap location will be stored before an attempt is made to read it, or that an argument to a procedure will have been computed before an attempt is made to use it. Even so, many researchers report that exploiting even small threads has a significant impact on performance [Ian88b, Joh84, BHY88]. The results presented here, which rely on only a very simple threading algorithm requiring no interprocedural analysis, confirm this.

The remainder of this paper describes the multi-thread compiler and analyzes the performance of the code it produces. The compiler described here is inspired by the Berkeley TL0 compiler for Id [CSS+91], and in fact is implemented as a post-pass on the Threaded Abstract Machine (TAM) intermediate form produced by that compiler. The Threaded Abstract Machine is a multi-threaded abstract machine similar to the P-RISC abstract machine [NA89], which in turn was based on ideas found in Monsoon and in Iannucci's VNDF architecture [Ian88b]. Rather than present the compiler in terms of TAM, however, abstract dataflow graphs

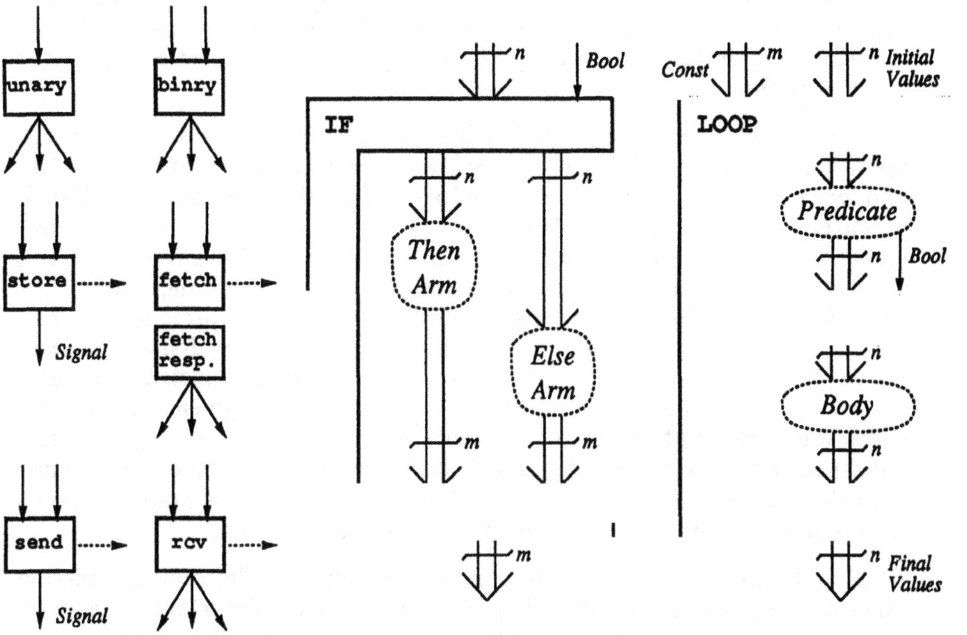

Figure 3: Summary of TTDA Graph Operators

(Section 2) are used as the starting point. This allows a more direct comparison between multi-thread style code and the more traditional dataflow style code, and also avoids many details of TAM which are not relevant to the code generation process for Monsoon, and which in fact must be removed by the compiler before proceeding to code generation. Section 3 defines the characteristics of a thread, and indicates how an abstract dataflow graph may be partitioned into threads. Section 4 describes multi-thread style compilation in detail. Sections 5 and 6 compare the efficiency of multi-thread style code with that of traditional dataflow style code for Monsoon, first by analysis and then by empirical observations of actual programs. Section 7 concludes.

2 Dataflow Graphs

Non-strict languages such as Id [Nik90] are compiled for dataflow machines by producing some sort of dataflow graph as an intermediate form. Graphs for the Tagged-Token Dataflow Architecture (TTDA) [AN90] provide a convenient starting point for understanding code generation for Monsoon, both in the traditional style and in the new multi-threaded style to be presented later. Compilation of Id into TTDA graphs is well understood [Tra86].

The constructs found in TTDA graphs are summarized in Figure 3, and include the following kinds of instructions:

- One- and two-input arithmetic, relational, and logical operators. Run-time system primitives for obtaining new activation frames and new regions of heap storage are included in this category, as they are implemented as supervisor call instructions.
- Global memory operations, including imperative *fetch* and *store*, the I-structure operations *I-fetch* and *I-store* [ANP86], and the M-structure operations *take* and *put* [Ste89]. Each is implemented as a split-phase transaction [AN90]: executing the instruction sends a request to a memory unit, freeing the processor to execute other instructions. In the case of a fetch request (*fetch*, *I-fetch*, or *take*), the memory unit will respond at a later time, sending the value fetched to the destinations of the fetch via the corresponding *fetch-response* instruction. In the case of a store request (*store*, *I-store*, or *put*), the memory unit generates no direct response (if the store instruction has a destination, that destination receives only an acknowledgment that the request was sent), but receipt of the store request by the memory unit may trigger responses to earlier, deferred fetch requests. Thus, there is a dynamic data dependence, not explicitly represented in the dataflow graph, between a store and the destinations of fetches to the same location.
- *Send* and *receive* instructions for procedure linkage. The *send* instruction takes a continuation (pair of code pointer and frame pointer) and a value to send, sending an argument to a called procedure or a result back to a caller. For convenience, *send* is parameterized by a small integer offset to be added to the code pointer. The *receive* instruction in principle may be any dataflow instruction that expects a single token as input; an identity instruction may be used when the actual destination does not fit this constraint.
- Instructions for controlling conditionals and loops, including the *switch* instruction and some specialized instructions for k-bounded loops [CA88]. The TTDA graphs used here represent these constructs abstractly as encapsulator instructions [Tra86], rather than with *switch* and other instructions that are specific to the dataflow style of code generation, for the latter instructions have no direct counterpart when conditionals and loops are compiled in the multi-thread style.

Graphs of this sort can serve as the basis for generating both traditional dataflow-style code for Monsoon as well as the multi-thread style presented here. Generating dataflow-style code from TTDA graphs is quite simple: mostly it involves inserting additional instructions to deal with machine constraints (for example, instructions on Monsoon can have at most two, and in some cases one, destination, whereas in the TTDA graphs infinite fan-out is assumed). More details are given in Section 5, where dataflow-style code is compared to multi-thread code. The generation of multi-thread code is taken up in the next two sections.

3 Threads

Throughout this paper, a thread will mean a subset of the instructions comprising a procedure body, such that:

- A compile-time instruction ordering can be determined for the thread which is valid for all contexts in which the containing procedure can be invoked.
- Once the first instruction in a thread is executed, it is always possible to execute each of the remaining instructions, in the compile-time ordering, without pause, interruption, or execution of instructions from other threads.

This is a more restrictive notion of thread than is adopted elsewhere [Tra91], where the second requirement is omitted. Note, too, that it is a *static* notion: threads are subunits of compiled code. Each of these two requirements leads to a function being compiled into more than one thread, for different reasons.

Because of the first requirement of a thread, that a compile-time instruction ordering valid for all invocations can be determined, non-strictness in the language can result in multiple threads. In the following function, for example:

```
def f x y = cons (x + 2) (y * 3);
```

the addition and multiplication may not be part of the same thread. This is because the function f can be invoked like this,

```
{a  = f 3 yy;
 yy = hd a;
 ...}
```

(the braces denote a "letrec" block of mutually recursive definitions) where the multiplication must follow the addition, and also like this,

```
{a  = f yy 3;
 yy = tl a;
 ...}
```

where the multiplication must precede the addition. The author's earlier work [Tra89, Tra91] discusses at length the conditions under which expressions cannot be placed in the same thread for reasons of data dependence, as in the example.

Because of the second requirement of a thread, that a thread must be executable to completion once initiated, split-phase memory transactions and procedure calls result in multiple threads. When a split-phase fetch is issued, an indeterminate amount of time may elapse before the response is received, either because of communication latency, or, in the case of an *I-fetch*, because of the dynamic dependence on the corresponding *I-store*. In any event, the response cannot be processed by the same thread issuing the request, as that might mean the suspension of the thread or the interleaved execution of some other thread. A similar situation exists when an argument is sent to a called procedure: other threads may need to execute before the result is received.

While the analysis required to form large threads can be quite complex (and, in general, requires approximating the answers to undecidable questions) [Tra91], it is possible to obtain a reasonable partition of a procedure body into threads from a simple examination of the arcs in the procedure's TTDA graph. A variety of such methods have been reported [Ian88a, CSS+91, Eka86]. In general, these methods

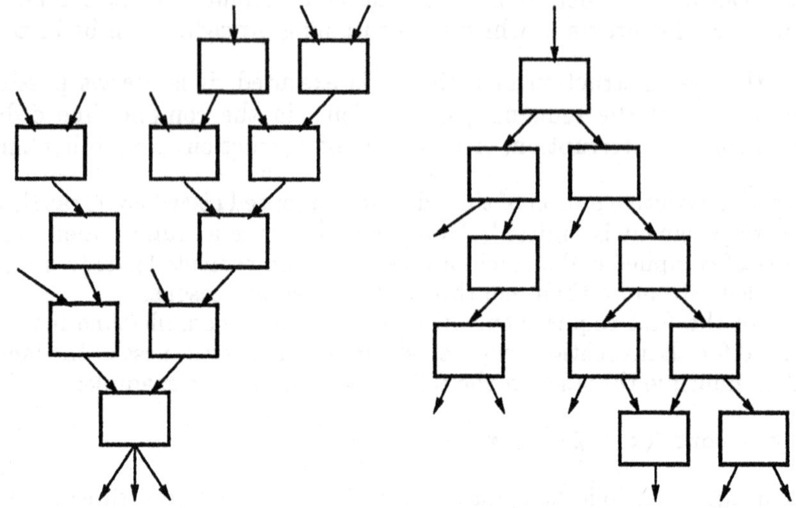

(a) (b)

Figure 4: DAGs Which May Always Be Single Threads

search the TTDA graph for one or both of the patterns illustrated in Figure 4. The first pattern is a directed acyclic graph (DAG) with many input arcs but only a single exit arc; the second is a DAG with many output arcs but only a single entry arc. Any such DAG may be compiled as a single thread, ordering it according to any topological sort of the intra-DAG dependence edges.[1]

The algorithms assume that dynamic dependence edges, shown as dashed lines in Figure 3, always span two threads. Thus, *store*, *fetch*, and *send* instructions are always the unique exit node when included in a thread matching Figure 4a, and *fetch-response* and *receive* instructions are always the unique entry node when included in a thread matching Figure 4b. To do otherwise would require sophisticated analysis to take advantage of calls to strict functions or compile-time determinable relationships between fetches and stores. Incidentally, this treatment of dynamic dependence automatically takes care of the second requirement of threads (execution to completion), as an *I-fetch* will never be in the same thread as the corresponding *fetch-response*, nor will a *send* to a procedure be in the same thread as the *receive* of the result.

The thread forming method used in this paper is the one embedded in Version 1.2 of the TL0 compiler from Berkeley [CSS+91].

[1]Such DAGs are called *strict regions* in [Tra91], where it is shown that no analysis of the surrounding context is necessary to show that they may be compiled as single threads. Briefly, the reason is that no dependence path between two different parts of the DAG can be completed through nodes outside the DAG, as such a path would have to be completed through the unique exit (entry) arc, and therefore would be part of a cycle.

3.1 Conditionals

Conditionals require special treatment during partitioning because of static cycles. Consider the following function, taken from [Tra89]:

```
def conditional_example x =
  {p = x > 0;
   a = if p then bb else 3;
   b = if p then 4 else aa;
   aa = a + 5;
   bb = b + 6;
   c = aa + bb;
   in
     c};
```

The TTDA graph will have a cycle involving two *IF* encapsulators and two additions for aa and bb. This is not an incorrect program, for at run time there will be no dependence cycle, but merely an exploitation of non-strictness. Some thread forming methods, such as Iannucci's [Ian88a], simply rule out such use of conditionals, altering the semantics of the source language. The TL0 compiler used in the present study correctly handles conditionals with the following two rules:

1. The arms of an *IF* encapsulator are treated as independent graphs, which are furthermore independent from the graph outside the encapsulator. Edges between these three graphs are ignored during thread formation, and their instructions are never mixed into the same thread.

2. When finding threads in each arm of an *IF*, the arcs entering the arm from outside the encapsulator are treated as dynamic arcs. When finding threads in the graph surrounding an *IF*, the arcs leaving the bottom of the *IF* are treated as dynamic arcs.

The first rule prevents the thread forming algorithm from seeing any static cycles in the TTDA graph, while the second prevents it from grouping together instructions in a way that is in conflict with the edges disregarded by the first rule. These rules are obviously more stringent than necessary, and a more sophisticated treatment could lead to better code for conditionals, particularly when no static cycles actually exist.[2]

A similar problem with cycles arises around function calls, when the result of a call is fed back into an argument. Due to the representation of a function call as separate *send* and *receive* instructions, though, this situation does not even appear as a static cycle in the TTDA graphs used here, and no special treatment is required.

[2]This description applies to the version of the Berkeley TL0 compiler used in this paper. Later versions of that compiler do indeed handle conditionals better [SCvE91].

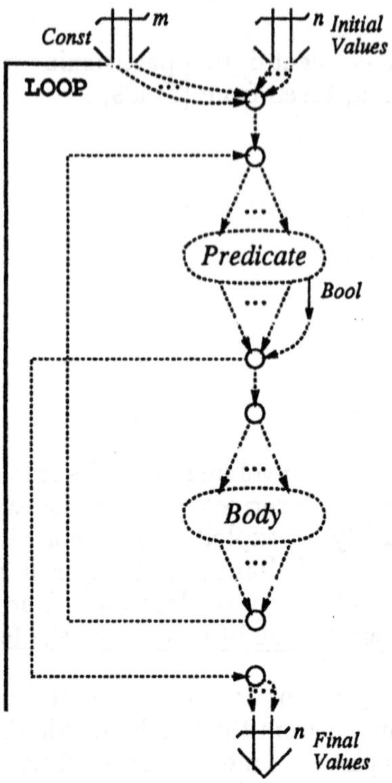

Figure 5: Compilation of Loops

3.2 Loops

The Id language gives special semantics to loops, which the Berkeley TL0 compiler exploits to yield particularly efficient code. This has a first-order effect on the results reported here.

Nominally, loops in Id have a semantics equivalent to recursion. But, there is an important restriction: it must be possible to evaluate completely all the expressions of one iteration of the loop before beginning any expression in the next iteration. This differs semantically from the tail recursive equivalent, as non-strict function calls may allow later iterations to begin execution before earlier ones complete. Loops are given a different semantics in Id to give the run-time system control over the resources consumed during execution of a loop, by *k-bounding* the loop to execute at most k iterations simultaneously [CA88].

The Berkeley TL0 compiler exploits this aspect of loop semantics by always compiling loops as one-bounded. The resulting code resembles ordinary von Neumann code for a loop, where there is a single conditional branch controlling the loop. In contrast, the k-bounded loop schema used in traditional dataflow code involves an elaborate complex of branches and termination trees, discussed in Section 5. The effect on the TTDA graph of compiling a loop as one-bounded is shown in Figure 5: as with conditionals, the subgraphs of the *LOOP* encapsulator are kept separate from each other and from the surrounding code, and six artificial nodes ("artificial" because they do not ultimately correspond to any instruction in the finished code) are added to sequentialize the loop. These induce exactly the DAG structure required for large threads, and in some cases, the body can be compiled as a single thread (if it is free of split-phase fetches, conditionals, and procedure calls).

4 Multi-Thread Code Generation

After partitioning, the procedure body is a network of threads, where each thread is a DAG that may be arbitrarily scheduled at compile time (respecting the intra-DAG dependence arcs, of course). In this section we present a code generation method that compiles each thread using standard von Neumann code generation techniques, resulting in a single sequential instruction sequence for each thread. By doing so, instructions within a thread may pass data to each other in frame slots or in registers, rather than on tokens, exploiting register addressing modes and the implied synchronization of sequential execution. Inter-thread communication will also be through frame slots, with tokens serving only to trigger the initiation of threads, not to pass data. This means that multiple tokens are not necessary when multiple data items are produced in one thread and consumed in another. The net effect will be, in many cases, more efficient code than is obtainable from a traditional dataflow style, as demonstrated in Sections 5 and 6.

Throughout this section, the inner loop of matrix multiplication is carried through as an example. In Id, this loop is:

```
{sum = 0;
 k = 1;
 in
   {while k <= n do
      next sum = sum + (a[i,k] * b[k,j]);
      next k = k + 1;
    finally sum}}
```

The TTDA graph for this loop is shown in Figure 6. Before reaching the TTDA graph stage, the compiler has linearized the array references and hoisted out invariant subexpressions. No induction variable elimination has been done, however, and so the subscript calculations are in terms of `k` and three loop constants (one a function of `i`, one a function of `j`, and a multiplier for `k` used in `a`'s subscript expression).

The multi-thread code generation method described here has two broad phases. The first handles inter-thread dataflow and control flow, introducing explicit operators for reading and writing inter-thread values in the activation frame, and explicit inter-thread control flow operators. After this phase, each thread is an independent acyclic dataflow graph. The second phase compiles efficient code from each thread's graph.

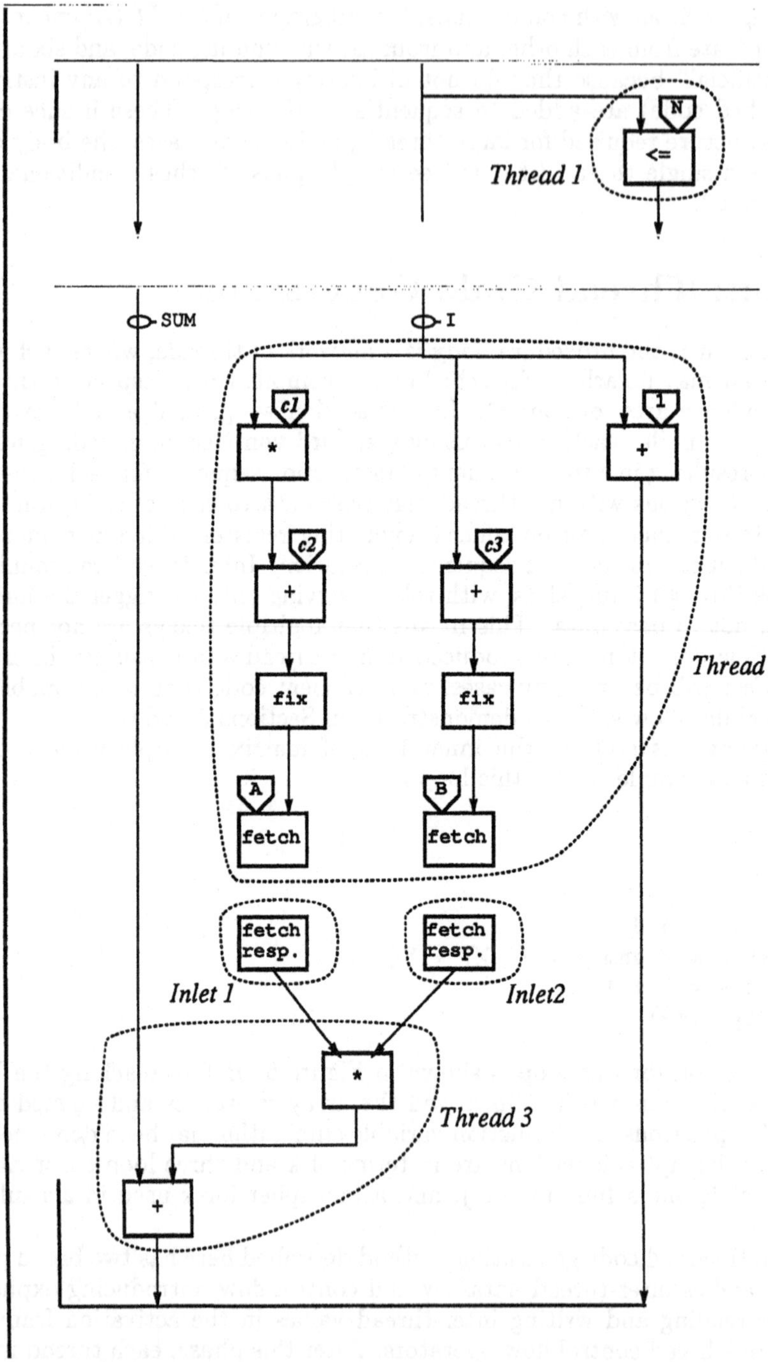

Figure 6: TTDA Graph for the Inner Loop of Matrix Multiply, with Thread Partitioning Indicated

4.1 Separating the Threads

There are three steps in obtaining an independent graph for each thread: separation of control flow from data flow, elimination of redundant control flow, and making control flow explicit. Prior to this step, the procedure body is the original TTDA graph with instructions grouped into threads (Figure 6), and arcs between threads represent a combination of both data and control flow. Because of hardware and calling convention constraints, each *fetch-response* and *receive* instruction is placed into a separate thread called an *inlet* [CSS+91], even if the thread forming algorithm was able to group them with other instructions.

To separate data flow from control flow, a distinct activation frame slot is allocated for each value that is produced by one thread and used by others; that is, for the output of a binary, unary, *fetch-response*, or *receive* instruction that has an inter-thread dataflow arc. Each inter-thread data flow arc is converted to a control flow arc by inserting a *frame-store* instruction where the value is produced and a *frame-fetch* instruction in each thread where the value is consumed. The *frame-store* and *frame-fetch* instructions are not split-phase transactions, but simply placeholders that cause the code generator to use addressing modes that imperatively move data to and from the current activation frame. Inter-thread signal arcs from *store*-like and *send* instructions may be considered control flow arcs without any further modification, as they carry no data. While each control flow arc was originally a dataflow arc between two instructions, the source and destination of a control flow arc are not individual instructions within two threads, but the threads themselves.

IF and *LOOP* encapsulators require special treatment during this step. First, the frame slots assigned to the values consumed and produced in the interior subgraphs must be consistent with those outside the encapsulators: for example, if in the graph surrounding an *IF* a particular input arc to the *IF* was converted to a *frame-store*(*slot5*) instruction, then within each arm the corresponding arcs are converted to *frame-fetch*(*slot5*) instructions. For loops, each circulating variable occupies the same frame slot within the predicate and body as it does outside the loop. Satisfying these assignment constraints occasionally requires the insertion of an *identity* instruction (*i.e.*, a `MOV` in the finished code). Second, control flow arcs are added from the thread computing the predicate of a conditional to each thread in each arm, and across loops as suggested in Figure 5.

The next step removes redundant control flow arcs. If in the original TTDA graph there were several values passed from Thread A to Thread B, then at this point there will be as many control flow arcs between these two threads. As the control flow arcs carry no data, only a single arc between A and B is required. Also, transitive control flow arcs are redundant: if there is a control flow arc (A, C) and a path $A, \ldots, B, \ldots, C$ then (A, C) is redundant and can be removed. For the purposes of removing redundant control flow arcs, there is considered to be a control flow arc between every *fetch*-like instruction and its corresponding *fetch-receive*. Similarly, there is considered to be a control flow arc between the *send* that sends the return address to a called procedure and each *receive* from that procedure, but without further analysis no control flow relationships may be assumed between the arguments' *send*s and any of the *receives*. Figure 7 shows the inner loop of matrix multiply after control flow has been made explicit; the

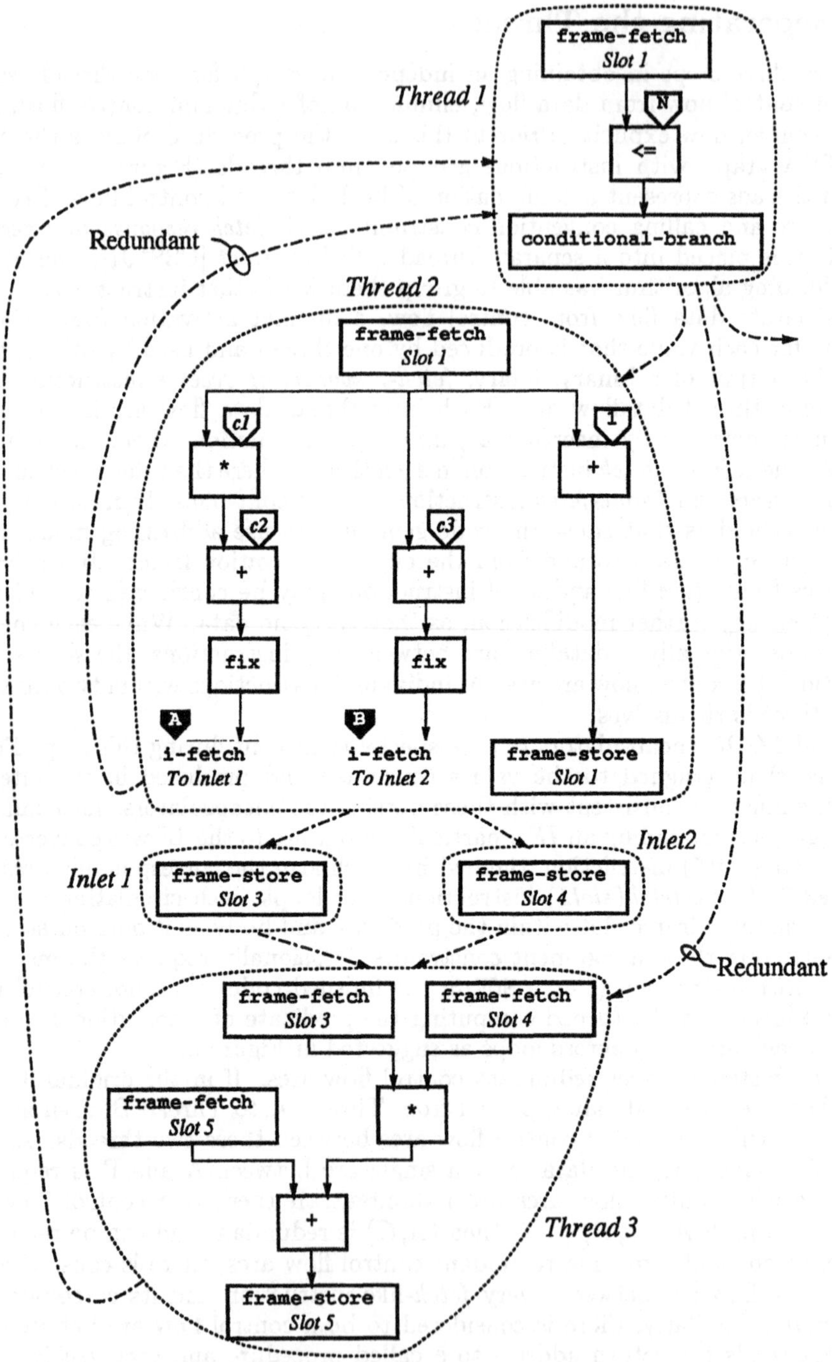

Figure 7: Threads with Explicit Control Flow

dot-and-dashed lines indicate control flow. There are two redundant control flow edges in that graph.

At this point, control flow operations are made explicit through the introduction of *fork* and *join* operators. For every control flow arc (A, B), a *fork* instruction naming B as its target is introduced into thread A. No *fork* instruction is required for the arc from an *I-fetch* to its associated inlet thread, however, for when the *I-fetch* is eventually compiled it will indicate the inlet thread as the place where the response should be sent; similarly, no *fork* is required for an arc from a *send* to a corresponding *receive*. For this reason, the redundant control flow removal phase should prefer to retain these arcs when there is a choice. Where more than one control flow arc enters a thread, a *join* instruction is introduced, parameterized by the number of incoming arcs.

Additional arcs called *scheduling arcs* are now introduced within each thread to insure proper instruction scheduling. By now, a thread is a forest of DAGs, perhaps containing a *join*, several *fork*s, and several expression DAGs whose entry nodes are *frame-fetch*es and whose exit nodes are *frame-store*, *store*-like, *send*, and *fetch*-like instructions.[3] Scheduling arcs are added:

- From the *join* to every other instruction in the thread.
- From the *frame-store* instruction of each value escaping the thread via a particular *fork*, to that *fork* instruction. The values escaping on a particular *fork* are determined by consideration of the dataflow arcs from whence the *fork*'s control flow arc was originally derived, taking into account the control flow paths that were combined during redundant control flow arc removal. *Fetch*- and *send*-like instructions are given similar treatment since they act as forks to the associated inlet thread.
- When a thread has a *frame-fetch* and *frame-store* instruction naming the same frame slot, a scheduling arc is added from the fetch to the store. This can only arise in loops, where the current value of a circulating variable must be fetched before the new value is stored back into the frame.

4.2 Compiling the Threads

At this point, a thread is a self-contained expression DAG (or DAG forest), operating on frame slots, and there are no arcs of any kind between threads. The arcs in the thread's DAG are dataflow arcs and scheduling arcs. Each thread may now be compiled independently. The basis of thread compilation is Waite's well-known technique of partitioning into trees [ASU86]: the instructions in a thread are partitioned such that two instructions A and B are in the same partition if and only if A has a dataflow arc leading to B, and that is A's only outgoing dataflow arc. The root of each tree is therefore either an arithmetic or *frame-fetch* instruction with more than one outgoing dataflow arc, or an instruction with no outgoing

[3] Given that threads are obtained by finding DAGs as shown in Figure 4, there will generally be only one expression DAG in a thread. An exception occurs in loop bodies, where several independent expression DAGs can be grouped in a thread because of the artificial dependences illustrated in Figure 5. Of course, a more sophisticated partitioning algorithm might group independent DAGs into a single thread, even outside of loops.

dataflow arcs: a *join*, *frame-store*, *I-store*, *I-fetch*, *send*, or *fork*. Code generation then proceeds in three steps: scheduling, register allocation, and code output.

Scheduling is done by a topological sort of the trees according to inter-tree dataflow and scheduling arcs; in the finished code, all instructions belonging to one tree will be contiguous. The topological sort is guided by some heuristics that attempt to minimize the total number of temporary registers used within the thread.

After inter-tree scheduling, register allocation assigns a register to the value exiting every tree that produces a value (*i.e.*, to every tree whose root has outgoing dataflow arcs). Register allocation for values whose lifetimes are entirely within one tree is done during code output; the register allocation phase only takes note of the number of additional registers needed by each tree, and reserves that number for later use. A "register" here is either an actual Monsoon T-register or a new activation frame slot. The activation frame slots used as intra-thread registers must be unique over threads, as different threads may be executing in different interleaves of the pipeline on Monsoon.[4] On the other hand, within a thread a given slot may be used for several values having disjoint lifetimes. Registers are allocated such that a value is held in exactly one location over its lifetime within a thread. This was done for expediency, to avoid tackling the issue of spilling from T-registers to frame slots; but in practice it seems a reasonable policy due to the small size of threads obtained from Id. The current register allocator gives priority in assigning the T-registers to intra-tree temporaries, and if there are any left over it gives priority to the inter-tree temporaries referenced the greatest number of times within the thread.

Special treatment is given to *frame-fetch* instructions during register allocation. If it was decided to place the output of *frame-fetch* in a T-register, then the *frame-fetch* instruction will be compiled as a `MOV` instruction. If, on the other hand, its output was assigned to a frame temporary, no `MOV` will be generated, and the destination instructions will fetch the value directly from the location named by the *frame-fetch*. The latter decision is always taken when the *frame-fetch* has only one outgoing dataflow arc, and so an inter-thread value is moved to a register only when used more than once within a thread.

In loops, the special register allocation for *frame-fetch* instructions can interfere with the strategy of compiling trees contiguously in the following way. As described earlier, a scheduling arc is added between a *frame-fetch* and *frame-store* to the same frame slot; this can only occur within loops. Now if a T-register is not allocated for the *frame-fetch*, it is the trees using the output of the *frame-fetch* that will actually fetch from the frame, not the *frame-fetch*'s tree. So the scheduling arcs must be added between those trees and the *frame-store*. This can introduce a cycle of scheduling arcs, preventing scheduling. The solution is to break the cycle by forcing the output of *frame-fetch* to be placed in a temporary. The scheduling arcs can then emanate from the *frame-fetch*, and a cycle will no longer exist. An example of this is seen in Figure 7: the tree that increments `k` cannot be scheduled after the *I-fetch*es, as threads enabled by those fetches need to see the new value of `k`, but it cannot be scheduled before, as the threads containing the *I-fetch*es need

[4] By considering the inter-thread control flow, it would be possible to recycle these slots. That analysis is currently not done.

to use the old value of k. Forcing the old value of k to be placed in a temporary solves the problem.

Once registers are assigned, code for each tree is produced, in the order given by the schedule determined earlier. Trees are compiled using the standard depth-first algorithm [ASU86] which minimizes the number of new temporaries required. The value carried on a token is treated as a register during tree evaluation, and so an actual temporary is only needed when both inputs to a binary instruction are subtrees (as opposed to constants or inter-tree arcs). Appropriate conditional branches are inserted around the forks from the predicate to the arms of a conditional, and from the predicate to the body of a loop. Peephole optimization follows the generation of code for all trees. A more detailed description of the code is deferred until the next section, where it is compared with traditional dataflow-style code.

5 Comparison to Dataflow Code Generation

While Monsoon's instruction set is highly geared toward traditional dataflow-style code, multi-thread style code often yields more efficient code. This is true even without using the T-registers. There are three factors contributing to this:

- A value that is used several times within a thread need not be "fanned out" by *identity* instructions.
- Redundant forking and joining between threads can be eliminated.
- Because of one-bounded loops, redundant control flow elimination always results in only one conditional branch for each loop.

All these factors exploit the implicit synchronization present in linear instruction sequences.

This section presents a comparative analysis of the efficiency of multi-thread style code versus traditional dataflow style code. The measure of efficiency used here is the sum of the number of machine cycles required for execution of all instructions, which is equivalent to the number of tokens that enter the Monsoon pipeline. For a joining binary instruction (*e.g.*, the typical dataflow two-input *plus* instruction), two cycles are counted. This reflects the fact that the first token to arrive, while performing no arithmetic, occupies a pipeline interleave for the pipeline's full length. On the other hand, the machine cycle measure does not take into account the number of idle cycles—cycles when no token enters the pipeline. This is related to the parallelism exposed by the code, and is influenced not only by how a given thread is compiled but also by what other parts of the program may or may not be executing concurrently.

5.1 Threaded Code Without Registers

Dataflow and multi-thread code for a procedure are compared through a hierarchical decomposition of the original TTDA graph, taking advantage of the TTDA graph's being the common ancestor of finished code in both styles. The TTDA graph may be viewed as divided into subgraphs according to the thread partitioning used for multi-thread code, with the stipulation that each *fetch-response* and *receive* instruction is an inlet thread of its own. Each of these thread subgraphs may be further viewed as divided into expression trees. By definition, each non-root node of a tree has exactly one outgoing dataflow arc, to another node in the same tree. Each root node has either zero outgoing dataflow arcs, one outgoing dataflow arc which must be an inter-thread arc (if it were intra-thread, the node could not be the root of a tree), or more than one outgoing dataflow arc of which zero or more are intra-thread and zero or more are inter-thread. The comparison of the two styles is performed by counting the cycles required to evaluate each tree (excluding inlet threads), then considering the additional code required to glue the trees together. For the multi-thread style, this "glue" includes the *frame-fetch*, *frame-store*, *fork*, and *join* instructions inserted during multi-thread code generation.[5] For the dataflow style, the "glue" mostly consists of extra *identity* instructions for fan-out, *switch* instructions in conditionals and loops, and other loop control operators. Of course, the way the graph is partitioned only has an effect on the multi-thread count, not on the dataflow count.

The code produced for trees in both styles is summarized in Figure 8 (the notation $c(E)$ is used to mean the number of cycles to execute a segment of code E). The nine rows of the figure, plus three symmetric cases not shown, define a graph grammar that generates all expression trees. For the dataflow style, the leaves of the tree (black dots in the graph grammar) are distinct tokens sent to the tree, and the output is produced on a token. Note that an equal number of tokens must be sent into a tree regardless of whether some of the values originated from the same instruction. For the multi-thread style, the leaves of the tree are values held in frame slots, and the output is produced on a token. In the case of multiply used values, the same frame slot will be read several times at the leaves. Leaf nodes where all operands are constants require an additional trigger token in the dataflow style [Tra86], and so an additional cycle must be charged for the trigger's fan-out tree. In the multi-thread style, this triggering is implicit in the sequential control flow. In all but one case, the multi-thread style requires no more cycles than the dataflow style.

To compose a program from compiled expression trees, code must be inserted to take care of inter-tree data and/or control flow. In dataflow-style code, this means fan-out instructions. In the multi-thread style, there are *frame-store* instructions, plus explicit *fork* and *join* instructions. Note that *frame-fetch* instructions do not result in any instructions when T-registers are not used—the code compiled for trees fetches directly from the frame. There are three cases to be analyzed, according to the TTDA instruction at the root of the tree. The code for each case is given in Figure 9. In each case, the following notation is used to quantify the connectivity of the tree to other trees: *LD* is the number of outgoing dataflow arcs (*i.e.*, arcs in the TTDA graph) from the tree's root to other trees in the same thread, *GD* is the number of outgoing dataflow arcs to trees in other threads, and *GC* is the number of control flow arcs in the multi-thread style corresponding to the outgoing dataflow arcs, counting only those that remain after redundant control

[5] To avoid confusion, it should be emphasized that "trees" in this section are subgraphs of the original TTDA graph, and do not include these four multi-thread glue instructions.

TTDA Graph	Dataflow Style Code	Dataflow Style Cycles	Thread Style Code	Thread Style Cycles
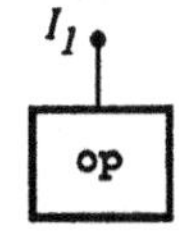	`op V`	1	`op [`I_1`]`	1
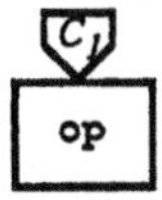	*; fanout from trigger* `op [`C_1`]L`	2	`op [`C_1`]L`	1
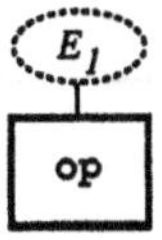	*; code for* E_1 `op V`	$c(E_1)+1$	*; code for* E_1 `op V`	$c(E_1)+1$
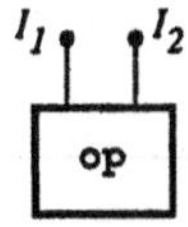	`lab [*]: op VL, VR`	2	`MOV [`I_1`],V` `op V,[`I_2`]`	2
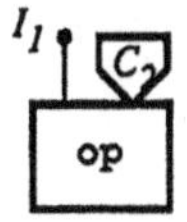	`op V, [`C_2`]L`	1	`MOV [`I_1`],V` `op V,[`C_2`]L`	2
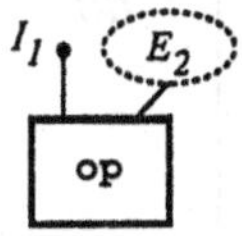	*; code for* E_2 `|| JUMP lab.R` `lab [*]: op VL, VR`	$c(E_2)+2$	*; code for* E_2 `op [`I_1`],V`	$c(E_2)+1$

	*; fanout from trigger*
	`MOV [`C_1`]L, V`
	`op V, [`C_2`]L`
		3	`MOV [`C_1`]L,V`
			`op V,[`C_2`]L`
				2

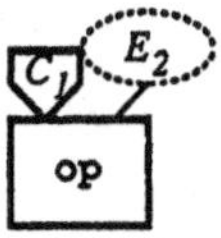	*; code for* E_2 `op [`C_1`]L, V`	$c(E_2)+1$	*; code for* E_2 `op [`C_1`]L,V`	$c(E_2)+1$

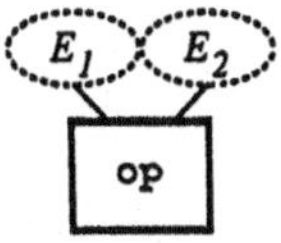	*; code for* E_1 `|| JUMP lab.L`
	; code for E_2 `|| JUMP lab.R`
	`lab [*]: op VL, VR`
		$c(E_1)+c(E_2)+2$	*; code for* E_1
			`MOV V,[tmp]`
			; code for E_2
			`op [tmp],V`
				$c(E_1)+c(E_2)+2$

Figure 8: Code Generated for Expression Trees in the Dataflow and Multi-thread Styles

<table>
<tr><th>TTDA Graph</th><th>Dataflow Style Code</th><th>Cycles</th><th>Thread Style Code</th><th>Cycles</th></tr>
<tr>
<td>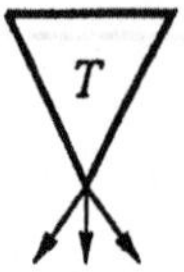
LD+GD Arcs</td>
<td>LD = 0; GD = 1:
; Code for T || FORK $dest_1$

LD + GD = 2:
; Code for T || FORK $dest_1$
; Code for $dest_2$

LD + GD > 2:
; Code for T || FORK $dest_1$
FORK $dest_2$
...
FORK $dest_{LD+GD-2}$
FANOUT $dest_{LD+GD-1}$, $dest_{LD+GD}$</td>
<td>c(T)

c(T)

c(T) + LD + GD − 2</td>
<td>GC = 0:
; Code for T
MOV V,[loc]

GC > 0:
; Code for T
MOV V,[loc] || FORK thr_1
FORK thr_2
...
FORK thr_{GC}</td>
<td>c(T) + 1

c(T) + GC</td>
</tr>
<tr>
<td>
(Signal)</td>
<td>; Code for T || JUMP dest</td>
<td>c(T)</td>
<td>; Code for T || FORK thr</td>
<td>c(T)</td>
</tr>
<tr>
<td>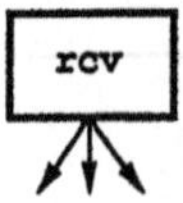
GD Arcs</td>
<td>GD = 1:
JUMP dest

GD = 2:
FANOUT $dest_1$, $dest_2$

GD > 2:
FANOUT $dest_1$,12
...
12: FORK $dest_2$
...
FORK $dest_{GD-2}$
FANOUT $dest_{GD-1}$, $dest_{GD}$</td>
<td>1

1

GD − 1</td>
<td>GC = 1:
MOV V,[loc] || JUMP thr_1

GC > 1:
MOV V,[loc] || JUMP 12
...
12: FORK thr_1
...
FORK thr_{GC-2}
FANOUT thr_{GC-1}, thr_{GC}</td>
<td>1

GC</td>
</tr>
</table>

Figure 9: "Glue" Code Generated Between Trees in the Dataflow and Multi-thread Styles

Tree is not last in thread:

LD=0

GC \ GD	0	1	2	3	4
0	×	0/1	0/1	1/1	2/1
1	×	0/1	0/1	1/1	2/1
2	×	×	0/2	1/2	2/2
3	×	×	×	1/3	2/3
4	×	×	×	×	2/4

LD=1

GC \ GD	0	1	2	3	4
0	×	0/1	1/1	2/1	3/1
1	×	0/1	1/1	2/1	3/1
2	×	×	1/2	2/2	3/2
3	×	×	×	2/3	3/3
4	×	×	×	×	3/4

LD=2

GC \ GD	0	1	2	3	4
0	0/1	1/1	2/1	3/1	4/1
1	×	1/1	2/1	3/1	4/1
2	×	×	2/2	3/2	4/2
3	×	×	×	3/3	4/3
4	×	×	×	×	4/4

Tree is last in thread:

LD=0

GC \ GD	0	1	2	3	4
0	×	×	×	×	×
1	×	0/1	0/1	1/1	2/1
2	×	×	0/2	1/2	2/2
3	×	×	×	1/2	2/2
4	×	×	×	×	2/3

LD=1

GC \ GD	0	1	2	3	4
0	×	×	×	×	×
1	×	0/1	1/1	2/1	2/1
2	×	×	1/2	2/2	3/2
3	×	×	×	2/2	3/2
4	×	×	×	×	3/3

Key

d
m

d = Glue cycles, dataflow style

m = Glue cycles, multi-thread style

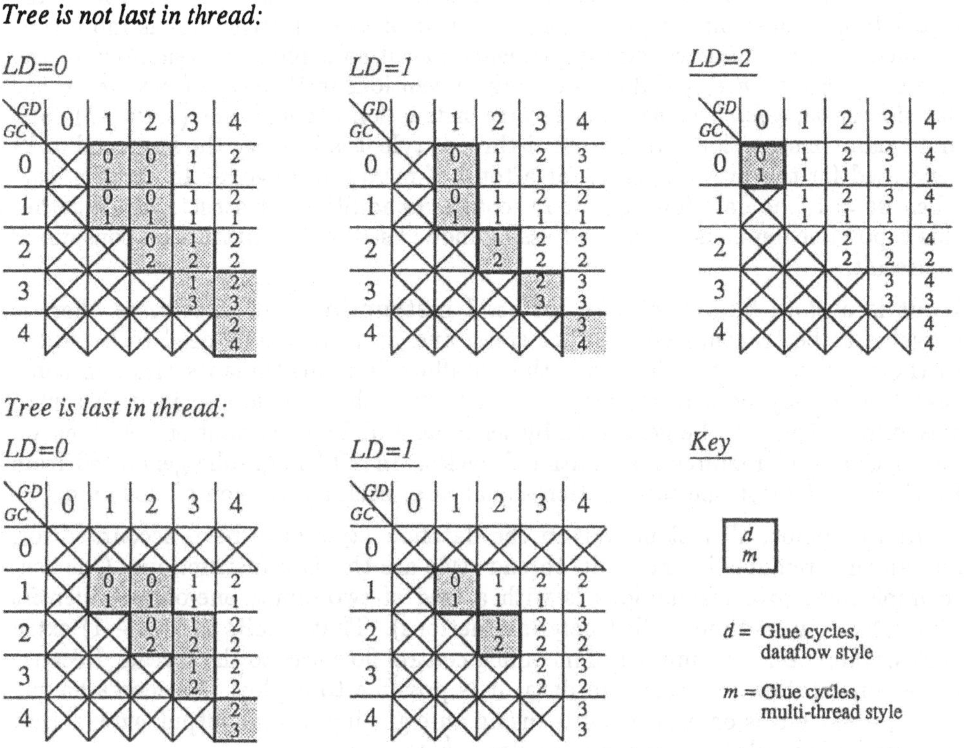

Figure 10: Comparison of Cost of Glue Code, Root of Tree is a Binary or Unary Instruction

---

flow elimination.

Root is a binary or unary instruction. In this case, a value is produced by the tree and sent to one or more other trees, in the same thread or in different threads. In the dataflow style, $LD + GD$ tokens must be produced bearing the value computed by the tree, requiring $\max(0, LD + GD - 2)$ fork and fanout instructions. In the multi-thread style, an instruction to store into the frame is always required, plus $\max(0, GC - 1)$ additional fork instructions, for a total of $\max(1, GC)$ extra cycles. Note that in the dataflow style, the compiler has an extra degree of freedom in that it can always place one of the destinations of tree T immediately following the root of T. In the multi-thread style, the code must continue to the next tree in the thread, which is not necessarily a destination of T. There is a savings of one instruction in the multi-thread style when T is the last tree in a thread.

The comparison of these formulae is shown in Figure 10, where the region enclosed by the thick line is where the dataflow style is superior. For values of LD greater than shown in the figure, the dataflow style is never superior. By definition of a tree, either $LD + GD \geq 2$ or $LD = 0$ and $GD = 1$, and because of redundant control flow elimination $GC \leq GD$; these constraints are reflected by the blocked-out regions of the charts in the figure.

Root is a *fetch-response* or *receive* instruction. The code generated for these instructions is just fan-out, but the placement of these instructions is more constrained, due to the hardware implementation of split-phase transactions in the case of *fetch-response*, and due to calling conventions in the case of *receive*. In the dataflow style, a *fetch-response* or *receive* instruction becomes $\max(1, GD-1)$ `fork` and `fanout` instructions. In the multi-thread style it is just like the store and forks generated for the previous case, for a total of $\max(1, GC)$ cycles. In certain cases when $GD = 1$, the dataflow style may require no additional instructions. Whether this is possible depends on the addressing mode used by the instruction consuming the result.

Root is a *store*-like, *fetch*-like, or *send* instruction. In most cases, there is no value to be transmitted to other trees, and no instructions need to be added to the code for the tree in either the dataflow or multi-thread styles. In some cases, there may be a termination signal leaving the instruction; in both styles, this extra output can be generated by selecting a different variant of the Monsoon instruction, and requires no additional cycles. In TTDA graphs generated from Id, there is at most one termination signal from each instruction of this kind.

At this point, all instructions in the dataflow style have been accounted for, and all that remains in the multi-thread style are the *join* instructions. One way to implement *join* instructions is with a tree of two-input, one-output *identity* instructions (sometimes called *gate* instructions). That results in $2(IC - 1)$ extra cycles, where IC is the number of incoming control flow arcs to the thread. Because these control flow arcs carry no data, it is possible to exploit Monsoon's having three presence bits on each word by using an eight-input, one-output *gate*; if that instruction is used, the number of cycles is $\frac{8}{7}(IC - 1)$.

This accounting of instructions in the dataflow and multi-thread styles is complete, but it is somewhat difficult to summarize them as they are highly dependent on the connectivity of the TTDA graph. Balanced trees result in the same number of cycles in both styles, while unbalanced trees favor multi-thread compilation. Inter-tree dataflow is more complex. In the worst case, every inter-tree dataflow arc is an inter-thread arc, and there is no redundant control flow. In that case, each new inter-tree arc results in one cycle in the dataflow style, and three cycles in the multi-thread style (one for a fork, and two for a join). This statement is true only in the limit, as the first one or two arcs added to the graph do not necessarily require a new fork instruction (mathematically, this is expressed by the max operators in the formulae). On the other hand, threading can tilt this comparison in favor of the multi-thread style if a sufficient number of the inter-tree arcs are contained within one thread, or if redundant control flow elimination succeeds in a sufficient number of cases, or if a combination of both occurs.

5.2 Conditionals

The multi-thread style of code generation has the potential for a great deal of savings, because there is often redundant control flow associated with the *switch* instructions employed in traditional dataflow style code generation. Unfortunately, the conservative algorithm used by the Berkeley TL0 compiler, which treats each variable entering and leaving a conditional as a dynamic arc, prevents much of this redundant control flow from being detected.[6] This has a doubly negative effect: not only is there as much switching overhead as in the dataflow style, but the dynamic arcs result in small threads in the arms of the conditional. Small threads imply that GC is comparable to LD + GD, and so multi-thread style code will have more instructions than dataflow style code.

5.3 Loops

Unlike conditionals, the bounded loop schemas used in dataflow style code generation [CA88] have a considerable overhead which is avoided in the multi-thread style. In the one-bounded dataflow loop schema, there is the following overhead for each circulating variable: a *switch* instruction (2 cycles), a corresponding fan-out from the predicate (1 cycle), a *gate* at the bottom of the loop body (2 cycles), and termination trees for both the body and the gates (6 cycles, including a fan-out from a *switch* for the body's termination tree, and a fan-out from that tree to the *gate*). The total is 11 additional cycles per circulating variable. The k-bounded loop schema does not have the body's termination tree, so its overhead totals 6 cycles per circulating variable.

In contrast, in the multi-thread style there are no termination trees required for bounding the loop, as the synchronization is implicit in the sequential control flow. Because of the way loop bounding affects the dependence graph (Figure 5), there is a great deal of opportunity for redundant control flow elimination. In particular, only one conditional branch instruction is needed, regardless of how many circulating variables there are. Furthermore, the number of threads remains quite small—only the presence of dynamic dependence arcs will cause multiple threads to be produced—which means that GC $<<$ LD + GD for many expression trees in the body. From the previous analysis, this results in quite efficient code for the body relative to the dataflow style.

5.4 Threaded Code With Registers

The use of T-registers can reduce the cost of multi-thread code even further. As suggested in Figure 1, the savings results from the more powerful addressing modes permitted with registers. Essentially, the registers permit a three-address style of code generation. One quirk of the Monsoon hardware is that the move of a result into the destination register is actually part of the instruction following the one computing the result. This has no material effect on a long sequence of three-address operations, but does affect the way register addressing modes sometimes conflict with activation frame addressing modes.

Addressing mode conflicts make it difficult to count analytically the number of cycles executed by register code. Roughly speaking, registers allow most of the `MOV` instructions in Figures 8 and 9 to be eliminated. When both register and activation frame operands are involved in the same thread, however, there may be conflicts which prevent the removal of a `MOV`. These come about because

[6] Again, a later version of the TL0 compiler, not available at the time of this study, has an improved algorithm.

of limitations on the number of bits in a Monsoon instruction, preventing the simultaneous specification of a frame operand, register operands, and a `JUMP` or `FORK` destination.

6 Empirical Results

This section compares the multi-thread and dataflow styles through measurement of actual Id program performance on a one-processor Monsoon system. Programs were compiled four ways: dataflow style code using the one-bounded dataflow loop schema, dataflow style code using the k-bounded loop schema, multi-thread style without using the T-registers, and multi-thread style using three T-registers (the maximum permitted by the hardware). The dataflow compiler is the MIT Id Compiler, which in most cases is able to generate the best possible dataflow style code as described in the previous section. The multi-thread compiler relies on the Berkeley TL0 compiler to partition the program into threads and to eliminate redundant control flow. While the Berkeley compiler in many cases is able to achieve the results suggested in Sections 3 and 4, some threads are not as large as they could be, and not all redundant control flow is eliminated. This is primarily because only a very preliminary version of the Berkeley compiler was available for this study, which had known algorithmic bugs. Also, the multi-thread compiler is implemented as a post-pass to the Berkeley compiler, and so it must reconstruct the partitioned dataflow graph from TL0 code. In some cases, artifacts of TL0 are retained in the finished code; these would not be present if the compiler directly implemented the method outlined earlier. Finally, while both compilers have the same suite of target-independent optimizations, the Berkeley compiler has a slightly different type system that results in subscript expressions being calculated with floating point arithmetic. While floating point operations do not take any more cycles than integer operations on Monsoon, an additional conversion operation is inserted before each indexed fetch instruction. Of course, these deficiencies only exist because the use of the preliminary version of the Berkeley compiler was the most expedient option. In all cases, they result in a conservative comparison, in the sense that the multi-thread results are poorer than they could be.

The experimental methodology was to run the compiled programs on a one-processor Monsoon system, and use the hardware statistics registers to obtain a count of the machine cycles executed. Most of the programs have a nested, iterative structure, and so it is possible to obtain a polynomial expression for the number of cycles in terms of the input parameter. Each term of the polynomial gives the total number of cycles for all loops at a given level of nesting. In all cases, the polynomial thus obtained had integer coefficients, and its predictive power was verified against several other data points.

The result are tabulated in Figure 11. The first set of programs is designed to measure the instructions required by expression trees. For example, `expr4b` is the following program:

```
def expr4b x = ((x * x) * (x * x));
```

`Expr8b` is similar, but with eight occurrences of `x`, *etc.* The u-suffixed programs have an unbalanced tree of operators. (Common subexpression elimination was

Program	Dataflow style, loops are One-Bounded	k-Bounded	Multi-thread style, T-Regs are not used	used
expr4b	21	—	27	24
expr8b	33	—	36	28
expr16b	57	—	53	50
expr4u	21	—	24	24
expr8u	33	—	28	28
expr16u	57	—	36	36
iterma5	$87n + 103$	$64n + 560$	$46n + 64$	$44n + 63$
iterma6	$101n + 115$	$73n + 584$	$49n + 67$	$47n + 66$
recma5	$164n + 66$	—	$270n + 142$	$267n + 139$
recma6	$174n + 72$	—	$288n + 153$	$285n + 150$
matmult	$31n^3 + 261n^2 + 657n + 1575$	$34n^3 + 617n^2 + 2148n + 3282$	$26n^3 + 219n^2 + 578n + 3496$	$23n^3 + 215n^2 + 573n + 3493$

Figure 11: Empirical Results

disabled for this set of programs.) The absolute numbers in Figure 11 for each of these programs are not too interesting, as most of the cycle count is due to procedure linkage overhead. The interesting comparison is between, say, `expr4b` and `expr8b` in each style: as the number of occurrences of `x` increases, the number of cycles required in the multi-thread style increases more slowly than the dataflow style, as predicted in Section 5. The use of T-registers improved the comparison between `expr4b` and `expr8b`, but not between `expr8b` and `expr16b`, as `expr16b` does not fit within three registers. T-registers did not improve any of the unbalanced expressions, because at any point there is only one live intermediate value.

The next set of programs attempt to measure the cost of loops, conditionals, and procedure calls. `Iterma5` computes a five-point moving average of a vector, with the following loop:

```
{for i <- 1.0 to n do
   v5 = a[i];
   b[i] = (v1+v2+v3+v4+v5)/5.0;
   next v1 = v2;
   next v2 = v3;
   next v3 = v4;
   next v4 = v5;
 finally b}
```

`Iterma6` is similar, but is a six-point average. By taking the difference between the two, the overhead associated with each circulating variable is measured. For the dataflow style and one-bounded loops, the difference is 14: the 11 overhead cycles counted in Section 5.3, two cycles for a `plus` instruction, and one for an additional fan-out from the variable's `switch` to feed that `plus`. For the dataflow style and k-bounded loops, the overhead drops from 11 to 6, and the total difference is 9. On the other hand, the k-bounded loop schema has much more expensive setup and cleanup code, which is reflected in the larger lower-order terms. In the multi-thread style, the difference is only 3: a fetch from the frame, a `plus`, and a store to the frame. The next two programs are recursive versions, which for each circulating variable have an additional formal parameter, an argument to the recursive call, and a variable entering the conditional that terminates the recursion. The dataflow style is superior in this case: as discussed in Section 5.2 the overhead of the conditional is not any less due to the way it is handled by the Berkeley compiler's thread partitioner, and the resulting threads fall in the regions of Figure 10 where the multi-thread style requires more cycles.

The final program is a matrix multiply program, which includes two calls to a procedure that creates and fills a new matrix, the matrix multiply, and a procedure that sums all the elements of the product matrix. All of these procedures are implemented with loops, and all contribute to every term of the polynomials, save the cubic term which only counts the inner loop of the matrix multiplication itself. In the terms that correspond to loops, the multi-thread style performs about 15–20% better than the dataflow style. If the Berkeley compiler had the same type system as the MIT compiler, the coefficient of the cubic term for the multi-thread style would be 24 without T-registers or 21 with T-registers.

7 Conclusion

A method of compiling non-strict programs for dataflow architectures is presented, which takes a view of the dataflow machine as a general multi-threaded architecture. Simple algorithms requiring no interprocedural analysis are capable of finding sequential threads in non-strict programs. These threads may be statically scheduled at compile time, allowing the compiler to exploit the implicit control flow of a sequential code stream. By passing operands in the activation frame and in temporary registers, control flow is separated from data flow, which in turn permits the elimination of redundant control flow. Threads are compiled by introducing explicit operations to move data to and from the activation frame and explicit control flow operations; the resulting thread is a DAG for which standard code generation techniques apply.

Both analytic and empirical results show that if there is sufficient redundant control flow, multi-thread style code can perform significantly better than traditional dataflow style code. This is because fewer forking and joining operations are necessary. The compiler is most effective at removing redundant control flow in loops, by exploiting the strict, one-bounded semantics given them in the Id language.

There are several areas in which the present compiler could be improved. As already noted, the results here were obtained from a very preliminary version of the threading and control flow algorithms embedded in the Berkeley TL0 compiler. Better algorithms could lead to larger threads with fewer control flow operations. It is an open question whether a sophisticated threading analysis, which took into account procedure strictness and data structure dependence information, could yield significantly larger threads than the simple graph traversals described here. Even without interprocedural analysis, there is a great deal of improvement possible in the way that conditionals are handled.

One very important consideration is the parallelism exposed in multi-thread style object code. The whole point in building dataflow architectures, of course, is that dataflow programs typically expose large amounts of parallelism, which not only help to utilize large parallel machines, but also help individual processors tolerate the latency of global memory operations [ACM88]. As presented here, the multi-thread compilation seeks the most sequential code possible, as that results in the greatest savings in the total number of cycles. In particular, the use of one-bounded loops eliminate the largest source of parallelism in scientific programs. The best code generation strategy must expose sufficient parallelism to keep the machine busy, while not introducing so much that an inordinate amount of cycles are spent in redundant forking and joining. For the matrix multiply example, a good policy might be to compile the inne⁻ loop the multi-thread style, for efficiency, while the outer loops could be k-bounded, for parallelism. Exploring the tradeoff between efficiency and parallelism and formulating practical policies is an important area to be investigated.

Finally, the analysis summarized in Figures 8, 9, and 10 give a very precise indication of when dataflow style code is preferable to that of the multi-thread style. Specifically, if the result of an expression is not used more than once within the thread where it is computed (*i.e.*, $\text{LD} \leq 1$), and if each of the other uses is in a separate thread ($\text{GC} \approx \text{GD}$), then it may be profitable to pass that value on tokens rather than through the activation frame. By considering this sort of tradeoff, it should be possible to arrive at a hybrid style of code generation which by using each style in the appropriate situation, arrives at object code for dataflow architectures that is superior to both the traditional dataflow style and to the multi-thread style.

Acknowledgments

The author wishes to express his deep appreciation to David Culler for providing the TL0 compiler and much of the inspiration for this work, to his students Thorsten von Eicken and Klaus Erik Schauser for their assistance in understanding the threading and control flow algorithms, and to Venkat Natarajan of MCRC for porting the TL0 compiler onto the author's computer. The ideas in this paper benefited from helpful discussions with Arvind and Greg Papadopoulos.

References

[ACM88] Arvind, D. E. Culler, and G. K. Maa. Assessing the benefits of fine-grained parallelism in dataflow programs. *International Journal of Supercomputer Applications*, 2(3):10–36, 1988.

[AN90] Arvind and R. S. Nikhil. Executing a program on the MIT tagged-token dataflow architecture. *IEEE Transactions on Computers*, 39(3):300–318, March 1990.

[ANP86] Arvind, R. S. Nikhil, and K. K. Pingali. I-structures: Data structures for parallel computing. In *Graph Reduction*, volume 279 of *Lecture Notes in Computer Science*, pages 336–369. Springer-Verlag, October 1986.

[ASU86] A. V. Aho, R. Sethi, and J. D. Ullman. *Compilers: Principles, Techniques, and Tools.* Addison-Wesley, Reading MA, 1986.

[BHY88] A. Bloss, P. Hudak, and J. Young. Code optimizations for lazy evaluation. *Lisp and Symbolic Computation*, 1(2):147–164, September 1988.

[CA88] D. E. Culler and Arvind. Resource requirements of dataflow programs. In *Proceedings of the 15th Annual International Symposium on Computer Architecture*, pages 141–150. IEEE, June 1988.

[CSS+91] D. E. Culler, A. Sah, K. E. Schauser, T. von Eicken, and J. Wawrzynek. Fine-grain parallellism with minimal hardware support: A compiler-controlled threaded abstract machine. In *Fourth International Conference on Architectural Support for Programming Languages and Operating Systems*, pages 164–175. Association for Computing Machinery, April 1991.

[Eka86] K. Ekanadham. Multi-tasking on a dataflow-like architecture. Research Report RC 12307, IBM T. J. Watson Research Center, Hawthorne NY, November 1986.

[Ian88a] R. A. Iannucci. A dataflow/von Neumann hybrid architecture. Technical Report TR-418, Massachusetts Institute of Technology Laboratory for Computer Science, Cambridge MA, May 1988.

[Ian88b] R. A. Iannucci. Toward a dataflow/von Neumann hybrid architecture. In *Proceedings of the 15th Annual International Symposium on Computer Architecture*, pages 131–140. IEEE, June 1988.

[Joh84] T. Johnsson. Efficient compilation of lazy evaluation. *ACM SIGPLAN Notices*, 19(6):58–69, June 1984. (Proceedings of the SIGPLAN 84 Symposium on Compiler Construction).

[NA89] R. S. Nikhil and Arvind. Can dataflow subsume von Neumann computing? In *Proceedings of the 16th Annual International Symposium on Computer Architecture*, pages 262–272. IEEE, June 1989.

[Nik90] R. S. Nikhil. Id version 90.0 reference manual. Computation Structures Group Memo 284-1, Massachusetts Institute of Technology Laboratory for Computer Science, Cambridge MA, September 1990.

[PC90] G. M. Papadopoulos and D. E. Culler. Monsoon: an explicit token store architecture. In *Proceedings of the 17th Annual International Symposium on Computer Architecture*, pages 82–91. IEEE, 1990.

[PT91] G. M. Papadopoulos and K. R. Traub. Multithreading: A revisionist view of dataflow architectures. In *Proceedings of the 18th Annual International Symposium on Computer Architecture*, pages 342–351. IEEE, May 1991.

[SCvE91] K. E. Schauser, D. E. Culler, and T. von Eicken. Compiler-controlled multithreading for lenient parallel languages. In *Functional Programming Languages and Computer Architecture*, 1991. (To Appear).

[Ste89] K. Steele. An i-structure memory controller. Master's thesis, Massachusetts Institute of Technology, Cambridge MA, December 1989.

[Tra86] K. R. Traub. A compiler for the MIT tagged-token dataflow architecture. Technical Report TR-370, Massachusetts Institute of Technology Laboratory for Computer Science, Cambridge MA, August 1986.

[Tra89] K. R. Traub. Compilation as partitioning: A new approach to compiling non-strict functional languages. In *Functional Programming Languages and Computer Architecture*, pages 75–88. Association for Computing Machinery, September 1989.

[Tra91] K. R. Traub. *Implementation of Non-Strict Functional Programming Languages*. Pitman Publishing, London, 1991. Also published by MIT Press, Cambridge MA.

GAML : a Parallel Implementation of Lazy ML

Luc Maranget

INRIA Rocquencourt, BP 105, 78153 LE CHESNAY CEDEX, FRANCE.

Abstract

We present a new parallel implementation of lazy ML. Our scheme is a direct extension of the G-machine-based implementation of lazy ML. Parallelism is introduced by *fork* annotations inserted by the programmer. We discuss the interference of such user annotations with strictness annotations generated by our compiler. The system has been implemented on a Sequent Balance computer. We also address the main practical issues involved, including stack and heap management.

1 Introduction

The object of this work is to demonstrate that a lazy runtime system such as the G-machine may be implemented efficiently on a parallel shared-memory computer.

It is natural to consider parallelism in a language without side effects. Its semantics guarantee that it is possible to evaluate subexpressions in any order (Church-Rosser property). From a more operational point of view it can be observed that a lazy runtime system already provides facilities for delaying evaluations and that it should be relatively easy to adapt them to the concurrent evaluation of delayed tasks.

Therefore, our starting point is to allow several G-machines to reduce the same graph concurrently. We choose "standard" G-machines for their elegance and simplicity. The performance of our system is competitive with similar implementations [4, 13], taking memory management time into account.

2 A brief tour of GAML

The language implemented by GAML is the ML language with lazy semantics, very close to lazy ML of Göteborg [3, 8]. The syntax is actually closer to the one of CAML [14].

Unlike LML, GAML implements lazy pattern matching as defined by [9, 12]. LML relies on a more classical left-to-right evaluation order of the discriminating expression [3]. Lazy pattern matching, adapts the evaluation order to each set of patterns, guaranteeing termination whenever possible. GAML also has a simple module system which allows type-safe separate compilation.

Compiling lazy ML language to the G-machine has been extensively described in the literature [3, 8, 11]. However, we shall examine this notions first, in order to make our extensions easier to understand.

2.1 Simplified GAML

We consider the language defined by the following grammar :

programs :

p ::= **let rec** $f_1^{n_1}$ $[!]x_1 \ldots [!]x_{n_1} = e_1$
and ...
...
and $f_m^{n_m}$ $[!]x_1 \ldots [!]x_{n_m} = e_m$
in e

expressions :

e ::= $x\ e_1 \ldots e_n$
| $f\ e_1 \ldots e_n$
| $c_k^n\ e_1 \ldots e_n$
| **match** e **with** $c_1{}^{k_1}\ x_1 \ldots x_n$ -> e_1 | ...
| **let** [**rec**] $x_1 = e_1$ **and** ... **in** e
| $!e$
| $?x$

We write f^n for a function of arity n, x for a local variable and c_k^n for a constructor of arity n, identified by its constructor number k. The notation [item] expresses an optional item. This language is the intermediate language between the front end of the compiler and the G-code generator. Actually, this language is a subset of the GAML source language. The front end consists of a sequence of source-to-source transformations, such as pattern matching compilation, strictness analysis and lambda-lifting. Some restrictions should be emphasized : The λ-lifting transformation has been applied to the original source code, as a consequence functions exist at the program level only and constructors cannot be partially applied. Strictness annotations, written "!" and "?", are generated by the strictness analyzer. The exclamation mark "!" has two meanings :

- In **let rec** $f\ !x = \ldots$, it means that the function f is strict in its argument x.
- As an expression, $!e$ means that e can be evaluated eagerly.

The annotation ? applied to a variable x means that the expression bound to x is already reduced.

GAML is a lazy language. Expressions are reduced to weak head normal form, or canonical form. A canonical form is either the partial application of a function or a constructed value :

canonical forms :

r ::= $f^n\ e_1 \ldots e_m \quad 0 \leq m < n$
| $c_k^n\ e_1 \ldots e_n \quad 0 \leq n$

Arguments to functions and constructors are left unevaluated.

2.2 Compilation

$$c_1 \quad \mathcal{F}[\![f\ x_1 \ldots x_n = e]\!] \ = \ \text{LABEL } f;\ \mathcal{A}[\![x_1, \ldots x_n]\!];\ \text{LABEL } \_f;\ \mathcal{R}[\![e]\!]\ [x_1 = n \ldots x_n = 1]\ n \quad (n > 0)$$

$$c_{1b} \quad \mathcal{A}[\![x_1, \ldots\ !x_i, \ldots\ x_n]\!] = \ldots;\ \text{PUSH } i-1;\ \text{EVAL};\ \text{POP } 1;\ \ldots$$

$$c_2 \quad \mathcal{R}[\![e]\!]\ \rho\ d \quad = \mathcal{E}[\![e]\!]\ \rho\ d;\ \text{UPDATE } (d+1);\ \text{POP } d;\ \text{UNWIND}$$

$$c_3 \quad \mathcal{E}[\![c_k\ e_1 \ldots e_n]\!] \quad = \mathcal{C}[\![c_k\ e_1 \ldots e_n]\!] \quad (n \geq 0)$$

$$c_4 \quad \mathcal{E}[\![\textbf{match } e \textbf{ with } c_1{}^n\ x_1 \ldots x_n \text{ -> } e_1 \ldots]\!]\ \rho\ d \ = \ \mathcal{E}[\![e]\!];\ \text{CASE } (l_1, l_2, \ldots);\ \text{LABEL } l_1;\ \text{SPLIT};\ \mathcal{E}[\![e_1]\!]\ \rho[x_1 = d+n, \ldots x_n = d+1]\ (d+n);\ \text{SQUEEZE } 1\ n\ ;\ \text{JUMP } l\ ; \ldots\ \text{LABEL } l$$

$$c_5 \quad \mathcal{E}[\![\textbf{let } x_1 = e_1 \textbf{ and} \ldots x_n = e_n \textbf{ in } e]\!]\ \rho\ d \ = \ \mathcal{C}[\![e_1]\!]\ \rho\ d;\ \ldots;\ \mathcal{C}[\![e_n]\!]\ \rho\ (d+n-1)\ ;\ \mathcal{E}[\![e]\!]\ \rho[x_1 = d+1, \ldots x_n = d+n]\ (d+n);\ \text{SQUEEZE } 1\ n$$

$$c_6 \quad \mathcal{E}[\![\textbf{let rec } x_1 = e_1 \textbf{ and} \ldots x_n = e_n \textbf{ in } e]\!]\ \rho\ d \ = \ \text{ALLOC}^{n\dagger};\ \mathcal{C}[\![e_1]\!]\ \rho_r\ (d+n);\ \text{UPDATE } n;\ \ldots\ \mathcal{C}[\![e_n]\!]\ \rho_r\ (d+n);\ \text{UPDATE } 1;\ \mathcal{E}[\![e]\!]\ \rho_r\ (d+n);\ \text{SQUEEZE } 1\ n\ (\text{where } \rho_r = \rho[x_1 = d+1, \ldots x_n = d+n])$$

$$c_7 \quad \mathcal{E}[\![?x]\!]\ \rho\ d \quad = \text{PUSH } d - \rho(x)$$

$$c_8 \quad \mathcal{E}[\![e]\!]\ \rho\ d \quad = \mathcal{C}[\![e]\!]\ \rho\ d;\ \text{EVAL}$$

$$c_9 \quad \mathcal{C}[\![f^n\ e_1 \ldots e_m]\!]\ \rho\ d = \begin{cases} \mathcal{C}[\![e_m, \ldots e_1]\!]\ \rho\ d;\ \text{PFUN } f;\ \text{MKRAP}^{m\dagger} & (m < n) \\ \mathcal{C}[\![e_m, \ldots e_1]\!]\ \rho\ d;\ \text{PFUN } f; \text{MKRAP}^{(n-1)\dagger};\ \text{MKAP}^{(m-n+1)\dagger} & (m \geq n) \end{cases}$$

$$c_{10} \quad \mathcal{C}[\![e_f\ e_1 \ldots e_n]\!] \quad = \mathcal{C}[\![e_n, \ldots e_1]\!]\ \rho\ d;\ \mathcal{C}[\![e_f]\!]\ \rho\ (d+n);\ \text{MKAP}^n$$

$$c_{11} \quad \mathcal{C}[\![e_n, \ldots e_1]\!]\ \rho\ d \quad = \mathcal{C}[\![e_n]\!]\ \rho\ d;\ \ldots \mathcal{C}[\![e_1]\!]\ \rho\ (d+n-1)$$

$$c_{12} \quad \mathcal{C}[\![c_k^n\ e_1 \ldots e_n]\!]\ \rho\ d = \mathcal{C}[\![e_n, \ldots e_1]\!]\ \rho\ d;\ \text{MKCONSTR } c_k^n$$

$$c_{13} \quad \mathcal{C}[\![x]\!]\ \rho\ d \quad = \text{PUSH } d - \rho(x)$$

$$c_{14} \quad \mathcal{C}[\![f]\!]\ \rho\ d \quad = \text{PFUN } f$$

$$c_{15} \quad \mathcal{C}[\![!\, e]\!]\ \rho\ d \quad = \mathcal{E}[\![e]\!]\ \rho$$

† ALLOC^n, MKRAP^n and MKAP^n stand for ALLOC, MKRAP and MKAP repeated n times.

Figure 1: Simplified compilation scheme of GAML

The figure above explicits the GAML compilation scheme. There are four different compilation functions $\mathcal{F}$, $\mathcal{R}$, $\mathcal{E}$ and $\mathcal{C}$. All these functions take an expression or program as argument and give a sequence of G-code as result. The $\mathcal{R}$, $\mathcal{E}$ and $\mathcal{C}$ functions take an environment ρ and a stack depth d as additional arguments, to manage bindings :

1. $\mathcal{F}[\![\text{f}\ x_1 \ldots x_n = e]\!]$: Compile the definition of a supercombinator f. There are two entry points to a function f, labeled f and $\_f$. When entered as $\_f$, the function assumes that its strict arguments are already reduced. When entered as f, it must reduce its possibly non-canonical strict arguments in a prelude generated by the $\mathcal{A}$ scheme (rule c_{1b}). The strictness analyzer

replaces a call to f by a call to $\_f$ whenever appropriate.

2. $\mathcal{R}[\![e]\!]\ \rho\ d$: Evaluate e and return from a function (rule c_2).

3. $\mathcal{E}[\![e]\!]\ \rho\ d$: Evaluate to weak head normal form. This scheme is initially called by $\mathcal{R}$. It is recursively called on the strict parts of the language constructs (c_4 to c_6), on primitives (such as arithmetic operations) and on expressions annotated by the ! annotation (rule c_{15}).

4. $\mathcal{C}[\![e]\!]\ \rho\ d$: Construct a graph. This scheme is invoked on the arguments to functions and constructors, as well as on expressions bound by a **let** (rules c_{11} and c_5–c_6). While compiling function application, when the arity of the function is known at compile time, RAP nodes are introduced to represent partial applications (rule c_9),

The actual compiler implements more sophisticated schemes, that perform most usual optimizations : tail calls in the $\mathcal{R}$ scheme by the DISPATCH instruction, direct calls in the $\mathcal{E}$ scheme by the CALL instruction [11]. Neither do we consider functions of zero arguments.

A program **let rec** f ... **in** e is compiled by calling the $\mathcal{F}$ scheme on the function definitions f. Its execution consists of evaluating the expression e to normal form. This is done by the usual "printing" mechanism, which basically is a repeated application of evaluation to weak head normal form in a deep-first, left-to-right traversal.

2.3 The G-machine

The nodes in the graph are :

- Binary application nodes, AP n_1 n_2. The real implementation also uses vector application nodes, which represent functions applied to the right number of arguments in a compact way. In the simplified model, AP nodes are the only non-canonical nodes.

- Reduced application nodes, RAP n_1 n_2. They represent partial application, which are canonical forms (rule e_2 in figure 2).

- Function nodes, FUN (C, a), where C is the compiled code of the function and a its arity.

- Constructor nodes CONSTR c_k^a $n_1 \ldots n_a$.

The G-machine reduces expression graphs to weak head normal form. Its state is described by a 4-tuple $<C, s, G, D>$, where C is the code being executed, s is the main stack, G is the graph and D is the *dump* —a stack saving machine states when the G-machine is called recursively by an EVAL instruction. The initial state of the machine is $<\mathsf{EVAL}.(), n.(), G[n = N], ()>$, where n is a pointer to a graph representation N of the expression to be reduced, $G[n = N]$ is a graph containing N and () stands for the empty sequence.

e_1 <EVAL.C, $n.s$, $G[n = \mathrm{AP}\ n_1\ n_2]$, D> $\Rightarrow$ <UNWIND.(), $n.()$, $G[\ldots]$, $(C,s).D$>

e_2 <EVAL.C, $n.s$, G, D>, and n canonical $\Rightarrow$ <C, $n.s$, G, D>

e_3 <UNWIND.(), $n.s$, $G[n = \mathrm{(R)AP}\ n_1\ n_2]$, D> $\Rightarrow$ <UNWIND.(), $n_1.n.s$, $G[\ldots]$, D>

e_4 <UNWIND.(), $n_0.n_1.\ldots.n_k.s$, $G[n_0 = \mathrm{FUN}\ (C_f, k)$, $n_1 = \mathrm{AP}\ n'_1\ n''_1, \ldots n_k = \mathrm{AP}\ n'_k\ n''_k\ ]$, D>
$\Rightarrow$ <C_f, $n''_1.\ldots.n''_k.n_k.s$, $G[\ldots]$, D>

e_5 <UNWIND.(), $n_0.n_1.\ldots.n_k.()$, $G[n_0 = \mathrm{FUN}\ (C_f, a)]$, $(C,s).D$> and $a < k$ $\Rightarrow$
<C, $n_k.s$, $G[n_0 = \mathrm{FUN}\ (C_f, a)]$, D>

e_6 <UNWIND.(), $n.()$, $G[n = \mathrm{CONSTR}\ c^a_k\ n_1 \ldots n_a]$, $(C,s).D$> $\Rightarrow$ <C, $n.s$, $G[\ldots]$, D>

e_7 <UPDATE $d.C$, $n_0.n_1\ldots n_d.s$, $G[n_0 = N_0,\ n_d = N_d]$, D> $\Rightarrow$
<C, $n_1\ldots n_d.s$, $G[n_0 = N_0,\ n_d = N_0]$, D>

e_8 <PUSH $d.C$, $n_0.\ldots n_d.s$, G, D> $\Rightarrow$ <C, $n_d.n_0\ldots n_d.s$, G, D>

e_9 <PFUN $f.C$, s, $G[n = \mathrm{FUN}\ (C_f, a)]$, D> $\Rightarrow$ <C, $n.s$, $G[n = \mathrm{FUN}\ (C_f, a)]$, D>

e_{10} <POP $d.C$, $n_1.\ldots.n_d.s$, G, D> $\Rightarrow$ <C, s, G, D>

e_{11} <SQUEEZE $d\ m.C$, $n_1\ldots n_{d+m}.s$, G, D> $\Rightarrow$ <C, $n_1\ldots n_d.s$, G, D>

e_{12} <ALLOC.C, s, G, D> $\Rightarrow$ <C, $n.s$, $G[n = \mathrm{HOLE}]$, D>

e_{13} <MKAP.C, $n_1.n_2.s$, G, D> $\Rightarrow$ <C, $n.s$, $G[n = \mathrm{AP}\ n_1\ n_2]$, D>

e_{14} <MKCONSTR $c^a_k.C$, $n_1.\ldots.n_a.s$, G, D> $\Rightarrow$ <C, $n.s$, $G[n = \mathrm{CONSTR}\ c^a_k\ n_1 \ldots n_a]$, D>

e_{15} <CASE $(l_1, l_2\ldots)\ldots$LABEL $l_k.C$, $n.s$, $G[n = \mathrm{CONSTR}\ c^a_k\ n_1 \ldots n_a]$, D> $\Rightarrow$
<C, $n.s$, $G[\ldots]$, D>

e_{16} <SPLIT.C, $n.s$, $G[n = \mathrm{CONSTR}\ c^a_k\ n_1 \ldots n_a]$, D> $\Rightarrow$ <C, $n_1\ldots n_a.s$, $G[\ldots]$, D>

Figure 2: Transitions of the sequential G-machine

The transitions of the sequential G-machine are summarized in figure 2. The typical reduction process, started by EVAL applied to a "root" AP node (e_1), repeatedly applies rule e_3 to "unwind the spine" on the S stack. Once the function at the bottom of the spine is reached, and if there are enough arguments on the stack (e_4), the code for this function is entered. This code, as compiled by rule c_2 in figure 1, constructs a new graph in canonical form, updates the root (e_7) and resumes the unwinding process.

The G-code is expanded into native machine code in the efficient way presented in [3]. Our sequential compiler is similar to the Chalmers LML compiler [3, 8], in design and performance.

3 Parallelism at the source level

The parallel extension preserves the deterministic lazy semantics of GAML. The reduction of expressions is organized in a different way, so that some parts of the evaluation process may be performed simultaneously.

3.1 Annotations

Idealy, the compiler should determine where parallel computations can be started, without user intervention. As a first step, we have chosen to rely on user annotations in the source program, indicating subcomputations to be performed in parallel. Automatic parallelization can be added later on as a source to source transformation. The advantage of source to source transformations is that they give the user a precise idea of what the compiler is doing.

Parallelism annotations come in addition to strictness annotations. Consider, for instance, Takeushi's function :

```
let rec tak x y z =  match  x < y with
      true -> z
    | false ->
       tak
         (tak (x-1) y z)
         (tak (y-1) z x)
         (tak (z-1) x y) in
tak 18 12 6
```

It is compiled as follows :

```
let rec tak !x !y !z = match  ?x < ?y with
      false ->
       _tak
         !(_tak !(int._sub ?x 1) ?y ?z)
         !(_tak !(int._sub ?y 1) ?z ?x)
         !(_tak !(int._sub ?z 1) ?x ?y)
    | true -> ?z in
_tak 18 12 6
```

Strictness analysis successfully infers that the **tak** function is strict in its three arguments. As a consequence, all calls to the **tak** function are made directly without constructing a graph, since the optimized $\mathcal{E}$ scheme, induced by the ! annotation compile them with a CALL instruction. Furthermore all calls are made through the **_tak** entry of the function, so that the arguments are not tested for canonical form.

3.2 An annotation for parallelism

We use a *fork* annotation "#", such an annotation is also called *spark* following [11]. The expression #*e* means that *e* is to be reduced in parallel with the current thread of computation. This makes sense only if #*e* can be referenced later. A first case is when #*e* is an argument to a constructor. This constructor can be destructured later, by a **match** construct or by the printing mechanism, so that the value of *e* can be retrieved. A second case is when #*e* is bound to a variable. That is, #*e* is an argument in a function call, or bound by a **let** construct. Consider, for instance :

```
let rec fib = fun n -> match n with
   0 -> 1
 | 1 -> 1
 | _ -> let v = #(fib (n-1)) in 1 + fib (n-2) + v in
fib 30
```

The programmer specifies that the call `(fib (n-1))` should be done in parallel. When the computation needs the result of this call, it will find it bound to variable `v`. Synchronization is easily expressed by the syntax of the expressions itself.

It is not always obvious to decide when to fork exactly. Consider :

```
let K x y = x
and F x = fib x + fib (x/2) in
K 0 (F #(F (F 2)))
```

It is not clear when `#(F (F 2))` should be forked : while constructing the graph for the whole expression `(F #(F (F 2)))` ? Or while reducing it, that is while performing the outermost call to `F` (which, in this case, will not happen) ? The second solution gives the programmer more precise control on fork time. Thus, $\#e$ means "start reducing e in parallel at the time when this expression is bound". An expression is bound either by a **let** construct or by reducing a function call. To do so, the compiler introduces a new function `G` and rewrites the example above as :

```
let K x y = x
and F x = fib x + fib (x/2)
and G x = F #(F (F x)) in
K 0 (G 2)
```

This transformation allows to choose the "fork at binding time" semantics without any special node in the graph. It also applies to annotated **let** bindings. The $\mathcal{E}$ scheme is the only one that deals with parallel bindings, $f\ \ldots\ \#e\ \ldots$ and **let** $x = \#e$ **in**....

The case of the constructors is less ambiguous, the expression $c_k^n \ldots \#e \ldots$ just means : "fork at the time when the value is actually constructed", both the $\mathcal{C}$ and $\mathcal{E}$ compilation schemes construct this value.

3.3 Treatment of # by the compiler

The presence of the spark annotation does not inhibit strictness-based optimizations. Moreover, these optimizations are combined with another source to source transformation expressing load control at runtime.

On a real computer with a limited number of CPUs, it is likely that an expression will not be reduced as soon as it is forked. It can happen that a forked expression is not yet reduced when its parent computation thread needs it. In this case, the parent thread reduces the unevaluated expression as it would do in the sequential case. This is the simplest and most efficient solution. Waiting for someone else to do the reduction is both wasteful and difficult to implement safely.

This "advisory fork" mechanism has additional benefits. Since a possibly forked expression can be reduced by its parent, it is not necessary to actually fork it when

c'$_1$	$\mathcal{C}[\![\#e]\!]\ \rho\ d = \mathcal{C}[\![e]\!]$; FORK	
c'$_2$	$\mathcal{C}[\![f^n\ e_1 \ldots e_m]\!]\ \rho\ d =$	
	$\mathcal{C}[\![e_m, \ldots e_1]\!]\ \rho\ d$; PFUN f; MKRAP^m	$(m < n)$
	$\mathcal{C}[\![e_m, \ldots e_1]\!]\ \rho\ d$; PFUN f; MKRAP$^{(n-1)}$; MKAP$^{(m-n)}$; MKSAP	$(m \geq n)$
c'$_3$	$\mathcal{C}[\![e_f\ e_1 \ldots e_n]\!]\ \rho\ d = \mathcal{C}[\![e_n, \ldots e_1]\!]\ \rho\ d$; $\mathcal{C}[\![e_f]\!]\ \rho\ (d+n)$; MKAP$^{(n-1)}$; MKSAP	

Figure 3: Compilation of parallel GAML

the computer load is too high. This can be expressed at the source level. The compiler transforms the Fibonacci example above :

```
let rec fib !n = match ?n with
      0 -> 1
    | 1 -> 1
    | _ -> match ?sys.forkNow with
          true ->
           let v_3 = #(_fib !(int._sub ?n 1)) in
           let b_5 = !(_fib !(int._sub ?n 2)) in
           let b_6 = !v_3 in
           int._add (int._add 1 ?b_5) ?b_6
        | false ->
           let b_7 = !(_fib !(int._sub ?n 2))
           and b_8 = !(_fib !(int._sub ?n 1)) in
           int._add (int._add 1 ?b_7) ?b_8 in
_fib 30
```

Here `sys.forkNow` is a boolean system variable set to `true` by the runtime system when the load is low. This example shows the main advantage of expressing load control at the source level. In the case when no fork is not done (the `false` branch), strictness optimizations apply, and the call `!(_fib (int._sub ?n 1))` is compiled into a direct call by the optimized $\mathcal{E}$ scheme. This would not be possible if the decision whether or not to fork were done by the runtime system alone.

Another point is that the programmer does not need to worry about the order of evaluation of strict expressions. In the Fibonnaci example, the programmer specifies that the expression `(_fib !(int._sub ?n 1))` should be forked. The compiler introduces annotated `let` bindings, expressing the fork (binding `v_3`), evaluate the other needed subexpression (binding `b_5`) and synchronize (binding `b_6`) evaluation order. This order is implicitly meant by the programmer when he puts the # annotation.

4 The parallel G-machine

4.1 Compilation to the parallel G-machine

A parallel G-machine is best described as one of several G-machines operating on the same graph.

A given subgraph cannot be reduced by more than one G-machine at a time. This could lead to inconsistent graphs. And such duplication of work wastes resources. Therefore, when applied to an AP node, the EVAL and UNWIND instructions change its tag to a new tag, the RUN tag. Another machine will not perform an EVAL or UNWIND instruction on a RUN node. As several machines may attempt to change an AP node into a RUN node simultaneously, the tag test and change sequence must be atomic. This is done by using a lock associated to the memory address of the tag. Locking is always expensive, even on the architectures where any memory address can be viewed as a lock, which is not the case in our Sequent Balance system. Thus, we try to avoid this penalty as much as possible.

The atomic change from AP to RUN state is not needed if the AP node is not shared. This leads us to distinguish between possibly shared application nodes SAP and certainly unshared application nodes AP. It does not matter whether a partial application RAP node is shared or not, since these nodes are never modified.

Possibly shared expressions are the ones bound by a **let**, the arguments in an application, and the arguments to a constructor. All these expressions are compiled with the $\mathcal{C}$ scheme (figure 1, rules $\mathbf{c}_5$, $\mathbf{c}_6$, and $\mathbf{c}_9$ to $\mathbf{c}_{12}$). Thus, the $\mathcal{C}$ scheme is modified : rules $\mathbf{c}_9$ and $\mathbf{c}_{10}$ are replaced by the new rules $\mathbf{c'}_2$ and $\mathbf{c'}_3$ (figure 3). The new rules generate a SAP node when called on a (possibly) non-canonical expression.

Obviously this criterion is not optimal. In some cases, a bound expression is not shared. Some sharing analysis could be used to determine unshared variables [7, 5]. This analysis seems not very useful in our case, because the spark annotation introduces a lot of sharing. For instance, in the Fibonacci function, variable **v** is shared between the parent thread and the child thread, whereas it is obviously not shared in a sequential implementation.

4.2 A parallel G-machine model

In this section we explain how several G-machines cooperate. A concurrent G-machine state is a 6-tuple $<C, s, D, G, R, F>$. The components C, s, G and D are the same as in the sequential case. We will explain the *run pool* R and the *fork pool* F later. The components C, s and D are local to each G-machine, whereas G, R and F are shared between the cooperating G-machines. The transitions of the parallel G-machine are shown in figure 4. Transitions $\mathbf{e'}_1$–$\mathbf{e'}_4$ and $\mathbf{e'}_8$–$\mathbf{e'}_{10}$ comes in addition to the transitions of the sequential G-machine. Whereas transition $\mathbf{e'}_5$ replaces transition $\mathbf{e}_5$ and transitions $\mathbf{e'}_6$–$\mathbf{e'}_7$ replaces transition $\mathbf{e}_7$.

The graph G has two new types of nodes :

- the shared application node, SAP n_1 n_2, created by the MKSAP instruction.
- the RUN node, RUN p n_2. A RUN node is created by overwriting a SAP node. This is the reason why a RUN node has two fields, though only the first one p is used.

When a machine forks an expression, it just puts the graph representing it in the *fork pool* F (transition $\mathbf{e'}_8$), where idle machines can pick it up ($\mathbf{e'}_{10}$). When a machine attempts to EVAL or UNWIND a node being processed by another

$$\text{e'}_1\quad <\text{EVAL}.C,\ n.s,\ D,\ G[n=\text{SAP}\ n_1\ n_2],\ R,\ F> \ \Rightarrow$$
$$<\text{UNWIND}.(),\ n_1.n.(),\ (C,s).D,\ G[n=\text{RUN}\ ()\ n_2],\ R,\ F>$$

$$\text{e'}_2\quad <\text{EVAL}.C,\ n.s,\ D,\ G[n=\text{RUN}\ p],\ R,\ F> \Rightarrow$$
$$<(),\ (),\ (),\ G[n=\text{RUN}\ (<\text{EVAL}.C,\ n.s,\ D>.p)],\ R,\ F>$$

$$\text{e'}_3\quad <\text{UNWIND}.(),\ n.s,\ D,\ G[n=\text{SAP}\ n_1\ n_2],\ R,\ F> \ \Rightarrow$$
$$<\text{EVAL}.(),\ n.(),\ (\text{UNWIND}.(),n.s).D,\ G[\ldots],\ R,\ F>$$

$$\text{e'}_4\quad <\text{UNWIND}.(),\ n.s,\ D,\ G[n=\text{RUN}\ p],\ R,\ F> \ \Rightarrow$$
$$<(),\ (),\ (),\ G[n=\text{RUN}\ (<\text{UNWIND}.(),\ n.s,\ D>.p)],\ R,\ F>$$

$$\text{e'}_5\quad <\text{UNWIND}.(),\ n_0.\ldots.n_k.(),\ (C,s).D,\ G[n_0=\text{FUN}\ (C_f,a)\ ],\ R,\ F>\ \text{and}\ a<k\Rightarrow$$
$$<\text{UPDATE}\ 1.C,\ n.n_k.s,\ D,\ G[\ n_0=\ldots,\ n=\text{RAP}\ n_{k-1}*(n_k+2)],\ R,\ F>$$

$$\text{e'}_6\quad <\text{UPDATE}\ d.C,\ n_0.n_1\ldots.n_d.s,\ D,\ G[n_0=N_0,\ n_d=\text{RUN}\ p],\ R,\ F> \ \Rightarrow$$
$$<C,\ n_1\ldots.n_d.s,\ D,\ G[n_0=N_0,\ n_d=N_0],\ R[p],\ F>$$

$$\text{e'}_7\quad <\text{UPDATE}\ d.C,\ n_0.n_1\ldots.n_d.s,\ D,\ G[n_0=N_0,\ n_d\neq\text{RUN}\ p],\ R,\ F> \ \Rightarrow$$
$$<C,\ n_1\ldots.n_d.s,\ D,\ G[n_0=N_0,\ n_d=N_0],\ R,\ F>$$

$$\text{e'}_8\quad <\text{FORK}.C,\ n.s,\ D,\ G,\ R,\ F> \ \Rightarrow <C,\ n.s,\ D,\ G,\ R,\ F[n]>$$

$$\text{e'}_9\quad <(),\ (),\ (),\ G,\ R[p=<C,\ s,\ D>],\ F> \ \Rightarrow <C,\ s,\ D,\ G,\ R,\ F>$$

$$\text{e'}_{10}\quad <(),\ (),\ (),\ G[n=\text{SAP}\ n_1\ n_2],\ R,\ F[n]> \ \Rightarrow <\text{EVAL}.(),\ n.(),\ (),\ G[\ldots],\ R,\ F>$$

Figure 4: Transition rules of the concurrent G-machine

machine, it finds a node with a RUN tag. Evaluation of the current task cannot be pursued. Therefore, its state is saved as a process structure $<C,\ s,\ D>$ and queued on the p field of the RUN node (e'$_2$ and e'$_4$). The machine then enters the idle state $<(),\ (),\ (),\ G,\ R,\ F>$. When the machine processing the RUN node overwrites it with its canonical form (instruction UPDATE), it will awake the processes on this node (transition e'$_6$). These awakened processes become runnable, they are put in the *run pool* R, where idle machines can pick them up (transition e'$_9$).

In the parallel G-machine, UPDATE is a generic instruction just like EVAL or UNWIND : its effect depends upon the nodes it operates on (transitions e'$_6$ and e'$_7$). A new UPDATE instruction has to be inserted when an UNWIND instruction fails (transition e'$_5$). In this case, the root node to be updated (N_k) can be a RUN node, so its tag must be changed into RAP and the suspended processes queued in the p field must be awakened.

A complete system is made of several G-machines. Initially, one machine is in the state $<\text{EVAL}.(),\ n.(),\ D,\ G[\ n=\ldots],\ (),\ ()>$, where n is a pointer to the expression to compute. The others machines are in idle state, waiting for the initiator machine to put something in the fork pool.

4.3 Implementation

The fork pool is a statically allocated area of memory holding pointers to forked expressions. It is not accessed in an exclusive manner, so that some forked expressions may be lost (if two machines forks simultaneously) or picked up more than once. This does not compromise the correctness of the implementation, since spark is advisory and the RUN tag already prevents several machine from reducing the same sub-graph. This non-locked access mechanism is crucial for the efficiency of the parallel G-machines. Another important point is that the fork pool is statically allocated, so that the FORK operation does not allocate memory. These two points make a FORK instruction very cheap : it takes between 9 and 20 machine instructions (including testing buffer overflow).

Unlike the fork pool F, the run pool R needs exclusive access. Once started, a reduction must be completed, otherwise the whole computation could stop before completion. The run pool is implemented as a linked list of processes. A lock can be used to guard a global pool, or each machine can have its own private RUN pool. This choice is not critical, since few EVAL or UNWIND instructions find nodes in RUN state. Therefore the RUN pool is empty most of the time.

4.4 Scheduling

In figure 4 no scheduling policy is imposed idle machines can take either transaction e'_9 or e'_{10}.

In the best case, all forked expressions are eventually required (conservative parallelism) and the scheduling strategy is only a matter of efficiency. If a process does not terminate, neither will the complete program, since the non-terminating process computes a needed value.

Experimentation shows that the scheduler should look at the run pool first to avoid creating a new process when an already existing process is runnable (non-running processes waste stack and heap resources). The strategy governing the run pool itself has little impact, because the run pool is empty most of the time. If the run pool is local to each machine, then it can be checked just once per call to the scheduler.

The best strategy for the fork pool is a LIFO strategy : the fork buffer is a bounded stack of 128 pointers. Other alternatives tested are the linked list, the circular buffer and various "random" policies. Experiments indicate that the evaluation of forked expressions should not be delayed too much. This seems to help to keep the number of suspended tasks low and avoid reductions of forked tasked by their parents.

When some forked expression may not be needed (speculative parallelism), we must make sure that the processes computing the normal reduction are not blocked for ever by speculative tasks. This can be done by pre-emptive fair scheduling. We plan to design a more clever implementation, where a "token" is passed through the running processes, so that the process holding the token is computing the normal order branch of reduction, and that the process holding the token is always running.

Another important point is the management of the `forkNow` variable. A simple policy gives good results. When an idle machine finds the fork pool empty it sets `forkNow` to `true`. When a forking machine finds the fork pool full it sets `forkNow` to `false`.

5 Heap management

Heap management is the hidden cost the previous parallel G-machine implementations. Usually they use a sequential garbage collector. That is, one processor is collecting the memory using a traditional algorithm while the others are idle. This is a waste of CPU power.

5.1 Calling the parallel collector

We want to keep the efficiency and simplicity of stop & copy garbage collectors. In this section we present a parallel version of this algorithm. Our algorithm is parallel in the sense that all running processors take part in the collection. Collection is not performed concurrently with the main program however. Therefore, this approach does not require complicated synchronization between processors executing user code and processors collecting memory as in [2].

The heap space is divided in two spaces, the from-space and the to-space. The processors request to-space pages from a global memory manager, which is a critical section. After getting a page, each processor allocates in it without any further synchronization. As described in [8, page C-18], a request for the heap space needed by a basic block is made at the beginning of the block. When there is not enough memory left in the current page to satisfy a request, the processor asks for a new heap page. Thus, large heap pages are desirable, to minimize synchronization. If a memory request is more than one page large, then it should be broken into smaller ones, by shortening basic blocks. If large objects such as arrays are to be allocated (this is not the case in GAML), then several contiguous pages can be given by the memory manager.

If a request for a new page fails, then the requesting machine enters collector state. All the others allocating machines will end up having consumed their own pages. We experimentally checked that it was not worth the trouble for the allocating processors to try to enter collector state before running out of space naturally. However, when a machine is polling on the fork queue or performing a non-allocating computation, it does not allocate any memory. Such machines periodically check a shared variable. When a machine enters collector state, it sets this variable, so that non-allocating machines join it for starting collection. We cannot use very large pages, because the larger the page, the longer the delay for starting garbage collection. In practice $4Kb$ is a good tradeoff.

5.2 Safe copying in parallel

Once all the processors are in collector state, the collection begins. The to-space and the from-space are swapped. Then each processor starts a traditional stop & copy algorithm, allocating memory page by page in the new to-space. To preserve the structure of the graph, no object can be copied by more than one processor. Therefore synchronization is needed. More precisely, while tracing referenced objects, a collector repeatedly invokes the `copyObj` function to copy object into its own to-space pages. We give the C code for the `copyObj` function, that copies objects, and then, overwrite their old locations with a forward reference to their new locations.

```
word pointer *last;  /* Next free position   */

void INCRLAST(n);     /* Handle memory allocation */

word MemLock(obj);    /* Lock obj, return its tag */

word MemUnlock(obj,newTag);  /* UnLock obj, change its tag */

word *copyObj(obj)
word *obj;
{
 word *tag,*newObj,oldObj;

 tag = (word *)*obj;
 switch (tag) {
  ....
  case SAP:                      /* not yet copied */
   tag = (word *)MemLock(obj);
   if (tag == MOVED) {           /* lost race */
    MemUnlock(obj,MOVED);
    return((word *)*(obj+1));   /* return forward pointer */
   } else {                      /* won race */
    INCRLAST(3);                 /* three words needed */
    newObj = last; oldObj = obj++;
    *last++ = SAP;  *last++ = *obj; /* fill first two words */
    *obj++ = newObj;             /* set forward pointer */
    MemUnlock(oldObj,MOVED);
    *last++ = *obj;              /* copy last word */
    return(newObj);
  }
   ....
  case MOVED:                   /* already copied  */
   return ((word *)*(obj+1)); /* return forward pointer */
   ....
 }
}
```

The tag check and the setting of the forwarding pointer have to be performed atomically : This is done by using the already present mechanism of tags as locks from section 4.1 (cf functions MemLock and MemUnlock). In the source code above, the SAP tag is changed this way into a new MOVED tag identifying pointers to moved nodes. The overhead for locking is paid only when the object has a chance to be copied, i.e. no mutual exclusion is necessary to access the forwarding pointer in a MOVED node, or to retrieve the statically allocated version of a node, as it is the case for FUN nodes and CONSTR nodes with zero argument.

5.3 The roots for the GC

At the beginning of the GC, the roots considered are the stacks of the running processes, plus the runnable processes in the run pool. As the GC proceeds, the processes suspended on RUN nodes are discovered . The stacks of suspended processes are also scanned as roots. All theses processes are said to be active, their stacks have to be scanned since they are running or may run in the future.

The fork pool also has to be scanned. But it is not part of the roots, the pointers to the graph in the fork pool are "weak pointers" : if an object is pointed to from the fork pool only, then it is garbage, since it is not referenced to by any active process. This is done by scanning the fork pool after the main collection has been completed, not collecting objects not copied at this stage and replacing pointers to them by a pointer to a dummy object. The scanning of the fork pool itself is done in parallel, which is easy since the fork pool is a contiguous zone of memory.

5.4 Distributing the work

As all machines cooperate to collect unused space it is important to distribute the work to be done as evenly as possible, to maximize parallelism. We do this by distributing the roots to be scanned between the processors.

A first idea is just to have each processor scan its own running process (if any), and then let it scan the suspended processes as they are found in the heap, queued on RUN nodes. This solution does not lead to good balancing : some processors are idle while others are scanning large stacks. To improve on this, we divide the job of scanning a stack into "scanning tasks". We fix a granularity constant T. A scanning task consists of a base pointer sp and of an offset o less than T. Completing a scanning task is scanning a stack, starting at location $sp + o$, skipping T by T.

When a processor has a stack to scan, it puts the corresponding scanning tasks in a global pool. As this pool is not accessed with mutual exclusion (for efficiency reasons), the initiator of tasks must then try to complete them, in case they are lost in the pool. This absence of synchronization also implies that several processors may start completing the same scanning task. But it is easy for a processor completing a scanning task to know that this task has already been completed or is being completed by another processor : as long as it has not yet been examined, a pointer to the heap is a pointer to the from-space ; once the pointed object has been copied, the pointer is changed into a pointer to the to-space. So, a processor scanning a portion of stack gives up when it encounters a pointer to the to-space.

The choice of the granularity constant T is critical. If it is too small, the distribution of the work is poor. If it is too big there are too many tasks and the stacks are not efficiently scanned. Our benchmarks gives best results with T between 8 and 16.

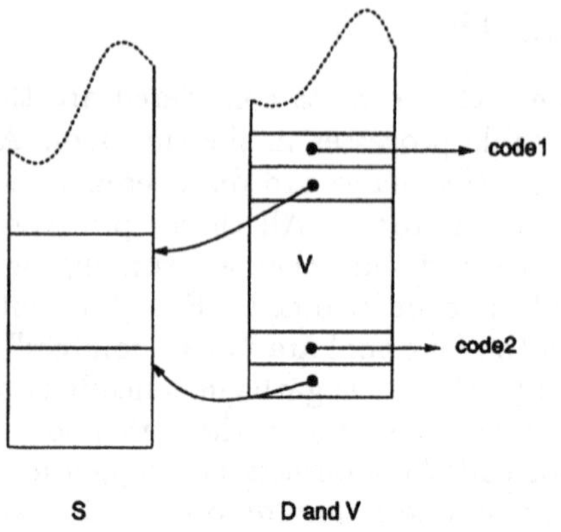

Figure 5: Stacks in the sequential implementation

6 Implementation of the stacks

The theoretical G-machine has tree stacks : The S stack, that is used to unwind the spine, the V stack, for the intermediate results of arithmetic computations, and the dump or D stack. In our parallel implementations, stack space is given to a G-process on its explicit demand. This implies that a machine has to check stack overflow, so that it can ask for more stack space when needed. In our parallel implementation, this mechanism is needed for one real stack only, and the stack overflow check is not done so often.

6.1 The V stack

Traditionally, arithmetic expressions are compiled with a stack model in mind. That is, arithmetic operators pop their arguments from a stack and push their results on it. The G-machine has the V stack for this purpose. We omitted the V stack from our description of the G-machine for the sake of simplicity.

The V stack is a stack of integers or other basic values, which the garbage collector must not consider as pointers. This is the reason why it is convenient to implement the V and S stacks as separate stacks : the garbage collector simply ignore the V stack. If we want to have one stack only, and still not use a conservative garbage collector, then the garbage collector must be able to distinguish a pointer from a non-pointer value. This can be achieved by *tagging* : one bit per word is reserved to indicate its pointer or non-pointer status, see [6, p. 50] for instance. This information can be stored somewhere else than in the word itself [1, 4, 13]. These solutions imply important modifications of the runtime system.

Fortunately, a simpler solution is already given in [3, p. C-27–C-29] : the V stack can be made empty each time the heap is checked. More precisely, intermediate arithmetic results are stored in the S stack when they survive basic blocks. This is achieved by a source-to-source transformation : the V stack elimination. It

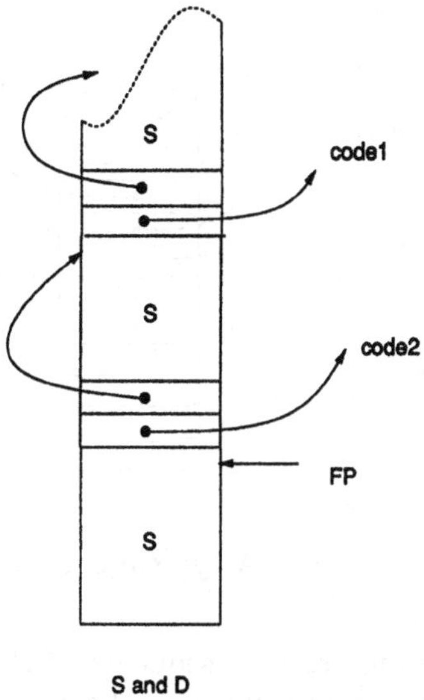

Figure 6: Stacks in the parallel implementation

lifts expressions that compile into an EVAL out of arithmetic expressions, replacing them by fresh variables bound by a strict **let** :

```
fib (n-1) + fib (n-2) + 1
```

will be transformed into :

```
let a = !(fib (n-1))
and b = !(fib (n-2)) in
?a+?b+1
```

Since a process gets suspended by evaluating a RUN node, the V stack will always be empty at that time. Therefore, the V stack is not part of the saved state of a process.

6.2 The D stack

The D stack is used to remember G-machine states, that is, pairs (S, C) of S stacks and return addresses. In the sequential implementation, all the S stacks are allocated contiguously on one real stack. A saved state is two entries on the dump, one pointing to the code and the other pointing to the beginning of the S stack starting just below the saved S stack (cf figure 5, stacks are growing from top to bottom). In our parallel implementation, we store a pointer to the beginning of the current S stack in the FP (frame pointer) register. Of course, when a new S stack is started, the EVAL instruction has to save the old frame pointer, it just pushes it on the real stack with the return address. Therefore, the only real stack

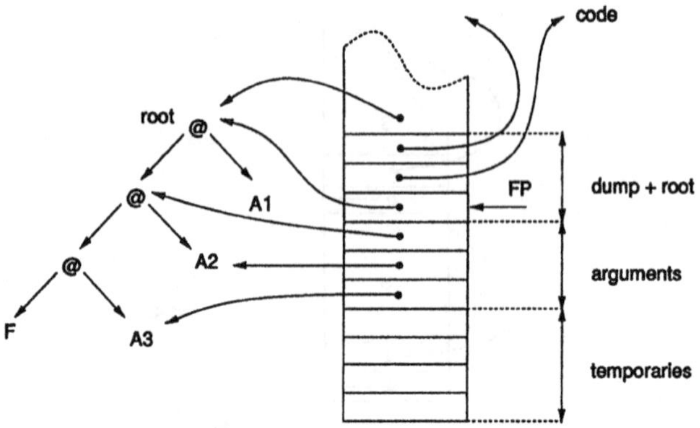

Figure 7: A typical S stack

used will look as depicted in figure 6 : a sequence of S stacks separated by pairs of saved frame pointers and program counters. The garbage collector easily retrieves the pointers to the heap from such a stack, either by following the saved frame pointers or by just checking all words in the stack against heap bounds.

6.3 Checking stack overflow

Thus, there is only one real stack per process. We simply call it "the stack". In a strict language checking stack overflow needs be performed at the beginning of the functions only : each function checks whether there is enough room on the stack to hold its local variables and temporaries. This does not work in GAML, because the EVAL and UNWIND instructions may use an amount of stack that cannot be bounded by a local analysis. But, for a given program, the depth of the S stacks can bounded by a constant depending upon the program only.

Consider a typical S stack, such as the one in figure 7. Assume that this stack was started to compute the expression $E = F\ A_1\ A_2 \ldots A_n$, where F is a supercombinator and A_1,A_2,...A_n are arbitrary expressions. From top to bottom, first, there are three slots for the old frame pointer, the return address and a pointer to the root node of E. Then, n stack entries hold the arguments that were *given* to F. These arguments were put on the stack while unwinding the spine. The remaining entries, up to the stack pointer, are filled with the temporaries and local variables of F. This description also applies when F is invoked from another supercombinator via UNWIND.

The code generator can easily compute an upper bound temp(F) of the number of temporaries used by the function F. In ML, which is a typed language, an upper bound args(F) of the number of arguments than can be given to F, can also be computed. Suppose that F has a non-polymorphic type, then F cannot be invoked with more arguments then specified by its type. For instance, the curried addition on integers, of type int $\rightarrow$ int $\rightarrow$ int, cannot be applied to more than two arguments. But types in ML may be polymorphic. Fortunately, as observed by Andrew Appel [1], each function is used with a finite number of different ground types. David Lester [10] states that these monomorphic types can be computed while type-checking the program, by conserving all the instances of polymorphic type schemes. Consider the program :

```
let I x = x in I I 1
```

The polymorphic function I of type $\forall\alpha \rightarrow \alpha$ is used with the type instances "(int $\rightarrow$ int) $\rightarrow$ int $\rightarrow$ int" and "int $\rightarrow$ int". Here, $\text{args}(I) = 2$. Some generic variables may remain in the type instances. As they cannot be instantiated any further, this has no impact on the computation of $\text{args}(F)$. For instance, in `let I x = x in I I`, the type instances are $(\alpha \rightarrow \alpha) \rightarrow \alpha \rightarrow \alpha$ and $\alpha \rightarrow \alpha$, and $\text{args}(I) = 2$.

Therefore, for a program P, the S stack will never grow to more than $N = 3 + \max(\text{args}(F)) + \max(\text{temp}(F))$ elements, where F ranges over the supercombinators defined by P. This upper bound can be computed at compile time. Thus, before starting a new S stack, the EVAL instruction checks that there is at least N free entries on the real stack. If not, it asks a new stack chunk from global memory manager, and changes the return address in the new S stack, so that the stack chunk will be freed while returning from EVAL. In this way, the activation records of the functions are stack-allocated.

Unfortunately, the computation of N in the presence of separate compilation requires to put *all* the instances of polymorphic types in the public part of the modules. This appears quite inconvenient, if not prohibitive. In practice, we only use the fact that the N upper bound exists, and fix it to a hopefully large enough value. In our benchmarks 32 is large enough. If more safety is required, the stack must be checked each time EVAL or UNWIND pushes something on it, and at the beginning of the functions.

7 Performance

7.1 Overall performance

There are four benchmarks. The sources are given in the appendix. The *nfib30*, *primes* and *queens* benchmarks exhibit the same good performance in speedup (figure 8). The *euler* test gives a disappointing result. Namely, not only the *euler* test uses more memory than the others, but it also generate parallelism in a different way.

	nfib30	primes	queens	euler
sequential	130 (1.00)	139 (1.00)	337 (1.00)	314 (1.00)
parallel	213 (1.63)	199 (1.43)	467 (1.39)	430 (1.37)

In the table above, we give the wall clock time performance of the parallel implementation relatively to the sequential implementation (comparable with LML 0.99). Combined with the speedup figures, these data show that parallelism leads to real benefits, as soon as more than one processor is used.

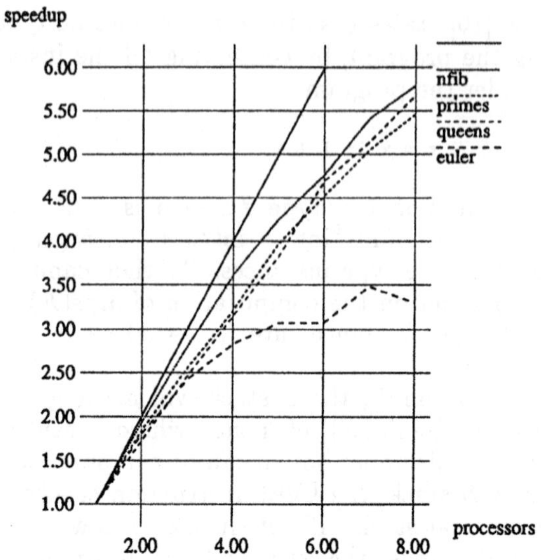

Figure 8: Speedups relative to one processor.

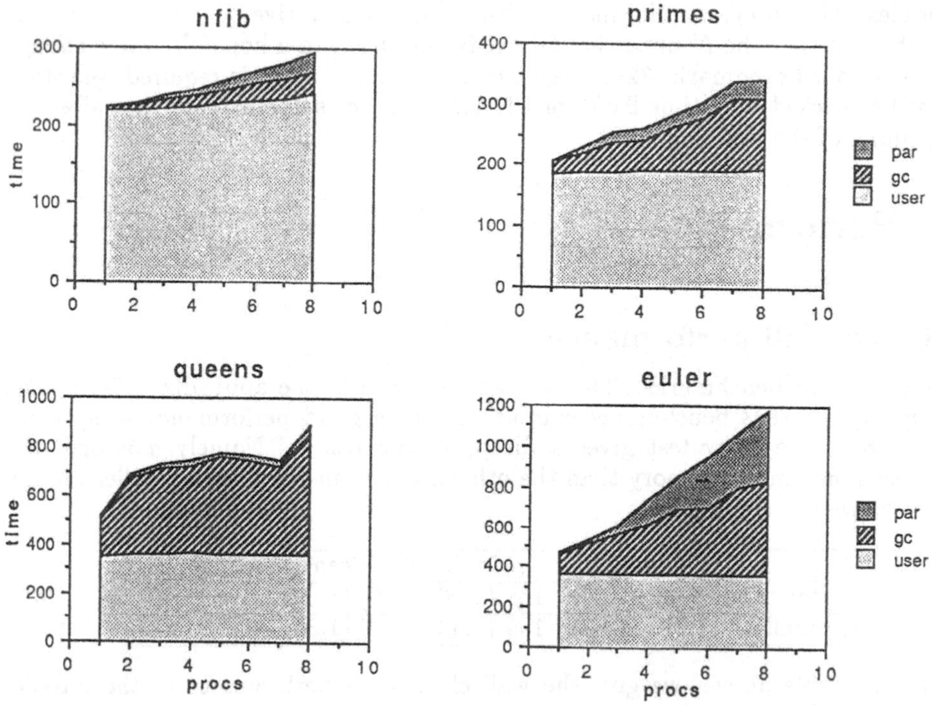

Figure 9: Distribution of CPU time.

The figure 9 shows how the total CPU time and its distribution evolves as the number of processors increases. Total CPU time is the sum of the CPU time of all the cooperating processors. This time is divided in three categories, according to where it is spent :

- **user** corresponds to the code of the user functions,
- **gc** is the garbage collector,
- **par** accounts for the scheduler loop and the management of the Unix processes implementing the cooperating G-machines.

In all the tests, the **user** time slightly increases with the number of processors, because of some synchronization costs in the EVAL, UNWIND and UPDATE instructions. In addition, for the *nfib30* the strictness optimizations (in the `false` branch of the `forkNow` test, section 3.3) may apply less often.

For the first three tests, the **par** time stays marginal. There is little polling on the fork queue, because these programs can fork tasks evenly. For the *euler* test the parallelism is generated by scanning the list of the first 1000 integers. For each cons in the list, two tasks are forked, one for a large computation and the other for treating the next cell in the list. If a scanning task gets lost —which is likely when the fork buffer has less than twice as many elements as the list—, the scanning of the list is stopped. Scanning will restart once the normal reduction order has reached the point where scanning stopped. This introduces delays.

7.2 Efficiency of the GC

We deliberately choose a relatively small heap size (one megabyte), to get closer to the behavior of real programs, for which the time spent in garbage collection is significant.

As the number of processors increases, so does the percentage of running time spent in garbage collection. This is not only because garbage collection is not parallelized as efficiently as the GAML programs themselves. Parallelism has a cost in terms of memory. The number of calls to the GC does not increase much with parallelism though. The slight increase in the total memory allocated comes from process structures (but there are few of them), and extra graphs created to be put in the fork pool. But the increase in the number of processes has an indirect effect : there are more stacks to scan, furthermore there are more live objects in the heap, i.e., the heap occupancy rate increases as shown in the table below :

procs	nfib30	primes	queens	euler
1	0.10	7.09	11.92	5.74
4	0.36	7.07	12.41	9.63
8	0.62	7.04	13.94	14.04

Hence, our stop & copy-based GC, has more objects to copy. This effect depends upon the benchmark considered.

Acknowledgments

I thank Xavier Leroy and Georges Gonthier for their editorial work. I also thank Robert Ehrlich who made the *gproff* Unix profiling utility work for parallel programs.

References

[1] Andrew W. Appel, *Runtime Tags Aren't Necessary*, Lisp and Symbolic Computation, vol 2 1989.

[2] Andrew W. Appel, John R. Ellis, and Kai Li, *Real-time Concurrent Collection on Stock Multiprocessors*, PLDI'88.

[3] Lennart Augustsson, *Compiling Lazy Functional Languages Part II*, Ph. D. Thesis, Chalmers University of Technology, 1987.

[4] Lennart Augustsson and Thomas Johnsson, *Parallel Graph Reduction with the <ν, G>-machine*, FPCA'89.

[5] Alain Deutsch, On determining lifetime and aliasing of dynamically allocated data in higher order functional specifications POPL'90.

[6] *Report on the Programming Language Haskell*, Version 1.0, YALEU/DCS/RR-77.

[7] Paul Hudak, *A Semantic Model of Reference Counting and its Abstraction*, in *Abstract Interpretation of Declarative Languages*, Ellis Horwood 1987.

[8] Thomas Johnsson, *Compiling Lazy Functional Languages*, Ph. D. Thesis, Chalmers University of Technology, 1987.

[9] Alain Laville, *Implementation of Lazy Pattern Matching Algorithms*, ESOP'88, LNCS 300.

[10] David Lester, *Stacklessness : Compiling Recursion for a Distributed Architecture*, FCPA'89.

[11] S. L. Peyton Jones, *The Implementation of Functional Programming Languages*, Prentice-Hall, 1987.

[12] Laurence Puel, Ascánder Suárez, Compiling Pattern Matching by Term Decomposition, LFP'90.

[13] Simon L. Peyton-Jones, John Salkild, *The Spineless Tagless G-machine*, FPCA'89.

[14] Pierre Weis, *The CAML Reference manual* Version 2.6.1, INRIA Technical Report 121.

Appendix : source of the benchmarks

primes : primes numbers up to 1000.

```
let filter f =  let rec f_rec l = match l with
      []    -> []
    | x::xs -> if f x then x::#(f_rec xs) else f_rec xs in f_rec in

let rec sieve l = match l with
    []    -> []
  | p::xs ->  p::sieve (filter (fun x ->x mod p <> 0) xs) in

sieve (count 2 10000)
```

queens : the 10 queens problem

```
let concmap f =  let rec c_rec m = match m with
      []    -> []
    | x::xs -> append (f x) #(c_rec xs) in  c_rec in

let filter f = let rec filter_rec l =  match l with
    []    -> []
  | x::xs -> if f x then x::#(filter_rec xs) else filter_rec xs in filter_rec in

let rec safe x d l = match l with
  []     -> true
| q::qs -> x<>q  & x<>q+d & x<>q-d & safe x (d+1) qs in

let ok l =  match l with  []     -> true | x::xs -> safe x 1 xs in

let rec gen n = match n with
  0 -> [[]]
| _ -> concmap
        (fun b ->filter ok (map (fun q ->q::b) (count 1 10)))
        (gen (n-1)) in

length (gen 10)
```

euler : the euler totient function

```
let map f =  let rec map_rec l = match l with
    []     -> []
  | x::xs -> #(f x)::#(map_rec xs) in map_rec in

let rec gcd x y = match y with 0 -> x | _ -> gcd y (x mod y) in
let relprime x y = gcd x y = 1 in
let euler n =  length (filter (relprime n) (fromto 1 (n-1))) in

sum (map euler (count 1 1000))
```

Functional Programming with Bananas, Lenses, Envelopes and Barbed Wire

Erik Meijer * Maarten Fokkinga † Ross Paterson ‡

Abstract

We develop a calculus for lazy functional programming based on recursion operators associated with data type definitions. For these operators we derive various algebraic laws that are useful in deriving and manipulating programs. We shall show that all example functions in Bird and Wadler's "Introduction to Functional Programming" can be expressed using these operators.

1 Introduction

Among the many styles and methodologies for the construction of computer programs the Squiggol style in our opinion deserves attention from the functional programming community. The overall goal of Squiggol is to *calculate* programs from their specification in the way a mathematician calculates solutions to differential equations, or uses arithmetic to solve numerical problems.

It is not hard to state, prove and use laws for well-known operations such as addition, multiplication and —at the function level— composition. It is, however, quite hard to state, prove and use laws for arbitrarily recursively defined functions, mainly because it is difficult to refer to the recursion scheme in isolation. The algorithmic structure is obscured by using unstructured recursive definitions. We crack this problem by treating various recursion schemes as separate higher order functions, giving each a notation of its own independent of the ingredients with which it constitutes a recursively defined function.

This philosophy is similar in spirit to the 'structured programming' methodology for imperative programming. The use of arbitrary goto's is abandoned in favour of structured control flow primitives such as conditionals and while-loops that replace fixed patterns of goto's, so that reasoning about programs becomes feasible and sometimes even elegant. For functional programs the question is which recursion schemes are to be chosen as a basis for a calculus of programs. We shall consider several recursion operators that are naturally associated with algebraic type definitions. A number of general theorems are proven about these operators and subsequently used to transform programs and prove their correctness.

Bird and Meertens [4, 18] have identified several laws for specific data types (most notably *finite* lists) using which they calculated solutions to various programming problems. By embedding the calculus into a categorical framework, Bird and Meertens' work on lists can be extended to arbitrary, inductively defined data types [17, 12]. Recently the group of Backhouse [1] has extended the calculus to a relational framework, thus covering indeterminancy.

*University of Nijmegen, Department of Informatics, Toernooiveld 6525 ED Nijmegen, e-mail: erik@cs.kun.nl
†CWI, Amsterdam & University of Twente
‡Imperial College, London

Independently, Paterson [21] has developed a calculus of functional programs similar in contents but very dissimilar in appearance (like many Australian animals) to the work referred to above. Actually if one pricks through the syntactic differences the laws derived by Paterson are the same and in some cases slightly more general than those developped by the Squiggolers.

This paper gives an extension of the theory to the context of lazy functional programming, i.e., for us a type is an ω-cpo and we consider only continuous functions between types (categorically, we are working in the category CPO). Working in the category SET as done by for example Malcolm [17] or Hagino [14] means that finite data types (defined as initial algebras) and infinite data types (defined as final co-algebras) constitute two different worlds. In that case it is not possible to define functions by induction (catamorphisms) that are applicable to both finite and infinite data types, and arbitrary recursive definitions are not allowed. Working in CPO has the advantage that the carriers of initial algebras and final co-algebras coincide, thus there is a single data type that comprises both finite and infinite elements. The price to be paid however is that partiality of both functions and values becomes unavoidable.

2 The data type of lists

We shall illustrate the recursion patterns of interest by means of the specific data type of cons-lists. So, the definitions given here are actually specific instances of those given in §4. Modern functional languages allow the definition of cons-lists over some type A by putting:

$$A* \ ::= \ \mathsf{Nil} \mid \mathsf{Cons}\ (A \| A*)$$

The recursive structure of this definition is employed when writing functions $\in A* \to B$ that destruct a list; these have been called *catamorphisms* (from the greek preposition $\kappa\alpha\tau\alpha$ meaning "downwards" as in "catastrophe"). *Anamorphisms* are functions $\in B \to A*$ (from the greek preposition $\alpha\nu\alpha$ meaning "upwards" as in "anabolism") that generate a list of type $A*$ from a seed from B. Functions of type $A \to B$ whose call-tree has the shape of a cons-list are called *hylomorphisms* (from the Aristotelian philosophy that form and matter are one, $\upsilon\lambda o$ meaning "dust" or "matter").

Catamorphisms

Let $b \in B$ and $\oplus \in A \| B \to B$, then a list-catamorphism $h \in A* \to B$ is a function of the following form:

$$\begin{aligned} h\,\mathsf{Nil} &= b \\ h\,(\mathsf{Cons}\,(a, as)) &= a \oplus (h\ as) \end{aligned} \tag{1}$$

In the notation of Bird&Wadler [5] one would write $h = \mathsf{foldr}\ b\ (\oplus)$. We write catamorphisms by wrapping the relevant constituents between so called banana brackets:

$$h \ = \ (\!| b, \oplus |\!) \tag{2}$$

Countless list processing functions are readily recognizable as catamorphisms, for example $\mathsf{length} \in A* \to \mathsf{Num}$, or $\mathsf{filter}\ p \in A* \to A*$, with $p \in A \to \mathsf{bool}$.

$$\begin{aligned} \mathsf{length} &= (\!| 0, \oplus |\!) \ \mathit{where}\ a \oplus n = 1 + n \\ \mathsf{filter}\ p &= (\!| \mathsf{Nil}, \oplus |\!) \\ & \quad \mathit{where}\ a \oplus as = \mathsf{Cons}\,(a, as), \quad p\ a \\ & \qquad\qquad\qquad\ \ = as, \qquad\qquad\quad \neg p\ a \end{aligned}$$

Separating the recursion pattern for catamorphisms $(\!|\_|\!)$ from its ingredients b and $\oplus$ makes it feasible to reason about catamorphic programs in an algebraic way. For example the *Fusion Law* for catamorphisms over lists reads:

$$f \circ (\!|b,\oplus|\!) = (\!|c,\otimes|\!) \;\Leftarrow\; f\,b = c \,\wedge\, f\,(a \oplus as) = a \otimes (f\,as)$$

Without special notation pinpointing catas, such as $(\!|\_|\!)$ or foldr, we would be forced to formulate the fusion law as follows.

Let h, g be given by

$$\begin{array}{rcl} h\,\mathrm{Nil} &=& b \\ h\,(\mathrm{Cons}\,(a,as)) &=& a \oplus (h\,as) \end{array} \qquad \begin{array}{rcl} g\,\mathrm{Nil} &=& c \\ g\,(\mathrm{Cons}\,(a,as)) &=& a \otimes (g\,as) \end{array}$$

then $f \circ h = g$ if $f\,b = c$ and $f\,(a \oplus as) = a \otimes (f\,as)$.

A clumsy way of stating such a simple algebraic property.

Anamorphisms

Given a predicate $p \in B \to \mathrm{bool}$ and a function $g \in B \to A\|B$, a list-anamorphism $h \in B \to A*$ is defined as:

$$\begin{array}{rcll} h\,b &=& \mathrm{Nil}, & p\,b \\ &=& \mathrm{Cons}\,(a, h\,b'), & \mathrm{otherwise} \\ && \mathrm{where}\ (a,b') = g\,b & \end{array} \qquad (3)$$

Anamorphisms are not well-known in the functional programming folklore, they are called unfold by Bird&Wadler, who spend only few words on them. We denote anamorphisms by wrapping the relevant ingredients between concave lenses:

$$h = [\!(g,p)\!] \qquad (4)$$

Many important list-valued functions are anamorphisms; for example $zip \in A*\|B* \to (A\|B)*$ which 'zips' a pair of lists into a list of pairs.

$$\begin{array}{rcl} zip &=& [\!(g,p)\!] \\ p\,(as,bs) &=& (as = \mathrm{Nil}) \vee (bs = \mathrm{Nil}) \\ g\,(\mathrm{Cons}\,(a,as), \mathrm{Cons}\,(b,bs)) &=& ((a,b),(as,bs)) \end{array}$$

Another anamorphism is iterate f which given a, constructs the infinite list of iterated applications of f to a.

$$\mathrm{iterate}\ f = [\!(g, \mathrm{false}^\bullet)\!]\ \mathrm{where}\ g\,a = (a, f\,a)$$

We use $c^\bullet$ to denote the constant function $\lambda x.c$.

Given $f \in A \to B$, the map function $f* \in A* \to B*$ applies f to every element in a given list.

$$\begin{array}{rcl} f*\mathrm{Nil} &=& \mathrm{Nil} \\ f*(\mathrm{Cons}\,(a,as)) &=& \mathrm{Cons}\,(f\,a, f*as) \end{array}$$

Since a list appears at both sides of its type, we might suspect that map can be written both as a catamorphism and as an anamorphisms. Indeed this is the case. As catamorphism: $f* = (\!|\mathrm{Nil},\oplus|\!)$ where $a \oplus bs = \mathrm{Cons}\,(f\,a, bs)$, and as anamorphism $f* = [\!(g,p)\!]$ where $p\,as = (as = \mathrm{Nil})$ and $g\,(\mathrm{Cons}\,(a,as)) = (f\,a, as)$.

Hylomorphisms

A recursive function $h \in A \to C$ whose call-tree is isomorphic to a cons-list, i.e., a linear recursive function, is called a hylomorphism. Let $c \in C$ and $\oplus \in B \| C \to C$ and $g \in A \to B \| A$ and $p \in A \to \mathit{bool}$ then these determine the hylomorphism h

$$\begin{aligned} h\,a &= c, \qquad\qquad p\,a \\ &= b \oplus (h\,a'), \ \ \mathit{otherwise} \\ &\quad\ \mathit{where}\ (b, a') = g\,a \end{aligned} \tag{5}$$

This is exactly the same structure as an anamorphism except that Nil has been replaced by c and Cons by $\oplus$. We write hylomorphisms by wrapping the relevant parts into envelopes.

$$h \;=\; [\![(c, \oplus), (g, p)]\!] \tag{6}$$

A hylomorphism corresponds to the composition of an anamorphism that builds the call-tree as an explicit data structure and a catamorphism that reduces this data object into the required value.

$$[\![(c, \oplus), (g, p)]\!] \;=\; (\!| c, \oplus |\!) \circ [\!(g, p)\!]$$

A proof of this equality will be given in §15.

An archetypical hylomorphism is the factorial function:

$$\begin{aligned} \mathit{fac} &= [\![(1, \times), (g, p)]\!] \\ p\,n &= n = 0 \\ g\,(1+n) &= (1+n, n) \end{aligned}$$

Paramorphisms

The hylomorphism definition of the factorial maybe correct but is unsatisfactory from a theoretic point of view since it is not inductively defined on the data type $\mathit{num} ::= 0 \mid 1 + \mathit{num}$. There is however no 'simple' φ such that $\mathit{fac} = (\!|\varphi|\!)$. The problem with the factorial is that it "eats its argument and keeps it too" [27], the brute force catamorphic solution would therefore have fac' return a pair $(n, n!)$ to be able to compute $(n+1)!$.

Paramorphisms were investigated by Meertens [19] to cover this pattern of primitive recursion. For type num a paramorphism is a function h of the form:

$$\begin{aligned} h\,0 &= b \\ h\,(1+n) &= n \oplus (h\,n) \end{aligned} \tag{7}$$

For lists a paramorphism is a function h of the form:

$$\begin{aligned} h\,\mathit{Nil} &= b \\ h\,(\mathit{Cons}\,(a, as)) &= a \oplus (as, h\,as) \end{aligned}$$

We write paramorphisms by wrapping the relevant constituents in barbed wire $h = \{\!| b, \oplus |\!\}$, thus we may write $\mathit{fac} = \{\!| 1, \oplus |\!\}$ where $n \oplus m = (1+n) \times m$. The function $\mathit{tails} \in A* \to A{*}{*}$, which gives the list of all tail segments of a given list is defined by the paramorphism $\mathit{tails} = \{\!| \mathit{Cons}\,(\mathit{Nil}, \mathit{Nil}), \oplus |\!\}$ where $a \oplus (as, tls) = \mathit{Cons}\,(\mathit{Cons}\,(a, as), tls)$.

3 Algebraic data types

In the preceding section we have given specific notations for some recursion patterns in connection with the particular type of cons-lists. In order to define the notions of cata-, ana-, hylo- and paramorphism for arbitrary data types, we now present a generic theory of data types and functions on them. For this we consider a recursive data type (also called 'algebraic' data type in Miranda) to be defined as the least fixed point of a functor[1].

Functors

A bifunctor $\dagger$ is a binary operation taking types into types and functions into functions such that if $f \in A \to B$ and $g \in C \to D$ then $f \dagger g \in A \dagger C \to B \dagger D$, and which preserves identities and composition:

$$\begin{aligned} id \dagger id &= id \\ f \dagger g \circ h \dagger j &= (f \circ h) \dagger (g \circ j) \end{aligned}$$

Bifunctors are denoted by $\dagger, \ddagger, \S, \ldots$

A monofunctor is a unary type operation F, which is also an operation on functions, $\mathsf{F} \in (A \to B) \to (A\mathsf{F} \to B\mathsf{F})$ that preserves the identity and composition. We use $\mathsf{F}, \mathsf{G}, \ldots$ to denote monofunctors. In view of the notation $A*$ we write the application of a functor as a postfix: $A\mathsf{F}$. In §5 we will show that $*$ is a functor indeed.

The data types found in all current functional languages can be defined by using the following basic functors.

Product The (lazy) product $D \| D'$ of two types D and D' and its operation $\|$ on functions are defined as:

$$\begin{aligned} D \| D' &= \{(d, d') \mid d \in D, d' \in D'\} \\ (f \| g)\,(x, x') &= (f\,x, g\,x') \end{aligned}$$

Closely related to the functor $\|$ are the projection and tupling combinators:

$$\begin{aligned} \grave{\pi}\,(x, y) &= x \\ \acute{\pi}\,(x, y) &= y \\ (f \vartriangle g)\,x &= (f\,x, g\,x) \end{aligned}$$

Using $\grave{\pi}, \acute{\pi}$ and $\vartriangle$ we can express $f \| g$ as $f \| g = (f \circ \grave{\pi}) \vartriangle (g \circ \acute{\pi})$. We can also define $\vartriangle$ using $\|$ and the doubling combinator $\Delta\,x = (x, x)$, since $f \vartriangle g = f \| g \circ \Delta$.

Sum The sum $D \mid D'$ of D and D' and the operation $\mid$ on functions are defined as:

$$\begin{aligned} D \mid D' &= (\{0\} \| D) \cup (\{1\} \| D') \cup \{\bot\} \\ (f \mid g)\,\bot &= \bot \\ (f \mid g)\,(0, x) &= (0, f\,x) \\ (f \mid g)\,(1, x') &= (1, g\,x') \end{aligned}$$

[1]We give the definitions of various concepts of category theory only for the special case of the category CPO. Also 'functors' are really endo-functors, and so on.

The arbitrarily chosen numbers 0 and 1 are used to 'tag' the values of the two summands so that they can be distinguished. Closely related to the functor | are the injection and selection combinators:

$$\begin{aligned} \grave{\imath}\, x &= (0,x) \\ \acute{\imath}\, y &= (1,y) \\ (f \triangledown g)\ \bot &= \bot \\ (f \triangledown g)\ (0,x) &= f\ x \\ (f \triangledown g)\ (1,y) &= g\ y \end{aligned}$$

with which we can write $f \mid g = (\grave{\imath} \circ f) \triangledown (\acute{\imath} \circ g)$. Using ∇ which removes the tags from its argument, $\nabla\ \bot = \bot$ and $\nabla\ (i,x) = x$, we can define $f \triangledown g = \nabla \circ f \mid g$.

Arrow The operation $\rightarrow$ that forms the function space $D \rightarrow D'$ of continuous functions from D to D', has as action on functions the 'wrapping' function:

$$(f \rightarrow g)\ h \ = \ g \circ h \circ f$$

Often we will use the alternative notation $(g \leftarrow f)\ h = g \circ h \circ f$, where we have swapped the arrow already so that upon application the arguments need not be moved, thus localizing the changes occurring during calculations. The functional $(f \overset{F}{\leftarrow} g)\ h = f \circ hF \circ g$ wraps its F-ed argument between f and g.

Closely related to the $\rightarrow$ are the combinators:

$$\begin{aligned} \mathit{curry}\ f\ x\ y &= f\ (x,y) \\ \mathit{uncurry}\ f\ (x,y) &= f\ x\ y \\ \mathit{eval}\ (f,x) &= f\ x \end{aligned}$$

Note that $\rightarrow$ is contra-variant in its first argument, i.e. $(f \rightarrow g) \circ (h \rightarrow j) = (h \circ f) \rightarrow (g \circ j)$.

Identity, Constants The identity functor I is defined on types as $DI = D$ and on functions as $fI = f$. Any type D induces a functor with the same name $\underline{D}$, whose operation on objects is given by $C\underline{D} = D$, and on functions $f\underline{D} = id$.

Lifting For mono-functors F, G and bi-functor † we define the mono-functors FG and F†G by

$$\begin{aligned} x(FG) &= (xF)G \\ x(F\dagger G) &= (xF) \dagger (xG) \end{aligned}$$

for both types and functions x.

In view of the first equation we need not write parenthesis in xFG. Notice that in (F†G) the bi-functor † is 'lifted' to act on functors rather than on objects; (F†G) is itself a mono-functor.

Sectioning Analogous to the sectioning of binary operators, $(a\oplus)\ b = a \oplus b$ and $(\oplus b)\ a = a \oplus b$ we define sectioning of bi-functors †;

$$\begin{aligned} (A\dagger) &= \underline{A}\dagger I \\ (f\dagger) &= f \dagger id \end{aligned}$$

hence $B(A\dagger) = A \dagger B$ and $f(A\dagger) = id \dagger f$. Similarly we can define sectioning of $\dagger$ in its second argument, i.e. $(\dagger B)$ and $(\dagger f)$.

It is not too difficult to verify the following two properties of sectioned functors:

$$
\begin{aligned}
(f\dagger) \circ g(A\dagger) &= g(B\dagger) \circ (f\dagger) \qquad \text{for all } f \in A \to B & (8)\\
(f\dagger) \circ (g\dagger) &= ((f \circ g)\dagger) & (9)
\end{aligned}
$$

Taking $f \dagger g = g \to f$, thus $(f\dagger) = (f\circ)$ gives some nice laws for function composition.

Laws for the basic combinators

There are various equations involving the above combinators, we state nothing but a few of these. In parsing an expression function composition has least binding power while $\|$ binds stronger than $|$.

$$
\begin{aligned}
\grave{\pi} \circ f \| g &= f \circ \grave{\pi} & f \mid g \circ \grave{\imath} &= \grave{\imath} \circ f\\
\grave{\pi} \circ f \vartriangle g &= f & f \triangledown g \circ \grave{\imath} &= f\\
\acute{\pi} \circ f \| g &= g \circ \acute{\pi} & f \mid g \circ \acute{\imath} &= \acute{\imath} \circ g\\
\acute{\pi} \circ f \vartriangle g &= g & f \triangledown g \circ \acute{\imath} &= g\\
(\grave{\pi} \circ h) \vartriangle (\acute{\pi} \circ h) &= h & (h \circ \grave{\imath}) \triangledown (h \circ \acute{\imath}) &= h \Leftarrow h \text{ strict}\\
\grave{\pi} \vartriangle \acute{\pi} &= id & \grave{\imath} \triangledown \acute{\imath} &= id\\
f \| g \circ h \vartriangle j &= (f \circ h) \vartriangle (g \circ j) & f \triangledown g \circ h \mid j &= (f \circ h) \triangledown (g \circ j)\\
f \vartriangle g \circ h &= (f \circ h) \vartriangle (g \circ h) & f \circ g \triangledown h &= (f \circ g) \triangledown (f \circ h) \Leftarrow f \text{ strict}\\
f \| g = h \| j &\equiv f = h \wedge g = j & f \mid g = h \mid j &\equiv f = h \wedge g = j\\
f \vartriangle g = h \vartriangle j &\equiv f = h \wedge g = j & f \triangledown g = h \triangledown j &\equiv f = h \wedge g = j
\end{aligned}
$$

A nice law relating $\vartriangle$ and $\triangledown$ is the *abides law*:

$$
(f \vartriangle g) \triangledown (h \vartriangle j) = (f \triangledown h) \vartriangle (g \triangledown j) \qquad (10)
$$

Varia

The one element type is denoted **1** and can be used to model constants of type A by nullary functions of type $\mathbf{1} \to A$. The only member of **1** called *void* is denoted by $()$.

In some examples we use for a given predicate $p \in A \to bool$, the function:

$$
\begin{aligned}
p? &\in A \to A \mid A\\
p?\, a &= \bot, \quad p\, a = \bot\\
&= \grave{\imath}\, a, \quad p\, a = true\\
&= \acute{\imath}\, a, \quad p\, a = false
\end{aligned}
$$

thus $f \triangledown g \circ p?$ models the familiar conditional **if** p **then** f **else** g **fi**. The function VOID maps its argument to void: VOID $x = ()$. Some laws that hold for these functions are:

$$
\begin{aligned}
\text{VOID} \circ f &= \text{VOID}\\
p? \circ x &= x \mid x \circ (p \circ x)?
\end{aligned}
$$

In order to make recursion explicit, we use the operator $\mu \in (A \to A) \to A$ defined as:

$$
\mu\, f = x \text{ where } x = f\, x
$$

We assume that recursion (like $x = f\ x$) is well defined in the meta-language.

Let F, G be functors and $\varphi_A \in AF \to AG$ for any type A. Such a φ is called a *polymorphic* function. A *natural transformation* is a family of functions φ_A (omitting subscripts whenever possible) such that:

$$\forall f : f \in A \to B : \varphi_B \circ fF = fG \circ \varphi_A \tag{11}$$

As a convenient shorthand for (11) we use $\varphi \in F \dot{\to} G$ to denote that φ is a natural transformation. The "Theorems For Free!" theorem of Wadler, deBruin and Reynolds [28, 9, 22] states that any function definable in the polymorphic λ-calculus is a natural transformation. If φ is defined using μ, one can only conclude that (11) holds for strict f.

Recursive types

After all this stuff on functors we have finally armed ourselves sufficiently to abstract from the peculiarities of cons-lists, and formalize recursively defined data types in general.

Let F be a monofunctor whose operation of functions is continuous, i.e., all monofunctors defined using the above basic functors or any of the map-functors introduced in §5. Then there exists a type L and two strict functions $in_F \in LF \to L$ and $out_F \in L \to LF$ (omitting subscripts whenever possible) which are each others inverse and even $id = \mu(in \overset{F}{\leftarrow} out)$ [6, 23, 16, 24, 30, 12]. We let μF denote the pair (L, in) and say that it is "the least fixed point of F". Since in and out are each others inverses we have that LF is isomorphic to L, and indeed L is — upto isomorphism — a fixed point of F.

For example taking $XL = \mathbf{1} \mid A \| X$, we have that $(A*, in) = \mu L$ defines the data type of cons-lists over A for any type A. If we put $Nil = in \circ \grave{\imath} \in \mathbf{1} \to A*$ and $Cons = in \circ \acute{\imath} \in A\|A* \to A*$, we get the more familiar $(A*, Nil \triangledown Cons) = \mu L$. Another example of data types, binary trees with leaves of type A results from taking the least fixed point of $XT = \mathbf{1} \mid A \mid X\|X$. Backward lists with elements of type A, or snoc lists as they are sometimes called, are the least fixed point of $XL = \mathbf{1} \mid X\|A$. Natural numbers are specified as the least fixed point of $XN = \mathbf{1} \mid X$.

4 Recursion Schemes

Now that we have given a generic way of defining recursive data types, we can define cata-, ana-, hylo- and paramorphisms over arbitrary data types. Let $(L, in) = \mu F$, $\varphi \in AF \to A$, $\psi \in A \to AF$, $\xi \in (A\|L)F \to A$ then we define

$$(\!|\varphi|\!)_F = \mu(\varphi \overset{F}{\leftarrow} out) \tag{12}$$
$$[\!(\psi)\!]_F = \mu(in \overset{F}{\leftarrow} \psi) \tag{13}$$
$$[\![\varphi, \psi]\!]_F = \mu(\varphi \overset{F}{\leftarrow} \psi) \tag{14}$$
$$\{\!|\xi|\!\}_F = \mu(\lambda f.\ \xi \circ (id \vartriangle f)F \circ out) \tag{15}$$

When no confusion can arise we omit the F subscripts.

Definition (13) agrees with the definition given in §2; where we wrote $(\!|e, \oplus|\!)$ we now write $(\!|e^\bullet \triangledown (\oplus)|\!)$.

Definition (14) agrees with the informal one given earlier on; the notation $[\!(g, p)\!]$ of §2 now becomes $[\!((VOID \mid g) \circ p?)\!]$.

Definition (15) agrees with the earlier one in the sense that taking $\varphi = c^\bullet \triangledown \oplus$ and $\psi = (\mathrm{VOID} \mid g) \circ p?$ makes $[\![(c^\bullet, \oplus), (g, p)]\!]$ equal to $[\![\varphi, \psi]\!]$.

Definition (15) agrees with the description of paramorphisms as given in §2 in the sense that $\{b, \oplus\}$ equals $\{b^\bullet \triangledown (\oplus)\}$ here.

Program Calculation Laws

Rather than letting the programmer use explicit recursion, we encourage the use of the above fixed recursion patterns by providing a shopping list of laws that hold for these patterns. For each Ω-morphism, with $\Omega \in \{\text{cata, ana, para}\}$, we give an *evaluation rule*, which shows how such a morphism can be evaluated, a *Uniqueness Property*, a canned induction proof for a given function to be a Ω-morphism, and a *fusion law*, which shows when the composition of some function with an Ω-morphism is again an Ω-morphism. All these laws can be proved by mere equational reasoning using the following properties of general recursive functions. The first one is a 'free theorem' for the fixed point operator $\mu \in (A \to A) \to A$

$$f\,(\mu g) = \mu h \quad \Leftarrow \quad f \text{ strict} \wedge f \circ g = h \circ f \tag{16}$$

Theorem (16) appears under different names in many places[2] [20, 8, 2, 15, 7, 25, 13, 31]. In this paper it will be called *fixed point fusion*.

The strictness condition in (16) can sometimes be relaxed by using

$$f\,(\mu g) = f'\,(\mu g') \quad \Leftarrow \quad f \perp = f' \perp \wedge f \circ g = h \circ f \wedge f' \circ g' = h \circ f' \tag{17}$$

Fixed point induction over the predicate $P(g, g') \equiv f\ g = f'\ g'$ will prove (17).

For hylomorphisms we prove that they can be split into an ana- and a catamorphism and show how computation may be shifted within a hylomorphism. A number of derived laws show the relation between certain cata- and anamorphisms. These laws are not valid in SET. The hylomorphism laws follow from the following theorem:

$$\mu(f \overset{F}{\leftarrow} g) \circ \mu(h \overset{F}{\leftarrow} j) = \mu(f \overset{F}{\leftarrow} j) \quad \Leftarrow \quad g \circ h = id \tag{18}$$

Catamorphisms

Evaluation rule The *evaluation rule* for catamorphisms follows from the fixed point property $x = \mu f \Rightarrow x = f\ x$:

$$(\!|\varphi|\!) \circ in \;=\; \varphi \circ (\!|\varphi|\!)_L \tag{CataEval}$$

It states how to evaluate an application of $(\!|\varphi|\!)$ to an arbitrary element of L (returned by the constructor in); namely, apply $(\!|\varphi|\!)$ recursively to the argument of in and then φ to the result.

For cons lists $(A*, \mathrm{Nil} \triangledown \mathrm{Cons}) = \mu L$ where $X_L = \mathbf{1} \mid A \| X$ and $f_L = id \mid id \| f$ with catamorphism $(\!|c \triangledown \oplus|\!)$ the evaluation rule reads:

$$(\!|c \triangledown \oplus|\!) \circ \mathrm{Nil} \;=\; c \tag{19}$$
$$(\!|c \triangledown \oplus|\!) \circ \mathrm{Cons} \;=\; \oplus \circ id \| (\!|c \triangledown \oplus|\!) \tag{20}$$

[2]Other references are welcome.

i.e. the variable free formulation of (1). Notice that the constructors, here $\mathsf{Nil} \triangledown \mathsf{Cons}$ are used for parameter pattern matching.

UP for catamorphisms The *Uniqueness Property* can be used to prove the equality of two functions without using induction explicitly.

$$f = (\!|\varphi|\!) \equiv f \circ \bot = (\!|\varphi|\!) \circ \bot \;\wedge\; f \circ in = \varphi \circ f_L \qquad \text{(CataUP)}$$

A typical induction proof for showing $f = (\!|\varphi|\!)$ takes the following steps. Check the induction base: $f \circ \bot = (\!|\varphi|\!) \circ \bot$. Assuming the induction hypothesis $f_L = (\!|\varphi|\!)_L$ proceed by calculating:

$$\begin{aligned}
& f \circ in = \ldots = \varphi \circ f_L \\
= & \quad \text{induction hypothesis} \\
& \varphi \circ (\!|\varphi|\!)_L \\
= & \quad \text{evaluation rule (CataEval)} \\
& (\!|\varphi|\!) \circ in
\end{aligned}$$

to conclude that $f = (\!|\varphi|\!)$. The schematic set-up of such a proof is done once and for all, and built into law (CataUP). We are thus saved from the standard ritual steps; the last two lines in the above calculation, plus the declaration that 'by induction' the proof is complete.

The $\Rightarrow$ part of the proof for (CataUP) follows directly from the evaluation rule for catamorphisms. For the $\Leftarrow$ part we use the fixed point fusion theorem (17) with $f := (f\circ)$, $g := g' := in \overset{L}{\leftarrow} out$ and $f' := (\!|\varphi|\!)$. This gives us $f \circ \mu(in \overset{L}{\leftarrow} out) = (\!|\varphi|\!) \circ \mu(in \overset{L}{\leftarrow} out)$ and since $\mu(in \overset{L}{\leftarrow} out) = id$ we are done.

Fusion law for catamorphisms The *Fusion Law* for catamorphisms can be used to transform the composition of a function with a catamorphism into a single catamorphism, so that intermediate values can be avoided. Sometimes the law is used the other way around, i.e. to split a function, in order to allow for subsequent optimizations.

$$f \circ (\!|\varphi|\!) = (\!|\psi|\!) \;\Leftarrow\; f \circ \bot = (\!|\psi|\!) \circ \bot \;\wedge\; f \circ \varphi = \psi \circ f_L \qquad \text{(CataFusion)}$$

The fusion law can be proved using fixed point fusion theorem (17) with $f := (f\circ)$, $g := \varphi \overset{L}{\leftarrow} out$, $g' := in \overset{L}{\leftarrow} out$ and $f' := ((\!|\psi|\!)\circ)$.

A slight variation of the fusion law is to replace the condition $f \circ \bot = (\!|\psi|\!) \circ \bot$ by $f \circ \bot = \bot$, i.e. f is strict.

$$f \circ (\!|\varphi|\!) = (\!|\psi|\!) \;\Leftarrow\; f \text{ strict} \;\wedge\; f \circ \varphi = \psi \circ f_L \qquad \text{(CataFusion')}$$

This law follows from (16). In actual calculations this latter law is more valuable as its applicability conditions are on the whole easier to check.

Injective functions are catamorphisms Let $f \in A \to B$ be a strict function with left-inverse g, then for any $\varphi \in A_F \to A$ we have

$$f \circ (\!|\varphi|\!) = (\!|f \circ \varphi \circ g_F|\!) \;\Leftarrow\; f \text{ strict} \;\wedge\; g \circ f = id \qquad (21)$$

Taking $\varphi = \mathrm{in}$ we immediatly get that any strict injective function can be written as a catamorphism.

$$f = (\!|f \circ \mathrm{in} \circ g_F|\!)_F \;\; \Leftarrow \;\; f \text{ strict} \wedge g \circ f = id \tag{22}$$

Using this latter result we can write out in terms of in since $\mathrm{out} = (\!|\mathrm{out} \circ \mathrm{in} \circ \mathrm{in}_L|\!) = (\!|\mathrm{in}_L|\!)$.

Catamorphisms preserve strictness The given laws for catamorphisms all demonstrate the importance of strictness, or generally of the behaviour of a function with respect to $\perp$. The following "poor man's strictness analyser" for that reason can often be put into good use.

$$\mu F \circ \perp = \perp \;\; \Leftarrow \;\; \forall f :: F\, f \circ \perp = \perp \tag{23}$$

The proof of (23) is by fixed point induction over $P(F) \equiv F \circ \perp = \perp$.

Specifically for catamorphisms we have

$$(\!|\varphi|\!)_L \circ \perp = \perp \;\; \equiv \;\; \varphi \circ \perp = \perp$$

if L is strictness preserving. The $\Leftarrow$ part of the proof directly follows from (23) and the definition of catamorphisms. The other way around is shown as follows

$$
\begin{array}{ll}
 & \perp \\
= & \quad \text{premise} \\
 & (\!|\varphi|\!) \circ \perp \\
= & \quad \mathrm{in} \circ \perp = \perp \\
 & (\!|\varphi|\!) \circ \mathrm{in} \circ \perp \\
= & \quad \text{evaluation rule} \\
 & \varphi \circ (\!|\varphi|\!)_L \circ \perp \\
= & \quad L \text{ preserves strictness} \\
 & \varphi \circ \perp
\end{array}
$$

Examples

Unfold-Fold Many transformations usually accomplished by the unfold-simplify-fold technique can be restated using fusion. Let $(\mathrm{Num}*, \mathrm{Nil} \triangledown \mathrm{Cons}) = \mu L$, where $X_L = \mathbf{1} \mid \mathrm{Num}\|X$ and $f_L = id \mid id\|f$ be the type of lists of natural numbers. Using fusion we derive an efficient version of $\mathrm{sum} \circ \mathrm{squares}$ where $\mathrm{sum} = (\!|0^\bullet \triangledown +|\!)$ and $\mathrm{squares} = (\!|\mathrm{Nil} \triangledown (\mathrm{Cons} \circ SQ\|id)|\!)$. Since sum is strict we just start calculating aiming at the discovery of a ψ that satisfies the condition of (CataFusion').

$$
\begin{array}{ll}
 & \mathrm{sum} \circ \mathrm{Nil} \triangledown (\mathrm{Cons} \circ S\|id) \\
= & (\mathrm{sum} \circ \mathrm{Nil}) \triangledown (\mathrm{sum} \circ \mathrm{Cons} \circ SQ\|id) \\
= & \mathrm{Nil} \triangledown ((+) \circ id\|\mathrm{sum} \circ SQ\|id) \\
= & \mathrm{Nil} \triangledown ((+) \circ SQ\|id \circ id\|\mathrm{sum}) \\
= & \mathrm{Nil} \triangledown ((+) \circ SQ\|id) \circ \mathrm{sum}_L
\end{array}
$$

and conclude that $\mathit{sum} \circ \mathit{squares} = (\!|\mathsf{Nil} \triangledown ((+) \circ \mathsf{SQ} \| \mathsf{id})|\!)$.

A slightly more complicated problem is to derive a one-pass solution for

$$\mathit{average} \;=\; \mathsf{DIV} \circ \mathit{sum} \vartriangle \mathit{length}$$

Using the tupling lemma of Fokkinga [10]

$$(\!|\varphi|\!)_L \vartriangle (\!|\psi|\!)_L \;=\; (\!|(\varphi \circ \grave{\pi}_L) \vartriangle (\psi \circ \acute{\pi}_L)|\!)$$

a simple calculation shows that $\mathit{average} = \mathsf{DIV} \circ (\!|(0^\bullet \triangledown (+) \circ \mathsf{id} \| \grave{\pi}) \vartriangle (0^\bullet \triangledown (+1) \circ \acute{\pi}|\!)$.

Accumulating Arguments An important item in the functional programmer's bag of tricks is the technique of *accumulating arguments* where an extra parameter is added to a function to accumulate the result of the computation. Though stated here in terms of catamorphisms over cons-lists, the same technique is applicable to other data types and other kind of morphisms as well.

$$\begin{array}{l} (\!|c^\bullet \triangledown \oplus|\!)\ l = (\!|(c\otimes)^\bullet \triangledown \ominus|\!)\ l\ \nu_\oplus \text{ where } (a \ominus f)\ b = f\ (a \odot b) \\ \Leftarrow \\ a \otimes \nu_\oplus = a \ \wedge\ \bot \otimes a = \bot \ \wedge\ (a \oplus b) \otimes c = b \otimes (a \odot c) \end{array} \qquad (24)$$

Theorem (24) follows from the fusion law by taking $\mathit{Accu} \circ (\!|c^\bullet \triangledown \oplus|\!) = (\!|(c\oplus)^\bullet \triangledown \ominus|\!)$ with $\mathit{Accu}\ a\ b = a \otimes b$.

Given the naive quadratic definition of $\mathit{reverse} \in A* \to A*$ as a catamorphism $(\!|\mathit{Nil}^\bullet \triangledown \oplus|\!)$ where $a \oplus as = as \mathbin{+\!\!+} (\mathit{Cons}\ (a, \mathit{Nil}))$, we can derive a linear time algorithm by instantiating (24) with $\oplus := \mathbin{+\!\!+}$ and $\odot := \mathit{Cons}$ to get a function which accumulates the list being reversed as an additional argument: $(\!|\mathit{id} \triangledown \ominus|\!)$ where $(a \ominus as)\ bs = as\ (\mathit{Cons}\ (a, bs))$. Here $\mathbin{+\!\!+}$ is the function that appends two lists, defined as $as \mathbin{+\!\!+} bs = (\!|\mathit{id}^\bullet \triangledown \oplus|\!)\ as\ bs$ where $a \oplus f\ bs = \mathit{Cons}\ (a, f\ bs)$.

In general catamorphisms of higher type $L \to (I \to S)$ form an interesting class by themselves as they correspond to *attribute grammars* [11].

Anamorphisms

Evaluation rule The evaluation rule for anamorphisms is given by:

$$\mathsf{out} \circ [\!(\psi)\!] \;=\; [\!(\psi)\!]_L \circ \psi \qquad \text{(AnaEval)}$$

It says what the result of an arbitrary application of $[\!(\psi)\!]$ looks like: the constituents produced by applying out can equivalently be obtained by first applying ψ and then applying $[\!(\psi)\!]_L$ recursively to the result.

Anamorphisms are real old fusspots to explain. To instantiate (AnaEval) for cons list we define:

$$\begin{array}{rcl} \mathit{hd} &=& \bot \triangledown \grave{\pi} \circ \mathsf{out} \\ \mathit{tl} &=& \bot \triangledown \acute{\pi} \circ \mathsf{out} \\ \mathit{is\_nil} &=& \mathit{true}^\bullet \triangledown \mathit{false}^\bullet \circ \mathsf{out} \end{array}$$

Assuming that $f = [\!(\mathsf{VOID} \mid (h \vartriangle t) \circ p?)\!]$ we find after a little calculation that:

$$\begin{array}{rcl} \mathit{is\_nil} \circ f &=& p \\ \mathit{hd} \circ f &=& h \Leftarrow \neg p \\ \mathit{tl} \circ f &=& t \Leftarrow \neg p \end{array}$$

which corresponds to the characterization of unfold given by Bird and Wadler [5] on page 173.

UP for anamorphisms The UP for anamorphisms is slightly simpler than the one for catamorphisms, since the base case does not have to be checked.

$$f = [\![\varphi]\!] \quad \equiv \quad \mathrm{out} \circ f = f_L \circ \varphi \qquad \text{(AnaUP)}$$

To prove it we can use fixed point fusion theorem (16) with $f := (\circ f)$, $g := \mathrm{in} \overset{L}{\leftarrow} \mathrm{out}$ and $h := \mathrm{in} \overset{L}{\leftarrow} \psi$. This gives us $\mu(\mathrm{in} \overset{L}{\leftarrow} \mathrm{out}) \circ f = \mu(\mathrm{in} \overset{L}{\leftarrow} \psi)$ and again since $\mu(\mathrm{in} \overset{L}{\leftarrow} \mathrm{out}) = \mathrm{id}$ we are done.

Fusion law for anamorphisms The strictness requirement that was needed for catamorphisms can be dropped in the anamorphism case. The dual condition of $f \circ \bot = \bot$ for strictness is $\bot \circ f = \bot$ which is vacuously true.

$$[\![\varphi]\!] \circ f = [\![\psi]\!] \quad \Leftarrow \quad \varphi \circ f = f_L \circ \psi \qquad \text{(AnaFusion)}$$

This law can be proved by fixed point fusion theorem (16) with $f := (\circ f)$, $g := \mathrm{in} \overset{L}{\leftarrow} \varphi$ and $h := \mathrm{in} \overset{L}{\leftarrow} \psi$.

Any surjective function is an anamorphism The results (21) and (22) can be dualized for anamorphisms. Let $f \in B \to A$ a surjective function with right-inverse g, then for any $\psi \in A \to A_L$ we have

$$[\![\psi]\!] \circ f = [\![g_L \circ \psi \circ f]\!] \quad \Leftarrow \quad f \circ g = \mathrm{id} \qquad (25)$$

since $\psi \circ f = f_L \circ (g_L \circ \psi \circ f)$. The special case where ψ equals out yields that any surjective function can be written as an anamorphism.

$$f = [\![g_L \circ \mathrm{out} \circ f]\!]_L \quad \Leftarrow \quad f \circ g = \mathrm{id} \qquad (26)$$

As in has right-inverse out, we can express in using out by $\mathrm{in} = [\![\mathrm{out}_L \circ \mathrm{out} \circ \mathrm{in}]\!] = [\![\mathrm{out}_L]\!]$.

Examples

Reformulated in the lense notation, the function $\mathit{iterate}\ f$ becomes:

$$\mathit{iterate}\ f \quad = \quad [\![\acute{\imath} \circ \mathrm{id} \vartriangle f]\!]$$

We have $[\![\acute{\imath} \circ \mathrm{id} \vartriangle f]\!] = [\![\mathrm{VOID} \mid \mathrm{id} \vartriangle f \circ \mathit{false}^\bullet?]\!] (= [\![\mathrm{id} \vartriangle f, \mathit{false}^\bullet]\!]$ in the notation of section 2).

Another useful list-processing function is $\mathit{takewhile}\ p$ which selects the longest initial segment of a list all whose elements satisfy p. In conventional notation:

$$\begin{aligned} \mathit{takewhile}\ p\ \mathit{Nil} &= \mathit{Nil} \\ \mathit{takewhile}\ p\ (\mathit{Cons}\ a\ as) &= \mathit{Nil}, && \neg p\ a \\ &= \mathit{Cons}\ a\ (\mathit{takewhile}\ p\ as), && \mathit{otherwise} \end{aligned}$$

The anamorphism definition may look a little daunting at first:

$$\mathit{takewhile}\ p \quad = \quad [\![\grave{\imath} \triangledown (\mathrm{VOID} \mid \mathrm{id} \circ (\neg p \circ \grave{\pi})?) \circ \mathrm{out}]\!]$$

The function $f\ \mathit{while}\ p$ contains all repeated applications of f as long as predicate p holds:

$$f\ \mathit{while}\ p \quad = \quad \mathit{takewhile}\ p \circ \mathit{iterate}\ f$$

Using the fusion law (after a rather long calculation) we can show that $f\ \mathit{while}\ p = [\![\mathrm{VOID} \mid (\mathrm{id} \vartriangle f) \circ \neg p?]\!]$.

Hylomorphisms

Splitting Hylomorphisms In order to prove that a hylomorphism can be split into an anamorphism followed by a catamorphism

$$[\![\varphi, \psi]\!] \quad = \quad (\!|\varphi|\!) \circ [\!(\psi)\!] \qquad \text{(HyloSplit)}$$

we can use the total fusion theorem (18).

Shifting law Hylomorphisms are nice since their decomposability into a cata- and an anamorphism allows us to use the respective fusion laws to shift computation in or out of a hylomorphism. The following *shifting law* shows how computations can be shifted within a hylomorphism.

$$[\![\varphi \circ \xi, \psi]\!]_L = [\![\varphi, \xi \circ \psi]\!]_M \;\Leftarrow\; \xi \in L \dot{\rightarrow} M \qquad \text{(HyloShift)}$$

The proof of this theorem is straightforward.

$$\begin{array}{ll} & [\![\varphi \circ \xi, \psi]\!]_L \\ = & \quad \text{definition hylo} \\ & \mu(\lambda f.\varphi \circ \xi \circ f_L \circ \psi) \\ = & \quad \xi \in L \dot{\rightarrow} M \\ & \mu(\lambda f.\varphi \circ f_M \circ \xi \circ \psi) \\ = & \quad \text{definition hylo} \\ & [\![\varphi, \xi \circ \psi]\!]_M \end{array}$$

An admittedly humbug example of (HyloShift) shows how left linear recursive functions can be transformed into right linear recursive functions. Let $f_L = id \mid f \| id$ and $f_R = id \mid id \| f$ define the functors which express left respectively right linear recursion, then if $x \oplus y = y \oplus x$ we have

$$\begin{array}{ll} & [\![c \triangledown \oplus, f \mid (h \vartriangle t) \circ p?]\!]_L \\ = & [\![c \triangledown \oplus \circ SWAP, f \mid (h \vartriangle t) \circ p?]\!]_L \\ = & \quad SWAP \in L \dot{\rightarrow} R \\ & [\![c \triangledown \oplus, SWAP \circ f \mid (h \vartriangle t) \circ p?]\!]_R \\ = & [\![c \triangledown \oplus, f \mid (t \vartriangle h) \circ p?]\!]_R \end{array}$$

where $SWAP = id \mid (\acute{\pi} \vartriangle \grave{\pi})$.

Relating cata- and anamorphisms

From the splitting and shifting law (HyloShift), (HyloSplit) and the fact that $(\!|\varphi|\!) = [\![\varphi, out]\!]$ and $[\!(\psi)\!] = [\![in, \psi]\!]$ we can derive a number of interesting laws which relate cata- and anamorphisms with each other.

$$(\!|in_M \circ \varphi|\!)_L = [\!(\varphi \circ out_L)\!]_M \;\Leftarrow\; \varphi \in L \dot{\rightarrow} M \qquad (27)$$

Using this law we can easily show that

$$(\!|\varphi \circ \psi|\!)_L = (\!|\varphi|\!)_M \circ [\![\psi \circ out_L]\!]_M \Leftarrow \psi \in L \dot{\to} M \quad (28)$$
$$= (\!|\varphi|\!)_M \circ (\!|in_M \circ \psi|\!)_L \Leftarrow \psi \in L \dot{\to} M \quad (29)$$

$$[\![\varphi \circ \psi]\!]_M = (\!|in_M \circ \varphi|\!)_L \circ [\![\psi]\!]_L \Leftarrow \varphi \in L \dot{\to} M \quad (30)$$
$$= [\![\varphi \circ out_L]\!]_M \circ [\![\psi]\!]_L \Leftarrow \varphi \in L \dot{\to} M \quad (31)$$

This set of laws will be used in §5.

From the total fusion theorem (18) we can derive:

$$[\![\psi]\!]_L \circ (\!|\varphi|\!)_L = id \Leftarrow \psi \circ \varphi = id \quad (32)$$

Example: Reflecting binary trees

The type of binary trees with leaves of type A is given by $(tree\ A, in) = \mu L$ where $X_L = \mathbf{1} \mid A \mid X \| X$ and $f_L = id \mid id \mid g \| g$. Reflecting a binary tree can be defined by: $reflect = (\!|in \circ SWAP|\!)$ where $SWAP = id \mid id \mid (\acute{\pi} \vartriangle \grave{\pi})$. A simple calculation proves that $reflect \circ reflect = id$.

$$reflect \circ reflect$$
$$= \quad SWAP \circ f_L = f_L \circ SWAP$$
$$[\![SWAP \circ out]\!] \circ (\!|in \circ SWAP|\!)$$
$$= \quad SWAP \circ out \circ in \circ SWAP = id$$
$$id$$

Paramorphisms

The *evaluation rule* for paramorphisms is

$$\{\varphi\} \circ in = \varphi \circ (id \vartriangle \{\varphi\})_L \quad \text{(ParaEval)}$$

The *UP* for paramorphisms is similar to that of catamorphisms:

$$f = \{\varphi\} \equiv f \circ \bot = \{\varphi\} \circ \bot \wedge f \circ in = \varphi \circ (id \vartriangle f)_L \quad \text{(ParaUP)}$$

The *fusion law* for paramorphisms reads

$$f \circ \{\varphi\} = \{\psi\} \Leftarrow f \text{ strict} \wedge f \circ \varphi = \psi \circ (id \| f)_L \quad \text{(ParaFusion)}$$

Any function f (of the right type of course!) is a paramorphism.

$$f = \{f \circ in \circ \grave{\pi}_L\}$$

The usefulness of this theorem can be read from its proof.

$$
\begin{array}{ll}
& \{f \circ in \circ \grave{\pi}_L\} \\
= & \quad \text{definition (15)} \\
& \mu(\lambda g.f \circ in \circ \grave{\pi}_L \circ (id \vartriangle g)_L \circ out) \\
= & \quad \text{functor calculus} \\
& \mu(\lambda g.f \circ in \circ out) \\
= & \\
& f
\end{array}
$$

Example: composing paramorphisms from ana- and catamorphisms

A nice result is that any paramorphism can be written as the composition of a cata- and an anamorphism. Let $(L, in) = \mu L$ be given, then define

$$
\begin{array}{rcl}
X_M & = & (L \| X)_L \\
h_M & = & (id \| h)_L \\
(M, IN) & = & \mu M
\end{array}
$$

For natural numbers we get $X_M = (Num\|X)_L = \mathbf{1} \mid Num\|X$, i.e. $(Num*, in) = \mu M$, which is the type of lists of natural numbers.

Now define $preds \in L \to M$ as follows:

$$preds = [\![\Delta_L \circ out_L]\!]_M$$

For the naturals we get $preds = [\![id \mid \Delta \circ out]\!]$, that is given a natural number $N = n$, the expression $preds\ N$ yields the list $[n-1, \ldots, 0]$.

Using $preds$ we start calculating:

$$
\begin{array}{ll}
& (\![\varphi]\!)_M \circ preds \\
= & (\![\varphi]\!)_M \circ [\![\Delta_L \circ out_L]\!]_M \\
= & \mu(\lambda f.\varphi \circ f_M \circ \Delta_L \circ out_L) \\
= & \mu(\lambda f.\varphi \circ (id\|f)_L \circ (id \vartriangle id)_L \circ out_L) \\
= & \mu(\lambda f.\varphi \circ (id \vartriangle f)_L \circ out_L) \\
= & \{\varphi\}_L
\end{array}
$$

Thus $\{\varphi\}_L = (\![\varphi]\!)_M \circ preds$. Since $(\![IN]\!)_M = id$ we immediately get $preds = \{IN\}_L$.

5 Parametrized Types

In §2 we have defined for $f \in A \to B$, the map function $f* \in A* \to B*$. Two laws for $*$ are $id* = id$ and $(f \circ g)* = f* \circ g*$. These two laws precisely state that $*$ is a functor. Another characteristic property of map is that it leaves the 'shape' of its argument unchanged. It turns out that any *parametrized* data type comes equipped with such a map functor. A parametrized type is a type defined as the least fixed point of a sectioned bifunctor. Contrary to Malcolms approach [17] map can be defined both as a catamorphism and as an anamorphism.

Maps

Let $\dagger$ be a bi-functor, then we define the functor $*$ on objects A as the parametrized type $A*$ where $(A*, in) = \mu(A\dagger)$, and on functions $f \in A \to B$ as:

$$f* \;=\; (\!|in \circ (f\dagger)|\!)_{(A\dagger)} \tag{33}$$

Since $(f\dagger) \in (A\dagger) \to (B\dagger)$, from (27) we immediately get an alternative version of $f*$ as an anamorphism:

$$f* \;=\; [\!((f\dagger) \circ out)\!]_{(B\dagger)}$$

Functoriality of $f*$ is calculated as follows:

$$\begin{array}{ll} & f* \circ g* \\ = & \quad \text{definition } * \\ & (\!|in \circ (f\dagger)|\!) \circ (\!|in \circ (g\dagger)|\!) \\ = & \quad (29) \\ & (\!|in \circ (f\dagger) \circ (g\dagger)|\!) \\ = & \quad (9) \\ & (\!|in \circ ((f \circ g)\dagger)|\!) \\ = & \quad \text{definition } * \\ & (f \circ g)* \end{array}$$

Maps are shape preserving. Define SHAPE = VOID$*$ then SHAPE $\circ f* =$ VOID $\circ f* =$ SHAPE.

For cons-list $(A*, Nil \triangledown Cons) = \mu(A\dagger)$ with $A \dagger X = \mathbf{1} \mid A \| X$ and $f \dagger g = id \mid f \| g$ we get $f* = [\!(f \dagger id \circ out)\!]$. From the UP for catas we find that this conforms to the usual definition of map.

$$\begin{aligned} f* \circ Nil &= Nil \\ f* \circ Cons &= Cons \circ f \| f* \end{aligned}$$

Other important laws for maps are *factorization* [26] and *promotion* [4].

$$(\!|\varphi|\!) \circ f* \;=\; (\!|\varphi \circ (f\dagger)|\!) \tag{34}$$

$$f* \circ [\!(\psi)\!] \;=\; [\!((f\dagger) \circ \psi)\!] \tag{35}$$

$$(\!|\varphi|\!) \circ f* \;=\; g \circ (\!|\chi|\!) \;\Leftarrow\; g \circ \chi = \varphi \circ f \dagger g \;\wedge\; g \text{ strict} \tag{36}$$

$$f* \circ [\!(\psi)\!] \;=\; [\!(\xi)\!] \circ g \;\Leftarrow\; \xi \circ g = f \dagger g \circ \psi \tag{37}$$

Now we know that $*$ is a functor, we can recognize that $in \in \imath\dagger* \dot{\to} *$ and $out \in * \dot{\to} \imath\dagger*$ are natural transformations.

$$\begin{aligned} f* \circ in &= in \circ f \dagger f* \\ out \circ f* &= f \dagger f* \circ out \end{aligned}$$

Iterate promotion

Recall the function $iterate\ f = [\!(\imath \circ id \vartriangle f)\!]$, the following law turns an $\mathcal{O}(n^2)$ algorithm into an $\mathcal{O}(n)$ algorithm, under the assumption that evaluating $g \circ f^n$ takes n steps.

$$g* \circ iterate\ f = iterate\ h \circ g \;\Leftarrow\; g \circ f = h \circ g \tag{38}$$

Law (38) is an immediate consequence of the promotion law for anamorphisms (37).

Interestingly we may also define iterate as a cyclic list:

$$\text{iterate f x} = \mu(\lambda xs.\text{Cons}\ (x, f{*}xs))$$

and use fixed point fusion to prove (38).

Map-Reduce factorization

A data type $(A{*}, in) = \mu(A\dagger)$ with $A \dagger X = A \mid X_F$ is called a *free* F-type over A. For a free type we can always write *strict* catas $(\!|\psi|\!)$ as $(\!|f \triangledown \varphi|\!)$ by taking $f = \psi \circ \grave{\imath}$ and $\varphi = \psi \circ \acute{\imath}$. For f∗ we get

$$\begin{aligned} f{*} &= (\!|in \circ f \mid id|\!) \\ &= (\!|tau \mid join \circ f \mid id|\!) \\ &= (\!|tau \circ f \triangledown join|\!) \end{aligned}$$

where $tau = in \circ \grave{\imath}$ and $join = in \circ \acute{\imath}$.

If we define the *reduction* with φ as

$$\varphi/ = (\!|id \triangledown \varphi|\!) \qquad (39)$$

the factorization law (34) shows that catamorphisms on a free type can be factored into a map followed by a reduce.

$$\begin{aligned} & (\!|f \triangledown \varphi|\!) \\ = \ & (\!|id \triangledown \varphi \circ f \mid id|\!) \\ = \ & (\!|id \triangledown \varphi|\!) \circ f{*} \\ = \ & \varphi/ \circ f{*} \end{aligned}$$

The fact that tau and join are natural transformations give evaluation rules for f∗ and $\varphi/$ on free types.

$$\begin{aligned} f{*} \circ tau &= tau \circ f & \qquad \varphi/ \circ tau &= id \\ f{*} \circ join &= join \circ f{*}_F & \qquad \varphi/ \circ join &= \varphi \circ (\varphi/)_F \end{aligned}$$

Early Squiggol was based completely on map-reduce factorization. Some of these laws from the good old days; *reduce promotion* and *map promotion*.

$$\begin{aligned} \varphi/ \circ join/ &= \varphi/ \circ (\varphi/){*} \\ f{*} \circ join/ &= join/ \circ f{*}{*} \end{aligned}$$

Monads

Any free type gives rise to a monad [17], in the above notation, $({*}, tau \in I \dot{\to} {*}, join/ \in {*}{*} \dot{\to} {*})$ since:

$$\begin{aligned} join/ \circ tau &= id \\ join/ \circ tau{*} &= id \\ join/ \circ join/ &= join/ \circ join/{*} \end{aligned}$$

Wadler [29] gives a thorough discussion on the concepts of monads and their use in functional programming.

6 Conclusion

We have considered various patterns of recursive definitions, and have presented a lot of laws that hold for the functions so defined. Although we have illustrated the laws and the recursion operators with examples, the usefulness for practical program calculation might not be evident to every reader. Unfortunately we have not enough space here to give more elaborate examples.

There are more aspects to program calculation than just a series of combining forms (like $(\!|\_|\!)$, $[\!(\_)\!]$, $\{\!|\_|\!\}$, $[\![\_,\_]\!]$) and laws about them. For calculating large programs one certainly needs high level algorithmic theorems. The work reported here provides the necessary tools to develop such theorems. For the theory of lists Bird [3] has started to do so, and with success.

Another aspect of program calculation is machine assistance. Our experience —including that of our colleagues— shows that the size of formal manipulations is much greater than in most textbooks of mathematics; it may well be comparable in size to "computer algebra" as done in systems like MACSYMA, Maple, Mathematica etc. Fortunately, it also appears that most manipulations are easily automated and, moreover, that quite a few equalities depend on natural transformations. Thus in several cases type checking alone suffices. Clearly machine assistance is fruitful and does not seem to be too difficult.

Finally we observe that category theory has provided several notions and concepts that were indispensable to get a clean and smooth theory; for example, the notions of functor and natural transformation. (While reading this paper, a category theorist may recognize several other notions that we silently used). Without doubt there is much more categorical knowledge that can be useful for program calculation; we are just at the beginning of an exciting development.

Acknowledgements Many of the results presented here have for the case SET already appeared in numerous notes of the STOP Algorithmics Club featuring among others Roland Backhouse, Johan Jeuring, Doaitse Swierstra, Lambert Meertens, Nico Verwer and Jaap van der Woude. Graham Hutton provided many useful remarks on draft versions of this paper.

References

[1] Roland Backhouse, Jaap van der Woude, Ed Voermans, and Grant Malcolm. A relational theory of types. Technical Report ??, TUE, 1991.

[2] Rudolf Berghammer. On the use of composition in transformational programming. Technical Report TUM-I8512, TU München, 1985.

[3] R. Bird. An introduction to the theory of lists. In M. Broy, editor, *Logic of Programming and Calculi of Discrete Design*, pages 3–42. Springer Verlag, 1987. Also Technical Monograph PRG-56, Oxford University, October 1986.

[4] Richard Bird. Constructive functional programming. In M. Broy, editor, *Marktoberdorf International Summer school on Constructive Methods in Computer Science*, NATO Advanced Science Institute Series. Springer Verlag, 1989.

[5] Richard Bird and Phil Wadler. *Introduction to Functional Programming*. Prentice-Hall, 1988.

[6] R. Bos and C. Hemerik. An introduction to the category-theoretic solution of recursive domain equations. Technical Report TRCSN 88/15, Eindhoven University of Technology, October 1988.

[7] Manfred Broy. *Transformation parallel ablaufender Programme.* PhD thesis, TU München, München, 1980.

[8] A. de Bruin and E.P. de Vink. Retractions in comparing Prolog semantics. In *Computer Science in the Netherlands 1989*, pages 71–90. SION, 1989.

[9] Peter de Bruin. Naturalness of polymorphism. Technical Report CS 8916, RUG, 1989.

[10] Maarten Fokkinga. Tupling and mutumorphisms. *The Squiggolist*, 1(4), 1989.

[11] Maarten Fokkinga, Johan Jeuring, Lambert Meertens, and Erik Meijer. Translating attribute grammars into catamorphisms. *The Squiggolist*, 2(1), 1991.

[12] Maarten Fokkinga and Erik Meijer. Program calculation properties of continuous algebras. Technical Report 91-4, CWI, 1991.

[13] C. Gunter, P. Mosses, and D. Scott. Semantic domains and denotational semantics. In *Marktoberdorf International Summer school on Logic, Algebra and Computation*, 1989. to appear in: Handbook of Theoretical Computer Science, North Holland.

[14] Tasuya Hagino. Codatatypes in ML. *Journal of Symbolic Computation*, 8:629–650, 1989.

[15] J.Arsac and Y Kodratoff. Some techniques for recursion removal. *ACM Toplas*, 4(2):295–322, 1982.

[16] D.J. Lehmann and M.B. Smyth. Algebraic specification of data types: a synthetic approach. *Math. Systems Theory*, 14:97–139, 1981.

[17] Grant Malcolm. *Algebraic Types and Program Transformation.* PhD thesis, University of Groningen, The Netherlands, 1990.

[18] Lambert Meertens. Algorithmics — towards programming as a mathematical activity. In *Proceedings of the CWI symposium on Mathematics and Computer Science*, pages 289–334. North-Holland, 1986.

[19] Lambert Meertens. Paramorphisms. To appear in Formal Aspects of Computing, 1990.

[20] John-Jules Ch. Meyer. *Programming calculi based on fixed point transformations: semantics and applications.* PhD thesis, Vrije Universiteit, Amsterdam, 1985.

[21] Ross Paterson. *Reasoning about Functional Programs.* PhD thesis, University of Queensland, Brisbane, 1988.

[22] John C. Reynolds. Types abstraction and parametric polymorphism. In *Information Processing '83.* North Holland, 1983.

[23] David A. Schmidt. *Denotational Semantics.* Allyn and Bacon, 1986.

[24] M.B. Smyth and G.D. Plotkin. The category-theoretic solution of recursive domain equations. *SIAM Journal on Computing*, 11(4):761–785, November 1982.

[25] Joseph E. Stoy. *Denotational Semantics, The Scott-Strachey Approach to Programming Language Theory.* The MIT press, 1977.

[26] Nico Verwer. Homomorphisms, factorisation and promotion. *The Squiggolist*, 1(3), 1990. Also technical report RUU-CS-90-5, Utrecht University, 1990.

[27] Phil Wadler. Views: A way for pattern matching to cohabit with data abstraction. Technical Report 34, Programming Methodology Group, University of Göteborg and Chalmers University of Technology, March 1987.

[28] Philip Wadler. Theorems for free ! In *Proc. 1989 ACM Conference on Lisp and Functional Programming*, pages 347–359, 1989.

[29] Philip Wadler. Comprehending monads. In *Proc. 1990 ACM Conference on Lisp and Functional Programming*, 1990.

[30] M. Wand. Fixed point constructions in order enriched categories. *Theoretical Computer Science*, 8, 1979.

[31] Hans Zierer. Programmierung mit funktionsobjecten: Konstruktive erzeugung semantische bereiche und anwendung auf die partielle auswertung. Technical Report TUM-I8803, TU München, 1988.

A Strongly-Typed Self-Applicable Partial Evaluator

John Launchbury
Computing Science Department
Glasgow University
jl@dcs.glasgow.ac.uk

Abstract

When attempting self-application of a partial evaluator written in and for a strongly-typed language several problems arise that do not seem to occur in the untyped world. These problems have hindered the production of a self-applicable partial evaluator in such languages for a number of years. In this paper we report on what is, to the best of our knowledge, the first successful attempt to produce such a partial evaluator and, in the process, we discuss some theoretical aspects of partial evaluation raised by strong-typing.

1 Introduction

Since the first self-applicable partial evaluator was produced at DIKU, Copenhagen, in the mid-eighties [JSS85], many derivatives have followed. The original was implemented in a first-order subset of Scheme [Dyb87], and since then there have been others in a wide variety of settings, ranging from λ-calculus to Prolog to imperative languages [Bon90, Con88, GJ89, GJ91, Bon89, FA88]. However, each of these partial evaluators have the following property in common: they are all implemented in and for untyped languages.

Self-application in the context of a partial evaluator does not correspond to the sort of self-application that occurs in, for example, the usual definition of the fixed point combinator in the λ-calculus. Instead it more closely corresponds to the familiar bootstrapping technique of using a compiler to compile itself, for which strong typing causes no problems. However, even though there are no obvious theoretical difficulties introduced by strong-typing, it has remained an open question whether it would be possible to write a self-applicable partial evaluator in and for a typed language.

In this paper we are able to answer this question in the affirmative by describing a partial evaluator written in and for LML [Aug84], a strongly-typed functional language with algebraic datatypes. We include examples to demonstrate that successful self-application has been achieved.

There are a couple of reasons why the challenge of producing a partial evaluator in a language such as LML is of interest. Firstly, typed languages are very popular in many different programming paradigms, since strong-typing leads to benefits for both correctness and efficiency. Given this popularity, it is useful to know whether typed languages are suitable as a vehicle for partial evaluation or not. Secondly, types often force issues into the open that may be overlooked in the untyped world. By addressing the problem of constructing a self-applicable partial evaluator in LML we have had to face these issues, with a consequent illumination of principles that underly partial evaluation, even in the untyped world.

1.1 The Key Problems

As we shall see in some detail in Sections 4 and 7, there are two main problems in the construction of a self-applicable partial evaluator, *mix*, in languages such as LML. They may be summarised as follows.

- At self-application, *mix*'s second parameter receives a double encoding. As a consequence of this, a naive implementation of *mix* would be grossly inefficient at self-application, and some encoding effort is necessary to avoid this.
- All values manipulated by *mix* have to be represented within a single, universal datatype. Using current *mix* technology this results in the specialised versions of *mix* also being based around a single universal datatype—a sign of *mix*'s inability to remove the layer of interpretation completely.

The first problem has to be addressed in order to obtain any plausibly efficient implementation of *mix* in strongly-typed languages. The second is not of itself a hindrance to successful self-application, but its solution has important efficiency implications.

1.2 Purpose and Organisation

This paper has two purposes.

- To report that a self-applicable partial evaluator has now been successfully implemented in a strongly-typed language, in this case LML;
- To explore some principles of partial evaluation and self-application which strong-typing forced us to consider.

The paper is organised as follows. In Section 2 we give a brief introduction to partial evaluation, with an emphasis on self-application, and in Section 3 a brief overview of the program defining *mix*. In Section 4 we focus on the origin of the double encoding problem that the use of typed languages introduces, and go on to look at different solutions, varying from the naive to the more elaborate, following this with Section 5 where we present an example of self-application. We go on to show in Section 6 that the problem of double encoding is not limited to typed languages. Section 7 contains a discussion of the non-removal of a complete layer of interpretation with some suggestions for future research, and Section 8 concludes.

There are many aspects of partial evaluation that are not addressed here in order not to confuse the account. For example, the version of the partial evaluator we present here does not use partially-static structures which, even though well understood, do introduce added complications. Similarly, although the partial evaluator described here is written in and for LML, we scarcely consider laziness and ignore polymorphism completely, these being far less well understood. Finally, we leave any discussion of higher-orderness until the closing sections, and address the first-order case only in the body of the paper.

2 Partial Evaluation

At its simplest, partial evaluation may be thought of as *currying on programs*. From a program describing a function $f : A \times B \rightarrow Y$ and a value $a \in A$, a partial evaluator produces a program describing the corresponding specialised function $f_a : B \rightarrow Y$. Thus[1],

$$f_a = mix\ f\ a$$

The new, or *residual* program is to be an optimised version of the old, having taken the input value into account. It is a very powerful technique: its best known application perhaps that of automatically generating compilers from interpreters (see [Mog86, CD89, Sun91] for examples of other applications). Generally, the language in which f_a is defined (that is, *mix*'s output language) is the same as the language in which f was defined (*mix*'s input language), but this is not necessarily the case [Hol88].

The portion of the input data supplied for partial evaluation is called the *static* data, the remainder is *dynamic*. Any computations within the definition of f that depend solely on the static data may be performed, leaving behind only those that require the dynamic data.

For example, suppose that *int* is an interpreter, that is, a function which takes an input program and its input data, interprets the program on the input data, and returns the results. Partially evaluating the program defining the interpreter with respect to a particular input program produces a residual function which, when given the input data, returns the corresponding results. That is, it is a program in the output language of *mix* that behaves exactly like the input program to the interpreter (which was written in the interpreter's input language).

Depending on the program used to define *int*, the partial evaluation may remove some or even all of the original interpretation overhead, so producing an efficient equivalent of the input program in *mix*'s output language. In effect, partially evaluating an interpreter with respect to some input program compiles that input program from the input language of the interpreter to the output language of *mix*.

The most important requirement for the partial evaluation to be successful is that the program being specialised should contain a good separation between static and dynamic computations. In this case, the static computations may be performed independently of any computation requiring dynamic values.

For example, if an interpreter implemented dynamic scoping of variables, for example, then it is highly unlikely that the variable names would eliminated from the resulting "compiled" program. In contrast, if the interpreter implemented static

[1] The notation we use in this section is somewhat informal. It is tightened up in Section 4

scoping, there is every possibility that all computations requiring the variable names would be performed during partial evaluation. Thus, variable names would not be present in the residual program, making for greater efficiency.

2.1 Self-Application

The partial evaluator *mix* works by interpreting the program given as its first argument, in an environment binding static names to the static values supplied as its second. It is clearly going to be expensive to interpret a given input program f repeatedly, perhaps on a whole series of different static inputs $a_1 \ldots a_n$,

$$\begin{aligned} f_{a_1} &= mix\ f\ a_1 \\ &\vdots \\ f_{a_n} &= mix\ f\ a_n \end{aligned}$$

For example, in the case where f is itself an interpreter, it is far from ideal to have to re-interpret this interpreter on each of the input programs $a_1 \ldots a_n$. By specialising *mix* to its input program we may (in principle, at least) produce an optimised version of *mix* in which the layer of interpretation has been removed.

To achieve this specialisation, we use *mix* itself: we apply *mix* to its own defining program and to that of the interpreter, and obtain the specialised version of *mix*. Thus,

$$mix_f = mix\ mix\ f$$

The resulting program mix_f will, when given an input program in the input language of the interpreter, produce a compiled version in *mix*'s output language. That is,

$$\begin{aligned} f_{a_1} &= mix_f\ a_1 \\ &\vdots \\ f_{a_n} &= mix_f\ a_n \end{aligned}$$

In other words, mix_f is acting as a compiler. This potential of self-application was noted first by Futamura [Fut71].

As before, the degree of success achieved by self-application will depend crucially on how many of the computations in the definition of *mix* may be performed statically, that is, on whether the program defining *mix* itself has a good separation between static and dynamic computations. If the bulk of the control decisions made during the execution of *mix* depend solely on the program being partially-evaluated, then much of the interpretive overhead of *mix* may be removed by specialisation. In contrast, if *mix* bases many of its decisions on both its input program *and* on that program's static input data, then little reduction will be possible, as the program's static input data is not present at self-application—the result will be little better than that obtained by a simple partial application.

Using this criterion, we may broadly divide partial evaluators into two camps: static partial evaluators, which make most or all of their control decisions statically, that is, solely on the program being partially evaluated; and dynamic partial evaluators, which make the decisions dynamically, that is, using both the input program and its static data (these have also been called respectively *offline* and *online* partial evaluators [Bon90, WCRS90]). From the foregoing discussion it is clear that it is the static partial evaluators that may be most successfully self-applied.

This highlights the role of binding-time annotations. These are annotations inserted into the input program, so enabling *mix* to make its decisions statically. The binding-time annotations may be used as a specification of which conditionals and case expressions should be reduced, which function calls should be unfolded, and which expressions in the input program are static and so may be completely evaluated (it is, of course, possible to compute this information on-the-fly, but it is both more efficient and easier to understand when presented in the form of annotations [BJMS88]).

3 Overview of the Partial Evaluator

In order to be able to describe the methods used to achieve self-application of the strongly-typed partial evaluator, we must have some knowledge of its overall structure. This knowledge will enable us to understand the reasons for the various coding methods and why they should be effective. The basic design we use for the partial evaluator is that pioneered by the DIKU group (see [Ses86] for example).

A partial evaluator is first and foremost an interpreter—in our case a self-interpreter as we shall specify *mix*'s input, output and definition languages all to be LML. We distinguish between expressions and values, and correspondingly, have two distinct forms of interpretation: `eval` whose result is a value, and `reduce` whose result is an expression.

```
eval   :: Prog -> Static_Env -> Value
reduce :: Prog -> Static_Enc -> Dynamic_Env -> Exp
```

As the name `reduce` indicates, it performs a step-by-step reduction of the expression (including eliminating conditionals/case-expressions whose condition/discriminant is completely static and so may be evaluated) until no further reductions are possible. In contrast, `eval` is only applied to those expressions that may be completely evaluated. Thus one difference between `reduce` and `eval` is that while `reduce` needs two environments (one binding static parameters to values, the other binding dynamic parameters to expressions), `eval` only requires one (binding static parameters to values).

The main loop of the partial evaluator is based around the function `spec`, which takes as arguments the program being specialised, a *pending-list* and a *done-list*. The pending-list is a list of pairs, each pair consisting of a function name and a list of values destined for that function's static parameters. These pairs describe what specialisation is still to be performed. The done-list has exactly the same form and records what specialisations have already been performed. If the pending-list is empty, `spec` returns the empty list as result. If it is not empty, the first element is compared with the contents of the done-list. If present, it is discarded in order to avoid duplicated work (and resulting possible non-termination of `spec`).

Given a function name and a list of its static arguments, `spec` obtains the function definition from the program. This consists of two lists of parameters, the static and the dynamic, and the function's body. A static environment is constructed by binding the static parameters to the static values, and a dynamic environment by binding the dynamic parameters to their own names. Using these environments, the body of the function is reduced, resulting in a residual expression. This residual expression forms the body of the residual function. It is scanned for any residual function calls that may indicate the need for further specialisation.

3.1 Values and Expressions

In order for *mix* to be able to partially evaluate all (first-order) LML programs, the type of values must be able to represent all (first-order) LML values. That is, it must act as a universal type. Even if the user defines new algebraic types, the same value type must be sufficient. We define this type of all values as follows.

```
type Value = Num Int
           + Str String
           + Constr String (List Value)
```

This defines a type called `Value` having three summands, with `Num`, `Str` and `Constr` as the constructors of the type. Numbers and strings are treated specially to avoid introducing unnecessary overheads. The (small) price we shall pay is to disallow the use of pattern matching over these two types, and to use nested conditionals along with the equality test instead. Elements of other (algebraic) types will be represented as an element of the universal value domain using the constructor `Constr`. Thus the list `[Foo; Baz 4]`[2] would be represented by:

```
Constr "." [Constr "Foo" [];
            Constr "." [Constr "Baz" [Num 4];
                        Constr "[]" [] ]]
```

In addition to a type of values, we need a type of expressions. This may be defined along the following lines.

```
type Exp = Val Value
         + Parm String
         + EConstr String (List Exp)
         + Case Exp (List (String # List String # Exp))
         + If Exp Exp Exp
         + Prim String (List Exp)
         + Call String (List Exp) (List Exp)
         + Static Exp
```

The `Val` variant allows us to express values as (constant) expressions. `Parm` indicates a parameter of the function, and `EConstr` represents an application of a constructor. The only distinction between `Constr` and `EConstr` is that the arguments of the latter represent expressions in need of evaluation, whereas the arguments of the former are already values.

The first argument to the `Case` constructor is the expression over which the case analysis is to proceed. The final argument is a list of the case-clauses, each clause being a triple of constructor name, list of variables, and right-hand-side. We assume

[2] In LML, the list element separator is ; and . is used for cons

that all case expressions have been expanded to match the outer constructor only. This is not only for simplicity, but as Bondorf argues, it is important for being able to remove completely the interpretive layer during self-application (see [Bon90] pages 107-108).

The `If` constructor is obvious.

`Prim` is used to represent primitive function calls (like + or * etc.) while, in contrast, `Call` is used for user-defined functions. The parameters to a user-defined function are split up into static and dynamic parameters.

Any sub-expressions occurring in the body of a function that depend solely on the function's static parameters are tagged with the `Static` constructor. The sub-expression may be merely an occurrence of a static parameter, or it may be much more.

3.2 Reducing Expressions

The following is a (slightly simplified[3]) fragment of `reduce`[4].

```
reduce prog s_env d_env exp
 = case exp in
      Val v : exp
   || Parm x : lookup d_env x
   || EConstr c es :
        EConstr c (map (reduce prog s_env d_env) es)
   || Case e cls :
        if (static e) then
          case (eval prog s_env e) in
            Constr c vs :
              match_reduce prog s_env d_env (c,vs) cls
          end
        else
          Case (reduce prog s_env d_env e)
               (reduce_clauses prog s_env d_env cls)
   :
  ||  Static e : Val (eval prog s_env e)
  end
```

Values are already completely reduced so are returned unchanged. By assumption, the only parameters examined by `reduce` are dynamic parameters, and the expressions to which they are bound are contained in the dynamic environment. Also by assumption, arguments to `EConstr` might not be completely reduced, so the result is also expressed by `EConstr`. In contrast, in the definition of `eval` we assume that all the arguments can be completely evaluated and so will use `Constr` for the result.

When a case-expression is encountered, the binding-time annotation of its first argument is used to decide whether to completely evaluate that argument and so

[3]Because we do not use partially-static structures, each environment will have to be separated into two components (a name list and a value list) to obtain good results when `reduce` is itself being specialised. Furthermore, unless higher-order functions are handled the call to `map` will have to be hand specialised in the obvious way.

[4]In LML layout is not significant. Instead the syntactic marker || is used to separate the various case clauses.

reduce the case-expression, or whether to construct a residual case-expression. In the former case, the result of the evaluation (which is bound to return a constructor value) is decomposed into the constructor name, and its arguments. Then in `match_reduce`, the clauses are scanned for an occurrence of the constructor, and when one is found the corresponding right-hand side is reduced in an appropriately extended environment.

Finally, a completely static sub-expression is evaluated using `eval`. Note that `eval` only requires the static environment.

4 Double Encoding

In Section 1 we stated that in a strongly-typed language the specialisation of *mix* requires that the partial evaluator's second argument must be encoded twice. We shall now consider the reason why.

It is vital in any discussion of self-application in partial evaluation to distinguish between a *program text* and *the function that the program defines*[5]. Both may be viewed as semantic objects, of course, but they have very different semantic properties. We adopt the following convention. If f is a function then $\overline{f}$ is a program defining that function. Note that overbar is not a mapping from functions to programs as there may be many distinct programs that compute f. Rather f and $\overline{f}$ are distinct lexical symbols whose meanings are related by the semantics of the language (i.e. $\mathcal{E}[\![\overline{f}]\!] = f$). This convention emphasises the semantic level and makes semantic points easy to stress[6].

Using this convention we note that while *mix* is a partial evaluation function, $\overline{mix}$ is a partial evaluation program.

We can usefully extend the notation to types. If $a \in A$ then we say that $\overline{a} \in \overline{A}$. In terms of the Hindley-Milner type system as used in LML, for example, all objects of the form $\overline{a}$ are going to be elements of the universal value domain `Value`. The form $\overline{A}$ refers to a subtype of this universal type and is useful for expository purposes, but plays no part within either the code or type of the partial evaluator.

As we have already described, the partial evaluator *mix* takes a program (for simplicity we may assume it to be a two-argument program) and some input for that program (again, we may assume the input is the program's first argument), and produces a program defining a function of the remaining argument whose behaviour is equivalent to the original when given all the input. The type of *mix* may be expressed as follows.

$$mix \;:\; \overline{A \times B \to C} \times \overline{A} \to \overline{B \to C}$$

where A, B and C may be instantiated to any types. Note that *mix*'s second argument is a representation, or encoding, of the static value, it is not the value

[5] This is precisely what we did not do in Section 2.

[6] The alternative is to emphasis the syntactic level, and to use evaluation functions to produce the corresponding semantic objects. Unfortunately, while this approach has some benefits it becomes very clumsy if done consistently. For example, we would be unable even to assert that *1* + *2* = *3*, as the default assumption would be that *1* + *2* and *3* are syntactic objects. To describe the equality would necessitate something akin to $\mathcal{E}[\![\mathit{1} + \mathit{2}]\!] = \mathcal{E}[\![\mathit{3}]\!]$. Furthermore, we shall need to express multiple levels of encoding, and this is easier if we work from the semantic level.

itself. In an untyped language, an alternative is normally used, namely that,

$$mix \; : \; \overline{A \times B \rightarrow C} \; \times \; A \; \rightarrow \; \overline{B \rightarrow C}$$

Unfortunately, this alternative is not available to us in most strongly-typed languages. The first argument to *mix* is a program which is just an element of some fixed type. The second argument, however, varies its type according to the precise *value* of the first argument. Quite elaborate dependent types would be needed to express this relationship. Certainly there is no facility within the Hindley-Milner type system that is sufficiently powerful.

The apparently innocuous use of $\overline{A}$ in the first type for *mix* has serious consequences. Suppose we were to apply *mix* to $\overline{mix}$ (that is, to its own defining program). We instantiate A to $\overline{A \times B \rightarrow C}$, B to $\overline{A}$, and C to $\overline{B \rightarrow C}$, and obtain the following instance of the type of *mix*.

$$mix \; : \; \overline{\overline{A \times B \rightarrow C} \times \overline{A} \rightarrow \overline{B \rightarrow C}} \; \times \; \overline{\overline{A \times B \rightarrow C}} \; \rightarrow \; \overline{\overline{A}} \; \rightarrow \; \overline{\overline{B \rightarrow C}}$$

The first argument to *mix* is a single encoding of *mix*, that is, its defining program $\overline{mix}$. The second argument, however, is a double encoding of the program to which $\overline{mix}$ is being specialised. Thus, rather than just passing the defining program for an interpreter, we also have to embed that program into the universal value domain.

Exactly the same feature arises when we specialise *mix* to $\overline{mix}$ (that is, compute $mix\ \overline{mix}\ \overline{\overline{mix}}$). The resulting function, often called *cogen* (it is a compiler generator), has type

$$cogen \; : \; \overline{\overline{A \times B \rightarrow C}} \; \rightarrow \; \overline{\overline{A}} \; \rightarrow \; \overline{\overline{B \rightarrow C}}$$

so it also requires its input program to be doubly encoded.

For completeness we may notice that in the untyped world this problem does not arise if we define a *mix* having the second type given above. In this case the instantiation is,

$$mix \; : \; \overline{\overline{A \times B \rightarrow C} \times A \rightarrow \overline{B \rightarrow C}} \; \times \; \overline{A \times B \rightarrow C} \; \rightarrow \; \overline{A \; \rightarrow \; \overline{B \rightarrow C}}$$

The second argument to *mix* is just the interpreter program—it does not need to be further embedded into the universal value domain.

4.1 Size Explosion

To embed programs into the universal value domain we have to be able to encode expressions as values. We define a coding function `term`,

```
term e = case e in
            Val v : Constr "Val" [val v]
         || Parm x : Constr "Parm" [Str x]
         || EConstr c ts :
               Constr "EConstr" [Str c; lst (map term ts)]
          :
         || Static e : Constr "EConstr" [term e]
         end
```

Given an expression, `term` produces a value which describes the structure of the expression. It uses auxiliary functions such as `val` which codes up a value as a value, and `lst` which codes a list of values as a value. Unfortunately, `val` cannot be the identity function as the coding must be one-to-one, in order to ensure that we are able to retrieve the original value from the coded version. If `val` was just the identity function then distinct levels of representation would become confused. Instead it must be defined along the lines of,

```
val v = case v in
            Num n : Constr "Num" [Num n]
         || Str s : Constr "Str" [Str s]
         || Constr c vs :
               Constr "Constr" [Str c; lst (map val vs)]
         end
```

Now the fundamental problem with this encoding scheme may be seen. A simple expression in LML such as `Foo x` will be represented as an expression by,

```
EConstr "Foo" [Parm "x"]
```

This may be seen as just the abstract syntax tree of the expression. However, when we code this expression as a value we obtain the following.

```
Constr "EConstr"
         [Str "Foo"; Constr "." [Constr "Parm" [Str "x"];
                                  Constr "[]" []]]
```

It is clear that were we to use this encoding on the whole of the program defining *mix*, we would obtain a huge data structure. This is precisely what happens when we compute $mix\ \overline{mix}\ \overline{\overline{int}}$. The price we pay is twofold. First, there is inordinate heap usage corresponding to the existence of this gigantic data structure, with all the obvious efficiency implications such as increased frequency of garbage collection and/or memory paging. Secondly, whenever a residual version of a function with a static program argument is produced (such as `eval` or `reduce`) the program argument needs to be compared with the program arguments in all other specialisations of the same function (all recorded in the `done` list) to ensure that work is not duplicated. The time taken by the equality test is directly proportional to the size of the objects being compared, and so this part of the process of specialisation is also much less efficient.

4.2 Delaying Expansion

At first it might be thought that laziness would help in reducing the heap usage as the expansion of expressions would only happen when needed. Unfortunately the equality test mentioned above would force the evaluation, so laziness is no help here. Instead we need to explicitly delay the expansion ourselves.

Initially, we assumed that it was important to have cheap encodings of numbers and strings as values. We achieved this by adding a variant to the `Value` type which enabled the original number or string to be embedded by simple tagging. We can use the same technique for expressions. We extend the value type with a variant for expressions.

```
type Value = Num Int
           + Str String
           + Constr String (List Value)
           + Term Exp
```

However, this is only part of the solution. We were willing to give up pattern matching on numbers and strings as the price of their efficient encoding, but we are certainly not willing to do so for such a rich type as expressions. While the equality test is sufficient for the simple types, something more is needed over expressions.

We redefine the encoding function `term` so that it expands an expression by one level, and delays expansion beyond. Thus,

```
term e = case e in
            Val v : ("Val",[val v])
         || Parm x : ("Parm",[Str x])
         || EConstr c ts :
              ("EConstr",[Str c; lst (map Term ts)])
          :
         || Static e : ("Static",[Term e])
         end
```

Rather than expand the arguments to the constructor `c` by a call to `term`, the arguments are simply injected into `Value` by tagging with the `Term` constructor. Whereas we would previously have applied `term` to the input program before specialisation, now we do so within the definition of `reduce` (and also of `eval`). It occurs in the handling of case expressions, as follows.

```
:
if (static e) then
  case (eval prog s_env e) in
     Constr c vs : match_reduce prog s_env d_env (c,vs) cls
  || Term t : match_reduce prog s_env d_env (term t) cls
  end
else
:
```

If the result of evaluating the discriminant is already in the expanded form (i.e. uses `Constr`) then the matching can proceed directly. If not, `term` is applied to the expression to give a one-level expansion into a form in which matching may proceed.

The cost of this delayed encoding is the possibility of repeated on-line expansion. Because a given static value might be examined by many case expressions the term might often be expanded. However, this cost is far outweighed by the benefits that accrue. The fact that the static expression values are around one fifth of their previous size means that the heap is used less and the equality tests are faster. In practice this means that the time taken to compute $mix\ \overline{mix}\ \overline{\overline{mix}}$, for example, is reduced from hours to minutes.

The same technique may be usefully applied to other types used in the definition of *mix*, and to lists in particular. Being such a ubiquitous type it can prove advantageous to introduce a variant `Lst` into `value` and handle it like `Term`.

There is a close relationship between S-expressions and this technique for controlling encoding-explosion in that the constructor `Term` acts very much like `quote` in S-expressions. The presence of both `Term` and `Constr` means that we have two ways of expressing a single value as an element of the universal value domain. For example, both `Term (Parm "x")` and `Constr "Parm" [Str "x"]` are representations of the same term. The same can happen with S-expressions: `(quote (a.b))` is the same as `(cons (quote a) (quote b))`, for example. Because of this, it is quite common for partial evaluators based on S-expressions to have two sets of rules for reducing primitive operations. For example, there may be pairs of rules of the form

```
(car (cons a b)) -> a
(car '(a.b)) -> 'a
```

This duplication of rules corresponds directly with what we have done above.

5 Example

In this section we present an example of the partial evaluator in action. In order to keep things simple we will use a stock example, namely Ackerman's function. It is in the nature of Ackerman's function that the benefit obtainable by partial evaluation is far outweighed by the inherent cost of computing its results. Nonetheless, as a pedagogic tool it provides a great deal of insight.

We begin with a module defining Ackerman's function. The function is defined in standard LML except for the addition of binding-time annotations. It is well known how to add these annotations (see [Ses86, Mog88, Lau89, Bon90] for example), so we will not discuss them in great detail. The annotation ‘ is used to indicate a completely static parameter or sub-expression, and $ indicates a residual function call.

```
module
rec   ack ‘m n = if ‘(m=0) then n+1 else
                 if n=0 then ‘(ack (m-1) 1) else
                 $ack ‘(m-1) ($ack ‘m (n-1))
end
```

If we use the partial evaluator to specialise ack to 2, we obtain the following program, as usual.

```
module
export ack_a;
rec   ack_a n = if n=0 then 3 else ack_b (ack_a (n-1))
and   ack_b n = if n=0 then 2 else ack_c (ack_b (n-1))
and   ack_c n = n+1
end
```

where `ack_a` is what we previously would have called ack_2.

More interestingly, we will specialise `mix` itself to the module defining `ack`, and so obtain a "compiler" for `ack`. That is, compute

$$\overline{mix_{\overline{ack}}} = mix\ \overline{mix}\ \overline{\overline{ack}}$$

The result is given in Figure 1. The first four functions constitute machinery from `mix` that are little changed (except that the residual version of `spec` contains a nested conditional comparing `f` against all the functions in the original program—in this example, there is only `ack`). Two of the functions used in this `mix` machinery, namely `tidy` and `search` are defined in the module `aux` of auxiliary functions.

The main benefit of the specialisation is seen in the residual versions of `reduce` and `eval`. Recall that in `mix` the functions `reduce` and `eval` are used to interpret expressions in the input program, and whereas `reduce` is used to reduce non-static expressions, resulting in residual code, `eval` is given only completely static expressions and returns a value. The specialisation of `mix` produces either a residual version of `reduce` or of `eval` (or both) for each function in the program module depending on whether that function appears statically or dynamically.

In the case of the module defining `ack`, for example, the function `ack` occurs once completely statically (giving rise to a residual version of `eval`) and twice with dynamic parameters (giving rise to a residual version of `reduce`). Thus, within the text of the specialised version of `mix`, we have now two versions of `ack`, one for computing static values, the other for building residual code. These differing tasks of `eval_f` and `reduce_e` may be seen from their types:

```
eval_f   :: List Value -> Value
reduce_e :: List Value -> List Exp -> Exp
```

The form of `eval_f` follows closely that of `ack` itself, except that all the values are tagged, and all the parameters are pachaged into a single list. For clarity, if we perform arity raising ([Ses86]), and then tag-removal ([Lau89]), we obtain

```
eval_f m n = if m=0 then n+1 else
             if n=0 then eval_f (m-1) 1 else
             eval_f (m-1) (eval_f m (n-1))
```

which has exactly the form of `ack`. The corresponding tidied-up version of `reduce_e` is as follows.

```
reduce_e m p = if m=0 then Prim "+" [p; Val (Num 1)] else
               If (Prim "=" [p; Val (Num 0)])
                  (Val (Num (eval_f (m-1) 1)))
                  (Call "ack"
                        [Val (Num (m-1))]
                        [Call "ack"
                              [Val (Num m)]
                              [Prim "-" [p; Val (Num 1)]]])
```

Note that while much of `reduce` is devoted to code-construction, there are decisions it takes (e.g. `if m=0 ...`) and values it computes (e.g. the call to `eval_f`).

When the residual program of Figure 1 is compiled and executed, these residual versions of `ack` will run at compiled speed rather than having to be evaluated via a level of interpretation. This shows the value of successful self-application of `mix`, and demonstrates why a "compiler" obtained in this way has the potential of outperforming plain partial evaluation. Of course, the tagging etc. will entail some degradation compared with optimum performance, but the improvement is still significant.

```
module
#include "aux.t"
export mix_a;

rec  mix_a f args = tidy (spec_b [(f,args)] [])

and  spec_b pend done
      = case pend in
          []   : [] ||
         p.ps : if mem p done then spec_b pns done else
                case p in
                  (f,args) : spec1_c ps (p.done) f args
                end
        end

and  spec1_c pend done f sargs
      = if f="ack" then
          spec2_d pend done "ack" args ["n"]
                                        (reduce_e args [Parm "n"])
        else fail ("spec1: Could not find function: " @ f)

and  spec2_d pend done f svs ps e
      = (f, svs, ps, e) . spec_b (pend @ search e) done

and  reduce_e svs vs
      = if hd svs = Num 0 then Prim "+" [hd vs; Val (Num 1)] else
        If (Prim "=" [hd vs; Val (Num 0)])
           (Val (eval_f [Num (unN (hd svs)-1); Num 1]))
           (Call "ack"
                 [Val (Num (unN (hd svs)-1))]
                 [Call "ack"
                       [Val (hd svs)]
                       [Prim "-" [hd vs; Val (Num 1)]]]])

and  eval_f svs
      = if hd svs = Num 0 then Num (unN (hd (tl svs))+1) else
        if hd (tl svs) = Num 0 then
          eval_f [Num (unN (hd svs)-1); Num 1]
        else
        eval_f [Num (unN (hd svs)-1);
                eval_f [hd svs; Num (unN (hd (tl svs))-1)]]
end
```

Figure 1: mix specialised to ack

6 Double Encoding in Untyped Languages

Originally it was the presence of the Hindley-Milner type system that forced us to consider double encoding. However, it turns out that to some extent the issue is not about types at all. Exactly the same problem occurs in the untyped λ-calculus! Assume initially that there are no constants. We will demonstrate that in this setting double encoding occurs in exactly the same way. Furthermore, we will demonstrate that it is only by the addition of suitable constants to the calculus, and by restricting the generality of the partial evaluator, that double encoding may be avoided.

Using Barendregt's notation [Bar81], we will discuss λ-terms such as $\ulcorner \lambda x.\lambda y.x \urcorner$. Such a term is a representation of the λ-term $\lambda x.\lambda y.x$, but is very different from it. Without going outside the λ-calculus we could not examine the structure of the latter—apart from passing it around as an argument to other functions, all we could do with it is apply it. In contrast, we can examine the structure of the first and decompose it accordingly. Note that using standard encoding methods, the λ-term $\ulcorner \lambda x.\lambda y.x \urcorner$ is about an order-of-magnitude larger than the term $\lambda x.\lambda y.x$.

It is an important property of the λ-calculus that there exists a self-interpreter, which we shall call *L_int*. Given the representation of any λ-term, *L_int* is able to produce the corresponding function. Thus, for example,

$$L\_int \ \ulcorner \lambda x.\lambda y.x \urcorner \;=\; \lambda x.\lambda y.x$$

(where the equality is extensional). In other words, *L_int* is able to drop a layer of representation. Clearly *L_int* is not one-to-one as there are many distinct l-terms which are extensionally equal, and so it is not invertible. Even more importantly, there is in general *no* λ-term which, given another λ-term as argument, is able to return its representation. Such a "function" would not be referentially transparent, of course. Consequently we see a fundamental asymmetry between moving down from the level of representation and moving back up. The former is possible, the latter is not.

Now consider a trivial partial evaluator. It takes a λ-term and an argument for the outermost λ, and performs no real computation but merely returns a partial application. So, for example, given the λ-term $\ulcorner \lambda x.\lambda y.x \; y \urcorner$, and the input $\ulcorner \lambda z.z \urcorner$ the trivial *mix* produces as a result the λ-term $\ulcorner (\lambda x.\lambda y.x \; y) \; (\lambda z.z) \urcorner$. While trivial, this result is clearly correct, and it enables us to see the crucial point that even this trivial *mix* requires its input data to be a representation of the static data, and not the static data itself. Had we omitted the meta-quotes from the argument $\ulcorner \lambda z.z \urcorner$ we would not have been able to construct the residual λ-term from within the λ-calculus.

This is not merely a consequence of using a trivial *mix*. Even quite elaborate partial evaluators will, on occasion, insert static data into the residual program, and so must able to produce a representation of the static data. Only if the static data is passed around as a representation, will there be no problem. However, this immediately entails the problem of double encoding[7].

---

[7]It should be clear that a similar encoding technique to that used in the LML partial evaluator would also work in the λ-calculus, so the cost of the double encoding could be largely overcome.

6.1 Adding Constants

Given the above discussion, how is it that double encoding is not present in the partial evaluators listed in the introduction? The answer lies in the addition of constants. While it is impossible in general to take a λ-term and produce its representation, it is possible to do so for constants: in some sense they are just compact representations for λ-terms anyway. By restricting the static data to be constants, it becomes possible (in the untyped world) to manipulate these constants directly during partial evaluation while still retaining the ability to include them in the residual program.

As soon as we go outside the world of such constants we would expect to have to manipulate representations, even in the untyped world. Experience bears this out. Similix is a partial evaluator for a higher-order subset of Scheme [Bon90]. Ground static values are manipulated as themselves: no representation is introduced. In stark contrast, all higher-order static values are manipulated by explicit representation. Apparently in contrast is λ-mix [GJ91], a partial evaluator for the untyped λ-calculus extended with S-expressions as constants. Here functions are *not* encoded, but are passed around as functions. However, the binding-time analysis in λ-mix is defined by type rules, where the types are given by *type* ::= *base* | *type* → *type* | *code*, and the only method for producing a *code* value from a non-*code* value is through the use of the *lift* operator. But this has type *lift* : *base* → *code*, that is, it will only lift base constants to code and not functions.

7 Removing a Complete Layer of Interpretation

So far in the paper we have only addressed the first of the problems raised by typed languages. In this section we will briefly consider the second, namely that *mix* is unable to remove all the interpretive overhead particularly when specialising itself, and some possible solutions.

In the Ackerman example above, the original interpretation left a residue in the specialised versions of `eval` and `reduce`. This was in two forms: all the parameters occurred in a list, and all the values were tagged to inject them into the universal type. Both of these are easy to deal with using partially static structures—the spine of the list is static, as is the tag on the value—and a result corresponding to the hand-tidied example could be obtained automatically.

However, things are much harder when we consider a program defined over some type unknown within the definition of `mix`. For example, if the Ackerman example is rewritten using an algebraic type for numbers as follows,

```
module
rec  ack ‘m n = case ‘m in
                    Zero   : Succ n
                 || Succ j : case n in
                                Zero   : ‘(ack j (Succ Zero))
                             || Succ k : $ack ‘j ($ack ‘m k)
                             end
                 end
end
```

then the residual version of reduce is,

```
reduce_e svs vs =
 = case hd svs in
     Constr name args :
       if "Zero" = name then
         Constr "Succ" [hd vs]
       else
       if "Succ" = name then
         Case (hd vs)
           [("Zero", [], eval_f [hd args;
                                 Constr "Succ"
                                        [Constr "Zero" []]]);
           ("Succ", ["k"], Call "ack"
                                 [hd args]
                                 [Call "ack"
                                       [hd svs]
                                       [Parm "k"]])]
       else
       fail ("Could not match " @ n)
   end
```

The static value of m (contained in the head of svs) is coded using Constr. Note that, unlike the case of numbers, this is not simply a tagging of a value to include it into the universal datatype, but is an invasive encoding. One consequence of this is that the residual version of reduce contains a nested conditional to implement the original case expression. While the form of the program is close to that of the original, the detail is quite different and loses out on two counts. First, the test on the constructor's name is performed as a string match in this residual version of reduce, and secondly, the original case expression would have been compiled to a single test and a multiway jump, whereas here we have a linear nesting of conditionals (in a datatype with many more variants this difference would become quite significant).

The first of these problems may be overcome by modelling constructor names with integers, for example, and performing the equality tests on these. The second problem is much harder to deal with, however. Because it is impossible to provide an upper bound on the size of every datatype appearing in programs submitted to mix, it is not possible to implement pattern matching in a self-interpreter by a single case-expression. Consequently, no naive residual version of eval or reduce will contain case expressions over user-defined datatypes. Of course, a postprocessing phase could detect the particular pattern of nested ifs and relace it with a case over the representation of constructors used in mix.

One possible route for recovering user datatypes is *type specialisation*. The universal value domain is used to code up many user types. In particular, the Constr constructor may in principle be specialised to each of the values to which it is applied. Thus, in the example above, we would obtain Constr_Zero and Constr_Succ. Assuming that the list-structure of their arguments is also static, usual arity-raising may be performed. Then Constr_Zero would have no arguments, whereas `Constr_Succ` would have one. A necessary consequence of this specialisation is that the linear nesting of `if`s would have to be replaced by an appropriate case expression. The details of all this are the subject of current research.

The invasive encoding of user-defined datatypes has an impact on the use of external functions. In Similix, for example, compiled modules containing external functions may be supplied, and any external function having completely static parameters may be called during partial evaluation. There is one exception to this, namely that higher-order external functions will *not* be called. The reason for this is that, as we have already noted, Similix manipulates explicit closures when interpreting higher-order functions. In contrast, since ground values are manipulated as themselves, these may be passed directly as parameters to external functions.

It would be fairly easy to do likewise in the LML `mix` for the types that receive special treatment in the universal value domain, but in general there is a problem. Not only are `mix`'s representation of values from user defined datatypes in the wrong form for external functions to use, but the necessary injection and projection functions could not be built into `mix`. Instead, the user would have to supply these along with any module of external functions, and this is unreasonable because it demands additional effort from the user before `mix` may be used.

One obvious solution is to provide the text of the external functions for `mix` to interpret. This is not as bad as it seems at first sight because `mix` is self-applicable. As we saw in the Ackerman example, functions which would interpreted during straightforward partial evaluation become incorporated into the text of the specialised version of `mix`, and here they require no interpretation.

8 Conclusion

The primary conclusion we may draw is that it is possible to write a self-applicable partial evaluator in a strongly-typed language such as LML. There are currently a number of distinct versions in existence, each containing different degrees of sophistication within the `Value` type.

It is interesting to note that a partial evaluator written in and for the untyped λ-calculus suffers from exactly the same data-explosion problem and, unless appropriate constants are added, techniques such as those described in this paper are required here also. This demonstrates that the double-encoding problem is only partly related to strong-typing, and it can show itself in untyped contexts also. However, by the judicious use of appropriate coding techniques, double encoding need not be a source of insuperable inefficiency. The problems of representational explosion encountered here are similar to those found in reflection [Smi84].

Currently, the requirement (imposed by strong-typing) that *mix* use a universal type to represent its data means that residual versions of *mix* manipulate tagged data, or worse. How to overcome this in general is still an open problem. A possible approach might be through the use of a type `Dynamic` [ACPP89], though the details are far from clear. If it is actually possible for this tagging problem to be overcome then, because programs in untyped languages actually manipulate tagged data, rather than strong-typing being a hindrance to partial evaluation, the residual versions of *mix* will actually be able to take advantage of their type system.

9 Acknowledgements

A number of people have been most helpful in achieving the results here. In particular Anders Bondorf, John Hughes, and Carsten Kehler Holst all assisted me in the production of the first self-applicable version of *mix* for LML. Subsequently, they, along with Mary Sheeran and others at Glasgow have made many useful suggestions analysing and improving first version, and Ryszard Kubiak has kindly helped me to debug the latest versions of my partial evaluator. Finally, Neil Jones and Torben Mogensen have continually provided me with useful ideas and feedback, and Simon Peyton Jones and Phil Wadler made useful suggestions for improving the presentation.

This work was carried out under funding from ESPRIT basic research action *Semantique.*

References

[ACPP89] M.Abadi, L.Cardelli, B.Pierce and G.Plotkin. *Dynamic Typing in a Statically-Typed Language.* Proc. POPL89, Austin, Texas, 1989.

[Aug84] L.Augustsson. *A Compiler for Lazy ML.* Proceedings of Lisp and Functional Programming Conference, Austin, Texas, 1984.

[Bar81] H.Barendregt, *The Lambda Calculus*, Studies in Logic, Vol 103, North-Holland, 1981.

[BEJ88] D.Bjørner, A.P.Ershov and N.D.Jones eds, *Partial Evaluation and Mixed Computation*, Proceedings IFIP TC2 Workshop, Gammel Avernæs, Denmark, October 1987,North-Holland, 1988.

[Bon89] A.Bondorf, *A Self-Applicable Partial Evaluator for Term Rewriting Systems*, in TAPSOFT 89, eds. J.Diaz and F.Orejas, LNCS 352, Springer-Verlag, 1989.

[Bon90] A.Bondorf, *Self-Applicable Partial Evaluation*, Ph.D. Thesis, DIKU, Copenhagen, 1990.

[BJMS88] A.Bondorf, N.D.Jones, T.Mogensen and P. Sestoft, *Binding Time Analysis and the Taming of Self-Application*, Tech Report, DIKU, Copenhagen, 1988.

[CD89] C.Consel and O.Danvy, *Partial Evaluation of Pattern Matching in Strings*, Inf. Proc. Lett. 30, pages 79-86, 1989.

[Con88] C.Consel, *New Insights into Partial Evaluation: the Schism Experiment*, ESOP 88, ed. H.Ganzinger, LNCS 300, Springer-Verlag, 1988.

[Dyb87] R.K.Dybvig, *The SCHEME Programming Language*, Prentice-Hall Inc., New Jersey, 1987.

[FA88] D.A.Fuller and S.Abramsky, *Mixed Computation of Prolog Programs*, In *New Generation Computing*, Vol 6, No 2,3, pages 119-141, Springer-Verlag, 1988.

[Fut71] Y.Futamura, *Partial Evaluation of Computation Process—An Approach to a Compiler-Compiler*, Systems, Computers, Controls, Vol. 2, No. 5, pages 45-50, 1971.

[GJ89] C.Gomard and N.D.Jones, *Compiler Generation by Partial Evaluation: A Case Study*, Tech Report, DIKU, Copenhagen, 1989.

[GJ91] C.Gomard and N.D.Jones, *A Self-Applicable Partial Evaluator for the Untyped Lambda Calculus*, J. of Functional Programming, CUP, Jan 1991.

[Hol88] C.Kehler Holst, *Language Triplets: The AMIX Approach*, in [BEJ88], pages 167-186, 1988.

[JSS85] N.D.Jones, P.Sestoft and H.Søndergaard, *An Experiment in Partial Evaluation: The Generation of a Compiler Generator*, Rewriting Techniques and Applications, Dijon, France, ed. J.-P.Jouannaud, LNCS 202, 1985.

[Lau89] J.Launchbury, *Projection Factorisations in Partial Evaluation*, Ph.D. Thesis, University of Glasgow, Nov 1989. Distinguished Dissertations in Computer Science, Vol 1, C.U.P., 1991.

[Mog86] T.Mogensen, *The Application of Partial Evaluation to Ray-Tracing*, Master's Thesis, DIKU, University of Copenhagen, 1986.

[Mog88] T.Mogensen, *Partially Static Structures in a Self-Applicable Partial Evaluator*, in [BEJ88], pages 325–347, 1988.

[Ses86] P.Sestoft, *The Structure of a Self-Applicable Partial Evaluator*, in *Programs as Data Objects*, editors H. Ganzinger and N.D. Jones, LNCS 217, pages 236-256, 1986.

[Sun91] R.S.Sundaresh and P.Hudak, *A Theory of Incremental Computation and its Application*, Proc. POPL 91, Orlando, Florida, 1991.

[Smi84] B.C.Smith, *Reflection and Semantics in Lisp*, Proc. POPL 84, Salt Lake City, Utah, 1984.

[WCRS90] D.Weise, R.Conybeare, E.Ruf and S.Seligman, *Automatic Online Partial Evaluation*, draft paper, Computer Systems Lab, Stanford Univ, 1990.

Automatic Online Partial Evaluation*

Daniel Weise
Roland Conybeare
Erik Ruf
Scott Seligman

Computer Systems Laboratory
Margaret Jacks Hall
Stanford University
Stanford, CA 94305-2140

Abstract: We have solved the problem of constructing a fully automatic online program specializer for an untyped functional language (specifically, the functional subset of Scheme). We designed our specializer, called *Fuse*, as an interpreter that returns a trace of suspended computations. The trace is represented as a graph, rather than as program text, and each suspended computation indicates the type of its result. A separate process translates the graph into a particular programming language. Producing graphs rather than program text solves problems with code duplication and premature reduce/residualize decisions. Fuse's termination strategy, which employs online generalization, specializes conditional recursive function calls, and unfolds all other calls. This strategy is shown to be both powerful and safe.

1 Introduction

Program specialization (also called *partial evaluation*) transforms a program and a description of the *valid inputs* to the program into a *specialized program* that is optimized to work on those inputs. Program specializers employ a very simple transformational technique: the selective symbolic execution of the program. Expressions that can be reduced are reduced, while those that cannot be reduced appear in the specialized program. Program specialization has been investigated as an artificial intelligence tool [2, 17], and is a proven technique for creating compilers and compiler generators [20], rediscovering important algorithms [12], speeding up computations by two orders of magnitude [5], parallelizing scientific code [3], and optimizing programs [4]. Program specialization is less powerful than

*This research supported in part by NSF Contract No. MIP-8902764, and in part by Defense Advanced Research Projects Agency Contract No. N00014-87-K-0828. Erik Ruf is supported by an AT&T Bell Laboratories Ph.D. Scholarship.

other transformational techniques such as the unfold/unfold transformation of [9] and the driving transformations of supercompilation [30]. Nonetheless, it is still a very powerful transformation technique. Unlike fold/unfold, it is automatic, and unlike supercompilation, it is rapid.

Research in the 1960's and 1970's stressed the optimizing properties of program specialization [2, 17, 21, 22]. Specializers were tools for optimizing programs. Research emphasized improving the quality of specialized programs, and operating on programs that were not written with the specializer in mind. Because the quality of a specialized program depends upon the number of reductions performed by the specializer, much effort was expended to gather as much information as possible. Toward this goal, symbolic type systems, conditional contexts, and conditional side-effects were developed [17]. Relatively little research was done on automatic termination or automatic prevention of code duplication. The contributions of this period were both theoretical, *e.g.*, the development of the Futamura projections [14, 15], and practical, *e.g.*, the exhibition that program specialization is a powerful tool.

Research in the 1980's stressed self-application [19, 20, 8]. The contributions of this period were the development of automatic termination strategies, and of Binding Time Analysis (BTA), which allowed the construction of efficient self-applicable partial evaluators. The cost of achieving self-application and compiler generation was less optimization and generality, as it was discovered that self-application required a very simple *specialization kernel*. To keep the kernel small, it was reduced to making reduce/residualize/generalize decisions based upon binding time information, and not based upon actual data values. The type systems, conditional contexts, and side-effect handling of the 70's were abandoned. Another proven benefit of BTA based systems was speed of specialization. For example, the *action trees* of [13] provided a highly tuned method for performing specialization very rapidly.

Our goals match those of the 70's: strong optimization for a wide range of programs and programming styles. Rather than striving for self-application at the cost of accuracy, our goal is to make specializers that produce highly specialized programs, and do so for programs that are not designed with specialization in mind. In particular, we are interested in ***online program specialization***, where the reduce/residualize/generalize decision is made during specialization using actual data values, rather than *offline program specialization*, where the reduce/residualize/generalize decision is made using binding time information. The major cost of achieving our goal is the speed of specialization: online methods will often be slower than offline methods.

Four major issues must be addressed when designing a program specializer.

Residual program structure: Specializers beta substitute the program text itself. When a formal parameter appears more than once, code may be duplicated. Code duplication expands code size, and can change the time complexity of an algorithm [28]. Obviously, a specializer should avoid duplicating code.

Termination: Specializers symbolically execute code and explore program paths that may not be explored at runtime. When a specializer explores an infinite program path that may not be explored at runtime, it will fail to terminate.

(Failing to terminate if the program itself would fail to terminate is considered acceptable behavior.) The tension is between performing too little exploration, thereby producing a very poor specialization, and performing too much exploration, thereby risking divergence. Arbitrary cutoff methods usually produce poor specializations.

Information usage: There are many sources of information about data values that can be used during symbolic execution. Examples include information provided by the user when invoking a specializer; constants within the program being specialized; paths that lie on the true or false branches of `if` expressions, which allow the specializer to assume the truth or falsity of the `if` expression's predicate; and properties of the residual code created during specialization, such as the type or structure of the values the residual code will return at runtime. All specializers make use of the first two sources of information, while the other sources are used depending upon the ambition and goal of the specializer.

Polyvariance: A given program point may be specialized in many different ways, each using different information. The best specializations are produced when there is no *a priori* limit on the types or numbers of specializations that can be generated from a given program point. Some specializers only produce one specialization per program point (these are rare), some limit the specializations according to a given template (usually the offline specializers that employ BTA), and some set no limit (usually the online specializers). We will call a specializer that sets no limits on the types of specializations *completely polyvariant.*

The attraction of online program specialization is its simplicity and power. Structured values are as easy to reason about as scalars are, and higher order functions are only slightly more complicated. Online specializers usually create completely polyvariant specializations. Because online specializers aren't self-applicable, they can have the ability to reason about residual code [31], employ conditional contexts [17], aggressively reuse specializations [26], and have a safe yet powerful termination strategy. Also, for structured objects constructed during specialization, the reduce/residualize decision can effectively be postponed until after specialization is complete, resulting in better specializations (c.f., Section 4).

The problem, until now, has been to create a fully automatic online specializer that produces highly specialized programs and solves the code duplication problem. Previous online partial evaluators either required user provided annotation to guide termination and code duplication [17, 27], or had weak or non-existent automatic termination methods [16, 21] and only worked on a small range of programs. In his (re-)examination of program specialization, Jones [18] described his concerns regarding the construction of an automatic online specializer. Jones was concerned that online methods would be too expensive, would not be general enough to be practical, would be very hard to make terminate, would not use nonlocal information, and would not be amenable to self-application. Except for not being amenable to self-application, the problems that he cites are all solved by this research. We show that the extra expense yields better specializations, that online methods can be made both general and practical, that termination can be accomplished, and that nonlocal information can be used.

This paper focuses on Fuse's solution to code duplication, and its termination method. To us, the problem of code duplication is not avoiding it, *per se*, but to do so without compromising the accuracy of the specializer. A specializer can't know with 100% accuracy what code is duplicated without first "duplicating" the code. Ideally, code duplication should effectively be ignored during specialization to allow highly specialized programs to be constructed. Fuse achieves this ideal through its use of *graphs*. Specialized programs are represented as graphs, not as program text. Computations are represented by nodes, and the flow of values by directed edges. A value that is needed in many places in the residual program will appear as a node with multiple fanout. Such nodes represent values that need to be bound with a `let` expression at code generation time. During specialization, reductions are made regardless of code duplication or the specialized program's eventual structure. Scalar and structured values (cons cells and closures) are handled identically. The code generator also reconstructs the necessary lexical structure to express the block structure possessed by graphs.

The termination properties of an automatic specializer lie in its handling of function calls [28]. It makes a *reduce/residualize/generalize* decision when applying a function: whether to reduce the call, *i.e.*, invoke the function on its arguments, or to create a *residual call* to a specialized function. When it chooses to produce a specialized function a *generalize* decision must be made: how much of the known information to use when creating the specialization. Choosing to reduce too few calls, or to use too little information, results in trivial specialization, whereas reducing too many calls, or using too much information, often leads to nontermination. The task is to get both choices right.

Fuse's termination strategy is based upon specializing closures that are used recursively, and upon online generalization. Fuse specializes the application of a closure when the application represents a recursive call that will be conditionally executed at runtime. Fuse specializes a closure on the generalization of the current arguments and the arguments from a pending (active) call, thereby building a specialization that can be used for the current and pending call. This strategy is very safe, but sometimes prone to premature termination. Special generalization rules are used lessen the amount of generalization performed, thereby yielding better specializations without risking divergence.

This paper has six sections. Section 2 presents an overview of the structure of Fuse. It discusses *symbolic values*, basic computational elements of Fuse. Fuse's termination strategy is given in Section 3. The benefit of graphs, and generating code from them, is presented in Section 4. Related research is discussed in Section 5. We conclude with Section 6.

2 Overview of Fuse

Fuse is designed primarily as an interpreter and secondarily as a program transformer. The specialized program is generated almost as an afterthought of interpretation. Functions are applied to *symbolic values* and return symbolic values. The structure of Fuse is very similar to an interpreter for an untyped functional language [1]. The major difference is the handling of `if` expressions and `call` expressions (applications). The change for `if` expressions is very minor, whereas the change handling for `call` expressions is very large, because termination decisions are made here. We will first discuss symbolic values, then discuss the structure of Fuse.

2.1 Symbolic Values

Symbolic values represent both the type of object that will be produced at run time and the code to produce the value. The result of interpreting (specializing) any expression is a symbolic value. Each symbolic value has a ***value attribute*** and a ***code attribute***. The value attribute represents a subset of *VAL*, the value domain of the language whose programs are specialized. Besides representing a subset of *VAL*, the value attribute is also a value that is operated upon. For example, during partial evaluation the `car` operation takes the car of the value attribute of the symbolic value it is applied to. We say that a symbolic value represents a *known value*, or, more simply, *is* a known value, when the set it represents contains only one value. Otherwise, it is called an *unknown value*. Value attributes range over the Scheme values supported by Fuse, and over the special markers `a-value`, `a-list`, `a-natural`, `a-boolean`, and `a-function`. (In the implementation these markers are represented by tagged values, not as Lisp symbols. For simplicity of exposition, this technical distinction is not made in the rest of this paper.) These markers are interpreted as representing all values in the type. The marker `a-value` represents all values. Any symbolic value whose value attribute is `a-value` is called *completely unknown* or *completely unconstrained*. Because symbolic values are first class objects, constructing structured symbolic values, such as the value that represents all pairs whose first element is a boolean and whose second element is a natural, is simple.

(Our notions of "known" and "unknown" differ significantly from the BTA terms "static" and "dynamic". "Static" and "dynamic" refer to expressions, such as identifiers and `if` expressions, not to values. An expression is ***static*** if all the specialization time values it denotes are *known*. An expression is ***dynamic*** when it may denote an *unknown* value during specialization. BTA terminology uses the term ***partially static structure*** to refer to an expression that always returns a structured value where certain slots will be known during specialization. We have no special terminology for a structured value that contains unknowns, we simply call them structured values.)

The code attribute specifies how the value represented by the symbolic value is computed from the formal parameters of the procedure (or, when block structure is employed, procedures) being specialized. Symbolic values are very similar to IBL's *partial values* [27], except that the code attribute of a partial value is program text, whereas ours is a *graph structure*. The code specifying the creation of a value V only appears in the specialized program when V itself must be constructed at runtime. Code is either (1) an identifier, (2) an `if` expression, (3) a `call` expression, or (4) a value. When a symbolic value represents a known value, the code attribute is the value attribute. The two major benefits of using symbolic values are propagation of type information, and postponement of many reduce/residualize choices until code generation time. We will write a symbolic value using angle brackets, for example, a symbolic value with value attribute v and code attribute c will be written $\langle$v,c$\rangle$. A more detailed description of symbolic values appears in [31].

Example symbolic values include:

⟨4,4⟩. The number 4.

⟨a-natural,a⟩. A number whose name is a.

⟨(⟨4,4⟩ . ⟨a-natural,a⟩),(cons 4 a)⟩. The cons of the above 2 items. Cons pairs are written (a . b).

⟨(⟨a-boolean,(car (f a))⟩ . ⟨a-natural,(cdr (f a))⟩),(f a)⟩. A pair to be created by a runtime call to f.

Fuse is invoked on a program and symbolic values. The user constructs symbolic values using the unary function known-value, which is applied to numbers and booleans, the niladic functions a-natural, a-value, a-boolean, and the binary function a-cons. The symbolic values so constructed have empty code slots. Before starting symbolic execution Fuse *instantiates* the symbolic values, initializing their code slots. Instantiation makes the code slots of unknown scalar values be the formal parameter the symbolic value is bound to. For pairs, it operates recursively, making the code slots of the car and cdr of a symbolic pair take the car and cdr of the symbolic pair itself. (Actually, the code slot is set to take the tc-car and tc-cdr of the parent pair. The tc- functions are described later.)

2.2 Fuse's Structure

Fuse is structured as an interpreter for an untyped functional language [1]. It differs from a standard interpreter in it handling of if expressions and call expressions (Figure 1), and the operations of its primitive functions.

A syntactic preprocessor transforms input programs into a semantically equivalent program that uses just six different expression types. (See [29] for a motivation and implementation of using a small number of expression types for reasoning about programs.) The six primitive expression types are: Constant, Variable, If, Letrec, Call, and Lambda. Four of the six, Constant, Variable, Letrec, and Lambda, simply execute as normal. Lambda builds closures that contain an extra slot for caching the specializations of the closure. For If expressions, the predicate is partially evaluated. If it evaluates to either *true* or *false*, then the consequent or alternate is specialized. If the predicate evaluates to an unknown value, then a new symbolic value is created whose value attribute is a-value and whose code slot contains a residual if expression. Call expressions are the subject of Section 3.

The primitive functions, such as +, cons, and cdr operate on symbolic values and produce symbolic values. Known symbolic values produce known symbolic values, while unknown symbolic values cause the creation of a new symbolic value whose code slot indicates the primitive function to be called at runtime. The primitive functions also perform type checking, and create code at the appropriate safely level. For example, when + is handed a-value and 5, it issues the + function, but when it is handed a-natural and 5, it issues the tc-+ (TypeChecked-+) function. The tc- functions know that their arguments have been typechecked, and do not perform redundant type checking.

The function cons always constructs a cons pair. When known values are paired together, the code slot contains the pair, otherwise it contains an instruction to

```
(define peval
  (lambda (exp env stack)
    (cond ((constant? exp) exp)
          ((var? exp) (lookup exp env))
          ((if? exp)
           (let ((pred (peval (if-pred exp) env stack)))
             (cond ((true? pred) (peval (if-then exp) env stack))
                   ((false? pred) (peval (if-else exp) env stack))
                   (else
                     (let ((then-sv (peval (if-then exp) env (mark-stack stack)))
                           (else-sv (peval (if-else exp) env (mark-stack stack))))
                       (make-sv *a-value*
                                (make-code 'if (list pred then-sv else-sv))))))))
          ((lambda? exp) (create-closure exp env))
          ((call? exp) (papply (peval (call-head exp) env stack)
                               (peval (call-arg exp) env stack)
                               stack))
          ((letrec? exp) (peval (letrec-body exp)
                                (recursive-extend-env (letrec-bindings exp) env)
                                stack)))))
```

Figure 1: The specializing interpreter. The variable **stack** is used for termination. This interpreter differs from the standard interpreter in the handling of **if**-expressions and the application of closures.

cons together the arguments at runtime. When handed a pair, both car and cdr simply return the car or cdr of its value attribute, respectively. The functions `car` and `cdr` only produce new code when handed `a-value` or `a-list`. The other structured value constructors, `vector` and `lambda`, also always construct objects during specialization.

3 Termination

Termination in all automatic program specializers is based upon some form of loop detection. At selected "program points," a cache is kept of the specializations made from the program point indexed by the states that produced the different specializations. Whenever the program point is to be specialized rather than unfolded, the cache is checked. If there is a hit, the cache entry is used as the specialization, otherwise, a new specialization is made and entered in the cache. Unless arbitrary bounds are used, automatic specialization only terminates when all loops that arise during partial evaluation are either self-terminating or broken by a cache hit.

The element of specialization (program point) in Fuse is the closure. Specializing a closure produces a *specialized closure* that contains three elements: a new name, the arguments that produced the specialized closure, and a symbolic value that contains the type returned by the specialized closure and the code of the specialized closure. We refer to the code of a specialized closure as a graph, and draw it as such (c.f., Section 4).

Fuse detects loops when detected when applying closures. For each closure, a cache is maintained that contains the specializations of the closure *indexed* by the types of the arguments that generated the specializations. Each time a closure is applied, its cache is checked; if the arguments have the same type as an index, then, instead of applying the closure, a residual call to the specialized closure is created and returned. (To maximize sharing of specializations, Fuse also maintains information that allows a specialization to be reused, without any information loss, when the arguments don't exactly match the cache index [26].)

Ensuring cache hits requires choosing to residualize certain calls to create cache entries of specialized closures, and abstracting the arguments to ensure a finite number of cache entries. When not enough calls are residualized, the specializer loops endlessly for lack of hitting in the cache; when the abstraction doesn't discard enough information, the specializer builds an infinite number of specializations. For example, consider the "counting down" implementation of the factorial function:

```
(define (fact n)
  (letrec ((loop (lambda (n)
                   (if (= n 0) 1 (* n (loop (- n 1)))))))
    (loop n)))
```

When specialized on an unknown number, the call sequence looks like

```
(fact <a-natural, n>)
(loop <a-natural, n>)
(loop <a-natural, (- n 1)>)
```

```
(loop <a-natural, (- (- n 1) 1)>)
...
```

If the none of the calls to `loop` are residualized, the specializer will loop. Residualizing one of the calls will effect termination because hits are based on type information. Before a closure is specialized, an entry is made in the specialization cache to hold the specialization that will be produced. When the recursive call is encountered while specializing the closure, a cache hit will occur, terminating the loop.

It would seem that residualizing all calls to closures would solve the problem of deciding which ones to specialize. Unfortunately, no information is gleaned from a residual call expression,[1] so information would be lost. The problem could be avoided somewhat by carefully writing code to be partially evaluated, but this would go against our goal of specializing as large a class of programs as possible.

Sometimes the arguments that a closure is specialized on must be abstracted before specialization. Otherwise, an infinite number of specializations will be made. Consider, for example, the "counting up" implementation of the factorial function:

```
(define (fact n)
  (letrec ((loop (lambda (m ans)
                   (if (> m n)
                       ans
                       (loop (1+ m) (* m ans))))))
    (loop 1 1)))
```

When "counting up" factorial is specialized on an unknown number, the calls to `loop` appear as

```
(fact <a-natural, n>)
(loop <1,1> <1,1>)
(loop <2,2> <1,1>)
(loop <3,3> <2,2>)
(loop <4,4> <6,6>)
(loop <5,5> <24,24>)
...
```

Clearly, deciding to residualize any given call, or all of them, would not ensure termination. In this example, termination is not an issue of unfold versus residualize, and specializers that rely only on unfold or residualize strategies will fail to terminate. To ensure termination, the arguments must be abstracted. Abstraction maps a value to a value that represents more values. For example, an abstraction of `1` is `a-natural`, and an abstraction of `a-natural` is `a-value`. In this example, abstracting both arguments to `a-natural` before specializing would achieve termination.

Fuse's primary termination strategy unfolds a recursive call (applies a closure) only when there is no match in the cache, and when it can prove that if the program made the previous call then it would also make the current call (Figure 2).

[1][31] describes an extension to Fuse that allows type information to propagate out of residual expressions. Given such a feature, a specializer could residualize every call, and use a postpass to collapse trivial calls. Such a mechanism, however, extracts an additional specialization time cost, as would the collapsing postpass.

```
(define (apply-closure cl args stack)
  (cond ((lookup-specialization-cache cl args)
         (make-residual-call (lookup-specialization-cache cl args) args))
        ((specialize? cl args stack)
         (let ((<args' stack'> (generalize-argument cl args stack)))
          (if (lookup-specialization-cache cl args')
              (make-residual-call (lookup-specialization-cache cl args') args')
              (make-residual-call (specialize-closure cl args' stack') args))))
        (else (primitive-apply-closure cl args stack))))

(define (specialize-closure cl args stack)
  (let ((sc (make-specialized-closure
              (gen-name)
              arg
              "to be replaced")))
    (cache! (closure-spec-cache cl) args sc)
    (set-specialized-closure-body sc (primitive-apply-closure cl args stack))
    sc))

(define (make-residual-call sc args)
  (make-sval *a-value* (make-code sc args)))

(define (primitive-apply-closure cl args stack)
  (let ((<formals body env> cl))
   (peval body
          (extend-env formals args env)
          (cons (cons cl args) stack))))
```

Figure 2: Application of compound procedures. Termination and specialization decisions are made here.

To do so, it maintains a stack containing all active calls to closures, and the arguments the closures were applied to. The stack also contains *conditional markers*. The specializer places them on the stack when specializing the arms of `if` expressions whose predicates did not evaluate to either true or false. These markers indicate that the specializer has entered a *speculative region* of the computation: the program at runtime may or may not perform the computations being specialized. Before a closure is applied, the cache is checked. If the arguments match the index of specialized closure S, then a residual call to S is created. Otherwise, the stack is examined starting from the most recent entry. If there is no active call to the same closure, or there is no conditional marker before the most recent call to the same closure, then the call is unfolded. If there is a conditional marker before the most recent call to the same closure, it means that the call about to be made is speculative, and that unfolding it may lead to specializer loops that don't correspond to runtime loops.

When such a call is detected, Fuse elects to specialize rather than unfold. Abstraction of arguments occurs at this point, because merely specializing the closure may lead to infinite numbers of specializations. Fuse attempts to perform the minimal amount of abstraction while still ensuring termination. It does so by comparing the arguments of the call being specialized against all arguments of all active calls to the same closure. It finds the invocation whose arguments are the most similar to those of the current call, and then *generalizes* these together to form a new set of arguments. If the new arguments don't hit in the cache, a new specialization is created for the generalized arguments.

Generalization maps two symbolic values *s1* and *s2* into a new symbolic value S representing (at least) all the objects that *s1* and *s2* represent. Fuse's termination strategy uses generalization to discard information about values to ensure that only a finite number of specializations are made. When either of *s1* or *s2* are scalars, S's value attribute is the least upper bound of *s1* and *s2*'s value attributes. When both *s1* and *s2* are pairs, their cars are generalized and their cdrs are generalized. The code slots are created via instantiation.

As as example, we will show how Fuse specializes the Iota program (named after the operator of the same name from APL):

```
(define (iota n)
  (letrec ((loop (lambda (m)
                   (if (= m n) '() (cons m (loop (1+ m)))))))
    (loop 0)))
```

The stack starts as

```
(iota <a-natural, n>)
```

and after the first call to `loop` is

```
(iota <a-natural, n>)
(loop <0,0>)
```

and before the second call to `loop` is

```
(iota <a-natural, n>)
(loop <0,0>)
*conditional-marker*
```

Therefore, Fuse discovers that the second call to *loop* is speculative. Since there is no cache entry that this call hits, Fuse creates a specialization based on the generalization of the current argument <1, 1> and the previous argument, <0,0>, yielding <a-natural, m>. Loop is now specialized on this value, and with a cache entry indexed by the type a-natural to hold the result of the specialization. Specialization proceeds with the stack

```
(iota <a-natural, n>)
(loop <a-natural, m>)
```

At the next call to loop, its argument is <a-natural, (1+ m)> whose type, a-natural, hits in the cache. A residual call to the specialized closure in the cache is created, the creation of the specialized closure is completed. The final code is (with a little cleaning of variable names):

```
(define (iota1 n)
  (if (= 0 n)
      '()
      (cons
        0
        (letrec ((loop1 (lambda (m)
                          (if (= m n)
                              '()
                              (cons m (loop1 (1+ m)))))))
          (loop1 1)))))
```

This strategy produces "surplus" code because loops aren't specialized until the recursive call is hit, at which time the loop has already been unrolled once. Fuse heuristically eliminates this extra preamble. Whenever the arguments of active call A on the stack are generalized against some other arguments, it means that call A will be a preamble to a specialization. Therefore, when the invocation A is finished, instead of returning its result, Fuse returns a residual call to the specialization that was created. Applying this heuristic to the example yields the code that Fuse produces:

```
(define (iota1 n)
  (letrec ((loop1 (lambda (m)
                    (if (= m n)
                        '()
                        (cons m (loop1 (1+ m)))))))
    (loop1 0)))
```

(Offline systems that use a monovariant BTA that does not duplicate code, and therefore assigns one BTA signature per function definition, do not produce preambles.)

Fuse's strategy is very safe. For example, it avoids divergence in the presence of *counters* (called "static values under dynamic control" in [18]), which are values that are always known, but that don't affect control flow. Speculative loops that perform a test before iterating are eventually halted through the generalization mechanism. Fuse will fail to terminate only when the program being specialized itself fails to terminate for any valid input, or when the program contains a non-terminating region regardless of input. However, in its eagerness to terminate,

Fuse will sometimes terminate too early because it generalizes away too much information.

To the basic termination strategy Fuse adds rules that either allow unfolding where specialization had before been required, or that prevent generalization when specialization is chosen. In either case, the rule is not allowed to change the termination properties of Fuse: any program which Fuse would terminate on without the extra rules it must terminate on when new rules are used.

As an example of premature termination, consider compiling a program P written in language L by specializing an interpreter I for L on P. To ensure that the constituent elements of conditional expressions in P are compiled, the arms of the conditional statement within I must be specialized even though the predicate of the conditional will not be known until runtime. More concretely, a the fragment of I that interprets conditional statements in L may appear as

```
(if (conditional-expression? exp)
    (if (eval (predicate exp) env)
        (eval (then-arm exp) env)
        (eval (else-arm exp) env))).
```

To fully compile the program, all calls to `eval` in this fragment must be unfolded (or specialized) without losing the value of `exp`. Unfortunately, the calls to `eval` in the consequent and alternative of the inner if are speculative, and generalization here loses the value of `exp`.

We have two approaches to solving this problem, one that is fairly standard, and one that is novel, but unimplemented. The standard approach is based upon detecting structural inductions in the program [28]: unfold instead of specialize when there is some bounded argument that gets smaller on each recursive call . At each subsequent recursive call, the same argument must get smaller for unfolding to be performed again.

The other method exploits the observation that we want the specializer to "consume" all of the inputs. The purpose of program specialization when compiling programs is to translate the entire source program into the language the interpreter is written in. Therefore, a method for achieving the goal of traversing all input structures is to remember which objects are part of the input (of which there are only a finite number), and which are created during specialization. When unfolding a speculative call, it is safe to unfold when patterns of input values are different from previous patterns of input values. Since there are only a finite number of input values, this strategy will not cause the partial evaluator terminate any less often than before. Considering the interpreter fragment above, `eval` will be unfolded as long as different pieces of the input appear in `exp`. Only when the same value reappears in `exp` will a specialization occur, at which point the environment will be generalized.

The termination strategy is adequate for programs which, when specialized, produce a graph without residual unspecialized closures. However, some programs produce higher-order residual code; in this case, unspecialized closure objects will appear in the final graph whenever a closure is an argument in a residual function call. Because of Fuse's design, these closures must be specialized before the code generator that turns graphs into target code can run. When specialization is complete, a postpass finds each residual unspecialized closure and specializes it on completely unknown inputs. (A similar technique is proposed in [24].) It would be more accurate to specialize each closure on an approximation to the arguments of all its potential call sites, but we haven't yet implemented the pass to collect this information.

Stream-like objects, such as the Y operator, cause a minor problem because specializing a closure may result in a new residual closure, whose specialization produces a new residual closure, etc. For example, consider

```
(define (evolve-system f s)
  (let loop ((s s))
    (cons s (lambda () (loop (f s))))))
```

Specializing this function on unknown values produces a graph with a residual closure. Specializing that closure will yield yet another closure.

The termination strategy described above fails in this case, because it relies on the presence of a conditional expression with unknown test to signal entry into a speculative region, thus pushing a conditional marker and forcing generalization. In this case, specializing the residual closure is speculative, not because the specializer was unable to decide a conditional, but because it cannot prove that the residual closure will indeed be applied at runtime.

At the moment, Fuse relies on a heuristic which forces the pushing of a conditional marker when specializing a residual closure. Using this heuristic, specializing `evolve-system` on `1+` and 0 will produce

```
(define (evolve-system1 f s)
  (cons 0 (let loop ((s 1))
            (cons s (lambda () (loop (1+ s)))))))
```

There is a preamble before the loop, as usual, but the proper loops are formed. This mechanism also properly handles the Y operator.

This solution is not ideal; although it works in many common cases, such as that shown above, it is sometimes overly conservative, and fails to terminate in some pathological cases. We are actively researching a better strategy. Other specializers that handle higher order programs [11, 7] avoid this termination problem through the use of monovariant BTAs.

4 Graphs

Using graphs to represent code in a program specializer was pioneered by Berlin [3, 5]. This technique allows program structure to be ignored during specialization without risking code duplication. A postpass constructs executable code from the graph, at which time the proper binding constructs are inserted into the generated code. The important differences between our graphs and Berlin's graph are that our graphs may be cyclic so that they can express loops, and may themselves contain subgraphs so that they can express block structure.

A node in a graph (Figure 3) is either a primitive function, an application node (written as `@`), an `if` node, or a `lambda` node, which corresponds to a specialized closure. Our graphical representation solves code duplication problems, as well as allows the delaying of some reduce/residualize decisions until after specialization is complete. The cost of this added power is the cost of generating executable code from the graph. If we assume that the specialized program is compiled before being executed, then this additional cost is relatively small, because the work performed by our code generator is a subset of the work that a compiler performs. The major algorithm run by the code generator is computing dominators, a standard compiler task.

4.1 Code Duplication

During conventional program specialization there is a substitution of formal parameters by actual parameters. Some of the actual parameters will be represented by the code that computes them. If these expressions are substituted wherever formal parameters occur, then code will be duplicated when a formal parameter appears more than once. This can change both a program's complexity [28], and, in the presence of side-effects, its meaning.

However, in order to achieve the best specialization, it is often (especially in scientific code [5]), necessary to perform reductions that risk such duplication. For example, consider the function for adding two complex numbers represented in rectangular coordinates:

```
(define (+complex x y)
  (make-complex (+ (real x) (real y))
                (+ (imag x) (imag y))))
```

We would like the specialization of

```
(define (+complex3 x y z)
   (+complex x (+complex y z)))
```

to produce

```
(lambda (x y z)
  (make-complex (+ (real x) (real y) (real z))
                (+ (imag x) (imag y) (imag z))))
```

This result can only be obtained if multiple substitutions are allowed, because the original definition of `+complex` has multiple occurrences of both `x` and `y`. But allowing such substitutions may lead to code duplication, because one cannot tell if there is duplicated code until after all substitutions and simplifications have been performed.

Because Fuse builds graphs, and produces program text in a separate pass, it avoids these problems. Graphs express shared values, so that the control part of the specializer need not worry about sharing or duplication. The code generator introduces the necessary binding constructs (`let` expressions) to avoid code duplication.

Specializers that operate by pure beta-reduction either can't reproduce this result because they outlaw duplication on the same control thread (e.g., [8]), or can reproduce this result but run the risk of really being left with duplicate code (e.g., [28], which allows some duplication in carefully controlled instances).

4.2 Delaying the Reduce/Residualize Decision

One major benefit of symbolic values is that because structured objects are built at specialization time, with the code to construct them attached to them, only when specialization is complete is the decision to produce residual code made. If a value is fully consumed during specialization, it will not appear in the output graph, and the code to construct it need not be issued. For example, consider the following program fragment.

```
(let ((local-f (lambda (x y) (+ (* x x) (* y y)))))
  (if (pred42 z)
      (local-f z (g z))
      (list 1+ local-f)))
```

The question is whether to leave the `let` binding residual or to reduce it. A specializer cannot make the correct choice until after the evaluation of `pred42`. When `(pred42 y)` evaluates to *true* then reducing the binding allows the function to be run and discarded at partial evaluation time. Otherwise the lambda expression must appear in the specialized program. Symbolic values solve this problem, because they denote both the closure and the code to build it.

This example can be repeated for other types of structured values, such as pairs and vectors. In general, the specializer doesn't need to be aware of the reduce/residualize decision for structured values, as the symbolic value will represent both the object and the code to construct it. (Schooler's , *partial values* [27] also had this property.)

Most importantly, a structured value can be both used and left residual. For example, consider representing conditionals in the lambda calculus, where *true* is $\lambda xy.x$, *false* is $\lambda xy.y$ and a conditional is $\lambda pca.pca$. When there are residual conditionals left in specialized code, the `lambda` expressions representing *true* and *false* must also remain residual (unless transformations not usually performed by a specializer are employed). If having the *true* and *false* lambda expressions be residual prevents any reduction of *true* or *false*, no conditionals can be reduced, resulting in very poor specializations. Consider, for example, the following code.

```
(lambda (x y z)
  (let ((true (lambda (x y) x))
        (false (lambda (x y) y))
        (fif (lambda p c a) (p c a)))
    (let ((f> (lambda (x y) (if (> x y) true false))))
      (+ (fif (f> x y) 3 4)
         (fif (f> y z) 3 9)))))
```

If this code were specialized for `x` being 10, `y` being 20, and `z` being unknown, we would want the specializer to reduce `(fif (f> x y) 3 4)` to 4. But it could only do this if it could both apply true and leave its construction residual. Using symbolic values and graphs allows this to happen in Fuse.

4.3 Generating Programs from Graphs

The main issues in generating code are translating the parallel meaning of graphs into serial code (*i.e.*, choosing orderings in which to do things) and rediscovering

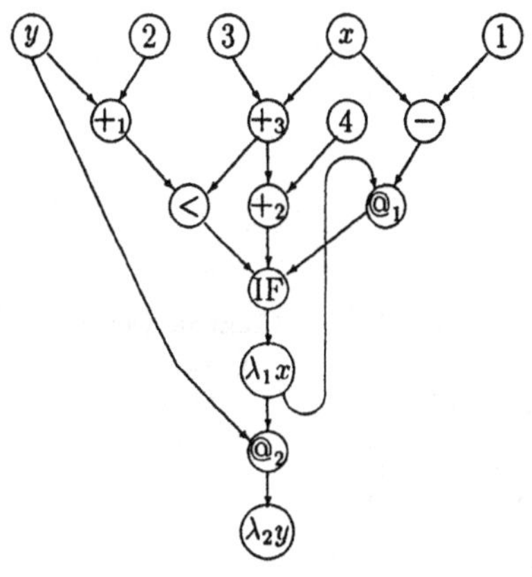

Figure 3: A Fuse graph. The λ nodes represent procedures (specialized closures). The node labeled $\lambda_1 x$, for example, represents a procedure λ_1 with a single formal parameter x, whose body is represented by the IF node. The @ nodes represent procedure applications. Nodes labeled + represent generic primitive operators.

---

block structure and lexical scoping. Translating a parallel graph into serial code is difficult because order of evaluation must be reestablished: the dataflow IFs of graphs must be permuted into the control IFs of serial programming languages. This problem is compounded by large fanout and reconvergences of the possible execution paths and data values. The Fuse code generator currently produces both Scheme and C programs.

Graphs have several characteristics that distinguish them from the style of program representation of our target languages. Graphs show only the dataflow of a program. The control information needed to evaluate the program is implicit and, in general, not uniquely determined. As an illustration, consider the graph of Figure 3. For brevity we refer to the computation represented by the node rooted at $+_2$, for example, simply as "$+_2$". There is no indication as to which of $+_1$ and $+_3$ should be evaluated first. Indeed, if the target language allowed parallelism to be explicitly represented, there would be cases for which we would not wish to specify the relative ordering of the computations. Also, although it is possible (in this simple example, trivial) to deduce that $+_3$ must be evaluated before the IF node, this ordering is not indicated explicitly.

Conditional nodes of graphs differ from the conditional expressions of many conventional languages in that the consequent, for example, may need to be evaluated even if the predicate is false (because the consequent may have multiple fanout, ie, be used in more than once place). This allows more flexibility when constructing the target program, at the cost of deciding for each node not only *where* but also *if* it is to be evaluated. We can introduce memoization (delay and force constructs) into the target program to allow more precise control over the computation.

Although graphs contain procedures (specialized closures), there is no explicit indication as to which computations are performed when a particular closure is applied. In the illustration we can see that, whereas $+_3$ must be evaluated on each application of λ_1, multiple applications of λ_1 for which the value y does not change

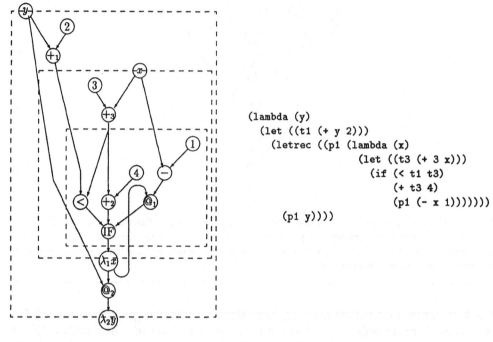

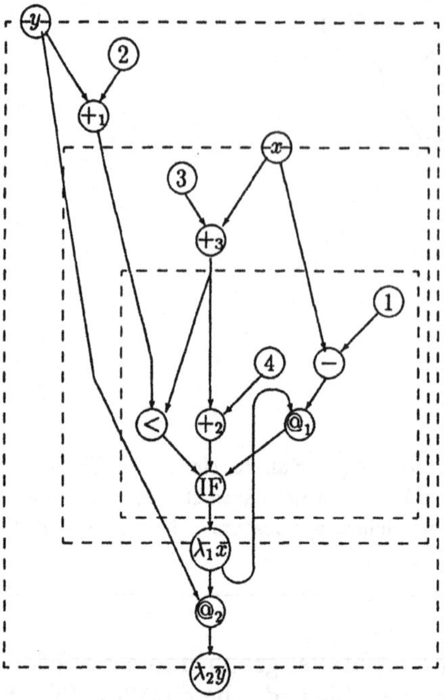


```
(lambda (y)
  (let ((t1 (+ y 2)))
    (letrec ((p1 (lambda (x)
                   (let ((t3 (+ 3 x)))
                     (if (< t1 t3)
                         (+ t3 4)
                         (p1 (- x 1)))))))
      (p1 y))))
```

Figure 4: The augmented counterpart to Figure 3's graph, and the corresponding Scheme code.

can make use of a single evaluation of $+_1$. Performing computation outside the body of a closure in this manner is analogous to hoisting code out of loops as done by standard optimizing compilers.

We named the nodes in the example graphs for reference only; these names have no other significance. Names are generally used in conventional languages to allow values to be used repeatedly. These languages must therefore provide a rule, such as lexical scoping, for determining the value corresponding to a particular use of a name. Graphs use edges with arbitrarily large fanout rather than names to indicate such dependencies between nodes, so there is no need to represent within a graph any lexical structure or scoping.

The essence of code generation is making explicit the information left implicit or unspecified by a graph. As an illustration of how such information might be represented, examine the *augmented graph* of Figure 4. This is the same graph as appeared in Figure 3, with boxes overlayed to indicate a block-like structuring of the computation. The box passing through each λ node delineates the entirety of that procedure. We can now see that $+_1$ is not a part of the body of λ_1, and that its evaluation should precede that of $+_3$ (which *is* a part of the body of λ_1).

Each box corresponds to some computation, with values crossing into the box corresponding to the free variables of that computation. The two edges leading from $+_3$ into the inner box have been coalesced into a single edge that forks at the box's boundary. Such an edge indicates a value that will be assigned to a variable in the target program, and the point at which it crosses into a box corresponds to the point where its value will be named. This, along with the tree-like nesting of

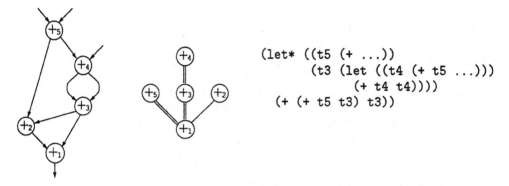

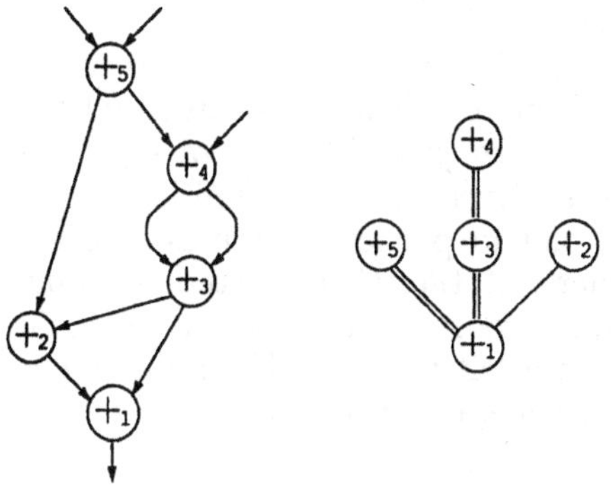

```
(let* ((t5 (+ ...))
       (t3 (let ((t4 (+ t5 ...)))
             (+ t4 t4))))
  (+ (+ t5 t3) t3))
```

Figure 5: A graph fragment, its def-point tree, and the generated Scheme code.

---

the boxes, forms a lexical structure that aids deriving the lifetimes and scopes of the values in the target program.

Finally, the tree-like structure within each box allows for a straight-forward reading of the sequence of those computations. The correspondence between the augmented graph and the Scheme code in Figure 4 should be clear. The main task of code generation is to (effectively) produce augmented graphs.

4.3.1 The Def-Point Tree

To impose structure on a graph, we introduce the *def-point tree.* The def-point tree of a graph is the skeleton of the structure of its target program. It is essentially a representation of the information found in the augmented graph described above. Its nodes are exactly the nodes of the graph, and its root is the root node of the graph. A node's parent in this tree is that node's *def-point*, short for *definition point.* The target program is structured so as to ensure that each node is *defined*—that is, the code for computing the node's value is evaluated—before or as part of the definition of its def-point.

The sharing of nodes between a graph and its corresponding def-point tree is a potential source of ambiguity when referring to these structures. To avoid confusion, we adopt the following terminology. The terms *producer* and *consumer* specify relations within a graph. A node is a consumer of each of the nodes on whose value it directly depends, and is a producer for each of the nodes that directly depend on it. In the graph representing the summation of nodes X and Y, for example, the $+$ node consumes both X and Y. The terms *parent* and *child* specify relations within the def-point tree, with *ancestor* and *descendant* being their respective transitive closures. Children of the same parent are *siblings.* A node is said to be *shallower* than any of its proper descendants, and *deeper* than any of its proper ancestors.

As an illustration of def-point trees, consider the graph fragment of Figure 5. The figure also shows a fragment of the corresponding def-point tree. There are two types of edges. The single edge between $+_1$ and $+_2$ indicates that $+_1$ is the only consumer of $+_2$'s value and that $+_2$ is not being hoisted (more on hoisting later). In this case the code for $+_1$ will include the code for $+_2$.

A double edge indicates that the parent must be defined in an environment in which the child has already been defined. Thus the figure indicates that the definition of $+_4$ precedes that of $+_3$, which in turn precedes that of $+_1$. The ordering in which siblings are defined is also significant. The definition of $+_5$, for example, must precede all of the others, and in particular it must precede that of $+_3$, a consumer of one of $+_5$'s consumers. Rather than cluttering up our illustrations by drawing these ordering relations, we instead choose to draw the tree such that it is safe to define the siblings from left to right. The right side of Figure 5 shows the Scheme code that would be generated from this tree.

4.3.2 Choices in Building the Def-Point Tree

A unique choice of def-point for a particular node may not exist, but a single def-point must be assigned. Several, sometimes conflicting, factors guide the selection process. It is desirable to keep environments as small as possible and to minimize the live ranges of the values manipulated by the target program. For example, the intermediate results of a computation should often be used as soon as they have been determined. This argues for placing some nodes deep in the tree. On the other hand, code hoisting out of loops is achieved through the shallow placement of some nodes.

The placement of nodes in the def-point tree affects the termination properties of the resulting target program. We choose not to require that all computations performed by the unspecialized program be performed by the specialized one. Thus the specialized program may terminate more often than the unspecialized one. Since, in general, evaluating a node may be expensive or even nonterminating, we ensure that no computation is performed by the specialized program unless it is likewise performed by the unspecialized one.

A conditional node is said to *guard* nodes that may be evaluated on one arm of the conditional but not the other. Such a conditional is referred to as a *guard.* A node must be deeper than any of its guards. Otherwise, we say that a guard has been *violated*, possibly allowing the evaluation of a node not evaluated in the unspecialized program. The prohibition against violating the guards of conditionally executed code prevents the specialized program from executing code that would not have been executed by the corresponding unspecialized program. If a node appears only in the consequent of a conditional node, for example, it may not be shallower than the conditional node.

This restriction has two unfortunate consequences. Expressions that are invariant across multiple calls to a procedure may be evaluated repeatedly, and opportunities for the specialized program to avoid needless computations performed by the corresponding unspecialized program may be lost. The code generator safely hoists conditional code by employing memoization. Unfortunately, a description of the mechanism by which it detects and hoists invariant conditional code is beond the scope of this paper.

4.3.3 Assigning Def-Points

The algorithm for finding the def-points of the nodes in a graph begins with a graph traversal starting at the root node. The root is unique in having no parents, and it therefore has no real def-point. To get the recursive algorithm rolling, we assign the root node a fictitious def-point, and make it the first member and root of the def-point tree that we construct as the algorithm progresses.

Once a node's parents have all been added to the def-point tree, the def-point of the node itself can be found. First a bit of terminology. We can think of the def-point tree as being partitioned into procedures, with node N belonging to procedure P if P is the first procedure node on the direct path from N's parent to the root. A node is *definable* within a procedure if each free variable on which the node depends is a formal parameter of some procedure node on the direct path from the node to the root. Now we can formulate a preliminary version of the rule for determining a node's def-point. Recall that we must ensure that a node is defined before it is used, and that no computation is performed by the target program unless it would also be performed by the source program. In addition, we wish to minimize the lifetimes of the intermediate results of computations, and we wish to hoist code out of loops where possible. For the def-point of a node, therefore, we choose the deepest common ancestor within the shallowest procedure for which the node is definable, and for which no guards are violated. The phrase "common ancestor" refers to an ancestor of all of the node's parents.

The above rule is not sufficient, however, since it does not properly manage cycles in the graph. Progress is stalled when each of the nodes that has not yet been added to the def-point tree has a parent that likewise has not yet been added. We account for this by having the specializer keep track of procedure-level lexical structure as it builds the graph. This information is used to break the cycles.

5 Related Research

5.1 Related Automatic Termination Research

The other realistic research on automatic termination methods has been for offline specializers. These methods fall into two classes, which we shall call the Mix [28] approach and the Similix [8] approach. Both methods perform a Binding Time Analysis (BTA) to determine binding time information, ie, which expressions will be dynamic during specialization and which will be static. Mix employs a pass that uses the binding time information to annotate each call with an instruction to the specializer whether to unfold or specialize the call. This pass considers both termination and code duplication when annotating the program. Similix hoists `if` expressions whose predicates are dynamic (called *dynamic ifs*) into their own procedures, and then always specializes these and only these procedures. Both methods usually terminate equally often, but the specializations produced by Similix can be better because Similix generally performs more unfolding. We view Similix as the more powerful method. Similix, like Fuse, builds residual specializations for only the speculative portions of the computation.

Where the offline termination strategies differ most from Fuse's strategy is in the lack of online generalization. Both Mix and Similix overload binding time information to play the role of an abstraction function. When residualization/specialization is chosen, any variable whose binding time value is *dynamic* is effectively boosted to `a-value` before specialization occurs, regardless of its actual value. Specializers that use binding time information as the abstraction function when producing specializations of program points fail to terminate on *counters*, values that are always known and change, but don't affect control flow. For example, we know of no offline specializer that terminates on the "counting up" factorial program or the `iota` program when given an unknown input. They correctly choose to residualize, but then produce an infinite number of specializations. Jones [18] proposed a method for performing further lifting of binding time values to solve this problem, but, there seems to be no published results regarding its use, nor has it been extended along with BTA to handle partially static structures and first class functions.

Although Fuse terminates more often than the offline methods, it sometimes prematurely terminates. We believe that with the additional structual unfolding rule, Fuse explores as much of a computation as Mix does while terminating more often. There are examples where Similix explores more of a computation than Fuse does and still terminates. This is to be expected: since Similix is willing to terminate less often, it can be more aggressive. The major difference between Fuse and Similix is that, when infinite specializations won't arise, Fuse does not know this and prematurely terminates, whereas Similix doesn't prematurely terminate. However, when infinite specializations do arise, Fuse stops, but Similix doesn't. Which strategy is superior depends on the specialization task at hand. We are investigating much more powerful termination strategies that would allow Fuse to continue unfolding in many more instances than it does now. These strategies, incorporated into an experimental specializer called *Melt*, would allow Fuse to dramatically increase the depth of exploration it could do without sacrificing termination.

5.2 Comparing Symbolic Values with *Partial Values* and *Q-tuples*

Symbolic values are closely related to IBL's *partial values* [27] and REDFUN-2's *q-tuples* [17]. (We collectively refer to these objects as *type/code objects.*) All solve the problem of associating type information (as well as other information) with residual code. The differences involve the status of the type/code object itself, what an individual type/code object can represent, and the representation of residual code.

Fuse and IBL, which are interpreters, treat type/code objects as first class values: *i.e.*, they are members of data structures, arguments to functions, and results of functions. Describing structured objects with partially known slots is easy: one simply constructs the object (which is itself a type/code object) out of type/code objects. REDFUN-2, which is designed as part of a "Program Manipulation System," treats type/code objects as the result of a transformation, they are not values passed to a program (though the known values they represent can be passed to a program). In particular, they cannot be elements of data structures, which prevents REDFUN-2 from representing, say, a three element list whose first element is the symbol a and whose other elements are integers. Another drawback is that information is lost during simplification. Consider `(cons x y)` where is it known that x is either 7 or 8. This information is lost when the q-tuple representing the residual cons expression is constructed. If the car of the q-tuple is taken, the symbol x is produced, but it is no longer known that its value is either 7 or 8.

IBL's partial values are not as first class as Fuse's symbolic values. There is no method for the user to create them, or to direct specialization using them. This is because IBL is viewed as an adjunct to a compiler, not as a stand-alone specializer.

The type structure of q-tuples is richer in some ways than that of symbolic values or partial values. Although q-tuples do not express structured values, they can represent arbitrary sets of values, which symbolic values and partial values do not do. For example, a q-tuple can represent the set $\{3, 4, 7\}$, or the set {`alice`, `mary`, `john`}. A q-tuple can also represent specific values that will never be produced at runtime. This richer type structure allows for more accurate specializations.

Both partial values and q-tuples represent code as a tree. This results in code duplication. For the experiments Schooler performed, this duplication was quite a problem. Because symbolic values represent code as graphs, code duplication is not a problem.

5.3 Graphs and Specialization

Perlin [25] uses what he terms *Call Graphs* as the target of partial evaluation. His system differs from FUSE in that it doesn't have typed values, the graphs it produces must correspond to straight-line programs (their control can't depend on the unknown inputs), call graphs cannot call each other directly, and the user controls how the graph is built. It doesn't appear as if intermediate data structures are eliminated. His system has the advantage of interpreting the graphs directly instead of translating them into program text. By remembering the results of computations, his system can incrementally evaluate programs under changing inputs, an important feature for aritificial intelligence production systems, which were Perlin's domain.

6 Conclusions and Future Research

We have solved our goal of constructing a fully automatic and powerful online program specializer. Fuse has excellent termination properties and produces highly specialized programs. We have replicated many of the published experiments in partial evaluation. In [31] we show Fuse compiling programs, and doing so for a naturally written interpreter. We are also now capable of reproducing the work reported in [5] completely automatically. That original work, which dramatically applied program specialization to compiling scientific code, was performed using a manually guided specializer.

Fuse scores well on the issues of residual program structure (code and call duplication) termination, information usage, and polyvariance. Symbolic values allow the propagation of type information, and a graph representation for code allows reductions to be made without concern for program structure. In FUSE, the only decisions made during specialization involve termination, not program representation. Only after the program is partially evaluated do considerations of program layout arise. Because of this separation, FUSE performs extremely thorough specialization. Fuse's termination strategy correctly handles counters, while allowing for completely polyvariant specializations. Our decision to separate termination decisions from residual program structure will continue to pay benefits as Fuse is extended to make use of more information sources, such as the predicates of conditional statements.

We claimed in the introduction that the simplicity of online partial evaluation was a major attraction. Our experiences in using and extending Fuse bears this out. For example, Fuse has no difficulty with, or much knowledge of structured values that contain unknowns. Indeed, somewhat surprisingly, Fuse is virtually the first fully automatic specializer to handle pairs (cons cells) that may themselves contain unknown values. Mogensen [24], who first investigated *partial statics,* apparently never hooked his BTA directly to a specializer (his experiments were performed using hand written call annotations [23], although Sestoft's automatic call annotator [28] could have been used), and Schism [10, 11] is not automatic. While Similix-2 [6] can encode pairs as closures, its monovariant BTA, which doesn't duplicate code at BTA time, makes this encoding method a very fragile mechanism: information can be very easily lost. Another instance of Fuse's power is, that in the presence of higher order functions, Fuse's complete polyvariance can yield much better specializations than Similix-2 or Schism [11] can. (And does so without using macros to manually duplicate code.) These comparisons do not indicate that Fuse is better than Similix-2 or Schism, only that there is a tradeoff between self-applicability (which entails offline strategies) and simple, general, online methods that are not easily amenable to self-application. The other specializers listed here can specialize themselves, while the same cannot be said for Fuse.

Fuse solves many of the problems in constructing an online specializer that Jones anticipated. In particular, we have shown that online specialization is extremely practical, can be made to terminate, uses nonlocal information when it generalizes arguments with previous calls, and is not too expensive.

We have reported on only the basic elements of Fuse. Fuse has several interesting extensions. First, it reasons about residual code to determine the types of values that residual expressions will produce at runtime [31]. This additional information produces much better specialization for a wide class of programs. Second, it avoids redundant specializations [26]. Redundant specialization occurs when two different sets of arguments produce the same specialization. This has not yet been a major problem because specializers have used very weak descriptions of partial objects. As the descriptive system gets more powerful, for example, by the inclusion of a type system such as Fuse's, redundant specialization becomes a more severe problem. Solving redundant specializations also ameliorates some of the difficulty with reasoning about residual code, which requires computing fixed points. The cost of computing these fixed points drops dramatically when redundant specializations are avoided.

We want Fuse to incorporate more of the Scheme programming language. Scheme includes object identity, side-effects, and continuations. We intend to make side-effects explicit in the graph. This means having all side-effects take the resources they mutate (*e.g.*, the store, ports, and identity markers) as arguments and return the mutated resources. This approach turns control flow constraints into dataflow constraints, and simplifies reasoning about side-effects.

References

[1] H. Abelson, G. J. Sussman, and J. Sussman. *Structure and Interpretation of Computer Programs.* MIT Press, 1985.

[2] L. Beckman et al. A partial evaluator and its use as a programming tool. *Artificial Intelligence*, 7(4):291–357, 1976.

[3] A. Berlin. A compilation strategy for numerical programs based on partial evaluation. Master's thesis, Massachusetts Institute of Technology, Cambridge, MA, July 1989. Published as Artificial Intelligence Laboratory Technical Report TR-1144.

[4] A. Berlin. Partial evaluation applied to numerical computation. In *Proceedings of the 1990 ACM Conference on Lisp and Functional Programming*, Nice, France, 1990.

[5] A. Berlin and D. Weise. Compiling scientific programs using partial evaluation. *IEEE Computer Magazine*, 23(12):25–37, December 1990.

[6] A. Bondorf. Automatic autoprojection of higher order recursive equations. In N. Jones, editor, *Proceedings of the 3rd European Symposium on Programming*, pages 70–87. Springer-Verlag, LNCS 432, 1990.

[7] A. Bondorf. *Self-Applicable Partial Evaluation.* PhD thesis, DIKU, University of Copenhangen, Copenhagen, Denmark, December 1990.

[8] A. Bondorf and O. Danvy. Automatic autoprojection for recursive equations with global variables and abstract data types. DIKU Report 90/04, University of Copenhagen, Copenhagen, Denmark, 1990.

[9] R. M. Burstall and J. Darlington. A transformation system for developing recursive programs. *Journal of the ACM*, 24(1):44–67, January 1977.

[10] C. Consel. New insights into partial evaluation: the SCHISM experiment. In *Proceedings of the 2nd European Symposium on Programming*, pages 236–246. Springer-Verlag, LNCS 300, 1988.

[11] C. Consel. Binding time analysis for higher order untyped functional languages. In *Proceedings of the 1990 ACM Conference on Lisp and Functional Programming*, pages 264–272, Nice, France, 1990.

[12] C. Consel and O. Danvy. Partial evaluation of pattern matching in strings. *Information Processing Letters*, 30(2):79–86, 1989.

[13] C. Consel and O. Danvy. From interpreting to compiling binding times. In N. Jones, editor, *Proceedings of the 3rd European Symposium on Programming*, pages 88–105. Springer-Verlag, LNCS 432, 1990.

[14] A. P. Ershov. On the partial computation principle. *Information Processing Letters*, 6(2):38–41, April 1977.

[15] Y. Futamura. Partial evaluation of computation process—an approach to a compiler-compiler. *Systems, Computers, Controls*, 2(5):45–50, 1971.

[16] M. A. Guzowski. Towards developing a reflexive partial evaluator for an interesting subset of LISP. Master's thesis, Dept. of Computer Engineering and Science, Case Western Reserve University, Cleveland, Ohio, January 1988.

[17] A. Haraldsson. *A Program Manipulation System Based on Partial Evaluation.* PhD thesis, Linköping University, 1977. Published as Linköping Studies in Science and Technology Dissertation No. 14.

[18] N. D. Jones. Automatic program specialization: A re-examination from basic principles. In D. Bjørner, A. P. Ershov, and N. D. Jones, editors, *Partial Evaluation and Mixed Computation*, pages 225–282. North-Holland, 1988.

[19] N. D. Jones, P. Sestoft, and H. Søndergaard. An experiment in partial evaluation: The generation of a compiler generator. In *Rewriting Techniques and Applications*, pages 124–140. Springer-Verlag, LNCS 202, 1985.

[20] N. D. Jones, P. Sestoft, and H. Søndergaard. Mix: A self-applicable partial evaluator for experiments in compiler generation. *Lisp and Symbolic Computation*, 1(3/4):9–50, 1988.

[21] K. M. Kahn. A partial evaluator of Lisp written in Prolog. Technical Report 17, UPMAIL, Department of Computing Science, Uppsala University, Uppsala, Sweden, February 1983.

[22] L. A. Lombardi and B. Raphael. Lisp as the language for an incremental computer. In Berkeley and Bobrow, editors, *The Programming Language Lisp*, pages 204–219. MIT Press, Cambridge, MA, 1964.

[23] T. Mogensen. Partially static structures. In D. Bjørner, A. P. Ershov, and N. D. Jones, editors, *Partial Evaluation and Mixed Computation*, pages 325–347. North-Holland, 1988.

[24] T. Mogensen. *Binding Time Aspects of Partial Evaluation.* PhD thesis, DIKU, University of Copenhangen, Copenhagen, Denmark, March 1989.

[25] M. Perlin. Call-graph caching: Transforming programs into networks. In *Proceedings of the 11th International Joint Conference on Artificial Intelligence*, pages 122–128, 1989.

[26] E. Ruf and D. Weise. Using types to avoid redundant specialization. In *Proceedings of the 1991 ACM SIGPLAN Symposium on Partial Evaluation and Semantics-Based Program Manipulation*, New Haven, CN, June 1991.

[27] R. Schooler. Partial evaluation as a means of language extensibility. Master's thesis, MIT, Cambridge, MA, August 1984. Published as MIT/LCS/TR-324.

[28] P. Sestoft. Automatic call unfolding in a partial evaluator. In D. Bjørner, A. P. Ershov, and N. D. Jones, editors, *Partial Evaluation and Mixed Computation*, pages 485–506. North-Holland, 1988.

[29] G. L. Steele Jr. Rabbit: A compiler for Scheme. Technical Report AI-TR-474, MIT Artificial Intelligence Laboratory, Cambridge, MA, 1978.

[30] V. Turchin. The concept of a supercompiler. *ACM Transactions on Programming Languages and Systems*, 8(3):292–325, 1986.

[31] D. Weise and E. Ruf. Computing types during program specialization. Technical Report CSL-TR-90-441, Computer Systems Laboratory, Stanford University, Stanford, CA, 1990.

Assignments for Applicative Languages

Vipin Swarup* The MITRE Corporation

Uday S. Reddy† University of Illinois at Urbana-Champaign

Evan Ireland‡ Massey University

Abstract

We propose a theoretical framework for adding assignments and dynamic data to functional languages without violating their semantic properties. This differs from semi-functional languages like Scheme and ML in that values of expressions remain static and side-effect-free. A new form of abstraction called *observer* is designed to encapsulate state-oriented computation from the remaining purely applicative computation. The type system ensures that observers are combined linearly, allowing an implementation in terms of a global store. The utility of this extension is in manipulating *shared dynamic data* embedded in data structures. Evaluation of well-typed programs is Church-Rosser. Thus, programs produce the same results whether an eager or lazy evaluation order is used (assuming termination). A simple, sound logic permits reasoning about well-typed programs. The benefits of this work include greater expressive power and efficiency (compared to applicative languages), while retaining simplicity of reasoning.

Keywords Functional languages, imperative programming, lambda calculus, type systems, strong normalization, Church-Rosser property, referential transparency, continuation-passing style.

1 Introduction

Functional languages are popular among computer scientists because of their strong support of modularity. They possess two powerful glues, higher-order functions and laziness, that permit programs to be modularized in new, useful ways. Hughes [Hug90] convincingly argues that "...lazy evaluation is too important to be relegated to second-class citizenship. It is perhaps the most powerful glue functional programmers possess. One should not obstruct access to such a vital tool." However, side-effects are incompatible with laziness: programming with them requires knowledge of global context, defeating the very modularity that lazy evaluation is designed to enhance.

* Address: The MITRE Corporation, Burlington Road, Bedford, MA 01730; E-mail: swarup@mitre.org; Supported by NASA grant NAG-1-613 (while at the University of Illinois at Urbana-Champaign).

† Address: Department of Computer Science, University of Illinois at Urbana-Champaign, Urbana, IL 61801; E-mail: reddy@cs.uiuc.edu; Supported by a grant from Motorola Corporation.

‡ Address: School of Information Sciences, Massey University, Palmerston North, New Zealand; E-mail: E.Ireland@massey.ac.nz

Pure functional languages have nice properties that make them easy to reason about. For instance, + is commutative, = is reflexive, and most other familiar mathematical properties hold of the computational operators. This is a consequence of expressions representing *static* values: values that do not change over time. Thus, an expression's value is independent of the order in which its subexpressions are evaluated. Side-effects are incompatible with these properties, as side-effects change the values of other expressions, making the order of evaluation important.

Assignments are a means of describing *dynamic* data : data whose values change over time. In their conventional form, assignments have side-effects on their environment, making their order of evaluation important. Not only are such assignments incompatible with laziness, but they also destroy the nice mathematical properties of pure languages. Hence lazy functional languages shun assignments.

However, since assignments directly model the dynamic behavior of a physical computer's store, they yield efficient implementations of dynamic data. In contrast, one models dynamic data in functional languages by representing the state explicitly or, possibly, by creating streams of states. Compilation techniques and language notations have been proposed to permit explicit state manipulation to be implemented efficiently [HB85, GH90, Wad90b, Wad90a]. Unfortunately, these methods do not achieve all the effects of true dynamic data. For instance, dynamic data may be "shared", i.e., embedded in data structures and accessed via different access paths. When shared dynamic data are updated using assignments, the change is visible to all program points that have access to the data. In contrast, when state is being manipulated explicitly, updating shared data involves constructing a fresh copy of the entire data structure in which the data are embedded, and explicitly passing the copy to all program points that need access to the data. This tends to be tedious and error-prone, and results in poor modularity. One particularly faces this difficulty while encoding graph traversal algorithms such as topological sort, unification and the graph reduction execution model of lazy functional languages.

In this paper, we propose a theoretical framework for extending functional languages with dynamic data and assignments while retaining the desirable properties of static values. The resulting language has the following key properties:

- Expressions have static values.
  State-dependent and state-independent expressions are distinguished via a type system. The former are viewed as functions from states to values and the functions themselves are static. (Such functions are called *observers* and resemble classical continuations [Sto77, SW74]). The type system ensures that this view can be consistently maintained, and limits the interaction between observers in such a way that expressions do not have side-effects [1].

- The language is a strict extension of lambda calculus.
  Function abstraction and application have precisely the same meaning as in

[1] In the contemporary functional programming community, the terms "assignment" and "side-effect" are sometimes used synonymously. We use the term "side-effect" in its original meaning: an expression has a side-effect if, in addition to yielding a value, it changes the state in a manner that affects the values of other expressions in the context. Assignments in our proposed language do not have such side-effects. Similar comments apply to terms like "procedure" and "object".

lambda calculus. This is a key property that is not respected by call-by-value languages like Scheme (even in the absence of side-effects). The operational semantics is presented as a reduction system that consists of the standard reduction rules of lambda calculus together with a set of additional rules; these rules exhibit symmetries similar to those of lambda calculus. The reduction system is *confluent* (or, equivalently, Church-Rosser), and recursion-free terms are *strongly normalizing.*

This work can also be given a logical interpretation: it extends the correspondence between logic and programming to include dynamic data. Entities that describe dynamic data, namely references, play a role similar to that of variables in conventional logic. The language described in this paper is the language of constructions for a suitably formulated constructive logic. This dual aspect is treated elsewhere [SR91, Swa91].

The utility of the language is characterized by the following properties:

- Shared dynamic data are available.
  Dynamic data are represented by typed objects called *references.* References can refer to other references as well as to functions. They can be embedded in data structures and used as inputs and outputs of functions.

- Dynamic data may be implemented by a store.
  This is achieved by a type system that sequentializes access to regions of the state, much as in effect systems [GL86] and the languages based on linear logic [GH90, Wad90b, Wad91].

- The language is higher-order.
  References, data structures, functions and observers are all permissible as arguments and results of functions. This permits, for instance, the definition of new control structures, new storage allocation mechanisms, and an object-oriented style of programming.

- The language is integrated symmetrically.
  The applicative sublanguage and the imperative sublanguage are equally powerful and they embed each other. Not only can applicative terms be embedded in imperative terms, but imperative terms can also be embedded in applicative terms. This allows the definition of functions that create and use state internally but are state-independent externally.

The remainder of this paper is organized as follows. Section 2 presents a core formal language called Imperative Lambda Calculus (ILC) that is an extension of the typed lambda calculus. Section 3 studies ILC's use in programming. Section 4 discusses the motivation and design issues behind ILC's type system. Section 5 presents the formal semantics of ILC. This includes a typed denotational semantics and an operational semantics presented as reduction rules. Various formal properties are established, such as type soundness, confluence and strong normalization. Section 6 demonstrates the utility of ILC with an extended example: the unification of first-order terms. Finally, Section 7 compares ILC with related work in the literature.

2 Imperative Lambda Calculus (ILC)

Imperative Lambda Calculus (ILC) is an abstract formal language obtained by extending the typed lambda calculus [Mit90] with imperative programming features. Its main property is that, in spite of this extension, its applicative sublanguage has the same semantic properties as the typed lambda calculus (eg. confluence and strong normalization). Furthermore, these same properties also hold for the entire language of ILC.

2.1 Types

Let β represent the primitive types of ILC. These may include the natural numbers, characters, strings etc. The syntax of ILC types is as follows:

$$
\begin{array}{lcll}
\tau & ::= & \beta \mid \tau_1 \times \tau_2 \mid \tau_1 \rightarrow \tau_2 & \text{(Applicative types)} \\
\theta & ::= & \tau \mid \texttt{Ref}\ \theta \mid \theta_1 \times \theta_2 \mid \theta_1 \rightarrow \theta_2 & \text{(Mutable types)} \\
\omega & ::= & \theta \mid \texttt{Obs}\ \tau \mid \omega_1 \times \omega_2 \mid \omega_1 \rightarrow \omega_2 & \text{(Observer types)}
\end{array}
$$

The type system is stratified into three layers. The *applicative* layer τ contains the types of the simply typed lambda calculus (extended with pairs). These applicative types include the primitive types β and are closed under product and function space constructions. Note that we use the term "applicative" to refer to the *classical* values manipulated in lambda calculus; semantically, all three layers of ILC are applicative.

The *mutable* layer θ extends the applicative layer with objects called *references*. References are typed values that refer (i.e. point) to values of a particular type. ($\texttt{Ref}\ \theta$) denotes the type of references that refer to values of type θ. References are used to construct a mutable world (called a *store*) that is used for imperative programming. The world itself is mutable and goes through *states*. The mutable layer includes all applicative types and is closed under the type constructors $\times, \rightarrow$ and **Ref**. Note that references can point to other references, thereby permitting linked data structures. Tuples of references denote mutable records, while reference-returning functions denote mutable arrays.

Finally, the world of the mutable layer needs to be manipulated. In ILC, we take the position that the only manipulation needed for states is *observation* (i.e. inspection). Consider the fact that in the typed lambda calculus, environments are implicitly extended and observed (via the use of variables), but are never explicitly manipulated. Similarly, in ILC, states are implicitly extended and observed (via the use of references), but are never explicitly manipulated. Thus, in a sense, *the world exists only to be observed.* A state differs from an environment in that it may be mutated while being observed; the mutation is restricted to the observation and is not visible to expressions outside the observation.

Observation of the state is accommodated in the *observer* layer ω. This layer includes all applicative and mutable types. In addition, it includes a new type constructor denoted "$\texttt{Obs}\ \tau$". A value of type $\texttt{Obs}\ \tau$ is called an *observer.* Such a value observes (i.e. views or inspects) a state and returns a value of type τ. It is significant that the value returned in this fashion is of an applicative type τ. Since a state exists only to be observed, all information about the state is lost when its observation is completed. So, the values observed in this fashion should be meaningful independent of the state, i.e., they should be applicative. An observer type `Obs` τ may be viewed as an implicit function space from the set of states to the type τ.

The three layers can be characterized as ***kinds*** and given category-theoretic semantics. The product and function space constructions have the same meaning in all three layers (cf. Section 5). Thus, there is no ambiguity involved in treating τ types as also being θ and ω types. The name "Imperative Lambda Calculus" is justified by the property that the semantics of functions in all three layers is the same as that of lambda calculus.

2.2 Terms

The abstract syntax of unchecked "preterms" is as follows:

$$\begin{array}{lcl} e & ::= & k \mid x \mid v^* \mid \lambda x{:}\,\omega.e \mid f(e) \mid \langle e_1, e_2\rangle \mid e.1 \mid e.2 \\ & & \mid \texttt{letref}\ v^*{:}\,\texttt{Ref}\ \theta := e\ \texttt{in}\ t \\ & & \mid \texttt{get}\ x{:}\,\theta \Leftarrow l\ \texttt{in}\ t \\ & & \mid l := e\ ;\ t \end{array}$$

where k are constants, x, v^* are variables, e, e_1, e_2, f, l, t are terms and ω, θ are types.

The constants of ILC ***are limited to be of applicative type.*** Permissible constants include numbers, booleans, characters and primitive functions on these values. No imperative constants (i.e. no constants involving mutable or observer types) are permitted. This permits us to carefully control the creation and use of the state. We (partially) relax this restriction in section 5.1.

The terms of ILC use two countable sets of variables: ***conventional variables*** and ***reference variables***. Conventional variables are the usual variables of the typed lambda calculus. Reference variables are a new set of variables that share all the properties of conventional variables. Further, distinct reference variables within a term always denote distinct references. References are always introduced by binding them to reference variables; conventional variables can then be bound to such references. This property permits us to reason about the equality of references without recourse to reference constants (which are absent from the language). In the formal presentation, we use an asterisk superscript to distinguish reference variables u^*, v^*, w^* from conventional variables x, y, z. Since the context of a variable determines whether it is a reference or conventional variable, we do not use asterisk superscripts in any of our examples.

Figure 1 presents the context sensitive type syntax of ILC terms. The syntax is expressed as inference rules for judgements of the form $(\Gamma \vdash e{:}\,\pi)$, where e is a term, π is a type (of any kind τ, θ or ω), and Γ is a sequence of typing assumptions of the forms $(x{:}\,\pi)$ or $(v^*{:}\,\texttt{Ref}\ \theta)$. Γ contains typing assumptions for all the free variables in e.

ILC includes the simply-typed lambda calculus extended with pairs. These terms have their usual meaning in all three layers (rules ***→-intro***, ***→-elim***, ***×-intro***,

Constant

$$\Gamma \vdash k : \tau$$
(if k is a constant of type τ)

Weakening

$$\frac{\Gamma \vdash e : \pi}{\Gamma, x : \pi' \vdash e : \pi}$$

Variable hypothesis

$$\Gamma, x : \pi, \Gamma' \vdash x : \pi$$

Reference hypothesis

$$\Gamma, v^* : \mathtt{Ref}\ \theta, \Gamma' \vdash v^* : \mathtt{Ref}\ \theta$$

→-intro

$$\frac{\Gamma, x : \pi_1 \vdash e : \pi_2}{\Gamma \vdash (\lambda x : \pi_1 . e) : \pi_1 \rightarrow \pi_2}$$

→-elim

$$\frac{\Gamma \vdash f : \pi_1 \rightarrow \pi_2 \quad \Gamma \vdash e : \pi_1}{\Gamma \vdash f(e) : \pi_2}$$

×-intro

$$\frac{\Gamma \vdash e_1 : \pi_1 \quad \Gamma \vdash e_2 : \pi_2}{\Gamma \vdash \langle e_1, e_2 \rangle : \pi_1 \times \pi_2}$$

×-elim

$$\frac{\Gamma \vdash e : \pi_1 \times \pi_2}{\Gamma \vdash e.i : \pi_i} \quad \text{for } i = 1, 2$$

Obs-intro

$$\frac{\Gamma \vdash t : \tau}{\Gamma \vdash t : \mathtt{Obs}\ \tau}$$

Obs-elim

$$\frac{\Gamma \vdash t : \mathtt{Obs}\ \tau}{\Gamma \vdash t : \tau} \quad \text{(if } \Gamma \text{ has only } \tau \text{ types)}$$

Creation

$$\frac{\Gamma, v^* : \mathtt{Ref}\ \theta \vdash e : \theta \quad \Gamma, v^* : \mathtt{Ref}\ \theta \vdash t : \mathtt{Obs}\ \tau}{\Gamma \vdash (\mathtt{letref}\ v^* : \mathtt{Ref}\ \theta := e\ \mathtt{in}\ t) : \mathtt{Obs}\ \tau}$$

Dereference

$$\frac{\Gamma \vdash l : \mathtt{Ref}\ \theta \quad \Gamma, x : \theta \vdash t : \mathtt{Obs}\ \tau}{\Gamma \vdash (\mathtt{get}\ x : \theta \Leftarrow l\ \mathtt{in}\ t) : \mathtt{Obs}\ \tau}$$

Assignment

$$\frac{\Gamma \vdash l : \mathtt{Ref}\ \theta \quad \Gamma \vdash e : \theta \quad \Gamma \vdash t : \mathtt{Obs}\ \tau}{\Gamma \vdash (l := e\ ;\ t) : \mathtt{Obs}\ \tau}$$

Figure 1: Type inference rules

and $\times$-*elim*). In addition, ILC contains three new observer terms to create a new reference (*creation*), access a reference's content (*dereference*), and modify a reference's content (*assignment*). We now discuss these terms in more detail.

We have seen that there are no reference constants in the language. All references have to be explicitly allocated and bound to a reference variable. This is done by the `letref` construct:

$$\texttt{letref } v^*\texttt{: Ref } \theta := e \texttt{ in } t$$

Such a term is an observer of the same type as t (rule *Creation*). When used to observe a state, it extends the state by creating a new reference, extends the environment by binding v^* to the reference, initializes the reference to the value of e in the extended environment, and finally observes the value of t in the extended environment and state.

The mutable world of references may be inspected by dereferencing a reference, i.e. by inspecting the value that the reference points to, or, using alternate terminology, by inspecting the reference's *content*. If l is a reference-valued expression of type $\texttt{Ref } \theta$, then a term of the form

$$\texttt{get } x\texttt{: }\theta \Leftarrow l \texttt{ in } t$$

binds x to the content of l, and denotes the value of t in the extended environment. Here, t must be an observer of type $\texttt{Obs } \tau$, and the entire term is again an observer of type $\texttt{Obs } \tau$ (rule *Dereference*).

Finally, the content of a reference may be modified via assignment observers of the form

$$l := e \, ; \, t$$

where l is of type $\texttt{Ref } \theta$ and e is of type θ, for some θ (rule *Assignment*). When used to observe a state, an assignment observer modifies the reference l to refer to e, and observes the value of t in the modified state. Note that "$l := e$" is not a term by itself as in conventional languages. The state is modified *for* the observer t, and the entire construct is again an observer.

The lifetime of a mutable world (i.e. a collection of references) is limited to its observation. So, the creation of v^* and the modification of l are observable only within the bodies t of the creation and assignment observers respectively, and there are no side effects produced by the observers. If there are no free occurrences of reference variables or other state-dependent variables in an observer term, then the term is a trivial observer that is independent of any state. Such an observer can be coerced to an applicative term (rule *Obs-elim*). Conversely, every applicative term (every term of a τ type) is trivially an observer (rule *Obs-intro*).

It is important to note that all the primitive constructions on observers (get, letref and assignment) involve exactly one subterm of an observer type. This reflects the requirement that manipulations of state should be performed in a sequential fashion, similar in spirit to the proposal of single-threaded lambda calculus [GH90]. Even though it is possible to express functions which accept more than one observer, the state manipulations of such observers have to be eventually sequentialized because there are no multi-ary primitives on observers. (Recall that there are no constants of mutable and observer types). This fact has two consequences. First, programming in the imperative sublanguage of ILC requires a continuation-passing style. Second, the state can be implemented efficiently by means of a global store. We return to these issues in section 4.

3 ILC as a Programming Language

ILC can be used as a programming language in different styles. It can be used as a purely applicative language by restricting oneself to applicative types. It can be used as a purely imperative language by mainly using observers (this requires a continuation-passing style of programming). These styles correspond to traditional programming paradigms.

ILC also permits an interesting new style of programming. It permits closed imperative observers to be embedded in applicative terms (via the rule *Obs-elim*). Applicative terms can be freely embedded in imperative observers (via the rule *Obs-intro*). Higher-order functions and laziness can be used to glue together both imperative and applicative subcomputations, though imperative computation is restricted to continuation-passing style.

One extreme of this paradigm is to use ILC with imperative observers at the top level, but with nontrivial applicative subcomputations involving higher-order functions. This use is similar to that of Haskell where state-oriented input/output operations are usually carried out at the top level. More generally, ILC can be used with imperative observers embedded in applicative expressions (via the rule *Obs-elim*). This corresponds to the use of side-effect-free function procedures in Algol-like languages.

The examples in this paper further illustrate this style of programming. Example 1 (factorial) displays how imperative computations can be embedded in applicative terms. Example 2 (a movable point object) exhibits how imperative computations can be encapsulated as closures. The unification example of Section 6 demonstrates how the laziness of observers permits them to be passed to functions and returned as results.

3.1 Syntactic sugar for dereferencing

The need to use get's for dereferencing is rather tedious: it forces us to choose new names, and more importantly, it clutters up the code. The tedium can be alleviated to a large extent through a simple notational mechanism.

Abbreviation: If ($\mathbf{get}\ x \Leftarrow l\ \mathbf{in}\ t[x]$) is an observer term with no occurrence of x in a proper observer subterm of t, then we allow it to be abbreviated as $t[l\uparrow]$. $l\uparrow$ may be read informally as "the current content of reference l".

Expansion: If t is an observer term with a particular occurrence of $l\uparrow$, then it is expanded by introducing a "get" at the smallest observer subterm of t containing the occurrence of $l\uparrow$.

The intuition behind this abbreviation is that an observer term ($\mathbf{get}\ x \Leftarrow l\ \mathbf{in}\ t$) is a program point at which the content of l is observed, while occurrences of x in

t are program points at which that content is used. If l is never modified between the point of dereference and a point of use, then we can safely view the dereference as taking place at the point of use. For example,

$$\begin{aligned}&(p := n\uparrow * p\uparrow;\ n := n\uparrow -1;\ c)\\ &\quad = \texttt{get}\ x \Leftarrow n\ \texttt{in}\ \texttt{get}\ y \Leftarrow p\ \texttt{in}\\ &\qquad\quad p := x * y;\\ &\qquad\quad \texttt{get}\ z \Leftarrow n\ \texttt{in}\\ &\qquad\qquad\quad n := z - 1;\ c\end{aligned}$$

$$l\uparrow\uparrow = (\texttt{get}\ x \Leftarrow l\ \texttt{in}\ x\uparrow) = (\texttt{get}\ x \Leftarrow l\ \texttt{in}\ \texttt{get}\ y \Leftarrow x\ \texttt{in}\ y)$$

$$f(l\uparrow) = (\texttt{get}\ x \Leftarrow l\ \texttt{in}\ f(x)) \qquad \text{if} f : \tau_1 \rightarrow \texttt{Obs}\ \tau_2$$

$$f(l\uparrow) = f(\texttt{get}\ x \Leftarrow l\ \texttt{in}\ x) \qquad \text{if} f : \texttt{Obs}\ \tau_1 \rightarrow \texttt{Obs}\ \tau_2$$

3.2 Examples

For our examples, we assume that ILC is enhanced with user-defined type constructors and record types (drawn from standard ML [MTH90]). We also assume that ILC is enhanced with *explicit* parametric polymorphism with types ranging over the universe of applicative (τ) types. Implicit polymorphism is problematic in the presence of references and assignments [Tof88] — explicit polymorphism does not suffer from these problems. In our examples, we erase explicit type quantification and type application, and leave it to the reader to fill in the missing information.

We also assume primitives such as `case`, `let`, `letrec` and `if-then-else` for all types. Note that these primitives violate our earlier prohibition of primitives over mutable and observer types. In section 5.1, we shall see that such primitives are indeed permissible.

Example 1: Factorial

This trivial example is meant to provide an initial feel for the language, and illustrate how imperative observers can be embedded in applicative expressions. This example is not meant to illustrate the benefits of ILC; indeed, a preferred solution is to write this as a tail-recursive applicative function and have the compiler optimize the code into an iterative loop.

```
factorial  =  λm:nat. letref n:Ref nat := m in
                      letref acc:Ref nat := 1 in
                      letrec fact:Obs nat =  if (n↑< 2) then acc↑
                                             else acc := n↑ * acc↑;
                                                  n := n↑ -1;
                                                  fact
                      in fact
```

The function `factorial` has no free references or state-dependent variables, and so has the applicative type (`nat` → `nat`). This means that `factorial` can be freely embedded in applicative expressions even though it contains imperative subcomputations.

Example 2: Points

We implement a point object that hides its internal state and exports operations. Let `Point` be the type of objects that represent movable planar points.

$$\begin{aligned}\texttt{Point} \;=\; \{&\text{x\_coord} : (\texttt{Real} \rightarrow \texttt{Obs}\ T) \rightarrow \texttt{Obs}\ T,\\ &\text{y\_coord} : (\texttt{Real} \rightarrow \texttt{Obs}\ T) \rightarrow \texttt{Obs}\ T,\\ &\text{move} : (\texttt{Real} \times \texttt{Real}) \rightarrow \texttt{Obs}\ T \rightarrow \texttt{Obs}\ T,\\ &\text{equal} : \texttt{Point} \rightarrow (\texttt{Bool} \rightarrow \texttt{Obs}\ T) \rightarrow \texttt{Obs}\ T\}\end{aligned}$$

The function `mkpoint` implements objects of type `Point`.

$$\begin{aligned}\texttt{mkpoint} \;:\;& (\texttt{Real} \rightarrow \texttt{Real} \rightarrow (\text{Point} \rightarrow \texttt{Obs}\ T) \rightarrow \texttt{Obs}\ T)\\ =\;& \lambda x.\ \lambda y.\ \lambda k.\\ & \texttt{letref}\ xc\text{:}\,\texttt{Real} := x\ \texttt{in}\\ & \texttt{letref}\ yc\text{:}\,\texttt{Real} := y\ \texttt{in}\\ & k(\{\text{x\_coord} = \lambda k.\ k(xc\uparrow),\\ & \quad \text{y\_coord} = \lambda k.\ k(yc\uparrow),\\ & \quad \text{move} = \lambda(dx, dy).\ \lambda c.\ xc := xc\uparrow + dx;\ yc := yc\uparrow + dy;\ c,\\ & \quad \text{equal} = \lambda\{x\_coord, y\_coord, move, equal\}.\ \lambda k.\\ & \qquad\qquad x\_coord(\lambda x.\ y\_coord(\lambda y.\\ & \qquad\qquad\quad k(x = xc\uparrow\ \text{and}\ y = yc\uparrow)))\\ & \quad \})\end{aligned}$$

Note, first of all, that the `mkpoint` operation cannot simply yield a value of type `Point` because it is not an applicative value. The extent of xc and yc is limited to the bodies of the `letrefs` which allocate these references; hence the entire computation which uses these references must occur in these bodies. Therefore, `mkpoint` is defined to accept a point observer function k and pass it the newly created point. This is similar to the continuation-passing style of programming. Observers here play the role of continuations.[2] Such continuation-passing style functions can be defined more conveniently using Wadler's monad comprehension notation [Wad90a]. Note that each operation in the object is similarly defined in the continuation-passing style.

This example demonstrates that state-encapsulating closures are available in ILC, albeit in the continuation-passing style. Such closures are also representable in semi-functional languages like Scheme and Standard ML, but usually involve side-effects.

---

[2] Technically speaking, observers are not continuations because they return values. But, they can be thought of as continuations in the imperative sublanguage so that the "answers" produced can then be consumed in the applicative sublanguage.

4 Discussion of ILC

The motivation behind ILC's type system is threefold. First, we wish to exclude imperative terms that "export" their local effects. Consider the unchecked preterm ($\texttt{letref}\ v := 0\ \texttt{in}\ v$). This term, if well-typed, would export the locally created reference v outside its scope resulting in a dangling pointer. Closures that capture references are prohibited for the same reason — they export state information beyond its local scope. The type system prohibits such terms by requiring the value returned by an observer to be applicative and hence free of state information. (Recall that observer types are of the form $\texttt{Obs}\ \tau$ where τ is an applicative type).

Second, we wish to ensure that the imperative sublanguage can be implemented efficiently without causing side-effects. Consider the unchecked preterm

$$v := 0\ ;\ ((v := 2\ ;\ \texttt{get}\ x \Leftarrow v\ \texttt{in}\ x) + (\texttt{get}\ x \Leftarrow v\ \texttt{in}\ x))$$

In a language with a global store and global assignments (eg. ML or Scheme), the value of the term depends on the order of evaluation of +'s arguments. Further, the term has the side-effect of changing the value of the global reference v to 2. On the other hand, if assignments are interpreted to have local effects, then the value of the term would be 2 regardless of the order of evaluation, and the term would not have any side-effects. However, the state can no longer be implemented by a (global) store. The state needs to be copied and passed to each argument of +, making the language quite inefficient.

The type system of ILC excludes such terms from the language by requiring that all state-manipulations be performed in a sequential fashion. Well-typed terms of ILC do not require the state to be copied, and hence the state can be implemented by a (global) store. The only legal way to express the above example in ILC, is to sequentialize its assignments. For example,

$$v := 0\ ;\ \texttt{get}\ x \Leftarrow v\ \texttt{in}\ (v := 2\ ;\ \texttt{get}\ y \Leftarrow v\ \texttt{in}\ (y + x))$$

is a well-typed term.

ILC distinguishes between state-dependent observers and applicative values. Both observers and values can be passed to functions and returned as results — it is not necessary to evaluate an observer to a value before passing it. In fact, an observer of the form ($\texttt{get}\ x \Leftarrow l\ \texttt{in}\ t$) is in head normal form, just as a lambda expression is in head normal form (see section 5.2). This is a form of laziness and, in fact, directly corresponds to Algol's call by name. However, an observer passed to a function can only be evaluated in a single state due to the single-threaded nature of the type system. So, the ambiguities caused by Algol's call-by-name are not shared by ILC.

Finally, we wish the type system to ensure that all recursion-free terms are strongly normalizable, i.e., their evaluation always terminates. We postpone a discussion of this issue to section 5.2. For now, we merely note that strong normalization is achieved by making observers non-storable values. If strong normalization is not considered critical, the θ and ω layers may be conflated.

The type system described thus far is overly restrictive. It prohibits all nonsequential combinations of observers in order to ensure that the state is never copied.

For example, a term of the form

$$(v := 0\ ;\ (\texttt{get}\ x \Leftarrow v\ \texttt{in}\ x) + (\texttt{get}\ x \Leftarrow v\ \texttt{in}\ x))$$

is excluded because the observer arguments of + are combined nonsequentially. However, this term does not require the state to be copied since the arguments of + do not locally modify the state. This suggests that the type system could be relaxed by distinguishing between:

- *creators*, that locally extend the state;
- *pure observers*, that observe the state without locally extending or modifying it; and
- *mutators*, that locally modify the state.

The type system could then permit certain state-dependent terms to be combined. For example, two pure observers could be safely combined. To be effective, such a solution would also have to incorporate a comprehensive type system that captures "effects" of expressions on "regions" of references (similar to that of FX [LG88]). This would permit combining mutators that mutate disjoint regions of the state. We do not explore this solution in this paper because it is orthogonal to the issues considered here. It is also clear that such a type system does not completely eliminate the need for sequencing.

5 Semantics of ILC

We present the denotational and operational semantics of ILC, and sketch the proofs of several important properties including soundness, strong normalization and confluence.

5.1 Denotational semantics

The denotational semantics is defined using complete partial orders (cpo's) as domains. For every primitive type β, choose a domain D_β. $D_{\tau\times\tau}$ and $D_{\tau\to\tau}$ are defined by the standard product and continuous function space constructions on cpo's.

For every reference type $\texttt{Ref}\ \theta$, choose a countable flat domain $D_{\texttt{Ref}\ \theta}$. The defined elements of a $D_{\texttt{Ref}\ \theta}$ domain should be disjoint from those of any other such domain. The defined elements of these domains may be thought of as "locations". $\texttt{State}$ is the set of partial mappings σ from $\bigcup_\theta D_{\texttt{Ref}\ \theta}$ to $\bigcup_\theta D_\theta$ with the constraint that, whenever $\alpha \in D_{\texttt{Ref}\ \theta}$, $\sigma(\alpha) \in D_\theta$ and $\sigma(\bot_{\texttt{Ref}\ \theta}) = \bot_\theta$. The subset of $\bigcup_\theta D_{\texttt{Ref}\ \theta}$ mapped by σ is denoted $dom(\sigma)$. σ_0 is the "empty" state, i.e., $dom(\sigma_0)$ contains only $\bot_{\texttt{Ref}\ \theta}$ elements.

The domain for an observation type is $D_{\texttt{Obs}\ \tau} = [\texttt{State} \to D_\tau]$.

An environment η is a mapping from variables to $\bigcup_\omega D_\omega$. If Γ is a type assignment, we say that η satisfies Γ if $\eta(x) \in D_\omega$ for every $x{:}\,\omega \in \Gamma$, $\eta(v^*) \in D_{\texttt{Ref}\ \theta}$ for every $v^*{:}\,\texttt{Ref}\ \theta \in \Gamma$, and $\eta(v^*) \neq \eta(w^*)$ for every $v^*, w^*{:}\,\texttt{Ref}\ \theta \in \Gamma$.

$$
\begin{array}{lcl}
[\![\Gamma \vdash x{:}\,\omega]\!]\,\eta & = & \eta x \\
[\![\Gamma \vdash (\lambda x{:}\,\omega_1.e){:}\,\omega_1 \to \omega_2]\!]\,\eta & = & \lambda v \in D_{\omega_1}.[\![\Gamma, x{:}\,\omega_1 \vdash e{:}\,\omega_2]\!]\,(\eta[x \to v]) \\
[\![\Gamma \vdash f(e){:}\,\omega_2]\!]\,\eta & = & ([\![\Gamma \vdash f{:}\,\omega_1 \to \omega_2]\!]\,\eta)([\![\Gamma \vdash e{:}\,\omega_1]\!]\,\eta) \\
[\![\Gamma \vdash \langle e_1, e_2\rangle{:}\,\omega_1 \times \omega_2]\!]\,\eta & = & \langle [\![\Gamma \vdash e_1{:}\,\omega_1]\!]\,\eta, [\![\Gamma \vdash e_2{:}\,\omega_2]\!]\,\eta\rangle \\
[\![\Gamma \vdash e.1{:}\,\omega_1]\!]\,\eta & = & \mathtt{fst}([\![\Gamma \vdash e{:}\,\omega_1 \times \omega_2]\!]\,\eta) \\
[\![\Gamma \vdash e.2{:}\,\omega_2]\!]\,\eta & = & \mathtt{snd}([\![\Gamma \vdash e{:}\,\omega_1 \times \omega_2]\!]\,\eta)
\end{array}
$$

$$
\begin{array}{lcl}
[\![\Gamma \vdash e{:}\,\tau]\!]\,\eta & = & [\![\Gamma \vdash e{:}\,\mathtt{Obs}\ \tau]\!]\,\eta\,\sigma_0 \\
[\![\Gamma \vdash e{:}\,\mathtt{Obs}\ \tau]\!]\,\eta & = & \lambda\sigma.[\![\Gamma \vdash e{:}\,\tau]\!]\,\eta
\end{array}
$$

$$
\begin{array}{lcl}
\multicolumn{3}{l}{[\![\Gamma \vdash (\mathtt{letref}\ v^*{:}\,\mathtt{Ref}\ \theta := e\ \mathtt{in}\ t){:}\,\mathtt{Obs}\ \tau]\!]\,\eta} \\
 & = & \lambda\sigma.[\![\Gamma, v^*{:}\,\mathtt{Ref}\ \theta \vdash t{:}\,\mathtt{Obs}\ \tau]\!]\,(\eta[v^* \to \alpha])\,(\sigma[\alpha \to v_e]) \\
 & & \text{where } \alpha \text{ is any element of } D_{\mathtt{Ref}\ \theta} \text{ not in } dom(\sigma) \\
 & & \text{and } v_e = [\![\Gamma, v^*{:}\,\mathtt{Ref}\ \theta \vdash e{:}\,\theta]\!]\,(\eta[v^* \to \alpha]) \\
\multicolumn{3}{l}{[\![\Gamma \vdash (\mathtt{get}\ x{:}\,\theta \Leftarrow l\ \mathtt{in}\ t){:}\,\mathtt{Obs}\ \tau]\!]\,\eta} \\
 & = & \lambda\sigma.[\![\Gamma, x{:}\,\theta \vdash t{:}\,\mathtt{Obs}\ \tau]\!](\eta[x \to \sigma([\![\Gamma \vdash l{:}\,\mathtt{Ref}\ \theta]\!]\eta)])\,\sigma \\
[\![\Gamma \vdash (l{:}= e; t){:}\,\mathtt{Obs}\ \tau]\!]\,\eta & = & \lambda\sigma.[\![\Gamma \vdash t{:}\,\mathtt{Obs}\ \tau]\!]\,\eta\,(\sigma[v_l \to v_e]) \\
 & & \text{where } v_l = [\![\Gamma \vdash l{:}\,\mathtt{Ref}\ \theta]\!]\eta \text{ and } v_e = [\![\Gamma \vdash e{:}\,\theta]\!]\eta
\end{array}
$$

Figure 2: Denotational semantics

The denotational semantics of ILC (see figure 2) is defined by induction on type derivations. The meaning of an expression ($\Gamma \vdash e{:}\,\omega$) is a mapping from environments satisfying Γ to D_ω. (See [Mit90] for a discussion of this notation).

Lemma 1 $[\![\Gamma \vdash e{:}\,\omega]\!]$ *is well-defined.*

This involves showing that continuous functions in the interpretation of λ are unique and that the choice of α in the interpretation of `letref` is immaterial.

Proposition 2 $[\![\Gamma \vdash e{:}\,\omega]\!]\eta \in D_\omega$ *whenever* η *satisfies* Γ.

This is proved by a simple induction on type derivations. The main property to be verified is that η and σ are always extended or modified in a manner type-consistent with Γ. We present the proof case for `letref` terms; other cases can be verified similarly. Assume that η satisfies Γ.

- $[\![\Gamma \vdash (\mathtt{letref}\ v^*{:}\,\mathtt{Ref}\ \theta := e\ \mathtt{in}\ t){:}\,\mathtt{Obs}\ \tau]\!]\,\eta \in D_{\mathtt{Obs}\ \tau}$
  Let $\alpha \in D_{\mathtt{Ref}\ \theta}$. Then, since η satisfies Γ, $(\eta[v^* \to \alpha])$ satisfies $\Gamma, v^*{:}\,\mathtt{Ref}\ \theta$. Thus, by induction hypothesis, $[\![\Gamma, v^*{:}\,\mathtt{Ref}\ \theta \vdash t{:}\,\mathtt{Obs}\ \tau]\!]\,(\eta[v^* \to \alpha]) \in D_{\mathtt{Obs}\ \tau}$ and $v_e = [\![\Gamma, v^*{:}\,\mathtt{Ref}\ \theta \vdash e{:}\,\theta]\!]\,(\eta[v^* \to \alpha]) \in D_\theta$. Thus, $(\sigma[\alpha \to v_e])$ is a well-formed state, and hence $\lambda\sigma.[\![\Gamma, v^*{:}\,\mathtt{Ref}\ \theta \vdash t{:}\,\mathtt{Obs}\ \tau]\!]\,(\eta[v^* \to \alpha])\,(\sigma[\alpha \to v_e]) \in D_{\mathtt{Obs}\ \tau}$ as desired.

This property ensures that every expression of an applicative type τ is free of state information. It also shows that observers (of type `Obs` τ) do not have any visible side-effects. This proves our claim that ILC is free of side-effects.

We note that the semantics uses the state in a single-threaded fashion [Sch85]. Whenever a state is updated, the old state is discarded. Thus, the semantics can indeed be realized by a global store and no side effects need enter the implementation through the "back door".

At this stage, we can also point out what kind of primitive constants of mutable and observer types may be added to the language without violating the basic framework. The acceptable constants should be purely *combinatorial*, i.e., they should not use any information about the semantic interpretations of their parameters. For example, the constants $if_{\texttt{Obs}\ \tau}\colon \texttt{Bool} \times \texttt{Obs}\ \tau \times \texttt{Obs}\ \tau \longrightarrow \texttt{Obs}\ \tau$ defined by

$$if_{\texttt{Obs}\ \tau}(p, t_1, t_2) = \begin{cases} t_1, & \text{if } p = true \\ t_2, & \text{if } p = false \end{cases}$$

are acceptable because they are not dependent on the semantic interpretation of the $\texttt{Obs}\ \tau$ parameters. On the other hand, the constant *add*: $\texttt{Obs}\ \tau \times \texttt{Obs}\ \tau \longrightarrow \texttt{Obs}\ \tau$ defined by

$$add(t_1, t_2) = \lambda\sigma.\,(t_1\sigma + t_2\sigma)$$

is not acceptable as it interprets $\texttt{Obs}\ \tau$ parameters to be functions of type $[\texttt{State} \rightarrow D_\tau]$.

5.2 Reduction semantics

We now present reduction rules for terms of ILC. These rules are meant to reduce terms to normal form such that every closed term of a primitive type β reduces to a constant of that type. Let $V(t)$ be the set of free variables of term t.

The reduction rules presented in figure 3 propagate **get** terms outward until they encounter a **letref** or assignment, and then discharge the **get** construct. The **letref** and assignment constructs can be discharged only after the state observation in their body is completed, i.e., after the body reduces to applicative term. At that stage, the body would be a "value term" of the form k, $\lambda x\colon\omega.e_1$ or $\langle e_1, e_2\rangle$. Rules (3) and (6) handle this situation.

Let $\stackrel{*}{\longrightarrow}$ be the reflexive, transitive closure of $\longrightarrow$. We can easily show that one step reduction preserves types, and by induction, so does $\stackrel{*}{\longrightarrow}$.

Lemma 3 (Type preservation) *If* $(\Gamma \vdash s\colon\omega)$ *is a term, and* $s \longrightarrow t$*, then* $(\Gamma \vdash t\colon\omega)$ *is a term.*

We can also show that one step reduction preserves meaning.

Proposition 4 (Soundness) *Let* $(\Gamma \vdash s\colon\omega)$ *and* $(\Gamma \vdash t\colon\omega)$ *be terms, and let* $s \longrightarrow t$*. Then*

$$[\![\Gamma \vdash s\colon\omega]\!]\,\eta \equiv [\![\Gamma \vdash t\colon\omega]\!]\,\eta$$

Proof: Rules (1) and (2) are classical. For (3) and (6), note that if u is of the stated form, it can only be a trivial observer which is also of an applicative type τ. (Nontrivial observers have a **letref**, **get** or ":=" at their principal position.)

Let $u ::= k \mid \lambda x{:}\,\omega.e_1 \mid \langle e_1, e_2\rangle$

(1)	$(\lambda x{:}\,\omega.e_1)(e_2)$	$\longrightarrow$	$e_1[e_2/x]$	
(2)	$\langle e_1, e_2\rangle.i$	$\longrightarrow$	e_i	for $i = 1, 2$
(3)	$\mathtt{letref}\ v^*{:}\,\mathtt{Ref}\ \theta := e\ \mathtt{in}\ u$	$\longrightarrow$	u	if $v^* \notin V(u)$
(4)	$\mathtt{letref}\ v^*{:}\,\mathtt{Ref}\ \theta := e\ \mathtt{in}$ $\mathtt{get}\ x{:}\,\theta' \Leftarrow v^*\ \mathtt{in}\ t$	$\longrightarrow$	$\mathtt{letref}\ v^*{:}\,\mathtt{Ref}\ \theta := e$ $\mathtt{in}\ t[e/x]$	
(5)	$\mathtt{letref}\ v^*{:}\,\mathtt{Ref}\ \theta := e\ \mathtt{in}$ $\mathtt{get}\ x{:}\,\theta' \Leftarrow w^*\ \mathtt{in}\ t$	$\longrightarrow$	$\mathtt{get}\ x'{:}\,\theta' \Leftarrow w^*\ \mathtt{in}$ $\mathtt{letref}\ v^*{:}\,\mathtt{Ref}\ \theta := e$ $\mathtt{in}\ t[x'/x]$	if $v^* \neq w^*$ and $x' \notin V(e) \cup V(t)$
(6)	$v^* := e\ ;\ u$	$\longrightarrow$	u	
(7)	$v^* := e\ ;$ $\mathtt{get}\ x{:}\,\theta \Leftarrow v^*\ \mathtt{in}\ t$	$\longrightarrow$	$v^* := e\ ;\ t[e/x]$	
(8)	$v^* := e\ ;$ $\mathtt{get}\ x{:}\,\theta \Leftarrow w^*\ \mathtt{in}\ t$	$\longrightarrow$	$\mathtt{get}\ x'{:}\,\theta \Leftarrow w^*\ \mathtt{in}$ $v^* := e\ ;\ t[x'/x]$	if $v^* \neq w^*$ and $x' \notin V(e) \cup V(t)$

Figure 3: Reduction rules

Hence, u is state-independent. For example,

$$\begin{array}{ll} & [\![\Gamma \vdash (\mathtt{letref}\ v^*{:}\,\mathtt{Ref}\ \theta := e\ \mathtt{in}\ u){:}\,\mathtt{Obs}\ \tau]\!]\ \eta \\ = & \lambda\sigma.[\![\Gamma, v^*{:}\,\mathtt{Ref}\ \theta \vdash u{:}\,\mathtt{Obs}\ \tau]\!](\eta[v^* \to \alpha])(\sigma[\alpha \to v_e]) \\ & \quad \text{where } \alpha \text{ is any element of } D_{\mathtt{Ref}\ \theta} \text{ not in } dom(\sigma) \\ & \quad \text{and } v_e = [\![\Gamma, v^*{:}\,\mathtt{Ref}\ \theta \vdash e{:}\,\theta]\!]\ (\eta[v^* \to \alpha]) \\ = & \lambda\sigma.[\![\Gamma, v^*{:}\,\mathtt{Ref}\ \theta \vdash u{:}\,\tau]\!]\ \eta[v^* \to \alpha] \\ = & \lambda\sigma.[\![\Gamma \vdash u{:}\,\tau]\!]\ \eta \qquad \text{since } v^* \notin V(u) \\ = & [\![\Gamma \vdash u{:}\,\mathtt{Obs}\ \tau]\!]\ \eta \end{array}$$

For (4) and (5), recall that v^* and w^* are "reference variables" which are only bound in letref constructs. By the denotational semantics, any two such variables denote distinct references unless they are syntactically identical. For example,

$$\begin{array}{ll} & [\![\Gamma \vdash (\mathtt{letref}\ v^*{:}\,\mathtt{Ref}\ \theta := e\ \mathtt{in}\ (\mathtt{get}\ x{:}\,\theta \Leftarrow v^*\ \mathtt{in}\ t)){:}\,\mathtt{Obs}\ \tau]\!]\ \eta \\ = & \lambda\sigma.[\![\Gamma, v^*{:}\,\mathtt{Ref}\ \theta \vdash (\mathtt{get}\ x{:}\,\theta \Leftarrow v^*\ \mathtt{in}\ t){:}\,\mathtt{Obs}\ \tau]\!](\eta[v^* \to \alpha])(\sigma[\alpha \to v_e]) \\ & \quad \text{where } \alpha \text{ is any element of } D_{\mathtt{Ref}\ \theta} \text{ not in } dom(\sigma) \\ & \quad \text{and } v_e = [\![\Gamma, v^*{:}\,\mathtt{Ref}\ \theta \vdash e{:}\,\theta]\!]\ (\eta[v^* \to \alpha]) \\ = & \lambda\sigma.[\![\Gamma, v^*{:}\,\mathtt{Ref}\ \theta, x{:}\,\theta \vdash t{:}\,\mathtt{Obs}\ \tau]\!]\ (\eta[v^* \to \alpha][x \to v_e])(\sigma[\alpha \to v_e]) \\ = & \lambda\sigma.[\![\Gamma, v^*{:}\,\mathtt{Ref}\ \theta \vdash t[e/x]{:}\,\mathtt{Obs}\ \tau]\!]\ (\eta[v^* \to \alpha])(\sigma[\alpha \to v_e]) \\ = & [\![\Gamma \vdash (\mathtt{letref}\ v^*{:}\,\mathtt{Ref}\ \theta := e\ \mathtt{in}\ t[e/x]){:}\,\mathtt{Obs}\ \tau]\!]\ \eta \end{array}$$

Rules (7) and (8) are similar. □

Strong normalization is considered to be a desirable property of typed programming languages. It asserts that the evaluation of a well-typed recursion-free term *always* terminates. Conceptually, its significance is that all terms are meaningful;

there are no undefined terms [Pra71]. Its pragmatic implication is that nontermination is limited to explicit recursion. Strong normalization is ensured in ILC by making observers non-storable. If observers were storable, **Ref Obs nat** would be a well-formed type and the language would contain the following infinite reduction sequence:

$$\begin{aligned}&(\texttt{letref}\ u^* : \texttt{Ref Obs}\ T := (u^* \uparrow)\ \texttt{in}\ u^* \uparrow)\\ &\quad\longrightarrow (\texttt{letref}\ u^* : \texttt{Ref Obs}\ T := (u^* \uparrow)\ \texttt{in}\ u^* \uparrow)\\ &\quad\longrightarrow \ldots\end{aligned}$$

Since u^* : **Ref Obs nat**, we can store in it an observation of itself ($u^* \uparrow$). Indeed, recursion is defined in Scheme by a similar device [RC86].

Proposition 5 (Strong Normalization) *Let* $(\Gamma \vdash t : \omega)$ *be a recursion-free term. Then there is no infinite reduction sequence* $t \longrightarrow t_1 \longrightarrow t_2 \longrightarrow \ldots$ *of well-typed* ILC *terms.*

Proof: The proof of the above proposition is quite elaborate and uses twin induction on types and terms, along the classical lines of [Tai75, GLT89]. The proof may be found in [Swa91].

The Church-Rosser property for the reduction system may be established as follows. Let V be a countably infinite set of reference variables. Treat the reduction rules (4) and (7) as schematic rules representing an infinite set of rules, one for each $v^* \in V$. Similarly, the rules (5) and (8) may be treated as being schematic for an infinite set of rules, one for each distinct pair of $v^*, w^* \in V$. The resulting reduction system has no "critical overlaps", i.e., no left hand side has a common instance with a subterm of another left hand side, unless the subterm is a metavariable. So, it follows that:

Lemma 6 (Local Confluence) *If* $(\Gamma \vdash r : \omega)$ *is a term, and if* $r \longrightarrow s_1$ *and* $r \longrightarrow s_2$, *then there is a term* $(\Gamma \vdash t : \omega)$ *such that* $s_1 \xrightarrow{*} t$ *and* $s_2 \xrightarrow{*} t$.

Hence, by Newman's Lemma, we have

Proposition 7 (Confluence) *If* $(\Gamma \vdash r : \omega)$ *is a term, and if* $r \xrightarrow{*} s_1$ *and* $r \xrightarrow{*} s_2$, *then there is a term* $(\Gamma \vdash t : \omega)$ *such that* $s_1 \xrightarrow{*} t$ *and* $s_2 \xrightarrow{*} t$.

This result can be extended to the language with recursion as follows. Add the following reduction rule

$$(9) \quad \text{fix}\, e \quad\longrightarrow\quad e(\text{fix}\, e)$$

where *fix* is the least fixed point operator for each type ω. The resulting system still has no critical overlaps. Further, it is left-linear, i.e., there are no repeated occurrences of metavariables on any left hand side. Hence, by Huet [Hue80], Lemma 3.3, we have

Proposition 8 *The reduction system (1-9) is confluent.*

This property, which is equivalent to the Church-Rosser property, gives further evidence of the side-effect-freedom of ILC. If there were side effects, then the evaluation of a subexpression would affect the meaning of its context, and the normal forms would be dependent on the evaluation order.

The independence of results on the evaluation order means, in particular, that call-by-value and call-by-name evaluations produce the same results. This observation must be interpreted carefully. In the lambda calculus setting, the distinction between call-by-value and call-by-name refers to when the arguments to a function are *evaluated*. We are using these terms in the same sense. However, in the imperative programming framework, the terms call-by-value and call-by-name are used to make a different distinction — the question of when the arguments to a function are *observed*. In the terminology of ILC, this involves a coercion from a type `Obs` τ to a type τ. Since `Obs` τ represents the function space [`State` $\rightarrow D_\tau$], such a coercion involves change of semantics. ILC permits no such coercion. Thus, in the imperative programming sense, ILC's parameter passing is call-by-name. However, the linearity of observer constructions means that a function accepting an observer can use it to observe at most one state. This contrasts with Algol 60, where a call-by-name parameter can be used to observe many states with quite unpredictable effects.

6 Extended Example : Unification

To illustrate the expressive power and usability of the language, we implement unification by an algorithm that performs *shared updates* on a data structure. Unification [Rob65] is a significant problem that finds applications in diverse problems including type inference, implementation of Prolog and theorem provers, and natural semantics.

Figure 4 contains an ILC program that computes the most general common instance of two terms t_1 and t_2. A *term* is either a variable or a pair denoting the application of a function symbol to a list of subterms. A variable is represented by a *reference*. The reference may contain either a term (if the variable is already bound), or the special value `Unbound`. This representation of terms illustrates the notion of *shared dynamic data* mentioned in Section 1; a function accepting a term has indirect access to all the references embedded in the term.

We assume the existence of a global reference called `sigma` that accumulates the list of references bound during an attempt at unification. If the unification is successful, this yields the most general unifier, while the representations of the terms t_1 and t_2 correspond to the most general common instance. On failure, this list is used to reset the values of the references to `Unbound`.

The function `unify` attempts to compute the most general common instance of two terms `t` and `u`. If the unification is successful, it instantiates both `t` and `u` to their most general common instance (by updating the references embedded in them), and evaluates the success continuation `sc`. If the unification is unsuccessful, it leaves the terms unchanged and evaluates the failure continuation `fc`. Internally, it uses the auxiliary function `unify-aux` which updates the terms in both cases. By providing the failure continuation `(undo fc)` to this function, terms are restored to their original values upon failure. The function `unify-lists` unifies two lists of terms `(lt, lu)`, `bind` unifies a variable `v` with a term `u`, `occurs` checks whether a variable `v` occurs free in a term `u`, and `undo` resets the values of variables that

```
datatype  term  =  Var of Ref var
                |  Apply of (symbol × List term)

    and   var   =  Unbound | Bound of term

unify: term × term × Obs T × Obs T → Obs T
    = λ(t, u, sc, fc). unify-aux(t, u, sc, undo(fc))

unify-aux: term × term × Obs T × Obs T → Obs T
    = λ(t, u, sc, fc).
          case (t, u) of
             (Var(v1), Var(v1)) ⇒ sc
           | (Var(v1), Apply(f, ts)) ⇒ bind(v1, u, sc, fc)
           | (Apply(f, ts), Var(v2)) ⇒ bind(v2, t, sc, fc)
           | (Apply(f, ts), Apply(g, us)) ⇒
                  if (f = g) then unify-lists(ts, us, sc, fc) else fc

unify-lists: List term × List term × Obs T × Obs T → Obs T
    = λ(lt, lu, sc, fc). case (lt, lu) of
                             ([], []) ⇒ sc
                           | (t :: ts, u :: us) ⇒
                                  unify-aux(t, u, unify-lists(ts, us, sc, fc), fc)
                           | (_, _) ⇒ fc

bind: Ref var × term × Obs T × Obs T → Obs T
    = λ(v, u, sc, fc). case v↑ of
                             Unbound ⇒ occurs(v, u, fc, (v := Bound(u);
                                                          sigma := v :: sigma↑;
                                                          sc))
                           | Bound(t) ⇒ unify-aux(t, u, sc, fc)

undo: Obs T → Obs T
= λfc. case sigma↑ of
           [] ⇒ fc
         | v :: vs ⇒  v := Unbound;
                      sigma := vs;
                      undo(fc)

occurs: Ref var × term × Obs T × Obs T → Obs T
    = ···
```

Figure 4: Unification of first-order terms

have been bound during a failed attempt at unification. The definition of `occurs` is straightforward and has been omitted.

The significant aspect of this program is that when an unbound variable is unified with a term that does not contain any free occurrence of the variable, unification succeeds by *assigning* the term to the reference that represents the variable (see function `bind`). This modification is visible via other access paths to the reference. It is this information sharing that affects the unification of subsequent subterms, even though no values are *passed* between these program points. In contrast, in a pure functional language, every computed value needs to be passed explicitly to all program points which need it. In the unification example, this means that whenever a variable is modified, the modified value needs to be passed to all other subterms that are yet to be unified, an expensive proposition indeed.

7 Related Work

In this section, we compare our research with related work. We organize this comparison based on the broad approach taken by the related work.

Linearity Substantial research has been devoted to determining when values of pure functional languages can be modified destructively rather than by copying. Guzman and Hudak [GH90] propose a typed extension of functional languages called *single threaded lambda calculus* that can express the sequencing constraints required for the in-place update of array-like data structures. Wadler [Wad90b] proposes a similar solution using types motivated by Girard's Linear Logic and, later, shows the two approaches to be equivalent [Wad91]. He also proposes an alternate solution inspired by monad comprehensions [Wad90a].

These approaches differ radically from ours in that they do not treat references as values. Programming is still done in the functional style (that is, using our τ types). Shared updates cannot be expressed, and *pointers* (references to references) and *objects* (mutable data structures with function components) are absent. Although it is possible to represent references as indices into an array called the store, the result is a low-level "Fortran-style" of programming, and it is not apparent how references of *different types* can be accommodated.

Continuation-based effects Our approach to incorporating state changes is closely related to (and inspired by) continuation-based input/output methods used in functional languages [HW90, Kar81, Per90, MH]. The early proposal of Haskell incorporated continuation-based I/O as a primitive mechanism, but Haskell version 1.0 defines it in terms of stream-based I/O [HW90, HS88]. Our `Obs` types are a generalization of the Haskell type `Dialog`. In ILC, `Dialog` can be defined as `Obs Unit` where `Unit` is a one-element type.

Effect systems An effect system of Gifford and Lucassen [GL86] is a type system that describes the side-effects that expressions can have. A compiler can then use this information to determine when expressions can be evaluated in parallel, or when they may be memoized without altering the meaning of the program. The side-effect information computed by Gifford and Lucassen assumes an eager order of evaluation; this contrasts with our goal of handling assignments in lazy languages.

Equational axiomatizations Felleisen [Fel88, FF87, FH89], Mason and Talcott [MT89a, MT89b] give equational calculi for untyped Scheme-like languages with side effects. The calculi are based on the notion of *observational equivalence*: two terms are equivalent if they yield the same result in all contexts of atomic type. Our reduction system bears some degree of similarity to these calculi. However, the calculi are considerably more complex than our reduction system because of the possibility of side effects. We are investigating the formal relationships between the different approaches.

Laws of programming In a recent paper, Hoare et. al. [HHJ+87] present an equational calculus for a simple imperative language without procedures. The equations can be oriented as reduction rules and used to normalize recursion-free command phrases. Our work is inspired, in part, by this equational calculus.

Algol-like languages In a series of papers [Rey81, Rey82], Reynolds describes a language framework called *Idealized Algol* which is later developed into the programming language *Forsythe* [Rey88]. Forsythe has a two-layered operational semantics: the reduction semantics of the typed lambda calculus, and a state transition semantics. The former expands procedure calls to (potentially infinite) normal forms, while the latter executes the commands that occur in the normal forms. Forsythe is based on the principle that the lambda calculus layer is independent of the state transition layer. In particular, references to functions are not permitted because assignments to such references would affect β-expansion.

In contrast, our operational semantics involves a single *unified* reduction system that includes both β-expansion and command execution. Therefore, Forsythe's restrictions do not appear in our formulation. At the level of terms, ILC contains an applicative sublanguage (in terms of τ types) which is absent in Forsythe. Further, ILC permits state-independent imperative terms to be coerced to applicative types thereby allowing functions that create and use local state. No similar coercion is available in Forsythe.

8 Conclusion

We have presented a formal basis for adding mutable references and assignments to applicative languages without violating the principle of referential transparency. This is achieved through a rich type system that distinguishes between state-dependent and state-independent expressions and sequentializes modifications to the state. The language possesses the desired properties of applicative languages such as strong normalization and confluence. At the same time, it allows the efficient encoding of state-oriented algorithms and linked data structures.

We hope this work forms the beginning of a systematic and disciplined integration of functional and imperative programming paradigms. Their differing strengths are orthogonal, but not conflicting. Much further work remains to be done regarding the approach presented here. The issues of polymorphism over mutable and observer types must be investigated. A complete equational calculus must be found for supporting formal reasoning. This, in turn, requires a formalization of the models of ILC and the development of proof methods like logical relations. The incorporation of an effect system and use of the monad comprehension notation would make the language more flexible and convenient to use. Finally, the issues of implementation need to be addressed.

Acknowledgements We thank John Gray, Jim Hook, Matthias Felleisen, Sam Kamin, Dave MacQueen, Ian Mason, John Ramsdell, John Reynolds, Peter Sestoft, Harald Sondergard, Carolyn Talcott, Satish Thatte and Phil Wadler for numerous discussions which led to vast improvements in our presentation.

References

[Fel88] M. Felleisen. lambda-v-cs: An extended lambda-calculus for scheme. In *ACM Symp. on LISP and Functional Programming*, 1988.

[FF87] M. Felleisen and D. P. Friedman. A calculus for assignments in higher-order languages. In *ACM Symp. on Principles of Programming Languages*, pages 314–325, 1987.

[FH89] M. Felleisen and R. Hieb. The revised report on the syntactic theories of sequential control and state. Technical Report COMP TR89-100, Rice University, 1989.

[GH90] J.C. Guzman and P. Hudak. Single-threaded polymorphic lambda calculus. In *IEEE Symp. on Logic in Computer Science*, pages 333–343, 1990.

[GL86] D.K. Gifford and J.M. Lucassen. Integrating functional and imperative programming. In *ACM Symp. on LISP and Functional Programming*, pages 28–38, 1986.

[GLT89] Jean-Yves Girard, Yves Lafont, and Paul Taylor. *Proofs and Types.* Cambridge University Press, 1989.

[HB85] P. Hudak and A. Bloss. The aggregate update problem in functional programming systems. In *ACM Symp. on Principles of Programming Languages*, pages 300–314, 1985.

[HHJ+87] C. A. R. Hoare, I. J. Hayes, He Jifeng, C. C. Morgan, A. W. Roscoe, J. W. Sanders, I. H. Sorensen, J. M. Spivey, and B. A. Sufrin. Laws of programming. *Communications of the ACM*, 30(8):672–686, August 1987.

[HS88] P. Hudak and R. Sundaresh. On the expressiveness of purely functional I/O systems. Technical Report YALEU/DCS/RR665, Yale University, Dec 1988.

[Hue80] G. Huet. Confluent reductions: abstract properties and applications to term rewriting systems. *Journal of the ACM*, 27(4):797–821, October 1980. (Previous version in *Proc. Symp. Foundations of Computer Science*, Oct 1977).

[Hug90] J. Hughes. Why functional programming matters. In *Research Topics in Functional Programming*, Univ. of Texas at Austin Year of Programming Series, chapter 2, pages 17–42. Addison-Wesley, 1990.

[HW90] P. Hudak and P. Wadler (editors). Report on the programming language Haskell, A non-strict purely functional language (Version 1.0). Technical Report YALEU/DCS/RR-777, Dep. of Computer Sc., Yale University, Apr 1990.

[Kar81] K. Karlsson. Nebula, A functional operating system. Tech. report, Chalmers University, 1981.

[LG88] J.M. Lucassen and D.K. Gifford. Polymorphic effect systems. In *ACM Symp. on Principles of Programming Languages*, pages 47–57, 1988.

[MH] L. M. McLoughlin and S. Hayes. Interlanguage working from a pure functional language. Functional Programming mailing list, Nov 1988.

[Mit90] J. C. Mitchell. Type systems for programming languages. In J. van Leeuwen, editor, *Handbook of Theoretical Computer Science*. North-Holland, Amsterdam, 1990. (also Report No. STAN-CS-89-1277, Department of Computer Science, Stanford University).

[MT89a] I. A. Mason and C. Talcott. Axiomatizing operational equivalence in the presence of side effects. In *IEEE Symp. on Logic in Computer Science*, pages 284–293. IEEE, 1989.

[MT89b] I. A. Mason and C. Talcott. A sound and complete axiomatization of operational equivalence between programs with memory. Technical Report STAN-CS-89-1250, Stanford University, 1989. (to appear in *Theoretical Computer Science*).

[MTH90] R. Milner, M. Tofte, and R. Harper. *The definition of Standard ML*. The MIT Press, Cambridge, Massachusetts, 1990.

[Per90] N. Perry. *The Implementation of Practical Functional Programming Languages*. PhD thesis, Imperial College of Science, Technology and Medicine, University of London, 1990.

[Pra71] D. Prawitz. Ideas and results in proof theory. In *Proc. Second Scandinavian Logic Symposium*, 1971.

[RC86] J. Rees and W. Clinger (editors). Revised^3 report on the algorithmic language scheme. *ACM SIGPLAN Notices*, 21(12):37–79, Dec 1986.

[Rey81] J. C. Reynolds. The essence of Algol. In J. W. de Bakker and J. C. van Vliet, editors, *Algorithmic Languages*, pages 345–372. North-Holland, 1981.

[Rey82] J. C. Reynolds. Idealized Algol and its specification logic. In Neel. D., editor, *Tools and Notions for Program Construction*, pages 121–161. Cambridge Univ. Press, 1982.

[Rey88] J.C. Reynolds. Preliminary design of the programming language Forsythe. Technical Report CMU-CS-88-159, Carnegie Mellon University, June 1988.

[Rob65] J. A. Robinson. A machine-oriented logic based on the resolution principle. *Journal of the ACM*, 12:23–41, 1965.

[Sch85] D. A. Schmidt. Detecting global variables in denotational specifications. *ACM Transactions on Programming Languages and Systems*, 7(2):299–310, Apr 1985.

[SR91] V. Swarup and U.S. Reddy. A logical view of assignments. In *Conf. on Constructivity in Computer Science*, 1991. (To appear).

[Sto77] J. E. Stoy. *Denotational Semantics: The Scott–Strachey Approach to Programming Language Theory.* MIT Press, 1977.

[SW74] C. Strachey and C. P. Wadsworth. Continuations - a mathematical semantics for handling full jumps. Tech. Monograph PRG-11, Programming Research Group, University of Oxford, 1974.

[Swa91] V. Swarup. *Type theoretic properties of assignments.* PhD thesis, University of Illinois at Urbana-Champaign, 1991. (To appear).

[Tai75] W. W. Tait. A realizability interpretation of the theory of species. In R. Parikh, editor, *Proceedings of Logic Colloquium*, volume 453 of *Lecture Notes in Mathematics*, pages 240–251. Springer, Berlin, 1975.

[Tof88] M. Tofte. *Operational semantics and polymorphic type inference.* PhD thesis, Edinburgh University, 1988. Available as Edinburgh Univ. Lab. for Foundations of Computer Science Technical Report ECS-LFCS-88-54.

[Wad90a] P. Wadler. Comprehending monads. In *ACM Symp. on LISP and Functional Programming*, 1990.

[Wad90b] P. Wadler. Linear types can change the world. In *IFIP Working Conf. on Programming Concepts and Methods*, Sea of Gallilee, Israel, Apr 1990.

[Wad91] P. Wadler. Is there a use for linear logic? In *Proc. ACM SIGPLAN Conf. on Partial Evaluation and Semantics-Based Program Manipulation*, New York, 1991. ACM. (SIGPLAN Notices, to appear).

Linearity and Laziness

David Wakeling and Colin Runciman
University of York*

Abstract

A criticism often levelled at functional languages is that they do not cope elegantly or efficiently with problems involving changes of state. In a recent paper [26], Wadler has proposed a new approach to these problems. His proposal involves the use of a type system based on the linear logic of Girard [7]. This allows the programmer to specify the "natural" imperative operations without at the same time sacrificing the crucial property of referential transparency.

In this paper we investigate the practicality of Wadler's approach, describing the design and implementation of a variant of Lazy ML [2]. A small example program shows how imperative operations can be used in a referentially transparent way, and at the same time it highlights some of the problems with the approach. Our implementation is based on a variant of the G-machine [15, 1]. We give some benchmark figures to compare the performance of our machine with the original one. The results are disappointing: the cost of maintaining linearity in terms of lost optimisations at compile-time, and the extra data structures that must be created at run-time more than cancels out the gains made by using linear types to reduce the amount of garbage collection. We also consider how the language and the implementation can be extended to accommodate aggregates such as arrays. Here the results are more promising: linear arrays are usually more efficient than trailered ones, but they are less efficient than destructively-updated ones. We conclude that larger aggregates are the most promising area of application for Wadler's type system.

1 Introduction

For many years researchers have advocated the use of functional programming languages because of their mathematical tractability, their economy of expression and their suitability for programming parallel computers. But functional languages do not cope "naturally" with real world situations involving changes of state, such as

*Authors' address: Department of Computer Science, University of York, Heslington, York Y01 5DD, United Kingdom. Electronic mail: `dw@uk.ac.york.minster`, `colin@uk.ac.york.minster`

altering a pixel on a bit-mapped display or updating a record in a database. Where the imperative solution to these problems is concise and efficient, the functional one is verbose and inefficient. Any function altering a bit-mapped display, for example, must take the bit-map as one of its arguments and return a new bit-map as part of its result. The verbosity of this solution is annoying, but even worse is its manifest inefficiency: the implementation cannot update the display directly without sacrificing referential transparency, and so it must copy the bit-map after each pixel has been altered.

In situations like these an optimising compiler is a double-edged sword. It may improve performance dramatically, for example by detecting that the bit-map *can* be updated directly without the loss of referential transparency, but in doing so it also turns a program which is inefficient into one which is inefficient in *unpredictable* ways : a small change to the program might (by fooling the compiler's analysis) lead to a large decrease in its efficiency which is hard to trace. It is most unfortunate that the behaviour of a functional program should depend so heavily on the cleverness of the compiler. The functional programmer should not be expected to know that it is better to write a program in one way rather than another just so that it can be compiled more efficiently.

In a recent paper [26], Wadler has proposed a new approach to problems involving changes of state. His approach does not try to reduce the verbosity of the functional solution to these problems, but it does try to increase its efficiency and predictability.

All implementations of lazy functional languages employ some notion of *sharing*, whether it is achieved indirectly by using an environment or directly by using pointers. One view is that sharing is essential to an efficient implementation, saving time by avoiding the recomputation of values and saving space by having only one copy of each value. But another view is that sharing is a source of inefficiency because the possibility of sharing prevents the implementation from re-using storage space immediately. Instead, storage space which is no longer in use must eventually be recovered for re-use by an expensive process known as *garbage collection.* Wadler has developed a type system, based on the linear logic of Girard [7], that attempts to reconcile these two viewpoints by giving the programmer greater control over storage management. In Wadler's type system there are two distinct families of types, *conventional types* and *linear types.* A value of a conventional type may be shared, as in `share x = (x,x)` or it may be thrown away, as in `throw x = ()`. A value of a linear type, on the other hand, must obey the *linearity constraint*: it cannot be shared and it cannot be thrown away.

At the implementation level, there may be many pointers to a conventional value (it may be *duplicated*), or there may be none at all (it may be *discarded*); there is always exactly one pointer to a linear value. Conventional storage can only be safely recovered for re-use by garbage collection, but linear storage can be recovered directly as a result explicit instructions in the compiled code for the program.

Wadler's idea is that the programmer should specify whether a new type is conventional or linear when it is declared — a trade-off between flexibility and efficiency. There are no restrictions on the use of values of a conventional type, but they cannot be updated directly and they require garbage collection. Conversely, values of a linear type must be used exactly once, but they can be updated directly and they avoid the overhead of garbage collection.

The rest of this paper is organised into six sections. Section 2 briefly reviews Wadler's type system, and Section 3 describes a functional programming language that makes use of it. Section 4 gives a small example program. Section 5 is concerned with various aspects of the implementation of this language, and Section 6 describes how the language and the implementation can be extended to incorporate aggregate structures such as arrays. Finally, Section 7 reviews some closely related work, and Section 8 concludes.

2 Wadler's Type System

In Wadler's type system two distinct families of types coexist. A *conventional type* can be either a base type, a function type or a pair type:

$$T,\ U,\ V ::= K \mid (U \to V) \mid (U \times V)$$

where K ranges over conventional base types and T, U and V range over conventional types. A *linear type* can also be either a base type, a function type or a pair type:

$$P,\ Q,\ R ::= J \mid (Q \multimap R) \mid (Q \otimes R)$$

and in this case, J ranges over linear base types and P, Q and R range over linear types. Wadler's *nonlinear type system* combines these two families of types:

$$T,\ U,\ V ::= !K \mid (U \to V) \mid (U \times V) \mid K \mid (U \multimap V) \mid (U \otimes V)$$

Here $!K$ ranges over conventional base types, K ranges over linear base types and T, U and V range over types.

The *nonlinear λ-calculus* is a variant of the λ-calculus that combines the terms of the *conventional λ-calculus* and the *linear λ-calculus* (in which all bound variables must be used exactly once) in an analogous way*:

*In his paper Wadler adopts an *inverse* "!" *convention*: terms from the *linear* λ-calculus are annotated with the symbol "¡". Our notation follows the tradition of linear logic.

$$
\begin{array}{rl}
t,\, u,\, v ::= & x \\
| & (!\lambda x : U\, .v) \\
| & (\lambda x\ : U\, .v) \\
| & (!t\ u) \\
| & (t\ u) \\
| & (!C\ t_1 \ldots t_n) \\
| & (C\ t_1 \ldots t_n) \\
| & (\text{case}\ u\ of\ !C_1\ x_{11} \ldots x_{1n} \rightarrow v_1 \mid \ldots\ !C_m\ x_{m1} \ldots x_{mn} \rightarrow v_m) \\
| & (\text{case}\ u\ of\ C_1\ x_{11} \ldots x_{1n} \rightarrow v_1 \mid \ldots\ C_m\ x_{m1} \ldots x_{mn} \rightarrow v_m) \\
| & (\text{fix}\ t)
\end{array}
$$

Here x ranges over variables and t, u and v range over terms. The novel feature of this calculus is that it allows algebraic type declarations of the form

$$K = C_1\ T_{11}\ \ldots\ T_{1p} \mid \cdots \mid C_n\ T_{n1}\ \ldots\ T_{nq}$$

where K is a new base type name, the C_i are new constructor names, and the T_{ij} are types.

Figure 1 gives the typing rules for the nonlinear λ-calculus in the usual style. Wadler discusses these rules in detail, but for the purposes of this paper the important points to note are:

- Each assumption in A about a linear variable must be used exactly once in the typing (rule VAR). An assumption list is nonlinear if each assumption $x : T$ in it has nonlinear T. In other words, the type-checker enforces the linearity constraint.
- The closure of a conventional function may not incorporate a linear value (rule $\rightarrow \mathcal{I}$). This is because there are no restrictions on the use of conventional functions. If the closure could bind a linear value there would be no restriction on the use of this value either, and so this binding must be disallowed.
- The two rules for applications (rule $\rightarrow \mathcal{E}$ and rule $\multimap \mathcal{E}$) make it clear that no linear variable may appear in both the function and argument portion of an application. Clearly, if each linear variable in t occurs exactly once in A and each linear variable in u occurs exactly once in B then each linear variable in the conjunction of the two lists, $A.B$ occurs exactly once in $(t\ u)$.
- A conventional data structure may not have any linear components (rule $!K\mathcal{I}$). This is because updating any component of a data structure updates the structure itself, and the updating of conventional data structures must be disallowed.

$$\text{VAR}\ \frac{}{A.x : T \vdash x : T}\ \text{nonlinear } A$$

$$\rightarrow\mathcal{I}\ \frac{A,\ x : U \vdash v : V}{A \vdash (!\lambda x : U\ .v) : U\ \rightarrow\ V}\ x \notin A,\ \text{nonlinear } A \qquad \multimap\mathcal{I}\ \frac{A,\ x : U \vdash v : V}{A \vdash (\lambda x : U\ .v) : U \multimap V}\ x \notin A$$

$$\rightarrow\mathcal{E}\ \frac{A \vdash t : U \rightarrow V \quad B \vdash u : U}{A \vdash (!t\ u) : V} \qquad \multimap\mathcal{E}\ \frac{A \vdash t : U \multimap V \quad B \vdash u : U}{A, B \vdash (t\ u) : V}$$

$$!K\mathcal{I}\ \frac{A_1 \vdash t_1 : T_1\ \ \ldots\ \ A_n \vdash t_n : Tn}{A_1,\ \ldots\ A_n \vdash (!C\ t_1\ \ldots\ t_n) : K}\ \text{nonlinear } T_i \qquad K\mathcal{I}\ \frac{A_1 \vdash t_1 : T_1\ \ \ldots\ \ A_n \vdash t_n : Tn}{A_1,\ \ldots\ A_n \vdash (C\ t_1\ \ldots\ t_n) : K}$$

Figure 1: Typing rules for the nonlinear λ-calculus

3 A Functional Language

Although the nonlinear λ-calculus is both simple and elegant, the syntax is so Spartan that only a fanatic would advocate using it to program a computer. We have developed a functional programming language with a more agreeable syntax which is based on the nonlinear λ-calculus and uses the nonlinear type system. This language is called Nonlinear Lazy ML (NLML), and it is a variant the language Lazy ML (LML) developed at Chalmers University by Augustsson and Johnsson [2]. In this section we shall be concerned mainly with the type system and type inference, an area where there are significant and interesting differences between the two languages.

3.1 Types

In NLML the conventional base types are `Int`, `Bool` and `Char`, and there are no linear base types. One of the first decisions taken in the design of NLML was that providing linear versions of the basic types was not worthwhile. This decision was partly the result of reading Lafont's work [16, 17], and partly the result of our unsuccessful attempts to write useful functions using linear integers.

Conventional type variables are written as `!*a` and linear type variables are written as `*a`. Conventional functions are constructed with the `->` arrow and linear functions are constructed with the `-o` arrow. The requirement that the closure of a conventional function must not incorporate a linear value means that the function

```
signature f: *a->(!*b->*a);
f x y = x
```

is type-incorrect because it allows a linear value to be used many times (every time the conventional function (f v) is applied to a conventional argument, the implementation duplicates the linear value v). There would be no problem, and the type-checker could be more permissive, if it could guarantee that the function (f v) would be applied only once. This, of course, is what the -o arrow is used for, and the following definition is type-correct.

```
signature g: *a->(!*b-o*a);
g x y = x
```

On first acquaintance linear functions appear to be exotic beasts. Their role in NLML, however, is a very minor one: they serve only to placate the type-checker by restricting the use of partial applications, ensuring the integrity of linear values. In our experience, the programming style that results from a more ambitious use of linear functions is not to be recommended. Lafont [17], for example, makes extensive use of them and his programs are rather difficult to understand.

NLML allows the programmer to declare algebraic data types. There are two different kinds of type declaration, conventional ones and linear ones. For example,

```
type Clist !*a = Cnil + Ccons !*a (Clist !*a)
```

declares the type of a conventional list of conventional values. There are no restrictions on lists of this type; they may be used any number of times. The declaration

```
linear type Llist !*a = Lnil + Lcons !*a (Llist !*a)
```

declares the type of a linear list of conventional values. A list of this type must be used exactly once; it cannot be shared or thrown away. The use of the list *items*, though, is unrestricted. The linear type announces that the programmer is prepared to trade flexibility in exchange for a more efficient implementation. Flexibility is lost because the type system insists that linear lists should be used exactly once, but efficiency is gained because the implementation can re-use the space occupied by linear list cells explicitly, so avoiding the overhead of garbage collection.

In NLML, the explicit recovery of storage is accomplished by ***destructive case-analysis***. Consider the following definition of a concatenation function for linear lists:

```
signature nconc: (Llist !*a)->(Llist !*a)-o(Llist !*a);
   nconc Lnil ys = ys
|| nconc (Lcons x xs) ys = Lcons x (nconc xs ys)
```

Here pattern-matching is being used to perform *case-analysis* of the first argument. When one of the two clauses has been chosen, the space occupied by the linear list cell that was examined can safely be recovered — the type system guarantees that it is not referred to elsewhere. Thus, the `nconc` function *destroys* its first argument in computing its result.

3.2 Type-checking

In NLML type-checking takes place after the program has been translated into the nonlinear λ-calculus using techniques similar to those described in Peyton Jones' book [21]. During this translation, information from any type signatures in the program, along with information about the types of the primitive operations, is used to annotate the resulting terms. So, for example, the function

```
signature id: !*a->!*a;
id x = x
```

is translated into

$$id = ((\lambda x.x :!X) :!X \to !X)$$

Type-checking is then performed in two stages. The first stage uses a simple variant of Milner's archetypal type-checking algorithm $\mathcal{W}$ [20] using information supplied in the type signatures. At this stage, a function is considered to be type-incorrect if it is *ambiguous*. For example, if its type signature is omitted, then `id` is ambiguous because it can have four possible types ($X \to X$, $!X \to !X$, $X \multimap X$ and $!X \multimap !X$). The programmer must often write type signatures to resolve ambiguities for the type-checker.

In the second stage, the type-checker ensures that all variables declared to have a linear type obey the linearity constraint. This is a simple syntactic check, performed by following each possible path through a function and counting the occurrences of the variables with linear types. Some additional checks ensure that linear values are never incorporated in cyclic structures created with `let rec`, that they cannot appear in the closures of conventional functions, and that they cannot appear as the components of conventional data structures.

This two stage implementation is largely a matter of convenience. A direct implementation of the typing rules given in Section 2 involves reference counting the assumption lists maintained by the type-checker, and this turns out to be rather awkward.

From the above description it might seem that type-checking is quite straightforward. However, there are many pitfalls for the unwary. Consider, for example, the following function which increments the nth element of a linear list.

```
signature inc: Int->(Llist Int)->(Llist Int);
inc n Lnil = Lnil
inc 1 (Lcons x xs) = Lcons (x+1) xs
inc n (Lcons x xs) = Lcons x (inc (n-1) xs)
```

Using the pattern-matching transformation described by Wadler in Peyton Jones' book [21], this function is translated into the nonlinear λ-calculus as follows (type annotations have been omitted for the sake of clarity):

$$
\begin{array}{l}
inc = \lambda A1.\lambda A2. \\
\quad case\ A2\ in \\
\quad\quad Lnil : Lnil \\
\quad \| \quad Lcons\ x\ xs : \\
\quad\quad\quad case\ A1\ in \\
\quad\quad\quad\quad 1 : case\ A2\ in \\
\quad\quad\quad\quad\quad\quad Lnil : ERROR \\
\quad\quad\quad\quad\quad \| \quad Lcons\ x\ xs : Lcons\ (x + 1)\ xs \\
\quad\quad\quad \| \quad n : case\ A2\ in \\
\quad\quad\quad\quad\quad\quad Lnil : ERROR \\
\quad\quad\quad\quad\quad \| \quad Lcons\ x\ xs : Lcons\ (inc\ (n - 1))\ xs
\end{array}
$$

The problem here is the repeated case-analysis of *A2*. It must be a linear list, yet in the translation it may be used twice, and this is a type-incorrect. As Wadler points out, it is straightforward to improve the translation of pattern-matching to avoid the repeated case-analysis of a single variable. However, there are other more subtle problems that cannot be solved in this way, as we shall now show.

In NLML, as in LML, argument patterns are always matched strictly. (This differs from languages like Miranda[†] where tuple patterns are matched *lazily*: the argument is not evaluated unless one of its components is required during evaluation of the right-hand side.) But some form of lazy pattern-matching is essential, and in both NLML and LML this is achieved using the binding mechanism of the `let`-expression. Consider an expression of the form

`let` $p = q$ `in` r

When this expression is evaluated, no check is made that q matches the pattern p until the value of one of the variables in p is required in r. Now suppose we declare two linear types as follows.

```
linear type Lpair *a *b = Lpr *a *b

linear type Signal = S Bool Signal
```

[†]Miranda is a trademark of Research Software Limited

The first is the type of pairs of linear values and the second is the type of infinite sequences of booleans. There is nothing sinister about these two declarations, but now we use them to define the function `divide` which copies a `Signal`:

```
signature divide: Signal->(Lpair Signal Signal);
divide (S x xs) =
    let (Lpr xs1 xs2) = divide xs in Lpr (S x xs1) (S x xs2)
```

This function is translated into the nonlinear λ-calculus so that the pattern-matching in the `let`-expression is lazy (once again, type annotations have been omitted for the sake of clarity):

```
divide = λA1.
    case A1 in
        S x xs :
            let rec t = divide xs
            and xs1 = case t in
                          Lpr u v : u
                      || _ : ERROR
            and xs2 = case t in
                          Lpr u v : v
                      || _ : ERROR
            in Lpr (S x xs1) (S x xs2)
    || _ : ERROR
```

This will not type-check either. Here the local variable t introduced during the pattern-matching transformation must be a linear pair, and yet it is used by two case-expressions, each of which discards one of its linear components.

Now, it is an entertaining, if somewhat futile, exercise to attempt to translate the `divide` function into the nonlinear λ-calculus — where, remember, there is no pattern-matching of any kind — while preserving both the linearity and the laziness suggested by the original definition. It cannot be done: linearity demands that the result of *(divide xs)* must not be shared at all; laziness demands that it must be shared among the selectors for *xs1* and *xs2*. The problem evinced by `divide` is in fact very serious: at one time, this simple function seemed to throw our whole enterprise into jeopardy. We do have a solution of sorts, but since it depends on details of the implementation we shall postpone discussion of it until Section 5.

Worrying as they are, these problems with type-checking have not prevented us from writing several interesting NLML programs. One of these is described below.

4 An Example: Generating the Mandelbrot Set

The Mandelbrot set [19] is a set of complex numbers governed by the iterative formula $z \leftarrow z^2 + k$. If this formula converges for an initial z of (0,0) then the point k is within the set, otherwise it is not. Unfortunately, it is impossible to find all and only those points for which the iteration converges. However, it is possible to find an *approximation* to the set by making use of a simple and sufficient condition for *divergence*: the sequence of iterations will diverge if the size of the complex number z, written $|z|$, exceeds 2. Any point for which the iteration has not diverged after a fixed finite number of iterations is assumed to lie within the set. When enough points set have been computed they can be plotted on a graph of the complex plane, as in Figure 2.

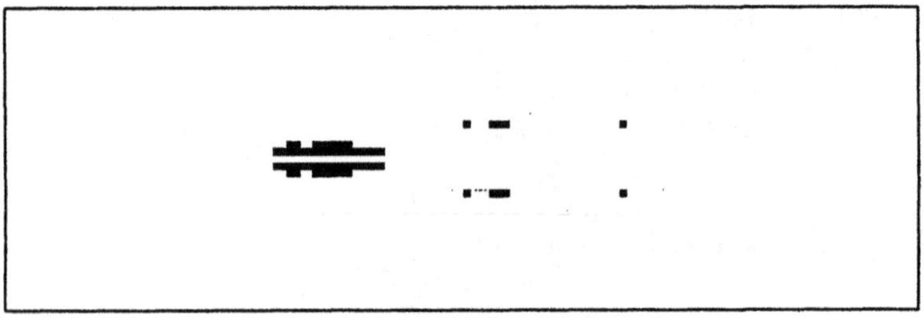

Figure 2: An Approximation of the Mandelbrot set

At the heart of our program to generate the set is an implementation of the iteration $z \leftarrow z^2 + k$. Trading flexibility for efficiency, we shall make the type of complex numbers a linear one

```
linear type Complex = C Float Float
```

allowing a true assignment to be used in the iterative loop, just as it would be in an imperative programming language. We can now define the central function `inset` which returns `true` if the point `k` is still with in the set after a certain predefined number of iterations, and `false` otherwise.

```
signature inset: Complex->Bool;
inset k = inset1 0 (C 0.0 0.0) k
```

The `inset` function uses an auxiliary `inset1` to compute its result. The three arguments that it gives to this function are an initial value for the iteration counter, an initial value for `z` and the point `k`. The iterations stop when either the iteration count reaches the predefined maximum, `NITER`, or |z| exceeds 2. The first clause of the `inset1` function tests the iteration counter:

```
inset1 NITER z k = yes z k
```

If the number of iterations has reached NITER, then the point k is assumed to be within the set and the result is true. Unfortunately, it would not be type-correct simply to return true immediately — that would involve discarding two linear values, z and k. Instead, an intermediate function yes is required:

```
signature yes: Complex->Complex-oBool;
yes (C r1 i1) (C r2 i2) = true
```

This function returns true only after using up both of its arguments during destructive case-analysis; the function no is similar. The second clause of the inset1 function tests for $|z| > 2$ and it is rather more complicated:

```
inset1 n z k =
    let (Lpr z1 z2) = copy_complex z in
    if squared_size z1 >= 4.0 then
        no z2 k
    else
        let (Lpr k1 k2) = copy_complex k in
        inset1 (n+1) (add_complex (sqr_complex z2) k1) k2
```

The size of a complex number is found by squaring each of its parts, adding them together and taking the square root of the sum. However, since we only want the size of z in order to compare it with 2, we avoid the square root operation by comparing with 4 instead. The function squared_size returns the square of the size of a complex number:

```
signature squared_size: Complex->Float;
squared_size (C r i) = (r .* r) .+ (i .* i)
```

Complex numbers are represented by a linear type and so every operation on a complex number, including squared_size, consumes it by destructive case-analysis. Thus, we must take a copy of z before testing it so that we can use it again afterwards. Assuming that z fails the test, we can carry out another iteration, which involves computing the value of z*z + k. To do this we must explicitly copy k in order to satisfy the type-checker which insists that all linear values must be used exactly once. We can avoid copying z by specialising the function mul_complex of two arguments to a function sqr_complex of one:

```
signature sqr_complex: Complex->Complex;
sqr_complex (C r i) =
    C ((r .* r) .- (i .* i)) ((r .* i) .+ (r .* i))
```

The Mandelbrot set itself may now be obtained by mapping the `inset` function over a grid of complex numbers represented by a list.

This program illustrates many of the problems that we have encountered while writing programs in NLML. The loss of flexibility that results from using linear types is dramatic. Extra functions must often be written to copy or throw away linear values, and in order to avoid writing these artificial functions, one often resorts to programming in unnatural and devious ways.

Having to supply type signatures can be irksome, especially for quite simple functions. More seriously, type signatures can lead to a creeping loss of polymorphism. A signature which is appropriate for a function in the context of the program being developed can mask its true polymorphic nature, something which a system performing pure type inference would reveal.

Our implementation has no built-in linear types or library functions to process them. In this particular example, the programmer has to define linear pairs explicitly. In time, of course, it is likely that some linear types would become built-in to the implementation, and some functions for processing them would find their way into libraries. But many of these new library functions would just be imitations of existing ones which process conventional types. This need to provide "two of everything" complicates life for both the programmer and the implementor.

Overall, programming in NLML is quite laborious. The programs are more cumbersome and there is a significant loss of flexibility when compared with a conventional language like LML. The restrictive nature of the type-system means that the prods that one receives from the type-checker during program development are both frequent and sharp, and many of the problems that it finds can be hard to correct.

5 Implementation

This section describes the implementation of NLML using an abstract machine called the *nonlinear G-machine*. The nonlinear G-machine is closely related to Johnsson and Augustsson's G-machine [15, 1], and in what follows we shall refer to their machine as the *conventional G-machine*. Some familiarity with the idea of programmed graph reduction and the conventional G-machine is assumed in this section; for those without such familiarity an excellent tutorial description can be found Peyton Jones' book [21].

5.1 The Nonlinear G-machine

After type-checking and lambda-lifting [15], the NLML compiler compiles every function into code for the nonlinear G-machine. This abstract machine has instructions to construct and manipulate graphs representing expressions. It can be thought of as a finite-state machine with the following components:

I, the instructions remaining to be executed;

S, a stack of pointers;

V, a stack of basic values;

C, the conventional partition of the graph;

L, the linear partition of the graph;

E, a global environment;

D, a dump stack.

Together, these seven components specify the entire state of the abstract machine, written as

$$\langle \text{I, S, V, C, L, E, D} \rangle$$

The effect of each abstract machine instruction is described by a state transition rule. So, for example, the effect of the PUSH instruction is described by the rule:

$$\langle \mathsf{PUSH}\ m.\text{I},\ n_0 \cdots n_m.\text{S, V, C, L, E, D} \rangle \Rightarrow \langle \text{I},\ n_m.n_0 \cdots n_m.\text{S, V, C, L, E, D} \rangle$$

An important difference between the nonlinear G-machine and the conventional one is that the nonlinear G-machine *partitions* the graph with respect to the type of the vertices. The single graph, G, that appears in the state of the conventional G-machine is replaced by two graphs, C and L, in the state of the nonlinear G-machine. This partition is essential to support linear data structures. However, it is not the only difference between the two machines.

5.2 Destructive Case Analysis

Case analysis of both conventional and linear data structures is performed using a single CASE instruction. Two further instructions are used for accessing the components of a data structure: LSPLIT pushes the components of a linear data structure onto the stack, and CSPLIT does the same for a conventional one. The only difference between these two instructions is the effect that they have on the data structure node. The LSPLIT instruction destroys it — although the components can subsequently be accessed on the stack, the node itself has vanished from the graph. The understanding here is that its storage has also been recovered for re-use. The CSPLIT instruction behaves in a similar manner, but the node that it operates on remains in the graph. A small example serves to illustrate the use of the CASE and LSPLIT instructions to implement destructive case analysis. We can define the tail function on linear lists as

```
signature tail: (Llist !*a)->(Llist !*a);
tail (Lcons x xs) = xs
```

This function compiles into the following instructions:

```
tail: PUSH 0
      EVAL
      CASE (Lnil,L1) (Lcons,L2)
L1:   STOP
L2:   LSPLIT 2
      PUSH 1
      UPDATE 3
      POP 2
      UNWIND
```

The CASE instruction examines the value at the top of the stack and selects the appropriate label. If control reaches L2 then the LSPLIT instruction destroys the Lcons node and pushes its components onto the stack.

5.3 The Protection Mechanism

In Section 3 we showed that the function divide is translated into a type-incorrect form in the nonlinear λ-calculus, and we also noted that it is impossible to translate this function into a form that exhibits both the linearity and the laziness suggested by the original definition. Our solution to this problem allows the transformation of lazy pattern-matching to take place unhindered. A run-time *protection mechanism* is then used to delay the destruction of linear nodes until they are no longer shared. This works as follows:

- when the linear node becomes shared, a *protection count* is attached to it. This protection count is set to the number of pointers sharing the node;
- every time the node is accessed by one of the selectors the protection count is decremented;
- when the node is accessed by one of the selectors and the protection count is one, it is destroyed.

The compiler determines the protection count by examining the lazily matched pattern. In the case of *divide*, for example, the protection count is two. This solution can easily be generalised to more complicated patterns than pairs. However, it only works properly when all of the variables in the pattern are used at least once. Otherwise it leads to a space leak because the protection count attached to the shared linear node is never reduced to one. This weakness means that lazy pattern-matching must be used with care. Nevertheless, we have found the protection mechanism to be a workable solution to an extremely difficult problem.

To implement the protection mechanism another variant of the SPLIT instruction must be added to the nonlinear G-machine. The PSPLIT instruction is like LSPLIT except that it respects the protection count of the linear graph node that it operates on. If the protection count is greater than one the PSPLIT instruction causes it to be decremented, but the node itself is still protected and so it remains in the graph. Otherwise, the node is destroyed. The compiler detects case-expressions that are being used to select components of shared linear values and it uses PSPLIT instead of LSPLIT for them.

Other run-time solutions to the problem of lazy pattern-matching are also possible. For example, the LSPLIT instruction could be modified to update all references to the components of the node that it destroys. There would then be no need for PSPLIT. Unfortunately, it is hard to implement such schemes using only the source-to-source transformations employed by the NLML compiler.

5.4 Heap Organisation and Garbage Collection

The nonlinear G-machine has two heaps: a *conventional heap* managed using the classic scheme suggested by Fenichel and Yochelson [6], and a *linear heap* which is is divided into a number of *free-lists*, one for each possible linear graph node size. There is also a *non-volatile storage area* for graph nodes representing compile-time constants such as integers and strings. This avoids having to allocate space for them on the heap whenever they are needed (see Figure 3). The conventional heap

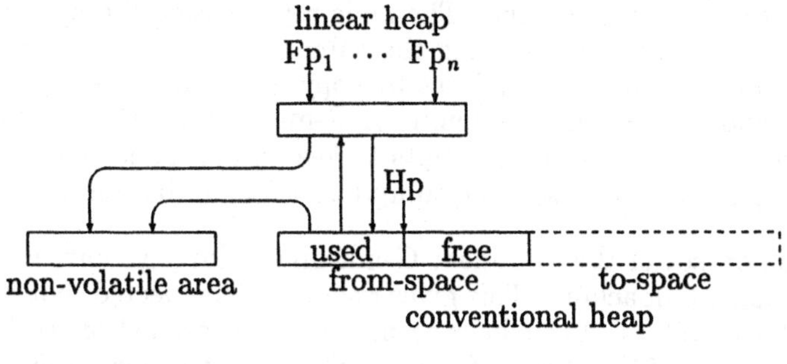

Figure 3: The conventional and linear heaps

supports the implicit destruction of disused nodes by garbage collection, while the free-list organisation of the linear heap supports the explicit destruction of disused nodes by destructive case-analysis.

5.5 The Simulated Stack and Free-list

One of the most important optimisations performed by Augustsson and Johnsson's LML compiler involves the use of a *simulated stack*. When an abstract machine instruction such as PUSHINT 3 is encountered, no machine code is emitted; instead the value 3 is pushed onto a simulated stack maintained by the code generator. During code generation, operands are taken from simulated stack if possible; otherwise some machine code is emitted to take them from the real stack at run-time.

The NLML compiler retains this optimisation and adds a *simulated free-list*. When a node is destroyed by destructive case analysis, no machine code is emitted to link it back onto the appropriate free-list; instead it is stored on a simulated free-list maintained by the code generator. During code generation, space for new linear nodes is allocated by re-using nodes on the simulated free-list if possible; otherwise code to acquire a new cell from the appropriate free-list must be emitted.

Some care is required in managing the simulated stack and the simulated free-list in the presence of destructive operations. For example, the components of a linear node that has been the subject of destructive case analysis must be saved in registers or on the real stack, bypassing the simulated stack. Disaster ensues if references to them via the destroyed node appear on the simulated stack because this node may have been reallocated in the meantime. It is equally important to ensure that the simulated free-list is "flushed" to the real one to avoid space leaks.

5.6 Updating and Sharing

Apart from during type-checking, the nonlinear G-machine treats linear functions and their applications in exactly the same way as conventional ones. This means that the graph nodes representing all functions and their applications are stored in the C partition of the graph. But a problem arises when the result of a function application is a linear value. The node representing the application must be updated with the node representing the value in order to ensure lazy evaluation. The conventional G-machine updates by copying the root node of the result over application node. However, the nonlinear G-machine clearly cannot do this: that would make a nonsense of its attempts to keep graph nodes partitioned by type. Instead the compiler must arrange to update using an indirection node.

The instruction set of the nonlinear G-machine is largely borrowed from that of the conventional G-machine. This gives rise to an unexpected, but benign, form of sharing of linear values. As we have seen, the PUSH instruction works by *copying* a pointer to the top of the stack. If that pointer is to a linear value, then the linear value becomes shared. Fortunately, the linear value will only ever be accessed via this new pointer during execution. In fact, such sharing causes a problem only during garbage collection, where the garbage collector must be prepared to encounter pointers to linear nodes that have already been destroyed.

5.7 Benchmarks for List Structures

Four benchmark programs were written in NLML and compiled with our prototype compiler. With minor alterations (omitting the extra functions required to maintain linearity), the same four programs were written in LML and compiled with the Chalmers LML compiler, version 0.95. The four benchmark programs were as follows.

- *adder*: a gate-level simulation of a four-bit ripple-carry performing 20,000 additions.
- *mandelbrot*: generates a crude view of the Mandelbrot set on an ordinary terminal.
- *turtle*: draws 20 Hilbert curves using simple turtle graphics.
- *qsort*: a quicksort of a list of 4,000 random numbers.

The benchmark figures given below were recorded on a lightly loaded SUN 3/280 file-server with 16M bytes of memory running version 3.5 of the SUN UNIX operating system. For both implementations the total heap space was limited to 1Mbyte in order to force a significant number of garbage collections. The NLML compiler was instructed to generate code for a version of the nonlinear G-machine in which 20% of the total heap space was reserved for the linear heap, and the remainder was divided into two semispaces for the conventional heap. The LML compiler was similarly instructed to generate code for a version of the conventional G-machine in which the total heap space was divided into two semispaces for the single conventional heap. For each of the benchmarks we measured the total execution time, the amount of time spent garbage collecting, the number of garbage collections, and the amount of storage allocated from the heap(s). Execution time was measured in seconds, and the storage allocated was measured in bytes. Table 1 gives the results for the programs produced by the NLML compiler, and Table 2 gives the results for the programs produced by the LML compiler.

These benchmark figures are very disappointing. The performance of the NLML programs is generally much worse than that of the LML ones. There are several reasons for this.

The first is the need to apply extra functions to share linear values (by explicit copying) and to throw them away (by explicit case analysis). These functions are costly in terms of both space and time. The graphs representing their applications must be built in the heap and later garbage collected. This is a particular problem in both the *adder* and *mandelbrot* programs, and in both cases it is exacerbated

	execution time		GCs	heap storage allocated	
	total	GC		conventional	linear
adder	44.34	0.27	89	34,003,380	13,120,876
mandelbrot	29.73	0.08	36	14,553,948	3,098,952
turtle	44.32	0.70	68	10,806,240	1,931,280
qsort	17.98	3.17	23	7,026,112	5,037,568

Table 1: Results for NLML programs using linear lists

	execution time		GCs	heap storage allocated
	total	GC		conventional
adder	21.16	0.08	48	22,482,252
mandelbrot	20.18	0.03	22	11,116,536
turtle	40.24	0.59	54	10,754,160
qsort	15.30	5.19	34	8,915,200

Table 2: Results for LML programs using conventional lists

by the fact that the extra functions are in the "inner loop" of the entire program. Notice the increase in the number of garbage collections in both cases.

One of the advantages of the conventional G-machine's semispace heap organisation is that only a single test for heap exhaustion has to be made before a sequence of allocations. The free-list organisation of the linear heap means that a test for free-list exhaustion must be made before every allocation. However, the cost of this test is actually quite low: omitting it produces only a 4% speed up at most. The reason is that the simulated free-list optimisation is quite effective: the speed up from using it can be as much as 11%.

Programming in NLML often involves passing around tuples instead of single values in order to maintain linearity. These tuples are expensive for two reasons. Firstly, there is the obvious cost of creating and destroying them. This cost should not be underestimated: in the *mandelbrot* program 12% of the storage allocated in the linear heap is for tuples whose sole purpose is to maintain linearity; in the *adder* program, the figure rises to 39%. Secondly, and more insidiously, these tuples exact a significant cost in terms of lost opportunities for compile-time optimisation. The upshot of this is that the nonlinear G-machine builds many graphs at run-time that were optimised away for the conventional G-machine at compile-time.

6 Aggregate Structures

Problems involving large aggregates, such as arrays and file systems, have always been something of a *bête noir* for function languages. It is difficult for the implementation to allow the aggregate to be updated while maintaining both referential transparency and acceptable efficiency. In the past, a number of solutions to this *aggregate update problem* have been proposed including run-time checks [10], syntactic restrictions [23], and abstract interpretation [13, 3]. In this section we shall give yet another solution by showing how the nonlinear type system can be used in the implementation of arrays.

6.1 Implementation

The literature describes two implementation techniques for conventional arrays, *trailered arrays* and *destructively-updated arrays*. Trailered arrays require run-time checks to maintain referential transparency when they are updated; destructively-updated arrays require compile-time checks. Bloss describes both techniques in [3]. She shows that trailered arrays are very expensive at run-time and that destructively-updated arrays are very expensive at compile-time.

Linear arrays offer a solution to this dilemma. If an array is declared to have a linear type then the single-threaded use of that array will be verified at compile-time by the type-checker; at run-time all updates to the array can then be done destructively.

A linear array is created in much the same way as conventional one. In NLML the operation

```
array: (List !*a)->(Array !*a)
```

allocates space for a linear array whose elements are drawn from a list. The update operation

```
update: (Array !*a)->Int-o!*a-o(Array !*a)
```

is similar to that for conventional arrays, but the index operation

```
index: (Array !*a)->Int-o(Xpair !*a (Array !*a))
```

is rather different. The nonlinear type system prevents a linear array from being thrown away, and so the index operation must return the array as part of its result. The type `Xpair` simply pairs a conventional value with a linear one.

```
linear type Xpair !*a *b = Xpr !*a *b
```

If an array really is to be disposed of, then this must be done explicitly. The operation

```
yarra: (Array !*a)->(List !*a)
```

destroys an array and returns a list of its elements.

From this brief description of the linear array primitives it is not obvious how the destructive update operations are sequenced so that the program remains "safe". Consider the function swap which swaps two elements in a linear array.

```
swap: (Array !*a)->Int-oInt-o(Array !*a);
swap a i j =
    let (Xpr x a) = index a i  in
    let (Xpr y a) = index a j  in
    update (update a i y) j x
```

Here, the data dependencies are all that is required to ensure that the indexing operations are performed prior to the updates. No extra machinery, such as the sequential `let!` of [26] or the sequential `let*` of [9] is necessary.

Although the most obvious place to store linear arrays would be in the linear heap, our implementation actually stores them in the conventional heap and garbage collects them because of the complexities of managing a free-list for objects whose size cannot be determined at compile-time.

6.2 Benchmarks for Arrays

Four benchmark programs were written in NLML and compiled with our prototype compiler. With minor alterations (no result tuples were used to maintain linearity), the same four programs were written in LML and compiled with two modified versions of the Chalmers LML compiler, the first with trailered arrays and the second with destructively-updated arrays. In all cases, a strict `let` was used to sequence the update operations correctly.

The four benchmark programs were as follows.

- *histogram*: counts occurrences in a list of 40,000 random decimal digits.
- *warshall*: finds the transitive closure of 18 identical 26-node graphs.
- *life*: charts the evolution of 20 generations of a small colony of cells on a 32×32 board.

- *qsort*: an in-place quicksort of an array of 4,000 random numbers.

The benchmarks were recorded in the same conditions as those described in Section 4, except that the total heap size was raised to 2M bytes. Table 3 gives the results for the programs produced by the NLML compiler using linear arrays, Table 4 gives the results for the programs produced by the LML compiler using trailered arrays and Table 5 gives the results for the programs produced by the LML compiler using destructively-updated arrays.

	execution time		GCs	heap storage allocated	
	total	GC		conventional	linear
histogram	11.43	6.39	17	4,960,544	640,000
life	44.23	18.13	29	18,937,568	3,605,440
warshall	14.94	0.24	13	10,421,928	2,905,344
qsort	9.40	0.48	7	4,303,620	2,280,928

Table 3: Results for NLML programs using linear arrays

	execution time		GCs	heap storage allocated
	total	GC		conventional
histogram	13.35	7.93	21	5,920,544
life	24.83	1.11	24	17,895,280
warshall	15.23	0.26	15	11,816,424
qsort	9.27	0.61	8	4,632,828

Table 4: Results for LML programs using trailered arrays

	execution time		GCs	heap storage allocated
	total	GC		conventional
histogram	11.01	6.34	17	4,960,544
life	23.81	0.98	23	17,428,336
warshall	13.52	0.20	13	10,421,928
qsort	8.22	0.52	7	4,303,620

Table 5: Results for LML programs using destructively-updated arrays

We found that linear arrays are usually faster than trailered arrays, but slower than destructively-updated ones. They fare particularly badly in programs like *qsort* and *life* — both of these programs perform an order of magnitude more indexing than updating operations. The reason for this, of course, is the need to pass tuples around in order to maintain linearity. As was the case with fine-grained data structures, these tuples exact a high cost in terms of lost optimisations at compile-time and extra work that must be performed at run-time.

7 Related Work

One of the things that prompted Wadler to develop the nonlinear λ-calculus and the nonlinear type system was the observation that languages based on the linear λ-calculus have several shortcomings. We know of two such languages, one developed by Lafont and the other by Holmström.

In his thesis [17], Lafont describes the implementation of a small functional programming language based on the linear λ-calculus. However, instead of attempting to apply what he calls the "brutish" compilation scheme of his published papers [8, 16] to an ordinary functional language, he designs his own linear functional language, called LIVE. This language exposes the programmer to the full rigours of the linear λ-calculus, and only a few "small" types (such as integers) are permitted to escape the linearity constraint. LIVE is implemented using a linear variant of the Categorical Abstract Machine [4] called the Linear Abstract Machine. The advantage of this machine is that it does not require garbage collection. However, there are also two obvious disadvantages: the grain of reduction is very small (similar to that of the SK reduction machine [24]), and the results of computations are never shared because the machine was designed to implement a linear language without any sharing at all. This can be very inefficient.

Holmström [11] has described another functional programming language based on the linear λ-calculus. In his language all functions and data types inherit the linearity constraint from the linear λ-calculus. However, Holmström considers this constraint to be unacceptable in general, and so he provides a way to lift it which works for all types, not just those with a propitious machine representation. Unfortunately, Holmström has found that his language still exhibits the same fundamental lack of flexibility that Lafont's does [12]. Holmström sketched an implementation of his language using a linear variant of Landin's SECD machine [18]. This machine performs direct interpretation of the program source code. It is of interest because it allows a restricted form of sharing, and thus requires garbage collection. However, there is still no mechanism for sharing the result of a computation and, as we remarked before, this can be very inefficient.

Guzmán and Hudak [9] have developed a variant of the λ-calculus capable of expressing destructive operations, together with a type system which ensures that these operations do not compromise referential transparency. In their paper, they reject an approach based purely on linear logic, such as the one described here, as being too constraining. Instead, their type system captures the notion of state by annotating the type of each function in one of seven possible ways to indicate how it uses its argument. The resulting type system is more complex than the nonlinear one, but it controls destructive operations with considerably more precision, allowing non-destructive operations in contexts where destructive ones are permitted (but not vice versa). Guzmán and Hudak [9] plan to implement an extension of Haskell [14] based on their ideas.

Wadler has proposed a `let!`-expression based on the observation that it is perfectly safe to have more than one reference to a linear value temporarily, so long as only one reference exists when it is updated. The expression

```
let! (x) y = u in v
```

is used to grant "read-only" access to a linear value x within u. Unfortunately, this construction comes with a number of extremely ad-hoc restrictions: for example, the evaluation of u should be hyperstrict, and it must not be possible for u (or any component of u) to evaluate to x (or any component of x). Wadler formalises these requirements [26], but he is still unsure of how they relate to any existing theory [27]. We have avoided this construction on the grounds of its complexity, its poor interaction with lazy evaluation, and its dubious theoretical foundation. Wadler is currently trying to bridge the gap between theory and practice; his latest paper [25] attempts to establish the connection between the theoretically-based work of Lafont and Holmström and the more practically-based work of Guzmán and Hudak.

A more detailed account of our own work can be found in the first author's DPhil thesis [28].

8 Conclusions and Future Work

In this paper we have described the design and implementation of a functional language based on Wadler's approach to problems involving changes of state. Our work has revealed a number of drawbacks of the approach. Broadly, these are as follows.

The right to use destructive operations is accompanied by the onerous responsibility to maintain linearity. This leads to a significant loss of flexibility, and programming in NLML is rather difficult. What is needed is some extension of the underlying nonlinear λ-calculus such as the read-only access granted by Wadler's `let!`-expression. Unfortunately, the logical foundation of this expression is unclear and so there is a need for further research to find either a logical justification of the `let!`-expression, or some similar construction with such a justification. Another possible approach would be to follow Guzmán and Hudak [9] by adopting a more sophisticated type system whose connection with linear logic is of a looser kind.

The nonlinear G-machine is an attempt to implement NLML using the graph reduction technique that is used so successfully in the implementation of LML. Its performance is disappointing. More research is needed into abstract machine architectures suitable for implementing languages like NLML. We particularly favour an approach based on a machine that can make better use of sharing information, such as the TIM [5] or the Spineless Tagless G-machine [22].

It has been suggested to us that it might be better to dispense with the run-time machinery for dealing with linear values. Instead, all values would be stored in a single garbage-collected heap. Destructive operations on linear values would then be restricted to those which could be detected at compile-time using the simulated free-list. With this restriction, it would be pointless to pass tuples around to maintain linearity, and so there would be no lost optimisations at compile-time or extra data structures created at run-time. This suggestion amounts to a weakening of the linearity constraint: linear values still cannot be shared, but they can now be thrown away. In other words, they are ***single-threaded*** [23]. Single-threaded type systems are a promising area for future research, but they represent a departure from Wadler's original proposal which we have not investigated yet.

Our linear array implementation shows some promise. Linear arrays are usually more efficient than trailered ones, but they are less efficient than destructively-updated ones. We are firmly convinced that larger aggregates are the most promising area of application for the nonlinear type system, and we intend to continue our work on arrays and file systems.

Acknowledgements

We have benefitted greatly from correspondence with Lennart Augustsson and Thomas Johnsson, whose work on the LML compiler and the G-machine served as the basis for much of our own, and from correspondence with Yves Lafont, Sören Holmström and Phil Wadler, whose papers first introduced us to linear logic. We are also grateful for the comments of Neil Jones, Paul Hudak and Simon Peyton Jones.

Wakeling was funded by a research studentship from the Science and Engineering Research Council of Great Britain.

References

[1] L. Augustsson. *Compiling Lazy Functional Languages, Part II.* PhD thesis, Chalmers University of Technology, S-412 96 Göteborg, November 1987.

[2] L. Augustsson and T. Johnsson. *Lazy ML Users Manual*, July 1989. (Distributed with the LML compiler, version 0.95).

[3] A. Bloss. Update analysis and the efficient implementation of functional aggregates. In *Proceedings of the 1989 Conference on Functional Programming Languages and Computer Architecture*, pages 26–38. ACM Press, September 1989.

[4] G. Cousineau, P.-L. Curien, and M. Mauny. The categorical abstract machine. *Science of Computer Programming*, 8:173–202, 1987.

[5] J. Fairbairn and S. Wray. TIM: A simple, lazy abstract machine to execute supercombinators. In *Proceedings of the 1987 Conference on Functional Programming Languages and Computer Architecture*, pages 34–45. Springer-Verlag, September 1987. LNCS 274.

[6] R. R. Fenichel and J. C. Yochelson. A LISP garbage-collector for virtual-memory computer systems. *CACM*, 12(11):611–612, November 1969.

[7] J.-Y. Girard. Linear logic. *Theoretical Computer Science*, 50(1):1–101, 1987.

[8] J.-Y. Girard and Y. Lafont. Linear logic and lazy computation. In *Proceedings of the International Joint Conference on Theory and Practice of Software Development (TAPSOFT'87)*, pages 52–66. Springer-Verlag, March 1987. LNCS 250.

[9] J. C. Guzmán and P. Hudak. Single-threaded polymorphic lambda calculus. In *Proceedings of the Fifth Annual IEEE Symposium on Logic In Computer Science*, pages 333–343, June 1990.

[10] S. Holmström. A simple and efficient way to handle large data structures in applicative languages. In *Proceedings of the SERC/Chalmers Workshop on Declarative Programming*, pages 185–187. University College London, April 1983.

[11] S. Holmström. A linear functional language. In *Proceedings of the Workshop on the Implementation of Lazy Functional Languages, Aspenäes*, pages 13–32, September 1988. Report 53, Programming Methodology Group, Chalmers University of Technology, S-412 96 Göteborg.

[12] S. Holmström. Quicksort in a linear functional language. PMG Memo. 65, Chalmers University of Technology, S-412 96 Göteborg, January 1989.

[13] P. Hudak. A semantic model of reference counting and its abstraction. In S. Abramsky and C. Hankin, editors, *Abstract Interpretation of Declarative Languages*, pages 45–62. Ellis Horwood, 1987.

[14] P. Hudak and P. Wadler (editors). Report on the programming language Haskell, a non-strict purely functional language (Version 1.0). Technical report, University of Glasgow, Department of Computer Science, April 1990.

[15] T. Johnsson. *Compiling Lazy Functional Languages.* PhD thesis, Chalmers University of Technology, S-412 96 Göteborg, February 1987.

[16] Y. Lafont. The linear abstract machine. *Theoretical Computer Science*, 59:157–180, 1988.

[17] Y. Lafont. *Logiques, Catégories et machines.* PhD thesis, Université de Paris 7, 1988.

[18] P. J. Landin. The mechanical evaluation of expressions. *Computer Journal*, 6(4):308–320, 1964.

[19] B. B. Mandelbrot. *The Fractal Geometry of Nature.* W. H. Freeman, 1983.

[20] R. Milner. A theory of type polymorphism in programming. *Journal of Computer and System Sciences*, 17(3):348–375, 1978.

[21] S. L. Peyton Jones. *The Implementation of Functional Programming Languages.* Prentice-Hall, 1987.

[22] S. L. Peyton Jones and J. Salkild. The Spineless Tagless G-machine. In *Proceedings of the 1989 Conference on Functional Programming Languages and Computer Architecture*, pages 184–201. ACM Press, September 1989.

[23] D. A. Schmidt. Detecting global variables in denotational specifications. *ACM Transactions on Programming Languages and Systems*, 7(2):299–310, April 1985.

[24] D. A. Turner. A new implementation technique for applicative languages. *SOFTWARE — Practice and Experience*, 9(1):31–50, January 1979.

[25] P. Wadler. Is there a use for linear logic? Technical report, Department of Computing Science, University of Glasgow, December 1990.

[26] P. Wadler. Linear types can change the world! In *IFIP Working Conference on Programming Concepts and Methods*, Sea of Gallilee, Israel, April 1990.

[27] P. Wadler. Private communication, February 1990.

[28] D. Wakeling. Linearity and laziness. DPhil thesis, Department of Computer Science, University of York, November 1990. Technical Report YCST 90/07.

Syntactic Detection of Single-Threading using Continuations*

Pascal Fradet
IRISA / INRIA
Campus de Beaulieu, 35042 Rennes Cedex, France
fradet@irisa.fr

Abstract

We tackle the problem of detecting global variables in functional programs. We present syntactic criteria for single-threading which improves upon previous solutions (both syntactic and semantics-based) in that it applies to higher-order languages and to most sequential evaluation strategies. The main idea of our approach lies in the use of continuations. One advantage of continuation expressions is that evaluation ordering is made explicit in the syntax of expressions. So, syntactic detection of single-threading is simpler and more powerful on continuation expressions. We present the application of the analysis to the compilation of functional languages, semantics-directed compiler generation and globalization-directed transformations (i.e. transforming non-single-threaded expressions into single-threaded ones). Our results can also be turned to account to get single-threading criteria on regular λ-expressions for different sequential evaluation orders.

1 Introduction

Single-threading is a property allowing function parameters or semantics domains to be implemented by a global variable. This optimization can have drastic effects on the efficiency of both functional language and semantics-directed compilers. In particular, single-threading can be exploited for register allocation and for the efficient implementation of contiguous data structures.

Imperative language compilers make great use of registers [1], whereas functional language compilers do not take much advantage from register allocation because of frequent context switching. A function which is single-threaded in its argument (we will say that the argument is globalizable) can be compiled using a global register to hold its argument value. A recursive call with a new argument results in a register updating and registers are used throughout the reduction of recursive functions without having to be saved in the stack.

Contiguous data structures, such as arrays, are useful because they can be accessed in constant time. A functional implementation of arrays involves making a new copy before each update (since the original array can be referenced later on). This can clearly be a source of extreme inefficiency. A program using an array in a single-threaded fashion can be implemented using destructive updates on a global array variable. This optimization has a counterpart in semantics-directed compiler generation [11]: the store appears as an argument of the semantic function and a naïve implementation involves a duplication of the store each time the update function is called. In order to derive realistic compilers from denotational specifications one should detect that the store can safely be modified in place. This can be done by checking that the semantic definition is single-threaded in its store domain.

Two approaches have been considered for the detection of single-threading: syntactic analysis [19] and semantic analysis (or abstract interpretation) [2,3,9,18]. In both cases, analyses are approxi-

* Part of this research was done during a visit to Kansas State University (thanks to David Schmidt).

mate since single-threading is not a decidable property. Abstract interpretation often produces more precise results at the cost of an exponential worst case complexity. For this particular problem, it is not clear whether the gain is worth the cost. Syntactic analysis turns out to be sufficient in most common cases and we choose it here for two reasons:

- it is typically a linear time analysis,
- in case of failure, it indicates the faulty subexpression and detects (for free) subexpressions satisfying the property. One can take advantage of this information to perform program transformations (section 4.3) or local optimizations (section 4.1).

The main idea of our approach lies in the use of continuations. Single-threading depends heavily on the evaluation strategy; for example a single-threaded expression using left-to-right call-by-value may turn out to be non single-threaded using right-to-left call-by-value. One advantage of continuation expressions is that evaluation ordering is made explicit in the syntax of expressions. Therefore, syntactic detection of properties depending on the computation rule is likely to be simpler and more powerful on this kind of expressions. We should point out that we do not consider here continuations as a programming tool (in particular, we are not interested in first-class continuations) but as a way of formalizing part of the implementation process, namely the evaluation strategy. Our analysis applies to continuation expressions that are supposed to be produced by a continuation passing style (CPS) transformation. However, our results can be turned to account to get single-threading criteria on regular λ-expressions for different evaluation orders. This is one important advantage of our approach: it can be applied to most sequential evaluation strategies.

Section 2 introduces the syntax of continuation expressions and studies their reduction. In section 3, we present our criteria for single-threading and the associated global variable transformation. Section 4 is devoted to the application of the analysis to functional language implementation, semantics-based compilation and goal-directed transformation. Section 5 describes the generation of sufficient conditions for single-threading on ordinary λ-expressions according to several evaluation orders. We conclude with an overview of related works and a discussion on possible extensions.

2 Continuation expressions

Continuations have been primary used in denotational semantics to model unrestricted jumps [21,22]. Continuation semantics take an additional argument (a continuation) representing control, that is, the evaluation ordering of program constructs. The same concept is used to compile the computation rule of functional programs [4,5,14,16]. CPS transformations produce continuation expressions reducible without dynamic search for the next redex. Typically, a CPS compiler transforms an expression E into an expression E_c taking a continuation as argument and applying it to the result of evaluating E. For example, each operator *opm* such that $opm\ V_1 \ldots V_m \rightarrow_\delta N$, is transformed into a new operator *opmc* such that $opmc\ C\ V_1 \ldots V_m \rightarrow_\delta C\,N$.

The language used in this paper is described in Figure 1. It is general enough to support the compilation of most sequential evaluation orders and standard optimizations of CPS transformations.

Expressions	**Types**
$V^\nu ::= K^\beta \mid v^\nu \mid opmc^{(\nu \rightarrow \kappa) \rightarrow \nu 1 \ldots \rightarrow \nu m \rightarrow \kappa} \mid \lambda c^{\kappa 1}.C^{\kappa 2} \mid rec\ f^\nu = V^\nu$	$\nu ::= \beta \mid \kappa_1 \rightarrow \kappa_2 ;\quad \beta ::= bool \mid int \mid [int] \mid \ldots$
$C^\kappa ::= fin^{\nu \rightarrow \mathcal{A}} \mid c^\kappa \mid (ifc\ C_1^\kappa\ C_2^\kappa)^{bool \rightarrow \kappa} \mid \lambda v^\nu.C^\kappa \mid C^{\nu \rightarrow \kappa}\, V^\nu \mid V^{\kappa 1 \rightarrow \kappa 2}\, C^{\kappa 1}$	$\kappa ::= \mathcal{A} \mid \nu \rightarrow \kappa$

Figure 1 Syntax of Continuation Expressions

Type β stands for first-order types, ν for value types, κ for continuation types and $\mathcal{A}$ for answers. An expression is either a value V^{ν} or a continuation C^{κ}. A value is either a first-order constant K, a variable v, a strict operator of arity m *opmc*, a functional value $\lambda c^{\kappa 1}.C^{\kappa 2}$ or a recursive definition (note that values are weak normal forms). A continuation is either the final continuation $fin^{\nu \rightarrow \mathcal{A}}$, a continuation variable with the unique name c, a conditional *ifc* taking two continuation expressions and a boolean, a functional continuation $\lambda v^{\nu}.C^{\kappa}$ or an application ($V^{\kappa 1 \rightarrow \kappa 2}\ C^{\kappa 1}$ or $C^{\nu \rightarrow \kappa}\ V^{\nu}$). In the remainder of the paper we often omit types to make reading easier.This syntax generalizes usual continuation expressions in two ways:

- One standard CPS optimization, which is very important in practice, is to avoid to introduce a continuation for each λ-abstraction. For example, if an expression $\lambda v_1 \ldots \lambda v_n.E$ is known to be fully applied to n arguments, then a single continuation is sufficient and the transformed expression is of the form $\lambda c.\lambda v_1 \ldots \lambda v_n.E_c$. Thus, function values which usually have type $\kappa \rightarrow \nu \rightarrow \mathcal{A}$ (that is, take a continuation, a value and yields an answer) have here the generalized type $\kappa \rightarrow \nu_1 \rightarrow \ldots \rightarrow \nu_n \rightarrow \mathcal{A}$. For the same concerns, continuation types, usually of the form $\nu \rightarrow \mathcal{A}$, are generalized to $\nu_1 \rightarrow \ldots \rightarrow \nu_n \rightarrow \mathcal{A}$.
- Usually, continuation expressions are of the form $E_1 \ldots E_n$ (E_is being weak normal forms) Here, we allow nested applications in continuations. Expressions can be of the form $V\ C\ V_1 \ldots V_n$, C being itself of the form $U\ C'\ U_1 \ldots U_n$.

The factorial function can be written in this continuation passing style language as follows:

rec factc = $\lambda c.\lambda n.$ *eqc (ifc (c 1) (subc (factc (multc c n)) n 1)) n 0*

The reduction rules for this language are the following:

(β) $\quad (\lambda x.E)F \rightarrow_{\beta} E[F/x]$

(fix) $\quad rec\ f = V \rightarrow_{fix} V[rec\ f = V/f]$

(δ) $\quad opmc\ C\ V_1 \ldots V_m \rightarrow_{\delta} C\ N \qquad ifc\ C_1\ C_2\ True \rightarrow_{\delta} C_1 \qquad ifc\ C_1\ C_2\ False \rightarrow_{\delta} C_2$

No reduction rule is specified for the continuation *fin* and expressions *fin V* are considered as normal forms.

The key property (Property 1) of those expressions is that they can be evaluated using a simpler evaluation order than normal order. It is sufficient to reduce at each step the head operator thus avoiding the need of a dynamic search for the next redex. This evaluation scheme, called First, is formally defined (Figure 2) by a set of axioms (no inference rule is needed).

$$opmc\ C\ V_1 \ldots V_m\ V_{m+1} \ldots V_n \xrightarrow[F]{1} C\ N\ V_{m+1} \ldots V_n$$

$$ifc\ C_1\ C_2\ True\ V_1 \ldots V_n \xrightarrow[F]{1} C_1\ V_1 \ldots V_n$$

$$ifc\ C_1\ C_2\ False\ V_1 \ldots V_n \xrightarrow[F]{1} C_2\ V_1 \ldots V_n$$

$$(\lambda x.E)\ F\ V_1 \ldots V_n \xrightarrow[F]{1} E[F/x]\ V_1 \ldots V_n$$

$$(rec\ f = V)\ V_1 \ldots V_n \xrightarrow[F]{1} V[rec\ f = V/f]\ V_1 \ldots V_n$$

Figure 2 First evaluation strategy

Property 1 *An expression E has a weak head normal form (whnf) W iff E has a whnf W' (W cnv W') such that* $E \xrightarrow[F]{*} W'$.

Proof: Using the standardization theorem and the fact that any expression of type ν is a wnf. The only kind of expression being a First normal form without being a whnf is a strict operator applied to unevaluated arguments (e.g. *plus 1 (plus 2 3)*). But syntactic restrictions (Figure 1) enforce that strict operators always have their arguments in normal form (e.g. the former expression would be written *plusc (plusc fin 1) 2 3*), so First normal form and whnf are equivalent for our language.

Example: We describe here the first steps of the reduction by First of the factorial function applied to the continuation *fin* and argument 1.

(rec factc = λc.λn. eqc (ifc (c 1) (subc (factc (multc c n)) n 1)) n 0) fin 1

$\xrightarrow[F]{}$ *eqc (ifc (fin 1) (subc ((rec factc = λc.λn...)(multc fin 1)) 1 1)) 1 0*

$\xrightarrow[F]{}$ *ifc (fin 1) (subc ((rec factc = λc.λn...) (multc fin 1)) 1 1)) False*

$\xrightarrow[F]{}$ *subc ((rec factc = λc.λn...) (multc fin 1)) 1 1*

$\xrightarrow[F]{}$ *(rec factc = λc.λn...) (multc fin 1) 0*

... and so on until ...$\xrightarrow[F]{}$ *fin 1*

It is often helpful to look at continuation expressions operationally. An expression $V\,C\,V_1 \ldots V_n$ can be seen as a stack machine sate, *V* being the instruction to reduce, the continuation *C* representing the remainder of the program, and $V_1,\ldots,V_n$ the stack. Actually, after a few supplementary transformations (e.g. abstraction using combinators), one can get true generic stack machine code from those expressions [5,6]. The important point for the single-threading detection is that for any application $V^{\kappa 1 \rightarrow \kappa 2}\, C^{\kappa 1}$ we know that *V* is evaluated first and then applies continuation *C* to its result. We show in the next section how this information can be exploited.

3 Single-Threading Detection and Globalization Transformation

Let us take an example to introduce the problem and our solution. Let f be a recursive function defined by:

rec f = λa.λi.λp. if (eq i 0) a (f (update a i p) (sub i 1) (mult p (access a i)))

Function *f* can be used to replace each element *a[i]* of the array *a* by the product of its successors; for example *f [4,3,2] 3 1= [6,2,1]*. A naïve implementation of *f* would produce code copying the array before each update. We want to detect whether the first argument can be globalized and updated destructively. First, we should notice that the entity to be represented by a global variable is the sequence of arrays (*a, update a i p, update (update a i p) (i-1) (a[i]*p),...*). We rely on types to characterize single-threading properties. Let ρ → int → int → ρ be the type of *f*, therefore each element of the above sequence has type ρ and the problem is to detect whether type ρ can be implemented by a global variable. (Throughout the paper, type ρ denotes the candidate for globalization. We sometimes say that a function is single-threaded in an argument (or parameter) assuming that this argument can be characterized by its type). Assuming a call-by-value (cbv) implementation of function *f*, two cases arise:

- the update is done before the access (left-to-right cbv). In this case, f is not single-threaded and we cannot use destructive updates,

- the access is done before the update (right-to-left cbv) and the array can be modified in place.

Such cases are easily detected on CPS versions of f. Considering left-to-right call-by-value, f is transformed into:

rec f = $\lambda c.\lambda a.\lambda i.\lambda p.$ *eqc (ifc (c a) (updatec (subc (accessc (multc (f c) p) a i) i 1) a i p)) i 0*

We will say that an expression F *modifies* ρ if its reduction may involve the creation of a new instance of type ρ. In particular, an operator *opmc* of type $(\rho \to \kappa_1) \to \kappa_2$, which yields an element of type ρ (since its continuation has type $\rho \to \kappa_1$), will be a modifier (of ρ). The criterion used here to detect that f is not single-threaded in ρ is that a free variable of type ρ (namely a) appears in the continuation of a modifier (*updatec*). In other words, the structure would be modified whereas it is still referenced (by a free variable); therefore it cannot be updated in place.

Using right-to-left call-by-value, f becomes:

rec f = $\lambda c.\lambda a.\lambda i.\lambda p.$ *eqc (ifc (c a) (accessc (multc (subc (updatec (f c) a i p) i 1) p) a i)) i 0*

Here, no free variable of type ρ appears in the continuation of the modifier *updatec*, and we will see later that this expression is indeed single-threaded in ρ.

3.1 Single-threading criteria

Our criteria are in the form of a predicate Δ such that $\Delta_\rho(E)$ implies that E is single-threaded in type ρ. Before giving a formal and comprehensive account of Δ, let us introduce it in a more intuitive way.

Let $V^{\kappa 1 \to \kappa 2}\, C^{\kappa 1}\, V_1 \ldots V_n$ be the expression to analyze. Operationally, single-threading implies that every element of type ρ in the stack $V_1 \ldots V_n$ can be represented by a single global variable throughout the reduction. First, we must check that all elements of type ρ present in the stack are equal. To this purpose, predicate Δ always keeps the last encountered ρ-value. A new value or a modification will be accepted only when

(i) There is no reference (free variables) to an "old" ρ-value occurring in the continuation. Predicate $nfv_\tau(E)$ indicates that E does not contain free variables of type τ (we also use $fv_\tau(E)$ to denote the opposite).

(ii) No ρ-value occurs in the stack. This is checked on the type of $(V\ C)^{\kappa 2}$ by predicate $nt_\rho(\kappa 2)$ defined by $n_\beta(\tau) = if\ \tau \equiv \tau_1 \to \tau_2\ then\ \tau_1 \not\equiv \beta \wedge nt_\beta(\tau_2)\ else\ True$. Thus $nt_\rho(\kappa 2)$ means that there is no ρ-value among $V_1,\ldots,V_n$.

This explains the three following criteria:

- General expressions of the form $V^{\kappa 1 \to \kappa 2}\, C^{\kappa 1}$ are single-threaded in ρ if V and C are single-threaded in ρ and if V modifies ρ then its continuation C does not contain free variables of type ρ (rule (Δ9)). For example, expression $\lambda c.\lambda x^\rho.\ succ^{(\rho \to \mathcal{A}) \to \rho \to \mathcal{A}}\,(succ\ c\ x^\rho)\ x^\rho$ violates the criterion since *succ* is a modifier (produces $(x+1)^\rho$) and a free ρ-typed variable appears in its continuation. On the other hand, expression $\lambda c.\lambda x^\rho.\ chr^{(char \to \mathcal{A}) \to \rho \to \mathcal{A}}\,(succ\ c\ x^\rho)\ x^\rho$ satisfies the criterion since *chr* does not create a new ρ-typed value.

- Expression $C^{\rho \to \kappa} K^{\rho}$ is single-threaded if C is single-threaded, and if K is different from the last encountered ρ-value then no ρ-typed elements should appear in the stack (i.e. $nt_{\rho}(\kappa)$) and no free ρ-typed variables should occur in C (i.e. $nfv_{\rho}(C)$) (rule (Δ6)). For example, expressions *plusc fin* $1^{\rho}\ 2^{\rho}$ and $\lambda c.\lambda x^{\rho}.\ plusc\ c\ x^{\rho}\ 1^{\rho}$ violate the criterion.
- The reduction of an operator yielding a ρ-value $opmc^{(\rho \to \nu m+1 \to \ldots \to \nu n \to \mathcal{A}) \to \kappa}\ C\ V_1 \ldots V_m\ V_{m+1} \ldots V_n \xrightarrow[F]{1} C\ N^{\rho}\ V_{m+1} \ldots V_n$ entails that no element of type ρ should occur in $\{V_{m+1}, \ldots, V_n\}$. (i.e. $nt_{\rho}(\nu_{m+1} \to \ldots \to \nu_n \to \mathcal{A})$ (rule (Δ1)). For example, expression $\lambda c.\lambda x^{\rho}.\ succ^{(\rho \to \rho \to \mathcal{A}) \to \rho \to \rho \to \mathcal{A}}\ (plusc\ c)\ x^{\rho}\ x^{\rho}$ violates the criterion (after reduction of *succ* there will be two different ρ-values ($x+1$ and x) in the stack).

Two problems arise with closures:

- In general we do not know when the closure will be applied, so we enforce that no free ρ-typed variable occurs in closures.

- In an expression $v\ C$ we do not know if variable v will be bound to a modifying expression or not. One solution is to find a sufficient condition P such that $P(\tau)$ implies that any closure of type τ is not a modifier of ρ. So, considering the expression $v^{\kappa 1 \to \kappa 2}\ C$, if $P(\kappa 1 \to \kappa 2)$ then we can deduce that v will not be bound to a modifying expression and C can contain free variables of type ρ; otherwise no free variables of type ρ should occur in C. Here we choose, to be coherent with operator types, $P(\tau) = (\tau \not\equiv (\rho \to \kappa_1) \to \kappa_2)$ (Δ1) and P is made into a sufficient condition by rule (Δ8).

Recursive functions could have been treated in the same way as closures. However, the associated criterion can be less conservative because we know that the expression $rec\ f = V$ will be bound to variable f. To this aim, recursive functions are assumed to bear different names. An expression $rec\ f = V$ is single-threaded if its body V is single-threaded assuming that variable f is single-threaded (rule (Δ5)). To check that a function does not modify ρ, the assumption is that f is not a modifier.

Our single-threading predicate Δ_{ρ}^{r} is recursively defined on the structure of expressions. We assume that type ρ is a first-order type and that primitive operators act on their arguments in a single-threaded fashion. Superscript r represents the last ρ-typed value encountered; initially r is set to a special value Ω different from any other value. Figure 3 gathers the criteria for single-threading.

Definition 2 *An expression E is said single-threaded in type ρ if* $\Delta_{\rho}^{\Omega}(E)$.

$\Delta_{\rho}^{r}(E^{\tau})$ iff:

(Δ1) $E^{\tau} \equiv fin^{\kappa} \vee c^{\kappa}$

(Δ2) $E^{\tau} \equiv (v^{\nu} \vee opmc^{\nu}) \wedge (\nu \equiv (\rho \to \kappa_1) \to \kappa_2 \Rightarrow nt_{\rho}(\kappa_1))$

(Δ3) $E^{\tau} \equiv ifc\ C_1\ C_2 \wedge \Delta_{\rho}^{r}(C_1) \wedge \Delta_{\rho}^{r}(C_2)$

(Δ4) $E^{\tau} \equiv \lambda x.F \wedge \Delta_{\rho}^{r}(F)$

(Δ5) $E^{\tau} \equiv rec\ f = V \wedge nfv_{\rho}(V) \wedge ((\Delta_{\rho}^{\Omega}(f) \vdash \Delta_{\rho}^{\Omega}(V)) \vee (\Theta_{\rho}^{\Omega}(f) \vdash \Theta_{\rho}^{\Omega}(V)))$

(Δ6) $E^{\tau} \equiv C^{\rho \to \kappa} K^{\rho} \wedge \Delta_{\rho}^{K}(C) \wedge (K \equiv r \vee (nfv_{\rho}(C) \wedge nt_{\rho}(\kappa)))$

(Δ7) $E^{\tau} \equiv C^{\rho \to \kappa} v^{\rho} \wedge \Delta_{\rho}^{r}(C)$

(Δ8) $E^{\tau} \equiv C^{\sigma \to \kappa} V^{\sigma} \wedge \Delta_{\rho}^{r}(C) \wedge nfv_{\rho}(V) \wedge \text{if } \sigma \not\equiv (\rho \to \kappa_1) \to \kappa_2 \text{ then } \Theta_{\rho}^{\Omega}(V) \text{ else } \Delta_{\rho}^{\Omega}(V)$

(Δ9) $E^{\tau} \equiv V^{\kappa 1 \to \kappa 2} C^{\kappa 1} \wedge ((\Theta_{\rho}^{r}(V) \wedge \Delta_{\rho}^{r}(C)) \vee (nfv_{\rho}(C) \wedge \Delta_{\rho}^{r}(V) \wedge \Delta_{\rho}^{\Omega}(C)))$

Figure 3 Single-threading criteria on continuation expressions (Predicate Δ)

Intuitively, $\Delta_\rho^K(E)$ means that E is single-threaded provided that the global variable implementing ρ-values has previously being initialized to K (and $\Delta_\rho^\Omega(E) \Rightarrow \forall K\, \Delta_\rho^K(E)$). In the remainder of the paper, σ stands for a value type different from ρ. The non-modification criteria $\Theta_\rho^r(E)$ means that E is single-threaded and does not create new instances of type ρ. That is to say that E does not contain (except in closures of type $(\rho \to \kappa_1) \to \kappa_2$) expressions of the form $v^{(\rho \to \kappa 1) \to \kappa 2}\, C$, $opmc^{(\rho \to \kappa 1) \to \kappa 2}$ or $C\, K^\rho$ with $K \not\equiv r$. Θ_ρ^r is formally defined in Figure 4.

Θ_ρ^r (E) iff:

$E^\tau \equiv fin^\kappa \vee c^\kappa$

$E^\tau \equiv (v^\nu \vee opmc^\nu) \wedge \nu \not\equiv (\rho \to \kappa_1) \to \kappa_2$

$E^\tau \equiv ifc\ C_1\ C_2 \wedge \Theta_\rho^r(C_1) \wedge \Theta_\rho^r(C_2)$

$E^\tau \equiv \lambda x.F \wedge \Theta_\rho^r(F)$

$E^\tau \equiv rec\ f = V \wedge nfv_\rho(V) \wedge (\Theta_\rho^\Omega(f) \vdash \Theta_\rho^\Omega(V))$

$E^\tau \equiv C^{\rho \to \kappa}\, K^\rho \wedge \Theta_\rho^r(C) \wedge K \equiv r$

$E^\tau \equiv C^{\rho \to \kappa}\, v^\rho \wedge \Theta_\rho^r(C)$

$E^\tau \equiv C^{\sigma \to \kappa}\, V^\sigma \wedge \Theta_\rho^r(C) \wedge nfv_\rho(V) \wedge \text{if } \sigma \not\equiv (\rho \to \kappa_1) \to \kappa_2 \text{ then } \Theta_\rho^\Omega(V) \text{ else } \Delta_\rho^\Omega(V)$

$E^\tau \equiv V^{\kappa 1 \to \kappa 2}\, C^{\kappa 1} \wedge \Theta_\rho^r(V) \wedge \Theta_\rho^r(C)$

Figure 4 Non-modification criteria on continuation expressions (Predicate Θ)

We can now check by applying the Δ-rules that the function

rec f = λc.λa.λi.λp. eqc (ifc (c a) (accessc (multc (subc (updatec (f c) a i p) i 1) p) a i)) i 0

is single-threaded in ρ. As an example, we describe a few steps of the analysis of subexpression *subc (updatec (f c) a i p) i 1*:

$\Delta_\rho^\Omega(subc^{(\sigma \to \kappa 1) \to \kappa 2}\, (\ldots)\, i^\sigma\, 1^\sigma)$

$\Leftrightarrow \Delta_\rho^\Omega(subc^{(\sigma \to \kappa 1) \to \kappa 2}\, (\ldots)\, i^\sigma) \wedge nfv_\rho(1^\sigma) \wedge \Theta_\rho^\Omega(1)$ (Δ8)

$nfv_\rho(1^\sigma) \wedge \Theta_\rho^\Omega(1)$ is trivially true and the same applies to i thus

$\Leftrightarrow \Delta_\rho^\Omega(subc^{(\sigma \to \kappa 1) \to \kappa 2}\, (\ldots))$

$\Leftrightarrow \Theta_\rho^\Omega(subc^{(\sigma \to \kappa 1) \to \kappa 2}) \wedge \Delta_\rho^\Omega(updatec\ (f\ c)\ a^\rho\ i\ p)$ (Δ9)

and so on.

One important property of Δ is that it is preserved by the reduction by First.

Property 3 $(\forall E^{\mathcal{A}})\ \Delta_\rho^r(E) \wedge E \overset{*}{\underset{F}{\Rightarrow}} F \Rightarrow \Delta_\rho^r(F)$

Proof: Showing $\Delta_\rho^r(E) \wedge E \overset{1}{\underset{F}{\Rightarrow}} F \Rightarrow \Delta_\rho^r(F)$ for each rule of First. The only tedious part is the proof that the predicate is preserved by β-reduction; the following lemmas (each one is proved by structural induction) resolve this point:

- $\Delta_\rho^r((\lambda c.C_1)\, C_2) \Rightarrow \Delta_\rho^r(C_1[C_2/c])$
- $\Delta_\rho^K((\lambda v.C)\, K^\rho) \Rightarrow \Delta_\rho^K(C[K/v])$ *and* $\Theta_\rho^K((\lambda v.C) K) \Rightarrow \Theta_\rho^K(C[K/v])$
- $\Delta_\rho^r((\lambda v.C)\, V^\sigma) \Rightarrow \Delta_\rho^r(C[V/v])$ *and* $\Theta_\rho^r((\lambda v.C) V) \Rightarrow \Theta_\rho^r(C[V/v])$

We tried to keep the criteria from being too complex and did not mention some less conservative but more intricate options. One potential source of failure lies in our treatment of closures. Our requirement (if $\sigma \not\equiv (\rho \to \kappa_1) \to \kappa_2$ then $\Theta_\rho^\Omega(V)$ else $\Delta_\rho^\Omega(V)$) is somewhat simplistic and better solutions could have been chosen. The best way would be to perform a closure analysis to detect the set of closures that each higher-order variable v may be bound to; non-modification has to be enforced on those closures only if really needed (for example if expression $v\ C$ has free ρ-typed variables). This may be too costly an analysis and one might prefer alternative solutions relying on types. For each closure V^{σ} we might check $\Delta_{\rho}^{r}(V) \wedge \neg\Theta_{\rho}^{r}(V)$ constructing this way a set of modifying closure types $\mathcal{M}$ (i.e. $\sigma \in \mathcal{M}$ iff there is a closure V of type σ such that $\Delta_{\rho}^{r}(V) \wedge \neg\Theta_{\rho}^{r}(V)$). An expression $v^{\nu}\ C$ with free ρ-typed variables could be single-threaded only if type ν does not belong to $\mathcal{M}$. Another case of failure occurs when a free ρ-typed variable is enclosed. There are ways to relax this restriction. For instance, when the closure application time (or a safe approximation of it) is known, it is sufficient to enforce that no modification occurs until then.

3.2 Global variable transformation

Property 3 does not state that ρ can indeed be implemented by a global variable. In order to show that globalization can be performed on single-threaded expressions we now give a formal specification of this optimization. Global variable transformation has been expressed using a Simula-like class [19] or by adding explicit assignments [18]. We choose here to stay in the functional framework and to describe the globalization in terms of program transformations. The transformation produces expressions of the form $V\ C\ R\ V_1 \ldots V_n$ where the extra argument R plays the role of a global variable. Operationally, expressions can still be seen as a stack machine state where R denotes a register. Transformation $\mathcal{R}$ (Figure 5) removes variables of type ρ (rules *(R5)*,*(R8)*) and replaces the creation of new ρ-values by destructive updates (rules *(R3)*,*(R7)*). Applications are transformed to take into account the global variable (rules *(R10)*, *(R11)*). If the global expression yields a result of type σ (different from ρ) then continuation *fin* removes the global variable before returning the answer (rule *(R2)*). Destructive versions of operators are introduced; for example:

$$plusd\ C\ R\ V \rightarrow_{\delta} C\ (R+V)$$

$$updated\ C\ [a_1,\ldots a_i,\ldots a_m]\ i\ V \rightarrow_{\delta} C\ [a_1,\ldots,a_{i-1},V,\ldots a_m]$$

More generally, operators *opmc* such that $opmc\ C\ V_1^{\sigma 1} \ldots V_i^{\rho} \ldots V_m^{\sigma m} \rightarrow_{\delta} C\ N^{\sigma}$ are transformed into operators *opmd* such that $opmd\ C\ V_i^{\rho}\ V_1^{\sigma 1} \ldots V_{i-1} V_{i+1} \ldots V_m^{\sigma m} \rightarrow_{\delta} C\ V_i^{\rho}\ N^{\sigma}$. Modifiers *opmc* such that $opmc\ C\ V_1^{\sigma 1} \ldots V_i^{\rho} \ldots V_m^{\sigma m} \rightarrow_{\delta} C\ N^{\rho}$ are transformed into operators *opmd* such that $opmd\ C\ V_i^{\rho}\ V_1^{\sigma 1} \ldots V_{i-1} V_{i+1} \ldots V_m^{\sigma m} \rightarrow_{\delta} C\ N^{\rho}$. That is to say, if *opmc* takes *m* arguments, *n* being ρ-typed, *opmd* takes only *(m-n)+1* arguments (single-threading enforces the *n* ρ-typed elements to be equal) and yields the same value as *opmc*, updating the global variable if the result is of type ρ (rule *(R3)*). The conditional is treated in the same way *(R4)*

(R1)	$\mathcal{R}_{\rho}(a) = a$ if $a \equiv v, c, K$ or $fin^{\rho \rightarrow \mathcal{A}}$	*(R2)*	$\mathcal{R}_{\rho}(fin^{\sigma \rightarrow \mathcal{A}}) = \lambda r.\ fin$
(R3)	$\mathcal{R}_{\rho}(opc) = opd$	*(R4)*	$\mathcal{R}_{\rho}(ifc\ C_1\ C_2) = ifd\ \mathcal{R}_{\rho}(C_1)\ \mathcal{R}_{\rho}(C_2)$
(R5)	$\mathcal{R}_{\rho}(\lambda v^{\rho}.\ C) = \mathcal{R}_{\rho}(C)$	*(R6)*	$\mathcal{R}_{\rho}(\lambda v^{\sigma}.\ C) = \lambda r.\lambda v.\mathcal{R}_{\rho}(C)\ r$
(R7)	$\mathcal{R}_{\rho}(E\ K^{\rho}) = \lambda r.\mathcal{R}_{\rho}(E)\ K$	*(R8)*	$\mathcal{R}_{\rho}(C\ v^{\rho}) = \mathcal{R}_{\rho}(C)$
(R9)	$\mathcal{R}_{\rho}(\lambda c.\ V) = \lambda c.\mathcal{R}_{\rho}(V)$	*(R10)*	$\mathcal{R}_{\rho}(V\ C^{\kappa}) = \mathcal{R}_{\rho}(V)\ \mathcal{R}_{\rho}(C)$

(R11) $\mathcal{R}_{\rho}(C\ V^{\sigma}) = \lambda r.\ \mathcal{R}_{\rho}(C)\ r\ \mathcal{R}_{\rho}(V)$ or using a convenient combinator = push $\mathcal{R}_{\rho}(V)\ \mathcal{R}_{\rho}(C)$ (push $V\ C\ R \underset{F}{\rightarrow} C\ R\ V$)

Figure 5 Global Variable Transformation $\mathcal{R}$

The expressions produced by this transformation contain at most one free occurrence of ρ-typed variables. Operationally, this means that no ρ-value will ever be pushed on the stack. The correctness property (Property 4) states that if an expression $E^{\mathcal{A}}$ is single-threaded then its reduction and the reduction of its transformed version produce equivalent results.

Property 4 *For all closed* $E^{\mathcal{A}}$ *such that* $\Delta_\rho^\Omega(E)$, *if E has a whnf, i.e.* $E \xrightarrow[F]{*} fin\ N$ *then* $(\forall R^\rho)\ \mathcal{R}_\rho(E)\ R \xrightarrow[F]{*} fin\ \mathcal{R}_\rho(N)$

Proof: Induction requires a stronger property that we do not describe here for the sake of brevity. The structure of the proof is as before by showing the property for one reduction step using lemmas ($\mathcal{R}_\rho(E)[\mathcal{R}_\rho(C^\kappa)/c] \equiv \mathcal{R}_\rho(E[C^\kappa/c])$, $\mathcal{R}_\rho(E)[\mathcal{R}_\rho(V^\sigma)/v] \equiv \mathcal{R}_\rho(E[V^\sigma/v])$) which are themselves proved by structural induction; Property 3 is then used for the induction on the length of the reduction.

Example: The application of the global variable transformation to function *f*

rec f = λ*c*.λ*a*.λ*i*.λ*p*. *eqc (ifc (c a) (accessc (multc (subc (updatec (f c) a i p) i 1) p) a i)) i 0*

yields

rec f = λ*c*.λ*r*.λ*i*.λ*p*. *push 0 (push i (eqd (ifd (c) (push i (accessd (push p (multd (push 1 (push i (subd (push p (push i (updated (f c))))))))))))))) r*

The array argument has been replaced by the global variable *r*. We describe below some of the reduction steps of the application of this function to arguments *fin*, $[4,3,2]^\rho$, *3*, *1*.

(rec f = λ*c*.λ*r*.λ*i*.λ*p*. *push 0 (push i (eqd (ifd (c) (push i (...)))) r) fin [4,3,2] 3 1*

$\xrightarrow[F]{}$ *push 0 (push 3 (eqd (ifd (fin) (push 3 (...))))) [4,3,2]*

$\xrightarrow[F]{}$ *push 3 (eqd (ifd (fin) (push 3 (...)))) [4,3,2] 0*

$\xrightarrow[F]{}$ .... $\xrightarrow[F]{}$ *updated ((rec f =...) fin) [4,3,2] 3 1 2 2* {destructive update of the 3rd element}

$\xrightarrow[F]{}$ *(rec f* =λ*c*.λ*r*.λ*i*.λ*p*....*) fin [4,3,1] 2 2*

$\xrightarrow[F]{}$ .... $\xrightarrow[F]{}$ *updated (f fin) [4,3,1] 2 2 1 6* {destructive update of the 2nd element}

$\xrightarrow[F]{}$ *(rec f* =λ*c*.λ*r*.λ*i*.λ*p*....*) fin [4,2,1] 1 6* $\xrightarrow[F]{}$ ....

$\xrightarrow[F]{}$ *updated ((rec f =...)fin) [4,2,1] 1 6 0 24* {destructive update of the 1st element}

$\xrightarrow[F]{}$ *(rec f* =λ*c*.λ*r*.λ*i*.λ*p*....*) fin [6,2,1] 0 24*

$\xrightarrow[F]{}$ ... $\xrightarrow[F]{}$ *ifd (fin) (push 0 (...)) [6,2,1] True* $\xrightarrow[F]{}$ *fin [6,2,1]*

Criteria Δ and transformation $\mathcal{R}$ extend trivially to single-threading in several types $\rho_1,...\rho_i$. The transformed expressions would have several explicit global variables and would be of the form $V\ C\ R_1 ... R_i\ V_1 ... V_n$.

4 Applications

In this section we describe several applications of the analysis: the compilation of functional languages (section 4.1), semantics-directed compilation (section 4.2) and globalization-based transformations (section 4.3).

4.1 Compilation of functional languages

The primarily goal of our work was to improve the compilation of functional programs. We are currently working on the integration of our analysis in a transformation-based compiler [5,6]. The first step of this compiler is the compilation of the computation rule; call-by-value, call-by-need and even mixed evaluation orders (e.g. call-by-need with strictness information) are compiled using CPS transformations; single-threading is then detected on the resulting continuation expressions. Preliminary results indicate that this optimization is very effective for iterative functions where the use of registers can reduce execution time up to *50* per cent and, of course, for the implementation of arrays. Our criteria is also helpful for non single-threaded functions since they detect single-threaded subexpressions which can be locally transformed by $\mathcal{R}$.

However, there are cases where a standard type annotation would not fit well with the analysis. For example, when two parameters have the same type, we would try to detect if both of them can be implemented using a single global variable. In most cases this would fail whereas they can be implemented in two different variables. Let *itfact* be the iterative version of the factorial function:

$$rec\ itfact = \lambda c^{int \rightarrow \mathcal{A}}.\lambda x^{int}.\lambda y^{int}.\ eqc\ (ifc\ (c\ y)\ (multc\ (subc\ (itfact\ c)\ x\ 1)\ x\ y))\ 0\ x$$

Δ_{int} fails because *itfact* is obviously not single-threaded in type *int*.

We are primarily interested in globalizing parameters of recursive functions, a simple solution consists in annotating types so that each parameter has a different type. A recursive function of type $(\kappa \rightarrow \mathcal{A}) \rightarrow \nu \rightarrow \nu \rightarrow \mathcal{A}$ is typed $(\kappa \rightarrow \mathcal{A}) \rightarrow \nu 1 \rightarrow \nu 2 \rightarrow \mathcal{A}$. Type inference will be performed using this information and assuming that τi matches the unannotated type τ (e.g. $int1 \rightarrow int$ and $int \rightarrow int2$ are unified into $int1 \rightarrow int2$).

If the factorial function is given type $(int \rightarrow \mathcal{A}) \rightarrow int1 \rightarrow int2 \rightarrow \mathcal{A}$ then type inference produces new types for operators and the type of *itfact* becomes $(int2 \rightarrow \mathcal{A}) \rightarrow int1 \rightarrow int2 \rightarrow \mathcal{A}$.

$$\begin{aligned} rec\ itfact = \lambda c^{int2 \rightarrow \mathcal{A}}.\lambda x^{int1}.\lambda y^{int2}.\ eqc\ (ifc\ (c\ y^{int2})\\ (multc^{(int2 \rightarrow \mathcal{A}) \rightarrow int1 \rightarrow int2 \rightarrow \mathcal{A}} (subc^{(int1 \rightarrow int2 \rightarrow \mathcal{A}) \rightarrow int1 \rightarrow int \rightarrow int2 \rightarrow \mathcal{A}}\\ (itfact^{(int2 \rightarrow \mathcal{A}) \rightarrow int1 \rightarrow int2 \rightarrow \mathcal{A}}\ c)\ x^{int1}\ 1)\ x^{int1}\ y^{int2}))\ 0\ x^{int1} \end{aligned}$$

Using this annotation, Δ_{int1} and Δ_{int2} detect that *itfact* is single-threaded in types *int1* and *int2*.

Type inference must be extended a bit to be able to type functions like $rec\ f = \lambda c.\lambda x^{int}.\lambda y^{int}$... *subc (f c y) y 1*... If f has type $(int \rightarrow \mathcal{A}) \rightarrow int1 \rightarrow int2 \rightarrow \mathcal{A}$, then $f\ c\ y$ can not be typed. To solve this point, an operator *Idc*, with reduction rule $Idc\ C\ V \rightarrow C\ V$, is introduced. The previous expression becomes *Idc (f c) y* and function f can now be typed:

$$rec\ f = \lambda c.\lambda x^{int1}.\lambda y^{int2}....\ subc\ (Idc^{(int1 \rightarrow int2 \rightarrow \mathcal{A}) \rightarrow int2 \rightarrow int2 \rightarrow \mathcal{A}}\ (f\ c)\ y^{int2})\ y^{int2}\ 1)...$$

If a function is single threaded in type ρ_1 and ρ_2 then an operator $Idc^{(\rho 1 \rightarrow \kappa) \rightarrow \rho 2 \rightarrow \kappa}$ corresponds to the affectation $R_1 := R_2$, R_1 and R_2 being the global variables implementing ρ_1 and ρ_2.

This heuristic for annotating types fits our needs but is not optimal in that it would fail to detect when several arguments can indeed be implemented by a single global variable. As mentionned in section 6.2, a better solution would be to use the information provided by the single-threading criteria to choose the annotation.

4.2 Semantics-directed compiler generation

We plan to integrate our analysis into a semantics-directed compiler generator which would also include a CPS transformation. Starting from a direct denotational semantics, a first step is the defunctionalization of the store introducing a first-order data structure (e.g. an array). The second step is the compilation of the computation rule using a CPS transformation. Call-by-value is chosen if the semantics uses a strict λ-calculus or if we can infer (using a strictness analysis) that the valuation functions are strict; otherwise call-by-need is used. Single-threadedness of the store domain is then analyzed on the resulting continuation expressions and the globalization transformation is applied if possible. The next step is the partial evaluation of the semantics function applied to a particular program. Let us take an example to illustrate these steps; let $\mathcal{P}$ be a specification of a small imperative language (cf. Figure 6). The valuation functions are assumed to be strict in their arguments.

$\mathcal{P}$: Program → Store → Store

$\mathcal{P}[\![C.]\!] = \mathcal{C}[\![C]\!]$

$\mathcal{C}$: Command → Store → Store

$\mathcal{C}[\![I:=E]\!] = \lambda s.\ \text{update}\ s\ [\![I]\!]\ (\mathcal{E}[\![E]\!]\ s)$

$\mathcal{C}[\![C_1;C_2]\!] = \lambda s.\ \mathcal{C}[\![C_2]\!]\ (\mathcal{C}[\![C_1]\!]\ s)$

$\mathcal{C}[\![\textbf{if}\ B\ \textbf{then}\ C_1\ \textbf{else}\ C_2]\!] = \lambda s.\ \text{if}\ (\mathcal{B}\ [\![B]\!]\ s)\ (\mathcal{C}\ [\![C_1]\!]\ s)\ (\mathcal{C}[\![C_2]\!]\ s)$

$\mathcal{C}[\![\textbf{while}\ B\ \textbf{do}\ C]\!] = (\text{rec loop} = \lambda s.\ \text{if}\ (\mathcal{B}\ [\![B]\!]\ s)\ (\text{loop}\ (\mathcal{C}\ [\![C]\!]\ s))\ s)$

$\mathcal{E}$: Expression → Store → Int

$\mathcal{E}[\![E_1 * E_2]\!] = \lambda s.\ \text{mult}\ (\mathcal{E}[\![E_1]\!]\ s)\ (\mathcal{E}[\![E_2]\!]\ s)$ {same thing for $E_1 - E_2$, $E_1 + E_2$,...}

$\mathcal{E}[\![I]\!] = \lambda s.\ \text{access}\ s\ [\![I]\!]$

$\mathcal{E}[\![N]\!] = \lambda s.\ \mathcal{N}[\![N]\!]$

$\mathcal{B}$: Expression → Store → Bool (omitted)

Figure 6 Denotational Semantics of a Small Imperative Language (extract)

These functions are first transformed using a CPS conversion (e.g. $\mathcal{V}$ described in section 5). For instance, the first equation describing commands becomes $\lambda c.\lambda s.\ \mathcal{E}[\![E]\!]\ (updatec\ c\ s\ [\![I]\!]\ )s$. Predicate Δ_{Store} is then applied to check that command equations are single-threaded in their store domain. For the equation above, we have to check $\Theta_{Store}(\mathcal{E}[\![E]\!]\ )$ since this expression has a free store-typed variable in its continuation. Transformation $\mathcal{R}$ is applied and the first command equation is now $\lambda c.\lambda r.\ \mathcal{E}[\![E]\!]\ (\lambda r.\ push\ [\![I]\!]\ \ (updated\ c)\ r)\ r$; the global variable r is suppressed by η-reduction and we get $\lambda c.\mathcal{E}[\![E]\!]\ (push\ [\![I]\!]\ \ (updated\ c))$. Figure 7 gathers the transformed equations after globalization.

$\mathcal{P}$: Program → Cmdcont → Cmdcont

$\mathcal{P}[\![C.]\!] = \mathcal{C}[\![C]\!]$

$\mathcal{C}$: Command → Cmdcont → Cmdcont

$\mathcal{C}[\![I{:=}E]\!] = \lambda c.\ \mathcal{E}[\![E]\!]\ (\mathrm{updated}_{[\![I]\!]}\ c)$ (updated$_{[\![I]\!]}$ being an abbreviation for push [[I]] o updated)

$\mathcal{C}[\![C_1;C_2]\!] = \lambda c.\ \mathcal{C}[\![C_1]\!]\ (\mathcal{C}[\![C_2]\!]\ c)$

$\mathcal{C}[\![\text{if B then } C_1 \text{ else } C_2]\!] = \lambda c.\ \mathcal{B}\ [\![B]\!]\ (\mathrm{ifc}\ (\mathcal{C}\ [\![C_1]\!]\ c)\ (\mathcal{C}[\![C_2]\!]\ c))$

$\mathcal{C}[\![\text{while B do C}]\!] = (\mathrm{rec\ loop} = \lambda c.\ \mathcal{B}\ [\![B]\!]\ (\mathrm{ifc}\ (\mathcal{C}\ [\![C_1]\!]\ (\mathrm{loop}\ c))\ c))$

$\mathcal{E}$: Expression → ExprCont → Cmdcont

$\mathcal{E}[\![E_1 * E_2]\!] = \lambda c.\ \mathcal{E}[\![E_2]\!]\ (\mathcal{E}[\![E_1]\!]\ (\mathrm{multd}\ c))$

$\mathcal{E}[\![I]\!] = \lambda c.\ \mathrm{accessd}_{[\![I]\!]}\ c$

$\mathcal{E}[\![N]\!] = \mathrm{push}\ \mathcal{N}[\![N]\!]$

$\mathcal{B}$: Expression → ExprCont → Cmdcont (omitted)

Figure 7 Semantics after CPS and globalization transformations

This semantics applied to a program is simplified by partial evaluation. For that particular semantics, this step is straightforward since it amounts to β-reduce continuations. The expressions obtained can be seen as generic stack machine code. For example:

$$\mathcal{P}[\![X{:=}2;Y{:=}Y*X.]\!] = \lambda c.\ \mathcal{C}[\![X{:=}2]\!]\ (\mathcal{C}[\![Y{:=}Y*X]\!]\ c) = \ldots$$

$$= \lambda c.\ push\ 2\ (updated_{[\![X]\!]}\ (accessd_{[\![X]\!]}\ (accessd_{[\![Y]\!]}\ (multd\ (updated_{[\![Y]\!]}\ c)))))$$

This method produces very good quality code for such toy languages. This would not be the case if environments and procedures were added to the language. Much work remains to be done in order to automatically derive efficient compilers for real life languages.

4.3 Globalization-directed transformations

We are interested in this section in non single-threaded functions. No extension of the criteria could help, however our analysis returns information which can be turned to account to transform non single-threaded functions into single-threaded ones. One of the most common cases of non single-threadedness is when arguments are not evaluated in a proper order. The evaluation strategy enforces a specific order which may invalidate single-threading, whereas arguments of strict functions can be evaluated in any order. In order to deal with this problem, we define program transformations which can be seen as local modifications of the evaluation ordering. Let us come back to the *f* function defined in section 3.

$$rec\ f = \lambda c.\lambda a.\lambda i.\lambda p.\ eqc\ (ifc\ (c\ a)\ (accessc\ (multc\ (subc\ (updatec\ (f\ c)\ a\ i\ p)\ i\ 1)\ p)\ a\ i))\ i\ 0$$

Function *f* is not single-threaded in its third argument which is modified while still referenced. Let ρ be the type of the third argument; Δ_ρ points out that *f* is not single-threaded in ρ because there are occurrences of ρ-typed free variable *i* in the continuation of modifier *subc*. The idea is to postpone the evaluation of *subc* until it can be done in a single-threaded fashion or it becomes necessary.

Let Π be a function such that:

$$\Pi_i(F^V) = j \Rightarrow (\forall C,V_1,\ldots,V_i)\ (F\ C\ V_1 \ldots V_i \overset{*}{\underset{F}{\nrightarrow}} C\ U_1 \ldots U_{j-1} V_i) \vee (F\ C\ V_1 \ldots V_i = \bot)$$

Intuitively, this function indicates that the *ith* element of the stack is not needed by F and will be at position j in the stack after the execution of F. Of course, Π is a partial function which yields only a safe approximation ($\perp$ or an integer). We do not describe it here and we just give the rule that is needed for our example:

$\Pi_i(opmc) = i\text{-}m\text{+}1$ *if* $i>m$ otherwise $\perp$

Using this function, safe adjustments of the evaluation ordering can be performed. One basic transformation is:

$$F\,(E\;C\;V_1 \ldots V_p) \leftrightarrow E\;(\lambda v_1. \ldots \lambda v_{n-1}.\,F\,(C\;v_1 \ldots v_{n-1}))\;V_1 \ldots V_p \qquad \text{if } \Pi_{p+1}(E) = n > 0$$

with $p \geq 0$ and $v_1,\ldots,v_{n-1}$ being fresh variables.

Evaluations of F and E are inverted and it is easy to prove that both expressions are operationally equivalent. This transformation is worth applying when non single-threading comes from free variables in the continuation of a modifier, that is when $\neg\Theta_\rho(F) \wedge fv_\rho(C)$ is detected. The above transformation is used to delay the reduction of the modifier until it is needed or, hopefully, until the free variables are eventually consumed.

When analyzing the subexpression *subc (updatec (f c) a i p) i 1*, we get Δ_ρ *(subc)* $\wedge fv_\rho$*(updatec (f c) a i p)* and Π_4*(updatec)* = 2, thus the transformation can be applied and returns *updatec* (λ*v. subc (f c v)) a i p i 1*. Function *f* is now single-threaded in its second and third arguments.

5 Single-threading detection on source expressions

All the results described so far apply to continuation expressions. It is not however compulsory and we describe in this section how to use Δ to get criteria on regular λ-expressions according to different computation rules. The idea is to design a CPS conversion $\mathcal{C}$ mapping source expressions to continuation expressions according to a specific evaluation scheme $\mathcal{E}$. Transformation $\mathcal{C}$ must produce expressions whose reduction by First models the reduction by $\mathcal{E}$ of the original expressions. By simplifying $\Delta \circ \mathcal{C}$ one can get single-threading criteria on source expressions for the evaluation ordering $\mathcal{E}$. Figure 8 describes a transformation compiling left-to-right call-by-value. For the sake of brevity, we consider here a λ-calculus extended with constants and operators only.

- $\mathcal{V}(v^\tau) = \lambda c.c^{\bar{\tau} \to \mathcal{A}}\,v^{\bar{\tau}}$
- $\mathcal{V}(op^\tau) = \lambda c.c^{\bar{\tau} \to \mathcal{A}}\,op\,c^{\bar{\tau}}$
- $\mathcal{V}(\lambda v^{\tau1}.F^{\tau2}) = \lambda c.c^{\overline{(\tau1 \to \tau2)} \to \mathcal{A}}\,(\lambda c.\lambda v^{\overline{\tau1}}.\mathcal{V}(F)\,c^{\overline{\tau2} \to \mathcal{A}})$
- $\mathcal{V}(E_1^{\tau1 \to \tau2}\,E_2^{\tau1}) = \lambda c^{\overline{\tau2} \to \mathcal{A}}.\mathcal{V}(E_1)\,(\lambda f^{(\overline{\tau2} \to \mathcal{A}) \to \overline{\tau1} \to \mathcal{A}}.\mathcal{V}(E_2)\,(f\,c))$

With the associated transformation on types defined by: $\overline{\beta} = \beta$ and $\overline{\tau1 \to \tau2} = (\overline{\tau2} \to \mathcal{A}) \to \overline{\tau1} \to \mathcal{A}$

Figure 8 CPS transformation for left-to-right call-by-value ($\mathcal{V}$)

The proof that $\mathcal{V}$ models properly left-to-right call-by-value is beyond the scope of this paper. The interested reader may refer to [6] which presents such a proof.

We proceed by simplifying $\Delta \circ \mathcal{V}$ to get criteria defined on the syntax of source expressions. We do not describe the simplification process which is straightforward; for example, the first rule (if E is an atom then E is single-threaded) follows from: $\Delta_\rho \circ \mathcal{V}(v) = \Delta(\lambda c.c^{\tau \to \mathcal{A}}\,v^{\tau}) = True$ and $\Delta \circ \mathcal{V}(op^\tau) = \Delta(\lambda c.c^{\tau \to \mathcal{A}}\,op\,c^{\tau}) = True$ (since $nt_\rho(\mathcal{A})$). For all expression E, $(\Theta_\rho \circ \mathcal{V})\,E$ can be shown equivalent to: $(\Delta_\rho \circ \mathcal{V})\, E \wedge$ (*E does not contain active expressions of type* ρ *different from an identifier*), where an expression is said *active* if it is not properly contained within a λ-abstraction. The resulting predicate is described in Figure 9.

$\Delta_\rho \circ \mathcal{V}(E)$ iff:

- $E \equiv$ atom (v or op)
- $E \equiv \lambda v^{\tau 1}.F^{\tau 2} \wedge \Delta_\rho \circ \mathcal{V}(F) \wedge$
  - (i) $\tau 1 \equiv \rho \Rightarrow$ all free ρ-typed identifiers in F are v^ρ
  - (ii) $\tau_1 \not\equiv \rho \Rightarrow$ F has no active ρ-typed expressions
  - (iii) $\tau_2 \not\equiv \rho \Rightarrow$ E does not contain active expressions of type ρ different from an identifier.
- $E \equiv E_1^{\tau 1 \rightarrow \tau 2}\, E_2^{\tau 1} \wedge \Delta_\rho \circ \mathcal{V}(E_1) \wedge \Delta_\rho \circ \mathcal{V}(E_2) \wedge$

  $fv_\rho(E_2) \Rightarrow$ all occurrences of active ρ-typed expressions in E_2 are occurrences of identifiers.

Figure 9 Single-threading criteria for λ–calculus using left-to-right cbv $(\Delta_\rho \circ \mathcal{V})$

If right-to-left call-by-value is used, the associated CPS conversion $\mathcal{V}_r$ remains the same except for the application rule which becomes:

$$\mathcal{V}_r(E_1\, E_2) = \lambda c^{\overline{\tau 2} \rightarrow \mathcal{A}}.\mathcal{V}(E_2)\, (\lambda a^{\overline{\tau 1}}.\mathcal{V}(E_1)\, (\lambda f.f^{(\overline{\tau 2} \rightarrow \mathcal{A}) \rightarrow \overline{\tau 1} \rightarrow \mathcal{A}}\, c\, a))$$

The criteria remain the same except for the last one which becomes:

- $E \equiv E_1^{\tau 1 \rightarrow \tau 2}\, E_2^{\tau 1} \wedge \Delta_\rho \circ \mathcal{V}_r(E_1) \wedge \Delta_\rho \circ \mathcal{V}_r(E_2) \wedge$
  - (i) $\tau_1 \equiv \rho \Rightarrow$ all occurrences of active ρ-typed expressions in E_1 are occurrences of identifiers
  - (ii) $fv_\rho(E_1) \Rightarrow$ all occurrences of active ρ-typed expressions in E_2 are occurrences of identifiers.

In order to introduce as few continuations as possible, efficient transformations often use the following optimizations [6]:

- $\mathcal{V}(opm\ V_1 \ldots V_m) = \lambda c.\ \mathcal{V}(V_m)\ (\ldots (\mathcal{V}(V_1)\ (opmc\ c))\ldots)$
- $\mathcal{V}((\lambda v_1. \ldots \lambda v_n. F_1)\ F_2 \ldots F_n) = \lambda c.\ \mathcal{V}(F_n)\ (\ldots (\mathcal{V}(F_2)\ (\lambda v_1. \ldots \lambda v_n.\ \mathcal{V}(F_1)\ c))\ldots)$

This amounts to introducing multi-applications in the language and single-threading detection takes a great benefit from it. For example, the expression $\lambda x^\rho.\lambda y x$ would not be single-threaded in general: it can be applied to one argument and yields a closure $\lambda y.x[K^\rho/x]$ containing ρ-typed elements (and one can check that $(\Delta_\rho \circ \mathcal{V})\lambda x^\rho.\lambda y x = False$). This would have drastic effects on single-threading since only the last parameter of functions would be a candidate for globalization. However, if the expression is known to be fully applied, no closure has to be built. Taking into account the above optimizations, we get an improved version of our criteria. For example:

- $E \equiv (\lambda v_1. \ldots \lambda v_n. F_1)\ F_2 \ldots F_n \wedge \Delta_\rho \circ \mathcal{V}(F_1) \wedge \ldots \wedge \Delta_\rho \circ \mathcal{V}(F_n) \wedge$

$fv_\rho(F_i) \Rightarrow$ all occurrences of active ρ-typed expressions in $F_{i-1}, \ldots, F_1$ are occurrences of identifiers.

Using this criterion, the expression $\lambda x^\rho.\lambda y x$ applied to two arguments is detected as single-threaded

It would also be possible to get criteria for call-by-need but they would be of little use since most parameters would be enclosed, and few globalizable variables would be found. However, a call-by-need with strictness information can benefit from single-threading analysis. Let us assume that $\underline{E_1}\ E_2$ indicates that E_1 is strict and $\underline{v}$ means that v is defined by a strict λ-abstraction $\lambda v.E$. Then a CPS transformation for call-by-need can make use of these pieces of information in order to evaluate arguments of strict functions before calling them (cf. Figure 10).

- $\mathcal{N}(v) = v$
- $\mathcal{N}(\underline{v}) = \lambda c.c\ v$ {v is already evaluated}
- $\mathcal{N}(op) = \lambda c.c\ opc$
- $\mathcal{N}(\lambda v.F) = \lambda c.c\ (\lambda c.\lambda v.\mathcal{N}(F)\ c)$
- $\mathcal{N}(E_1\ E_2) = \lambda c.\mathcal{N}(E_1)\ (\lambda f.f\ c\ \mathcal{N}(E_2))$
- $\mathcal{N}(\underline{E_1}\ E_2) = \lambda c.\mathcal{N}(E_2)\ (\lambda a.\mathcal{N}(E_1)\ (\lambda f.f\ c\ a))$ {E_1 is strict; its argument is evaluated}

Figure 10 CPS transformation for call-by-need with strictness annotations ($\mathcal{N}$)

Therefore, by simplifying $\Delta \circ \mathcal{N}$, we can get criteria for call-by-need with strictness annotations.

This method of deriving criteria on source expressions is general (at least for sequential computation rules) and quite simple. However, to insure its correctness one has to check that the CPS transformation models the underlying implementation properly; in particular, the sequencing of variable definitions and uses must be identical.

6 Conclusions

We have presented sufficient syntactic criteria to detect the single-threading property on both continuation expressions and standard λ-expressions. Syntactic analysis is attractive by its low cost and by the information it provides. The approach is general enough to be applied to the compilation of functional languages, semantics-directed compiler generation and goal-directed transformations. Our work improves upon previous solutions (both syntactic and semantics-based) in that it applies to higher-order languages and to most sequential evaluation strategies.

6.1 Related Works

The closest related work is Schmidt's [19] which performs a syntactic analysis on a λ-calculus with a call-by-value semantics. His criteria can be described as the predicate $\mathcal{S}_\rho$ in Figure 11.

S_ρ iff:

- $E \equiv$ atom (v or op)
- $E \equiv \lambda v^\tau.F \wedge \mathcal{S}_\rho(F) \wedge$
  - (i) $\tau \equiv \rho \Rightarrow$ all free ρ-typed identifiers in F are v^ρ
  - (ii) $\tau \not\equiv \rho \Rightarrow$ F has no active ρ-typed expressions
- $E \equiv (E_1\ E_2)^\tau \wedge \mathcal{S}_\rho(E_1) \wedge \mathcal{S}_\rho(E_2) \wedge$
  - (i) $\tau \equiv \rho \Rightarrow$ if both E_1 and E_2 contain one or more active ρ-typed expressions then all of the active ρ-typed expressions in E are occurrences of the same identifier
  - (ii) $\tau \not\equiv \rho \Rightarrow$ all occurrences of active ρ-typed expressions in E are occurrences of the same identifier

Figure 11 Schmidt's single-threading criteria (call-by-value)

Our criteria combined with transformations $\mathcal{V}$ or $\mathcal{V}_r$ turns out to be less conservative than $\mathcal{S}$. Formally stated:

Property 5 $\mathcal{S}_\rho(E) \Rightarrow (\Delta_\rho^\Omega \circ \mathcal{V}(E)) \wedge (\Delta_\rho^\Omega \circ \mathcal{V}_r(E))$

This property is easily shown by structural induction using definitions of $\Delta_\rho \circ \mathcal{V}$ and $\Delta_\rho \circ \mathcal{V}_r$ (section 5). Actually, Property 5 would hold for any transformation $\mathcal{V}$ compiling a call-by-value reduction strategy. The main reason is that $\mathcal{S}_\rho$ does not rely upon a particular version of call-by-value. $\mathcal{S}_\rho$ is valid for any sequential or parallel version of call-by-value and therefore does not take advantage of a particular evaluation order. If this loss of information may be accepted in semantics-directed compiling (where a language designer may make conscious use of the criteria), it would spoil many optimization opportunities when used in a functional language compiler. Another drawback of S_ρ is that multi-applications (cf. Section 5) are not considered and it detects only functions that are single-threaded in their last parameter. This work has been extended in order to analyse combinator languages [15].

Most of the other single-threading detection methods are based on abstract interpretation with some kind of operational semantics describing the sequencing of definitions and uses of variables. [13] builds a lifetime grammar to detect global variables in procedural programs. Bloss [2] uses the notion of path semantics to analyze a lazy first order functional language. [3] considers the same kind of language but accepts call-by-need with strictness information; this analysis, while still in exponential time, is faster than Bloss'. Sestoft [18] focuses on function parameters and considers a strict higher order functional language. The single-threading criteria are defined by an interference analysis on a definition-use grammar constructed from a path semantics. This approach is quite different from ours and a formal assessment of their relative power is difficult to achieve. However, since Sestoft's analysis includes a closure analysis it might detect globalizable parameters that we fail to detect. On the other hand, multi-applications are not considered and this analysis has the same shortcoming as Schmidt's. A notable difference is that Sestoft's work does not rely on types and therefore is well-suited for untyped languages. This work has been extended recently in order to detect globalizable parameters that may be captured in closures [7]. It is worth mentioning that they also found the need to make the order of evaluation explicit on the syntax level, although not using continuations but *let*-construct. Experimental results would be helpful to have a better idea of the relative costs and powers of these analyses.

Another approach is to allow the programmer to make space reutilization explicit [8,23]. New constructs are added to the language to express sequentiality and destructive updates. A type system, inspired from linear logic, is needed to insure that referential transparency is preserved. Wadler proposed another solution based on monad comprehension [24]; in this case no new typing discipline is necessary. Under this approach the programmer is able and has to reason about order of evaluation and space utilization of the program. This may be regarded as a benefit or as a drawback.

Related are also the work done by Raoult and Sethi [17] who have studied single-threading using a pebble game on a program tree. Let us also mention studies aiming at reducing storage allocations for dynamic data structures [10,12] by doing a sharing analysis on strict, first order, languages.

6.2 Future work

We did not consider product types in this paper. There are several ways to extend this work to deal with such constructs. One straightforward solution is to treat tuples the same way as closures but other approaches should be investigated.

We focused on recursive function parameters because the use of registers seems the most useful in this case. However, Δ may also be used for more general register allocation (e.g. using registers to store intermediate results); Δ can be applied not only to check but also to choose type annotations. For example, let C be a continuation expression containing no free variables of types ρ_1 or ρ_2, then when analyzing the expression

$$plusc^{(\alpha\to\kappa)\to\rho2\to\rho1\to\kappa}\,(plusc^{(\beta\to\kappa)\to\rho2\to\alpha\to\kappa}\,C\,y^{\rho2})\,y^{\rho2}\,x^{\rho1}$$

where α and β are type variables, we deduce that the condition for single-threading is $\alpha \not\equiv \rho_2$. Thus $\alpha \equiv \rho_1 \wedge (\beta \equiv \rho_1 \vee \beta \equiv \rho_2)$ are possible choices for implementing those intermediate values by global variables. Predicate Δ would produce a register-interference graph which could be used by classic register allocation algorithms [1].

We believe that the continuation-based approach is also promising for other syntactic analyses. Many properties depend on the evaluation ordering and it is clear that continuations provide valuable information to this respect. We plan to study along these lines stack-single-threading [20] (e.g. detecting when closures or lists can be allocated on a stack) and the introduction of safe destructive updates for list management.

References

1. A.V. Aho, R. Sethi and J.D. Ullman. *Compilers: Principles, Techniques, and Tools*. Addison-Wesley, 1986.

2. A. Bloss. Update analysis and the efficient implementation of functional aggregates. In *FPCA'89*, pp. 26-38, ACM Press, 1989.

3. M. Draghicescu and S. Purushothaman. A compositional analysis of evaluation order and its application. In *Proc. of 1990 Conf. on Lisp and Func. Prog.*, ACM Press, pp. 242-250, 1990.

4. M. J. Fisher. Lambda-calculus schemata. In *Proc. of the ACM Conf. on Proving Properties about Programs*, Sigplan Notices, Vol. 7(1), pp. 104-109,1972.

5. P. Fradet and D. Le Métayer. Compilation of λ-calculus into functional machine code. In *Proc. TAPSOFT'89*, LNCS vol. 352, pp. 155-166, 1989.

6. P. Fradet and D. Le Métayer. Compilation of functional languages by program transformation. *ACM Trans. on Prog. Lang. and Sys.*, 13(1), pp. 21-51, 1991.

7. C.K. Gomard and P. Sestoft. Globalization and live variables. In *Proc. of ACM Symposium on Partial Evaluation and Semantics-Based Program Manipulation,* Yale, June 1991. (to appear in Sigplan Notices)

8. J.Guzmán and P. Hudak. Single-threaded polymorphic lambda-calculus. In *IEEE Symposium on Logic in Computer Science*, June 1990.

9. P. Hudak. A semantic model of reference counting and its abstraction. In *Proc. of Conf. on Lisp and Func. Prog.*, ACM Press, pp. 351-363, 1986.

10. K. Inoue, H. Seki and H. Yagi. Analysis of functional programs to detect run-time garbage cells. *ACM Trans. on Prog. Lang. and Sys.*, 10(4), 1988, 555-578.

11. N.D. Jones Ed. *Semantics-Directed Compiler Generation. LNCS Vol. 94*, 1980.

12. S.B. Jones and D. Le Métayer. Compile-time garbage collection by sharing analysis. In *FPCA'89*, pp.54-74, ACM Press, 1989.

13. U. Kastens and M. Schmidt. Lifetime analysis for procedure parameters. In *ESOP 86, LNCS Vol. 213*, pp.53-69, 1986.

14. D. Kranz, R. Kelsey, J. Rees, P. Hudak, J. Philbin and N. Adams. Orbit: An optimizing compiler for Scheme. In *proc. of 1986 ACM SIGPLAN Symp. on Comp. Construction*, 219-233, 1986.

15. D. Lass. Detection of single-threading properties in combinator notations. Ph.D. Thesis, Iowa State University, 1991.

16. G.D. Plotkin. Call-by-name, call-by-value and the λ-calculus. *Theoretical Computer Science 1*, pp. 125-159, 1975.

17. J.-C. Raoult and R. Sethi. The global storage needs of a subcomputation. In *Proc. ACM Symp. on Princ. of Prog. Lang.*, 1984, 148-157.

18. P. Sestoft. Replacing function parameters by global variables. In *FPCA'89*, ACM Press, pp.39-53, 1989. (see also Tech. Report 88-7-2, University of Copenhagen, 1988.)

19. D.A. Schmidt. Detecting global variables in denotational specifications. *ACM Trans. on Prog. Lang. and Sys.*, vol. 7, 1985, 299-310.

20. D.A. Schmidt. Detecting stack-based environments in denotational definitions. *Science of Computer Programming, 11(2)*, 1988.

21. D.A. Schmidt. *Denotational Semantics. A Methodology for Language Development.* Allyn & Bacon, 1986.

22. J.E. Stoy. *Denotational Semantics: The Scott-Strachey Approach to Programming Language Theory*, MIT Press, Cambridge, Mass.,1977.

23. P. Wadler. Linear types can change the world! In *IFIP Working Conf. on Programming Concepts and Methods*, North Holland, 1990.

24. P. Wadler. Comprehending monads. In *Proc. of 1990 Conf. on Lisp and Func. Prog.*, *ACM Press*, pp. 61-78, 1990.

A Projection Model of Types

D.J. Lillie P.G. Harrison

Abstract

We present an intuitive model of polymorphic recursive types and subtypes based on a metric space of projections. We show this model to be semantically equivalent to types as strong ideals although requiring less structure in the semantic framework and allowing a more concise analysis. We present a new set of type inference rules for a combinatorial language and prove the rules correct with respect to our model. An algorithm embodying these rules has been implemented.

1 Introduction

Recent proposals for models of types for functional programming languages, such as [AP90, ABL86], have returned to the idea of types as Scott-domains, although the first successful model of polymorphic recursive types, the ideal model presented in [MPS86], did not have this property.

Here we present a new model of polymorphic recursive types based on projections, in which the elements of the types again form domains. The model follows that of [MPS86] in using metric space properties to solve recursive equations, but the equational semantics of the type constructors, together with the rich algebraic properties of projections allow us to give extremely elegant proofs of soundness for type inference rules.

Section 2 introduces the basic concepts and notations we shall require, together with some key propositions from earlier work. Section 3 describes the complete metric space of projections stressing the importance of the contractive functions over it. In section 4 we show how common type constructors are contractive and hence how they can be used in the specification of recursive types. Section 5 shows that our projection model is semantically equivalent to the strong ideals of [MPS86].

In section 6 we present a weakly-typed higher-order combinatorial language and a novel set of type inference rules for it which we prove to be sound.

Finally we conclude in section 7 with a brief comparison with other recent models and an outline of some possible future directions for the work presented here.

The remainder of this section motivates the rest of the paper and outlines the way in which our model operates.

1.1 Recursive Types

Modern functional programming languages such as ML [GMW79] and HOPE [BMS80] allow the programmer to define non-primitive data types (and functions over them) using mutually recursive 'equations' in much the same way as functions are defined. For example, a data type *stack* consisting of stacks of numbers (of type *num*) might be defined in HOPE as follows:

data *stack == Empty ++ Push(num X stack)*

The theoretical basis for such definitions requires a model of types in which such arbitrary recursively defined data types can be given meaningful semantics. (Informally we distinguish between a syntactic definition of a data type and the semantic interpretation of the same, which we term a type.) To model *stack*, we need a type S such that if E is the type modelling *Empty* and N is the type modelling *num*, then

$$S = E + (N \times S)$$

holds, where $+$ and $\times$ are suitably defined sum and product operations on types. In some models, isomorphism is acceptable where we have equality.

A solution to this equation for S is clearly a fixed point of the function *Stack* defined by

$$Stack(s) = E + (N \times s) \qquad (*)$$

i.e. $stack = Stack(stack)$. *Stack* is called a type constructor for *stack*, and our model provides a semantics of types such that equations such as $(*)$, associated with syntactically correct data type definitions, always have a fixed point. In fact our model provides these type constructors with *unique* fixed points.

The next section informally describes how this is done.

1.2 Solving Recursive Type Equations

There are several classical fixed point theorems, applying to various abstract structures. The one we use to guarantee the existence of fixed points of type constructors is Banach's fixed point theorem [Ban22], which concerns 'contractive' functions over 'complete metric spaces'. The bulk of the paper is spent showing that this theorem is always applicable.

In outline, we define the 'distance' $d(t, t')$ between two types t and t' as a measure of the complexity of objects which distinguish between t and t'. See section 3 for the details.

This distance function has the properties defining a *metric*, and we show that the metric space of types is complete.

For function f mapping types into types, define the sequence

$$\begin{aligned} t_0 &= \bot_T \qquad \text{the least type in our model} \\ t_{n+1} &= f(t_n) \end{aligned}$$

Some functions will have the property that

$$\forall m \geq 0 \cdot \exists n \geq 0 \cdot \forall i, j \geq n \cdot d(t_i, t_j) < m$$

so the points of the sequence $\langle t_i \rangle$ generally get closer together (the sequence *contracts*); in other words, the further along the sequence one looks, one needs more and more complex objects in order to distinguish between points of the sequence.

Banach's fixed point theorem states that such 'contractive' functions on a complete metric space have unique fixed points.

Section 4 is devoted to showing that some standard type constructors satisfy this criterion of contractiveness, and thus that equations such as $(*)$ always have a (unique) fixed point in our model. As noted above, this fixed point models the programmer-defined data type.

1.3 Projections, Strictness Analysis and Types

The possibility of using projections to represent types, for us, came from the work of Wadler and Hughes [WH87] rather than from Scott as one might think. [WH87] introduces the notion of a function's strictness depending on the context in which it appears:

Definition 1 *A function f is β-strict in context α if $\alpha \circ f = \alpha \circ f \circ \beta$*

This is written as $f : \alpha \Rightarrow \beta$, reminiscent of type notation. The idea is that the projection β will evaluate some part of the argument to f, and the equation states that if α will be applied to the result then we may as well perform the β evaluation before calling f. For suitable choice of α and β this is strictness analysis.

From the point of view of types, the definition of $\alpha \Rightarrow \beta$ above is not quite a type. The equation reads as "if α happens next, doing β now changes nothing." For function types the standard interpretation is "if we have α already, we end up with β" for a function $f : \alpha \rightarrow \beta$, which is arguing the other direction. We can express this as an equation in the same terms as above as follows:

Definition 2 $f : \alpha \rightarrow \beta \iff f \circ \alpha = \beta \circ f \circ \alpha$

Note that the roles of α and β are reversed here.

The formal definition of exponential types appears in section 4.3, together with a proof that it follows the above intuition.

As we shall see, projections have rich algebraic properties making them easy to reason with, and they form a complete lattice which makes subtyping easier to handle.

2 Basic Concepts

In this section we introduce the basic definitions we use in the theory to follow. The framework for our semantics is the well known one of Scott domains, with which we assume the reader is familiar. Our work is based on [MPS86] and when we use propositions given there unchanged we do not repeat the proofs.

[MPS86] briefly review how semantics of programming languages can be captured denotationally by building a solution to a recursive domain equation, for example

$$D = B_1 + \cdots + B_m + (D + D) + (D \times D) + [D \to D]$$

where the B_i are basic domains such as truth values and natural numbers, as a sequence of approximations (or unfoldings)

$$\begin{aligned} D_0 &= \{\bot\} \\ D_{n+1} &= B_1 + \cdots + B_m + (D_n + D_n) + (D_n \times D_n) + [D_n \to D_n] \end{aligned}$$

which has a limit $D = \lim_{n \geq 0} D_n$ and this provides a concrete space in which to define the semantics. This theory is from [SP82], based on earlier work by Scott.

The *finite* elements of constructed domains can be expressed in terms of the finite elements of their constituents; for sums and products we have simple formulae:

$$\begin{aligned} (D \times E)^o &= D^o \times E^o \\ (D + E)^o &= \{\text{in}_1(x) | x \in D^o\} \cup \{\text{in}_2(y) | y \in E^o\} \end{aligned}$$

For the function space we first define the continuous *step function* $(a \to b)$ for $a \in D^o, b \in E^o$:

$$(a \to b)x = \begin{cases} b\,, & a \sqsubseteq x \\ \bot, & \text{otherwise} \end{cases}$$

and then a finite functions is one formed by taking the supremum of a finite number of step functions.

An important proposition for both [MPS86] and ourselves concerns the structure of the finite elements of each domain construction. For each finite element x in the limit domain D, define the rank of x, $r(x)$, to be the least n such that $x \in D_n$ (we are omitting injections to improve readability).

Proposition 1 *For domains D, E we have:*

1. $r(x) = 0 \iff x = \bot$

2. $r(x \sqcup y) \leq \max\{r(x), r(y)\}$ *assuming $x \sqcup y$ exists.*

3. $z \in (D \times E)^o \Longrightarrow \exists x \in D^o, y \in E^o \cdot z = \langle x, y\rangle \ \wedge\ r(x) < r(z) \ \wedge\ r(y) < r(z)$

4. $z \in (D + E)^o \Longrightarrow$
$(\exists x \in D^o \cdot z = \text{in}_1(x) \ \wedge\ r(x) < r(z)) \vee (\exists y \in E^o \cdot z = \text{in}_2(y) \ \wedge\ r(y) < r(z))$

5. $f \in [D \to E]^o \Longrightarrow$
$\exists\{a_1,\ldots,a_n\} \subseteq D^o, \{b_1,\ldots,b_n\} \subseteq E^o \cdot$
$f = \bigsqcup\{(a_i \to b_i) | 1 \leq i \leq n\} \wedge \forall i \leq n \cdot r(a_i) < r(f) \ \wedge \ r(b_i) < r(f)$

Proof

The proof is given in [MPS86, p. 109].

2.1 Projections

Definition 3 *A* projection *on domain D is a function* $p \in [D \to D]$ *satisfying* $p \circ p = p$ *(idempotence) and* $p \sqsubseteq ID_D$.

We will be modelling types by certain projections, saying that if type t is modelled by projection p then an object x has type t ($x : t$) if and only if $px = x$. The concept of subtype is easily modelled by the approximation ordering on projections as continuous functions. In what follows we will not normally distinguish between types and projections, denoting them by the same identifier. Thus the notation $x : p$ is equivalent to the assertion $px = x$.

The set of all projections on a domain D will be written PRJ_D. The set $DCP_D \subseteq PRJ_D$ will denote the set of all projections with downward-closed range. Only projections in DCP_D will be allowed as types; motivation for this can be found as far back as [Mil78, p.360] (which cites [Sco76]...). The importance of this choice for our model will become apparent in section 4.3. For most of this paper, D will be a fixed domain (a solution toan equation such as the one above) and we will omit the subscripts.

Projections have many algebraic properties which we will find useful as we expound our theory. Here we record some of the basic facts as a proposition.

Proposition 2 *For* $p, q \in PRJ$ *and* $P \subseteq PRJ$ *we have the following:*

1. $\bigsqcup P$ *and* $\bigsqcap P$ *both exist and are in* PRJ, *i.e.* PRJ *is a complete lattice.*

2. *If we also have* $P \subseteq DCP$, *then* $\bigsqcup P, \bigsqcap P \in DCP$, *i.e.* DCP *is also a complete lattice.*

3. $\{px | x \in D\} = \{x \in D | px = x\}$, *i.e. the range and fixed-point set of a projection are equal.*

4. *The range $\{px|x \in D\}$ of p is closed under arbitrary suprema (where they exist).*

5. *If $p \sqsubseteq q$ then $p = p \sqcap q = p \circ q = q \circ p$.*

Proof

Most of these are well-known; we cite proofs for brevity. Note that the terminology of [GHK+80] differs from ours — our projections are called (continuous) kernel operators there, and their projections are not required to be $\sqsubseteq ID_D$.

1. See [WH87, p389].

2. This follows immediately from the above proof and the fact that in $[D \to D]$ suprema and infima are calculated pointwise.

3. An easy consequence of idempotence ($p \circ p = p$).

4. See [GHK+80, prop. O-3.12(i)].

5. Firstly, $p = p \sqcap q$ is equivalent to $p \sqsubseteq q$ in any lattice. Now if $p \sqsubseteq q$ then for any x we have $px \sqsubseteq qx \sqsubseteq x$, so by monotonicity of p, $p(px) \sqsubseteq p(qx) \sqsubseteq p(x)$. But $p \circ p = p$ so we have $px \sqsubseteq (p \circ q)x \sqsubseteq px$ and hence $p = p \circ q$. Also, by monotonicity of q we have $q(px) \sqsubseteq px$, but $p \sqsubseteq q$ gives $px = p(px) \sqsubseteq q(px)$ so $p = q \circ p$.

We have a further proposition which shows that the set of elements having a given type forms a domain, a subdomain of the value space.

Proposition 3 *If $p \in DCP_D$ then $\{pd|d \in D\}$ is a subdomain of D.*

Proof

Write pD for the range of p. That pD is a consistently-complete cpo is easy; $p\bot = \bot$ gives a least element, and proposition 2(4) gives suprema of increasing sequences and bounded subsets.

For ω-algebraicity, it can be seen that any ω-finite element of pD is also ω-finite in D and hence we have a countable basis, and for $x \in pD$ we have $(\downarrow x)^o \subseteq pD$ by downward-closure of pD and hence $x = \bigsqcup(\downarrow x)^o$ as required.

3 Complete Metric Spaces of Projections

3.1 Metric Spaces

Following [MPS86], we wish to use Banach's Fixed Point Theorem [Ban22] to establish solutions to our type equations. We proceed by constructing the framework of metric spaces in which we work.

Definition 4 *A* metric space *is a set M together with a function $d_M : M^2 \to \mathcal{R}^+$ (non-negative real numbers) satisfying the following for all x, y and z in M:*

1. $d_M(x, y) = 0 \iff x = y$
2. $d_M(x, y) = d_M(y, x)$
3. $d_M(x, z) \leq d_M(x, y) + d_M(y, z)$

Such a d_M is called a metric *on M. If d_M satisfies the stronger condition*

4. $d_M(x, z) \leq \max(d_M(x, y), d_M(y, z))$

then d_M is an ultrametric *and M is an* ultrametric space.

Definition 5 *If p, $q \in CF_D$, then a* witness *for p and q is any finite element $x \in D$ such that $px \neq qx$. The* closeness *$c(p, q)$ of p and q is the least possible rank of a witness for p and q, or ∞ if none exists.*

We have the following proposition analagous to [MPS86, proposition 2]:

Proposition 4 *The closeness function c defined above has the following properties, for all projections p, q, r:*

1. $c(p, q) = \infty \iff p = q$
2. $c(p, q) = c(q, p)$
3. $c(p, r) \geq \min(c(p, q), c(q, r))$

Proof

1. $c(p, q) = \infty \iff$ for all finite $x, px = qx \iff p = q$.
2. By definition — a witness for p, q is also a witness for q, p.

3. Immediate if $c(p,r)=\infty$. Otherwise let b be a witness of minimum rank for p,r. Then b must be a witness either for p,q or for q,r, and hence we have the inequality required.

[MPS86, section 3.2] explains how given a closeness function with these properties, one can define an ultrametric thus: $d(p,q)=2^{-c(p,q)}$, with the usual convention that $2^{-\infty}=0$.

3.2 Completeness and Contractive Functions

We use the same idea as [MPS86] to solve recursive equations, by associating such an equation with a function over the metric space DCP and proving that this function has a fixed point — such a fixed point then 'satisfies' the equation.

Instead of proving the existence of a fixed point for each equation, we use a general theorem and show that all our type constructors satisfy the conditions of the theorem.

First some more definitions:

Definition 6 *Let (M,d_M), $(M',d_{M'})$ be metric spaces.*

1. *A* Cauchy sequence *is a is a sequence $\langle p_i\rangle_{i\geq 0}$ in M such that*

$$\forall \varepsilon>0\cdot\exists n\cdot\forall i,j\geq n\cdot\ d_M(p_i,p_j)<\varepsilon \qquad (\dagger)$$

2. *M is a* complete metric space *if every Cauchy sequence $\langle p_i\rangle_{i\geq 0}$ in M converges, i.e.*

$$\forall m\geq 0\cdot\exists n\geq 0\cdot\forall i\geq n\cdot c(p_i,q)>m \qquad (\ddagger)$$

3. *A function $f:M\rightarrow M'$ is* contractive *if there is a real number $0\leq k<1$ such that for all x and x' in M we have*

$$d_{M'}(fx,fx')\leq k d_M(x,x')$$

This generalises to functions of several variables thus:

$$d_{M'}(f(x_1,\ldots,x_n),f(x'_1,\ldots,x'_n))\leq k\max\{d_M(x_i,x'_i)|1\leq i\leq n\}$$

Contractive functions satisfy the condition given in section 1.2, and Banach's fixed-point theorem ([Ban22]) states that every contractive function on a complete metric space has a unique fixed point.

Thus, we show that DCP is complete as a metric space and (in section 4) that the functions by which we model type constructors are contractive. Then any recursive type equation built using our constructors is guaranteed to have a (unique) fixed point, and hence a solution.

To facilitate the proofs, we relate the above definitions to our closeness function. The Cauchy criterion (†) can be expressed in terms of the closeness function thus:

$$\forall m \geq 0 \cdot \exists n \geq 0 \cdot \forall i, j \geq n \cdot \ c(p_i, p_j) > m \tag{§}$$

From [MPS86] we have the following characterisation of contractive functions in terms of our closeness function:

Proposition 5 *A function $f : PRJ^n \rightarrow PRJ$ is contractive if and only if for all projections $p_1, \ldots, p_n, q_1, \ldots, q_n$ with some $p_i \neq q_i$ we have*

$$c(f(p_1, \ldots, p_n), f(q_1, \ldots, q_n)) > \min\{c(p_i, q_i) | 1 \leq i \leq n\}$$

Proof

The proof given in [MPS86, propostion 5] carries across unchanged.

Now we prove the cornerstone of our theory:

Theorem 1 *The metric space of projections is complete.*

Proof

For Cauchy sequence $\langle p_i \rangle_{i \geq 0}$ define the function q as follows:

$$qx = y \iff \forall^\infty i \cdot p_i x = y$$

where $\forall^\infty$ is the notation we use for 'almost all', meaning 'all but finitely many'.

We proceed by showing that q is well-defined, that $\langle p_i \rangle$ converges to q, and that q is continuous.

1. Well-defined:

   For given x, we show that y such that $\forall^\infty i \cdot p_i x = y$ is uniquely defined. First we prove that there is such a y. We dispose of $x = \bot$ by noting that $\forall i \cdot p_i \bot = \bot$. For $x \neq \bot$, suppose for contradiction that

$$\nexists y \cdot \forall^\infty i \cdot p_i x = y \tag{¶}$$

So for all n, an infinite number of i's exist such that $p_n x \neq p_i x$. Let $m = r(x) + 1$. By (§) we can choose $n \geq 0$ such that $\forall i \geq n \cdot c(p_i, p_n) > m$. But by (¶), $\exists i > n \cdot p_i x \neq p_n x$, so $r(x) \geq c(p_i, p_n) > m > r(x)$. This is a contradiction, so (¶) is false. It is clear that this y is unique, since if $\forall^\infty i \cdot p_i x = y$, then only a finite subset of the p_i's can map x elsewhere, and so our function q is indeed well-defined.

2. Convergence:
Let m be given, and choose n by condition (§). Take $i \geq n$ arbitrarily, and let x be a witness for q, p_i of least rank, so $c(p_i, q) = r(x)$. If there is no witness, $c(p_i, q) = \infty > m$ trivially. Otherwise $\forall^\infty j \cdot p_j x = qx \neq p_i x$ so $\exists j > i \cdot c(p_i, p_j) \leq r(x)$, and we have $c(p_i, q) = r(x) \geq c(p_i, p_j) > m$ and hence (‡).

3. Continuity:
Let $X = \{x_\lambda | \lambda \in \Lambda\}$ be directed with supremum x. Noting that $\forall^\infty i \cdot qx = p_i x \wedge \forall^\infty i \cdot qx_\lambda = p_i x_\lambda$ implies $\forall^\infty i \cdot (qx = p_i x \wedge qx_\lambda = p_i x_\lambda)$, we can choose for each $\lambda \in \Lambda$, an i_λ such that $qx = p_{i_\lambda} x$ and $qx_\lambda = p_{i_\lambda} x_\lambda$. Define functions

$$\begin{aligned} u &= \sqcup_{\lambda \in \Lambda} p_{i_\lambda} \\ v &= \sqcap_{\lambda \in \Lambda} p_{i_\lambda} \end{aligned}$$

Then u and v are continuous since PRJ is a complete lattice. Now $\forall \lambda \in \Lambda \cdot vx_\lambda \sqsubseteq p_{i_\lambda} x \sqsubseteq qx_\lambda \sqsubseteq ux_\lambda$, and also we have $vx = qx = ux$. But then by continuity of u, v we have:

$$qx = vx = \bigsqcup_\lambda (vx_\lambda) \sqsubseteq \bigsqcup_\lambda (qx_\lambda) \sqsubseteq \bigsqcup_\lambda (ux_\lambda) = ux = qx$$

So $qx = \sqcup_\lambda (qx_\lambda)$ and so q is continuous.

It remains only to show that q is a projection when all the p_i are. By idempotence of projections, $y = qx$ must be a fixed point of almost all p_i, and thus $qy = y$, so q is idempotent also. It is clear that $q \sqsubseteq ID$, for given any x, $qx = p_i x \sqsubseteq x$ for at least one i.

Corollary 2 *The metric space DCP of projections with downward-closed fixed-point sets is complete.*

Proof

Clearly it suffices to show that if $\langle p_i \rangle_{i \geq 0}$ is a Cauchy sequence in DCP, then q defined as above is also in DCP. If $x = qx$ then for almost all i, $p_i x = x$. So if $y \sqsubseteq x$ we have that for almost all i, $p_i y = y$ since all the p_i are in DCP. But this means that $qy = y$ by definition of q.

4 Contractive Type Constructors

In order to use Banach's fixed point theorem to provide solutions to our type equations, we must prove that our type constructors are contractive. In the following sections, we shall define several common type constructors and prove that they are contractive as functions over DCP. Most of our constructors are in fact contractive over PRJ also. We will implicitly appeal to propositions 1 and 5, and in the interests of brevity we will not explicitly itemize each proposition of contractiveness.

4.1 Product

We define $p \times q$ as in [MPS86], thus:

$$(p \times q)\langle a, b\rangle = \langle pa, qb\rangle$$

Let x be a witness of least rank for $p \times q$, $p' \times q'$, so $(p \times q)(x) \neq (p' \times q')(x)$. Now $x = \langle y, z\rangle$, otherwise both projections give $\bot$, and $\langle py, qz\rangle \neq \langle p'y, q'z\rangle$. Assume without loss of generality that $py \neq p'y$. So $r(x) > r(y) > \min(c(p, p'), c(q, q'))$, so the product is contractive.

4.2 Sum

We define

$$(p + q)x = \begin{cases} px, & \mathrm{is}_1 x \\ qx, & \mathrm{is}_2 x \\ \bot & \text{otherwise} \end{cases}$$

Let x be a witness of least rank for $p + q, p' + q'$. Then x is either $\mathrm{in}_1(a)$ with $r(a) < r(x)$, or $\mathrm{in}_2(b)$ with $r(b) < r(x)$, by proposition 1. Assume without loss of generality that $x = \mathrm{in}_1(a)$. Then

$$(p+q)x = pa \neq p'a = (p'+q')x$$

So a is a witness for p, p' of lower rank than x, so $+$ is contractive.

4.3 Exponential

We considered exponential types in section 1.3, with regards to projections for strictness analysis. Here, before we define our exponential type, we consider the ideal type constructor $\boxed{\rightarrow}$ in [MPS86], defined thus:

$$I \boxed{\rightarrow} J = \{f \in [D \rightarrow D] | f(I) \subseteq J\}$$

The condition on f is that $x : I \Longrightarrow (fx) : J$, without restricting f on arguments not of type I, which is the standard interpretation as in 1.3.

In our model, substituting projections p and q for ideals I and J, this condition reads as $px = x \Longrightarrow q(fx) = fx$. But by proposition 2 the range and fixed point set of p coincide, so $px = x \iff x = py$ for some y. So we have

$$\begin{array}{ll} & \forall y \cdot x = py \Longrightarrow q(fx) = fx \\ \text{i.e.} & \forall y \cdot q(f(py)) = f(py) \\ \text{i.e.} & q \circ f \circ p = f \circ p \end{array}$$

This equation then characterises functions in essentially the same way as the ideals construct; in section 5 we make this more precise. To turn this equation into a projection we need to resort to approximations (which means we need proposition 7 to maintain our intuition):

Definition 7 *The exponential type of types p and q is defined as follows:*

$$(p \Rightarrow q)f = \bigsqcup\{g \sqsubseteq f | g \circ p = q \circ g \circ p\}$$

Since this is the only section in which we use the fact that our projections are drawn from DCP rather than PRJ, we will draw the reader's attention to the points where we make use of this.

Proposition 6 *For $p, q \in PRJ$, $(p \Rightarrow q) \in PRJ$. Furthermore, if $q \in DCP$ then $(p \Rightarrow q) \in DCP$.*

Proof

By proposition 7 it suffices that when $f \circ p = q \circ f \circ p$ and $g \sqsubseteq f$ we have $g \circ p = q \circ g \circ p$. But for all $x = py$ we have that $gx \sqsubseteq fx = q(fx)$, and hence since $q \in DCP$[1] and fx is in the range of q, gx is in the range of q, i.e. $gx = q(gx)$. Thus $g \circ p = q \circ g \circ p$ as required.

The following proposition allows us to use the intuitive equational characterisation from 1.3 (and above) in proofs:

Proposition 7 *For $p, q \in PRJ$ and $f \in [D \to D]$ we have*

$$(p \Rightarrow q)f = f \iff f \circ p = q \circ f \circ p$$

Proof

1. $(\Leftarrow)$
   $f \circ p = q \circ f \circ p$
   so $f \in \{g \sqsubseteq f | g \circ p = q \circ g \circ p\}$
   thus $f = \bigsqcup\{g \sqsubseteq f | g \circ p = q \circ g \circ p\} = (p \Rightarrow q)f$

2. $(\Rightarrow)$
   $(p \Rightarrow q)f = f$
   so $\forall x \cdot fx = \bigsqcup\{gx | g \sqsubseteq f \wedge g \circ p = q \circ g \circ p\}$
   thus we calculate $\forall x$:

$$\begin{aligned}(f \circ p)x &= \bigsqcup\{(g \circ p)x | g \sqsubseteq f \wedge g \circ p = q \circ g \circ p\}\\ &\qquad \text{by definition of } \bigsqcup \text{ on } [D \to D]\\ &= \bigsqcup\{(q \circ g \circ p)x | g \sqsubseteq f \wedge g \circ p = q \circ g \circ p\}\\ &= (q \circ f \circ p)x\\ &\qquad \text{by continuity of } q\end{aligned}$$

We now present two lemmas to aid our proof of contractiveness (proposition 10).

Lemma 8 *If $q \in DCP$ and $g \in [D \to D]$ then $g \circ p = q \circ g \circ p \iff \forall h \in (\downarrow g)^o \cdot h \circ p = q \circ h \circ p$.*

Proof

The implication $\Rightarrow$ is an easy consequence of propositions 7 and 6. The converse holds by continuity of composition and the fact that $[D \to D]$ is a domain.

---

[1] Use of *DCP*.

Lemma 9 *If* $[p \Rightarrow q] \neq [p' \Rightarrow q']$ *then there is a finite* h *of least rank such that*

$$h \circ p \neq q \circ h \circ p, \quad h \circ p' = q' \circ h \circ p'$$

or vice versa.

Proof

We are given $\exists f \cdot [p \Rightarrow q]f \neq [p' \Rightarrow q']f$. Then from the definition of $[\cdot \Rightarrow \cdot]$ there is some $g \sqsubseteq f$ such that without loss of generality

$$g \circ p \neq q \circ g \circ p, \quad g \circ p' = q \circ g \circ p'$$

But then by lemma 8 there is some finite h with the same equality and inequality holding, as required.

Proposition 10 $[\cdot \Rightarrow \cdot]$ *is contractive on DCP.*

Proof

We utilize the fact [MPS86, section 4.1] that on an ultrametric space such as the one we are dealing with, a function is contractive if it is contractive in each argument separately.

1. 1st Arg:
   Suppose $[p \Rightarrow q] \neq [p' \Rightarrow q]$. Then by lemma 9 without loss of generality there is a finite h of least rank such that

   $$h \circ p \neq q \circ h \circ p, \quad h \circ p' = q \circ h \circ p'$$

   Then $h = \sqcup_{1 \leq i \leq n}(a_i \rightarrow b_i)$ with $r(a_i) < r(h)$ and $r(b_i) < r(h)$ for all i. Now there exists a finite x of least rank such that $(h \circ p)x \neq (q \circ h \circ p)x$. Write $z = px$. Note that since p is idempotent, $pz = z$ Let $a = \sqcup\{a_i | a_i \sqsubseteq z\}$, $b = \sqcup\{b_i | a_i \sqsubseteq z\}$. Then $r(a) < r(h)$, $r(b) < r(h)$ and $ha = hz = b$. Also, $a \sqsubseteq z$ and since p is in DCP[2] we have $pa = a$. Since $ha = hz = (h \circ p)x$ we have $(h \circ p)a = (h \circ p)z = (h \circ p)x$. But $(h \circ p)x \neq (q \circ h \circ p)x$ so $(h \circ p)a \neq (q \circ h \circ p)a$, and so $b \neq qb$. That is, $ha \neq (q \circ h)a$, and so $p'a \neq a$ since $(h \circ p') = (q \circ h \circ p')$. So $p'a \neq pa$ and a is a witness for p, p' of lower rank than h, which is to say that $[\cdot \Rightarrow \cdot]$ is contractive in its first argument.

[2]Use of *DCP*. The use here is the essential one.

2. 2nd Arg:
Given $[p \Rightarrow q] \neq [p \Rightarrow q']$, again choose h finite of least rank such that

$$h \circ p \neq q \circ h \circ p, \quad h \circ p = q' \circ h \circ p$$

Then there exists a finite x of least rank such that

$$(q \circ h \circ p)x \neq (q' \circ h \circ p)x$$

Write $z = px$. Note that since p is idempotent, $pz = z$ Let $a = \sqcup\{a_i | a_i \sqsubseteq z\}$, $b = \sqcup\{b_i | a_i \sqsubseteq z\}$. Then $r(a) < r(h)$, $r(b) < r(h)$ and $b = ha = hz = (h \circ p)x = (q \circ h \circ p)x = qb$, and we have $qb \neq q'b$. Thus b is a witness for q, q' of rank lower than $r(h)$, which is to say that $[\cdot \Rightarrow \cdot]$ is contractive in its second argument.

Thus $[\cdot \Rightarrow \cdot]$ is contractive on DCP.

4.4 Bounded Quantification

For $f : PRJ^{n+1} \rightarrow PRJ$, the *bounded universal quantification* of f with respect to $p \in PRJ$ (often denoted by $\forall q \leq p \cdot f(q)$ for unary f) is the function $(\forall^{\leq p} f)$: $PRJ^n \rightarrow PRJ$, defined as follows:

$$(\forall^{\leq p} f)(q_1, \ldots, q_n) = \sqcap \{f(q, q_1, \ldots, q_n) | q \in PRJ \wedge q \sqsubseteq p\}$$

and the bounded existential quantification of f is defined as follows:

$$(\exists^{\leq p} f)(q_1, \ldots, q_n) = \sqcup \{f(q, q_1, \ldots, q_n) | q \in PRJ \wedge q \sqsubseteq p\}$$

Note that ordinary unbounded quantification can be derived by setting the bound p to be ID in either case.

Proposition 11 *If f as above is contractive in its last n arguments, then for all projections p, $(\forall^{\leq p} f)$ and $(\exists^{\leq p} f)$ are also contractive.*

Proof

We prove the universal case, the existential case being proven by the same proof substituting $\exists$ for $\forall$ and $\sqcap$ for $\sqcup$.

Take $\underline{q}, \underline{q}' \in PRJ^n$, not equal. Let x be a witness of least rank for $(\forall^{\leq p} f)\underline{q}$ and $(\forall^{\leq p} f)\underline{q}'$. So $(\forall^{\leq p} f)\underline{q}(x) \neq (\forall^{\leq p} f)\underline{q}'(x)$.

Thus $(\sqcap\{f(q,\underline{q})\})x \neq (\sqcap\{f(q,\underline{q}')\})x$

so $\sqcap\{f(q,\underline{q})x\} \neq \sqcap\{f(q,\underline{q}')x\}$

Therefore $\exists q \cdot f(q,\underline{q})x \neq f(q,\underline{q}')x$, i.e. x is a witness for $f(q,\underline{q})$ and $f(q,\underline{q}')$.

$$
\begin{aligned}
\text{Thus } c((\forall^{\leq p} f)\underline{q}, (\forall^{\leq p} f)\underline{q}') &= r(x) \\
&\geq c(f(q,\underline{q}), f(q,\underline{q}')) \\
&> \min c(q_i, q'_i)
\end{aligned}
$$

since f is contractive in its last n arguments.

Thus $(\forall^{\leq p} f)$ is contractive, as required.

4.5 Fixed points

The fixed point constructor μ operates on functions of the form $f : (X \times Y_1 \times \cdots \times Y_n) \rightarrow X$ contractive in the first argument. Then $(\mu f) : (Y_1 \times \cdots \times Y_n) \rightarrow X$ is defined by taking $(\mu f)(y_1, \ldots, y_n)$ to be the unique x such that $x = f(x, y_1, \ldots, y_n)$ as guaranteed by Banach's fixed point theorem.

This is the same operator as defined in [MPS86], and the proof of contractiveness given there is valid in a general complete metric space, and so carries directly across to our case.

4.6 An Example: Sequences

One of the most common data types used in functional programming is the sequence or list. It is usual to restrict lists to elements of a particular type t and call them "lists of t," denoted by various notations such as $[t]$, List t, $t\star$, t list etc.

Here we take a slightly different approach from these homogenous lists, and to avoid confusion we will consistently use the name *sequences* rather than lists. We do not require all elements of a sequence to have a particular type, instead we give in effect a sequence of types corresponding to the positions of elements in the sequence. The notation we will use is angle brackets $\langle\ \rangle$ for sequence objects and double angle brackets $\ll\ \gg$ for sequence types.

This kind of sequence is similar in many ways to record types or structures familiar from many imperative languages, and is a combination of products (tuples) and homogenous lists. (cf. FP sequences in [Bac78], and our section 6).

There is a natural ordering on the sequence objects which derives from viewing (finite) sequences as products. In this ordering, only sequences of the same length are comparable, and those sequences are compared lexicographically. However we will use an equally natural ordering which derives from viewing sequences as lists. Here, we do not require sequence objects to be of the same length in order to be comparable; we merely compare lexicographically. Shorter sequences take precedence in case one is an extension of the other. [3]

This ordering has been considered carefully by Cardelli [Car88] in a rather different context.

Formally, we begin by defining sequence objects and the appropriate selection operators.

Definition 8 *For objects $x_1, \ldots, x_n$ we define $\langle x_1, \ldots, x_n \rangle$ to be a* sequence object, *and on any sequence object the* selectors π_j *are defined for* $1 \leq j$ *such that*

$$\pi_j\langle x_1, \ldots, x_n \rangle = \begin{cases} x_j, & j \leq n \\ \bot & j > n \end{cases}$$

Definition 9 *For sequence objects $\langle x_1, \ldots, x_n \rangle$ and $\langle y_1, \ldots, y_m \rangle$ we define*

$$\langle x_1, \ldots, x_n \rangle \sqsubseteq \langle y_1, \ldots, y_m \rangle \iff n \leq m \ \wedge\ \forall 1 \leq i \leq n \cdot x_i \sqsubseteq y_i$$

Definition 10 *Given types $t_1, \ldots, t_m$ we define the* sequence type $\ll t_1, \ldots, t_m \gg$ *to be the type including all sequence objects $\langle x_1, \ldots, x_n \rangle$ with $m \leq n$ such that for $1 \leq i \leq m$, $x_i : t_i$ (i.e. x_i has type t_i). In terms of projections, we have the following projection type:*
$\ll \alpha_1, \ldots, \alpha_m \gg \langle x_1, \ldots, x_n \rangle =$

$$\textbf{if } n < m \textbf{ then } \bot \quad \textbf{else } \langle \alpha_1 x_1, \ldots, \alpha_m x_m, x_{m+1}, \ldots, x_n \rangle$$

Before we proceed to put this example to use in our type inference rules, we give some properties which will be useful later.

Proposition 12 *For projections α_i, $1 \leq i \leq n$ and β_i, $1 \leq i \leq m$:*

$$\ll \alpha_i \gg_{1 \leq i \leq n} \sqsubseteq \ll \beta_i \gg_{1 \leq i \leq m} \iff m \leq n \ \wedge\ 1 \leq i \leq m \Rightarrow \alpha_i \sqsubseteq \beta_i$$

[3] It is interesting to note that this ordering is closer to dictionary order than the usual lexicographic ordering on products, since the dictionary places words of unequal length in this order whereas the product ordering would put all three-letter words separate from (and indeed incomparable with) all four-letter words.

Proof

Similar to products and omitted.

Proposition 13 *For all projections α_i and continuous functions f_i, where i runs between 1 and some arbitrary (but finite) n we have:*

$$\ll \alpha_1, \ldots, \alpha_n \gg \circ [f_1, \ldots, f_n] = [\alpha_1 \circ f_1, \ldots, \alpha_n \circ f_n]$$

Proof

For all x we calculate:

$$\begin{aligned} \ll \alpha_1, \ldots, \alpha_n \gg \circ [f_1, \ldots, f_n]\ (x) &= \ll \alpha_1, \ldots, \alpha_n \gg (\langle f_1 x, \ldots, f_n x \rangle) \\ &= \langle \alpha_1(f_1 x), \ldots, \alpha_n(f_n x) \rangle \\ &= \langle \alpha_1 \circ f_1(x), \ldots, \alpha_n \circ f_n(x) \rangle \\ &= [\alpha_1 \circ f_1, \ldots, \alpha_n \circ f_n]\,(x) \end{aligned}$$

Finally we show that our sequence type constructor is contractive:

Proposition 14 *The sequence type constructor $\ll\ \gg$ is contractive.*

Proof

Similar to products and omitted.

5 Relationship with the Ideal Model

We now show that our projection model is semantically equivalent to types as strong ideals, as in the appendix of [MPS86]. Note, however, that [MPS86] required *primal* domains in order to give a strong ideal semantics, whereas we only use finite elements.

For every ideal we define a projection with analogous properties, and in fact for the strong ideals the sets corresponding to the types modelled by the ideal and associated projection coincide.

For $I \subseteq D$ an ideal we make the following definition:

Definition 11

$$[I]x = \bigsqcup\{y \in I^o | y \sqsubseteq x\} = \bigsqcup(I^o \cap (\downarrow x)^o)$$

Proposition 15 *For any ideal I, $[I]$ is a projection such that $I \subseteq \{[I]d | d \in D\}$, with equality attained iff I is strong.*

Proof

We take the proof in three stages:

1. Continuity:
   Take $X = \{x_\lambda | \lambda \in \Lambda\}$ directed in D. Then

$$\begin{aligned}
[I](\bigsqcup X) &= \bigsqcup\{y \in I^o | y \sqsubseteq \bigsqcup X\} \\
&= \bigsqcup(I^o \cap \downarrow \bigsqcup X) \\
&= \bigsqcup(I^o \cap (\downarrow \bigsqcup X)^o) \\
&= \bigsqcup(I^o \cap \bigcup_\lambda (\downarrow x_\lambda)^o) \\
&= \bigsqcup(\bigcup_\lambda (I^o \cap (\downarrow x_\lambda)^o)) \\
&= \bigsqcup_\lambda(\bigsqcup(I^o \cap (\downarrow x_\lambda)^o)) \\
&= \bigsqcup_\lambda([I]x_\lambda)
\end{aligned}$$

   Hence $[I]$ is continuous.

2. Projection:
   That $[I]x \sqsubseteq x$ is trivial; for idempotence we have:

$$\begin{aligned}
[I]([I]x) &= \bigsqcup\{y \in I^o | y \sqsubseteq [I]x\} \\
&= \bigsqcup\{y \in I^o | y \sqsubseteq \bigsqcup\{z \in I^o | z \sqsubseteq x\}\} \\
&= \bigsqcup\{y \in I^o | \exists z \in I^o \cdot y \sqsubseteq z \sqsubseteq x\} \\
&= \bigsqcup\{y \in I^o | y \sqsubseteq x\} \\
&= [I]x
\end{aligned}$$

   showing that $[I]$ is a projection.

3. $I \subseteq [I](D)$:
   Take $x \in I$. Then

$$[I]x = \bigsqcup\{y \in I^o | y \sqsubseteq x\} = \bigsqcup(\downarrow x)^o = x$$

   and so $I \subseteq [I](D)$ as claimed. For strong ideals we have for all $x \in D$ that $\{y \in I^o | y \sqsubseteq x\}$ is a directed subset of I, so $[I]x = \sqcup X \in I$ as ideals are closed under suprema of directed subsets, giving an equality $I = [I](D)$. Conversely, if this equality holds then as the image of a projection I is closed under finite suprema by proposition 2, and hence is strong as claimed.

The correspondence between projections and strong ideals is in fact one-one; this is a corollary of the following proposition:

Proposition 16 *Projections $p, q \in PRJ_D$ having the same range $p(D) = q(D)$ are equal ($p = q$).*

Proof

By monotonicity, and the fact that for projections the range and set of fixed points coincide, we calculate:

$$\begin{array}{lllllll} qx & \sqsubseteq & x & \Longrightarrow & qx & = & p(qx) \sqsubseteq px \\ px & \sqsubseteq & x & \Longrightarrow & px & = & q(px) \sqsubseteq qx \end{array}$$

and hence $px = qx$.

Proposition 17 *If strong ideals I and J are the fixed-point sets of projections p and q, then*

$$f \in (I \boxed{\rightarrow} J) \iff (f \circ p) = (q \circ f \circ p)$$

Proof

First we show that $f \in I \boxed{\rightarrow} J$ implies that $(q \circ f \circ p) = (f \circ p)$. Assume that $\forall x \in I \cdot fx \in J$.

$$\begin{array}{llll} (q \circ f \circ p)x & = & (q \circ f \circ p)(px) & \text{since } p \text{ idempotent} \\ & = & (f \circ p)(px) & \text{since } px \in I \\ & = & (f \circ p)x & \end{array}$$

It remains to show that whenever $(q \circ f \circ p) = (f \circ p)$ we have $f \in I \boxed{\rightarrow} J)$. Take $x \in I$. Then $px = x$ so:

$$fx = (f \circ p)x = (q \circ f \circ p)x = (q \circ f)x = q(fx)$$

Thus $fx \in J$ since J is the fixed-point set of q. Therefore $f \in I \boxed{\rightarrow} J)$ as required.

6 Example Language and Type Inference Rules

Tables 1 and 2 summarise the syntax and semantics of a typical higher-order combinatorial language similar to Backus' FP [Bac78] and Curien's CCL [Cur86].

Expressions e are either constants of some base type, sequences of expressions, a function, or the application of a function to an expression. Functions f are

f	$::=$	$f_1 \circ f_2$	composition
	$\mid$	$f_1 \rightarrow f_2; f_3$	conditional
	$\mid$	$[f_1, \ldots, f_n]$	construction
	$\mid$	Λf	currying
	$\mid$	$@$	apply
	$\mid$	$\mathbf{Y} f$	recursion

Table 1: Example Syntax

described by the syntax shown in table 1 and have semantics based on table 2. Note that in the semantics of currying, the λ-term is intended to mean that if $[\![\Lambda f]\!]\, x$ is applied to an argument which is a sequence object, then the result is the λ-body, otherwise the result is $\perp$.

The inference rules, summarized in table 3 are novel in that they do not need an environment of variables and associated types; the language does not have variables, but uses rather more categorical ideas to build functions. In particular, we have the **Y** combinator to compute least fixed points for recursion and the Λ combinator to express functional abstraction. We differ from FP principally in these two combinators, and we also allow applications (using the @ combinator).

The rules use only the exponential and sequence type constructors, together with the sup and inf operations. We suggest that in any model of types supporting these operations (and in particular any model providing a complete lattice of types) these rules will remain valid. We proceed to prove the soundness of the rules in our projection model. Notice the simplifications possible by using the algebraic properties of projections; we have given more detail than is strictly necessary in the proofs, a level of detail which is unusual in this field.

6.1 Composition

$$[\text{COMP}] \quad \frac{f : \beta' \rightarrow \gamma \quad g : \alpha \rightarrow \beta}{(f \circ g) : \alpha \rightarrow \gamma} \quad \text{with } \beta \leq \beta'$$

$$
\begin{aligned}
[\![f_1 \circ f_2]\!]\, x &= [\![f_1]\!]\,([\![f_2]\!]\, x) \\
[\![f_1 \to f_2; f_3]\!]\, x &= \begin{cases} [\![f_2]\!]\, x, & [\![f_1]\!]\, x = \mathtt{tt} \\ [\![f_3]\!]\, x, & [\![f_1]\!]\, x = \mathtt{ff} \\ \bot, & \text{otherwise} \end{cases} \\
[\![[f_1, \ldots, f_n]]\!]\, x &= \langle [\![f_1]\!]\, x, \ldots, [\![f_n]\!]\, x \rangle \\
[\![\Lambda f]\!]\, x &= \lambda \langle x_1, \ldots, x_n \rangle \cdot ([\![f]\!]\, \langle x, x_1, \ldots, x_n \rangle) \\
[\![f@x]\!] &= [\![f]\!]\, [\![x]\!] \\
[\![\mathbf{Y} f]\!] &= \mathbf{Y}[\![f]\!] \\
[\![e]\!] &= e \text{ for other expressions}
\end{aligned}
$$

Table 2: Example Semantics

$$
\begin{aligned}
\gamma \circ f \circ g \circ \alpha &= \gamma \circ f \circ \beta \circ g \circ \alpha \\
&= \gamma \circ f \circ \beta' \circ \beta \circ g \circ \alpha \qquad \text{since } \beta \sqsubseteq \beta' \\
&= f \circ \beta' \circ \beta \circ g \circ \alpha \\
&= f \circ \beta \circ g \circ \alpha \\
&= f \circ g \circ \alpha
\end{aligned}
$$

6.2 Conditional

$$
[\text{COND}] \quad \frac{p : \alpha \to \mathbf{bool}\,, \quad g : \beta \to \delta\,, \quad h : \gamma \to \varepsilon}{(p \to g; h) : (\alpha \sqcap \beta \sqcap \gamma) \to (\delta \sqcup \varepsilon)}
$$

From table 2 we see that there are three possible results for $(p \to g; h)x$, namely gx, hx or $\bot$. We take each case separately.

1. $(\delta \sqcup \varepsilon) \circ g \circ (\alpha \sqcap \beta \sqcap \gamma)(x)$

$$
\begin{aligned}
&= (\delta \sqcup \varepsilon) \circ g \circ \beta \circ (\alpha \sqcap \beta \sqcap \gamma)(x) && \text{since } (\alpha \sqcap \beta \sqcap \gamma) \sqsubseteq \beta \\
&= (\delta \sqcup \varepsilon) \circ \delta \circ g \circ \beta \circ (\alpha \sqcap \beta \sqcap \gamma)(x) && \text{by assumption on } g \\
&= \delta \circ g \circ \beta \circ (\alpha \sqcap \beta \sqcap \gamma)(x) && \text{since } \delta \sqsubseteq (\delta \sqcup \varepsilon) \\
&= g \circ \beta \circ (\alpha \sqcap \beta \sqcap \gamma)(x) \\
&= g \circ (\alpha \sqcap \beta \sqcap \gamma)(x)
\end{aligned}
$$

2. As above, $(\delta \sqcup \varepsilon) \circ h \circ (\alpha \sqcap \beta \sqcap \gamma) = h \circ (\alpha \sqcap \beta \sqcap \gamma)$

[COMP]	$\dfrac{f:\beta' \to \gamma \quad g:\alpha \to \beta}{(f \circ g):\alpha \to \gamma}$ with $\beta \leq \beta'$
[COND]	$\dfrac{p:\alpha \to \mathbf{bool}\ ,\ \ g:\beta \to \delta\ ,\ \ h:\gamma \to \varepsilon}{(p \to g; h):(\alpha \sqcap \beta \sqcap \gamma) \to (\delta \sqcup \varepsilon)}$
[CSTR]	$\dfrac{f_i:\alpha_i \to \beta_i\ ,\ \ 1 \leq i \leq n}{[f_1,\ldots,f_n]:\sqcap\alpha_i \to \ll \beta_1,\ldots,\beta_n \gg}$
[CURR]	$\dfrac{f:\ll \alpha,\beta_1,\ldots,\beta_n \gg \to \gamma}{\Lambda(f):\alpha \to (\ll \beta_1,\ldots,\beta_n \gg \to \gamma)}$
[APPL]	$\dfrac{f:\alpha \to \beta\ ,\ \ x:\alpha}{f@x:\beta}$
[RECN]	$\dfrac{f:\alpha \to \alpha}{\mathbf{Y}\ f:\alpha}$

Table 3: Summary of Inference Rules

3. $\bot$ is a fixed point of every projection, so $(\delta \sqcup \varepsilon) \circ \bot \circ (\alpha \sqcap \beta \sqcap \gamma) = \bot \circ (\alpha \sqcap \beta \sqcap \gamma)$

Using the laws

$$\begin{aligned} (p \to g; h) \circ f &= p \circ f \to g \circ f; h \circ f \\ f \circ (p \to g; h) &= p \to f \circ g; f \circ h \end{aligned}$$

from [Bac78] we can combine these three cases to give

$$(\delta \sqcup \varepsilon) \circ (p \to g; h) \circ (\alpha \sqcap \beta \sqcap \gamma) = (p \to g; h) \circ (\alpha \sqcap \beta \sqcap \gamma)$$

6.3 Construction

[CSTR] $\dfrac{f_i:\alpha_i \to \beta_i\ ,\ \ 1 \leq i \leq n}{[f_1,\ldots,f_n]:\sqcap\alpha_i \to \ll \beta_1,\ldots,\beta_n \gg}$

$$\begin{aligned}
\ll \beta_i \gg \circ [f_i] \circ \sqcap\alpha_j &= [\beta_i \circ f_i \circ \sqcap\alpha_j] && \text{by proposition 13}\\
&= [\beta_i \circ f_i \circ \alpha_i \circ \sqcap\alpha_j] && \text{since } \sqcap\alpha_j \sqsubseteq \alpha_i\\
&= [f_i \circ \alpha_i \circ \sqcap\alpha_j]\\
&= [f_i \circ \sqcap\alpha_j]\\
&= [f_i] \circ \sqcap\alpha_j
\end{aligned}$$

6.4 Curry

[CURR] $$\frac{f :\ll \alpha, \beta_1, \ldots, \beta_n \gg\rightarrow \gamma}{\Lambda(f) : \alpha \rightarrow (\ll \beta_1, \ldots, \beta_n \gg\rightarrow \gamma)}$$

Now $[\ll \beta_i \gg\Rightarrow \gamma] \circ \Lambda f \circ \alpha = \Lambda f \circ \alpha$
$\Longleftrightarrow \forall x \cdot (\Lambda f \circ \alpha)\, x$ is a fixed point of $[\ll \beta_i \gg\Rightarrow \gamma]$
$\Longleftrightarrow \forall x \cdot \gamma \circ (\Lambda f \circ \alpha : x) \circ \ll \beta_i \gg = (\Lambda f \circ \alpha : x) \circ \ll \beta_i \gg$

We use an extensionality argument. First suppose that $\ll \beta_i \gg y = \perp$, either because y is not a sequence or y is a sequence of length less than n. Then we have:

$$\begin{aligned}
(\gamma \circ ((\Lambda f)(\alpha x)) \circ \ll \beta_i \gg)y &= (\gamma \circ ((\Lambda f)(\alpha x)))\perp\\
&= \gamma\perp\\
&= \perp\\
&= (((\Lambda f)(\alpha x)) \circ \ll \beta_i \gg)y
\end{aligned}$$

For $y = \langle y_1, \ldots, y_m \rangle$ with $m \geq n$ we calculate:

$$\begin{aligned}
(\gamma \circ ((\Lambda f)(\alpha x)) \circ \ll \beta_i \gg)y &= (\gamma \circ ((\Lambda f)(\alpha x)))\langle \beta_1 y_1, \ldots, \beta_n y_n, y_{n+1}, \ldots, y_m \rangle\\
&= \gamma(f\langle \alpha x, \beta_1 y_1, \ldots, \beta_n y_n, y_{n+1}, \ldots, y_m \rangle)\\
&= (\gamma \circ f \circ \ll \alpha, \beta_1, \ldots, \beta_n \gg)\langle x, y_1, \ldots, y_m \rangle\\
&= (f \circ \ll \alpha, \beta_1, \ldots, \beta_n \gg)\langle x, y_1, \ldots, y_m \rangle\\
&= (((\Lambda f)(\alpha x)) \circ \ll \beta_i \gg)y
\end{aligned}$$

as required.

6.5 Apply

[APPL] $$\frac{f : \alpha \rightarrow \beta\ ,\quad x : \alpha}{f@x : \beta}$$

For all $x : \alpha$,

$\beta(f@x) = \beta(fx) = (\beta \circ f)x = (\beta \circ f)(\alpha x) = (\beta \circ f \circ \alpha)x = (f \circ \alpha)x = f(\alpha x) = fx = f@x$

6.6 Recursion

[RECN] $$\frac{f : \alpha \to \alpha}{\mathbf{Y}\ f : \alpha}$$

First note that when $f : (\alpha \Rightarrow \alpha)$ (which is our semantic interpretation of the syntactic assumption $f : \alpha \to \alpha$) we have

$$\begin{aligned} \alpha x = x &\Longrightarrow \alpha \circ f(x) = f(x) \\ &\Longrightarrow \alpha(fx) = fx \end{aligned}$$

Thus $x : \alpha \Longrightarrow (fx) : \alpha$.

Now if we define the sequence $\langle z_i \rangle$ as follows:

$$\begin{aligned} z_0 &= \bot \\ z_{n+1} &= f z_n \end{aligned}$$

By the property noted above, since $\alpha\bot = \bot$ for all α, every element of this sequence is a fixed point of α.

We have $\mathbf{Y}f = \bigsqcup z_i$ by definition; but the sequence is increasing, and thus directed, and so by continuity of α we have $\alpha(\mathbf{Y}f) = \mathbf{Y}f$ as required.

7 Conclusions

We have seen how projections can be used to model types and how contractive functions over projections allow us to define recursive types. The equational nature of our type constructors leads to types having intuitive properties. Moreover projections have rich algebraic properties which lead to elegant proofs. In section 5 we showed that the strong ideal model of [MPS86] is semantically equivalent to our model, but we needed fewer restrictions on the semantic framework, notably our domains need not be primal.

7.1 Models of Types

Three recent proposals for modelling types are [ABL86, CZ86, AP90]. [ABL86] also uses projections to model types, but restricts admissible projections to the finitary ones, i.e. those with range isomorphic to a domain. Our projections are also finitary, but we have a rather nice equational characterisation of types and our approach is very different. It seems clear that characterising types by projections is a fruitful notion. It is in their use of projections to solve *higher-order* domain equations that [ABL86] have made real progress, the key being their lemma 2.4.

Of the two papers on per models of types, [CZ86, AP90], the latter imposes sufficient restrictions on 'good' pers to make the type represented by such a per again isomorphic to a domain. The authors then concentrate on applying a standard construction ([See87]) to generate a model for the second-order typed λ-calculus before considering (briefly) the possibility of using metric considerations with pers.

[CZ86] offer a general relational model of types and then consider various restrictions, including pers, and show how the ideal model of [MPS86] can be embedded into a relational model. We have not explored the relationship between our projection model and the relational framework of [CZ86] fully, but it seems probable that metric considerations will lead to a combined model along the lines suggested in [AP90] as mentioned above.

An important application for our type inference system is to strengthen certain theorems in equational program transformation by deducing contextual information [FH88, part 3]. The axioms in such systems are typically expressed in a weakly typed language such as we consider in this paper and theorems tend to be sufficiently weak that they apply to expressions of arbitrary type. We propose to use our type system to deduce additional information in order to identify opportunities to apply more powerful but more restricted theorems.

Other directions for future work include investigating metric considerations of projections as used in other fields, such as strictness analysis. [WH87] use projections to model strictness analysis for first-order functions, and their work has recently been extended to the higher-order case using pers in place of projections [Hun90]. Neither paper considers metrics. Another direction in which this work may be taken is to give a more explicitly categorical view. As well as highlighting the similarities and differences with [AP90], the categorical approach to metric spaces presented in [AR89] may provide a useful generalised framework for this kind of model.

7.2 Type Inference

Turning to our novel inference system, most researchers have only considered type inference for various extensions of the λ-calculus, with more or less syntactic sugar. Our rules for a combinatory language appear to be entirely new. We have implemented (in HOPE) an algorithm embodying these rules which seems correct, and the formal verification is in progress. We hope to publish the algorithm and proof shortly. The language considered in this paper has a number of deficiencies which should also be rectified; for instance it would probably be better to use only pairs rather than sequences, as this makes writing recursive functions easier. The language used in our implementation also has constants.

Notice that primitive operations in a weakly typed language, such as FP's selection functions, have types involving universal quantification; this is the only way our implementation introduces quantified types. The quantifiers are explicit, leading to deep types rather than the shallow types permitted in ML etc. This is possible because we have no generalisation rule to introduce quantifiers.

Another problem with traditional type inference which can be dealt with more cleanly in our system is the distinction between `let`-bound and λ-bound variables, the former being given generic types and the latter restricted to monotypes. Combinatorial languages and algebraic manipulation go hand in hand and researchers are used to calculating improved versions of programs using equations. We can use these same equations to infer additional inference rules such as:

$$\frac{[f_1 \circ g, \ldots, f_n \circ g] : \alpha}{[f_1, \ldots, f_n] \circ g : \alpha}$$

which is valid whenever g is strict.

Such rules may also be deduced for the λ-calculus, but combinatorial languages already have a repertoire of such equations and they are easily implemented as souce-level rewrites within the type checker. The careful reader will notice that the above rule applies exactly where a λ-abstraction could be replaced by a `let` construct.

Acknowledgements

We are grateful to an anonymous referee for the proof of proposition 16.

References

[ABL86] R. Amadio, K. B. Bruce, and G. Longo. "The Finitary Projection Model for Second Order Lambda Calculus and Solutions to Higher Order Domain Equations". In *IEEE Symposium on Logic in Computer Science*, 1986.

[AP90] M. Abadi and G. Plotkin. "A Per Model of Polymorphism and Recursive Types". In *IEEE Symposium on Logic in Computer Science*, 1990.

[AR89] P. America and J. Rutten. "Solving Reflexive Domain Equations in a Category of Complete Metric Spaces". *Journal of Computer and System Sciences*, 39:343–375, 1989.

[Bac78] J. Backus. "Can Programming be Liberated from the von Neumann Style? A Functional Style and its Algebra of Programs". *Communications of the ACM*, 21(8), 1978.

[Ban22] S. Banach. "Sur les operations dans les ensembles abstraits et leurs applications aux equations integrales". *Fund. Math.*, 3:7–33, 1922.

[BMS80] R. M. Burstall, D. B. MacQueen, and D. T. Sanella. "Hope: an Experimental Applicative Language". In *Lisp Conference*, pages 136–143. A.C.M., August 1980.

[Car88] L. Cardelli. "A Semantics of Multiple Inheritance". *Information and Computation*, 76:138–164, 1988.

[Cur86] P.-L. Curien. *Categorical Combinators, Sequential Algorithms and Functional Programming*. Pitman, 1986.

[CZ86] M. Coppo and M. Zacchi. "Type Inference and Logical Relations". In *IEEE Symposium on Logic in Computer Science*, 1986.

[FH88] A. J. Field and P. G. Harrison. *Functional Programming.* Addison-wesley Publishing Company, 1988.

[GHK+80] G. Gierz, K. H. Hofmann, K. Keimel, J. D. Lawson, M. Mislove, and D. S. Scott. *A Compendium of Continuous Lattices.* Springer-Verlag, 1980.

[GMW79] M. J. Gordon, A. J. Milner, and C. P. Wadsworth. *Edinburgh LCF, LNCS.* Number 78 in LNCS. Springer-Verlag, 1979.

[Hun90] S. Hunt. "PERs Generalise Projections for Strictness Analysis". In *Third Annual Glasgow Workshop on Functional Programming, Draft Proceedings*, pages 156–168, 1990.

[Mil78] R. Milner. "A Theory of Type Polymorphism in Programming". *Journal of Computer and System Sciences*, 17:348–375, 1978.

[MPS86] D. MacQueen, G. Plotkin, and R. Sethi. "An Ideal Model for Recursive Polymorphic Types". *Information and Control*, 71:95–130, 1986.

[Sco76] D.S. Scott. "Data Types as Lattices". *SIAM Journal on Computing*, 5(3):522–587, 1976.

[See87] R.A.G. Seely. "Categorical Semantics for Hiugher-Order Polymorphic Lambda Calculus". *Journal of Symbolic Logic*, 52(4), 1987.

[SP82] M. B. Smyth and G. D. Plotkin. "The Category-Theoretic Solution of Recursive Domain Equations". *SIAM Journal on Computing*, 11:761–783, 1982.

[WH87] P. Wadler and R.J.M. Hughes. "Projections for Strictness Analysis". In *Functional Programming and Computer Architecture, LNCS*, vol. 274, pages 386–406, 1987.

What is an Efficient Implementation of the λ-calculus?

Gudmund S. Frandsen *†
Department of Computer Science, Aarhus University

Carl Sturtivant
Department of Computer Science, University of Minnesota

Abstract

We propose to measure the efficiency of any implementation of the λ-calculus as a function of a new parameter ν, that is itself a function of any λ-expression.

Complexity is expressed here as a function of ν just as runtime is expressed as a function of the input size n in ordinary analysis of algorithms. This enables implementations to be compared for worst case efficiency.

We argue that any implementation must have complexity $\Omega(\nu)$, i.e. a linear lower bound. Furthermore, we show that implementations based upon Turner Combinators or Hughes Super-combinators have complexities $2^{\Omega(\nu)}$, i.e. an exponential lower bound.

It is open whether any implementation of polynomial complexity, $\nu^{O(1)}$, exists, although some implementations have been implicitly claimed to have this complexity.

Introduction

Objectives

The aim of this paper is to provide a theoretical basis for efficiency considerations in the implementation of functional languages.

So far, people working in this area have approached the subject as programmers. That is to say, they have taken an intuitive approach to efficiency backed up by empirical trials once some new implementation has been created (e.g. measuring the runtimes of benchmark programs). Their major concerns have been to increase the expressive power of functional languages and to create more efficient implementations so that functional languages are usable.

From our standpoint, the implementation problem for functional languages is just another algorithmic problem, albeit one of some difficulty. In other areas

*This research was partially carried out, while visiting Dartmouth College, New Hampshire

†This research was partially carried out, while supported by the Danish Natural Science Research Council (grant No. 11-7991) and while supported by the ESPRIT II Basic Research Actions Program of the EC under contract No. 3075 (project ALCOM).

of algorithm design, there is a sound theoretical framework: the notion of input size, n; measuring the worst case and average case runtimes of an algorithm on inputs of size n in O-notation; and the idea of an optimal algorithm as one whose runtime as a function of n is of minimum growth. Such tools are not presently available to implementers of functional languages. Whilst it is not necessarily true that theoretically "fast" algorithms are the best in practice, nevertheless an investigation of various theoretically fast algorithms provides a good starting point for practical implementation considerations.

It is our aim to provide an analogous quantitative theoretical framework in which to assess the complexities of implementations of functional languages. This would ensure that the same tools are available to implementers of functional languages as are available to other algorithm designers.

Once such a framework is in place, we will be able to define the notion of an optimal implementation. This has importance in understanding what the complexity of a functional program is, as is discussed next.

The Complexity of a Functional Program

Currently, it is not known how to analyse the complexity of a functional program in an implementation independent way. Indeed, it is not clear that the complexity of a functional program is in any sense implementation independent. This is in marked contrast to programs written in common imperative languages. Here it is informally understood that all good implementations endow any given program with essentially the same complexity (in O-notation).

Clearly, there are bad implementations of imperative languages in which the complexities of some programs are degraded below their "true" complexities. Thus the reason that the complexity of programs in imperative languages is well defined is that we have identified the good implementations (i.e. optimal implementations in O-terms), and we regard these implementations as defining *the* complexity of a program. Consequently, the complexity of an imperative program is implicitly implementation independent in this sense.

If we wish to arrive at a similar situation in regard to the complexity of functional programs, then we need to know what an optimal implementation of a functional language is.

We introduce a complexity theoretic definition of the efficiency of any implementation of a functional language. Using this definition, we define what an optimal implementation is. A basic acquaintance with the lambda calculus is assumed[Chu32, Ros84, Bar81].

The first half of the paper is concerned with philosophical and motivational considerations, and gives an informal discussion of the technical results given in full detail in the second half of the paper.

Philosophical Considerations

In this paper we propose to consider the problem of implementing the pure λ-calculus, which may be regarded as a (rather difficult to use) functional programming language. We give a complexity theoretic framework for considering the efficiency of such implementations. We argue below why this then provides a complexity theoretic framework for understanding the efficiency of implementations of *any* functional language. Hereafter, we will use the phrase "*lambda*-calculus" to mean the pure *lambda*-calculus.

Why Study the Pure Lambda Calculus?

The reader may ask how it is that pure lambda expressions can reflect the computational power of their favorite functional languages. In particular, the reader may say that the reader's favorite functional language has a lot of added primitives (functions, data structures, etcetera) that are not present in the pure lambda calculus, and thus why are results about the pure lambda calculus applicable to these extensions?

Our reply is an argument to establish informally that these features may be encoded into the pure λ-calculus in such a way that there is an implementation of the pure λ-calculus endowing these features with a certain complexity if and only if there is an implementation of the functional language directly endowing the features with the same complexity (up to a constant factor). The argument proceeds as follows:-

We fix some machine model of sequential computation (there are some technical difficulties with the RAM model of computation: see the appendix for a complete discussion of this argument). Then we give an encoding of any machine in this model as a pure λ-expression, with the property that a constant number of β-reduction steps simulate an atomic step of the machine and these involve only a bounded amount of work. (The constant may depend upon the machine being encoded. In fact, it can be arranged that the expression encoding a machine follows exactly the steps that the machine would take if a normal order reduction strategy is used.) Thus particular functions and data structures may be embedded naturally in the pure λ-calculus along with their imperative implementations.

At this point, the reader may agree that many of the features of the reader's favorite functional language can be encoded in the pure λ-calculus in such a way as to retain the potential for efficient implementation. Consider an arbitrary program in the reader's favorite functional language. Even if we strip away all its syntactic sugar of the above forms, and replace it with λ-encodings, what remains may not be a simple λ-expression. The reader may say that what remains is what may be termed "a mutually recursive λ-program": i.e. a series of mutually recursive definitions in the pure λ-calculus. (In fact there may be some additional control structures, etcetera, but hopefully the reader will be convinced that these can be encoded as simple λ-expressions whilst retaining the possibility of equally efficient implementation.)

A careful investigation of the sizes of the expressions in the multiple fixed point theorem ([Bar81] p.142) shows that such a mutually recursive λ-program defines a λ-expression whose size is linear in the size of the original program. Thus an efficient implementation of λ-expressions would provide an efficient implementation of λ-programs. (We have not discussed the input to the functional program — we assume that it is a part of the program here. For further discussion of this point see below.)

We have given an informal argument why any functional programming language may be encoded as pure λ-expressions whilst maintaining the possibility of equally efficient implementation. Without a formal definition of a functional language, it is not possible to prove our contention. For this reason we refer to it as the ***implementation thesis*** for functional languages.

The Implementation Thesis:

> Any functional programming language may be efficiently compiled into the pure λ-calculus in such a way as to retain the possibility of equally efficient implementation.

The converse of this thesis is also a matter of definition: any functional language has the power to directly define an arbitrary pure λ-expression—one may take this as a part of the definition of a functional language. (N.B. Presumably some strongly typed languages do not have this property—these are possibly weaker than the pure λ-calculus in computational power, and this may improve their implementability.) In any case we have argued that the efficient implementation problem for functional languages is at most as difficult as the implementation problem for pure λ-expressions (in a theoretical sense), and for those functional languages that contain the pure λ-calculus as a sub-language, the problems are equally hard.

One detail that has been glossed over is that real programs tend to be separated from their inputs. By using pure λ-expressions as the canonical model of a functional language we, loose this. The program and input (if any) are both λ-expressions, and we consider the cost of reducing the expression consisting of the first applied to the second (or just the first). However, this just amounts to taking the cost of "compilation" and the cost of "run" together, and is no disadvantage from a theoretical standpoint. (Of course in practice a program may be compiled and used on many different inputs. We regard this as a different issue, and ignore it.)

In the case of an interactive program, not all of the input is available as the run proceeds. This restricts the implementation possibilities, and therefore can only make life harder than the problem we consider.

The Pure λ-Calculus

In this paper we propose to consider the following problem, that we call λ-expression normal form computation (LENF). Input to LENF is a λ-expression in the standard syntax, and the corresponding output is the normal form of that expression if such exists, and otherwise is empty (a solution being allowed not to halt in this case).

Currently there seems to be a belief that there is neither a canonical way of simulating reduction in the λ-calculus efficiently nor a canonical way to define formally what efficiently should mean. This is best illustrated by a citation:

There have been some studies about the relative efficiencies of various implementation techniques for applicative languages, but there are no clear winners. This should not be surprising at all, if we consider the generality of the problem. We are dealing with the efficiency of the process of evaluating arbitrary partial recursive functions. Standard complexity theory is clearly not applicable to such a broad class of computable functions. The time-complexity of such a universal procedure cannot be bounded by any computable function of the size of the input. ... Complexity theory is concerned with the inherent difficulty of the problems (or classes of problems) rather than the overall performance of some particular model of a universal computing device. [Rév88, page 131]

Furthermore, the result that no strategies that choose optimal reduction sequences are recursive [Bar81, ch. 13] may mislead if not examined closely, because of its dependence upon λ-expressions with no normal form. In fact the problem

Input: A λ-expression M with a normal form

Output: A minimal length reduction sequence to normal form for M

has an algorithmic solution: simply explore all reduction sequences that use up to the number of reductions which the leftmost strategy takes to reach normal form, and choose a minimal one.

We do not claim that this procedure is efficient; however, its runtime is bounded by some recursive function of the number of β-reductions in the normal order reduction sequence to normal form. Furthermore, this is also true if we extend the input set to include all λ-expressions, since those with no normal form have infinite normal order reduction sequences.

This suggests that a change of the definition of "input size" to include some measure of the length of reduction chains may make it possible to bound the runtime of an implementation of LENF by some recursive function of the new input size. This would also hold in the case of λ-expressions with no normal form, since their input size would be infinity. This is the approach we take. In the next section we discuss our precise definition of the new input size.

Definition of the New Input Size Parameter

Lévy proposed an optimal implementation to be one in which "work is not duplicated". He has given a formal definition in terms of a parallel reduction step for a labelled version of the λ-calculus [Lév80, Lév88]. We do not take up his notion of optimality since our aim is not to minimise the number of some kind of reduction steps, but rather to minimise the overall runtime. However, we do adopt his notion of parallel reduction.

Let L be any λ-expression. We define $\mu_\pi(L)$ to be the minimum number of parallel reduction steps required to reduce L to normal form (infinity if L has no normal form).

We define the new input size parameter ν of the λ-expression L with normal form N to be the size of L plus the size of N plus $\mu_\pi(L)$ ($\nu = \infty$ if L has no normal form).

The philosophy behind this definition is as follows—We wish to put a complexity measure on λ-expressions and to do this we must arrange the definition of the input size parameter ν so that it conforms with the ***bounded runtime principle***; namely that there exists an implementation whose runtime is bounded above by some recursive function of ν. (Recursive functions are considered to be extended to map infinity to infinity.)

The size of L must appear in ν because if the input is already in normal form, then this must be verified by any implementation. In general, this must take time proportional to the size of L.

A measurement of the length of some sort of canonical reduction chain to normal form must be included in ν because otherwise expressions with no normal form constitute a family of inputs in conflict with the bounded runtime principle. Lambda-expressions defining arbitrarily complex functions will also give violations of the bounded runtime principle if the input size parameter does not involve such a measure of reduction. We choose μ_π as this measure. Some other candidates that spring to mind are the minimum number of β-reductions to reach normal form, μ_β, or the length of the normal order reduction sequence to normal form, l_{normal}. (We ignore η reduction here; our justification stems from corollary 15.1.6 and the first part of the proof of corollary 15.1.5 in [Bar81].)

Finally, the length of the normal form N should be present since there are many families of λ-expressions with the property that the size of the normal form is exponential in the number of reduction steps to normal form. (This is analogous to an algorithm whose output size is exponential—the runtime is exponential for trivial reasons.) Thus the absence of the size of N would automatically imply an exponential lower bound on all implementations: we would like a definition that does not impose such trivial limitations.

These three arguments justify most of the definition of ν, excepting the choice of μ_π as a measurement of reduction chain length.

Of the two other obvious candidates given above (μ_β and l_{normal}), l_{normal} is not remotely optimal for some λ-expressions. Later in the paper (proposition 3) we give an example of a family of λ-expressions for which applicative order gives the minimum length reduction chain to normal form. For this family, Normal order reduction gives exponentially longer chains to normal form. Thus, measuring the complexity of an implementation using l_{normal} can give unrealistically optimistic assessments. For this reason, we rule out l_{normal}.

We choose μ_π rather than μ_β for a number of reasons. First, it is known that μ_π is always less than or equal to μ_β. Second, an optimal strategy is known for parallel reductions—normal order [Lév80], whereas none such is known for the optimal β-reduction sequence. Thus, by using μ_π we get a harsher measure of complexity; however, this is nevertheless consistent with the bounded runtime principle: a naive simulation of the normal order parallel reduction sequence to normal form has a runtime that is bounded by a recursive function of ν, as the reader may verify.

Furthermore μ_π and μ_β may be significantly different. Until recently we knew of no λ-expression for which they differ by more than a factor of three. However, in the second part of the paper, we give an infinite family of λ-expressions which seems to have the property that μ_β is significantly greater than μ_π. In particular, the third member of the family has μ_β greater than five times μ_π. We conjecture for this family that μ_β is not bounded by any constant multiple of μ_π. Whether μ_β can be as much as exponentiallly different from μ_π, we do not know, but we think this may well be so.

The interesting positive factor about using parallel reductions instead of β-reductions is that parallel reduction was defined as a kind of improved β-reduction in which work was not duplicated (in the sense of doing several reductions instead of one because of copying of redices). To hope for an implementation of the λ-calculus of low (say polynomial $\nu^{O(1)}$) complexity, is therefore to take an optimistic view that perhaps the duplication of work that sometimes seems unavoidable in ordinary β-reduction is unnecessary in a general implementation.

Thus we optimistically adopt μ_π, whilst not being dogmatic in our choice. Should it transpire that all implementations must have very high complexity under this definition of input size ν, then it may be useful to change to a larger notion of input size ν. However, such a result would in itself be a great step forward in our understanding of the inherent complexity of implementations of the λ-calculus, and would seem to justify an initial choice of μ_π.

The Complexity of an Implementation

Now that we have defined the input size parameter ν, it remains to define the complexity of an implementation $\mathcal{I}$, in the obvious way. Informally, the complexity of $\mathcal{I}$ is just the time taken by $\mathcal{I}$ to compute the normal form of a λ-expression, expressed as a function of ν. However, as in everyday analysis of algorithms, this conceals the important choice of whether we take worst-case or some sort of average-case complexity to be the fundamental measure.

Just as in the usual setting, a problem with average-case complexity is the question of which probability distribution one should use over inputs of a given size. This problem is particularly pronounced in the case of implementations of the λ-calculus, because it may be important to focus on large sub-classes of expressions. For example, the kind of arguments given in the section on philosophical considerations, as to how various features of some functional programming language may be efficiently encoded in the pure λ-calculus, would certainly lead to a bizarrely biased collection of λ-expressions, depending very much upon the features of that language. Merely choosing λ-expressions of the form "program" applied to "input" would also bias the distribution. Thus naive assumptions such as taking the uniform distribution over λ-expressions with a given ν, are likely to be meaningless.

For that reason, we take the worst-case complexity as the canonical measure of the complexity of an implementation of the λ-calculus.

Having made the choice to use the worst-case complexity, we then secure the benefit that if the implementation $\mathcal{I}$ has been proven to have some complexity as a function of ν then there are no "bad" families of inputs that violate this bound—we are absolutely assured that whatever we use the λ-calculus for, in whatever encoding, we will obtain the guaranteed performance.

In particular, suppose we have a λ-expression consisting of a "program" applied to an "input" (perhaps encoded as a binary list), where the input is of size n. If we now obtain the normal form of this expression using the implementation $\mathcal{I}$, then the worst case complexity of $\mathcal{I}$ provides for a relationship between the conventional complexity expressed as a function of n and the complexity of the implementation.

Summary of Technical Results and Open Problems

In the second part of the paper, we define formally the input size parameter ν and the complexity of an implementation of the λ-calculus, in accordance with the principles discussed above. We argue that any implementation must have complexity $\Omega(\nu)$. Furthermore, we give lower bounds of $2^{\Omega(\nu)}$ on implementations based upon Turner combinators or Hughes super-combinators.

We give a λ-expression for which μ_β is greater than five times μ_π. This λ-expression is the third member of an infinite family of λ-expressions for which μ_β seems significantly greater than μ_π. However, we do not know the values of μ_β or μ_π for all of this family. The problem of finding a bound for μ_β in terms of μ_π in general (i.e. that holds for all λ-expressions) remains unresolved.

Many other implementations of the λ-calculus exist that have not been analysed. Furthermore, some authors ([Sta82, Lam90]) have claimed their implementations optimal in the sense of Lévy, (i.e. that they do not simulate more than μ_π reduction steps), However, optimality in this sense does not impose significant constraints on the complexity of an implementation. Hence, the existence of a polynomial time ($\nu^{O(1)}$) implementation remains an open question.

Preliminaries and Definitions

Definition 1

λ-expressions

The set of λ-expressions, Λ, is defined inductively,

- variables: $x_i \in \Lambda$ for all $i \in \{0, 1, 2, 3, \dots\}$
- abstraction: if $l \in \Lambda$ then $(\lambda.l) \in \Lambda$
- application: if $l_1, l_2 \in \Lambda$ then $(l_1 l_2) \in \Lambda$

We adopt the convention that

$$l_1 l_2 l_3 \dots l_n = (\dots((l_1 l_2) l_3) \dots l_n)$$

and let I denote the identity expression:

$$I = (\lambda.x_0)$$

In the original syntax for λ-expressions [Chu32], the variable bound in the abstraction is written explicitly in the prefix, e.g. $\lambda x.l$ denotes that the specific variable x is bound. However, we adopt deBruijn's convention for naming variables [deB72] according to which an occurrence of x_i denotes the variable that is bound at the $(i+1)$'th enclosing abstraction (if such exists). Hence it is unnecessary to specify a variable name in the abstraction prefix.

As an example consider the least fixed point operator,

$$\lambda f.(\lambda x.f(xx))(\lambda x.f(xx))$$

as described with named variables. In deBruijn's notation it is

$$\lambda.(\lambda.x_1(x_0x_0))(\lambda.x_1(x_0x_0)).$$

Both notations are described in [Bar81]. The deBruijn-syntax is often preferable for formal reasoning since name clashes do not arise (and α-reduction becomes obsolete), whereas the syntax with names facilitates human perception. We use either of the two notations at our discretion.

Definition 2

β-reduction

- A *redex* is a λ-expression of the form $(\lambda.l_1)l_2$.
- A specific occurrence of a variable x_i in the expression l is *free* if this occurrence has less than $i+1$ enclosing abstractions.
- A redex may be transformed in a *β-reduction*

  $$(\lambda.l_1)l_2 \rightarrow_\beta l_1'$$

  where l_1' is formed from l_1 by the following sequence of transformations.

  1. All occurrences of the abstracted variable (i.e. those x_i in l_1 that have precisely i surrounding abstractions in l_1), are replaced by specially modified versions of l_2, viz. in the replacement of x_i, free variables of l_2 have their indices incremented by i to reflect the modified number of enclosing abstractions.
  2. All other free occurrences of variables in l_1 have their index decremented by 1.

- Let $l = l_1[r]$ denote that the λ-expression l contains the subexpression r in the context l_1. If $l = l_1[r]$ and $r \rightarrow_\beta r'$ then $l_1[r] \rightarrow_\beta l_1[r']$.
- The notation $\rightarrow_\beta^*$ denotes the reflexive and transitive closure of $\rightarrow_\beta$.
- A λ-expression that contains no redex is in *normal form*. A *normal order* reduction sequence $l_0 \rightarrow_\beta l_1 \rightarrow_\beta \ldots \rightarrow_\beta l_n$ is one in which the leftmost outermost redex is chosen for transformation at each step.
- A reduction sequence $l_0 \rightarrow_\beta l_1 \rightarrow_\beta \ldots \rightarrow_\beta l_n$, where l_n is in normal form, is *complete* and l_n is the normal form of l_0.

- The notation $\mu_\beta(l)$ denotes the length of the shortest possible complete reduction sequence starting from l. If no such sequence exists the value is ∞.

By the Church Rosser property (simple proof in [Ros84]), the normal form of a λ-expression is unique. If an expression l has a normal form then a normal order reduction sequence will eventually lead to it, but not necessarily in the smallest possible number of steps.

Definition 3

Parallel Reductions

- The set of *labels* L is defined in terms of an infinite set of atomic labels A.
  1. $A \subseteq L$
  2. If $u, v \in L$ then $uv \in L$
  3. If $u \in L$ then $\underline{u} \in L$
- A *labelled* λ-expression has a label attached to every subexpression. In an *initial* expression all labels are atomic and mutually different.
- In a β-reduction labels are modified according to the following rule (M, N denote λ-expressions and u, v denote labels):
  1. $((\lambda x.M)^u N)^v \rightarrow_\beta (M^{\underline{u}}[x \rightarrow N^{\underline{u}}])^v$

  Multiple labels are concatenated into a single label:

  2. $(M^u)^v \rightarrow M^{uv}$

  (When using the named λ-calculus, we assume that renaming has occurred so as to avoid name clashes).
- Given two labelled λ-expressions l_0, l_1 such that l_0 is initial and $l_0 \rightarrow^*_\beta l_1$, we say that two redices r_1, r_2 in l_1 are *equivalent* with respect to l_0 if they have identical labels, i.e. if $r_1 = ((\lambda x.M_1)^{u_1} N_1)^{v_1}$ and $r_2 = ((\lambda y.M_2)^{u_2} N_2)^{v_2}$ then $u_1 = u_2$
- A *parallel* reduction sequence $l_0 \rightarrow_\pi l_1 \rightarrow_\pi \ldots \rightarrow_\pi l_n$ is a sequence in which all redices in precisely one equivalence class with respect to l_0 are reduced in a single step. (The ordinary reductions in this step are done from the bottom up until no more reductions with the same label are possible. This process always terminates.)
- A parallel reduction sequence is *normal order* if in each step the equivalence class being reduced contains the syntactically leftmost redex.
- A *complete* parallel reduction sequence ends with a λ-expression in normal form.

- The notation $\mu_\pi(l)$ denotes the length of the shortest complete parallel reduction sequence starting from l. If no such sequence exists the value is ∞.

Two equivalent redices may overlap syntactically, so the notion of a parallel reduction step must be defined with great care. See [Lév80] for details. Our condensed definition is due to [Klo80] and described in [Fie90]. The original investigation of parallel reduction is due to Lévy [Lév80, Lév88].

Intuitively a parallel reduction sequence avoids duplication of work. All "identical" redices are reduced in a single step, where two redices are "identical" if for some regular reduction sequence they arise as copies (i.e. ***residuals***) of a single redex.

It is known that a complete parallel normal order reduction sequence for a λ-expression l has length $\mu_\pi(l)$ (i.e. normal order is an optimal strategy) and $\mu_\pi(l) \leq \mu_\beta(l)$ for all λ-expressions l [Lév80].

Definition 4

The Complexity of an Implementation of the λ-calculus.

- A procedure $\mathcal{I}$ is an ***implementation*** of the λ-calculus if $\mathcal{I}$ on input a λ-expression M outputs N, the normal form of M (if M has no normal form then $\mathcal{I}$ need not halt).

- The ***input-size*** parameter $\nu : \Lambda \rightarrow \mathbf{N} \cup \{\infty\}$ is given by

$$\nu(M) = |M| + \mu_\pi(M) + |N|$$

  for all $M \in \Lambda$ where N is the normal form of M, and the norm denotes expression size. (If M has no normal form then $\nu(M) = \infty$).

- An implementation $\mathcal{I}$ of the λ-calculus has ***worst-case complexity*** $T(\nu)$ if $T : \mathbf{N} \rightarrow \mathbf{N}$ satisfies

$$T(\nu) = \text{Max}\{\text{run time of } \mathcal{I} \text{ on input } M \mid M \in S_\nu\}$$

  when $S_\nu \neq \emptyset$ and where $S_\nu = \{M \in \Lambda | \nu(M) = \nu\}$.

- An implementation $\mathcal{J}$ of the λ-calculus of worst case complexity $T_\mathcal{J}(\nu)$, is an ***optimal*** implementation if for any implementation $\mathcal{I}$ of the λ-calculus of worst case complexity $T_\mathcal{I}(\nu)$, we have $T_\mathcal{J}(\nu) = O(T_\mathcal{I}(\nu))$.

The complexity of an implementation is well defined, since the sets S_ν are always finite, and there is a number ν_0 such that for $\nu > \nu_0$, S_ν is always non empty.

A Linear Lower Bound

Proposition 1

Any implementation of the λ-calculus has complexity $\Omega(\nu)$.

Outline Proof: In the appendix we give an encoding of an arbitrary (imperative) computation as a λ-expression with the property that $\mu_\pi = \mu_\beta = l_{normal}$, and each step of the computation is simulated by a constant number of reductions which in turn can be implemented in such a way as to take only a bounded amount of work. Thus the existence of an implementation with complexity $o(\nu)$ would immediately give rise to a method of speeding up an arbitrary computation. QED.

Exponential Lower Bounds for some Combinator-based Implementations

Proposition 2

Implementations of the λ-calculus based on Turner combinators or Hughes super combinators are exponentially inefficient.

Proof: We shall exhibit a family of λ-expressions for which both a translation to Turner combinators and a translation to Hughes super combinators results in exponentially inefficient executions.

The construction will exploit the fact that a combinator may take more than one argument, and the reduction rules for such a combinator can not be used unless all arguments are present. In contrast the original λ-expression can be partially evaluated, since each abstraction $(\lambda x.M)$ refers to only one variable.

Define a family $\{A_n\}$ of λ-expressions by

$$A_0 = (\lambda x.I)$$

$$A_n = (\lambda h.(\lambda w.wh(ww))A_{n-1}) \text{ for } n \geq 1$$

By induction we may prove that $A_n \rightarrow_\beta^{4n} A_0$. The case $n = 0$ is obvious. The induction step is proved by considering the following sequence of reductions:

$$\begin{aligned} A_n &= (\lambda h.(\lambda w.wh(ww))A_{n-1}) \\ &\rightarrow_\beta^{4(n-1)} (\lambda h.(\lambda w.wh(ww))A_0) \\ &\rightarrow_\beta (\lambda h.A_0h(A_0A_0)) \\ &\rightarrow_\beta (\lambda h.I(A_0A_0)) \\ &\rightarrow_\beta (\lambda h.A_0A_0) \\ &\rightarrow_\beta (\lambda h.I) \\ &= A_0 \end{aligned}$$

The exponentially bad behaviour will be obtained for the family $\{B_n\}$, where $B_n = A_nI$. We see that $\mu_\beta(B_n) \leq 4n + 1$ using the result above. Hence $\nu \leq |B_n| + \mu_\beta(B_n) + |I| = O(n)$

Let us first consider a translation to Turner combinators. The following 8 combinators are used:

$$
\begin{aligned}
\mathbf{S}abc &= ac(bc)\\
\mathbf{K}ab &= a\\
\mathbf{I}a &= a\\
\mathbf{B}abc &= a(bc)\\
\mathbf{C}abc &= acb\\
\mathbf{S}'abcd &= a(bd)(cd)\\
\mathbf{B}'abcd &= ab(cd)\\
\mathbf{C}'abcd &= a(bd)c
\end{aligned}
$$

The combinators **S** and **K** alone suffice, but to avoid any critique saying that the exponentially bad behaviour was caused by not using a specific combinator, we include all 8 above.

The translation process is described by rewrite rules:

1. $(\lambda x.x) \rightarrow \mathbf{I}$
   $(\lambda x.y) \rightarrow \mathbf{K}y$ for y being a variable $y \neq x$.
   $(\lambda x.MN) \rightarrow \mathbf{S}(\lambda x.M)(\lambda x.N)$
2. The following rules should be used whenever they apply to some intermediate expression generated by the rules in (1) (A, B are arbitrary expressions):

   $$
   \begin{aligned}
   &\mathbf{S}(\mathbf{K}A)(\mathbf{K}B) \rightarrow \mathbf{K}(AB)\\
   &\mathbf{S}(\mathbf{K}A)\mathbf{I} \rightarrow A\\
   &\mathbf{S}(\mathbf{K}A)B \rightarrow \mathbf{B}AB\\
   &\mathbf{S}A(\mathbf{K}B) \rightarrow \mathbf{C}AB
   \end{aligned}
   $$

3. Whenever an intermediate expression is formed to which one of the following rules apply, use it: (A, B, K are arbitrary expressions)

   $$
   \begin{aligned}
   &\mathbf{S}(\mathbf{B}KA)B \rightarrow \mathbf{S}'KAB\\
   &\mathbf{B}(KA)B \rightarrow \mathbf{B}'KAB\\
   &\mathbf{C}(\mathbf{B}KA)B \rightarrow \mathbf{C}'KAB
   \end{aligned}
   $$

The rules (1) suffice, but the additional rules makes the generated code more efficient for some λ-expressions.

The λ-expression $\{B_n\}$ translates into combinator expressions $\{\mathcal{B}_n\}$ that may be described recursively:

$$
\begin{aligned}
&\mathcal{A}_0 = \mathbf{KI}\\
&\mathcal{A}_n = \mathbf{C}(\mathbf{C}'\mathbf{S}(\mathbf{CI})(\mathbf{SII}))\mathcal{A}_{n-1} \text{ for } n \geq 1\\
&\mathcal{B}_n = \mathcal{A}_n\mathbf{I}
\end{aligned}
$$

Let $S(n)$ denote the minimal number of combinator reduction steps that brings $\mathcal{A}_n x$ to its normal form **I** (independent of expression x). Clearly $S(0) = 1$ and $S(n)$ may be found by an inductive argument:

$$\begin{aligned}
\mathcal{A}_n x &= \mathbf{C}(\mathbf{C'S}(\mathbf{CI})(\mathbf{SII}))\mathcal{A}_{n-1}x \\
&\rightarrow \mathbf{C'S}(\mathbf{CI})(\mathbf{SII})x\mathcal{A}_{n-1} \\
&\rightarrow \mathbf{S}(\mathbf{CI}x)(\mathbf{SII})\mathcal{A}_{n-1} \\
&\rightarrow \mathbf{CI}x\mathcal{A}_{n-1}(\mathbf{SII}\mathcal{A}_{n-1}) \\
&\rightarrow \mathbf{I}\mathcal{A}_{n-1}x(\mathbf{SII}\mathcal{A}_{n-1}) \\
&\rightarrow \mathcal{A}_{n-1}x(\mathbf{SII}\mathcal{A}_{n-1}) \\
&\rightarrow^{S(n-1)} \mathbf{I}(\mathbf{SII}\mathcal{A}_{n-1}) \\
&\rightarrow \mathbf{SII}\mathcal{A}_{n-1} \\
&\rightarrow \mathbf{I}\mathcal{A}_{n-1}(\mathbf{I}\mathcal{A}_{n-1}) \\
&\rightarrow \mathcal{A}_{n-1}(\mathbf{I}\mathcal{A}_{n-1}) \\
&\rightarrow^{S(n-1)} \mathbf{I}
\end{aligned}$$

The above reduction is optimal because we are forced to copy the complex expression for $\mathcal{A}_{n-1}$ since it is irreducible (though extensionally equivalent to $\mathcal{A}_0$). From the recurrence relation $S(n) = 2S(n-1) + 8$ and the initial condition above, we obtain $S(n) = 9 \cdot 2^n - 8$, which also is the number of steps necessary to reduce $\mathcal{B}_n$. Hence we conclude that an implementation of the λ-calculus based on Turner combinators has complexity $2^{\Omega(\nu)}$.

Next we consider super combinators. Instead of using a fixed set of combinators we customise "super" combinators to the specific λ-expression at hand. In the translation process we first eliminate occurrences of free variables within the body of a single λ-expression, by possibly binding more than one variable to a single λ. In B_n the only affected subexpression is $(\lambda w.wh(ww))$ that is converted into $(\lambda w'w.ww'(ww))h$. For the translation of B_n the following $n+2$ super combinators will be formed $(\mathbf{L}, \mathbf{M}_0, \mathbf{M}_1, \mathbf{M}_2, .., \mathbf{M}_n)$:

$$\begin{aligned}
&\mathbf{L}w'w = ww'(ww) \\
&\mathbf{M}_j h = \mathbf{L}h\mathbf{M}_{j-1} \text{ for } 1 \leq j \leq n \\
&\mathbf{M}_0 h = \mathbf{I}
\end{aligned}$$

B_n is translated into $\mathbf{M}_n\mathbf{I}$.

Let $T(n)$ denote the number of reduction steps needed to reduce $\mathbf{M}_n x$ to $\mathbf{I}$ (independent of expression x). Clearly $T(0) = 1$. By an inductive argument, we can find $T(n)$:

$$\begin{aligned}
\mathbf{M}_n x &\rightarrow \mathbf{L}x\mathbf{M}_{n-1} \\
&\rightarrow \mathbf{M}_{n-1}x(\mathbf{M}_{n-1}\mathbf{M}_{n-1}) \\
&\rightarrow^{T(n-1)} \mathbf{I}(\mathbf{M}_{n-1}\mathbf{M}_{n-1}) \\
&\rightarrow \mathbf{M}_{n-1}\mathbf{M}_{n-1} \\
&\rightarrow^{T(n-1)} \mathbf{I}
\end{aligned}$$

The order of reduction applied here is optimal, since we are forced to copy the irreducible combinator $\mathbf{M}_{n-1}$. From the recurrence relation $T(n) = 2T(n-1) + 3$ and the initial condition above we obtain $T(n) = 4 \cdot 2^n - 3$ and conclude that also super combinators lead to an implementation of complexity $2^{\Omega(\nu)}$. QED.

The combinators **S**,**K**,**I**,**B**,**C** were first defined by Schönfinkel [Sch24] under the names **S**,**C**,**I**,**Z**,**T**. Turner introduced the combinators $\mathbf{S}', \mathbf{B}', \mathbf{C}'$ [Tur79a]. Functional abstraction (the translation process) is described in [Sch24, CuFe58, Tur79a].

Application of combinators to functional programming is described in [Tur79b]. Super combinators and their application to functional programming are described in [Hug82, Hug84].

The exponential inefficiency relies in both cases on the existence of combinator expressions that are irreducible but extensionally equivalent to much simpler expressions. One may extend combinatory logic with axioms for extensionality [CuFe58, Bar81], but it seems unlikely that it would be computationally feasible to deal with extensionality in any combinator-based implementation of the λ-calculus such that this exponentially bad worst-case behaviour is eliminated.

Previous critiques of combinator-based translation have focused on a potentially quadratic size blow up in the translation from λ-expressions to Turner combinators and devised techniques to avoid this phenomenon [Bur82, Nos85, KeSl87]. Hughes proved that his super combinators have at most a quasi-linear size blow up during translation from λ-expressions to combinators [Hug84].

The Relation Between l_{normal} and μ_β

Proposition 3

There is an infinite family $\{A_k\}$ of λ-expressions such that $l_{normal}(A_k) = 2^{\Omega(\mu_\beta(A_k))}$

Proof:

We construct the expressions A_k such that reduction in applicative order is exponentially more efficient than reduction in normal order.

Let

$$\begin{aligned} A_k &= (\lambda x.xx)A_{k-1} \\ A_0 &= I \end{aligned}$$

Let S(k) and T(k) denote the number of β-reduction steps needed to transform A_k to normal form using normal and applicative order respectively. It is easy to obtain the recurrence equations

$$\begin{aligned} S(k) &= 2 \cdot S(k-1) + 2 \\ S(0) &= 0 \\ T(k) &= T(k-1) + 2 \\ T(0) &= 0 \end{aligned}$$

that have solutions

$$\begin{aligned} S(k) &= 2^{n+1} - 2 \\ T(k) &= 2 \cdot n \end{aligned}$$

from the which the proposition follows.

The Relation Between μ_β and μ_π

Proposition 4

There is a λ-expression A such that

$$\mu_\beta(A) > 5 \cdot \mu_\pi(A)$$

Proof: It will suffice to take A to be A_3 in the following infinite family of λ-expressions:

$$\begin{array}{rcl} A_0 & = & I \\ A_1 & = & (\Delta(\lambda h_1.h_1 I)) \\ A_2 & = & (\Delta(\lambda h_2.\Delta(\lambda h_1.h_2(h_1 I)))) \end{array}$$

and in general

$$A_n = (\Delta(\lambda h_n.(...(\Delta(\lambda h_1.h_n(...(h_1 I)...)))...)))$$

where $\Delta = (\lambda x.xx)$.

Computer simulations show the following values

n:	0	1	2	3
$\mu_\pi(A_n)$:	0	4	9	24
$\mu_\beta(A_n)$:	0	4	12	122

QED.

We have not been able to derive an explicit formula for $\mu_\beta(A_n)$ or $\mu_\pi(A_n)$, but we conjecture that

$$\lim_{n\to\infty} \frac{\mu_\beta(A_n)}{\mu_\pi(A_n)} = \infty.$$

and there is possibly an exponential relationship of the kind exposed in proposition 3.

The expression A_2 is one of the simplest λ-expressions for which μ_β is strictly larger than μ_π. Slightly modified versions of A_2 are presented in [Lév88, Fie90, Lam90].

Conclusion

- We have defined a notion of complexity with which to measure the efficiency of an implementation of the λ-calculus. In terms of this, the ***complexity*** of a functional program can be given a precise meaning.
- We show that all implementations must have at least linear complexity.
- We have devised a technique (as exemplified in proposition 2) for proving combinator based implementations inefficient.

Open Problems

- Does there exist an optimal implementation? If yes, what is its complexity?
- What are the complexities of various well known implementations? (e.g. graph reduction.)
- Does there exist an implementation of polynomial ($\nu^{O(1)}$) or linear ($O(\nu)$) complexity?
- Is μ_β bounded in terms of μ_π?

Appendix

Naturally Embedding Imperative Computations in the λ-calculus whilst Conserving Complexity

We want to show that a conventional machine model can be simulated in the λ-calculus with only a constant amount of overhead.

Choice of Machine Model.

The most realistic choice would be a RAM. However, there are several variants differing in their basic instruction sets and their complexity measures. It seems that the idea of a "unit-cost" RAM is flawed from a theoretical standpoint, unless its arithmetic instruction set is restricted to contain only the successor function, and no shift operations are permitted (see [Sch80] for discussion and references). An alternative is the "logarithmic cost" RAM. However, this model also seems flawed in that it seems unable to read and store its input in linear time (see [Sch88] for details).

The Turing Machine (TM) is a more basic model, for which the choice of a basic instruction set does not influence the complexity measure. However, the TM is unrealistically slow, because its storage tapes only allow sequential access. Schönhages Storage Modification Machine overcomes this deficiency, but seems too powerful for our purposes. (See [HBTCS, ch.1] for a presentation and discussion of all these models).

We introduce a strengthed version of the TM. Our version uses trees rather than tapes as a storage medium. The tree TM has a complexity measure that is closely related to the RAM measures. Yet, the tree TM has the same simple instruction set as the conventional TM with tape storage.

Definition A.1

k-tree Turing Machine

A k-tree Turing machine consists of two i/o tapes, k work-trees and a finite control. The input tape contains initially a string over $\{0,1\}$ terminated by a '#' and one head positioned at the left end of the tape. The head may read symbols and move to the right (and nothing else). The output tape is initially empty and has one head positioned at the left end of the tape. The head may write symbols {0,1,#} and move to the right, but nothing else. Both trees are initially empty, i.e. all cells contain the blank symbol, and each tree has one head that may both read and write in addition to moving stepwise in one of the directions {1,2,3}. In each step, a k-tree Turing machine reads the cell symbol under each of the $(k+1)$ heads that are allowed to read, inspects the state, and based upon the transition function, the control changes the state, overwrites the symbol under each of the the $(k+1)$ heads that are allowed to write and moves some (or none) of the $(k+2)$ heads in legal directions.

A k-tree Turing machine M is said to compute a function $f : \{0,1\}^n \rightarrow \{0,1\}^m$ whenever the following holds:

For all $(a_1, a_2, ..., a_n)$ in $\{0,1\}^n$, we have $f(a_1, a_2, ..., a_n) = (b_1, b_2, ..., b_m)$ if and only if M started on an input tape '$a_1, a_2, ..., a_n, \#$' stops with output tape '$b_1, b_2, ..., b_m, \#$'.

The complexity $T_M(n)$ of the machine M is the maximum number of steps taken before halting on any input of length n. The size of a k-tree Turing Machine with q states and s symbols is $q \cdot s^k \cdot log(q \cdot s^k)$.

It should be clear to the reader that the complexity measure defined by the k-tree TM is very close to that defined by the various RAM models. More or less all the models discussed above define complexities that differ by at most a log factor. Informally, a k-tree TM may be used to simulate a RAM by using one of its trees to simulate the RAM's memory with binary addressing in the intuitive way. A second tree may be used to assist with bookkeeping and arithmetic instructions. Thus a similar complexity measure to the logarithmic cost RAM is obtained, but at much greater simplicity. The reasons for our choice of the k-tree TM will become apparent.

Definition A.2

Control and data structures encoded as λ-expressions

We give specific names to some very useful λ-expressions:

- The truth-values:

$$\begin{aligned} \mathbf{t} &= (\lambda xy.x) \\ \mathbf{f} &= (\lambda xy.y) \end{aligned}$$

These are conveniently used for a conditional control expression

$$\texttt{if } c \texttt{ then } L \texttt{ else } N \texttt{ fi}$$

to be coded as

$$(cLN)$$

We may also encode an iterative (recursive) control expression

$$Pl_0$$

where

$$PL = \texttt{if } (cL) \texttt{ then } (P(pL)) \texttt{ else } (qL) \texttt{ fi}$$

using the least fixed point combinator Y from definition 1:

$$P = Y(\lambda f.\lambda L.(cL)(f(pL))(qL))$$

- The data structure *list*

$$\begin{aligned} [\,] &= (\lambda x.I) \\ [M_0, M_1, \ldots, M_n] &= (\lambda x.xM_0[M_1, \ldots, M_n]) \end{aligned}$$

with the indexing functions

$$\begin{aligned} tl_n &= (\lambda x.x\mathbf{ff}\ldots\mathbf{f}) \\ hd_n &= (\lambda x.(tl_n x)\mathbf{t}) \end{aligned}$$

where the defining expression for tl_n contains n copies of $\mathbf{f}$ and

$$\begin{aligned} tl_k[M_0, M_1, ..., M_n] &= [M_k, ..., M_n] \\ hd_k[M_0, M_1, ..., M_n] &= [M_k] \end{aligned}$$

- Unary integers.

$$u_n = hd_n$$

Definition A.3

λ-programs

Let $f : \{0,1\}^* \to \{0,1\}^*$ be a partial function on Boolean strings. A λ-expression N computes f when

1. if $f(b_1, ..., b_n) = (c_1, ..., c_m)$ then $L = (N[u_{b_1}, ..., u_{b_n}, u_2])$ has the normal form $[u_{c_1}, ..., u_{c_m}, u_2]$.
2. if $f(b_1, ..., b_n)$ is undefined then L has no normal form.

Proposition A.4

Efficient simulation of tree Turing Machines in the λ-calculus

For every 2-tree TM M there is a λ-expression N and a constant c such that N and M compute identical functions and if M on input $(b_1, ..., b_n)$ halts after t steps then the λ-expression $L = (N[u_{b_1}, ..., u_{b_n}, u_2])$ satisfies that $\mu_\pi(L) = \mu_\beta(L) = l_{normal}(L) \leq c \cdot t$.

Proof

For a given 2-tree Turing Machine M we construct a λ-program as follows.

Both symbols and states are represented by unary numbers such that for ***symbols***

1. u_0 and u_1 denote the bit-symbols 0 and 1.
2. u_2 denote the tape end-marker #.
3. u_3 denotes the blank symbol.

and for ***states***

1. u_0 denotes the initial state.
2. u_1 denotes the unique halt state.

An instantaneous description of the 2-tree Turing Machine is kept as a list of five elements

$$\mathbf{id} = [\mathbf{state}, \mathbf{tree}_1, \mathbf{tree}_2, \mathbf{tape}_i, \mathbf{tape}_o]$$

One may regard a tree as having a root at the head position and being directed away from this root, in which case each node in the tree has two outgoing edges and one incoming edge except for the root that has three outgoing edges and no incoming edges. Every subtree may be represented as the symbol at the subtree-root combined with a subtree for each edge that goes out of the root. For simplicity, we take a subtree for each incident edge:

$$\mathbf{tree} = [\mathbf{t}, \mathbf{symbol}, \mathbf{tree}_1, \mathbf{tree}_2, \mathbf{tree}_3]$$

where in the case of an incoming edge, the corresponding tree is empty, represented by

$$tree_e = [\mathbf{f}, u_3]$$

The empty tree is also used as a representation of unexplored subtrees that have blank symbols at all nodes. The truth-value occurring as the first element in the list representation of a tree is used to distinguish the empty tree.

A tape is represented by a recursive list

$$\mathbf{tape} = [\mathbf{symbol}, \mathbf{tape}]$$

that may be empty

$$tape_e = [u_2]$$

Too see how a single step of a computation on the 2-tree Turing Machine may be simulated, we look at a representative example. Assume that in the current **id**, we must make the following changes

1. The finite state control goes into *state'*.
2. $symbol'_1$ is written under the head of $tree_1$, which stays.
3. $symbol'_2$ is written under the head of $tree_2$, which moves one step in direction 1.

4. The head of the input tape is moved one step (necessarily to the right).
5. *symbol'* is written on the output tape (and the head is moved one step to the right).

The following λ-expression will applied to an **id** reduce to a modified **id** as prescribed above.

$$
\begin{array}{ll}
(\lambda x.[& state', \\
 & [\mathbf{t}, symbol'_1, tl_2(hd_1\,x)], \\
 & [\quad \mathbf{t}, \\
 & \quad hd_1(hd_2(hd_2\,x)), \\
 & \quad [\mathbf{t}, symbol'_2, tree_e, tl_3(hd_2\,x)], \\
 & \quad hd_0(hd_2(hd_2\,x))\; tl_3(hd_2(hd_2\,x))\; [tree_e, tree_e] \\
 &] \\
 & tl_1(hd_3\,x), \\
 & [symbol', hd_4\,x] \\
])
\end{array}
$$

The most complicated part of the above expression is the modification of $tree_2$. It is here necessary to provide two alternative sub-actions according to whether the subtree in direction 1 has been visited before or not. The choice is made by the truth-valued expression $hd_0(hd_2(hd_2\,x))$.

The state and symbols under the heads in the present **id** determines which action to take. All possible actions are therefore organised in a 4-dimensional array *transitiontable* that is indexed by

1. state
2. symbol under head of $tree_1$
3. symbol under head of $tree_2$
4. symbol under input head

The simulation of one single transition step may thus be done by the following λ-expression that updates its argument (an **id**) appropriately:

$$F = (\lambda x.hd_0(tl_3x)(hd_1(tl_2x)(hd_1(tl_1x)(hd_0x\; transitiontable)))x)$$

We are now in a position to describe the whole simulation. For control purposes we define a constant expression

$$halt = [\mathbf{f}, \mathbf{t}, \mathbf{f}, \mathbf{f}, \ldots, \mathbf{f}]$$

with the property that 'u_i *halt*' reduces to **t** precisely when u_i denotes the halt state (The size of the expression for halt is proportional to the number of states in the machine M). Assume the λ-program G on argument *id* reduces to the output tape eventually computed if *id* leads to a halting configuration, and otherwise G does not reduce to a normal form. This G may be characterised recursively: $G = (\lambda x.hd_0x\; halt(hd_4x)(G(Fx)))$, i.e. if the present configuration contains a halt state then the result consists in the present output tape (hd_4x), otherwise apply G to the result of yet another iteration, $G(F\,x)$. Hence G may be defined by

$$G = Y(\lambda g.\lambda x.hd_0\, x\; halt\; (hd_4 x)\; (g(F\,x))).$$

G gives the output tape in reverse order, and then we need a list reversal function. Define first the constant expression

$$end = [\mathbf{f}, \mathbf{f}, \mathbf{t}, \mathbf{f}, \mathbf{f}, \ldots, \mathbf{f}]$$

with the property that 'u_i *end*' reduces to **t** precisely when u_i denotes the tape end marker #. The reversal function is

$$Rev = (\lambda z.Y(\lambda h.\lambda x.\lambda y.hd_0\, y\; end\; x\; (h[hd_0\, y, x](tl_1\, y)))\;\; [u_2]\; z)$$

i.e. $Rev[u_{i_1}, u_{i_2}, \ldots, u_{i_n}, u_2]$ reduces to $[u_{i_n}, u_{i_{n-1}}, \ldots, u_{i_1}, u_2]$ where $i_j \neq 2$.

Define

$$id_0 = (\lambda x.[u_0, [\mathbf{t}, u_3, tree_e, tree_e, tree_e], [\mathbf{t}, u_3, tree_e, tree_e, tree_e], x, [u_2]])$$

which applied to an input tape $[u_{b_0}, \ldots, u_{b_n}, u_2]$ reduce to the initial **id** of the 2-tree Turing Machine. Finally define the λ-program

$$N = (\lambda x.Rev(G(id_0 x)))$$

that computes the same function as the 2-tree Turing Machine M does.

It should be clear from the construction that the number of β-reduction steps needed for the simulation of a single TM-step is bounded by a constant. We find also that regular β-reduction in any order is as efficient as normal order parallel reduction, essentially because a list indexing function forces an order of reduction by creating only one redex at a given time. Where more than one indexing function is enabled the corresponding reduction steps are independent and may be done in any order. Hence $\mu_\pi(L) = \mu_\beta(L) = l_{normal}(L)$.

QED.

References

[Bar81] Barendregt, H. P., *The Lambda Calculus. Its Syntax and Semantics.* North Holland, 1981.

[Bur82] Burton, F. W., A Linear Space Translation of Functional Programs to Turner Combinators. *Information Processing Letters, 14 (1982), pp. 201-204.*

[deB72] de Bruijn, N. G., Lambda Calculus Notation with Nameless Dummies, a Tool for Automatic Formula Manipulation. *Indag Math, 34 (1972), pp. 381-392.*

[Chu32] Church, A., A Set of Postulates for the Foundation of Logic. *Annals of Math. 33, 2nd series (1932), pp. 346-366.*

[CuFe58] Curry, H. B. and Feys, R. *Combinatory Logic, Vol. 1.* North Holland, 1958.

[Fie90] Field, J., On Laziness and Optimality in Lambda Interpreters: Tools for Specification and Analysis. In [PoPL90], pp. 1-15.

[HBTCS] *the Handbook of Theoretical Computer Science, vol A* (ed. J. van Leeuwen). Elsevier, Amsterdam, 1990.

[Hug82] Hughes, R. J. M., Super Combinators: A New Implementation Method for Applicative Languages. In *Proceedings of the 1982 ACM Symposium on Lisp and Functional Programming, pp.1-10.*

[Hug84] Hughes, R. J. M., *The Design and Implementation of Programming Languages.* Ph.D. Thesis, Oxford University, 1984. (PRG-40)

[KeSl87] Kennaway, J. R. and Sleep, M. R., Variable Abstraction in $O(n\log(n))$ Space. *Information Processing Letters, 24 (1987), pp. 343-349.*

[Klo80] Klop, J. W., *Combinatory Reduction Systems.* Mathematical Centre Tracts 127. Mathematisch Centrum, Amsterdam, 1980.

[Lam90] Lamping, J., An Algorithm for Optimal Lambda Calculus Reduction. In [PoPL90], pp. 16-30.

[Lév80] Lévy, Jean-Jacques, Optimal Reductions in the Lambda-Calculus. In Seldon, J. P. and Hindley, J. R. (editors), *To H. B. Curry: Essays on Combinatory Logic, Lambda Calculus and Formalism,* Academic Press, 1980, pp. 159-191.

[Lév88] Lévy, Jean-Jacques, Sharing in the Evaluation of Lambda Expressions. In Fuchi,K. and Kott,L. (editors), *Programming of Future Generation Computers II,* North Holland, 1988, pp. 183-189.

[Nos85] Noshita, K., Translation of Turner Combinators in $O(n\log(n))$ Space. *Information Processing Letters, 20 (1985), pp. 71-74.*

[PoPL90] Proceedings of Seventeenth Annual ACM Symposium on Principles of Programming Languages. ACM, New York, 1990.

[Rév88] Révész, G. E., *Lambda-Calculus, Combinators and Functional Programming.* Cambridge University Press, 1988.

[Ros84] Rosser, J. B., Highlights of the History of the Lambda-Calculus. *Annals of the History of Computing 6 (1984), pp. 337-349.*

[Sch24] Schönfinkel, M., Über die Bausteine der mathematischen Logik. *Matematische Annalen, 92 (1924), pp. 305-316.*

[Sch80] Schönhage, A., Storage Modification Machines. *SIAM Journal on Computing 9 (1980), pp. 490-508.*

[Sch88] Schönhage, A., A Nonlinear Lower Bound for Random-Access Machines under Logarithmic Cost. *Journal of the ACM 35 (1988), pp. 748-754.*

[Sta82] Staples, J., Two-Level Expression Representation for Faster Evaluation. In Ehrig,H., Nagl,M. and Rozenberg,G. (editors), *Proceedings from 2nd International workshop "Graph Grammars and their Application to Computer Science"*. Springer Verlag (LNCS 153), 1983, pp. 392-404.

[Tur79a] Turner, D. A., Another Algorithm for Bracket Abstraction. *The Journal of Symbolic Logic 44 (1979), pp. 267-270.*

[Tur79b] Turner, D. A., New Implementation Techniques for Applicative Languages. *Software: Practice & Experience. 9 (1979), pp. 31-49.*

Outline of a proof theory of parametricity

*Harry G. Mairson**
Department of Computer Science
Brandeis University
Waltham, Massachusetts 02254

Abstract

Reynolds' Parametricity Theorem (also known as the Abstraction Theorem), a result concerning the model theory of the second order polymorphic typed λ-calculus (F_2), has recently been used by Wadler to prove some unusual and interesting properties of programs. We present a purely syntactic version of the Parametricity Theorem, showing that it is simply an example of formal theorem proving in second order minimal logic over a first order equivalence theory on λ-terms. We analyze the use of parametricity in proving program equivalences, and show that structural induction is still required: parametricity is not enough.

As in Leivant's transparent presentation of Girard's Representation Theorem for F_2, we show that algorithms can be extracted from the proofs, such that if a λ-term can be proven parametric, we can synthesize from the proof an "equivalent" parametric λ-term that is moreover F_2-typable. Given that Leivant showed how proofs of *termination*, based on inductive data types and structural induction, had computational content, we show that inductive data types are indeed parametric, hence providing a connection between the two approaches.

1 Introduction

In a recent interesting and beguiling paper, "Theorems for free!" Philip Wadler showed how to use Reynolds' Abstraction Theorem [Rey83] to prove program equivalences. "Write down the definition of a polymorphic function on a piece of paper. Tell me its type, but be careful not to let me see the function's definition. I will tell you a theorem that the function satisfies."[Wad89] He gives the example of a function $r \in \forall A.A^* \rightarrow A^*$, where A^* denotes the type of lists over elements of type A, and claims for all $f \in X \rightarrow Y$ and $\ell \in X^*$, we must have the equality

$$\mathbf{map}_{XY}\ f\ (r_X\ \ell) = r_Y\ (\mathbf{map}_{XY}\ f\ \ell). \tag{1}$$

Intuitive justifications of such an equation are clear: the function r is constrained by its type to rearrange, duplicate, and remove elements of its input in a data-independent manner. However, a more formal means of justification does not appear obvious. What Wadler did was to identify Reynolds' Abstraction Theorem, heretofore used as a means of relating values in different models of programming languages, as a key to showing such equivalences: as such it becomes a tool for program verification and proving properties of programs. When a function is typable in the second-order polymorphic typed λ-calculus invented by Girard and Reynolds [Gir72, Rey74] (henceforth called F_2), Wadler showed that the interpretation of the function in the *frame models* of Bruce, Meyer, and Mitchell [BMM90] satisfies a technical condition called *parametricity*. Parametricity enforces the *denotational* equivalence of terms such as in equation (1) above.

*Supported by NSF Grant CCR-9017125, and grants from Texas Instruments and from the Tyson Foundation.

A variety of questions immediately come to mind concerning this program of deriving "free theorems," presumably so named because much of the work seems to be done effortlessly by the Abstraction Theorem, and because of the surprising absence of induction arguments. First and foremost: do we really need model theory and denotational semantics to prove such equivalences, either from the point of true mathematical necessity, or from the perspective of clarity? There is a lurking suspicion that program equivalences such as (1) above may be compromised by models that are not fully abstract, since λ-terms not β-convertible may be denotationally equated in a model that is not fully abstract. Furthermore, generations of computer scientists have been taught that the *append* function is associative, and that the *reverse* function computes an involution, all without recourse to model theory (see, for example, [BW88]): are these new theorems qualitatively different, and how so? In fact, proofs of the former theorems are standard examples of the use of structural induction. No induction arguments appear in Wadler's free theorems: are they implicitly hidden, unnecessary, or incorrectly absent? Finally, little attention is given by Wadler to the *language* in which programs are written, or at least to the programming *style*: observe F_2-typable functions do not admit unbounded recursion (i.e., a fixpoint operator), an unusual constraint on expressiveness. Wadler concludes his paper with a suggestion that this *terra incognita* be explored further.

In this paper, we show how to derive Wadler's free theorems in a purely syntactic way, without recourse to any model theory. The logical calculus we use is just second order logic over a first-order equational theory of λ-terms. The syntactic view not only does away with unnecessary model theory, it also clarifies the constructive (and indeed, computational) nature of parametricity arguments, as well as explaining what parts of such proofs are mathematical, and what parts are metamathematical. One consequence of this clarification is that we uncover the genuine need for *structural induction* in proving equivalences such as (1) above, underlining part of the hidden cost of free theorems. The proof theory we develop is a straightforward syntactic rendition of *logical relations*, inspired by the Curry-Howard "propositions as types" analogy [How80]. The Curry-Howard analogy has been used in analysis of the constructive nature of logical calculi, where types are propositions, and λ-terms are proofs. What is more or less irrelevant in this development is what the propositions are *about*: in this paper, we show the propositions can be interpreted as statements about how the term may be used.

We relate the syntactic presentation of parametricity to work of Daniel Leivant, who has given particularly transparent and simple explanations and extensions of Girard's Representation Theorem for F_2 [Gir72] as well as Gödel's Dialectica Theorem [Göd58]. In this framework, type inference for a term becomes merely the homomorphism of a proof in second order logic about the use of the term, in other words the familiar work of proving properties of programs. In his paper, "Contracting proofs to programs," Leivant shows that type inference in F_2 can be viewed as termination proofs for a programming language over inductive data types [Lei90].[1] For instance, we can code map as

$$\mathbf{map}\ f\ \mathbf{nil} \;=\; \mathbf{nil} \tag{2}$$

$$\mathbf{map}\ f\ (\mathbf{cons}\ x\ \ell) \;=\; \mathbf{cons}\ (f\ x)\ (\mathbf{map}\ f\ \ell) \tag{3}$$

in the usual style, and we demonstrate map is a total function by proving the theorem[2]

$$\mathcal{M}(\mathbf{map}) \equiv \forall AB.\forall f.(\forall x.A(x) \to B(fx)) \to \forall \ell.A^*(\ell) \to B^*(\mathbf{map}\ f\ \ell), \tag{4}$$

where for any unary relation T, we define

$$T^*(\ell) \equiv \forall P.(\forall yt.T(y) \to P(t) \to P(\mathbf{cons}\ y\ t)) \to P(\mathbf{nil}) \to P(\ell). \tag{5}$$

Of course, T^* is the familiar axiom of structural induction over lists of "type" T. Leivant showed how from the *proof* of $\mathcal{M}$(map) we can extract an *algorithm* (λ-term) computing map which is

[1] This result also appears in [BB85].

[2] We write $\forall A \ldots$, using capital letters, to denote second-order quantification (respectively, quantification over type variables), and $\forall x \ldots$, using small letters, to denote first-order quantification over terms.

F_2-typable, such that substituting the λ-term for **map** satisfies the recursive equations used as the initial definition of the function, and indeed such equations can be checked constructively by β-reduction. The parametricity of the solutions follows immediately. We therefore argue that in some sense proving *termination* is conceptually prior to proving *parametricity*, in that the latter follows formally and logically from the former in the case of inductive data types. Complementing Leivant's extraction of programs from proofs, we show a similar contraction whereby parametric programs can be extracted from proofs of parametricity.

Finally, since part of the beauty of "free theorems" is the (relative!) absence of *induction*, we present a style of "free programs" which exhibit surprising expressive power in the absence of *recursion*. The style is not new, however we believe that the type-free presentation we give is particularly lucid, and should be completely understandable to functional programming enthusiasts who have not been immersed in the type theory literature.

The preference of the author for proof theory over model theory is merely a taking of sides in a longstanding philosophical debate about the nature and foundations of mathematics: for a short exposition of the two semantic traditions, sometimes ascribed to Tarski and Heyting, see [GLT89]. The reduction we give to *logic* we believe is primary, and has a long tradition including Boole (who reduced "laws of thought" to logic), Russell and Whitehead (who reduced mathematics to logic), and more recently Curry and Howard (who, unbeknownst to them, reduced computation to logic). What we present is firmly in the tradition of the Curry-Howard "propositions as types" analogy.

We wish to emphasize our belief that there is no "right answer" in this debate. As a consequence, the work presented here is not meant to contradict Wadler's results, rather to complement them: we develop a simple and constructive framework for proving equalities about programs. Among the virtues of this constructive framework is that one could easily envision a formal proof checking system in which these equalities could be developed. Not coincidentally, it is this kind of goal which prompted the initial development of ML. What we are trying to explain simply and in a straightforward manner is that programs are just first order equational theories, and polymorphic types are theorems in second order logic about those theories. A not very surprising consequence is that types can be used to prove properties of programs.

As background references, for a description of F_2, we recommend [GLT89, PDM89, Sc90, Rey90]; for relevant ideas and notation from logic, especially sequent calculus and natural deduction, we recommend [vanD79]. A good introduction to logical relations can be found in [Sta85, Mit91].

2 Constructing proofs of parametricity from type inferences

The slogan generally associated with *parametricity* is that "programs evaluated in related environments have related results." We now formalize this notion in a very straightforward manner, using binary relations and second-order logic. Given the derivation of a type judgement $\Gamma \rhd E{:}\,\sigma$ using the type inference rules of F_2, we can synthesize a proof concerning the parametric properties of E. Said otherwise, type judgements are homomorphic contractions of parametricity proofs.

Definition 2.1 *If E is an (untyped) λ-term, we define E' to be the term derived by replacing each free variable x of E by x'. Similarly, we define E'' by replacing each free variable x of E by x''.*

Definition 2.2 *If σ is an F_2 type and E is a λ-term, we define the proposition $\mathcal{R}^\sigma(E',E'')$ inductively as:*

$$\mathcal{R}^A(E',E'') \equiv A(E',E'') \qquad \text{if } \sigma\equiv A \text{ is a type variable} \tag{6}$$

$$\mathcal{R}^{\sigma\to\tau}(E',E'') \equiv \forall x'x''.\mathcal{R}^\sigma(x',x'') \to \mathcal{R}^\tau((Ex)',(Ex)'') \tag{7}$$

$$\mathcal{R}^{\forall A.\sigma}(E',E'') \equiv \forall A.\mathcal{R}^\sigma(E',E''). \tag{8}$$

The propositions in the above Definition specify relations between terms E' and E'' that are identical except for their free variables. The slogan associated with parametricity now takes on particular meaning in that we can consider such propositions as ***hypotheses*** about terms (i.e., an environment), and deduce similar propositions about other terms. This perspective motivates the next definition.

Definition 2.3 *If* Γ *is a type context, we define the set* $\tilde{\Gamma}$ *of propositions as:*

$$\tilde{\Gamma} = \{\mathcal{R}^{\sigma}(x', x'') \mid x{:}\sigma \in \Gamma\}. \tag{9}$$

Each kind of type inference rule can now be interpreted as the contraction of a second order logical deduction. We consider in turn each of the F_2 inference rules.

Rule (*var*). For the type inference rule

$$(var) \qquad \frac{}{\Gamma \cup \{x{:}\alpha\} \rhd x{:}\alpha}$$

we have the logical rule

$$[hyp] \qquad \frac{}{\tilde{\Gamma} \cup \{\mathcal{R}^{\alpha}(x', x'')\} \vdash \mathcal{R}^{\alpha}(x', x'')}$$

Rule (*app*). For the type inference rule

$$(app) \qquad \frac{\Gamma \rhd M{:}\alpha \rightarrow \beta \qquad \Gamma \rhd N{:}\alpha}{\Gamma \rhd MN{:}\beta}$$

we have the logical rule

$$[\rightarrow E] \qquad \frac{\tilde{\Gamma} \vdash \forall x'x''.\mathcal{R}^{\alpha}(x', x'') \rightarrow \mathcal{R}^{\beta}((Mx)', (Mx)'') \qquad \tilde{\Gamma} \vdash \mathcal{R}^{\alpha}(N', N'')}{\tilde{\Gamma} \vdash \mathcal{R}^{\beta}(M'N', M''N'')}$$

Rule (*abs*). For the type inference rule

$$(abs) \qquad \frac{\Gamma \cup \{x{:}\alpha\} \rhd M{:}\beta}{\Gamma \rhd \lambda x.M{:}\alpha \rightarrow \beta}$$

we have the logical rule

$$[\rightarrow I] \qquad \frac{\tilde{\Gamma} \cup \{\mathcal{R}^{\alpha}(x', x'')\} \vdash \mathcal{R}^{\beta}(M', M'')}{\tilde{\Gamma} \vdash \forall x'x''.\mathcal{R}^{\alpha}(x', x'') \rightarrow \mathcal{R}^{\beta}((\lambda x.M)'x', (\lambda x.M)''x'')}$$

Rule (*inst*). For the type inference rule

$$(inst) \qquad \frac{\Gamma \rhd M{:}\forall A.\Phi(A)}{\Gamma \rhd M{:}\Phi(\sigma)}$$

we have the logical rule

$$[\forall^2 E] \qquad \frac{\tilde{\Gamma} \vdash \forall A.\mathcal{R}^{\Phi(A)}(M', M'')}{\tilde{\Gamma} \vdash \mathcal{R}^{\Phi(\sigma)}(M', M'')}$$

Rule (*gen*). Finally, for the type inference rule

$$(gen) \qquad \frac{\Gamma \rhd M{:}\,\Phi(A) \qquad [A \notin FV(\Gamma)]}{\Gamma \rhd M{:}\,\forall A.\Phi(A)}$$

we have the logical rule

$$[\forall^2 I] \qquad \frac{\tilde{\Gamma} \vdash \mathcal{R}^{\Phi(A)}(M', M'') \qquad [A \notin FV(\tilde{\Gamma})]}{\tilde{\Gamma} \vdash \mathcal{R}^{\forall A.\Phi(\sigma)}(M', M'')}$$

Comments.

1. Unlike the usual presentation of type inference rules for F_2, we have omitted any type information in the λ-terms. For instance, we write M instead of $M\,[\sigma]$ in the conclusion to rule (*inst*), and M instead of $\Lambda A.M$ in the conclusion to rule (*gen*). The reason is to separate cleanly type information from their associated pure λ-terms, to parallel the logical deductions about such terms.
2. Observe that the logical interpretation of the inference rules for F_2 sometimes requires several logical steps. For example, the interpretation of (*app*) requires $\forall^1$-elimination as well as *modus ponens*.
3. Rule (*abs*) in its logical interpretation assumes $(\lambda x.M)'x' = M'$ and $(\lambda x.M)''x'' = M''$, hence an underlying first order theory of equality on λ-terms. We can safely limit this theory to a set of equations $M = N$, where M and N are equivalent modulo at most one β-reduction. (Observe, then, how computation is related to proof.)

Proposition 2.4 *The logical rules given are all sound.*

Lemma 2.5 *(Fundamental Theorem of Logical Relations [Sta85, Mit91]) If $\Gamma \rhd E{:}\,\sigma$ is a derivable type judgement, then $\tilde{\Gamma} \vdash \mathcal{R}^{\sigma}(E', E'')$ is a derivable sequent.*

Proof. By induction on the inference of the type judgement. ∎

Definition 2.6 *When $\vdash \mathcal{R}^{\sigma}(E, E)$ is a provable sequent, we say the λ-term E is* parametric. *(We remark that in this case, E must be a closed term, hence $E \equiv E' \equiv E''$.)*

Corollary 2.7 *If $\Gamma \rhd E{:}\,\sigma$ is a derivable type judgement, and E is a closed λ-term, then E is parametric.*

There is nothing particularly significant about binary relations: the above syntactic presentation could be carried out for any arity.

Theorem 2.8 *If $\Gamma \vdash \mathcal{R}^{\sigma}(E', E'')$ is a provable sequent, then there exists a λ-term P and context Γ_P where $\Gamma_P \rhd P{:}\,\sigma$ is a derivable type judgement.*

Proof. (sketch) We take the proof of $\Gamma \vdash \mathcal{R}^{\sigma}(E', E'')$ and *contract* it by removing all first-order information, in the style of Leivant [Lei90]. For example, the axiom of induction for integers,

$$\mathsf{Int}(k) \equiv \forall P.(\forall x.P(x) \to P(\mathbf{succ}\ x)) \to P(\mathbf{zero}) \to P(k), \qquad (10)$$

contracts to $\forall P.(P \to P) \to P \to P$, the inductive type representation of integers. By attaching labels to the hypotheses in sequents, we derive a type inference for a λ-term P describing the structure of the proof of the sequent. ∎

3 Applications of parametricity and induction to proving program equivalence

Parametricity can be used in a straightforward way to prove properties of programs. Here is a simple example:

Proposition 3.1 *If* $\triangleright f\colon \forall A.A \to A$ *is a derivable* F_2 *type judgement, then* $\vdash \forall x.fx = x$ *is a provable sequent in minimal second order logic.*

Proof. Observe that f need not be $\lambda x.x$, only that it *act like* the identity function. The intuition is clear: for *any* type A, f must input an x of type A, and output fx of type A. Since f has no information as to what operations equip type A, it can perform no useful computation with x, and is constrained to simply output the input.

Since the type judgement $\triangleright f\colon \forall A.A \to A$ has no assumptions, f is a closed λ-term. By Corollary 2.7, using the *unary* version of parametricity, we then know $\vdash \forall A.\forall x.A(x) \to A(fx)$ is a derivable sequent. By quantifier elimination and introduction, we derive $\vdash \forall A.A(x) \to A(fx)$, the familiar "Leibniz equality" in second order logic. Instantiating A as $A(z) \equiv z = x$, we have $\vdash x = x \to fx = x$. We derive $\vdash \forall x.fx = x$ by use of the identity axiom, modus ponens, and quantifier introduction. ∎

There are many other identities that we can similarly prove, for instance $\triangleright k\colon \forall AB.A \to B \to A$ implies $\vdash \forall xy.kxy = x$, or $\triangleright b\colon \forall A.A \to A \to A$ implies $\vdash \forall xy.bxy = x \vee bxy = y$. In these examples, "implies" indicates a metamathematical statement about proofs in the formal systems. Of course, the former example attests to the "uniqueness" of the K combinator, and the latter characterizes the coding of Boolean values. Again, the intuitions are straightforward, but more interesting is that the logic provides a completely mechanical way of deriving the identities.

More problematic, however, is the mechanization of such proofs when the underlying datatypes are infinite and defined inductively: integers, lists, trees, queues, and so on – in short, the building blocks of abstract data types. Parametricity does not seem to be powerful enough for reasoning about these more complex data types. We now attempt to explain why.

3.1 An example: Wadler's "map theorem"

Wadler gives the following example of the use of parametricity: let **m** and **map** both be F_2-typable terms with type $\forall AB.(A \to B) \to A^* \to B^*$, where for any type T we define $T^* \equiv \forall P.(T \to P \to P) \to P \to P$, and let **id** be the usual identity function with polymorphic type $\forall A.A \to A$. Then for any $f \in X \to Y$ and $\ell \in X^*$, we must have

$$\mathbf{map}\ f\ (\mathbf{m}\ \mathbf{id}\ \ell) = \mathbf{m}\ \mathbf{id}\ (\mathbf{map}\ f\ \ell) \tag{11}$$

$$\mathbf{m}\ f\ \ell = \mathbf{map}\ f\ (\mathbf{m}\ \mathbf{id}\ \ell) \tag{12}$$

In trying to prove these equations, we will assume that **m** and **map** satisfy parametricity conditions dictated by the specified type, and the usual equational axioms for **map**. We first try and reproduce Wadler's derivation of the first equation in second-order logic, observing the logical syntax carefully to analyze why the assumptions are insufficient. We then prove the second equation, using logical assumptions which replace parametricity with a higher-order form of induction. In this analysis, types play the role of predicates, and the first-order terms are program fragments. Thus types are propositions about programs. No "intuition" (semantics) is used about what the fragments mean.

We imagine programs to be defined axiomatically via an equational theory, for example

$$\mathbf{map}\ f\ \mathbf{nil} \;=\; \mathbf{nil} \tag{13}$$
$$\mathbf{map}\ f\ (\mathbf{cons}\ x\ \ell) \;=\; \mathbf{cons}\ (f\ x)\ (\mathbf{map}\ f\ \ell) \tag{14}$$

where boldface denotes *constants* and italic face denotes (universally quantified) *variables.*

Let's begin by trying to prove (11), assuming the parametricity conditions $\Psi(\mathbf{map})$ and $\Psi(\mathrm{m})$, where

$$\begin{aligned}\Psi(g) \;\equiv\; & \forall AB.\forall hh'.(\forall xx'.A(x,x') \rightarrow B(hx, h'x')) \rightarrow \\ & \forall \ell\ell'.\mathcal{R}^{A^*}(\ell,\ell') \rightarrow \mathcal{R}^{B^*}(g\ h\ \ell, g\ h'\ \ell'),\end{aligned} \tag{15}$$

and for any binary relation A, we define $\mathcal{R}^{A^*}(\ell,\ell')$ as:

$$\begin{aligned}& \forall P.\forall cc'.(\forall xx'.A(x,x') \rightarrow \forall rr'.P(r,r') \rightarrow P(c\ x\ r, c'\ x'\ r')) \rightarrow \\ & \forall nn'.P(n,n') \rightarrow P(\ell\ c\ n, \ell'\ c'\ n').\end{aligned} \tag{16}$$

(This logical relation comes from the F_2 coding $A^* \equiv \forall P.(A \rightarrow P \rightarrow P) \rightarrow P \rightarrow P$ for lists.) Let $A(z,z') \equiv B(z,z') \equiv z' = fz$ and $h = h' = \mathbf{id}$; then from $\Psi(\mathrm{m})$ we derive

$$(\forall xx'.x' = fx \rightarrow \mathbf{id}\ x' = f(\mathbf{id}\ x)) \rightarrow \forall \ell\ell'.\mathcal{R}^{A^*}(\ell,\ell') \rightarrow \mathcal{R}^{B^*}(\mathrm{m}\ \mathbf{id}\ \ell, \mathrm{m}\ \mathbf{id}\ \ell'). \tag{17}$$

By the (added!) assumption $\mathbf{id}\ x = x$, the premise is true; we have

$$\forall \ell\ell'.\mathcal{R}^{A^*}(\ell,\ell') \rightarrow \mathcal{R}^{B^*}(\mathrm{m}\ \mathbf{id}\ \ell, \mathrm{m}\ \mathbf{id}\ \ell'). \tag{18}$$

Now let $\ell' = \mathbf{map}\ f\ \ell$: we get

$$\mathcal{R}^{A^*}(\ell, \mathbf{map}\ f\ \ell) \rightarrow \mathcal{R}^{B^*}(\mathrm{m}\ \mathbf{id}\ \ell, \mathrm{m}\ \mathbf{id}\ (\mathbf{map}\ f\ \ell)). \tag{19}$$

We can rewrite $\mathcal{R}^{A^*}(\ell, \mathbf{map}\ f\ \ell)$, given our earlier assumption that $A(z,z') \equiv z' = fz$, as

$$\begin{aligned}& \forall P.\forall cc'.(\forall xrr'.P(r,r') \rightarrow P(c\ x\ r, c'\ (f\ x)\ r')) \rightarrow \\ & \forall nn'.P(n,n') \rightarrow P(\ell\ c\ n, (\mathbf{map}\ f\ \ell)\ \ c'\ n').\end{aligned} \tag{20}$$

Let's ask a simpler question: how could we prove (20) not for *all* ℓ, but for simply $\ell \equiv \mathbf{nil}$? Observe that the first premise is irrelevant; what we really want to prove is (observing $\mathbf{map}\ f\ \mathbf{nil} = \mathbf{nil}$):

$$\forall nn'.P(n,n') \rightarrow P(\mathbf{nil}\ c\ n, \mathbf{nil}\ c'\ n'). \tag{21}$$

This is easy as long as we add the assumption

$$\mathbf{nil}\ x\ y \;=\; y. \tag{22}$$

In general, to prove (18) we need an assumption that ℓ is a list of "type" A, i.e., the induction axiom:

$$A^*(\ell) \equiv \forall Q.(\forall yt.A(y) \rightarrow Q(t) \rightarrow Q(\mathbf{cons}\ y\ t)) \rightarrow Q(\mathbf{nil}) \rightarrow Q(\ell). \tag{23}$$

We then choose $Q(z) \equiv \mathcal{R}^{A^*}(z, \mathbf{map}\ f\ z)$: note our "simple example" above was proof of the basis $Q(\mathbf{nil})$. For the inductive step, we need to prove $Q(\mathbf{cons}\ y\ t)$ given the additional assumptions

$A(y)$ and $Q(t)$. But $Q(t)$ is

$$\forall P.\forall cc'.(\forall x r r'.P(r,r') \rightarrow P(c\ x\ r, c'\ (f\ x)\ r')) \rightarrow \\ \forall n n'.P(n,n') \rightarrow P(t\ c\ n, (\mathbf{map}\ f\ t)\ c'\ n'), \tag{24}$$

while $Q(\mathbf{cons}\ y\ t)$ is defined as

$$\forall P.\forall cc'.(\forall x r r'.P(r,r') \rightarrow P(c\ x\ r, c'\ (f\ x)\ r')) \rightarrow \\ \forall n n'.P(n,n') \rightarrow P((\mathbf{cons}\ y\ t)\ c\ n, (\mathbf{map}\ f\ (\mathbf{cons}\ y\ t))\ c'\ n'). \tag{25}$$

We now recall that $\mathbf{map}\ f\ (\mathbf{cons}\ y\ t) = \mathbf{cons}\ (f\ y)\ (\mathbf{map}\ f\ t)$; in addition, we add the assumption

$$(\mathbf{cons}\ z\ w)\ x\ y \ = \ x\ z\ (w\ x\ y). \tag{26}$$

Observe that using λ-notation, assumptions (22) and (26) can be rewritten as the familiar inductive type definitions

$$\mathbf{nil} \ \equiv \ \lambda x.\lambda y.y \tag{27}$$

$$\mathbf{cons} \ \equiv \ \lambda z.\lambda w.\lambda x.\lambda y.x\ z\ (w\ x\ y). \tag{28}$$

Adding assumption (26), we observe that the conclusion in (25) can be rewritten as:

$$P(c\ y\ (t\ c\ n), c'\ (f\ y)\ ((\mathbf{map}\ f\ t)\ c'\ n')). \tag{29}$$

Using the premises of (25) in assumption (24), we can derive $P(t\ c\ n, (\mathbf{map}\ f\ t)\ c'\ n')$; we use the assumptions in (25) further to prove (29). From the induction assumption (23) we then derive $\mathcal{R}^{A^*}(\ell, \mathbf{map}\ f\ \ell)$, hence from (19) we get $\mathcal{R}^{B^*}(\mathbf{m\ id}\ \ell, \mathbf{m\ id}\ (\mathbf{map}\ f\ \ell))$, namely:

$$\forall P.\forall cc'.(\forall y r r'.P(r,r') \rightarrow P(c\ y\ r, c'\ (f\ y)\ r')) \rightarrow \\ \forall n n'.P(n,n') \rightarrow P(\mathbf{m\ id}\ \ell\ c\ n, \mathbf{m\ id}\ (\mathbf{map}\ f\ \ell)\ c'\ n'). \tag{30}$$

If we choose $P(z,z') \equiv z' = \mathbf{map}\ f\ z$ and $c = c' = \mathbf{cons}$, $n = n' = \mathbf{nil}$, then the premises in (30) become

$$r' = \mathbf{map}\ f\ r \rightarrow \mathbf{cons}\ (f\ y)\ r' = \mathbf{map}\ f\ (\mathbf{cons}\ y\ r) \tag{31}$$

$$\mathbf{nil} = \mathbf{map}\ f\ \mathbf{nil}, \tag{32}$$

the familiar equational definitions of **map**; we then derive

$$\mathbf{m\ id}\ (\mathbf{map}\ f\ \ell)\ \mathbf{cons\ nil} \ = \ \mathbf{map}\ f\ (\mathbf{m\ id}\ \ell\ \mathbf{cons\ nil}). \tag{33}$$

It then remains to show

$$\mathbf{m\ id}\ (\mathbf{map}\ f\ \ell)\ \mathbf{cons\ nil} \ = \ \mathbf{m\ id}\ (\mathbf{map}\ f\ \ell) \tag{34}$$

$$\mathbf{map}\ f\ (\mathbf{m\ id}\ \ell\ \mathbf{cons\ nil}) \ = \ \mathbf{map}\ f\ (\mathbf{m\ id}\ \ell) \tag{35}$$

To prove (35) we need to show $\mathbf{m\ id}\ \ell\ \mathbf{cons\ nil} = \mathbf{m\ id}\ \ell$, which we demonstrate by induction on $\mathbf{m\ id}\ \ell$—but to do so, we need to know that it is indeed a list! Hence we must make the additional assumption that $\mathbf{m}$ is totally defined and maps lists to lists, i.e., $\mathcal{M}(\mathbf{m})$, where

$$\mathcal{M}(g) \equiv \forall AB.\forall f.(\forall x.A(x) \rightarrow B(fx)) \rightarrow \forall \ell.A^*(\ell) \rightarrow B^*(g\ f\ \ell). \tag{36}$$

(Recall (23) for the definition of A^* and B^*.) In the course of the induction proof of (35), the "iterator equalities" (22) and (26) are used again. The proof of (34) is similar.

Retrospective

What added assumptions become apparent in this proof? Recall the slogan that motivated Wadler's theorems: "You give me the type, and I'll give you a theorem." From the *type* of m came the "free" proof of the *parametricity* of m, but we needed to assume its *totality* as well, namely that m mapped lists of one "type" to lists of another "type." Induction axioms for lists were also essential; again, assumptions that lists are parametric did not seem strong enough. Also, we required the iterator equalities for **cons** and **nil**.

The induction hypotheses used by Wadler (essentially, the instantiations of A and B) were entirely correct; what we have tried to do is formalize some of the inductive machinery. What we discover is that from assuming m (and, of course, map) is *total* and mapping lists to lists, the assumptions of parametricity and, as we shall see shortly, the iterator equalities are not needed either. The inductions needed to finish a parametricity-based proof, however superfluous they seem to be, depend on a proof that m is a total function mapping lists to lists. This condition on m seems stronger than its mere parametricity. The reason is in part given by the following proposition:

Proposition 3.2 $\forall xy.\mathbf{nil}\ x\ y = x, \forall xyzw.(\mathbf{cons}\ z\ w)\ x\ y = x\ z\ (w\ x\ y) \vdash A^*(\ell) \rightarrow \mathcal{R}^{A^*}(\ell)$.

Proof. We instantiate the induction axiom $A^*(\ell)$ with a parametricity relation. ∎

We can generalize the proposition to:

Theorem 3.3 *If the constructors of an inductive data type* τ *satisfy equations of primitive recursion, then the terms of type* τ *are parametric.*

(The converse does not seems obvious.) Furthermore, the truth of the program equivalences described above depend on the style in which lists are typically encoded in F_2 (see Section 4): the "map theorem" is then dependent on a particular coding.

3.2 Another interesting equality, using a simpler proof method

We now proceed to prove Wadler's second equation. In place of parametricity, the logical assumption made about m we write as $\mathcal{M}_2(\mathrm{m})$, where $\mathcal{M}_2(g)$ is defined as:

$$\begin{aligned}\mathcal{M}_2(g) \equiv\ & \forall AB.\forall hh'.(\forall xx'.A(x,x') \rightarrow B(h\ x, h'\ x')) \rightarrow \\ & \forall \ell\ell'.\mathcal{S}^{A^*}(\ell,\ell') \rightarrow \mathcal{S}^{B^*}(g\ h\ \ell, g\ h'\ \ell'). \end{aligned} \tag{37}$$

This proposition introduces relations $\mathcal{S}^{A^*}$ and $\mathcal{S}^{B^*}$, where for any binary relation A we define $\mathcal{S}^{A^*}$ as:

$$\begin{aligned}\mathcal{S}^{A^*}(\ell,\ell') \equiv\ & \forall P.(\forall yy'tt'.A(y,y') \rightarrow P(t,t') \rightarrow P(\mathbf{cons}\ y\ t, \mathbf{cons}\ y'\ t')) \rightarrow \\ & P(\mathbf{nil},\mathbf{nil}) \rightarrow P(\ell,\ell'). \end{aligned} \tag{38}$$

Hence if $\mathcal{S}^{A^*}(\ell,\ell')$ is provable, ℓ and ℓ' must have the same length, where the elements of the two lists are pairwise related by relation A. It is this logical statement which corresponds to Wadler's informal definition (in [Wad89]) of relations between lists; this informal definition is not precisely captured by the logical relation defined by the type of lists.

Observe that if $\mathcal{M}(g)$ is provable in second order logic, so is $\mathcal{M}_2(g)$. To construct $\mathcal{M}_2(g)$ from $\mathcal{M}(g)$, we replace unary relations by binary relations, and replace each first-order quantified variable by two such variables: the first variable is used in the first coordinate of binary relations, and the second variable in the second coordinate of the relations. The (metamathematical) transformation of the associated proof of $\mathcal{M}(g)$ into a proof of $\mathcal{M}_2(g)$ is similar. Just as parametricity is a general notion which can be expressed over relations of any arity, so we may generalize inductively defined relations to any arity. Since inductively defined relations are fundamentally induction axioms in the logic, programs like **m** and **map** induce *higher order* inductively defined relations (they map inductions axioms to induction axioms).

Given $\mathcal{M}_2(\mathbf{m})$, let $A(z,z') \equiv z' = z$, $B(z,z') \equiv z' = fz$, $h = \mathbf{id}, h' = f$, and let $\ell' = \ell$; we derive

$$(\forall xx'.x = x' \to fx' = f(\mathbf{id}\ x)) \to \mathcal{S}^{A^*}(\ell,\ell) \to \mathcal{S}^{B^*}(\mathbf{m\ id}\ \ell, \mathbf{m}\ f\ \ell). \tag{39}$$

The first premise is a tautology; we prove $\mathcal{S}^{A^*}(\ell,\ell)$ by induction on ℓ, recalling the induction axiom

$$A^*(\ell) \equiv \forall Q.(\forall yt.A(y) \to Q(t) \to Q(\mathbf{cons}\ y\ t)) \to Q(\mathbf{nil}) \to Q(\ell), \tag{40}$$

taking $Q(z) \equiv \mathcal{S}^{A^*}(z,z)$. We omit this proof, which is quite straightforward: observe that it does not use iterator equations. We then derive $\mathcal{S}^{B^*}(\mathbf{m\ id}\ \ell, \mathbf{m}\ f\ \ell)$, namely:

$$\forall P.(\forall ytt'.P(t,t') \to P(\mathbf{cons}\ y\ t, \mathbf{cons}\ (f\ y)\ t')) \to P(\mathbf{nil},\mathbf{nil}) \to P(\mathbf{m\ id}\ \ell, \mathbf{m}\ f\ \ell). \tag{41}$$

Take $P(z,z') \equiv z' = \mathbf{map}\ f\ z$; we get

$$\begin{aligned}(\forall yt.\mathbf{cons}\ (f\ y)\ (\mathbf{map}\ f\ t) = \mathbf{map}\ f\ (\mathbf{cons}\ y\ t)) \to \\ \mathbf{nil} = \mathbf{map}\ f\ \mathbf{nil} \to \mathbf{m}\ f\ \ell = \mathbf{map}\ f\ (\mathbf{m\ id}\ \ell).\end{aligned} \tag{42}$$

We then prove $\mathbf{m}\ f\ \ell = \mathbf{map}\ f\ (\mathbf{m\ id}\ \ell)$ using the equational definition of **map** and *modus ponens.*

3.3 Comparison of the two proof methods

In what sense can our proof methods be considered simpler? The key insight of Wadler was that the parametricity of **m** is *almost* a higher-order form of induction, and the second order instantiations in his proofs are essentially induction hypotheses. It may seem that the substitutions used in both proofs are without motivation, but one should remember that induction indeed requires insight. However, the substitutions we have used can be derived almost mechanically by unification of parts of the "goal" equation with the terms of the final atomic formula in $\mathcal{M}_2(\mathbf{m})$ (respectively, $\Psi(\mathbf{m})$).

We observe that Wadler leaves out some of the logical machinery needed to push through these inductive assertions, and this machinery seems to be the difference between parametric and inductive assumptions. While these proofs can be carried out by assuming that *lists* are parametric when viewed as primitive recursive *iterators*, an additional assumption is then needed at the end that lists are *inductive*–not at all surprising, since lists are a standard example of inductive data types. Our simplification is to largely dispense with parametricity, and work directly with induction axioms.

However, it should be remarked that parametricity defines a logical relation which can be generated from *any* type inference for a closed term, while our "inductively defined relations" seem to make sense for only a restricted subset of terms (those inductively defined). Furthermore, the higher order inductively defined relations (like $\mathcal{M}_2(\mathbf{m})$) require some ingenuity to prove, and do not follow mechanically from type inferences. In this sense, parametricity seems to be a more general notion, but not necessarily more powerful. There are indeed bizarre terms which are parametric, for example, the simulation of Turing Machines in [HM91], employing a programming style completely orthogonal to the inductive-type style illustrated, for example, in [PDM89]; nonetheless, it seems unclear what program equivalences can be proven from them using parametricity. In the case of programming over inductively defined types, we have shown that logical machinery based on inductively defined relations is a much straighter path to the goal.

3.4 Proof theory and cut elimination

There is an added benefit from the approach we have advocated: the "map theorems" we have proven are not restricted to the second-order polymorphic lambda calculus. More specifically, our derived equalities hold for any programming language, including ones having a fixpoint operator, where we can prove $\mathcal{M}(\mathbf{m})$, $\mathcal{M}(\mathbf{map})$, and $A^*(\ell)$. Without loss of generality, we can let the first-order terms be over an algebra with variables, constants (**cons**, **nil**, **m**, **map**, etc.), and a first order theory which is not about β-reduction, but *any* equational theory. For instance, we can describe **map** by the standard equational presentation, with similar definitions for **m**. As long as we can prove the relevant higher order induction propositions about the relevant programs, the result holds. Equivalents of the "map theorem" can easily be stated for other inductive datatypes, where (for example) we replace lists with trees: what changes is the form of the induction axioms.

What, then, does any of this have to do with F_2, the second-order polymorphic lambda calculus? Leivant has shown that by analyzing the *proofs* of $\mathcal{M}(\mathbf{m})$ and $\mathcal{M}(\mathbf{map})$, we can extract F_2-typable *algorithms* for computing these functions, where the "map theorem" holds for these algorithms. In the case of **map**, the algorithm we synthesize is:

$$\mathbf{map} = \lambda f.\lambda \ell.\ell\ (\lambda x.\mathbf{cons}\ (f\ x))\ \mathbf{nil}. \tag{43}$$

Written with F_2 type information, this can be rewritten:

$$\begin{aligned}\mathbf{map} \;=\; & \Lambda A.\Lambda B.\lambda f{:}\, A \to B.\\ & \quad \lambda \ell{:}\, \forall P.(A \to P \to P) \to P \to P.\\ & \qquad \ell\ [\forall Q.(B \to Q \to Q) \to Q \to Q]\\ & \qquad\quad (\lambda x{:}\, A.\mathbf{cons}[B]\ (f\ x))\ \mathbf{nil}[B],\end{aligned} \tag{44}$$

where

$$\begin{aligned}\mathbf{cons} \;=\; & \Lambda A.\lambda x{:}\, A.\lambda \ell{:}\, \forall P.(A \to P \to P) \to P \to P.\\ & \quad \Lambda Q.\lambda c{:}\, A \to Q \to Q.\lambda n{:}\, Q.\\ & \qquad c\ x\ (\ell[Q]\ c\ n)\end{aligned} \tag{45}$$

$$\mathbf{nil} = \Lambda A.\Lambda Q.\lambda c{:}\, A \to Q \to Q.\lambda n{:}\, Q.n. \tag{46}$$

Written in "logical" form, the totality of the **map** function could be written as:

$$\begin{aligned}\mathbf{map} \;=\; & \Lambda A.\Lambda B.\lambda f{:}\, \forall x.A(x) \to B(fx).\\ & \quad \lambda \ell{:}\, \forall P.(\forall yt.A(y) \to P(t) \to P(\mathbf{cons}\ x\ t)) \to P(\mathbf{nil}) \to P(\ell).\\ & \qquad \ell\ [\forall Q.(\forall yt.B(y) \to Q(t) \to Q(\mathbf{cons}\ x\ t) \to Q(\mathbf{nil}) \to Q(\ell)]\\ & \qquad\quad (\lambda x{:}\, A(x).\mathbf{cons}\ (f\ x))\ \mathbf{nil}{:}\, Q(\mathbf{nil}).\end{aligned} \tag{47}$$

While the "logical" notation above is a bit fanciful, it is meant to suggest the Curry-Howard isomorphism: namely, that λ-bound variables are the names of *parcels* of logical hypotheses, where function application is deduction.

Finally, we mention that our proofs of the "map theorems" have an additional computational content: not only do they prove equalities of certain terms, but they ensure that these terms are convertible, and moreover encode the conversion. Syntactic equalities ensure truth in all models, hence in the term model, but we can in addition "provably" convert both sides of the equalities (for fixed f and ℓ, with proper substitutions for the second-order variables) by performing cut elimination on the resultant proof.

3.5 An analysis of Reynolds' isomorphism

Using parametricity, we can as well give a syntactic explanation of an isomorphism discussed by Reynolds in [Rey83] and later by Wadler. The syntactic analysis is interesting because it makes explicit an encoding of existential quantification. Let $\mathrm{i} \equiv \lambda x.\lambda g.gx$ and $\mathrm{j} \equiv \lambda h.h(\lambda x.x)$, with F_2 typings $\mathrm{i}: A \to \tilde{A}$ and $\mathrm{j}: \tilde{A} \to A$, where $\tilde{A} \equiv \forall X.(A \to X) \to X$. By pure equational reasoning (i.e., using β-reduction only) one can easily prove $\forall x.\mathrm{j}(\mathrm{i}\,x) = x$, but not $\forall h.\mathrm{i}(\mathrm{j}\,h) = h$: by equational reasoning, the best one can do is $\mathrm{i}(\mathrm{j}\,h) = \lambda g.g(h(\lambda x.x))$. However, if $\mathrm{i}(\mathrm{j}\,h)$ is F_2-typable, then $h: \tilde{A}$, so that we can indeed prove $\forall h.\mathcal{R}^{\tilde{A}}(h) \to \mathrm{i}(\mathrm{j}\,h) = h$ in second order logic. Recall that the *unary* relation $\mathcal{R}^{\tilde{A}}(h)$ is defined as

$$\mathcal{R}^{\tilde{A}}(h) \equiv \forall X.\forall g.(\forall a.A(a) \to X(ga)) \to X(hg); \tag{48}$$

instantiating X as $X(z) \equiv \exists b.z = gb \wedge A(b)$, from a proof of $\mathcal{R}^{\tilde{A}}(h)$ one can then derive

$$(\forall a.A(a) \to \exists b.ga = gb \wedge A(b)) \to \exists b.hg = gb \wedge A(b). \tag{49}$$

The premise is clearly provable, and from $hg = gb$ we can deduce $\lambda g.hg = \lambda g.gb$; assuming a λ-theory with η-equality, we then have $\exists b.h = \lambda g.gb \wedge A(b)$. Note that while our goal is to prove an equality *for all h*, there is really only one *interesting h* (modulo the value b). By equational reasoning we then can prove

$$\exists b.\mathrm{i}(\mathrm{j}\,h) = \mathrm{i}\,b = \lambda g.gb = h \wedge A(b). \tag{50}$$

The fact that we instantiate X using existential quantifiers should come as no surprise, since in second order logic we can prove

$$\vdash \exists y.A(y) \longleftrightarrow \forall X.(\forall y.A(y) \to X) \to X; \tag{51}$$

see ([vanD79], pp. 160–162). Ignoring first-order information, we have the propositional theorem $\vdash A \leftrightarrow \forall X.(A \to X) \to X$. The functions i and j code, in the style of the Curry-Howard correspondence, an introduction and elimination of existential quantifiers: viewed from a propositional perspective; they code the "iff" of the above propositional tautology.

4 Programs for free!

Since the subject of this paper has been parametricity, induction, and the synthesis of F_2-typable terms from parametricity and induction proofs, we provide a brief compendium of the functional programmer's favorite functions, written in a form which admits F_2 typing. The method is not new (see, for instance, [PDM89]), but *how* these functions work is easier to see for the first time if we ignore typing information. We call these "free programs" because they do not use recursion explicitly, but rather a form of *primitive recursion*, although (as in Wadler's analysis) they *do* hide a form of (structural) induction. The examples assume the usual λ-calculus coding of Boolean values, pairing, and projection.

4.1 Integers

Integers are represented by the familiar Church numerals, where the integer k is given by $\lambda s.\lambda z.s^k z$.

$$\begin{aligned}
\textbf{zero} &= \lambda s.\lambda z.z && (52)\\
\textbf{succ} &= \lambda n.\lambda s.\lambda z.s\ (n\ s\ z) && (53)\\
\textbf{plus} &= \lambda m.\lambda n.m\ \textbf{succ}\ n && (54)\\
\textbf{times} &= \lambda m.\lambda n.m\ (\textbf{plus}\ n)\ \textbf{zero} && (55)\\
\textbf{expt} &= \lambda b.\lambda e.e\ (\textbf{times}\ b)\ (\textbf{succ zero}) && (56)\\
\textbf{pred} &= \lambda n.\pi_2\ (n\ (\lambda p.\langle \textbf{succ}\ (\pi_1\ p), \pi_1\ p\rangle)\ \langle \textbf{zero}, \textbf{zero}\rangle) && (57)\\
\textbf{minus} &= \lambda m.\lambda n.n\ \textbf{pred}\ m && (58)\\
\textbf{zero?} &= \lambda n.n(\lambda x.\textbf{false})\ \textbf{true} && (59)\\
\textbf{equal?} &= \lambda m.\lambda n.\textbf{and}\ (\textbf{zero?}\ (\textbf{minus}\ m\ n))\ (\textbf{zero?}\ (\textbf{minus}\ n\ m)) && (60)
\end{aligned}$$

4.2 Lists

Church numerals are very familiar, but note that the following presentation of lists can be thought of as "Church lists," where lists are represented as:

$$[x_1, x_2, \ldots, x_k] \equiv \lambda c.\lambda n.c\ x_1\ (c\ x_2\ \cdots\ (c\ x_k\ n)\cdots).$$

Observe how **nil** is like **zero**, **cons** is like **succ**, **tail** is like **pred**, and **append** is like **plus**. Church numerals are just lists where the cells in the list cannot contain any information. Observe as well how lists abstract control structure.

$$\begin{aligned}
\textbf{nil} &= \lambda c.\lambda n.n && (61)\\
\textbf{cons} &= \lambda x.\lambda \ell.\lambda c.\lambda n.c\ x\ (\ell\ c\ n) && (62)\\
\textbf{head} &= \lambda \ell.\ell\ (\lambda x.\lambda y.x)\ \textbf{nil} && (63)\\
\textbf{tail} &= \lambda \ell.\pi_2\ (\ell\ (\lambda x.\lambda p.\langle \textbf{cons}\ x\ (\pi_1\ p), \pi_1\ p\rangle)\ \langle \textbf{nil}, \textbf{nil}\rangle) && (64)\\
\textbf{append} &= \lambda \ell_1.\lambda \ell_2.\ell_1\ \textbf{cons}\ \ell_2 && (65)\\
\textbf{append-lists} &= \lambda L.L\ \textbf{append nil} && (66)\\
\textbf{map} &= \lambda f.\lambda \ell.\ell\ (\lambda x.\textbf{cons}\ (f\ x))\ \textbf{nil} && (67)\\
\textbf{length} &= \lambda \ell.\ell\ (\lambda x.\textbf{succ})\ \textbf{zero} && (68)\\
\textbf{tack} &= \lambda x.\lambda \ell.\ell\ \textbf{cons}\ (\textbf{cons}\ x\ \textbf{nil}) && (69)\\
\textbf{reverse} &= \lambda \ell.\ell\ \textbf{tack nil} && (70)\\
\textbf{filter} &= \lambda \ell.\lambda test.\ell\ (\lambda x.(test\ x)\ (\textbf{cons}\ x)\ (\lambda y.y))\ \textbf{nil} && (71)
\end{aligned}$$

The interested reader should try to code insertion of an integer into a sorted list of integers: insertion sort can then be coded as **sort** $= \lambda \ell.\ell$ **insert nil**.

4.3 Binary trees

$$\begin{aligned}
\textbf{leaf} &= \lambda x.\lambda n.\lambda \ell.\ell\ x && (72)\\
\textbf{node} &= \lambda L.\lambda R.\lambda n.\lambda \ell.n\ (L\ n\ \ell)\ (R\ n\ \ell) && (73)\\
\textbf{flatten} &= \lambda t.t\ \textbf{append}\ (\lambda x.\textbf{cons}\ x\ \textbf{nil}) && (74)\\
\textbf{sum-leaves} &= \lambda t.t\ \textbf{plus}\ (\lambda x.x) && (75)\\
\textbf{map-leaves} &= \lambda t.\lambda f.t\ \textbf{node}\ (\lambda x.\textbf{leaf}\ (f\ x)) && (76)
\end{aligned}$$

5 Conclusions

Polymorphic types give a great deal of information about λ-terms. They guarantee strong normalization, and can also prove termination in a stricter sense, i.e., ensuring particular inductively defined relations between (inductive type) inputs and outputs. Polymorphic types also encode parametricity. Given such properties as a consequence of having a polymorphic type, it should come as no surprise that type inference is so computationally difficult!

While it might have seemed that parametricity allows us to 'read off' unusual program equivalences, we have shown that proofs of these equivalences still seem to require structural induction, as well as stronger assumptions than parametricity. What Wadler's analysis does suggest, however, is a kind of structural induction argument over arbitrary relations, as in axiom $\mathcal{S}^{A^*}(\ell, \ell')$ for lists. Theorem provers should consequently rest assured that theorems are not free: proving properties of programs requires induction. The use of "unary" parametric assumptions, on the other hand, seems appropriate for proving that there is "only one" λ-term of a given type.

We have put the case quite strongly for looking to syntactic methods for understanding parametricity and proving program equivalences, but really this is just a matter of taste. What this perspective forces on the analyst is to make (near all) matters of proof explicit and constructive. By way of analogy, consider Gödel's theorem that the consistency of the Peano axioms cannot be demonstrated by constructive, finitary means—yet there is a naive proof of exactly that consistency by considering a plausible model (the integers as we know them), and reflection that the Peano axioms are indeed true in the model, and hence are consistent. While this example is far more sophisticated than anything presented in this paper, there is a powerful analogy in that Wadler's analysis, by focusing on model theory, neglected some of the hard work (or boring drudgery?) in formally carrying out what are essentially induction hypotheses.

Several questions merit further attention. We have seen that closed, typable λ-terms are parametric; is the converse true? Are parametric data types inductive? Can the syntactic presentation of parametricity shown in Section 2 be used to give a term model for F_2 that is not incestuous, but of genuine interest? Does the perspective on data types presented here give any further insight into the complexity of type inference? These will be topics of future research.

Acknowledgements. I would like to thank Daniel Leivant for his patience and kindness far beyond the call of duty, in his answering a seemingly interminable barrage of questions about his paper "Contracting Proofs to Programs," as well as providing further encouragement and advice on the current work. Phil Wadler has also been extremely generous with his time and energy, explaining a lot to me that I didn't understand. I also want to thank Luca Cardelli, Qingming Ma, John Reynolds, Don Smith, and Mitch Wand for their encouragement of this research, and comments on earlier versions of the paper.

References

[BW88] R. Bird and P. Wadler. **Introduction to Functional Programming.** Prentice-Hall, 1988.

[BB85] C. Böhm and A. Berarducci. *Automatic synthesis of typed λ-programs on term algebras.* **Theoretical Computer Science** 39, pp. 135–154.

[BMM90] K. Bruce, J. C. Mitchell, and A. R. Meyer. *The semantics of second-order lambda-calculus.* In **Logical Foundations of Functional Programming**, ed. G. Huet, pp. 213–272. Addison Wesley, 1990.

[vanD79] D. van Daalen. **Logic and Structure.** Springer-Verlag, 1979.

[Gir72] J.-Y. Girard, *Interprétation Fonctionelle et Elimination des Coupures de l'Arithmetique d'Ordre Superieur.* Thèse de Doctorat d'Etat, Université de Paris VII, 1972.

[GLT89] J.-Y. Girard, Y. Lafont, and P. Taylor. **Proofs and Types.** Cambridge University Press, 1989.

[Göd58] K. Gödel. *Über eine bisher noch nict benüte Erweiterung des finiten Standpunktes.* **Dialectica** 12 (1958), pp. 280–287. Republished with English translation and explanatory notes by A. S. Troelstra in **Kurt Gödel: Collected Works** (Oxford University Press, 1990), vol. II, ed. S. Feferman.

[How80] W. Howard. *The formulae-as-types notion of construction.* In **To H. B. Curry: Essays on Combinatory Logic, Lambda Calculus, and Formalism**, ed. J. Seldin and R. Hindley, pp. 479–490. Academic Press, 1980.

[Lei90] D. Leivant. *Contracting proofs to programs.* In **Logic and Computer Science**, ed. P. Odifreddi, pp. 279–328. Academic Press, 1990.

[HM91] F. Henglein and H. Mairson. *The complexity of type inference for higher-order typed lambda calculi.* **Proceedings of the 18-th ACM Symposium on the Principles of Programming Languages**, January 1991, pp. 119–130.

[Mit91] J. C. Mitchell. *Type systems for programming languages.* **Handbook of Theoretical Computer Science**, van Leeuwen et al., eds. North-Holland, 1990, pp. 365–458.

[PDM89] B. Pierce, S. Dietzen, and S. Michaylov. *Programming in higher-order typed lambda calculi.* Technical Report CMU-CS-89-111, Carnegie Mellon University, March 1989.

[Rey74] J. C. Reynolds. *Towards a theory of type structure.* In **Proceedings of the Paris Colloquium on Programming**, Lecture Notes in Computer Science 19, Springer Verlag, pages 408–425, 1974.

[Rey90] J. C. Reynolds. *Introduction to polymorphic lambda-calculus.* In **Logical Foundations of Functional Programming**, ed. G. Huet, pp. 77–86. Addison Wesley, 1990.

[Rey83] J. C. Reynolds. *Types, abstraction, and parametric polymorphism.* In **Information Processing 83**, ed. R. E. A. Mason, pp. 513–523. Elsevier, 1983.

[Sc90] A. Scedrov. *A guide to polymorphic types.* In **Logic and Computer Science**, ed. P. Odifreddi, pp. 387–420. Academic Press, 1990.

[Sta85] R. Statman. *Logical relations and the typed lambda calculus.* **Information and Control** 65 (1985), pp. 85–97.

[Wad89] P. Wadler. *Theorems for free!* In **4th International Symposium on Functional Programming Languages and Computer Architecture**, London, September 1989.

Reasoning about Simple and Exhaustive Demand in Higher-Order Lazy Languages

Allen Leung *Prateek Mishra**
Department of Computer Science
The State University of New York at Stony Brook
Stony Brook, NY 11794
allen@sbcs.sunysb.edu, mishra@sbcs.sunysb.edu

Abstract

In this work we describe an innovative strictness analysis method for reasoning about simple and exhaustive demand in higher-order lazy languages. By reasoning about simple demand, we mean determining whether a function requires its input in head normal form whenever its output is so required, i.e., is the function *strict*? Similarly, by exhaustive demand we mean determining whether a function requires its input in normal form whenever its output is so required, i.e., is the function *fully strict*?.

Our method, which is based on type inference, supports reasoning about strictness and full-strictness within a unified framework by making essential use of subtypes. In contrast to previous proposals, our method does not require fixpoint iteration and hence should be more amenable to practical use. Furthermore, our method can handle such features as pattern-matching and user-defined datatypes which are important in practical programming. The insight behind our results is that program properties such as strictness can be treated as *types* possessed by programs. As a consequence, we are able to design an inference algorithm, which given program *P* constructs a representation for all possible "strictness" types deducible for *P*. This representation takes the form of a set of *constraints*. We show that strictness and full-strictness properties of *P* can be derived, in a precise formal sense, from this set of constraints. We include a systematic comparison between our techniques and results and those of higher-order abstract interpretation.

***This work has been partially supported by NSF CCR-8706973 and by an REU supplement for Allen Leung.**

1 Introduction

One of the most significant and challenging problems in strictness analysis has been the development of *practical* analysis techniques for higher-order languages. The techniques for higher-order abstract interpretation described in the literature [BHA86, Abr85, Mau85, HY86] constitute significant and impressive contributions but are all based on extending Mycroft's first-order algorithm to the higher-order case. An essential aspect of Mycroft's method is the use of fixpoint iteration to solve for function strictness. This must involve repeated equality checking of functions over the abstract domain. In the higher-order case, this involves determining the equality of expressions defined over higher-order domains, and, as we will show below, may be arbitrarily complex. As a consequence, despite considerable research into the problem of equality checking [MH87, Hun89], these methods have had only limited impact on implementations.

In this work, we describe an new analysis technique for reasoning about simple and exhaustive demand in a higher-order lazy language. Our technique requires no fixpoint iteration and hence should be amenable to practical use. Our techniques support reasoning about both forms of demand within a *unified framework* by making essential use of subtypes. Our techniques require *no fixpoint iteration* and can cope with such features as pattern-matching and user-defined datatypes.

By reasoning about simple demand, we mean determining whether a function requires its input in head normal form whenever its output is so required, i.e., is the function *strict?* similarly, by exhaustive demand we mean determining whether a function requires its input in normal form whenever its output is so required, i.e., is the function *fully strict?* Simple and exhaustive demand are fundamental forms of demand that arise naturally during lazy evaluation. Simple demand arises from contexts where a minimally defined value is needed: the operator position in an application or the argument of a strict function. Exhaustive demand arises from contexts where a completely evaluated data-structure is needed, such as the result of sorting lists or multiplying matrices. A strict function under simple demand may safely have its arguments pre-evaluated to head normal form; a similar optimization is available for fully strict functions under exhaustive demand. The importance of these forms of demand and their use in optimizing lazy evaluation has been extensively described in the literature [Myc80, Lin86, SPR90, LLD87].

Our results are based on the insight, first reported in [KM87], that program properties such as strictness can be considered to be *types* possessed by a program. Subsequently, in [KM89b] we used the techniques and tools of type inference and gave a framework (and algorithms that avoid fixpoint iteration) for reasoning about strictness properties of higher-order programs. In this work, our main result is the extension of our framework to include reasoning about full-strictness in a higher-order language that includes pattern-matching and user-defined datatypes. The technical difficulties in making such an extension lie in the interaction between the concept of "lack of normal form" and the concepts of pattern-matching and tupling and in developing a powerful notion of subtyping to support reasoning about both forms of demand within the same framework.

1.1 Overview of Results

The specification of a type language and a set of inference rules is fundamental to our approach. The type language of interest consists of the constants $\top, \bot, \Omega$ that stand for the set of all terms, looping terms and terms without normal form, respectively, and the type constructors "function" and "tuple". Thus, the type $\bot \to \bot$ describes the set of strict programs and the addition function possesses properties $\top \times \bot \to \bot$ and $\bot \times \top \to \bot$. Higher-order properties such as $(\Omega \to \Omega) \to \Omega \to \Omega$ – "maps fully strict functions to fully strict functions" – are also expressible. The inference rules describe the deduction of types for higher-order programs and consist of conventional rules as found in [DM82] extended with a subtype rule and rules for pattern-matching.

Our inference algorithm, given a program P, simulates all possible derivations for P using the inference rules and constructs a set of *constraints* in a single traversal of P. All the strictness and full-strictness properties of P that are provable using the inference system can be derived, in a precise formal sense, from the set of constraints.

1.1.1 Representing Program Properties by Constraints

A higher-order program will in general have many strictness properties just as it may have many types in standard type systems. We use *strictness expressions* to represent sets of strictness properties; this is analogous to using "generic" type expressions to represent a set of types possessed by a term[DM82].

A strictness expression is an extension of the notation used in the literature for subtype inference [FM90, FM89] and consists of a pair (C, τ) where C is a set of *inclusions* between type expressions and τ is a type expression. For example, properties of the *Twice* combinator $\lambda f.\lambda x.f(f\ x)$ are represented by the strictness expression: $\{\alpha \subseteq \beta\}$, $(\beta \to \alpha) \to \beta \to \alpha$. It is easy to see that we can deduce the following properties of *Twice* by suitably instantiating the type variables α and β by substitutions that respect the constraint $\alpha \subseteq \beta$:

$(\top \to \bot) \to (\top \to \bot)$	$(\bot \to \bot) \to (\bot \to \bot)$	$(\Omega \to \Omega) \to (\Omega \to \Omega)$
Twice is strict on f	*Twice* f is strict, whenever f is strict	*Twice* f is fully strict, whenever f is fully strict

1.1.2 Pattern Matching and Tupling

Reasoning about exhaustive demand in the context of pattern-matching and tupling poses challenges in terms of the inference rules required and the expressive power of strictness expressions. Consider the pattern-abstraction:

$$M \equiv \lambda(c^k(x_1, x_2) \Rightarrow c^k(x_1, x_2))$$

which is the identity function on two-tuples $c^k(M_1, M_2)$. One natural property we expect M to possess is full-strictness, i.e., $M \in \Omega \to \Omega$. To prove this, we must show that $M \in \top \times \Omega \to \Omega$ and $M \in \Omega \times \top \to \Omega$; i.e., if the input value lacks normal form then either x_1 lacks normal form or x_2 lacks normal form and in each case the body of the lambda-abstraction lacks normal form.

Thus, in general, when proving that a pattern abstraction possesses some property α, we may need to reason about the *set* of types possessed by the abstraction. In contrast, all other expressions P have the property that in order to show they possess some property τ, we only need prove *single properties* $\tau_1, \ldots, \tau_n$ of the subterms $P_1, \ldots, P_n$ of P. In Section 4, we will show that we can represent reasoning about sets of types by the use of a *finite conjunction* operator on sets of inclusions.

1.1.3 Subtypes and Consistency Checking

Subtypes play an essential role in extracting strictness and full-strictness properties from a single set of constraints. Subtypes support reasoning of the form: if a value is looping ($\perp$) then it is strict ($\perp \rightarrow \perp$); if a program has type $\Omega \rightarrow \perp$ then it also has type $\perp \rightarrow \perp$ and $\Omega \rightarrow \Omega$. This can also be viewed as a general technique for connecting together distinct but related analysis techniques so that each can make use of the other.

In general, the problem of deducing strictness property α from strictness expression (C, τ) requires determining whether the set of inclusions $C \cup \{\tau \subseteq \alpha\}$ is *consistent*. By consistency we mean: can we find a substitution S mapping variables to type constants that satisfies each inclusion in $C \cup \{\tau \subseteq \alpha\}$. We describe a consistency checking procedure CON which we prove to be sound and complete. We prove CON terminates for a class of inclusions that do not include "cyclic" inclusions. In practice, a restricted class of cyclic inclusions arises from the presence of recursive datatypes in programs. For such inclusions we describe a sound extension to the consistency checking procedure.

1.1.4 Reasoning about Recursion

In reasoning about recursive functions and data-structures (infinite lists) our algorithms does not utilize fixpoint iteration. This is possible because we *constrain* the class of strictness properties expressible in our type system. As a consequence, our method will not report certain "inductive" strictness properties that abstract interpretation is theoretically capable of reporting.

1.2 Related Work

As stated above, while the approaches described in the literature [BHA86, Abr85, Mau85, HY86] constitute significant and impressive contributions, two outstanding problems remain:

- These approaches develop a *specific* computational technique that extends Mycroft's first-order algorithm to the higher-order case. An essential aspect of Mycroft's method is the use of fixpoint iteration to solve for function strictness. This must involve repeated equality checking of functions over the abstract domain. In the first-order case, this appears to be reasonable though it is exponential in the number of function arguments[HY86].

  In the higher-order case, equality checking appears to be intractable. For example, in [HY86] higher-order strictness properties are represented by a syntax that consists of lambda-expressions *augmented* with a union and intersection operator on lambda-terms. Equality checking of expressions belonging to such a syntax appears to be very difficult even for simple higher-order programs. For example, the presence of union and intersection operators suggests that expressions may not even have unique normal forms. Furthermore, Statman [Sta79] has shown that even small typed-lambda terms can create arbitrarily long computations and that the general problem of checking the equality of typed-lambda terms lies outside the primitive recursive functions. As typed lambda-terms are a proper subset of the syntax used in [HY86], this suggests that equality checking of expressions in this syntax may be arbitrarily complex.

The approach taken in [BHA86] avoids working with a rich syntactic representation but instead deals directly with higher-order functions spaces on the abstract domain. Equality checking over such higher-order function spaces also appears intractable: for example, the trivial higher-order domain $(3 \rightarrow 3) \rightarrow 3 \rightarrow 3$, where 3 is the linearly ordered three point domain $(\perp, \Omega, \top)$ already contains over 10^5 elements and it is not difficult to find ([Hun89],p.8) simple examples with over 10^6 elements. As a consequence, despite considerable research into the problem of equality checking [MH87, Hun89], these methods have had little impact on implementations.

- While these methods [HY86, BHA86] allow the deduction of first-order strictness properties in the presence of higher-order functions, they *do not* support the deduction of higher-order properties themselves. In the example above, we have shown that in our framework we can prove that *Twice* maps strict functions to strict functions and fully strict functions to fully strict functions. *It is not clear how such properties could be derived in the abstract interpretation framework.* This is because these frameworks directly use lambda-terms to represent program properties (e.g., properties of *Twice* would be represented by *Twice* itself). Any deduction takes the form of symbolic execution using $\top, \perp, \Omega$ and the lambda-term. Thus, the only property of *Twice* we could prove using higher-order abstract interpretation is that *Twice* $\perp = \perp$, i.e., *Twice* is strict.

The concept of exhaustive demand (written d^e) was first introduced by Lindstrom [Lin86] where he describes inference rules for "demand propagation" for a first-order language. In [SPR90] Lindstrom's framework was extended to include pattern-matching and the problem was explicitly set up in terms of Mycroft's original formulation. Both frameworks[Lin86, SPR90] are based on abstract interpretation and therefore do not yield a practical higher-order analysis method. Other more sophisticated notions of demand relevant to data-structures have been discussed in [Wad87, WR87, Bur90]. These works describe techniques for reasoning about such notions of demand and their application to compilation in the context of first-order languages.

1.3 How to read this Paper

The remainder of the paper is organized as follows: Section 2 provides definitions for the language and type system as well as semantics. Section 3 describes the inference rules and inclusion theory for strictness properties. Section 4 describes the syntax for representing strictness types and the type inference algorithm. Section 5 describes an algorithm for consistency checking. Concluding remarks may be found in Section 6.

2 Framework

2.1 Operational Semantics

We will work with an applied lambda-calculus that explicitly supports tupling and pattern-matching:

$$M ::= x \mid f \mid M_1 M_2 \mid c^k(M_1, \ldots, M_n)\ , n \geq 0 \mid \lambda(p_1 \Rightarrow M_1 \| \ldots \| p_n \Rightarrow M_n)$$
$$p ::= x \mid c^k(x_1, \ldots, x_n)\ , n \geq 0$$

The expression $c^k(e_1, \ldots, e_n)$ denotes an n-tuple of expressions e_i with constructor $c^k \in \mathcal{C}$ at the outermost-level and lambda abstraction includes one level pattern matching into which more complex pattern matching can be compiled [PJ87, PS90]. We will often abbreviate $\lambda(y \Rightarrow M)$ by the more familiar $\lambda y.M$. Primitive functions $f \in \mathcal{F}$ include integers, booleans, arithmetic and logical operators as well as *fix*. The operational semantics of our language is given by the set of reduction rules given below:

$$\begin{array}{lrcl}
(\beta 1) & \lambda(\cdots \| x \Rightarrow M \| \cdots) N & \longrightarrow & [N/x]M \\
(\beta 2) & \lambda(\cdots \| c^k() \Rightarrow M \| \cdots) c^k() & \longrightarrow & M \\
(\beta 3) & \lambda(\cdots \| c^k(x_1, \cdots, x_n) \Rightarrow M \| \cdots) c^k(N) & \longrightarrow & [\pi_i^n(N)/x_i]M \\
\\
(\textbf{fix}) & \textbf{fix}\ M & \longrightarrow & M(\textbf{fix}\ M) \\
(\pi) & \pi_i^n(M_1, \cdots, M_n) & \longrightarrow & M_i \\
\\
(\delta) & +m & \longrightarrow & +_m \\
 & +_m n & \longrightarrow & m + n \\
 & \text{etc} & &
\end{array}$$

Figure 1: Reduction Rules

A **redex** is a term which has the form found on the left-hand-side of the reduction rules. A term M **reduces** to N in one step, $M \longrightarrow N$, if we replace one occurrence of a redex in M by the corresponding term on the right-hand-side of the reduction rule and results in N. In such a case, we say that the redex in M has been contracted. Let the $=$ relation be the reflexive, symmetric and transitive closure of $\longrightarrow$ and thus by $M = N$ will mean that we can go from M to N by a sequence of steps that involve expanding or contracting redexes.

In this paper, we choose **head evaluation with constants** as the evaluation mechanism. This is an extension of the classical notion of head evaluation[Wad76] that has been used for the pure λ-calculus.[1] The **head redex** of a term is defined as follows:

The head redex of

- x, is undefined
- $c^k(N_1, \ldots, N_m)$, is undefined
- f, is undefined
- $\lambda(p_1 \Rightarrow M_1 \| \ldots \| p_n \Rightarrow M_n)$, is the head redex of any M_i
- MN,
  - if MN is a redex, then it is MN
  - if $M \equiv f$ then it is the head redex of N
  - if $M \equiv \lambda(p_1 \Rightarrow M_1 \| \ldots \| p_n \Rightarrow M_n)$ then it is the head redex of N
  - otherwise, it is the head redex of M

A term is in **head normal form** if it has no head redex. A term is in **normal form** if it has no subterm which is a redex. Head evaluation is defined to be the repeated contraction of the head redex. If evaluation succeeds, the evaluator yields a term in head normal form as its final result. It is not difficult to see that head evaluation defines a partial function from terms to terms in head normal form.

Rules **(**β**2),(**β**2)** in Figure 1 implement a *lazy product matching* rule as described in [PJ87]: tuples are only evaluated to head normal form. It would be straightforward to incorporate *strict product matching* in our system; this would entail modifying **(**β**2),(**β**3)** to force tuple components to be evaluated to head normal form.

Finally, we will assume that subterms of the form $\lambda(p_1 \Rightarrow M_1 \| \ldots \| p_n \Rightarrow M_n)(c^k(N_1, \ldots, N_p))$ with $p_i \not\equiv c^k(\ldots)$ and $p_i \not\equiv x$ do not occur in any term. This corresponds to the notion that functions defined by pattern matching are defined exhaustively over all "reasonable" input values and are applied only to such values. Checking for exhaustiveness of pattern-matching is routinely included in compilers for languages like standard ML and thus it appears to be reasonable constraint to impose on our language semantics.

2.2 Type System

The language of type expressions α is given by the following syntax rule:

$$\text{[type]} \quad \alpha ::= \top \mid \bot \mid \Omega \mid \alpha_1 \rightarrow \alpha_2 \mid \alpha_1 \times \cdots \times \alpha_n$$

Type expression α will be interpreted as denoting the set of terms with property α.

[1] Strictness analysis for pure λ-calculus has previously been studied, see [Mis88, KM89a].

Definition 1

$$\begin{array}{rcl}
\bot & = & \{M \mid M \textit{ lacks hnf }\} \\
\Omega & = & \{M \mid M \textit{ lacks normal form }\} \\
\top & = & \{\textit{all terms }\} \\
\alpha \rightarrow \beta & = & \{M \mid \forall N \in \alpha, MN \in \beta\} \\
\alpha_1 \times \cdots \times \alpha_n & = & \{M \mid M = c^k(M_1, \cdots, M_n), \forall c^k \in \mathcal{C},\ \forall i. M_i \in \alpha_i\} \cup \bot \\
 & & \cup \{M \mid M = c^k N, \forall c^k \in \mathcal{C},\ \forall N \in \alpha_1 \times \cdots \times \alpha_n\}
\end{array}$$

Base types $\top$ ("all"), $\bot$ ("undefined") and Ω ("incomplete") are all closed under $=$ and may therefore be reasonably considered to be semantic properties or types. It is not difficult to verify that the tupling and function type constructors preserve semantic properties. One consequence of our "tag-free" definition of tuples is the need to maintain a distinction between one-tuples of types $(\alpha)_1$ and plain types α: i.e., the type $\bot$ denotes the set of looping terms, while $(\bot)_1$ denotes the set of terms formed out of one-ary constructors with a nested looping term.

Using type expressions α we can express strictness properties of programs with data structures. For instance, the function *reverse*, which reverses a list, has type $\Omega \rightarrow \Omega$, and the function *sumlist*, which sums up the elements in a list, has type $\Omega \rightarrow \bot$. Higher order strictness is also expressible. For example the function *map*, which constructs a new list by applying a function f to each element,

```
map f nil            = nil
map f (cons(h,t))  = cons(f h,map f t)
```

has types $(\Omega \rightarrow \Omega) \rightarrow \Omega \rightarrow \Omega$, and $\top \rightarrow \bot \rightarrow \bot$.

We will also be interested in the strictness properties of a term under some assumptions about its free variables' strictness properties. For example, under the assumption that $f \in \bot \rightarrow \bot$ and $x \in \bot$, we have $f(fx)$ is in $\bot$. We shall use the notation $\{f : \bot \rightarrow \bot, x : \bot\} \models f(fx) : \bot$ to denote this fact. In general, we can define the relation $A \models M : \alpha$ by the following :

Definition 2 $\{x_1 : \alpha_1, \cdots, x_n : \alpha_n\} \models M : \alpha$ *iff* $\forall N_i \in \alpha_i, [N_i/x_i]M \in \alpha$

Whenever necessary, we shall assume that in $A \models M : \alpha$ the domain of A is exactly the set of free variables of M.

3 Inference Rules

Figure 2 specifies an inference system for reasoning about strictness properties of programs. If A_1 and A_2 are two type assumptions then $A_1 ++ A_2$ is their sequential union: first, consider the bindings in A_2, then those in A_1. Function AS, which maps pattern-type pairs into a set of bindings for each pattern component, is defined by:

$$\begin{array}{rcl}
AS(x)(\tau) & = & \{\{x : \tau\}\} \\
AS(c^k())(\tau) & = & \{\emptyset\}
\end{array}$$

(const)

$$A \vdash c : \alpha_c$$

(var)

$$A \vdash x : \alpha, \;\; x : \alpha \in A$$

(app)

$$\frac{A \vdash M : \alpha \to \beta; A \vdash N : \alpha}{A \vdash MN : \beta}$$

(tuple)

$$\frac{A \vdash M_i : \alpha_i}{A \vdash c^k(M_1, \cdots, M_n) : \alpha_1 \times \cdots \times \alpha_n}$$

(rule1)

$$A \vdash c^k() \;\Rightarrow\; M : \Omega \to \bot$$

(rule2)

$$A \vdash c^k(x_1, \cdots, x_n) \;\Rightarrow\; M : \bot \to \bot$$

(lambda1)

$$\frac{\forall \bar{A} \in AS(p)(\tau), A +\!\!+ \bar{A} \vdash e : \sigma}{A \vdash p \Rightarrow e : \tau \to \sigma}$$

(lambda2)

$$\frac{\forall i, A \vdash p_i \;\Rightarrow\; N_i : \alpha \to \beta}{A \vdash \lambda(p_1 \;\Rightarrow\; e_1 \| \ldots \| p_n \;\Rightarrow\; e_n) : \alpha \to \beta}$$

(coerce)

$$\frac{A \vdash M : \alpha; \alpha \subseteq \beta}{A \vdash M : \beta}$$

Figure 2: Inference Rules

$$\begin{aligned} AS(c^k(x_1,\cdots,x_n))(\Omega) &= \bigcup_{1\le i\le n} \{\{x_i:\Omega, x_{j,j\neq i}:\top\}\} \\ AS(c^k(x_1,\cdots,x_n))(\tau_1\times\cdots\times\tau_n) &= \{\{x_i:\tau_i\}\} \\ AS(c^k(x_1,\cdots,x_m))(\tau_1\times\cdots\times\tau_n) &= \{\},\ m\neq n \\ AS(c^k(x_1,\cdots,x_n))(\top) &= \{\{x_i:\top\}\} \end{aligned}$$

Most of the inference rules are standard and only the rules for pattern matching require elaboration. Rules $(rule1), (rule2)$ describe strictness properties induced by the shape of the pattern alone. $(lambda1)$ is a generalization of the traditional rule for lambda-abstraction extended to cope with the interaction of Ω and patterns. For an example of its use, consider the derivation for $c^k(x,y) \Rightarrow c^k(x,y) : \Omega \rightarrow \Omega$:

$$\begin{array}{llcll} 1 & \{x:\top, y:\Omega\} & \vdash & (x,y):\top\times\Omega & \\ 2 & \{x:\top, y:\Omega\} & \vdash & (x,y):\Omega & (coerce) \\ 3 & \{x:\Omega, y:\top\} & \vdash & (x,y):\Omega\times\top & \\ 4 & \{x:\Omega, y:\top\} & \vdash & (x,y):\Omega & (coerce) \\ 5 & & \vdash & c^k(x,y) \Rightarrow c^k(x,y):\Omega\rightarrow\Omega & (lambda1) \end{array}$$

3.1 Inclusion Theory

Types, when viewed as sets of terms, have a natural inclusion relation between them. For example, since every looping term is a term, we have $\bot \subseteq \top$. A term which maps every term to a looping term will also map every looping term to a looping term; thus $\top \rightarrow \bot \subseteq \bot \rightarrow \bot$.

The formal system in Figure 3 is a description of the inclusion relation for types α. In other work[KM89a], we have shown that this formal system is both sound and complete, i.e. $\vdash \alpha \subseteq \beta$ iff $\alpha \subseteq \beta$ for reasoning about types built out of $\bot, \top$. Therefore we will only argue correctness of rules that involve Ω. Rule **(component)** is justified by observing that if any component of a constructor term lacks normal form, then so does the term itself. Similarly, rule (Ω) is based on the observation that if term M has property $\top \rightarrow \Omega$ then it must be equal to $\lambda x.N$ where $N \in \Omega$. To see that the converse of (Ω) does not hold observe that $Y(= fix\ \lambda\, x.x) \in \Omega$ but $(Y\ \lambda\, x.\lambda\, y.y) = \lambda\, y.y$.

3.2 Types of Primitive Functions

Primitive functions often have many types, sometimes even infinitely many. In the presence of the (coerce) rule, we need only **minimal types** for axioms but unfortunately, many of the primitive functions do not have a unique minimal types. Some, e.g., *fix*, even have infinitely many minimal types. Some of the (const) axioms are listed here :

$$\begin{array}{ll} A \vdash 0 : \top & A \vdash true : \top \\ A \vdash Succ : \bot \rightarrow \bot & A \vdash Zerop : \bot \rightarrow \bot \\ A \vdash Add : \Omega \rightarrow \bot & A \vdash Or : \Omega \rightarrow \bot \\ A \vdash Add : \top \rightarrow \Omega \rightarrow \bot & A \vdash Or : \top \rightarrow \Omega \rightarrow \bot \\ A \vdash Not : \bot \rightarrow \bot & A \vdash fix : (\alpha \rightarrow \alpha) \rightarrow \alpha \end{array}$$

(reflex)

$$\vdash \alpha \subseteq \alpha$$

(bottom)

$$\vdash \bot \subseteq \alpha$$

(top)

$$\vdash \alpha \subseteq \top$$

($\top$)

$$\vdash \top \subseteq \top \rightarrow \top$$

($\bot$)

$$\vdash \top \rightarrow \bot \subseteq \bot$$

(Ω)

$$\vdash \top \rightarrow \Omega \subseteq \Omega$$

(trans)

$$\frac{\vdash \alpha \subseteq \beta \,;\, \vdash \beta \subseteq \gamma}{\vdash \alpha \subseteq \gamma}$$

(arrow)

$$\frac{\vdash \beta_1 \subseteq \alpha_1 \,;\, \vdash \alpha_2 \subseteq \beta_2}{\vdash \alpha_1 \rightarrow \alpha_2 \subseteq \beta_1 \rightarrow \beta_2}$$

(component)

$$\frac{\exists i, \vdash \alpha_i \subseteq \Omega}{\vdash \alpha_1 \times \ldots \times \alpha_i \times \ldots \times \alpha_n \subseteq \Omega}$$

(tuple)

$$\frac{\forall i, \vdash \alpha_i \subseteq \alpha'_i}{\vdash \alpha_1 \times \ldots \times \alpha_n \subseteq \alpha'_1 \times \ldots \times \alpha'_n}$$

Figure 3: Formal System for $\subseteq$

It is useful to observe that the projection functions π_i each possess property $\Omega \rightarrow \top$; i.e., no information about Ω is preserved by these functions. This motivates our treatment of pattern-matching as a primitive notion.

3.3 Soundness Theorem

Theorem 1 $A \vdash M : \alpha \;\Rightarrow\; A \models M : \alpha$

Proof: Induction on the structure of M.

■

3.4 Normal Proof

By considering the structure of proof trees, it is easy to see that all inference rules, except the (coerce) rule, are used according to the structure of programs. As any notion of inclusion must be transitive, at most one (coerce) step is needed after the application of a structural rule. By examining the structure of proofs, it is not difficult to see that the (coerce) rule is needed only on certain steps in the proof, namely:

- a final coercion step at the end of the proof.
- a coercion between the type of the argument and the domain type of the operator in an application (rule (app)).
- coercion step in each branch of the proof tree before the application of (lambda1). The proof for $\vdash c^k(x,y) \;\Rightarrow\; c^k(x,y) : \Omega \rightarrow \Omega$, shown above, demonstrates the necessity of such coercion steps.

The coercion step at the end of the proof can simply be deferred, this is called "lazy instance" in [FM89], and therefore it is necessary to apply coercion steps only at application nodes and for rules in a lambda-abstraction. A proof satisfying the above criteria will be called a *normal proof*; the following theorem will allow our type inference procedure to simulate only normal proofs, rather than all proofs, without any loss of strictness properties.

Theorem 2 $A \vdash M : \alpha \;\Rightarrow\; \exists \beta, \beta \subseteq \alpha$ *and* $A \vdash M : \beta$ *has a normal proof*

3.5 Example

Table 1 shows a normal proof for $\vdash map : (\Omega \rightarrow \Omega) \rightarrow \Omega \rightarrow \Omega$ where

$$map \equiv fix(\lambda f.\lambda g.\lambda(nil \Rightarrow nil \| cons(x,y) \Rightarrow \; cons(g\; x, f\; g\; y)))$$

Bold edges denote the use of the **(coerce)** rule.

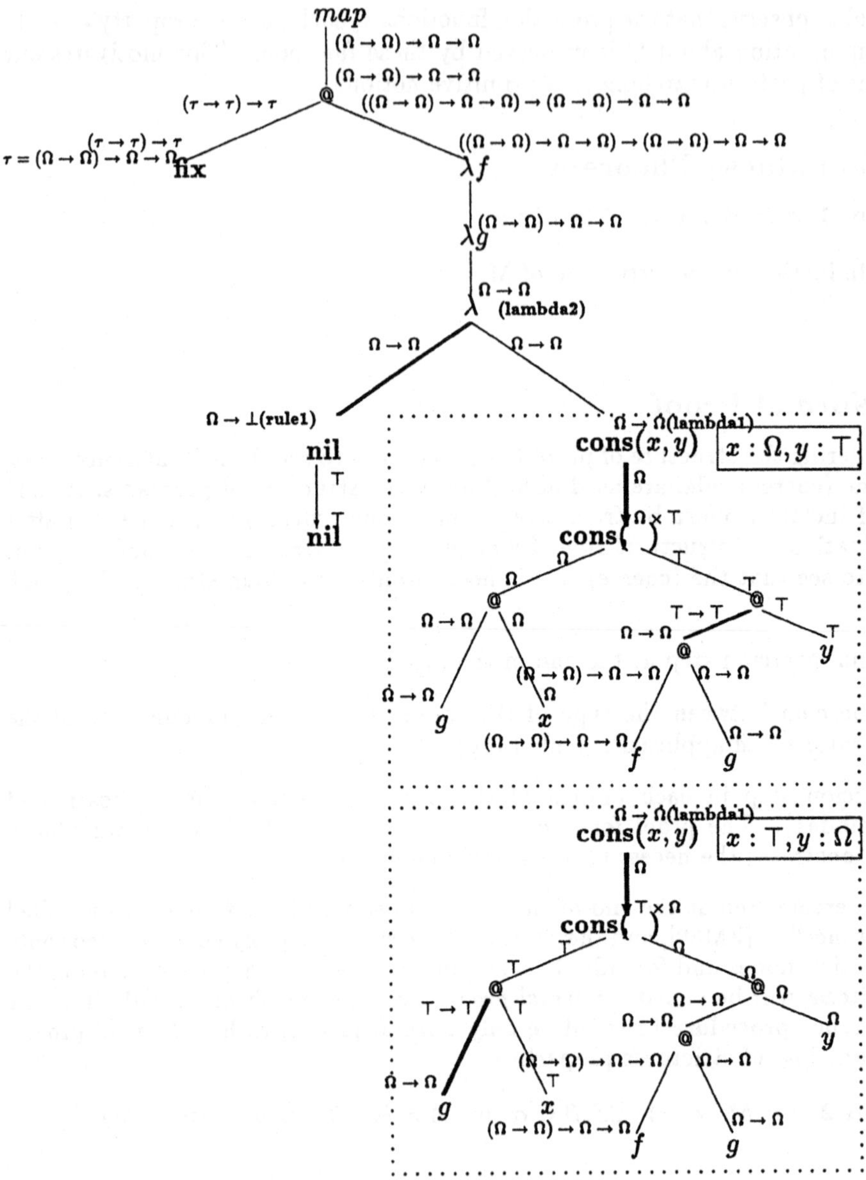

Table 1: Normal proof for $\vdash map : (\Omega \to \Omega) \to \Omega \to \Omega$.

3.6 Extension to Wadler's Four Point Domain

One important characteristic of the deductive systems presented above is that they may be easily extended to include types that describe other more expressive strictness properties. For example, Wadler [Wad87] describes a system for computing the following strictness properties: (i) Does a function map all infinite lists to $\perp$? and, (ii) Does a function map all lists, with the property that some head or tail is $\perp$, to $\perp$? These properties cannot be expressed in the type system we have described above though it should be noted that property (ii) is closely related to $\Omega \rightarrow \perp$.

We can extend our type system to express such information by introducing two new type constants, ∞ and $list_{\exists\perp}$, which stand for "infinite list" and "list with undefined head or tail", respectively, to the type language. The interpretations for such constants is as follows:

$$\begin{array}{rcl} \infty & = & \{M \mid M = cons(M_1, M_2), M_2 \in \infty\} \cup \perp \\ list_{\exists\perp} & = & \{M \mid M = cons(M_1, M_2), M_1 \text{ lacks hnf } \} \cup \\ & & \{M \mid M = cons(M_1, M_2), M_2 \in list_{\exists\perp}\} \cup \perp \end{array}$$

For example, the function *length*, which computes the length of a list, has type $\infty \rightarrow \perp$, while the function *map* has types $(\perp \rightarrow \perp) \rightarrow list_{\exists\perp} \rightarrow list_{\exists\perp}$ and $\top \rightarrow \infty \rightarrow \infty$. Such information can be used for more sophisticated forms of program optimization. For instance, since functions like *length* loop on infinite lists, it is safe to completely pre-evaluate the "spine" of their argument lists.

To accomodate reasoning about ∞ and $list_{\exists\perp}$, *no* alteration of the inference system given in Figure 2 is necessary. However, function *AS* must be extended to model the interaction between pattern matching and the two new type constants.

$$\begin{array}{rcl} AS(cons(x_1, x_2))(\infty) & = & \{\{x_1 : \top, x_2 : \infty\}\} \\ AS(cons(x_1, x_2))(list_{\exists\perp}) & = & \{\{x_1 : \perp, x_2 : \top\}, \{x_1 : \top, x_2 : list_{\exists\perp}\}\} \end{array}$$

We will also need to extend the inclusion theory described in Figure 3 with the following axioms:

($\infty list_{\exists\perp}$)

$$\vdash \infty \subseteq list_{\exists\perp}$$

(∞1)

$$\vdash \top \times \infty \subseteq \infty$$

(∞2)

$$\vdash \infty \subseteq \top \times \infty$$

$(list_{\exists\bot}1)$

$$\vdash list_{\exists\bot} \subseteq \Omega$$

$(list_{\exists\bot}2)$

$$\vdash \bot \times \top \subseteq list_{\exists\bot}$$

$(list_{\exists\bot}2)$

$$\vdash \top \times list_{\exists\bot} \subseteq list_{\exists\bot}$$

4 Implementation Issues

4.1 Representing Strictness Types

A compact syntactic representation is needed to keep track of all inferable strictness properties of a term. Following the literature on type inference, [DM82, FM90] the combination of types with variables (parametrized types) and a set of inclusions provides one such representation. Unfortunately, such a representation isn't powerful enough to model all types possessed by programs in our framework.

First, some programs possess types that cannot be represented by a single (C, τ) pair. One such example is:

$$if \equiv \lambda(true \Rightarrow \lambda x.\lambda y.x \| false \Rightarrow \lambda x.\lambda y.y)$$

which possesses types:

$$\Omega \rightarrow \top \rightarrow \top \rightarrow \bot \qquad \alpha \rightarrow \beta \rightarrow \beta \rightarrow \beta$$

This can be remedied by the use of a *finite set* of (C, τ) pairs. A second source of complexity arises when reasoning about pattern abstractions. As shown in Section 3, in determining whether program $\vdash \lambda(c^k(x_1, x_2) \Rightarrow c^k(x_1, x_2)) : \Omega \rightarrow \Omega$, we need to verify that $\vdash \lambda(c^k(x_1, x_2) \Rightarrow c^k(x_1, x_2)) : \top \times \Omega \rightarrow \Omega$ and $\vdash \lambda(c^k(x_1, x_2) \Rightarrow c^k(x_1, x_2)) : \Omega \times \top \rightarrow \Omega$. In general, when reasoning about a pattern abstraction which occurs as a subterm in some program, we may need to reason about the *set* of types possessed by the abstraction. In contrast, all other expressions P have the property that to show they possess some property τ, we only need prove *single properties* $\tau_1, \ldots, \tau_n$ of the subterms $P_1, \ldots, P_n$ of P. To model reasoning about pattern-abstractions we explicitly introduce a finite conjunction operator defined over individual inclusion sets. This remarks motivate the following definition of **strictness expressions:**

[parameterized type]	τ	::=	$\bot \mid \Omega \mid \top \mid \alpha \mid \tau_1 \rightarrow \tau_2 \mid \tau_1 \times \cdots \times \tau_n$
[coercion set]	C	::=	$\{\tau_1 \subseteq \tau_2, \ldots, \tau_1' \subseteq \tau_2'\} \mid \wedge_{\tau_1 \mid \tau_2} C$
[strictness expression]	σ	::=	$\{(C_i, \tau_i)\}$

where α is the set of type variables.

Definition 3 *A coercion set* $\bigwedge_{\tau_1 \mid \tau_2} C$ *is satisfiable under substitution* S *such that for all* $R \in \tau_1 \mid S(\tau_2)$*:*

- $C \equiv \{\tau_1 \subseteq \tau_2, \ldots, \tau_1' \subseteq \tau_2'\} : \forall(\tau_1 \subseteq \tau_2) \in C \Rightarrow\ \vdash S \circ R(\tau_1) \subseteq S \circ R(\tau_2)$.
- $C \equiv \bigwedge_{\tau_1' \mid \tau_2'} C' : \bigwedge_{\tau_1' \mid \tau_2'} C'$ *is satisfiable under substitution* $S \circ R$.

The pattern decomposition operator $\mid$ is modeled after AS, and takes a parametrized type and a type expression as argument and returns a set of substitutions:

$$\begin{aligned}
\tau_1 \times \cdots \times \tau_n \mid \bot &= \{[\bot/\tau_i]\} \\
\tau_1 \times \cdots \times \tau_n \mid \top &= \bigcup \{[\alpha_i/\top]\} \\
\tau_1 \times \cdots \times \tau_n \mid \Omega &= \bigcup_{1 \le i \le n} \{[\Omega/\tau_i][\top/\tau_{j, j \neq i}]\} \\
\tau_1 \times \cdots \times \tau_n \mid \sigma_1 \times \cdots \times \sigma_n &= \{[\sigma_i/\tau_i]\} \\
\tau_1 \times \cdots \times \tau_m \mid \sigma_1 \times \cdots \times \sigma_n &= \{\},\ m \neq n
\end{aligned}$$

A coercion set C is consistent if there exists substitution S which satisfies C.

Definition 4 *Type* β *is an instance of strictness expression* (C_i, τ_i)*, written* $\beta \in \mathcal{I}(C_i, \tau_i)$*, if there exists a substitution* S *such that, for some* j*,* $\beta = S(\tau_j)$ *and* S *satisfies* C_j*.*

Thus the pair (C, τ) stands for the set of types derived by appropriately instantiating τ, and a strictness expression $\sigma = \{(C_1, \tau_1), \cdots, (C_n, \tau_n)\}$ represents the union of all such sets.

4.2 Side-Constraints: Optimizing Strictness Expressions

In practice, a number of simple changes to the representation have a significant impact on the efficiency of the type inference and the consistency checking algorithms. First, conjunctions $\bigwedge_{\tau \mid \tau'}$ are coupled with the constraint sets of the pattern-abstraction from which they are derived. This significantly reduces the size of the coercion set over which conjunctions must be taken. Thus, in algorithm *TYPE* below, a coercion set may contain both inclusions *and* nested coercion sets that are derived from pattern-abstractions. Further, the inclusions in coercion sets C_i's generated during type inference for some program P are for the most part identical and the parametrized types τ_i all have the same "shape". The sets C_i's differ only in that each incorporates different choices made for types of constants and pattern-abstractions. Our type inference algorithm incorporates this insight and represents sets (C_i, τ_i) by the *triple* $(C, S \equiv \{S_i\}, \tau)$. Each S_i is a *disjunction* of coercion sets $\bigvee_j D_j$ each disjunct of which corresponds to the different choices that could be made for an occurrence of a constant or pattern-abstraction. The idea here is that the image of each (C_i, τ_i) is equivalent to that of some $(C \cup \bigcup_{D_{k_j} \in S_j} \{D_{k_j}\}, \tau)$ and that the explicit construction of C_i can be deferred till later. For example, the strictness properties of the *add* operator would be represented by the triple:

$$(\emptyset, \alpha \rightarrow \beta \rightarrow \gamma, \{\{\{\alpha \subseteq \Omega, \gamma \subseteq \Omega\}, \{\beta \subseteq \Omega, \gamma \subseteq \Omega\}\}\}$$

With the use of side-constraints and the association of conjunctions with appropriate sub-constraint sets, a constraint set constructed by algorithm *TYPE* contains two types of constraints, one of the following forms:

$$[\text{constraint}]\ C ::= \tau_1 \subseteq \tau_2 \mid \bigwedge_{\tau_1 \mid \tau_2} (C, S)$$

where S is a side-constraint.

4.3 Type Inference Algorithm

Algorithm *TYPE* (Figure 4), takes an expression and a set of assumptions as input and computes a strictness expression. We assume that the initial set of assumptions contains types for all constants. TYPE generates a "parametrized" normal proof and generates constraints between parametrized types by applying coercions at application subterms and at pattern-abstractions. The algorithm constructs the strictness expression (C, S, τ) in a single traversal over the input program; the size of C is bounded by the number of application subterms and pattern abstractions occurring in the program; the size of S by the total number of constants and pattern abstractions.

Each clause in *TYPE* is commented with the inference rules used. Observe the use of side constraint in the rules for pattern abstractions, wherein the effect of $(rule1)$ and $(rule2)$ is modeled by additions to the side constraint.

Theorem 3 (Completeness and Soundness)
$(C, S, \tau) = TYPE(A, e), \gamma \in \mathcal{I}(C, S, \tau) \iff A \vdash e : \gamma$

Proof: Induction over proof tree of program input to TYPE.

■

5 Consistency Checking

The consistency checking problem is: given coercion set C determine whether there exists substitution S which satisfies C. Such a procedure can be used to determine whether program P possesses strictness property α, by checking whether $(C \cup \{\tau \subseteq \alpha\}, S)$ is consistent, where $(C, S, \tau) = TYPE(A, P)$. Algorithm *CON* takes a coercion set and returns true only if there exists an interpretation such that all the coercions in the set are provably true. We shall reserve the letters α and β for type variables, and $\delta, \gamma, \tau, \sigma$ etc. for arbitrary type expressions. In the course of consistency checking it may be necessary to introduce new variables. We shall write them as α_i, for some integers i.

We will need the notion of **high** and **low** variables in *CON*. Intuitively, a high variable, written as $\overline{\alpha}$, is a type variable that can only be instantiated by any expression τ such that $\Omega \subseteq \tau$. Similarly, a low variable, written as $\underline{\alpha}$, is one that can only be instantiated by type expressions τ such that $\tau \subseteq \Omega$. Variables that lacks such constraints are written without bars and we call such **unconstrained** variables. High and low variables are only created in the process of consistency checking, and these we shall call **constrained** variables.

(* (const) *) $TYPE\ A\ [\![c]\!] = NEW(lookup\ (A, c))$

(* (var) *) $TYPE\ A\ [\![x]\!] = lookup\ (A, x)$

(* (app), (coerce) *) $TYPE\ A\ [\![e_1 e_2]\!] =$

Let

$$(C_1, S_1, \tau_1) = TYPE\ A\ [\![e_1]\!]$$
$$(C_2, S_1, \tau_2) = TYPE\ A\ [\![e_2]\!]$$
$$\alpha = \text{new\_variable}()$$

in

$$(\{\tau_1 \subseteq \tau_2 \rightarrow \alpha\} \cup C_1 \cup C_2, S_1 \cup S_2, \alpha)$$

end

(* (tuple) *) $TYPE\ A\ [\![c^k(e_1, \cdots, e_n)]\!] =$

Let

$$(C_i, S_i, \tau_i) = TYPE\ A\ [\![e_i]\!]$$

in

$$(\bigcup_{1 \leq i \leq n} C_i, \bigcup_{1 \leq i \leq n} S_i, \tau_1 \times \cdots \times \tau_n)$$

end

(* (lambda2), (coerce) *) $TYPE\ A\ [\![\lambda(pat_1 \Rightarrow e_1 \mid \cdots \mid pat_n \Rightarrow e_n)]\!] =$

Let

$$(C_i, S_i, \tau_i) = TYPE\ A\ [\![pat_i \Rightarrow e_i]\!]$$
$$\alpha, \beta = \text{new\_variable}()$$

in

$$(C \cup (\bigcup_{1 \leq i \leq n} C_i) \cup \{\tau_i \subseteq \alpha \rightarrow \beta\}, S \cup (\bigcup_{1 \leq i \leq n} S_i), \alpha \rightarrow \beta)$$

end

(* (rule1),(lambda1) *) $TYPE\ A\ [\![c^k() \Rightarrow e]\!] =$

Let

$$(C, S, \tau) = TYPE\ A\ [\![e]\!]$$
$$\alpha = \text{new\_variable}()$$

in

$$(C, S \cup \{\{\{\top \rightarrow \tau \subseteq \alpha\}, \{\Omega \rightarrow \bot \subseteq \alpha\}\}, \alpha)$$

end

(* (rule2),(lambda1) *) $TYPE\ A\ [\![c^k(x_1, \cdots, x_m) \Rightarrow e]\!] =$

Let

$$\sigma_i, \alpha, \beta = \text{new\_variable}()$$
$$(C, S, \tau) = TYPE\ (A +\!\!+ \{x_i : \sigma_i\})\ [\![e]\!]$$

in

$$(\{\bigwedge_{\sigma_1 \times \cdots \times \sigma_n \mid \alpha}(C \cup \{\tau \subseteq \beta\}\},$$
$$S \cup \{\{\{\tau \subseteq \alpha \rightarrow \beta\}, \{\bot \rightarrow \bot \subseteq \alpha \rightarrow \beta\}\}\}, \alpha \rightarrow \beta)$$

end

(* (lambda1) *) $TYPE\ A\ [\![x \Rightarrow e]\!] =$

Let

$$\alpha = \text{new\_variable}()$$
$$(C, S, \tau) = TYPE\ (A +\!\!+ \{x : \alpha\})\ [\![e]\!]$$

in

$$(C, S, \alpha \rightarrow \tau)$$

end

Figure 4: Algorithm TYPE

5.1 Algorithm

We present *CON* as a function defined by the following set of rules:

$$
\begin{array}{lll}
(1) & CON\{\top \subseteq \bot\} \cup A & = \textit{false} \\
(2) & CON\{\top \subseteq \Omega\} \cup A & = \textit{false} \\
(3) & CON\{\Omega \subseteq \bot\} \cup A & = \textit{false} \\
(4) & CON\{\Omega \subseteq \Omega\} \cup A & = CON\,A \\
(5) & CON\{\bot \subseteq \tau\} \cup A & = CON\,A \\
(6) & CON\{\top \subseteq \overline{\alpha}\} \cup A & = CON\,[\top/\overline{\alpha}]A \\
(7) & CON\{\top \subseteq \underline{\alpha}\} \cup A & = \textit{false} \\
(8) & CON\{\top \subseteq \alpha\} \cup A & = CON\,[\top/\alpha]A \\
(9) & CON\{\top \subseteq \tau \to \sigma\} \cup A & = CON\{\top \subseteq \sigma\} \cup A \\
(10) & CON\{\Omega \subseteq \overline{\alpha}\} \cup A & = CON\,A \\
(11) & CON\{\Omega \subseteq \underline{\alpha}\} \cup A & = CON\,[\Omega/\underline{\alpha}]A \\
(12) & CON\{\Omega \subseteq \alpha\} \cup A & = CON\,[\overline{\alpha_1}/\alpha]A \\
(13) & CON\{\overline{\alpha} \subseteq \Omega\} \cup A & = CON\,[\Omega/\overline{\alpha}]A \\
(14) & CON\{\underline{\alpha} \subseteq \Omega\} \cup A & = CON\,A \\
(15) & CON\{\alpha \subseteq \Omega\} \cup A & = CON\,[\underline{\alpha_1}/\alpha]A \\
(16) & CON\{\overline{\alpha} \subseteq \bot\} \cup A & = \textit{false} \\
(17) & CON\{\underline{\alpha} \subseteq \bot\} \cup A & = CON\,[\bot/\underline{\alpha}]A \\
(18) & CON\{\alpha \subseteq \bot\} \cup A & = CON\,[\bot/\alpha]A \\
(19) & CON\{\tau_1 \times \cdots \times \tau_n \subseteq \bot\} \cup A & = \textit{false} \\
(20) & CON\{\tau \to \sigma \subseteq \bot\} \cup A & = CON\{\top \subseteq \tau, \sigma \subseteq \bot\} \cup A \\
(21) & CON\{\tau_1 \times \cdots \times \tau_n \subseteq & \\
 & \quad \sigma_1 \times \cdots \times \sigma_n\} \cup A & = CON\,(\bigcup_{1\le i\le n}\{\tau_i \subseteq \sigma_i\} \cup A) \\
(22) & CON\{\tau \to \sigma \subseteq \gamma \to \delta\} \cup A & = CON\{\gamma \subseteq \tau, \sigma \subseteq \delta\} \cup A \\
 & & \quad \text{if } \textit{nontop}\ \delta \\
(23) & CON\{\overline{\alpha} \subseteq \underline{\beta}\} \cup A & = CON\,[\Omega/\overline{\alpha}][\Omega/\underline{\beta}]A \\
(24) & CON\{\alpha \subseteq \underline{\beta}\} \cup A & = CON\,[\underline{\alpha_1}/\alpha](\{\alpha \subseteq \underline{\beta}\} \cup A) \\
(25) & CON\{\underline{\alpha} \subseteq \overline{\beta}\} \cup A & = CON\,A \\
(26) & CON\{\tau \subseteq \sigma\} \cup A & = CON\,A \text{ if } \textit{top}\ \sigma \\
(27) & CON\{\alpha \subseteq \tau \to \sigma\} \cup A & = CON\,[\alpha_1 \to \alpha_2/\alpha](\{\alpha \subseteq \tau \to \sigma\} \cup A) \\
 & & \quad \text{if } \textit{nontop}\ \sigma \\
(28) & CON\{\Omega \subseteq \tau_1 \times \cdots \times \tau_n\} \cup A & = CON\,(\bigcup_{1\le i\le n}\{\top \subseteq \tau_i\} \cup A) \\
(29) & CON\{\tau_1 \times \cdots \times \tau_n \subseteq \Omega\} \cup A & = \bigvee_{1\le i\le n} CON\{\tau_i \subseteq \Omega\} \cup A \\
(30) & CON\{\Omega \subseteq \tau \to \sigma\} \cup A & = CON\{\top \subseteq \sigma\} \cup A
\end{array}
$$

$$
\begin{array}{lll}
(31) \quad CON\,\{\tau \rightarrow \sigma \subseteq \Omega\} \cup A & = & CON\,\{\top \subseteq \tau, \sigma \subseteq \Omega\} \cup A \\
(32) \quad CON\,\{\overline{\alpha} \subseteq \tau \rightarrow \sigma\} \cup A & = & CON\,\{\top \subseteq \sigma\} \cup A \\
(33) \quad CON\,\{\underline{\alpha} \subseteq \tau \rightarrow \sigma\} \cup A & = & CON\,[\top \rightarrow \alpha_1/\underline{\alpha}(\{\underline{\alpha} \subseteq \tau \rightarrow \sigma\} \cup A)] \\
 & & \text{if } \mathit{nontop}\,\sigma \\
(34) \quad CON\,\{\overline{\alpha} \subseteq \tau_1 \times \cdots \times \tau_n\} \cup A & = & CON\,(\bigcup_{1 \leq i \leq n} \{\top \subseteq \tau_i\} \cup A) \\
(35) \quad CON\,\{\alpha \subseteq \tau_1 \times \cdots \times \tau_n\} \cup A & = & CON\,[\alpha_1 \times \cdots \times \alpha_n/\alpha](\{\alpha_i \subseteq \tau_i\} \cup A) \\
 & & \vee(CON\,[\bot/\alpha]A) \\
 & & \text{if } \mathit{nontop}\,(\tau_1 \times \cdots \times \tau_n)
\end{array}
$$

$$
\begin{array}{ll}
(36) & CON\,\{\underline{\alpha} \subseteq \tau_1 \times \cdots \times \tau_n\} \cup A \;= \\
 & CON\,[\alpha_1 \times \cdots \times \alpha_n/\underline{\alpha}](\{\underline{\alpha_i} \subseteq \tau_1 \times \cdots \times \tau_i, \alpha_1 \times \cdots \times \alpha_n \subseteq \Omega\} \cup A) \\
 & \qquad\qquad \vee CON\,[\bot/\alpha]A \\
 & \qquad\qquad \text{if } \mathit{nontop}\,(\tau_1 \times \cdots \times \tau_n) \\
(37) & CON\,\{\tau \rightarrow \sigma \subseteq \underline{\alpha}\} \cup A \;= \\
 & CON\,[\top \rightarrow \underline{\alpha_1}/\underline{\alpha}](\{\tau \rightarrow \sigma \subseteq \underline{\alpha}\} \cup A) \vee CON\,[\Omega/\underline{\alpha}](\{\tau \rightarrow \sigma \subseteq \underline{\alpha}\} \cup A) \\
(38) & CON\,\{\tau_1 \times \cdots \times \tau_n \subseteq \underline{\alpha}\} \cup A \;=\; CON\,[\Omega/\underline{\alpha}](\{\tau_1 \times \cdots \times \tau_n \subseteq \Omega\} \cup A) \vee \\
 & \bigvee_{1 \leq i \leq n}(CON\,[\alpha_1 \cdots \alpha_{i-1} \times \underline{\alpha_i} \times \alpha_{i+1} \cdots \alpha_n/\underline{\alpha}](\{\tau_1 \times \cdots \times \tau_n \subseteq \underline{\alpha}\} \cup A)
\end{array}
$$

$$
\begin{array}{lll}
(39) \quad CON\,\bigwedge_{\alpha_1 \times \cdots \times \alpha_n \,|\, \top} C & = & CON\,[\top/\alpha_i]C \\
(40) \quad CON\,\bigwedge_{\alpha_1 \times \cdots \times \alpha_n \,|\, \bot} C & = & CON\,[\bot/\alpha_i]C \\
(41) \quad CON\,\bigwedge_{\alpha_1 \times \cdots \times \alpha_n \,|\, \tau_1 \times \cdots \times \tau_n} C & = & CON\,[\tau_i/\alpha_i]C \\
(42) \quad CON\,\bigwedge_{\alpha_1 \times \cdots \times \alpha_n \,|\, \Omega} C & = & \bigwedge_{1 \leq i \leq n}(CON\,[\Omega/\tau_i][\top/\tau_{j, j \neq i}]C) \\
(43) \quad CON\,\bigwedge_{\alpha_1 \times \cdots \times \alpha_n \,|\, \beta} C & = & CON\,[\bot/\beta]\bigwedge_{\alpha_1 \times \cdots \times \alpha_n \,|\, \beta} C \\
 & & \vee CON\,[\top/\beta]\bigwedge_{\alpha_1 \times \cdots \times \alpha_n \,|\, \beta} C \\
 & & \vee CON\,[\gamma_1 \times \cdots \times \gamma_n/\beta]\bigwedge_{\alpha_1 \times \cdots \times \alpha_n \,|\, \beta} C \\
 & & \vee CON\,[\Omega/\beta]\bigwedge_{\alpha_1 \times \cdots \times \alpha_n \,|\, \beta} C \\
(44) \quad CON\,\bigwedge_{\alpha_1 \times \cdots \times \alpha_n \,|\, \overline{\beta}} C & = & CON\,[\top/\overline{\beta}]\bigwedge_{\alpha_1 \times \cdots \times \alpha_n \,|\, \overline{\beta}} C \\
 & & \vee CON\,[\Omega/\overline{\beta}]\bigwedge_{\alpha_1 \times \cdots \times \alpha_n \,|\, \overline{\beta}} C \\
(45) \quad CON\,\bigwedge_{\alpha_1 \times \cdots \times \alpha_n \,|\, \underline{\beta}} C & = & CON\,[\bot/\underline{\beta}]\bigwedge_{\alpha_1 \times \cdots \times \alpha_n \,|\, \underline{\beta}} C \\
 & & \vee CON\,[\Omega/\underline{\beta}]\bigwedge_{\alpha_1 \times \cdots \times \alpha_n \,|\, \beta} C) \\
 & & \vee CON\,[\gamma_1 \times \cdots \times \gamma_n/\underline{\beta}] \\
 & & \quad \bigwedge_{\alpha_1 \times \cdots \times \alpha_n \,|\, \underline{\beta}} \{\gamma_1 \times \cdots \times \gamma_n \subseteq \Omega\} \cup C \\
(46) \quad CON\,\bigwedge_{\alpha_1 \times \cdots \times \alpha_m \,|\, \tau_1 \times \cdots \times \tau_n} C & = & \mathit{true}\,,\; m \neq n \\
(47) \quad CON\,A & = & \mathit{true}\,,\;\; \text{otherwise}
\end{array}
$$

where,

$$
\begin{array}{lll}
\mathit{nontop}\,\top & = & \mathit{false} \\
\mathit{nontop}\,\bot & = & \mathit{true} \\
\mathit{nontop}\,\Omega & = & \mathit{true} \\
\mathit{nontop}\,\alpha & = & \mathit{false} \\
\mathit{nontop}\,\underline{\alpha} & = & \mathit{true} \\
\mathit{nontop}\,\overline{\alpha} & = & \mathit{false} \\
\mathit{nontop}\,(\tau \rightarrow \sigma) & = & \mathit{nontop}\,\sigma \\
\mathit{nontop}\,(\tau_1 \times \cdots \times \tau_n) & = & \bigvee_{1 \leq i \leq n} \mathit{nontop}\,\tau_i
\end{array}
$$

and

$$
\begin{array}{lcl}
top\ \top & = & true \\
top\ \bot & = & false \\
top\ \Omega & = & false \\
top\ \alpha & = & false \\
top\ \underline{\alpha} & = & false \\
top\ \overline{\alpha} & = & false \\
top\ (\tau \rightarrow \sigma) & = & top\ \sigma \\
top\ (\tau_1 \times \cdots \times \tau_n) & = & \bigwedge_{1 \leq i \leq n} top\ \tau_i
\end{array}
$$

The function *nontop* returns true only if the type expression is definitely not equal to $\top$, and the function *top* returns true only if the type expression is definitely equal to $\top$. It is worth noting that they are not negations of each other with the presence of variables.

During consistency checking, high and low variables are introduced only at rules (13) and (16). It is worth noting that high and low variables are used here as an notational convenience. For instance, the set $\{\underline{\alpha} \subseteq \tau\} \cup A$ can be considered as an abbreviation for $\{\alpha \subseteq \tau, \alpha \subseteq \Omega\} \cup A'$ where $A' = [\alpha/\underline{\alpha}]A$. Since coercions of the form $\Omega \subseteq \alpha$ and $\alpha \subseteq \Omega$ cannot be easily eliminated in consistency checking, high and low variables seem necessary in order to express the algorithm *CON* with only patterns involving single coercions.

CON terminates (47) when the coercion set cannot be simplified or decomposed any further. The final coercion set contains coercions of either of the two forms:

$$
\begin{array}{lcl}
\tau & \subseteq & \sigma \text{ and } not(nontop\ \sigma) \\
\underline{\alpha} & \subseteq & \underline{\beta}
\end{array}
$$

It is easy to see that the interpretation in which every high and unconstrained variable is $\top$ and every low variable is Ω is trivially valid for these coercion sets.

5.2 Soundness and Termination

Definition 5 *Two type expressions τ and σ are* **matching** *if and only if*

(i) *both τ and σ are constants or type variables,*

(ii) *$\tau = \tau_1 \rightarrow \tau_2$ and $\sigma = \sigma_1 \rightarrow \sigma_2$ where τ_1, σ_1 are matching and τ_2, σ_2 are matching,*

(iii) *$\tau = \tau_1 \times \cdots \times \tau_n$ and $\sigma = \sigma_1 \times \cdots \times \sigma_n$ and τ_i, σ_i are matching for all i's.*

In essence, two type expressions are matching if they have the same structure. We say a coercion $\tau \subseteq \sigma$ is matching if τ and σ are matching.

Definition 6 *A coercion set C is* **matchable** *if there exists a ground substitution S such that for all $\tau \subseteq \sigma \in S(C)$ are matching and each τ and σ are matching; if $C \equiv \bigwedge_{\tau_{1i} \mid \tau_{2i}} \cdots C'$ then τ_{1i} matches $S(\tau_{2i})$.*

Definition 7 *A coercion set C is* **virtually matchable** *if we replace each occurrence of the type constants c_i in C by a distinct variable α_i and the resulting set C' is matchable.*

Theorem 4 *CON is sound and will terminate given coercion sets that are virtually matchable. CON is complete with respect to virtually matchable input;i.e. if C is virtually matchable then $CON\ C = true \iff C$ is consistent.*

5.3 Cyclic Coercion Sets

Most inclusions generated by *TYPE* for well-typed programs are virtually matching. However, certain restricted forms of cyclic (non virtually matching) inclusions arise from recursive datatypes and recursive definitions. For example, the strictness expression reported by *TYPE* for the following program

$$fix(\lambda ones.cons(1, ones))$$

consists of:

$$(\{(fix \rightarrow fix) \rightarrow fix \subseteq (\alpha \rightarrow \top \times \alpha) \rightarrow \tau\}, \tau)$$

The set $\{(fix \rightarrow fix) \rightarrow fix \subseteq (\alpha \rightarrow \top \times \alpha) \rightarrow \tau\}$ is not virtually matchable: no instantiation of the variable α and fix can make the set match. In the algorithm *CON* cyclic variables run into the danger of being expanded without terminating by repeated use of Rule (35).

An useful and relatively inexpensive heuristic to guarantee the termination of *CON* in the presence of cyclic coercions is to assign an unique **expansion count** to each type variable. For example, let $E(\alpha)$ be the expansion count of α. When variable α is expanded to $\alpha_1 \times \cdots \times \alpha_n$ within *CON* , we increase the count on each α_i to $E(\alpha) + 1$. Variables that have expansion counts which exceed a preset maximum are prohibited from further expansion. Since each variable and each variable's expansion can only be expanded a finite number of times, it is easy to see that such a heuristic prevents non-termination. This can also be seen as a technique for carrying out"breadth-first" search of a potentially infinite proof tree.

6 Conclusion

We have exhibited an inference system that is a modest extension of traditional type inference systems [DM82], and yet describes complex reasoning about higher-order strictness properties. For one specific type language, based on the primitive notions of "all", "looping" and "lacking normal form", we have given algorithms to compute strictness expressions and carry out consistency checking. The systematic use of a subtype notion allows the deduction of strictness and full-strictness properties in the same framework. Our inference algorithms avoids fixpoint iteration and hence may be amenable to practical use. Further details of algorithms and their use in an implementation may be found in [Leu91].

From a different point of view, our inference system can be used (with modest extension) for many different type systems; for example, we have presented the extensions necessary for a type system based on the concepts in [Wad87]. If we were interested in foundational theoretical results concerning the power of our inference system, we could even consider incorporating quantification or conjunction[CDV81, Lei86] in our type system. In this respect our framework is *parametrized* with respect to the relative power of the type language and can be used with many possible type languages. This should provide another perspective on the differences between our approach and higher-order abstract interpretation.

6.1 Acknowledgements

We thank Geoffrey Burn and Marc Neuberger for their valuable comments on early drafts of this paper.

References

[Abr85] Samson Abramsky. Strictness Analysis And Polymorphic Invariance. In *LNCS 217: Workshop on Programs as Data Objects*, 1985.

[BHA86] G. L. Burn, C. L. Hankin, and S. Abramsky. Strictness Analysis of Higher-Order Functions. *Science of Computer Programming*, 7, 1986.

[Bur90] G. Burn. Using Projection Analysis in Compiling Lazy Functional Programs. In *ACM Symposium on Lisp and Functional Programming*, 1990.

[CDV81] M. Coppo, M. Dezani-Ciancaglini, and B. Venneri. Functional Characters of Solvable Terms. *Zeitschr. f. math. Logik und Grundlagen d. Math.*, 27:45–58, 1981.

[DM82] L. Damas and R. Milner. Principal Type Schemes for Functional Programs. In *ACM Symposium on Principles of Programming Languages*, pages 207–212, 1982.

[FM89] You-Chin Fuh and Prateek Mishra. Polymorphic Subtype Inference: Closing the Theory-Practice Gap. In *TAPSOFT-89*, March 1989.

[FM90] You-Chin Fuh and Prateek Mishra. Type Inference with Subtypes. *Theoretical Computer Science*, 73:155–175, 1990.

[Hun89] S. Hunt. Frontiers and Open Sets in Abstract Interpretation. In *ACM-IFIP Conference on Functional Programming Languages and Computer Architecture*, September 1989.

[HY86] P. Hudak and J. Young. Higher-Order Strictness Analysis in Untyped Lambda Calculus. In *ACM Symposium on Principles of Programming Languages*, 1986.

[KM87] Tsung-Min Kuo and Prateek Mishra. On Strictness and its Analysis. In *ACM Symposium on Principles of Programming Languages*, 1987.

[KM89a] Tsung-Min Kuo and Prateek Mishra. Inferring Strictness Properties of the Pure λ-Calculus: Completeness and Incompleteness Theorems. Technical Report 89/28, Submitted to LICS 91, SUNY at Stony Brook, 1989.

[KM89b] Tsung-Min Kuo and Prateek Mishra. Strictness Analysis : A New Perspective Based on Type Inference. In *ACM-IFIP Conference on Functional Programming Languages and Computer Architecture*, September 1989.

[Lei86] Daniel Leivant. Typing and Computational Properties of Lambda Expressions. *Theoretical Computer Science*, 44:51–68, 1986.

[Leu91] A. K. T. Leung. *Reasoning with Simple and Exhaustive Demands In Higher Order Functional Languages.* Master's thesis, The State University of New York at Stony Brook, 1991.

[Lin86] G. Lindstrom. Static Evaluation of Functional Programs. In *SIGPLAN86 Symposium on Compiler Construction*, 1986.

[LLD87] G. Lindstrom, G. Lal, and Y. Dowming. Generating Efficient Code from Strictness Annotations. In *LNCS 250: TAPSOFT 87*, 1987.

[Mau85] D. Maurer. Strictness Computation Using Special λ-expressions. In *LNCS 217: Workshop on Programs as Data Objects*, 1985.

[MH87] C. Martin and C. Hankin. Finding Fixed Points in Finite Lattices. In *LNCS 274: Functional Programming Languages and Computer Architecture*, pages 426–445, 1987.

[Mis88] Prateek Mishra. Strictness Analysis of the Untyped λ-calculus. *Information Processing Letters*, 28:121–125, 1988.

[Myc80] A. Mycroft. The Theory and Practice of Transforming Call-by-need into Call-by-value. In *LNCS 83*, 1980.

[PJ87] S.L. Peyton Jones. *The Implementation of Functional Programming Languages.* Prentice Hall, 1987.

[PS90] L. Puel and A. Suarez. Compiling Pattern Matching by Term Decomposition. In *ACM Symposium on Lisp and Functional Programming*, pages 273–281, 1990.

[SPR90] R.C. Sekar, S. Pawagi, and I.V. Ramakrishnan. Small Domains Spell Fast Strictness Analysis. In *ACM Symposium on Principles of Programming Languages*, 1990.

[Sta79] R. Statman. The Typed λ-calculus is not Elementary Recursive. *Theoretical Computer Science*, 9:73–81, 1979.

[Wad76] C. P. Wadsworth. The Relation between Computational and Denotational Properties for Scott's D_∞-models of the Lambda-calculus. *SIAM J. of Computation*, 5(3), 1976.

[Wad87] P. Wadler. Strictness Analysis over Non-flat Domains. In *Abstract Interpretation of Declarative Languages*, Ellis Horwood, 1987.

[WR87] Philip Wadler and Hughes R.J.M. Projections for Strictness Analysis. In *ACM-IFIP Conference on Functional Programming Languages and Computer Architecture*, 1987.

Strictness Analysis in Logical Form

Thomas P. Jensen*

Imperial College†

Abstract

This paper presents a framework for comparing two strictness analysis techniques: Abstract interpretation and non-standard type inference. The comparison is based on the representation of a lattice by its ideals. A formal system for deducing inclusions between ideals of a lattice is presented and proved sound and complete. Viewing the ideals as *strictness properties* we use the formal system to define a program logic for deducing strictness properties of expressions in a typed lambda calculus. This *strictness logic* is shown to be sound and complete with respect to the abstract interpretation, which establishes the main result that strictness analysis by type-inference and by abstract interpretation are equally powerful techniques.

1 Introduction

Abstract interpretation is a well-established technique for static analysis of programs. Its virtue is its strong connection with denotational semantics which provides a means of proving the analysis correct. Its vice is that the process of doing abstract interpretation is quite costly in terms of computation time, although developments in the area of algorithms for finding fixpoints have improved the situation substantially [7]. Recently, a number of researchers have suggested that analyses be based on non-standard type systems. Examples include Wadler's linear types [14] and Kuo and Mishra's strictness types [11]. The advantage of this approach is that there exist efficient algorithms for checking and inferring types of programs. However, the correctness of these analyses has received rather less attention than the implementation aspects and to the best of our knowledge there has not been given a satisfactory explanation of what can be achieved by abstract interpretation but not by the type system and *vice versa*.

The purpose of this paper is to present a framework for relating abstract interpretations to non-standard type systems. We will concentrate on strictness analysis in this paper but the framework is applicable to other analyses as well. The basic

*This work was partially supported by ESPRIT grant BRA 3124 SEMANTIQUE

†Author's address: Department of Computing, Imperial College, 180 Queen's Gate, London SW7 2BZ, U.K. Email: tpj@doc.ic.ac.uk

idea is to view these non-standard type systems as program logics. The relationship between abstract interpretation and non-standard type inference can then be seen as a special case of the relationship between denotational and axiomatic semantics. This topic has been investigated by a number of researchers and we shall be following a line similar to that of [1].

We begin with a section in which we describe the kind of properties we shall be using in the strictness logic. Essentially these properties are those that are given by downwards closed subsets of the strictness domains. We prove the important fact that our abstract domains can equally well be presented as an ordered set of elements or as a collection of properties of the domain, because these presentations determine each other. We then give a formal system that axiomatises the entailment relation between the strictness properties and we prove that the formal system is sound and complete with respect to the interpretation of properties as subsets of an ordered set. Section 4 reviews strictness analysis by abstract interpretation and introduces a program logic for deducing strictness properties of programs. We give a proof of the main theorem, that the strictness logic can prove exactly those strictness properties that we could find by abstract interpretation. Section 5 concludes with relating the present work to that of others and sketching some directions for future developments.

2 The ideal representation of lattices

This section presents some lattice-theoretic facts that will form the basis for our comparison between abstract interpretation and program logics. We discuss what a property over an abstract domain is and show how the order structure on the domain can be used to single out certain properties of interest. We shall see that a lattice-theoretic result concerning the representation of a semilattice by its ideals can be interpreted as saying that an abstract domain is fully determined by a certain kind of properties definable over the domain together with the logical entailment relation associated with these properties.

In this paper we shall take an abstract interpretation to be a denotational semantics (see *e.g.*, [13]) for which the denotation of any program is effectively computable. One way of achieving effectiveness is by requiring the domains used in the interpretation to be finite. This on the other hand introduces a loss of information that in general makes it impossible to calculate the condition in a branching expression. The interpretation of a branching expression is therefore usually taken to be a combination of the interpretations of the branches. The ability to combine denotations is ensured by requiring the domain to have binary joins. A least element, $\bot$, is added for the interpretation of fixpoint operators. We summarise this in a definition.

Definition 1 *A* join-semilattice *(or* $\sqcup$*-semilattice) is an ordered set* $(S, \sqsubseteq)$ *with a binary join operator* $\sqcup : S \times S \rightarrow S$ *and a distinguished element* $\bot \in S$ *such that*

- $a \sqcup b$ *is the least upper bound of* a *and* b *in* S.
- $\bot$ *is the least element in* $(S, \sqsubseteq)$.

The category of all finite join–semilattices with order–preserving maps as morphisms is denoted by $\mathbf{JSL}_f$. For the rest of the paper we shall take our domains to be objects in $\mathbf{JSL}_f$. We note that a finite join–semilattice actually is a complete lattice, but we shall not use this fact in this section.

Similarly a meet–semilattice is an ordered set with a greatest lower bound operator, $\wedge$, and a greatest element, $\top$. The category of finite meet–semilattices is denoted by $\mathbf{MSL}_f$.

In ordinary set–based logic a property can be identified with the subset of elements satisfying the property, and, conversely, any subset determines a property. Property P then entails property Q if the set of elements satisfying P is contained in the set of elements satisfying Q. With an ordering imposed on the set of elements it is possible to restrict attention to a smaller set of properties by only studying subsets satisfying certain constraints related to the order structure. *E.g.* with a two–point domain $\{\bot, \top\}$ with $\bot$ denoting non–termination and $\top$ denoting termination, we initially have properties $\{\bot\}$, $\{\top\}$ and $\{\bot, \top\}$ where the latter property corresponds to the "empty" property satisfied by all elements. If we are not interested in whether a program definitely terminates, *i.e.*, satisfies property $\{\top\}$, we can require our propositions to be subsets downwards closed with respect to the ordering on the domain. This will give us the two properties $\{\bot\}$ and $\{\bot, \top\}$ with $\{\bot\}$ entailing $\{\bot, \top\}$. This is exactly the kind of properties on which we shall build a program logic in the following sections. We formalise this notion of property using the concept of an *ideal* of a semilattice.

Definition 2 *An* ideal *of a join–semilattice S is a non–empty subset $I \subseteq S$ satisfying*

- *I is down–closed,* i.e., *$x \in I$ and $x \sqsubseteq y$ implies $y \in I$.*
- *I is closed under binary joins* i.e., *$x, y \in I$ implies $x \sqcup y \in I$.*

An ideal is principal *if it is the down–closure of a single element a. In this case we write I as $\downarrow(a)$*

What structure do we have on the collection of ideals? The union of two ideals is in general not an ideal but the intersection is. Furthermore the intersection of two ideals A and B is the greatest ideal contained in both A and B. There is also an ideal that contains all other ideals of S namely S itself. In other words the set of ideals of S forms a meet–semilattice with set intersection as the meet operation. If S is finite so is the set of ideals of S. We thus have a mapping $\mathsf{Idl} : \mathbf{JSL}_f \rightarrow \mathbf{MSL}_f$ which maps a join–semilattice to its meet–semilattice of ideals.

Under the assumption that a join–semilattice S is finite we can say more. As all ideals are finite and closed under finite joins every ideal must contain a maximal element, hence all ideals are principal and the mapping $a \rightarrow \downarrow(a)$ is a bijective correspondence between the elements of the join–semilattice S and the meet–semilattice $\mathsf{Idl}(S)$.

So far we have taken the domain as starting point and constructed a collection of properties over the domain. The next question is: Is this process reversible? Can we reconstruct the original join–semilattice from the meet–semilattice of properties? The answer is yes and we show this by giving a general method for constructing a domain from a set of properties we want to be definable over the domain. The key idea here is that *an element should be fully described by the properties it satisfies.* Following this idea we construct a new lattice, the elements of which are sets of properties. However, only sets satisfying certain consistency requirements should be considered. The sets must be closed under implication and conjunction, because if property P_1 holds of an element p and P_1 implies P_2, then P_2 will hold of p as well. Similarly, if properties P_1 and P_2 hold of an element p then so does $P_1 \wedge P_2$. This is formalised by the notion of a filter of a meet–semilattice.

Definition 3 *A* filter *of a meet–semilattice M is a non–empty subset $F \subseteq M$ that satisfies*

- *F is upwards closed.*
- *$P_1, P_2 \in F \Rightarrow P_1 \wedge P_2 \in F$.*

A filter is called *principal* if it is the upwards closure of a single element. Note that a filter of a meet–semilattice M turns into an ideal if the ordering on M is reversed. This means that many of the results about ideals in join–semilattices can be translated into results about filters in meet–semilattices "by duality". Especially it is easy to see that the filters of a finite meet–semilattice are upwards closures of single elements (*i.e.*, they are principal filters).

We take filters of properties to be the elements of a domain. The ordering on the elements is determined by the set of properties in the filter. The key observation here is that *the more properties an element satisfies, the less defined it is.* In particular the least defined element is the element satisfying all properties. So we order the filters by reverse inclusion and the least upper bound operation then becomes set intersection. This gives a mapping $\mathsf{Fil} : \mathbf{MSL}_f \to \mathbf{JSL}_f$ that sends a meet–semilattice to its join–semilattice of filters.

How does a join–semilattice L relate to the join–semilattice $\mathsf{Fil}(\mathsf{Idl}(L))$ obtained from the closed subsets of L? There is an obvious embedding $\eta : L \to \mathsf{Fil}(\mathsf{Idl}(L))$ defined by

$$\eta(a) = \{I \in \mathsf{Idl}(L) \mid a \in I\}.$$

This maps a to the set of ideals containing a, or in logical terms, to the set of properties satisfied by a.

Proposition 1 *The mapping $\eta : L \to \mathsf{Fil}(\mathsf{Idl}(L))$ is a $\mathbf{JSL}_f$–isomorphism*

Proof. First observe that the set $\{I \in \mathsf{Idl}(L) \mid a \in I\}$ is equal to the set of ideals containing the ideal $\downarrow(a)$. In other words $\eta(a) = \uparrow(\downarrow(a))$, so $\eta(a)$ is a (principal) filter. On the other hand, every filter is principal because of finiteness, so every filter is of the form $\uparrow(I)$ for some ideal I, and every ideal is principal so $I = \downarrow(a)$ for some a, so every filter is of the form $\uparrow(\downarrow(a))$, ie η is surjective. Injectivity follows from the fact that for two different elements, $a_1 \neq a_2$ of L there exists an ideal containing one but not the other, hence $\eta(a_1) \neq \eta(a_2)$. Finally we must show that η is order-preserving:

$$\begin{aligned} a_1 \sqsubseteq a_2 &\Rightarrow \downarrow(a_1) \sqsubseteq \downarrow(a_2) \\ &\Rightarrow \uparrow(\downarrow(a_1)) \sqsubseteq \uparrow(\downarrow(a_2)) \\ &\Rightarrow \eta(a_1) \sqsubseteq \eta(a_2) \qquad \blacksquare \end{aligned}$$

The conclusion of this is that our abstract domains can equally well be presented as a join-semilattice of elements or as a meet-semilattice of properties in the sense that these two structures determines each other up to isomorphism.

3 Strictness domains presented axiomatically

The next step is to apply the domain representation defined in the previous section to the domains encountered in abstract interpretation used for strictness analysis. The strictness analysis employs a set of types defined by the grammar:

$$\sigma ::= \mathbf{2} \mid \sigma_1 \rightarrow \sigma_2$$

To each type is associated a lattice as defined by the function $D : \mathbf{Types} \rightarrow \mathbf{JSL}_f$

$$D(\mathbf{2}) = \{0, 1\} \text{ with } 0 \sqsubseteq 1$$

$$D(\sigma_1 \rightarrow \sigma_2) = D(\sigma_1) \rightarrow_m D(\sigma_2)$$

where the symbol $\rightarrow_m$ denotes the space of order-preserving (monotone) maps. From the previous section we have the representation of any $D(\sigma)$ by its meet-semilattice of ideals. However, we do not have a proper syntactic description of $\mathsf{Idl}(D(\sigma))$. The purpose of this section is to provide an axiomatic system that precisely defines the meet-semilattice of ideals for all $D(\sigma)$. For every type σ we define a logical theory

$$\mathcal{L}(\sigma) = (L(\sigma), \wedge, \leq, =)$$

where $L(\sigma)$ is a set of formulae (denoting properties), the binary operator $\wedge$ is conjunction, $\leq$ corresponds to entailment and $=$ is logical equivalence between formulae. We shall see that the ordered set of propositions $\mathcal{L}(\sigma)$ quotiented by logical equivalence is order-isomorphic to the meet-semilattice of ideals of $D(\sigma)$, thus providing a purely axiomatic description of $\mathsf{Idl}(D(\sigma))$.

There are several ways of axiomatising meet-semilattices. The most concise presentation would formalise arbitrary, finite (including empty) meets. We have chosen to introduce some redundancy by explicitly naming certain elements in the meet-semilattices of ideals. We do this to make the presentation easier to read and to obtain a formal system close to that of [11]. *E.g.* the top element, $\mathbf{t}$, in every meet-semilattice is in effect the empty meet, so by axiomatising the top

element separately we only have to define binary meets to obtain all finite meets. Similarly we introduce a formula for the least ideal, $\mathtt{f} = \{\bot\}$. Of course the price we have to pay is that we have to add as extra axioms all facts provable about these formulae in the original system.
The sets of formulae are defined inductively as follows:

$$\bullet\ \mathtt{t}, \mathtt{f} \in L(\sigma) \qquad \bullet\ \frac{\phi, \psi \in L(\sigma)}{\phi \wedge \psi \in L(\sigma)}$$

$$\bullet\ \frac{\phi \in L(\sigma), \psi \in L(\tau)}{\phi \to \psi \in L(\sigma \to \tau)}$$

The following axioms and rules define the semilattice structure on each $L(\sigma)$.

$$\bullet\ \varphi \leq \varphi \qquad \bullet\ \frac{\varphi \leq \psi, \psi \leq \chi}{\varphi \leq \chi}$$

$$\bullet\ \frac{\varphi \leq \psi_1, \varphi \leq \psi_2}{\varphi \leq \psi_1 \wedge \psi_2}$$

$$\bullet\ \varphi \wedge \psi \leq \varphi \qquad \bullet\ \varphi \wedge \psi \leq \psi$$

$$\bullet\ \frac{\varphi \leq \psi, \psi \leq \varphi}{\varphi = \psi} \qquad \bullet\ \frac{\varphi = \psi}{\varphi \leq \psi, \psi \leq \varphi}$$

$$\bullet\ \varphi \leq \mathtt{t} \qquad \bullet\ \mathtt{t}_{\sigma \to \tau} \leq \mathtt{t}_\sigma \to \mathtt{t}_\tau$$

$$\bullet\ \mathtt{f} \leq \varphi \qquad \bullet\ \mathtt{t}_\sigma \to \mathtt{f}_\tau \leq \mathtt{f}_{\sigma \to \tau}$$

$$\bullet\ \varphi \to \psi_1 \wedge \varphi \to \psi_2 \leq \varphi \to (\psi_1 \wedge \psi_2)$$

$$\bullet\ \frac{\varphi' \leq \varphi, \psi \leq \psi'}{\varphi \to \psi \leq \varphi' \to \psi'}$$

The connection between this logical system defining $\mathcal{L}(\sigma)$ and the collection of ideals of $D(\sigma)$ is established by means of semantic functions $[\![\_]\!]_\sigma : \mathcal{L}(\sigma) \to \mathsf{Idl}(D(\sigma))$:

$$\begin{array}{lcl}
[\![\mathtt{t}]\!]_\sigma & = & D(\sigma) \\
[\![\mathtt{f}]\!]_\sigma & = & \{\bot_{D(\sigma)}\} \\
[\![\bigwedge_{i \in I} \psi_i]\!]_\sigma & = & \bigcap_{i \in I} [\![\psi_i]\!]_\sigma \\
[\![\varphi \to \psi]\!]_{\sigma \to \tau} & = & \{f \in D(\sigma \to \tau) \mid f([\![\varphi]\!]) \subseteq [\![\psi]\!]\}
\end{array}$$

We now set out to give a characterisation of the connection between the ideals in the domains and the formal system defined above. The following theorems state that all ideals of a domain are indeed definable in the logical system and that the logic is sound and complete, *i.e.*, that all inclusions that hold between ideals in the domains can be proved in the logic (completeness) and no inclusions but those that hold can be proved (soundness).
Before we embark on proving the theorems we need some results about how functions on lattices can be approximated by simpler objects. For these results it is

important that for finite join–semilattices it is possible to define a greatest lower bound operator, *i.e.*, they are in reality complete lattices. It is well known [1] from Domain Theory that all continuous functions between two Scott-domains can be expressed using some simple functions called ***step-functions***. These step functions are used to approximate functions from below. We shall be concerned with approximating functions (on lattices) from above, hence we study the dual to a step function:

Definition 4 *Let* A, B *be lattices and assume that* $(a,b) \in A \times B$. *The* co–step function $\lfloor(a,b)\rfloor : A \rightarrow B$ *is defined by*

$$\lfloor(a,b)\rfloor(x) = \begin{cases} b & \textit{if } x \sqsubseteq a \\ \top & \textit{otherwise} \end{cases}$$

We shall also use this notation for the greatest lower bound of a set of co–step functions. Let $u = \{(a_i, b_i) \mid i \in I\}$ be a set of pairs drawn from $A \times B$. The function $\lfloor u \rfloor$: A $\rightarrow$B induced by u is defined by

$$\lfloor u \rfloor(a) = \sqcap\{b_i \mid a \sqsubseteq a_i\}$$

Any function is the greatest lower bound of the co–step functions greater than function itself, so this gives a way of using co–step functions to build other functions. In fact we can be a bit more economical with the set of approximants due to the following lemma:

Lemma 1 *Let* $f : A \rightarrow B$ *Then*

$$f = \lfloor\{(a, f(a)) \mid a \in A\}\rfloor = \sqcap\{\lfloor(a, f(a))\rfloor \mid a \in A\}$$

The usefulness of co–step functions is due to the fact that the principal ideal generated by the co–step function $\lfloor$(a,b)$\rfloor$ is the set of functions that map ideal $\downarrow$(a) into the ideal $\downarrow$(b). We generalise this fact in the following lemma:

Lemma 2 *Let* $u = \{(a_i, b_i) \mid i \in I\}$. *Then*

$$\downarrow(\lfloor u \rfloor) = \cap_{i \in I}\{f : A \rightarrow B \mid f(\downarrow(a_i)) \subseteq \downarrow(b_i)\}$$

Proof: $f \sqsubseteq \lfloor u \rfloor$

$\Leftrightarrow \ \forall a \in A. f(a) \sqsubseteq \sqcap\{b_i \mid a \sqsubseteq a_i\}$

$\Leftrightarrow \ \forall i \in I. \forall a \in A. a \sqsubseteq a_i \Rightarrow f(a) \sqsubseteq b_i$

$\Leftrightarrow \ \forall i \in I. f \sqsubseteq \lfloor(a_i, b_i)\rfloor$

$\Leftrightarrow \ f \in \cap_{i \in I}\{\downarrow(\lfloor(a_i, b_i)\rfloor)\}$

$\Leftrightarrow \ f \in \cap_{i \in I}\{f : A \rightarrow B \mid f(\downarrow(a_i)) \subseteq \downarrow(b_i)\}$ ∎

The following theorem states that all ideals can be denoted by a formula from our formal system. In the formulation of the theorem we use the fact that all ideals are principal *i.e.*, downwards closures of a single element.

Theorem 1 (Definability) *For all elements $a : D(\sigma)$ there exist a $\varphi_a \in \mathcal{L}(\sigma)$ such that*

$$\downarrow(a) = [\![\varphi_a]\!]_\sigma$$

Proof. The proof works by structural induction over the type σ. For the base type **2** it is straightforward to see that the two elements 0 and 1 corresponds to the formulae $\mathbf{f}$ and $\mathbf{t}$, respectively. Now, let $f \in D(A \to B)$. Then we have:

$$\begin{aligned}\downarrow(f) &= \downarrow(\lfloor\{(a, f(a)) \mid a \in A\}\rfloor) \quad \text{by lemma 1}\\ &= \textstyle\bigcap_{a \in A}\{g : A \to B \mid g(\downarrow(a)) \subseteq \downarrow(f(a))\} \quad \text{by lemma 2}\\ &= [\![\textstyle\bigwedge_{a \in A} \varphi_a \to \varphi_{f(a)}]\!] \quad \text{where } \varphi_a \text{ and } \varphi_{f(a)} \text{ are given by the ind. hyp.} \quad \blacksquare\end{aligned}$$

Theorem 2 (Soundness) *For all elements $\varphi, \psi \in \mathcal{L}(\sigma)$:*

$$\varphi \leq \psi \;\Rightarrow\; [\![\varphi]\!]_\sigma \subseteq [\![\psi]\!]_\sigma$$

Proof. The proof amounts to check that each axiom and rule is sound, which can be done using simple set-theoretical arguments. ■

Theorem 3 (Completeness) *For all elements $\varphi, \psi \in \mathcal{L}(\sigma)$:*

$$[\![\varphi]\!]_\sigma \subseteq [\![\psi]\!]_\sigma \;\Rightarrow\; \varphi \leq \psi$$

Proof. Induction over the structure of σ. For the base case **2** we can easily prove the only non-trivial inclusion $[\![\mathbf{f}]\!] \subseteq [\![\mathbf{t}]\!]$ using either the rule $\varphi \leq \mathbf{t}$ or $\mathbf{f} \leq \varphi$. For the inductive step we let $\bigwedge_{i \in I}(\varphi_i \to \psi_i)$ and $\bigwedge_{j \in J}(\varphi_j \to \psi_j)$ be two elements of $\mathcal{L}(\sigma \to \tau)$ and let a_n, b_n be such that $\downarrow(a_n) = [\![\varphi_n]\!]$ and $\downarrow(b_n) = [\![\psi_n]\!]$. Dropping subscripts on the conjunctions we have:

$$\begin{aligned}&[\![\textstyle\bigwedge(\varphi_i \to \psi_i)]\!] \subseteq [\![\textstyle\bigwedge(\varphi_j \to \psi_j)]\!]\\ \Leftrightarrow\;& \textstyle\bigcap[\![\varphi_i \to \psi_i]\!] \subseteq \textstyle\bigcap[\![\varphi_j \to \psi_j]\!]\\ \Leftrightarrow\;& \textstyle\bigcap\downarrow(\lfloor(a_i, b_i)\rfloor) \subseteq \textstyle\bigcap\downarrow(\lfloor(a_j, b_j)\rfloor)\\ \Leftrightarrow\;& \downarrow(\lfloor\{(a_i, b_i)\}\rfloor) \subseteq \downarrow(\lfloor\{(a_j, b_j)\}\rfloor)\\ \Leftrightarrow\;& \lfloor\{(a_i, b_i)\}\rfloor \sqsubseteq \lfloor\{(a_j, b_j)\}\rfloor\\ \Leftrightarrow\;& \forall j.\exists i. a_j \sqsubseteq a_i \;\&\; b_i \sqsubseteq b_j\\ \Leftrightarrow\;& \forall j.\exists i.[\![\varphi_j]\!] \subseteq [\![\varphi_i]\!] \;\&\; [\![\psi_i]\!] \subseteq [\![\psi_j]\!] \quad \text{by definition of } a_i, a_j, b_i \text{ and } b_j\\ \Leftrightarrow\;& \forall j.\exists i.\varphi_j \leq \varphi_i \;\&\; \psi_i \leq \psi_j \quad \text{by the induction hypothesis}\\ \Leftrightarrow\;& \forall j.\exists i.\varphi_i \to \psi_i \leq \varphi_j \to \psi_j\\ \Leftrightarrow\;& \textstyle\bigwedge(\varphi_i \to \psi_i) \leq \textstyle\bigwedge(\varphi_j \to \psi_j)\end{aligned}$$

We leave it to the reader to check the cases where the formulae $\mathbf{t}_{\sigma \to \tau}$ and $\mathbf{f}_{\sigma \to \tau}$ form part of the conjunction. ■

It should be noted that the formula guaranteed to exist by the Definability Theorem is not unique. In general there are many formulae that denote the same ideal. However, the Completeness Theorem tells us that these formulae are all logically equivalent. Hence, by quotienting the set of formulae by logical equivalence we get a structure which is in bijective correspondence with the ideals of the domain $D(\sigma)$. This quotient structure is also known as the *Lindenbaum algebra* $\mathcal{LA}(\sigma)$ of the logical structure $\mathcal{L}(\sigma)$:

$$(\mathcal{LA}(\sigma), \leq_{\mathcal{LA}(\sigma)}) = (\mathcal{L}(\sigma)/=_{\mathcal{L}(\sigma)}, \leq_{\mathcal{L}(\sigma)} / =_{\mathcal{L}(\sigma)}).$$

The Soundness and Completeness Theorems tells us that this bijection respects the order on the lattices so it is in fact a order–preserving bijection. By the results in the previous section we can conclude that for every type σ:

$$D(\sigma) \cong \mathsf{Fil}(\mathsf{Idl}(D(\sigma))) \cong \mathsf{Fil}(\mathcal{LA}(\sigma)).$$

This is the precise description of the relation between the strictness domains and the formal system. It expresses the fact that there is a bijective correspondence between elements of the domain and sets of formulae closed under conjunction and entailment.

4 Strictness analysis

This section applies the developments in the previous sections to strictness analysis. We briefly review strictness analysis by abstract interpretation and then go on to define a program logic for strictness analysis which is then proved sound and complete with respect to the abstract interpretation. For a general introduction to abstract interpretation see *e.g.*, [2].

We shall be using the simply typed lambda calculus with constants including a conditional and a fixpoint operator. The set of terms, Λ_T, of the language is given by the grammar:

$$e = x \mid c \mid \lambda x.e \mid e_1 e_2 \mid \mathsf{fix}(e) \mid \mathsf{cond}(e_1, e_2, e_3)$$

The typing rules for the language are entirely standard and omitted. The standard denotational semantics, denoted by $[\![\_]\!]^{std}$, interprets each type as a complete partial order (cpo) and each term as an element of the partial order corresponding to the type of the term. Specifically, terms of function type are interpreted as functions between cpo's.

A function f is said to be *strict* iff its result is undefined whenever its argument is undefined. This can be expressed in the standard semantics by saying that $[\![f]\!]^{std}(\bot) = \bot$, where $\bot$ stands for the smallest element in the appropriate domains. The term strictness analysis is used to denote the class of program analyses aimed at detecting when a given function is strict. We shall not go into the details of how strictness information can be used to optimise functional programs, but only refer to [12] and [3].

4.1 Strictness analysis by abstract interpretation

Strictness analysis by abstract interpretation works by interpreting the terms of Λ_T over non–standard domains built up from the two–point domain **2** interpreting the type constructor $\rightarrow$ as the domain of continuous functions. The abstract interpretation of a term f of type $Int \rightarrow Int$ would then be a function $[\![f]\!] : \mathbf{2} \rightarrow \mathbf{2}$. The function $[\![\_]\!]$ takes as arguments a term in Λ_T and an environment mapping variables to values and returns as result the abstract value of the term. It is defined as follows:

$$\begin{array}{lcl}
[\![x]\!]\rho & = & \rho(x) \\
[\![c]\!]\rho & = & \lambda x_1 . \ldots \lambda x_n . \sqcap\{x_1, \ldots, x_n\} \quad \text{where } n \geq 0 \text{ is the arity of } c \\
[\![\lambda x.e]\!]\rho & = & \lambda v.[\![e]\!]\rho[x \mapsto v] \\
[\![e_1 e_2]\!]\rho & = & [\![e_1]\!]\rho([\![e_2]\!]\rho) \\
[\![\mathsf{fix}(e)]\!]\rho & = & \bigsqcup_{n \in \omega} ([\![e]\!]\rho)^n(\bot) \\
[\![\mathsf{cond}(e_1, e_2, e_3)]\!]\rho & = & \begin{cases} \bot & \text{if } [\![e_1]\!]\rho = \bot \\ [\![e_2]\!]\rho \sqcup [\![e_3]\!]\rho & \text{otherwise} \end{cases}
\end{array}$$

The main result in [4] is that if the abstract interpretation of a term denotes a strict function then the standard interpretation of the function is strict as well, *i.e.*, by studying the abstract version of the function we can get information about the strictness properties of the function itself. As all domains are finite, this gives an effective method for detecting strictness properties of functions definable in the typed lambda calculus.

4.2 Strictness logic

We now define a program logic for the simply typed λ-calculus based on the formal system of strictness properties. It is shown that the program logic is equivalent to the abstract interpretation presented above in the sense that all strictness properties that holds of an abstract interpretation of a function can be proved in the strictness logic. The strictness logic is defined by the following rules

$$\textbf{Conj}\ \frac{\Gamma \vdash E : \psi_1 \quad \Gamma \vdash E : \psi_2}{\Gamma \vdash E : \psi_1 \wedge \psi_2} \qquad \textbf{Weak}\ \frac{\Gamma \leq \Delta \quad \Delta \vdash E : \phi \quad \phi \leq \psi}{\Gamma \vdash E : \psi}$$

$$\textbf{Taut}\ \ \Gamma \vdash E : \mathbf{t} \qquad \textbf{Var}\ \ \Gamma[x \mapsto \phi] \vdash x : \phi$$

$$\textbf{Abs}\ \frac{\Gamma[x \mapsto \phi] \vdash E : \psi}{\Gamma \vdash \lambda x.E : (\phi \rightarrow \psi)} \qquad \textbf{App}\ \frac{\Gamma \vdash E_1 : (\phi \rightarrow \psi) \quad \Gamma \vdash E_2 : \phi}{\Gamma \vdash E_1 E_2 : \psi}$$

$$\textbf{Fix}\ \frac{\Gamma \vdash E : \phi \rightarrow \phi}{\Gamma \vdash \mathsf{fix}(E) : \phi}$$

$$\textbf{Cond-1}\ \frac{\Gamma \vdash E_1 : \mathbf{f}}{\Gamma \vdash \mathsf{cond}(E_1, E_2, E_3) : \mathbf{f}} \qquad \textbf{Cond-2}\ \frac{\Gamma \vdash E_2 : \phi \quad \Gamma \vdash E_3 : \phi}{\Gamma \vdash \mathsf{cond}(E_1, E_2, E_3) : \phi}$$

Other constants (including built–in functions) can be treated by adding more rules. A function like addition which is strict in both arguments is defined by the rule

$$\vdash + : \mathtt{f}{\rightarrow}\mathtt{t}{\rightarrow}\mathtt{f} \wedge \mathtt{t}{\rightarrow}\mathtt{f}{\rightarrow}\mathtt{f}.$$

The following proof demonstrates the use of the proof system. The function we analyse is taken from [11], where it was used to demonstrate the limitations of a type system without conjunctive types. It is defined as:

$$f\ x\ y\ z = \textit{if}\ (z = 0)\ \textit{then}\ x + y\ \textit{else}\ f\ y\ x\ (z - 1)$$

Written in our language it looks like $\mathsf{fix}(\lambda f.\lambda x.\lambda y.\lambda z.\mathsf{cond}(z = 0, x{+}y, fyx(z{-}1)))$. We want to show that this function is strict in x and y separately, which in our logic is expressed by the formula

$$\mathtt{f}{\rightarrow}\mathtt{t}{\rightarrow}\mathtt{t}{\rightarrow}\mathtt{f} \wedge \mathtt{t}{\rightarrow}\mathtt{f}{\rightarrow}\mathtt{t}{\rightarrow}\mathtt{f}$$

For notational convenience denote this formula by ψ and let similarly ψ_1 and ψ_2 denote $\mathtt{f}{\rightarrow}\mathtt{t}{\rightarrow}\mathtt{t}{\rightarrow}\mathtt{f}$ and $\mathtt{t}{\rightarrow}\mathtt{f}{\rightarrow}\mathtt{t}{\rightarrow}\mathtt{f}$, respectively. Furthermore, let E denote the term

$$\lambda x.\lambda y.\lambda z.\mathsf{cond}(z = 0, x + y, f\ y\ x\ (z - 1)).$$

and let Γ be the environment $[f : \psi, x : \mathtt{t}, y : \mathtt{f}, z : \mathtt{t}]$.
We then get the proof tree:

$$\dfrac{\dfrac{\begin{array}{c}\vdots\\ [f:\psi]\vdash E:\psi_1\end{array} \qquad \dfrac{\dfrac{\dfrac{\Gamma\vdash x:\mathtt{t} \quad \Gamma\vdash y:\mathtt{f}}{\Gamma\vdash x+y:\mathtt{f}} \quad \dfrac{\dfrac{\Gamma\vdash f:\psi}{\Gamma\vdash f:\psi_1} \quad \Gamma\vdash y:\mathtt{f} \quad \Gamma\vdash x:\mathtt{t} \quad \Gamma\vdash (z-1):\mathtt{t}}{\Gamma\vdash f\ y\ x\ (z-1):\mathtt{f}}}{\Gamma\vdash \mathsf{cond}(z=0, x+y, f\ y\ x\ (z-1)):\mathtt{f}}\ \mathrm{Cond-2}}{[f:\psi]\vdash E:\psi_2}\ \mathrm{Abs}}{\dfrac{[f:\psi]\vdash \lambda x.\lambda y.\lambda z.\mathsf{cond}(z=0, x+y, f\ y\ x\ (z-1)):\psi}{\dfrac{\vdash \lambda f.\lambda x.\lambda y.\lambda z.\mathsf{cond}(z=0, x+y, f\ y\ x\ (z-1)):\psi{\rightarrow}\psi}{\vdash \mathsf{fix}(\lambda f.\lambda x.\lambda y.\lambda z.\mathsf{cond}(z=0, x+y, f\ y\ x\ (z-1))):\psi}\ \mathrm{Fix}}\ \mathrm{Abs}}\ \mathrm{Conj}$$

4.3 Soundness and Completeness

Before stating the main theorem that relates the program logic to the abstract interpretation we introduce some notation:

Notation Let σ be a type, e a term of type σ and FV(e) the set of free variables in e. Assume that $d \in D(\sigma), \psi \in \mathcal{LA}(\sigma)$ and let ρ and Γ be environments mapping variables to values and properties respectively.

We write:

$$\begin{array}{lcl} d \models \varphi & \equiv & d \in [\![\varphi]\!] \\ \rho \models \Gamma & \equiv & \forall x : \rho(x) \models \Gamma(x) \\ \Gamma \models e : \varphi & \equiv & \forall \rho \models \Gamma : [\![e]\!]\rho \models \varphi \end{array}$$

i.e., we overload the symbol $\models$ to mean *i*) a value satisfies a formula, *ii*) an environment of values satisfies an environment of formulae and *iii*) the denotation of a term e satisfies formula φ when e is evaluated in an environment satisfying environment Γ. The main theorem linking the abstract interpretation with the strictness logic can then be stated as follows:

Theorem 4 (Soundness & Completeness of the program logic) *Let e be a term of type σ and assume that Γ is an environment mapping free variables to propositions. For φ a formulae belonging to $\mathcal{LA}(\sigma)$ we have:*

$$\Gamma \vdash e : \varphi \Leftrightarrow \Gamma \models e : \varphi$$

Proof The soundness (the "$\Rightarrow$" in the biimplication) is proved by induction on the length of the proof. The completeness (the "$\Leftarrow$") of the logic is proved by structural induction on the term e. We treat a few of the rules here:

Soundness. For the soundness it suffices to prove that if the premises of a given rule are valid in the semantics then the conclusion is valid too. Induction then gives us that all provable facts are indeed semantically valid.

Abstraction. $\Gamma[x : \varphi] \models e : \psi$

$$\begin{array}{ll} \Rightarrow & \forall \rho \models \Gamma . \forall d \models \varphi . [\![e]\!]\rho[x \mapsto d] \in [\![\psi]\!] \\ \Rightarrow & \forall \rho \models \Gamma . \forall d \in [\![\varphi]\!] . [\![\lambda x.e]\!]\rho(d) = [\![e]\!]\rho[x \mapsto d] \in [\![\psi]\!] \\ \Rightarrow & \Gamma \models \lambda x.e : \varphi \rightarrow \psi \end{array}$$

Fixpoints. $\Gamma \models e : \psi \rightarrow \psi$

$$\begin{array}{ll} \Rightarrow & \forall \rho \models \Gamma . \forall i \in \omega . [\![e]\!]^i \rho(\bot) \in [\![\psi]\!] \quad \text{since } \bot \in [\![\psi]\!] \\ \Rightarrow & \forall \rho \models \Gamma . [\![\mathsf{fix}(e)]\!]\rho \in [\![\psi]\!] \quad \text{since } [\![\psi]\!] \text{ is closed under } \sqcup \\ \Rightarrow & \Gamma \models \mathsf{fix}(e) : \psi \end{array}$$

Cond-1. $\Gamma \models e_1 : \mathbf{f}$

$$\begin{array}{ll} \Rightarrow & \forall \rho \models \Gamma . [\![e_1]\!]\rho = \bot \\ \Rightarrow & \forall \rho \models \Gamma . [\![\mathsf{cond}(e_1, e_2, e_3)]\!]\rho = \bot \\ \Rightarrow & \Gamma \models \mathsf{cond}(e_1, e_2, e_3) : \mathbf{f} \end{array}$$

Completeness Completeness amounts to showing (by structural induction over the terms) that all facts that hold in the semantics can be proved in the logic.

Application. $\Gamma \models e_1 e_2 : \psi$

$\Rightarrow \forall \rho \models \Gamma . [\![e_1 e_2]\!]\rho = [\![e_1]\!]\rho([\![e_1]\!]\rho) \in [\![\psi]\!]$

$\Rightarrow \forall \rho \models \Gamma . d \in \downarrow([\![e_2]\!]\rho) \Rightarrow [\![e_1]\!]\rho(d) \in [\![\psi]\!]$

$\Rightarrow \forall \rho \models \Gamma . \exists \varphi . [\![e_2]\!]\rho \in [\![\varphi]\!] \;\&\; [\![e_1]\!]\rho \in [\![\varphi \to \psi]\!]$ (Definability Theorem)

$\Rightarrow \Gamma \vdash e_1 : \varphi \to \psi \;\&\; \Gamma \vdash e_2 : \varphi$ by induction hypothesis

$\Rightarrow \Gamma \vdash e_1 e_2 : \psi$

Abstraction. $\Gamma \models \lambda x . e : \varphi \to \psi$

$\Rightarrow \forall \rho \models \Gamma . [\![\lambda x . e]\!]\rho \in [\![\varphi \to \psi]\!]$

$\Rightarrow \forall \rho \models \Gamma . \exists d_1, d_2 . [\![\varphi]\!] = \downarrow(d_1) \;\&\; [\![\psi]\!] = \downarrow(d_2) \;\&\; [\![e]\!]\rho[x \mapsto d_1] \sqsubseteq d_2$

$\Rightarrow \Gamma[x : \varphi] \models e : \psi$

$\Rightarrow \Gamma \vdash \lambda x . e : \varphi \to \psi$

Fixpoints. $\Gamma \models \mathsf{fix}(e) : \psi$

$\Rightarrow \forall \rho \models \Gamma . \downarrow([\![\mathsf{fix}(e)]\!]\rho) \subseteq [\![\psi]\!]$

Now, let φ be such that $[\![\varphi]\!] = \downarrow([\![\mathsf{fix}(e)]\!]\rho)$. As $[\![\varphi]\!] \subseteq [\![\psi]\!]$ we have from the completeness theorem for the domain logic that $\varphi \leq \psi$, so we can deduce as follows:

$[\![e]\!]\rho([\![\mathsf{fix}(e)]\!]\rho) = [\![\mathsf{fix}(e)]\!]\rho$

$\Rightarrow \Gamma \vdash e : \varphi \to \varphi$ by induction hypothesis

$\Rightarrow \Gamma \vdash \mathsf{fix}(e) : \varphi \;\&\; \varphi \leq \psi$

$\Rightarrow \Gamma \vdash \mathsf{fix}(e) : \psi$ by the rule **Weak** ■

By combining this theorem with the isomorphism between semantic domains and filters of formulae $\eta_\sigma : D(\sigma) \to \mathsf{Fil}(\mathcal{LA}(\sigma))$ we can give a precise characterisation of the correspondence between the abstract interpretation and the strictness logic. We have that for an expression e of type σ and for environments $\rho \models \Gamma$

$$[\![e]\!]\rho = \eta^{-1}\{\varphi \mid \Gamma \vdash e : \varphi\}$$

i.e., that the denotation of an expression given by the abstract interpretation is determined and determines the set of formulae provable of e in the strictness logic.

5 Conclusion

We have presented a framework for relating abstract interpretation and non-standard type systems. The presentation took the abstract interpretation as starting point and developed a program logic equivalent to the interpretation. It is important to notice that this process is reversible, because this is the basis for demonstrating that the two methods are equally powerful. We believe that the representation of lattices by certain classes of subsets (here ideals) is the basis for relating denotationally and axiomatically formulated program analyses. It should be noted that the representation of join–semilattices by their ideals presented here is a particular instance of a general mathematical construction known as *Stone duality*. In fact the proposition linking the strictness domains $D(\sigma)$ with the formal system $\mathcal{L}(\sigma)$ is a first step towards establishing a natural transformation forming an adjunction between the two functors Fil and Idl. It is well outside the scope of this paper to go into more details about this subject and we shall only refer the reader to [1], [5] and [9].

The work reported here is of course inspired by previous work on strictness analysis via type inference reported by Kuo and Mishra in [11]. The difference between our work and theirs is that whereas they concentrate on obtaining a good implementation of their type system, we have addressed the question of how these type systems arise and why they give correct results. Thus we see our work as complementary to the work in [11]. It is evident that the developments reported here are of limited use if they are not accompanied by advances in the technology of implementing these program logics. Fortunately, work is going on in this area, see *e.g.*, [6].

We have not made any attempt to prove the strictness logic correct with respect to a standard semantics for the language. This is because once we have established the equivalence to the abstract interpretation we can rely on previous correctness results for the abstract interpretation. Still, abstract interpretation uses abstraction maps from the standard to the abstract domains to establish the correctness of the analysis, and an obvious question is what is the corresponding concept on the logical side? It is a fact that we can represent a Scott–domain by the so–called irreducible, closed subsets. We conjecture that it should be possible from an axiomatic semantics based on these irreducible, closed subsets to view abstraction as equating certain closed sets in the standard domain. On the logical side this means that abstraction simply amounts to introducing logical equivalences between properties in the standard semantics, but this needs further investigation.

Finally it would be a natural continuation of the work reported here to apply similar ideas to other program analyses. We are currently investigating the relationship between the binding–time analysis via type–inference described in [10] and the PER–based abstract interpretation presented in [8]. Another analysis worth considering is the system of use–types suggested in [14] which is aimed at estimating how many times a given value is used during execution of a program. There is currently no corresponding abstract interpretation for this kind of analysis so it would be an interesting exercise to see whether the principles presented in this paper can be used to design such an abstract interpretation.

Acknowledgements

Thanks are first and foremost due to Sebastian Hunt for his continued interest in the work reported here. His insight and his helpful comments have been a great support during the whole work process. Thanks are also due to Geoff Burn, Chris Hankin, Dave Sands and the partners in the SEMANTIQUE project for listening to my ideas and suggesting improvements.

References

[1] S. Abramsky. Domain theory in logical form. *Journal of Pure and Applied Logic*, 1990.

[2] S. Abramsky and C. Hankin. *Abstract Interpretation of Declarative Languages.* Ellis Horwood, 1987.

[3] G.L. Burn. *Abstract Interpretation and the Parallel Evaluation of Functional Languages.* PhD thesis, Imperial College, University of London, 1987.

[4] G.L. Burn, C.L. Hankin, and S. Abramsky. The theory and practice of strictness analysis for higher order functions. *Science of Computer Programming*, 7:249–278, 1986.

[5] B.A. Davey and H.A. Priestley. *Introduction to Lattices and Order.* Cambridge University Press, 1990.

[6] C. K. Gomard. Partial type inference for untyped functional programs. In *Lisp and Functional Programming '90*, pages 282–287. ACM, 1990.

[7] S. Hunt and C. Hankin. Fixed points and frontiers: A new perspective. *Journal of Functional Programming*, 1(1), 1991.

[8] S. Hunt and D. Sands. Binding time analysis: A new PERspective. In *Proc. ACM SIGPLAN Symposium on Partial Evaluation and Semantics-Based Program Manipulation*, 1991.

[9] P. T. Johnstone. *Stone Spaces*, volume 3 of *Cambridge Studies in Advanced Mathematics.* Cambridge University Press, Cambridge, 1982.

[10] N. Jones, C. Gomard, A. Bondorf, O. Danvy, and T. Mogensen. A self-applicable partial evaluator for the lambda calculus. In *International Conference on Computer Languages.* IEEE Computer Society, 1990.

[11] T-M Kuo and P. Mishra. Strictness analysis : A new perspective based on type inference. In *Proc. 4th. Int. Conf. on Functional Programming and Computer Architecture.* ACM Press, 1989.

[12] A. Mycroft. *Abstract Interpretation and Optimising Transformation for Applicative Programs.* PhD thesis, Univ. of Edinburgh, 1981.

[13] D. A. Schmidt. *Denotational Semantics.* Allyn and Bacon, 1986.

[14] P. Wadler. Is there a use for linear logic? In *Proc. ACM SIGPLAN Symposium on Partial Evaluation and Semantics-Based Program Manipulation*, 1991.

A Note on Abstract Interpretation of Polymorphic Functions

Gebreselassie Baraki
Computing Science Department
University of Glasgow
Glasgow G12 8QQ
Scotland

Abstract

Strictness analysis of monomorphic functional programs by abstract interpretation has been extensively studied. Abramsky's work describes the extension to polymorphic functions. However, if different instances of a polymorphic function are used in a program, we have to re-analyse to compute abstract functions at each instance used. In the first-order case, Hughes showed how to compute the needed abstract functions without re-analysis. In this paper we develop a method of computing safe approximations to abstract functions of higher-order functions. The approximations are computed from abstract functions of simple instances of polymorphic functions. In the first-order case, the method gives exact values.

1 Introduction

One of the compile-time analyses of functional programs, on which a significant amount of work has been done, is *strictness analysis*. Abstract interpretation is one technique for performing such an analysis. Many algorithms have been developed, together with their proofs of correctness [Mycroft 81, BHA 86, Wadler 87]. But there still is considerable scope for further work, especially where the efficiency of the algorithms is concerned. This is particularly important in the case of polymorphic languages with higher-order functions.

In his work on polymorphic invariance of strictness analysis, Abramsky showed that if the analysis detects that an instance of a polymorphic function is strict then it will detect that every other instance is also strict [Abramsky 85]. Therefore, to determine if an instance is strict, it is sufficient to consider the simplest instance. However, polymorphic invariance does not enable us to compute the abstract function of one instance from that of another. If different instances of the same function occur in an expression, then during the analysis of the expression the abstract functions corresponding to each instance used need to be computed, perhaps requiring multiple analyses of the function body. Obviously, this is inefficient especially when the functions are recursive.

Hughes developed a method by which an abstract function of an instance can be computed from that of the simplest instance [Hughes 88], in the first-order case. The method relies on the semantic relationship between the different instances of a polymorphic function. The semantics of the first-order polymorphic language he considered was defined on the category of domains and continuous functions. Monotypes are interpreted as domains, monomorphic functions as continuous functions and type constructors are viewed as covariant functors. In this framework, a polymorphic function is interpreted as a natural transformation. The difficulty with the higher-order case comes from the contravariance of the function type functor with respect to its first argument.

In an attempt to extend Hughes' work, Abramsky worked in a different category [Abramsky 88]. In this category, the functor corresponding to the function type constructor is covariant. But it is shown that the techniques used by Hughes, for computing the abstract function of any instance from the simplest instance, do not work for higher-order functions. In this paper, we use a slightly different category of domains. We first establish a semantic relationship between different instances of polymorphic functions, weaker than naturality. This relationship will be exploited in building a relationship between the abstract functions of different instances. In particular, we show that a safe approximation to an abstract function of an instance can be computed from that of the simplest.

In Section 2, we introduce the definitions and properties of some mathematical structures which will be used in the remaining sections. An object language and its semantics are described in Section 3. Computation for strictness analysis is done on finite lattices. We will, therefore, study a category of finite lattices and the relationship between abstract functions of different instances of polymorphic functions in Section 4. In Section 5 we prove a weaker version of semantic polymorphic invariance.

2 Preliminaries

The category of domains and continuous functions is adequate to define the semantics of a polymorphically typed functional language with some form of the Hindley-Milner type system. However, in the case of higher-order functions it is difficult to establish a simple semantic relationship between different instances of a polymorphic function. In a paper about semantic polymorphic invariance and strictness, Abramsky used a more suitable category [Abramsky 88]. It was hoped that in such a category, polymorphic functions would be natural transformations. One of the consequences of this would have been the semantic polymorphic invariance of strictness—either all instances of a polymorphic function would be strict, or all instances would be non-strict. However, Abramsky has discovered that there are problems in the proofs of naturality; it was not possible to prove that all polymorphic functions were natural transformations. But working in a slightly different category, the category of domains and embedding-closure pairs, we are able to prove some useful semantic properties of polymorphic functions. In fact, we will also prove a weaker version of the semantic polymorphic invariance of strictness.

Before we study the structures over which the semantics is defined, we will introduce some general definitions.

2.1 Categories

Definition 2.1 *A category* $\mathbf{K}$ *is a structure defined by the following set of data and properties.*

(i) *We have a collection* $Obj(\mathbf{K})$ *of objects.*

(ii) *For every pair of objects* A *and* B *in* $Obj(\mathbf{K})$, *there is a set* $\mathbf{Hom_K}(A, B)$, *called the set of morphisms from* A *to* B.

(iii) *Given* $f \in \mathbf{Hom_K}(A, B)$ *and* $g \in \mathbf{Hom_K}(B, C)$, *we may form the composite* $g.f \in \mathbf{Hom_K}(A, C)$.

(iv) *For every object* A *there is a morphism* $id_A \in \mathbf{Hom_K}(A, A)$, *called the identity morphism.*

(v) *The composition defined in (iii) is associative.*

(vi) *For every* $f \in \mathbf{Hom_K}(A, B)$, *we have* $f.id_A = f$ *and* $id_B.f = f$

Examples

(i) The collection of sets forms a category where sets are objects, functions are morphisms, ordinary function composition is the composition and the identity function is the identity morphism.

(ii) The collection of domains forms a category where domains are objects, continuous functions are morphisms, ordinary function composition becomes the composition of morphisms and the identity function becomes the identity morphism.

Given a category $\mathbf{K}$, its **opposite category**, $\mathbf{K^{op}}$ is defined to be the category with the same objects as $\mathbf{K}$, and for every pair of objects A and B, $f \in \mathbf{Hom_{K^{op}}}(A, B)$ if and only if $f \in \mathbf{Hom_K}(B, A)$. Now it is easy to see how the composition should be defined, and then verifying that $\mathbf{K^{op}}$ is indeed a category is also easy.

Definition 2.2 *A functor* F *from a category* $\mathcal{C}$ *to a category* $\mathcal{D}$ *is a function which maps objects of* $\mathcal{C}$ *to objects of* $\mathcal{D}$, *and for every pair of objects* A *and* B *in the category* $\mathcal{C}$, F *maps every morphism* $f \in \mathbf{Hom}_{\mathcal{C}}(A, B)$ *to* $F(f) \in \mathbf{Hom}_{\mathcal{D}}(F(A), F(B))$ *and satisfies the following conditions:*

$$\begin{aligned} F(id_A) &= id_{F(A)} \text{ for every object } A \in Obj(\mathcal{C}) \\ F(g.f) &= F(g).F(f) \text{ whenever } g.f \text{ is defined in } \mathcal{C} \end{aligned}$$

Such functors are called *covariant* functors. If instead of the second condition above, F satisfies the condition : $F(g.f) = F(f).F(g)$, then F is called a *contravariant* functor.

Definition 2.3 *Let* F *and* G *be two functors from the category* $\mathcal{C}$ *to the category* $\mathcal{D}$. *Let* $\{f_A\}$ *be a collection of morphisms indexed by the objects of the category* $\mathcal{C}$, *and each* $f_A \in \mathbf{Hom}_{\mathcal{D}}(F(A), G(A))$. *The collection* $\{f_A\}$ *is called a natural* *transformation from F to G if for every pair of objects A and B in the category $\mathcal{C}$, and any morphism h in* $\mathbf{Hom}_{\mathcal{C}}(A, B)$ *we have :*

$$f_B.F(h) = G(h).f_A$$

2.2 The category of domains and embedding-closure pairs

We shall denote the category of domains and continuous functions by $\mathcal{C}$. Consider the category $\mathcal{C}^{ec}$ whose objects are the same as that of $\mathcal{C}$ and with morphisms of the form $(e, c) : A \lhd B$ where $e : A \rightarrow B$ and $c : B \rightarrow A$ are morphisms in $\mathcal{C}$, with $c.e = id$ and $e.c \sqsupseteq id$. If (e_1, c_1) and (e_2, c_2) are morphisms in $A \lhd B$ and $B \lhd C$ respectively, then their composition $(e_2, c_2).(e_1, c_1) : A \lhd C$ is defined as $(e_2.e_1, c_1.c_2)$. It is trivial to check that this is indeed a morphism. $\mathcal{C}^{ec}$ is called *the category of domains and embedding-closure pairs.* If (e, c) is a morphism, we shall call s an *embedding* and c a *closure.* For a morphism f in $A \lhd B$ we will write $f = (f^e, f^c)$, where f^e is the embedding and f^c is the closure.

Remark

If h and k are morphisms in $A \lhd B$ then

- $h^e.h^c$ is a closure on B, in the sense used in [Scott 76].
- h^e is *one-to-one* and h^c is strict and *onto.*
- h^e is $\bot$*-reflecting,* i.e. $h^e(a) = \bot \Rightarrow a = \bot$.
- $h^e \sqsubseteq k^e$ if and only if $h^c \sqsupseteq k^c$, and hence h^e is uniquely determined by h^c and *vice-versa.*

Functors

Since we want to model type constructions by functors, we will only consider a certain inductively defined class of functors. We will call such functors *type functors.* Corresponding to product and function space constructors we define $\times$ and $[. \rightarrow .]$ as follows.

(*i*) $\times : \mathcal{C}^{ec} \times \mathcal{C}^{ec} \rightarrow \mathcal{C}^{ec}$

$$\begin{aligned} \times(A, B) &= A \times B \\ \times(f, g) &= (f^e \times g^e, f^c \times g^c) \end{aligned}$$

(*ii*) $[. \rightarrow .] : \mathcal{C}^{ec} \times \mathcal{C}^{ec} \rightarrow \mathcal{C}^{ec}$

$$\begin{aligned} [. \rightarrow .](A, B) &= [A \rightarrow B] \\ [. \rightarrow .](f, g) &= (\lambda h.g^e.h.f^c, \lambda h.g^c.h.f^e) \end{aligned}$$

Here, $A \times B$ denotes the product of A and B in $\mathcal{C}$, and $[A \rightarrow B]$ denotes the space of continuous functions from A to B. We shall write $[f \rightarrow g]$ for $[. \rightarrow .](f, g)$. In general, corresponding to type constructors which involve n type variables we define functors from $(\mathcal{C}^{ec})^n$ to $\mathcal{C}^{ec}$. This will include the identity functor Id and constant functors. For any type functor F defined in this way there are two functors F^e and F^c from $(\mathcal{C}^{ec})^n$ to $\mathcal{C}$ and $\mathcal{C}^{op}$ respectively. On objects both functors act like F. On morphisms, F^e selects the embedding and F^c selects the closure.

It is possible to introduce an ordering on $A \lhd B$ by letting $f \sqsubseteq g$ whenever $f^e \sqsubseteq g^e$. Thus, it makes sense to talk about monotonicity of functors. For example, we have the following proposition about the function type functor.

Proposition 2.1 *The functors* $[. \to .]^e$ *and* $[. \to .]^c$ *are monotonic in their second and first argument respectively. On the other hand, they are anti-monotonic with respect to their first and second argument respectively.*

For any type functors F and G, we define the type functors $F \times G$ and $F \to G$ by

(*i*)

$$\begin{aligned}(F \times G)(A) &= F(A) \times G(A)\\ (F \times G)(h) &= ((F^e \times G^e)(h), (F^c \times G^c)(h))\end{aligned}$$

(*ii*)

$$\begin{aligned}(F \to G)(A) &= [F(A) \to G(A)]\\ (F \to G)(h) &= (\lambda k.G^e(h).k.F^c(h), \lambda k.G^c(h).k.F^e(h))\end{aligned}$$

Proposition 2.2 *If F is a first-order type functor then F^e is monotonic and F^c is anti-monotonic.*

Definition 2.4 *If F and G are functors and f is a family $\{f_A\}$ of morphisms indexed by domains and $f_A : F(A) \to G(A)$, we say that f is a lax natural transformation if for any morphism $h : A \lhd B$ we have :*

$$G^c(h).f_B \sqsubseteq f_A.F^c(h)$$

In such cases we shall write $f : F \stackrel{\cdot}{\longrightarrow}_{\sqsubseteq} G$.

Remark

- the f_A's are continuous functions between domains, not embedding-closure pairs.
- the inequality in the definition above is equivalent to

$$f_B.F^e(h) \sqsubseteq G^e(h).f_A$$

- If equality holds, in the definition of lax natural transformations, for the collection $\{f_A\}$, then f becomes a natural transformation from G^c to F^c.

In the next section, we will show that polymorphic functions are lax natural transformations. In the first-order case we have natural transformations.

3 The Object Language

As in [Abramsky 88] we only consider polymorphic functional programs which are built from the constants id, Ap, fst, snd, fix and variables by the constructors <.,.>, ., and Λ. Let A, B and C be domains. Now, the semantics of instances of the polymorphic functions may be given by :

$$\begin{aligned}
\mathtt{fst}_{A,B}(x,y) &= x \\
\mathtt{snd}_{A,B}(x,y) &= y \\
<\mathtt{f},\mathtt{g}>_{A,B,C}(x) &= (f(x),g(x)) \\
\mathtt{Ap}_{A,B}(f,x) &= f(x) \\
\Lambda_{A,B,C}(f)(x)(y) &= f(x,y) \\
\mathtt{fix}_A(f) &= \bigsqcup_{n\in\omega} f^n(\perp)
\end{aligned}$$

Now, in the first-order case polymorphic functions are natural transformations. However, this does not hold for higher-order functions. What we can prove, though, is that polymorphic functions are lax natural transformations. The statement of the theorem will be similar to the one that appears in [Abramsky 88] except that here we have lax natural transformations.

Theorem 3.1 **(i)** fst *:* $F \xrightarrow{\cdot}_{\sqsubseteq} G$ *is a lax natural transformation. Here,* $F, G : (\mathcal{C}^{sr})^2 \rightarrow \mathcal{C}^{sr}$ *are defined by* $F(A,B) = A \times B$ *and* $G(A,B) = A$.

(ii) *Similarly,* snd, Ap *and* fix *are lax natural transformations.*

(iii) *If* f *:* $F \xrightarrow{\cdot}_{\sqsubseteq} G$ *and* g *:* $F \xrightarrow{\cdot}_{\sqsubseteq} H$ *are lax natural transformations then;* <f,g> *:* $F \xrightarrow{\cdot}_{\sqsubseteq} (G \times H)$ *is a lax natural transformation.*

(iv) *If* f *:* $(F \times G) \xrightarrow{\cdot}_{\sqsubseteq} H$ *is a lax natural transformation then;* Λ(f) *:* $F \xrightarrow{\cdot}_{\sqsubseteq} (G \rightarrow H)$ *is a lax natural transformation.*

Proof

Throughout the proof it will be assumed that A, B, C and D are domains, $h_1 : A \lhd C$ and $h_2 : B \lhd D$ are morphisms. It is very simple to verify that fst and snd are lax natural transformations. Therefore, we will start with (ii).

(ii) To prove that Ap is a lax natural transformation, we need to show that

$$\mathtt{Ap}_{A,B}.((\lambda.k.h_2^c.k.h_1^e) \times h_1^e) \;\sqsupseteq\; h_2^c.\mathtt{Ap}_{C,D}$$

But for any f and x

$$\begin{aligned}
(\mathtt{Ap}_{A,B}.((\lambda.k.h_2^c.k.h_1^e) \times h_1^e))(f,x) &= h_2^c(f(h_1^e(h_1^c(x)))) \\
&\sqsupseteq h_2^c(f(x)) \\
&= (h_2^c.\mathtt{Ap}_{C,D})(f,x)
\end{aligned}$$

Thus Ap is a lax natural transformation.

To prove that fix is a lax natural transformation, we need to show that

$$\mathtt{fix}_A.(\lambda.k.h_1^c.k.h_1^e) \;\sqsupseteq\; h_1^c.\mathtt{fix}_C$$

But for any f

$$\begin{aligned}(\mathtt{fix}_A.(\lambda.k.h_1^c.k.h_1^e))(f) &= \mathtt{fix}_A(h_1^c.f.h_1^e)(f) \\ &= \bigsqcup_{n\in\omega}(h_1^c.f.h_1^e)^n(\bot) \\ &\sqsupseteq \bigsqcup_{n\in\omega}(h_1^c.f^n.h_1^e)(\bot)\end{aligned}$$

Moreover,

$$\begin{aligned}\bigsqcup_{n\in\omega}(h_1^c.f^n.h_1^e)(\bot) &\sqsupseteq \bigsqcup_{n\in\omega}(h_1^c(f^n(\bot))) \\ &= h_1^c(\bigsqcup_{n\in\omega}(f^n(\bot))) \\ &= h_1^c(\mathtt{fix}_C(f))\end{aligned}$$

Thus we have the desired result.

(iii) We skip this because its proof is very simple.

(iv) From the hypothesis, we have

$$\mathtt{f}_A.(F^c(h_1)\times G^c(h_1)) \sqsupseteq H^c(h_1).\mathtt{f}_C$$

Thus, for any x and y we have

$$(\mathtt{f}_A.(F^c(h_1)\times G^c(h_1)))(x,y) \sqsupseteq (H^c(h_1).\mathtt{f}_C)(x,y)$$

which means

$$\mathtt{f}_A.(F^c(h_1)(x), G^c(h_1)(y)) \sqsupseteq H^c(h_1)(\mathtt{f}_C(x,y))$$

We want to show that

$$\Lambda(\mathtt{f}_A).F^c(h_1)(x)(y) \sqsupseteq (G\to H)^c(h_1).\Lambda(\mathtt{f}_C)(x)(y)$$

But it can be shown that this is equivalent to

$$\mathtt{f}_A(F^c(h_1)(x),y) \sqsupseteq H^c(h_1)(\mathtt{f}_C(x, G^e(h_1)(y)))$$

From the definition of embedding-closure pairs we get

$$\mathtt{f}_A(F^c(h_1)(x),y) = \mathtt{f}_A(F^c(h_1)(x), G^c(h_1)(G^e(h_1)(y)))$$

By hypothesis, we have

$$\mathtt{f}_A(F^c(h_1)(x), G^c(h_1)(G^e(h_1)(y)) \sqsupseteq H^c(h_1)(\mathtt{f}_C(x, G^e(h_1)(y)))$$

Combining these two statements we obtain the desired inequality. Thus, $\Lambda(\mathtt{f})$ is a lax natural transformation. □

Remark

Only in the parts of the proof of the theorem which involve higher-order functions do we have inequalities. Therefore, first-order polymorphic functions are natural transformations.

4 The category of finite lattices and embedding-closure pairs

During strictness analysis, calculation is performed on finite lattices. Therefore, we will more closely study the category $\mathcal{A}^{ec}$ of finite lattices as a subcategory of $\mathcal{C}^{ec}$. Of special interest will be the morphisms from the two-element domain $\mathbf{2}(=\{0,1\}$, with $0 \sqsubseteq 1)$ to other finite lattices and their images under the various functors.

Definition 4.1 *Let A be a finite lattice and $a \in A$ different from the top element, $\top_A$, of A. The functions $h_a^e : \mathbf{2} \to A$ and $h_a^c : A \to \mathbf{2}$ are defined by*

$$h_a^e(x) = \begin{cases} a & \text{if } x = 0 \\ \top_A & \text{if } x = 1 \end{cases}$$

$$h_a^c(x) = \begin{cases} 0 & \text{if } x \sqsubseteq a \\ 1 & \text{otherwise} \end{cases}$$

It is now simple to show that $h = (h_a^e, h_a^c)$ is a morphism in $\mathbf{2} \lhd A$. Moreover, every morphism in $\mathbf{2} \lhd A$ has this form. This is because if (f,g) is a morphism, then by letting $a = f(0)$, it is easy to show that $(f,g) = (h_a^e, h_a^c)$. Although the definitions of h_a^e and h_a^c would make sense if a were $\top_A$, (h_a^e, h_a^c) would not be a morphism in $\mathbf{2} \lhd A$.

Type functors which do not involve the function space constructor will be referred to as *first-order type functors*. We will now state and prove a number of properties of functors and transformations.

Proposition 4.1 *Let F be a first-order type functor. Let A be a finite lattice with $a, b \in A$. Suppose $h : \mathbf{2} \lhd A$ is a morphism. Then*

(i)

$$\begin{aligned} F^e(h_{a \sqcap b}) &= F^e(h_a) \sqcap F^e(h_b) \\ F^c(h_{a \sqcap b}) &= F^c(h_a) \sqcup F^c(h_b). \end{aligned}$$

(ii) *$F^e(h)$ is distributive over both $\sqcup$ and $\sqcap$.*
$F^c(h)$ is distributive over $\sqcup$.

Proof
We will use induction on the structure of the functors.

(i) In the cases where $F = Id$ or F is a constant functor it is trivial to show that the properties hold. Suppose $F = G \times H$ and assume that the properties hold for G and H. Then,

$$\begin{aligned} F^e(h_{a \sqcap b}) &= G^e(h_{a \sqcap b}) \times H^e(h_{a \sqcap b}) \\ &= (G^e(h_a) \sqcap G^e(h_b)) \times (H^e(h_a) \sqcap H^e(h_b)) \\ &= (G^e(h_a) \times H^e(h_a)) \sqcap (G^e(h_b) \times H^e(h_b)) \\ &= F^e(h_a) \sqcap F^e(h_b) \end{aligned}$$

Replacing e and, where appropriate, $\sqcap$ by c and $\sqcup$ respectively in the above proof yields a proof of the second statement.

(ii) Again, the cases where $F = Id$ or F is a constant functor are trivial. Suppose $F = G \times H$ and assume that the properties hold for G and H. Let $x, y \in F(2)$.Then,

$$\begin{aligned} F^e(h)(x \sqcup y) &= G^e(h)(x \sqcup y) \times H^e(h)(x \sqcup y) \\ &= (G^e(h)(x) \sqcup G^e(h)(y)) \times (H^e(h)(x) \sqcup H^e(h)(y)) \\ &= (G^e(h) \times H^e(h))(x) \sqcup (G^e(h) \times H^e(h))(y) \\ &= F^e(h)(x) \sqcup F^e(h)(y) \end{aligned}$$

The other statements can also be proved in a similar way.
To see why $F^c(h)$ does not in general distribute over $\sqcap$ consider the case where $F = Id$ and h in $\mathbf{2} \lhd (\mathbf{2} \times \mathbf{2})$ is the embedding-closure pair (h^e, h^c) with h^e taking 0 to $(0,0)$ and 1 to $(1,1)$. Now, h^c maps $(0,0)$ to 0 and the rest to 1. Letting $x = (0,1)$ and $y = (1,0)$ we have $F^c(h)(x \sqcap y) = 0$ but $F^c(h)(x) \sqcap F^c(h)(y) = 1$.

In abstract interpretation, we have the operators $\sqcup$ and $\sqcap$ which may be regarded as polymorphic functions. The semantics of instances of such operators, *i.e.* $\sqcup_A : A \times A \to A$ and $\sqcap_A : \mathbf{2} \times A \to A$, may be defined in the usual way for finite lattices A. Now, it is easy to show that the operators are natural transformations.

Recall that, our aim is to be able to establish certain relationships between different components or instances of transformations. In particular, we would like to express the components corresponding to big domains in terms of those of smaller ones. This is unfortunately not possible, but once we know what the smaller instances are, then we can use them to obtain approximate values for the other instances.

Now we come to an important result. It is a result which establishes some relationship between any component of a lax natural transformation and the component corresponding to the lattice 2. More precisely, we have the following.

Theorem 4.1 *If f is a lax natural transformation between functors F and G, and A is any finite lattice then we have :*

$$f_A \sqsubseteq \textstyle\bigsqcap_a G^e(h_a).f_2.F^c(h_a)$$

where a ranges over the non-top elements of A.

Proof
Let h be any morphism in $\mathbf{2} \lhd A$. Then,

$$\begin{aligned} & f_A.F^e(h) \sqsubseteq G^e(h).f_2 \\ \Rightarrow\ & f_A.F^e(h).F^c(h) \sqsubseteq G^e(h).f_2.F^c(h) \\ \Rightarrow\ & f_A \sqsubseteq G^e(h).f_2.F^c(h) \end{aligned}$$

Since h is arbitrary, we have :

$$f_A \sqsubseteq \textstyle\bigsqcap_a G^e(h_a).f_2.F^c(h_a) \qquad \square$$

In strictness analysis it is always safe to replace an abstract function by an overestimate. From the theorem above, if f_A is the abstract function of some instance of a polymorphic function then, it is safe to use $\prod_a G^e(h_a).f_2.F^c(h_a)$ instead. Thus, from f_2 we obtain an approximate value for f_A. The greatest lower bound is taken over n–1 functions, where n is the size of the lattice A. In the first-order case, some optimisations which cut down the number of functions involved exist. Moreover, if we are dealing with natural transformations, what we obtain is not an overestimate but an exact value. We will state a property of embedding-closure pairs before we prove this fact.

Proposition 4.2 *Let F be a first-order functor and A be a finite lattice. Then*

$$\textstyle\prod_a F^e(h_a).F^c(h_a) \;=\; id_{F(A)}$$

We now consider the case of natural transformations between first-order type functors.

Proposition 4.3 *Let F and G be first-order type functors and A be a finite lattice. If f is a natural transformation from F to G then*

$$f_A \;=\; \textstyle\prod_a G^e(h_a).f_2.F^c(h_a)$$

where a ranges over all non-top elements of A.

Proof

Since f is a natural transformation, for any a in A we have

$$G^c(h_a).f_A \;=\; f_2.F^c(h_a)$$

This implies

$$G^e(h_a).G^c(h_a).f_A \;=\; G^e(h_a).f_2.F^c(h_a)$$

since a is arbitrary

$$\textstyle\prod_a G^e(h_a).G^c(h_a).f_A \;=\; \prod_a G^e(h_a).f_2.F^c(h_a)$$

But, from the preceding proposition we have

$$\textstyle\prod_a G^e(h_a).G^c(h_a) \;=\; id_{G(A)}$$

Therefore

$$f_A \;=\; \textstyle\prod_a G^e(h_a).f_2.F^c(h_a)$$

This statement is significant because we already know that first-order polymorphic functions are natural transformations.

The following proposition will be used in minimising the number of functions involved in the computation of approximations to abstract functions.

Proposition 4.4 *Let F and G be first-order type functors and f be a lax natural transformation from F to G. If a and b are elements of a finite lattice A then*

$$G^e(h_a).f_2.F^c(h_a) \sqcap G^e(h_b).f_2.F^c(h_b) \sqsubseteq G^e(h_{a \sqcap b}).f_2.F^c(h_{a \sqcap b}).$$

Proof
Since the functors are first-order, we have

$$\begin{aligned} G^e(h_{a\sqcap b}).f_2.F^c(h_{a\sqcap b}) &= (G^e(h_a) \sqcap G^e(h_b)).f_2.F^c(h_{a\sqcap b}) \\ &= G^e(h_a).f_2.F^c(h_{a\sqcap b}) \sqcap G^e(h_b).f_2.F^c(h_{a\sqcap b}) \\ &\sqsupseteq G^e(h_a).f_2.F^c(h_a) \sqcap G^e(h_b).f_2.F^c(h_b) \end{aligned}$$ □

One of the corollaries of this proposition is the following whose proof is trivial.

Corollary 4.1 *If F,G,f and A are as in preceding proposition then*

$$\textstyle\bigsqcap_a G^e(h_a).f_2.F^c(h_a) = \bigsqcap_t G^e(h_t).f_2.F^c(h_t)$$

where a ranges over elements of A-$\{\top_A\}$ and t ranges over elements of $\{x \in A : x \sqsubset y \Rightarrow y = \top_A\}$.

5 Semantic Polymorphic Invariance

In practice, the polymorphic invariance of strictness analysis which was proved in [Abramsky 85] is satisfactory as long as the analysis is done by an abstract interpretation of the type described in the same paper. But if more powerful methods of analysing programs are developed, then polymorphic invariance has to be studied again in relation with the new methods. This is because it does not provide any information about functions whose strictness could not be decided by the abstract interpretation. It is conceivable that other methods may succeed in detecting the strictness of some instances of these functions. What can one say about the remaining instances? Although we do not have a complete answer to this question, we will prove a partial result which roughly states that the strictness of simple instances implies the strictness of the more complex ones.

Proposition 5.1 *Let $f : F \stackrel{\cdot}{\longrightarrow}_{\sqsubseteq} G$ be a lax natural transformation. Suppose there is a morphism $h \in \mathbf{2} \lhd A$. Then, if f_2 is strict then so is f_A.*

Proof
The morphism $h = (h^e, h^c)$ may be chosen so that h^e is strict. For any type functor H, if h^e is strict then $H^e(h)$ is also strict. Suppose f_2 is strict.
Since f is a lax natural transformation, we have

$$f_A.F^e(h) \sqsubseteq G^e(h).f_2$$

This implies that

$$f_A(F^e(h)(\bot)) \sqsubseteq G^e(h)(f_2(\bot))$$

Since f_2, $F^e(h)$ and $G^e(h)$ are all strict,

$$f_A(\bot) = \bot$$ □

6 Conclusion

One of the consequences of our choice of the structures over which we defined the semantics of the language is a weaker version of semantic polymorphic invariance of strictness. More importantly, we have described a method of finding safe approximations for abstract functions of instances of polymorphic functions. These approximations are expressed in terms of the abstract function of the simplest instance. However, a good approximation is obtained by computing the greatest lower bound of several functions. The number of the functions may be large, making the computation expensive. Currently, we are investigating efficient ways of computing the greatest lower bound.

Acknowledgement

I am very grateful to John Hughes, my supervisor, for his help and encouragement. He made several useful comments and suggestions on a draft of this paper.

References

[Abramsky 85] S. Abramsky. *Strictness Analysis and Polymorphic Invariance.* In *Programs as Data Objects*, LNCS 217, 1985.

[AH 87] S. Abramsky and C.L. Hankin (eds). *Abstract Interpretation of Declarative Languages.* Ellis-Horwood, 1987.

[Abramsky 88] S. Abramsky. *Notes on Strictness Analysis for Polymorphic Functions.* Draft paper, 1988.

[BHA 86] G.L. Burn, C.L. Hankin and S. Abramsky. *Strictness Analysis for Higher-Order Functions.* Science of Computer Programming, 7, 1986.

[Hughes 88] R.J.M. Hughes. *Abstract Interpretation of First-Order Polymorphic Functions.* Proceedings of the 1988 Glasgow Workshop on Functional Programming, Research Report 89/R4, University of Glasgow, 1989.

[Mycroft 81] A. Mycroft. *Abstract Interpretation and Optimising Transformations for Applicative Programs.* Ph.D. Thesis, University of Edinburgh, 1981.

[Scott 76] D. Scott. *Data Types as Lattices.* SIAM Journal of Computing, Vol 5, No. 3, 1976.

[Wadler 87] P. Wadler. *Strictness Analysis on Non-Flat Domains by Abstract Interpretation.* In [AH 87].

Incremental Polymorphism

Shail Aditya   Rishiyur S. Nikhil
Laboratory for Computer Science, MIT.

Abstract

The Hindley/Milner polymorphic type system has been adopted in many programming languages because it provides the convenience of programming languages like Lisp along with the correctness guarantees that come with static type-checking. However, programming environments for such languages are still not as flexible as those for Lisp. In particular, the style of incremental, top-down program development possible in Lisp is precluded because the type inference system is usually formulated as a "batch system" that must examine definitions before their uses. This may require large parts of the program to be recompiled when a small editing change is performed.

In this paper, we attempt to strike a balance between the apparently conflicting goals of incremental, top-down programming flexibility and static type-checking. We present an incremental typing mechanism in which top-level phrases can be compiled one by one, in any order, and repeatedly (due to editing). We show that the incremental type system is sound and complete with respect to the more traditional "batch system". The system derives flexibility from the inherent polymorphism of the Hindley/Milner type system and minimizes the overhead of book-keeping and recompilation. Our system is implemented and has been in use by dozens of users for more than two years.

1 Introduction

Modern computing environments strive for several desirable features: the environments should support the development of reliable programs, *i.e.*, they should be able to detect as many programming errors as early as possible; the environments should be robust, *i.e.*, they must gracefully report all errors and exceptions as and when they occur; finally, the environments should have flexible and interactive facilities for editing, testing and debugging of programs.

Strongly typed languages meet the first goal by guaranteeing that "type-consistent" programs will not incur run-time type-errors. Recent programming languages based on the Hindley/Milner type system [4, 8] also provide the convenience

---

Current address for both authors: Laboratory for Computer Science, Massachusetts Institute of Technology, 545 Technology Square, Cambridge, Massachusetts 02139. Current Internet e-mail address: shail@abp.lcs.mit.edu and nikhil@abp.lcs.mit.edu.

This paper describes research done at the Laboratory for Computer Science of the Massachusetts Institute of Technology. Funding for the Laboratory is provided in part by the Advanced Research Projects Agency of the Department of Defense under Office of Naval Research contract N00014-89-J-1988.

of type polymorphism and automatic type inference. But most programming environments for such languages have to compromise the flexibility of incremental, top-down program development in order to achieve this "type-consistency" over the whole program. This is because the Hindley/Milner type system is usually formulated as a "batch system" that must examine the definitions before they can be used and the complete program before any of its parts can be exercised. The problem is further complicated due to polymorphism where the meaning of "type-consistency" is one of inclusion, rather than equality.

In this paper, we will address the issue of providing a robust and interactive programming environment for Id, which is a polymorphic, strongly typed, incrementally compiled, parallel programming language developed at the Laboratory for Computer Science, MIT [11]. Id's typing mechanism is based on the Hindley/Milner type inference system, but it differs from its traditional description in that it is "incremental" in nature. We have modified and extended the standard Hindley/Milner type inference algorithm to facilitate incremental development and testing of programs. In this paper, we will describe this incremental algorithm used in Id. We will also show its correctness (soundness and completeness) with respect to the standard formulation of the Hindley/Milner type inference algorithm that examines the complete program. Our goal is to produce the same typings as obtained *via* the standard algorithm, only that we produce them incrementally. For convenience, we will refer to the traditional type inference mechanism as the "batch system" and our mechanism as the "incremental system" throughout the paper.

The paper is organized as follows. Section 2 discusses a few other interactive programming environments and motivates the incremental approach taken in Id. Section 3 establishes the notations used in this paper. Section 4 describes the issues in incremental type inference under an interactive environment *via* several examples. Section 5 describes our incremental type inference system in detail. In Section 6 we show its correctness. Section 7 extends the incremental algorithm to handle complex editing situations. In Section 8 we discuss the complexity of our system and briefly describe some possible optimizations that are detailed in appendix A. Finally, in Section 9 we summarize our results and compare them with the related work in this field.

2 Background

Nikhil in [10] pointed out the disparity between the goals of an incremental programming environment, and ML-like type inference system. ML [2, 9] is interactive, but a session in ML is essentially a large lexically nested ML program. Each toplevel definition has the rest of the session as its scope. Thus, editing an earlier definition may force the user to recompile and reload all the intermediate definitions that used it[1]. In building large systems, the recompilation and reloading of large pieces of potentially unrelated code, just to recreate the same environment every time a small error is detected, is at best, quite annoying.

In Miranda [16, 17], this problem is resolved by making the unit of compilation

[1]SML's module mechanism gives some relief in this respect, due to separate compilation.

to be a whole file (also called a "Miranda script"). Definitions within a file may appear in any order and the compiler is responsible for reordering them during compilation. The interactive session only evaluates expressions using definitions from the current script. But, definition level incrementality has been lost, and editing forces entire files to be recompiled.

In contrast, Lisp programming environments smoothly integrate the editor, the compiler, and the read-evaluate-print loop. The unit of compilation in these systems is a single top-level definition. They allow the user to furnish multiple top-level definitions, either together, or one by one in any order, resolving global references to other definitions automatically by dynamic linking. The user can test, debug, and edit these definitions incrementally, without waiting to write the complete program or having to recompile a substantial fraction of the definitions already supplied.

In Id, we attempt to achieve the flexibility of Lisp-like environments along with static type-checking. The programming environment for Id, called "Id World"[12], smoothly integrates the editor, the Id compiler, and the underlying execution vehicle. Like Lisp, our unit of compilation is a single top-level definition. Each compiled definition is accumulated into a flat global environment, implying that edited definitions are immediately and automatically made available to other definitions that use them. Simple interprocedural book-keeping maintains type-consistency between the definition and the uses of each top-level identifier. The book-keeping mechanism derives flexibility from the polymorphism of the definitions, flagging only inconsistent definitions for recompilation. As a consequence, we permit out of order compilation, redefinition, and editing with minimum overhead, while still guaranteeing type correctness before program execution. We also allow executing partially defined Id programs, where the undefined identifiers simply generate an exception if actually used at run-time. Again, the incremental book-keeping mechanism helps in incorporating the missing parts as and when they become available with minimum overhead.

3 Syntax and Notation

In this section, we present a brief overview of the notation used in this paper. Readers are referred to [5, 14] for details. Those already familiar with the Hindley/Milner type system may just skim this section for the notation — there are no new concepts introduced here.

3.1 The Expression Mini-Language

The basic expression language used in describing the Hindley/Milner type system is fairly small. We use the same formulation as in [4, 14] with only slight modifications to suit our incremental system. The syntax of the mini-language appears below:

$$x, y, z \in \text{Identifiers} \tag{1}$$

$$c \in \text{Constants} \quad ::= \quad \{\texttt{true}, \texttt{false}, 1, 2, \ldots\} \tag{2}$$

$$
\begin{array}{rcll}
e \in \text{Expressions} & ::= & c & (3)\\
& | & x & \\
& | & \lambda x.\, e_1 & \\
& | & e_1\, e_2 & \\
& | & \texttt{let}\ x = e_1\ \texttt{in}\ e_2 & \\
B \in \text{Bindings} & ::= & x = e & (4)\\
P \in \text{Programs} & ::= & B_1;\ B_2; \cdots;\ B_n;\ \texttt{it} = e & (5)
\end{array}
$$

The above mini-language retains the notion of top-level, independent bindings as units of compilation. A complete program is a set of such bindings. The final binding is special[2] in that it represents a program query and is also evaluated after being compiled within the current environment.

We will freely (and informally) use tuple expressions and tuple bindings in this mini-language because tuples can always be simulated by the function type constructor ($\rightarrow$) alone.

3.2 The Type Language

The standard Hindley/Milner type language is inductively defined as follows:

$$
\begin{array}{rcll}
\pi \in \text{Type-Constructors} & = & \{int, bool, \ldots\} & (6)\\
\alpha, \beta \in \text{Type-Variables} & = & \{\texttt{*0}, \texttt{*1}, \ldots\} & (7)\\
\tau \in \text{Types} & ::= & \pi & (8)\\
& | & \alpha & \\
& | & \tau_1 \rightarrow \tau_2 & \\
\sigma \in \text{Type-Schemes} & ::= & \tau & (9)\\
& | & \forall \alpha.\, \sigma_1 &
\end{array}
$$

3.3 Type Notation

A **Type Environment** maps identifiers to type-schemes. All type variables of a type τ are considered to be **free** in that type. The quantified type-variables of a type-scheme are taken to be **bound** in that type-scheme and the other type-variables are taken to be **free**. This definition extends pointwise to type environments. We will denote the free type-variables of T by $tyvars(T)$, where T could either be a type, a type-scheme, or a type environment.

A **Substitution** S maps type-variables to types. By extension, we can apply substitutions to types, type-schemes, or type environments, in each case only operating on their free type-variables. Given a type-scheme $\sigma = \forall \alpha_1 \cdots \alpha_n.\, \tau$, an **Instantiation** $\sigma \succ \tau'$ is defined by a substitution S for the bound variables of σ so that $S\tau = \tau'$. The instantiation $\sigma_1 \succeq \sigma_2$ is valid if $\sigma_1 \succ \tau_2$ (where $\sigma_2 = \forall \beta_1 \cdots \beta_m.\, \tau_2$) and no β_j is free in σ_1. The key point to remember is that substitutions affect only free type-variables, while instantiations operate only on bound type-variables.

---

[2]This is adapted from the ML interactive runtime environment where the last expression evaluated is referred to as "it".

Given a type τ and a type environment TE, we define $close(TE,\tau) = \forall\alpha_1\cdots\alpha_n.\tau$ where $\{\alpha_1,\ldots,\alpha_n\} = tyvars(\tau) - tyvars(TE)$. When $tyvars(TE) = \phi$, we may also write simply $close(\tau)$ instead of $close(TE,\tau)$.

4 Issues in Incremental Typing

In this section, we will describe the various issues that need to be addressed during incremental type inference by means of simple examples[3].

4.1 Forward References

In Id, all top-level definitions are compiled into a single global environment. So, it is possible and convenient to use functions that are defined later, as the following example shows[4]:

```
def f x = (x+1):(g x);                    % int -> (list int)
def g x = x:nil;                          % *0 -> (list *0)
```

We have shown the inferred type for each of the definitions as a comment appearing to the right of the definition[5]. Assuming that the above definitions are compiled in the order of their appearance, the function `f` uses `g` inside its body as a function with type `(int -> (list int))` without actually knowing anything about it.

When `g` is compiled, `f` "sees" its definition and the system should make sure that all its previous uses are "consistent" with its definition. In later sections, we will describe in detail how this consistency check is formulated and verified. For now, it suffices to say that use of an identifier should have a type that is an instance of the type inferred at its definition. In the above example, it is indeed the case, the type of `g`, `(int -> (list int))`, used within `f` is an instance of the defined type of `g`, `(*0 -> (list *0))`[6]. Therefore, `f` need not be recompiled even though it used `g` before it was defined.

4.2 Editing

Going a step further, we may edit `g` as follows:

```
def g x = x:(x-1):nil;                    % int -> (list int)
```

This restricts the type of `g`, but its use inside `f` is still valid, and no recompilation is necessary. On the other hand, if we had redefined `g` as,

---

[3]Even though all our analysis is based on the mini-language given in section 3, our examples use the full Id syntax for convenience and clarity. In [5], we show a simple translation from Id to this mini-language.

[4]In Id, toplevel function definitions are introduced with the keyword `def` and terminated by a semi-colon (`;`). Also, colon (`:`) is the infix cons operator. Text following a percent (`%`) is taken to be a comment and is ignored.

[5]The type variables appearing in a type are assumed to be implicitly universally quantified at the outermost unless otherwise stated or clear by the context.

[6]This instantiation uses the simple substitution $S = \{*0 \mapsto \texttt{int}\}$ for the bound type-variable `*0`.

```
def g x = x-1;                               % int -> int
```

then the inferred type of g no longer matches its use inside f and the system should detect it and report an error. Note that this analysis is independent of the order of the original definition of f and g, or for that matter, any other definitions that appear temporally in between the definitions of f and g. Such independent definitions are never disturbed; all recompilation requirements, if any, apply only to the definitions that fail the consistency check.

4.3 Mutual Recursion

The situation becomes more complicated with mutually recursive functions, which have to be type-checked together in the Hindley/Milner type system. In the incremental system, such definitions may be compiled separately. We have to either rule out such cases by requiring that mutually recursive definitions be supplied together, or incrementally detect definitions that become mutually recursive and handle them appropriately. Simple book-keeping, as described in section 4.1, may fail to catch type-errors embedded across mutually recursive definitions, as the following example shows:

```
def f x = g f;                               % *0 -> *1
...
def g x = f g;                               % *2 -> *3
```

The above two definitions are mutually recursive and are rejected by the batch system[7]. The incremental system infers the type of f to be `(*0 -> *1)`, as shown above, assuming the type of g to be `(*0 -> *1) -> *1)`. Similarly, when g is compiled, its type is obtained as `(*2 -> *3)`, assuming the type of f to be `((*2 -> *3) -> *3)`. Note that in both cases, the assumed types are instances of their corresponding inferred types, and the simple consistency checking used in section 4.1 is not sufficient to catch the type-error in the above program.

The following example shows that without explicit book-keeping of mutually recursive definitions, the incremental system may, in fact, compute unsound types even when there is no overall type-error.

```
def K x y = x;                               % *0 -> *1 -> *0

def f x = (g f) x;                           % *2 -> *3

def g x = K x (x:(f x));                     % *4 -> *4
```

The K function simply returns its first argument. The inferred types of f and g individually are as shown. The uses of both f and g are instances of their inferred types, so no consistency error is present. But when supplied together and taking into account that f and g are mutually recursive, the correctly computed Hindley/Milner type of g should be `((*4 -> (list *4)) -> (*4 -> (list *4)))` and that of f should be `(*4 -> (list *4))`.

---

[7]The Hindley/Milner type system does not handle infinite types and flags them as type-errors. In this example, the type of both f and g are infinite.

4.4 Editing and Type Relaxation

It is possible during editing that the type of a definition gets relaxed and therefore must be reflected in other definitions that use it. Consider the following example:

```
def f x y = (x+1);                        % int -> *0 -> int

def g x y = f x (y+1);                    % int -> int -> int
```

The type of f constrains the type of g's argument x to be int. Now, if we decide to edit the function f so as to relax its type,

```
def f x y = x;                            % *1 -> *0 -> *1
```

the type of g that was earlier constrained to be (int -> int -> int) can now also be relaxed to (*2 -> int -> *2). The system should be able to detect this as well. Note that this relaxation does not create unsound types but may render the original types as incomplete or non-principal.

Constraint relaxation may also occur due to a change in mutual recursion among definitions. Consider the following example:

```
def fst (x,y) = x;                        % (*0,*1) -> *0

def h x = if true then
            x
          else fst (t x x);               % *2 -> *2

def t x y = h x,h y;                      % *2 -> *2 -> (*2,*2)
```

Since h and t are mutually recursive, the type of the two arguments of t are constrained to be the same. Now, if we edit the definition for h to be the simple identity function,

```
def h x = x;                              % *2 -> *2
```

then the constraint on the arguments of t is no longer present since h can now be instantiated differently. Therefore, the type of t can be relaxed to (*3 -> *4 -> (*3,*4)). The system should be able to detect this and flag the recompilation of t.

5 The Incremental Type Inference System

Our incremental system is based on the standard Hindley/Milner inference rules given in the literature [4, 3, 14], so we will not describe those inference rules again. We follow the description of [14] which expresses the rules for Instantiation and Generalization implicitly. This has the advantage of making the inference rules completely deterministic[8], and we always infer a type for an expression instead of a type-scheme[9].

In this section, we will describe our incremental book-keeping strategy and the incremental type inference algorithm that uses it.

---

[8]This means that exactly one rule will apply to a given expression.

[9]The equivalence of the rules appearing in [4] and those in [14] has been shown in [3].

5.1 Incremental Book-Keeping

The basic idea in incremental compilation is to be able to compute some desired compile-time properties for an aggregate of identifiers in an incremental fashion. This aggregate forms the **identifier namespace** that we operate in. For our purposes, this is the set of all top-level identifiers. Our first step is to define a "property".

Definition 1 *A* **property** $\mathcal{P} = (\mathcal{D}, \sqsubseteq)$ *is characterized by a domain of values* $\mathcal{D}$ *partially ordered*[10] *by the relation* $\sqsubseteq$. *Given two values,* $v_1, v_2 \in \mathcal{D}$ *for a property* $\mathcal{P} = (\mathcal{D}, \sqsubseteq)$, *we say that* v_1 *is consistent with* v_2 *if and only if* $v_1 \sqsubseteq v_2$.

The domain of values is simply a syntactic set of values with some structural relationship defined among its elements. The domain must also contains a special element "$\perp$" (read "bottom") that corresponds to the default property value assigned to as yet undefined identifiers in the namespace.

The interdependences among the properties of identifiers at various times during incremental compilation is maintained *via* sets of "assumptions" defined below.

Definition 2 *An* **assumption** $(x, y, v_y) \in \mathcal{A}$ *is a triple consisting of an* **assumer** x, *an* **assumee** y, *and an* **assumed-value** $v_y \in \mathcal{D}$, *for the assumee's property* $\mathcal{P} = (\mathcal{D}, \sqsubseteq)$. $\mathcal{A}$ *is termed as the* **assumption domain**. *An* **assumption set** A_x *for the assumer* x *is a set of all such assumptions made by* x *and can be written as a map from the assumees to their assumed-values.*

Each assumption domain has an associated consistency checking function. An **assumption check** C *is a predicate that verifies the assumed-value* v_y *of an assumee from a given assumption set against its current value* v'_y *available in the environment for consistency. This check may use the property predicate* $\sqsubseteq$ *for this purpose.*

Assumption domains are characterized by the properties they record and the assumption checks they employ in order to verify consistency. Several assumption domains may be associated with the same property that use different assumption checks. We will see examples of this later on. Also note that an assumption set for an assumer may contain several assumptions for the same assumee corresponding to its various occurrences in the definition of the assumer.

The union of all the property mappings of namespace identifiers to their property values constitutes a **compilation environment**. The sets of assumptions associated with each assumer identifier make up the book-keeping overhead of the compilation environment.

5.2 Overall Plan for Incremental Analysis

The overall scheme for incremental property computation and maintenance appears in Figure 1. Essentially, we process each top-level binding individually, accumulating its assumptions and property values in the current environment.

[10] A partial order on a domain is a reflexive, transitive, and anti-symmetric binary relation on the elements of the domain.

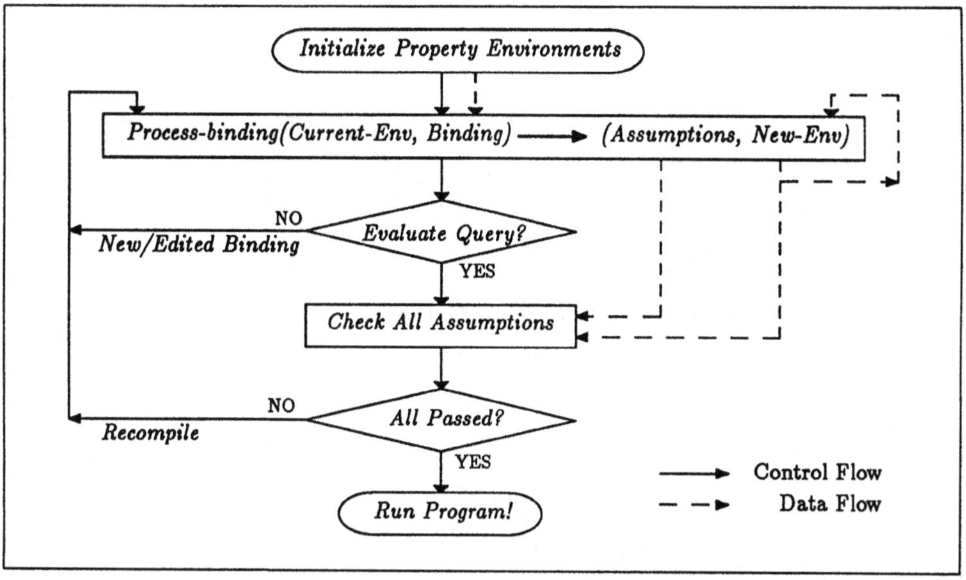

Figure 1: Overall Plan for Incremental Property Maintenance.

If we need to evaluate a query, we first check whether all the accumulated assumptions are consistent with respect to the latest environment, and proceed to evaluate the query only if all the assumptions pass their checks. Otherwise, the failing definitions are flagged for recompilation.

The success or failure of the above mechanism in computing the desired properties correctly and efficiently depends upon several factors. These factors include, the semantic characteristics of the accumulated property domains, their interdependences and computation algorithms, the various kinds of assumptions collected and their respective assumption checks, and the incremental compilation environment history and its maintainance. Now, we will use this incremental property maintenance strategy to compute the types of top-level definitions within the well defined framework of Hindley/Milner type inference system.

5.3 Properties and Assumptions

As a start, we consider only out-of-order compilations, *i.e.*, we will assume that editing of previously defined bindings is not permitted, though, new bindings can still be added incrementally. This is done to ensure monotonicity of the compilation environment and will be relaxed in a later section. We still allow the compiler to issue recompilations of previously encountered bindings if necessary, but the user is not allowed to edit them.

We maintain the following compilation properties and assumptions in this system.

Property – *Type* = (Type-Schemes, $\succeq$) (see Figure 2 (a)). This property records the type of all the identifiers. The "bottom" element of the domain is the

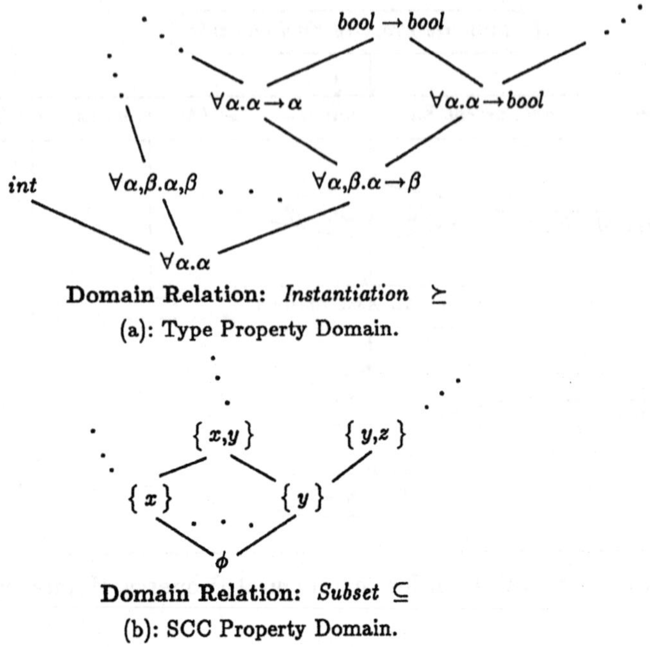

Figure 2: Compilation Properties used in the Incremental System.

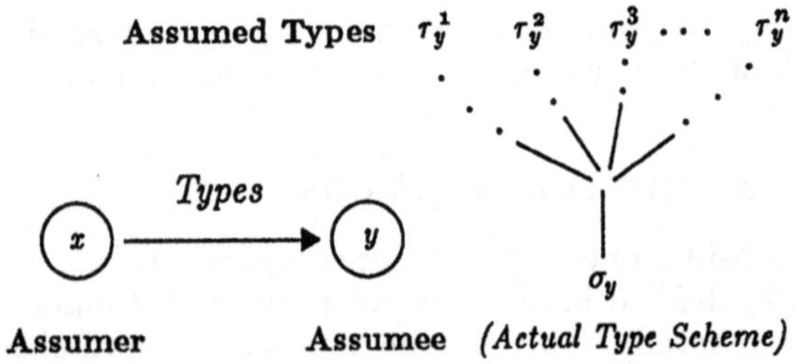

Figure 3: The Upper Bound Type Assumptions used in the Incremental System.

most general type-scheme $\forall\alpha.\alpha$. As stated earlier, we denote the mapping of identifiers to their types in a Type-Environment (TE).

Property – *Strongly-Connected-Components* = (*powerset*(Identifiers), $\subseteq$) (see Figure 2 (b)). The ***strongly connected component*** (SCC) of an identifier is the set of all identifiers in the static call graph that are mutually recursive with the given identifier. We denote the mapping of the identifiers to their recursive sets in a SCC-Environment (SE).

Assumption – We define an assumption domain $\mathcal{M}$ called the *Upper-Bound-Type-Assumptions* that is used to record the actual type instance of each use of a free generic identifier in a top-level definition (see Figure 3).

$$\begin{array}{l}\text{COLLECT: } M_x = \{(y \mapsto \tau_y)\}, \quad \forall \text{ occurrences of } y \in (\mathit{free}(e_x) - SCC_x) \\ \text{CHECK: } \forall (y \mapsto \tau_y) \in M_x,\ \ TE(y) \succeq \tau_y\end{array} \tag{10}$$

These assumptions are called the upper bound type assumptions because in the partially ordered domain of type instances of the assumee's type-scheme, the recorded instances appear as an upper bound of useful instances used by the assumer. We collect a set of such assumptions for each assumer identifier defined on the left hand side of a top-level binding. The associated assumption check tests if these assumed types are valid instances of the latest type-scheme assigned to the assumee identifiers in some later type environment *TE*.

The upper bound type assumption checks ensure that the final type-scheme of an assumee identifier in the environment *TE* is at least as polymorphic as it was assumed when its assumer definition was compiled. If any of these checks fail, we may conclude that the assumee's type-scheme has changed significantly since the compilation of its assumer, and therefore, the assumer definition should be recompiled. For example, after the second redefinition of function **g** in section 4.2, its latest type `(int -> int)` can no longer instantiate the assumed type `(int -> (list int))` recorded in the upper bound type assumptions of the function `f`, which will then be flagged for recompilation by the system.

5.4 Incremental Algorithm

Our identifier namespace consists of the set $X = \{x_1, x_2, \ldots, x_n\} \cup \{\texttt{it}\}$ of identifiers bound in the LHS of the top-level bindings in a complete program as defined by equation 5. The initial property environments TE_0 and SE_0, assign the bottom elements of their respective domains to all the identifiers in the namespace.

$$TE_0 = TE_{lib} \cup \{x_k \mapsto \forall\alpha.\alpha\} \qquad \forall x_k \in X. \tag{11}$$

$$SE_0 = \{x_k \mapsto \phi\} \qquad \forall x_k \in X. \tag{12}$$

TE_0 also includes a standard library type environment TE_{lib} that maps all the standard library function identifiers, predefined operators etc. to their appropriate type-schemes. There are no free type-variables in this environment by assumption.

Def $W_1(TE_{i-1}, SE_{i-1}, B_i) =$
Let B_i *be the binding* '$x = e_x$'.
Construct the current call graph G_i *using the free identifiers of* B_i.
Let $SCC_x^i = \{z_1, \ldots, x, \ldots, z_n\}$ *be the current SCC of* x *in* G_i.
SCC Environment:
$$SE_i = SE_{i-1} \setminus_{SCC_x^i} + \{z_k \mapsto SCC_x^i\} \qquad \forall z_k \in SCC_x^i.$$
for each *top-level identifier* $z_k \in SCC_x^i$ **do**
Let e_{z_k} *be the RHS expressions associated with* z_k.
Let $\beta_{k1}, \ldots, \beta_{kn}$ *be new type-variables.*
$New\text{-}TE_k^i = TE_{i-1} \setminus_{SCC_x^i} + \{z_1 \mapsto \beta_{k1}, \ldots, z_n \mapsto \beta_{kn}\}$.
$(S_k^i, \tau_{z_k}^i, A_k^i) = W'(New\text{-}TE_k^i, e_{z_k})$.
endfor.

$$U_i = Unify\text{-}Columns \begin{pmatrix} S_1^i(\beta_{11}) & \cdots & S_1^i(\beta_{1k}) & \cdots & S_1^i(\beta_{1n}) \\ \vdots & & \vdots & & \vdots \\ S_n^i(\beta_{n1}) & \cdots & S_n^i(\beta_{nk}) & \cdots & S_n^i(\beta_{nn}) \\ \tau_{z_1}^i & \cdots & \tau_{z_k}^i & \cdots & \tau_{z_n}^i \end{pmatrix}$$

Type Environment:
$$TE_i = TE_{i-1} \setminus_{SCC_x^i} + \{z_k \mapsto close(U_i \tau_{z_k}^i)\} \qquad \forall z_k \in SCC_x^i.$$
Upper-bd Type Assumptions:
$$M_{z_k} = U_i A_k^i \setminus_{SCC_x^i} \qquad \forall z_k \in SCC_x^i.$$
Return (TE_i, SE_i).

Figure 4: The Incremental Algorithm W_1.

Our incremental type inference algorithm[11] W_1 appears in Figure 4. This algorithm corresponds to the *process-binding* function of Figure 1. With each invocation of W_1, we compute the compilation properties and the assumptions of a single top-level binding and accumulate them in the compilation environment.

The first step in algorithm W_1 is to compute the static call graph[12] of the current binding $x = e_x$ (also denoted by B_i, corresponding to the i-th invocation of W_1), using the currently reachable nodes. Then, we partition this graph into its strongly connected components using standard graph theoretic techniques [1]. We record the strongly connected component SCC_x^i for the top-level identifier x within the SCC environment.

In our incremental system, we treat all the bindings contained within a SCC as a single *supernode* of the static call graph and type all of them together, each time

[11] The notation $A\setminus_B$ used in the algorithm represents the mapping A with its domain restricted to elements other than those in set B.

[12] A Static Call graph is a directed graph where each top-level binding is a node, and there is an edge from binding $x = e_x$ to binding $y = e_y$ in the graph whenever there is an occurrence of y inside e_x, or in other words, whenever x *uses* y.

```
Def W'(TE,e) =
  case e of
    x          ⇒ let
                    ∀α1 ··· αn. τ = TE(x).
                    β1, ..., βn be new type-variables.
                    τ' = {αi ↦ βi}τ.
                 in
                    (ID,τ',{(x ↦ τ')}).
    λx. e1     ⇒ let
                    β be a new type-variable.
                    TE' = TE + {x ↦ β}.
                    (S1, τ1, A1) = W'(TE', e1).
                 in
                    (S1, S1β → τ1, A1\{x}).
    e1 e2      ⇒ let
                    (S1, τ1, A1) = W'(TE, e1).
                    (S2, τ2, A2) = W'(S1(TE), e2).
                    β be a new type-variable.
                    S3 = U(S2τ1, τ2 → β).        (may fail)
                 in
                    (S3S2S1, S3β, S3(S2A1 ∪ A2)).
    let x = e1 in e2 ⇒
                 let
                    (S1, τ1, A1) = W'(TE, e1).
                    TE' = S1(TE) + {x ↦ close(S1(TE), τ1)}.
                    (S2, τ2, A2) = W'(TE', e2).
                 in
                    (S2S1, τ2, S2A1 ∪ A2\{x}).
  endcase.
```

Figure 5: Pseudo-code for the Inference Algorithm W'.

any one of them changes. This is necessary in order to correctly identify and type the definitions that become mutually recursive incrementally. For instance, the examples of section 4.3 will all be typed correctly when the last definition in their strongly connected component is encountered. This may require keeping track of the actual code of each definition as it is compiled, which is not too difficult to maintain in the integrated editor-compiler environment of Id.

The set of bindings $z_k = e_{z_k}$ for each $z_k \in SCC_x^i$ are type-checked in two phases. First, we type-check each of the RHS expressions e_{z_k} independent of the types of other top-level identifiers of SCC_x^i. We also collect upper bound type assumptions for each z_k from its RHS. Then in the second phase, we unify the defined type $\tau_{z_k}^i$ obtained from typing each RHS, with the type of z_k as used by other bindings of the same SCC. We do this operation as one giant unification of all the terms corresponding to the same top-level identifier. This operation effectively simulates the task of the fixpoint constructor necessary to model recursive definitions in the

Incremental System	Batch System
$TE_0 = TE_{lib} + \{x_i \mapsto \forall\alpha.\alpha\}$:	$TE^t_{x_1} = TE_{lib}$:
$x_1 = e_1$	let $x_1 = e_1$ in
TE_1 :	$TE^t_{x_2} = TE^t_{x_3}$:
$x_2 = e_2$	let $x_2, x_3 = e_{23}$ in
⋮	⋮
TE_{i-1} :	$TE^t_{x_i}$:
$x_i = e_i$	let $x_i = e_i$ in
TE_i :	⋮
⋮	$TE^t_{e_{main}}$:
$\texttt{it} = e_{main}$	e_{main}.
TE_f.	$TE_t = TE^t_{e_{main}} + \{\texttt{it} \mapsto \sigma_{e_{main}}\}$.

Figure 6: A user session in the Incremental System and the Batch System.

batch system.

The algorithm W' that actually computes the type of each top-level RHS expression and records its type assumptions, is shown in Figure 5. It recursively collects all type instances generated for each use of a freely occuring identifier into a set of type assumptions for the current assumer. We will show some assertions about these collected assumptions in the next section. Apart from this extra book-keeping, the algorithm is exactly the same as the standard type inference algorithm W of [14]. Consequently, the theorems of soundness and completeness of the type computed by W with respect to the standard Hindley/Milner inference rules (see [4, 14]) are also valid for W'.

6 Correctness

In this section we outline the proof of correctness for our incremental type inferencing system. The detailed proofs of the lemmas and theorems appearing below are given in [5].

We need to show a correspondence between the incremental type inference strategy outlined in the previous section and the batch-mode Hindley/Milner type system that infers types for complete expressions. As given in equation 5, a program in the incremental system is an unordered sequence of bindings with the program query at the end. In the batch system, one would have to appropriately group mutually recursive bindings, reorder these groups bottom up according to their calling order, and process all of them together as a giant nested expression, with the program query occurring innermost. These two situations are contrasted in Figure 6. The incremental system corresponds to an interactive user session, while the batch system processes entire programs.

We intend to show that the type environment created in the batch system after typing the innermost program query "e_{main}" is exactly the same as the final environment reached in the incremental system after all the bindings have been processed and all their assumption checks have been passed in that environment, *i.e.*, $TE_f = TE_t$.

6.1 Some Results on Type Assumptions

Before we show the correspondence between the incremental system and the batch system, it is instructive to identify the importance of assumptions and assumption checks. The upper bound type assumptions collected *via* the algorithm W' serve as an exact type specification of the interface between the current top-level definition and other definitions. Thus, by recording them, we capture all the external type requirements of the given definition in the form of a type signature, which can be used later to reconstruct its type derivation in a different environment, simply by checking if all these assumptions were satisfied in that environment. This notion of assumption based type derivation tree is defined as follows.

Definition 3 *Given a typing* $TE \vdash e : \tau$ *and its associated derivation tree, we write* $A^{TE} \vdash e : \tau$*, or simply* $A \vdash e : \tau$ *(when TE is clear by context), as another typing representing the same derivation tree that explicitly records all type instances of its free (external) identifiers.* $A^{TE} = assumptions(e)$ *is the set of assumptions constructed inductively as follows:*

$$
\begin{array}{l}
\texttt{Def}\ \mathit{assumptions}(e) = \\
\quad \texttt{case}\ e\ \texttt{of} \\
\quad\quad x \quad \Longrightarrow \{(x \mapsto \tau)\} \\
\quad\quad \lambda x.\, e_1 \Longrightarrow \texttt{let}\ TE' = TE + \{x \mapsto \tau_2\}\ ; \\
\quad\quad\quad\quad\quad\quad\quad A^{TE'} \ = \ \mathit{assumptions}(e_1) \\
\quad\quad\quad\quad\quad\quad \texttt{in} \\
\quad\quad\quad\quad\quad\quad\quad A^{TE'} \backslash_{\{x\}} \\
\quad\quad e_1\ e_2 \ \Longrightarrow \texttt{let}\ A_1^{TE} \ = \ \mathit{assumptions}(e_1)\ ; \\
\quad\quad\quad\quad\quad\quad\quad A_2^{TE} \ = \ \mathit{assumptions}(e_2) \\
\quad\quad\quad\quad\quad\quad \texttt{in} \\
\quad\quad\quad\quad\quad\quad\quad A_1^{TE} \cup A_2^{TE} \\
\quad\quad \texttt{let}\ x \ = \ e_1\ \texttt{in}\ e_2 \Longrightarrow \\
\quad\quad\quad\quad\quad\quad \texttt{let}\ TE' = TE + \{x \mapsto \mathit{close}(TE, \tau_1)\}\ ; \\
\quad\quad\quad\quad\quad\quad\quad A_1^{TE} \ = \ \mathit{assumptions}(e_1)\ ; \\
\quad\quad\quad\quad\quad\quad\quad A_2^{TE'} \ = \ \mathit{assumptions}(e_2) \\
\quad\quad\quad\quad\quad\quad \texttt{in} \\
\quad\quad\quad\quad\quad\quad\quad A_1^{TE} \cup A_2^{TE'} \backslash_{\{x\}} \\
\quad \texttt{endcase.}
\end{array}
$$

Note that there may be several type instances recorded in A^{TE} for the same identifier x corresponding to its various occurrences within e. Also note that A^{TE} is not a type environment in itself, but it serves as a cumulative record of the use of the free identifiers of the expression e during the derivation of the typing $TE \vdash e : \tau$.

The range of an assumption set A^{TE} is a set of types, so we can apply substitutions to assumption sets just like we do to type environments. The only restriction is that substitutions do not apply to those type-variables in the range that were "closed" *via* the generalization operation during the typing of expression e. We call such type-variables $genvars(A^{TE})$. This restriction has the same effect as in the case of type environments, where by definition, substitutions do not apply to the bound type-variables in their range. The algorithm W' achieves this automatically by always using fresh type-variables to instantiate a previously closed type-variable. Thus, at each stage of the typing derivation, the substitutions used at that point never interfere with the previously closed type-variables.

The following lemma forms the backbone of the assumption based reasoning in the subsequent proofs for correctness of our incremental system.

Lemma 1 *Let* $A^{TE} \vdash e : \tau$ *be a typing corresponding to* $TE \vdash e : \tau$ *defined via definition 3. Then for any substitution* S *that does not involve* $genvars(A)$ *in its domain or range,* $S(A^{TE}) \vdash e : S\tau$ *is also a valid typing corresponding to* $S(TE) \vdash e : S\tau$.

The above lemma provides a way to use the assumption sets to obtain new correct typings from old typings for the same expression.

Now we come back to the algorithm W' (refer Figure 5) and show that the assumptions collected there actually correspond to the typing generated by the algorithm. The proof of this lemma is by structural induction on e and uses lemma 1.

Lemma 2 *If assumption set* A *is collected in the invocation* $W'(TE, e) = (S, \tau, A)$ *then* $A \vdash e : \tau$ *is a valid typing that corresponds to the typing* $S(TE) \vdash e : \tau$ *generated using structural induction on* e *under the type environment* TE.

The above lemma shows that the assumptions collected by algorithm W' are sound in the sense that they denote a valid typing.

6.2 Correctness of Algorithm W_1

The correctness of algorithm W_1 is established in two phases. First, we show that it is complete, *i.e.*, at all times the type environment resulting from type-checking a binding is a generalization of the final type environment TE_t obtained in the batch system.

Lemma 3 *If* TE_t *is the final type environment in the batch system with the type-scheme obtained for the final program query being assigned to the special variable "*`it`*", then for every* $i \geq 0$, $TE_i \succeq TE_t$.

The above lemma implies that starting with the most general type-scheme $\forall\alpha.\alpha$, the type-schemes of the top-level identifiers get constantly refined as their definitions are type-checked, but at each stage they remain complete with respect to their actual type-schemes. The proof of this lemma requires a similar statement regarding the SCC of top-level identifiers, that they grow monotonically from the empty set ϕ stablizing at their actual SCC.

The second step in proving the correctness of algorithm W_1 is to show that the process of incrementally refining the compilation environment eventually terminates, and when it does, it exactly corresponds to the compilation environment obtained in the batch system. As noted in section 5.2, we stop further compilation only when all the assumption checks collected during the various invocations to W_1 are passed successfully by the existing property-values in the current compilation environment. The assumption checks play an important role here in guaranteeing that only a sound compilation environment is acceptable, otherwise the process of incremental refinement continues. Termination is shown by proving that the assumptions checks are eventually passed by some environment.

Lemma 4 *In the sequence of type environments $TE_0, \ldots, TE_i, \ldots$ generated from the various invocations to W_1, there exists an environment TE_f (and every environment after that) that passes all the upper bound type assumptions (M) for all the top-level identifiers, i.e.,*

$$\forall x \in X,\ \forall(y \mapsto \tau_y^i) \in M_x,\ \ TE_f(y) \succeq \tau_y^i$$

and moreover, $TE_t \succeq TE_f$.

The proof of this lemma uses the earlier lemmas 1 and 2 about the properties of assumptions collected. This also requires a similar lemma for the soundness of SCC environment.

The soundness of the types obtained in our incremental system depends on whether all the upper bound type assumptions checks have been passed or not. We state this in the form of a termination strategy.

Termination Strategy 1 *Assuming that all the top-level definitions in the given program are compiled at least once, the incremental compilation system terminates when all the upper bound type assumptions (M) for each of the top-level identifiers pass their check in the latest compilation environment.*

Finally, we state the correctness theorem.

Theorem 5 *Given a complete and type-correct program, when the incremental system terminates, it has computed exactly the same type and SCC environments as computed in a batch system.*

Proof: The incremental system starts in an empty compilation environment (TE_0 and SE_0) as given by equations 11 and 12. So the completeness lemma 3 is applicable. The termination strategy ensures that the system terminates in an environment (TE_f and SE_f) that satisfies the soundness lemma 4. Combining the result of these lemmas we straightaway obtain $SE_f = SE_t$ and $TE_f = TE_t$. □

7 Extensions to Algorithm W_1

7.1 Complete Programs

Uptil now we dealt with a given set of top-level definitions supplied incrementally that were assumed to form a complete program. Actually, the notion of a complete program depends on the program query. Only those definitions that are called by the program query, directly or indirectly, need to be supplied and checked for consistency. The status of other definitions that are unrelated to the given query, is unimportant. Therefore, in the incremental system, we perform the consistency checks only for the minimal set of definitions that are self contained with respect to the given program query. This set can be computed by looking at the minimal call graph rooted at the given query, that does not have any dependency edges going out of it. This can enormously reduce the number of definitions that need to be checked.

7.2 Constraint Relaxation

The other problem that we have not yet addressed is editing that leads to constraint relaxation. The completeness lemma 3 implies that the compilation environment of the incremental system is never allowed to be more constrained than the final environment of the batch system. This may not always be the case due to editing when some constraints on the bindings may get relaxed as shown in section 4.4. It is the user's responsibility to recompile a definition after editing it, but it is the compiler's responsibility to propagate those changes throughout the rest of the program and warn the user accordingly while maintaining soundness and completeness of the derived types.

We can detect these constraint relaxations by using some additional property assumptions and checks as defined below. We can collect these extra assumptions along with the upper bound type assumptions already collected in algorithm W_1.

Assumption – We define an assumption domain $\mathcal{N}$ called the ***Lower-Bound-Type-Assumptions*** that is used to record the actual type-schemes of free generic identifiers used within a top-level definition.

$$\begin{array}{ll}\text{COLLECT: } N_x = \{y \mapsto TE(y)\}, & \forall y \in (free(e_x) - SCC_x) \\ \text{CHECK: } \forall (y \mapsto \sigma_y) \in N_x,\ \sigma_y \succeq TE(y) & \end{array} \tag{13}$$

These assumptions are called the lower bound type assumptions because the recorded assumee type-scheme is a lower bound for the assumee type instances used by the assumer according to the partial order of the type domain. Note that the assumption check uses the same subsumption test as for the upper bound type assumptions, but in the reverse direction. The check fails if the assumee type-scheme becomes more polymorphic than it was assumed to be when the assumer was compiled. This enables the assumer to be flagged for recompilation in order to adjust its type according to the latest assumee type-scheme.

Assumption – We also define an assumption domain $\mathcal{Q}$ called ***SCC-Assumptions*** that is used to record the SCC of each identifier used directly by another identifier from within its own SCC.

$$\begin{array}{ll}\text{COLLECT: } Q_x = \{y \mapsto SCC_y\}, & \forall y \in (free(e_x) \cap SCC_x) \\ \text{CHECK: } \forall (y \mapsto SCC_y) \in Q,\ SCC_y = SE(y) & \end{array} \tag{14}$$

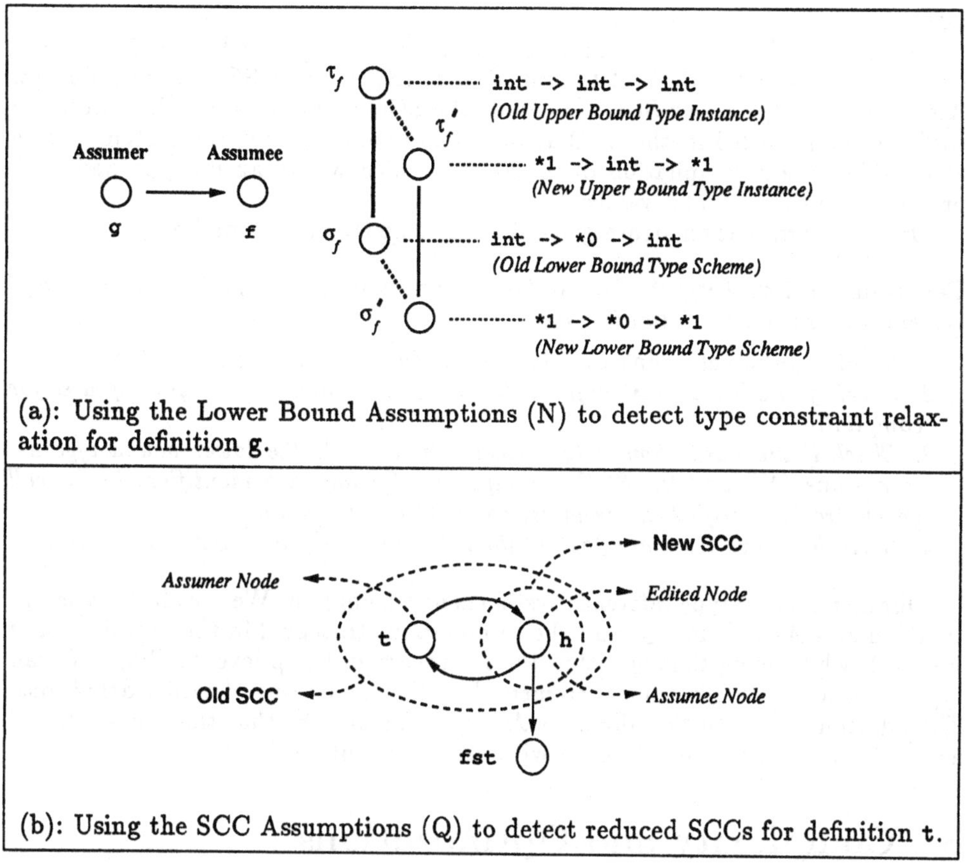

(a): Using the Lower Bound Assumptions (N) to detect type constraint relaxation for definition g.

(b): Using the SCC Assumptions (Q) to detect reduced SCCs for definition t.

Figure 7: Examples of additional assumptions being used to detect Constraint Relaxation during editing.

> The consistency check in this case is a test of (set) equality. This ensures that if the SCC of one of the identifiers changes, then all identifiers that were excluded from its old SCC during this change will fail this check and will be flagged for recompilation.

To see how these additional assumptions help in detecting constraint relaxation, we apply them to the examples given earlier in section 4.4.

The situation for the first example of section 4.4 is pictorially depicted in Figure 7 (a). The function g uses function f with type instance (int -> int -> int) derived from its initial type-scheme (int -> *0 -> int) which is recorded in the lower bound assumption set of g. After function f is edited, its new type-scheme becomes (*1 -> *0 -> *1) which fails the lower bound assumption check against the type-scheme recorded in g's lower bound assumption set. Therefore, the system will be able to flag the recompilation of function g, so that it may benefit from the relaxed type of function f. Note that this type relaxation of f can not be detected *via* the upper bound type assumptions of g because f's type instance recorded there remains an instance of the relaxed type-scheme of `f`.

Looking at the second example given in section 4.4 (see Figure 7 (b)), the function `t` records the SCC of the function `h`, {`h,t`}, in its SCC assumption set. After `h` is edited, its new SCC, {`h`}, fails the SCC assumption check against the earlier value recorded in the SCC assumption set of `t`. Thus, the system will be able to flag the recompilation of function `t` which will relax its type and SCC properties to their correct values.

Our new termination strategy is now only slightly more complex.

Termination Strategy 2 *To test for termination of the extended incremental system, we execute the following steps.*

1. *Build a static call graph with the query binding "*`it` $= e_{main}$*" as the root.*
2. *Check if any leaf identifier from the above call graph has not yet appeared for compilation.*
3. *Check if the upper bound type assumptions (M), the lower bound type assumptions (N), and the SCC assumptions (Q) for each identifiers in the call graph are all satisfied in the latest compilation environment.*
4. *If all the above tests are passed, then the incremental system terminates.*

Our incremental type inference system is now complete. We use all the assumption domains $\mathcal{M}$, $\mathcal{N}$, and $\mathcal{Q}$, and the termination strategy 2 in the overall plan of Figure 1, while using the algorithm W_1 to process each top-level binding. We can type-check a set of definitions incrementally, allowing editing of earlier definitions. The additional assumption domains $\mathcal{N}$ and $\mathcal{Q}$ make sure that the types inferred are both sound and complete even with arbitrary editing.

8 Complexity and Optimizations

8.1 Complexity of the Incremental System

Apart from the inherent complexity of the Hindley/Milner type system, which is known to be exponential [6], our incremental system incurs book-keeping and recompilation overheads. The book-keeping cost can be included within the regular cost of compiling a program. Therefore, we will only focus on the number of recompilations necessary in our incremental system to arrive at the correct typings.

Incremental changes in the program potentially affect all the topologically preceding definitions starting from the point of change in the call graph. Our mechanism of maintaining upper and lower bound assumptions attempts to reduce this set of affected definitions. When the definition of an identifier appearing later in the incremental sequence of compilations falls within the assumed bounds, no recompilation is flagged. Even when these assumptions fail, we can localize the retyping to just the assumer identifier and its SCC instead of the whole program. But, in the worst case, each such recompilation can give rise to more failures in the topologically preceding SCCs and we may end up recompiling the whole program.

As an example, consider the set of definitions given in Figure 8 (a). The call graph in this case is a simple chain as shown in (b). The upper bound type assumptions of the identifier `h` fail the assumption checks as soon as `m` is defined, and

```
def f x = g x;

def g x = h x;

def h x = m x;

def m x = x:nil;
```

(a)

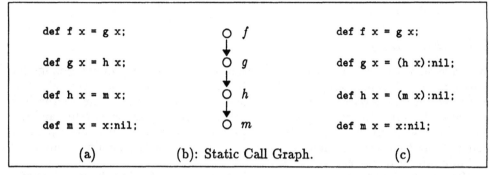

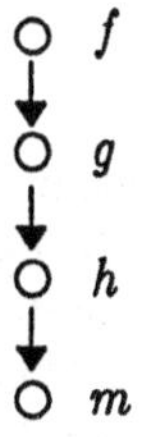

(b): Static Call Graph.

```
def f x = g x;

def g x = (h x):nil;

def h x = (m x):nil;

def m x = x:nil;
```

(c)

Figure 8: Example program to illustrate the high number of Recompilations.

h has to be recompiled. The recompilation of h propagates the type information of m onto h and causes the failure of assumption checks of g and so on. This example shows that the cost of an incremental change to the program could be linear in its size.

Recompiling a definition as soon as some of its assumptions fail, may not be the best strategy. The definitions given in Figure 8 (c) will incur quadratic number of recompilations following this strategy, because every time a new definition is encountered, the upper bound type assumptions of all the preceding definitions fail. It is possible to amortize the cost of recompilation over several assumption failures by adopting a lazy recompilation strategy. If we postpone all recompilations until all the definitions have been encountered, a single sweep of recompilations in the reverse order will settle all the types to their correct values. We have adopted this lazy strategy in Id by postponing all recompilations until we are ready to evaluate a program query (see Figure 1).

8.2 Optimizations

It is possible to further reduce the cost of an incremental change to the program, if it does not affect the properties of other nodes. In our current scheme, whenever a node is flagged for recompilation, we recompile all the definitions in its latest SCC. This is necessary when the new SCC of the node is different from its old one. But this may be wasteful if the editing changes do not affect the SCC or the type properties of the node. Indeed, the only computation really necessary in such cases is the compilation of the edited node itself.

Even when the type of the edited node is different but its SCC is the same, it may not be necessary to recompile all the other definitions in its SCC. This is because type-checking a given definition does not use any information about other definitions in its SCC (apart from the fact that they are all in the same SCC) until the latter part of algorithm W_1 when we unify all the assumed types of the definitions with their computed types in a unification matrix (see Figure 4). Therefore, if we save the assumed types of SCC identifiers while typing a given definition, we can use them directly in the latter part of the W_1 algorithm when some other identifier from the same SCC is being recompiled. The details of these optimizations and a modified inference algorithm W_2 appear in appendix A.

9 Conclusions

9.1 Summary

We have shown that it is possible to obtain correct Hindley/Milner typings for programs of a ML-like language when placed in an incrementally compiled environment geared towards easy editing, debugging and testing. Our approach is guided by Lisp-like environments that offer definition level incrementality and dynamic linking. A single toplevel definition forms a convenient unit of compilation and inter-unit consistency maintenance both in terms of maintaining modularity and minimizing book-keeping overhead.

We have achieved this incremental flexibility by maintaining the interface of a top-level definition with respect to the other definitions in a consistent fashion. We described a general mechanism of incremental property collection and consistency maintenance, which was applied in our case to maintaining the types and the strongly connected components of top-level definitions of a program. We took advantage of the inherent polymorphism of the type system by keeping only the upper and lower bounds of type usage and maintaining the definitions within those bounds.

We should mention that the automatic, incremental book-keeping mechanism we described in the preceding pages is independent of the program granularity it is applied to. It could very well be applied to program modules consisting of groups of definitions, or to complete files, or at a finer grain, to individual subexpressions inside a top-level definition.

9.2 Comparison with Related Work

Some other systems [7, 13, 15] also provide incremental compilation. The GLIDE system [15] comes closest to our philosophy of incremental type inference because it is also based on the ideas presented by Nikhil in [10], but it differs significantly in approach.

The GLIDE system employs an automatic, lazy loading strategy at run-time whereby definitions are automatically compiled and loaded into the run-time environment only as needed by the currently executing expression. It also does retyping of old definitions on the fly, if necessary. In sharp contrast, our system has clearly distinguishable phases of compilation, loading, consistency checking, and execution. Each phase is explicitly initiated by the user which gives him/her complete control over scheduling of various definitions through the individual phases.

The lazy loading mechanism of GLIDE has the advantage of touching only those definitions that are actually needed at run-time, but it forces the system to perform all the necessary consistency checks and resulting retypings immediately as each new definition is loaded. This must be done in order to detect any fresh type errors caused by the changed or new definition before the execution can resume. As pointed out in section 8.1, such a strategy may end up in quadratic number of retypings for programs resembling the example in Figure 8 (c). The GLIDE system attempts to reduce the work involved in such retypings by sharing type information between multiple retypings of the same definition.

In contrast, our system permits early loading of definitions and puts all retyping under explicit user control. The user is guided by the errors reported during consistency checking in appropriately scheduling the retypings so that no definition needs to be retyped more than once. Note that the consistency checks now have to be performed for each definition in the static call graph of the query expression rather than the definitions actually used in its execution.

Probably the most important difference between our system and the GLIDE system is in the actual framework for consistency checking and maintenance. We have been able to formalize an independent system of incremental property maintenance, and have used it successfully to maintain type and SCC properties of top-level definitions. The GLIDE system, on the other hand, has a specific incremental type inference system built into it. Our type consistency checks use the inherent polymorphism of the language to advantage and avoid retyping where simple syntactic interference checks as used in GLIDE may not be able to do so. And finally, we collect and maintain incremental type information only at the granularity of top-level definitions and no record is kept for internal subexpressions. The GLIDE system, on the other hand, maintains type information at all subexpressions so that it may be reused during retyping.

9.3 Status

Finally, we should point out that the incremental type inference system for Id described in this paper has been implemented in the Id compiler and has been in use for the last two years.

10 Acknowledgements

We would like to express our thanks to Zena Ariola, Boon Ang, Alejandro Caro, and Steve Glim, from the Computation Structures Group at Laboratory for Computer Science, MIT, for their insightful comments and help in proof-reading this paper.

A Optimizations for Algorithm W_1

As mentioned in section 8.2, we can optimize the algorithm W_1 by saving the type instances used by each top-level identifier and using them later while typing other top-level identifiers from the same SCC. Essentially, we need to save all the type information necessary to reproduce the unification matrix in the latter half of algorithm W_1 (see Figure 4). We will use our incremental property maintenence system to record this information as compilation properties of the corresponding top-level identifiers. Note that these properties are "local", *i.e.*, they are independently computed for each identifier in a SCC and do not use any information

Def $W_2(TE_{i-1}, SE_{i-1}, B_x) =$

PHASE I:

Let B_x *be the binding* '$x = e_x$'.

Construct the current call graph G_i *using the free identifiers (FId) property.*

$SCC_x^i = \{z_1, \ldots, x, \ldots, z_n\}$ *be the current SCC of* x *in* G_i.

if $SCC_x^i \neq SE_{i-1}(x)$ **then**

SCC Environment: $SE_i = SE_{i-1} \setminus_{SCC_x^i} + \{z_k \mapsto SCC_x^i\} \qquad \forall z_k \in SCC_x^i$.

for each *top-level identifier* $z_k \in SCC_x^i$ **do**

Let e_k *be the RHS expressions associated with* z_k.

SCC Assumptions: $Q_{z_k} = \{y \mapsto SCC_x^i\} \qquad \forall y \in (free(e_{z_k}) \cap SCC_x^i)$.

Let $\beta_{k1}, \ldots, \beta_{kn}$ *be new type-variables.*

$New\text{-}TE_k^i = TE_{i-1} \setminus_{SCC_x^i} + \{z_1 \mapsto \beta_{k1}, \ldots, z_n \mapsto \beta_{kn}\}$.

$W'(New\text{-}TE_k^i, e_k) = (S_k^i, \tau_{z_k}^i, A_k^i)$.

Local Assumptions: $A_k^{local} = \{z_1 \mapsto S_k^i\beta_{k1}, \ldots, z_n \mapsto S_k^i\beta_{kn}\}$.

endfor.

Local Assumption Environment:

$AE_i = AE_{i-1} \setminus_{SCC_x^i} + \{z_k \mapsto A_k^{local}\} \qquad \forall z_k \in SCC_x^i$.

Local Type Environment:

$WE_i = WE_{i-1} \setminus_{SCC_x^i} + \{z_k \mapsto \tau_{z_k}^i\} \qquad \forall z_k \in SCC_x^i$.

else

SCC Assumptions: $Q_x = \{y \mapsto SCC_x^i\} \qquad \forall y \in (free(e_x) \cap SCC_x^i)$.

Let $\beta_1, \ldots, \beta_n$ *be new type-variables.*

$New\text{-}TE_x^i = TE_{i-1} \setminus_{SCC_x^i} + \{z_1 \mapsto \beta_1, \ldots, z_n \mapsto \beta_n\}$.

$W'(New\text{-}TE_x^i, e_x) = (S_x^i, \tau_x^i, A_x^i)$.

Local Assumptions: $A_x^{local} = \{z_1 \mapsto S_x^i\beta_1, \ldots, z_n \mapsto S_x^i\beta_n\}$.

Local Assumption Environment: $AE_i = AE_{i-1} \setminus_{\{x\}} + \{x \mapsto A_x^{local}\}$.

Local Type Enironment: $WE_i = WE_{i-1} \setminus_{\{x\}} + \{x \mapsto \tau_x^i\}$.

endif.

Figure 9: PHASE I of the Updated Incremental Algorithm W_2.

about other identifiers from the same SCC. Therefore, we do not need to maintain any assumption checks for them. We maintain the following two local properties.

Local property – *Local Type* = (Types, =). For each identifier x, we record its local type τ_x^i computed in the invocation of W'. We save this property in a map from identifiers to types called Local-Type-Environment WE.

Local property – *Local Assumptions* = (Local-Type-Environments, =). For each identifier x, its local assumption set A_x^{local} is a map from the identifiers in its SCC to their types as inferred from the invocation of W'. We collect this property in Local-Assumption-Environment AE.

The updated algorithm W_2 appears in Figures 9 and 10, where we have also incorporated the collection of the SCC and the lower bound type assumptions introduced in section 7. The algorithm now operates in two phases.

PHASE II:

$$U_i = \textit{Unify-Columns}\begin{pmatrix} AE_i(z_1)(z_1) & \cdots & AE_i(z_1)(z_k) & \cdots & AE_i(z_1)(z_n) \\ \vdots & & \vdots & & \vdots \\ AE_i(z_n)(z_1) & \cdots & AE_i(z_n)(z_k) & \cdots & AE_i(z_n)(z_n) \\ WE_i(z_1) & \cdots & WE_i(z_k) & \cdots & WE_i(z_n) \end{pmatrix}$$

Type Environment:

$TE_i = TE_{i-1} \setminus_{SCC_x^i} + \{z_k \mapsto close(U_i WE_i(z_k))\}$ $\quad \forall z_k \in SCC_x^i$.

if *only x was type-checked in PHASE I* **then**

Upper Bound Type Assumptions: $M_x = U_i A_x^i \setminus_{SCC_x^i}$.

Lower Bound Type Assumptions:

$N_x = \{y \mapsto TE_{i-1}(y)\}$ $\quad \forall y \in (free(e_x) - SCC_x^i)$.

else

Upper Bound Type Assumptions: $M_{z_k} = U_i A_k^i \setminus_{SCC_x^i}$ $\quad \forall z_k \in SCC_x^i$.

Lower Bound Type Assumptions:

$N_{z_k} = \{y \mapsto TE_{i-1}(y)\}$ $\quad \forall y \in (free(e_k) - SCC_x^i), \forall z_k \in SCC_x^i$.

endif.

Return (TE_i, SE_i).

Figure 10: PHASE II of the Updated Incremental Algorithm W_2.

The first phase computes the SCC of the given definition and compares it with its earlier value. If the SCC has changed then we proceed as before, compiling each of the definitions belonging to the new SCC afresh and accumulating their properties. We also record the locally inferred type of each identifier and its local type assumptions about the other identifiers in its SCC for future use. If the SCC has not changed from its earlier value, then it implies that only the current binding needs to be compiled and we can use previously saved local properties of the other identifiers of that SCC in the second phase, instead of computing all of them afresh.

The second phase, as before, constructs a unification matrix using the freshly computed or previously saved local properties of all the identifiers of the SCC and updates their type properties. It also records the upper and the lower bound type assumptions for the identifiers compiled in the first phase.

References

[1] Alfred V. Aho, John E. Hopcroft, and Jeffrey D. Ullman. *The Design and Analysis of Computer Algorithms.* Addison-Wesley, 1974.

[2] Andrew W. Appel and David B. MacQueen. *Standard ML Reference Manual.* Princeton University and AT&T Bell Laboratories, Preliminary edition, 1989. Distributed along with the Standard ML of New Jersey Compiler.

[3] D. Clément, J. Despeyroux, T. Despeyroux, and G. Kahn. A Simple Applicative Language: Mini-ML. In *Proceedings of the ACM Symposium on LISP and Functional Programming*, pages 13–27, August 1986.

[4] L. Damas and R. Milner. Principle Type Schemes for Functional Programs. In *Proceedings of the 9th ACM Symposium on Principles of Programming Languages*, pages 207–212, 1982.

[5] Shail Aditya Gupta. An Incremental Type Inference System for the Programming Language Id. Technical Report MIT/LCS/TR-488, Laboratory for Computer Science, 545 Technology Square, MIT, Cambridge, MA 02139, November 1990. First published as the author's Master's thesis.

[6] Harry G. Mairson. Deciding ML Typability is Complete for Deterministic Exponential Time. In *Proceedings of the 17th ACM Symposium on Principles of Programming Languages*, pages 382–401, January 1990.

[7] Lambert Meertens. Incremental Polymorphic Type Checking in B. In *Proceedings of the 10th ACM Symposium on Principles of Programming Languages*, January 1983.

[8] Robin Milner. A Theory of Type Polymorphism in Programming. *Journal of Computer and System Sciences*, 17:348–375, 1978.

[9] Robin Milner, Mads Tofte, and Robert Harper. *The Definition of Standard ML*. The MIT Press, Cambridge, Massachusetts, 1990.

[10] Rishiyur S. Nikhil. Practical Polymorphism. In *Proceedings of the Conference on Functional Programming Languages and Computer Architectures, Nancy, FRANCE*, volume 201 of *Lecture notes in Computer Science*. Springer-Verlag, September 1985.

[11] Rishiyur S. Nikhil. Id Version 90.0 Reference Manual. Technical Report CSG Memo 284-1, MIT Laboratory for Computer Science, 545 Technology Square, Cambridge, MA 02139, July 1990.

[12] Rishiyur S. Nikhil, P. R. Fenstermacher, J. E. Hicks, and R. P. Johnson. *Id World Reference Manual*. Computation Structures Group, MIT Laboratory for Computer Science, 545 Technology Square, Cambridge, MA 02139, revised edition, November 1989.

[13] Aaron Sloman and the Poplog Development Team. POPLOG V14 - A portable, multi-language, interactive software development environment with X11R4 interface. School of Cognitive and Computing Sciences, Sussex University, Brighton, BN1 9QH England, December 1990. (Overview description obtained *via* personal communication).

[14] Mads Tofte. *Operational Semantics and Polymorphic Type Inference*. PhD thesis, University of Edinburgh, Department of Computer Science, 1988. Also published as ECS-LFCS-88-54.

[15] Ian Toyn, Alan Dix, and Colin Runciman. Performance Polymorphism. In *Functional Programming Languages and Computer Architecture*, volume 274 of *Lecture Notes in Computer Science*, pages 325–346. Springer-Verlag, 1987. Proceedings of the FPCA Conference held in Portland, Oregon, 1987.

[16] David A. Turner. Miranda: A non-strict functional language with polymorphic types. In *Proceedings of the Conference on Functional Programming Languages and Computer Architectures, Nancy, FRANCE*, volume 201 of *Lecture Notes in Computer Science*. Springer-Verlag, September 1985.

[17] David A. Turner. An Overview of Miranda. *SIGPLAN Notices*, 21(12):158–166, December 1986.

Dynamics in ML

Xavier LEROY
Ecole Normale Supérieure*

Michel MAUNY
INRIA Rocquencourt*

Abstract

Objects with dynamic types allow the integration of operations that essentially require run-time type-checking into statically-typed languages. This paper presents two extensions of the ML language with dynamics, based on what has been done in the CAML implementation of ML, and discusses their usefulness. The main novelty of this work is the combination of dynamics with polymorphism.

1 Introduction

Static typing (compile-time enforcement of the typing rules for a programming language) is generally preferred over dynamic typing (the production of run-time tests to check the rules), since static typing reports type violations earlier, and allows for generation of more efficient code. However, one has to revert to dynamic typing for programs that cannot be recognized type-safe at compile-time. This situation often reveals weaknesses of the type system used. Dynamic typing could be avoided, then, by employing more advanced type systems. For instance, it had long been believed that generic functions (functions that can be applied to arguments of different types) can only be supported by dynamically-typed languages, such as Lisp, until the advent of polymorphic type disciplines, such as the one of ML, that permit static typing of such functions.

In contrast, there are programming situations that seem to require dynamic typing in an essential way. A first example is the `eval` function (and similar meta-level operations), that takes a character string, evaluates it as an expression of the language, and returns its value. The type of the returned value cannot be known at compile-time, since it depends on the expression given as argument. Another example is structured input/output. Some runtime systems provide an `extern` primitive, that takes an object of any type, and efficiently outputs a low-level representation of the object to persistent storage. The object can be read back later on, possibly in another process, by the `intern` primitive. The `extern` function can easily be typed in a polymorphic type system; but this is not the case for the `intern` function, since the type of its result depends on the contents of the file being read. In order to guarantee type safety, it is clear that the values

*Authors' address: INRIA Rocquencourt, projet Formel, B.P. 105, 78153 Le Chesnay, France. `Xavier.Leroy`, `Michel.Mauny@inria.fr`

returned by `eval` or by `intern` must carry some type information at run-time, and that this type information must be dynamically checked against the type expected by the context.

As demonstrated above, dynamic typing cannot be avoided for a few highly specific functions. But we would like to retain static typing for the huge majority of functions that can be typechecked at compile-time. What we need is a way to embed dynamic typechecking within a statically-typed language. The concept of *objects with dynamic types* (or *dynamics*, for short) is an elegant answer to this need. A dynamic is a pair of a value v and a type expression τ, such that value v has type τ. From the standpoint of static typing, all dynamics belong to the built-in type **dyn**. Type **dyn** represents those values that are self-described as far as types are concerned; that is, those values on which run-time type checking is possible.

Continuing the examples above, function `eval` naturally returns dynamics, so its static type is `string` → **dyn**. Similarly, `intern` has type **io_channel** → **dyn**, and the `extern` function will be made to accept arguments of type **dyn** only, since the external representation of an object should now include its type.

Two constructs are provided to communicate between type **dyn** and the other types in the language. One construct creates dynamics by taking an object of any type and pairing it with its static type. The other construct checks the internal type of a dynamic against some static type τ, and, in case of success, gives access to the internal value of the dynamic with type τ.

In this paper, we consider the integration of dynamics, as described above, into the ML language [12]. The main novelty of this work is the combination of dynamics with a polymorphic type discipline. This combination raises interesting issues that have not been addressed yet. The main published references on dynamics have only considered first-order types [1], or first-order types with subtyping [4]. Polymorphism gets mentioned in [2], but very briefly and very informally. An early, unpublished work by Mycroft [13] is said to consider the extension of ML with dynamics, but we were unable to find this draft.

The two extensions of ML with dynamics we present here are not mere proposals. The simpler one has been fully integrated into the CAML system [18], the ML implementation developed at INRIA, for more than two years. It has grown to the point of stability where dynamics are used inside the CAML system. The second, more ambitious extension was also extensively prototyped in CAML. This practical experience enables us to discuss the main implementation issues involved by dynamics. It also gives some hints on the practical usefulness of dynamics in an ML system, both for user-level programming and system-level programming.

The remainder of this paper is organized as follows. Section 2 presents a first extension of ML with dynamics. After an informal presentation, we formalize typing and evaluation rules for dynamics within a small subset of ML, and discuss type inference and compilation issues. Section 3 extends the system previously described with the ability to destructure dynamics (both the type part and the value part), and rebuild dynamics with the components of the structure. We adapt the typing and evaluation rules of section 2 to this extension. Section 4 discusses the practical usefulness of the two systems, based on some significant uses of dynamics in the CAML environment. Finally, we give a few concluding remarks in section 5.

2 Simple dynamics

This section describes dynamics as they are implemented in CAML release 2.6 and later [18, chapter 8].

2.1 Presentation

The new construct `dynamic` a is provided to create dynamics. This construct evaluates a, and pairs it with (the representation of) the principal type inferred for a. For instance, `dynamic 1` evaluates to `(1, int)`, and `dynamic true` to `(true, bool)`. In any case, the expression `dynamic` a is of type `dyn`, without any mention of the internal type of the dynamic.

Objects with polymorphic types can be put in dynamics, provided their type is *closed*: none of the type variables free in their type should be free in the current typing environment. For instance, `dynamic(function x` $\rightarrow$ `x)` is perfectly legal, since the identity function has type $\alpha \rightarrow \alpha$, and α is a fresh type variable, that does not appear anywhere else. The resulting dynamic value is (`function x` $\rightarrow$ `x`, $\forall\alpha.\ \alpha \rightarrow \alpha$). The explicit quantification over α emphasizes the fact that the internal type of the dynamic is closed, and suggests that the internal value is really polymorphic: it will be possible to use it with several types.

On the other hand, `function x` $\rightarrow$ `dynamic x` is rejected: `dynamic x` is typed in the environment `x` : α, where `x` does not have a closed type. In this case, it is problematic to determine at compile-time the exact type of the object put into the dynamic: static typing says it can be any instance of α, that is, any type. To correctly evaluate the function above, the actual type to which α is instantiated would have to be passed at run-time. Since polymorphic functions can be nested arbitrarily, this means that all polymorphic functions, even those that do not build dynamics directly, would have to take type expressions as extra parameters, and correctly propagate these types to the polymorphic functions they call. We would loose one major benefit of static typing: that run-time type information is not needed except inside dynamic objects. Such is the reason why dynamics are required to be created with closed types.

To do anything useful with a dynamic, we must gain access to its internal value, bringing it back to the statically-typed world. A run-time type check is needed at that point to guarantee type safety. This check must ensure that the internal type of the dynamic does match the type expected by the context. This operation is called *coercion* of a dynamic. Coercion is customarily presented as a special syntactic construct (the `typecase` construct in [1]). This construct binds the internal value of the dynamic to some variable. It also handles the case where the run-time type check fails, and another coercion must be attempted, or an exception raised.

In ML, these two aspects, binding and failure handling, are already covered by the pattern-matching mechanism. Hence, instead of providing a separate coercion construct, we integrate dynamic coercion within pattern-matching. Namely, we introduce a new kind of pattern, the dynamic patterns, written **dynamic**$(p : \tau)$. This pattern selects all dynamics whose internal value matches the pattern p, and whose internal type agrees with the type expression τ. For instance, here is a function that takes a dynamic, and attempts to print a textual representation for it:

```
let print = function
      dynamic(x : int) → print_int x
    | dynamic(s : string) → print_string s
    | dynamic((x,y) : int × int) →
        print_string "("; print_int x; print_string ",";
        print_int y; print_string ")"
    | x → print_string "?"
```

For type matching, two behaviors can be considered. The first one is to require that the internal type of the dynamic is exactly the same as the expected type, up to a renaming of type variables. The other behavior is to also accept any dynamic whose internal type is more general than the expected type. For instance, **dynamic** [], whose internal type is $\forall \alpha.\ \alpha$ `list`, matches the pattern **dynamic** (`x : int list`) with the latter behavior, but not with the former. We have retained the latter behavior, since it seems more coherent with the statically-typed part of the ML language (where e.g. the empty list can be used in any context that expects a list of integers).

Type patterns are allowed to require a polymorphic type, as in **dynamic**(`f` : $\alpha \rightarrow \alpha$). This pattern matches any dynamic whose internal type is as general or more general than the type in the pattern (e.g. $\beta \rightarrow \beta$, or $\beta \rightarrow \gamma$). As a consequence of these semantics, identifier `f` can safely be used with any instance of the type $\alpha \rightarrow \alpha$ in the right-hand side of the pattern-matching:

```
function dynamic(f : α → α) → f f
```

The type matching semantics guarantee that `f` will be bound at run-time to a value that belongs to all type instances of the type scheme $\alpha \rightarrow \alpha$. This is the only case in ML where a variable bound by a `function` construct can be used with several types inside the function body.

In the example above, the type variable α is not a regular pattern variable such as `f`: it is implicitly quantified universally by the dynamic pattern, and therefore cannot be instantiated during the matching process. For instance, the pattern **dynamic**(`x` : α `list`) only matches a dynamic of the polymorphic empty list, not any dynamic of any list. As a consequence, a type pattern τ more general than a type pattern τ' will match less dynamics than τ', in contrast with regular ML patterns. This means that in a dynamic matching, the most general type patterns must come first. To catch polymorphic lists as well as integer lists, one must write

```
function dynamic(x : α list) → ...
       | dynamic(x : int list) → ...
```

instead of the more intuitive definition

```
function dynamic(x : int list) → ...
```

$\mid$ `dynamic(x :` α `list)` $\rightarrow$ ...

In the latter definition, the second case would never be selected, since the first case also matches dynamics with internal type α `list`.

2.2 Syntax

We now formalize the ideas above, in the context of the core ML language, enriched with pattern-matching and dynamics. The syntax of the language is as follows:

$$\begin{array}{rcl}
\tau & ::= & \texttt{int} \parallel \alpha \parallel \tau \rightarrow \tau' \parallel \tau \times \tau' \parallel \text{dyn} \\
p & ::= & x \parallel i \parallel (p, p') \parallel \texttt{dynamic}(p : \tau) \\
a & ::= & x \parallel i \parallel \texttt{function}\, p_1 \rightarrow a_1 \mid \ldots \mid p_n \rightarrow a_n \parallel a\ a' \parallel (a, a') \\
 & & \parallel \texttt{let}\ p = a\ \texttt{in}\ a' \parallel \texttt{dynamic}\ a
\end{array}$$

Type expressions (with typical elements τ, σ) are either atomic types such as the type `int` of integers; type variables α; function types; product types; or the type dyn of dynamics.

Patterns (typical elements p,q) are either variables x; integer constants i; pairs of patterns; or dynamic patterns `dynamic`$(p : \tau)$.

Finally, for expressions (typical elements a,b), we have variables x; integer constants i; functions with pattern matching on the argument; function application; pair construction; the `let` binding with pattern matching on the first expression; and the `dynamic` construct to build dynamics.

2.3 Typechecking

The typing rules for this calculus are given in figure 1. Most of the rules are just those of the core ML language, revised to take pattern-matching into account in the `function` and `let` constructs. Two additional rules present the creation and coercion of dynamics.

The rules define the predicate $E \vdash a : \tau$, meaning "expression a has type τ in the typing environment E". An auxiliary predicate, $\vdash p : \tau \Rightarrow E$, is used, meaning "pattern p has type τ and enriches the type environment by E". Here, E stands for a sequence of typing assumptions of the format $x : \Sigma$, where Σ is a type scheme: a type expression τ with zero, one or more type variables α_k universally quantified.

$$E \;::=\; (x : \forall \alpha_1 \ldots \alpha_n . \tau)^*$$

We write $E(x)$ for the type associated to x in E. If x is bound several times, we consider the rightmost binding only. We write $FV(\tau)$ for the free variables of type expression τ, and $FV(E)$ for the union of the free variables of all type schemes in E. Finally, $Clos(\tau, V)$ stands for the closure of type τ with respect to those type variables not in the set V. It is defined by:

$$Clos(\tau, V) = \forall \alpha_1 \ldots \alpha_n . \tau$$

$$(1)\quad E \vdash i : \mathtt{int} \qquad\qquad (2)\quad \frac{E(x) = \forall \alpha_1 \ldots \alpha_n.\tau}{E \vdash x : \tau[\alpha_k \leftarrow \tau_k]}$$

$$(3)\quad \frac{\vdash p_k : \sigma \Rightarrow E_k \qquad E, E_k \vdash a_k : \tau}{E \vdash \mathtt{function}\ p_1 \rightarrow a_1 \mid \ldots \mid p_n \rightarrow a_n : \sigma \rightarrow \tau}$$

$$(4)\quad \frac{E \vdash a : \sigma \rightarrow \tau \qquad E \vdash b : \sigma}{E \vdash a\ b : \tau} \qquad\qquad (5)\quad \frac{E \vdash a : \sigma \qquad E \vdash b : \tau}{E \vdash (a, b) : \sigma \times \tau}$$

$$(6)\quad \frac{E \vdash a : \sigma \qquad \vdash p : \sigma \Rightarrow E' \qquad E, Clos(E', FV(E)) \vdash b : \tau}{E \vdash \mathtt{let}\ p = a\ \mathtt{in}\ b : \tau}$$

$$(7)\quad \frac{E \vdash a : \sigma \qquad FV(\sigma) \cap FV(E) = \emptyset}{E \vdash \mathtt{dynamic}\ a : \mathrm{dyn}}$$

$$(8)\quad \vdash x : \tau \Rightarrow x : \tau \qquad\qquad (9)\quad \vdash i : \mathtt{int} \Rightarrow \epsilon$$

$$(10)\quad \frac{\vdash p : \tau \Rightarrow E \qquad \vdash p' : \tau' \Rightarrow E'}{\vdash (p, p') : \tau \times \tau' \Rightarrow E, E'} \qquad (11)\quad \frac{\vdash p : \tau \Rightarrow E}{\vdash \mathtt{dynamic}(p : \tau) : \mathrm{dyn} \Rightarrow Clos(E, \emptyset)}$$

Figure 1: Typing rules

where $\{\alpha_1, \ldots, \alpha_n\}$ is $FV(\tau) \setminus V$. The *Clos* operator is extended pointwise to type environments.

The only new rules are rule 7, that deals with dynamic creation, and rule 11, that deals with dynamic coercion. Rule 7 says that the expression $\mathtt{dynamic}\ a$ has type dyn, provided that a has a closed type τ: none of the free variables of τ are free in the current typing environment E.

Rule 11 says that the pattern $\mathtt{dynamic}(p : \tau)$ matches values of type dyn, provided p matches values of type τ. Assume p binds variables $x_1 \ldots x_n$ to values of types $\tau_1 \ldots \tau_n$. Then, $\mathtt{dynamic}(p : \tau)$ binds the same variables to the same values. As described above, all type variables free in $\tau_1 \ldots \tau_n$ can be generalized. Hence, we take that $\mathtt{dynamic}(p : \tau)$ binds $x_1 \ldots x_n$ to values of types $Clos(\tau_1, \emptyset) \ldots Clos(\tau_n, \emptyset)$.

2.4 Type inference

The type system presented above enjoys the principal type property, just as the one of ML. The principal type is computed by a trivial extension of the Damas-Milner type inference algorithm [5] to handle the dynamic construct and dynamic patterns. For the $\mathtt{dynamic}\ a$ construct, the only difficulty is to ensure that the type of a is closed. It would not be correct to infer the most general type τ for a, and fail immediately if some variables in τ are free in the current typing environment: these variables may become instantiated to monomorphic types later. Consider the expression `(function x → dynamic x) 1`. Assuming the function part of the application is typed before the argument, the function is given type $\alpha \rightarrow \mathrm{dyn}$, and

$$(12)\quad e \vdash x \Rightarrow e(x) \qquad\qquad (13)\quad e \vdash i \Rightarrow i$$

$$(14)\quad e \vdash \texttt{function} \ldots \mid p_k \rightarrow a_k \mid \ldots \Rightarrow [e, \ldots \mid p_k \rightarrow a_k \mid \ldots]$$

$$(15)\quad \frac{e \vdash a \Rightarrow [e', \ldots \mid p_k \rightarrow a_k \mid \ldots] \quad e \vdash b \Rightarrow v \qquad \vdash v < p_k \Rightarrow e'' \quad e', e'' \vdash a_k \Rightarrow w \quad k \text{ minimal}}{e \vdash a\ b \Rightarrow w}$$

$$(16)\quad \frac{e \vdash a \Rightarrow v \quad e \vdash b \Rightarrow w}{e \vdash (a, b) \Rightarrow (v, w)} \qquad (17)\quad \frac{e \vdash a \Rightarrow v \quad \vdash v < p \Rightarrow e' \quad e, e' \vdash b \Rightarrow w}{e \vdash \texttt{let}\ p = a\ \texttt{in}\ b \Rightarrow w}$$

$$(18)\quad \frac{e \vdash a \Rightarrow v \quad \mathit{Type}(a) = \tau}{e \vdash \texttt{dynamic}\ a \Rightarrow \texttt{dynamic}(v : \tau)}$$

$$(19)\quad \vdash v < x \Rightarrow x \leftarrow v \qquad\qquad (20)\quad \frac{\vdash v < p \Rightarrow e \quad \vdash v' < p' \Rightarrow e'}{\vdash (v, v') < (p, p') \Rightarrow e, e'}$$

$$(21)\quad \vdash i < i \Rightarrow \epsilon \qquad\qquad (22)\quad \frac{\vdash v < p \Rightarrow e \quad \theta\tau = \sigma}{\vdash \texttt{dynamic}(v : \tau) < \texttt{dynamic}(p : \sigma) \Rightarrow e}$$

Figure 2: Evaluation rules

dynamic x appears to build a dynamic with non-closed type α. But when the application is typed, α gets instantiated to **int**, and we know that the dynamic is created with internal type **int**. Hence, the closedness check must be delayed to the end of type inference. The CAML implementation proceeds as follows: when typing **dynamic** a, all type variables that are free in the inferred type for a and in the current typing environment are collected in a list, and prevented from being generalized. At the end of typechecking, all type variables in the list must be instantiated by ground types.

For dynamic patterns **dynamic**$(p : \tau)$, the expected type τ is given explicitly in the pattern, so there is actually nothing to infer. We just check that the pattern p is of type τ, and record the (polymorphic) types of the variables bound by p. We have considered inferring τ from the pattern p and the right-hand side a of the pattern-matching, but this seems quite difficult, since variables bound by p can be used with several different types in a.

2.4.1 Evaluation

We now give call-by-value operational semantics for our calculus. Expressions are mapped to values, that is, terms with the following syntax:

$$v ::= i \parallel (v, v') \parallel \texttt{dynamic}(v : \tau) \parallel [e, p_1 \rightarrow a_1 \mid \ldots \mid p_n \rightarrow a_n]$$
$$e ::= (x \leftarrow v)^*$$

A value is either an integer i; a pair of values; a dynamic value **dynamic**$(v : \tau)$ (a pair of a value v and a type expression τ); or a closure $[e, p_1 \to a_1 \mid \ldots \mid p_n \to a_n]$ of function body $p_1 \to a_1 \mid \ldots \mid p_n \to a_n$ by evaluation environment e. Evaluation environments map identifiers to values in the same way as typing environments map identifiers to types. For dynamic values, all type variables in the type part are considered universally quantified there; hence, two dynamic values are identified up to a renaming of their type variables.

The evaluation rules are given in figure 2. They closely follow the structure of the typing rules. A first set of rules define the predicate $e \vdash a \Rightarrow v$, meaning "expression a evaluates to value v in environment e". The remaining rules define the auxiliary predicate $\vdash v < p \Rightarrow e$, meaning "value v matches pattern p, binding variables in p to values as described by e".

Since most rules are classical, we only detail the two rules dealing with dynamics. Rule 18 expresses that evaluating `dynamic` a amounts to evaluating a, and pairing its value with the static type of a. The type of a is not mentioned in the expression `dynamic` a, so there are some technicalities involved in defining precisely what it is. We assume all expressions a considered here are subterms of a given closed, well-typed term a_0 (the program). Let $\mathcal{D}$ be the principal type derivation for a_0 (the one that is built by the type inference algorithm). For each subterm a of a_0, $\mathit{Type}(a)$ is defined as the type given to a in $\mathcal{D}$. (In practice, dynamic expressions are annotated with their types during typing.)

Rule 22 defines the semantics of pattern matching over dynamics. The internal type τ of the dynamic is required to be more general than the type σ expected by the pattern: there must exist a substitution θ of types for type variables such that $\theta\tau$ is σ. The internal value of the dynamic is recursively matched against the value part of the dynamic pattern.

2.5 Compilation

In the current CAML implementation, internal types of dynamics are represented by the following term-like structure:

```
type gtype = Gvartype of int
           | Gconsttype of int × gtype list
```

Type constructors are identified by unique stamps instead of names to correctly handle type redefinition. Type variables are also encoded as integers. The code generated for `dynamic` a simply pairs the value of a with the structured constant representing $\mathit{Type}(a)$ as a **gtype**. For pattern matching, CAML provides a library function **ge_gtype**, that takes two types and tests whether the first one is more general than the second one. The code generated for pattern matching on dynamics simply calls **ge_gtype** with the internal type of the dynamic, and the expected type (again, a structured constant of type **gtype**). Only when **ge_gtype** returns true is the sequence of tests matching the internal value against the pattern entered. Those tests were compiled assuming that the value being tested belongs to the expected type for the dynamic; therefore, it would be incorrect to match the internal value first, and then the internal type.

Little effort went into making run-time type tests faster. We have not yet encountered CAML programs that need to perform dynamic coercions inside tight loops. In case coercion speed becomes an important issue, we could first switch to the following representation for internal types of dynamics:

```
type gtype = Gvartype of gtype option ref
           | Gconsttype of int × gtype list
```

This representation makes it possible to perform instantiations by physical modifications on the type, which is more efficient than recording them separately as a substitution. (These physical modifications are undone at the end of the matching.)

Then, we could perform partial evaluation on the **ge_gtype** predicate, since its second argument is always known at compile-time. Conventional pattern-matching compilation techniques [14] do not apply directly, however, since they consist in specializing term-matching predicates on their first argument (the more general term), not on the second one (the less general term). Specializing a matching predicate such as **ge_gtype** on its second argument turns out to be just as hard as the more general problem of specializing a unification predicate on one of its arguments. The latter problem has been extensively studied in the context of Prolog compilation. A popular solution is the Warren Abstract Machine and its compilation scheme [17, 9]. Most of the techniques developed there apply to our problem. We shall detail this issue at the end of section 3.6.

3 Non-closed types in dynamic patterns

This section presents an extension of the system presented above that makes it possible to match dynamic values against dynamic patterns with incomplete type information. This enables destructuring dynamics without specifying their exact type.

3.1 Presentation

With the previous system, the internal value of a dynamic can only be extracted with a fixed type. This turns out to be insufficient in some cases. Let us continue the `print` example of section 2.1. For product types, we would like to have a single case that matches all dynamics of pairs, prints the parentheses and comma, and recursively calls the `print` function to print the two components of the pair. This cannot be done with the system above: the pattern `dynamic((x, y)` $: \alpha \times \beta)$ will only match dynamics whose internal type is at least as general as $\forall\alpha\forall\beta.\,\alpha \times \beta$, definitely not all dynamics whose internal type is a pair type. What we need is to have type variables in dynamic patterns that are not universally quantified, but rather existentially quantified, so that they can be bound to the corresponding parts of the internal type of the dynamic.

We now give a more complete version of the `print` function, with explicit universal and existential quantification for type variables in dynamic patterns. We will use it as a running example in this section.

```
type fun_arg  =  Arg of string in
```

```
let rec print = function
    dynamic(i : int) →                                                      (1)
        print_int i
  | dynamic(s : string) →                                                   (2)
        print_string "\""; print_string s; print_string "\""
  | ∃α.∃β.dynamic((x, y) : α × β) →                                         (3)
        print_string "("; print(dynamic x); print_string ",";
        print(dynamic y); print_string ")"
  | ∃α.dynamic([] : α list) →                                               (4)
        print_string "[]"
  | ∃α.dynamic(x :: l : α list) →                                           (5)
        print(dynamic x); print_string " :: "; print(dynamic l)
  | ∀α.dynamic(f : α → α) →                                                 (6)
        print_string "function x → x"
  | ∃α.∀β.dynamic(f : α → β) →                                              (7)
        print_string "function x → ⊥"
  | ∀α.∃β.dynamic(f : α → β) →                                              (8)
        let s = gensym() in
          print_string "function "; print_string s;
          print_string " → "; print(dynamic(f (Arg s)))
  | dynamic(Arg(s) : fun_arg) →                                             (9)
        print_string s
  | ∃α.∃β.dynamic(f : α → β) →                                              (10)
        print_string "function x → ..."
  | d →                                                                     (11)
        print_string "?"
```

Typing existential quantification

Let us detail first how these existentially quantified type variables behave when typing the right-hand side of the pattern-matching. Such a variable α can be bound to any actual type at run-time. Hence, at compile-time, we should make no assumptions about type α, and treat it as an abstract type. That is, type α does not match any type except itself; and type α must not escape the scope of the pattern-matching that binds it: α is not allowed to be free in the type of the returned value. As a consequence, the following two functions are rejected:

```
function ∃α. dynamic(x : α) → x = 1
function ∃α. dynamic(x : α) → x
```

while this one is perfectly legal:

```
function ∃α. dynamic((f, x) : (α → int) × α) → f x
```

and can be applied to `dynamic(succ, 2)` as well as to `dynamic(int_of_string, "3")`.

There is one important difference between existentially bound type variables and abstract types: the actual type bound to such a type variable is available at run-time. Given an object a whose static type contains a variable α existentially bound, it is possible to build a dynamic from this object. The internal type of the dynamic will be the "true" type for a: its static type where the binding of α has been performed. Cases (3) and (5) in the `print` function illustrates this feature: when the matching with $\exists\alpha$. dynamic(`x :: l` : α `list`) succeeds, two dynamics are created, `dynamic x` with internal type the type τ bound to α; and `dynamic l` with internal type τ `list`. This transforms a dynamic of a non-empty list into the dynamic of its head, and the dynamic of its tail, thus allowing recursion on the list.

Mixed quantifications

Existentially quantified variables can be freely mixed with universally quantified variables inside type patterns. Then, the semantics of the matching depends on the relative order in which these variables are quantified. This is illustrated by cases (7) and (8) in the `print` example — two modest attempts at printing functional values.

In case (7), the pattern is $\exists\alpha.\forall\beta$.dynamic(`f` : $\alpha \rightarrow \beta$). Since α is bound before β, variable α only matches type expressions that do not depend on β. For instance, a dynamic with internal type $\gamma \rightarrow \gamma$ is rejected. The functions selected by the pattern above are exactly those returning a value of type β for all β. Since no such value exists in ML, the selected functions never terminate (or always raise an exception), hence they are printed as `function x` $\rightarrow \perp$.

In case (8), the pattern is $\forall\alpha.\exists\beta$.dynamic (`f` : $\alpha \rightarrow \beta$). Here, β is bound after α; hence β can be instantiated by type expressions containing α. For instance, this pattern matches a dynamic with type $\gamma \rightarrow \gamma$ `list`, binding β to α `list`. This pattern catches a class of functions that operate uniformly on arguments of any type. These functions cannot test or destructure their argument, but only put it in data structures or in closures. Therefore, if we apply such a function to a symbolic name `x`, and recursively print the result, we get a representation of the function body, with `x` standing for the function parameter[1]. (Actually, the printed function is extensionally equivalent to the original function, assuming there are no side-effects.)

In the presence of mixed quantification, the rules for typing the right-hand side of pattern-matchings outlined above have to be strengthened: it is not always correct to treat an existentially quantified type variable as a new abstract atomic type. Consider:

$$\texttt{function}\ \forall\alpha.\exists\beta.\text{dynamic}(\texttt{f} : \alpha \rightarrow \beta)\ \rightarrow\ \texttt{f 1} = \texttt{f true}$$

Assuming `f` : $\forall\alpha.\ \alpha \rightarrow \beta$, the expression `f 1 = f true` typechecks, since both applications of `f` have type β. Yet, when applying the function above to `dynamic (function x` $\rightarrow$ `x)`, the matching succeeds, `f 1` evaluates to `1`, `f true` evaluates to `true`, and we end up comparing `1` with `true` — a run-time type violation. Since the actual value of β is allowed to depend on α, static typechecking has to

[1]To avoid any confusion between the formal parameter and constants mentioned in the function body, formal parameters are represented by a local type `fun_arg = Arg of string`. This ensures that the given function cannot create any terms of type `fun_arg`, unless it is the `print` function itself. Fortunately, the self-application `print(dynamic print)` selects case (10) of the definition.

assume that β does depend over α, and treat two occurrences of β corresponding to different instantiations of α as incompatible.

This is achieved by taking β in the right-hand side of the matching to be a type constructor parameterized by α. To avoid confusion, we shall write $\overline{\beta}$ for the type constructor associated to type variable β. Therefore, we now assume $\texttt{f} : \forall\alpha.\ \alpha \rightarrow \overline{\beta}(\alpha)$ for the typing of $\texttt{f 1} = \texttt{f true}$, and this leads to a static type error, since the two sides of the equal sign have incompatible types $\overline{\beta}(\texttt{int})$ and $\overline{\beta}(\texttt{bool})$. However, $\texttt{f 1} = \texttt{f 2}$ is well-typed, since both sides have type $\overline{\beta}(\texttt{int})$. The general rule is: for the purpose of typing the right-hand side of a pattern-matching, existentially quantified type variables β are replaced by the type expression $\overline{\beta}(\alpha_1, \ldots, \alpha_n)$, where $\alpha_1 \ldots \alpha_n$ is the list of those type variables that are universally quantified before β in the pattern. This transformation is known in logic as Skolemization.

Multiple dynamic matching

Type variables are quantified at the beginning of each case of the pattern-matching, not inside each dynamic pattern. This makes no difference for universally quantified variables. However, existentially quantified variables can be shared among several dynamic patterns, expressing sharing constraints between the internal types of several dynamics. For instance, the "dynamic function application" example of [1] can be written as:

$$\texttt{function}\ \exists\alpha.\exists\beta.\ (\texttt{dynamic}(\texttt{f} : \alpha \rightarrow \beta),\ \texttt{dynamic}(\texttt{x} : \alpha)) \rightarrow \\ \texttt{dynamic(f x)}$$

This function takes a pair of two dynamics, applies the first one (which should contain a function) to the second one, and returns the result as a dynamic. It ensures that the type of the argument is compatible with the domain type of the function.

Type variables can be shared among two dynamic patterns of the same matching; but we shall prohibit sharing between patterns belonging to different matchings (curried dynamic matching). In other terms, all cases in a pattern matching are required to be closed: all type variables contained in dynamic patterns should be quantified at the beginning of the corresponding matching. For instance, it is not possible to write the dynamic apply function in the following way (as it originally appears in [1]):

$$\texttt{function}\ \exists\alpha.\exists\beta.\ \texttt{dynamic}(\texttt{f} : \alpha \rightarrow \beta) \rightarrow \texttt{function dynamic}(\texttt{x} : \alpha) \rightarrow \\ \texttt{dynamic(f x)}$$

This violates the requirement above, since α is bound by the outermost matching, and mentioned in the innermost one. The reasons for this restriction are mostly pragmatic: curried dynamic matching, in conjunction with polymorphic dynamics, can require postponing some type matching in an outer dynamic matching until an inner dynamic matching is performed. Our closedness condition on pattern matching cases rules out these nasty situations, without significantly reducing the expressive power of the language: curried dynamic application can still be written as

```
function df → function dx → match (df,dx) with ...
```

$$(23)\quad \frac{Q_k \vdash p_k : \sigma \Rightarrow E_k \quad E, E_k \vdash a_k : \tau \quad FSC(\tau) \cap BV(Q_k) = \emptyset}{\texttt{function } Q_1 p_1 \rightarrow a_1 \mid \ldots \mid Q_n p_n \rightarrow a_n : \sigma \rightarrow \tau}$$

$$(24)\quad Q \vdash x : \tau \Rightarrow x : \tau \qquad\qquad (25)\quad Q \vdash i : \texttt{int} \Rightarrow \epsilon$$

$$(26)\quad \frac{Q \vdash p : \tau \Rightarrow E \quad Q \vdash p' : \tau' \Rightarrow E'}{Q \vdash (p, p') : \tau \times \tau' \Rightarrow E, E'}$$

$$(27)\quad \frac{FV(\tau) \subseteq BV(Q) \quad Q \vdash p : \tau \Rightarrow E \quad \theta = S(\epsilon, Q)}{Q \vdash \texttt{dynamic}(p : \tau) : \texttt{dyn} \Rightarrow Clos(\theta\tau, \emptyset)}$$

Figure 3: Typing rules with explicit quantification in type patterns

at the expense of a later error detection, in case df is not a dynamic of function.

3.2 Syntax

The only syntactic change is the introduction of a sequence of quantifiers in front of each case in pattern matchings.

$$\begin{array}{rcl} a & ::= & \ldots \parallel \texttt{function } Q_1 p_1 \rightarrow a_1 \mid \ldots \mid Q_n p_n \rightarrow a_n \\ Q & ::= & \epsilon \parallel \forall \alpha . Q \parallel \exists \alpha . Q \end{array}$$

We will always assume that variables are renamed so that quantifier prefixes Q never bind the same variable twice. We write $BV(Q)$ for the set of variables bound by prefix Q.

3.3 Typechecking

We introduce the Skolem constants at the level of types. To each type variable α, we associate the type constructor $\overline{\alpha}$, with variable arity.

$$\tau \;::=\; \ldots \parallel \overline{\alpha}(\tau_1, \ldots, \tau_n)$$

Skolem constants are not permitted in the type part of dynamic patterns, nor in the internal types of dynamic values. We shall write τ^0, σ^0 for type expressions free of Skolem constants. We define $FSC(\tau)$, the free Skolem constants of type τ, as the set of all variables α such that type constructor $\overline{\alpha}$ appears in τ.

The new typing rules for functions and for patterns are shown in figure 3. For each case $Qp \rightarrow a$ in a function definition, the pattern p is typed taking Q into account. The proposition $\vdash p : \sigma \Rightarrow E$ now takes Q as an extra argument, becoming $Q \vdash p : \sigma \Rightarrow E$. The Q prefix is carried unchanged through all rules, and it is used only in the rule for dynamic patterns. There, in the types of all identifiers bound by the pattern, we replace existentially quantified type variables by the corresponding Skolem functions. This is performed by the substitution

$$(28)\quad e \vdash \mathbf{int} \Rightarrow \mathbf{int} \qquad (29)\quad e \vdash \alpha \Rightarrow \alpha \qquad (30)\quad e \vdash \mathbf{dyn} \Rightarrow \mathbf{dyn}$$

$$(31)\quad \frac{e \vdash \sigma \Rightarrow \sigma^0 \quad e \vdash \tau \Rightarrow \tau^0}{e \vdash \sigma \rightarrow \tau \Rightarrow \sigma^0 \rightarrow \tau^0} \qquad (32)\quad \frac{e \vdash \sigma \Rightarrow \sigma^0 \quad e \vdash \tau \Rightarrow \tau^0}{e \vdash \sigma \times \tau \Rightarrow \sigma^0 \times \tau^0}$$

$$(33)\quad \frac{e(\alpha) = [\alpha_1 \ldots \alpha_n].\tau^0 \quad e \vdash \tau_k \Rightarrow \tau_k^0}{e \vdash \overline{\alpha}(\tau_1 \ldots \tau_n) \Rightarrow \tau^0[\alpha_k \leftarrow \tau_k^0]}$$

$$(34)\quad \frac{e \vdash \tau \Rightarrow \tau^0 \quad e \vdash a \Rightarrow v}{e \vdash \texttt{dynamic}\ a \Rightarrow \texttt{dynamic}(v : \tau^0)}$$

$$(35)\quad \frac{\begin{array}{c} e \vdash a \Rightarrow [e_1, \ldots \mid Q_k p_k \rightarrow a_k \mid \ldots] \quad e \vdash b \Rightarrow v \quad k \text{ minimal} \\ Q_k \vdash v < p_k \Rightarrow e_2\,;\Gamma \quad Solve(Q_k, \Gamma) = e_3' \quad e_1, e_2, e_3 \vdash a_k \Rightarrow w \end{array}}{e \vdash a\ b \Rightarrow w}$$

$$(36)\quad Q \vdash v < x \Rightarrow x \leftarrow v\,;\epsilon \qquad (38)\quad \frac{Q \vdash v < p \Rightarrow e\,;\Gamma \quad Q \vdash v' < p' \Rightarrow e'\,;\Gamma'}{Q \vdash (v, v') < (p, p') \Rightarrow e, e'\,;\Gamma, \Gamma'}$$

$$(37)\quad Q \vdash i < i \Rightarrow \epsilon\,;\epsilon$$

$$(39)\quad \frac{Q \vdash v < p \Rightarrow e\,;\Gamma \quad FV(\tau) \cap BV(Q) = \emptyset}{Q \vdash \texttt{dynamic}(v : \tau) < \texttt{dynamic}(p : \sigma) \Rightarrow e\,;\Gamma, \tau = \sigma}$$

Figure 4: Evaluation rules with explicit quantification in type patterns

$\theta = S(\epsilon, Q)$, defined inductively on Q as follows:

$$\begin{array}{rcl} S(\alpha_1 \ldots \alpha_n, \epsilon) & = & id \\ S(\alpha_1 \ldots \alpha_n, \forall\alpha.Q) & = & S(\alpha_1 \ldots \alpha_n \alpha, Q) \\ S(\alpha_1 \ldots \alpha_n, \exists\alpha.Q) & = & [\alpha \leftarrow \overline{\alpha}(\alpha_1, \ldots, \alpha_n)] \circ S(\alpha_1 \ldots \alpha_n, Q) \end{array}$$

Typing of action a proceeds as previously. We simply check that the type of τ does not contain any Skolem constants corresponding to variables bound by Q.

3.4 Evaluation

The introduction of existential type variables in dynamic patterns significantly complicates the semantics of the language, both for dynamic creation, and for dynamic matching. The modified evaluation rules are shown in figure 4.

For dynamic creation (rule 34), the evaluation of `dynamic` a now has to transform the static type τ inferred for a before pairing it with the value of a. Skolem constants representing existentially bound type variables are replaced by the actual types bound to these variables, properly instantiated. These bindings of type variables are recorded in the evaluation environment e. Hence the new syntax for evaluation environments:

$$e \ ::= \ (x \leftarrow v \parallel \alpha \leftarrow [\alpha_1, \ldots, \alpha_n]\tau^0)^*$$

Since existential type variables may depend upon universal variables, existential variables are actually bound to a type context (a type expression with holes) instead of a simple type expression. We write type contexts as $[\alpha_1, \ldots, \alpha_n]\tau^0$, where type variables $\alpha_1 \ldots \alpha_n$ are names for the holes. Rules 28–33 define the evaluation relation on types $e \vdash \tau \Rightarrow \tau^0$, mapping a type expression τ to a type expression τ^0 without Skolem constants.

For dynamic matching during function application (rule 35), it is not possible anymore to perform dynamic type matching separately for each dynamic pattern, since patterns may share existentially quantified variables. Therefore, all dynamic type constraints are collected first, as a set of equations $\tau = \sigma$, where τ is the internal type of a dynamic, and σ a type pattern. The pattern-matching predicate becomes $Q \vdash v < p \Rightarrow e\,;\Gamma$, where Γ is the sequence of equations between types described above, and Q is the quantifier prefix for the matching (rules 36–39). The Q prefix is used in rule 39 to rename the internal types of dynamics, if necessary, so that their free type variables are not bound by Q. In a second phase, the function $Solve$ is called to resolve the equations on types Γ, taking prefix Q into account. The precise definition of $Solve$ is postponed to the next section. When the type matching succeeds, $Solve$ returns the correct bindings for existentially quantified type variables. Then, evaluation of the right-hand side of the matching proceeds as usual.

3.5 Unification

The run-time matching between type patterns and internal types of dynamics amounts to a certain kind of unification problem, called *unification under a prefix.* This problem is studied extensively in [11], though in the very general setting of higher-order unification, while we only deal with first-order terms here. The first-order problem also appears in [10]. In our case, the problem consists in checking the validity of propositions of the format

$$q_1\alpha_1 \ldots q_n\alpha_n.\ \sigma = \tau,$$

where the q_k are either universal or existential quantifiers, and σ, τ are first-order terms of a free algebra. Unification under mixed prefix generalizes the well-known matching problem ("given two terms σ, τ, find a substitution θ such that $\theta\sigma = \tau$") and the unification problem ("given two terms σ, τ, find a substitution θ such that $\theta\sigma = \theta\tau$"): writing $\alpha_1 \ldots \alpha_n$ for the variables of σ, and $\beta_1 \ldots \beta_n$ for the variables of τ, the matching problem is equivalent to

$$\forall\beta_1 \ldots \forall\beta_n \exists\alpha_1 \ldots \exists\alpha_n.\ \sigma = \tau,$$

and the unification problem to

$$\exists\beta_1 \ldots \exists\beta_n \exists\alpha_1 \ldots \exists\alpha_n.\ \sigma = \tau.$$

For the purpose of dynamic matching, we not only want to know whether the problem $Q.\ \sigma = \tau$ is satisfiable (Q is a quantifier prefix), but also to find minimal assignments for the variables existentially quantified in Q that satisfy the proposition. From now on, we shall treat variables universally bound in Q as constants. That is, we add such variables as term constructors with arity zero to the initial signature (int and dyn of arity zero, $\rightarrow$ and $\times$ of arity two).

Definition 1 *A substitution θ is a Q-substitution iff for all variables α, all constants β contained in the term $\theta\alpha$ are bound before α in prefix Q.*

Definition 2 *A substitution θ is a Q-unifier of σ and τ iff $\theta\sigma = \theta\tau$, and θ is a Q-substitution. If such a substitution exists, σ and τ are said to be Q-unifiable.*

Proposition 1 *The proposition $Q.\ \sigma = \tau$ is satisfiable if and only if σ and τ are Q-unifiable.*

Proposition 2 *Two terms σ and τ are Q-unifiable if and only if σ and τ are unifiable, and their most general unifier is a Q-substitution.*

Proof: The "if" part is obvious. For the "only if" part, let θ be a Q-unifier of σ and τ. Since $\theta\sigma = \theta\tau$, the terms σ and τ are unifiable. Let μ be their most general unifier. Let ϕ be a substitution such that $\theta = \phi \circ \mu$. For all variables α, the constants contained in $\mu\alpha$ are a subset of those contained in $\theta\alpha$. Since θ is a Q-substitution, all constants in $\mu\alpha$ are also bound before α in Q. Hence μ is a Q-substitution. □

This result trivially gives an algorithm to compute the most general Q-unifier of σ and τ: compute the most general unifier of σ and τ, using Robinson's algorithm, and check that it is a Q-substitution.

We can now define the function *Solve* used in evaluation rule 32. It takes a prefix Q and a set Γ of equations $\sigma_1 = \tau_1 \ldots \sigma_n = \tau_n$. Since Q binds the variables in the τ_k only, prefix Q is first completed to bind the variables in the σ_k also. Let $\alpha_1 \ldots \alpha_m$ be the variables in the σ_k. We take $Q' = Q.\exists\alpha_1 \ldots \exists\alpha_m$. (None of the α_k is bound by Q, and they can be instantiated to any type.) Let μ be the most general Q'-unifier of $\sigma_1 \times \ldots \times \sigma_n$ and $\tau_1 \times \ldots \times \tau_n$, as computed by the algorithm above. Substitution μ is transformed into an evaluation environment, by adding bindings for the variables that are existentially quantified in Q. More precisely, we take $Solve(Q, \Gamma)$ to be $s(\mu, \epsilon, Q)$, where s is the run-time counterpart of the Skolemization function S used for static typing in section 3.3:

$$\begin{aligned}
s(\mu, \alpha_1 \ldots \alpha_n, \epsilon) &= \epsilon \\
s(\mu, \alpha_1 \ldots \alpha_n, \forall\alpha.Q) &= s(\mu, \alpha_1 \ldots \alpha_n\alpha, Q) \\
s(\mu, \alpha_1 \ldots \alpha_n, \exists\alpha.Q) &= \alpha \leftarrow [\alpha_1, \ldots, \alpha_n]\mu\alpha,\ s(\mu, \alpha_1 \ldots \alpha_n, Q)
\end{aligned}$$

3.6 Compilation

The semantics given above are quite complicated, so it is no surprise their implementation turns out to be delicate. The main difficulty is unification under a prefix

Q. Efficient algorithms are available for the regular unification phase. It remains to quickly check that the resulting substitution is a Q-substitution. This check can actually be integrated within the occur check, at little extra cost. The idea is to reflect dependencies by associating ranks (integers) to type variables. Variables bound by Q are statically given ranks $0, \ldots, n$ from left to right. Other variables (i.e. those in the internal types of dynamics) are considered bound at the end of Q, and therefore given rank ∞. When identifying two variables α and β, the resulting variable is given rank $min(rank(\alpha), rank(\beta))$. Then, binding existential variable α to a constructed type τ is legal iff:

1. (occur check) α does not occur in τ
2. (rank check) τ does not contain any universal type variable whose rank is greater than the rank of α.

As in the case of simple dynamics (section 2.5), the easiest way to implement type matching is to call at run-time a unification primitive, with the type pattern (annotated by rank information) as a constant argument. Partial evaluation of the unification primitive on the type pattern is desirable, not only to speed up type matching, but also to provide a cleaner handling of run-time type environments: after specialization, the bindings for the existential type variables could be recorded e.g. on the stack or in registers, as for regular variables; without specialization, the unification primitive would return a data structure containing these bindings, and less efficient code would be generated to access these bindings.

Specializing unification on one of its arguments is not much harder than specializing matching on its second argument (section 2.5). The techniques developed for the Warren Abstract Machine [17, 9] directly apply, with the exception of the extra rank check. For instance, the WAM does not perform occur check for the initial binding of an existential variable, while we have to check ranks even in this case. Another difference is that backtracking is always "shallow", in the WAM terminology, since ML pattern-matching is deterministic. This simplifies the handling of the trail.

During the summer of 1988, the first author integrated a prototype unification compiler in the CAML system, following the ideas above. The CAML pattern-matching compiler was modified to implement unification semantics as well as matching semantics, depending on flags put on the patterns. This low-level mechanism allowed performing unification on some parts of a data structure, and regular pattern-matching on the other parts. Then, dynamic patterns $\mathtt{dynamic}(p : \tau)$ were simply expanded after type inference into product patterns $(p, \mathtt{repr}(\tau))$, where $\mathtt{repr}(\tau)$ is the pattern that matches all internal representations of types matching τ. The pattern $\mathtt{repr}(\tau)$ is marked to use unification semantics.

The only missing feature from what we have described above was rank check. At that time, we considered only dynamic patterns where all universal type variables come first, followed by all existential variables. Rank check could have been added with little modifications.

Dynamic matching benefited from all optimizations performed by the pattern-matching compiler, including factorization of tests between cases, and utilization of typing informations. As a consequence, dynamic matching was performed quite efficiently. However, we agreed that this efficiency was not worth the extra complication of the compiler, and this prototype was never carried to the point it could be released.

4 Assessment

This section discusses the practical usefulness of the two propositions above, drawing from our practical experience with the CAML system.

4.1 Interfacing with system functions

Dynamics makes it possible to provide an interface with a number of system functions that cannot be given a static type in ML. Without dynamics, these functions could not be made available to the user in a type-safe way. In the CAML system, these functions include:

- `extern` : `extern_channel` $\times$ `dyn` $\rightarrow$ `unit` and `intern` : `intern_channel` $\rightarrow$ `dyn`, to efficiently write and read data structures on persistent storage, preserving sharing inside the structure. A typical use is, for a separate compiler, to communicate compiled object code with its linker, and to save and reload symbol tables representing compiled module interfaces.
- `eval_syntax` : `ML` $\rightarrow$ `dyn`, to typecheck, compile, and evaluate a piece of abstract ML syntax (type `ML`). This makes it easy to provide CAML as an embedded language inside a program. For instance, the Calculus of Construction [8], a proof development environment, provides the ability to interactively define proof tactics written in CAML, and to apply them on the fly. The CAML macro facility [18, chapter 18] also makes use of `eval_syntax`, since a macro body is an arbitrary CAML expression whose evaluation leads to the substituted text.
- `MLquote` : `dyn` $\rightarrow$ `ML`, which is one of the constructors of the datatype representing abstract syntax trees. This constructor embeds constants of arbitrary types inside syntax trees. These constants are produced by compile-time evaluation (e.g. macro expansion and constant folding).
- `print` : `dyn` $\rightarrow$ `unit`, to print a dynamic value in ML syntax. CAML cannot provide a polymorphic printing function with type $\alpha \rightarrow$ `unit`, due to some optimizations in the data representation algorithm, that makes it impossible to decipher the representation of a data without knowing its type.

In these examples, the returned dynamics are generally coerced to fully known types, usually monomorphic. Therefore, we do not see the need for existential type variables there, and the simpler dynamic system presented in section 2 seems largely sufficient. In practice, the restriction encountered first is not that dynamics can only be coerced to closed types, but that dynamics can only be created with closed types. This prevents the `print` function from being called by a polymorphic function to print its polymorphic argument, for instance. This is often needed for debugging purposes.

4.2 Ad-hoc polymorphism

ML polymorphism is uniform: polymorphic functions operate in the same way on arguments of several types. In contrast, ad-hoc polymorphism consists in having generic functions that accept arguments of several types, but operate differently on objects of different types. Prime examples are the print function or the equal predicate: different algorithms are used to print or compare integers, strings, lists, or references. Several extensions of functional languages have been proposed, that support the definition of such generic functions, including type classes [16] and run-time overloading [15].

Dynamics provide a naive, but easy to understand, way to define generic functions. As demonstrated above in the print example, dynamics permit joining predefined functions on atomic types (print_int, print_string) and functions on data structures (pairs, lists), that recurse on the components of the structures — the main operation in defining generic functions. Another important aspect of generic functions is extensibility: whenever a new datatype is defined, they can be extended to deal with objects of the new type as well. This can also be supported in the dynamic implementation, by keeping in a reference a list of, say, printing functions with type dyn → unit, to be applied until one succeeds whenever none of the standard cases apply.

```
exception Cannot_print;;
type fun_arg  =  Arg of string in
let printers  =  ref ([] : (dyn → unit) list) in
let rec print  =  function
    ...
  | d →
      let rec try_print  =  function
        []  →  print_string "?"
      | f :: rest  →  try f d with Cannot_print → try_print rest
      in try_print !printers
and new_printer f  =
    printers  :=  f :: !printers
```

Assuming, for instance, that type foo = A | B of int × foo has been defined, we could add a printer for type foo as follows:

```
new_printer (function
    dynamic(A : foo)  →  print_string "A"
  | dynamic(B(x,y) : foo)  →
      print_string "B("; print (dynamic x); print_string ",";
      print (dynamic y); print_string ")"
  | x  →  raise Cannot_print)
```

It should be pointed out that this implementation of generic functions with dynamics has several major drawbacks. First, because of the restrictions on dynamic creation, polymorphic functions that need to call print have to take dynamics themselves. This is not too serious for print, but would be prohibitive for heavily used generic functions, such as equal: all functions on sets, association lists, etc., would have to operate on dynamics, thus dramatically reducing accuracy of static typing and efficiency of compiled code. Moreover, nothing statically prevents the `print` function from being applied to objects that have no printing method defined. This important class of type errors will only be detected at run-time. Finally, such an implementation of generic functions is rather inefficient, since dynamics are built and coerced at each recursive call.

Type classes and run-time overloading techniques seem more realistic in this respect. They statically guarantee that generic functions can only be applied to objects on which they are defined. They perform type matching at compile-time whenever possible. And run-time type information can usually be arranged as dictionaries of methods, allowing faster method selection than dynamic type matching.

5 Conclusions

We have presented two extensions of ML with dynamic objects. The simpler one has proved quite successful for interfacing user code with some important system functions in a type-safe way. Its implementation cost remains moderate. The other extension, that generalizes the dynamic patterns to include both universal and existential variables in the type part, makes it possible to work on dynamics without coercing them to fixed types. Its semantics are more delicate, and therefore harder to implement. We lack strong evidence of its practical usefulness. We have presented one promising application: writing generic functions such as `print` in a way that is conceptually simpler than type classes. However, the usability of these functions is limited by the restriction that dynamics must be created with closed types. This restriction can be lifted, either by passing type information at run-time to all polymorphic functions, or by examining the call chain at dynamic creation time to reconstruct the instantiations of type variable — a technique developed for tagless garbage collection [3, 6]. It remains to estimate the run-time penalty incurred.

References

[1] Martín Abadi, Luca Cardelli, Benjamin Pierce, and Gordon Plotkin. Dynamic typing in a statically-typed language. In *Proc. Symp. Principles of Programming Languages*, 1989.

[2] Martín Abadi, Luca Cardelli, Benjamin Pierce, and Gordon Plotkin. Dynamic typing in a statically-typed language. Research report 47, DEC Systems Research Center, 1989. Extended version of [1].

[3] Andrew Appel. Run-time tags aren't necessary. *Lisp and Symbolic Computation*, 2(2):153–162, June 1989.

[4] Luca Cardelli. Amber. In *Combinators and Functional Programming Languages*, volume 242 of *Lecture Notes in Computer Science*. Springer-Verlag, 1986.

[5] Luis Damas and Robin Milner. Principal type-schemas for functional programs. In *Proc. Symp. Principles of Programming Languages*, 1982.

[6] Benjamin Goldberg. Tag-free garbage collection for strongly typed programming languages. In *SIGPLAN conference on Programming Language Design and Implementation*, 1991.

[7] Michael Gordon. Adding `eval` to ML. Privately circulated note, circa 1980.

[8] Gérard Huet. The Calculus of Constructions, documentation and user's guide. Technical report 110, INRIA, 1989.

[9] David Maier and David S. Warren. *Computing with logic: logic programming with Prolog.* Benjamin/Cummings, 1988.

[10] Dale Miller. Lexical scoping as universal quantification. In *Proceedings of the sixth international conference for logic programming*, 1989.

[11] Dale Miller. Unification under a mixed prefix. Draft, 1990.

[12] Robin Milner, Mads Tofte, and Robert Harper. *The definition of Standard ML.* The MIT Press, 1990.

[13] Alan Mycroft. Dynamic types in ML. Draft, 1983.

[14] Simon Peyton-Jones. *The implementation of functional programming languages.* Prentice-Hall, 1987.

[15] François Rouaix. Safe run-time overloading. In *Proc. Symp. Principles of Programming Languages*, 1990.

[16] Philip Wadler and Stephen Blott. How to make ad-hoc polymorphism less ad-hoc. In *Proc. Symp. Principles of Programming Languages*, 1989.

[17] David H.D. Warren. An abstract Prolog instruction set. Technical note 309, SRI International, 1983.

[18] Pierre Weis. The CAML reference manual, version 2.6.1. Technical report 121, INRIA, 1990.

Implementing Regular Tree Expressions

Alexander Aiken
IBM Almaden Research Center
650 Harry Rd.
San Jose, CA 95120
aiken@ibm.com

Brian R. Murphy
Computer Science Department
Stanford University
Stanford, CA 94305
brm@cs.stanford.edu

Abstract

Regular tree expressions are a natural formalism for describing the sets of tree-structured values that commonly arise in programs; thus, they are well-suited to applications in program analysis. We describe an implementation of regular tree expressions and our experience with that implementation in the context of the FL type system. A combination of algorithms, optimizations, and fast heuristics for computationally difficult problems yields an implementation efficient enough for practical use.

1 Introduction

Regular tree expressions are a natural formalism for describing the sets of tree-structured values that commonly arise in programs. As such, several researchers have proposed using (variations on) regular tree expressions in type inference and program analysis algorithms [JM79, Mis84, MR85, HJ90, HJ91, AM91]. We are not aware of any implementations based on regular tree expressions, however, except for our own work on type analysis for the functional language FL [B+89].

A previous paper described the theoretical basis for our FL type inference system, in which types are represented by regular tree expressions [AM91]. This paper describes an implementation of regular tree expressions and our experience with that implementation in the context of the FL type system. Implementing regular tree expressions efficiently is challenging, because some of the basic operations have exponential time complexity [Sei89]. Even some operations with polynomial time algorithms perform poorly in practice. The fundamental operations on regular tree expressions are: computing fixed points, union, intersection, negation, and testing inclusion (including solving sets of inclusion constraints). Of these, both negation and inclusion require exponential time in general. This is particularly troublesome in the case of inclusion, because in our system it is by far the most commonly used operation, and we would expect the same to be true for most applications.

We give an abstract description of a complete implementation of regular tree expressions, including algorithms, heuristics (where necessary), and a number of optimizations. We also present the results of performance measurements on our implementation. The performance measurements show that the amortized cost per regular tree operation is nearly constant in our system.

We begin in Section 2 with a straightforward definition of regular tree expressions; we use this representation to illustrate their usefulness. In Section 3, we introduce the representation used in our system: *leaf-linear systems of equations* [GS84, MR85]. We discuss why leaf-linear systems are better suited to implementation than the representation of Section 2. Section 4 outlines an incremental algorithm to test whether a leaf-linear system is empty. The next several sections describe, at a high level, implementations of the operations on regular tree expressions. For brevity, we call these operations *regular tree operations.* In Section 6, we present a fast heuristic for testing inclusion of leaf-linear systems. The heuristic is conservative: the result is either "yes, the containment holds" or "don't know." This heuristic works surprisingly well in our application; in almost a year of use in the FL type analysis system, we have yet to find a practical example where the quality of information produced by the system is affected by the use of this heuristic.

Section 7 covers two simple optimizations that substantially improve the performance of intersection, union, negation, and testing inclusion. Both optimizations focus on avoiding computations whenever possible. The first optimization comes from facts such as $(A \subseteq B) \Leftrightarrow (A \cap B = A)$. If it is known that $A \subseteq B$, then we can save time and space by not computing $A \cap B$ but just returning A. Applying similar ideas uniformly dramatically improves performance. The second optimization is to use *memoization* to record and reuse the results of operations [Mic68]. While the usefulness of this optimization depends on the particular application, in our system it is very common for the same operations to be performed again and again. The performance of the system with these two optimizations is more than two orders of magnitude faster than without them. Measurements and discussion of the system's performance are also presented in Section 7.

It is worth explaining our choice of the term "regular tree expression". In [MR85], a regular tree is what we term a regular tree expression. We use a different name because the term "regular tree" is usually a finite or infinite tree with a finite number of subtrees [Cou83]. Using this definition, a regular tree expression together with a substitution denotes a set of regular trees. Regular tree expressions can also be thought of as tree automata with free variables; we discuss this view in Section 3.

2 Regular Tree Expressions

In this section, we introduce regular tree expressions, describe some of their properties, and develop a few examples. The representation shown here is not the one used for implementation; however, we present it first because it is easy to understand and illustrates the important operations. We begin with some basic definitions. Let $C = \{b, c, \ldots\}$ be a set of constructors, each with an arity $a(c)$. We assume this set is constant hereafter.

E ::=	0	$\Psi(0,\sigma)$	$=$	$\emptyset$
|	1	$\Psi(1,\sigma)$	$=$	H
|	α	$\Psi(\alpha,\sigma)$	$=$	$\sigma(\alpha)$
|	$E_1 \vee E_2$	$\Psi(E_1 \vee E_2,\sigma)$	$=$	$\Psi(E_1,\sigma) \cup \Psi(E_2,\sigma)$
|	$E_1 \wedge E_2$	$\Psi(E_1 \wedge E_2,\sigma)$	$=$	$\Psi(E_1,\sigma) \cap \Psi(E_2,\sigma)$
|	$\neg E_1$	$\Psi(\neg E_1,\sigma)$	$=$	$H - \Psi(E_1,\sigma)$
|	$\mathit{fix}\ \alpha.E_1$	$\Psi(\mathit{fix}\ \alpha.E_1,\sigma)$	$=$	least T s.t. $T = \Psi(E_1, \sigma[\alpha \leftarrow T])$
|	$c(E_1,\ldots,E_n)$	$\Psi(c(E_1,\ldots,E_n),\sigma)$	$=$	$\{c(t_1,\ldots,t_n) \| t_i \in \Psi(E_i,\sigma)\}$

Figure 1: Syntax and semantics of regular tree expressions.

Definition 2.1 Let C^0 be the set of zero-ary constructors in C. The Herbrand universe is the least set of terms H such that

$$H = C^0 \cup \{c(t_1,\ldots,t_{a(c)}) | c \in C, t_i \in H\}$$

Definition 2.2 A *substitution* σ is a function from some set of variable symbols V to the power set of H. We define $\sigma \uparrow \Delta$ to be the substitution σ restricted to the set of variables Δ.

Regular tree expressions denote sets of terms of the free algebra H. A syntax and semantics for regular tree expressions is given in Figure 1. The meaning function Ψ maps an expression under an environment σ to a subset of H. A variable α is *bound* in an expression if it appears in the scope E of a *fix* $\alpha.E$; otherwise the variable is *free.* We restrict the negation operator to argument expressions with no free variables; this ensures that Ψ is monotonic in its second argument, and thus the least fixed-point operator is well-defined.

Other proposals for program analysis systems based on regular tree expressions adopt slightly different definitions, depending upon the application. For example, Mishra and Reddy restrict the use of disjunction in a type inference algorithm for a statically typed functional language [MR85], and Heintze and Jaffar use projection functions in a program analysis for logic programs [HJ90]. Almost all of our implementation design would apply to these other systems with little or no modification.

The following examples illustrate the usefulness of regular tree expressions. Let c be a binary constructor and let b be a zero-ary constructor. If we interpret c as describing a Lisp `cons` operation and b as describing the atom `nil`, then the set of Lisp lists is $\mathit{fix}\ \alpha.c(1,\alpha) \vee b$. Similarly, the set of binary trees with leaves described by β is $\mathit{fix}\ \alpha.c(\alpha,\alpha) \vee \beta$. A more sophisticated example uses regular tree expressions to infer the types of recursively defined functions. Consider a recursive function $\mathit{def}\ f \equiv e(f)$. If we assume that f may return a member of the set α and prove from this assumption that $e(f)$ returns a term in the set $E(\alpha)$, we can conclude that f returns any term in $\mathit{fix}\ \alpha.E(\alpha)$.

The grammar of Figure 1 illustrates most of the important operations on regular tree expressions (least fixed-points, union, intersection, and negation). It is also possible to add a greatest fixed-point operation, but this introduces no new ideas in an implementation, so we we do not consider it here. Two other important algorithms test emptiness and inclusion relationships. In the type inference example above, it may be useful to know if $\mathit{fix}\ \alpha.E(\alpha)$ is empty, since this amounts to a proof that f is a non-terminating function (i.e., f's set of possible results is empty). A more general method to determine the results of recursive functions involves the solution of inclusion constraints on regular tree expressions [AM91].

In the sections that follow, we describe a high-level implementation of these operations with considerable attention to efficiency. As a rule, we state results needed to justify our algorithms, but omit the proofs for brevity. Many of these results may be found in the literature [GS84, MR85, HJ90, AW91].

3 Systems of Equations

Regular tree expressions are easy to understand, but are not well suited to the implementation of some algorithms. The algorithms we present are formalized as transformations on sets of equations of the form $\{x_i = \mathit{Rhs}_i\}$, where the x_i are variables and the Rhs_i are regular tree expressions not using the *fix* operator. To discuss the correctness of such transformations, we use the following definition.

Definition 3.1 Let $S = \{x_i = \mathit{Rhs}_i\}$ be a set of equations. We define the following functions on S: $\mathit{Vars}(S)$ is the set of variables in S, $\mathit{Bound}(S)$ is the set of *bound* variables x_i appearing on the left-hand side of equations, and $\mathit{Free}(S)$ is the set of *free* variables $\mathit{Vars}(S) - \mathit{Bound}(S)$.

Throughout this paper, we uniformly use x_i for bound variables, greek letters for free variables, and v for an arbitrary free or bound variable. We also assume that every system of equations contains an equation $x_H = \bigvee_{c \in C} c(x_H, \ldots)$. This allows a concise description of negation (see Section 4). Note that $\mathit{Rhs}_H = 1$.

Definition 3.2 The set of *solutions* $\mathcal{S}(S)$ of S is the set of substitutions for variables in $\mathit{Vars}(S)$ that satisfy the equations:

$$\mathcal{S}(S) = \{\sigma | \Psi(x_i, \sigma) = \Psi(\mathit{Rhs}_i, \sigma)\}$$

Two sets of equations S_1 and S_2 are *equivalent* (written $S_1 \equiv S_2$) if $\mathcal{S}(S_1) = \mathcal{S}(S_2)$. S_1 and S_2 are equivalent over a set of variables Δ if their solutions are the same over those variables:

$$S_1 \equiv_\Delta S_2 \qquad \Leftrightarrow \qquad \{\sigma \uparrow \Delta | \sigma \in \mathcal{S}(S_1)\} = \{\sigma \uparrow \Delta | \sigma \in \mathcal{S}(S_2)\}$$

The inputs and outputs of our algorithms are *leaf-linear systems of equations* [MR85] or *regular* ΣX*-grammars* [GS84]. These are systems of equations with conjunction and disjunction operators syntactically restricted. A syntax and semantics for leaf-linear systems is given in Figure 2. The following theorem shows that the semantics is well-defined [AW91].

Theorem 3.3 Let S be a leaf-linear system. Then for any substitution σ for variables $\mathit{Free}(S)$, there is exactly one substitution σ' for variables $\mathit{Vars}(S)$ such that σ' extends σ and $\sigma' \in \mathcal{S}(S)$.

$S ::= \{x_1 = Rhs_1, \ldots, x_n = Rhs_n\}$ $C ::= \{b, c, \ldots\}$ $Rhs ::= 0 \mid G \wedge T \mid Rhs_1 \vee Rhs_2$ $G ::= \alpha_1 \wedge \ldots \wedge \alpha_k$ where $\alpha_i \in Free(S)$ $T ::= 1 \mid c(y_1, \ldots, y_{a(c)})$ where $y_i \in X, c \in C$	$\Psi_S(x_j, \sigma) = \Psi(x_j, \sigma')$ where σ' is the unique substitution such that $\sigma' \uparrow Free(S) = \sigma \uparrow Free(S)$ and, for all $(x_i = Rhs_i) \in S$, $\Psi(x_i, \sigma') = \Psi(Rhs_i, \sigma')$

Figure 2: Syntax and Semantics of Systems of Leaf-Linear Equations

In other words, each substitution for the free variables determines a substitution for the bound variables. Regular tree expressions and leaf-linear systems are equivalent in a strong sense [MR85]:

Theorem 3.4 For any regular tree expression R there is a leaf-linear system of equations S, and for any leaf-linear system of equations S there is a regular tree expression R such that

$$\forall \sigma \; \Psi(R, \sigma) \;=\; \Psi_S(x_1, \sigma)$$

Thus far, we have treated a leaf-linear system as a system of equations; however, a leaf-linear system also can be viewed as a tree automaton [GS84]. We occasionally adopt this view to make use of results from automata theory. When a leaf-linear system is viewed as a tree automaton, an equation represents a state and the transition function for that state. By convention, x_1 is the initial state. The variable on the left-hand side of an equation is the name of the state, and the right-hand side represents the possible transitions. A disjunction corresponds to non-determinism; the automaton may choose one of several transitions. A constructor transition $c(x_1, \ldots, x_{a(c)})$ accepts if the input is of the form $c(t_1, \ldots, t_{a(c)})$ and each x_i accepts t_i. A 1 transition accepts everything; a 0 transition rejects everything. Given some substitution σ for the free variables in a leaf-linear system S, the language $\mathcal{L}(S)$ accepted by a leaf-linear system S is just $\Psi_S(x_1, \sigma)$.

Representing regular tree expressions by leaf-linear systems in an implementation has two significant advantages. First, leaf-linear systems allow sharing among equations, whereas subexpressions are not shared in regular tree expressions. This is obviously more economical. Second, two of the most important algorithms, testing emptiness and containment, are more easily expressed and efficiently implemented using leaf-linear systems. The potential disadvantage of using leaf-linear systems is that they may be, in the worst case, exponentially larger than the smallest equivalent regular tree expression. We have found that, in practice, all of this potential size explosion can be avoided by using the algorithms and optimizations presented here.

As an example, the expression *fix* $\alpha.c(1,\alpha) \vee b$ (the set of Lisp lists) is represented by the leaf-linear system:

$$\begin{aligned} x_1 &= c(x_2, x_1) \vee b \\ x_2 &= 1 \end{aligned}$$

Our system implements leaf-linear systems almost exactly as described here. A system of equations is represented by an array. Free and bound variables are indices into the array, and right-hand sides of equations are the entries in the array. There are four types of right-hand sides: one each for 0, 1, free variables, and disjunctions of constructor expressions. As operations are performed, new equations may be added, extending the array, and free variables may be instantiated, in which case the corresponding index of the array acquires a new entry.

4 Testing Emptiness

One fundamental problem is determining whether an expression denotes the empty set under all substitutions for free variables. More formally, for a given leaf-linear system S, we wish to test the predicate $\forall \sigma \in \mathcal{S}(S)\ \Psi_S(E,\sigma) = \emptyset$. Testing emptiness is useful for two reasons. First, it can be an important part of the application. For example, in our type inference algorithm for FL, proving that a function is type-safe is reduced to proving that a regular tree expression is empty [AM91]. Second, emptiness testing is important for the efficiency of the system. It is wasteful, both of time and space, to build and maintain expressions of the form $c(Y,X)$ or $Y \wedge X$ where Y is empty. The following easy lemma shows that the problem of testing emptiness in all substitutions reduces to the problem of testing emptiness in one particular substitution.

Lemma 4.1 Let τ be the substitution $\forall v\ \tau(v) = H$. Then

$$\forall \sigma\ \Psi_S(E,\sigma) = \emptyset \qquad \Leftrightarrow \qquad \Psi_S(E,\tau) = 0$$

To test whether $\Psi_S(x_i,\tau) = \emptyset$, we use the function Φ_S defined in Figure 3. This definition is a straightforward adaptation of algorithms for reachability and emptiness for finite automata [HU79, GS84].

Lemma 4.2 Let $S = \{x_1 = \mathit{Rhs}_1, \ldots, x_k = \mathit{Rhs}_k\}$ be a leaf-linear system, and let Φ_S be defined as in Figure 3. Then

$$\Phi_S(x_i) = \perp \qquad \Leftrightarrow \qquad \Psi_S(x_i,\tau) = \emptyset$$

Proof: [sketch] It is easy to show by induction on the height of terms t that

$$\Phi_S(x_i) = \perp \qquad \Leftrightarrow \qquad \forall t\ \mathit{height}(t) \leq k \Rightarrow t \notin \Psi_S(x_i,\tau)$$

To finish the proof, we observe that the language of a tree automaton of k states is non-empty if and only if it accepts a term of height at most k [GS84]. □

Φ_S is the least function (under the ordering $\bot \leq \top$) s.t.

$$\begin{array}{rcl}
\Phi_S(x_i) & = & \Phi_S(Rhs_i) \\
\Phi_S(1) & = & \top \\
\Phi_S(0) & = & \bot \\
\Phi_S(c(E_1,\ldots,E_n)) & = & \begin{cases} \top & \text{if } \forall i\ \Phi_S(E_i) = \top \\ \bot & \text{otherwise} \end{cases} \\
\Phi_S(E_1 \wedge E_2) & = & \begin{cases} \top & \text{if } \Phi_S(E_1) = \top \text{ and } \Phi_S(E_2) = \top \\ \bot & \text{otherwise} \end{cases} \\
\Phi_S(E_1 \vee E_2) & = & \begin{cases} \top & \text{if } \Phi_S(E_1) = \top \text{ or } \Phi_S(E_2) = \top \\ \bot & \text{otherwise} \end{cases} \\
\Phi_S(\alpha) & = & \top \text{ if } \alpha \in \mathit{Free}(S)
\end{array}$$

Figure 3: Testing for emptiness

Let n be the total number of symbols appearing in a leaf-linear system S. The function Φ_S is computable for every equation in the system in $\mathcal{O}(n^2)$ time using a standard fixed-point computation. Initially, $\Phi_S(x_i)$ is assumed to be $\bot$ for all x_i. Iteratively updating Φ_S requires at most $\mathcal{O}(n)$ passes to compute a fixed point, and each iteration requires examining $\mathcal{O}(n)$ right-hand side symbols.

In our application, we found that up to a third of expressions turn out to be empty. Consequently, our system maintains the following invariant:

Invariant 4.3 Let $S = \{x_i = Rhs_i\}$, and let E be any subexpression appearing in a Rhs_i.

$$\forall \sigma \in \mathcal{S}(S)\ \Psi_S(E, \sigma) = \emptyset \quad \Rightarrow \quad (E = 0)$$

Thus if x_i is empty in all solutions, then $Rhs_i = 0$. This makes testing whether an equation is empty very cheap; it is empty if its right-hand side is 0. In the rest of this section, we describe the incremental algorithm used to maintain this invariant.

The function Φ_S is the basis for the first transformation on sets of equations.

$$S \cup \{x_i = Rhs_i\} \;\equiv\; S \cup \{x_i = 0\} \qquad \text{if } \Phi_S(x_i) = \bot \tag{1}$$

This transformation enforces Invariant 4.3 for entire right-hand sides. To enforce the invariant for every expression, we introduce a group of equivalences given in Figure 4. These are obvious simplifications, and, when regarded as rewrite rules from left to right, form a confluent rewrite system that is noetherian up to the commutativity of $\wedge$ and $\vee$. For an expression E, $\mathit{Simp}(E)$ is the normalization of expressions under the rules of Figure 4. The complexity of computing $\mathit{Simp}(E)$ is potentially exponential in the size of E due to the rules for intersection and negation; however, in practice right-hand sides of equations are quite small, so this has not been a problem in our implementation. Using these simplifications, the rest of Invariant 4.3 is enforced by the following transformation.

$$S \cup \{x_i = 0, x_j = E(x_i)\} \;\equiv\; S \cup \{x_i = 0, x_j = \mathit{Simp}(E(0))\} \tag{2}$$

For efficiency, we would like to locate the equation x_j in Rule (2) quickly. The set $\mathit{Users}(x)$, defined in Figure 5, is the set of all equations that mention x on the

$$
\begin{array}{rcl}
E_1 \wedge E_2 & = & E_2 \wedge E_1 \\
E_1 \vee E_2 & = & E_2 \vee E_1 \\
E \wedge 0 & \Rightarrow & 0 \\
E \wedge 1 & \Rightarrow & E \\
E \wedge E & \Rightarrow & E \\
E \vee 0 & \Rightarrow & E \\
E \vee 1 & \Rightarrow & 1 \\
E \vee E & \Rightarrow & E \\
c(E_1, \ldots, E_{a(c)}) \wedge c(E'_1, \ldots, E'_{a(c)}) & \Rightarrow & c(E_1 \wedge E'_1, \ldots, E_{a(c)} \wedge E'_{a(c)}) \\
c(\ldots) \wedge d(\ldots) & \Rightarrow & 0 \text{ if } c \neq d \\
c(\ldots, 0, \ldots) & \Rightarrow & 0 \\
\neg 0 & \Rightarrow & 1 \\
\neg 1 & \Rightarrow & 0 \\
\neg\neg E & \Rightarrow & E \\
\neg(E_1 \wedge E_2) & \Rightarrow & \neg E_1 \vee \neg E_2 \\
\neg(E_1 \vee E_2) & \Rightarrow & \neg E_1 \wedge \neg E_2 \\
\neg(c(E_1, \ldots, E_{a(c)})) & \Rightarrow & \bigvee_{d \in C - \{c\}} d(x_H, \ldots) \\
 & & \vee \bigvee_{1 \leq i \leq a(c)} c(\ldots, x_H, \neg E_i, x_H, \ldots)
\end{array}
$$

Figure 4: Simplifying expressions.

$$
\begin{array}{rcl}
\mathit{Vars}(E) & = & \mathit{Free}(E) \cup \mathit{Bound}(E) \\
\mathit{Users}(v) & = & \{x_i | v \in \mathit{Vars}(\mathit{Rhs}_i)\} \\
\mathit{AllUsers}(v) & = & \text{least } V = \mathit{Users}(v) \cup \{x_i | x_i \in \mathit{Users}(v'), v' \in V\}
\end{array}
$$

Figure 5: Simple functions on leaf-linear systems.

right-hand side. Our system incrementally maintains *Users*(x) for each equation, thus allowing candidates for the application of Rule (2) to be located in constant time.

Lemma 4.4 Let S' be any leaf-linear system closed under application of Rules (1) and (2). Then S' satisfies Invariant 4.3.

As an example, consider the following system.

$$\begin{aligned} x_1 &= d(x_2, x_2) \\ x_2 &= c(x_2) \end{aligned}$$

Both x_1 and x_2 are empty in all substitutions. Rule (1) sets x_2 to 0, then Rule (2) sets x_1 to 0.

Given any leaf-linear system, we can apply Rules (1) and (2) to produce a leaf-linear system that satisfies the invariant. However, a more practical situation is that a leaf-linear system S satisfying the invariant is modified in one equation to produce a slightly different system S', and then we wish to enforce the invariant for S'.

We briefly describe an incremental version of this algorithm that solves this problem efficiently. Let $x_i = Rhs_i$ be the equation of S that is modified to produce S'. The meaning of an equation can change as a result of this modification only if it depends, directly or indirectly, on x_i. The function *AllUsers*, defined in Figure 5, captures the set of equations that depend on a particular variable. A straightforward restriction of the function Φ_S to *AllUsers*(x_i) is all that is required. We add one new clause to the definition in Figure 3:

$$\Phi_S(x_j) = \top \text{ if } x_j \notin \{x_i\} \cup \mathit{AllUsers}(x_i)$$

In practice, an incremental algorithm is important, because the size of *AllUsers*(x_i) is small (typically tens) compared to the number of equations in the system (typically thousands). Our implementation computes *AllUsers* using the obvious $O(n^3)$ fixed-point computation.

5 Construction, Or, And, Fix, and Not

In this section we show how to perform the operations given in Section 2 on leaf-linear systems. Section 7 covers the optimization of these algorithms. In the following, $E_1, \ldots, E_n$ are regular tree expressions, S is a leaf-linear system where

$$\forall\sigma\ \Psi_S(x_i, \sigma) = \Psi(E_i, \sigma)$$

and x is a fresh variable. For each operation $f(E_1, \ldots, E_n)$, we show how to extend S to a leaf-linear system S' with an equation $x = E'$ such that

$$\forall\sigma\ \Psi_S(x, \sigma) = \Psi(f(E_1, \ldots, E_n), \sigma)$$

For each case, unless otherwise noted, it is necessary to enforce Invariant 4.3 for all new and modified equations. We begin with the base cases and constructor expressions. If E_1 is a free variable α, we define $S' = S \cup \{x = \alpha \wedge 1\}$. If E_1 is 0 or 1, we define $S' = S \cup \{x = 0 \text{ or } 1\}$.

5.1 Constructors

Constructors are the easiest operations to implement using leaf-linear systems. Consider a regular tree expression $c(E_1, \ldots, E_{a(c)})$. We define a leaf-linear system $S' = S \cup \{x = c(x_1, \ldots, x_n)\}$. This is a constant time operation.

5.2 Or

Union is also a constant-time operation on leaf-linear systems. Consider a regular tree expression $E_1 \vee E_2$. We define a new leaf-linear system S' as follows:

$$S' = S \cup \{x = \mathit{Rhs}_1 \vee \mathit{Rhs}_2\}$$

Clearly $x = x_1 \vee x_2$, as desired. Furthermore, S' is in leaf-linear form, because the disjunction of right-hand sides is still a valid right-hand side. Finally, if S satisfies Invariant 4.3, then S' satisfies Invariant 4.3 without any additional work.

5.3 And

Intersection is easy if we are not concerned with efficiency. Consider a regular tree expression $E_1 \wedge E_2$. To build a leaf-linear system with an equation representing $x_1 \wedge x_2$, we may add all equations of the form

$$x_i \wedge x_j = \mathit{Simp}(\mathit{Rhs}_i \wedge \mathit{Rhs}_j)$$

and then replace conjunctions of bound variables $x_i \wedge x_j$ by new variable names [MR85]. This is wasteful, however, because many of these equations may not be required to express the desired intersection, and this algorithm always uses $\Theta(n^2)$ time and space. Thus a series of only m intersections of systems of n equations consumes $\Theta(n^m)$ time and space.

While we cannot improve on the worst-case time and space complexity, a different algorithm does much better in the typical case. The idea is to generate only those conjunctions of bound variables that are needed to express the result. We define a system S' as follows:

$$S' = S \cup \{x = \mathit{Simp}(\mathit{Rhs}_1 \wedge \mathit{Rhs}_2)\}$$

S' is not necessarily a leaf-linear system, but only a limited violation of leaf-linearity can occur in S'.

Lemma 5.1 Let Rhs_i and Rhs_j be right-hand sides in leaf-linear form. Then, if $\mathit{Simp}(\mathit{Rhs}_i \wedge \mathit{Rhs}_j)$ is not in leaf-linear form, it contains subexpressions of the form $c(\ldots, x_h \wedge x_k, \ldots)$.

The only way $\mathit{Simp}(\mathit{Rhs}_i \wedge \mathit{Rhs}_j)$ can fail to be leaf-linear is if it contains conjunctions of pairs of bound variables inside of constructors. We use two transformations to eliminate the conjunctions of bound variables. These transformations use an auxiliary set of equations A.

$$S \cup \{x_i = E(x_j \wedge x_k)\} \cup A \equiv_{Vars(S)} \begin{array}{l} S \cup \{x_i = E(x'), x' = Simp(Rhs_j \wedge Rhs_k)\} \\ \cup A \cup \{x' = x_j \wedge x_k\},\ x' \text{ new} \end{array} \quad (3)$$

$$\begin{array}{c} S \cup \{x_i = E(x_j \wedge x_k)\} \\ \cup A \cup \{x' = x_j \wedge x_k\} \end{array} \equiv S \cup \{x_i = E(x')\} \cup A \cup \{x' = x_j \wedge x_k\} \quad (4)$$

To transform S' into leaf-linear form, we repeatedly apply Rules (3) and (4) to equations that are not leaf-linear. For efficiency (and to guarantee termination) Rule (4) is always chosen in preference to (3) when both apply. It is easy to prove by induction on the number of transformations performed by this algorithm that if $x_i \wedge x_j$ is a conjunction of bound variables introduced by a transformation, then $x_i = Rhs_i$ and $x_j = Rhs_j$ are equations in S'. Thus, this algorithm terminates because there are only $\mathcal{O}(|\,Vars(S)|^2)$ possible conjunctions of bound variables. Finally, we can drop the set A of auxiliary equations.

Lemma 5.2 Suppose a leaf-linear system $S' \cup A$ is obtained by application of Rules (3) and (4) to $S \cup \emptyset$, as directed above. Then $S \cup \emptyset \equiv_{Vars(S)} S' \cup A$ and $S' \equiv_{Vars(S)} S' \cup A$.

5.4 Fix

This case is easy enough that the solution can be given directly, without additional rules. Consider a regular tree expression $fix\ \alpha.E_1$, and let S be a leaf linear system with free variable α such that

$$\forall \sigma\ \Psi_S(x_1, \sigma) = \Psi(E_1, \sigma)$$

We define a new leaf-linear system

$$S' = S \cup \{\alpha = Least(\alpha, Rhs_1)\} \text{ where}$$

$$Least(\alpha, Rhs) = \begin{cases} Least(\alpha, W) & \text{if } Rhs = W \vee (\alpha \wedge Y) \text{ for } Y \neq 0 \\ Rhs & \text{otherwise} \end{cases}$$

The system S' differs from S in that α becomes a bound variable and there is one new equation. The function *Least* is needed because $\alpha = W \vee (\alpha \wedge Y)$ has (potentially) many solutions for every substitution of the free variables $Free(S) - \{\alpha\}$; however, because *fix* is a least fixed-point operator, we are interested only in the least solution. The following lemma makes this precise.

Lemma 5.3 Consider a set of equations S with free variable α. Given a substitution π for $Free(S) - \alpha$, let σ be the least substitution that extends π to $Vars(S)$ such that $\sigma \in \mathcal{S}(S \cup \{\alpha = Rhs_1\})$. Then $\sigma \in \mathcal{S}(S \cup \{\alpha = Least(\alpha, Rhs_1)\})$.

The equation $\alpha = Least(\alpha, Rhs_1)$ is in leaf-linear form, because *Least* removes any occurrences of the newly bound variable from a guard in the right-hand side of the equation. Other equations in S' may not be in leaf-linear form because they contain α in intersections. The algorithm for intersection is used to restore leaf-linear form to the equations in $Users(\alpha)$. As an aside, a greatest fixed point operator is obtained by using

$$Grtst(\alpha, Rhs) = \begin{cases} Grtst(\alpha, W) \vee Grtst(\alpha, Y) & \textit{if } Rhs = W \vee (\alpha \wedge Y) \textit{ for } Y \neq 0 \\ Rhs & \text{otherwise} \end{cases}$$

in place of *Least*.

5.5 Negation

Let S be a leaf-linear system for the regular tree expression E_1, which contains no free variables. A system S' for $\neg E_1$ is

$$S' = S \cup \{x = Simp(\neg Rhs_1)\}$$

The approach used to put S' into leaf-linear form is very similar to the algorithm for intersection. The transformations are:

$$\begin{array}{rcll} S \cup \{x_i = E(\neg x_j)\} \cup A & \equiv_{Vars(S)} & S \cup \{x_i = E(x'), x' = Simp(\neg Rhs_j)\} & (5) \\ & & \cup A \cup \{\neg x_j = x'\} \; x' \text{ new} & \\ S \cup \{x_i = E(\neg x_j)\} & \equiv & S \cup \{x_i = E(x')\} \cup A \cup \{\neg x_j = x'\} & (6) \\ \cup A \cup \{\neg x_j = x'\} & & & \end{array}$$

As with the algorithm for intersection, these transformations are iterated until neither applies, and then the set of auxiliary equations is dropped. However, the resulting system may not be leaf-linear, because these transformations may introduce intersections of bound variables. These are eliminated as before using the algorithm for intersection.

Computing a leaf linear system for $\neg E$ may require time and space exponential in the size of E, and we have found that this does, occasionally, become a problem in practice. To compensate, we allow the computed negation to be either a subset or superset of the exact result, depending on which direction is conservative for the context in which the result is used. The heuristic we use is bounding the depth to which negations are computed; beyond this fixed depth k, the result is either 0 or 1, depending on the context. The following revised rules express the idea.

$$\begin{array}{rcl} S \cup \{x_i = E(\neg_0^+ x_j)\} \cup A & \Rightarrow & S \cup \{x_i = Simp(E(1))\} \\ S \cup \{x_i = E(\neg_0^- x_j)\} \cup A & \Rightarrow & S \cup \{x_i = Simp(E(0))\} \\ S \cup \{x_i = E(\neg_k^d x_j)\} \cup A & \equiv_{Vars(S)} & S \cup \{x_i = E(x'), x' = Simp(\neg_{k-1}^d Rhs_j)\} \\ & & \cup A \cup \{x' = \neg x_j\} \; x' \text{ new, if } k > 0 \\ S \cup \{x_i = E(\neg_k^d x_j)\} & \equiv & S \cup \{x_i = E(x')\} \cup A \cup \{x' = \neg x_j\} \text{ if } k > 0 \\ \cup A \cup \{x' = \neg x_j\} & & \end{array}$$

Note that it is necessary to discard the set of assumptions A in the first two transformations, because when the approximation rules are used the constraints in A may no longer hold.

6 Testing Inclusion

Given a set of equations S and two expressions E_1 and E_2, we often wish to test the predicates $\forall\sigma\ \Psi_S(E_1,\sigma) \subseteq \Psi_S(E_2,\sigma)$ and $\exists\sigma\ \Psi_S(E_1,\sigma) \subseteq \Psi_S(E_2,\sigma)$. Performing these tests is critical in our application. The first predicate arises when type analysis proves that a function is always applied to an argument in its appropriate domain (i.e., that the actual arguments are a subset of the appropriate domain). The second predicate arises in analyzing recursive functions, when it becomes necessary to solve constraints to assign types to recursive functions [AM91] (in this case, it is necessary to actually compute a substitution σ that satisfies the constraints). A fast algorithm for containment has a third application: it can dramatically increase the performance of the other regular tree operations (see Section 7). Given the importance of testing inclusion, the following result is discouraging.

Theorem 6.1 Evaluating the predicates

$$\forall\sigma\ \Psi_S(E_1,\sigma) \subseteq \Psi_S(E_2,\sigma)$$

$$\exists\sigma\ \Psi_S(E_1,\sigma) \subseteq \Psi_S(E_2,\sigma)$$

is exponential-time hard [AW91].

For the first predicate, $\forall\sigma\ \Psi_S(E_1,\sigma) \subseteq \Psi_S(E_2,\sigma)$, a decision procedure is known with the restrictions upon negation used here [Mur90]. This algorithm proved impractical in an implementation. The predicate $\exists\sigma\ \Psi_S(E_1,\sigma) \subseteq \Psi_S(E_2,\sigma)$ is computable in general, and in fact it is possible to compute all substitutions that make the inclusion relationship true [AW91]. Unfortunately, this algorithm runs in non-deterministic exponential time.

In this section, we present a single mechanism implementing a conservative heuristic for both inclusion tests. As we discuss below, this heuristic has worked very well in our implementation. The heuristic is formalized using a logic with theorems of the form $A \vdash E_1 \subseteq E_2$. The set A contains constraints on the free variables that make the inclusion relationship true. The predicate $\forall\sigma\ \Psi_S(E_1,\sigma) \subseteq \Psi(E_2,\sigma)$ is reduced to the question $\emptyset \vdash E_1 \subseteq E_2$, while the $\exists\sigma\ \Psi_S(E_1,\sigma) \subseteq \Psi_S(E_2,\sigma)$ predicate reduces to finding any A such that $A \vdash E_1 \subseteq E_2$. The logic is not complete; that is, there may be no proof $A \vdash E_1 \subseteq E_2$, even if there exists a substitution for which the inclusion relationship holds.

The axioms and inference rules for proving inclusion relationships are given in Figure 6. Several of the rules in Figure 6 could be combined to give a more concise system; however, because we are presenting an implementation, we prefer to describe the cases that are actually handled by the algorithm. To help explain these rules, we make the following definition. For a set of constraints A, $F(A)$ is the subset of A consisting of constraints of the form $\alpha \subseteq E$ or $E \subseteq \alpha$. Note that the only other possible constraints are between bound variables (rule [BASSUME]).

Our implementation uses a proof procedure based on these rules. This proof procedure is goal-oriented; it begins with a fact to prove, and runs the inference rules backward to axioms, building up the needed assumptions as it goes. Figure 7 gives an example of a simple proof derived by our proof procedure using the logic.

$\overline{\emptyset \vdash E \subseteq 1}$	[ONE]	$\overline{\emptyset \vdash 0 \subseteq E}$	[ZERO]
$\dfrac{A \vdash Rhs_H \subseteq E}{A \vdash 1 \subseteq E}$	[LONE]	$\overline{\emptyset \vdash E \subseteq E}$	[TAUT]
$\overline{\{x_1 \subseteq x_2\} \vdash x_1 \subseteq x_2}$	[BASSUME]	$\dfrac{A \cup \{x_i \subseteq x_j\} \vdash Rhs_i \subseteq Rhs_j}{A \vdash x_i \subseteq x_j}$	[REC]
$\overline{\{\alpha \subseteq E_2\} \vdash \alpha \subseteq E_2}$	[VASSUM1]	$\overline{\{E_1 \subseteq \alpha\} \vdash E_1 \subseteq \alpha}$	[VASSUM2]
$\overline{\emptyset \vdash \alpha \wedge E \subseteq \alpha}$	[LVAR]	$\dfrac{A \vdash \alpha \subseteq E}{A \vdash \alpha \subseteq \alpha \wedge E}$	[RVAR]
$\dfrac{\forall i\ A_i \vdash E \subseteq E_i}{\bigcup_i A \vdash E \subseteq \bigwedge_i E_i}$	[AND]	$\dfrac{A \vdash \alpha \subseteq E_1 \vee E_3,\quad \Psi_S(E_3,\sigma) = H - \Psi_S(E_2,\tau)}{A \vdash \alpha \subseteq \alpha \wedge E_2 \subseteq E_1}$	[VAR]
$\dfrac{\forall i\ A_i \vdash x_{1i} \subseteq x_{2i}}{\bigcup_i A_i \vdash c(\ldots,x_{1i},\ldots) \subseteq c(\ldots,x_{2i},\ldots)}$	[CONS]	$\dfrac{\exists i\ A \vdash x_i \subseteq 0}{A \vdash c(\ldots,x_i,\ldots) \subseteq 0}$	[ZCONS]
$\dfrac{\forall i\ A_i \vdash E_i \subseteq E}{\bigcup_i A_i \vdash \bigvee_i E_i \subseteq E}$	[LOR]	$\dfrac{\exists i\ A \vdash E \subseteq E_i}{A \vdash E \subseteq \bigvee_i E_i}$	[ROR]

Figure 6: Inference rules for testing inclusion.

$$\underline{\{\alpha \subseteq \gamma\} \vdash \alpha \subseteq \gamma} \text{ [VASSUM1]} \qquad \underline{\{x_1 \subseteq x_2\} \vdash x_1 \subseteq x_2} \text{ [BASSUME]}$$

$$\underline{\{\alpha \subseteq \gamma, x_1 \subseteq x_2\} \vdash c(\alpha, x_1) \subseteq c(\gamma, x_2)} \text{ [CONS]} \qquad \underline{\emptyset \vdash b \subseteq b} \text{ [CONS]}$$

$$\underline{\{\alpha \subseteq \gamma, x_1 \subseteq x_2\} \vdash c(\alpha, x_1) \subseteq c(\gamma, x_2) \vee b} \text{ [ROR]} \qquad \underline{\emptyset \vdash b \subseteq c(\gamma, x_2) \vee b} \text{ [ROR]}$$

$$\underline{\{\alpha \subseteq \gamma, x_1 \subseteq x_2\} \vdash c(\alpha, x_2) \vee b \subseteq c(\gamma, x_2) \vee b} \text{ [LOR]}$$

$$\{\alpha \subseteq \gamma\} \vdash x_1 \subseteq x_2 \text{ [REC]}$$

$$\begin{aligned} x_1 &= c(\alpha, x_1) \vee b \\ x_2 &= c(\gamma, x_2) \vee b \end{aligned}$$

Figure 7: An inclusion example.

The rules in Figure 6 almost define a deterministic proof procedure. To eliminate non-determinism, axioms [TAUT], [ONE], and [ZERO] are always applied in preference to all other rules. An assumption on bound variables is introduced by [BASSUME] if and only if there is a [REC] step to eliminate the assumption; this constraint guarantees that the conclusion of a proof has the form $A \vdash x_i \subseteq x_j$ where A contains assumptions only on free variables (i.e., $F(A) = A$).

When both sides of an inclusion are disjunctions, [LOR] is applied to break up the left-hand side before [ROR] is used. This is the order used in Figure 7. Inference rules [LVAR] or [RVAR] are used, if applicable, before [VASSUM1] or [VASSUM2]. This guarantees that in a proof there are no assumptions of the form $\alpha \subseteq \alpha \wedge E$ or $\alpha \wedge E \subseteq \alpha$ in $F(A)$. Finally, the last source of non-determinism is the order in which possibilities are considered in [ZCONS] and [ROR]; in our implementation, this order is fixed to be from left to right.

6.1 Computing Substitutions from Constraints

A proof of $A \vdash x_i \subseteq x_j$ does not necessarily yield a substitution that makes the relationship $x_i \subseteq x_j$ true. For example, it is entirely possible to have a proof

$$\{\alpha \subseteq 0, 1 \subseteq \alpha\} \vdash x_i \subseteq x_j$$

In this case, the set of constraints implies (by transitivity) that $1 \subseteq 0$; that is, the set of constraints is inconsistent. The following definition identifies the sets of constraints that do yield substitutions.

Definition 6.2 A set of constraints A is *closed* if·

$$\{X \subseteq \alpha, \alpha \subseteq Y\} \subseteq A \Rightarrow A \vdash X \subseteq Y$$

Let $A \vdash x_i \subseteq x_j$. If A is not closed, choose constraints $\{X \subseteq \alpha, \alpha \subseteq Y\} \subseteq A$ that do not satisfy Definition 6.2 and and find a proof $A' \vdash X \subseteq Y$. Repeat this procedure on $A \cup A'$ until the set is closed, or an inconsistency is discovered. This process terminates because constraints are built only from existing expressions and

$$A \cup \{\alpha \subseteq E_1, \alpha \subseteq E_2\} \equiv A \cup \{\alpha \subseteq E_1 \wedge E_2\}$$
$$A \cup \{E_1 \subseteq \alpha, E_2 \subseteq \alpha\} \equiv A \cup \{E_1 \vee E_2 \subseteq \alpha\}$$

Figure 8: Simplifying sets of constraints.

expressions introduced by [VAR]. An easy calculation shows that the total number of such expressions is finite, and thus so is the set of possible constraints. The set of constraints in Figure 7 is closed.

A closed set of constraints is simplified using the rules in Figure 8 so that there is at most one upper and one lower bound per free variable. We also add trivial constraints $0 \subseteq \alpha$ and $\alpha \subseteq 1$ to guarantee that there is exactly one upper and lower bound per free variable. In Figure 7, there is only one constraint; adding the trivial constraints yields the constraints $\{0 \subseteq \alpha \subseteq \gamma, \alpha \subseteq \gamma \subseteq 1\}$. In the case where constraints are between free variables only, our system performs a small optimization and does not add trivial constraints for both variables. In this case, the set of constraints produced by our system is $\{\alpha \subseteq \gamma \subseteq 1\}$.

Theorem 6.3 Let $A \vdash x_i \subseteq x_j$ be a proof where A is closed and

$$A = \{L_i \subseteq \alpha_i \subseteq U_i | \alpha_i \textit{ free in } S\}$$

Let $\beta_1, \ldots, \beta_n$ be fresh variables, and let S' be the set of equations S extended with the additional equations (for each α_i)

$$\alpha_i = L_i \vee (\beta_i \wedge U_i)$$

Then $\forall \sigma\ \Psi_{S'}(x_i, \sigma) \subseteq \Psi_{S'}(x_j, \sigma)$.

The proof of this theorem is difficult; see [AW91]. The intuition behind the construction is that the free variable β_i allows the actual value of α_i to be anything "in between" the lower and upper bounds L_i and U_i. Referring again to Figure 7, using the constraints $\{\alpha \subseteq \gamma \subseteq 1\}$ our system produces the system of equations

$$\begin{aligned} x_1 &= c(\alpha, x_1) \vee b \\ x_2 &= c(\gamma, x_2) \vee b \\ \gamma &= \alpha \vee \beta \end{aligned}$$

6.2 Discussion

For the most part, the rules in Figure 6 have the property that the conclusion holds if and only if the hypotheses hold. The two exceptions are the inference rules [VAR] and [ROR]. These two rules are the "heuristics" in our proof procedure. We explain the rational behind each below.

The rule [VAR] is an approximation of the fact $\alpha \wedge E_2 \subseteq E_1 \Leftrightarrow \alpha \subseteq E_1 \vee \neg E_2$. The problem is that $\neg E_2$ may not be expressible in our language—that is, it may introduce negations on free variables. As discussed in Section 2, we do not permit this because negation is not monotonic, and therefore admitting negations at this point makes it impossible to define a least fixed-point operator. If E_2 does not depend on free variables, then this rule is precise; the effect of [VAR] is to use the best approximation of E_2 that does not depend on free variables. In our system, when [VAR] is used E_2 rarely depends on free variables; thus, this heuristic appears to have little practical effect on our system.

Rule [ROR] states that to prove $C \subseteq D \vee E$, prove either $C \subseteq D$ or $C \subseteq E$. Many facts are not provable with this rule, such as

$$c(a \vee b) \subseteq c(a) \vee c(b)$$

In our application, [ROR] appears to be more than adequate. While we cannot completely explain this, one reason is that our system optimizes disjunctions $c(a) \vee c(b)$ into the equivalent $c(a \vee b)$. Similarly, $d(a, x) \vee d(b, x)$ becomes $d(a \vee b, x)$. Apparently this suffices to cover common cases missed by the [ROR] rule; our type analysis system builds very complex equations, and yet we have not found a practical example where this approximation fails to be accurate.

It is worth pointing out that there are much stronger rules than [ROR]. Consider the following lemma.

Lemma 6.4 Let S be a subset of $\{1, \ldots, n\}$ and let $\overline{S}$ be $\{1, \ldots, n\} - S$.

$$c(x, y) \subseteq \bigvee_{1 \leq i \leq n} c(x_i, y_i) \quad \Leftrightarrow \quad \forall S\ (x \subseteq \bigvee_{j \in S} x_j) \vee (y \subseteq \bigvee_{j \in \overline{S}} y_j)$$

See [Mur90] for a generalization to constructors of arbitrary arity. The problem with an inference rule based on Lemma 6.4 is that it consumes exponential time and space, since it generates exponentially many new regular tree expressions. For an implementation, the rules in Figure 6 have the advantage that, except for sets of assumptions, they consume no space.

7 Optimizations

The implementation we have described thus far is complete but still performs poorly in practice. This section covers the remaining performance problems and the optimizations that overcome them. In order to make the effectiveness of the optimizations clear and concrete, we use an example from our type inference system for FL. In the FL type inference algorithm, types are represented by regular tree expressions. In the process of analyzing a program, the type inference algorithm performs many (typically thousands) of regular tree operations. The FL type system is implemented on an IBM RT/PC in Lucid Common Lisp 3.0.

The example we use is a heapsort program written in FL. This program was written to exercise the type system, especially its ability to solve systems of constraints arising from recursively defined higher-order functions. The type system generates large and complex types while analyzing heapsort. The text of the heapsort program is about 60 lines of FL; after parsing and abbreviation elimination, the program that the type system actually analyzes has about 100 lines.

Using the algorithms described so far, the type system analyzes heapsort for about five minutes before the Lisp system crashes with a stack overflow. Just before it dies, the system has generated 12,948 equations, including one with a disjunction of 1040 constructors on the right-hand side! Inspection shows that the intersection algorithm is generating an enormous number of equations. Before the crash, the system computes 1407 intersections, which require a total of 84,409 applications of Rules (3) and (4), for an average of 60 rules per intersection computed. The cost of 60 rules per intersection is misleading—this cost grows rapidly during the computation and would presumably far exceed 60 rules per intersection if the Lisp system had more stack space. Although the cost of intersections dominates in this example, the inclusion and negations algorithms are also slow.

Analyzing the actual sequence of intersections, negations, and inclusion tests performed reveals part of the problem: many of the operations are being computed over and over again. *Memoization* is a simple optimization that caches and reuses the results of computations [Mic68]. We have already used something quite like memoization in the auxiliary systems of equations used for computing intersection and negation in Section 5. If fact, instead of discarding those auxiliary equations, they can be retained and reused if the same computations are performed again.

We formalize memos as a set of auxiliary equations. For regular tree operations, every memo is an equation of the form $x = f(x_1, \ldots, x_n)$ for a regular tree operation f. Whenever one of these operations is computed, the set of auxiliary equations is searched to see if the answer is already known. If so, the left-hand side of the equation is used instead of performing the computation again. If an auxiliary equation is not found, then the computation is performed and the result is recorded in the auxiliary equations. These memos cost only constant space and time; every memo is of constant size and corresponds to some result that must be computed anyway. Furthermore, lookup can be done in constant time if the auxiliary equations are implemented as a hash table.

Memos for inclusion are similar, but instead of auxiliary equations the memos are auxiliary constraints. Whenever the system proves a fact $\emptyset \vdash x_1 \subseteq x_2$, a constraint $x_1 \subseteq x_2$ is added to the system. During inclusion tests, if the subgoal $x_1 \subseteq x_2$ is in the list of auxiliary constraints, then that subgoal is discharged. Inclusion memos are more expensive than memos for regular tree operations. While the added time to search for a memo is still effectively constant with a hashtable implementation, the space consumed is potentially $\mathcal{O}(n^2)$ for a system of n equations.

With memoization of all regular tree operations and inclusion tests, the system performs somewhat better on heapsort. In this trial, the system nearly fills the Lisp memory and begins to thrash after running for two hours. Stopping the computation at this point, the system has 36,194 equations. Again, the main culprit is intersection, with an average of 45 rules per computation. The remaining problem is that many trivial operations add new equations. For example, to compute $E \wedge 1$, the system generates a new equation instead of just using the existing equation for E. Generalizing, if $E_1 \subseteq E_2$, then the result of computing $E_1 \wedge E_2$ should be just the equation for E_1, thus avoiding a possibly large number of redundant equations produced by using the intersection algorithm to compute $E_1 \wedge E_2$. We add the following rules to the intersection algorithm, which are applied

heapsort			
	operations	total steps	steps/operation
inclusion	3965	8591	2.17
intersection	1947	2493	1.28
negation	541	569	1.05
range for other trials			
	operations	total steps	steps/operation
inclusion	8098-29724	12765-55398	1.54-1.87
intersection	2190-8236	2894-11225	1.29-1.38
negation	506-2165	540-2325	1.05-1.08

Figure 9: Results of experiments.

in preference to all other rules.

$$S \cup \{x = E(x_i \wedge x_j)\} \equiv S \cup \{x = E(x_j)\} \text{ if } \emptyset \vdash x_i \subseteq x_j$$
$$S \cup \{x = E(x_i \wedge x_j)\} \equiv S \cup \{x = E(x_i)\} \text{ if } \emptyset \vdash x_j \subseteq x_i$$

Similarly, to compute the union $E_1 \vee E_2$, if $E_1 \subseteq E_2$ then the equation for E_2 is used, and if $E_2 \subseteq E_1$ then the equation for E_1 is used. If neither case applies, the equation given in Section 5.2 is added to the system.

Combining memoization and the inclusion optimizations results in a dramatic improvement. Using these optimizations, the system is able to analyze the heapsort program in just under two minutes. The system generates 5081 equations in this trial; the most complex equation has three constructors on the right-hand side.

The first half of the table in Figure 9 gives the number of operations, the number of steps, and the steps per operation for each of inclusion, intersection, and negation in this trial. For negation and intersection, the number of steps is the total number of equations added and successful memo lookups. For inclusion, it is the number of subgoals of the form $x_1 \subseteq x_2$ in proofs and the number of successful memo lookups. Thus, the measure for inclusion counts the total number of pairs of equations that are compared.

We have run the same experiment on ten other programs; these programs are between one hundred and five hundred lines long. The second half of Figure 9 gives the range of measurements in these trials. With the exception of inclusion, the amortized cost of each operation is about the same as in heapsort. Inclusion tests are noticeably cheaper in the general trial; presumably this is because heapsort was designed specifically to stress the inclusion algorithm. Overall, the result of this experiment shows that, with the optimizations, the amortized cost of regular tree operations is nearly constant in practice.

8 Conclusion

Regular tree expressions are a powerful tool for describing sets of terms of a free algebra; as such, several program analysis algorithms based on regular tree expressions have been proposed. We have described our implementation of regular tree expressions for a type inference system. Our experience is that, with carefully designed algorithms and some optimizations, regular tree operations can be efficiently implemented.

Acknowledgements

The authors would like to thank Jennifer Widom, John Williams, and Ed Wimmers for discussions and their comments on earlier versions of this paper.

References

[AM91] A. Aiken and B. Murphy. Static type inference in a dynamically typed language. In *Eighteenth Annual ACM Symposium on Principles of Programming Languages*, pages 279–290, Orlando, 1991.

[AW91] A. Aiken and E. Wimmers. A decision problem for set constraints. Research Report Forthcoming RJ, IBM, 1991.

[B+89] J. Backus et al. FL language manual, parts 1 and 2. Research Report RJ 7100, IBM, 1989.

[Cou83] B. Courcelle. Fundamental properties of infinite trees. *Theoretical Computer Science*, 25:95–169, 1983.

[GS84] F. Gecseg and M. Steinby. *Tree Automata.* Academei Kaido, Budapest, 1984.

[HJ90] N. Heintze and J. Jaffar. A finite presentation theorem for approximating logic programs. In *Seventeenth Annual ACM Symposium on Principles of Programming Languages*, pages 197–209, January 1990.

[HJ91] N. Heintze and J. Jaffar. Set-based program analysis. Draft manuscript, 1991.

[HU79] J. E. Hopcroft and J. D. Ullman. *Introduction to Automata Theory, Languages, and Computation.* Addison-Wesley, 1979.

[JM79] N. D. Jones and S. S. Muchnick. Flow analysis and optimization of LISP-like structures. In *Sixth Annual ACM Symposium on Principles of Programming Languages*, pages 244–256, January 1979.

[Mic68] D. Michie. 'Memo' functions and machine learning. *Nature*, (218):19–22, April 1968.

[Mis84] P. Mishra. Towards a theory of types in PROLOG. In *Proceedings of the First IEEE Symposium in Logic Programming*, pages 289–298, 1984.

[MR85] P. Mishra and U. Reddy. Declaration-free type checking. In *Proceedings of the Twelfth Annual ACM Symposium on the Principles of Programming Languages*, pages 7–21, 1985.

[Mur90] B. R. Murphy. A type inference system for FL. Master's thesis, MIT, 1990.

[Sei89] H. Seidl. Deciding equivalence of finite tree automata. In *6th Annual Symposium on Theoretical Aspects of Computer Science*. Lecture Notes in Computer Science, February 1989.

Efficient Type Inference for Higher-Order Binding-Time Analysis*

Fritz Henglein
DIKU
University of Copenhagen
Universitetsparken 1
2100 Copenhagen Ø
Denmark
Internet: henglein@diku.dk

Abstract

Binding-time analysis determines when variables and expressions in a program can be bound to their values, distinguishing between *early* (compile-time) and *late* (run-time) binding. Binding-time information can be used by compilers to produce more efficient target programs by *partially evaluating* programs at compile-time. Binding-time analysis has been formulated in abstract interpretation contexts and more recently in a type-theoretic setting.

In a type-theoretic setting binding-time analysis is a *type inference problem*: the problem of inferring a *completion* of a λ-term e with binding-time annotations such that e satisfies the typing rules. Nielson and Nielson and Schmidt have shown that every simply typed λ-term has a unique completion $\hat{e}$ that minimizes late binding in TML, a monomorphic type system with explicit binding-time annotations, and they present exponential time algorithms for computing such minimal completions.[1] Gomard proves the same results for a variant of his two-level λ-calculus without a so-called "lifting" rule. He presents another algorithm for inferring completions in this somewhat restricted type system and states that it can be implemented in time $O(n^3)$. He conjectures that the completions computed are minimal.

In this paper we expand and improve on Gomard's work in the following ways.

- We identify the combinatorial core of type inference for binding-time analysis in Gomard's type system with "lifting" by effectively characterizing it as solving a specific class of constraints on type expressions.
- We present normalizing transformations on these constraints that preserve their solution sets, and we use the resultant normal forms to prove constructively the existence of *minimal solutions*, which yield *minimal completions*; this sharpens the minimal completion result of Gomard and extends it to the full type system with "lifting".

*This research has been supported by Esprit BRA 3124, Semantique.

[1] A (minimal) completion is called a (best) decoration in the work of Nielson and Nielson and Schmidt.

- We devise a very efficient algorithm for computing minimal completions. It is a refinement of a fast unification algorithm, and an amortization argument shows that a fast union/find-based implementation executes in almost-linear time, $O(n\alpha(n,n))$, where α is an inverse of Ackermann's function.

Our results are for the two-level type system of Gomard, but we believe they are also adaptable to the Nielsons' TML. Our algorithm improves the computational complexity of computing minimal completions from exponential time to almost-linear time. It also improves on Gomard's polynomial time completion algorithm by a quadratic factor and as such appears to be the first efficient algorithm that provably computes minimal completions.

1 Introduction

Given information on the static or dynamic availability of data, binding-time analysis determines which operations can safely be evaluated "early" (statically, at compile-time) and which should be deferred until "late" (to be executed dynamically, at run-time). Instead of 'early' and 'late' we also use the common terms 'static' and 'dynamic', respectively. Binding-time information can be used to optimize the implementation of programming languages by scheduling operations with statically bound data at compile time (e.g., [JM76,JM78,JS80,Kro81,NN86] *etc*). Automatic binding-time analysis is usually beneficial for guiding the actions of program specializers, but it plays an especially important role in the generation of compilers from self-applicable partial evaluators [JSS85,JSS89,Con88, Rom87,JGB*90,Bon90a,GJ91] as a preprocessing phase to program specialization [BJMS88].

In the early work on partial evaluators a simple dichotomy static/dynamic was used (e.g., [Ses85]). This was generally too conservative for compound data types such as lists, and rewriting of a program was required to recover more static binding information. This was remedied by using more refined binding-time values [Lau87,Mog87], which Mogensen calls partially static structures. The relevance of this refinement is not limited to first-order data types. For example, if y is dynamic the function ($\lambda x.x@y$) is partially static: we can evaluate *statically* the application of $\lambda x.x@y$ to a (completely) dynamic argument z; yet we cannot evaluate statically the resulting application of x to y since x will be bound to z, which is completely dynamic.

Every function application can of course be evaluated late, which amounts to deferring all computation to run-time. Partial evaluation seeks to do as much computation at compile-time as is correct, possible and sensible. For this purpose binding-time analysis is used to find as many operations that can be evaluated ("bound") statically.

Early binding-time analysis work limited itself to first-order languages [JSS85, JSS89,Jon87,Mog89,Rom87,Lau87,Lau90], but, more recently, higher-order languages have also been analyzed: Mogensen [Mog89], Bondorf [Bon90a,Bon90b], Consel [Con90] and Hunt and Sands [HS91] describe higher-order binding time analysis in an abstract interpretation framework; Nielson and Nielson [NN88a], Schmidt [Sch87] and Gomard [Gom89,Gom90,GJ91] formalize it as a *type inference* (or *type annotation*) problem within two-level typed λ-calculus.

A two-level type system has an *early-binding* and a *late-binding* variant of every operator, which are distinguished by ***binding-time annotations.*** In Gomard's two-level typed λ-calculus there is a distinguished type Λ that represents unevaluated, *untyped* λ-terms[2], which are the result of late-binding operators at partial evaluation time. A late-binding syntactic operator (such as @, λ) is indicated by ***underscoring*** it (e.g., $\underline{@}, \underline{\lambda}$) whereas its early-binding counterpart has *no* underscore.

The main difference to the original two-level λ-calculus TML of Nielson [NN88b] is that in Nielson's work the represented λ-terms are also *typed*, which is reflected in a more complex type structure for (two-level) λ-terms denoting such unevaluated "object terms". Nielson and Nielson [NN88a] and Schmidt [Sch87] have shown that every *simply typed* λ-term has a *minimal* completion $\hat{e}$ in TML in the sense that all late-binding annotations (underscores in Gomard's system) in $\hat{e}$ occur in every completion of e with binding-time annotations, and they present exponential time algorithms for computing such minimal completions. Gomard proves the same results for *untyped* λ-terms in his two-level λ-calculus without a "lifting" rule [Gom89]. He presents a more efficient completion algorithm [Gom90] and states that this algorithm can be implemented in time $O(n^3)$ using Huet's fast unification algorithm [Gom89]. He conjectures that his algorithm computes minimal completions.

In this paper we expand and improve on Gomard's work in the following ways.

- We identify the combinatorial core of type inference for binding-time analysis in Gomard's type system with "lifting" by effectively characterizing it as solving a specific class of constraints on type expressions.
- We present normalizing transformations on these constraints that preserve their solution sets, and we use the resultant normal forms to prove constructively the existence of *minimal solutions*, which yield *minimal completions* for the type inference system; this sharpens the minimal completion result of Gomard and extends itto the full type system with "lifting".
- We devise a very efficient algorithm for computing minimal completions. It is a refinement of a fast unification algorithm, and an amortization argument shows that a fast union/find-based implementation executes in almost-linear time, $O(n\alpha(n,n))$, where α is an inverse of Ackermann's function.

Our results are for the two-level type system of Gomard (with "lifting"), but we believe they are also adaptable to the Nielsons' TML. Our algorithm improves the computational complexity of computing minimal completions from exponential time to almost-linear time. It also improves on Gomard's polynomial time algorithm by a quadratic factor and as such appears to be the first efficient algorithm that provably computes minimal completions.

We believe that the constraints used to characterize typability may be usable in describing other, similar type inference problems, thus providing a common "back-end" for a whole class of type inference problems. Furthermore, we expect

[2] In [Gom90] the type Λ type is actually called "untyped"; and in [Gom89] it is referred to as "code" because of its intended interpretation in the two-level λ-calculus.

the union/find-based implementation of our type inference algorithm to be implementable, adaptable and responsive in practice. This may well lay the foundation of a practical implementation technology for type-based program analyses.

In Section 2 we recall Gomard's type inference approach to binding time analysis. We present a characterization of completions by solutions of type constraint systems in Section 3. In Section 4 we show how these constraint systems can be normalized while preserving their solution sets. Section 5 shows how minimal completions are constructed. An efficient implementation of the constraint transformations is the basis of our almost-linear time constraint normalization in Section 6. In Section 7 we show how it can be used to implement an almost-linear time binding-time analysis algorithm. Finally, in Section 8 we briefly summarize our results and propose directions in which this kind of type-based analysis might be extended and generalized.

2 Binding-time analysis by type inference

We use a small, but paradigmatic higher-order language of *untyped λ-terms* for which we perform binding-time analysis; they are the terms e generated by the production

$$e ::= x \mid \lambda x.e' \mid e'@e'' \mid \mathbf{fix}\, e \mid \mathbf{if}\, e' \,\mathbf{then}\, e'' \,\mathbf{else}\, e''' \mid c \mid e' \,op\, e''$$

where x ranges over a class of variables, c is a class of given first-order constants, op stands for a set of given binary first-order operations, **fix** is a recursion (fixed-point) operator, and $\mathbf{if}\, e' \,\mathbf{then}\, e'' \,\mathbf{else}\, e'''$ is the usual conditional form.

In the type inference approach to binding-time analysis binding-time values are represented by *type expressions (types)*. Our types τ are generated by the production

$$\tau ::= B \mid \Lambda \mid \alpha \mid \tau' \rightarrow \tau''$$

The type constant B represents the binding-time value "static"; it denotes the set of (first-order) *base values*, such as the Boolean truth values and integers. The type constant Λ represents the binding-time value "dynamic"; extensionally it stands for the dynamic values: the set of unevaluated untyped λ-terms. A *type variable* α represents an arbitrary (fixed, but unknown) binding-time value. The function type $\tau_1 \rightarrow \tau_2$ represents a higher-order binding-time value; e.g., $\Lambda \rightarrow \Lambda$ represents a partially static function such as $(\lambda x.x@y)$ for dynamic y.

Binding-time information is represented explicitly by *operator, type*, and *lifting annotations* in λ-terms: a late-bound operator is distinguished from an early-bound operator by an underscore; an early-bound λ-abstraction carries an explicit type; and application of a lift operator represents turning a base value into a dynamic value. A λ-term with such annotations is called an *annotated* λ-term. Binding-time annotations are used to guide the actions of a partial evaluator: an early-bound operator is directly executed on its arguments, a late-bound operator is left uninterpreted (i.e., it results in constructing a piece of code from its (code) arguments), and a lift operator is interpreted by generating code representing the (static) value of its argument. We assume that base values, but not functions, can be made dynamic by application of the lift operator. As a consequence we distinguish in our type system between $B \to B$ and B even though both represent fully static binding-time values.

A binding-time proposition "expression e has binding-time value τ" is written as a *typing* $e : \tau$. Such typings are derived by a formal inference system.[3]

Figure 1 contains the inference rules for our *(two-level) type system* in natural deduction style. In it we use the following conventions: e, e', e'' range over λ-terms; x, x' over variables, τ, τ' over type expressions. A hypothesis that may be discharged at a rule application is written in square brackets; i.e., $[x : \tau']$. The introduction of a typing hypothesis for variable x "hides" all other typing hypotheses for x until it is discharged. In the following we write $A \vdash e : \tau$ if $e : \tau$ can be derived from the rules in Figure 1 and exactly one hypothesis for each free variable in e, the set of which is denoted by A. In this case we call e a *well-annotated* λ-term (w.r.t. A). For example, $(\lambda x : \Lambda.x\underline{@}y)@z$ is well-annotated w.r.t. $\{y : \Lambda, z : \Lambda\}$.

This type system is monomorphic and corresponds in expressive power roughly to what has been termed a "sticky" analysis in abstract interpretation. The inference rules consist of one rule each for every early-binding and late-binding operator, a rule for constants and the lifting rule. There are no compound (first-order) data types such as pairs and lists in our language, but they and their binding-time properties — formalized with our without partially static structures — could be added easily in the form of additional type inference rules.

Apart from inessential differences this type system is the same as Gomard's [Gom89,GJ91]. (Note that the type inference algorithm in [Gom90] is for the same type system, but without rule (LIFT).) The corresponding two-level type system for simply typed λ-terms is described in Nielson and Nielson [NN88a].

The *erasure* of an annotated λ-term e is the untyped λ-term in which all operator, type and lifting annotations are eliminated, but which is otherwise identical to e. A *completion* of an unannotated λ-term e w.r.t. typing assumptions A is a well-annotated λ-term $\bar{e}$ (w.r.t. A) whose erasure is e.

A set of typing assumptions is a *(first-order) binding-time assumption* for λ-term e if it contains exactly one typing assumption for every free variable in e, and all typing assumptions are of the form $x : B$ or $x : \Lambda$. In this context binding-time analysis is the problem of computing a *minimal* completion of an unannotated λ-term w.r.t. a given binding-time assumption in the intuitive sense that it has a minimum of late-binding operators (see Section 5 for a definition of minimality).

By using the erasures of annotated λ-terms in the "explicit" type system of Figure 1 we obtain an "implicit" type inference system for untyped λ-terms with the properties that: if $A \vdash e : \tau$ in the explicit system then $A \vdash e' : \tau$ in the implicit system where e' is the erasure of e; if $A \vdash e : \tau$ in the implicit system then there exists a completion $\bar{e}$ such that $A \vdash \bar{e} : \tau$ in the explicit system; and, in particular, for every type derivation for an untyped λ-term e there is a *unique* completion of e with an isomorphic derivation in the explicit type inference system. In other words, implicit type derivations, explicit type derivations and well-annotated λ-terms are

[3]Binding-time properties are semantic properties, and there is thus an arbitrary number of concrete conceivable "static" (recursive) analyses to approximate these quintessentially dynamic properties. The inference rules specify exactly the expressiveness of an analysis and thus determine the particular binding-time analysis problem to be solved without predetermining how to compute binding-time properties.

(ABSTR)
$$\frac{\begin{array}{l}[x : \tau']\\ e : \tau\end{array}}{\lambda x : \tau'.e : \tau' \rightarrow \tau}$$

(APPL)
$$\frac{\begin{array}{l}e : \tau' \rightarrow \tau\\ e' : \tau'\end{array}}{e@e' : \tau}$$

(FIX)
$$\frac{e : \tau \rightarrow \tau}{\mathbf{fix}\, e : \tau}$$

(IF)
$$\frac{\begin{array}{l}e : B\\ e' : \tau\\ e'' : \tau\end{array}}{\mathbf{if}\, e\, \mathbf{then}\, e'\, \mathbf{else}\, e'' : \tau}$$

(OP)
$$\frac{\begin{array}{l}e : B\\ e' : B\end{array}}{e\; op\; e' : B}$$

(CONST)
$$c : B$$

(LIFT)
$$\frac{e : B}{\mathit{lift}\, e : \Lambda}$$

(ABSTR-DYN)
$$\frac{\begin{array}{l}[x : \Lambda]\\ e : \Lambda\end{array}}{\underline{\lambda} x.e : \Lambda}$$

(APPL-DYN)
$$\frac{\begin{array}{l}e : \Lambda\\ e' : \Lambda\end{array}}{e\underline{@}e' : \Lambda}$$

(FIX-DYN)
$$\frac{e : \Lambda}{\underline{\mathbf{fix}}\, e : \Lambda}$$

(IF-DYN)
$$\frac{\begin{array}{l}e : \Lambda\\ e' : \Lambda\\ e'' : \Lambda\end{array}}{\underline{\mathbf{if}}\, e\, \underline{\mathbf{then}}\, e'\, \underline{\mathbf{else}}\, e'' : \Lambda}$$

(OP-DYN)
$$\frac{\begin{array}{l}e : \Lambda\\ e' : \Lambda\end{array}}{e\; \underline{op}\; e' : \Lambda}$$

Figure 1: Type inference system with type Λ

pairwise in natural one-to-one correspondences.

Since the lift operator and every variant — underscored and not underscored — of every syntactic operator have exactly one inference rule scheme (without side conditions) it follows that type *checking* for an annotated λ-term is (RAM-)linear-time equivalent to solving a unification problem [Wan87,Hen88a] and thus can be done efficiently in linear [PW78,MM82] or almost-linear time [Hue76,ASU86]. We will show that type *inference* for unannotated (or partially annotated) λ-terms and computation of minimal completions can actually be done in essentially the *same* time.

3 Type constraint characterization

Recall that the universe of type expressions is the class of terms $T(A, V)$ generated from the ranked alphabet $A = \{B, \rightarrow, \Lambda\}$ where B and Λ have arity (rank) 0 and $\rightarrow$ has arity 2; V is the set of type variables $\alpha, \alpha', \ldots, \beta, \gamma$ *etc.* We write $\tau = \tau'$ if τ and τ' are the same type expressions.

We define $\leq_b, \leq_f$ to be the "flat" partial orders that contain only the strict inequalities

$$B <_b \Lambda \qquad (1)$$

$$\Lambda \rightarrow \Lambda <_f \Lambda \qquad (2)$$

A *constraint system* C is a multiset of formal constraints of the form

- $\alpha' \rightarrow \alpha'' \overset{?}{\leq}_f \alpha$,
- $\beta \overset{?}{\leq}_b \alpha$,
- $\alpha \overset{?}{=} \alpha'$, and
- $\alpha \rhd \alpha'$.

where $\alpha, \alpha', \alpha_1, \ldots, \alpha_k, \beta$ are type variables or the type constant Λ; β can also be the type constant B. A substitution S (of type expressions for type variables) is a *solution* of C if

- for every constraint of the form $\alpha' \rightarrow \alpha'' \overset{?}{\leq}_f \alpha$ we have $S(\alpha' \rightarrow \alpha'') \leq_f S(\alpha)$;
- for every constraint of the form $\beta \overset{?}{\leq}_b \alpha$ we have $S(\beta) \leq_b S(\alpha)$;
- for every constraint of the form $\alpha \overset{?}{=} \alpha'$ we have $S(\alpha) = S(\alpha')$;
- for every constraint of the form $\alpha \rhd \alpha'$ we have that if $S(\alpha) = \Lambda$ then $S(\alpha') = \Lambda$;
- for every type variable α not occurring in C we have $S(\alpha) = \alpha$.[4]

[4]The last condition is a technical condition to guarantee that solutions S and S' are considered equal for a constraint system C whenever their restrictions to the variables actually occurring in C are equal.

We write Sol(C) for the set of all solutions of C.

Let e be a λ-term and A a binding-time assumption for e. We associate a type variable $\alpha_{x'}$ with every λ-bound variable x' occurring in e and unique type variables $\alpha_{e'}, \bar{\alpha}_{e'}$ for every λ-term occurrence e' in e (for an occurrence of a λ-bound variable x we take $\alpha_e = \alpha_x$). W.l.o.g. we assume that there are no two λ-bindings for any variable in e. We define the constraint system $C_A(e)$ by induction as follows.

1. If $e = \lambda x.e'$ then $C_A(e) = \{\alpha_x \rightarrow \bar{\alpha}_{e'} \overset{?}{\leq}_f \alpha_e, \alpha_e \overset{?}{\leq}_b \bar{\alpha}_e\} \cup C_A(e')$;
2. if $e = e'@e''$ then $C_A(e) = \{\bar{\alpha}_{e''} \rightarrow \alpha_e \overset{?}{\leq}_f \bar{\alpha}_{e'}, \alpha_e \overset{?}{\leq}_b \bar{\alpha}_e\} \cup C_A(e') \cup C_A(e'')$;
3. if $e =$ **fix** e' then $C_A(e) = \{\alpha_e \rightarrow \alpha_e \overset{?}{\leq}_f \bar{\alpha}_{e'}, \alpha_e \overset{?}{\leq}_b \bar{\alpha}_e\} \cup C_A(e')$;
4. if $e =$ **if** e' **then** e'' **else** e''' then $C_A(e) = \{B \overset{?}{\leq}_b \bar{\alpha}_{e'}, \alpha_e \overset{?}{=} \bar{\alpha}_{e''}, \alpha_e \overset{?}{=} \bar{\alpha}_{e'''}, \bar{\alpha}_{e'} \triangleright \alpha_e, \alpha_e \overset{?}{\leq}_b \bar{\alpha}_e\} \cup C_A(e') \cup C_A(e'') \cup C_A(e''')$;
5. if $e = c$ then $C_A(e) = \{B \overset{?}{\leq}_b \alpha_e, \alpha_e \overset{?}{\leq}_b \bar{\alpha}_e\}$;
6. if $e = e'$ *op* e'' then $C_A(e) = \{B \overset{?}{\leq}_b \bar{\alpha}_{e'}, \bar{\alpha}_{e'} \overset{?}{=} \bar{\alpha}_{e''}, \bar{\alpha}_{e''} \overset{?}{=} \alpha_e, \alpha_e \overset{?}{\leq}_b \bar{\alpha}_e\}$;
7. if $e = x$ (x a λ-bound variable) then $C_A(e) = \{\alpha_x \overset{?}{\leq}_b \bar{\alpha}_e\}$.
8. if $e = x$ (x a free variable with typing assumption $x : \tau$) then $C_A(e) = \{\tau \overset{?}{\leq}_b \bar{\alpha}_e\}$.

Every type derivation for an untyped λ-term e (in the implicit type inference system) corresponds uniquely to a *type labeling* of the syntax tree of e; that is, to a mapping of (λ-term) occurrences in e into type expressions. A type labeling that arises from a type derivation in this fashion, however, can equally well be viewed as a mapping from the canonical type variables associated above with the occurrences in e to type expressions. Consequently, every (implicit) type derivation for a λ-term e determines uniquely a *substitution* on these type variables by mapping every other type variable to itself. By induction on the syntax of λ-terms e it can be shown that such a substitution is a solution of the constraint system $C_A(e)$ and, vice versa, every solution of $C_A(e)$ is a substitution determined by a type derivation for e. Since every implicit type derivation of e corresponds to a unique completion of e we have the following theorem.

Theorem 1 *For every λ-term e and binding-time assumption A for e there is a one-to-one correspondence between the completions of e and the solutions of $C_A(e)$.*

Let us get an intuitive idea of why $C_A(e)$ captures exactly the type constraints necessary and sufficient for any completion of e w.r.t. A. First of all, the implicit version of our type inference system is useful since it describes well-typedness in terms of a given *unannotated* λ-term, which is all we have initially. In the implicit version of the type inference system of Figure 1 there are two rule schemes for every syntactic constructor (with the exception of constants and variables). Our goal is to translate the implicit system into a deterministic syntax-directed type system in which every construct has exactly one typing rule (scheme). The idea is to factor well-typedness into syntactic well-formedness plus satisfaction of (nonsyntactic) type constraints. Since syntactic well-formedness is presupposed in the input the solutions to the resulting type constraints characterize all the typings. For example, consider the implicit versions of the typing rules for λ-abstraction, (ABSTR) and (ABSTR-DYN), in Figure 1. They can be combined into the single rule

$$\text{(ABSTR-COMB)}\quad \frac{\begin{array}{l}[x : \tau'] \\ e : \tau \\ \tau' \to \tau = \tau'' \text{ or } \tau' = \tau = \tau'' = \Lambda\end{array}}{\lambda x.e : \tau''}$$

It is obvious that rule (ABSTR) is applicable if and only if the first disjunct in the side condition on types holds, and rule (ABSTR-DYN) is applicable if and only if the second disjunct holds. Since the disjunction is exclusive any rule application of (ABSTR-COMB) corresponds to an application of exactly one of the rules (ABSTR), (ABSTR-DYN), and it is easy to figure out to which. Note that $\tau' = \tau = \tau'' = \Lambda$ if and only if $\tau' \to \tau <_f \tau''$. Consequently we can write the disjunction as $\tau' \to \tau = \tau'' \vee \tau' \to \tau <_f \tau''$, viz. $\tau' \to \tau \leq_f \tau''$. Using the type variables associated with subterms in the construction of $C_A(e)$, rule (ABSTR-COMB) can be applied to a λ-abstraction $e = \lambda x.e'$ if and only if $\alpha_x \to \alpha_{e'} \overset{?}{\leq}_f \alpha_e$ is solvable; c.f. the constraints in $C_A(e)$ above.[5] Generally it is possible that a subterm is "lifted" using rule (LIFT). For occurrence e' the type variable $\alpha_{e'}$ represents the "immediate" type of e', and $\bar{\alpha}_{e'}$ represents its type after possible lifting. This explains the type constraints of the form $\alpha_{e'} \overset{?}{\leq}_b \bar{\alpha}_{e'}$ in the definition of $C_A(e)$.

Note that the inequalities $<_b, <_f$ do *not* induce inequalities on higher-order types because there is no analogue for "induced" lifting in the type inference system.

The constraint system $C_A(e)$ depends only on the language of type expressions, not the actual syntax of λ-terms. When adding additional language primitives or additional type expressions (such as a list-type and appropriate list manipulation primitives) it may be possible to modify the construction of the constraint system correspondingly without actually changing the class of constraints that are to be solved in an essential way. Thus any efficient method for solving constraint systems can conceivably be reused directly for (slightly) different program analyses. In the following two sections we show how constraint systems arising here can be solved efficiently. We view the initial translation of (a type inference problem for) a program term e into the "intermediate language" of constraints as the "front end" of our analysis and the algorithm(s) for solving these constraints as its "back end". We hope that, possibly after some suitable generalization, our constraints

[5] Similar considerations can be applied to other type inference problems to derive systematically reductions to solvability of type constraint systems; in particular, the reductions of Mitchell [Mit84], Wand [Wan87], Fuh and Mishra [FM88], Stansifer [Sta88], Henglein [Hen88b] can be derived in this fashion.

are both expressive enough to capture many interesting program analyses and still constrained enough to admit efficient computation of solutions.

4 Normalization of type constraints

In Section 3 we have seen that the type derivations for a λ-term e under binding-time assumption A — and thus its completions — can be characterized by the solutions of a constraint system $C_A(e)$. In this section we present transformations that preserve the set of solutions of such a constraint system. A constraint system that is in normal form with respect to these transformations will have the further property that it defines directly a solution with "minimality" property.

Our transformation rules define a labeled reduction relation $C \overset{S}{\Rrightarrow} C'$ where C and C' are constraint systems and S is a substitution. If the substitution is the identity substitution we simply write $C \Rrightarrow C'$. For substitution S and constraint system C, we denote applying S to all type expressions in C by $S(C)$. Let $G(C)$ be the directed graph on variables in constraint system C that contains an edge (α, β) if and only if there is an inequality constraint of the form $\alpha \to \alpha' \overset{?}{\leq}_f \beta$ or $\alpha' \to \alpha \overset{?}{\leq}_f \beta$ in C. If $G(C)$ contains a cycle we say C is *cyclic*; *acyclic* otherwise.[6] The transformation rules are given in Figure 2. The first two inequality constraint rules show how inequality constraints with *identical* right-hand sides are eliminated: If the left-hand sides have the *same* type constructor then these left-hand sides are equated in the "reduced" system (Rule 1a); if the left-hand sides have *different* left-hand side type constructors then the right-hand side is equated with Λ (Rule 1b) and the inequalities are eventually eliminated by Rules 1f and 1g.

The transitive closure of the transformation rules is defined by: $C \overset{S}{\Rrightarrow}+ C'$ if $C \overset{S}{\Rrightarrow} C'$ and $C \overset{S;S'}{\Rrightarrow}+ C''$ if $C \overset{S}{\Rrightarrow}+ C', C' \overset{S'}{\Rrightarrow}+ C''$ for some C', where $S; S'$ denotes the left-to-right composition of S and S'. We say C is a *normal form* (or *normalized*) constraint system if there is no C' such that $C \overset{S}{\Rrightarrow} C'$ for any S, and C *has* a normal form if there is a normal form C' such that $C \overset{S}{\Rrightarrow}+ C'$ for some substitution S. The correctness of the transformations is captured in the following theorem, which is easily proved by induction on the length of transformation sequences and by case analysis of the individual rules using elementary properties of $\leq_b, \leq_f$.

Theorem 2 *(Soundness and completeness of transformations)*
Let $C \overset{S}{\Rrightarrow}+ C'$. Then $Sol(C) = \{(S; S') \mid S' \in Sol(C')\}$.

The transformations can be used to derive an algorithm for normalizing constraint systems based on the following theorem.

---

[6]Constraints of the form $\alpha \overset{?}{=} \alpha'$ and $\alpha \overset{?}{\leq}_b \alpha'$ need not be considered in the definition of cyclicity since our transformation rules eliminate all equational constraints and $\leq_b$-inequality constraints remaining in a normal form constraint system are irrelevant.

1. (inequality constraint rules)

   (a) $C \cup \{\alpha \to \alpha' \overset{?}{\leq}_f \gamma, \beta \to \beta' \overset{?}{\leq}_f \gamma\} \Rightarrow C \cup \{\alpha \to \alpha' \overset{?}{\leq}_f \gamma, \alpha \overset{?}{=} \beta, \alpha' \overset{?}{=} \beta'\}$;
   (b) $C \cup \{\alpha \to \alpha' \overset{?}{\leq}_f \gamma, B \overset{?}{\leq}_b \gamma\} \Rightarrow C \cup \{\alpha \to \alpha' \overset{?}{\leq}_f \gamma, B \overset{?}{\leq}_b \gamma, \gamma \overset{?}{=} \Lambda\}$;
   (c) $C \cup \{\alpha \to \alpha' \overset{?}{\leq}_f \beta, \beta \overset{?}{\leq}_b \beta'\} \Rightarrow C \cup \{\alpha \to \alpha' \overset{?}{\leq} \beta, \beta \overset{?}{=} \beta'\}$;
   (d) $C \cup \{B \overset{?}{\leq}_b \alpha, \alpha \overset{?}{\leq}_b \alpha'\} \Rightarrow C \cup \{B \overset{?}{\leq}_b \alpha, B \overset{?}{\leq}_b \alpha', \alpha \rhd \alpha'\}$;
   (e) $C \cup \{B \overset{?}{\leq}_b \alpha', \alpha \overset{?}{\leq}_b \alpha'\} \Rightarrow C \cup \{B \overset{?}{\leq}_b \alpha, B \overset{?}{\leq}_b \alpha', \alpha \rhd \alpha'\}$;
   (f) $C \cup \{\alpha \to \alpha' \overset{?}{\leq}_f \Lambda\} \Rightarrow C \cup \{\alpha \overset{?}{=} \Lambda, \alpha' \overset{?}{=} \Lambda\}$;
   (g) $C \cup \{B \overset{?}{\leq}_b \Lambda\} \Rightarrow C$;
   (h) $C \cup \{\Lambda \overset{?}{\leq}_b \alpha\} \Rightarrow C \cup \{\Lambda \overset{?}{=} \alpha\}$.
   (i) $C \cup \{\alpha \overset{?}{\leq}_b \Lambda\} \Rightarrow C \cup \{B \overset{?}{\leq}_b \alpha\}$ if α is a type variable.

2. (equational constraint rules)

   (a) $C \cup \{\Lambda \overset{?}{=} \alpha\} \Rightarrow C \cup \{\alpha \overset{?}{=} \Lambda\}$ if α is a type variable;
   (b) $C \cup \{\Lambda \overset{?}{=} \Lambda\} \Rightarrow C$;
   (c) $C \cup \{\alpha \overset{?}{=} \alpha'\} \overset{S}{\Rightarrow} S(C)$ if α is a type variable and $S = \{\alpha \mapsto \alpha'\}$;

3. (dependency constraint rules)

   (a) $C \cup \{\alpha \rhd \Lambda\} \Rightarrow C$;
   (b) $C \cup \{\Lambda \rhd \alpha\} \Rightarrow C \cup \{\alpha \overset{?}{=} \Lambda\}$;

4. (occurs check rule)

   (a) $C \Rightarrow C \cup \{\alpha \overset{?}{=} \Lambda\}$ if C is cyclic and α is on a cycle in $G(C)$.

Figure 2: Transformation rules for constraint systems

Theorem 3 *(Normalization of constraint systems)*

1. *The transformations of Figure 2 are (weakly) normalizing; that is, every C has a normal form.*

2. *If C' is a normal form constraint system then*

   (a) *it has no equational constraints;*

   (b) *it is acyclic;*

   (c) *its constraints are of the form $\beta \rightarrow \beta' \overset{?}{\leq}_f \alpha, \gamma \overset{?}{\leq}_b \alpha$ or $\alpha \rhd \alpha'$ where: α, α' are type variables; β is a type variable or the type constant Λ; and γ is a type variable or the type constant B.*

   (d) *for every inequality constraint of the form $\beta \rightarrow \beta' \overset{?}{\leq}_f \alpha$ the type variable α does not occur on the right-hand side of other $\leq_f$-inequalities or on the left-hand side of $\leq_b$-inequalities;*

   (e) *for every inequality constraint of the form $B \overset{?}{\leq}_b \alpha$ the type variable α does not occur on the right-hand side of $\leq_f$-inequalities or on either side of $\leq_b$-inequalities.*

3. *If C contains no constraints of the form $\alpha \overset{?}{\leq}_b \alpha'$ where α is a type variable and $C \overset{S}{\Rightarrow}+ C'$ then C' contains no constraint of that form either.*

Proof: *1.* Define a megastep as follows: apply any applicable rule and then apply the equational constraint transformation rules exhaustively. It is easy to see that every megastep terminates and that after it terminates all equational constraints have been eliminated. Let c be the number of constraints; n the number of variables occurring in them; and v the number of inequality constraints with a variable on the left-hand side. It is easy to check that every megastep decreases the sum $c + n + 2v$ by at least one. Consequently every sequence of megasteps terminates.
2. By definition of normal form.
3. None of the rules introduce $\leq_b$-inequalities with a variable on the left-hand side. (End of proof) ■

Normal forms are unique modulo type variable renamings. A solution S of a constraint system C is a *ground solution* if it maps all types into ground types; that is, types that contain no type variables. We say that a ground solution S of a constraint system C is *minimal* if: it solves all $\leq_f$-inequality constraints equationally; and for every type variable α, if there is *any* (ground) solution S' such that $S'(\alpha) = B$ and S' solves all $\leq_f$-inequality constraints equationally then $S(\alpha) = B$. Clearly, a minimal solution is unique if it exists at all.

Theorem 4 *Every normal form constraint system C has a minimal solution.*

Proof: Interpret all inequalities in C as equations. Since C is a normal form constraint system, by Theorem 3, part 2, these equations have a most general unifier U [LMM87] . Let BS be the substitution that maps every type variable occurring in $U(C)$ to B. Since neither U nor BS substitutes Λ for any type variable, all the dependency constraints in C are trivially satisfied. Consequently, the substitution $U; BS$ is a ground solution that solves all $\leq_f$-constraints equationally. Let S' be any other solution with $S'(\alpha) = B$ that solves the $\leq_f$-constraints equationally. Since S' is a solution α cannot be the right-hand side of an $\leq_f$-constraint, and since it solves $\leq_f$-constraints equationally there is no sequence of type variables $\alpha_0, \ldots, \alpha_k$ such that $\alpha_0 = \alpha$, α_k is the right-hand side of an $\leq_f$-constraint, and $\alpha_{i-1} \overset{?}{\leq}_b \alpha_i$ or $\alpha_i \overset{?}{\leq}_b \alpha_{i-1}$ for $0 < i \leq k$. As a consequence U maps α to B or to a type variable. In either case $U; BS$ maps α to B. This shows that S is a minimal solution. (End of proof) ■

By extension we define as the minimal solution of an arbitrary constraint system C the substitution $S; U$ if $C \overset{S}{\Rightarrow}+ C'$, C' is a normal form, and U is the minimal solution of C'. This proposition shows that every constraint system is solvable, and in particular that the $\leq_f$-inequality constraints in a normal form constraint system can be interpreted as equational constraints without losing solvability. Note that this property holds for normal forms, but not for general constraint systems.

5 Minimal Completions

The minimal solution of $C_A(e)$ corresponds to a canonical "minimal" completion of e that has a minimum of late-binding operators and the "most static" type annotations possible. Formally, let $\sqsubseteq$ be the smallest partial order such that $B \sqsubseteq \tau, \tau' \sqsubseteq \Lambda$ for all τ, τ' and $\sigma_1 \rightarrow \tau_1 \sqsubseteq \sigma_2 \rightarrow \tau_2$ if $\sigma_1 \sqsubseteq \sigma_2, \tau_1 \sqsubseteq \tau_2$ (c.f., [Gom89]), and extend it point-wise to lists of type assumptions. A completion of e is minimal if the operator annotations occurring in it occur in *every* completion of e and every type annotation τ in any other completion with the *same* operator annotations has a type τ' in the corresponding position with $\tau \sqsubseteq \tau'$ (w.r.t. to a binding-time assumption A). For example, both $(\underline{\lambda} x.x\underline{@}y)\underline{@}z$ and $(\lambda x : \Lambda.x\underline{@}y)@z$ are completions of $(\lambda x.x@y)@z$ w.r.t. $\{y : \Lambda, z : \Lambda\}$, but only $(\lambda x : \Lambda.x\underline{@}y)@z$ is minimal.

Since the "="-part of an inequality constraint $\alpha \rightarrow \alpha' \overset{?}{\leq}_f \alpha''$ in constraint system $C_A(e)$ for λ-term e arises from applying an unannotated (early-binding) typing rule in Figure 1 whereas its "$<_f$"-part derives from the corresponding annotated (late-binding) type rule, the minimal solution of $C_A(e)$ translates into a completion of e (via Theorem 1) that has only operator annotations where every completion of e has one. This satisfies the first half of the minimal completion definition. From Theorem 4 it can be shown that it also "minimizes" the type annotations since every other completion with the same operator annotations also solves the $\leq_f$-inequality constraints equationally. Thus we have the following theorem.

Theorem 5 *(Minimal typing)*

Every λ-term e has a unique minimal completion w.r.t. any binding-time assumption A for e.

This theorem extends and sharpens Gomard's minimal completion result since his definition of minimality does not take type annotations into account and his result is for his type system without rule (LIFT) [Gom89].

6 Efficient constraint normalization

Since the transformations of Section 4 are normalizing they can be used to design an algorithm that first normalizes a constraint system and then extracts the minimal solution from it. Instead of using the naive normalization strategy described in the proof of Theorem 3 we present a fast algorithm using efficient data structures whose actions can be interpreted as implementations of (sequences of) transformation steps.

This algorithm only works on constraint systems with constraints of the form $\alpha \rightarrow \alpha' \overset{?}{\leq}_f \alpha'', B \overset{?}{\leq}_b \alpha, \alpha \overset{?}{=} \alpha'$ and $\alpha \triangleright \alpha'$ where $\alpha, \alpha', \alpha''$ are type variables or the type constant Λ. No constraints of the form $\alpha \overset{?}{\leq}_b \alpha'$ are permitted where α is a type variable. Since the type constructor ($\rightarrow$ or B) on the left-hand side of an inequality constraint identifies uniquely whether it is a $\leq_b$- or $\leq_f$-inequality we shall drop the subscripts in this section. At the end of this section it is indicated how our efficient constraint normalization algorithm algorithm can be refined to accommodate constraints of the form $\alpha \overset{?}{\leq}_b \alpha'$.

Term graphs with equivalence classes have been used for fast implementations of unification. We shall not go into details, but refer the reader to the literature; e.g. [HK71,AHU74,Hue76,PW78,MM82,ASU86]. The equivalence classes are represented by a system of equivalence class representatives (*ecr's*), and there are two operations available on ecr's: find(n) for node n is a function that returns the ecr of the equivalence class to which n belongs; union(n, n'), which can only be applied to distinct ecr's n, n', is a procedure that merges the equivalence classes of n and n' and returns an ecr of the merged equivalence class. An analysis of efficient union/find data structures can be found in [Tar83]. Our notation uses standard control structure dictions and some special operations, which are explained in Figure 3. All primitive operations, apart from union and find, can easily be implemented to execute in constant time.

A *term graph representation* of a constraint system C consists of

- a term graph, representing all terms in C;
- an equivalence relation on its nodes, representing a substitution;
- a *dependency* list dps(n) of nodes $[n_1, \ldots, n_k]$ associated with every variable-labeled equivalence class representative n, representing dependencies $n \triangleright n_i$;
- a nonvariable node leq(n) associated with every equivalence class representative n, representing the inequality constraints leq(n) $\overset{?}{\leq}_f$ n or leq(n) $\overset{?}{\leq}_b$ n;
- a worklist consisting of
  - inequality pairs (n <= n') with n non-variable-non-Λ-labeled, representing inequality constraints n $\overset{?}{\leq}_f$ n' or n $\overset{?}{\leq}_b$ n';
  - equality pairs (n = n'), representing equational constraints n $\overset{?}{=}$ n';

- a set dynned, implemented by a Boolean-valued map on nodes, for keeping track of those function-labeled nodes n whose children have already been set to Λ ("dynned"); that is, dynned(n) is set to true at the point when for all children c of n the equational constraints $c \stackrel{?}{=} \Lambda$ are added to the worklist.

Our algorithm delays checking for the conditions of the occurs check (see Figure 2) as long as possible since its applicability hinges upon a global condition of the constraint system; i.e., one that cannot be checked by simply looking at one or two constraints at a time. As a consequence it operates in four phases.

Phase 1: For constraint system C a term graph representation is constructed. It consists of: a term graph representing all terms occurring in C; the equivalence classes initialized to consist of one node each; all dependencies n $\triangleright$ n', n $\triangleright$ n", ... for n represented by initializing dps(n) to [n', n", ...]; leq(n) undefined for every node n; the worklist initialized to all inequality and equality constraints; dynned(n) set to false for every n.

Phase 2: Using the term graph representation constructed in Phase 1 a (term graph representation of a) normal form C' for the transformation rules *without* the occurs check rule is computed. See Figure 4.

Phase 3: A maximal strongly connected component analysis of (the representation of) $G(C')$ is performed and for every nontrivial strongly connected component an element α is taken and the pair $(\alpha = \Lambda)$ added to the worklist. (Not described here; see, e.g., [AHU74].)

Phase 4: Finally, the normalization of Phase 2 is performed again until a normal form is reached.

The possibly cyclic "quasi-normal" form reached after Phase 2 could be interpreted, analogous to Theorem 1, with rational (regular recursive) type expressions. Phase 3 implements a single application of the occurs-check rule 4a in Figure 2. Inserting the equations $\alpha \stackrel{?}{=} \Lambda$ for variables α that are on cycles in $G(C')$ will break all cycles since *all* variables on cycles will be substituted by Λ in Phase 4. The final result is guaranteed to be acyclic and thus (the representation of) a normal form constraint system. The proof of Theorem 5 shows how a minimal solution can be extracted from the normal form constraint system.

We analyze the asymptotic (time) complexity of our algorithm by amortization; that is, by averaging the complexity of each primitive operation over the whole sequence of operations executed by the algorithm for a given input [Tar83]. To accomplish this we associate a *computational potential* P with a data structure and calculate the amortized cost c_a of a primitive operation on that data structure by $c_a = c + \Delta P$ where c is the actual running time of the operation and ΔP is the difference in potential before and after the operation, which may in general be positive or negative. The cumulative amortized cost of a sequence of primitive operations is then the sum of their running times plus the difference in potential before and after applying them. As a special case we get that if the amortized cost of every primitive operation is zero and the potential of the data structure *after* executing them is nonnegative, then the total running time is bounded from

<table>
<tr><td>(General operations)</td><td></td></tr>
<tr><td>e = e'</td><td>returns true if e is equal to e'; false otherwise</td></tr>
<tr><td>e <> e'</td><td>returns true if e is not equal to e'; false otherwise</td></tr>
<tr><td>(Operations on lists)</td><td></td></tr>
<tr><td>remove e from W</td><td>removes an element from (nonempty) list W and assigns it to variable e</td></tr>
<tr><td>add v to W</td><td>adds element v to the list W</td></tr>
<tr><td>[]</td><td>denotes the empty list</td></tr>
<tr><td>L ++ L'</td><td>concatenates lists L and L' destructively and returns the result</td></tr>
<tr><td>for x in L do
<statement>
end for;</td><td>executes <statement> for every element x in list L where L is traversed from "left to right"</td></tr>
<tr><td>for x in L || x' in L' do
<statement>
end for;</td><td>executes <statement> for every pair of elements x, x' while simultaneously and synchronously iterating over lists L and L' (L and L' have the same length)</td></tr>
<tr><td>(Operations on nodes)</td><td></td></tr>
<tr><td>constr(n)</td><td>return the constructor of the nonvariable term represented by node n</td></tr>
<tr><td>children(n)</td><td>returns the list of children nodes of node n</td></tr>
<tr><td>dps(n)</td><td>returns a list of nodes dependent on ecr n (see dependency constraints)</td></tr>
<tr><td>leq(n)</td><td>if defined, for ecr n returns a node that must be $\leq_f$ n or $\leq_b$ n</td></tr>
<tr><td>dynned(n)</td><td>returns true if the children c of ecr n have already been "dynned"; i.e., pairs (c = dyn) added to the worklist</td></tr>
<tr><td>(Operations on equiv. classes)</td><td></td></tr>
<tr><td>find(n)</td><td>returns the ecr of the equivalence class to which n belongs</td></tr>
<tr><td>union(n, n')</td><td>merges the equivalence classes represented by the distinct ecrs n, n' and returns one of n, n' as the new ecr of the merged class; it returns a nonvariable-label node or a node with leq defined whenever possible</td></tr>
</table>

Figure 3: Operations used in fast constraint system normalization algorithm

```
while worklist <> [] do
   remove e from worklist;
   case e of
      (n <= n'):
         m := find(n); m' := find(n');
         if leq(m') undefined then
            leq(m') := m;
         else (* leq(m') is defined *)
            m'' := find(leq(m'));
            if constr(m) = constr(m'') then
               if m <> m'' then
                  _ := union(m, m'');
                  for c in children(m) || c' in children(m'') do
                     add (c = c') to worklist;
                  end for;
               end if;
            else (* constr(m) <> constr(m') *)
               add (m' = dyn) to worklist;
               if not dynned(m) then
                  dynned(m) := true;
                  for c in children(m) do
                     add (c = dyn) to worklist;
                  end for;
               end if;
               if not dynned(m'') then
                  dynned(m'') := true;
                  for c' in children(m'') do
                     add (c' = dyn) to worklist;
                  end for;
               end if;
            end if;
         end if;
      (n = n'):
         m := find(n); m' := find(n');
         if m <> m' then
            m'' := union(m, m');
            if m = dyn then
               (m, m') := (m', m);
            end if;
            if m' = dyn then
               for l in dps(m) do
                  add (l = dyn) to worklist;
               end for;
            else (* m' is variable *)
               dps(m'') := dps(m) ++ dps(m');
               if leq(m) defined and leq(m') defined then
                  (* assume w.l.o.g. m = m'' *)
                  add (leq(m') <= m'') to worklist;
               end if
            end if;
         end if;
   end case;
end while;
```

Figure 4: Phase 2 of efficient constraint system normalization algorithm

above by the *initial* potential. In the following we define a potential on the data structure manipulated in Phase 2 of our constraint normalization algorithm such that every operation (in Phase 2) has an amortized cost of zero.

The data structure at the beginning of Phase 2 consists of:

1. n nodes, with n' variable-labeled nodes, n'' non-variable-non-Λ-labeled nodes, and a node labeled by Λ; i.e., $n = n' + n'' + 1$;

2. m term edges represented by the set of children lists children(n) for non-variable-non-Λ-labeled nodes n;

3. i inequalities (n <= n');

4. e equations (n = n'); and

5. d dependencies, represented by the set of dependency lists dps(n).

The size of the input to the algorithm is $N = n+m+i+e+d$. We define the potential of the data structure manipulated in Phase 2 by associating a computational "chunk" with the following components: equalities (n = n') and inequalities (n <= n') in the worklist, and variable-labeled and non-variable-non-Λ-labeled ecr's in the term graph. The potential of the whole term graph representation is then the sum of all its associated chunks. We denote these chunks by $c_e, c_i, c_v(m), c_n(m)$, respectively, and we write c_{uf} for the cost of one union- or find-operation.

$$\begin{aligned} c_e &= 3c_{uf} + O(1) \\ c_i &= 3c_{uf} + O(1) \\ c_v(n) &= |dps(n)|(c_e + O(1)) + c_i + O(1) \\ c_n(n) &= |children(n)|(2c_e + O(1)) + O(1) \end{aligned}$$

The chunks for equalities and inequalities are constant whereas the chunks for ecr's depend on the ecr itself. The total potential at the beginning of Phase 2 is

$$\begin{aligned} P_0 &= \Sigma_{n'}c_v + \Sigma_{n''}c_n + ic_i + ec_e \\ &= d(c_e + O(1)) + n'c_i + O(n') + m(2c_e + O(1)) + O(n'') + ic_i + ec_e \\ &= (d + n' + 2m + i + e)c_e + O(d) + O(n') + O(m) + O(n'') \\ &\leq 6Nc_{uf} + O(N) \end{aligned}$$

It can be verified that the amortized cost of every operation in Phase 2 is zero. Under common assumptions on the presentation of the input Phase 1 takes linear time. Since the potential is never negative, the combined running times of Phases 2 and 4 is bounded by P_0 by our considerations above. Phase 3 can be implemented in linear time [Tar72]. Finally, using *path compression* and *union by rank* (or similar union/find heuristics; see [Tar83]) for Phase 2 we get the following theorem.

Theorem 6 *A constraint system can be normalized in time $O(N\alpha(N,N))$ on a pointer machine, where N is the size of the input.*

Since $G(C)$ may be cyclic it does not appear that any of the linear-time unification algorithms can be adapted to our problem. Consequently it remains to be seen whether there is a linear-time algorithm for solving our constraint-systems. Note, however, that the factor $\alpha(n,n)$ can be treated as a small constant in practice. We believe that our algorithm is not only asymptotically fast, but also implementable, efficient, adaptable and responsive in practice. In particular it appears to be well-suited for adaptation in an incremental environment (see following section).

We conclude this section by sketching an extension of the fast constraint normalization algorithm to handle constraints of the form $\alpha \overset{?}{\leq}_b \alpha'$, too. First we "prenormalize" a constraint system with respect to rules 1c, 1d, and 1e. This can be accomplished with a linear-time reachability algorithm. During full constraint normalization substituting Λ for a type variable α by rule 2c triggers the following actions: for all α', α'' with $\alpha' \overset{?}{\leq}_b \alpha$ and $\alpha \overset{?}{\leq}_b \alpha''$ we add $(B <= \alpha')$ and $(\Lambda = \alpha')$ to the worklist. The cost of adding these constraints to the worklist and subsequently processing them is dominated by the other operations of the constraint normalization algorithm. So Theorem 6 also holds for constraint systems with "pure variable" constraints $\alpha \overset{?}{\leq}_b \alpha'$.

7 Efficient binding-time analysis

The constraint system normalization algorithm of Section 6 forms the core of efficient binding-time analysis. Theorem 5 guarantees that every λ-term e has a unique minimal completion given any binding-time assumption A for e. Our binding-time algorithm computes a minimal completion as follows.

1. (Construction) Construct a type constraint system $C_A(e)$ as described in Section 3.
2. (Normalization) Normalize the constraint system according to the transformation rules of Figure 2 using the fast constraint normalization algorithm of Section 6.
3. (Minimal solution) Construct a minimal solution as described in Section 4.
4. (Annotation) Annotate (the syntax-tree of) e with operator, type and lifting annotations using the minimal solution to get the minimal completion of e as described in Section 5.

Every type variable in the constraint normalization system is associated with a node in the syntax-tree. The binding-time annotations of the minimal completion of e can be computed in a single pass over the syntax-tree of e. Thus all but the constraint normalization can be done in linear time with respect to the size of e. This proves the following theorem.

Theorem 7 *The minimal completion of e w.r.t. binding-time assumption A (for e) can be computed in time $O(n\alpha(n,n))$ where n is the size of e.*[7]

[7] The cost of displaying the type annotations in string form is not included since the string representation of the type expressions may be exponentially bigger than the original input. Note this is also the case for simple type inference and for unification!

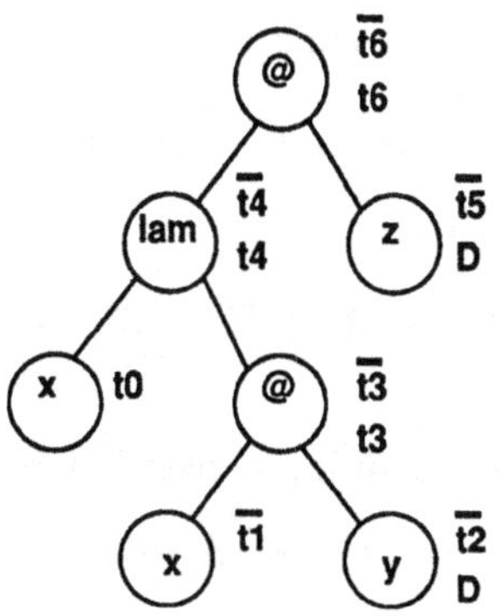

Figure 5: A syntax tree with type variables

Our constraint normalization algorithm can easily be adapted to an algorithm that operates on-line under additions of constraints to a constraint system without loss in efficiency. As a consequence the construction of the constraint normalization system and its normalization can be interleaved efficiently. For example, it is possible to display immediately the annotations of an untyped λ-term in an interactive environment as it is being typed in at an "almost-constant" cost per character typed. (This does *not* hold for *deletions*!) The flexibility of the constraint normalization algorithm should make it also possible to devise a "toolbox" of binding-time analyses for different environments by modularizing such an analysis into input and output actions, constraint construction and constraint normalization. Notice specifically that constraint normalization is independent of the syntax of the λ-terms unlike syntax-oriented algorithms that have to be modified every time the syntax is modified or enhanced.

We conclude this section with an illustration of how our binding-time analysis algorithm proceeds on the λ-term

$$(\lambda x.x@y)@z$$

w.r.t. the binding-time assumption $\{y : \Lambda, z : \Lambda\}$. Its syntax tree with associated type variables is displayed in Figure 5.

The constraint system constructed from this syntax tree is[8]

$$\begin{array}{rcl} t0 & \stackrel{?}{\leq}_b & \overline{t1} \\ \Lambda & \stackrel{?}{\leq}_b & \overline{t2} \\ \Lambda & \stackrel{?}{\leq}_b & \overline{t5} \\ \overline{t2} \rightarrow t3 & \stackrel{?}{\leq}_f & \overline{t1}, \quad t3 \stackrel{?}{\leq}_b \overline{t3} \\ t0 \rightarrow \overline{t3} & \stackrel{?}{\leq}_f & t4, \quad t4 \stackrel{?}{\leq}_b \overline{t4} \\ \overline{t5} \rightarrow t6 & \stackrel{?}{\leq}_f & \overline{t4}, \quad t6 \stackrel{?}{\leq}_b \overline{t6} \end{array}$$

[8]In Figure 5 we write "D" instead of Λ.

Normalization produces the single constraint

$$\Lambda \to \Lambda \overset{?}{\leq_f} t4$$

and the substitution expressed by

$$\begin{array}{lcl} t0, \overline{t1}, \overline{t2}, t3, \overline{t3}, \overline{t5}, t6, \overline{t6} & \mapsto & \Lambda \\ \overline{t4} & \mapsto & t4. \end{array}$$

The minimal solution of the remaining constraint is the substitution

$$t4 \mapsto \Lambda \to \Lambda.$$

Thus the minimal competion of $\lambda x.x@y)@z$ is the well-annotated λ-term

$$(\lambda x : \Lambda.x\underline{@}y)@z.$$

These annotations signal to a partial evaluator that the outer application can be evaluated statically whereas the inner application is deferred until the values for y and z become available.

8 Summary and directions for future research

Higher-order binding-time analysis can be viewed as a type inference problem for unannotated or partially annotated λ-terms in a two-level λ-calculus. We have shown that this type inference problem can be factored into: construction of type constraint systems with equational, conditional-equational, and specialized kinds of inequality constraints; transformation of this system into a normal form; and extraction of a "canonical" solution from the normal form. We have presented a higher-order binding-time analysis algorithm that can be implemented in almost-linear time. This improves on previous work in that our algorithm is guaranteed to produce minimal completions, yet its running time is almost linear; as such it is asymptotically more efficient than previous binding-time analysis algorithms. Since the data structures we use are known to behave well in practice, we expect our algorithm to be also very fast in practice.

The class of type constraint systems in this paper and our efficient constraint system normalization algorithm are of independent interest since they can be used to solve other analyses; in particular, we have applied it successfully to the description and design an efficient type inference algorithm for a dynamic typing discipline [Hen91].

Several problems might be addressed as a continuation of this work:

- Binding-time analysis has been cast in different conceptual frameworks: abstract interpretation, projection analysis, and type inference. What is their relative expressiveness for a given language? What is the computational complexity of these various problem formulations of binding-time analysis, and what is the complexity of already existing formulations?

- Can the type system with type Λ be generalized to an ML-style polymorphic system? What are its properties?

- In our system "lifting" is restricted to first-order values. But higher-order lifting is both possible and useful in practice, as exemplified in Similix [Bon90b]. What happens when lifting for static functions and "induced" lifting for arbitrary partially static structures and functions are also permitted?

Acknowledgments

I would like to express my thanks: to Carsten Gomard for many hours of explaining the use of his type inference system in binding-time analysis, for providing me with a copy of his Master's thesis, for listening patiently to the ideas presented in this paper as they were evolving, and for stimulating comments and suggestions on this work and possible continuations; to Neil Jones for clarifying and rectifying my understanding of binding-time analysis, for detailed comments, critical suggestions and several corrections[9] on earlier drafts of this paper, and for explaining to me the importance of the lift-operator in partial evaluation; to Johnny Chang for fine-combing through the fast constraint normalization algorithm and finding several small errors in it; to Anders Bondorf for suggesting valuable improvements to the presentation of this paper and for sharing some of his extensive practical knowledge of self-applicable partial evaluators with me; and to the TOPPS group at DIKU as a whole for providing active feedback and a generally stimulating environment.

References

[AHU74] A. Aho, J. Hopcroft, and J. Ullman. *The Design and Analysis of Computer Algorithms.* Addison-Wesley, 1974.

[ASU86] A. Aho, R. Sethi, and J. Ullman. *Compilers: Principles, Techniques, and Tools.* Addison Wesley, 1986. Addison-Wesley, 1986, Reprinted with corrections, March 1988.

[BJMS88] A. Bondorf, N. Jones, T. Mogensen, and P. Sestoft. Binding time analysis and the taming of self-application. Sep. 1988. To appear in Transactions on Programming Languages and Systems (TOPLAS).

[Bon90a] A. Bondorf. Automatic autoprojection of higher order recursive equations. In N. Jones, editor, *Proc. 3rd European Symp. on Programming (ESOP '90), Copenhagen, Denmark*, pages 70–87, Springer, May 1990. Lecture Notes in Computer Science, Vol. 432.

[Bon90b] A. Bondorf. *Self-Applicable Partial Evaluation.* PhD thesis, DIKU, University of Copenhagen, Dec. 1990.

[Con88] C. Consel. New insights into partial evaluation: the Schism experiment. In *Proc. 2nd European Symp. on Programming (ESOP), Nancy, France*, pages 236–246, Springer, 1988. Lecture Notes in Computer Science, Vol. 300.

[9]Naturally, any remaining errors are completely my responsibility just as those that have already been corrected were since they shouldn't even have been in the paper in the first place.

[Con90] C. Consel. Binding time analysis for higher order untyped functional languages. In *Proc. LISP and Functional Programmin (LFP), Nice, France*, ACM, July 1990.

[FM88] Y. Fuh and P. Mishra. Type inference with subtypes. In *Proc. 2nd European Symp. on Programming*, pages 94–114, Springer-Verlag, 1988. Lecture Notes in Computer Science 300.

[GJ91] C. Gomard and N. Jones. A partial evaluator for the untyped lambda-calculus. *J. Functional Programming*, 1(1):21–69, Jan. 1991.

[Gom89] C. Gomard. *Higher Order Partial Evaluation – HOPE for the Lambda Calculus.* Master's thesis, DIKU, University of Copenhagen, Denmark, September 1989.

[Gom90] C. Gomard. Partial type inference for untyped functional programs (extended abstract). In *Proc. LISP and Functional Programming (LFP), Nice, France*, July 1990.

[Hen88a] F. Henglein. Simple type inference and unification. Oct. 1988. New York University, Computer Science Department, SETL Newsletter 232.

[Hen88b] F. Henglein. Type inference and semi-unification. In *Proc. ACM Conf. on LISP and Functional Programming (LFP), Snowbird, Utah*, pages 184–197, ACM, ACM Press, July 1988.

[Hen91] F. Henglein. Dynamic typing. March 1991. Semantique note 90, DIKU, University of Copenhagen.

[HK71] J. Hopcroft and R. Karp. *An Algorithm for Testing the Equivalence of Finite Automata.* Technical Report TR-71-114, Dept. of Computer Science, Cornell U., 1971.

[HS91] S. Hunt and D. Sands. Binding time analysis: a new PERspective. In *Proc. ACM/IFIP Symp. on Partial Evaluation and Semantics Based Program Manipulation (PEPM), New Haven, Connecticut*, June 1991.

[Hue76] G. Huet. *Résolution d'equations dans des langages d'ordre 1, 2, ..., omega.* PhD thesis, Univ. Paris VII, Sept. 1976.

[JGB*90] N. Jones, C. Gomard, A. Bondorf, O. Danvy, and T. Mogensen. A self-applicable partial evaluator for the lambda calculus. In *1990 International Conference on Computer Languages, New Orleans, Louisiana, March 1990*, pages 49–58, IEEE Computer Society, 1990.

[JM76] N. Jones and S. Muchnick. Binding time optimization in programming languages: some thoughts toward the design of the ideal language. In *Proc. 3rd ACM Symp. on Principles of Programming Languages*, pages 77–94, ACM, Jan. 1976.

[JM78] N. Jones and S. Muchnick. *TEMPO: A Unified Treatment of Binding Time and Parameter Passing Concepts in Programming Languages.* Volume 66 of *Lecture Notes in Computer Science*, Springer, 1978.

[Jon87] N. Jones. Automatic program specialization: a re-examination from basic principles. In D. Bjorner, A. Ershov, and N. Jones, editors, *Proc. Partial Evaluation and Mixed Computation*, pages 225–282, IFIP, North-Holland, Oct. 1987.

[JS80] N. Jones and D. Schmidt. Compiler generation from denotational semantics. In N. Jones, editor, *Semantics-Directed Compiler Generation, Aarhus, Denmark*, pages 70–93, Springer, 1980. Lecture Notes in Computer Science, Vol. 94.

[JSS85] N. Jones, P. Sestoft, and H. Sondergard. An experiment in partial evaluation: the generation of a compiler generator. *SIGPLAN Notices*, 20(8), Aug. 1985.

[JSS89] N. Jones, P. Sestoft, and H. Sondergaard. Mix: a self-applicable partial evaluator for experiments in compiler generation. *LISP and Symbolic Computation*, 2:9–50, 1989.

[Kro81] H. Kröger. Static-Scope-Lisp: splitting an interpreter into compiler and run-time system. In W. Brauer, editor, *GI — 11. Jahrestagung, Munich, Germany*, pages 20–31, Springer, Munich, Germany, 1981. Informatik-Fachberichte 50.

[Lau87] J. Launchbury. Projections for specialisation. In D. Bjorner, A. Ershov, and N. Jones, editors, *Proc. Workshop on Partial Evaluation and Mixed Computation, Denmark*, pages 465–483, North-Holland, Oct. 1987.

[Lau90] J. Launchbury. *Projection Factorisations in Partial Evaluation.* PhD thesis, University of Glasgow, Jan. 1990.

[LMM87] J. Lassez, M. Maher, and K. Marriott. Unification revisited. In J. Minker, editor, *Foundations of Deductive Databases and Logic Programming*, Morgan Kauffman, 1987.

[Mit84] J. Mitchell. Coercion and type inference. In *Proc. 11th ACM Symp. on Principles of Programming Languages (POPL)*, 1984.

[MM82] A. Martelli and U. Montanari. An efficient unification algorithm. *ACM Transactions on Programming Languages and Systems*, 4(2):258–282, Apr. 1982.

[Mog87] T. Mogensen. Partially static structures in a self-applicable partial evaluator. In D. Bjorner, A. Ershov, and N. Jones, editors, *Proc. Workshop on Partial Evaluation and Mixed Computation, Denmark*, pages 325–347, North-Holland, Oct. 1987.

[Mog89] T. Mogensen. Binding time analysis for polymorphically typed higher order languages. In J. Diaz and F. Orejas, editors, *Proc. Int. Conf. Theory and Practice of Software Development (TAPSOFT), Barcelona, Spain*, pages 298–312, Springer, March 1989. Lecture Notes in Computer Science 352.

[NN86] H. Nielson and F. Nielson. Semantics directed compiling for functional languages. In *Proc. ACM Conf. on LISP and Functional Programming (LFP)*, 1986.

[NN88a] H. Nielson and F. Nielson. Automatic binding time analysis for a typed lambda calculus. *Science of Computer Programming*, 10:139–176, 1988.

[NN88b] H. Nielson and F. Nielson. Two-level semantics and code generation. *Theoretical Computer Science*, 56, 1988.

[PW78] M. Paterson and M. Wegman. Linear unification. *J. Computer and System Sciences*, 16:158–167, 1978.

[Rom87] S. Romanenko. A compiler generator produced by a self-applicable specializer can have a surprisingly natural and understandable structure. In D. Bjorner, A. Ershov, and N. Jones, editors, *Proc. Workshop on Partial Evaluation and Mixed Computation, Denmark*, pages 465–483, North-Holland, Oct. 1987.

[Sch87] D. Schmidt. Static properties of partial evaluation. In D. Bjorner, A. Ershov, and N. Jones, editors, *Proc. Workshop on Partial Evaluation and Mixed Computation, Denmark*, pages 465–483, North-Holland, Oct. 1987.

[Ses85] P. Sestoft. The structure of a self-applicable partial partial evaluator. In H. Ganzinger and N. Jones, editors, *Programs as Data Objects, Copenhagen, Denmark*, pages 236–256, Springer, 1985. published in 1986, Lecture Notices in Computer Science, Vol. 217.

[Sta88] R. Stansifer. Type inference with subtypes. In *Proc. 15th ACM Symp. on Principles of Programming Languages*, pages 88–97, ACM, San Diego, California, Jan. 1988.

[Tar72] R. Tarjan. Depth-first search and linear graph algorithms. *SIAM J. Comput.*, 1(2), June 1972.

[Tar83] R. Tarjan. *Data Structures and Network Flow Algorithms*. Volume CMBS 44 of *Regional Conference Series in Applied Mathematics*, SIAM, 1983.

[Wan87] M. Wand. A simple algorithm and proof for type inference. *Fundamenta Informaticae*, X:115–122, 1987.

Finiteness Analysis

Carsten Kehler Holst *
Department of Computing Science,
University of Glasgow
kehler@dcs.glasgow.ac.uk

Abstract

This paper address quasi-termination (or finiteness) in general and termination of poly-variant partial evaluation in particular. A program is quasi-terminating if it only goes through finitely many different states. A terminating program is a special case of a quasi-terminating program, only going through finitely many states. Furthermore a quasi-terminating program can easily be converted into a terminating program that gives the same result except where the original program was non-terminating.

The following observation makes quasi-termination interesting when it comes to partial evaluation. Partial evaluation of a program will terminate iff the program is quasi-terminating in the static part of the state, *i.e.*, only finitely many statically different states can be reached.

This paper develops a finiteness analysis, and shows how its results can be used to ensure termination of partial evaluation. The finiteness analysis is an abstraction of a transition semantics consisting of a dependency and a size analysis. It determines various kinds of inductive properties such as increasing, decreasing, and *in situ* increasing/decreasing arguments. Sufficient conditions for quasi-termination is then stated in terms of these properties.

Using the result of the finiteness analysis the binding time annotation of a program can be changes (parts of the static data are made dynamic) such that the resulting program is quasi-terminating in the remaining static part of the state. This guarantees that partial evaluation of the program will terminate. Our experiments have shown this algorithm to be powerful enough to handle complicated interpreters and self-applicable partial evaluators with good results.

Keywords: Finiteness, termination, quasi-termination, abstract interpretation, transition analysis, induction, memoisation, partial evaluation.

*Supported by University of Copenhagen, The Danish Research Academy, and ESPRIT BRA 3124 SEMANTIQUE

1 Introduction

This paper addresses quasi-termination in general and termination of poly-variant partial evaluation in particular. Both termination and quasi-termination are important properties, but undecidable properties. The best we can hope for is an algorithm that gives a safe approximation; identify a large and interesting subset of the terminating programs. Termination of partial evaluation in itself is trivial. The proof of Kleene's S-m-n theorem [10] gives a trivial terminating algorithm for doing partial evaluation. The problem is making a non-trivial *terminating* partial evaluator. Partial evaluators like Mix [9], Similix [1], Schism [3], and LambdaMix [7] are all non-trivial and *often* terminating.

In this paper we present an analysis that identify various kinds of inductive arguments and we give a condition that guarantee quasi-termination, which again guarantee termination of partial evaluation. For example if the argument to a function gets smaller, in some well-founded ordering, at each call then, eventually, the function must terminate.

Termination is very hard to prove automatically, and the information that "The analyser could not prove that your program terminates" is not very useful. This is probably the reason why termination analysis has received so little attention. We do not aim at developing a "useful" termination analysis in this paper. Instead we develop a finiteness analysis that makes it possible to ensure termination of non-trivial partial evaluation. The work presented here was inspired by some ideas of Neil D. Jones [5], and to a lesser extent by the work of Neil D. Jones and Tine Andersen [6], on implementing a safe binding time analysis for partial evaluation.

Computation is often defined as a sequence of transitions, or a sequence of states related by a transition relation. In the λ-calculus the state is a λ-expressions and the transitions are β-reductions; in machine language the content of memory is the state and each machine instruction is a transition. We use a variation over this theme. Instead of a transition sequence we describe a computation as a transition tree. The language is that of first-order recursion equations. A state is a function call, signifying a computation, and transitions relate computations to their sub-computations. A transition describes how a function call gives rise to other function calls.

It takes only finitely long to compute a transition, so a computation with a finite number of transitions terminates, and a computation with an infinite sequence (or tree) of transitions is non-terminating. There are essentially two kinds of non-terminating computations. A computation is quasi-terminating iff it only enters finitely many different states. So a program that is non-terminating and quasi-terminating must have transition sequences that enter the same state again and again, *i.e.*, the transition sequences must contain cycles. if the program is not even quasi-terminating the computation reaches infinitely many different states.

The transition model of computation is well known; it is used in Turing-machines, λ-calculus, small-step operational semantics, and many other models of computation. The following theorem, well known from term-rewriting, see Dershowitz [4], defines an easy way of proving termination of transition systems.

Theorem 1. Given a transition system with transitions $\tau_1, \ldots, \tau_n$, and a well-founded ordering on states ($\sqsubseteq$) such that:

$$\tau_i(s) \sqsubset s \quad \text{or} \quad s_0 \xrightarrow{\tau_{i_1}} s_1 \xrightarrow{\tau_{i_2}} s_2 \ldots \Rightarrow s_0 \sqsupset s_1 \sqsupset s_2 \sqsupset \ldots$$

then the transition system is strongly terminating. □

Corollary 2. Given a transition system with transitions $\tau_1, \ldots, \tau_n$, and an well-founded ordering on states ($\sqsubseteq$) such that: $\tau_i(s) \sqsubseteq s$ then the transition system is quasi-terminating. □

These theorems are the inspirational starting point for the work in this paper. The idea is to find a weaker condition that still guarantees quasi-termination. We look for some kind of structurally inductive argument. The example below shows how an inductive argument can ensure termination.

Example 3. Consider the definition of append given below. There is only one way a call to append can give rise to a call to append in one step.

```
append x y = if (null? x) y
                (cons (hd x) (append (tl x) y))
```

We have a one-step transition from append to append where the first argument gets smaller and the second argument stays the same. Taking the transitive closure of the set of transitions we end up with an infinite set of transitions, for all of which the first argument gets smaller and the second arguments stays the same. This transition respect the sub-term ordering which is a well-founded ordering, so according to theorem 1 the recursion can only be finitely deep, thus all calls to append with well defined and finitely large arguments must terminate. This argument relies heavily on the fact that the language is strict and that only finite data structures exist. □

1.1 Outline

We start out giving a sufficient condition for a program to be quasi-terminating. The condition is: if all the transitions, defined by program p, that have an *in situ* increasing argument also have an *in situ* decreasing argument in a *safe* argument position then the program is quasi-terminating. The precise definition of *in situ* increasing, *in situ* decreasing, and safe together with a detailed proof of the correctness of this condition is given in section 2. In section 3 we consider poly-variant partial evaluation. We show that if the condition holds for for a program where the dynamic argument positions are blanked out then partial evaluation of that program will terminate. Furthermore we show how it is possible to guarantee termination of partial evaluation by changing the binding time annotations, by making more arguments dynamic, until the program fulfills the condition for the static arguments. Finally we address the problem of designing an automated test procedure, checking if a program fulfills the condition. This is done in section 4 which starts out giving a transition semantics for a small strict first-order language. Using abstract interpretation techniques we collect a finite safe approximation of the set of transitions defined by the program in question. This approximation is then checked against the condition, instead of the infinite concrete set of transitions. Of course this test cannot spot all quasi-terminating programs, after all, quasi-termination is an undecidable property. One could fear that the method described was too conservative. The experiments we have performed, some of which is reported in section 5, indicates that this is not the case. In the conclusion, section 6, our approach to termination of poly-variant partial evaluation is compared with others, we suggest future improvements, and extensions of the analysis, as example we show how the analysis can be used as a termination analysis.

1.2 Prerequisites

Some familiarity with abstract interpretation and domain theory is assumed. In parts of the paper, some knowledge about partial evaluation will be useful.

2 Quasi-Termination

The "grand finale" of this section will be theorem 15 stating a sufficient condition for programs to be quasi-terminating. We start out developing a model of computation based on transitions. Analysing this model we end up with theorem 15.

The intuition behind the theorem can be stated fairly simply. In order to have an infinite loop (here meaning reaching infinite many different argument values) some argument has to "grow" unboundedly many times. The condition of the theorem states a very liberal bound on how many times an argument can grow.

The power of the theorem is twofold. First it is a strong theorem; many non-trivial programs can be proven to be quasi-terminating, secondly it is easy to test the condition of the theorem thus prove quasi-termination.

2.1 Transition Relations

A program p defines a locally finite transition relation R_p which relates $f\boldsymbol{x}$ to $g\boldsymbol{y}$ if a call of f with input tuple $\boldsymbol{x}$ gives rise to a direct call of g with argument tuple $\boldsymbol{y}$ (a bold $\boldsymbol{x}$ is the tuple $(x_1, \ldots, x_n)$) . The domain of R_p is $\bigcup_i f_i \times D^{m_i}$, where f_i is a function name in p; and m_i is the arity of f_i.

Definition 4. A *transition relation* R is a relation that is *locally finite*, *i.e.*,

$$\forall a \in \mathrm{Dom}(R) : \{\, b \mid a\ R\ b \,\} \text{ is finite}$$

□

Given a transition relation R_p for some program p and an input tuple $\boldsymbol{i}$ we can define an *evaluation tree*, $ET(R_p, \boldsymbol{i})$. The root of $ET(R_p, \boldsymbol{i})$ is $f\boldsymbol{i}$ where f is the goal function in p and each node, $g\boldsymbol{y}$ is the offspring of $f_i\boldsymbol{x}$ iff $f_i\boldsymbol{x}\ R_p\ g\boldsymbol{y}$.

By identifying identical nodes an evaluation tree can be folded into an *evaluation graph*, $EG(R_p, \boldsymbol{i})$.

Definition 5. A transition relation, R, is *terminating* if all evaluation trees for R are finite.

$$\forall \boldsymbol{i} \in D^n : ET(R, \boldsymbol{i}) \text{ is finite}$$

Likewise, R is *quasi-terminating* if all evaluation graphs for R are finite.

$$\forall \boldsymbol{i} \in D^n : EG(R, \boldsymbol{i}) \text{ is finite}$$

Note: a finite evaluation graph may correspond to an infinite evaluation tree. If one wants to avoid introducing trees and graphs one can define a relation as terminating if it is well-founded and quasi-terminating if the transitive closure $(R)^+$ of of the relation R is locally finite. □

It should be clear that if the transition relation R_p defined by program p is (quasi) terminating then the program is (quasi) terminating.

2.2 A Size Relation on Data

We are going to leave the data domain D unspecified. A *size relation*, $(\leq \subseteq D^2)$, on D is a reflexive and transitive relation which has the finite downwards closure property. The downward closure operation is defined as

$$\downarrow(x) = \{\ y \in D \mid y \leq x\ \}$$

Definition 6. A relation $(\leq)$ has *finite downward closures* iff

$$\forall d \in D :\ \downarrow(d) \text{ is finite}$$

□

The downward closure operations extends in the natural way to subsets of D.

$$\downarrow(X) = \bigcup_{x \in X} \downarrow(x)$$

An example of a data domain and a size relation could be finite terms and the sub term relation.

2.3 Transition Sequences

Given an evaluation tree, or an evaluation graph, a *transition sequence*, (τ_i), is a path in the graph. Whenever we talk about a transition sequence we assume that it is a path in $ET(R, \boldsymbol{i})$ for a given transition relation R and input, $\boldsymbol{i}$. We immediately have the following lemma.

Lemma 7. Let R be a non-terminating transition relation. Then there exist a evaluation tree with an infinite path. Likewise if R is a non-quasi-terminating transition relation there exist an evaluation graph with a non-trivial infinite path, *i.e.*, a path where all the argument tuples are different.

Proof: This is a simple consequence of König's lemma which says: There exist non-trivial infinite paths in locally finite infinite graphs. □

2.4 One-step Transitions

Given transition relations R, and R', R approximates R' iff $R' \subseteq R$. It follows trivially that if R approximates R' and R is (quasi) terminating then R' is (quasi) terminating.

In the rest of this paper we are going to be interested in a special form of transition relations. Namely transition relations which can be described a a set of transitions $\{\tau_1, \ldots, \tau_m\}$ where each transition is is a function typed with the names of the functions it is mediating between, like: $\tau_i : f \to g$. The transition relation $R_{\{\tau_1,\ldots,\tau_m\}}$ is defined as follows

$$fx \; R_{\{\tau_1,\ldots,\tau_m\}} \; gy \Leftrightarrow \exists \tau_i : f \to g : \tau_i x = y$$

If the set of transitions is finite the relation is locally finite. Given program p we can get such a relation by making a transition for each of the direct function calls textually occuring in the program. Let 1-$trans_p$ be the set of one-step transitions.

2.5 Properties a Transition might have

Let π_i be the *i'th* projection ($\pi_i x = x_i$). Position i in transition τ depends on position j iff

$$\exists c_i, a, b : \pi_i(\tau(c_1, \ldots, c_{j-1}, a, c_{j+1}, \ldots, c_n)) \neq \pi_i(\tau(c_1, \ldots, c_{j-1}, b, c_{j+1}, \ldots, c_n))$$

Transition, τ, is *decreasing* in position i iff the value of position i is smaller than one of the input arguments. More formally this means

$$\exists j \; \forall x \in D : \pi_i(\tau x) < \pi_j x$$

If the weaker relation ($\leq$) holds the transition is only *weakly decreasing* in position i.

A transition is *increasing* in position i iff is is neither constant nor weakly decreasing in position i, *i.e.*, if the value is not bounded neither by the values in the input tuple or the constant arguments in the program.

A *path* in a transition sequence, (τ_i) is a sequence of indexes $(i_n, \ldots, i_{n+m})$ such that position i_{n+j+1} of τ_{n+j+1} depends on position i_{n+j}. This sounds more complicated than it is. Intuitively a path in a transition sequence is a sequence of argument positions such that each argument position depends on the previous argument position in the sequence.

Given a path in a transition sequence, (τ_i), a value increase n times along the path if there are n indexes, $(i_{j_1}, \ldots, i_{j_n})$, in the sequence of indexes, such that transition τ_{j_l} is increasing in position i_{j_l}.

Lemma 8. Let (τ_i) be a non-quasi-terminating transition sequence. For arbitrary N we can find a path in (τ_i) along which a value is increased more than N times.

Proof: Assume that x is the first argument tuple. Let C be the set of constants defined by the transitions. $C$is the set of values of the constant positions in the set of transtions. More operationally C is the set of constant arguments in the program.

Let $RV^0(x) = \downarrow(C) \cup \bigcup_i \downarrow(x_i)$. $RV^0(x)$ is the set of argument values that can be reached using transitions without increasing positions, *i.e.*, using only weakly decreasing or constant transitions. There are only finitely many one-step transitions and hence only finitely many increasing one-step transitions. Let $RV^{n+1} = \bigcup_{\tau \in 1\text{-}trans_p} \downarrow(\tau(RV^n))$. So RV^n is finite for all n and to get a value outside RV^n we need a path with at least $n+1$ increasing transitions. An infinite non-quasi-terminating transition sequence contains infinitely many argument values (all in RV^ω), so it must contain argument values outside RV^n for arbitrary n. □

Beware that though arbitrary long sequences exists it is not always possible to find an infinite sequence. Figure 1 shows a non-quasi-terminating program that has no path along which the value increase infinitely many times.

```
f(x,y) = if y == 0 then f(1,x)
                   else f(x+1,y-1)
```

Figure 1: A non-quasi-terminating program

2.6 Composite Transitions

Transitions compose in the natural way. The composition of transitions $\tau : f \to g$ and $\sigma : g \to h$ is the transition $\sigma \circ \tau : f \to h$. An *endo-transition* is a transition of type $f \to f$, *i.e.*, a call path from a function to itself. Let $trans_p$ be the transitive closure of the one-step transitions $(1\text{-}trans_p)^+$.

The only difference between composite transitions and one-step transitions is the definition of being increasing. A composite transition is increasing in position i iff there is a path from the input to position i along which the value increases at least once.

Being increasing is a stronger property than (weakly) decreasing, so a transition can only be (weakly) decreasing in position i if it is not increasing in position i. This definition is made to avoid that the composition of an increasing and a decreasing transition should end up being decreasing.

A sequence of transitions can be collapsed into a sequence of composite transitions as follows.

Definition 9. Given a transition sequence (τ_i), we say that a sequence (τ_i') is a collapsed version of (τ_i) iff

$$\exists n \in \mathbb{N}^{\omega *} : n_i < n_{i+1} \quad \wedge \quad \tau_i' = \tau_{n_{i+1}-1} \circ \ldots \circ \tau_{n_i+1} \circ \tau_{n_i}$$

Which is a complicated way of saying that we compose some of the transitions in the transitions sequence. The resulting transition sequence is a more coarse grain description of the same computation. □

Proposition 10. An infinite non-quasi-terminating transition sequence (τ_i) can be collapsed into an infinite non-quasi-terminating endo-transition sequence (τ_i').

Proof: Trivial, as there are only finitely many function in the program. □

Definition 11. An endo-transition is *in situ* decreasing in position i iff position i is less than position i in its input tuple.

$$\forall x \in D^n : \pi_i(\tau x) < \pi_i x$$

Again the transition is *in situ* weakly decreasing if the weak size relation ($\leq$) holds.

An endo-transition is *in situ* increasing in position i iff it is neither weakly decreasing nor constant in position i and if position i depends on position i in the input tuple.

A composite endo-transition is *in situ* increasing if there is a path from position i in the input tuple to position i along which the value increase at least once. □

Lemma 12. Let (τ_i) be a non-quasi-terminating endo-transition sequence. Then (τ_i) can be collapsed into a endo-transition sequence (τ_i') such that for arbitrary N there is a path in (τ_i') along which the value increase at least N times.

Proof: For each function f we can make the maximal endo-transition sequence (τ_i^f). Maximal in the sense that all other endo-transition sequences looping around that function are collapsed versions of (τ_i^f); we simply make the composite transitons such that they start and end in f, but does not go through f. So if (τ_i^f) has no path along which the value increase more than N_f times then neither will any of the other endo-transition sequences looping around f. This gives a maximum number, M, of times a value can increase along a path in an endo-transition sequence which is a collapsed version of (τ_i). But, if the program has F functions, we can find a path in (τ_i) along which the value increases more than $2MF$ times. We can then collapse the transition sequence (τ_i) such that the path is increasing in each step. This collapsed path of length $> 2MF$ must go through some function g at least $2M$ times which contradicts with the assumption that a value can increase a maximum of M times along a path. □

Lemma 13. Let (τ_i) be a endo-transition sequence such that for arbitrary N there is a path in (τ_i) along which the value increases at least N times. Then, for arbitrary M, we can collapse (τ_i) into (τ_i') such that (τ_i') is longer than M and *in situ* increasing in position j at every step.

Proof: Let A be the arity of the argument tuples. A path of length MA must go through the same argument position, say j, at least M times. □

A trivial consequence of this is that for arbitrary M a non-quasi-terminating sequence can be collapsed into a endo-transition sequence longer than M which is *in situ* increasing in position j at every step.

Definition 14. Let f be a function in program p. Position i in f is *bounded* iff there exists a function $B : D \to \mathsf{P}D$ such that for any input argument tuple $\boldsymbol{i}$, $B(\boldsymbol{i})$ is a finite set, and position i in f-nodes in the evaluation graph $EG(R_p, \boldsymbol{i})$ only takes on values in $B(\boldsymbol{i})$. □

We are going to define an argument position as *safe* if no transitions are *in situ* increasing in that position and if it only depends on safe argument positions. A safe argument position cannot contain values outside $RV^{FA}(\boldsymbol{i})$ where F is the number of functions, and A is the number of argument positions. Safe argument positions are bounded.

Given a transition sequence (τ_i) we define the diagonal transition family, $\Delta(\tau_i)$, as

$$\Delta(\tau_i) = (\tau'_j) \text{ where } \tau'_j = \tau_j \circ \ldots \circ \tau_1$$

Beware that $\Delta(\tau_i)$ is not a transition sequence, but the family of transitions, consisting of compositions of all prefixes of (τ_i).

Theorem 15. If all transitions in $trans_p$ with an *in situ* increasing argument position has a bounded *in situ* decreasing argument position then the transition relation R_{trans_p} is quasi-terminating. Implying that program p is quasi-terminating. In formal notation the transition relation is quasi-terminating iff

$$\forall \tau \in trans_p : (\exists i : \text{ISI}_i(\tau)) \Rightarrow (\exists j \in \text{Bounded} : \text{ISD}_j(\tau)) \tag{1}$$

where $\text{ISI}_i(\tau)$ means τ is *in situ* increasing in position i, and $\text{ISD}_j(\tau)$ means τ is *in situ* decreasing in position j.

Proof: Assume R_{trans_p} is non-quasi terminating.

There must exist input $\boldsymbol{i}$ such that there is a non-quasi-terminating transition sequence (τ_i) in $EG(R_{trans_p}, \boldsymbol{i})$.

Lemma 12 gives us an endo-transition sequence (τ'_i) that is a collapsed version of (τ_i) such that this sequence, for arbitrarily M, have path along which the value increase at least M times. (τ'_i) is a endo-transition sequence looping around f and it starts with the input tuple $\boldsymbol{i}'$. The bounded positions of f are bounded by $RV^A(\boldsymbol{i}')$ where A is the arity of the argument tuple of f.

We shall prove that two of the argument tuples in that transition sequence must be equal. That way we arrive at a contradiction and must conclude that our assumption was false and the program is quasi-terminating. Part of the proof obligation will be to show that M can be determined given the program, p, and the input tuple, $\boldsymbol{i}'$.

Given the endo-transition sequence, (τ_i), of length M with an an argument position that is *in situ* increasing for all the transitions the proof goes by induction in the number of non-constant argument positions in (τ).

Induction Hypothesis : Given a sufficiently long, say of length M, endo-transition sequence, with at most n non-constant argument positions, there must be at least two argument tuples in the transition sequence that are equal.

0 (Base case) : If there are no non constant argument positions all the argument tuples are equal, hence if $M > 1$ there must be two argument tuples that are equal.

$n+1$ (Induction step) : Consider $\Delta(\tau_i)$ since (τ_i) is *in situ* increasing in, say, position i, all the transitions in $\Delta(\tau_i)$ must be *in situ* increasing in position i. The hypothesis (1) tells us that all the transitions in $\Delta(\tau_i)$ must be *in situ* decreasing in some argument position. If A is the number of argument positions there must be an argument position, say j, such that at least M/A of the transitions in $\Delta(\tau_i)$ are *in situ* decreasing in position j. We can now collapse (τ_i) getting (τ_i') such that all the transitions in $\Delta(\tau_i')$ is *in situ* decreasing in argument position j. If (τ_i') starts with argument tuple v this means that position j can take on only values in $\downarrow(v_j)$ so there must be at least $M/(A\,|\downarrow(v_j)|)$ argument tuples that coincide at position j. So we can collapse (τ_i') getting (τ_i^c) that is constant in position j and has at least length $M/(A\,|\downarrow(v_j)|)$.

The fact that argument position j is bounded, *i.e.*, $v_j \in B(i)$, means that it is possible to make $M/(A\,|\downarrow(v_j)|)$ arbitrarily large. The choice of M influence the value v_j so if v_j was not bounded it might not be possible to make $M/(A\,|\downarrow(v_j)|)$ sufficiently large.

(τ_i^c) has only n non-constant argument positions so by the induction hypothesis at least two of the argument tuples in (τ_i^c) must be equal and thus at least two of the argument tuples in (τ_i).

□

The above theorem does indeed give us a sufficient condition for a program to be quasi-terminating and, as we shall see in the next section, it also gives us a handle on how to ensure termination of partial evaluation. The usefulness of this theorem depends on two things: how easy it will be to collect a reasonably precise approximation to $trans_p$ the transitive closure of the transitions, and how precise the analysis are going to be, *i.e.*, can we make partial evaluation terminate without loosing too much of the power?

3 How to Make Partial Evaluation Terminate

Given program p with transition relation R_p we can generate a set of transitions $\{\tau_1, \ldots, \tau_m\} \supseteq R_p$. Typically by making a transition for each function call textually occurring in the program. If we can show that $\{\tau_1, \ldots, \tau_m\}$ fulfills the condition in theorem 15 the program is bound to be quasi-terminating. Furthermore, the finite evaluation graph can be generated in finite time using the minimal function graph approach described by Jones and Mycroft [8].

Poly-variant partial evaluation with static binding time analysis could be performed by first using the minimal function graph approach to generate the evaluation graph and then produce the residual program from the information in the graph. We "prove" that this approach terminates if the program being partial evaluated is quasi-terminating in the static positions. Later we discuss the differences between our, operational not very efficient, algorithm and an actual implementation as described in Sestoft [13] and in Jones [9] and how the differences affect termination.

3.1 Binding Times and Congruent Divisions

Assume that we have been given a program, p, annotated with congruent mono-variant binding time information. Mono-variant meaning that each function argument is annotated either as *static* or *dynamic*. Congruent means that the value of static arguments can be computed from the value of static arguments alone. This is the congruence condition defined in Jones [5].

By blanking out the dynamic arguments it is now possible to generate the evaluation graph, $EG(p, i)$, where i is the partial input, using the minimal function graph approach, Jones [8]. Of course it is necessary to follow both branches of a conditional if the condition is dynamic. It should be realised that it is the congruence of the binding time annotation that makes it possible to generate the evaluation graph with the dynamic positions blanked out, congruence guarantee that the value of the dynamic arguments will not be needed to compute the value of the static arguments. In figure 2 we have shown the evaluation graph for append with static first argument and dynamic second argument. The last node occurs because we have chosen to follow all calls. In partial evaluation the last node would not occur.

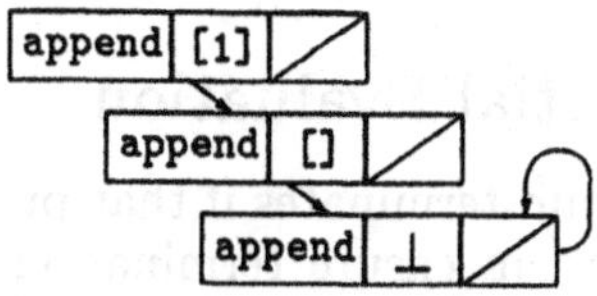

Figure 2: The evaluation graph for append

Algorithm 16. The residual program is now generated from the minimal function graph as follows.

1. Make a residual function for each call configuration in the minimal function graph which have a dynamic argument. The residual function will have the dynamic arguments as arguments. The static arguments is substituted into the body.

2. Transform calls with dynamic argument to calls to the corresponding residual function.

3. Substitute function calls where all arguments are static with their return value as found in the minimal function graph.

4. The resulting residual program can be improved by unfolding some of the residual functions, typically the ones to which there are only one call, and by performing various algebraic transformations in the body of the residual functions.

□

3.2 When does Partial Evaluation Terminate?

Partial evaluation is guaranteed to terminate if the evaluation graph is finite, *i.e.*, if the program is quasi-terminating in the static positions. A program is quasi-terminating in the static positions if it is quasi-terminating when we forget everything about the value of the dynamic positions and just compute the evaluation graph for the static positions. It is possible to do so because the binding time annotation is congruent. The only difference from the standard semantics is that we follow both branches of a conditional with dynamic test.

Observation 17. If all branches of conditionals are followed in the analysis of the program then the result we get by considering the static positions are safe, independently of the binding time division, as long as the binding time division is congruent.

This is the case, because in a congruent binding time division the static arguments only depends on the static arguments, so the dynamic arguments that is blanked out have not got any influence on the static arguments being considered.

This means that we only need to perform the analysis once. Changing the binding time division does not mean that we need to redo the analysis. □

3.3 Terminating Partial Evaluation

Partial evaluation of a program terminates if that program is quasi-terminating in its static arguments. So we can ensure termination of the partial evaluation by making arguments dynamic until the program is quasi-terminating in the remaining static arguments.

Algorithm 18. Given program p and initial division of the arguments into static and dynamic. We arrive at a congruent division, that is quasi-terminating in the static arguments, as follows.

1. All arguments that are *in situ* increasing in a transition where there are no safe *in situ* decreasing argument position becomes dynamic.
2. All arguments that depends on arguments that are dynamic becomes dynamic. This ensures congruence of the resulting annotation.

Proof: It is obvious that the division is congruent. Furthermore, it never makes a safe *in situ* decreasing argument position dynamic because safe positions does not depend on *in situ* increasing argument positions neither direct nor indirect and we only change *in situ* increasing argument positions or argument positions that depended on *in situ* increasing argument positions to dynamic. So, algorithm 18 gives a congruent binding time division of p such that p is quasi-terminating in the static argument positions in a one-step process. □

3.4 A "Real" Partial Evaluator

The partial evaluator described in Jones [9], and Sestoft [13] bears some resemblance with the minimal functional graph algorithm we described. But, for reasons of efficiency, it differ in some respects. Instead of describing this partial evaluator here we list the differences that are important with respect to termination.

- Function calls with completely static arguments are evaluated using an ordinary interpreter. This means that infinite loops of any kind in the completely static parts of the program being partially evaluated will result in the partial evaluator being non-terminating. This can be remedied either by demanding that the completely static parts of the program have to be terminating, our analysis could be used to show this, or to change the partial evaluator such that it memoise calls when evaluating completely static expressions.

- Only calls that are explicitly marked as residual are left as calls to residual functions, *i.e.*, put into the evaluation graph. All other calls are unfolded on the fly. This gives the risk of infinite unfolding; unfolding around a cycle in the evaluation graph. Again there are two solutions. Either one analyse the program and make sure that all unfolding paths are finite, this is the approach taken in Sestoft [14], or the partial evaluator use some kind of memoising strategy when unfolding function calls.

As it can be seen from this list it is very small changes to the partial evaluator that are needed in order to guarantee termination if the program being partial evaluated is quasi-terminating in its static arguments.

4 The Transition Semantics

This section gives a transition semantics for a strict, first-order language. The language has constants, variables, basic operations, conditionals, and function calls. The syntax of the language is given in 3.

The transition semantics will be a safe approximation of the partial evaluation semantics. During partial evaluation calls from both branches of dynamic conditionals will be collected. In the transition semantics calls from both branches of *all* conditionals will be collected. This makes the result of the transition semantics independent of the particular binding time division. Since ordinary evaluation is a special case of partial evaluation, everything is static, the transition semantics also approximates ordinary evaluation. The result of the transition semantics will normally be an infinite set of transitions. So we define a finite domain of abstract transitions and use abstract interpretation to approximate the transition semantics. This way we are guaranteed to terminate with a finite set of approximating transitions. We can then use these approximating transitions to check the condition in theorem 15 to establish if the program is quasi-terminating, or we apply algorithm 18 to get a congruent binding time annotation that guarantees termination of partial evaluation of the analysed program.

In figure 4 a transition semantics that collects a superset, $trans_p$, of the transitions defined by program p is defined. The semantic function $\mathcal{E}$ assigns meanings to expressions in the ordinary way. Basic operations are given meaning by the oracle $\mathcal{O}$. The meaning of an expression deviates slightly from the standard meaning. The meaning is not a function from the environment to a value, instead it is a function from the argument tuple to a value. This avoids referring to names[1]. The 1-step transitions are collected by the semantic function $\mathcal{CE}$. Because the transitions

[1]The cost is that the semantics, as we have written it, is context sensitive.

$x, x_i, \ldots \in$ Var, $e, e_i, \ldots \in$ Exp, $f, f_i, \ldots \in$ Fnames,
$o \in$ Operators, $c \in$ Constants.

$$\text{Prog} ::= f_1(x_1, \ldots, x_{n_{f_1}}) = e_1, \ \ldots, \ f_m(x_1, \ldots, x_{n_{f_m}}) = e_m$$

$$\text{Exp} ::= c \mid x_i \mid o(e_1, \ldots, e_{n_o}) \mid e_1 \rightarrow e_2 \mid e_3 \mid f(e_1, \ldots, e_{n_f})$$

Figure 3: Syntax

are collected independently of the values of the input transitions in both branches of conditionals are collected. The domain of f's argument tuple is S_f which is isomorphic to S^n where f has arity n. S_* is the sum $S_{f_1} + \ldots + S_{f_m}$. Programs are given meaning by $\mathcal{EP}$. The meaning is the function environment ϕ, and the full set of transitions ψ, or *trans*$_p$ defined as the transitive closure of the 1-step transitions under composition. The normal meaning of the program is the meaning of the first function, $\phi(f_1)$.

Definition 19. A finite product with n components consist of n selection functions: $\pi_1, \ldots, \pi_n$ functions and a construction function $\langle \_, \ldots, \_ \rangle$, such that the following holds:

$$\begin{aligned} \pi_j(x_1, \ldots, x_n) &= x_j \\ \langle f_1, \ldots, f_n \rangle\ x &= \begin{cases} \bot & \text{if some } f_i\ x = \bot \\ (f_1\ x, \ldots, f_n\ x) & \text{otherwise} \end{cases} \end{aligned}$$

□

The value $\bot$ is used both in the sense of run-time error and in the sense "non-terminating". A program is considered as terminating if it makes a run-time error; operations like `(hd nil)` give run-time errors.

4.1 An Approximating Semantics

There is one problem with the transition semantics given in figure 4, the set of transitions *trans*$_p$ will normally be infinite. So, instead of collecting *trans*$_p$, we are going to collect a finite approximation to *trans*$_p$ that gives us the needed information.

There are two logically independent kinds of information that we need about the transitions. First, which argument positions that depends on which, *i.e.*, a dependency analysis. Second, how the size of a position relates to the size of the input positions, particularly if it is smaller than one of these.

In this paper we are not going to present the dependency analysis as it is fairly simple. The dependency analysis basically collect the variables that occurs in an expression. Instead we are going to describe the size analysis in some details.

$$
\begin{aligned}
\text{Val} &= S_* \to S \\
\text{Trans} &= \mathrm{P}(S_* \to S_*) \\
\text{Fenv} &= \text{Fnames} \to \text{Val} \\
\mathcal{O} &= \text{Operators} \to \text{Val}
\end{aligned}
$$

$$\mathcal{EP} :: \text{Programs} \to (\text{Fenv} \times \text{Trans})$$

$$
\begin{aligned}
&\mathcal{EP}[\![\, f_1(x_1,\ldots,x_n) = e_1,\ \ldots, f_m(x_1,\ldots,x_n) = e_m \,]\!] = (\phi,\psi) \\
&\quad \text{where}\quad \psi = \mathit{fix}\ \lambda\psi.\{f_i \xrightarrow{\sigma\circ\tau} f_j \mid f_i \xrightarrow{\tau} f_k, f_k \xrightarrow{\sigma} f_j \in \psi\} \cup \psi \cup \psi_0 \\
&\qquad\qquad \psi_0 = \textstyle\bigcup_{i=1}^{m} \mathcal{CE}_{f_i}[\![\, e_i \,]\!]\phi \\
&\qquad\qquad \phi = \mathit{fix}\ \lambda\phi.[f_1 \mapsto \mathcal{E}[\![\, e_1 \,]\!]\phi, \ldots, f_m \mapsto \mathcal{E}[\![\, e_m \,]\!]\phi]
\end{aligned}
$$

$$\mathcal{E} :: \text{Exp} \to \text{Fenv} \to \text{Val}$$

$$
\begin{aligned}
\mathcal{E}[\![\, c \,]\!]\,\phi &= \lambda x.c = \mathrm{K}_c \\
\mathcal{E}[\![\, x_i \,]\!]\,\phi &= \pi_i \\
\mathcal{E}[\![\, o(e_1,\ldots,e_n) \,]\!]\,\phi &= \mathcal{O}(o) \circ \langle \mathcal{E}[\![\, e_1 \,]\!]\,\phi,\ldots,\mathcal{E}[\![\, e_n \,]\!]\phi\rangle \\
\mathcal{E}[\![\, e_1 \to e_2 \ \|\ e_3 \,]\!]\,\phi &= \lambda x.\mathcal{E}[\![\, e_1 \,]\!]\,\phi x \to \mathcal{E}[\![\, e_2 \,]\!]\,\phi x \ \|\ \mathcal{E}[\![\, e_3 \,]\!]\,\phi x \\
\mathcal{E}[\![\, f(e_1,\ldots,e_n) \,]\!]\,\phi &= \phi(f) \circ \langle \mathcal{E}[\![\, e_1 \,]\!]\,\phi,\ldots,\mathcal{E}[\![\, e_n \,]\!]\,\phi\rangle
\end{aligned}
$$

$$\mathcal{CE}_* :: \text{Exp} \to \text{Fenv} \to \text{Trans}$$

$$
\begin{aligned}
\mathcal{CE}_{f_i}[\![\, c \,]\!]\,\phi &= \emptyset \\
\mathcal{CE}_{f_i}[\![\, x \,]\!]\,\phi &= \emptyset \\
\mathcal{CE}_{f_i}[\![\, o(e_1,\ldots,e_n) \,]\!]\,\phi &= \textstyle\bigcup_{i=1}^{n} \mathcal{CE}_{f_i}[\![\, e_i \,]\!]\,\phi \\
\mathcal{CE}_{f_i}[\![\, e_1 \to e_2 \ \|\ e_3 \,]\!]\,\phi &= \textstyle\bigcup_{i=1}^{3} \mathcal{CE}_{f_i}[\![\, e_i \,]\!]\,\phi \\
\mathcal{CE}_{f_i}[\![\, f(e_1,\ldots,e_n) \,]\!]\,\phi &= \textstyle\bigcup_{i=1}^{n} \mathcal{CE}_{f_i}[\![\, e_i \,]\!]\,\phi \\
&\quad \cup\{\langle \mathcal{E}[\![\, e_1 \,]\!]\,\phi,\ldots,\mathcal{E}[\![\, e_n \,]\!]\,\phi\rangle : f_i \to f\,\}
\end{aligned}
$$

Figure 4: Transition Semantics

4.2 Size Analysis

The size analysis is an abstract version of the transition semantics. The end goal is to find inductive arguments or arguments that are bounded in size. First an abstract domain is defined, capable of expressing facts like: The first argument gets smaller at each recursive call. Then an abstract version of the transition semantics is defined, collecting information like: there is a transition from a function to itself where the first argument gets smaller, or better, the first argument gets smaller in all the transitions. The append function defined in the introduction is a good example of such a function.

4.3 The Size of Data Objects

We assume that $(S, \sqsubseteq)$ is a flat domain and the size relation $(S, \leq)$ is transitive, antisymmetric, and reflexive, furthermore we assume that it has the finite downwards closure property, and that the size relation obeys the domain ordering $(\sqsubseteq) \subseteq (\leq)$, *i.e.*, $\forall s \in S : \bot \leq s$.

4.4 An Abstraction of Function Spaces

A transition is a function between tuples of values. We want to express facts about transitions like: The j'th part of the result is always smaller than the i'th part of the input. Let ${}^{j}\!<^{i}$ be the set of functions whose j'th part of the result is less than the i'th part of the input.

Definition 20. Let ${}^{j}\!\leq^{i}$, and ${}^{j}\!<^{i}$ be subsets of $(S^n \to S^m)$ defined as follows:

$$\begin{aligned} {}^{j}\!\leq^{i} &= \{\phi \in (S^n \to S^m) \mid \forall s \in S\backslash\{\bot\} : \pi_j(\phi(s)) \preceq \pi_i(s)\} \\ {}^{j}\!<^{i} &= \{\phi \in (S^n \to S^m) \mid \forall s \in S\backslash\{\bot\} : \pi_j(\phi(s)) \prec \pi_i(s)\} \end{aligned}$$

□

Lemma 21. The sets ${}^{j}\!\leq^{i}$, ${}^{j}\!<^{i}$, $\bot_{\mathcal{S}^m_n} = \{\bot\}$, and $\top_{\mathcal{S}^m_n} = (S^n \to S^m)$ are Scott-closed.

Proof: Trivial in the flat case, since the size relation obeys the domain ordering. □

So $\mathcal{S}^m_n$, can be defined as a sub-domain of the Hoare (lower) power domain as follows.

Definition 22. Let $\mathcal{S}^m_n$ be the sub-domain of the Hoare power domain formed by closing the set $\{{}^{j}\!\leq^{i}, {}^{j}\!<^{i} \mid i \in \{1,\ldots,n\}, j \in \{1,\ldots,m\}\} \cup \{\bot, \top\}$ under $\sqcup$. $\mathcal{S}^m_n$ inherits the subset ordering from the Hoare power domain. The bottom element is $\bot_{\mathcal{S}^m_n}$, and the top element is $\top_{\mathcal{S}^m_n}$. $\mathcal{S}^m_n$ is a finite, complete lattice. □

4.5 Size Analysis by Abstract Interpretation

Following Burn, Hankin, and Abramsky [2] we define an abstraction function and later an abstract version of the transition semantics.

$$\begin{aligned} \mathrm{Abs_S} &: (S^n \to S^m) \to \mathcal{S}^m_n \\ \mathrm{Abs_S}\, f &= \sqcap\{p \in \mathcal{S}^m_n \mid f \in p\} \end{aligned}$$

$\mathrm{Abs_S}$ is continuous and the concretisation function $\mathrm{Con_S}$ is the identity.

In the transition semantics, transitions are built from these basic operations using composition and pairing. Again following Burn, Hankin, and Abramsky we define abstract versions of these constructions.

Definition 23. Composition and pairing in $\mathcal{S}^m_n$ is defined as:

$$\_ \circ^\sharp \_ : \mathcal{S}^m_k \times \mathcal{S}^k_n \to \mathcal{S}^m_n$$

$$q \circ^\sharp p = \bigsqcup\{\mathrm{Abs_S}(\psi \circ \phi) \mid \psi \in \mathrm{Con_S}(q),\ \phi \in \mathrm{Con_S}(p)\}$$

$$\langle \_,\ldots,\_ \rangle^\sharp : (\mathcal{S}^1_m)^n \to \mathcal{S}^n_m$$

$$\langle p_1,\ldots,p_n \rangle^\sharp = \bigsqcup\{\mathrm{Abs_S}(\langle \phi_1,\ldots,\phi_n \rangle) \mid \phi_i \in \mathrm{Con_S}(p_i)\}$$

□

The size analysis is given as an abstract interpretation in figure 5. The size analysis has the same structure as the transition analysis, except for the conditional where the least upper bound of the two branches is taken since the truth value of the condition is unknown. Again the domain and co-domain of the transitions will be indicated by the types of the transitions, and $\mathcal{S}_*$ will be the sum of the relevant $\mathcal{S}_n^m$ including $\mathcal{S}_n^1$.

$$\begin{array}{lcl} \text{Size} & = & \mathcal{S}_* \\ \text{TransS} & = & \mathsf{P}(\mathcal{S}_*) \\ \text{Fenv} & = & \text{Fnames} \rightarrow \mathcal{S}_* \end{array}$$

$$\mathcal{SP} :: \text{Programs} \rightarrow (\text{Fenv} \times \text{TransS})$$

$$\mathcal{SP}[\![\, f_1(x_1,\ldots,x_n) = e_1,\ \ldots, f_m(x_1,\ldots,x_n) = e_m \,]\!] = (\phi, \psi)$$

$$\begin{array}{ll} \text{where} & \psi = \mathit{fix}\ \lambda\psi.\{f_i \xrightarrow{\sigma \circ^! \tau} f_j \mid f_i \xrightarrow{\tau} f_k, f_k \xrightarrow{\sigma} f_j \in \psi\} \cup \psi \cup \psi_0 \\ & \psi_0 = \bigcup_{i=1}^{m} \mathcal{CS}_{f_i}[\![\, e_i \,]\!]\ \phi \\ & \phi = \mathit{fix}\ \lambda\phi.[f_1 \mapsto \mathcal{S}[\![\, e_1 \,]\!]\ \phi, \ldots, f_m \mapsto \mathcal{S}[\![\, e_m \,]\!]\ \phi] \end{array}$$

$$\mathcal{S} :: \text{Exp} \rightarrow \text{Fenv} \rightarrow \mathcal{S}_*$$

$$\begin{array}{lcl} \mathcal{S}[\![\, c \,]\!]\ \phi & = & \top \\ \mathcal{S}[\![\, x_i \,]\!]\ \phi & = & {}^{1}\!\leq^{i} \\ \mathcal{S}[\![\, o(e_1,\ldots,e_n) \,]\!]\ \phi & = & \text{Abs}_\text{S}(\mathcal{O}(o)) \circ^\sharp \langle \mathcal{S}[\![\, e_1 \,]\!]\ \phi, \ldots, \mathcal{S}[\![\, e_n \,]\!] \phi\rangle^\sharp \\ \mathcal{S}[\![\, e_1 \rightarrow e_2 \mid e_3 \,]\!]\ \phi & = & \mathcal{S}[\![\, e_2 \,]\!]\ \phi \sqcup \mathcal{S}[\![\, e_3 \,]\!] \phi \\ \mathcal{S}[\![\, f(e_1,\ldots,e_n) \,]\!]\ \phi & = & \phi(f) \circ^\sharp \langle \mathcal{S}[\![\, e_1 \,]\!]\ \phi, \ldots, \mathcal{S}[\![\, e_n \,]\!]\ \phi\rangle^\sharp \end{array}$$

$$\mathcal{CS}_* :: \text{Exp} \rightarrow \text{Fenv} \rightarrow \text{TransS}$$

$$\begin{array}{lcl} \mathcal{CS}_{f_i}[\![\, c \,]\!]\ \phi & = & \emptyset \\ \mathcal{CS}_{f_i}[\![\, x \,]\!]\ \phi & = & \emptyset \\ \mathcal{CS}_{f_i}[\![\, o(e_1,\ldots,e_n) \,]\!]\ \phi & = & \bigcup_{i=1}^{n} \mathcal{CS}_{f_i}[\![\, e_i \,]\!]\ \phi \\ \mathcal{CS}_{f_i}[\![\, e_1 \rightarrow e_2 \mid e_3 \,]\!]\ \phi & = & \bigcup_{i=1}^{3} \mathcal{CS}[\![\, e_i \,]\!]\ \phi \\ \mathcal{CS}_{f_i}[\![\, f(e_1,\ldots,e_n) \,]\!]\ \phi & = & \bigcup_{i=1}^{n} \mathcal{CS}_{f_i}[\![\, e_i \,]\!]\ \phi \\ & & \cup \{\langle \mathcal{S}[\![\, e_1 \,]\!]\ \phi, \ldots, \mathcal{S}[\![\, e_n \,]\!]\ \phi\rangle^\sharp : f_i \rightarrow f\ \} \end{array}$$

Figure 5: Size Analysis

Observation 24. Let $size_p$ be the size relations collected by the size analysis, ψ in figure 5. By construction, $size_p$ is closed under composition.

The size analysis gives a safe approximation of the transition semantics in the following sense. If $\tau \in trans_p$ then there exist a $\sigma \in size_p$ such that $\text{Abs}_\text{S}(\tau) \sqsubseteq \sigma$. Furthermore $size_p$ is computable because $\mathcal{S}_n^m$ is finite. □

4.6 Interpreting the Abstract Transitions

The abstract interpretation just defined combined with the dependency analysis, which we have only sketched, makes it possible to collect a finite set of abstract transitions. An abstract transition, $\tau = (\delta, \sigma)$, is a pair consisting of dependency information, δ, and size information σ. δ is safe in the following sense: if δ show that position i depends on position j this means that position i *might* depend on position j. Likewise, if δ show that position i does not depend on position j then it means that position i definitely does not depend on position j.

It is obvious that if an abstract transition, τ, says that a position is decreasing (*in situ* decreasing) then this information is safe, *i.e.*, all the transitions in $\mathrm{Con}(\tau)$ will be decreasing (*in situ* decreasing). It is less obvious that the abstract transitions are safe for composite transitions. Remember that our definition of increasing for a composite transition depended on the way in which the transition was composed. A composite transition was increasing in position i if there was a path ending in position i along which the value increased. Fortunately our abstract transitions are safe. If we have a composite transition $(\tau_n \circ \ldots \circ \tau_1)$ that is increasing (*in situ* increasing) in position i then $(\mathrm{Abs}(\tau_n) \circ^{\sharp} \ldots \circ^{\sharp} \mathrm{Abs}(\tau_1))$ are going to be increasing (*in situ* increasing) in position i.

5 Results

The analysis devised in the previous sections has been tested on several programs with good results. The main use has been, given a program, to find binding time annotations that guaranteed that partial evaluation of the program terminated. The analysis can also be used to establish termination properties of programs in general. The analysis has been implemented in LML and is quite efficient.

5.1 Ackermann's Function

Ackermann's function, shown in figure 6, is a small non-trivial example. It terminates, but is not primitive recursive. In the example program we have used unary numbers (a number n is represented by a list of length n); the functions `zero`, `add1`, and `sub1` have the obvious definitions.

```
> analyse " ack (n,m) = if zero(n) add1(m)
                         if zero(m) ack(sub1(n),'1)
                            ack(sub1(n),ack(n,sub1(m)))"

  ack (Bounded, Unbounded)
    --> (in situ decreasing, in situ increasing),
        (in situ weakly decreasing, in situ decreasing)
```

Figure 6: Analysis of Ackermann's function

The result of the analysis tells us that the first argument position is bounded while the second is potentially unbounded. Furthermore it tells us that the transitions either have an *in situ* decreasing first argument and a possibly *in situ* increasing second argument, or an *in situ* weakly decreasing first argument and an *in situ* decreasing second argument. Ackerman's function fulfills the conditions in theorem 15: in all transitions where there is an *in situ* increasing argument there is also an *in situ* decreasing argument, and is therefore quasi-terminating. Given that the size ordering is well-founded Ackerman's function can even be shown to be terminating, using the collected information it is easy to see that the transitions obey a lexicographical order so theorem 1 guarantees that the evaluation tree are going to be finite and thus that the program therefore is terminating.

5.2 The Function Length

Partial evaluation, as described in Jones [9], and Sestoft [13], often suffers from termination problems. In this section it is shown how these problems occur and how algorithm 18 solves these problems. Part of the problem is that partial evaluation is strict in dynamic conditionals, *i.e.*, it evaluates both branches. Given a part of the input (the static data) a partial evaluator collects the set of possible function calls, and for each function call it generates a new function specialised with respect to the value of the known arguments (the static arguments) in that function call. The problem is that the set of possible function calls could be infinite in which case partial evaluation does not terminate.

We illustrate with the following two definitions of length. Suppose the argument is dynamic, then the inductive version of length terminates under partial evaluation, generating exactly one specialised version. While the tail recursive version with an accumulating arguments perpetuates, generating infinitely many different versions of "`len`", specialised with respect to `a` = 0, 1, *etc.*

```
> analyse "    length (l) = if null(l) '0
                               add1(length(tl(l)))"
  length (Bounded)
    -->  (in situ decreasing)

> analyse "    length (l) = len(l,'0)
               len (l,a)  = if null(l) a
                               len(tl(l),add1(a))"
  length -->
  len (Bounded, Unbounded)
    -->  (in situ decreasing, in situ increasing)
```

Figure 7: Analyses of Two Length Functions

The partial evaluator described in Jones [9] would go into an infinite loop on a program containing the second definition of length. User guidance would be needed, to tell that the second argument to "`len`" had to be dynamic to avoid generating infinitely many versions of `len`. Algorithm 18 would spot that the static *in situ* increasing argument is not bound by a static *in situ* decreasing argument, since the first argument is dynamic, so it would make the second argument dynamic.

5.3 Interpreters and Self-Applicable Partial Evaluators

An important objective has been to keep the strength of partial evaluation, as defined by Jones [9], while ensuring termination. This means that analysis of interpreters and, in particular, of the partial evaluator itself must not be too conservative; it must not change too many arguments from static to dynamic. We have applied our analysis to several interpreters and partial evaluators. In most cases only the arguments that were dynamic initially were forced to be dynamic. In very involved cases some arguments, which could safely have been kept as static, were transformed to dynamic. The functions spotted were variants of copy; the generated structure, though equivalent to the input, were built by functions with accumulating arguments.

6 Conclusion

We have basically done three things in this paper. We have given a sufficient condition (theorem 15) for a program to be quasi-terminating. The condition is easy to check and it is easy to check if the program is quasi-terminating in a congruent subset of the arguments. We observed that partial evaluation of a program will terminate if the program is quasi-terminating in it's static arguments. Thus we could guarantee terminating of partial evaluation by forcing unsafe arguments to be dynamic. Finally we have used abstract interpretation techniques to collect an approximation of the transitions.

We believe that the important contributions of this work is decoupling the termination problem from the binding time analysis, and the application of abstract interpretation to the termination problem. Furthermore we find theorem 15 quite pleasant.

6.1 Related Works

The history of this work deserves a few words. On and off the problem of non-terminating partial evaluation has been attacked by the Copenhagen MIX group. Peter Sestoft [14] addressed the problem of deciding which program points to specialise to avoid infinite unfolding. Neil D. Jones took a more general approach to the problem in his "re-examination" paper [5] where he introduced the idea of finding inductive arguments, and arguments that took on only values that were substructures of the original input. It was this work that was the inspirational starting point of this paper.

The work being reported on enforcing termination of partial evaluation can be divided into two categories. The work that tries to enforce termination on the fly. A brute force approach is depth bounds, but also more sophisticated approaches have been seen, like Turchin's [15] generalisations which aims at choosing a finite set of values to specialise with respect to.

Another approach to termination analysis, is to consider it as a dual to strictness analysis. This approach has been too weak to have had any success.

A lot of work has been done in proving the termination of term rewriting systems. Almost all of this work have been in developing proof methods, although some has been done in the area of automatic termination analysis.

The prolog community has also been interested in termination problems and to a lesser extend in quasi-termination. Lutz Plümer [12] gives an interesting, but complex, ordering using linear inequalities which are potentially stronger than the fairly trivial ordering proposed in this paper.

6.2 Future Work

There are several natural extensions to this work:

- Defining even weaker quasi-termination conditions.
- Considering other kinds of size relations.
- Making a more fine grain transition analysis, *e.g.*, considering data structures other than argument tuples. This will be important when we want to guarantee termination of partial evaluators with partially static structures like Mogensen's [11].
- Higher-order languages. The problem is to define a size relation on closures. Like for partially static structures this is going to be important when we consider partial evaluators like Similix [1].
- Lazy languages. Here the problem is the existence of infinite and partial data objects.

Another area which ought to be addressed is that of termination. In this paper we have focused on quasi-termination, but the analysis can also detect termination. Ackermann's function is a good example of this.

One area of use is abstract interpretation with infinite high domains. One could hope to use this analysis to ensure termination of such abstract interpretations in much the same way as it was done here with partial evaluation.

Acknowledgments

Thanks to my supervisor John Hughes and to John Launchbury who have dragged me out of pits and traps in the area of abstract interpretation (and hopefully will continue to do so), and who have given several valuable suggestions about presentation. Thanks also to Neil D. Jones who laid out the basis for this work, and to Torben Mogensen with whom I discussed the first vague ideas.

References

[1] Anders Bondorf. Automatic autoprojection of higher order recursive equations. In Neil D. Jones, editor, *3rd European Symposium on Programming (ESOP '90),*

volume 432 of *Lecture Notes in Computer Science*, pages 70–87, Copenhagen, Denmark, May 1990. Springer-Verlag.

[2] G. L. Burn, C. L. Hankin, and S Abramsky. The theory of strictness analysis for higher order functions. In H. Ganzinger and N. D. Jones, editors, *Programs as Data Structures*, pages 42–62. Lecture Notes in Computer Science, October 1985.

[3] Charles Consel. New insights into partial evaluation: The schism experiment. In Harald Ganzinger, editor, *2nd European Symposium on Programming, (ESOP '88)*, volume 300 of *Lecture Notes in Computer Science*, pages 236–247, Nancy, France, 1988. Springer-Verlag.

[4] Nachum Dershowitz. Termination of rewriting. *Journal of Symbolic Computation*, 3:69–116, 1987.

[5] Neil D. Jones. Automatic program specialization: A re-examination from basic principles. In A.P. Ershov D. Bjørner and N.D. Jones, editors, *Partial Evaluation and Mixed Computation*, pages 225–282. North-Holland, 1988.

[6] Neil D. Jones and Tine Andersen. Notes on a safe binding time analysis. Internal note., 1989.

[7] Neil D. Jones, Carsten K. Gomard, Anders Bondorf, Olivier Danvier, and Torben Æ. Mogensen. A self-applicable partial evaluator for the lambda-calculus. In *1990 Interational Conference on Computer Languages.* IEEE computer Society, 1990.

[8] Neil D. Jones and Allan Mycroft. Data flow analysis of applicative programs using minimal function graphs. In *Thirteenth ACM Symposium on Principles of Programming Languages, St. Petersburg, Florida*, pages 296–306. ACM, 1986.

[9] Neil D. Jones, Peter Sestoft, and Harald Søndergaard. Mix: A self-applicable partial evaluator for experiments in compiler generation. *Lisp and Symbolic Computation*, 2(1):9–50, 1989.

[10] S. C. Kleene. *Introduction to Metamathematics.* D. van Nostrand, Princeton, New Jersey, 1952.

[11] Torben Æ. Mogensen. Partially static structures in a self-applicable partial evaluator. In A.P. Ershov D. Bjørner and N.D. Jones, editors, *Partial Evaluation and Mixed Computation*, pages 325–347. North-Holland, 1988.

[12] Lutz Plümer. *Termination Proofs for Logic Programs*, volume 446 of *Lecture Notes in Artificial Intelligence.* Springer-Verlag, 1990.

[13] Peter Sestoft. The structure of a self-applicable partial evaluator. In Harald Ganzinger and Neil D. Jones, editors, *Programs as Data Objects*, volume 217 of *Lecture Notes in Computer Science*, pages 236–256, Copenhagen, Denmark, 1986. Springer-Verlag.

[14] Peter Sestoft. Automatic call unfolding in a partial evaluator. In A.P. Ershov D. Bjørner and N.D. Jones, editors, *Partial Evaluation and Mixed Computation*, pages 485–506. North-Holland, 1988.

[15] V. F. Turchin. The algorithm of generalization in the supercompiler. In A.P. Ershov D. Bjørner and N.D. Jones, editors, *Partial Evaluation and Mixed Computation*, pages 531–549. North-Holland, 1988.

For a Better Support of Static Data Flow

Charles Consel
Yale University *
(consel@cs.yale.edu)

Olivier Danvy
Kansas State University †
(danvy@cis.ksu.edu)

Abstract

This paper identifies and solves a class of problems that arise in binding time analysis and more generally in partial evaluation of programs: the approximation and loss of static information due to dynamic expressions with static subexpressions. Solving this class of problems yields substantial binding time improvements and thus dramatically better results not only in the case of partial evaluation but also for static analyses of programs — this last point actually is related to a theoretical result obtained by Nielson. Our work can also be interpreted as providing a solution to the problem of conditionally static data, the dual of partially static data.

We point out which changes in the control flow of a source program may improve its static data flow. Unfortunately they require one to iterate earlier phases of partial evaluation. We show how these changes are subsumed by transforming the source program into continuation-passing style (CPS). The transformed programs get specialized more tightly by a higher-order partial evaluator, without iteration. As a consequence, static values get frozen according to the specialization strategy and not due to the structure of the source programs.

Our approach makes it possible to get better results without changing our partial evaluator, by using its higher-order capabilities more thoroughly. By construction, transforming source programs into CPS makes it yield better results, even in the particular case of self-application. New problems can even be tackled such as static deforestation by partial evaluation, specialization of contexts, and conditionally static data.

This development concerns applicative order, side-effect free functional languages because we consider existing self-applicable partial evaluators. We conjecture a similar improvement for lazy functional languages, based on the normal order CPS transformation.

Keywords

Partial evaluation, binding times, continuation-passing style, Scheme,
compilation of pattern matching, deforestation,
partially static data, conditionally static data.

---

*Department of Computer Science, Yale University, P.O. Box 2158, New Haven, CT 06520, USA. This research was supported by DARPA under grant N00014-88-k-0573. Part of it was carried out while visiting Kansas State University in 1990.

†Department of Computing and Information Sciences, Kansas State University, Manhattan, KS 66506, USA. Part of this work was carried out while visiting Yale University in 1990.

1 Introduction

Partial evaluation is a program transformation technique that aims at specializing programs with respect to part of their input. By definition, running the residual program on the remaining input yields the same result as running the source program on the complete input if they both terminate.

A partial evaluator reduces expressions in the source program as much as allowed by the available input, and reconstructs irreducible expressions, *i.e.*, expressions whose reduction depends on the unavailable parts of the input. Also, depending on the partial evaluation strategy and to ensure termination of the specialization process, an expression may be reconstructed even though it depends only on the available input; this issue goes beyond the scope of this paper but it is addressed in published work on self-applicable partial evaluation [26, 6, 3].

As initiated in the MIX project [25], the static and dynamic semantics of partial evaluation are best separated into two phases. The first phase — binding time analysis (BTA) — determines (a safe approximation of) the binding times of each source expression in a program, for a given division (known/unknown) of its input. The second phase — specialization — simply follows the binding time information: it reduces static expressions and reconstructs the other expressions.

Much of the work on partial evaluation has been devoted to improving the quality of residual programs. Indeed, partial evaluation occurs only once, whereas residual programs may run many times. In essence, this line of work aims at keeping track of the static parts of the data flow as accurately as possible, since the more static data are preserved throughout partial evaluation, the more source expressions get evaluated and therefore the less need to be executed in the residual program. However, this strategy does not address control structures whose specialization may freeze some static values as well as the computations that depend on these values.

As a simple example, let us consider the following applicative order expression

$$(\underline{\mathbf{if}}\ \underline{e_1}\ \underline{\mathbf{then}}\ \overline{e_2}\ \underline{\mathbf{else}}\ \overline{e_3})\ \underline{+}\ \overline{e_4}$$

where, for clarity, sub-expressions are annotated *à la* Nielson and Nielson. That is, an expression that is bound statically is overlined, otherwise it is bound dynamically and it is underlined.

Because the test expression e_1 cannot be evaluated at partial evaluation time, the conditional expression will be reconstructed. Therefore, the static values resulting from e_2 and e_3 will be frozen in the residual conditional expression although, outside, the second operand of the addition is static. As a consequence, the addition gets delayed until run time, despite the early binding time of both its operands.

Such losses of compile time values arise in many applications. For instance, in definitional interpreters, type checking operations get frozen; in pattern matchers, static knowledge about substitutions gets ignored.

Probably this problem can be solved by introducing more complicated mechanisms in the specialization process. We do not want to pursue this direction because the specialization technique described above is simple and yet effective enough to yield, *e.g.*, non-trivial self-applicable partial evaluators.

Therefore, we propose to keep the same partial evaluator but to transform the control flow of the source program to prevent static values from being frozen. Such a meaning-preserving transformation amounts to reordering threads of execution in the source program to make use of the compile time values at compile time. Getting back to the example above, such a transformation would result in distributing the context (that is, the pending computations) in the conditional branches, thereby making the two instances of the addition executable at partial evaluation time.

$$\underline{\textbf{if}}\ \underline{e_1}\ \underline{\textbf{then}}\ (\overline{e_2} \mathbin{\overline{+}} \overline{e_4})\ \underline{\textbf{else}}\ (\overline{e_3} \mathbin{\overline{+}} \overline{e_4})$$

Generalizing this approach based on reordering threads of execution is expensive since it requires one to iterate earlier phases of partial evaluation (*cf.* Section 3.) On the other hand, all threads could be reordered, thereby alleviating the need for iteration.

Regarding the extent of this radical transformation for a functional program, a more general version is actually well-known: it consists of translating the source program from direct style into continuation-passing style (CPS). From the point of view of partial evaluation, CPS programs appear to have numerous interesting properties: A CPS program is tail-recursive, thus, values are always passed forward; the resulting control flow improves on preserving the static parts of data flow with respect to the original source program. Further, because the CPS transformation essentially brings producers and consumers of intermediary data together, it becomes possible, at partial evaluation time, to eliminate the production and consumption of these data. Section 5 illustrates this strategy with a new approach to the deforestation problem [46]. Another novel aspect of this approach is the polyvariant specialization of contexts: each continuation is specialized with respect to different possible values.

Overview

The rest of this paper is organized as follows. Section 2 illustrates and characterizes the problem. Section 3 describes a solution based on a preliminary transformation of the source program into CPS and illustrates its effectiveness. Section 4 reviews the consequences of CPS for partial evaluation. Section 5 illustrates how partial evaluation can contribute to solving the deforestation problem and how contexts can be multiply specialized. Section 6 recasts our work as solving the problem of conditionally static data, the dual of partially static data. Finally, after a comparison with related work, our approach is put into perspective.

2 The Problem

This section illustrates the very common situation where the control flow in a source program hinders its static data flow. Then, we characterize the situations where the problem occurs by introducing a notion of context.

Our source and residual programs are expressed in Scheme [39]. We are using Schism, a self-applicable, binding time-based partial evaluator for pure Scheme programs extended with user-defined data types [8]. Schism handles higher order functions as well as partially static data.

```
(defineType Pattern
  (PatCst c)
  (PatVar v)
  (PatSeq l))
```

```
(defineType Result
  (Unit)
  (Subst s))
```

```
(defineType Substitution
  (EmptySubst)
  (ExtendSubst v d s))
```

Figure 1: Schism data types for pattern matching in lists.

2.1 An example: linear pattern matching in lists

Pattern matching is a typical problem where partial evaluation applies well [2]. The idea is to compile a pattern by specializing a pattern matcher with respect to a pattern. The function computed by a compiled pattern expects a datum and attempts to match it. We consider pattern matching in pure Lisp lists. A pattern either declares a constant, introduces a variable, or specifies a sequence of (sub)patterns. Matching a pattern against a datum yields either an indication of failure, represented by the one-point type *Unit*, or a substitution. A substitution associates variables with values.

Figure 1 displays the data types of the pattern matcher. Figure 2 displays the executable specification of the pattern matcher, written with an accumulator holding the substitutions so far. It takes a pattern and a datum, and returns *Unit* or a list of substitutions. A constant pattern matches a datum if the constant equals the datum. A variable pattern yields the substitution of the datum for the variable. A sequence matches the corresponding list of data, recursively.

However specializing this program with respect to a pattern does not produce satisfactory compiled patterns (*cf.* Figure 3), for the following reasons.

The program is specialized with respect to a pattern: its first argument is available at partial evaluation time whereas its second argument will only be available at run time. Correspondingly, the syntactic analysis of the pattern will be performed at partial evaluation time whereas any computation involving the data will be performed at run time.

Matching a pattern against a datum either yields a substitution or *Unit*, depending on whether the match succeeds or fails. At partial evaluation time, the result of a match cannot be determined since the datum is not known until run time. As a consequence, the domain *Result* is dynamic. Because the pattern matcher is driven by the results of the matches to continue the computation, its control flow is dynamic as well. This is captured in the following binding time signatures:

$$\texttt{match} : \overline{Pattern}\ \overline{\times}\ \underline{Data}\ \overline{\times}\ \widetilde{Subst} \Rrightarrow \underline{Result}$$

$$\texttt{match-Seq} : \overline{List(Pattern)}\ \overline{\times}\ \underline{Data}\ \overline{\times}\ \widetilde{Subst} \Rrightarrow \underline{Result}$$

where static (partial evaluation time) domains are overlined, dynamic (run time) domains are underlined, and partially static domains are marked with a tilde. Here are the corresponding domains:

```
;;; Pattern * Data -> Result
(define (main p d)
  (match p d (EmptySubst)))

;;; Pattern * Data * Substitution -> Result
(define (match p d s)
  (caseType p
    [(PatCst c) (if (equal? c d) (Subst s) (Unit))]
    [(PatVar v) (Subst (ExtendSubst v d s))]
    [(PatSeq l) (match-Seq l d s)]))

;;; List(Pattern) * Data * Substitution -> Result
(define (match-Seq l d s)
  (if (null? l)
      (if (null? d) (Subst s) (Unit))
      (if (null? d)
          (Unit)
          (caseType (match (hd l) (hd d) s)
            [(Unit) (Unit)]
            [(Subst s) (match-Seq (tl l) (tl d) s)]))))
```

Figure 2: Linear pattern matching in lists, direct style with accumulator.

$$\begin{array}{rcl} \widetilde{Subst} & = & \overline{EmptySubst} \mathbin{\overline{+}} \left(\overline{Variable} \mathbin{\overline{\times}} \underline{Data} \mathbin{\overline{\times}} \widetilde{Subst}\right) \\ \underline{Result} & = & \overline{Unit} \mathbin{\underline{+}} \widetilde{Subst} \end{array}$$

Because domain *Result* is dynamic, it is impossible to distinguish between *Unit* and a substitution statically. Therefore, residual programs such as the one in Figure 3 construct and decode intermediary results explicitly. The following section characterizes this pathological situation.

2.2 The problem of dynamic compound expressions

This section characterizes precisely when static subexpressions yield static values that get frozen in a dynamic expression, out of reach for a potential consumer. We outline the BNF of a Scheme program and introduce a notion of context. We formalize this notion with a BNF definition. Distinguishing between static, dynamic, and critical contexts, we pinpoint the possible loss of static information as a consequence of both the structure of a source program and the specialization strategy.

The syntactic categories of Scheme are predefined constants, identifiers, primitive calls, conditional expressions, applications, and abstractions. For simplicity, we leave blocks out of the discussion, since the **let** construct is a syntactic sugar

```
;;; for all d, (main0 d) == (main '(PatSeq ((PatVar x) (PatCst 3))) d)

;;; Data -> Result
(define (main0 d)
  (if (null? d)
      (Unit)
      (caseType (Subst (ExtendSubst 'x (hd d) (EmptySubst)))
        [(Unit) (Unit)]
        [(Subst s)
         (let ([d2 (tl d)])
           (if (null? d2)
               (Unit)
               (caseType (if (equal? 3 (hd d2))
                             (Subst s)
                             (Unit))
                 [(Unit) (Unit)]
                 [(Subst s) (if (null? (tl d2))
                                (Subst s)
                                (Unit))]))))])))
```

Figure 3: Specialized version of the direct style pattern matcher w.r.t. a pattern.

This code was pretty-printed by hand. It is equivalent to the output of Schism. Obviously this program can be evaluated statically further, essentially by reducing the case expressions and propagating the corresponding information across the other conditional expressions. Nevertheless the specializer did not perform these simplifications, based on the too conservative information accumulated by the binding time analysis.

for β-redexes and nested **letrec** expressions can be eliminated by lambda-lifting [24], yielding a set of mutually recursive functions as in Figure 2.

e ::= **cst**(c) | **ide**(i) | **cond**(e_1, e_2, e_3) |
prim(op, (e_1, ..., e_m)) | **lam**((i_1, ..., i_n), e) |
app(e_0,(e_1, ..., e_n))

Specialization rules are simple: expressions either are reduced or they are reconstructed. Reducing a conditional expression depends on whether its test is static or dynamic. The precise treatment of primitive operations depends on how partially static structures are handled. The decision to unfold or to residualize function calls is taken independently by the specializer. Static arguments are transmitted to the callee.

Such program transformations can freeze static values when a compound expression gets reconstructed. This possibility can be characterized syntactically, since static expressions yield static values. The following two definitions capture the relationship between an expression and a sub-expression.

Definition 1 *The* context *of an expression is its immediate ancestor in the abstract syntax tree.*

For example, in the expression **cond**(e_1, e_2, e_3), the context of e_1 is **cond**([ ], e_2, e_3).

We can derive the following context constructors from the BNF of Scheme expressions. With a slight abuse of notation, let us specify them using a BNF format:

E[ ] ::= **cond**([ ], e_2, e_3) | **cond**(e_1, [ ], e_3) | **cond**(e_1, e_2, [ ]) |
prim(op, (e_1, ..., [ ], ..., e_m)) | **lam**((i_1, ..., i_n), [ ]) |
app([ ],(e_1, ..., e_n)) | **app**(e_0,(e_1, ..., [ ], ..., e_n))

where the e_i denote Scheme expressions. In the following, we will refer to this as the "BNF of contexts."

Definition 2 *A* compound *expression* E[e] *is obtained by filling a context* E[ ] *with an expression* e.

For example, given the expressions e_1, e_2, and e_3, the compound expression **cond**(e_1, e_2, e_3) can be built out of e_1 and the context **cond**([ ], e_2, e_3); e_2 and **cond**(e_1, [ ], e_3); and, e_3 and **cond**(e_1, e_2, [ ]).

Contexts make it possible to relate siblings in an abstract syntax tree. The following definition generalizes binding times to contexts.

Definition 3 *The context* E[ ] *of an expression* e *is* static *if the corresponding compound expression* E[e] *is reduced during specialization, and* dynamic *if it is reconstructed during specialization.*

For example, if e_1 is bound statically, the context **cond**(e_1, [ ], e_3) is static since given the expression e_2, the corresponding compound expression **cond**(e_1, e_2, e_3) is reduced independently of what happens to e_2 and e_3. Correspondingly, if e_1 is bound dynamically, the context **cond**(e_1, [ ], e_3) is dynamic.

As can be noticed, a static context does not necessarily yield a static value. For example, a conditional expression whose test is static and branches are dynamic forms a static context with respect to its test. However, reducing this conditional expression yields a dynamic value.

Let us now connect the binding time of an expression with the binding time of its context.

Definition 4 *The context* E[ ] *of an expression* e *is* critical *if the corresponding compound expression* E[e] *is reduced or reconstructed depending on whether* e *is static or dynamic. We then say that e* determines E[ ].

For example, if e_2 is bound statically, the context **prim**(+, ([ ], e_2)) of the expression e (*i.e.*, the corresponding compound expression is **prim**(+, (e, e_2))) is critical because it is reduced or reconstructed depending on whether e is static or dynamic. For another example, the context **cond**(e_1, [ ], e_3) is not critical.

Now, following Strachey, we can view each expression in an abstract syntax tree as producing a value, and we can identify how these expressible values are *consumed* by their context: as a test in a conditional expression; as an operand in a primitive operation; and as a function in an application. The other expressions only *transmit* values: as a conditional branch; and as an argument to a function.

We can even view the path between an expression and its consumer in the abstract syntax tree as a construction where the constructors are contexts. For example, the path between e_3 and the consumer **prim**(+, ([ ], e_4)) in the expression **prim**(+, (**cond**(e_1, e_2, e_3), e_4)) is a construction where the constructors are **cond**(e_1, e_2, [ ]) and **prim**(+, ([ ], e_4)).

Definition 5 *A context is* critical in a path *if it is critical and occurs in this path.*

In the expression **prim**(+, (**cond**(e_1, e_2, e_3), e_4)), if e_4 is bound statically, the context **cond**([ ], e_2, e_3) is critical in the path between **prim**(+, (**cond**(e_1, e_2, e_3), e_4)) and e_1. On the other hand, the context **cond**(e_1, [ ], e_3) is not critical in the path between this expression and e_2.

Property 1 *An expression that determines its critical context can itself be compound.*

Proof: *cf.* BNF of contexts. □

In other terms, several contexts can be critical on the same path. An expression e may not determine its context E[ ], but the corresponding compound expression E[e] may determine its own context. Assuming E[ ] to be reduced statically, e actually may determine the context of E[e]. Looking back at the previous example, e_2 and e_3 actually determine **prim**(+, ([ ], e_4))

This syntactic non-locality of semantic dependence makes it possible to have interferences in the static data flow, as captured in the following property.

Property 2 *A static expression can be separated from its consumer (a test, a primitive operation, or an application) by a dynamic context which is not critical in the path between the expression and the consumer.*

Proof: *cf.* BNF of contexts (or more simply, the previous example.) □

A static expression that is separated from its consumer by a dynamic context gets frozen.

Consequence 1 *If a dynamic expression determines a critical context, all the siblings of this expression in the abstract syntax tree get frozen.*

This was the point of the example in the introduction:

$$\mathbf{prim}(+, (\mathbf{cond}(\underline{e_1}, \overline{e_2}, \overline{e_3}), \overline{e_4}))$$

Because of $\underline{e_1}$, $\overline{e_2}$ and $\overline{e_3}$ yield static values that are frozen. Similarly, $\overline{e_4}$ yields a value that is frozen.

In a nutshell, contexts are critical due to two distinct reasons: the specialization strategy and the structure of the source program. The former is understandable since partial evaluation subsumes constant propagation. The latter makes it clear why some programs "specialize better" than others.

3 A Solution

The problems listed in Section 2 have a common pattern: static values get frozen in residual expressions, out of reach for their consumers at partial evaluation time. Obviously, these static values and their consumers somehow should be put together despite the dynamic contexts in between. This could be achieved at different stages of partial evaluation, by changing either preprocessing (if there is any), or specialization, or postprocessing. In essence, such a strategy would amount to

1. identifying frozen static values and their consumers in an expression,
2. performing necessary transformations to bring them together, and
3. iterating the earlier phases of partial evaluation.

Static values get frozen in dynamic compound expressions because they cannot be reached by their consumers. Hence the idea, in step 2, is to distribute static contexts across dynamic compound expressions. This transformation makes sense because the present problem arises from the very structure of source programs, not from their specialization. However, the classification of static and dynamic constructs is determined by the structure of the program. Changing this structure requires one to re-analyze the binding times of the program, which in turn, may trigger new distributions of static contexts inside dynamic compound expressions, requiring a new binding time analysis, and so on — hence step 3. The number of iterations required depends on a given application.

A radical strategy would amount to bringing all potential values and corresponding consumers together, regardless of the binding times of these values. This would remove the need for iterating because repeated transformations are necessary only to propagate newly available values, which is done once and for all by the radical transformation that distribute *all* contexts inside *all* dynamic expressions, even function calls. This is an extreme approach, because presumably not all contexts need to be distributed; however, it yields definite results: further modifications of the program or iterations of the binding time analysis are not required. Since this radical transformation occurs before partial evaluation, it improves the static data flow of a program without any modification of the partial evaluator.

Let us first analyze how the radical transformation is naturally achieved by CPS transformation. Then, we will illustrate its effect on the pattern matching example, and finally take a critical look at the whole process.

3.1 Continuation-passing style

Transforming a program into CPS essentially amounts to representing each context as a lambda-expression, distributing this "continuation" across all control structures, and in particular passing it as an extra argument to each function of the original program [38, 15]. As a net effect, CPS programs are tail-recursive. Further, when a call is specialized, static values still are passed to the callee to specialize it — including what is static in the continuation.

Here is a BNF of CPS terms.

$$\begin{aligned}
e &::= \mathbf{cond}(t, e_2, e_3) \mid \mathbf{app}(t_0,(t_1, ..., t_n,t_{n+1}))\\
t &::= \mathbf{cst}(c) \mid \mathbf{ide}(i) \mid \mathbf{prim}(op, (t_1, ..., t_m)) \mid\\
&\quad \mathbf{lam}((i_1, ..., i_n,i_{n+1}), e) \mid \mathbf{lam}((i_1, ..., i_n,i_{n+1}), t)
\end{aligned}$$

A continuation has been added as an extra argument to functions. The terms t are "trivial" [40], *i.e.*, evaluating them cannot loop. In terms of "sub-problems" and "reductions" popular in the Scheme community [19], all the sub-problems amount to evaluating trivial expressions.

Following Section 2.2, let us derive the BNF of contexts for a CPS program.

$$\begin{aligned}
E[\,] &::= \mathbf{lam}((i_1, ..., i_n,i_{n+1}), [\,]) \mid \mathbf{cond}(t, [\,], e_3) \mid \mathbf{cond}(t, e_2, [\,])\\
T[\,] &::= \mathbf{cond}([\,], e_2, e_3) \mid\\
&\quad \mathbf{app}([\,],(t_1, ..., t_n,t_{n+1})) \mid \mathbf{app}(t_0,(t_1, ..., [\,], ..., t_n,t_{n+1})) \mid\\
&\quad \mathbf{prim}(op, (t_1, ..., [\,], ..., t_m)) \mid \mathbf{lam}((i_1, ..., i_n,i_{n+1}), [\,])
\end{aligned}$$

where the e_i and t_i are defined by the BNF above.

This BNF of contexts reveals a crucial property that parallels Property 1:

Property 3 *All the expressions that determine a critical context are trivial.*

Proof: by cases. □

Lemma 1 *Only trivial terms can be consumed.*

Proof: *cf.* BNF of CPS expressions. □

The following property parallels Property 2.

Property 4 *The only possible context which is not critical in the path between a static expression and its consumer is* $\mathbf{app}(t_0,(t_1, ..., [\,], ..., t_n,t_{n+1}))$

Proof: *cf.* BNF of contexts. □

The following consequences parallel Consequence 1.

Consequence 2 *There is no dynamic context in the path between a static expression and its consumer.*

No static value is frozen by a context on the path to its consumer since there is no compound expressions anymore but function calls. (Remember that by definition of the class of partial evaluators we are considering, static arguments are transmitted to the callee.)

Consequence 3 *A static value gets frozen because its consumer is a primitive operation and one of the siblings of the static value is dynamic.*

In other terms, if a static value has a static consumer, it will reach this consumer and be consumed. Otherwise a static value has a dynamic consumer; it will reach this consumer and be frozen.

Consequence 4 *The decision to reduce or to reconstruct a term only depends on the specialization strategy and not on the structure of the source program.*

To sum up, the problem described in Section 2, by construction, cannot occur for CPS terms. Since the CPS transformation is meaning-preserving, this motivates the transformation of source programs into CPS.

3.2 Example (continued): linear pattern matching in lists

```
;;; Pattern * Data -> Answer
(define (main p d)
  (match p d (EmptySubst) (lambda (r) r)))

;;; Pattern * Data * Substitution * [Result -> Answer] -> Answer
(define (match p d s k)
  (caseType p
    [(PatCst c) (if (equal? c d) (k (Subst s)) (k (Unit)))]
    [(PatVar v) (k (Subst (ExtendSubst v d s)))]
    [(PatSeq l) (match-Seq l d s k)]))

;;; List(Pattern) * Data * Substitution * [Result -> Answer] -> Answer
(define (match-Seq l d s k)
  (if (null? l)
      (if (null? d) (k (Subst s)) (k (Unit)))
      (if (null? d)
          (k (Unit))
          (match (hd l) (hd d) s (lambda (r)
                                     (caseType r
                                       [(Unit) (k (Unit))]
                                       [(Subst s) (match-Seq (tl l)(tl d) s k)]))))))
```

Figure 4: Linear pattern matching in lists, continuation-passing style with accumulator.

This program is the CPS counterpart of the program of Figure 2. It was obtained automatically using the CPS transformation for λ_v-terms [15].

Transforming the program of Figure 2 into CPS yields the program displayed in Figure 4 and the following domains, annotated as in Section 2.1:

$$
\begin{aligned}
\widetilde{\mathit{Subst}} &= \overline{\mathit{EmptySubst}} \mathbin{\overline{+}} (\overline{\mathit{Variable}} \mathbin{\overline{\times}} \underline{\mathit{Data}} \mathbin{\overline{\times}} \widetilde{\mathit{Subst}}) \\
\widetilde{\mathit{Result}} &= \overline{\mathit{Unit}} \mathbin{\overline{+}} \widetilde{\mathit{Subst}} \\
\underline{\mathit{Answer}} &= \overline{\mathit{Unit}} \mathbin{\underline{+}} \widetilde{\mathit{Subst}}
\end{aligned}
$$

The domain of results is now a static sum. Therefore whether a result is *Unit* or a substitution can be determined at partial evaluation time. As a consequence, all matching operations depending on the structure of patterns and on substitutions (syntactic analysis and propagation of intermediary substitutions) are performed at partial evaluation time. In fact, and as discovered in [14] and analyzed in Section 5, compiled patterns operate even better than when they are interpreted because all the structural tests occur first and the substitution is built only if the match succeeds, instead of incrementally, and potentially for nothing in case of

```
;;; for all d, (main0 d) == (main '(PatSeq ((PatVar x) (PatCst 3))) d)

;;; Data -> Answer
(define (main0 d)
  (if (null? d)
      (Unit)
      (let ([d2 (tl d)])
        (cond
          [(null? d2) (Unit)]
          [(equal? 3 (hd d2))
           (if (null? (tl d2))
               (Subst (ExtendSubst 'x (hd d) (EmptySubst)))
               (Unit))]
          [else (Unit)]))))
```

Figure 5: Specialized version of the CPS pattern matcher w.r.t. the same pattern as in Figure 3.

This dedicated program traverses its argument depth-first, iteratively. All the continuations of the source program depended on the structure of the pattern only and thus have been eliminated. There are no computation duplications because of the let expression. The substitution is built only if the match succeeds. Again, this code was pretty-printed by hand. It is equivalent to the output of Schism.

mismatch. This is illustrated by Figure 5 that displays the result of specializing the transformed pattern matcher with respect to the same pattern as in Figure 3.

4 Appraisal

Binding time analysis [26] abstracts the specialization semantics. As an abstract interpretation, it is less accurate that the semantics it abstracts. In other words, since binding time analysis does not operate on concrete values, it needs to approximate to yield "safe" information. Thus some expressions may be classified to be run time when they are actually compile time and therefore, fewer computations are performed during specialization. However, regarding CPS expressions, the only conservative effects of the BTA concern the final value, which is dynamic anyway.

The point of the CPS transformation is to bring contexts to expressions across conditional expressions and function calls. The CPS transformation brings partial evaluators that include a (necessarily approximate) BTA closer to the accuracy of those that do not include an explicit BTA at preprocessing time. Yet CPS transformation keeps the partial evaluators with an offline BTA more effective than the partial evaluators with an online discrimination because of the pre-computations based on the static binding time information. (Obviously, the best of both worlds is obtained with a partial evaluator that does not trust the dynamic binding time information, and analyzes the actual binding time of "dynamic" values online.)

Transforming the source program into CPS is a conservative action: as a source to source transformation, it does not introduce any new syntactic form that would require some special treatment.

However, transformation into CPS introduces a series of higher order functions that need to be treated explicitly, whereas implicit contexts were treated without ado. Still nothing there should frighten a higher order partial evaluator. Better, given a polyvariant one, *i.e.*, a partial evaluator that can produce multiple specialized versions of a function, pre-transforming the source program into CPS makes it possible to produce multiple specialized versions of source contexts and to eliminate intermediary data. This point is illustrated in Section 5.

Regarding termination, CPS programs introduce a new component to take into account: the continuation. In some cases the continuation needs to be generalized to ensure termination of partial evaluation. To examine this issue let us compare termination of partial evaluation for direct style and CPS programs in a typical case. Consider a recursive function with an induction variable bound dynamically. If this function is expressed in direct style, then, as described by Sestoft, for example [41], it should be specialized to delay recursion until run time (*i.e.*, when the value of the induction variable is available). If this function is expressed in CPS, then in addition to its specialization, the continuation has to be generalized. Indeed, the continuation may accumulate computations and thus cause infinite specialization. In other words, for CPS programs, not only is the control expressed by recursion, but it is also captured by the continuation. Thus, to freeze the control of a function at partial evaluation time, this function has to be specialized as well as generalized in its continuation argument.

In fact, this reasoning subsumes the traditional problems of accumulators as static values under dynamic control, [1] since accumulators are nothing but concrete representation of continuations [48]. Their (static) initial value always has required to be generalized to ensure termination of partial evaluation.

Let us apply this reasoning to the pattern matcher presented previously. First, notice that the pattern is the induction variable; also, recall that this variable is assumed to be bound statically. In that case, recursive calls can be unfolded and continuations propagated. If the pattern matcher was invoked with both a dynamic pattern and a dynamic datum, then recursive calls would have to be suspended and continuations generalized.

This generalization strategy can be refined using Chin's approach for removing higher order functions [5]. The idea is to propagate a functional argument — in our case a continuation — if the corresponding parameter is *variable-only*. Essentially a parameter of a function has this property if the corresponding argument in each recursive call to this function is made up of only variables. Of course, this property trivially holds for all parameters of non-recursive functions.

Chin uses this simple syntactic property to ensure successful folding of recursive expressions during deforestation. In the context of partial evaluation of CPS pro-

[1] Consider a recursive function computing the length of a list, using an accumulator. Specialize it w.r.t. the (static) initial value of the accumulator. This will provoke either infinite unfolding or the generation of infinitely many specialized functions, one for each static value of the accumulator.

grams, this property ensures that a continuation parameter will not cause infinite specialization because it is bound to finitely many functional values.

Finally, let us turn to self-application. CPS code has a very special property: it is completely tail-recursive. As a direct consequence, no value is ever returned but at the end. Thus if a static value gets frozen in a dynamic context, all outer contexts are dynamic. There is no outer critical context to be deprived of this static value. Hence the following proposition.

Proposition 1 *Let* run PE ⟨PE, ⟨p, _⟩⟩ *denote the self-application of* PE *to* p. *If* p *is a CPS program, the inner instance of* PE *need not be transformed into CPS.*

Proof. The only reason to transform a program is to bring critical contexts to static values. Since *p* is a CPS program, specializing each of its expressions never returns a value but at the end. Therefore there are no static contexts either, and thus no reason to transform *PE* into CPS.

This result parallels Shivers's static analyses that are in direct style because the analyzed programs are in CPS [42].

5 Applications

As is well-known, functional programs often make a momentary use of intermediary data.[2] A great deal of optimizations have been developed to eliminate the construction of these data [4, 46]. The wasteful programs can be reformulated into others that do not use intermediary data. The two following sections detail the elimination of four kinds of intermediary data.

5.1 Eliminating partially static data structures

As a static semantics processor, a partial evaluator produces and consumes static data structures, whether they are recursive (static fixpoints are unfolded) or not. For example, in an interpreter, the static part of the environment, lives at compile time; as such, it is a partially static structure that only exists at partial evaluation time. For another example, static injection tags live at partial evaluation time as well.

5.2 Eliminating dynamic data structures

Due to the CPS transformation, tuples holding dynamic results (*i.e.*, non recursive and dynamic data structures) are now passed forward to the continuation. As statically constructed data, they are eliminated, *e.g.*, by raising the arity [33] of the continuation.

However partial evaluation falls short and cannot handle dynamic, recursive data structures because they are built under dynamic control. This conflicts with fixed specialization strategies.

[2] This is referred to as the functional facet in Peter Mosses's Action Semantics [35].

5.3 Assessments

As reported in [14], CPS has considerable consequences both on source programs and on residual programs, in the case of pattern matching. In the source programs, (1) mismatching is solved statically as the application of the initial continuation; (2) the arity of the success continuation is raised by encoding the static tuples of results in the residual program; and (3) the static construction of static names and the static construction of dynamic values are separated. The new source program specializes very well with respect to any pattern. It yields tightly compiled patterns where (1) the list of names is built statically; (2) in the case of non-linear pattern matching, cross-references are solved statically; and (3) further, in the residual program, the substitution is built only if matching succeeds, instead of incrementally as in the source pattern matcher.

Finally let us turn to compiling and generating a compiler for strongly typed programs. As revealed by experience, scope resolution, storage calculation, and static type checking get processed at compile time [11].

6 Conditionally Static Values

This section presents an alternative motivation and development for CPS as providing a better support of static data flow. Essentially, we mirror Mogensen's separation of binding times in source programs [34].

The expressions specifying the components of data structures often are bound at different times. For example [11], in an interpreter for statically typed programs, a denotable value may be represented with a pair holding the type tag and the actual value. Because the language is statically typed, the type tag depends only on the program, whereas the actual value depends on both the program and its input. The expressions specifying the type tag are bound early (at compile time) whereas the expressions specifying the actual value are bound later (at run time). As pairs holding the type tag and the actual value, denotable values form an example of partially static data.

Definition 6 (Mogensen) *A* partially static datum *is a static product of (partially) static or dynamic data.*

In a partial evaluator that does not handle partially static data, any datum has the latest binding time of its components. In a partial evaluator that handles partially static data, a partially static datum has an early binding time, despite the late binding time of some of its components. This makes it possible to process partially static data at partial evaluation time.

Let us consider the dual of partially static data.

Definition 7 *A* conditionally static datum *is a dynamic sum of (conditionally or partially) static or dynamic data.*

N.B.: By the same token, we generalize partially static data to be static product of (partially or conditionally) static or dynamic data.

Conditionally static data results from dynamic conditional expressions. For example,

$$\mathbf{cond}(\underline{e_1}, \overline{e_2}, \overline{e_3}),\ \mathbf{cond}(\underline{e_1}, \underline{e_2}, \overline{e_3}),\ \text{and}\ \mathbf{cond}(\underline{e_1}, \overline{e_2}, \underline{e_3})$$

are three expressions yielding conditionally static data at partial evaluation time.

Conditionally static data are approximated with the latest binding time of their components by any existing binding time analysis. The following typical rule reflects that the result of a conditional expression is dynamic whenever its test is bound dynamically:

$$\frac{\Gamma \vdash e_1 : D}{\Gamma \vdash \mathbf{cond}(e_1, e_2, e_3) : D}$$

How can we process conditionally static data in a partial evaluator?

Let us continue the parallel with partially static data. They are processed either with an explicit representation [32, 7] or by separating binding times, *i.e.*, by rewriting the source program to separate the static and dynamic expressions that build the components of partially static structures [34]. Similarly, conditionally static data could be processed either with an explicit representation of sum values, or by separating binding times. In both cases, we need to represent contexts.

Transforming the source program in CPS offers an elegant solution. The context is represented with a function: the continuation. Polyvariant specialization routinely performs the specialization of each continuation with respect to each potential component of a sum value, thereby separating binding times.

This puts a new requirement upon BTA-based partial evaluators: to have a polyvariant BTA. This is necessary for specializing continuations with respect to values that are bound at different times.

To overcome the limitation of partial evaluators with monovariant BTA, a solution consists of duplicating contexts during the CPS transformation. For example, translating the following direct style Scheme expression

```
(f (if (if x y z) 4 5))
```

into CPS yields the following voluminous term:

```
(lambda (g47)
  (if x
      (if y (f 4 g47) (f 5 g47))
      (if z (f 4 g47) (f 5 g47))))
```

where contexts (conditional expression and function application) have been duplicated.

Compiler writers usually frown upon duplicating contexts and favor translation schemas which yield CPS terms that are linear in size with respect to the original direct style term. For example, without duplicating contexts, the expression above yields:

```
(lambda (g52)
  (let ([k53 (lambda (v54)
               (let ([k55 (lambda (v56)
                            (f v56 g52))])
                 (if v54 (k55 4) (k55 5))))])
    (if x (k53 y) (k53 z))))
```

However, for partial evaluation, duplicating contexts is a practical way to introduce a restricted form of polyvariance without using a polyvariant BTA, just as CPS transformation allows more thorough specialization while keeping the same specializer.

For completeness, let us list the four cases of building partially static and conditionally static data under static and under dynamic control:

	Product	Sum
Static context	(1)	(2)
Dynamic context	(3)	(4)

where by "static control" (resp. "dynamic control") we mean that the expression yielding the partially or conditionally static data occurs in a static (resp. dynamic) context (*cf.* Definition 2).

(1) corresponds to partially static data and is illustrated by

$$\overline{\mathbf{hd}}(\overline{\mathbf{cons}}(\mathrm{e}_1, \mathrm{e}_2))$$

where **cons** builds a product value and the context **hd**([ ]) is reduced statically, yielding a value with the same binding time as e_1.

(3) corresponds to a partially static datum whose construction is delayed until run time; it is illustrated by

$$\underline{\mathbf{equal}}(\underline{\mathrm{e}_1}, \overline{\mathbf{cons}}(\overline{\mathrm{e}_2}, \underline{\mathrm{e}_3}))$$

where **equal** denotes a primitive operation.

(4) corresponds to conditionally static data and is illustrated by

$$(\underline{\mathbf{if}}\ \underline{\mathrm{e}_1}\ \underline{\mathbf{then}}\ \overline{\mathrm{e}_2}\ \underline{\mathbf{else}}\ \underline{\mathrm{e}_3}) + \overline{\mathrm{e}_4}$$

(2) corresponds to the following irritant case:

$$(\underline{\mathbf{if}}\ \overline{\mathrm{e}_1}\ \underline{\mathbf{then}}\ \underline{\mathrm{e}_2}\ \underline{\mathbf{else}}\ \overline{\mathrm{e}_3})\ \underline{+}\ \overline{\mathrm{e}_4}$$

The binding time analysis cannot determine which expression e_2 or e_3 will be selected at specialization time. To ensure a safe approximation, the BTA assumes the result of the conditional expression to be dynamic, thereby freezing the siblings in the abstract syntax tree. Assuming e_1 to yield false statically, e_3 to yield 10, and e_4 to yield 20, the result of specializing this expression reads

$$10 + 20$$

which would not happen with a better support of static data flow such as the one offered by the CPS transformation.

Finally, let us conclude on partially *vs.* conditionally static data. Partially static data are built as products and essentially are treated using value-based strategies. Conditionally static data are built as sums and essentially are treated using continuation-based strategies. This is in pleasing relationship with Filinski's work on duality in programming languages [17].

7 Related work

Very early, experience with MIX has shown how some programs may "specialize better" than others [16]. But we are not aware of any formalization of this phenomenon in the context of partial evaluation, as presented in Section 2.2, though Nielson's work on data flow analysis in a denotational framework using abstract interpretation [36] relates to our endeavor. The most precise abstract interpretation is obtained by the Meet Over all Paths solution; in particular, Kam and Ullman have shown that in general it yields more precise results than the usual Maximal Fixed Point solution [29]. Considering the specification of an imperative language, Nielson has shown that the abstract interpretation of its direct style formulation usually leads to the Maximal Fixed Point solution whereas the abstract interpretation of a CPS formulation naturally leads to the Meet Over all Paths solution. This result actually forms a basis of our work because partial evaluation relates to the results of binding time analysis, which is an abstract interpretation; and because our pure version of Scheme (evaluation order nonwithstanding) is close to the metalanguage of denotational semantics. Anyway continuation-passing terms are independent of their evaluation order [40].

Jørring and Scherlis's staging transformations [28] closely relate to our approach. These source-to-source transformations aim at making a program more static. Static abstract syntax nodes are moved outwards in the abstract syntax tree. The transformation stops at conditional expressions. In contrast, transformation into CPS moves abstract syntax nodes inwards in the abstract syntax tree as this tree gets linearized. Also, CPS transformation does go through conditional expressions, thereby enabling considerably many more opportunities for actual specializations, but of course this is because we consider applicative order programs.

Mogensen's paper on separating binding times [34] is commonly referred to as addressing binding time improvements of programs. In fact, Mogensen's transformation uses the same binding time information as, say, a partial evaluator with partially static structures, to yield the same good results eventually. Separating binding times in a program does not improve its static data flow.

Nielson and Nielson aim at improving binding times of programs based on a static analysis identifying disagreement points [37]. For a class of higher-order programs, such information can be used to provide binding time improvements with respect to a fold/unfold strategy *à la* Burstall and Darlington.

This line of work is being pursued by Holst and Hughes who aim at applying Wadler's theorems for free (based on results about parametric polymorphism) to obtain binding time improvements [22, 47]. Our point is simpler and it is implemented. We identify a class of binding time improvements and stay within the framework of partial evaluation, based on the usual congruence between direct style programs and their continuation-passing counterpart.

Drawing a parallel between partial evaluation of eager programs and lazy evaluation, Holst and Gomard propose simple transformations to improve the sharing properties of a lazy program [20, 21]. This makes it possible for the evaluation of such fully lazy programs to match the efficiency obtained by partial evaluation of their eager counterpart. Holst and Gomard's hand transformations address first-order programs and are subsumed by the usual and automatic higher-order CPS transformation. It would be interesting to investigate the effects of a more radical pre-transformation into normal order CPS, as illustrated in the present paper for applicative order programs.

Writing source programs iteratively was known to contribute to their efficient specialization (see, *e.g.*, [9, 6].) Earlier works by the authors on compiling patterns [14] or processing the static and dynamic semantics of Algol and Prolog [11, 12] have motivated continuation-passing style as generalizing iterative style to circumvent the loss of compile time values in a higher-order, recursive setting. The present work integrates this style in the process of partial evaluation, thereby making it possible to handle a broader class of source programs more accurately.

Exhibiting continuations and keeping backtracking under static control, as suggested by the second author in [14], have already proven to be effective in the area of pattern matching: in [27], Jørgensen applies this technique to the compilation of patterns as encountered in a case expression; in [43], Smith exhibits both success and failure continuations of a logic program to compile pattern matching.

So far, continuation-passing style has been used to compile Scheme and Standard ML programs [44, 30, 1], to derive compilers from interpreters [49], and for transforming programs [48]. Let us address these three points. Shivers [42] develops a number of flow analyses for CPS Scheme programs, but does not motivate CPS as something else but a convenient intermediate representation. Deriving compilers from interpreters is achieved generically using a self-applicable partial evaluator [18, 26, 11] and the present paper motivates why CPS is "the right thing" indeed. Transforming programs using an explicit representation of contexts does not seem to have been applied to eliminate intermediary data, as addressed in Section 5. Similarly, the specific problem of specializing contexts had not been identified so far, even though *e.g.*, Launchbury mentions its effects in [31, pages 107–108].

Our work is based on the CPS transformation, as described by Plotkin in [38]. Further developments on this transformation are reported by Filinski and the second author in [15]: essentially, the binding times in Plotkin's CPS transformations can be improved, yielding more reasonable one-pass transformers; principally, the improvement is based on standardizing the sets of syntactic constructs yielded by a collecting interpretation.

Recent work by Weise and Ruf proposes "on the fly fixpoint iterations" to improve online partial evaluation [50] (this paper was brought to our attention after the present work was carried out.) We believe them to correspond to the iterations mentioned in Section 3. In the introduction of [50], Weise and Ruf also reject CPS as something incompatible with "termination extent strategies." We did not meet this problem.

Finally, Turchin's driving [45] is a program manipulation that also involves an explicit representation of the context. It is more general and powerful than partial evaluation in that a supercompiler actually can eliminate intermediary data structures, even if they are built under dynamic control, which partial evaluation cannot do (*cf.* Section 5). Yet our work can be seen as providing an explicit representation of the context (as a function: the continuation), besides improving its binding times.

8 Conclusions and Issues

This article identifies the problem of programs that specialize better than others as a structural instead of a conjectural one. Essentially, we propose to change the control flow of the source programs to support their static data flow better, thereby ensuring more thorough specialization while keeping the same higher-order specializer. We circumvent the need for iterating partial evaluation by systematically transforming the source program into CPS. This development is compatible with self-application. It makes it possible to improve on earlier applications such as compiling and compiler generation [18, 26, 11] and also to tackle new problems such as static deforestation, the specialization of contexts, and conditionally static data.

CPS transformation is excessive in that it does not guarantee the improvement of binding time properties of a source function. In other terms, not all of a source program need to be expressed in CPS. For example, completely static expressions obviously need not be transformed. For another example, if we write the pattern matcher of Figure 2 without accumulator but by appending intermediary substitutions, the function appending these substitutions need not be transformed into CPS. In the general case, it is not clear how to obtain this "ideal" representation of the source program swiftly — in particular without iterating the binding time analysis. We are currently weighting the relative merits of the total CPS transformation (simplicity, automatism, and transparency) and of some partial CPS transformation (increased opportunity to extract more substantial static and dynamic combinators [10].) The latter appear to require a termination analysis to discriminate between Reynolds's "serious" and "trivial" terms [40]. This could correspond to using strictness analysis for the normal order CPS transformation.

Residual programs in general are expressed in CPS. They can be mapped back into direct style, though not uniquely [38]. We are currently working on this issue.

In Section 4, we argue that our approach eliminates the approximations of the binding time analysis for conditional expressions. Indeed, CPS programs are tail-recursive: the context of a conditional expression is distributed over the branches. Beyond binding time analysis, this transformation appears applicable to other static analyses to circumvent similar approximations. This claim is supported by Nielson's results in [36] (*cf.* Section 7.)

Finally, we are currently investigating the connections between forward and backward static analyses [13, 23] and CPS. This might lay off grounds to backwards partial evaluation of programs, *i.e.*, the specialization of programs with respect to their context of use, instead of the current mere forward methods.

As a last word, let us stress that this work contributes to the relief from writing source programs in a contrived way, "to make them specialize better."

Acknowledgements

To Karoline Malmkjær, David Schmidt, and Andrzej Filinski. Thanks are also due to Siau Cheng Khoo, Olin Shivers, Don Smith, and the referee.

References

[1] A. W. Appel and T. Jim. Continuation-passing, closure-passing style. In *ACM Symposium on Principles of Programming Languages*, pages 293–302, 1989.

[2] D. Bjørner, A. P. Ershov, and N. D. Jones, editors. *Partial Evaluation and Mixed Computation*. North-Holland, 1988.

[3] A. Bondorf and O. Danvy. Automatic autoprojection of recursive equations with global variables and abstract data types. DIKU Research Report 90/04, University of Copenhagen, Copenhagen, Denmark, 1990. To appear in Science of Computer Programming.

[4] W. Burge. An optimizing technique for high level programming languages. Research Report RC 5834 (# 25271), IBM Thomas J. Watson Research Center, Yorktown Heights, New York, New York, 1976.

[5] W. N. Chin. *Automatic Methods for Program Transformation*. PhD thesis, University of London, Imperial College of Science, Technology and Medecine, London, UK, 1990.

[6] C. Consel. *Analyse de Programmes, Evaluation Partielle et Génération de Compilateurs*. PhD thesis, Université de Paris VI, Paris, France, June 1989.

[7] C. Consel. Binding time analysis for higher order untyped functional languages. In *ACM Conference on Lisp and Functional Programming*, pages 264–272, 1990.

[8] C. Consel. *The Schism Manual*. Yale University, New Haven, Connecticut, USA, 1990. Version 1.0.

[9] C. Consel and O. Danvy. Partial evaluation of pattern matching in strings. *Information Processing Letters*, 30(2):79–86, 1989.

[10] C. Consel and O. Danvy. From interpreting to compiling binding times. In N. D. Jones, editor, *ESOP'90, 3rd European Symposium on Programming*, volume 432 of *Lecture Notes in Computer Science*, pages 88–105. Springer-Verlag, 1990.

[11] C. Consel and O. Danvy. Static and dynamic semantics processing. In *ACM Symposium on Principles of Programming Languages*, pages 14–23, 1991.

[12] C. Consel and S. C. Khoo. Semantics-directed generation of a Prolog compiler. In *PLILP'91, 3rd International Symposium on Programming Language Implementation and Logic Programming*, 1991. To appear.

[13] P. Cousot. Semantic foundations of program analysis: Theory and applications. In S. S. Muchnick and N. D. Jones, editors, *Program Flow Analysis: Theory and Applications*. Prentice-Hall, 1981.

[14] O. Danvy. Semantics-directed compilation of non-linear patterns. *Information Processing Letters*, 37:315–322, March 1991.

[15] O. Danvy and A. Filinski. Representing control, a study of the CPS transformation. Technical Report CIS-91-2, Kansas State University, Manhattan, Kansas, USA, 1991.

[16] H. Dybkjær. Parsers and partial evaluation: An experiment. Diku student report 85-7-15, University of Copenhagen, Copenhagen, Denmark, 1985.

[17] A. Filinski. Declarative continuations: An investigation of duality in programming language semantics. In D.H. Pitt et al., editors, *Category Theory and Computer Science*, number 389 in Lecture Notes in Computer Science, pages 224–249, Manchester, UK, September 1989.

[18] Y. Futamura. Partial evaluation of computation process – an approach to a compiler-compiler. *Systems, Computers, Controls 2, 5*, pages 45–50, 1971.

[19] C. Hanson. Efficient stack allocation for tail-recursive languages. In *ACM Conference on Lisp and Functional Programming*, pages 106–118, 1990.

[20] C. K. Holst. Improving full laziness. In Simon L. Peyton Jones, Graham Hutton, and Carsten Kehler Holst, editors, *Functional Programming, Glasgow 1990. Workshops in Computing*, pages 71–82. Springer-Verlag, August 1990.

[21] C. K. Holst and C. K. Gomard. Partial evaluation is fuller laziness. In *Proceedings of the first ACM SIGPLAN and IFIP Symposium on Partial Evaluation and Semantics-Based Program Manipulation*, New Haven, Connecticut, June 1991. To appear in the SIGPLAN Notices.

[22] C. K. Holst and J. Hughes. Towards binding time improvement for free. In Simon L. Peyton Jones, Graham Hutton, and Carsten Kehler Holst, editors, *Functional Programming, Glasgow 1990. Workshops in Computing*, pages 83–100. Springer-Verlag, August 1990.

[23] J. Hughes and J. Launchbury. Towards relating forward and backwards analyses. In Simon L. Peyton Jones, Graham Hutton, and Carsten Kehler Holst, editors, *Functional Programming, Glasgow 1990. Workshops in Computing*, pages 101–113. Springer-Verlag, August 1990.

[24] T. Johnsson. Lambda lifting: Transforming programs to recursive equations. In J.-P. Jouannaud, editor, *Conference on Functional Programming Languages and Computer Architecture*, volume 201 of *Lecture Notes in Computer Science*, pages 190–203. Springer-Verlag, 1985.

[25] N. D. Jones, P. Sestoft, and H. Søndergaard. An experiment in partial evaluation: the generation of a compiler generator. In J.-P. Jouannaud, editor, *Rewriting Techniques and Applications, Dijon, France*, volume 202 of *Lecture Notes in Computer Science*, pages 124–140. Springer-Verlag, 1985.

[26] N. D. Jones, P. Sestoft, and H. Søndergaard. Mix: a self-applicable partial evaluator for experiments in compiler generation. *LISP and Symbolic Computation*, 2(1):9–50, 1989.

[27] J. Jørgensen. Generating a pattern matching compiler by partial evaluation. In Simon L. Peyton Jones, Graham Hutton, and Carsten Kehler Holst, editors, *Functional Programming, Glasgow 1990. Workshops in Computing*, pages 177–195. Springer-Verlag, August 1990.

[28] U. Jørring and W. L. Scherlis. Compilers and staging transformations. In *ACM Symposium on Principles of Programming Languages*, pages 86–96, 1986.

[29] J. B. Kam and J. D. Ullman. Monotone data flow analysis frameworks. *Acta Informatica*, 7:305–317, 1977.

[30] D. A. Kranz, R. Kelsey, J. A. Rees, P. Hudak, J. Philbin, and N. I. Adams. Orbit: an optimizing compiler for Scheme. *SIGPLAN Notices, ACM Symposium on Compiler Construction*, 21(7):219–233, 1986.

[31] J. Launchbury. *Projection Factorisation in Partial Evaluation.* PhD thesis, Department of Computing Science, University of Glasgow, Scotland, January 1990.

[32] T. Mogensen. Partially static structures in a self-applicable partial evaluator. In D. Bjørner, A. P. Ershov, and N. D. Jones, editors, *Partial Evaluation and Mixed Computation*, pages 325–348. North-Holland, 1988.

[33] T. Mogensen. *Binding Time Aspects of Partial Evaluation.* PhD thesis, DIKU, University of Copenhagen, Denmark, March 1989.

[34] T. Mogensen. Separating binding times in language specifications. In *FPCA'89, 4th International Conference on Functional Programming Languages and Computer Architecture*, pages 12–25. ACM Press, 1989.

[35] P. Mosses. *Action Semantics.* Cambridge University Press, 1991. draft textbook, in preparation.

[36] F. Nielson. A denotational framework for data flow analysis. *Acta Informatica*, 18:265–287, 1982.

[37] H. R. Nielson and F. Nielson. Eureka definitions for free! or disagreement points for fold/unfold transformations. In N. D. Jones, editor, *ESOP'90, 3rd European Symposium on Programming*, volume 432 of *Lecture Notes in Computer Science*, pages 291–305. Springer-Verlag, 1990.

[38] G. D. Plotkin. Call-by-name, call-by-value and the λ-calculus. *Theoretical Computer Science*, 1:125–159, 1975.

[39] J. Rees and W. Clinger, eds. Revised^3 report on the algorithmic language Scheme. *SIGPLAN Notices*, 21(12):37–79, December 1986.

[40] J. Reynolds. Definitional interpreters for higher order programming languages. In *ACM National Conference*, pages 717–740, 1972.

[41] P. Sestoft. Automatic call unfolding in a partial evaluator. In D. Bjørner, A. P. Ershov, and N. D. Jones, editors, *Partial Evaluation and Mixed Computation.* North-Holland, 1988.

[42] O. Shivers. The semantics of Scheme control-flow analysis. In *Proceedings of the first ACM SIGPLAN and IFIP Symposium on Partial Evaluation and Semantics-Based Program Manipulation*, New Haven, Connecticut, June 1991. To appear in the SIGPLAN Notices.

[43] D. A. Smith. Partial evaluation of pattern matching in CLP domains. In *Proceedings of the first ACM SIGPLAN and IFIP Symposium on Partial Evaluation and Semantics-Based Program Manipulation*, New Haven, Connecticut, June 1991. To appear in the SIGPLAN Notices.

[44] G. L. Steele, Jr. Rabbit: A compiler for Scheme. Technical Report AI-TR-474, Artificial Intelligence Laboratory, Massachusetts Institute of Technology, Cambridge, Massachusetts, May 1978.

[45] V. F. Turchin. The concept of a supercompiler. *ACM Transactions on Programming Languages and Systems*, 8(3):292–325, 1986.

[46] P. Wadler. Deforestation: Transforming programs to eliminate trees. In H. Ganzinger, editor, *ESOP'88, 2nd European Symposium on Programming*, volume 300 of *Lecture Notes in Computer Science*. Springer-Verlag, 1988.

[47] P. Wadler. Theorems for free! In *FPCA'89, 4th International Conference on Functional Programming Languages and Computer Architecture*, pages 347–359. ACM Press, 1989.

[48] M. Wand. Continuation-based program transformation strategies. *Journal of the ACM*, 27(1):164–180, January 1980.

[49] M. Wand. From interpreter to compiler: A representational derivation. In H. Ganzinger and N. D. Jones, editors, *Programs as Data Objects*, volume 217 of *Lecture Notes in Computer Science*, pages 306–324, 1985.

[50] D. Weise and E. Ruf. Computing types during program specialization. Technical Report 441, Stanford University, Stanford, USA, August 1990.

An Architectural Technique for Cache-level Garbage Collection

Tzi-cker Chiueh

Department of Electrical Engineering and Computer Science

University of California, Berkeley, CA 94720

Abstract

Cache performance is critical in high-speed computing systems. However, heap-intensive programs such as LISP codes typically have low cache performance because of inherently poor data locality. To improve the cache performance, the system should reuse heap cells while they are in cache, thus reducing the number of cache misses due to heap references. Furthermore, the system can adopt multi-threaded architecture to hide the cache miss overhead by switching to different control threads when a cache miss occurs. In this paper, a novel architectural scheme called *cache-level garbage collection* based on multi-threading is developed to improve the cache performance for heap-intensive programs. Consequently both the cache hit ratio is improved and the cache miss overhead is masked, thereby minimizing the total cache miss penalty. We present the garbage collection algorithm and its architectural support features, together with initial performance evaluation.

1. Introduction

Programs written in dynamic languages such as LISP reference heap memory extensively. Because of the unpredictable nature of heap references, they generally show poor cache-level locality, which can potentially destroy the usefulness of cache memory. Performance is lost because the processor pipeline is stalled when a cache miss arises. This pipeline-stall period is called *miss shadow* and the number of cycles in the miss shadow is called *miss overhead.* The *cache miss penalty* is determined by the cache miss ratio and the miss overhead. To minimize the cache miss penalty, one can either increase the cache hit ratio or to reduce the miss overhead. The miss overhead, unfortunately, is almost destined to become worse and worse as uniprocessor goes to superscalar or Very Long Instruction Word (VLIW) architecture, or the system moves from uniprocessor towards multiprocessor configurations. Typically this number ranges from 10 to 50 cycles. Although the miss ratio can be reduced by building a larger cache, larger caches also imply longer access time. So in some sense large caches simply trade off hit access time for miss overhead. The other approach is that instead of minimizing cache miss penalty, one can *tolerate* it. The idea is to switch to a different control thread when the current thread is stalled upon cache misses. This is similar to the notion of process suspension/switching induced by page faults in virtual memory systems. The difference is that the states of the control threads reside on the processor; therefore context switching only takes relatively small number of cycles.

Other than poor cache performance, which translates into wasted stalled processor cycles, heap memory also requires garbage collection activities running in background to put unused storage cells back to use, which in itself consumes an appreciable proportion of CPU time. Worse yet, the garbage collection procedure itself tends to pollute the contents of the cache of the running program, aggravating the already worse miss ratio. Combining these observations, the basic idea of this paper is then: since heap-intensive programs inherently cause higher cache miss ratio and leave numerous processor cycles wasted in the miss shadows, and heap-intensive programs also incur significant garbage collection overheads during execution, why not execute "overhead" task during the miss shadows ? Moreover, it has been shown that collecting garbage while they are still in cache can reuse the in-cache memory cells without going to main memory, therefore greatly improving the cache behavior. This scheme thus forms a positive feedback mechanism, which first aims at reducing the cache miss overhead, but as a side-effect, it also cuts down the cache miss ratio. Consequently the total cache miss penalty is minimized.

Putting this idea in the context of multi-threaded architecture, there are only two threads: one is used to perform *cache-level garbage collection,* and the other is dedicated to application programs. The garbage collection thread is called the *collector* and the application thread is called the *mutator.* The collector thread collects only *in-cache garbage* and is triggered whenever the mutator thread encounters a cache miss. By so doing, a lot of heap allocation requests can be satisfied right from the cache without resorting to the main memory. Furthermore, garbage write-backs and write-ins can be avoided. As a result, a substantial portion of cache misses are eliminated. The greatest beauty of this scheme is that the cache performance improvement is obtained for free because the CPU power put to garbage collection would have been wasted in a non-multithreaded architecture anyway.

The rest of this paper is organized as follows. In section two, the methods for cache performance optimization in the presence of extensive heap references are examined, which motivates the cache-level garbage collection scheme. Section three presents the architectural model and the algorithms for cache-level garbage collection. Related works in this area are reviewed in section four. We conclude in section five by pointing out planned future works and possible extensions of the proposed scheme.

2. Cache Performance Optimization For Heap-Intensive Programs

Previous garbage collection algorithms focused on improving collection efficiency and virtual memory locality. But to our knowledge, none actually took into account the presence of caches in the memory hierarchy. As data cache size increases, the impact of garbage collection on data caches becomes increasingly significant. The impact of garbage collection on data caches is very different from that on main memory. First, data caches are much smaller than main memory. One direct result is that the youngest generation in copy-based garbage collection algorithms does not fit into the cache, unless garbage collection is triggered frequently enough to keep the youngster's size small. Second, it is impossible to improve cache-level locality even by copy-based collectors or dynamic reorganization of address spaces because a cache block is too small to allow any flexibility of improving locality. Third, cache access time is closed tied with the processor speed. The size of data cache has a direct effect on its access time, which in turn determines the cycle time of the processor. Therefore, cache does not allow arbitrary increase in size as main memory, at least for first-level cache. Because of the relatively small size of data cache, traditional garbage collection algorithms usually do not make significant differences as far as cache performance is concerned [ZORN89]. This is largely due to the fact that conventional collectors deal with large-granularity data sets and tend to ignore the existence of cache. As data cache becomes an integral part of the processor system, a well-balanced garbage collector should take into account the dynamics of cache operation and aims at optimizing cache hit ratio as well as other metrics.

To gain some insight on the interaction between cache behavior and heap references, let's consider the following. We use LISP cells as example heap reference units. Suppose the number of heap memory allocation requests from a program is H_l, and the number of heap memory cells that are actually allocated in the address space is H_p. If there is no garbage collection, i.e., no re-use of heap memory, H_p is identical to H_l. In other words, $\frac{H_l}{H_p}$ is the average degree of re-use of a heap cell. Each time a heap cell is allocated, the average number of references to it before it is re-allocated is R_l. For each heap cell that has been allocated, the average total number of references to it is R_p. Because each heap cell can be used to satisfy more than one allocation request, R_p is generally greater than or equal to R_l. Suppose the cache line is one-heap-cell wide, and the heap cell never gets replaced and sent back to main memory, then the cache miss ratio for this heap cell is $\frac{1}{R_p}$. This is the lower bound on the cache miss ratio for heap memory references. With the cache line size W, the bound becomes $\frac{1}{W * R_p}$. It is important to note that this bound is *independent* of the cache size as long as the line size is fixed. Note also that this lower bound only accounts for the references to heap memory. The lower bound will become smaller if stack references are also incorporated. We will only consider the heap-related cache miss ratio hereafter.

To minimize the cache miss lower bound, R_p must be maximized, i.e., each heap cell should be re-used as many times as possible. However, maximizing R_p alone doesn't necessary lower the actual cache miss ratio. Consider a heap cell C that was brought into cache to satisfy an allocation request and then displaced back to main memory later on. While in memory, C becomes garbage and gets collected; later on it is brought into the cache again to satisfy another allocation request. In this scenario, although R_p can be made arbitrarily large, it does nothing to improve the cache performance. The problem is that C is collected in memory rather than in cache. As a result, C has to be transferred back and forth between cache and main memory, thus defeating the benefits of caching.

To remedy this inefficiency, consider how a typical heap-cell allocation request is processed through the cache: 1) ask for a heap cell from the memory allocator, 2) select a heap cell in the cache to displace, 3) send the chosen cell back to main memory if it is dirty, 4) bring the newly-allocated cell to the cache. These four steps can be significantly optimized as follows, if there is a way to detect which cells in the cache are garbage. Knowing the existence of in-cache garbage, the memory allocator can satisfy the memory request directly from the cache rather than looking to the main memory. As a result, the other three steps are eliminated altogether. We call this method *in-cache allocation.* When there is a cache miss, if possible the hardware first tries to replace garbage lines; otherwise uses normal replacement algorithms. This will always result in better cache performance because the garbage lines are by definition never going to be referenced in the future, and therefore will not cause any more misses because of their displacement. This is called *garbage-first replacement.* When a garbage line is selected to be displaced, the write-back can be skipped even if it is dirty because the garbage line will not be referenced any more. This optimization is called *write-back bypassing.* Lastly, when a cache line is just allocated and is to be brought into the cache, there is no reason to physically transfer the line from main memory if the system knows that the original contents of the line are to be overwritten, as in the case when the cell is just allocated. This optimization is called *write-in bypassing.*

It should be noted that in-cache allocation is much more powerful than the combined effect of garbage-first replacement, write-back and write-in bypassing. The reason is that in-cache allocation works at heap-cell level rather than cache-line level, thus allowing more flexibility. Furthermore, in-cache allocation directly recycles the in-cache garbage, as opposed to allocating *another* new line from the memory, finding a garbage line to displace, and skipping the write-in and write-back steps. In any case, all the above optimizations rest on the assumption that garbage cells can be detected and collected while they are still in the cache. That is, a cache-level garbage collector provides the underlying framework for all the cache performance optimizations. In the next section we discuss the architectural support and the detailed algorithm for cache-level garbage collection.

3. Cache-Level Garbage Collection

To minimize the overhead associated with cache-level garbage collection, the underlying architecture is dual-threaded, with one thread for the application program (the mutator) and the other for garbage collection (the collector). The processor switches to the collector thread when the mutator thread encounters a cache miss. In other words, the collector thread runs in the miss shadows of the mutator thread.

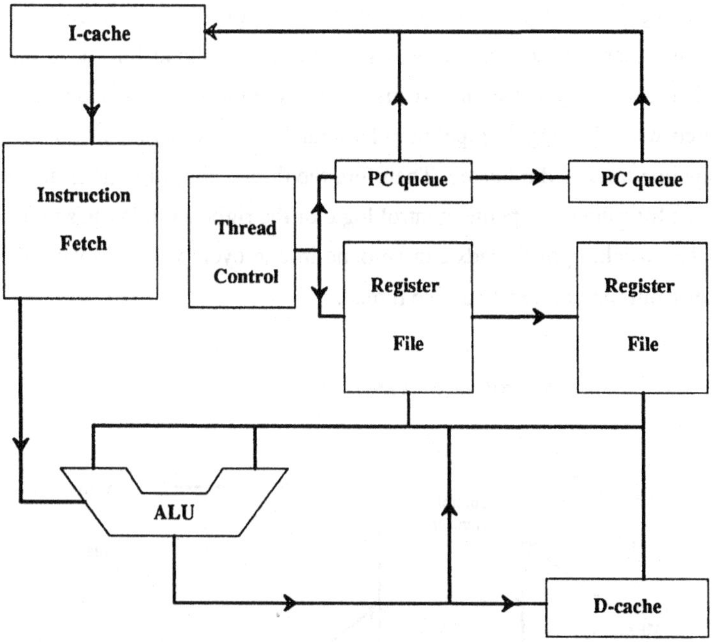

Figure 1 General Organization of Dual-threaded Architecture

3.1. The Architectural Model

Figure 1 shows the general architecture for a dual-threaded processor. Each thread has its own state in the form of a register file and a PC queue. The thread control logic coordinates the access to the data path by the two threads. Basically there are two ways for the threads to share the data path. The first method is called *static switching*, in which the processor is cyclically and periodically serving the threads one after another. Thread switching proceeds on a cycle-by-cycle basis, i.e., the processor initiates different instructions from different threads in each cycle. This scheme was used in Denelcor's HEP [SMIT78] and Horizon[SMIT88] The second approach, called *dynamic switching*, switches to different threads only when the current thread is stalled for some reason. The major application of dynamic switching is to mask memory latency by switching to another ready thread when the current thread issues a main memory request. This is exactly the same technique used in virtual memory systems when a page fault occurs, but at a thread level. Our architecture is based on dynamic switching. The triggering event for switching from the mutator to the collector is the cache miss in the mutator thread, and that for the other way is the completion signal for cache miss handling. The switching between threads typically entails certain overhead that is associated with flushing of pipeline intermediate results. To avoid this overhead, each pipeline latch is duplicated. Therefore the thread control logic is also responsible for informing the pipeline control logic of the right set of latches to use. As a result, the switching of threads can be done in one cycle without losing the intermediates from the previously active thread.

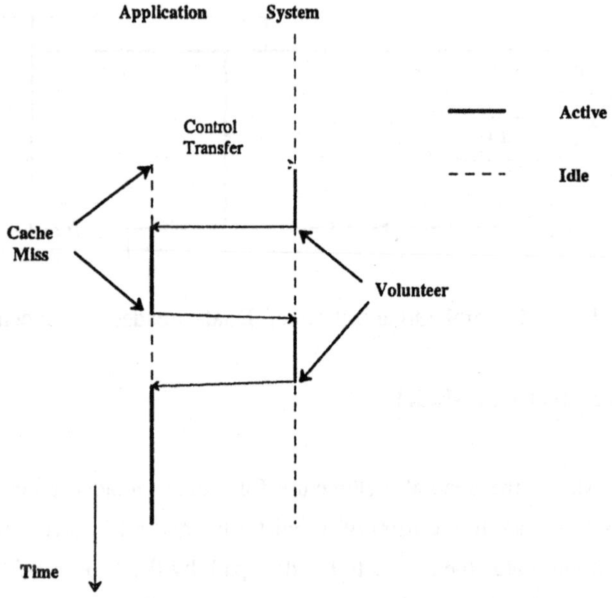

Figure 2 Asymmetry in The Two Threads in Asymmetric Multi-threading

The two threads in the processor actually share the data path in an *asymmetric* manner. Because the mutator gives in the processor only on cache misses, it occupies the processor most of the time. On the other hand, the collector gives in the processor voluntarily, i.e., when the corresponding cache miss handling completes, as shown in Figure 2. Another way to put it, the collector thread exploits the CPU cycles in the *cache miss delay slots* of the mutator thread. The same collector thread can work for different mutators at different time. As we will see later on, the collector thread has no knowledge of the semantics of the mutator. It simply interprets the requests made by the mutator. Because the collector runs a fixed program, it has its own instruction memory. Therefore in practice only the mutator will access the instruction cache shown in Figure 1. The thread states for the two threads also differ. The collector thread supports a larger register file that is used to emulate a queue. Furthermore, the collector thread can access the register file of the mutator, but not vice versa. As we will see in the next section, one of the nice properties of the collector-mutator dual-threaded architecture is that these two threads do not need to synchronize with each other except when the collector's queue is about to overflow. Moreover, the amount of work done in the collector thread is comparatively small with respect to the mutator, making the collection process completely transparent while taking full advantage of the unused cycles left in the cache miss shadows.

3.2. The Garbage Collection Algorithm

3.2.1. The Basic Principle

The goal of cache-level garbage collection is to collect and re-use garbage while they are still in cache. It makes no attempt to collect all the garbage generated by the applications. The difference between cache-level and ordinary garbage collection is that the former aims at reducing cache miss ratio and processor-memory traffic, whereas the latter focuses on avoiding running out of address space. By deferring cache-level garbage collection until there is a cache miss, some of the work that should have been performed in the mutator thread is shifted to the collector thread and done during miss shadows. Modern garbage collection algorithms are based on the idea of mark-and-sweep, with variations such as copy or non-copy, generational or non-generational, and incremental or stop-and-go. Mark-and-sweep is inherently *global* in the sense that the entire object reference graph must be explicitly (stop-and-do) or implicitly (generational) traversed. In contrast, *reference-count* based collection schemes are local because the reference status of each object is recorded on the fly with itself. Localness is an important requirement for our cache-level garbage collection scheme because it is supposed to run in miss shadows and therefore should not cause any more cache miss during collection. Reference-count collection schemes also have the property of detecting garbage *immediately*. As soon as the reference count drops to zero, the system knows that it is a garbage. This property is also essential for recycling in-cache garbage. Moreover, reference-count collection schemes do not need to access other cells other than the heap cells themselves; the cache interference caused by the garbage collection procedure can thus be kept to the minimum. For these reasons, the proposed cache-level garbage collection scheme is based on reference counting.

Pure reference-count garbage collection algorithms suffer from two flaws. First, circular structures can not be collected. Second, once the reference count reaches its maximum, the count will never be accurate. Both can be remedied by backing the reference counting scheme with a background garbage collector running a modern garbage collection algorithm. We will call it the *background* garbage collector. In our scheme three bits are associated with each heap cell (two memory words in LISP). When a heap cell's reference count reaches 7 (111), the cache-level garbage collector simply ignores it, i.e., neither decrements nor increments the count. Consequently both circular structures and high-reference-count cells are left to the background garbage collector. Furthermore, the heap cells in the main memory don't keep reference counts. Only when the heap cells reside in the cache do they have a reference count. When a heap cell is allocated and brought into the cache, the reference count is zero and increasing. Suppose a heap cell with non-zero reference count is displaced, its reference count does not go with the cell to main memory. As a result, when that cell is brought in again, its reference count is set by the hardware to be 7 (111), namely, it is not subject to cache-level garbage collection any more. This *conservativeness* policy does not affect the correctness of the cache-level garbage collection because the background garbage collector can always pick up the rest of the garbage. It does affect the amount of in-cache reuse because some of the garbage ignored under this policy would have been collected if each heap cell has its reference count as an integral part of itself. However, this policy offers several important advantages. First, it simplifies the cache-level garbage collection algorithm as shown in the next subsection. Second, it makes the cache-level garbage collection process completely transparent to the background garbage collector and the rest of the language system. In other words, language systems that do not support reference count fields can also run on this architecture without modification.

3.2.2. The Design

Pure reference counting schemes are inefficient in terms of space and performance overheads. Each heap cell needs to contain a reference-count field, which is a substantial amount of overhead in LISP because each allocated cell is small. This overhead is non-existent in our design because only heap cells that reside in cache have reference count fields. The organization of the data cache line is shown in Figure 3, where administrative bits refer to protection, reference and dirty bits. As for performance cost, every transaction that will affect the accessibility of a heap cell alters its reference count. This is especially intolerable when the cell referenced is not in the cache when the reference count change request is made.

In our scheme, the overhead is reduced in two ways. First, the handling of reference-count adjustment operations are deferred until miss shadows, making use of the would-have-otherwise-been-wasted processor cycles. Second, only when variables that affect the reference counts of some heap cells are stored to memory will reference-count adjustment requests be initiated. These variables include heap memory cells, and stack variables that are stored back to data cache for such reasons as context switching. In other words, heap-pointer manipulation among processor registers will not cause reference-count adjustment. When stack variables are recovered from the memory to the registers, the associated reference counts need to be adjusted accordingly. The second optimization is particularly important because the number of references from stack variables to heap memory is typically much greater than that of the references among heap memory cells.

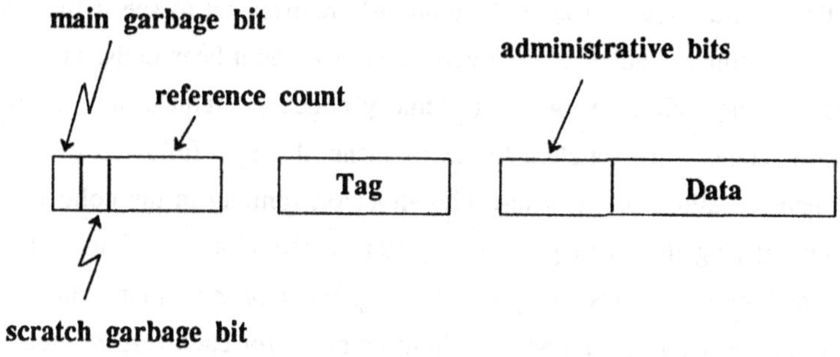

Figure 3 The Organization of Data Cache

Reference Count Adjustment

The compiler is responsible for annotating the mutator code to issue reference count adjustment requests to the collector thread. A special store instruction is provided, which fetches the original content of the address, *O*, and then stores the new word *N*. As a side effect of this store instruction, two reference-count adjustment requests, (d, O) and (i, N), are issued to a queue in the collector thread. A request consists of an increment/decrement flag and an address denoting the cell whose reference count needs to be modified. For example, (d,O) means a reference-count decrement for the cell denoted by O, and (i,N) an increment request for the cell N. Because the initiation of reference-count requests is a side effect of normal instruction processing, the impact on the performance of the mutator thread is negligible. The compiler uses this special store instruction when dealing with address manipulation. However it doesn't need to know whether the addressed word is in the cache because these adjustment requests are just hints.

These requests are stored in the collector's reference-count adjustment queue (RCAQ). When the mutator thread runs into a cache miss, the collector takes control of the processor and picks up the requests from RCAQ. The collector retrieves the reference count field associated with the cell designated by the address, increments/decrements the count, and stores it back. If the original reference count is 7 (111), the system ignores it and goes on to the next request. If the new reference count becomes zero, the system sets the main garbage bit. Note that at this point the cell with zero reference count is not necessarily a garbage cell because there may be stack variables in the register set that point to it. To be sure, the collector must scan through the mutator's register set to see if there are any registers pointing to cache-resident zero-reference-count heap cells. This scanning process is done lazily, i.e., when a memory allocation request arrives. Memory allocation requests are satisfied by an in-cache allocator followed by a conventional memory allocator. The in-cache allocator, running in the collector thread, starts by copying the main garbage bit map to the scratch garbage bit map, as shown in Figure 3. Assisted by a *register pointer bitmap* that indicates which registers in the mutator's register set hold pointers, for each zero-reference-count heap cell that is pointed by some register the in-cache allocator turns off its corresponding bit in the scratch garbage bitmap. Those cells whose bit in the scratch garbage bitmap is on is a garbage cell and can be recycled to satisfy the memory allocation requests. When a garbage cell is selected to be reused, its corresponding bits in the main and scratch garbage bitmaps are turned off, and a decrement reference count adjustment request is issued for the cell that it points to. If none of the bits in the scratch garbage bitmap is on, the conventional memory allocator is initiated and runs in the mutator thread. Note that the main garbage bit map is not affected by this scanning process, which allows those cells whose garbage bit is turned off during scanning to be collected later on.

If the cell designated in the adjustment request is not in cache, the system simply ignores the request and goes on to the next. This is because the reference count of these cells are assumed to be lost when they are moved out of the cache. Next time when they are brought back into the cache, their reference count will be 7 (111), which means that they are no longer subject to cache-level garbage collection. Had every heap cell kept its own reference count (even in main memory), the adjustment requests whose designated cells are not in the cache would need to be handled either by causing a cache miss to bring the cell in, or recirculating the request in RCAQ for the next trial. The former contradicts the requirement that cache-level garbage collection should never cause cache misses. The latter can potentially cause *false collection* because the recirculation affects the order in which the adjustment requests are issued by the mutator and therefore subtly changes the garbage collection semantics. Furthermore, with each cell keeping its reference count, the cache displacement operation becomes more complicated because the *dirtiness* criterion now includes the reference count field. Furthermore, since the reference count field is not updated right when the adjustment request is made, the "residual" reference count adjustment must be performed before it can be written back to the main memory. This essentially means that all the requests in RCAQ must be performed or scanned for each cache line displacement. By dictating that only the heap cells that are resident in cache can have reference counts, all the above complication are eliminated.

RCAQ Management

The RCAQ is implemented in a register file with two pointers HEAD and TAIL coordinating its operation, as shown in Figure 4. From the mutator's viewpoint, it has no knowledge of the collector's state. Therefore it simply issues requests with the queuing mechanism handled by the hardware in the collector. The first question of RCAQ management is the size of RCAQ. Ideally it should be

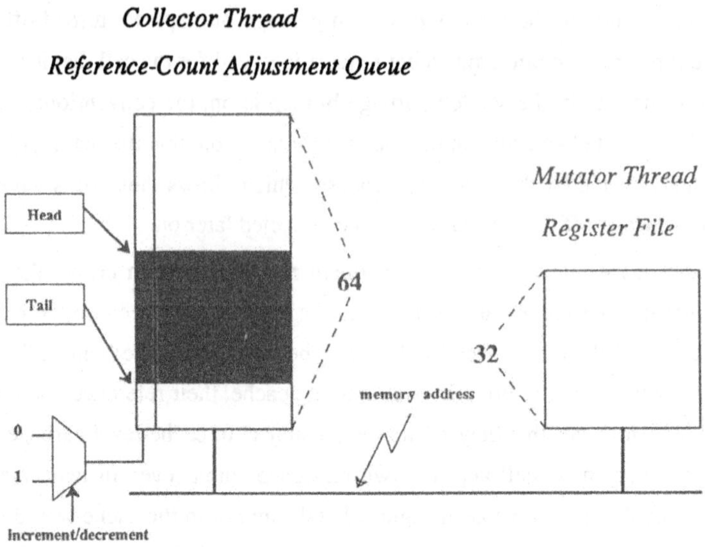

Figure 4 The Organization of Reference-Count Adjustment Queue

large enough to accommodate all reference-count operations between two cache misses. Suppose the cache miss ratio is 2%, that means there are roughly fifty references between two cache misses. Assuming CONS, RPLACA and RPLACD account for 7%, 0.5% and 3.5% respectively [CLAR77] [CLAR79], there are about 50 * (7% * 2 + 0.5% + 3.5%) = 9 references that entail reference-count adjustment. Here CONS is assumed to take two adjustment operations (for CAR and CDR). However, there are other sources for creating reference-count adjustment requests. First, when stack variables are moved from the registers to the data cache. Second, when a cell becomes garbage and get reused, a decrement adjustment request for the reference count of the cell that it points to is issued. Another factor to consider is the miss overhead, which determines the number of cycles in each collection round. If it is short, the requests from previous rounds may accumulate and overflow RCAQ. Further simulation studies are needed to determine the optimal value of this parameter.

The signal for switching from the collector thread to the mutator now becomes the combination of cache miss handling completion, and a flag which is set when the number of requests in RCAQ is below a certain threshold. In the case that an overflow in RCAQ does occur when the mutator thread is in control, a special trap will trigger the collector thread to take over and digest the adjustment requests in RCAQ until the collector-to-mutator switching signal is activated, in this case, until the number of requests in RCAQ is below the threshold. The number of entries in RCAQ is strictly decreasing because no more requests can be generated during the processing, thus guaranteeing the termination of the process.

Discussion

There are several performance optimizations that can be performed at compile-time[BART77]. They generally involve recognizing that corresponding pairs of increment-reference-count and decrement-reference-count requests can be canceled. It should be noted that in-cache garbage are maintained by the garbage bitmap associated with the data cache. They are not visible in the software free-list that is kept by the background garbage collector, which is typically initiated by the language run-time system or the operating system and runs in the mutator thread. In summary, the in-cache allocator and the cache-level garbage collector cooperate through the hardware garbage bitmap and both run in the collector thread, whereas the software memory allocator and the background cache-level garbage collector communicate through the free list and both run in the mutator thread. When the background garbage collector is initiated, it is important that the reference count field of the cells whose garbage bit is on be filled with 7 (111), making them no longer subject to cache-level garbage collection. This operation ensures that there is no overlap between the software-controlled free list and the hardware garbage bitmap, which in turn guarantees that the in-cache allocator and the software memory allocator will not cause inconsistency in the form of reusing cells that are currently in use.

In order to evaluate the proposed scheme, one needs to instrument the LISP run-time system to incorporate the in-cache allocator. Simply getting traces from existing LISP systems and run them against a simulator will not do the job because different memory allocator may result in very different memory reference traces. As a preliminary performance measure, [PeSo89] did a rough estimate on how much miss ratio reduction can one expect from this technique. They use a symbolic 3600-like software simulator to collect the traces and compare the cache miss ratios between the unoptimized case and the case where all memory allocations are assumed to be satisfied in the cache. Table 1 shows the miss ratio differences for a direct mapped cache of various organizations. It can be seen that in average 10-20 times of cache miss ratio reduction is achievable. The performance gain is more significant when the cache size is large and the line size is small. Of course, this estimate is optimistic and does not take into account the overhead involved. We are planning to simulate this technique on the SPUR machine [HILL86], a RISC-based processor designed for LISP processing, and measures the actual performance gain and its overhead.

Line Size (Words)	Case	Cache Size (Words)				
		1K	2K	4K	8K	16K
1	normal	31.1	28.1	27.4	26.4	25.7
	optimal	6.22	3.75	2.14	1.18	0.67
2	normal	16.3	15.2	14.3	13.9	13.5
	optimal	3.81	2.29	1.24	0.68	0.38
4	normal	9.1	8.1	7.5	7.0	6.7
	optimal	2.74	1.58	0.83	0.43	0.23
8	normal	5.5	4.6	3.9	3.2	3.0
	optimal	2.31	1.28	0.61	0.30	0.16
16	normal	3.8	2.7	2.1	1.7	1.2
	optimal	2.24	1.20	0.54	0.24	0.12
32	normal	3.1	2.2	1.4	1.1	0.9
	optimal	2.50	1.31	0.57	0.24	0.10

Table 1 Reduction of Cache Miss Ratio Using In-cache Allocation

4. Related Works

Peng and Sohi's work [PeSo89] on the potential performance gain from several cache optimization schemes motivates our investigation of cache-level garbage collection scheme. We borrowed some of the ideas from [DeBo76], which is developed for systems with multiple levels of storage, and large virtual address space. In particular, the delayed updating of reference counts is central to our mutator-collector dual threaded architecture. [KOOP90]'s measurement of cache behavior of functional programs provides an in-depth understanding of the impacts of cache organization parameters on the graph reduction efficiency. [RAM85][ABRA87] developed parallel garbage collection algorithms for virtual memory systems. The mutator and the collector are running on different processors. Special architectural support features are devised to synchronize the behavior of the the two processes and to enforce the consistency of the memories of the two processors. Burton Smith's HEP [SMIT78] pioneered the concept of multi-threaded architecture. The follow-on projects along the same approach includes Horizon[SMIT88] and TERA. These machines typically need a large number of threads to keep the pipeline busy. In practice it is difficult to sustain that much parallelism except in very large programs. We take an asymmetric approach to multithreading and keep only two threads. As a result a great deal of performance optimizations can be made to take advantage of this special arrangement.

5. Conclusion

Cache performance is crucial to high-performance processor design. Bigger caches do not solve the problem because processor cycle time is closely coupled with cache access time, which typically increases with the cache size. Multi -threaded architecture increases processor utilization efficiency by switching to the other thread when the current thread encounters a cache miss. However, increasing processor utilization efficiency is not equal to masking memory latency. Memory latency is only masked when the threads within a processor all belong to the same program. In this paper, we take a different view towards multi-threaded architecture. Instead of exploiting parallelism within a program, we exploit system/application parallelism by assigning one thread to the application and the other to the system. We call this architecture *asymmetric multi-threaded architecture.* It is asymmetric because the system thread is supposed to help the application thread, but not vice versa. In this paper, the system thread is carrying out a cache-level garbage collector, with an aim to detecting in-cache garbage as soon as possible. By detecting in-cache garbage immediately, the cache performance for heap-intensive programs can be drastically improved. Consequently multi-threading not only passively helps by masking the cache miss overhead, but actively decreasing the cache miss ratio and processor-memory traffic. We view this a synergetic effect resulting from combining the ideas of asymmetric multi-threading with cache-level garbage collection. The future research along this line includes investigating the possibility of applying this technique to distributed-memory multiprocessor configurations, where distributed garbage collection is typically based on reference-counting schemes. It is also conceivable that the system thread in an asymmetric multi-threaded architecture can be generalized to managing on-chip resources in a more general way, including such functions as maintaining cache coherence in large-scale multiprocessor systems. Finding the most suitable garbage collection algorithm for each level of the memory hierarchy that ranges from single data cache to multiple addresses spaces, and exploring the interaction and tradeoffs among the different algorithms is also an important and exciting area for more intellectual efforts.

REFERENCE

[ABRA87] S.G. Abraham, J.H. Patel, "Parallel Garbage Collection on A Virtual Memory System," Proceedings of 1987 International Conference on Parallel Processing, pp 243-246.

[BART77] J.M. Barth, "Shifting Garbage Collection Overhead to Compile Time," Communications of ACM, vol.20-7, pp 513-518, ACM, Jul. 1977.

[CLAR77] D.W. Clark, C.C. Green, "An Empirical Study of List Structures in LISP," Communications of ACM, vol. 20-2, pp 78-87, ACM, Feb. 1977.

[CLAR79] D.W. Clark, "Measurements of Dynamic List Structure Use in LISP," IEEE Transactions on Software Engineering, vol. 5-1, pp 51-59, IEEE, Jan. 1979.

[DeBo76] L.P. Deutsch, D.G. Bobrow, "An Efficient, Incremental, Automatic Garbage Collector," Communications of ACM, vol.19-9, pp 522-526, ACM, Sep. 1976.

[HILL86] M. Hill, et al., "SPUR: A VLSI Multiprocessor Workstation," IEEE Computer, 19(11):8-22, November 1986.

[KOOP90] P.J. Koopman, P. Lee, D.P. Siewiorek, "Cache Performance of Combinator Graph Reduction," Proceedings of 1990 International Conference of Computer Languages, pp 39-49.

[PeSo89] C.J. Peng, G.S. Sohi, "Cache Memory Design Considerations to Support Languages with Dynamic Heap Allocation," TR860, Computer Science Department, University of Wisconsin, Madison, Jul. 1989.

[RAM85] A. Ram, J.H. Patel, "Parallel Garbage Collection Without Synchronization Overhead," Proceedings of 1985 International Symposium on Computer Architecture, pp 84-90.

[SMIT78] B.J. Smith, "A Pipelined, Shared Resource MIMD Computer," Proceedings of 1978 International Conference on Parallel Processing, pp 6-8, 1978.

[SMIT88] B.J. Smith, "The Horizon Supercomputing System: Architecture and Software," Proceedings of 1988 Supercomputing Conference, pp 28-34.

[WILS90] P.R. Wilson, T.G. Moher, "Heap Management and Hierarchical Memories", To appear in SGPLAN Notices.

[ZORN89] B.G. Zorn, "Comparative Performance Evaluation of Garbage Collection Algorithms", Ph.D. Dissertation, University of California, Berkeley, November, 1989.

M-Structures: Extending a Parallel, Non-strict, Functional Language with State

Paul S. Barth, Rishiyur S. Nikhil and Arvind
Massachusetts Institute of Technology

Laboratory for Computer Science

545 Technology Square, Cambridge, MA 02139, USA

{barth,nikhil,arvind}@au-bon-pain.lcs.mit.edu

Abstract

Functional programs are widely appreciated for being "declarative" (algorithms are not *over-specified*) and implicitly parallel. However, when modeling state, both properties are compromised because the state variables must be "threaded" through most functions. Further, state "updates" may require much copying. A solution is to introduce assignments, as in ML and Scheme; however, for meaningful semantics, they resort to strict, sequential evaluation.

We present an alternative approach called *M-structures*, which are imperative data structures with implicit synchronization. M-structures are added to Id, a parallel non-strict functional language. We argue that some programs with M-structures improve on their functional counterparts in three ways: they are (1) more *declarative*; (2) more *parallel*; and (3) more *storage efficient*. Points (1) and (2) contradict conventional wisdom. We study two problems: histogramming a tree, and graph traversal, comparing functional and M-structure solutions.

1 Introduction

Functional programming is widely appreciated for its declarative nature. By "declarative" we mean that one does not have to *over-specify* the details of an algorithm. This is sometimes paraphrased as: "Say *what* you want done, not *how* you want it done".

However, some programs cannot be expressed naturally in a purely functional style. For example, a program to assign unique identifiers to the nodes in a tree must thread the supply of unique identifiers through the traversal of the tree; this "plumbing" can be quite messy. Another weakness of functional languages is that they are difficult to implement efficiently— there is too much copying of data structures.

A common approach to addressing these weaknesses is to extend a functional language with state. Both ML and Scheme are examples of this. However, in order that these imperative features have a meaningful semantics, the language is usually made into a strict, call-by-value, sequential language. For functional programs, this is an over-specification of the order of evaluation, and may thus be viewed as a loss of declarativeness.

Another issue is parallelism. In pure functional languages, parallelism is implicit. Annotations for parallelism may be used, but these can be viewed as hints and do not add to the intellectual burden of the programmer. However, in sequential functional languages with imperative extensions, parallelism is usually re-introduced through another layer of constructs such as threads, forks, semaphores, futures, *etc.* These features usually make the language more complex. Further, when two such parallel programs are composed, their parallelism does not compose, because of the underlying strict semantics. The difference in resulting parallelism can be exponential, as demonstrated in [14].

Parallelism can also be curtailed by the threading alluded to above. Threading ensures determinacy at the expense of serializing access to the shared data structure. For a large class of algorithms, determinacy can be ensured in the presence of asynchronous updates to a shared structure. For example, accumulation and set operations can use associative and commutative properties to produce determinate results under any sequence of operations. For such applications, only the *atomicity* of each operation need be guaranteed to ensure determinate results. Again, the threading required by functional programming over-specifies, by serializing, an inherently parallel algorithm.

Let us call the traditional approaches A and B:

> **Approach A:** purely functional (strict or non-strict) with implicit parallelism or annotations for parallelism.
>
> **Approach B:** strict functional + sequential evaluation + imperative extensions + threads and semaphores for parallelism.

In the literature, the landscape of functional programming techniques is normally defined by these two approaches. In this paper we would like to open up an entirely new frontier:

> **Approach C:** non-strict functional + implicitly parallel evaluation + M-structures + occasional sequentialization.

M-structures are mutable data structures manipulated with implicitly synchronized imperatives called *take* and *put*, which are quite different from the traditional assignment statement.

The main points we would like to demonstrate about Approach C are:

(1) Programs in Approach C are often more declarative than their functional counterparts, because they are less specific about the order in which things should be computed. By omitting this level of detail, programs in Approach C are often shorter and easier to read than the pure functional versions.

(2) Programs in Approach C often have much more parallelism than their functional counterparts.

(3) Programs in Approach C are often much more efficient than their functional counterparts in terms of heap storage used and total number of instructions executed.

The first two points come to us as a great surprise, because they contradict our previous intuitions (and, we believe, conventional wisdom)— we always took it for granted that functional programs are more declarative than programs with state, and that functional programs always had more parallelism than programs with state. See [3] for studies of implicit parallelism in functional Id programs.

In fact, point (2) is a very curious reversal of conventional wisdom. Whereas we always thought that programs with state needed powerful analysis (*i.e.*, dependence analysis) in order to recover the parallelism that is already evident in functional programs, we find here that it is the functional programs that would need powerful analysis to recover the parallelism that is evident in Approach C. To our knowledge, no such analysis techniques exist yet.

The final point, storage efficiency, is also an issue in sequential functional programs. Many analysis techniques have been developed which attempt to improve storage efficiency through reuse, such as abstract reference counting[10] and single-threadedness analysis. Unfortunately, most published techniques seem to be based on an underlying sequential, strict semantics, sometimes restricted to first-order languages and flat domains for data structures. Thus, non-strict, implicitly parallel languages are unlikely to benefit from these techniques.

We hasten to add that Approach C is not without its problems! As soon as one adds state, one loses referential transparency (RT), and any benefits that may go with it. For example, RT provides a foundation for equational reasoning, which may be used during compilation for common subexpression elimination, proofs of invariants used in loop optimization, *etc.* Equational reasoning may also be used to prove functional programs correct. Our intent is not to challenge this work, but rather to demonstrate some programs which benefit, in both declarativeness and efficiency, from violating RT. Such benefits have motivated other "functional" languages, such as ML and Scheme, to introduce imperative constructs. These languages, which comprise Approach B, are still considered to be functional languages because the style of programming in these languages is "mostly functional". We suggest the same for Approach C—programs are still written in a mostly functional style. Further, we claim that the non-strictness and implicit parallelism of Approach C yields a more functional programming style than Approach B with explicit parallelism constructs. Regardless, Approaches B and C will require the development of new foundations for proving correctness, such as proposed by [6].

In this paper, we will demonstrate our claims by comparing Approach A (functional programs) and Approach C (M-structures) for two example applications:

computing a histogram of values, and performing a graph traversal. The declarativeness of these programs is critiqued, and their performance measured on a parallel simulator. The rest of this paper is organized as follows: Section 2 describes the core functional language, its non-strict semantics and parallel execution model, the M-structure extensions, and our parallel simulator. Sections 3 and 4 explore the two example programs, respectively, in some detail. Section 5 discusses our results, and outlines a method for reasoning about M-structure programs. We conclude in Section 6.

2 Background

2.1 The core functional language

The core of Id is a non-strict functional language with implicit parallelism[13]. It has the usual features of many modern functional languages, including a Hindley/Milner type inference system, algebraic types and definitions with clauses and pattern matching, and list comprehensions. An Id block, which has *letrec* semantics, consists of a set of bindings and a body expression following the keyword `In`, *e.g.*:

```
{ x = 1:y ;
  y = 2:x ;
In
  x }
```

Here, ":" is an infix list constructor, and the block evaluates to a cyclic list whose infinite unfolding is `1:2:1:2:`··· Note that non-strict evaluation allows this cycle to be created with mutually recursive bindings; such bindings are meaningless under strict evaluation.

In addition, Id has extensive facilities for arrays, including array *comprehensions* for the efficient construction of functional arrays. For example, the expression

```
{array (1,5) of
 | [j] = 0 || j <- 1 to 5 }
```

creates an array with index range 1 to 5, with every location containing 0.

One form of array comprehension useful for computing histograms is the *accumulator.* For example, suppose we wish to build a histogram of numbers ranging from 1 to 5 drawn from a list of numbers `xs`. The result is an array with index range 1 to 5, such that the j'th cell of the array contains the number of occurrences of j in `xs`. Here is the program:

```
{array (1,5) of
 | [j] = 0 || j <- 1 to 5
 accumulate (+)
 | [j] = 1 || j <- xs }
```

Before the `accumulate` keyword is an array comprehension that specifies the initial contents of the array (zeroes). The rest of the construct specifies that for each j in `xs`, we increment element j of the histogram by 1.

In array and accumulator comprehensions, no order is specified for the array-filling computations. However, note that array comprehensions can be non-strict, whereas accumulator comprehensions must be strict. In array comprehensions, each slot is assigned at most once, *i.e.*, there is a single transition from $\perp$ to non-$\perp$ (or "unevaluated" to "evaluated", in graph reduction terminology). Thus, the array can be returned as soon as it has been allocated, with consumers automatically blocking on $\perp$ if necessary. However, in accumulator comprehensions, each slot may go through several intermediate non-$\perp$ states, and we cannot be sure that a slot has reached its final value until all the accumulations have been performed. Thus, the array cannot be returned to a consumer until it has been fully computed[1].

2.2 Non-strict, Implicitly Parallel Semantics

We are interested in non-strict semantics, not only for its expressive power, but also because it admits more parallelism than strict semantics [14]. Many evaluation orders implement non-strict semantics, with lazy evaluation being the most popular. Id, on the other hand, implements non-strict semantics by *eager* evaluation of most expressions. A precise description of Id's operational semantics using rewrite rules is given in [1, 15]. The flavor of Id's semantics is given here tc illustrate its expressive power and implicit parallelism. Briefly,

- In a block:

  ```
  { x1 = e1 ;
    ...
    xN = eN ;
  In
    eBody }
  ```

  all expressions (`e1`, ..., `eN` and `eBody`) are evaluated in parallel, and the value of `eBody` may be returned as soon as it is available (even if `e1`, ..., `eN` have not finished evaluating). Thus, the block has *letrec* semantics, with no implicit ordering on the evaluation of expressions, except as imposed by data dependencies.

- All expressions in an application (`e0 e1 ... eN`) may be evaluated in parallel. Suppose `e0` evaluates to a function `f` and we have a definition:

  ```
  def f x1 ... xN = eBody ;
  ```

  then the application can immediately be rewritten to:

[1] Array and accumulator comprehensions in Haskell were influenced by these array notations in Id[11].

```
{ x1 = e1 ;
  ...
  xN = eN ;
In
  eBody }
```

In other words, the function may be invoked as soon as `e0` is evaluated, and a result may be returned as soon as it is defined by the function, even if the arguments `e1`, ..., `eN` have not finished evaluating.

- In a conditional expression (`IF e1 THEN e2 ELSE e3`), `e1` is evaluated to a boolean value, after which *one* of the expressions `e2` or `e3` is evaluated.

Id's rewrite rules also take a precise position on *sharing* of computations and data structures, since this is also crucial in a language with state. Informally, an identifier such as `x1` above may not be substituted by `e1` until `e1` has been reduced to a variable or constant; this ensures that expressions do not get duplicated. Data structures are always referred to *via* labels, which may be regarded as abstract pointers. Thus, a constructor produces a single data structure that is shared among all its references.

Note that the operational semantics of Id are quite unique in that they are:

- Non-strict, but not lazy (blocks, constructors, and function applications may return values before any of their inputs are available), and

- Eager, but not call-by-value (evaluation of arguments is initiated whether they are needed or not).

As an example of eager, non-strict evaluation, consider the following. Given the function `f`

```
def f a b = (a+1,b+1) ;
```

we can evaluate the following block as sequence of rewrites:

```
{ (x,y) = f 3 x ;
In
   y}
```

First, the function application reduces to a nested block:

```
{(x,y) = { a = 3 ;
           b = x ;
         In
           (a+1,b+1) } ;
 In
   y}
```

In the rest of the sequence, nested block bindings are flattened into a single block, and tuple bindings are rewritten into identifier bindings. The block returns a value when the body identifier `y` is bound to a constant:

```
{ (x,y) = (a+1,b+1) ;  ==>  { x = a+1 ;  ==>  { x = 4 ;    ==>  5
  a     = 3 ;                 y = b+1 ;         y = b+1 ;
  b     = x ;                 a = 3 ;           a = 3 ;
In                            b = x ;           b = 4 ;
  y}                        In                In
                              y}                y}
```

This is perhaps an artificial example, but the cyclic binding establishes the point that *this is a non-strict language even though we do not use lazy evaluation.* To emphasize this further, we invite the reader to trace the evaluation of the function (due to Traub [18]):

```
def f b x y = { xx = if b then x  else yy ;
                yy = if b then xx else y  ;
              In
                xx + yy } ;
```

under the calls `(f True 10 20)` and `(f False 10 20)`. These expressions are undefined under strict semantics, but are perfectly meaningful in Id and other non-strict languages.

2.3 Non-strictness, yes, but why not lazy evaluation?

Consider the following function:

```
def f x = (e1, e2) ;
```

and suppose the expression `e1` contains a side-effect. In Id, we can immediately conclude that whenever `f` is called, the side-effect will occur.

In a lazy evaluator, on the other hand, we have to look at each application of `f` separately— the side-effect will occur only if the application is actually examined in a strict context and, further, that the first component of the resulting tuple is also examined in a strict context. For example, merely selecting the first component of the tuple and storing it into another data structure will not cause `e1` to be evaluated, so the side-effect will not occur. Thus, determining the conditions under which the side-effect will occur is as hard a problem as strictness analysis, requiring potentially global analysis. The presence of higher order functions only complicates matters further.

In Id, evaluation of an expression is controlled *only* by conditionals. Thus, determining the conditions under which a side-effect in a function `f` will occur requires only local analysis; we do not have to look at the contexts in which `f` is applied.

We believe that having such a *local* model of whether or not side-effects occur is essential in order to reason about programs with side-effects.

2.4 M-structures with *Take* and *Put* operations

As described, Id is a determinate language with no provision for side-effects. Its eager, non-strict semantics allows the efficient, parallel execution of functional programs. However, functional Id programs that share state suffer from the drawbacks alluded to earlier, *i.e.*, the loss of declarativeness and parallelism due to threading.

To support programs that share state, Id is extended with *M-structures*. M-structures are implicitly synchronized data structures that support atomic updates. We define two M-structure operations, called *take* and *put*, for reading and writing the components of an M-structure.[2]

Take and put operations are *implicitly synchronized*, *i.e.*, there is no separate notion of locks or semaphores. Rather, a state bit is associated with every M-structure element indicating whether it is *empty* or *full*. The empty state means that the element is currently taken and may not be read; the full state indicates that it is available. A *take* operation on a full element atomically reads its value and resets its state to empty, while a *take* on an empty element suspends. A *put* operation writes a new value to an empty (*i.e.*, taken) element;[3] if there are suspended *take* operations waiting for the element, one is resumed and the value communicated to it, and the element remains in the empty state. Otherwise, the value is written into the element and its state set to full.

For example, consider the following statement[4] that atomically increments an element of an M-structure array:

```
A![j] = A![j] + 1 ;
```

Here, the expression `A![j]` on the right hand side denotes a *take* operation on the j'th element of array `A`. This value is incremented by one; the expression `A![j]` on the left hand side denotes a *put* operation on the same element. Note that the strictness of the addition operator ensures that the *take* precedes the *put*. In general, the expression computing the value to be put into a cell should be strict in the value taken from the cell. Assuming this strictness, the M-structure synchronization guarantees that the cell update is atomic. For example, if k parallel computations attempt to execute the statement above, their access to the location will be properly serialized and the final value of the cell will be its original value plus k.

2.4.1 Explicit Sequencing

When writing parallel programs that share state, it is sometimes necessary to introduce explicit sequencing. For example, suppose we wish to reset an array location to 0 and return its old value, *e.g.*,

```
{ Aj = A![j] ;
  ---              % barrier
  A![j] = 0 ;
In
  Aj }
```

[2] An analogous pair of operations, called *E-fetch* and *E-store*, were developed independently by Milewski[12].

[3] A version in which multiple *put* operations are buffered has also been designed, allowing M-structures to act as producer-consumer channels. The examples in this paper will not use this feature.

[4] In Id, statements are included among a block's bindings

The first statement takes the old value out, and the second one puts the new value (0) back. The horizontal line is read as a sequentializing barrier, to ensure that the take occurs before the put. This is necessary since, by default, all components of a block are evaluated in parallel, and so there would be nothing to prevent the put occurring before the take. The barrier makes the put operation strict in the take.

A barrier in a block is more subtle than a simple sequencing form (the classical semicolon). It makes the statements following the barrier (including the body of the block) *hyperstrict* in the statements that precede the barrier. That is, no expressions following the barrier begin evaluation until all expressions before the barrier are completely evaluated, including procedure calls and all their expressions, recursively. This hyperstrict evaluation allows barriers to be used to sequence side-effects buried in procedure calls.

Unlike synchronization barriers in other parallel languages, an Id barrier is not a global barrier— it is entirely *local* to the block of bindings in which it appears, and it is reentrant, *i.e.*, each instance of the block has its own barrier. This not only makes them relatively easy to use, but they are also implemented very efficiently using "synchronization trees" (we do not have space to go into details here).

2.5 M-structures in Algebraic Types

As another example of an M-structure, consider a polymorphic list where each tail is updatable. The following type declaration defines such a list, where "`*0`" is a type variable and "`!`" denotes an updatable field (called an *m-field*):

```
type mlist *0 = MNil | MCons *0 !(mlist *0) ;
```

Although Id has pattern-matching on algebraic types, one usually does not use pattern-matching for types with m-fields, since pattern-matching and imperatives do not mix well. Thus, the fields of an algebraic type may also be selected using record syntax, with field names derived from the constructor and the field position. Ordinary fields, such as the head of the cons cell above, are selected using "dot" notation, *e.g.*, `x.MCons_1`. M-fields are taken using "bang" notation in an expression, as in `x!MCons_2`. A new value `v` may be put into an empty m-field using the statement:

```
x!MCons_2 = v
```

Type-checking ensures that m-fields and ordinary fields are accessed with the correct notation.

To compare the M-structure list with a functional list, consider the problem of inserting an integer `x` into a set `ys`, taking care not to insert duplicates. In the following functional solution, the set is represented as a list of integers and pattern matching is used:

```
typeof insert_f = (list int) -> int -> (list int) ;

def insert_f Nil    x = x:Nil
  | insert_f (y:ys) x = if (x == y) then
                          ys
                        else
                          y:(insert_f ys x) ;
```

Using record syntax instead of pattern matching, insert_f is:

```
def insert_f ys x = if (Nil? ys) then
                      Cons x Nil
                    else if (x == ys.Cons_1) then
                      ys
                    else
                      Cons ys.Cons_1 (insert_f ys.Cons_2 x) ;
```

For comparison, the following solution uses M-structure lists:

```
typeof insert_m = (mlist int) -> int -> (mlist int) ;

def insert_m ys x = if (MNil? ys) then
                      MCons x MNil
                    else if (x == ys.MCons_1) then
                      ys
                    else
                      { ys!MCons_2 = insert_m ys!MCons_2 x ;
                      In
                         ys } ;
```

The first two conditional clauses of insert_m mimic the functional solution. In the third clause, we take the tail of the list, insert x into it and put it back, and we *return the original list*. Note that insert_m is strict in ys (due to the conditional), so the take and put are properly ordered. The advantage of this program over the functional version is that it takes $O(1)$ heap store per insertion, instead of $O(n)$, where n is the length of the list.

Under non-strict semantics, insert_f has the attractive property that in the last line, the new cons cell can be returned even while we are inserting x into its tail. Thus, multiple insertions can be "pipelined", *i.e.*, a second insertion can run closely behind the first, automatically synchronizing on empty slots.

Note that insert_m has the same kind of "pipeline" parallelism as insert_f. In the last line, non-strictness allows us to return ys immediately. If a second insertion is attempted immediately, it can run closely behind the first, blocking on empty fields (due to takes) in the same manner as insert_f blocks on empty fields.

However, there is an interesting subtlety here. Consider the following two near-identical fragments:

```
zs = insert_f ys x1 ;          zs = insert_m ys x1 ;
ws = insert_f zs x2 ;          ws = insert_m zs x2 ;
```

and assume that neither x1 nor x2 is present in ys. In the functional case, despite the pipelined behavior, x2 is guaranteed to be inserted behind x1. The second insert_f can never "overtake" the first; if it tried to run faster, it would block at some point, waiting for a result from the first insert_f.

In insert_m, however, it is possible for the second insertion to overtake the first, inserting x1 behind x2. The reason is that in the parallel block in the last else clause, the first insert_m may return ys before it takes the MCons_2 field. Thus, when given ys, the second insert_m "races" with the first traversal to take of this field, and may potentially overtake it. If we want to prevent this overtaking, we have to delay returning ys until the take completes. This can be accomplished with a barrier:

```
def insert_m ys x = if ...
                    ...
                    else ...
                    ...
                    else
                      { ys' = ys!MCons_2 ;
                        ---
                        ys!MCons_2 = insert_m ys' x ;
                      In
                        ys } ;
```

Note that this expression does not wait for the put to take place before returning ys— that would make the insertion strict, eliminating pipelined behavior completely.

This subtlety highlights important differences between M-structures and their functional counterparts. First, atomicity is clearly a weaker property than determinacy. In the above example, both the M-structure and functional solutions are correct (neither make duplicate entries); however, the M-structure solution admits more parallelism through overtaking. Second, the M-structure solution can be modified to provide the sequencing property of the functional solution without the additional storage overhead. Finally, reasoning about the interaction of several concurrent operations is more difficult for M-structures than functional data structures. We address this issue in Section 5.

To conclude our discussion of the Id language and semantics, we make the following observation. In most approaches to parallel computing, one starts with a sequential language and adds parallel annotations. This is true even amongst functional languages, *e.g.*, the "future" annotation [8] and the "spark" annotation [7]. In contrast, we go in the opposite direction: we start with an implicitly parallel language and add sequentialization only where necessary. The degree to which we expose and exploit parallelism is thus much more aggressive.

2.6 Our Experiments

To determine the validity of our claims, we compare several Id programs written in a functional style (Approach A) against programs using M-structures (Approach C). These programs and our analysis are presented in the next two sections.

We evaluate the programs in several ways. First, we compare them subjectively in terms of declarativeness, *i.e.*, how well the structure of the program mirrors the structure of the problem. Second, we compare their efficiency in terms of storage use and number of instructions executed. Finally, their parallelism is compared. Since the parallelism exhibited by a program depends on many factors, this last measurement deserves some explanation.

Id programs compile into dataflow graphs, which constitute a parallel machine language (a partial order on instructions). The dataflow graphs respect the non-strict semantics and parallel evaluation order describe earlier in this section. The performance of these programs is measured on GITA, which is a dataflow simulator instrumented to take "idealized" performance measurements.[5] The GITA simulator executes dataflow graphs under the following idealized assumptions:

- No limit on the number of instructions that can be executed in parallel.
- An instruction is executed as early as possible, *i.e.*, as soon as all inputs are available.
- All instructions, including storage allocation "instructions", take 1 unit of time.
- No delay in communicating the output of one instruction to the input of another.

The purpose of idealized simulation is to give an upper bound on achievable performance, unconstrained by machine-specific characteristics, such as the number of processors, available memory, or scheduling policy. One important measure of idealized performance is the parallelism profile. This profile charts the number of parallel operations against time. Given the above assumptions, the parallelism profile exhibited under GITA describes the "inherent" parallelism of a program, *i.e.*, the program's limit of achievable parallelism. In this paper, we summarize these profiles as the average parallelism, which is the number of instructions divided by the time to completion.

Note that a major idealization in GITA is that each heap allocation takes one instruction. This hides the additional overhead of heap management encountered in a real system, such as garbage collection and initialization. In addition, storage management in a parallel system may also perform the task of load balancing. Thus, programs requiring more storage will, in fact, require more instructions than indicated by idealized performance measurements.

3 Histogramming a tree of samples

Consider the problem of histogramming numbers in the leaves of a tree. Given a tree T of numbers, where each number is in the range 1 to 5, the histogram H is an array of 5 elements such that H_i = the number of leaves containing number i.

[5] GITA is part of the "Id World" programming and simulation environment which has been in use at MIT and elsewhere since 1986.

This problem statement is a highly abstracted account of MCNP, an application program used by over 350 organizations in diverse industries such as oil exploration, automobiles, medical imaging, *etc.* [6] The program models the diffusion of subatomic particles from a radioactive probe through the surrounding material, using Monte Carlo simulation. For each original particle, the program follows it through events in its lifetime, such as motion in some direction, collision with a material boundary or another particle, *etc.* The tree structure arises because particles may split into two (and recursively, those particles may split again), after which the simulation follows each particle separately. When a particle finally dies, *i.e.*, reaches a leaf, some of its properties are collected in various histograms, such as final position and energy. MCNP has eluded easy parallelization in all conventional programming models, but is "embarassingly parallel", because the tree may have thousands of branches, and the events in a particle's life are decided purely locally, based on the toss of a coin.

In MCNP, no tree data structure is actually constructed. Rather, intermediate arguments and results are passed through the call/return tree. In our histogram example, the histogramming functions traverse a previously constructed tree, with the following type definition:

```
type tree = Leaf int | Node tree tree ;
```

The cost of creating this tree is not included in the measurements.

3.1 HA1: A Functional Solution

This program builds an initial array H0 containing 0 everywhere, and then performs a right-to-left traversal of the tree. At each leaf, the *i*'th element of the array is incremented by 1, where *i* is the number of the leaf. Since the functional solution may not use imperatives, incrementing this element requires building a new array, identical to the original, except that the *i*'th location is incremented. Here is the code:

```
typeof hist = tree -> (array int) ;

def hist T = { H0 = {array (1,5) of
                     | [j] = 0 || j <- 1 to 5 }
          In
            traverse T H0 } ;

typeof traverse = tree -> (array int) -> (array int) ;

def traverse (Leaf i)   H = incr H i
 | traverse (Node L R) H = traverse L (traverse R H) ;

typeof incr = (array int) -> int -> (array int) ;
```

[6]Los Alamos National Laboratory is developing a comprehensive version of MCNP in Id under the direction of Olaf Lubeck.

```
def incr H i = {array (1,5) of
               | [j] = if (i==j) then H[j]+1 else H[j] || j <- 1 to 5 } ;
```

Critique

In principle, the increments can be done in any order. However, since each increment creates a new array, the array must be "threaded" sequentially through the traversal. Threading requires that the recursive calls to `traverse` be composed, which imposes a particular order on the increment operations. In the original MCNP problem, threading is even worse, since many arguments and results are passed through the call/return tree. The threading required by functional programming obscures the independent nature of the accumulations.

This program also suffers from storage overhead, since the histogram array is copied at each leaf of the tree. Each copy of the array requires 5 loads and stores, while the problem requires only a single load and store per increment. Note that techniques for eliminating copying in functional programs, such as single-threadedness analysis and abstract reference counting, might determine that all the updates could occur in place. However, these analyses assume a *sequential* order of execution, and so preclude parallel execution.

3.2 HA2: A Functional Solution using Accumulators

In this example, we build an accumulator array with each element initialized to zero. The accumulation draws from a list produced by `traverse`, which collects all the numbers in the leaves of the tree. Here is the code:

```
typeof hist = tree -> (array int) ;

def hist T = {array (1,5) of
             | [j] = 0 || j <- 1 to 5
             accumulate (+)
             | i = 1 || i <- traverse T } ;

typeof traverse = tree -> (list int) ;

def traverse T = aux T Nil ;

typeof aux = tree -> (list int) -> (list int) ;

def aux (Leaf i)   is = i:is
 |  aux (Node L R) is = aux L (aux R is) ;
```

Critique

The use of an accumulator for the histogram eliminates the need to copy the array. In fact, the accumulator is quite declarative and modular: for each i drawn from the list of leaf numbers, the i'th element is incremented by one. The functions traverse and aux still require threading to construct the list of leaf numbers. However, non-strictness allows this list to be constructed in parallel and "piped" into the accumulator.

Although an improvement, the intermediate list read by the accumulator incurs storage overhead and overspecifies the order of accumulations. Accumulators use lists for modularity and composition; eliminating the list through compiler analysis requires global analysis to thread the accumulator through the generator function and its descendants.

The use of accumulators in an early version of the MCNP program corroborates these observations: the intermediate list complicated the program and introduced inefficiencies. The M-structure solution, presented next, retains the declarativeness of accumulators and eliminates the need for an intermediate list.

3.3 HC: An M-structure Solution

In this solution, the histogram H is represented as an M-array initialized to zero. The traverse function recursively passes H down to all leaves in parallel. Each leaf (containing i) atomically increments element H_i by taking the element, adding one, and putting it back. A sequential barrier is used to ensure that H is not returned until traverse completes. (Recall that this barrier is implicit in accumulators, since they may not return until all accumulations have been performed.) The M-structure program is below:

```
typeof hist = tree -> (m_array int) ;

def hist T = { H = {M_array (1,5) of
                    | [j] = 0 || j <- 1 to 5 } ;
               _ = traverse T H ;
               ---                                          % sequential barrier
             In
               H } ;

typeof traverse = tree -> (m_array int) -> void ;

def traverse (Leaf i)   H = { H![i] = H![i] + 1 }
  | traverse (Node L R) H = { _ = traverse L H ;
                              _ = traverse R H } ;
```

Bindings of the form "_ = e" are used to execute e for its side-effects and discard its result. Let blocks with no body expression return a meaningless value of type void, and are executed solely for side-effect.

Critique

This program requires no threading since the accumulation is performed by side-effects. Thus, the recursive calls to traverse are not composed, and the order of accumulations is not overspecified. The atomicity of each accumulation is is *locally* specified by the take and put operations and their implicit synchronization. In contrast to the functional programs, only storage for the result histogram is required, and each accumulation requires only a single load and store (take and put).

3.4 Other Functional Solutions

Several techniques for improving the performance of parallel and functional programs have been developed, such as parallel combining trees and tree-structured arrays. These techniques were used in three other functional solutions, which are summarized below:

HA3: Tree Accumulation. The program recursively descends in parallel to every leaf. At a leaf containing, say, 2, we produce the array `[0 1 0 0 0]`. At each node, we add the arrays from the two subtrees and return the new array. Thus, the top node produces the sum for the whole tree. Although this eliminates threading, its storage requirements are double that of HA1.

HA4: Parallel Traversal. The entire tree is traversed five times in parallel (once for each element in the histogram). The i'th traversal uses parallel tree accumulation to sum the number of leaves containing i. Since this accumulation computes an integer, it requires no additional storage. Finally, the histogram is constructed by storing the five sums into an array, which is returned. Although this has no threading and minimal storage, it executes a large number of instructions, because the entire tree is traversed for each element of the histogram.

HA5: Tree-Structured Histogram. The program is a modification of HA1, replacing the histogram array by a balanced tree. This reduces memory and instruction overhead by copying a single path of the tree ($O(\log b)$ instead of $O(b)$, where b is the number of elements in the histogram). Note that copying a path requires several memory allocations rather than one, as well as conditionals to route each increment to the appropriate leaf. Therefore, this solution is less efficient than HA1 for small histograms. Even with large histograms, threading still obscures the code and overspecifies the order of accumulations.

3.5 Experimental results

We ran the above programs on a full binary tree of depth 10, *i.e.*, 1024 leaves with an (almost) equal number of 1's, 2's, ... and 5's. The results are shown below:

Program version	Total instructions executed	Critical path	Avg. parallelism	Heap store used (words)
HA1	199,757	1,452	138	9,250
HA2	72,847	7,324	10	2,100
HA3	325,472	238	1368	18,423
HA4	266,223	195	1365	9
HA5	253,370	28,833	9	11,301
HC	60,496	589	103	9

3.5.1 Observations

Declarativeness: We believe the M-structure solution HC is more declarative than the functional solutions, since it does not overspecify accumulation order by threading.

Instruction count: HC requires the fewest number of instructions. The instruction overhead of copying in solutions HA1, HA3, and HA5 is significant when compared to HA2 (accumulators) and HC. The high instruction count in HA4 is due to the duplicate traversals of the tree.

Heap Store Used: Copying intermediate data structures in the functional solutions dominate their storage profiles. Imperative updates, as used in HC, allow storage use to be reduced by three orders of magnitude.

Parallelism: HA3 and HA4 have more parallelism than the other programs, but this is mostly due to redundant computation, such as copying arrays or multiple tree traversals. The poor parallelism in HA2 and HA5 comes from overserialization: the intermediate list in the case of accumulators, and copying the path of the tree in HA5. The parallelism in HC is limited by synchronization of take and put instructions. Because they are atomic, the number of parallel increment operations is bounded by the size of the histogram. Parallelism in this example exceeds 5 because these increments are overlapped with the tree traversal.

In summary, the M-structure solution to the histogramming problem is highly declarative, and combines instruction efficiency and low storage use with significant parallelism.

4 A Graph Traversal Problem

For a second comparison of functional and M-structure programs, consider a simple graph traversal problem. Suppose we are given a directed graph structure, *i.e.*, an interconnection of nodes:

```
type gnode = GNode int int (list gnode) ;
```

The first `int` field contains a unique identifier for the node, the second `int` field contains some numeric information, and the list of nodes represents the list of neighbors (possibly empty) of the current node.

The problem is this: given a node A in a graph, compute `rsum(A)`, the sum of the integer information in all nodes reachable from A.

The unique identifiers in the nodes highlight an important difference between graphs and trees: graphs can have can have shared substructures and cycles. Graph traversals need to take this into account to avoid repeated traversals of nodes and subgraphs. Therefore, traversal programs must be able to test equality between nodes. The notion of object equality differs between functional and imperative languages, but is not central to the issues in this paper. For clarity, the unique ID field in the graph nodes will be used to determine node equality.

Traditional graph traversal algorithms rely on "marking" visited nodes to avoid repeated traversals. For familiarity, we will begin this section with two M-structure programs that use imperative operations to mark visited nodes. This is followed by the functional solution and experimental results.

4.1 GC1: A Simple M-structure Solution

The traditional imperative solution to this problem involves extending the `node` type to contain a *mark* field, which is used to avoid repeated traversals of shared subgraphs. We assume that the mark field is initially set to `False`. The following program expresses this solution:

```
type gnode = GNode int int (list gnode) !bool ;

def rsum nd = if (marked? nd) then
                 0
               else
                 nd.GNode_2 + sum (map rsum nd.GNode_3) ;

def marked? nd = { m = nd!GNode_4 ;          % take the mark field
                    ---                       % sequentialize
                    nd!GNode_4 = True ;       % put True in mark field
                  In
                    m } ;
```

Note that in this solution, the unique ID field is not required.

Critique

The solution is very clear. The only subtle point is the atomicity of the `marked?` predicate. The value of the mark field is taken and returned, and set to `True` regardless of its previous value. Since the mark field is set to `True` the first time the node is visited, the node will be counted only once. As described earlier, the serialization barrier between the take and put guarantee that they happen in the correct order.

While this solution corresponds to most textbook algorithms, it has two drawbacks:

Mark initialization: We assumed that the marks in the graph were initialized to `False` before the traversal began. But, how do we achieve this? Traditionally, we have some *independent* access to all the nodes, such as an array or set of all nodes, and we iterate through this collection, resetting all marks. Note that resetting the marks cannot be overlapped with the traversal algorithm—this easily doubles the cost of the algorithm. Further, if the graph is large compared to the region traversed, resetting all marks may be more expensive than the traversal.

Multiple traversals: Suppose we are given two nodes A and B and want to compute the reachable sum from each of them, in parallel. GC1 cannot be used for this, since the marks from the A and B traversals may interfere, *i.e.*, nodes marked by A's traversal will not be counted by the traversal from B, and vice versa.

These drawbacks can be overcome by a simple extension of the "mark field" idea. Here, each traversal carries an additional parameter, a unique *traversal identifier*. Rather than marking nodes with a boolean, each node contains a list of traversal identifiers indicating who has visited the node. The `marked?` predicate checks and updates this list.

This solution allows multiple traversals to occur in parallel, since they have distinct traversal IDs and will not interfere. Also, node marks do not have to be reset, since a brand new traversal ID is issued for each traversal. However, the performance of this solution worsens as more and more traversals are performed, creating unused IDs that slow the `marked?` predicate and occupy storage. Because of this weakness, we will not pursue this idea any further.

4.2 GC2: A Solution Allowing Multiple Traversals

A better solution that allows multiple traversals uses a separate `visited` table to keep track of nodes already traversed. Rather than marking nodes directly, this table contains the unique IDs of visited nodes, and is updated as each new node is encountered. The original definition of graph nodes (without a mark field) is used:

```
type gnode = GNode int int (list gnode) ;
```

Here is the code for the reachable sum:

```
def rsum nd = { visited = mk_empty_table () ;

                def aux (GNode x i nbs) =
                  if (member?_and_insert  visited  x) then
                    0
                  else
                    i + sum (map aux nbs) ;
              In
                aux  nd } ;
```

The `member?_and_insert` function is analogous to the `marked?` function in GC1: it returns a boolean indicating whether `x` is present in the `visited` table, inserting `x` in the table if it is not.

Critique

The version of rsum given in GC2 is quite similar to GC1. There is no threading, and marking code is localized. The main difference between the programs is the modularity supplied by the visited table. It is shared by all calls to aux, but does not require threading or modification to the graphs. Further, its storage can be released after the traversal.

4.2.1 A Parallel Hash Table

We can implement the visited table in a number of ways. A parallel hash table is a good candidate, since it allows $O(1)$ access to the elements of a dynamically created set. An empty hash table of size N (for some suitable constant N) is constructed using an m-array comprehension:

```
def mk_empty_table () = {M_array (1,N) of
                         | [j] = MNil || j <- 1 to N} ;
```

Each bucket of the array is initialized to an empty mlist.

As with the marked? function in the GC1 solution, the member?_and_insert function must execute atomically to avoid duplicate traversals. This function tests whether an integer x is in the hash table and, if not, inserts it:

```
typeof member?_and_insert = (m_array (mlist int)) -> int -> bool ;

def member?_and_insert  table  x =
  { (l,u) = bounds table ;
    j = hash l x u;
    (b,ys') = member?_and_insert_list table![j] x ;
    table![j] = ys' ;
  In
    b } ;
```

In the first line in the block we extract l and u, the lower and upper index bounds of the table, and in the second line we hash the given integer index x into an index j in the range l to u (using some unspecified hash function). Then, we take the set of integers at index j and uses the member?_and_insert_list function to test if x is in that set and insert it if not. Finally, the (possibly) new set is put back and the boolean result returned.

Note that the list function that tests for membership, followed by conditional insertion, is *not* a simple composition of the member and insert functions on m-lists. The elements of the list must be tested and inserted in a single scan of the list to ensure atomicity. Otherwise, a node may be seen as unmarked by two processes, resulting in redundant traversals.

We modify our insert_m function from Section 2.5 to perform this simultaneous test for membership and insertion:

```
typeof member?_and_insert_list = (mlist int) -> int -> (bool,(mlist int)) ;

def member?_and_insert_list ys x =
  if (MNil? ys) then
    (False, MCons x MNil)
  else if (x == ys.MCons_1) then
    (True,ys)
  else
    { (b,ys') = member?_and_insert_list ys!MCons_2 x ;
      ys!MCons_2 = ys' ;
    In
      (b,ys) } ;
```

Note that the hash function can be applied to two integers `x1` and `x2` in parallel. If they hash to different indices, there is absolutely no interference between the two calls. Even if they hash to the same index, they may "pipeline" as discussed earlier.

GC2': A Mark Array

We can improve the implementation of the `visited` table even further if we know that the unique identifiers in the graph nodes are in some contiguous range, say 1 to N. In this case, the table can be implemented as an array of booleans, instead of a hash table, *i.e.*,

```
def mk_empty_table () = {m_array (1,N) of
                         | [j] = False || j <- 1 to N} ;

def member?_and_visited table x = { b = table![x] ;
                                    ---
                                    table![x] = True
                                  In
                                    b } ;
```

Note that in the pure functional program described next, the $O(1)$ access time of the hash and mark tables cannot be exploited. Implementing the `visited` table as a balanced binary tree is the best we can do.

4.3 GA1: A Functional Solution

Since nodes cannot be imperatively marked, the functional solution also uses a `visited` table to keep track of nodes that have already been traversed. This table is threaded through the traversal, as shown in the following program:

```
def rsum nd = { visited = TEmpty ;

                def aux (s,visited) (GNode x i nbs) =
                    if (member? x visited) then
                      (s,visited)
                    else
                      {  visited' = insert visited x ;
                      In
                         foldl  aux  (s+i,visited')  nbs } ;

                (s,visited') = aux (0,visited) nd
              In
                s } ;
```

The function `foldl` is similar to `map`, but passes partial results (the partial sum and visited table) to each successive call of `aux`. Here is the code for `foldl`:

```
def foldl f z Nil    = z
  | foldl f z (x:xs) = foldl f (f z x) xs ;
```

The `visited` table can be implemented as an ordered binary tree, with $\log n$ time for the `member?` and `insert` functions, assuming the tree is balanced:

```
type tree = TEmpty | TNode int tree tree ;

def member? TEmpty          x = False
  | member? (TNode y L R) x = if (x == y) then
                                True
                              else if (x < y) then
                                member? L x
                              else
                                member? R x ;

def insert TEmpty          x = TNode x TEmpty TEmpty
  | insert (TNode y L R) x = if (x == y) then
                               (TNode y L R)
                             else if (x < y) then
                               (TNode y (insert L x) R)
                             else
                               (TNode y L (insert R x)) ;
```

Critique

The `rsum` program is obscured by the "threading" the `visited` table through the traversal. Again, threading overspecifies the order in which the traversal is made; here, the order of insertions is determined by the function `foldl`. Conceptually, one imagines all outward edges from a node being explored in parallel, with a shared subnode being explored only by the first traversal that happens to arrive there (we don't care which one).[7]

[7] Readers who are familiar with parallel graph reduction will recognize that this is exactly what happens in a parallel graph reducer— a shared node is evaluated by the first process that arrives there, which also marks it as "in progress",

Note that here, unlike the histogram example, sharing is critical to ensure a polynomial time algorithm. Therefore, threading is unavoidable in purely functional solutions. In more complex problems, the threading required by functional programming further complicates the solution, adding extra parameters and return values and imposing unnecessary serialization.

The functional solution also introduces storage overhead. Each `insert` rebuilds the `visited` table along the path from the newly inserted leaf back to the root, allocating new tree nodes along the way. The total storage cost for the table over the complete graph traversal can therefore vary from $O(n \log n)$ to $O(n^2)$, depending on how well the tree is balanced. Including tree rebalancing operations introduces overhead that may be recouped over many operations.

4.4 Experimental Results

We ran tests on our simulator, running four versions of `rsum` on four graphs. The graphs each contained about 512 nodes, but differed widely in their topologies (amount of sharing). The four versions of `rsum` were:

GA1	The functional program with a `visited` table implemented as an ordered binary tree.
GC2	The M-structure program with a `visited` table implemented as a hash table of size 523.
GC2'	The M-structure program with a `visited` table, implemented as an array of booleans.
GC1	The M-structure program using mark fields in graph nodes.

For the functional version, the unique identifiers in the graph nodes were randomly generated so that the binary tree `visited` table would be roughly balanced, in order to show the numbers for the functional program in the best possible light. Random ID generation was also used for the hash and marks version, though it does not really matter for these versions. For the "array" version, IDs were integers in the range of 1 to n, the number of nodes in the graph, and the array of marks had the same index range.

The fundamental difference in heap store use for the four programs is in the `visited` tables. We modified the programs slightly from the text of the paper in order to measure this, *i.e.*, to separate heap usage for the `visited` table from heap usage for closures in higher order functions and tuples for multiple results. These changes do not affect the total instruction counts or parallelism very much.

The cost of originally building the graphs (storage and instructions) is not included because the graphs were built in a separate invocation before the application of `rsum`.

Figures 1 through 4 show the four graphs and the measurements for the four programs.

---

so that later-arriving processes will not duplicate the work.

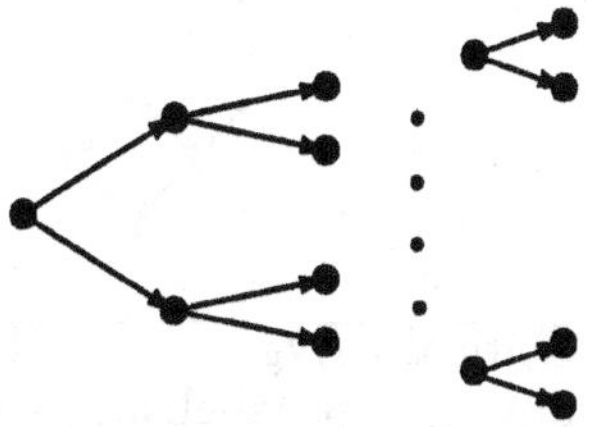

Program version	Total instructions executed	Critical path	Avg. parallelism	Heap store used (words)
GA1	480,123	90,605	5.3	15,934
GC2	102,244	4,280	23.9	2,072
GC2'	55,843	2,743	20.4	524
GC1	48,002	412	116.5	0

Figure 1: Reachable Sum on Graph0 (511 nodes).

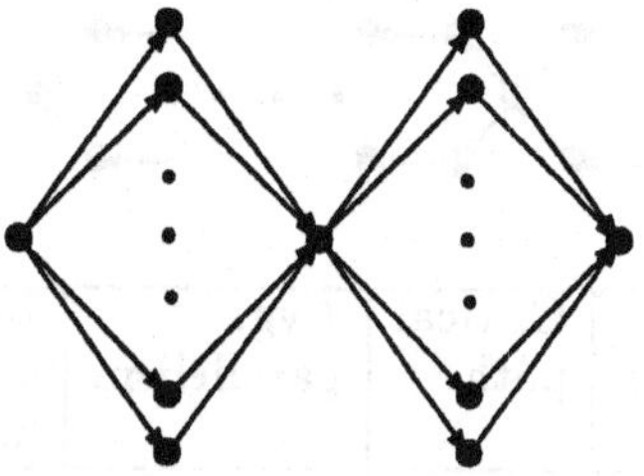

Program version	Total instructions executed	Critical path	Avg. parallelism	Heap store used (words)
GA1	594,323	124,276	4.8	17,305
GC2	177,062	9,271	19.1	2,959
GC2'	95,501	9,102	10.5	524
GC1	84,078	3,728	22.6	0

Figure 2: Reachable Sum on Graph1 (515 nodes).

Program version	Total instructions executed	Critical path	Avg. parallelism	Heap store used (words)
GA1	587,873	123,434	4.8	16,998
GC2	130,188	22,527	5.8	2,068
GC2'	68,933	12,799	5.4	524
GC1	59,902	11,596	5.2	0

Figure 3: Reachable Sum on Graph2 (511 nodes).

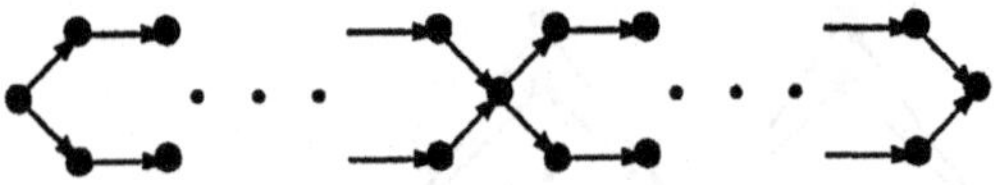

Program version	Total instructions executed	Critical path	Avg. parallelism	Heap store used (words)
GA1	549,169	103,917	5.3	18,550
GC2	103,456	28,844	3.6	2,076
GC2'	56,385	10,359	5.4	524
GC1	48,518	8,808	5.5	0

Figure 4: Reachable Sum on Graph3 (515 nodes).

4.4.1 Observations

Parallelism: Graph0 and Graph1 have a high degree of parallelism, *i.e.*, there is much branching without sharing; Graph2 is not very parallel (much branching, but also much sharing), and Graph3 is also not very parallel (not much branching). Nevertheless, the functional program is unable to exploit the parallelism in Graph0 and Graph1, because the threading of the `visited` table forces it to be practically sequential. All the other programs, however, were able to exploit the additional parallelism of those graphs.

Instruction count: The instruction counts for the functional program GA1 is highest, by over a factor of 10 from the most efficient version (marks).

Heap Store Used: The $O(n\log(n))$ heap store cost for the `visited` table in the functional program is apparent— it uses close to 10 times more heap store than its nearest rival (the hash program GC2). GC2 takes about 523 words for the hash array, plus 3 words (one cons cell) for each of the about 512 entries in the table, making a total of a little over 2000 words. The mark array GC2' program takes exactly 524 words for the array of booleans. GC1, which marks the nodes directly, allocates no store, but we should remember that we have already paid one word extra per graph node for the mark field, *i.e.*, a total of about 512 words.

Again, we point out that the functional program is being presented in it best possible light because (a) we are charging only one instruction for each heap allocation, and (b) we have set up the IDs to keep the `visited` tree balanced.

5 Discussion

In this section, our work on M-structures is put in the context of other work. First, we describe our preliminary experiences validating our simulation results on a real multiprocessor. Next, M-structures are briefly compared to other non-deterministic extensions to functional languages. Finally, a method for reasoning about M-structure programs is outlined.

5.1 Validation

In order to ensure that our simulations are reasonably accurate, we have also run all the above programs on Monsoon, a parallel machine with 64-bit, 10MIPS dataflow processors and 4 MWord I-structure memory units[16]. These processors are being built in partnership with Motorola, Inc. Our programs ran on a two-node prototype; a sixteen-node machine is expected to be available in June, 1991. The major unaccounted cost in our simulation is that of heap allocation, since the simulator counts each heap allocation as a single instruction. In Monsoon, therefore, instruction counts are higher than in our simulations, but the overall trends are the same (the Monsoon figures are too preliminary to publish at this time).

5.2 Nondeterminism in Other Languages

Since Approach C admits non-deterministic, parallel programs, it is interesting to compare it to Approaches A and B extended to allow non-determinacy. Several non-deterministic extensions have been proposed for Approach A, such as amb[19], streams[17], and managers[2, 4]. To retain the flavor of functional programming, these solutions are *process-oriented*: many processes share information over an *implicit* communication channel. This channel merges updates and synchronizes accesses. Each process can then be viewed as a state transformation function that maps successive values on the shared channel. Thus, each process can be analyzed as a function, with only the aggregate behavior producing non-determinism.

Approach B allows imperative operations but ensures determinacy through a sequential, strict control paradigm. Extensions for parallelism, such as fork and join in Scheme and ML, require explicit synchronization constructs to be used by the programmer. Proving such programs correct is difficult, and much of the original declarativeness of the program is destroyed.

M-structures are a *data-oriented* approach to non-determinism, which provides the efficiency of Approach B. In addition, M-structures provide the implicit synchronization, which guarantees the atomicity of operations on individual elements of data structures. This fine-grained atomicity allows for substantial parallelism in programs that share data without additional synchronization complexity. The result is highly declarative, efficient programs.

5.3 Reasoning about M-structure Programs

The attractiveness of an implicitly parallel, non-strict language like Id is that programmers can write parallel, determinate programs without annotations or explicit synchronization. Reasoning about determinate Id programs follows in the traditions of functional programming: functions map expressions to values, and correctness proved by equational reasoning.

M-structures introduce indeterminacy, and thus cannot use equational reasoning. Instead, the correctness of an M-structure program is related to the notion of serializability in databases. That is, correctness is defined in terms of the history of values held in an M-structure cell. In a correct program, the sequence of cell values is a member of an allowed set of sequences. Serializability is one notion of correctness, requiring that any parallel execution corresponds to some interleaving of its update operations. Serializability ensures that M-structure updates appear atomic and sequential.

Determining the possible histories of an M-structure cell requires an operational understanding of Id. The set of M-structure histories is determined by the possible orderings of take and put operations on the cell. Since Id is an implicitly parallel language, the order of operations is a partial order, formed by a precedence relation $\prec$ between operations. That is, given operations a and b in program P, if $a \prec b$, then a will execute before b under any correct execution of P. Precedence between two operations is determined by three things: data dependence, control constructs, and data structures.

Data dependence defines precedence between strict operators. For example,

```
{i = a+b;
 In
   i*i};
```

yields `+≺*`, since the multiplication is strict in the result of the addition.

Control constructs define precedence between a predicate and the selected expression. For example, in the following `if` expression,

```
if i==0 then
  i+1
else
  i+2
```

the equality test precedes the addition in both arms, *i.e.,* `==≺+`.

Finally, M-structures define a precedence relation, since a take is always preceded by some put. A formal description of precedence has been developed by the authors, based on operational semantics for Id given in [1].

We now outline a correctness proof of the histogram program HC that uses M-structures. We wish to show that each cell in the histogram contains the sum of the number of leaves in the tree with its index. We can prove this by showing that the histogram is initialized to 0, that each leaf is reached once, and that each update is atomic. Since the tree traversal is a simple recursion, the second step can be proved by traditional inductive means.

First, let us address the atomicity of the updates. When a leaf is reached, the expression `H![i] = H![i]+1` is evaluated. This corresponds to a take, an addition, and a put. Put and addition are strict in their arguments, therefore `take≺+≺put`. M-structure synchronization guarantees that exactly one take operation will get a value after a put. This value will be incremented and put back, as defined above, potentially satisfying another take. This continues until all increments complete. Thus, the precedence of this expression, and M-structure synchronization yield some interleaving of atomic updates.

To show that M-structure cells are initialized correctly. When an M-structure is allocated, its elements are initially empty; the constructor (the array comprehension) initializes these elements by putting a value in each element. In this case, the allocate is followed by a put with the value 0. Since any take must be preceded by a put, no increment operation will begin until the cell has been initialized.

Therefore, the history of histogram cell i is

`alloc≺put 0≺take≺+≺put≺take≺ +≺put≺ ··· ≺put`

which always corresponds to a serialization of the update operations. Since addition is commutative and associative, serialization is sufficient to determine that the cell has the correct count after the last put, regardless of the order of the increments. As expected, eager evaluation allows this proof strategy to use local assertions about initialization and update operations.

Note that M-structure synchronization enforces this precedence relation even if a take operation is invoked before a put operation, or several takes are issued simultaneously. The implicit synchronization provided by M-structures allows the set of all possible interleavings to be reduced to only the set allowed by the precedence relation. Proving the correctness of this set depends on the application.

Reasoning about M-structure programs involving more than a single cell is more complex, but follows the same principles. In this case, atomicity involves synchronizing several M-structure operations to prevent processes from interfering and to avoid deadlock. To aid the development of such programs, the authors are developing constructs for encapsulating M-structure operations to ensure atomicity. Such encapsulation has been shown to be useful elsewhere [6, 9] for reasoning about parallel programs that share state.

6 Conclusion

Although the results presented in this paper may be viewed as a recommendation to use Approach C in programming, it may also be viewed as a challenge for the functional programming community to come up with new purely functional notations and optimization analyses that match the declarativeness and efficiency of Approach C. There is some precedent for this kind of development. Some years ago, we proposed a non-functional construct called "I-structures", showing how they cleanly overcame certain limitations in expressive power and efficiency in functional languages [5]. This stimulated much debate and research, leading to the purely functional "array comprehension" notation in Id, which eliminates much of the need for I-structures. Perhaps this paper on M-structures can serve a similar role and lead to new developments in pure functional languages.

Acknowledgements: This paper describes research performed at the Laboratory for Computer Science of the Massachusetts Institute of Technology. Funding for the Laboratory is provided in part by the Advanced Research Projects Agency of the Department of Defense under the Office of Naval Research contract N00014-89-J-1988. Paul Barth is supported by a fellowship from Schlumberger Technology Corporation.

References

[1] Z. M. Ariola and Arvind. P-TAC: A Parallel Intermediate Language. In *Proceedings of the Fourth Conference on Functional Programming Languages and Computer Architecture, London*, pages 230–242, September 1989.

[2] Arvind and J. D. Brock. Resource Managers in Functional Programming. *Journal of Parallel and Distributed Computing*, 1(1), June 1984.

[3] Arvind, D. Culler, and G. Maa. Assessing the Benefits of Fine-Grained Parallelism in Dataflow Programs. *International Journal of Supercomputing Applications*, 2(3), 1988.

[4] Arvind, K. P. Gostelow, and W. Plouffe. Indeterminacy, Monitors and Dataflow. *Operating Systems Review (Proceedings of the Sixth ACM Symposium on Operating Systems Principles)*, 11(5), November 1977.

[5] Arvind, R. S. Nikhil, and K. K. Pingali. I-Structures: Data Structures for Parallel Computing. *ACM Transactions on Programming Languages and Systems*, 11(4):598–632, October 1989.

[6] F. W. Burton. Encapsulating Non-determinacy in an Abstract Type with Determinate Semantics. *Journal of Functional Programming*, 1(1), January 1991.

[7] C. Clack and S. L. Peyton Jones. The Four-Stroke Reduction Engine. In *Proceedings of the 1986 ACM Conference on Lisp and Functional Programming, Cambridge, Mass.*, pages 220–232, August 4-6 1986.

[8] R. H. Halstead. Multilisp: A Language for Concurrent Symbolic Computation. *ACM Transactions on Programming Languages and Systems*, 7(4):501–539, October 1985.

[9] C. A. R. Hoare. Monitors: An Operating System Structuring Concept. *Communications of the ACM*, 10(10):549–557, October 1974.

[10] P. Hudak. A Semantic Model of Reference Counting and Its Abstraction. In S. Abramsky and C. Hankin, editors, *Abstract Interpretation of Declarative Languages*, Computers and Their Applications, chapter 3, pages 45–62. Ellis Horwood Limited, Chichester, West Sussex, England, 1987.

[11] P. Hudak and P. Wadler (editors). Report on the Programming Language Haskell, A Non-strict Purely Functional Language (Version 1.0). Technical Report YALEU/DCS/RR777, Yale University, Department of Computer Science, Apr. 1990.

[12] J. Milewski. Functional Data Structures as Updatable Objects. *IEEE Transactions on Software Engineering*, 16(12):1427–1432, December 1990.

[13] R. S. Nikhil. Id (Version 90.0) Reference Manual. Technical Report CSG Memo 284-1, MIT Laboratory for Computer Science, 545 Technology Square, Cambridge, MA 02139, USA, July 1990.

[14] R. S. Nikhil. The Parallel Programming Language Id and its Compilation for Parallel Machines. In *Proc. Workshop on Massive Parallelism, Amalfi, Italy, October 1989*. Academic Press, 1990 (to appear).

[15] R. S. Nikhil and Arvind. *Programming in Id: a parallel programming language*. 1990. Textbook on implicit parallel programming. In preparation.

[16] G. M. Papadopoulos and D. E. Culler. Monsoon: An Explicit Token Store Architecture. In *Proc. 17th. Intl. Symp. on Computer Architecture, Seattle, WA*, May 1990.

[17] W. Stoye. Message-Based Functional Operating Systems. *Science of Computer Programming*, 6:291–311, 1986.

[18] K. R. Traub. Sequential Implementation of Lenient Programming Languages. Technical Report TR-417, MIT Laboratory for Computer Science, 545 Technology Square, Cambridge, MA 02139, May 1988. Ph.D. thesis.

[19] D. Turner. Functional Programming and Communicating Processes. In *Proceedings of PARLE: Parallel Architectures and Languages, Europe, Volume II, Eindhoven, The Netherlands, Springer-Verlag Lecture Notes In Computer Science, Volume 259*, pages 54–74, June 1987.

List Comprehensions in Agna, A Parallel Persistent Object System

Michael L. Heytens*
Rishiyur S. Nikhil†
Massachusetts Institute of Technology

Abstract

List comprehensions are structurally similar to SQL, the standard declarative query language for relational databases. Unlike SQL, they are more general, and are embedded seamlessly into powerful programming languages. Thus, functional languages with list comprehensions are attractive as query languages for persistent object systems, where database objects and queries are not distinguished from other objects and computations. We have implemented such a system, called AGNA. In this paper, we describe optimizations on list comprehensions in AGNA. We use techniques borrowed from relational databases, as well as techniques specific to our parallel implementation. Experimental results show a dramatic impact on performance. A comparison with a commercial relational database system and with an experimental parallel relational system indicates that the performance of AGNA approaches that of state of the art relational database systems.

1 Introduction

Many modern functional languages have a construct called the "list comprehension." While offering no fundamentally new expressive power, it provides an elegant and concise notation for expressing certain types of computations on lists.

The standard declarative database query language today is SQL, which evolved in the context of relational databases [10]. A strong similarity between SQL and list comprehensions has been recognized for some time [15]. List comprehensions are more powerful than SQL, however, because of their support for general computation. Also, they are well integrated with other parts of the language (*e.g.*, they may include arbitrary function calls and recursion, may be embedded within

*Room 36-667, 77 Massachusetts Avenue, Cambridge MA 02139, USA; Internet: heytens@caf.mit.edu
†Lab for Computer Science, 545 Technology Square, Cambridge, MA 02139, USA; Internet: nikhil@lcs.mit.edu

procedures, *etc.*), which is in marked contrast to the embedding of SQL in languages such as C or Ada. It is thus natural to consider a functional language with list comprehensions as a database query language ([15], see also [7]).

The close correspondence between list comprehensions and relational languages facilitates the application of relational optimization techniques to functional database systems. In his thesis, ([21]) Trinder shows how standard algebraic and implementation-based optimizations can be applied to list comprehension queries.

In this paper, we describe the optimization and translation of list comprehension queries in AGNA, a parallel persistent object system that we have built. We describe a number of standard optimizations, and some that are designed specifically for our parallel implementation. Experimental uniprocessor and multiprocessor results indicate the effectiveness of the optimizations. We compare our results with results obtained on a commercial relational database system and published results for other parallel database systems.

In Section 2 we describe the AGNA language (or at least that part of it that is relevant for this paper). In Section 3 we describe the optimizations for list comprehensions based on standard SQL optimizations, and we compare the uniprocessor performance of AGNA with that of a uniprocessor commercial relational database system. In Section 4 we describe the optimizations for list comprehensions based on our parallel.implementation, and compare the performance of AGNA on a parallel machine to published performance results of an experimental parallel relational database system. Finally, we conclude in Section 5 with some discussion of our results and prospects for the future.

2 Background

In AGNA, a database is viewed as a top-level persistent environment of bindings that associates names with persistent objects. The objects in the database may be of any type— scalars, complex objects, lists, procedures, indexed mappings, *etc.*

A transaction `(xact ...)` is a construct executed in this environment, and may contain definitions of new types, definitions of new bindings, declarative update specifications, and *queries* (expressions to be evaluated). In this paper we concentrate only on queries, which are pure functional expressions[1].

User-defined object types may be introduced into a database environment via the `type` form. For example, the following definitions introduce two new types and some of their fields (we currently use a Lisp-like notation to avoid detailed syntax design).

```
(type STUDENT (extent)
 ((name     <=>  STRING)
  (courses *<=>* COURSE)
  (gpa       =>  NUMBER)
  (year      =>  NUMBER)))
```

```
(type COURSE (extent)
 ((name   *<=> STRING)
  (number <=> STRING)
  (units   => NUMBER)))
```

[1]Briefly, an update specification is a declarative specification of the database visible to subsequent transactions, expressed as a function of its current state. For details, please see [17] and [12].

These declarations introduce new object type names `STUDENT` and `COURSE` along with the name and type of each field, whether they are single- or multi-valued, and whether they have single- or multi-valued inverses. For example, the student `name` field records a single string value, and supports a unique inverse mapping strings to students. The `courses` field is multi-valued, with a multi-valued inverse mapping a course to a collection of students. The basic operations available for manipulating structured objects, of both pre- and user-defined types, are allocation, field selection, and field definition. A field of an object may be read using the expression `(select` *object type field*`)`.

The `(extent)` qualifications in the type definitions declare that persistent extents containing all students and courses are to be maintained automatically, *i.e.*, every construction of a `student` or `course` object is automatically inserted into the corresponding system-maintained extent (these insertions are not visible in the current transaction). The expressions `(all student)` and `(all course)` use these extents, and evaluate to lists of all students and all courses, respectively. Such lists (extents of declared types) are also called "base extents" because they are automatically maintained by the system, in contrast to lists that are produced as results of some computation. While the system chooses efficient internal representations for base extents, they are accessed in programs exactly like other lists.

New functions may be introduced into the database environment using the `define` form. For example, the following transaction extends the top-level environment with a function `courses-with-name` that maps a string `s` to a list of courses with that name (using the generic `invert` form for inverted fields):

```
(xact
  (define courses-with-name
    (lambda (s) (invert course name s))))
```

List comprehensions in AGNA have the form:

```
(all  body-expression
      generator-or-filter
      ...
      generator-or-filter)
```

Each generator has the form `(`*identifier list-expression*`)`, and each filter has the form `(where` *boolean-expression*`)`. For example, here is a query to find the names of all first year students taking software engineering:

```
(xact
  (all (student-name s)
    (s (students-with-year 1))
    (c (courses-with-name "Software Engineering"))
    (where (member c (student-courses s)))))
```

While providing the conciseness and elegance of SQL, list comprehensions are more general because: (a) they allow arbitrary generator lists (that is, the lists over which identifiers such as `s` and `c` range may be arbitrary expressions, not just "base" extents), (b) they allow arbitrary predicates, not just arithmetic and string comparisons, and (c) the returned values can be of arbitrary type and computed using arbitrary functions, not just field projections. Further, since list comprehensions are expressions just like any other type of expression in the language, they may be embedded in procedures, embedded in recursive definitions, *etc.*

Non-strict, implicitly parallel, eager semantics

AGNA pursues parallelism very aggressively:

- In a block:

  ```
  (letrec ((x1 e1)
             ...
           (xN eN))
     eBody)
  ```

  all expressions `e1`, ..., `eN` and `eBody` are evaluated in parallel, and the value of `eBody` may be returned as soon as it is available, even if the other expressions have not finished evaluating.

- In a primitive application:

  ```
  (+ e1 e2)
  (cons e1 e2)
  ...
  ```

  all arguments are evaluated in parallel, and some primitives may even return a result value before the arguments have finished evaluating (for example, `cons` and other object constructors).

- In a function application:

  ```
  (ef e1 ... eN)
  ```

  all expressions are evaluated in parallel; the function (value of `ef`) may be invoked as soon as it is known, and it may even return a result, before the arguments are known.

- In a conditional expression:

  ```
  (if e1 e2 e3)
  ```

  the predicate `e1` is evaluated to a boolean value, after which one of the expressions `e2` or `e3` is evaluated and returned as the value of the expression.

In other words, *everything* is evaluated in parallel, except as controlled by conditionals and data dependencies. The semantics are:

- non-strict, but not lazy (we may evaluate expressions even if not needed for the result);
- eager, but not call-by-value (functions may be invoked before arguments are evaluated to values); and
- implicitly parallel (the programmer does not specify what must be done in parallel).

These semantics are borrowed from the Id programming language [16]. Programs evaluated under this regime often show massive amounts of parallelism. Id and AGNA are unique in this respect— we know of no other language that has these semantics or pursues parallelism this aggressively.

3 SQL-like optimizations

Compilation of AGNA transactions occurs in three major phases— source-to-source translation of the original transaction text, translation into dataflow program graphs, and translation into code for a multi-threaded abstract machine called P-RISC. Substantial code optimizations are performed at each stage.

The optimization and translation of list comprehensions takes place during the first phase of compilation. The primary function of this phase is to rewrite the input transaction text to a simpler form. While the AGNA query language is purely functional, some of the translations performed in this phase (and described in this paper) introduce non-functional constructs that are part of the internal intermediate languages.

Combination of unary operations

A well-known algebraic transformation performed in relational database systems combines sequences of unary operations, applying them as a group, in order to avoid multiple traversals over large collections of data. This general transformation is also useful for improving list comprehensions. For example, consider the following query to find the names of all students with a GPA of at least 3.9:

```
(all (select s student name)
  (s (all student))
  (where (>= (select s student gpa) 3.9)))
```

A straightforward translation of this query first filters the list of all students, producing an intermediate list, over which the name selection function is then mapped.

```
(map (lambda (s) (select s student name))                              (T1)
     (filter (lambda (s) (>= (select s student gpa) 3.9))
             (all student)))
```

While this translation is simple and elegant, it can be improved by eliminating the construction and traversal of the intermediate list. This can be accomplished by combining the list filtering and mapping (two unary operations), and performing them both in a single pass over the student list. Here is a translation which includes this improvement.

```
(letrec (((p s) (>= (select s student gpa) 3.9))
         ((t s) (select s student name))
         ((f l p t r) (if (nil? l)
                          r
                          (let ((x (hd l)))
                            (f (tl l) p t (if (p x) (cons (t x) r) r))))))
  (f (all student) p t nil))
```
(T2)

The three bindings define two unary functions `p` and `t` and one 4-argument, tail-recursive function `f` that performs the traversal.

We can summarize the principles behind this optimization in the laws given below (expressed using a more readable notation than our Lisp-like transaction language), which are used as rewrite rules. Each rule converts two list traversals into a single traversal.

```
map f ∘ filter p    = foldr (λ x ys.  IF p x THEN f(x):ys
                                      ELSE ys)
                            []

filter p ∘ map f    = foldr (λ x ys.  LET y = f(x)
                                      IN
                                        IF p y THEN y:ys
                                        ELSE ys)
                            []

map f ∘ map g       = map (f ∘ g)

filter p ∘ filter q = filter (λ x.  p x ∧ q x)
```

Related transformations to eliminate construction and traversal of intermediate data structures are described by Wadler in his more general "deforestation" technique [22].

In addition, we use the following transformation which is only valid when the order of elements in a list is not relevant (this is indeed the case in our database queries):

```
foldr (λ x ys.(f x)++ys) []   =   foldl (λ ys x.(f x)++ys) []
```

This transformation converts `foldr` into `foldl`, which is sometimes preferable because it is iterative instead of recursive.

Low-level filtering of base extents

For the filtering and transformation of an arbitrary list of objects, the translation scheme given above is optimal with respect to the number of cons operations performed to produce the result list (exactly one cons per output element). The value of the expression `(all student)` is obtained by scanning over the file that stores student objects and building a list in the volatile heap. When this list is available, it is then filtered and transformed in one scan.

However, a substantial improvement in performance can be obtained when the generator expression is a base extent, and the filters are simple predicates on the object fields. In this case, the filtering may be performed during file scanning, avoiding even the construction of the original list.

As in all database systems, AGNA is based on an "object storage system" that implements files and file scanning. The services provided by this module are similar to those provided in the Research Storage System (RSS) in System R [2], and WiSS, the Wisconsin Storage System [8]. The object storage system implements sequential object files, secondary BTREE and hash indexes, sequential and index object scans with predicates, and management of the cache of file pages. All persistent data access is performed through the object storage system, thereby insulating higher levels of the system from details of secondary storage such as data layout, whether access is through the OS file system or directly to a raw disk, *etc.*

The scan predicates supported by the object storage system are lists of conditions of the form $S\ \theta\ v$, where S is a field name, θ is a relational operator such as equality, and v is a value. We do not allow arbitrary AGNA predicates to be evaluated during the file scan because we would like predicate evaluation to be "quick", *i.e.,* matched to the speed at which the file scan is performed.

In the example query above, the condition describing the students of interest (GPA $\geq$ 3.9) is suitable for translation to such a low-level predicate, which we can then use in the scan of student objects. By performing the filtering within the storage system, a compact representation of the student extent (8K byte pages of objects) is scanned and filtered in an efficient manner. Here is a translation that incorporates this improvement:

```
(let ((pred (cons (make-condition gpa-slotid '>= 3.9) nil)))
  (map (lambda (s) (select s student name))                    (T3)
       (filter-extent STUDENT pred)))
```

The extent filtering is performed by primitive procedure `filter-extent`, which takes a type identifier and a predicate object (a list of condition objects). In this case the predicate consists of a single condition, which is created by procedure `make-condition`. As we shall see soon, this use of low-level filtering provides a significant improvement in performance.

Another kind of improvement is possible for this query. Since the body expression simply projects the name field out of the student objects, we could easily pass this information down to `filter-extent`, which could then build a list of names directly, eliminating the need for the second pass (the `map`). While AGNA currently does not perform this optimization, we could add it easily.

Use of indexes

One of the most important optimizations performed by relational systems is the use of efficient index structures. An index structure provides fast access to the records or objects in a file with a particular field value. Studies of relational systems have shown that the effective exploitation of indexes is essential for achieving good performance for a range of queries[5]. The experimental results presented in this paper indicate that the effective use of index structures is equally important for implementing list comprehension queries efficiently.

The object storage system in AGNA supports two types of secondary indexes—BTREE and hash. The decision to build an index on an object field is based on a user-supplied annotation in the type declaration. All user-defined object types have a "base" object file storing persistent objects. Index files for a field map field values to pointers to objects in the base file. By default, hash indexes are created for all fields with inverse mappings (*i.e.*, `*<=` and `<=` fields). This default behavior can be changed, however, by annotations in the `type` declaration. For example, if the student type were defined as follows:

```
(type STUDENT (extent)
  ((name   <=> STRING)
   (gpa     => FLOAT)
   (year  *<=> INTEGER (index btree))
   (bdate *<=> INTEGER (index btree))
   ...))
```

then three indexes would be created: a hash index on `name`, a BTREE index on `year`, and a BTREE index on `bdate`. In this example, BTREE indexes on year and birthdate may be preferred because of their ability to support range queries efficiently. For example, a BTREE index on `bdate` can be used to find all students with birthdates in a particular range, while a hash index can not be utilized in such a query. For the `name` field, on the other hand, a hash index may be preferred because of its ability to perform "exact match" name lookups more efficiently than a BTREE.

For a query which filters a base extent, there may be multiple "access paths" to the data. For example:

```
(all (select s student name)
  (s (all student))
  (where (and (== 1 (select s student year))
              (and (>= (select s student gpa) 3.9)
                   (< (select s student bdate) 720101)))))
```

There are at least three ways to implement this query: (1) scan the base `student` file with a predicate consisting of all three conditions; (2) use the index on `year` to locate first-year students, then apply the remaining conditions to the corresponding objects in the base file; and (3) use the index on `bdate` to locate students with birthdates before 1/1/72, then apply the remaining conditions to the corresponding objects in the base file.

Our compiler uses the following heuristics, listed in order of preference, to select an implementation strategy.

1. If a condition of the form $S = v$ exists on a field with a hash index, then use the index to find all objects with value v. Apply the remaining conditions to the objects returned. If conditions exist for more than one such field, then

choose a <= field (unique inverse) over a *<= field. If more than one possibility still exists, then pick one arbitrarily.

2. If a condition of the form $S\ \theta\ v$ exists on a field with a BTREE index and θ is not the inequality operator, then use the index to find objects satisfying all such conditions on S. Apply the remaining conditions to the objects returned. If conditions exist for more than one such field, say S_1 and S_2, then use the following four steps to select one. (1) If a condition involving the equality operator exists for one field and not the other then choose the field with the equality condition. (2) If one field has a single-valued inverse (<=) and the other has a multiple-valued inverse (*<=), then choose the one with the single-valued inverse. (3) Choose more restrictive condition sets over less restrictive ones. For example, $S_1 > v_1$ and $S_1 < v_2$ is more restrictive than $S_2 > v_1$. (4) Pick a field arbitrarily.

3. If Rules 1 and 2 are not applicable, then simply scan the entire base file for objects which satisfy all conditions.

More sophisticated strategies are certainly possible, taking into consideration such things as the number of objects in the base extent, the number of blocks or units of disk allocation occupied by the base and index files, histograms describing distributions of field values, *etc.*; AGNA does not currently implement them.

The access path selected by the compiler is passed as arguments to `filter-extent-inverted` indicating the unique field identifier and the type of index to use (there may be more than one). For the example query above, all first year students are located, and then the conditions on GPA and birthdate are applied. All three conditions are applied within the object storage system, rather than explicitly materializing lists and filtering them. Here is the translation:

```
(let ((pred (cons (make-condition year-slotid '== 1)
                  (cons (make-condition gpa-slotid '>= 3.9)
                        (cons (make-condition bdate-slotid '< 720101)      (T4)
                              nil)))))
  (map (lambda (s) (select s student name))
       (filter-extent-inverted STUDENT year-slotid BTREE pred)))
```

Experimental Results

To demonstrate the relative effectiveness of the optimizations discussed in this section, we executed the different list comprehension translations on a uniprocessor version of AGNA running on a Sun 4/490 workstation with 128 Mb of memory and an HP 97549 disk. The test database that we used contained 100,000 student objects. The student type was defined as follows:

```
(type STUDENT (extent)
((name    <=> (STRING 32))
 (gpa      => FLOAT)
 (bdate1 *<=> INTEGER (index btree))
 (bdate2   => INTEGER)))
```

The distribution of GPA values was such that 10000 students (10%) had GPAs of at least 3.9. The result lists were built in the heap and were not traversed by the top-level `print` procedure (*i.e.*, the timings do not include the time to print the result).

Translation T1 (build student list, filter and transform it):	163 seconds
Translation T2 (combine map and filter):	161 seconds
Translation T3 (filter during object retrieval):	20 seconds

The final experiment that we performed on the uniprocessor version of AGNA finds all students with birthdates in a particular range:

```
(all s
  (s (all student))
  (where (and (> (select s student bdate1) v1)
              (< (select s student bdate1) v2))))
```

Values v_1 and v_2 were chosen so that 1000 students were selected by the query (1% of all students). The query was also repeated using `bdate2` instead of `bdate1`. Fields `bdate1` and `bdate2` contained identical values, so that the answers were the same. In the first case, the optimizer exploits the `bdate1` index, whereas in the second case, the system must scan the entire file of student objects.

1% indexed selection (using `bdate1`):	0.25 secs
1% non-indexed selection (using `bdate2`):	9.00 secs

The results of these tests indicate the importance of efficient filtering and indexing in the implementation of list comprehension queries in AGNA.

Comparison with INGRES

We also ran these queries on INGRES version 6.3, a modern commercial relational database system. We built a corresponding database with the same size, and ran it on the same hardware platform (Sun 4/490, 128 Mb memory, HP 97549 disk). The SQL equivalent of the query on `gpa` is:

```
SELECT name
FROM   student
WHERE  gpa >= 3.9
```

The INGRES timings were:

`gpa` query:	5.9 secs
1% indexed selection (using `bdate1`):	0.4 secs
1% non-indexed selection (using `bdate2`):	5.0 secs

These results indicate that even on a uniprocessor, AGNA is well within shooting distance of commercial relational systems on comparable queries. Further, we have an advantage over SQL in that AGNA's list comprehensions are part of a full functional language, so that the user can smoothly extend queries to perform arbitrary computation.

4 Optimizations for parallelism

Our implementation of AGNA is designed primarily for MIMD multi-processors consisting of processor-memory elements (PMEs), with or without attached disks, interconnected via a high-speed network (see Figure 1). The network may be a bus, in small multiprocessors, or a switching network in larger machines.

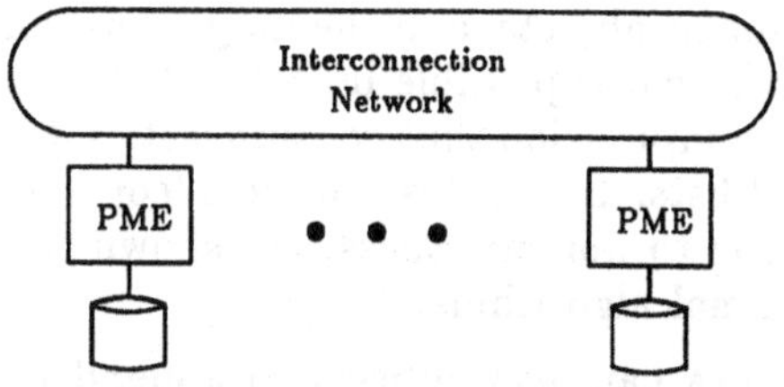

Figure 1: Machine organization.

While a number of object distribution strategies are possible, we currently distribute objects in a random fashion across all PMEs. In other words, `(allocate` *t*`)` allocates an object of type *t* on a PME chosen randomly. This strategy can be expected to provide a fairly uniform distribution of objects across the machine. The files at each PME (*i.e.*, the base and index files) are organized as described in the previous section.

Non-strictness, parallelism, and open lists

The non-strict semantics in AGNA provide many opportunities for parallel execution. Consider translation T1 from the previous section, repeated here:

```
(map (lambda (s) (select s student name))
     (filter (lambda (s) (>= (select s student gpa) 3.9))
             (all student)))
```

In a strict implementation, we must build the entire student list (*i.e.*, evaluate `(all student)`), filter it, and then perform the `map`. Each operation must execute entirely before the next one may begin. With the non-strictness in AGNA, as soon as the first cons cell in the student list is allocated, a reference to it can be returned as the result of `(all student)` (shown in Figure 2). A reference to a student object is stored in the head of the list, while the tail is left empty (⊥ in the figure).

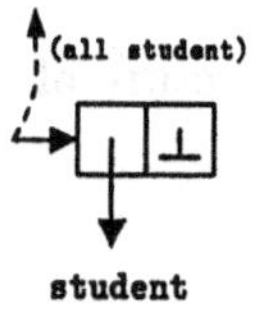

Figure 2: First cons cell in student list.

Construction of the remainder of the student list and the filter operation may then proceed in parallel. If the filter operation attempts to read the tail of a cons cell that is empty (*i.e.*, one that contains ⊥), then it simply blocks, waiting for a value to be stored there. When the write finally arrives, the blocked read operation is notified, allowing the list traversal to continue. Cons cells and other data structures in AGNA have single-assignment semantics, so we can be assured that all readers of a data structure element will receive the same value.

A similar kind of parallelism also exists between the filter operation, which produces a filtered list of student objects, and the map operation, which consumes it. In fact, this form of parallelism is possible in AGNA between *any* computation which produces a list, and a computation that consumes it, not just those involving extent lists, or filtered extent lists. In [1], this producer/consumer parallelism, and other forms of parallelism due to non-strictness, are shown to be pervasive, even in programs that use traditional algorithms.

The non-strictness in AGNA can also be used to append lists efficiently. Say, for example, that we want to append lists `L1` and `L2`. By choosing representations for `L1` and `L2` that embody two key ideas, we can append the lists in $O(1)$ time while using no additional storage. The first idea is to leave the tail of the last cons cell in each list empty. This will allow us to link the end of `L1` directly to the head of `L2` using no additional storage (*i.e.*, we don't have to build any intermediate lists). The second key idea is to maintain a direct reference not only to the first cons cell in each list, but also to the last one as well. This will allow us to locate the end of each list in constant time, so that we can link `L1` to `L2`, and terminate `L2` by storing `nil` in the tail of its last cons cell.

A representation for lists which includes these two ideas is called an *open list*. Open lists, which are closely related to difference lists in logic programming, can be represented as a cons cell containing two references A1 and A2, as shown in Figure 3. Internally, the structure consists of a list in which the tail of the last cons cell is empty. A1 points at the first cell and A2 points at the last cell (these may in fact be the same cell, if there is only one element in the list). With `L1` and `L2` represented as open lists, we can append them and return the result list as follows.

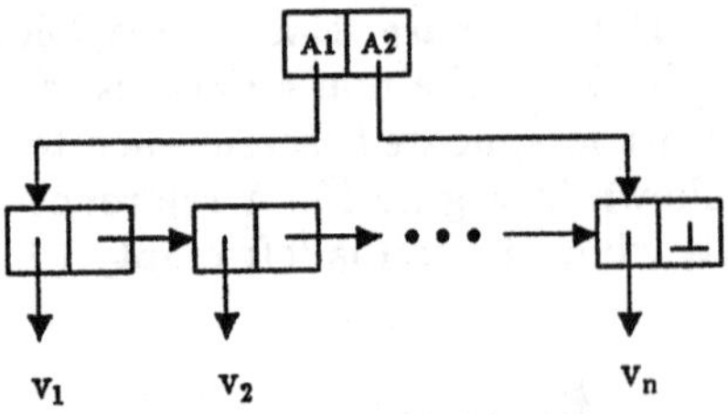

Figure 3: The structure of an open list.

```
(par
  (set-cons-tl (tl L1) (hd L2))
  (set-cons-tl (tl L2) Nil)
  (hd L1))
```

Par is a construct which evaluates all component expressions in parallel, returning the value of the last one. The first call to procedure `set-cons-tl` stores a reference to the head of `L2` in the last cons cell of `L1`. The second call to `set-cons-tl` terminates the list by storing `Nil` in the tail of the last cons cell in `L2`. The final expression returns the result list, which is not an open list.

Exploiting the locality of data

In a parallel environment, performance of a query can often be improved dramatically if the locality of the data being queried can be exploited. This is especially true in a persistent object system, where the volume of data may be large (*e.g.*, terabytes).

We start with a very simple example:

```
(all student)
```

i.e., an expression that simply evaluates to the list of all students. Student objects are distributed over the various PMEs of the parallel machine. The basic idea is for each PME to construct a list of all its students, and then to append these lists together. However, we would like the PMEs to work in parallel, and for the list-appending to be very efficient, *i.e.*, we wish to avoid constructing any intermediate lists.

Each PME executes the following procedure (we will see in a moment how it is persuaded to do this):

```
(local-extent2 STUDENT rest)
```

producing the result shown in Figure 4. Because of the non-strict semantics in

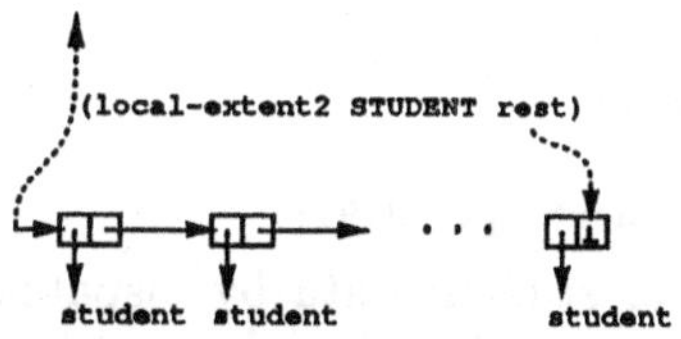

Figure 4: Local extent constructed on each PME.

AGNA we can construct the local list of student objects before we know the value of the `rest` argument. The last cons cell simply remains empty. As soon as the first cons cell is allocated, a reference to it can be returned as the result of `local-extent2`. When the value of `rest` arrives, which may be much later, it gets stored into the last cons cell.

Now, we step up one level to see the implementation of `(all student)`. Conceptually, the appending of the lists is accomplished by structuring the computation thus:

```
(foldr (lambda (j rest) (APPLY PME j local-extent2 STUDENT rest))
       Nil
       pmes)
```

`Pmes` is a list of PME numbers. The form:

```
(APPLY PME j f e1 ... eN)
```

evaluates the expression `(f e1 ... eN)` on PME j. Thus, the overall structure of the computation may be seen in Figure 5. The `foldr` computation runs on

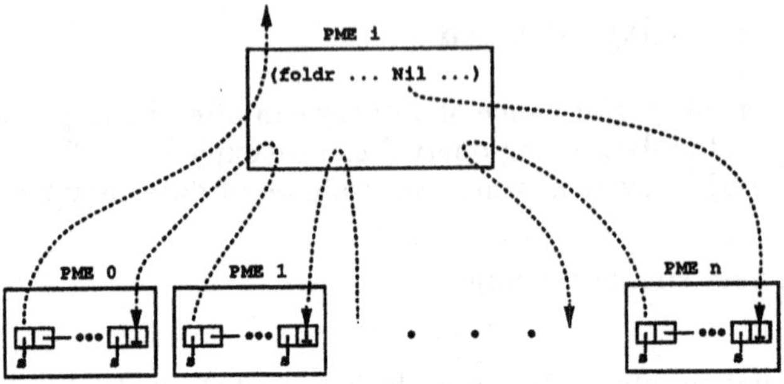

Figure 5: Local extent constructed on each PME.

some PME i, and initiates the `local-extent2` computations on each PME (including its own PME). Because of non-strictness, all these computations can proceed in parallel, even though each one does not yet have the value of its `rest` parameter. Further, each PME j can return the reference to the head of its sublist as soon as it is allocated; this reference is passed on by `foldr` as the `rest` parameter for the computation in PME $j-1$, where it is stored in the tail of the last cons cell.

The basic strategy used to implement `(all student)` can also be used to implement filtering of base extents. Consider the following query from the previous section.

```
(all (select s student name)
  (s (all student))
  (where (>= (select s student gpa) 3.9)))
```

We can exploit the locality of student data by dispatching the predicate to all PMEs on which student objects reside, where local extent filtering may then proceed in parallel using the techniques described in the previous section. The local result lists are appended efficiently as described above. Here is a translation which implements this strategy:

```
(let ((pred (cons (make-condition gpa-slotid '>= 3.9) Nil)))
  (foldr
    (lambda (j rest)                                              (T5)
      (APPLY PME j local-filter-extent STUDENT BASEFILE NOINDEX pred rest))
    Nil
    pmes))
```

Procedure `local-filter-extent` performs the local filtering and linking of sublists. Its first argument identifies the type extent to filter. Its second and third arguments indicate the access path chosen by the compiler. Constants `BASEFILE` and `NOINDEX` indicate that use of an index in this query is not possible, so the filter must be performed by scanning all student objects in the base file. When an index is available, the second argument identifies the field on which the index exists, while the third argument identifies which index to use (there may be more than one). The fourth argument to `local-filter-extent` is the predicate, expressed as a list of conditions, and the fifth argument is the remaining result list.

Here is the definition of `local-filter-extent`:

```
(define (local-filter-extent t ap index p rest)
  (let ((res (filter-extent3 t ap index p)))
    (if (nil? res)
        rest
        (par                                              ;; in parallel
          (set-cons-tl (tl res) rest)
          (hd res)))))
```

Local result lists are produced by primitive procedure `filter-extent3`, which is passed the type id, the access path, the index to use, and the predicate. Unlike procedure `filter-extent2` from the previous section (used in translation T4), `filter-extent3` returns either `nil`, if no local objects are found which satisfy the predicate, or an open list.

The use of an open list by `filter-extent3` allows all local result lists to be appended in an efficient manner by threading the head of the result list through each invocation of `local-filter-extent`. The overall structure of the computation is shown in Figure 6. Again, the `foldr` computation runs on some PME i, and initiates the `local-filter-extent` computations on each PME, including its own. The first invocation receives the initial result of `nil` through its `rest` argument, which it stores in the tail of its local result list. It then returns a reference to the head of the local list. The second invocation receives this reference, stores it in the tail of its local result list, and returns the new intermediate result list. This process continues until the last invocation is reached, which appends its local list and returns the final result to `foldr`. If a local inversion produces no result (*i.e.*, `filter-extent3` returns `nil`), then the incoming result list is simply passed along.

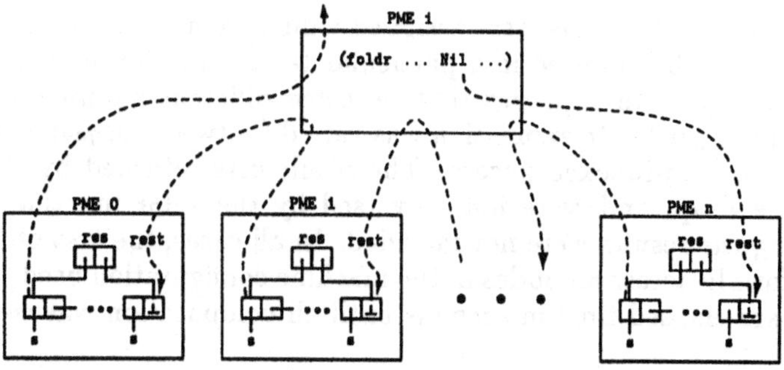

Figure 6: Local filtered extent constructed on each PME.

Experimental Results

We conducted three sets of experiments to evaluate the performance of simple list comprehensions in AGNA in a parallel environment. The tests were performed on an Intel iPSC/2 with 32 nodes. Each node consisted of an Intel 80386 processor, 8 megabytes of physical memory, and a 330 megabyte MAXTOR 4380 disk drive.

The experiments that we conducted varied the machine size (*i.e.*, number of PMEs), the problem size, or both. The first set of experiments evaluated performance relative to extent size by keeping the machine size constant while scaling up the problem size. The second set evaluated the scalability of the system by maintaining a constant problem size while increasing the number of PMEs in the machine configuration. Finally, the third set of experiments evaluated the ability of the system to maintain a constant response time as the problem size and machine size were increased proportionally. The design of our experiments was motivated by the performance study reported in [11].

The queries that we used were based on the selection queries in the Wisconsin benchmark [5]. All three sets of tests used the same object structure and query template. The object structure was:

```
(type TESTOBJ (extent)
 ((unique1  => INTEGER)
  (unique2 <=> INTEGER (index btree))
  (filler   => (STRING 200))))
```

and the query template was:

```
(all t
     (t (all testobj))
     (where (and (> (select t testobj unique1) v1)
                 (< (select t testobj unique1) v2))))
```

While the relation structure specified in the Wisconsin benchmark has more fields than the test object, only unique1 and unique2 were used by the part of the benchmark that we ran. Thus, we simply combined all unused fields into the filler field for simplicity. The total object length was the same as the Wisconsin benchmark relation width.

The unique1 and unique2 fields were assigned values from the range 1 - n, where n was the number of objects used in a particular test. This allowed values v_1 and v_2 to be varied easily to test queries that returned different numbers of objects. The field used in the predicate expression was varied (between unique1 and unique2) to test indexed vs. non-indexed access. The result lists returned by the queries were built in the heap, and were not traversed by the print function, *i.e.*, the times for printing the results were not included. In all cases, the test objects were distributed uniformly across all nodes in the machine configuration used. All query times reported are elapsed time in seconds until all computation was complete.

Performance relative to extent size

In this set of experiments, the machine configuration was kept constant at 32 PMEs while the extent size was increased from 100,000 to 10,000,000 objects. We ran two queries on `unique1` (the non-indexed field), selecting 1% of the objects in the base extent in the first one, and 10% in the second one. We also ran two queries on `unique2` (the indexed field), selecting 1% of the objects in the first one, and a single object in the second one.

Ideally, the increase in response time would not grow at a rate faster than the increase in extent size. The results are tabulated below.

Query Description	100,000	1,000,000	10,000,000
1% non-indexed selection	4.1	27.8	275
10% non-indexed selection	4.3	29.1	298
1% indexed selection	2.2	2.6	7.0
1 object using index	2.1	2.1	2.1

For the non-indexed selections, the increase in response time is almost perfectly matched with the increase in extent size from 1,000,000 to 10,000,000 objects (27.8 to 275 seconds, and 29.1 to 298 seconds). For the increase in extent size from 100,000 to 1,000,000 objects, this is not the case because with 100,000 objects the time it takes to begin a transaction, dispatch the local filter operations, append the local result lists, and end the transaction becomes more significant (almost half of the total time) relative to the time spent filtering on each node. Response time for the indexed selections is completely dominated by this overhead.

Speedup

In this set of experiments, we kept the extent size constant at 1,000,000 objects while the machine configuration was increased from 1 to 32 nodes. The ideal behavior in this case would be for response time to decrease (or speedup) proportionally with increases in machine size. Results for the 1% selection queries are shown in Figure 7. (We also ran the 10% selection query on a non-indexed field; the response time and speedup curves for it are almost identical to those for the 1% non-indexed selection.)

The speedup for non-indexed selections is slightly superlinear from 1 to 4 nodes, and then slightly sublinear from 4 to 32 nodes. For the indexed selection, good speedup is obtained from 1 to 8 nodes, but then response time levels off due to the additional time required to dispatch the local filter operations, and to append the local result lists.

Scaleup

In the final set of experiments, we increased the machine and extent sizes proportionally. The ideal behavior in this case would be for response time to remain constant. The results are shown in Figure 8.

Response time remains relatively constant throughout for selection on the non-indexed field. For the indexed selection, response time increases slowly with increases in the machine size due, again, to the additional transaction overhead.

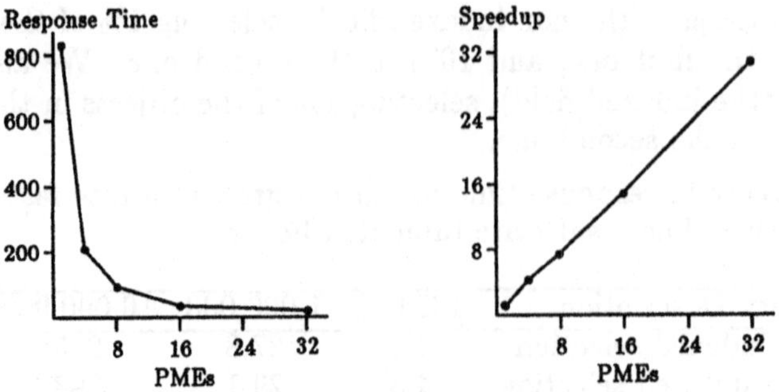

(a) 1% Non-indexed selection.

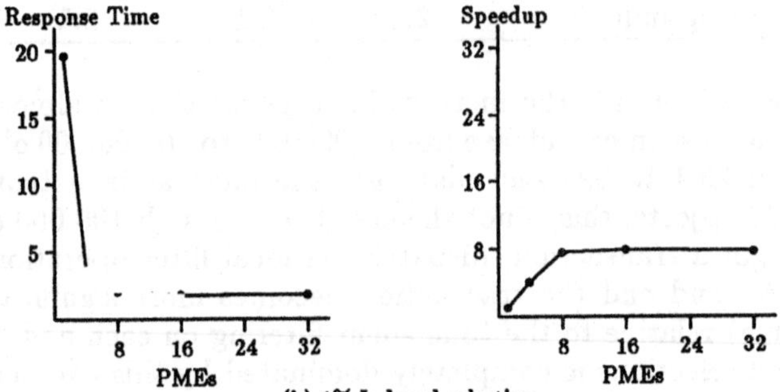

(b) 1% Indexed selection.

Figure 7: Speedup for 1% selection.

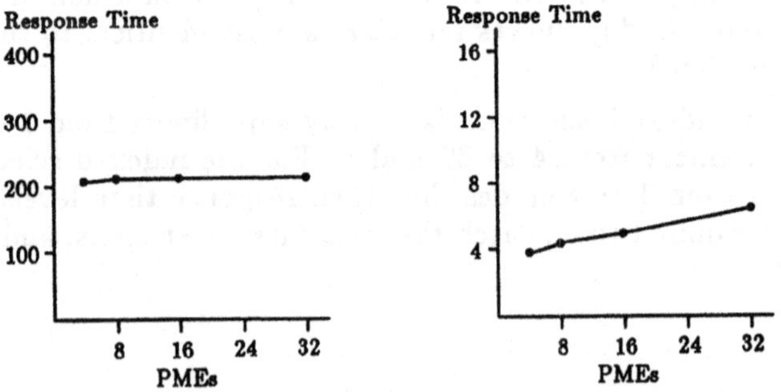

Figure 8: Scaleup for 1% selection with index (right) and without index (left).

Comparison with Gamma

The Gamma Parallel Relational Database Project (at the University of Wisconsin) has also reported results for the selection queries that we used in our experiments. A thorough performance evaluation of Gamma, on the same hardware platform, is reported in [11].

For queries that involve a significant amount of processing relative to the overhead of a transaction (*e.g.,* a non-indexed selection on all 32 nodes with an extent size of 10,000,000 objects), Gamma is anywhere from two to five times faster than AGNA. For very short transactions, the difference is more significant, often greater than a factor of ten. We believe that the differences in performance can be attributed to three things:

1. The P-RISC abstract machine, the target of the AGNA compiler, is currently emulated in software. Further, we know of numerous optimizations possible on P-RISC code that we have not yet had the opportunity to incorporate. From hand coded examples, we believe that these optimizations and better compilation can easily increase performance by a factor of 10 or more.

2. AGNA implements objects in a segmented, paged, virtual heap. The management of this heap, including its paging to disk, is implemented entirely in software which has not been optimized very much yet. Further, our heap structure is more complicated due to the more complex object model supported by AGNA.

3. Much less effort has gone into AGNA to date to tune the system.

We are very encouraged by our results, and believe that we are within shooting distance of parallel relational systems on comparable queries. Again, we have the advantage that in AGNA, the programmer can smoothly escalate to more complex objects and queries that involve general networks of objects and arbitrary computation.

5 Concluding Remarks

Some of the earliest connections between functional languages and database systems were made by Shipman in his work on the Functional Data Model [20], Buneman *et al.* in their work on FQL (Functional Query Language) [7] and Atkinson, Kulkarni *et al.* in their work on PS-Algol and the Extended Functional Data Model [3, 14]. Most of this work emphasized language design and all the implementations were sequential.

AGNA is related to object-oriented database systems (OODBs), a topic that has received much attention in the last few years. Several OODB products have even appeared on the market recently (*e.g.,* Gemstone [9]). Much of the recent activity in OODBs has emphasized language design— *e.g.,* designing static type systems and semantic models for inheritance, declarative query languages for objects, *etc.*

All the implementations that we know about are sequential implementations that have yet to match the overall performance of relational systems.

Trinder, in his thesis [21], has also studied the use of a non-strict functional language as a parallel database language. He examined parallelism in transactions by executing them on a simulator (running on a sequential machine) that models parallel execution and disk i/o in certain idealized ways. His results confirm our belief (a belief long held by our fellow dataflow researchers and substantiated by numerous experiments in dataflow architectures [1]) that non-strict parallel evaluation is a very promising method to exploit parallelism and to overcome the long latencies of disk i/o and communication in parallel machines.

Trinder and his colleagues are currently implementing his functional database model on GRIP, a parallel machine [19]. One difference from our work is that since GRIP does not have a parallel i/o system, the database will have to reside in main memory. In AGNA, we have addressed the issue of implementing a virtual heap that is much larger than main memory and of distributing objects onto multiple disks. A second difference is that GRIP is a shared memory architecture; we believe that our distributed memory model is not only physically easier to scale to much larger machines, but also operationally, because we have taken into account the increased latencies of larger machines.

FAD, designed at MCC [4], was another parallel functional database language. FAD did not have anything like list comprehensions; queries had to be composed explicitly using map and filter operators. In FAD, functions were not first class objects, and updates were completely imperative, so that a program with updates could produce non-deterministic results. FAD was to be implemented on Bubba, a parallel database machine [6] built on top of a Flex/32 multicomputer consisting of 40 PMEs (32 with local disks). We believe that only a relational subset of FAD (no inter-object references) was actually implemented before the end of the project; we do not know what optimizations were implemented or what performance was achieved.

Kato *et al.* [13] have designed a database language SPL based on list comprehensions. However, their approach seems quite different from ours. They have a compilation scheme where each generator and filter in the list comprehension is treated as a function from streams to streams. Each function is treated as a sequential process in a parallel system, and the streams are directly implemented as communication channels between these processes. With these restrictions, they have not had to deal with persistent heaps, and they do not utilize indexes for efficient access. Some problems that we see with this approach are that streams themselves are not first class objects, it is not so easy to deal with higher-order functions, and it is difficult to deal with updates.

In AGNA, we have not spent any time at all on concrete syntax design— with its heavily parenthesized notation, AGNA is by no means a user-friendly language. Further, we do not have any static type system, and this is clearly something desirable in the long run. Our main emphasis has been on studying the underlying constructs for implicit parallelism, and on efficient parallel implementation. Thus, the AGNA system may be viewed as an "engine" for a more humane database language (such as [18]).

To our knowledge, AGNA is the first real implementation of a *parallel* persistent object system, whether based on functional languages or not. Further, although functional languages have been proposed and prototyped as database query languages before, we believe that AGNA is the first implementation whose performance approaches that of state of the art relational database systems. The performance of AGNA relies heavily on:

- Optimization of list comprehensions, based on reducing the number of intermediate lists, use of indexes to combine generators and filters, and moving filters as close to disk i/o as possible.
- Aggressive pursuit of parallelism, based on fine grain, non-strict evaluation.

We plan to implement additional list comprehension optimizations in AGNA in the near future. One area of focus will be nested generators, the equivalent of join queries (cross-products) in relational systems. We plan to investigate traditional methods for implementing join queries, as well as new ones that can exploit the direct object references that are part of the AGNA object model.

We are also looking for other benchmark programs, especially ones that involve complex objects and general computation, and benchmark results from other persistent systems.

Acknowledgements

We thank Prof. David DeWitt of the University of Wisconsin, Madison, for giving us access to the Intel iPSC/2 at Wisconsin, and for assisting us in the actual use of the machine. We also thank Phil Trinder for his comments on an earlier draft. Funding for this work is provided in part by the Advanced Research Projects Agency of the Department of Defense under the Office of Naval Research contract N00014-89-J-1988. Support for the Michael Heytens is provided in part by an Intel Graduate Fellowship.

References

[1] Arvind, D. E. Culler, and G. K. Maa. Assessing the Benefits of Fine-grained Parallelism in Dataflow Programs. *Intl. J. of Supercomputer Applications*, 2(3), 1988.

[2] M. Astrahan et al. System R: Relational Approach to Database Management. *ACM Trans. on Database Systems*, 1(2), June 1976.

[3] M. P. Atkinson, K. Chisholm, and W. Cockshott. PS-Algol: An Algol with a Persistent Heap. *ACM SIGPLAN Notices*, 17(7):24–31, July 1981.

[4] F. Bancilhon, T. Briggs, S. Khoshafian, and P. Valduriez. FAD, a Powerful and Simple Database Language. In *Proc. 13th. Intl. Conf. on Very Large Databases, Brighton, England*, pages 97–105, September 1-4 1987.

[5] D. Bitton, D. J. DeWitt, and C. Turbyfill. Benchmarking Database Systems: A Systematic Approach. In *Proc. 1983 Conf. on Very Large Data Bases*, August 1983.

[6] H. Boral, W. Alexander, L. Clay, G. Copeland, S. Danforth, M. Franklin, B. Hart, M. Smith, and P. Valduriez. Prototyping Bubba, A Highly Parallel Database System. *IEEE Trans. on Knowledge and Data Engineering*, 2(1):4–24, March 1990.

[7] O. P. Buneman, R. E. Frankel, and R. S. Nikhil. An Implementation Technique For Database Query Languages. *ACM Trans. on Database Systems*, 7(2):164–186, June 1982.

[8] H.-T. Chou, D. J. DeWitt, R. H. Katz, and A. C. Klug. Design and Implementation of the Wisconsin Storage System. *Software—Practice and Experience*, 15(10):943–962, October 1985.

[9] G. Copeland and D. Maier. Making Smalltalk a Database System. In *Proc. ACM SIGMOD*, page 325, 1984.

[10] C. J. Date. *A Guide to the SQL Standard.* Addison-Wesley, Reading, MA, 1987.

[11] D. DeWitt, S. Ghandeharizadeh, D. Schneider, A. Bricker, H.-I. Hsiao, and R. Rasmussen. The Gamma Database Machine Project. *IEEE Trans. on Knowledge and Data Engineering*, 2(1):44–62, March 1990.

[12] M. L. Heytens. *The Design and Implementation of a Parallel Persistent Object System.* PhD thesis, MIT, 1991 (expected).

[13] K. Kato, T. Masuda, and Y. Kiyoki. A Comprehension-Based Database Language and its Distributed Execution. In *Proc. 10th Intl. Conf. on Distributed Computing Systems, Paris, France*, pages 442–449, May 28-June 1 1990.

[14] K. G. Kulkarni and M. P. Atkinson. Implementing Extended Functional Data Model Using PS-Algol. *Software: Practice & Experience*, 1986.

[15] R. S. Nikhil. Functional Databases, Functional Languages. In *Proc. 1985 Wkshp. on Persistence and Data Types, Appin, Scotland.* Dept. of Computing Science, Univ. of Glasgow, and Dept. of Computational Science, Univ. of St. Andrews, Scotland, July 1987 (revised).

[16] R. S. Nikhil. Id (Version 90.0) Reference Manual. Technical Report CSG Memo 284-1, MIT Laboratory for Computer Science, 545 Technology Square, Cambridge, MA 02139, USA, July 1990.

[17] R. S. Nikhil and M. L. Heytens. Exploiting Parallelism in the Implementation of AGNA, a Persistent Programming System. In *Proc. 7th IEEE Intl. Conf. on Data Engineering, Kobe, Japan*, April 8-12 1991.

[18] A. Ohori, O. P. Buneman, and V. Breazu-Tannen. Database Programming in Machiavelli— a Polymorphic Language with Static Type Inference. In *Proc. Intl. Conf. on the Management of Data, Portland, OR*, pages 46–57, June 1989.

[19] S. L. Peyton Jones, C. Clack, J. Salkild, and M. Hardie. GRIP - A High Performance Architecture for Parallel Graph Reduction. In *Proc. 3rd. Intl. Conf. on Functional Programming and Computer Architecture, Portland, OR*, September 1987.

[20] D. W. Shipman. The Functional Data Model and the Data Language DAPLEX. *ACM Trans. on Database Systems*, 6(1):140–173, March 1981.

[21] P. Trinder. A Functional Database. Oxford University D.Phil. Thesis, December 1989.

[22] P. Wadler. Deforestation: Transforming Programs To Eliminate Trees. In *European Symposium on Programming*, Nancy, France, January 1988.

GENERATING EFFICIENT CODE FOR LAZY FUNCTIONAL LANGUAGES

Sjaak Smetsers, Eric Nöcker, John van Groningen, Rinus Plasmeijer

Faculty of Mathematics and Computer Science,
University of Nijmegen,
Toernooiveld 1, 6525 ED Nijmegen, The Netherlands
E-mail: clean@cs.kun.nl

May 1991

Abstract

In this paper we will discuss how a good code generator can be built for (lazy) functional languages. Starting from Concurrent Clean, an experimental lazy functional programming language, code is generated for an intermediate abstract machine: the ABC machine. In this first pass many well-known optimisation techniques are included. However, we will also present some new ideas in this area, like the way in which strictness can be incorporated, and the implementation of higher order functions. In a second pass, the ABC code is translated to concrete target code for the Motorola MC680x0 processor. Again many optimisation methods appear to be applicable. Some of them (for example register allocation algorithms) are common for the implementation of other types of languages, but have to be adapted because of the specific properties of both source language and target machine. Other optimisations are specific for lazy functional languages, e.g. the implementation of higher order functions, efficient memory management and the optimised graph reduction. Measurements demonstrate that due to the optimisations of both passes very fast code can be generated. We have compared Concurrent Clean with two other functional languages, namely Lml and Hope, and also with the imperative language C. With respect to both functional languages this comparison clearly goes in favour of Concurrent Clean. Furthermore, we can conclude that, when using the presented compilation techniques, a lazy functional language is able to compete even with an imperative language such as C.

1. Introduction

It is very difficult to build an efficient implementation of a lazy functional language. In the recent years many compilation techniques have been presented, mostly with the aid of some abstract machine architecture. However, relatively little attention was spent on the methods to implement such an abstract machine (and therefore also the functional language) efficiently on a concrete machine.

In this paper we will discuss how a good code generator can be built for a lazy functional language. We describe a compiler for Concurrent Clean, an experimental lazy functional programming language (Brus (1987), Eekelen et al. (1990), Nöcker et al. (1991)). This language contains almost no syntactical sugar which enables us to concentrate fully on efficiency topics. We note that the compiler includes a strictness analyser, based on abstract reduction (Nöcker (1990)), which plays an essential role during the compilation process.

Concurrent Clean is compiled (Smetsers (1989)) first to code for an intermediate abstract machine: the ABC machine. The ABC machine (Koopman et al. (1990)) is a stack based graph reduction machine, similar to advanced G-machine like architectures (e.g. Johnsson (1987), Peyton Jones & Salkild (1989)). In a second pass the resulting ABC code is translated to concrete target code for the Motorola MC68020 processor (Groningen (1990)). Generating intermediate code has some advantages. The ABC machine by itself can easily be understood and implemented. Interpreters (Nöcker (1989)) as well as simple code generators (based on macro substitution of ABC instructions) are easily to build. As a consequence, it is easy to experiment with Concurrent Clean, the ABC machine or the compiler itself. A disadvantage of intermediate code is the possible loss of efficiency. The ABC code that is generated by the first pass seems to be clumsy. Furthermore, information needed by the second pass might no longer be available. However, we will show that it is very well possible to circumvent these problems and generate efficient code.

Overview of the paper

In the rest of this introduction we will give a very short overview of the language Concurrent Clean and the ABC machine. In section 2 we will treat the Concurrent Clean to ABC code compilation. The main task of this compilation pass is to derive and process type and strictness information as adequate as possible. In the second pass ABC code is translated to concrete machine code. Specific properties of a target machine are exploited. This is discussed in section 3. Note that we describe the generation of code for the Motorola MC68020 processor. It should be pointed out that most of the techniques are generally applicable. In section 4 we compare the implementation of Concurrent Clean with implementations other languages. Finally, we present conclusions and future work (section 5).

Concurrent Clean

Concurrent Clean is an experimental, lazy, higher-order functional programming language based on term graph rewriting (Barendregt et al. (1987), Plasmeijer & Eekelen (1991)). Concurrent Clean has many features in common with other lazy, higher-order functional languages, such as a Milner/Mycroft based polymorphic type system (including algebraic types, synonym types and abstract types) (Milner (1978), Mycroft (1984)). A key aspect of the language is that the main object that is manipulated by a program is a graph. Consequently, the programmer can explicitly indicate sharing of computations. For instance, cyclic objects can be created. The most important aspect of Concurrent Clean discussed in this paper is the way in which the order of evaluation can be controlled. Lazy evaluation can locally be changed to eager evaluation which has the advantage that it generally can be implemented considerably more efficiently than lazy evaluation. Even larger speed-up can be achieved by changing sequential evaluation into parallel evaluation. For this reason, Concurrent Clean also offers the possibility to indicate parallel execution by the use of annotations (Eekelen (1988), Eekelen et al. (1991)).

We will introduce Concurrent Clean by showing some well-known example functions (for more examples see Eekelen et al. (1990)). Consider the following definitions for the factorial function, and the function Map:

```
RULE
::   Fac !INT  ->   INT                          ;
     Fac 0     ->   1                            |
     Fac n     ->   *I n (Fac (--I n))           ;

::   Map (=> x y) ![x]  -> [y]                   ;
     Map f []           -> []                    |
     Map f [a|b]        -> [f a|Map f b]         ;

::   Start   -> [INT]                            ;
     Start   -> Map Fac [2,3,4]                  ;
```

Each function, optionally preceded by a type specification, consists of a number of alternatives. Square brackets are used for denoting lists: `[]` is an empty list, `[a|b]` denotes a list consisting of a list `b` prefixed with an element `a`. The example also shows that higher order functions can be used freely. There is no difference between the use of full and partial (curried) applications of functions. Types of higher order functions are specified using => (prefix notation) which corresponds to -> (infix notation) as used in most other functional languages.

The sequential flow of control can be influenced by means of so called *strict annotations*. Annotations can be placed in right hand sides of function definitions, in type specifications of functions, or in type definitions. Annotations in a type specification of a certain function are allowed to be placed before the type specification of either an argument on the left-hand-side or an argument of a tuple type appearing in a strict context. A tuple type is in a *strict context* if it has been supplied with a strict annotation itself or if it appears as the root node on the right-hand-side of the type rule. Intuitively, such a strict annotation indicates that the corresponding argument is always reduced to root normal form before the corresponding rule is applied. For example, the function `Fac` is made strict in its argument. It should be stated that this particular strictness property would also have been found by the strictness analyser.

Strict annotations may also be used in tuple types appearing in type synonym definitions The meaning of these annotated synonym types can be explained with the aid of a simple program transformation in which all occurrences of synonym types are replaced by their right-hand-sides (of course, annotations included). These annotated type definitions are a special case of the *partially strict data types* (Nöcker & Smetsers (1990)). An example of a partially strict tuple is the following definition of a complex number:

```
TYPE
::  Complex       -> (!REAL,!REAL)                ;

RULE
::  +C !Complex !Complex -> Complex               ;
    +C (r1,i1) (r2,i2)   -> (+R r1 r2,+R i1 i2)  ;
```

The annotations in the type definition for `Complex` provide that both the real and imaginary part of a complex number are computed immediately when the complex number appears in a strict context.

The ABC Machine

Since a complete, formal description of the ABC machine goes beyond the scope of this paper, we will give only a short introduction. In the sequel specific parts of the machine will be highlighted further if necessary. The ABC machine is a stack based graph reduction machine. Its main parts of interest are the three stacks (A, B and C stack) and the heap. The C stack is used for storing code addresses. The other two stacks are used for evaluating or building expressions, for passing arguments to functions and for returning results from functions. The A stack contains addresses of nodes in the heap, whereas the B stack contains values of basic types, such as integers or reals. Thus, basic values can be represented in two ways: as a node in the heap or as an item on the B stack. Graphs are stored in the heap. Conceptually, the heap consists of a collection of nodes. A node in the ABC machine represents a node of a Concurrent Clean graph. Hence, nodes in the ABC machine have a variable size.
The ABC instructions that will be used in this paper are almost self-explanatory. In any case, pieces of ABC code will be commented.

2. Concurrent Clean to ABC Code Generation

The main task of the Concurrent Clean compiler is to generate efficient ABC code. The syntax of Concurrent Clean is rather simple: no complex transformations like lambda lifting or the conversion of ZF-expressions are necessary. Many standard optimisation techniques are implemented: tail recursion removal, avoiding unnecessary evaluation calls and so on. In the sequel we will emphasize those parts of the compiler that differ from other well-known implementations.

2.1. The Basic Machinery

Conceptually, graph reduction takes place in the heap: whenever a graph has to be rewritten a new graph is built. The root node of the old graph will be overwritten with the root node of the new graph. Unfortunately, this scheme will not give efficient code. The goal of the compiler is to generate code in which graph building is prevented as much as possible. For generating such efficient code type and strictness information is necessary. Strictness information is used in two ways. First, it is used for deriving the evaluation order of right hand sides. Second it is used for parameter passing. The latter is treated in the next section. First we will discus how nodes are represented and reduced to head normal form.

The structure of nodes

Generally spoken, a node of a Concurrent Clean graph consists of a symbol with a certain number of arguments. Representing a node as a variable sized object causes problems with updating: the new node doesn't need to fit in the space of old one. This problem can be solved by introducing indirection nodes, but this will slow down the access to the contents of a node. In the ABC machine a node is split in a fixed and a variable sized part. The fixed size part contains a descriptor, a code pointer and a pointer to a variable sized part.

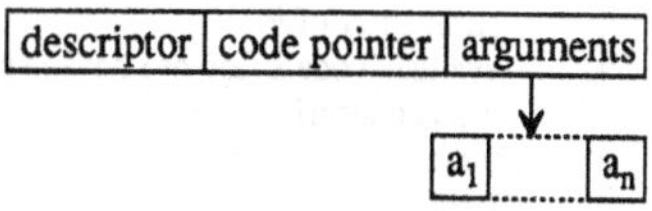

Fig 2.1 The node structure

The *descriptor* is a representation of a Clean symbol. Normally it is an index or pointer in a descriptor table. Descriptors are used in the following cases:

- pattern matching. Nodes contain the same symbol if they have the same descriptor.
- printing. The descriptor contains a string representing the symbol belonging to that descriptor.
- fetching arity. The arity is needed by the garbage collector, and by some ABC instructions.
- evaluating higher order functions (see further).

The code pointer refers to code with which the node can be evaluated to head normal form. This code is entered by a `jsr_eval` instruction. During reduction the code pointer can be changed. For example, after entering the node for evaluation a pointer to an error routine can be stored. If the node is ever entered again (indicating a non-terminating reduction) this code will be executed. If a node is updated with a head normal form value, the code pointer points to special code just containing a return statement:

```
_hnf_code:                    rtn
```

In the variable sized part the arguments of the node are stored. This means that the arguments have to be fetched via an extra indirection. On the other hand, updating a node is simple: update the fixed part, and allocate space for the arguments.

For nodes containing a basic value, e.g. an integer, the descriptor does not represent the Clean symbol (that would be the integer value itself). Instead, all integers share the same descriptor (e.g. INT). The integer value itself is stored in the argument reference part. For basic values that do not fit in the fixed part of a node (e.g. strings) a pointer to the value (for which space has to be allocated) is stored. Since basic nodes are always in normal form, they all contain the head normal form code pointer.

The evaluation of right hand sides

During the generation of code for the right hand side of an alternative, strictness information is used in order to derive what nodes are in a *strict context*. Generally, a node is in a strict context if it certainly has to be reduced. For a node in a strict context no intermediate graph needs to be built. Instead, the code that would have been stored in the node can be executed directly. Consider the following example:

```
F x y  ->   G n1 n2,
            n1: G x y,
            n2: G y x      ;
```

Suppose that `G` is only strict in its first argument. Then it is easy to see that nodes `n1` and `x` are in a strict context, and nodes `n2` and `y` are not. The root node itself is always in a strict context. This means that only node `n2` is built (node `y` is already available). The other two applications of `G` are implemented by direct calls to the code of `G`. If, at some time, node `n2` appears to be needed, it will be unpacked, whereafter also the code for `G` is executed. For this reason, the code for `G` has two entry points: the *node_entry* for the lazy evaluation, and the *strict_entry* for the strict one. For the node entry only the node itself is needed. The code unpacks the node, whereafter the strict entry is called. For the strict entry the arguments of the function are needed. They are passed via the stacks. How parameters are passed depends on the type of the function. This is discussed in the next section. The code for the right hand side of `F` would look as follows:

```
F:                                   | strict entry of F
        jsr_eval                     | evaluate node x (top of stack) to head normal from
        create                       | create node n2
        push_a 1                     | push x
        push_a 3                     | push y
        fill G nG 2 2                | fill node n2 with (G y x), x and y are removed
        create                       | create a node for the result of G
        push_a 3                     | push y
        push_a 3                     | push x
        jsr G                        | jsr to the strict entry of G (evaluation of node n1)
        update_a 1 3                 | clean the
        update_a 0 2                 | stacks: remove the old
        pop_a 2                      | x and y nodes
        jmp G                        | and jump to strict entry of G
```

Note that the last call to G is a direct jump instead of a subroutine call.

2.2. Passing Parameters and Returning Results

As mentioned before, the way the strict entry of a function expects its arguments and returns its result is determined by the type of this function. If a function is called (e.g. because its node is in a strict context), the calling code has to ensure that these calling conventions are obeyed.

The general calling convention is straightforward. Things become complicated if the type of a function contains basic types or strict tuples.

General way of parameter passing

We will start by considering the most general situation. Suppose a function F of arity n with type:

:: F T_1 ... T_n -> T_r ;

where none of the types is a basic type or a strict tuple. The above function F expects all its arguments and the node that has to be updated with the result on the A stack. So, if the function F is to be called, first the node to be updated has to be put on the stack. Thereafter, graphs for the arguments for F have to be built (if necessary) and pushed on the A stack. Strict arguments have to be reduced before calling F: the function *expects* them to be in head normal form.

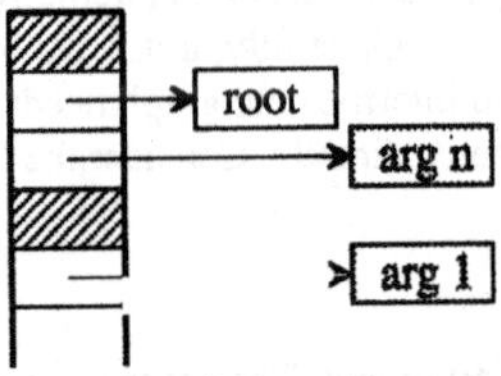

Fig 2.2: the A stack just before calling F.

The code for F takes care of the removal of the arguments. The updating of the root node is done only if it can be overwritten with a head normal form value. Consider for example the function:

```
F [] y    ->  G y y       |
F x  y    ->  [ x | y ]   ;
```

In the first alternative of F another function G is called. This function will get the same root node as F. This root node will either be updated by the code for G, or by another function that is called by G. In the second alternative the root node will be updated with a Cons node:

```
altl:                                  | entry for the first alternative
      update_a 1 0                     | replace topmost A stack element ([]) by y
      jmp sG                           | jump to the strict entry of G
alt2:                                  | entry for the second alternative
      fill Cons _hnf_code 2 2          | fill the root node with the cons (x and y removed)
      rtn                              | and return
```

Notice that because of the call to G is tail recursive, the A stack does not grow: the original arguments of F are replaced by the new ones for G.

Passing strict basic arguments

This general scheme changes if either one of the arguments or the result type is a strict basic type. As is the case for ordinary strict arguments, the caller has to reduce the strict arguments first. But instead of the A stack, the B stack is used now for passing values belonging to the strict basic types. For example:

```
::   F !INT [x] !REAL   ->   INT    ;
```

The basic integer and a real values needed by F are evaluated (if they have not been evaluated before) and pushed on the B stack, whereas the second argument is pushed on the A stack:

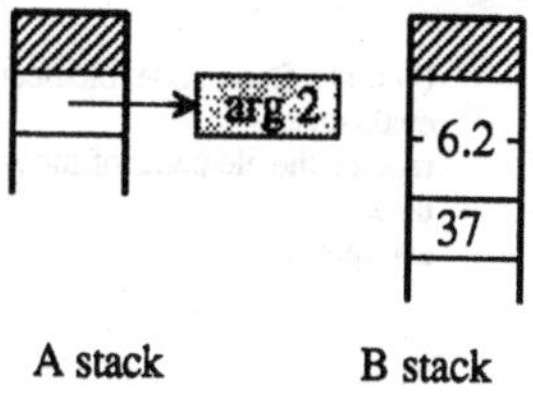

Fig 2.3: the stacks just before calling F.

Note that no root node is passed to F. The result value of F is returned via the B stack. The calling code itself decides what to do with it: it might use the value to fill a node, or pass it to another function.

Passing partially strict datatypes

For values that have a partially strict tuple type, it is exactly known at compile time how far the parts of the tuple have been reduced. So, whenever such a value is passed to another function it is sufficient to pass only the arguments of the tuple instead of the whole tuple. Consider, for example, the following function type:

```
:: F INT !(!INT,![CHAR]) -> (INT,!CHAR);
```

The function F requires two arguments. The first one is a non-strict integer. This value is passed via the A stack. The second argument is a strict tuple. Both elements of this tuple have to be reduced to head normal form before calling F. Then they can be passed to F via the stacks; the tuple itself needs not to be built. The integer is passed via the B stack, whereas the character list is passed via the A stack. The result value is handled in a similar way: only the elements of the tuple are returned. The first element, a non-strict integer, will be returned via the A stack, and the second, a strict character, via the B stack. In this way no intermediate tuple node is needed.

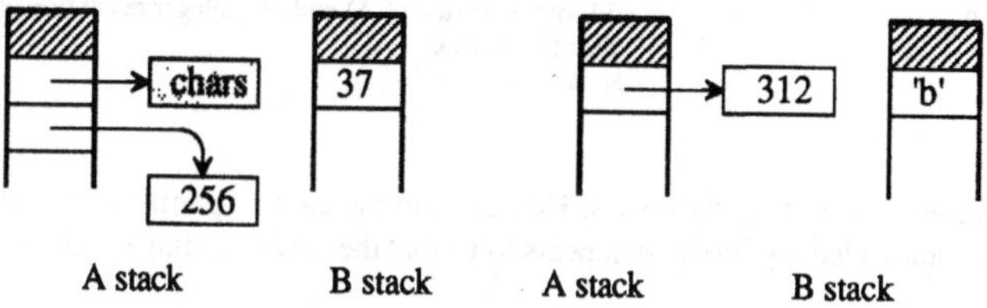

Fig 2.4: The stacks just before and after calling F

Selector functions

If the return type of a function is a single type variable that is bound in one of the argument types, we have another special case. Consider, for example, the function Hd that return the first element of a list:

```
::  Hd [x]       ->  x ;
    Hd [x | r]   ->  x ;
```

Functions with such a type are called *selector functions*: normally, they select an already existing node from a graph. Following the previous conventions, Hd will receive a root node for storing its result. The root node will be updated with the head normal form value of x:

```
Hd_alt1:                    | First alt of Hd: Cons node, elements and root on top of A
   jsr_eval                 | evaluate x
   fill_a 0 3               | update the root node with the contents of node x
   pop_a 3                  | clear the A stack
   rtn                      | and return
```

However, since node x already exists, it would be better to return that node itself. The calling code does not need to pass a root node to such a function which will prevent the creation of new, unnecessary nodes. The code for the right hand side of Hd becomes:

```
Hd_alt1:                    | First alt: Cons node, elements (no root!) on top of A
   jsr_eval                 | evaluate x
   update_a 0 2             | replace the elements of the A stack
   pop_a 2                  | by x
   rtn                      | and return
```

Coercions

The type of a function together with the strictness information determines the way this function expects the layout of the stacks when it is called. When the actual layout of the stack differs from the layout that the function expects at the strict entry there is a conflict. For example, such a conflict occurs in the node entry of a function: strict arguments (that still reside in the heap) have to be reduced and, in the case of basic types, pushed on the B stack. The conversion that is necessary to solve the conflicting situation is called a *coercion*. In the node entry, a coercion is also necessary if the result has a basic type: the root node has to be filled with the basic value that is returned via the B stack. Consider for example a function with type:

```
::  F !INT ![x] ->  INT  ;
```

The ABC code of the node entry would look as follows:

```
nF:                         | node entry of F: a node with symbol F on top of A stack
      push_args 0 2 2       | push the two arguments on the A stack
      push_a 1              | push the second argument on top
      jsr_eval              | and evaluate it
      pop_a 1               | clear the stack
      jsr_eval              | evaluate the first argument (on top of A)
      pushI_a 0 0           | and move the integer value from the node to the B stack
      pop_a 1               | remove the (integer) node form the A stack
      jsr sF                | call the strict entry of F (second arg on A, first arg on B)
      fillI 0 0             | fill root node (top of A) with the integer result (top of B)
      pop_b 1               | clear the B stack
      rtn                   | and return
```

The above kind of coercion is straightforward. However, in the case of partially strict datatypes coercions can become very complex pieces of code. It appears to us that the cases needing complicated coercions occur rather rarely.

2.3. Higher Order Functions

In Concurrent Clean symbols are defined with a fixed arity (from now on called the *formal arity*). However, each symbol can be applied to a number of arguments arguments (i.e. the *actual arity*) which is less than the formal arity (currying). Such a partial application can be represented as a spine of application nodes. However, a better way is to use *partial nodes*, i.e. nodes with a partially filled argument part. Such nodes are built as standard nodes, but contain special descriptors. This implies that for each Concurrent Clean symbol of arity n, n+1 descriptors are defined. In many respects, the ABC machine treats partial nodes in the same way as standard nodes. However, a partial node may be applied to another node with the *Apply* function (for convenience just called `Apply` here). The `Apply` function is a special built-in function with type:

```
::   Apply !(=> x y) x -> y  ;
```

It is inserted where hidden function applications appear. Consider, for example, the function Twice:

```
::   Twice (=> x x) x    -> x          ;
     Twice f x           -> f (f x)    ;
```

Its right hand side is internally transformed into:

```
     Twice f x           -> Apply f (Apply f x)     ;
```

For the first appearance of Apply a direct call to the Apply code is generated. The second application of Apply is not in a strict context: an Apply node will be built. The first thing the Apply code will do is an inspection of its first argument, the partial node. If that node needs precisely one more argument (being the second argument of the Apply), all arguments are available: the function of the partial node can now be called. Otherwise, a new partial node will be built. This new node is a copy of the original node, with one extra argument. The ABC code for the Apply function looks as follows:

```
apply_code:                 |   the strict entry of Apply
     get_node_arity 0       |   get the real arity of the partial node
     get_desc_arity 0       |   get the maximum arity of the symbol of the partial node
     subI                   |   subtract
     eqI_b +1 0             |   test if exactly one argument is needed
     jmp_false              |
args_needed
     push_ap_entry 0        |   yes, so push the code entry of the function on C stack
     pop_b 1                |   clear the B stack
     rtn                    |   jump to the code entry of the function
args_needed:
     create
     push_a 2               |   no, so create a new node
     add_args 2 1 1         |   get the argument to be added
     update_a 0 2           |   fill the new node with one extra argument
     pop_a 2                |
     pop_b 1                |   clear both
     rtn                    |   the stacks
                            |   and return
```

It will be clear that the Apply code needs to fetch the actual arity, the formal arity as well as a code address. This information is found via the descriptor which points to an entry of the descriptor table (see Fig 2.5):

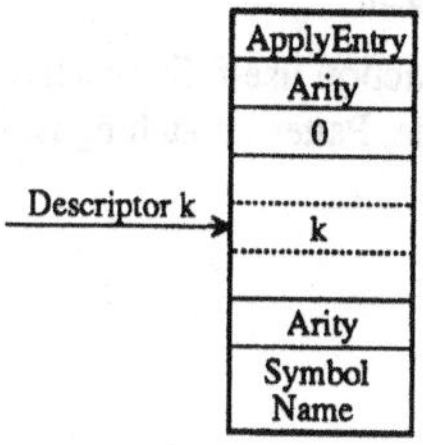

Fig 2.5: The layout of descriptors

The method is at a disadvantage in case long spines of Apply nodes are to be built: each of these intermediate nodes has to be updated by a partial node. However, such long spines occur very rarely. In other cases the method is very fast: the efficient representation of spines saves heap space, and no 'spine searching' is needed.

2.4. General Layout of the Code, Entry Points

The actual work of a function is done by the code of the strict entry. As discussed above, the strict entry expects the arguments of the function in the right form on the stacks. If these calling conventions cannot be applied directly, additional entry points are used. The code of these entry points will perform some coercions, whereafter execution proceeds with the strict entry. Earlier, we already introduced the node_entry. There are two other ways in which a function can be called.

Firstly, a function can be called via an application of the Apply function. This happens when a partial node is supplied with a sufficient number of arguments. The arguments of the function stored in the partial node have to be pushed on the A stack, whereafter they have to be coerced as required by the calling conventions of the function. The entry that does this work is called the *apply_entry*.

Secondly, also special things have to be done for exported functions. The exported type determines the calling convention outside the module. However, inside the module another calling convention may be more efficient. This is the case if abstract types are exported (hiding the internal representation), or if the strictness analyser finds more information than has been exported. So, for strict calls from outside an additional entry point is needed. This *external_strict_entry* converts the external to the internal calling conventions and continues with the internal strict entry.

So, in general the layout of the entry part of the code of a function with arity 'ar' is as follows:

```
apply_entry:
     repl_args ar-1 ar-1          | push the first (arity-1) args on the A stack
     jmp convert_code             | do coercions and execute strict code
node_entry:
     push_args ar ar 0            | push all the arguments on the A stack
convert_code:
     ...                          | convert strict args, unpack if necessary etc
     jmp strict_entry             | jump to the strict entry
external_strict_entry:
     ...                          | convert strict args, unpack if necessary etc
strict_entry:                     | and continue with strict entry
```

This layout is typical for a function that uses the general calling conventions. For other functions the layout is different. For example, if a function returns an integer value, the node entry itself has to provide that the root node (which initially contains the application of that function) is overwritten the integer result. The node entry for a function returning an integer would look as follows:

```
node_entry:
     push_args arity arity 0      | push all the arguments on the A stack
convert_code:
     ...                          | convert strict args, unpack if necessary etc
     jsr strict_entry             | jump-subroutine to the strict entry
     fillI 0 0                    | and fill the root node with the integer result
     pop_b 1                      | clear the B stack
     rtn                          | and return
```

The strict entry depends of course on the body of the function itself. For each alternative of the function there is a piece of match code, and code for the right hand side. Pattern matching is done straightforwardly.

```
strict_entry:
match_code_1:                  | matching code for the first alternative
    ...
alt_1:                         | code for the first alternative
    ...
    ...                        | other alternatives
match_code_n:
    ...                        | matching code for the last alternative
alt_n:
    ...                        | code for the last alternative
```

3. Generating Code towards Register Based Machines

In this section we will describe how abstract ABC code can be translated to real machine code. The ideas will be illustrated using a target machine based on the Motorola 68020 processor. A short introduction to this machine is given in the next section.
The most important aspects of implementing the ABC machine are:

- an efficient implementation of the components of the ABC machine state. As all computations take place in the heap and on the stacks, a good management of these structures is essential. This is handled in section 3.2.
- optimisation of ABC instruction sequences. It seems that the generated ABC code is not concerned with efficiency. For example, many ABC instructions require their arguments on top of the stack whereas on a real machine the arguments of corresponding instructions can be accessed more directly using one of the various addressing modes. This implies that the copy actions specified by the ABC instructions are not really necessary. How computations specified in ABC code can be optimised when generating machine code is described in section 3.3.
- use of registers, if possible. The MC68020 processors have the property that computations are performed much faster in registers than in memory. Registers can be used, for example, for implementing the ABC stacks and heap, for storing temporary values, and for passing arguments and return values. Register allocation is discussed in section 3.4.

3.1. The MC680x0 Family

There are two reasons that we have chosen for the Motorola 680x0 family of processors (68000, 68010, 68020, 68030, ...) as target machine (Motorola (1985,1984)). First of all, these kind of processors have been used in several widespread machines such as the SUN3, Apple Macintosh and Atari ST. Furthermore, the Motorola processors are very suited to serve as an actual target machine to illustrate how the ABC machine (and therefore functional languages in general) can be implemented efficiently. It should be no problem to use the presented ideas when generating actual target code for other register based processors (such as the Intel 80x86 family).

In this paper the MC68020 processor is used as example. It contains besides a program counter and a status register two kinds of general purpose registers, to wit data and address registers, eight of each kind. The data registers, often indicated by d0-d7, are mainly used in arithmetical operations whilst the address registers (indicated by a0-a7) can be used to access data structures that are kept in memory. An example of a data structure that can be implemented very efficiently with address registers is a stack. This is also due to the fact that address registers can be used in combination with many different addressing modes supported by these processors. Examples of such addressing modes are: address register indirect possible combined with post-increment, pre-decrement or displacement.

For the extend of this paper we do not require any knowledge about the specific structure of the MC68020 processor. Some familiarity with assembly languages will suffice to understand the examples of real code given in this section.

3.2. Representing the ABC Machine

Mapping the components of the ABC machine (i.e. ABC stacks, graph store (heap) and descriptors) onto the MC68020 does not cause many difficulties. Stacks can be implemented straightforwardly using some of the address registers. Implementing the heap takes some more doing. The structure of the descriptors mainly depends on how higher order functions are implemented. Their representation can be found later on in this section where the higher order functions are treated.

The C stack

For the C stack the system stack is taken (i.e. the stack used by the processor itself when performing a subroutine call). Therefore, the jump and return instructions of the ABC machine can be mapped directly on those of the MC68020 (of course, for the jsr_eval instructions other things have to be done, see further on). This implies that address register a7 (normally called *sp*) is reserved.

The A and B stack

The A and B stack are allocated in one contiguous area of memory where they can grow in opposite direction. In this way a check on stack overflow of both A and B stack can be done with a few instructions (just compare the two stack pointers and check whether their difference is not negative). The pointers to the tops of the stack are held in registers: for the A stack register a3 is reserved, for the B stack register a4 (for convenience we will refer to those registers by *asp* and *bsp* from now on).

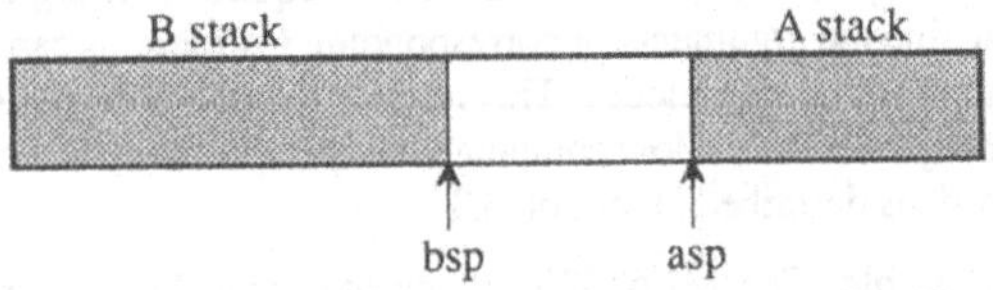

Fig 3.1: The layout of the combined A and B stack

The heap

For the heap a contiguous area of memory is reserved. The pointer to the free area is stored in register a6 (called *hp*), whereas the number of free heap cells (1 heap cell = 1 long word = 4 bytes) is stored in register d7 (*fh* from now on). With this representation the allocation of memory becomes cheap. Also, the filling of newly created nodes in the heap can be done efficiently as illustrated by the next example.

Suppose that a Cons node should be created that has two arguments. The references to both arguments are kept in the address registers a1 and a2. At the end a pointer to the new node is returned in register a0. First it has to be checked whether there is enough space in the heap. This is done by the following instructions:

```
    subq.l      #4,fh        ; we need 4 long words for storing the new node
    bcs         call_gc      ; call the garbage collector if not enough free heap
                             ; space is available
```

Now the heap pointer (held in register hp) refers to the first free long word in the heap. Filling the node by using hp is rather straightforward (for the actual representation of nodes see further):

```
return_from_gc:
    move.l      hp, d0           ; first the variable part is filled
                                 ; a pointer to it is temporarily stored in d0
    move.l      a1,  (hp)+       ; copy the pointer to the first argument to the new node
    move.l      a2,  (hp)+       ; copy the pointer to the second argument to the new node
    move.l      hp, a0           ; now the fixed part is treated.
                                 ; store a pointer to it in a0
    move.l   #Cons,  (hp)+       ; fill up the descriptor field with Cons
    move.l      d0,  (hp)+       ; copy the pointer to the variable part
```

Memory is recycled by a process called *garbage collection*. In our implementation a *copying garbage collector* is used which divides the memory available for the heap into two areas (*semispaces*). The nodes of the graph are stored in one semispace. When this area is filled up the garbage collector copies all the nodes still needed for the execution of the program to the other semispace leaving all the garbage behind.

Representation of nodes

As described earlier, a node in the ABC machine consists of a fixed and a variable sized part. The fixed size part consists of a pointer to a descriptor, a code pointer and a pointer to the variable sized part. A drawback of the ABC node structure is that the size of the nodes is relatively large: the fixed part would consist of 3 long words (12 bytes), one long word for each pointer. It is important that nodes are as small as possible: creating, filling and copying of nodes can be done faster and because less memory is consumed also the garbage collector will be called less often. We can observe that if a node is in head normal form, its code field points to the head normal form code so in fact only the pointer to the descriptor is of interest. On the other hand, if a node contains an (unevaluated) expression the descriptor is not used. This observation makes it possible to combine the descriptor and code field into one reducing the size of the fixed part by one third. However, one little problem has to be solved: the arity of a node is needed by the garbage collection. This arity, stored in the descriptor table, is not accessible when the descriptor is no longer available. The problem is solved by storing the arity not only in the descriptor table but also just before the node entry such that it can be accessed via the code pointer.

The new node structure is illustrated in the next picture. A disadvantage is that each node has to be supplied with a tag: the highest bit of the first word of the code/descr field (note that this field consists of two words) indicates whether it contains a descriptor or a code address. If this bit is set, the second word is an index in the descriptor table. Otherwise, the code/descr field contains a code pointer that is used to reduce the node to root normal form.

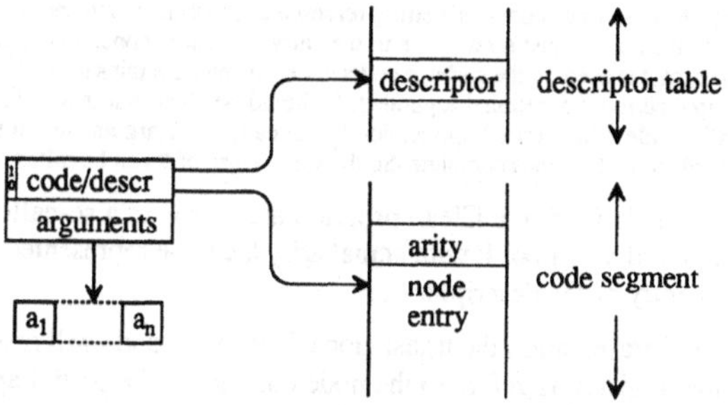

Fig 3.2: The structure of nodes

In the ABC machine nodes can be evaluated to root normal form by means of the `jsr_eval` instruction. This instruction fetches the code address from the node on top of the A stack and jumps to it. Due to the combined code/desc field we first have to check whether the node is already in root normal form before the jump to the evaluation code is made. The next piece of MC68020 code shows how this can be achieved (assume that register a1 is referring to the node that is going to be reduced):

```
    move.l    (a1), d6         ; get the code/desc field
    bmi    is_in_rnf           ; check whether the highest bit is set
    save_registers             ; save all the registers in use
    move.l    a1, a0           ; provide that a pointer to the node that
                               ; is going to  be evaluated is in reg. a0
    move.l    d6, a1           ; move the evaluation address in a1
    jsr       (a1)             ; call the evaluation code
    move.l    a0,a1            ; move the result of the evaluation back in a1
    restore_registers          ; restore the previously saved registers
 is_in_rnf:
    ...
```

Note that, in case of a node not in root normal form, this alternative representation leads to slightly less efficient code (an extra move instruction and a conditional branch are needed). But when the node is already in root normal form the code becomes much faster, for the saving and restoring of the registers is not needed anymore.

The descriptor table

In section 2.3 we described how partial (curried) function applications are implemented on the ABC machine. The ABC code shows that both the formal and actual arity of the node are needed. Furthermore, when all the arguments are available, the apply entry is also needed. The arities as well as the apply entry are found in the descriptor table that can be accessed via the descriptor stored in the node. A straightforward translation of the ABC apply code will result in rather inefficient MC68020 code. To increase efficiency, not only the actual arity of the curried application is stored in the descriptor but also a pointer to the code that should be executed when a partial application of the corresponding symbol is applied to an additional argument. This results in the following representation of symbol descriptors:

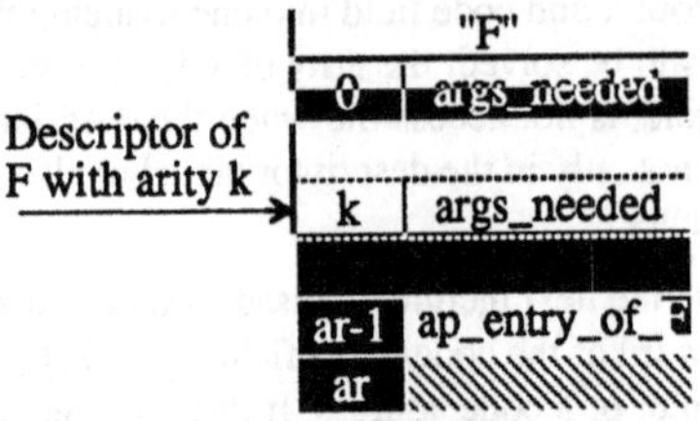

Fig 3.3: The lay-out of a descriptor in the descriptor table

`F` is a function with arity `ar`. The descriptor contains a string representation of the name and `ar`+1 entries. Now, the pointer stored in the descriptor field of the node is just a reference to the entry that corresponds to the arity with which F is actually applied. Besides this actual arity that is used by the garbage collector, each entry contains the code that should be reduced when a partial application of F is applied to an additional argument. It should be clear that this code is just the `args_needed` code as presented in section 2.3 unless the curried application has already `ar`-1 arguments. In that case the extra argument provides that this particular application becomes complete. So the apply entry of `F` can be called.

The descriptors of all symbols defined in a Clean program are stored in a so-called *descriptor table*. As a consequence, each application of a symbol F with actual arity k can be represented by an offset in this table that corresponds to the k-th entry of the descriptor of F.

With the aid of the previous representation the translation of the apply code will result in the following ABC instructions (we assume that register a1 refers to the node containing the partial application and register *st* refers to the beginning of the symbol table):

```
move    2(a1), a2   ; get the offset of the descriptor entry
add.l   st,    a2   ; add this offset to the beginning of the descriptor table
move.l  2(a2), a2   ; retrieve the reduction code
jsr     (a2)        ; call the reduction code
```

3.3. Generating MC68020 Code

A straightforward way of generating concrete machine code is by means of macro expansion: each ABC instruction is considered as a macro application that is substituted by a sequence of MC68020 instructions. The main disadvantage of this method is that when generation code for a certain instruction the context of that instruction is not taken into account. An illustrating example is given by the next piece of ABC code together with MC68020 code that might be the result of performing macro expansions:

Assume the following macro definitions:

```
#macro   push_b(n)   move.l  -((n+1)*4)(bsp), (bsp)+
#macro   addI        move.l  -(bsp),      d0
                     add.l   d0,          -4(bsp)
```

And the following ABC instructions:

```
push_b 0
push_b 2
addI
```

Applying the above standing macro definitions will result in:

```
move.l   -4(bsp),  (bsp)+
move.l   -12(bsp), (bsp)+
move.l   -(bsp),  d0
add.l    d0,     -4(bsp)
```

However, if all the three instruction were considered simultaneously, one could use that fact that the MC68020 `add` instruction does not require that the arguments are on top of the B stack. A more efficient code generator might compile the three abc instructions into three MC68020 instructions which are about 30% faster:

```
move.l -4(bsp),  d0
add.l  -8(bsp),  d0
move.l d0,       (bsp)+
```

So, before generating code it is useful to group ABC instructions into blocks. These so called *basic blocks* should have the property that they can be considered as atomic actions of the ABC machine. They specify state transitions that convert the state of the ABC machine (which is determined by the contents of the stacks and the graph store) at the beginning of these blocks into the final state at the end of the basic blocks. Now the task of a code generator becomes to implement such actions as efficient as possible. It is obvious that the largest gain will be achieved when it is tried to make these basic blocks as big as possible. In our code generator a basic block consist of the maximal sequence of ABC instructions that does not contain any label definitions or instructions that might change the flow of control (e.g. subroutine calls or conditional branches).

With the aid of basic blocks the compile-time analysis of ABC programs is simplified. A few examples:

- Flow of control: the original ABC instructions specify an evaluation order. Grouping these instructions into basic blocks allows us to deviate from this order as long as the new evaluation does not affect the final result at the end of the current basic block (i.e. the new code sequence should specify the same state transition). Changing the evaluation order makes it possible to improve the generated code as can be seen in the following example.

  Suppose we want to compute d0+d1 and d0+d2 in any register and d1 is used after these computations, but d0 and d2 not. First computing d0+d1 and then d0+d2:

  ```
  move.l    d0, d3
  add.l     d1, d3
  add.l     d2, d0
  ```

  But it would be better if d0+d2 was computed first. It saves not only one instruction but also one register:

  ```
  add.l     d0, d2
  add.l     d0, d1
  ```

  In the ideal case the code generator will determine an evaluation order of instructions such that the execution costs of the generated code are as low as possible. The execution costs can be found by simply adding the execution times of all the individual instructions (One should notice that the execution time of an instruction may depend on the preceding instructions). But the problem of finding an evaluation order in such a way that the total time is minimal is NP-complete which makes an algorithm based on this strategy useless. A different approach is to minimise the number of registers needed to evaluate basic block. This approach seems reasonable: since registers of a real processor are relatively sparse, the quality of the generated code strongly depends on how well they are utilised. Also, by decreasing the number of used registers generally less instructions are needed.

- Memory allocation: a basic block may contain instructions that reserve space in the heap. Such an instruction has to check whether the heap contains enough free cells. If this is not the case the garbage collector has to be called. As it is known compile time how many cells are actually needed in a certain basic block all these checks can be done at once instead of performing separate checks for each instruction (for an example see section 3.2).
- Optimising stack use: the generation of additional instructions for boundary checks of the stacks occurs inside a basic block can be avoided partially. For each block it can be determined how much the size of a stack will increase maximally which allows it to perform the testing in one time. The same counts for the adjustment of the stackpointer (due to the various `push` and `pop` instructions) which may involve additional `add` or `sub` instructions. Mostly these adjustments can be done on-the-fly using the post-increment or pre-decrement addressing modes. Another important improvement that might be obtained by using the post-increment or pre-decrement addressing modes is the disappearance of offsets.
- Compile time evaluation: since we are sure that a sub-sequence of instructions of basic block can only be reached via the beginning of this block we are free to substitute such a sequence by any piece piece of code having the same result. This allows us to replace instructions inside a basic block by other instructions which are executed faster than the original ones or to evaluate certain sub-expressions compile-time.

3.4. The Code Generation Process

The translation ABC programs into MC68020 code is quite complex so it is not reasonable to consider it as occurring in a single step. For this reason it has been partitioned into a number of phases. An overview of these phases is given in the next picture:

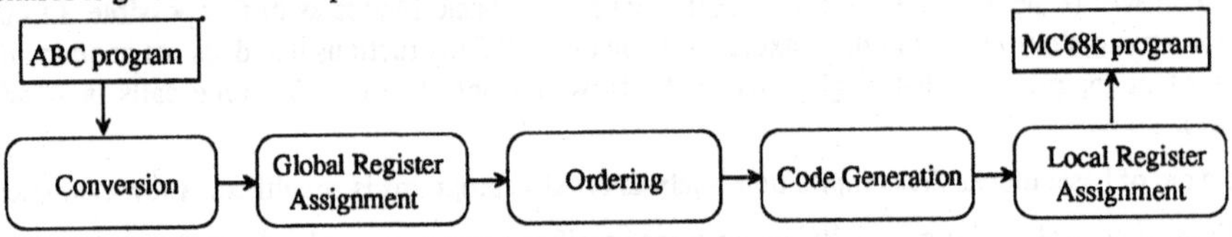

Fig 3.4: The code generation process

During the *conversion phase* the initial ABC program is divided into so-called basic blocks and converted into an internal representation using graphs. The *global register assignment phase* determines which entries of the A and B stacks are kept in registers at the beginning and at the end of these basic blocks. The *ordering phase* determines of all the sub-expressions the order in which these expressions should be evaluated. During the *code generation phase* (pseudo) MC68020 code is generated according to the order specified by the previous phase. The only difference between real MC68020 code and the generated code is that in the latter an unlimited amount of (virtual) registers is assumed. Finally, the *local register assignment phase* replaces virtual registers by real MC68020 registers.

The conversion phase

The correspondence between the initial stack frame S_b at the beginning of a basic block and the final stack frame F_b at the end is defined by the instructions of that basic block. A useful data structure for representing basic blocks such that automatic analysis of these blocks can be done more conveniently is a directed acyclic graph (hereafter called a *dag*). Such a dag gives a picture of how the value computed by each statement in a basic block is used in subsequent statements in the block. The dag representation of a basic block that we use has the following properties:

- The leaves either represent constants or entries of S_b
- All the other (interior) nodes represent applications of ABC instructions. The arguments of these nodes are the representations of the arguments of the corresponding instructions.

- If a node represents an instruction whereof the result appears in F_b this node is labelled with an identification of the corresponding entry in F_b. All the other nodes are not labelled.

The next example will serve as a guideline to illustrate the various phases of the ABC to MC68020 translation process. Consider the following Clean rewrite rule for F:

```
::   F !INT !INT    -> INT                   ;
     F a    b       -> -I (*I a b) (+I a 3)  ;
```

This rule is compiled into the following ABC instructions (only the strict entry is given):

```
sF:
   pushI +3
   push_b 1          |   push a on top of the stack
   addI              |   add b and 3
   push_b 2          |   push b on top of the stack
   push_b 2          |   push a on top of the stack
   mulI              |   multiply a and b
   update_b 1 3      |   update the b stack
   update_b 0 2
   pop_b 2
   subI              |   subtract the topmost elements
   rtn
```

The strict entry forms one basic block. The dag constructed according to this basic block is given in figure 3.5. The meaning of the additional information stored in the dag is explained later on.

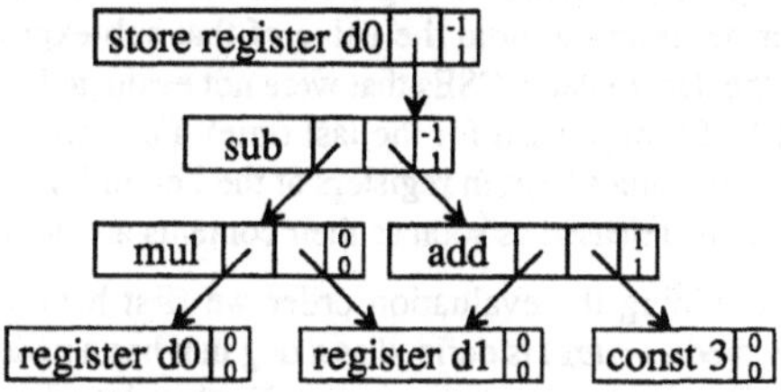

Fig 3.5: The dag of the strict entry

Note that the (superfluous) copying actions of stack entries do not appear in the dag.

The global register assignment phase

The so-called global register assignment specifies which values of the initial and final stackframes of each basic block are kept in registers. The information that is used to determine this assignment is obtained from the original Clean program. The Clean compiler uses the type information of the Clean rules to insert special ABC directives in the corresponding ABC program. These directives are placed at the beginning and the end of the basic blocks and specify the layouts of both the A and B stacks.

In section 2.2 we already mentioned that parameters and results of functions are passed via the A and B stacks. To increase efficiency the topmost elements of both stacks are kept in registers. So with the aid of this information the code generator reserves all the data and address register the are needed for storing these elements at the beginning of a basic block if such a basic blocks starts with a label that corresponds to an entry point of a function. The directives at the end of a basic block are used to provide that when a basic block is left at run-time, the results are kept on the right places (i.e. either in one of the register or one of the final stackframes itself). The latter may require that the contents of certain registers in use have to be saved on the stack.

The result of the global register assignment of a basic block is administered in the corresponding dag with the aid of two kinds of special nodes, namely, *register* and *store_register* nodes. A `register` node, which refers to an entry of the initial stackframe S_b, indicates that the value of that entry is kept in a register when entering the basic block (note that register node are always leaves of the dag). A `store_register` node, which refers to an entry of the final stackframe F_b, indicates that the value of that entry is held in a register when leaving the basic block. So `store_register` nodes are always labelled. For example, consider figure 3.5: due to the global register assignment parameters `a` and `b` are kept in resp. data register d1 and d0 and the final result should be stored in register d0. These register assignments are indicated with the aid of special `register` and `store_register` nodes.

The ordering phase

After executing a basic block all the entries of the final stack frame of that block have to be defined. So, the task of the code generator becomes to generate code for all the dags that are labelled. Under the assumption[1] that none of the instructions in a basic block, except the very last instruction may produce side effects the generation of code can be done independently of the original order of ABC instructions. The only requirement that has to be met is that when generating code for ca certain node of the dag all the other nodes that are reachable from this node have already been treated. So, we are free to change the original evaluation order as long as the previous requirement is fulfilled.

The aim of the ordering phase is to produce an evaluation order for a basic block for which the number of used registers is minimal. If a basic block does not contain any common subexpression (*CSE*), so the corresponding dag is free of sharing, the problem of determining the minimal number of registers is rather simple. An algorithm (which makes some assumptions about the registers and instructions of the target machine) has been given in Aho et al. (1986). The problem with common subexpressions is that the results of these expressions have to be stored somewhere until they are used the last time. This implies that after evaluating a certain sub-expression, the number of registers in use does not always increase by exactly one (due to the additional register necessary to hold the value of that sub-expression). It is possible that this increase is greater than one (if the dag contains CSEs that were not evaluated yet) or even smaller than one (if registers containing values of CSEs were used for the last time). Furthermore, the algorithm presented in Aho et al. (1986) cannot deal with values kept in registers at the beginning and at the end of a basic block. As with CSEs, such registers can be released as soon as their contents are not needed anymore.

To deal with CSEs when determining the evaluation order we first have to introduce some notions. A (rooted) connected dag (abbreviated as *cdag*) is defined as a dag that has a node r (called the root of the cdag) such that all the other nodes of this dag are reachable from r. Further, let n be the number of cdags that have to be evaluated and g_i denote the i-th cdag ($1 \le i \le n$). The evaluation order can be expressed by means of a permutation π of 1..n such that the cdag g_i is evaluated before a cdag g_j if $\pi^{-1}(i) < \pi^{-1}(j)$. Define $I(\pi,i)$ and $U(\pi,i)$ as:

$I(\pi,i)$ = the increase of the number of used registers due to the evaluation of $g_{\pi(i)}$ after evaluating $g_{\pi(1)},\ldots, g_{\pi(i-1)}$.

$U(\pi,i)$ = the (additional) number of registers required to evaluate $g_{\pi(i)}$ (also after evaluating $g_{\pi(1)},\ldots, g_{\pi(i-1)}$).

Note that $I(\pi,i)$ can be negative but $U(\pi,i)$ not and that $U(\pi,i) \ge I(\pi,i)$.

Given an evaluation order π, the maximum number of register is use during the evaluation of $g_{\pi(i)}$ is:

$$R(\pi,i) = U(\pi,i) + \sum_{k=1}^{i-1} I(\pi,k)$$

The number of registers necessary to evaluate all the graphs in an order specified by π is:

$$R_m(\pi) = \text{Maximum } \{R(\pi,i) \mid 1 \le i \le n\}$$

[1]From the (informal) definition of the notion basic block in this paper one could infer that the only instructions that have side effects are the instructions that can change the flow of control. This is not true. There are a few other ABC instructions which also have side effects and therefore have to be seen as instructions indicating the end of a basic block. An overview of these instructions can be found in Groningen (1990).

So finding an optimal evaluation order comes to the same as determining a permutation π_{min} such that for all other permutations π of 1..n: $R_m(\pi_{min}) \leq R_m(\pi)$.

A straightforward algorithm would generate all permutations π of 1..n and choose the one for which $R_m(\pi)$ is minimal. Unfortunately the complexity of such an algorithm is O(n!) which is, of course, unacceptable.

The algorithm that we have implemented estimates the values of $I(\pi,i)$ and $U(\pi,i)$ on forehand (i.e. before determining the evaluation order) by resp. I(i) and U(i). We require that the estimations are save which implies that for all permutations π both $I(\pi,i) \leq I(i)$ and $U(\pi,i) \leq U(i)$ must be valid. After determining I(i) and U(i), the evaluation order of the cdags is given by the following two rules:

- First evaluate all the cdags g_i with $I(i) \leq 0$ from low to high U(i)
- Then evaluate all the other cdags from high to low D (i), where D(i) is defined as U(i)-I(i).

It will be clear that the cdags g_i with $I(i) \leq 0$ have to be done first, for, after the evaluation of a graph with a non-positive I value some registers may become free. From the fact that we try to minimise the number of registers needed to evaluate the whole dag it immediately follows that these cdags should be treated in ascending U(i) order. Why all the other cdags are ordered according to their D value is more difficult to see. We will to illustrate this with an example (a correctness proof can be found in Groningen (1990)): Suppose we have three graphs g_1, g_2, and g_3 with I(1)=1, U(1)=2, I(2)=1, U(2)=2, I(3)=1 and U(3)=5. When we start with g_3 we will need 5 registers but if we start with one of the other two graphs at least 6 registers are necessary.

In Groningen (1990) these rules have been further refined. It also has been shown that the evaluation order gives a good approximation of the optimal order.

Registers on a MC68020

The two types of registers of the MC68020 processor are not generally exchangeable. Furthermore, not all registers are freely available: some of registers are dedicated to a special task. Due to this the number of address registers that we may use differs from the number of data register. Both facts make it necessary to adapt the algorithm described above. This is done in two stages. First, for each node of the dag it is decided whether this node is computed in an address register or in a data register. After that we determine for each cdag g_i two values of I(i): one for each register. Now, the total increase $I_t(i)$ is defined as:

$$I_t(i) = a*I_d(i) + d*I_a(i)$$

where a, I_a, d, I_d are resp. the number of address registers, the increase of address registers, the number of data registers and the increase of data registers.

In the same way we define $U_t(i)$ as:

$$U_t(i) = a*U_d(i) + d*U_a(i)$$

The evaluation order is obtained by applying the previous algorithm using the functions I_t and U_t instead of I and U.

Consider figure 3.5: each node is supplied with two numbers whereof the uppermost gives the I_d value of this node and the other number gives the U_d value. Since the I_a and U_a values do not matter they have been omitted . The negative I values (of the `sub` and the uppermost `register` nodes) are a consequence of the fact that the contents of the register d1 is not needed anymore after evaluating these nodes. The result of the `mul` node can be stored in register d0. So, in contrast with the `add` node, no additional registers are needed to compute the result of this node.

The code generation phase

During the code generation phase the dags of all the basic blocks are traversed. The order wherein all the cdags are treated is specified by the ordering phase For each of a cdag code is generated in a depth-first way: First, code is generated (recursively) for all of the arguments of a node (again in an order as specified by the ordering phase). Then the operation specified by the node is translated into one or more (pseudo) MC68020 instructions assuming an unlimited amount of (virtual) data and address register.

The local register assignment phase

Finally, during the last phase of the translation real registers are assigned to the virtual registers allocated by the code generation phase. The algorithm that determines the evaluation order tries to minimise the number of data and address registers that are needed to evaluate a basic block. However, it may be the case that one of these numbers exceeds the number of registers that are actually available (i.e. the number of virtual registers exceeds the number of real registers). In that case it will be necessary that at some point in the code the contents of a register of the required type has to be saved in memory so that it can be used again. The problem is which register has to be freed? The strategy we use is to choose the register of the required type whereof the contents that will not be used for the longest time.

Again using figure 3.5: during the last two phases code is generated for this dag. Actually, the very last phase is superfluous: there are enough registers available for allocating all the virtual registers. The final result of the code generation is shown below:

```
sF: muls.l d1,d0
    addq.l #3,d1
    sub.l  d1,d0
    rts
```

3.5 Other Improvements

Enlarging basic blocks

The gain in efficiency that can be achieved depends on the size of the basic blocks: large blocks offer more optimisation possibilities than small ones. In this section we describe two methods that can be used to extend basic blocks.

- Jsr_eval instructions: The `jsr_eval` instruction is translated into a sequence of MC68020 instructions which, amongst other things, investigate whether the corresponding node contains a descriptor or a pointer to the evaluation code. Since a `jsr_eval` instruction may change the flow of control it seems that a basic block containing such an instruction has to end at this point. However, this is not needed when the node that is going to be reduced is already in root normal form. An example of this can be found in section 3.2 in which the used registers are saved only when the evaluation code of the node is called.
- Code substitution: When calling a subroutine the current basic block is left. This, however, can be avoided if the subroutine call is substituted by the corresponding code. Note that this is only reasonable when the substituted code is relatively small. This optimisation is not yet implemented in our code generator (Though some code substitution mechanism has been implemented in the Concurrent Clean To ABC code compiler (Eekelen et al. (1990))).

Optimising booleans

In the ABC machine the conditional jump instructions (i.e. `jmp_true` and `jmp_false`) base their decision whether or not to jump on the (boolean) value that is on top of the B stack. If this boolean is the result of some comparison (which is indeed often the case) then it is not necessary to calculate this value explicitly. Instead, the conditional jump can use the condition codes of the concrete target machine that are set implicitly after performing the comparison. Take for example the following ABC instructions:

```
eqI_b      +10    0
jmp_false   label
```

The following code would have been generated if the boolean is calculated explicitly (assumed the top of the B stack is kept in register d0, register d1 is used to calculate the boolean and the value -1 and 0 represent resp. TRUE and FALSE):

```
cmpi.l #10,d0
seq    d1
extb.l d1
tst.l  d1
beq    label
```

Much better code is generated when using the condition codes of the MC68020:

```
cmpi.l #10,d0
bne    label
```

Using alternative instructions

On the MC68020 there are several instructions that, when applied to certain arguments, can be replaced by other instructions having the same effect but, with the advantage that their execution time is less. This replacement can easily be performed during the last phase of the MC68020 code generation or even by the assembler. Below examples of substitutions that have been implemented are given together with the gain in efficiency:

`move.l #data, Dn` can be replaced by `moveq #data, Dn` when $-128 \leq data \leq 127$. The gain is about 65%.
`muls.l #data, Dn` can be replaced by `lsl #n, Dn` when $data=2^n$. In this case the gain is 90%

The efficiency can also be increased by replacing instructions by combinations of other instructions with the same effect. Examples:

`cmpi.l #100,d0` can be substituted by `moveq #100,d1` followed by `cmp.l d1,d0`.
The same counts for `muls.l #10,d0` and the instructions `move.l d0,d1,lsl.l #2,d1,add.l d1,d0,add.l d0,d0`. The gains in efficiency are resp. about 30% and 75%.

Note that the alternative combinations of instructions need an extra data register. So one has to be sure that such a register is available.

4. Performance

We have compared the implementation of Concurrent Clean with implementations of Lml, Hope and C on the SUN3 (with a MC68020, 25Mhz processor). The Lml system is considered as a standard implementation of a lazy functional language. The Hope system is an example of a fast implementation of a strict functional language. The imperative languages are represented by C. It should be stated that, if possible, C has been used in an imperative way (i.e. using iteration instead of recursion). In our tests, the following implementations of these languages were used:

Lml	The Chalmers Lazy ML compiler, version 0.99.2, (90/08/20) (Augustsson & Johnsson (1989)).
Hope	The Hope+ compiler, release 3.2.1, August 1989 (Burstall et al. (1980)).
C	The gnu C compiler, version 1.36 (which generally gives faster code than the standard C compiler).

Measurements were done for the following test programs (see also the Appendix):

nfib	the well known nfib program with argument 30.
tak	the Takeuchi function, called with (tak 24 16 8).
sieve	a program which generates the first 10000 primes, using a quite optimal version of the sieve of Eratosthenes (outputs only the last one).
queens	counts all solutions for the (10) queens problem.
reverse	a program which reverses a list of 3000 elements 3000 times.
twice	four times the twice on the increment function.
revtwice	four times the twice of the reverse of a list of 30 elements.
rnfib	again the nfib program, but now working on real numbers, with argument 26.

fastfourier the fast fourier algorithm, on an array of 8K complex numbers. In the Concurrent Clean program a complex number is defined as a strict tuple of two reals.

	Clean	Lml	Clean (u!)	Hope	C	Clean (-!)
nfib	4.5	25	4.5	5.4	11	30
tak	4.9	40	4.9	7.2	11	36
sieve	8.1	25	6.8	9.1	4.5	12
queens	28	62	14	16	4.1	45
reverse	64	108	50	65	--	51
twice	1.7	SegFault	0.5	0.3	--	1.7
revtwice	27	OutOfHeap	9	12	--	39
rnfib	11	26	11	33	19	19
fastfourier	34	--	19	--	9.0	--

Table 5.1 Performance Overview (All times in seconds cpu time)

The following notes have to be made:

- The Lml versions of twice and revtwice resulted in run-time errors for these values.
- The reverse and twice programs have no sense in the context of C. The sieve and fast fourier programs are iterative versions. The other ones are inherently recursive.
- It has no sense to compute the fast fourier with the other functional languages: they all would run out of heap space.
- The times needed to generate an executable for the example programs vary widely. On an average, the Concurrent Clean implementation consumes about 3.5 seconds cpu time, the Lml system needs 6 seconds and the Hope system even 15 seconds.

The first two columns of the table compare a standard compilation of Concurrent Clean programs with Lml. The default reduction strategy is lazy, but strictness information is added automatically by the strictness analyser. It is obvious that in all cases Concurrent Clean outruns Lml.
The next two columns present a comparison between user annotated Clean, and Hope. User annotations are inserted at some places that are not indicated by the strictness analyser (see appendix A). The result is that functions become strict in more arguments (e.g. the sieve and queens programs), or return strict tuples (e.g. the fast fourier example). Concurrent Clean produces in almost all the cases the fastest code although the difference compared with Lml is not that great anymore. The only case in which Hope is faster is the twice example. This is mainly because Hope uses a smart integer representation. This is indicated by the revtwice program, which also tests the implementation of higher order functions but avoids the use of integers.
The recursive programs written in C appear to be slower than the ones written in Concurrent Clean. However, the iterative versions of the examples written in C are faster. But, in comparison with the past, the difference between execution times of on the one hand the functional languages and on the other hand the imperative languages has significantly decreased.
The last two rows of the table are measurements for real arithmetic. In fact, they show that of the functional languages only Concurrent Clean supports reals seriously.
Finally, the last column gives execution times for Concurrent Clean programs for which no annotations were added, neither automatically by the strictness analyser, nor by the programmer herself. From these figures we can conclude that in general strictness annotations increase the efficiency. The largest gain is achieved in programs which largely manipulate objects of basic types as is the case with tak and fast fourier.

5. Conclusions and Future Work

The figures presented in the previous section show that it is possible to obtain efficient implementations of lazy functional languages on conventional architectures. The division of the complicated compilation process into several stages has been proven to be fruitful. The first stage, wherein Concurrent Clean programs are translated into ABC code allowed us to concentrate our attention fully on the problem of how to avoid graph manipulations. During the second stage, in which the generated ABC instructions are grouped into basic blocks and translated to real target code, it appeared that all information needed to do this efficiently is still available in the ABC program; no essential information has been lost during the first stage. The performance comparison shows that optimisations presented in this paper give a significant increase in speed. The differences in speed between programs on the one hand written in Concurrent Clean and, on the other hand, written in imperative languages like C are now becoming acceptable.

However, the efficiency of the generated code can still be improved. With respect to the Concurrent Clean translation for instance, a so-called *application depended strictness analysis* can be added to the system. Such an analysis tries to determine whether eager evaluation of arguments for a certain application is safe because for this specific application it is known that these arguments will have been evaluated (inspite of the fact that the applied function is not known to be strict in these arguments for the general case). To the ABC to MC68020 code generator a more comprehensive global register allocator will be added. Also, the parameter passing of reals will be altered by using the floating point registers. Finally, the evaluation of lazy expressions and the implementation of the heap will be improved further and the in-line code substitution mechanism is going to be implemented.

Besides working on a sequential implementation we are also developing an parallel implementation of Concurrent Clean on transputers (Kesseler (1990)). At the moment a preliminary version is already available which allows interleaved multi-processing on a single transputer. This parallel system will be extended in the near future such that real speed-ups can be demonstrated. At UEA already some promising results have been obtained with a previous version of our Clean system (McBurney & Sleep (1990)).

References

Aho A.V., Sethi R., Ullman J.D. (1986), 'Compilers, Principles, Techniques and Tools', Bell Telephone Laboratories, Incorporated, Addison-Wesley.

Augustsson L., Johnsson T. (1989), 'The Chalmers Lazy-ML Compiler', The Computer Journal, Vol. 32, No. 2 1989.

Barendregt, H.P., Eekelen, M.C.J.D. van, Glauert, J.R.W., Kennaway, J.R., Plasmeijer, M.J., Sleep, M.R. (1987), 'Term Graph Reduction', Proceedings of Parallel Architectures and Languages Europe (PARLE), part II, Eindhoven, The Netherlands, LNCS Vol. 259, pp. 141-158, June 1987.

Brus T., Eekelen M.C.J.D. van, Leer M. van, Plasmeijer M.J. (1987), 'Clean - a Language for Functional Graph Rewriting', Proc. of the third International Conference on Functional Programming Languages and Computer Architecture (FPCA '87), Portland, Oregon, USA, Springer Lecture Notes on Computer Science 274, pp. 346-384.

Burstall, R.M., MacQueen, D.B., and Sanella, D.T. (1980), 'Hope: An Experimental Applicative Language', Proceedings of the 1980 LISP Conference, 136 - 143.

Eekelen, M.C.J.D. van (1988), 'Parallel Graph Rewriting, Some Contributions to its Theory, its Implementation and its Application', Ph.D. Thesis, University of Nijmegen, December 1988.

Eekelen M.C.J.D. van, Nöcker E.G.J.M.H., Plasmeijer M.J., Smetsers J.E.W. (1990), 'Concurrent Clean, version 0.6', Technical Report 90-21, University of Nijmegen, December 1990.

Eekelen, M.C.J.D. van, Plasmeijer, M.J., Smetsers, J.E.W. (1991). 'Parallel Graph Rewriting on Loosely Coupled Machine Architectures' proceedings of the workshop on CTRS'90. Montreal Canada. To appear in 1991.

Groningen J.H.G. van. (1990), 'Implementing the ABC-machine on M680x0 based architectures'. Master Thesis, University of Nijmegen, November 1990.

Johnsson Th. (1987), 'Compiling Lazy Functional Programming languages'. Dissertation at Chalmers University, Göteborg, Sweden. ISBN 91-7032-280-5.

Kesseler M.H.G., (1990), 'Concurrent Clean on Transputers', Master Thesis, University of Nijmegen, November 1990.

Koopman P.W.M., Eekelen M.C.J.D. van, Nöcker E.G.J.M.H., Smetsers J.E.W., Plasmeijer M.J. (1990). 'The ABC-machine: A Sequential Stack-based Abstract Machine For Graph Rewriting'. Technical Report no. 90-22, December 1990, University of Nijmegen.

McBurney D. and Sleep R. (1990), 'Concurrent Clean on Zapp', Proceedings of the Second International Workshop on Implementations of Functional Languages on Distributed Architectures, University of Nijmegen, November 1990.

Milner R.A. (1978). Theory of Type Polymorphism in Programming. *Journal of Computer and System Sciences*, Vol. 17, no. 3, 348 - 375.

Motorola, (1985, 1984), 'MC68020 32-Bit Microprocessor User's Manual', Second Edition, Motorola, Prentice Hall.

Mycroft A. (1984). Polymorphic type schemes and recursive definitions. Proc. of the 6th Int. Conf. on Programming, *Springer Lec. Notes Comp. Sci.* 167, 217 - 228.

Nöcker E.G.J.M.H., (1989). 'The PABC Simulator, v0.5. Implementation Manual'. University of Nijmegen, Technical Report 89-19.

Nöcker E.G.J.M.H. (1990). 'Strictness Analysis based on Abstract Reduction', in Proceedings of the Second International Workshop on Implementation of Functional Languages on Parallel Architectures, pp. 297-321, Technical Report no. 90-16, October 1990, University of Nijmegen.

Nöcker E.G.J.M.H., Smetsers J.E.W., (1990). 'Partially Strict Data Types', in Proceedings of the Second International Workshop on Implementation of Functional Languages on Parallel Architectures, pp. 237-255, Technical Report no. 90-16, October 1990, University of Nijmegen.

Nöcker E.G.J.M.H., Smetsers J.E.W., Eekelen, M.C.J.D. van, Plasmeijer (1991). 'Concurrent Clean', Proceedings of the Conference on Parallel Architectures and Languages Europe (PARLE '91), Eindhoven, The Netherlands, Lecture Notes on Computer Science, Springer Verlag, to appear in June 1991.

Peyton Jones S.L, Salkild J. (1989). 'The Spineless Tagless G-machine'. Proceedings of the Conference on Functional Programming Languages and Computer Architectures, Addison Wesley, pp 184 - 201.

Plasmeijer M.J., Eekelen M.C.J.D. van (1991). Functional Programming and Parallel Graph Rewriting. Lecture notes, University of Nijmegen, to appear at Addison Wesley 1991.

Smetsers J.E.W., (1989). 'Compiling Clean to Abstract ABC-Machine Code', University of Nijmegen, Technical Report 89-20, October 1989.

Appendix

Below follows a list a the benchmark programs used in section 4. The strictness annotations that were added by hand are in bold style.

```
||
||   The NFib Benchmark
||

::   Nfib INT        -> INT                                              ;
     Nfib n          -> IF   (<I n 2)
                             1
                             (++I (+I (Nfib (--I n)) (Nfib (-I n 2))))   ;

::   Start           ->  INT                                             ;
     Start           ->  Nfib 30                                         ;


||
||   The Takeuchi Benchmark
||

::   Tak INT INT INT    -> INT                                           ;
     Tak x y z          -> IF (<=I x y)
                               z
                               (Tak (Tak (--I x) y z)
                                    (Tak (--I y) z x)
                                    (Tak (--I z) x y))                   ;

::   Start -> INT                                                        ;
     Start -> Tak 24 16 8                                                ;
```

```
||
||   The Sieve Benchmark
||

::   Start          ->   INT                                        ;
     Start          ->   Select [2 | [3 | Primes]] 10000            ;

::   Primes         ->   [INT]                                      ;
     Primes         ->  primes: [5 | Sieve 7 4 primes]              ;

::   Sieve INT INT [INT]     -> [INT];
     Sieve g i prs           -> IF (IsPrime prs g (RTOI (SQRT (ITOR g))))
                                  [g | Sieve' g i prs]
                                  (Sieve (+I g i) (-I 6  i) prs)      ;

::   Sieve' INT INT [INT]    -> [INT];
     Sieve' g i prs          ->  Sieve (+I g i) (-I 6 i) prs          ;

::   IsPrime [INT] INT INT   ->  BOOL                                 ;
     IsPrime [f|r] pr bd     ->  IF (>I f bd)
                                TRUE
                                (IF (=I (MOD pr f) 0)
                                     FALSE
                                     (IsPrime r pr bd))               ;

::   Select [x] INT          -> x                                     ;
     Select [f|r] 1          -> f                                     |
     Select [f|r] n          -> Select r (--I n)                      ;

||
||   The Queens Benchmark
||

::   Start     -> INT                                                 ;
     Start     -> Length (Queens 1 [] [])  0                          ;

     BoardSize          -> 10                                         ;

::   Queens INT [INT] [[INT]]     -> [[INT]]                          ;
     Queens row board boards      -> IF (>I row BoardSize)
                                      [board | boards]
                                      (TryCols BoardSize row board boards);

::   TryCols INT !INT [INT] [[INT]]   -> [[INT]]                      ;
     TryCols 0 row board boards       -> boards                       |
     TryCols col row board boards     ->
          IF (Save col row board (--I row))
              (TryCols (--I col) row board queens)
              (TryCols (--I col) row board boards),
          queens: Queens (++I row) [col | board] boards               ;

::   Save !INT !INT [INT] INT     -> BOOL                             ;
     Save  c1 r1 [] 0             -> TRUE                             |
     Save  c1 r1 [c2|cols] r2     -> IF (Check r1 r2 (-I c1 c2))
                                         FALSE
                                         (Save c1 r1 cols (--I r2))   ;

::   Check !INT !INT INT          -> BOOL                             ;
     Check r1 r2 0                -> TRUE                             |
     Check r1 r2 cdiff            -> IF (=I cdiff (-I r1 r2))
                                         TRUE
                                         (=I cdiff (-I r2 r1))        ;

::   Length [x] INT               -> INT                              ;
     Length [a | r] n             -> Length r (++I n)                 |
     Length [] n                  -> n                                ;
```

```
||
||   The Reverse Benchmark
||

::   Rev_n INT [INT]          -> [INT]                              ;
     Rev_n 1 list             -> Rev list []                        |
     Rev_n n list             -> Rev_n (--I n) (Rev list [])        ;

::   Rev [INT]      [INT]     ->[INT]                               ;
     Rev [x|r]      list      -> Rev r [x | list]                   |
     Rev []    list           -> list                               ;

::   Reverse INT              -> INT                                ;
     Reverse n                -> Walk (Rev_n n (FromTo 1 n))        ;

::   Walk [INT]               -> INT                                ;
     Walk [x]                 -> x                                  |
     Walk [x|r]               -> Walk r                             ;

::   FromTo INT INT           -> [INT]                              ;
     FromTo a b               -> IF (=I a b)
                                     [a]
                                     [a | FromTo (++I a) b]         ;

::   Start                    -> INT                                ;
     Start                    -> Reverse 3000                       ;

||
||   The Twice Benchmark
||

::   Start               -> INT                              ;
     Start               -> Twice Twice Twice Twice ++I 0    ;

::   Twice (=> x x) x    -> x                                ;
     Twice f x           -> f !(f x)                         ;

||
||   The RevTwice Benchmark
||

::   RevList [INT]       ->[INT]                                    ;
     RevList l           -> Rev l []                                ;

::   Start     -> [INT]                                             ;
     Start     -> Twice Twice Twice Twice RevList (FromTo 1 30)     ;

||
||   The RNFib Benchmark
||

::   RNfib REAL     -> REAL                                  ;
     RNfib n   -> IF (<R n 1.5)
                     1.0
                     (+R (+R (RNfib (-R n 1.0))
                             (RNfib (-R n 2.0)))
                         1.0)                                ;

::   Start     ->  REAL                                      ;
     Start     ->  RNfib 26.0                                ;
```

```
||
||   The FastFourier Benchmark
||

TYPE

::   Complex   -> (!REAL,!REAL)                                          ;

RULE

::   +C Complex Complex       -> Complex                                 ;
     +C (a1, b1) (a2, b2)     -> (+R a1 a2, +R b1 b2)                    ;

::   -C Complex Complex       -> Complex                                 ;
     -C (a1, b1) (a2, b2)     -> (-R a1 a2, -R b1 b2)                    ;

::   *C Complex Complex       -> Complex     ;
     *C (a1, b1) (a2, b2)     -> (-R (*R a1 a2) (*R b1 b2),
                                     +R (*R a1 b2) (*R b1 a2))           ;

::   Root INT INT          -> Complex                                    ;
     Root j n              -> (COS z, SIN z),
                              z: /R (*R (ITOR j) 6.2831853) (ITOR n)     ;

     FastFourier com_array length      -> Fast com_array length          ;

::   Fast [Complex] INT       -> [Complex]                               ;
     Fast com 1               -> com                                     |
     Fast com length          -> Merge res_even res_odd length,
                                 (even, odd): Split com,
                                 res_even: Fast even next_length,
                                 res_odd:  Fast odd next_length,
                                 next_length: /I length 2                ;

::   Merge [Complex] [Complex] INT -> [Complex]                          ;
     Merge even odd n    -> Append low high,
                            (low, high): Merge2 even odd n 0             ;

::   Append [x] [x]           -> [x]                                     ;
     Append [a|x] y           -> [a |  Append x y]                       |
     Append [] y        -> y                                             ;

::   Merge' [Complex] [Complex] !INT !INT -> (![Complex], ![Complex])    ;
     Merge' [e|re] [o|ro] n i    -> ([!ui | urest], [!umi | umrest]),
                                (urest, umrest): !Merge' re ro n (++I i),
                                ri: Root i n    ,
                                prod: *C ri o,
                                ui: +C e prod,
                                umi: -C e prod                           |
     Merge' []      []      n i    -> ([], [])                           ;

::   Split [Complex]          -> (![Complex], ![Complex])                ;
     Split [a|[b|rest]]       -> ([a | even], [b | odd]),
                                 (even, odd):  !Split rest               |
     Split []                 -> ([], [])                                ;
```

Making Abstract Machines Less Abstract

JOHN HANNAN

DIKU, Department of Computer Science, University of Copenhagen
Universitetsparken 1, DK-2100 Copenhagen Ø, Denmark
hannan@diku.dk

ABSTRACT: We consider a class of abstract machines used for specifying the evaluation of intermediate-level programming languages, and demonstrate how various abstract aspects of these machines can be made concrete, providing for their direct implementation in a low-level microcoded architecture. We introduce the concept of stored programs and data to abstract machines. We demonstrate how machines that dynamically manipulate programs with abstract operations can be translated into machines that only need to read instructions from a fixed program. We show how familiar architectural features, such as a program counter, instruction register and a display can all be introduced very naturally into an abstract machine architecture once programs are represented as objects stored in memory. This translation lowers the level of the abstract machine, making it less abstract or, equivalently, more concrete. The resulting machines bear a close resemblance to a microcoded architecture in which the abstract machine instructions are defined in terms of a small set of micro-instructions that manipulate registers and memory. This work provides a further basis for the formal construction and implementation of abstract machines used for implementing programming languages. We demonstrate our results on an abstract machine that is a slight variant of the Categorical Abstract Machine.

1 Introduction

Abstract machines provide an intermediate level of representation for implementations of programming languages. The notion of intermediate is relative to high-level semantics in which the logic or language of the semantics encodes more details and low-level machine code implementations using native machine code stored in memory. These concrete representations of programs and data are influenced heavily by the available machine architectures, but also on the structure of the abstract machines.

In this paper we demonstrate that a particular class of abstract machines, called executors, can mechanically be compiled into a microcoded architecture. We perform this task in two phases. First we produce concrete machines from abstract machines. These differ from the abstract ones in their representation of programs and also their operations on programs. In an abstract machine, programs are represented as terms constructed from a set of constants. Term rewriting performs manipulations on programs, using pattern matching to destruct and construct programs. In a concrete machine programs are represented as objects stored in memory, and the only operation available (to the machine) is reading an instruction from memory into a register. An important contribution of this paper is the identification of a class of abstract machines from which concrete machines can easily be constructed. The execution of a stored program uses a program counter and instruction register, elements common to low-level machine architectures. The resulting concrete machine still uses pattern matching, but now only on the data being manipulated.

For the second step, we introduce a concrete representation of data and introduce low-level "micro-instructions" to perform data destruction and construction explicitly. The resulting architecture closely resembles a microcoded architecture in which the micro-language is essentially a register-transfer language, and the macro-instructions are the original abstract machine instructions, each defined now as a sequence of micro-instructions. While we do not attempt to translate this implementation further into a real machine language, we believe that such a process is nearly trivial as our micro-language is extremely simple.

This work can be seen as a continuation of the work presented in [Hannan and Miller, 1990] and further developed in [Hannan, 1991]. The former work considers the transformation of specifications given as sets of inference rules into abstract machines. The latter work considers the transformation of the resulting abstract machines, in the case of interpreters, to compilers and executors. We consider now a further translation to an even lower-level architecture, more closely resembling machine code. The overall goal of this work is to develop techniques for mechanically constructing provably correct and efficient implementations of programming languages based on operational semantics for languages.

We use a variant of the Categorical Abstract Machine as a prototypical example of the class of machines that we consider, and so our work has much in common with the work on the implementation of CAML [Cousineau *et al.*, 1987; Mauny and Suárez, 1986; Suárez, 1990]. In previous work we have given an account or derivation of a CAM-like machine using purely operational semantics (no categories). In the current work, we seek a lower-level representation for this machine and others like it.

This paper is organized as follows. In Section 2 we introduce abstract machines and define two classes of machines, interpreters and executors, briefly discussing their application and comparing them. In Section 3 we discuss how abstract programs, manipulated by abstract executors can be translated into concrete programs that are stored in memory. We then present a translation from abstract executors to concrete executors that operate on these concrete programs. In Section 4 we further refine our definition of concrete machine by eliminating pattern matching as a means for destructing data in favor of explicit operations on data, producing a microcoded architecture. Finally we summarize in Section 5.

2 Abstract Machines: Interpreters and Executors

We define abstract machines as term rewriting systems (TRS). We assume some familiarity with rewriting systems, its terminology and the notion of computation in a rewriting system. For our purposes, a TRS is a pair (Σ, R) such that Σ is a typed signature (a set of constants, each with a given type) and R is a set of directed equations $\{l_i \Rightarrow r_i\}_{i \in I}$ with $l_i, r_i \in T_\Sigma(X)$ and $FV(r_i) \subseteq FV(l_i)$. Here $T_\Sigma(X)$ denotes the set of first-order terms with constants from Σ and free variables from some set X, and $FV(t)$ denotes the set of free variables occurring in t. An abstract machine, then, is simply a TRS (Σ, R) in which the rules specify the transitions of the machine state. We shall restrict our attention to first-order, linear systems, i.e. Σ is a first-order signature and there are no repeated variables in the lefthand side of any rule. We provide general definitions for two classes of machines: interpreters and executors.

2.1 Interpreters

For a given programming language $\mathcal{L}$ we assume given a typed signature $\Sigma_{\mathcal{L}}$ used for constructing terms of type tm in a first-order abstract syntax, representing programs of $\mathcal{L}$. Furthermore, we require that if $k : \tau_1 \times \cdots \times \tau_n \rightarrow tm \in \Sigma_{\mathcal{L}}$ for $n \geq 1$, then $\tau_i = tm$ for all $i \in [n]$. That is, all subterms of a given term in the abstract syntax must also be terms in the abstract syntax. We define a class of machines specifying the interpretation of source programs. The essential characteristic of these machines is the use of instructions that operate on source programs, using the structure of these programs to distinguish various cases. For list notation we use constructors nil and :: (infix cons) and the operation @ (infix concatenation).

DEFINITION 2.1 (Abstract Interpreter) *An* Abstract Interpreter *for interpreting a language $\mathcal{L}$ is an abstract machine (Σ, R) such that*

(i) $\Sigma_{\mathcal{L}} \subset \Sigma$ *and* $k : \tau_1 \times \cdots \times \tau_n \rightarrow tm \in \Sigma$ *for* $n \geq 0$ *implies* $k \in \Sigma_{\mathcal{L}}$*;*

(ii) there exist a distinguished type ins *and a special constant* $ev : tm \rightarrow ins \in \Sigma$.

(iii) there exists some type $data$ *such that every rule is of the form* $\langle \alpha :: C,\ v \rangle \Longrightarrow \langle \alpha_1 :: \cdots :: \alpha_n :: C,\ w \rangle$ *for some terms* $\alpha, \alpha_1, \ldots, \alpha_n : ins, v, w : data$ *and variable* $C : (list\ ins)$.

We view $\langle \cdot,\ \cdot \rangle$ as a pairing construction so we can view the term $\langle u,\ v \rangle$ as a pair representing a *state* in the machine. The type $(list\ ins)$ is the type of instruction lists (lists whose elements are all of type ins), and the type $data$ represents the data that the instructions manipulate. When $n = 0$ we write the rule as $\langle \alpha :: C,\ v \rangle \Longrightarrow \langle C,\ w \rangle$. Note that the restriction on the structure of rules makes them *single-instruction oriented*, as each rule interprets the single instruction α with respect to the data v. The elements of Σ with target type ins are the *instruction symbols* of the machine.

The rules of R describe single reduction steps on states of the machine. A reduction sequence is a sequence $(\langle u_1,\ v_1 \rangle, \langle u_2,\ v_2 \rangle, \ldots, \langle u_n,\ v_n \rangle)$ such that $\langle u_i,\ v_i \rangle \Longrightarrow \langle u_{i+1},\ v_{i+1} \rangle$ is an instance of some rule in R. We assume that Σ contains an appropriate collection of constants for constructing pairs such that the state of a machine can always be represented as a pair.

Figure 1 contains the CLS machine, a variant of the SECD machine [Landin, 1964] and an example of an abstract interpreter for the untyped λ-calculus. This particular description is the one obtained in [Hannan and Miller, 1990] after applying a series of transformations to a specification of call-by-value evaluation given as a set of inference rules. The signature Σ_λ is $\{\hat{}: tm \times tm \rightarrow tm,\ \lambda : tm \rightarrow tm,\ 1 : tm,\ +1 : tm \rightarrow tm\}$. The syntax for λ-terms uses de Bruijn notation with '^' (infix) and λ as the constructors for application and abstraction, respectively, and 1 and +1 (postfix) as the constructors for de Bruijn indices. $\emptyset$ and '$\cdot$' are the environment constructors. $\emptyset$ is the empty environment and if e is an environment then

$$
\begin{array}{llcll}
\langle ev(M^\frown N) :: C, & (E :: L,\ S)\rangle & \Rightarrow & \langle ev(M) :: ev(N) :: ap :: C, & (E :: E :: L,\ S)\rangle \\
\langle\ ev(\lambda M) :: C, & (E :: L,\ S)\rangle & \Rightarrow & \langle\ C, & (L,\ \{E, \lambda M\} :: S)\rangle \\
\langle\ ev(1) :: C, & ((X{\cdot}E) :: L,\ S)\rangle & \Rightarrow & \langle\ C, & (L,\ X :: S)\rangle \\
\langle ev(n{+}1) :: C, & ((X{\cdot}E) :: L,\ S)\rangle & \Rightarrow & \langle\ ev(n) :: C, & (E :: L,\ S)\rangle \\
\langle\ ap :: C, & (L,\ X :: \{E, \lambda M\} :: S)\rangle & \Rightarrow & \langle\ ev(M) :: C, & ((X{\cdot}E) :: L,\ S)\rangle
\end{array}
$$

FIGURE 1
The CLS machine

$t{\cdot}e$ is the extension of the environment with the new element t. $\{e, t\}$ denotes the closure of term t with environment e. We overload the use of list constructors, using them to build instruction lists, environment lists and closure lists. The machine has two instruction symbols: $ev : tm {\rightarrow} ins$ and $ap : ins$. A state in the machine has the form $\langle c,\ (\ell, s)\rangle$ in which c is a list of instructions, ℓ is a list of environments, and s is a list of closures.

To evaluate a term t in an environment e we start the machine in the state $\langle ev(t) :: nil,\ (e :: nil,\ nil)\rangle$. A *successful* computation of the machine halts (i.e. no further rules applicable) in a state $\langle nil,\ (nil, \{e', t'\} :: nil)\rangle$ and the result is the closure $\{e', t'\}$. Note that a machine may halt in an unsuccessful state (one not in the above form) or it may never halt. In the latter case the instruction list may have a length of unbounded size.

Interpreters have the property that instructions may generate new instructions when rewritten by rules of the machine. For example, in the first rule of the CLS machine, an instruction sequence $ev(s^\frown t) :: \ell$ is rewritten to the sequence $ev(s) :: ev(t) :: ap :: \ell$. In terms of efficient implementation, this property poses two difficulties. First, the next instruction to be interpreted cannot be determined until the current instruction has been rewritten. Second, the length of the instruction list may not be bounded. It could grow arbitrarily large as the program is manipulated by rewrite rules. This property is typical of interpreters, with programs treated as data.

2.2 Executors

We can define an alternative class of abstract machines that does not suffer from the problems of interpreters and also resembles a typical machine architecture in some respects.

DEFINITION 2.2 (Abstract Executor) *An* Abstract Executor *is an abstract machine* (Σ, R) *such that*

(i) there exist a distinguished type ins *and a collection of constants* $\iota_i : ((list\ ins)_1 \times \cdots (list\ ins)_{n_i}) {\rightarrow} ins \in \Sigma$, $n_i \geq 0$, *for* $i \in [k]$ $(k \geq 1)$, *called instruction symbols.*

(ii) there exists some type $data$ *such that every rule is either of the form*

a. $\langle \iota_i(C_1, \ldots, C_{n_i}) :: C,\ v\rangle \Longrightarrow \langle C,\ w\rangle$ *or*

b. $\langle \iota_i(C_1, \ldots, C_{n_i}) :: C,\ v\rangle \Longrightarrow \langle C'@C,\ w\rangle$ *in which* C' *either occurs in* v *or is one of the* C_i,

$$
\begin{array}{llllll}
\langle & ap :: C, & (L,\ X :: \{E, \Lambda(B)\} :: S)\rangle & \Rightarrow & \langle B@C, & ((X{\cdot}E) :: L,\ S)\rangle \\
\langle & push :: C, & (E :: L,\ S)\rangle & \Rightarrow & \langle\ C, & (E :: E :: L,\ S)\rangle \\
\langle & lam(B) :: C, & (E :: L,\ S)\rangle & \Rightarrow & \langle\ C, & (L,\ \{E, \Lambda(B)\} :: S)\rangle \\
\langle & car :: C, & ((X{\cdot}E) :: L,\ S)\rangle & \Rightarrow & \langle\ C, & (L,\ X :: S)\rangle \\
\langle & cdr :: C, & ((X{\cdot}E) :: L,\ S)\rangle & \Rightarrow & \langle\ C, & (E :: L,\ S)\rangle
\end{array}
$$

FIGURE 2
The A-CAM machine

for some instruction symbol ι_i, *terms* v, w : $data$ *and variables* $C_1, \ldots, C_n, C, C'$: $(list\ ins)$ $(n_i \geq 0)$.

For an instruction of the form $\iota_i(C_1, \ldots, C_{n_i})$, we say that ι_i has arity n_i. When the arity is 0, we abbreviate $\iota()$ by ι. We can informally explain the action of these two kinds of rules as follows. Rules of the first kind perform the execution of an instruction, resulting in a state in which the data is now w and the following instruction can be executed. We call these rules *sequence* rules. Rules of the second kind perform a conditional jump to the start of instruction list C', with an implicit return to the instruction list C after completion of C'. The condition is determined by the instruction symbol ι and the data v. We call these rules *jsr* rules. The main goal of this paper is to demonstrate how these kinds of machines can be implemented in a low-level microcoded architecture in which programs are static objects stored in memory.

While abstract executors have a more restricted, but simpler, structure than abstract interpreters, they define a very useful class of abstract machine languages that provide an intermediate step between high-level languages and native machine code. In [Hannan, 1991] we explore the relationship between abstract executors and interpreters, demonstrating how an abstract executor and an associated compiler can be automatically constructed from an abstract interpreter. These executors, however, still contain a moderate amount of abstraction, when compared to traditional machine architectures. To understand this level of abstraction consider the necessary structure of a virtual machine for executors. We would need a machine that had primitives for performing term rewriting operations such as rule selection and pattern matching. Such a virtual machine seems far from a conventional architecture. (In practice we use Standard ML as our "virtual machine."

Figure 2 contains the A-CAM machine, a variant of the Categorical Abstract Machine (CAM) [Cousineau *et al.*, 1987] and an example of an abstract executor. We constructed this machine and an associated compiler from the definition of the CLS machine of Figure 1. A description of this construction can be found in [Hannan, 1991]. A state in the machine is similar to the state of the CLS machine, but the instructions are different. We will use this machine as our example in the next sections as we introduce less abstract versions of abstract machines.

In the next two sections we demonstrate how abstract executors can be made concrete so that the virtual machine required to implement these machines is very close to conventional von Neumann architectures, and in particular to a register transfer language.

3 Concrete Machines: Executing Stored Programs

The kinds of abstract machines presented so far are abstract in a number of ways. In this section we focus on a particular aspect: the representation of programs. We demonstrate how to shift our perspective from code-as-term to code-as-stored-instruction. This is done in two parts. First we examine the structure of programs manipulated by executors and present a concrete representation in which programs are considered objects addressed via memory locations. Second, we demonstrate how executors can be modified to exploit this representation. The resulting executors have a close resemblance to traditional machine architectures and include such features as a program counter, jump/return instructions and a simple display for maintaining return addresses.

3.1 A Concrete Representation for Programs

Our goal now is to represent a program as an object stored in memory. We use an idealized or abstract representation of memory, given as an array $\mathcal{M}$ of words or locations. The array is indexed by integers, but we assume no bounds on the size of the array. (It will always be large enough to store an entire program.) Each word is arbitrarily long, such that an instruction and all its arguments can always be stored in one word. The contents of the word at location i is denoted by $\mathcal{M}[i]$. Our model of memory, therefore, is still somewhat abstract, as we consider only a single address space and do not take word size into account, but this simplifies the presentation below. We later consider a slightly more concrete representation of memory, after describing our implementation on this abstract one.

An abstract executor manipulates programs given as lists of instructions. As stated above, an instruction can contain, as arguments, other programs (subroutines). This mutually recursive relationship between programs and instructions produces a nested structure of programs within programs within programs, etc. To map these abstract programs into concrete ones stored in a memory, we must "flatten" this nested structure. We use the idea that a concrete program is stored as a sequence of instructions in memory and is given by a pair $(\mathcal{M}, a)$ in which a is the address of the first instruction of the concrete program in memory $\mathcal{M}$. Often $\mathcal{M}$ will be left implicit as there will only be one memory $\mathcal{M}$. For example, if $a_1, \ldots, a_n$ are the addresses corresponding to the first instructions in the translations of programs $c_1, \ldots, c_n$, then the abstract instruction $\iota(c_1, \ldots, c_n)$ translates to the concrete instruction $\iota(a_1, \ldots, a_n)$, and this could be stored at a location in memory. We ignore any distinction between the abstract instruction symbol ι and its concrete representation. Both have the same arity, though the abstract one has arguments of type $(list\ ins)$ and the concrete one has arguments of type $address$. A list of abstract instructions will be translated into a sequence of concrete instructions stored consecutively in memory.

In addition to knowing the starting address of a program, we also need to know the ending point. In our abstract syntax, this corresponds to the end of the list representing the program. We need a corresponding delimiter at the end of a concrete program. Consider the structure of a *jsr* rule:

$$\langle \iota_i(C_1,\ldots,C_{n_i}) :: C,\ v\rangle \Longrightarrow \langle C'@C,\ v'\rangle.$$

When we start executing the program $C'@C$, we begin with the instructions of C' and continue until we have reached the end of this program, then we "resume" executing the program C. In our concrete representation of programs, we delimit the end of a program by introducing a new instruction ret that will occur at the end of a sequence of instructions. For example, the abstract program $push :: lam(car :: nil) :: lam(car :: nil) :: ap :: nil$ could be represented concretely as shown to the right.

address	contents
1 :	*push*
2 :	*lam 6*
3 :	*lam 8*
4 :	*ap*
5 :	*ret*
6 :	*car*
7 :	*ret*
8 :	*car*
9 :	*ret*

Rather than directly define a function translating from abstract programs to concrete programs, we first define a relation between the two.

DEFINITION 3.1 *For any abstract program c and concrete program $(\mathcal{M}, a)$ we define the relation $c \cong (\mathcal{M}, a)$ as the least relation such that*

$$\begin{array}{lll} nil \cong (\mathcal{M}, a) & \text{if} & \mathcal{M}[a] = ret \\ \iota(c_1,\ldots,c_n) :: c \cong (\mathcal{M}, a) & \text{if} & \mathcal{M}[a] = \iota(a_1,\ldots,a_n); \\ & & c_i \cong (\mathcal{M}, a_i) \ \text{ for } i \in [n]; \text{ and} \\ & & c \cong (\mathcal{M}, a{+}1). \end{array}$$

Note that because abstract programs are finite terms, they can only be related to concrete programs that do not contain cycles (when we view the concrete program as a graph). A concrete program may, however, contained "shared" nodes: more than one instruction may contain, as an argument, the same address. For example, in the example above we could change the contents of location *3* to be "lam *6*" to produce a concrete program equivalent to the same abstract program. Note that many concrete programs may be related to a single abstract program, but these concrete programs differ only in the choice of starting addresses.

We can extend this definition to abstract and concrete programs containing meta or schema variables, ranging over abstract programs and memory addresses, respectively, as found in rewrite rules. We assume given two sets of meta-variables C and $\mathcal{A}$, ranging over abstract programs and concrete addresses, respectively, and a bijective relation $\sim$ between these two sets. We then extend Definition 3.1 with the additional case

$$C \cong (\mathcal{M}, A) \ \text{ if } C \sim A.$$

It should be clear that for any abstract program c there exists a concrete program $(\mathcal{M}, a)$ such that $c \cong (\mathcal{M}, a)$. As a general notation, if $\alpha = \iota(c_1,\ldots,c_n)$ then we write $\overline{\alpha}$ for $\iota(a_1,\ldots,a_n)$ in which $c_i \cong (\mathcal{M}, a_i)$ for $i \in [n]$.

3.2 Executing Concrete Programs

Our original description of executors operated on terms in an abstract syntax, using pattern matching to destruct and construct terms. Such operations are not immediately available to our concrete representation of programs, but we can define corresponding operations that exploit the structure of these programs. We describe a systematic construction of such concrete executors based on their abstract descriptions. We focus on two aspects. First, the direct problem of executing a program stored in memory, including the introduction of auxiliary structures to facilitate this task. Later we consider the task of treating data as stored objects rather than abstract terms.

Recall from Definition 2.2, that an abstract executor consists of rules of the following two forms:

$$\langle \iota_i(C_1,\ldots,C_{n_i}) :: C,\ v\rangle \Longrightarrow \langle C,\ w\rangle \quad \text{and}$$
$$\langle \iota_i(C_1,\ldots,C_{n_i}) :: C,\ v\rangle \Longrightarrow \langle C'@C,\ w\rangle.$$

We can make some observations regarding the possible behavior of rules executing *concrete* programs based on the structure of these rules. Each rule executes a single concrete instruction that has a name (ι_i) and possibly some arguments (addresses). For rules of the first kind, if the current instruction is at location k then the next instruction in the *current sequence* is at location $k{+}1$. For rules of the second kind, if the current instruction is at location k then the next instruction to be executed is at some location A' such that $C' \cong (\mathcal{M}, A')$, and upon completing the code corresponding to C', execution should resume at location $k{+}1$ (corresponding to the code for C). From these observations we see that during execution the concrete code need never be modified: it can be a fixed and static object. The operations informally described above require simple maintenance of addresses for instructions. We can think of replacing the abstract operations over lists (*head*, *tail* and *concatenation*) with corresponding concrete operations. We begin by introducing a counter or register that contains the address of the next instruction to be executed. Then the concrete operations we need are (i) retrieving the instruction from memory addressed by this register (ii) incrementing this register by 1; (iii) changing the contents of this register to the start of some new piece of concrete code, while saving the old contents.

With these operations in mind, we propose a machine state for a concrete executor that includes:

(i) an *Instruction Register IR* that contains the instruction currently being executed (replaces *head*);

(ii) a *Program Counter PC* that contains the address of the next instruction to be executed (replaces *tail*);

(iii) a *Display D* that contains information for returning from "subroutines" (replaces *concatenation*).

The definition of instructions will still be given in terms of rewrite rules, but these will now operate on *IR*, *PC*, *D* and the data.

We describe a general transformation from an abstract executor to a concrete executor. This uses the relation between abstract programs and concrete programs given above, and also requires a relation between the data manipulated by an abstract executor and a concrete executor. Since the data manipulated by an abstract executor may contain occurrences of

$$\begin{array}{llll}
\langle PC, & ap, & D, (L, X :: \{E, \Lambda(A)\} :: S)\rangle & \Rightarrow \langle A{+}1, \mathcal{M}[A], PC :: D, ((X \cdot E) :: L, S)\rangle \\
\langle PC, & push, & D, (E :: L, S)\rangle & \Rightarrow \langle PC{+}1, \mathcal{M}[PC], D, (E :: E :: L, S)\rangle \\
\langle PC, & lam(A), & D, (E :: L, S)\rangle & \Rightarrow \langle PC{+}1, \mathcal{M}[PC], D, (L, \{E, \Lambda(A)\} :: S)\rangle \\
\langle PC, & car, & D, ((X \cdot E) :: L, S)\rangle & \Rightarrow \langle PC{+}1, \mathcal{M}[PC], D, (L, X :: S)\rangle \\
\langle PC, & cdr, & D, ((X \cdot E) :: L, S)\rangle & \Rightarrow \langle PC{+}1, \mathcal{M}[PC], D, (E :: L, S)\rangle \\
\langle PC, & ret, & A :: D, V\rangle & \Rightarrow \langle A{+}1, \mathcal{M}[A], D, V\rangle
\end{array}$$

FIGURE 3
C-CAM: a concrete version of A-CAM

abstract code, we need to modify this data to use addresses instead. To do this we replace each data constructor $k \in \Sigma$ that takes arguments of type $(list\ ins)$ with a new constructor k_c that takes corresponding arguments of type $address$. If v is a piece of abstract data then we obtain $\overline{v}$ by replacing each such k with k_c and each subterm c denoting abstract code with a such that $c \cong (\mathcal{M}, a)$. If Σ is a signature for an abstract machine then Σ_c is the corresponding signature in which the instruction symbols have arguments of type $address$ and the constructors like k have been replaced by k_c.

TRANSFORMATION 3.2 *Let $E_A = (\Sigma, R_A)$ be an abstract executor. The corresponding concrete executor E_C is $(\Sigma_c \uplus \{ret\}, R_C)$ such that R_C is the smallest set of rules including:*

(i) $(\langle PC,\ ret,\ A :: D,\ V\rangle \Longrightarrow \langle A{+}1,\ \mathcal{M}[A],\ D,\ V\rangle) \in R_C$;

(ii) if $(\langle \alpha :: C,\ v\rangle \Longrightarrow \langle C,\ w\rangle) \in R_A$ *then*
$(\langle PC,\ \overline{\alpha},\ D,\ \overline{v}\rangle \Longrightarrow \langle PC{+}1,\ \mathcal{M}[PC],\ D,\ \overline{w}\rangle) \in R_C$;

(iii) if $(\langle \alpha :: C,\ v\rangle \Longrightarrow \langle C'@C,\ w\rangle) \in R_A$ *then*
$(\langle PC,\ \overline{\alpha},\ D,\ \overline{v}\rangle \Longrightarrow \langle A'{+}1,\ \mathcal{M}[A'],\ PC :: D,\ \overline{w}\rangle) \in R_C$ *with* $C' \sim A'$.

In rewriting we identify terms $\mathcal{M}[a]$ with the contents of $\mathcal{M}$ at address a. So the occurrence of terms $\mathcal{M}[PC]$ and $\mathcal{M}[A']$ on the righthand sides of rules denotes the contents of the specified memory location. A state in a concrete executor is a tuple $\langle PC,\ IR,\ D,\ V\rangle$ in which PC is the program counter (address of the next instruction), IR is the instruction register (current instruction), D is the display (stack of saved addresses) and V is the data. Each rule of an abstract executor translates to one rule in a concrete executor. The concrete executor also has one additional rule defining the instruction ret. Implicit in the state of a concrete executor is the store $\mathcal{M}$ that contains the program being executed. As it is read-only we do not include it explicitly.

To start a concrete executor at address a (in store $\mathcal{M}$) on data v, we initialize the machine state to $\langle a{+}1,\ \mathcal{M}[a],\ nil,\ v\rangle$. The machine halts successfully in the state $\langle a',\ ret,\ nil,\ w\rangle$, for some address a'. Essentially this is the last return of the program, but the display is empty.

Applying Transformation 3.2 to the A-CAM of Figure 2 we obtain the C-CAM machine in Figure 3. The "data" parts of these two machines are essentially the same, except for the constructor Λ. In the A-CAM, the argument to Λ is a program c, but in the C-CAM, the

$$
\begin{aligned}
&\langle push : lam(car :: nil) :: lam(car :: nil) :: ap :: nil,\ (\emptyset :: nil,\ nil)\rangle \\
&\quad \Rightarrow\ \langle lam(car :: nil) :: lam(car :: nil) :: ap :: nil,\ (\emptyset :: \emptyset :: nil,\ nil)\rangle \\
&\quad \Rightarrow\ \langle lam(car :: nil) :: ap :: nil,\ (\emptyset :: nil,\ \{\emptyset, \Lambda(car :: nil)\} :: nil)\rangle \\
&\quad \Rightarrow\ \langle ap :: nil,\ (nil,\ \{\emptyset, \Lambda(car :: nil)\} :: \{\emptyset, \Lambda(car :: nil)\} :: nil)\rangle \\
&\quad \Rightarrow\ \langle car :: nil,\ ((\{\emptyset, \Lambda(car :: nil)\} \cdot \emptyset) :: nil,\ nil)\rangle \\
&\quad \Rightarrow\ \langle nil,\ (nil,\ \{\emptyset, \Lambda(car :: nil)\} :: nil)\rangle
\end{aligned}
$$

$$
\begin{aligned}
&\langle 2,\ push,\ nil,\ (\emptyset :: nil,\ nil)\rangle \\
&\quad \Rightarrow\ \langle 3,\ lam\,6,\ nil,\ (\emptyset :: \emptyset :: nil,\ nil)\rangle \\
&\quad \Rightarrow\ \langle 4,\ lam\,8,\ nil,\ (\emptyset :: nil,\ \{\emptyset, \Lambda(6)\} :: nil)\rangle \\
&\quad \Rightarrow\ \langle 5,\ ap,\ nil,\ (nil,\ \{\emptyset, \Lambda(8)\} :: \{\emptyset, \Lambda(6)\} :: nil)\rangle \\
&\quad \Rightarrow\ \langle 7,\ car,\ 5 :: nil,\ ((\{\emptyset, \Lambda(8)\} \cdot \emptyset) :: nil,\ nil)\rangle \\
&\quad \Rightarrow\ \langle 8,\ ret,\ 5 :: nil,\ (nil,\ \{\emptyset, \Lambda(8)\} :: nil)\rangle \\
&\quad \Rightarrow\ \langle 6,\ ret,\ nil,\ (nil,\ \{\emptyset, \Lambda(8)\} :: nil)\rangle
\end{aligned}
$$

address	contents
1 :	*push*
2 :	*lam 6*
3 :	*lam 8*
4 :	*ap*
5 :	*ret*
6 :	*car*
7 :	*ret*
8 :	*car*
9 :	*ret*

FIGURE 4
Reducing compiled form of $(\lambda x.x)(\lambda x.x)$ in A-CAM (top) and C-CAM (bottom)

argument is the address of the stored version of c. Figure 4 contains comparable reduction sequences using the example program from above.

We formalize the relation between abstract and concrete executors with the following theorem.

THEOREM 3.3 *Let E_A be an abstract executor and E_C be the concrete executor obtained via Transformation 3.2. Let c_0 and $(\mathcal{M}, a_0)$ be abstract and concrete programs, respectively, such that $c_0 \cong (\mathcal{M}, a_0)$. Then $\langle c_0,\ v\rangle \Longrightarrow^{*}_{E_A} \langle nil,\ w\rangle$ iff for some a', $\langle a_0{+}1,\ \mathcal{M}[a_0],\ nil,\ \overline{v}\rangle \Longrightarrow^{*}_{E_C} \langle a',\ ret,\ nil,\ \overline{w}\rangle$.*

To prove this theorem we shall use the following lemma that considers the "complete" execution of a single instruction.

LEMMA 3.4 *For abstract program c and concrete program $(\mathcal{M}, a)$ if $c \cong (\mathcal{M}, a)$ then for all d*

$$\langle \alpha :: c,\ v\rangle \Longrightarrow^{*}_{E_A} \langle c,\ w\rangle \text{ iff } \langle a,\ \overline{\alpha},\ d,\ \overline{v}\rangle \Longrightarrow^{*}_{E_C} \langle a{+}1,\ \mathcal{M}[a],\ d,\ \overline{w}\rangle.$$

PROOF The proof in the forward direction is by induction on the number n of *jsr* rules occurring in the $E_{\mathcal{A}}$-sequence.

base: $n = 0$. Then the reduction sequence contains only occurrences of sequence rules, and so it must be of length 1:

$$\langle \alpha :: c,\ v\rangle \Longrightarrow_{E_{\mathcal{A}}} \langle c,\ w\rangle.$$

Then by Transformation 3.2 and the equivalence $c \cong (\mathcal{M}, a)$, $E_{\mathcal{C}}$ must contain the rule

$$\langle a,\ \overline{\alpha},\ d,\ \overline{v}\rangle \Longrightarrow^{*}_{E_{\mathcal{C}}} \langle a{+}1,\ \mathcal{M}[a],\ d,\ \overline{w}\rangle$$

for arbitrary d and this satisfies the statement of the lemma.

step: $n > 0$. Assume the statement holds for all sequences containing fewer than n occurrences of *jsr* rules. Now consider a sequence

$$\langle \alpha :: c,\ v\rangle \Longrightarrow^{*}_{E_{\mathcal{A}}} \langle c,\ w\rangle$$

containing n occurrences of *jsr* rules. The first step in this sequence must be a *jsr* rule (otherwise the base case would apply, forcing $n = 0$). Assume this first step is of the form:

$$\langle \alpha :: c,\ v\rangle \Longrightarrow_{E_{\mathcal{A}}} \langle c'@c,\ v_1\rangle.$$

Then by Transformation 3.2 there is a reduction step

$$\langle a,\ \alpha,\ d,\ v\rangle \Longrightarrow^{*}_{E_{\mathcal{C}}} \langle a'{+}1,\ \mathcal{M}[a'],\ a :: d,\ v_1\rangle.$$

If $c' = \alpha_0 :: \alpha_1 :: \cdots :: \alpha_n :: nil$, then the remaining steps in the sequence can be described as:

$$\begin{aligned}
\langle \alpha_0 :: \alpha_1 :: \cdots :: \alpha_n :: c,\ v_1\rangle &\Longrightarrow^{*}_{E_{\mathcal{A}}} \langle \alpha_1 :: \cdots :: \alpha_n :: c,\ v_2\rangle\\
&\Longrightarrow^{*}_{E_{\mathcal{A}}} \langle \alpha_2 :: \cdots :: \alpha_n :: c,\ v_3\rangle\\
&\Longrightarrow^{*}_{E_{\mathcal{A}}} \ \ldots\\
&\Longrightarrow^{*}_{E_{\mathcal{A}}} \langle \alpha_n :: c,\ v_n\rangle\\
&\Longrightarrow^{*}_{E_{\mathcal{A}}} \langle c,\ w\rangle.
\end{aligned}$$

Each of these reduction sequences contains less than n occurrences of *jsr* rules, and so we can apply the induction hypothesis to each of these sequences. The translation of the abstract program $\alpha_0 :: \alpha_1 :: \cdots :: \alpha_n :: nil$ will be a concrete program $(\mathcal{M}, a_0)$, such that $\mathcal{M}[a_0{+}i] = \overline{\alpha_i}$ for $i \in [0..n]$ and $\mathcal{M}[a_0{+}n{+}1] = ret$. Thus, by the induction hypothesis we have the following reduction sequences:

$$\begin{aligned}
\langle a_0{+}1,\ \overline{\alpha_0},\ a :: d,\ \overline{v_1}\rangle &\Longrightarrow^{*}_{E_{\mathcal{C}}} \langle a_0{+}2,\ \overline{\alpha_1},\ a :: d,\ \overline{v_2}\rangle\\
&\Longrightarrow^{*}_{E_{\mathcal{C}}} \langle a_0{+}3,\ \overline{\alpha_2},\ a :: d,\ \overline{v_3}\rangle\\
&\Longrightarrow^{*}_{E_{\mathcal{C}}} \ \ldots\\
&\Longrightarrow^{*}_{E_{\mathcal{C}}} \langle a_0{+}n{+}1,\ \overline{\alpha_n},\ a :: d,\ \overline{v_n}\rangle\\
&\Longrightarrow^{*}_{E_{\mathcal{C}}} \langle a_0{+}n{+}2,\ ret,\ a :: d,\ \overline{w}\rangle.
\end{aligned}$$

Hence we can construct the reduction sequence

$$\begin{aligned}
\langle a,\ \alpha,\ d,\ \overline{v}\rangle &\Longrightarrow_{E_C} \langle a_0{+}1,\ \overline{\alpha_0},\ a :: d,\ \overline{v_1}\rangle \\
&\Longrightarrow^{*}_{E_C} \cdots \\
&\Longrightarrow^{*}_{E_C} \langle a_0{+}n{+}2,\ ret,\ a :: d,\ \overline{w}\rangle \\
&\Longrightarrow_{E_C} \langle a{+}1,\ \mathcal{M}[a],\ d,\ \overline{w}\rangle
\end{aligned}$$

which satisfies the statement of the lemma.

The proof in the reverse direction follows similarly, with the induction on the number of *jsr* rules occurring in an E_C-reduction sequence.

This concludes the proof of the lemma. □

PROOF [of Theorem 3.3] We just show the forward direction. Assume we have the reduction sequence $\langle c,\ v\rangle \Longrightarrow^{*}_{E_A} \langle nil,\ w\rangle$. If $c = nil$ then the statement holds immediately with both reduction sequences having length 0 and $v = w$, $\overline{v} = \overline{w}$, and $a' = a_0{+}1$. If $c = \alpha_0 :: \alpha_1 :: \cdots :: \alpha_n :: nil$ for $n \geq 0$, then we can decompose this sequence as follows:

$$\begin{aligned}
\langle \alpha_0 :: \alpha_1 :: \cdots :: \alpha_n :: c,\ v\rangle &\Longrightarrow^{*}_{E_A} \langle \alpha_1 :: \cdots :: \alpha_n :: nil,\ v_1\rangle \\
&\Longrightarrow^{*}_{E_A} \langle \alpha_2 :: \cdots :: \alpha_n :: nil,\ v_2\rangle \\
&\Longrightarrow^{*}_{E_A} \cdots \\
&\Longrightarrow^{*}_{E_A} \langle \alpha_n :: nil,\ v_n\rangle \\
&\Longrightarrow^{*}_{E_A} \langle nil,\ w\rangle.
\end{aligned}$$

To each of these reduction sequences we can apply Lemma 3.4, and so there exist reduction sequences

$$\begin{aligned}
\langle a_0{+}1,\ \overline{\alpha_0},\ nil,\ \overline{v}\rangle &\Longrightarrow^{*}_{E_C} \langle a_0{+}2,\ \overline{\alpha_1},\ nil,\ \overline{v_1}\rangle \\
&\Longrightarrow^{*}_{E_C} \langle a_0{+}3,\ \overline{\alpha_2},\ nil,\ \overline{v_2}\rangle \\
&\Longrightarrow^{*}_{E_C} \cdots \\
&\Longrightarrow^{*}_{E_C} \langle a_0{+}n{+}1,\ \overline{\alpha_n},\ nil,\ \overline{v_n}\rangle \\
&\Longrightarrow^{*}_{E_C} \langle a_0{+}n{+}2,\ ret,\ nil,\ \overline{w}\rangle.
\end{aligned}$$

and this satisfies the statement of the theorem. The reverse direction follows similarly, using Lemma 3.4 in the reverse direction. □

The concrete machines produced by Transformation 3.2 have certain properties that suggest how we can simplify them. First, note that we have essentially eliminated all non-trivial pattern matching on the program. The only place where pattern variables (to be matched against program parts) can occur is in the argument position of an instruction, and they must be variables. As such matching only depends on the instruction name (the arguments will always match the variables in the patterns), we can simplify the architecture by modifying our concrete representation of instructions: an instruction of the form $\iota(a_1, \ldots, a_n)$, stored in one word in our previous representation can alternatively be stored in $n{+}1$ contiguous words (starting at some address k) as shown to the right.

k :	ι
$k{+}1$:	a_1
$\vdots$	$\vdots$
$k{+}n$:	a_n

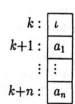

Transformation 3.2 can be modified to accommodate this change in representation, with the proof of the theorem changing only slightly. For example, the rule for *lam* in Figure 3 becomes

$$\langle PC,\ lam,\ D,\ (E :: L,\ S)\rangle \Longrightarrow \langle PC{+}2,\ \mathcal{M}[PC{+}1],\ D,\ (L,\ \{E, \Lambda(\mathcal{M}[PC])\} :: S)\rangle.$$

The argument to Λ is found in the memory location addressed by the current value of the *PC*. Now it should be clear that during execution of a program the pattern matching performed on the program only determines the name of the next instruction to be executed. All other required information is obtained relative to the address of that instruction or as part of the data. Thus, we can view an abstract machine as a set of rules, indexed by instruction names, specifying how data should be manipulated. Note that it may be possible for an instruction to be defined by more than one rule.

4 A Microcoded Machine

In the previous section we converted an abstract representation of a program (given by a list of instructions) into a concrete one stored in memory. In this section we consider the remaining abstract parts of the machine, namely the data and pattern matching, and demonstrate how these too can be made less abstract. As a first step we consider a suitable concrete representation for data in our machine. We then present a suitable set of operations over the concrete representation, replacing the operations over the abstract one.

4.1 A Concrete Representation for Data

In this section we convert abstract terms representing data into a stored representation. We choose an simple concrete representation of terms, using a record-like structure of contiguous memory locations whose first component is the name of the structure (e.g. **cons**), and whose remaining components are the addresses of the structure's arguments. Since the constructing of data on the righthand side of rules can involve any finite number of operations on abstract terms, creating larger terms than on the lefthand sides, we should expect that a concrete representation will require dynamic allocation of memory. This can be handled naively, by always allocating new memory for each new constructor. This is a very general method, though it may not be particularly efficient. Various optimizations to this representation have been presented in the literature [Appel and MacQueen, 1987], and most of these are beyond the scope of this paper. Our goal here is to provide a general method for representing data concretely.

Using this representation for data we can define an equivalence between abstract and concrete data as we did for programs in the previous section. Instead we shall consider one special case in which an efficient representation of constructors can be obtained. This case concerns the use of concrete lists, or stacks, to represent abstract lists. Using the general method outlined above to represent lists concretely we would introduce a three element record (three consecutive memory locations) with the first containing the label **cons**, the second containing the address of the head of the list and the third containing the address of the tail. It would be much simpler if we could represent an abstract list as a contiguous sequence of memory locations. This could eliminate the need for explicit constructor cells. Then the machine state would only maintain the address of the top of the stack, and operations such as push and pop would simply increment/decrement this address, storing or reading an item from memory.

Unfortunately, such a representation of abstract lists is not always possible. As an example of what can go wrong consider a rule that duplicates an abstract list, as in the rule for *push* in Figure 3. The variable E, representing the environment, is an abstract list. On the righthand side of this rule we have two occurrences of E. After applying this rule we will have two occurrences of the same environment. Subsequent rules could manipulate these two occurrences independently. Now if we represented environments as stacks then E would be given by an address and we would have two occurrences of this address in a machine state. Then, quite possibly, distinct applications of the *ap* rule could push different values onto each of these occurrences. This would cause one to overwrite the other. So representing environments as stacks in memory is not a good idea. However, such concrete lists, or stacks, are very useful when they safely implement abstract lists.

So when is a list a stack? We provide a sufficient condition for when a list structure, occurring in the state of an abstract machine can be represented as a concrete list. First we introduce the notion of context for machine states. A context $\mathcal{C}[\,]_1[\,]_2\cdots[\,]_n$ is a term containing n "holes" or meta-variables. We denote the filling or substitution for these holes with terms $t_1,\ldots,t_n$ by $\mathcal{C}[t_1]_1[t_2]_2\cdots[t_n]_n$ and for given a context we denote the ith hole by $\#i$. We give an example below.

DEFINITION 4.1 *Let (Σ, R) be an abstract machine. If there exists a context $\mathcal{C}[\,]_1[\,]_2\cdots[\,]_n$ for some $n > 0$ such that for every rule $r \in R$ there exist terms $t_1,\ldots,t_n,t'_1,\ldots,t'_n$ such that*

(i) r is $(\mathcal{C}[t_1]_1[t_2]_2\cdots[t_n]_n \Longrightarrow \mathcal{C}[t'_1]_1[t'_2]_2\cdots[t'_n]_n)$; and

(ii) $t_i = \alpha_1 :: \cdots \alpha_m :: L$, $t'_i = \alpha'_1 :: \cdots \alpha'_{m'} :: L$, for L a variable not free in any t_j, t'_j $(j \neq i)$ or α_k, α'_k $(k \in [m],\ k' \in [m'])$.

then we say that the ith position of the context $\mathcal{C}$ can be implemented as a stack.

The conditions of the definition ensure that the list is accessed only by destructing/constructing its topmost elements and that no duplication of the list can occur.

This definition provides only a sufficient condition for recognizing when lists are used in a stack-like fashion. Note that the environments manipulated by the rules in Figure 3 cannot be implemented using a stack (even if we had represented them abstractly using lists). As three examples of lists that satisfy this definition, consider the abstract machine of Figure 3 and the context $\mathcal{C} = \langle \#1,\ \#2,\ \#3,\ (\#4, \#5)\rangle$. By Definition 4.1 positions #3, #4 and #5 can all be implemented as stacks. Instead of presenting a formal description of how stacks can be implemented, we use an example below to convey the basic ideas. This leaves only the environment constructors: $\emptyset$ and '$\cdot$' and the closure constructor $\{\cdot,\cdot\}$, and these can be represented naively as described above. The nullary constructor $\emptyset$ (not explicitly used in the description in Figure 3) requires only a single word, while the binary constructors '$\cdot$' and $\{\cdot,\cdot\}$ require three words each. We introduce the new names `cons` and `closure` to be stored in the first word of records representing these constructors. We will make use of such a representation below.

4.2 Manipulating Concrete Data via Macro-instructions

With data in a concrete form we can no longer use pattern matching as a means for destructing and constructing data. Instead we will use explicit operations for accessing and updating the contents of memory. A machine state will still be a quadruple $\langle PC, IR, D, X\rangle$, in which

PC	is the address of the next instruction
IR	is the current instruction
D	is the address of top element on the Display stack
X	is the address of the root address of the data

We can think of each component as a register containing a value. (These registers could be reserved memory locations, for example).

We introduce some primitive instructions for manipulating registers and memory. Names beginning with **R** denote to registers. **RA** denotes a register whose contents is a memory address.

`move(R1,R2)`	move the contents of **R1** into **R2**.
`load(R,RA)`	copy the contents in memory at the address contained in **RA** into **R**.
`stor(R,RA)`	store the contents of **R** in memory at the address contained in **RA**.
`strc(C,RA)`	store the constant **C** in memory at the address contained in **RA**.
`inc(R)`	increment the contents of **R**.
`dec(R)`	decrement the contents of **R**.
`get(R,N)`	load **R** with the starting address of a new block of **N** new memory locations.
`heq(R,C)`	halt if contents of **R** equals constant **C**.
`hne(R,C)`	halt if contents of **R** does not equal constant **C**.

From these primitive instructions we can define some further instructions for manipulating stacks and constructing data. These are the *defined* instructions given in Figure 5. For the **psh** and **pop** instructions, the second argument is assumed to be the register whose contents is the address of the top of the stack. The bottom of a stack is denoted by a location containing the value **-1**. The **psh** instruction pushes the contents of **R1** and the result of a **pop** is left in **R1**.

Starting from a concrete machine and this set of micro-instructions, we can construct a microprogram that implements the machine. Each rule is translated into a sequence of micro-instructions that performs the operations on the concrete data corresponding to the abstract operations. This program consists of a fetch phase (that loads the instruction register and increments the program counter) and then an execute phase (essentially a large **case** statement indexed by the current instruction). We have not defined the **case** statement as a primitive, but its meaning should be obvious.

4.3 Microcoded CAM

As an example, we have translated the rewrite rules of Figure 3, and the corresponding microprogram is given in Figure 6. Each of the macro-instructions (**ap, push, lam, car, cdr, ret**) is defined in terms of micro-instructions. The first part of each definition performs the destructing of data. The **pop** instruction performs the proper check for a

```
pop(R1,R2) == load(R1,R2);
              heq(R1,-1);
              dec(R2)

psh(R1,R2) == inc(R2);
              stor(R1,R2)
```

```
mkcl(R,RA,RB) == get(R,3);
                 strc("clo",R);
                 inc(R);
                 stor(RA,R);
                 inc(R);
                 stor(RB,R)

mkcn(R,RA,RB) == get(R,3);
                 strc("cons",R);
                 inc(R);
                 stor(RA,R);
                 inc(R);
                 stor(RB,R)
```

FIGURE 5
Defined Instructions for Stacks and Data Construction

non-empty stack and the **hne** ("halt if not equal") command checks for a closure (in the definition of **ap**) and a non-empty environment (in the definition of **car** and **cdr**). Consider the rule for *ap* from Figure 3:

$$\langle PC,\ ap,\ D,\ (L,\ X :: \{E, \mathcal{A}(A)\} :: S)\rangle \Longrightarrow \langle A{+}1,\ \mathcal{M}[A],\ PC :: D,\ ((X{\cdot}E) :: L,\ S)\rangle.$$

The lefthand side of this rule destructs only the stack: it requires that the stack have two elements. The first element is assigned to X. The second element must be a closure and its two arguments are assigned to variables E and A. The remainder of the stack is assigned to S. This destructing is accomplished by the first seven instructions in the microcode definition of the macro-instruction **ap** in Figure 6. The first two **pop**s remove the top two elements from the stack, storing the first in register **X** and the second in register **T**. The stack register **S** is then left pointing to the remainder of the stack. The third instruction checks that **T** points to a closure, and then the following four instructions extract the first and second arguments of the closure, storing them in registers **E** and **A**, respectively.

The righthand side of the above rule performs the constructing of data. The term $(X{\cdot}E)$ is constructed and pushed onto the stack L, the *PC* is pushed onto the stack D, and the *PC* is updated with A. In the microcode version this is accomplished by the next four instructions of the definition of **ap**. The remaining rules are translated similarly. We have performed some optimizations that might not be immediately apparent from this reasonably simple-minded translation, but these were only to aid in readability. Further optimizations to the current description are possible and easily justified.

The process of compiling pattern matching as outlined here is straightforward, and more detailed descriptions can be found in the literature [Puel and Suárez, 1990]. We have considered only a very simple case of matching. In particular we ignored the case in which a macro-instruction may be defined by two or more rules. In this case after failing to match against a rule, the next rule should be tried. Again, we refer to the literature for more details on efficient methods for this kind of matching.

```
start: load(IR, PC);
       inc(PC);
       case IR :
         ap    =>  pop(X,S);
                   pop(T,S);
                   hne("clo",T);
                   inc(T);
                   load(E,T);
                   inc(T);
                   load(A,T);
                   mkcn(T,X,E);
                   psh(T,L);
                   psh(PC,D);
                   move(A,PC);
                   break;

         push  =>  load(X,L);
                   psh(X,L);
                   break;

         lam   =>  load(A,PC);
                   inc(PC);
                   pop(E,L);
                   mkcl(T,E,A);
                   psh(T,S);
                   break;

         car   =>  pop(T,L);
                   hne("cons",T);
                   inc(T);
                   load(X,T);
                   psh(X,S);
                   break;

         cdr   =>  pop(T,L);
                   hne("cons",T);
                   inc(T);inc(T);
                   load(X,T);
                   psh(X,L);
                   break;

         ret   =>  pop(PC,D)

       endcase;
       goto start
```

FIGURE 6
Microcode for the CAM

5 Summary

We have considered aspects of abstract machines that make them abstract and demonstrated how to define more concrete versions of them. We argued that the representation of programs and data as abstract terms, constructed from a set of constants, and the use of pattern matching to perform data destructing and constructing are the two principle features that make an abstract machine abstract. Rather than consider a very general class of abstract machines we focused on a class called executors. The programs executed by these machines have properties that provide for a direct translation into a simple concrete representation in which programs are fixed sequences of instructions stored in memory. The simple structure of these programs and the notion of control for the abstract machines also suggests the introduction of a program counter, an instruction register and a display to facilitate the manipulation of stored programs. Granted, our background in the implementation of languages has influenced certain choices made, but we feel that these were all justified choices, given our simple notion of memory.

We eliminated the use of pattern matching by introducing low-level operations for explicitly destructing and constructing data. This naturally gave rise to a set of macro-instructions (defining a programming language) defined in terms of a small set of micro-instructions. The resulting specification bears a close resemblance to a microcoded architecture, and we expect that the micro-instructions translate directly into the assembly language of most von Neumann architectures.

Our previous work in constructing abstract machines has shown that abstract executors form a natural class of machines for defining abstract machine languages. Furthermore, these machines and associated compilers can be constructed from abstract interpreters. The work presented here applies to this class of abstract executors, and is therefore potentially applicable to a wide variety of language implementation efforts based on abstract machines.

Acknowledgements. This work has been supported by a grant from the Danish Natural Science Research Council. I would like to thank Peter Koopman and the members of the programming language group at DIKU for discussions and comments that contributed to this work.

References

[Appel and MacQueen, 1987] A. Appel and D. MacQueen. A standard ML compiler. In G. Kahn, editor, *Proceedings of the Conference on Functional Programming and Computer Architecture*, Springer-Verlag LNCS, Vol. 274, 1987.

[Cousineau *et al.*, 1987] G. Cousineau, P-L. Curien, and M. Mauny. The categorical abstract machine. *The Science of Programming*, 8(2):173-202, 1987.

[Hannan, 1991] J. Hannan. Staging transformations for abstract machines. In J. Hughes, editor, *Proceedings of the ACM SIGPLAN Symposium on Partial Evaluation and Semantics Based Program Manipulation*, ACM Press, 1991.

[Hannan and Miller, 1990] J. Hannan and D. Miller. From operational semantics to abstract machines: preliminary results. In M. Wand, editor, *Proceedings of the 1990 ACM Conference on Lisp and Functional Programming*, pages 323-332, ACM, ACM Press, 1990.

[Landin, 1964] P. J. Landin. The mechanical evaluation of expressions. *Computer Journal*, 6(5):308-320, 1964.

[Mauny and Suárez, 1986] M. Mauny and A. Suárez. Implementing functional languages in the categorical abstract machine. In *Proceedings of the 1986 Symposium on Lisp and Functional Programming*, 1986.

[Puel and Suárez, 1990] L. Puel and A. Suárez. Compiling pattern matching by term decomposition. In M. Wand, editor, *Proceedings of the 1990 ACM Conference on Lisp and Functional Programming*, pages 273-281, ACM, ACM Press, 1990.

[Suárez, 1990] A. Suárez. Compiling ML into CAM. In G. Huet, editor, *Logical Foundations of Functional Programming*, chapter 4, pages 47-73, Addison-Wesley, 1990.

Unboxed values as first class citizens in a non-strict functional language

Simon L Peyton Jones and John Launchbury
Department of Computing Science, University of Glasgow G12 8QQ
{simonpj, jl}@dcs.glasgow.ac.uk

Abstract

The code compiled from a non-strict functional program usually manipulates heap-allocated *boxed* numbers. Compilers for such languages often go to considerable trouble to optimise operations on boxed numbers into simpler operations on their unboxed forms. These optimisations are usually handled in an *ad hoc* manner in the code generator, because earlier phases of the compiler have no way to talk about unboxed values.

We present a new approach, which makes unboxed values into (nearly) first-class citizens. The language, including its type system, is extended to handle unboxed values. The optimisation of boxing and unboxing operations can now be reinterpreted as a set of correctness-preserving program transformations. Indeed the particular transformations required are ones which a compiler would want to implement anyway. The compiler becomes both simpler and more modular.

Two other benefits accrue. Firstly, the results of strictness analysis can be exploited within the same uniform transformational framework. Secondly, new algebraic data types with unboxed components can be declared. Values of these types can be manipulated much more efficiently than the corresponding boxed versions.

Both a static and a dynamic semantics are given for the augmented language. The denotational dynamic semantics is notable for its use of *unpointed domains.*

1 Introduction

Most compilers have a phase during which they attempt to optimise the program by applying correctness-preserving transformations to it. Constant folding is a particular example of this sort of transformation; procedure inlining is another.

Functional languages are especially amenable to such transformation because of their simple semantics. Non-strict functional languages are nicest of all, because β-reduction (sometimes called unfolding in a transformational context) is always valid; in a strict language it is only valid if the body of the function being unfolded is guaranteed to evaluate the argument.

Several researchers have begun to express more and more of the work of the compiler in the form of correctness-preserving transformations (see Section 11). Such an approach has obvious advantages. Firstly, each transformation can be proved to be correct independent of the others. When more of the compiler takes the form of such transformations, it is easier to prove the compiler correct. Secondly, each transformation exposes opportunities for other transformations. The more that is done within a transformation phase, the more chance there is for such beneficial interactions.

There is an important class of optimisations for non-strict languages which has so far been beyond the scope of program transformation. These all relate to the treatment of so-called *unboxed values*, which we introduce in the next section. Instead, this family of optimisations is generally implemented in an *ad hoc* manner in the code generator.

Following some preliminaries (Sections 2 and 3), this paper makes four main contributions:

- Most important, we show how the class of unboxed-value optimisations can formulated as correctness-preserving transformations (Section 4). Unboxed values are made first-class citizens, distinguished from their boxed counterparts by the type system. These transformations do not generate much better code than current compilers do; our intention is only to present the optimisations in a new and elegant way.
- We show how to apply the same idea to express and exploit the results of strictness analysis in a uniform way (Section 5).
- We show how the approach can be generalised to other algebraic data types (Section 6). Declaring and using such unboxed data types gives a substantial performance improvement.
- We provide a formal underpinning for the approach, by giving both a static semantics and a denotational dynamic semantics for the language extended with unboxed values (Sections 7, 8, and 9). The dynamic semantics has the desirable property that the semantic equations are unchanged from those for the language without unboxed values, despite the extra strictness of the extended language. This effect is achieved by using *unpointed domains.*

We conclude by discussing some language-design issues, reviewing related work, and mentioning some areas for further work.

2 The problem

Consider the following function definition:

```
double x = x + x
```

In a non-strict language, `x` may be unevaluated when `double` is called, in which case a pointer to a heap-allocated *closure* (or suspension) for `x` is passed to `double`. When `double` needs `x`'s value (in this case right away), it *evaluates* the closure. As a side effect of this evaluation, the closure of `x` is overwritten with its value. Any further attempts to evaluate `x` will succeed immediately, returning its value. This way of ensuring that unevaluated closures are evaluated at most once is called *lazy evaluation.*

Unfortunately, lazy evaluation tends to make arithmetic horribly inefficient if some care is not taken. In particular, in a naïve implementation numbers are always represented by a pointer to a heap-allocated object which is either an unevaluated closure, or is a "box" containing the number's actual value, which has now overwritten the closure. This means that a simple arithmetic operation, which would take a single machine instruction in a strict language, requires quite a long sequence of instructions: the two operands are fetched from their boxes, the operation performed, a new box allocated to contain the result, and the result placed in it.

The bit-pattern representing the value itself, on which the built-in machine instructions operate, is called an *unboxed value*. Unboxed values come in a variety of shapes and sizes: 32-bit integers, 64-bit integers, single and double-precision floating point numbers, and so on, are all unboxed values. A pointer to a heap-allocated box containing an unboxed value is called a *boxed value*. Clearly it is vastly more efficient to manipulate unboxed values than boxed ones.

Quite a lot can be done. For example, consider again the definition of `double` given above. A naïve compiler would compile code for `double` which would evaluate `x`, extract its unboxed value, then evaluate `x` again and extract the value again, then add the two, and box the result. A slightly cleverer compiler would realise that it already had `x`'s value in hand, and refrain from the second evaluation. As another example, consider the following definition:

```
f x y z = x + (y * z)
```

A naïve compiler might generate code to box the value of `y*z`, only to unbox it again right away. A cleverer compiler can elide these unnecessary operations.

As a final example, consider the following call to `double`:

```
double (p+q)
```

The straightforward approach is to build a closure for `p+q` and pass it to `double` which will evaluate it. But `double` is clearly going to evaluate its argument so it is a waste to allocate the closure, only for `double` to evaluate it, and discard it for the garbage collector to recover later. It would be much better for the caller to evaluate `p` and `q`, add their values, and pass `p+q` to `double` in unboxed form.

3 The Core language

We begin with a few preliminaries, to set the scene for our new proposals.

Our compilation route involves the following steps:

1. The source language is HASKELL (Hudak et al. [1990]), a strongly-typed, non-strict, purely-functional language. HASKELL's main innovative feature is its support for systematic overloading, but we do not discuss this aspect at all here.

2. HASKELL is compiled to the *Core language*. All HASKELL's syntactic sugar has been compiled out, type checking performed, and overloading resolved. Pattern-matching has been compiled into case expressions, each of which performs only a single level of matching. Boxing and unboxing are explicit, as described below.

3. Program analyses and transformations are applied to the Core language. In particular, the boxing/unboxing optimisations are carried out here.

4. The Core language is translated to the STG language, the abstract machine code for the Spineless Tagless G-machine, our evaluation model. The Spineless Tagless G-machine was initially presented in Peyton Jones & Salkild [1989], but the latter has been completely rewritten as a companion to this paper (Peyton Jones [1991]).

5. The STG language is translated to "Abstract C". This is just an internal data type which can be simply printed out as C code and thence compiled to native code with standard C compilers. Abstract C can also serve serve as an input to a code generator, thereby generating native code directly, but we have not yet implemented this route.

In this paper we only concern ourselves with the Core language, which is introduced in the next section. However, since the Core language does not have explicit algebraic type declarations, we borrow HASKELL's syntax for this purpose when required.

3.1 The syntax of the Core language

The abstract syntax of the Core language is given in Figure 1. The *binds* constituting a *prog* should define `main`, which is taken to be the value of the program.

The concrete syntax we use is conventional: parentheses are used to disambiguate; application associates to the left and binds more tightly than any other operator; the body of a lambda abstraction extends as far to the right as possible; the usual infix arithmetic operators are permitted; the usual syntax for lists is allowed, with infix constructor ":" and empty list `[]`; and, where the layout makes the meaning clear, we allow ourselves to omit semicolons between bindings and case alternatives.

Notice that the bindings in `let(rec)` expressions are all simple; that is, the left hand side of the binding is always just a variable. Function bindings are expressed by binding a variable to a lambda abstraction. However, we permit ourselves the small liberty in the concrete syntax of writing the arguments of function bindings to the left of the = sign.

Similarly, the patterns in `case` expressions are all simple; nested pattern matching has been compiled to nested `case` expressions.

Here is an example program to illustrate these points:

```
fac n = case n of
        0  -> 1
        n' -> n * factorial (n-1)

main = fac 100
```

Program	*prog*	→	*binds*	
Bindings	*binds*	→	$bind_1$; … ; $bind_n$	$n \geq 1$
	bind	→	*var* = *expr*	
Expression	*expr*	→	$expr_1$ $expr_2$	Application
		|	`\` *var* `->` *expr*	Lambda abstract
		|	`case` *expr* `of` *alts*	Case expression
		|	`let` *bind* `in` *expr*	Local definition
		|	`letrec` *binds* `in` *expr*	Local recursion
		|	*con*	Constructor
		|	*var*	Variable
		|	*literal*	
Literal values	*literal*	→	*integer*	
		|	*float*	
Alternatives	*alts*	→	$calt_1$; … ; $calt_n$; `default` `->` *expr*	$n \geq 0$
		|	$lalt_1$; … ; $lalt_n$; *var* `->` *expr*	$n \geq 0$
Constructor alt	*calt*	→	*con* var_1 … var_n `->` *expr*	$n \geq 0$
Literal alt	*lalt*	→	*literal* `->` *expr*	$n \geq 0$

Figure 1: Syntax of the Core language

3.2 A semantics for the Core language

In this section we present a denotational semantics for well-typed Core language programs. We do so with a little more care than ususal, because we want it to form a basis for the denotational semantics of unboxed types later. We need to do two things:

- Give a *model*, which defines a domain $\mathcal{D}[\![\tau]\!]$ for each type τ in the language.
- Give a *valuation function* $\mathcal{E}[\![e]\!]$ which, for every expression e of type τ, gives its value in the domain $\mathcal{D}[\![\tau]\!]$.

3.3 The model

Beginning with the model, we give the syntax of types τ:

$$\begin{array}{rcll} \tau & ::= & \alpha & \\ & | & \texttt{Int} & \\ & | & \texttt{Float} & \\ & | & \tau_1 \rightarrow \tau_2 & \\ & | & \chi_n\ \tau_1 \ldots \tau_n & (n \geq 0) \end{array}$$

Here, α is a type variable, and χ_n ranges over type constructors of arity n. These type constructors arise from algebraic data type declarations made by the programmer. For example, the declaration

```
data Tree a = Leaf a | Branch (Tree a) (Tree a)
```

introduces a type constructor `Tree` with arity 1. Lists, booleans, pairs, and other types which usually come "built in" are all regarded as examples of such algebraic data types.

We define the domain corresponding to each type τ inductively, thus:

$$\begin{array}{lcl} \mathcal{D}[\![]\!] & : & \textit{Monotype} \rightarrow (\textit{Typevar} \rightarrow \mathbf{Dom}) \rightarrow \mathbf{Dom} \\ \mathcal{D}[\![\alpha]\!]\ \rho & = & \rho\ \alpha \\ \mathcal{D}[\![\texttt{Int}]\!]\ \rho & = & \{\text{The set of fixed-precision integers}\}_\perp \\ \mathcal{D}[\![\texttt{Float}]\!]\ \rho & = & \{\text{The set of fixed-precision floating-point numbers}\}_\perp \\ \mathcal{D}[\![\tau_1 \rightarrow \tau_2]\!]\ \rho & = & (\mathcal{D}[\![\tau_1]\!]\ \rho) \rightarrow (\mathcal{D}[\![\tau_2]\!]\ \rho) \\ \mathcal{D}[\![\chi_n\ \tau_1 \ldots \tau_n]\!]\ \rho & = & \chi_n\ (\mathcal{D}[\![\tau_1]\!]\ \rho) \ldots (\mathcal{D}[\![\tau_n]\!]\ \rho) \end{array}$$

The environment ρ maps type variables to domains; where the type τ has no free variables we write simply $\mathcal{D}[\![\tau]\!]$. Notice that the arrow on the left hand side of the fourth equation is part of the syntax of types, whereas on the right hand side it stands for the function space constructor (or functor) for domains. In just the same way, the χ_n stands for a domain constructor; so we must obviously say just how χ_n is defined for any given algebraic data type declaration. The general form of an algebraic data type declaration is as follows:

$$\texttt{data}\ \chi\ \alpha_1 \ldots \alpha_t \ = \ c_1\ \tau_{11} \ldots \tau_{1a_1}\ |\ \ldots\ |\ c_n\ \tau_{n1} \ldots \tau_{na_n}$$

Lifting	$A_\perp$	$=$	$\{\perp\} \cup \{\mathit{lift}\ a \mid a \in A\}$
Categorical sum	$A + B$	$=$	$\{\langle 0, a\rangle \mid a \in A\} \cup \{\langle 1, b\rangle \mid b \in B\}$
Categorical product	$A \times B$	$=$	$\{\langle a, b\rangle \mid a \in A, b \in B\}$

Figure 2: Definitions of domain constructions

where $t \geq 0$, $n > 0$ and $a_i \geq 0$. Corresponding to this declaration we give the following functor definition:

$$\begin{array}{rcl} \chi\ d_1 \ldots d_t & = & (s_1 + \ldots + s_n)_\perp \\ & & \text{where } \rho \ = \ [\alpha_1 \mapsto d_1,\ \ldots, \alpha_n \mapsto d_n] \\ & & \qquad s_i \ = \ \mathcal{D}[\![\tau_{i1}]\!]\ \rho \times \ldots \times \mathcal{D}[\![\tau_{ia_i}]\!]\ \rho \qquad (1 \leq i \leq n) \end{array}$$

The domain constructions are categorical product ($\times$) and sum ($+$), and lifting ($\cdot_\perp$); they are defined in Figure 2. This equation is more usually given using separated sum instead of categorical sum, and omitting the lifting, but the result is the same in either case, as is easily verified. The reason we choose this formulation is that it extends smoothly when we add unboxed types.

This construction gives rise to a mutually recursive set of functor definitions. These can be solved in the usual way to define a domain $\mathcal{D}[\![\tau]\!]$ for each type τ with no free variables. (See Smyth & Plotkin [1982] for a categorical account, or Schmidt [1986] for a more element-orientated treatment. The latter is particularly useful as it discusses unpointed (i.e. bottomless) domains, an aspect important later on.)

3.4 The semantic equations

That completes the description of the domains involved, so it remains only to give the definitions of the valuation functions. Figure 3, which gives these definitions, contains no surprises. The valuation function $\mathcal{P}[\![]\!]$ gives the meaning of programs, $\mathcal{E}[\![]\!]$ give the meaning of expressions, $\mathcal{B}[\![]\!]$ gives the meaning of groups of definitions, and $\mathcal{K}[\![]\!]$ (which is not further defined) give the meaning of literal constants.

The valuation function $\mathcal{E}[\![]\!]$ takes an *expression* and an *environment* and returns a *value*. We use **Env** for the domain of environments, and **Val** for the domain of values, defining them like this:

$$\begin{array}{rcl} \mathbf{Env} & = & \bigcup_\tau (\mathit{var}_\tau \to \mathcal{D}[\![\tau]\!]) \\ \mathbf{Val} & = & \bigcup_\tau \mathcal{D}[\![\tau]\!] \end{array}$$

The environment maps a variable of type τ to a value in the domain $\mathcal{D}[\![\tau]\!]$, and the domain of values is the union of all the $\mathcal{D}[\![\tau]\!]$. In these two equations τ ranges only over types with no free type variables.

$$\mathcal{P}[\![\mathit{program}]\!] : \mathbf{Val}$$
$$\mathcal{P}[\![\mathit{prog}]\!] \;=\; \mathcal{E}[\![\texttt{letrec}\ \mathit{prog}\ \texttt{in main}]\!]\ \rho_{init}$$

$$\mathcal{E}[\![\mathit{expr}]\!] : \mathbf{Env} \rightarrow \mathbf{Val}$$
$$\begin{array}{lcl}
\mathcal{E}[\![k]\!]\ \rho & = & \mathcal{K}[\![k]\!] \\
\mathcal{E}[\![x]\!]\ \rho & = & \rho\ x \\
\mathcal{E}[\![e_1\ e_2]\!] & = & (\mathcal{E}[\![e_1]\!]\ \rho)\ (\mathcal{E}[\![e_2]\!]\ \rho) \\
\mathcal{E}[\![\backslash x\texttt{->}e]\!]\ \rho & = & \lambda\epsilon.(\mathcal{E}[\![e]\!]\ (\rho \oplus \{x \mapsto \epsilon\})) \\
\mathcal{E}[\![\texttt{let}\ x\ \texttt{=}\ e\ \texttt{in}\ b]\!]\ \rho & = & \mathcal{E}[\![b]\!]\ (\rho \oplus \{x \mapsto \mathcal{E}[\![e]\!]\ \rho\}) \\
\mathcal{E}[\![\texttt{letrec}\ \mathit{binds}\ \texttt{in}\ e]\!]\ \rho & = & \mathcal{E}[\![e]\!]\ (\rho \oplus \mathit{fix}\ (\lambda\rho'.\mathcal{B}[\![\mathit{binds}]\!]\ (\rho \oplus \rho'))) \\
\mathcal{E}[\![c]\!]\ \rho & = & \lambda\epsilon_1.\ldots\lambda\epsilon_a.\langle c, \epsilon_1, \ldots, \epsilon_a\rangle
\end{array}$$

$$\mathcal{E}[\![\texttt{case}\ e\ \texttt{of}\ c_1\ x_{11}\ldots x_{1a_1}\ \texttt{->}\ e_1\texttt{;}\ \ldots\texttt{;}\ c_n\ x_{n1}\ldots x_{na_n}\ \texttt{->}\ e_n\texttt{;}\ \texttt{default}\ \texttt{->}\ e_d]\!]\ \rho$$
$$= \mathbf{case}\ E[\![e]\!]\ \rho\ \mathbf{of}$$
$$\begin{array}{lcl}
\perp & \rightarrow & \perp \\
\langle c_1, \epsilon_{11}, \ldots, \epsilon_{1a_1}\rangle & \rightarrow & \mathcal{E}[\![e_1]\!]\ (\rho \oplus \{x_{11} \mapsto \epsilon_{11}, \ldots, x_{1a_1} \mapsto \epsilon_{1a_1}\}) \\
\ldots & & \\
\langle c_n, \epsilon_{n1}, \ldots, \epsilon_{na_n}\rangle & \rightarrow & \mathcal{E}[\![e_n]\!]\ (\rho \oplus \{x_{n1} \mapsto \epsilon_{n1}, \ldots, x_{na_n} \mapsto \epsilon_{na_n}\}) \\
\mathit{else} & \rightarrow & \mathcal{E}[\![e_d]\!]\ \rho
\end{array}$$
$$\mathbf{end}$$

$$\mathcal{E}[\![\texttt{case}\ e\ \texttt{of}\ k_1\ \texttt{->}\ e_1\texttt{;}\ \ldots\texttt{;}\ k_n\ \texttt{->}\ e_n\texttt{;}\ x\ \texttt{->}\ e_d]\!]\ \rho$$
$$= \mathbf{case}\ E[\![e]\!]\ \rho\ \mathbf{of}$$
$$\begin{array}{lcl}
\perp & \rightarrow & \perp \\
\mathit{lift}\ k_1 & \rightarrow & \mathcal{E}[\![e_1]\!]\ \rho \\
\ldots & & \\
\mathit{lift}\ k_n & \rightarrow & \mathcal{E}[\![e_n]\!]\ \rho \\
\mathit{lift}\ \epsilon & \rightarrow & \mathcal{E}[\![e_d]\!]\ (\rho \oplus \{x \mapsto \epsilon\})
\end{array}$$
$$\mathbf{end}$$

$$\mathcal{B}[\![\mathit{binds}]\!] : \mathbf{Env} \rightarrow \mathbf{Env}$$
$$\mathcal{B}[\![x_1\texttt{=}e_1\texttt{;}\ \ldots\texttt{;}\ x_n\texttt{=}e_n]\!]\ \rho \;=\; \{x_1 \mapsto \mathcal{E}[\![e_1]\!]\ \rho, \ldots, x_n \mapsto \mathcal{E}[\![e_n]\!]\ \rho\}$$

Figure 3: Denotational semantics of the Core language

We need a notation for writing values in the domains corresponding to algebraic data types. Since only binary sum and product were defined, such values should formally consist of nested pairs, but these are rather tiresome to write. Instead we will permit ourselves the liberty of writing such values in the flattened form:

$$\langle c, \epsilon_1, \ldots, \epsilon_n \rangle$$

where c is a constructor of arity n, and ϵ_i are values from the appropriate argument domains.

The initial environment ρ_{init} contains bindings for all the built-in functions. For example, it contains the following binding for the addition function:

$$
\begin{array}{l}
+ \mapsto \lambda x.\lambda y.\textbf{case}\ x\ \textbf{of} \\
\quad \begin{array}{|lll}
\bot & \to & \bot \\
\mathit{lift}\ x' & \to & \textbf{case}\ y\ \textbf{of} \\
 & & \quad \begin{array}{|lll}
 \bot & \to & \bot \\
 \mathit{lift}\ y' & \to & \mathit{lift}(x' + y')
 \end{array} \\
 & & \textbf{end}
\end{array} \\
\quad \textbf{end}
\end{array}
$$

This definition also illustrates the semantic **case** construct which we use to discriminate among elements of a domain.

4 The main idea: exposing unboxed types to transformation

We are now ready to present the key idea of the paper. The big problem with earlier approaches to the boxing issue is this: *there is no way to talk about unboxed values in the Core language.* An immediate consequence is that *evaluation of numbers is implicit.* For example, in the definition:

```
f x y = y - x
```

x and y must be evaluated before they can be subtracted, but this fact is implicit, as is the *order* in which x and y are evaluated.

This implicit evaluation is in contrast with the situation for algebraic data types. For example, the `length` function might be defined like this:

```
length xs = case xs of
              x : xs -> 1 + length xs
              []     -> 0
```

Here, the evaluation of xs is completely explicit. In general, it is precisely case expressions (and nothing else) which perform evaluation of data structures.

This suggests an obvious improvement: perhaps the evaluation of numbers can be done by case expressions as well. Suppose we wrote the definition of f like this:

```
f x y = case y of
          Int y# -> case x of
                      Int x# -> case (y# -# x#) of
                                  t# -> Int t#
```

The idea is that the data type Int, of fixed-precision integers, is no longer primitive. Instead, we can imagine Int being declared in HASKELL like this:

```
data Int = Int Int#
```

That is, the Int type is an algebraic data type like any other, with a single constructor Int. (Here and elsewhere we will use the same name for the type and its constructor.) The Int constructor has one component, of type Int#, which is the primitive type of *unboxed* fixed-precision integers. A new primitive operator, -#, subtracts values of type Int#.

The outermost case expression in our new formulation of f serves to evaluate y and extract its unboxed component y#. The next case expression performs a similar function for x, giving x#. Next, the difference between y# and x# is computed and bound to t#, and finally, the function returns a value of type Int, obtained by applying the Int constructor to t#.

At first sight, the innermost case expression is rather curious. Why not just write the following instead?

```
Int (y# -# x#)
```

The reason we chose to use case for this purpose is to make explicit that the subtraction is performed before the result of the function is returned.

In general we will use a # sign to identify unboxed types, and to identify variables whose type is unboxed. This only serves to make the presentation clearer; the # annotations are ignored by the compiler which infers types as described later, in Section 8.

We note in passing that the transformation from the first form of f to the second can be carried out in a systematic way, merely by giving the following definition to the subtraction operator -, which was previously considered primitive:

```
(-) p q = case p of
            Int p# -> case q of
                        Int q# -> case (p# -# q#) of
                                    t# -> Int t#
```

Now the passage from one version of f to the other is just a matter of β-reduction, unfolding the application of - to its two arguments.

Now that Int has been expressed in terms of a more primitive type, its constructors, the integers 0, 1, and so on, must be regarded as short for Int 0#, Int 1#, and so on, where 0# and 1# are the unboxed constants for zero and one. Similarly, pattern matching against integers becomes a two-stage process. The function

```
f 1 = e1
f 2 = e2
f n = en
```

is shorthand for

```
f (Int 1#) = e1
f (Int 2#) = e2
f n        = en
```

The latter will get translated by the pattern-matching compiler to

```
f n = case n of Int n# -> case n# of
                              1# -> e1
                              2# -> e2
                              default -> en
```

This has a straightforward operational interpretation. The outer case evaluates n and extracts its unboxed contents, n#. The inner case scrutinises n# and selects the appropriate alternative.

Now that we can express programs involving unboxed values, we can demonstrate how the optimisations mentioned in Section 2 can be re-interpreted as program transformations.

4.1 Avoiding repeated evaluation

Consider the expression:

```
x+x
```

A naïve implementation would evaluate and unbox x twice. Let us see what the expression looks like when we unfold the application of +, just as we unfolded – in the previous section. It becomes this:

```
case x of
Int x1# -> case x of
           Int x2# -> case (x1# +# x2#) of
                      t# -> Int t#
```

Now, it is a simple observation that the inner case is scrutinising the same value as the outer case. In general, the following transformation holds:

case e of ... ; $c\ x_1 \ldots x_n$ -> ... case e of ... $c\ y_1 \ldots y_n$ -> *body* ... ; ...

$\Longrightarrow$

case e of ... ; $c\ x_1 \ldots x_n$ -> ... *body*$[x_1/y_1 \ldots x_n/y_n]$ ... ; ...

(There is a side condition: we assume that every binding site binds a distinct variable, so that the two occurrences of the expression e denote the same value.) Applying this transformation to the expression we are studying, we get:

```
case x of
Int x1# -> case (x1# +# x1#) of
           t# -> Int t#
```

which expresses precisely the optimisation we were seeking.

4.2 Eliding redundant boxing operations

As a second example, consider the expression

```
x + (y * z)
```

As mentioned earlier, we want to avoid wrapping a box around the value of y*z, because it will immediately be unwrapped by the enclosing addition. As before, let us see what the expression looks like when the applications of + and * are unfolded. It becomes this:

```
case x of
Int x# -> case ( case y of
                   Int y# -> case z of
                               Int z# -> case (y# *# z#) of
                                           t1# -> Int t1#
                 ) of
            Int w# -> case (x# +# w#) of t2# -> Int t2#
```

This expression does not look very promising, but it yields to the following well-known transformation:

$$\texttt{case (case } e \texttt{ of } p_1\texttt{->}e_1\texttt{; } \ldots\texttt{; } p_n\texttt{->}e_n\texttt{) of } alts$$
$$\Longrightarrow$$
$$\texttt{case } e \texttt{ of } p_1\texttt{-> (case } e_1 \texttt{ of } alts\texttt{)}; \ldots; p_n\texttt{-> (case } e_n \texttt{ of } alts\texttt{)}$$

(The same unique-binding side condition is necessary here too, to ensure that the meaning of *alts* is not changed by being moved into the scope of the patterns p_i.) Where the expression scrutinised by a case is itself a case expression, the cases can be interchanged, as shown. We call this the *case-of-case transformation*, for obvious reasons.

In general, there is a danger of duplicating code, because if the inner case has multiple alternatives, *alts* will be duplicated. Happily, in the expression we are transforming, the inner case has just one alternative. We can apply the transformation three times to give:

```
case x of
Int x# -> case y of
           Int y# -> case z of
                      Int z# -> case (y# *# z#) of
                                 t1# -> case (Int t1#) of
                                         Int w# -> case (x# +# w#) of
                                                    t2# -> Int t2#
```

Now another generally-useful transformation applies:

$$\texttt{case (} c\ x_1 \ldots x_n \texttt{) of } \ldots\texttt{; } c\ y_1 \ldots y_n \texttt{ -> } e \texttt{ ; } \ldots$$
$$\Longrightarrow$$
$$e[x_1/y_1 \ldots x_n/y_n]$$

That is, a case expression which scrutinises a constructor applied to some variables, can be replaced by the appropriate alternative after suitable renaming. (In general, a constructor which is applied to arbitrary expressions can be transformed to one applied to variables by introducing some let-bindings.) Using this transformation on the inner case expression gives:

```
case x of
Int x# -> case y of
              Int y# -> case z of
                            Int z# -> case (y# *# z#) of
                                          t1# -> case (x# +# t1#) of
                                                     t2# -> Int t2#
```

This final form refrains from boxing `t1#` and then taking it apart, just as we hoped. Instead, the result of the multiplication is used directly in the addition.

5 Strictness analysis and unboxed calls

Much effort has been devoted in the literature to *strictness analysis*, which detects whether or not a function is strict (Hankin & Abramsky [1986]). For a sequential implementation the significance is that strict arguments can be evaluated before the call. In particular, strict numeric arguments can be passed unboxed. In the following section we show how the results of strictness analysis can be exploited within our transformational framework.

5.1 Exploiting the results of strictness analysis

As with other aspects of boxing and unboxing, the exploitation of strictness analysis is usually left to the hapless code generator. Let us see how it can be expressed in our extended language. Consider the factorial function with an accumulating parameter, which in HASKELL might look like this:

```
afac a 0 = a
afac a n = afac (n*a) (n-1)
```

Translated into the Core language, it would take the following form:

```
afac a n = case n of
               Int n# -> case n# of
                             0#  -> a
                             n#' -> afac (n*a) (n-(Int 1#))
```

Integer constants have been replaces by the `Int` constructor applied to the corresponding unboxed constant, and pattern-matching have been translated into `case` expressions.

Suppose that a strictness analyser informs us that `afac` is strict in both its arguments. Then without (as yet) doing anything further to its body, we can transform it into the following pair of definitions:

```
afac a n = case a of Int a# -> case n of Int n# -> afac# a# n#

afac# a# n# = let n = Int n#
                  a = Int a#
              in
              case n of
```

```
Int n# -> case n# of
            0#  -> a
            n#' -> afac (n*a) (n-(Int 1#))
```

The "wrapper", afac, evaluates the arguments and passes them unboxed to the "worker", afac#. (Recall that the # annotations are merely present as cues to the human reader; the compiler ignores them.) The latter consists of a let-expression, whose bindings reconstruct the original arguments, and whose body is the unmodified body of the original afac.

Now we can go to work on the body of afac#. We unfold the definitions of *, -, and afac itself; and apply the transformations described earlier. One further related transformation is needed:

let x = $c\ x_1 \ldots x_n$ *in* ...(case x of ... ; $c\ y_1 \ldots y_n$ -> *body*; ...) ...
$\Longrightarrow$
let x = $c\ x_1 \ldots x_n$ *in* ...(*body*$[x_1/y_1 \ldots x_n/y_n]$)...

This transformation uses the auxilliary let bindings for a and n, after which no uses of a and n remain, so the let bindings for them can be dropped. A few moments work should convince you that the result is this:

```
afac# a# n# = case n# of
                0#  -> Int a#
                n'# -> case (n# *# a#) of
                         a1# -> case (n# -# 1#) of
                                  n1# -> afac# a1# n1#
```

Bingo! afac# is just what we hoped for: a strict, constant-space, efficient factorial function. Even the recursive call is made directly to afac#, rather than going via afac. Meanwhile, afac acts as an "impedence-matcher" to provide a boxed interface to afac#.

Now, much of the benefit of strictness comes from the fact that often the arguments are already partly or completely evaluated before the call. For example, consider the following call to afac:

```
if (x>10) then (afac 1 x) else 0
```

Here, x is already evaluated before we reach the call to afac. All we need to do to take advantage of this is to *always unfold calls to* afac (though not afac#!). This unfolding exposes the two evaluations which afac does. The transformations already discussed can then eliminate both of them, leaving a direct call to afac#.

To summarise, the results of strictness analysis can be uniformly incorporated into the transformation process by applying the following procedure to each strict function:

- Split the function into two: a *wrapper function* which evaluates the strict arguments and passes them to the *work function*. The work function uses let-bindings to reconstitute the original arguments, but is otherwise identical to the original function.
- Unfold all applications of the wrapper function wherever possible.
- Optimise using the transformations described earlier.

5.2 Strictness over non-numeric types

In fact, this is not quite the whole story. Firstly, a function can be strict in an argument whose type is a list. It is far from clear what the wrapper function should do in this case. Nor is it clear what the wrapper should do in the case of a function strict in a functional argument.

The most obvious cases where something useful can be done are these: *when the strict argument is of a data type which has just one constructor.* Then the wrapper can evaluate the object, extract its components, and pass them to the work function. (Actually, it is only necessary to pass the free variables of the work function's body to the work function. Components which are not used can be discarded by the wrapper.)

To take an example where the constructor has more than one component, consider the function

```
f t = case t of (x,y) -> (...)
```

It is clearly strict in its argument, which is a pair. Therefore we split it into two, thus:

```
f t = case t of (x,y) -> f# x y
f# x y  = let t = (x,y) in (...)
```

Now a call to `f` in which an explicit pair is given, thus

```
f (e1,e2)
```

will benefit from unfolding the wrapper for `f` and simplifying, giving

```
f# e1 e2
```

The example stands revealed as the standard currying transformation, another example of an *ad hoc* transformation appearing as a special case.

5.3 Unboxing results

The second addition to the strictness story can be seen by attempting the same transformation on the non-accumulating factorial function. Here is the original definition:

```
fac n = case n of
          Int n# -> case n# of
                      0#  -> Int 1#
                      n#' -> n * fac (n-(Int 1#))
```

Again, because `fac` is strict, we may split it into a wrapper and a worker, thus:

```
fac n = case n of Int n# -> fac# n#

fac# n# = case n# of
            0#  -> Int 1#
            n#' -> case (n# -# 1#) of
```

```
                        n1# -> case (fac# n1#) of
                                 Int m# -> case (n# *# m#) of
                                              r# -> Int r#
```

The point is that fac# has type Int# → Int, not Int# → Int#. Hence fac# contains code for taking apart the boxed integer returned by the recursive call to fac# (the next to innermost case does this).

It looks as if a new boxed Int is constructed in the heap for each recursive call, and this will indeed be the case for many implementations[1].

Can we avoid this problem? Observing that the result of a function call is always required (or else the call would not have been made), we can modify the way in which the split into wrapper and work functions is made. If the result of the original function is a single-constructor type (as in this case), we can split like this:

```
fac n = case n of Int n# -> case (fac1# n#) of t# -> Int t#

fac1# n# = let n = Int n#
           in
           case (...original body of fac...) of
           Int r# -> r#
```

Now fac1# has type Int# → Int#, and transformation turns it into

```
fac1# n# = case n# of
           0#   -> 1#
           n#'  -> case (n# -# 1#) of
                     n1# -> case (fac1# n1#) of m# -> n# *# m#
```

To conclude, the point of all this is not so much that any one alternative is obviously much better than any other, but that rather the new expressiveness offered by a language featuring unboxed types allows us to discuss and explore a wide range of options within a single uniform framework.

6 Generalising unboxed types

The presentation of Section 4 gave a definition for the Int type as an algebraic data type based on a primitive unboxed type, Int#. This is rather suggestive: can we generalise the idea to all algebraic data types, so that Int is not special, but rather a particular case of a general feature?

It turns out that we can indeed do so in two distinct ways:

- We can allow any constructor (and not just Int) to take arguments of unboxed type.
- We can allow any algebraic data type (and not just Int#) to be unboxed.

[1] It happens not to be the case for the Spineless Tagless G-machine, which returns even apparently boxed integers (among other things) in a register. The reason for this is that the only reason a boxed integer is ever evaluated is to unbox it. Even so, returning an unboxed value is still slightly more efficient than returning a boxed one.

6.1 Constructors with unboxed components

Consider the following (conventional) definition of a data type for complex numbers and a corresponding addition function:

```
data Cpx = Cpx Int Int   -- Real and imaginary parts

addCpx (Cpx r1 i1) (Cpx r2 i2) = Cpx (r1+r2) (i1+i2)
```

But, since all constructors are non-strict, what addCpx will do is to build a Cpx box containing pointers to an unevaluated closure for r1+r2 and another for i1+i2. Now this may be exactly what the programmer wanted — it allows values such as Cpx ⊥ ⊥, for example — but the implementation cost is heavy compared with a strict language which would simply build a Cpx box containing the *values of* r1+r2 and i1+i2.

The discussion of Section 4 suggests the following alternative:

```
data UCpx = UCpx Int# Int#

addUCpx (UCpx i1 r1) (UCpx i2 r2)
= case (i1 +# i2) of
  t1# -> case (r1 +# r2) of
         t2# -> UCpx t1# t2#
```

Now the components of the UCpx constructor are *unboxed* integers, and are therefore computed before the constructor is built.

6.2 Arbitrary unboxed algebraic data types

An *enumeration type* is an algebraic data type whose constructors all have zero arity. For example

```
data Boolean = False | True
data Colour = Red | Green | White | Blue
```

Objects of type Boolean and Colour are boxed; yet it makes sense to think of an unboxed boolean or colour, represented as one of a suitable set of bit-patterns. This observation provokes the question: can we allow the programmer to declare new *unboxed* enumeration types, perhaps like this:

```
data unboxed Colour# = Red# | Green# | White# | Blue#
data unboxed Boolean# = False# | True#
```

It would certainly be more efficient to represent a value of type Colour# or Boolean# than to represent one of type Boolean or Colour. As usual the # annotations are present only to clarify the presentation; it is the unboxed keyword which indicates that the enumeration should be unboxed.

The idea can be generalised further, by allowing *any* algebraic data type to be declared unboxed. For example:

```
data unboxed UPair# a b = UPair# a b
data unboxed UCpx# = UCpx# Int# Int#
data unboxed Maybe# a = Just# a | Nothing#
```

Each of these declarations has a natural operational reading. The type of unboxed pairs, UPair, is represented by a pair of pointers. These pointers are actually carried around together, rather then placing them in a heap-allocated box and carrying around a pointer to this box. Similarly the UCpx# type is represented by a pair of unboxed integers.

The Maybe# type is a little different, because it has more than one constructor. It can be represented by a bit to distinguish one constructor from the other, together with enough words to contain the components of any of the constructors (one, in this case). The implementation would be trickier here, and the efficiency gains might be less clear cut. Since the sole purpose of these unboxed types is to improve efficiency, it is not clear whether it it is worth implementing them in full generality.

Recursive unboxed types are even less plausible. For example:

```
data unboxed UTree a = ULeaf a | UBranch (UTree a) (UTree a)
```

Here, the size of an unboxed tree would be variable, and it is hard to imagine how it could ever be implemented efficiently. Accordingly, we impose the rule that there must be at least one boxed type involved in any recursive loop of types (see Section 7.3).

7 The semantics of unboxed types

So far we have motivated the introduction of unboxed types by showing a number of ways in which they can be useful. It is now time to give the idea some formal foundation.

We do so in two steps:

- We discuss the modifications necessary to the type system; that is, the static semantics (Section 8).
- We modify the dynamic semantics of the Core language to take account of unboxed values, and discuss the safety of program transformations in the presence of unboxed values (Section 9).

Before we begin this sequence, we discuss an important caveat. We are trying to make unboxed values into first-class citizens, but it turns out that we must make three significant restrictions on their use.

The first two of these restrictions certainly make writing programs involving unboxed types less convenient. But remember that we are talking here about the *Core* language, rather than about the *source* language in which the programmer writes. There are several steps we can take to reduce the impact of these restrictions on the programmer, by inserting implicit evaluations and coercions, but it is better to deal with one issue at a time. We therefore concentrate now on giving a semantics for the restricted language, while in Section 10, we discuss the language-design question.

7.1 Restriction 1: loss of polymorphism

Unboxed objects are dangerous beasts: if the garbage collector should ever treat one as a pointer to a heap object, the entire system might crash. Furthermore, the size of an unboxed object may vary with its type. An `Int#` object may be the same size as a pointer, but a `LongInt#` object would be larger, as would a 64-bit floating point number and an unboxed pair.

One approach would be to add tag bits to distinguish boxed and unboxed objects, and give size and layout information for unboxed objects. This would be intolerably slow. For example the simple function

```
head (x:xs) = x
```

would have to test the tag on the value `x` to find out how many bytes to move into the result location(s). This approach would largely obviate one of the major benefits of strong typing, namely the performance advantage of working with untagged data (Appel [1988]).

Accordingly, we assume that no tag bits distinguish boxed from unboxed objects, relying solely on the type system to keep them apart. It follows immediately that:

> **Restriction 1.** *Polymorphic functions cannot manipulate unboxed values.*

7.2 Restriction 2: explicit evaluation

Whenever an unboxed value is stored in a data structure or passed to a function, it must first be evaluated. Whilst this could be left implicit, we prefer to make it explicit. The main reason for doing so is that it allows the dynamic semantics to be much more straightforward, and ensures that most existing program transformations remain valid (Section 9).

There is a simple syntactic criterion which tells if an expression of unboxed type is in head normal form (HNF) or not: an expression of unboxed type is in HNF if it is:

- a literal constant,
- an application of an unboxed constructor, or
- a variable.

(An unboxed constructor is a constructor of an unboxed algebraic data type — see Section 6.2.) The only surprise here is that a variable is an HNF; this follows from the fact that unboxed variables are bound to the bit-pattern corresponding to the value, so then cannot be bottom. Since functions are all boxed, no partial application is an HNF of unboxed type.

Now we can formalise our restriction:

> **Restriction 2.** *An expression of unboxed type which appears as the argument of an application, or as the right-hand side of a binding, must be in HNF.*

As an example of this restriction, the expression

Polytype	σ	::=	$\forall\alpha.\,\sigma \mid \tau$	
Monotype	τ	::=	$\pi \mid \upsilon$	
Boxed type	π	::=	α	Type variable
		|	$\tau_1 \rightarrow \tau_2$	Function type
		|	$\chi\ \pi_1 \ldots \pi_n$	Parameterised boxed data type
Unboxed type	υ	::=	`Int#`	
		|	`Float#`	
		|	$\chi\#\ \pi_1 \ldots \pi_n$	Parameterised unboxed data type

Figure 4: Syntax of types

```
f (x +# y)
```

is illegal because `(x +# y)` is not an HNF. It must instead be written

```
case (x +# y) of t# -> f t#
```

The evaluation has thereby been made explicit.

Restriction 2 permits recursive definitions of unboxed values, which at first look unreasonable. They do not seem to be very useful, however, so we ignore them until Section 12.4.

7.3 Restriction 3: no recursive unboxed data types

For the reasons discussed above in Section 6.2, and to ensure the domain equations of Section 9 have a least solution, we prohibit recursive definitions of unboxed data types:

> **Restriction 3.** *There must be at least one boxed type involved in any recursive loop of types.*

This is rather similar to the usual rule that type synonyms must not be recursive.

8 The static semantics of unboxed types

Since all three restrictions are expressed in terms of types, it follows that the type system must be modified to embody them. Restriction 3 is a simple syntactic check, but Restrictions 1 and 2 are more interesting.

8.1 Types

The syntax for types is given in Figure 4. A monotype, τ, can be boxed or unboxed.

A boxed type, π, is a type variable, a function type, or a type constructor χ parameterised only over further boxed types. Each type constructor χ corresponds to a (boxed) algebraic data type declaration.

Functions are interesting. The argument and result of a function type can be any type, boxed or otherwise; but *the function itself is regarded as boxed* because it is represented by a pointer to a closure.

An unboxed type, υ, is either one of the built-in unboxed types such as `Int#` or `Float#`, or an unboxed type constructor $\chi\#$ parameterised over boxed types. Each such type constructor corresponds to an unboxed algebraic data type declaration.

The only surprise here is that data types cannot be parameterised over unboxed types. For example, does not the type `List Int#` (which would be written `[Int#]` in HASKELL) make perfect sense? The difficulty is that the garbage collector cannot tell that this particular list contains unboxed objects, which should not be treated as pointers; and furthermore, standard list cells might well be unable to accomodate, say, a double-precision floating pointer number. Another way to think of it is this: the list constructor "`:`" is polymorphic, and hence should not be applied to unboxed values (Restriction 1).

The only constructors which can have unboxed components are those which have been explicitly declared as such (such as `UCpx`). Notice that the type `UCpx` is a boxed type, despite having unboxed components. The restriction is that a polymorphic type cannot be *parameterised* with unboxed components.

8.2 Typing

We move on to consider how the type rules can be adjusted to accomodate the new constraints. Fortunately it is rather easy. Most type systems have a rule looking like this (for typical examples of complete typing rules see Damas & Milner [1982] or Hancock's chapter in Peyton Jones [1987]):

$$\text{SPEC}\quad \frac{A \vdash e : \forall\alpha.\, \sigma}{A \vdash e : \sigma[\tau/\alpha]}$$

This rule is used to instantiate polymorphic types, by substituting an arbitrary monotype τ for the type variable α in σ. All that we need to do to implement Restriction 1 is to ensure that polymorphic types are never instantiated with unboxed types, thus:

$$\text{SPEC'}\quad \frac{A \vdash e : \forall\alpha.\, \sigma}{A \vdash e : \sigma[\pi/\alpha]}$$

That is, only boxed types π should be substituted for α. Restriction 2 is also easy to embody. We need two rules for application instead of one:

$$\text{AP}\quad \frac{A \vdash e_1 : \pi \rightarrow \tau \qquad A \vdash e_2 : \pi}{A \vdash e_1\ e_2 : \tau} \qquad\qquad \text{AP\#}\quad \frac{A \vdash e_1 : \upsilon \rightarrow \tau \qquad A \vdash h : \upsilon}{A \vdash e_1\ h : \tau}$$

The *AP* rule applies to functions taking boxed arguments, while the *AP#* rule insists that an unboxed argument must be an HNF, h. The rule for `let` and `letrec` need to altered in a similar way.

And that is all! No further changes are required to the type system.

8.3 Type inference

Next, we consider what changes need to be made to a type inference system to accomodate the new rules and the accompanying two kinds of types.

SPEC is usually implemented in a type inference engine by substituting a fresh type variable for the universally quantified variable α. This is subsequently specialised as much as necessary by unification. To implement the new SPEC rule we therefore need to modify the unification process: *the unifier should fail to unify an unboxed type with a polymorphic type variable.* For example, consider the expression

```
id 4#
```

where `id` is the polymorphic identity function with type $\forall\alpha.\ \alpha \rightarrow \alpha$, and `4#` is an unboxed integer of type `Int#`. The type of `id` is instantiated to $\beta \rightarrow \beta$, where β is a fresh type variable. Then an attempt will be made to unify β with `Int#`, and at this point a type error will be reported.

This is not quite all we have to do. Consider the function definition

```
uInc x = x +# 1#
```

Function definitions are usually typed by adding the assumption `x` : α to the type environment, where α is a fresh type variable, and then typing the body. This yields a substitution which can be applied to α to give the argument type for `f`. In this case we do not want the type checker to complain at the unification of α with `Int#`; rather we want type inference to succeed in attributing to `uInc` the type `Int#` $\rightarrow$ `Int#`.

What is required is two forms of type variables: uncommitted ones, which can unify with anything; and boxed ones, which cannot unify with unboxed types. Function arguments are given uncommitted type variables, while boxed type variables are used to instantiate polymorphic types.

The same trick can be used to implement the two forms of AP rule. If the argument of the function is not simple variable, we unify the type of the argument with a boxed type variable. In effect, this tags the argument type (which might at this stage be only an uncommitted type variable), so that it can only subsequently unify with a boxed type, as required.

This completes our sketch of the modest changes required to a type inference system to accomodate unboxed types. It is a little surprising that the type *system* does not need two kinds of type variables; only the type *inferencer* does. It would be possible to introduce two kinds of type variables into the type system as well, and it might make it easier to prove soundness and completeness results if this was done.

9 The dynamic semantics of unboxed types

Next we consider what changes need to be made to the dynamic semantics of the Core language to accomodate unboxed types. As before, we need to give a domain model for each type, and we need to give the semantic equations.

9.1 The model

The first question is: what is the domain $\mathcal{D}[\![\texttt{Int\#}]\!]$, corresponding to the type of unboxed integers? Our first attempts to answer this question suggested that it should be the usual domain of integers, including $\bot$; but that meant that $\mathcal{D}[\![\texttt{Int}]\!]$, the domain of boxed integers, had to have an extra bottom. This double lifting gives rise to all sorts of complications, over which we draw a kindly veil.

A much better solution is to use *unpointed domains*, that is domains which lack a bottom element. (A good introduction is given by Schmidt [1986].) So the domain of unboxed integers is defined thus:

$$\mathcal{D}[\![\texttt{Int\#}]\!] = \{\text{The fixed-precision integers}\}$$

The domain has no bottom element, and the ordering relation is just the identity. The lack of a bottom element for unboxed domains corresponds nicely to our intution: a variable of unboxed type can never be bound to bottom, because the whole computation will diverge before the binding takes place.

The difference between the domains corresponding to Int and Int# is that the latter is not lifted. Now it is possible to see why we made the outermost lifting explicit in our model for algebraic data types in Section 3.3: it makes it easy to generalise the model to unboxed data types, merely by omitting the lifting. Specifically, for an unboxed algebraic data type declaration, of form

$$\texttt{data unboxed } \chi\#\ \alpha_1 \ldots \alpha_t \;=\; c_1\ \tau_{11} \ldots \tau_{1a_1} \mid \ldots \mid c_n\ \tau_{n1} \ldots \tau_{na_n}$$

we derive the following functor definition:

$$\begin{aligned} \chi\#\ d_1 \ldots d_t \;=\;& s_1 + \ldots + s_n \\ & \text{where } \rho = [\alpha_1 \mapsto d_1, \ldots, \alpha_t \mapsto d_t] \\ & \phantom{\text{where }} s_i = \mathcal{D}[\![\tau_{i1}]\!]\ \rho \times \ldots \times \mathcal{D}[\![\tau_{ia_i}]\!]\ \rho \qquad (1 \leq i \leq n) \end{aligned}$$

The only difference from the boxed case is the absence of the outermost lifting.

The inductive definition for $\mathcal{D}[\![]\!]$ from Section 3.3 goes through largely unchanged:

$$\begin{aligned} \mathcal{D}[\![\alpha]\!]\ \rho &= \rho\ \alpha \\ \mathcal{D}[\![\texttt{Int\#}]\!]\ \rho &= \{\text{The set of fixed-precision integers}\} \\ \mathcal{D}[\![\texttt{Float\#}]\!]\ \rho &= \{\text{The set of fixed-precision floating-point numbers}\} \\ \mathcal{D}[\![\tau \to \pi]\!]\ \rho &= (\mathcal{D}[\![\tau]\!]\ \rho) \to (\mathcal{D}[\![\pi]\!]\ \rho) \\ \mathcal{D}[\![\tau \to \upsilon]\!]\ \rho &= (\mathcal{D}[\![\tau]\!]\ \rho) \to (\mathcal{D}[\![\upsilon]\!]\ \rho)_\bot \\ \mathcal{D}[\![\chi_n\ \tau_1 \ldots \tau_n]\!]\ \rho &= \chi_n\ (\mathcal{D}[\![\tau_1]\!]\ \rho) \ldots (\mathcal{D}[\![\tau_n]\!]\ \rho) \\ \mathcal{D}[\![\chi\#_n\ \tau_1 \ldots \tau_n]\!]\ \rho &= \chi\#_n\ (\mathcal{D}[\![\tau_1]\!]\ \rho) \ldots (\mathcal{D}[\![\tau_n]\!]\ \rho) \end{aligned}$$

The main difference comes in the function space construction. A function returning an unboxed value may fail to terminate, so its result type must be lifted[8].

The resulting domain equations are well-founded provided Restriction 3 is observed, namely that every recursive loop of type declarations includes at least one boxed type.

9.2 The semantic equations

The major difference in the semantics of programs involving unboxed values is that unboxed arguments are evaluated before calling the function to which they are passed. At first it looks as though this will require a significant adjustment to the semantics, but this is the point at which Restriction 2 comes into its own. Because Restriction 2 has already made all evaluation explicit, *no changes whatsoever are required to the semantic equations of Figure 3.*

Whilst the equations themselves do not change, the definition of the domains **Val** and **Env** need to be adjusted in a somewhat subtle way.

First, the valuation of an expression of unboxed type may fail to terminate, and hence, as with function types, we need to lift the result domain:

$$\mathbf{Val} = \left(\bigcup_{\pi} \mathcal{D}[\![\pi]\!]\right) \cup \left(\bigcup_{v} \mathcal{D}[\![v]\!]_{\perp}\right)$$

Does the same need to be done for **Env**? No it does not, because we claim that *a variable of unboxed type can never be bound to bottom.* To justify this claim, consider all the places where a variable of unboxed type can be bound:

- The application of a lambda abstraction. Here the argument can only be a variable (Restriction 2), so if the claim is true of the argument it will also be true of the variable bound by the abstraction.
- The evaluation of a case alternative. Here variables are bound to the components of a constructor. But if any of these components is of unboxed type, then the corresponding argument at the call of the constructor will be a variable, and hence cannot be bottom.
- The evaluation of a case alternative. Here a variable is bound to the value which the case evaluates. But if this value is bottom then the case diverges, and so the binding never takes place.

This all corresponds directly to our intuition. The run-time environment will contain pointers to (perhaps as yet unevaluated) boxed values, and some unboxed values. The latter cannot be bottom! So we retain the same definition for **Env**:

$$\mathbf{Env} = \bigcup_{\tau}(var_{\tau} \rightarrow \mathcal{D}[\![\tau]\!])$$

[8] This decision is not as *ad hoc* as it may appear. The restricted form of function application permitted by Restriction 2 directly implements Kleisli composition over the lifting monad, where an arrow from A to B is a function from A to $B_{\perp}$ (Moggi [1989]).

9.3 Transforming programs involving unboxed types

The whole thrust of this paper has been to expose programs involving unboxed values to optimising transformations (cf Section 4). It is legitimate to ask whether all the transformations we know so well still apply in the new setting. This is not a trivial question. For example, suppose that we did not impose Restriction 2, so that unboxed arguments could be non-trivial expressions. Then β-reduction is no longer valid! For example, consider the expression:

```
(\x.3) (f 3)
```

where `f` has type `Int -> Int#`, and `f` happens diverges on argument 3. Then, because unboxed arguments must be evaluated before a call, this expression has value $\perp$. But a simple β reduction transforms this expression to 3, and hence changes the meaning.

The most important reason for Restriction 2 is to prevent this sort of problem. All the usual program transformations remain valid in the new setting. We can justify this claim by observing that *all the existing semantic equations remain unchanged, so if a transformation previously preserved correctness then it will do so in the extended language as well.* This sounds obvious, but many of our earlier attempts at a dynamic semantics required different semantic rules, and so the correctness of transformations was a matter for speculation.

There is a small caveat. We need to check that the result of a program transformation still obeys Restrictions 1 and 2; that is, they are still well-typed in the sense of Section 8.

10 Language design issues

The sole reason for introducing unboxed values in the first place is to improve efficiency. There are no programs which one can write using unboxed values which cannot be written equally easily without. It is therefore far from obvious whether unboxed values should be exposed to the programmer at all; it would be quite possible to use them solely as a convenient notation inside the compiler, helping to support the compilation-by-transformation paradigm as discussed in Sections 4 and 5.

Even so, there is a strong case for making unboxed values directly available to the programmer, including the generalisations proposed in Section 6, as we now discuss. (A possible compromise would be to make such language extensions available only to the *systems* programmer; for example, the person who writes the complex-number arithmetic package.)

Consider the `UCpx` data type introduced in Section 6.1. In principle, it is possible that a very clever program analyser could look at a program written in terms of `Cpx` and `addCpx` and figure out that it would not change the meaning of the program to rewrite it in terms of `UCpx` and `addUCpx`. In practice, this is far beyond what current compiler technology can do, because data can be placed in a data structure in one part of the program, and used somewhere else entirely. In any case, such an analysis would be impossible in the presence of separate compilation.

In short, the efficiency improvements arising from generalised unboxed algebraic data types cannot realistically be obtained without involving the programmer; yet these performance improvements can be substantial.

The other trouble with making unboxed values part of the source language is that Restrictions 1 and 2 are very tiresome. The remaining parts of this section consider how they may be alleviated.

10.1 Automatic evaluation

It is a simple matter to lift Restriction 2 in the source language, by transforming the program to obey the restriction after type inference is complete. For example, whenever a function is applied to a non-HNF argument of unboxed type, the application is enclosed in a `case` expression which evalutes the argument and binds it to a variable, which is then passed to the function.

Similarly, whenever a `let`-expression binds a non-HNF value of unboxed type, it is replaced with the corresponding `case` expression.

This transformation cannot be applied to `letrec` expressions, because there *is* no corresponding `case` expression. For the same reason, it cannot be applied to the top-level bindings of a program.

10.2 Automatic coercion

It is also possible to lift Restriction 1, which prohibits unboxed values from being passed to polymorphic functions, at least where there is a boxed form of the same data type, by coercing to and from the boxed form.

For example, a value of type `Int#` may be passed to a polymorphic function, by first being coerced type `Int` by applying the `Int` constructor to it. Similarly, a value of type `Int` can be coerced into one of type `Int#` by evaluating it and extracting its value. This is exactly the approach taken by Leroy [1991].

For example, the expression:

```
foldr (+#) 0# [4#, 5#]
```

would, after the coercions have been introduced, look like this:

```
case (foldr (\x. \y. case x of Int x# ->
                     case y of Int y# ->
                     case (+# x# y#) of t# -> Int t#)
        (Int 0#)
        [Int 4#, Int 5#])
of
Int t1# -> t1#
```

The unboxed contants have been boxed to make them compatible with the polymorphic functions `foldr` and the list constructor; the corresponding coercions have been done to the function passed to `foldr`; and the result of the `foldr` is then coerced back to `Int#`.

It is debatable whether all of this extra stuff should get introduced by the compiler, perhaps without the programmer realising that it is taking place. After all, the whole purpose of the exercise is to improve performance, so hidden perfomance losses are bad news.

The other problem is that, in general, it is possible to insert coercions in more than one place, and still obtain a correct program. Satish Thatte gives a good presentation of the issues (Thatte [1990]).

11 Related work

There is a long tradition of compilation by transformation, starting with Steele's Rabbit compiler (Steele [1978]), which pioneered continuation-passing style (CPS). CPS allows many representation decisions to be exposed, and expressed in the language being transformed, rather than being hidden in a black-box code generator. The Orbit compiler (Kranz [1988]) for Scheme is built on these ideas to make a production-quality optimising compiler.

Appel and MacQueen's Standard ML compiler is a further development in this line, with even greater modularity especially near the back end (Appel & Jim [1989]). Kelsey's thesis, entitled "Compilation by program transformation", is also CPS-based, but he handles imperative languages as well (Kelsey [1989]).

Fradet and LeMetayer describe another transformation-based compiler based on CPS (Fradet & Metayer [1990]; Fradet & Metayer [1988]). Their approach is unusual in that their target code is a continuation-based combinator language which has a direct reading either as a functional program or as a sequence of abstract machine instructions. The trouble is that they are thereby forced to make an early commitment to some low-level representation decisions, such as stack layout.

All of this work relates to compilation-by-transformation of languages with strict semantics. CPS is wonderful for such languages, because it makes explicit the order of evaluation which is implied by the semantics. For non-strict language, where the order of evaluation is demand-driven, CPS is not nearly so useful. A case expression is the nearest we get to it ("evaluate this expression and then continue in one of these ways, depending on the result you get").

The case-of-case transformation and its cousins (case-of-constructor, case-of-variable in a scope where the variable is bound to a constructor) are not new. They were the key transformations in the deforestation algorithm given by Wadler [1990], whose purpose is to eliminate intermediate data structures in functional programs. Indeed, the work described here could be seen as an exploration of the effects of exposing unboxed types to deforestation, the intermediate data structures in this case being the boxes around values.

None of these works directly addresses the main theme of this paper, namely the treatement of unboxed values in a non-strict language. The Clean compiler from Nijmegen (Brus et al. [1987]) does support unboxed values at the program level, but the details of what it does and how it works are not published.

Peterson's paper, whose title "Untagged data in tagged environments" is superficially similar to this paper, addresses a different, though related, problem (Peterson [1989]). Suppose that one took the ideas of this paper but dropped Restriction 1 (which restricts polymorphism), using tagging to identify unboxed data. Peterson then proposes an analysis to discover regions of the program in which the tags need not be attached to the unboxed values, which is of course much more efficient than manipulating the tagged representation. It is not clear how well his analysis would work in a non-strict language where the order of evaluation is much harder to predict.

Leroy's work has already been mentioned (Leroy [1991]). It deals with a strict language, and concentrates mainly on the coercion issues discussed in Section 10. It nicely complements this paper.

12 Further work

12.1 Overloading the built-in operators

In Section 6.1 we introduced the following example:

```
data Cpx = Cpx Int Int
addCpx (Cpx r1 i1) (Cpx r2 i2) = Cpx (r1+r2) (i1+i2)
```

Suppose that one had written the former definition of Cpx and addCpx, and then decided to make the components of Cpx unboxed. It would be nice if one could just replace Int with Int# in the definition of the Cpx data type, but make no change to the addCpx function, thus:

```
data Cpx = Cpx Int# Int#
addCpx (Cpx r1 i1) (Cpx r2 i2) = Cpx (r1+r2) (i1+i2)
```

(We are assuming that Restriction 2 is lifted as discussed above.) As things stand, addCpx and every other function which manipulates the components of a Cpx constructor, needs to be changed to use use unboxed operations instead of boxed ones:

```
addCpx (Cpx r1 i1) (Cpx r2 i2) = Cpx (r1 +# r2) (i1 +# i2)
```

This is a nuisance, and it would be nice if the compiler could figure such things out for itself. At first it seems that HASKELL's overloading mechanism might solve the problem, but this is defeated by Restriction 1. Hence we cannot declare an instance of the class Num for unboxed integers Int#.

12.2 Foreign-language interfacing

One of the reasons it is quite tricky to call subroutines written in another language (eg C) from a non-strict functional program is because other langauge generally manipulate unboxed values. Once we can manipulate unboxed values in the functional language, it is likely to become easier to build a direct interface to other imperative languages. We have not investigated this yet.

12.3 Unboxed functions

Does it make any sense to talk of unboxed *functions*? For example, a C program can pass code addresses around, and them call them.

In general, a function is represented by a code pointer and an environment. An unboxed function could perhaps be a code pointer together with a pointer to an environment. But then not much has been gained compared with making the code pointer just one more field in the environment.

The time that there would be a substantial benefit would be for functions which had no free variables; that is, no environment. Such functions can indeed be represented by just a code address, just like C.

12.4 Recursive definitions of unboxed values

Recursive definitions of unboxed values are permitted by Restriction 2, provided their right-hand sides are HNFs, and they even make sense! For example, given the type definitions

```
data unboxed Two# = Two# One Int#
data One = One Two#
```

the following recursive definition makes sense, attributing to `x` the type `UPair# Foo Int#`

```
x = Two# (One x) 3#
```

The way to understand such a definition is by naming each subexpression, and then, in the definition of each boxed variable, replacing each unboxed variable by its definition. This leaves a set of recursive definitions of boxed values, and some non-recursive definitions of unboxed values. In this example, the result is:

```
x = Two# y 3#
y = One (Two# y 3#)
```

Only the definition of `y` is recursive. We can always do this operation because of Restriction 3, provided there is no loop of the form

```
p# = q#
q# = p#
```

This rather unsatisfactory caveat is one reason we left this section under "Further work". In the light of the transformation given above, another approach would be to rule out recursive definitions of unboxed values.

Acknowledgements

When we were enmeshed in various rather complicated attempts at a dynamic semantics for unboxed values, John Hughes had the insight that we should try using unpointed domains. Kei Davis, Cordelia Hall, Will Partain, John Peterson, Kubiak Ryszard and Phil Wadler all made lots of very useful comments which helped to improve the presentation. Our grateful thanks to them.

This work was done with the support of the SERC GRASP project, and the ESPRIT Semantique Basic Research Action.

Bibliography

AW Appel [1988], "Runtime tags aren't necessary," CS-TR-142-88, Department of Computer Science, Princeton University.

AW Appel & T Jim [Jan 1989], "Continuation-passing, closure-passing style," in *Proc ACM Conference on Principles of Programming Languages*, ACM, 293-302.

TH Brus, MCJD van Eckelen, MO van Leer & MJ Plasmeijer [Sept 1987], "Clean - a language for functional graph rewriting," in *Functional programming languages and computer architecture, Portland*, G Kahn, ed., LNCS 274, Springer Verlag, 364–384.

LMM Damas & R Milner [1982], "Principal type schemes for functional programs," in *POPL*, 207–212.

P Fradet & D Le Metayer [1990], "Compilation of functional languages by program transformation," IRISA, Campus de Beaulieu, Rennes.

P Fradet & D Le Metayer [June 1988], "Compilation of lambda-calculus into functional machine code," INRIA.

[1986], in *Abstract Interpretation of Declarative Languages*, C Hankin & S Abramsky, eds., Ellis Horwood, Chichester, 246–265.

P Hudak, PL Wadler, Arvind, B Boutel, J Fairbairn, J Fasel, K Hammond, J Hughes, T Johnsson, R Kieburtz, RS Nikhil, SL Peyton Jones, M Reeve, D Wise & J Young [April 1990], "Report on the functional programming language Haskell," Department of Computing Science, Glasgow University.

R Kelsey [May 1989], "Compilation by program transformation," YALEU/DCS/RR-702, PhD thesis, Department of Computer Science, Yale University.

DA Kranz [May 1988], "ORBIT - an optimising compiler for Scheme," PhD thesis, Department of Computer Science, Yale University.

X Leroy [April 1991], "Efficient data representations in polymorphic languages," INRIA Research Report 1264, Rocquencourt.

E Moggi [June 1989], "Computational lambda calculus and monads," in *Logic in Computer Science, California*, IEEE.

J Peterson [Sept 1989], "Untagged data in tagged environments: choosing optimal representations at compile time," in *Functional Programming Languages and Computer Architecture, London*, Addison Wesley, 89–99.

SL Peyton Jones [1987], *The implementation of functional programming languages*, Prentice Hall.

SL Peyton Jones [Feb 1991], "The Spineless Tagless G-machine: a second attempt," Department of Computing Science, University of Glasgow.

SL Peyton Jones & Jon Salkild [Sept 1989], "The Spineless Tagless G-machine," in *Functional Programming Languages and Computer Architecture*, D MacQueen, ed., Addison Wesley.

DA Schmidt [1986], *Denotational semantics: a methodology for language development*, Allyn and Bacon.

MB Smyth & GD Plotkin [Nov 1982], "The category-theoretic solution of recursive domain equations," *SIAM Journal of Computing* 11, 761–783.

GL Steele [1978], "Rabbit: a compiler for Scheme," AI-TR-474, MIT Lab for Computer Science.

SR Thatte [1990], "Coercive type equivalence," Department of Maths and Computer Science, Clarkson University NY.

P Wadler [1990], "Deforestation: transforming programs to eliminate trees," *Theoretical Computer Science* 73, 231–248.

Lecture Notes in Computer Science

For information about Vols. 1–448
please contact your bookseller or Springer-Verlag

Vol. 449: M.E. Stickel (Ed.), 10th International Conference on Automated Deduction. Proceedings, 1990. XVI, 688 pages. 1990. (Subseries LNAI).

Vol. 450: T. Asano, T. Ibaraki, H. Imai, T. Nishizeki (Eds.), Algorithms. Proceedings, 1990. VIII, 479 pages. 1990.

Vol. 451: V. Marík, O. Stepánková, Z. Zdráhal (Eds.), Artificial Intelligence in Higher Education. Proceedings, 1989. IX, 247 pages. 1990. (Subseries LNAI).

Vol. 452: B. Rovan (Ed.), Mathematical Foundations of Computer Science 1990. Proceedings, 1990. VIII, 544 pages. 1990.

Vol. 453: J. Seberry, J. Pieprzyk (Eds.), Advances in Cryptology – AUSCRYPT '90 Proceedings, 1990. IX. 462 pages. 1990.

Vol. 454: V. Diekert, Combinatorics on Traces. XII, 165 pages. 1990.

Vol. 455: C.A. Floudas, P.M. Pardalos, A Collection of Test Problems for Constrained Global Optimization Algorithms. XIV, 180 pages. 1990.

Vol. 456: P. Deransart, J. Maluszyn´ski (Eds.), Programming Language Implementation and Logic Programming. Proceedings, 1990. VIII, 401 pages. 1990.

Vol. 457: H. Burkhart (Ed.), CONPAR '90 – VAPP IV. Proceedings, 1990. XIV, 900 pages. 1990.

Vol. 458: J.C.M. Baeten, J.W. Klop (Eds.), CONCUR '90. Proceedings, 1990. VII, 537 pages. 1990.

Vol. 459: R. Studer (Ed.), Natural Language and Logic. Proceedings, 1989. VII, 252 pages. 1990. (Subseries LNAI).

Vol. 460: J. Uhl, H.A. Schmid, A Systematic Catalogue of Reusable Abstract Data Types. XII, 344 pages. 1990.

Vol. 461: P. Deransart, M. Jourdan (Eds.), Attribute Grammars and their Applications. Proceedings, 1990. VIII, 358 pages. 1990.

Vol. 462: G. Gottlob, W. Nejdl (Eds.), Expert Systems in Engineering. Proceedings, 1990. IX, 260 pages. 1990. (Subseries LNAI).

Vol. 463: H. Kirchner, W. Wechler (Eds.), Algebraic and Logic Programming. Proceedings, 1990. VII, 386 pages. 1990.

Vol. 464: J. Dassow, J. Kelemen (Eds.), Aspects and Prospects of Theoretical Computer Science. Proceedings, 1990. VI, 298 pages. 1990.

Vol. 465: A. Fuhrmann, M. Morreau (Eds.), The Logic of Theory Change. Proceedings, 1989. X, 334 pages. 1991. (Subseries LNAI).

Vol. 466: A. Blaser (Ed.), Database Systems of the 90s. Proceedings, 1990. VIII, 334 pages. 1990.

Vol. 467: F. Long (Ed.), Software Engineering Environments. Proceedings, 1969. VI, 313 pages. 1990.

Vol. 468: S.G. Akl, F. Fiala, W.W. Koczkodaj (Eds.), Advances in Computing and Information – ICCI '90. Proceedings, 1990. VII, 529 pages. 1990.

Vol. 469: I. Guessarian (Ed.), Semantics of Systeme of Concurrent Processes. Proceedings, 1990. V, 456 pages. 1990.

Vol. 470: S. Abiteboul, P.C. Kanellakis (Eds.), ICDT '90. Proceedings, 1990. VII, 528 pages. 1990.

Vol. 471: B.C. Ooi, Efficient Query Processing in Geographic Information Systems. VIII, 208 pages. 1990.

Vol. 472: K.V. Nori, C.E. Veni Madhavan (Eds.), Foundations of Software Technology and Theoretical Computer Science. Proceedings, 1990. X, 420 pages. 1990.

Vol. 473: I.B. Damgård (Ed.), Advances in Cryptology – EUROCRYPT '90. Proceedings, 1990. VIII, 500 pages. 1991.

Vol. 474: D. Karagiannis (Ed.), Information Syetems and Artificial Intelligence: Integration Aspects. Proceedings, 1990. X, 293 pages. 1991. (Subseries LNAI).

Vol. 475: P. Schroeder-Heister (Ed.), Extensions of Logic Programming. Proceedings, 1989. VIII, 364 pages. 1991. (Subseries LNAI).

Vol. 476: M. Filgueiras, L. Damas, N. Moreira, A.P. Tomás (Eds.), Natural Language Processing. Proceedings, 1990. VII, 253 pages. 1991. (Subseries LNAI).

Vol. 477: D. Hammer (Ed.), Compiler Compilers. Proceedings, 1990. VI, 227 pages. 1991.

Vol. 478: J. van Eijck (Ed.), Logics in AI. Proceedings, 1990. IX, 562 pages. 1991. (Subseries in LNAI).

Vol. 480: C. Choffrut, M. Jantzen (Eds.), STACS 91. Proceedings, 1991. X, 549 pages. 1991.

Vol. 481: E. Lang, K.-U. Carstensen, G. Simmons, Modelling Spatial Knowledge on a Linguistic Basis. IX, 138 pages. 1991. (Subseries LNAI).

Vol. 482: Y. Kodratoff (Ed.), Machine Learning – EWSL-91. Proceedings, 1991. XI, 537 pages. 1991. (Subseries LNAI).

Vol. 483: G. Rozenberg (Ed.), Advances In Petri Nets 1990. VI, 515 pages. 1991.

Vol. 484: R. H. Möhring (Ed.), Graph-Theoretic Concepts In Computer Science. Proceedings, 1990. IX, 360 pages. 1991.

Vol. 485: K. Furukawa, H. Tanaka, T. Fullsaki (Eds.), Logic Programming '89. Proceedings, 1989. IX, 183 pages. 1991. (Subseries LNAI).

Vol. 486: J. van Leeuwen, N. Santoro (Eds.), Distributed Algorithms. Proceedings, 1990. VI, 433 pages. 1991.

Vol. 487: A. Bode (Ed.), Distributed Memory Computing. Proceedings, 1991. XI, 506 pages. 1991.

Vol. 488: R. V. Book (Ed.), Rewriting Techniques and Applications. Proceedings, 1991. VII, 458 pages. 1991.

Vol. 489: J. W. de Bakker, W. P. de Roever, G. Rozenberg (Eds.), Foundations of Object-Oriented Languages. Proceedings, 1990. VIII, 442 pages. 1991.

Vol. 490: J. A. Bergstra, L. M. G. Feljs (Eds.), Algebraic Methods 11: Theory, Tools and Applicatlons. VI, 434 pages. 1991.

Vol. 491: A. Yonezawa, T. Ito (Eds.), Concurrency: Theory, Language, and Architecture. Proceedings, 1989. VIII, 339 pages. 1991.

Vol. 492: D. Sriram, R. Logcher, S. Fukuda (Eds.), Computer-Aided Cooperative Product Development. Proceedings, 1989 VII, 630 pages. 1991.

Vol. 493: S. Abramsky, T. S. E. Maibaum (Eds.), TAPSOFT '91. Volume 1. Proceedings, 1991. VIII, 455 pages. 1991.

Vol. 494: S. Abramsky, T. S. E. Maibaum (Eds.), TAPSOFT '91. Volume 2. Proceedings, 1991. VIII, 482 pages. 1991.

Vol. 495: 9. Thalheim, J. Demetrovics, H.-D. Gerhardt (Eds.), MFDBS '91. Proceedings, 1991. VI, 395 pages. 1991.

Vol. 496: H.-P. Schwefel, R. Männer (Eds.), Parallel Problem Solving from Nature. Proceedings, 1991. XI, 485 pages. 1991.

Vol. 497: F. Dehne, F. Fiala. W.W. Koczkodaj (Eds.), Advances in Computing and Intormation - ICCI '91 Proceedings, 1991. VIII, 745 pages. 1991.

Vol. 498: R. Andersen, J. A. Bubenko jr., A. Sølvberg (Eds.), Advanced Information Systems Engineering. Proceedings, 1991. VI, 579 pages. 1991.

Vol. 499: D. Christodoulakis (Ed.), Ada: The Choice for '92. Proceedings, 1991. VI, 411 pages. 1991.

Vol. 500: M. Held, On the Computational Geometry of Pocket Machining. XII, 179 pages. 1991.

Vol. 501: M. Bidoit, H.-J. Kreowski, P. Lescanne, F. Orejas, D. Sannella (Eds.), Algebraic System Specification and Development. VIII, 98 pages. 1991.

Vol. 502: J. Bārzdiņš, D. Bjørner (Eds.), Baltic Computer Science. X, 619 pages. 1991.

Vol. 503: P. America (Ed.), Parallel Database Systems. Proceedings, 1990. VIII, 433 pages. 1991.

Vol. 504: J. W. Schmidt, A. A. Stogny (Eds.), Next Generation Information System Technology. Proceedings, 1990. IX, 450 pages. 1991.

Vol. 505: E. H. L. Aarts, J. van Leeuwen, M. Rem (Eds.), PARLE '91. Parallel Architectures and Languages Europe, Volume I. Proceedings, 1991. XV, 423 pages. 1991.

Vol. 506: E. H. L. Aarts, J. van Leeuwen, M. Rem (Eds.), PARLE '91. Parallel Architectures and Languages Europe, Volume II. Proceedings, 1991. XV, 489 pages. 1991.

Vol. 507: N. A. Sherwani, E. de Doncker, J. A. Kapenga (Eds.), Computing in the 90's. Proceedings, 1989. XIII, 441 pages. 1991.

Vol. 508: S. Sakata (Ed.), Applied Algebra, Algebraic Algorithms and Error-Correcting Codes. Proceedings, 1990. IX, 390 pages. 1991.

Vol. 509: A. Endres, H. Weber (Eds.), Software Development Environments and CASE Technology. Proceedings, 1991. VIII, 286 pages. 1991.

Vol. 510: J. Leach Albert, B. Monien, M. Rodríguez (Eds.), Automata, Languages and Programming. Proceedings, 1991. XII, 763 pages. 1991.

Vol. 511: A. C. F. Colchester, D.J. Hawkes (Eds.), Information Processing in Medical Imaging. Proceedings, 1991. XI, 512 pages. 1991.

Vol. 512: P. America (Ed.), ECOOP '91. European Conference on Object-Oriented Programming. Proceedings, 1991. X, 396 pages. 1991.

Vol. 513: N. M. Mattos, An Approach to Knowledge Base Management. IX, 247 pages. 1991. (Subseries LNAI).

Vol. 514: G. Cohen, P. Charpin (Eds.), EUROCODE '90. Proceedings, 1990. XI, 392 pages. 1991.

Vol. 515: J. P. Martins, M. Reinfrank (Eds.), Truth Maintenance Systems. Proceedings, 1990. VII, 177 pages. 1991. (Subseries LNAI).

Vol. 516: S. Kaplan, M. Okada (Eds.), Conditional and Typed Rewriting Systems. Proceedings, 1990. IX, 461 pages. 1991.

Vol. 517: K. Nökel, Temporally Distributed Symptoms in Technical Diagnosis. IX, 164 pages. 1991. (Subseries LNAI).

Vol. 518: J. G. Williams, Instantiation Theory. VIII, 133 pages. 1991. (Subseries LNAI).

Vol. 519: F. Dehne, J.-R. Sack, N. Santoro (Eds.), Algorithms and Data Structures. Proceedings, 1991. X, 496 pages. 1991.

Vol. 520: A. Tarlecki (Ed.), Mathematical Foundations of Computer Science 1991. Proceedings, 1991. XI, 435 pages. 1991.

Vol. 521: B. Bouchon-Meunier, R. R. Yager, L. A. Zadek (Eds.), Uncertainty in Knowledge-Bases. Proceedings, 1990. X, 609 pages. 1991.

Vol. 522: J. Hertzberg (Ed.), European Workshop on Planning. Proceedings, 1991. VII, 121 pages. 1991. (Subseries LNAI).

Vol. 523: J. Hughes (Ed.), Functional Programming Languages and Computer Architecture. Proceedings, 1991. VIII, 666 pages. 1991.